The BEAULIEU ENCYCLOPEDIA of the AUTOMOBILE

The BEAULIEU ENCYCLOPEDIA of the AUTOMOBILE

Volume 2
G-O

Editor in Chief
NICK GEORGANO

Foreword by
LORD MONTAGU
of **BEAULIEU**

FITZROY DEARBORN PUBLISHERS
CHICAGO · LONDON

© The Stationery Office 2000

Published in the United Kingdom by
The Stationery Office Limited, St Crispins, Duke Street, Norwich NR3 1PD.

Published in the United States of America by
Fitzroy Dearborn Publishers, 919 North Michigan Avenue, Chicago, Illinois 60611.

The information contained in this publication is believed to be correct at the time of manufacture. Whilst care has been taken to ensure that the information is accurate, the publisher can accept no responsibility for any errors or omissions or for changes to the details given.

A Cataloging-in-Publication record for this book is available from the Library of Congress.

ISBN 1-57958-293-1 Fitzroy Dearborn

First published 2000.

Reprinted with amendments 2001.

Produced and designed by The Stationery Office.

Design by Guy Myles Warren.

Reproductive services by Colourscript, Mildenhall, Suffolk.

Printed and bound by Butler & Tanner, Frome, Somerset.

Dedication

To the memory of George Ralph Doyle, John Pollitt, and Michael Sedgwick.

G.R.Doyle (1890–1961) was the first man to compile a worldwide address list of car manufacturers. *The World's Automobiles*, first published privately in 1932, stimulated the interest of countless enthusiasts. Without Doyle's pioneering work, the compilation of this encyclopedia would have been a near impossibility.

John Pollitt (1892–1958) was one of the most painstaking of researchers into motoring history. After his retirement from the Rover company in 1945, he devoted his entire time to investigations and correspondence on the subject, the fruits of which he wrote up in twenty eight files, running to several million words. These files, generously lent by the late Dennis C. Field) were among the most important cornerstones of the encyclopedia.

Michael Sedgwick (1926–1983) was the most tireless researcher into motoring history from the early 1960s to the day of his death in October 1983. He was Curator of the Montagu Motor Museum (today the National Motor Museum) from 1958 to 1966, and subsequently the Museum's Director of Research, Assistant Editor of *The Veteran & Vintage Magazine*, and a regular contributor to practically every old car magazine in the world. His enthusiasm and knowledge extended to any period and variety of road vehicle. He would have loved this book.

Contents

Dedication   v

Alphabetical List of Biographies   viii

Alphabetical List of Colour Illustrations in Volume 2   xi

Alphabetical List of Original Manufacturers'

  Promotional Images   xv

Foreword   xix

Acknowledgements   xxiii

Introduction   xxv

Terms and Abbreviations Used   xxxii

Colour Illustrations   *facing page* xxxii

Alphabetical List of Makes, G to O   601

Glossary   xxxiii

Contributors to the Encyclopedia   xxxix

Alphabetical List of Biographies included in Volume 1

Agnelli, Giovanni (Fiat)	537	Hershey, Frank (Ford)	566
Agnelli, Gianni (Fiat)	538		
Austin, Herbert (Austin)	102	Iacocca, Lee (Ford)	563
Bendix, Vincent (Bendix)	147	Jano, Vittorio (Alfa Romeo)	29
Bentley, W.O. (Bentley)	150	Jordan, Chuck (Chevrolet)	276
Benz, Karl (Benz)	155		
Borgward, Carl Freidrich Wilhelm (Borgward)	182	Keller, Kaufman T. (Chrysler)	286
Brown, David (Aston Martin)	86	Kettering, Charles Franklin (Cadillac)	234
Budd, Edward G. (Citroën)	301	Knudsen, William S. (Chevrolet)	274
Buehrig, Gordon (Cord)	334		
Bugatti, Ettore (Bugatti)	210	Lawson, Harry John (Daimler)	375
Buick, David Dunbar (Buick)	218	Leland, Henry (Cadillac)	232
		Lyons, Sir William (Jaguar)	778
Chevrolet, Louis (Chevrolet)	272		
Chrysler, Walter (Chrysler)	285	Marr, Walter L. (Buick)	219
Citroën, André (Citroën)	297	Martin, Lionel (Aston Martin)	85
Clément-Bayard, Adolphe (Clément-Bayard)	312	McPherson, Earle Steele (Ford)	564
Cord, Errett Lobban (Auburn)	94	Mitchell, William Leroy 'Bill' (Buick)	220
Daimler, Gottlieb (Daimler)	370	Nasser, Jacques (Ford)	581
De Causse, Frank (Franklin)	588		
De Dion, Count Albert (De Dion-Bouton)	398	Perry, Percival Lee Dewhurst (Ford)	574
De Lorean, John Zachary (DeLorean)	419		
Delage, Louis (Delage)	404	Rybicki, Irvin (Chevrolet)	278
Delahaye, Emile (Delahaye)	407		
Dodge, Horace (Dodge)	446	Scott-Montagu, The Hon. John (Daimler)	376
Dodge, John (Dodge)	446	Simms, Frederick Richard (Daimler)	373
Duesenberg, August (Duesenberg)	460	Stevens, Brooks (Excalibur (i))	512
Duesenberg, Frederick (Duesenberg)	460		
Durant, William Crapo (Durant)	469	Telnack, Jack (Ford)	567
Engel, Elwood (Ford)	570	Varlet, Amédée (Delahaye)	409
Ferrari, Enzo (Ferrari)	530	Walker, George (Ford)	568
Fiedler, Fritz (BMW)	172	Weiffenbach, Charles (Delahaye)	411
Ford, Henry (Ford)	558		
Ford, Henry, II (Ford)	561		
Gale, Thomas C. (Chrysler)	289		
Giacosa, Dante (Fiat)	542		

Alphabetical List of Biographies included in Volume 2

Ainsworth, Henry M. (Hotchkiss) 721

Birkigt, Marc (Hispano Suiza) 696

Chapin, Roy Dikeman (Hudson) 726
Chapin, Roy D., Jr (Hudson) 727
Chapman, Colin (Lotus) 926
Cherry, Wayne (Opel) 1151

Darrin, Howard 'Dutch' (Kaiser) 812
de Sakhnoffsky, Alexis (Nash) 1104
Dunham, George Willis (Hudson) 728

Earl, Harley (La Salle) 874
Edge, Selwyn Francis (Napier) 1098
Egan, John Leopold (Jaguar) 781

Fessia, Antonio (Lancia) 864
Ford, Edsel (Lincoln) 904
Frazer, Joe (Kaiser) 811

Gregorie, Bob (Lincoln) 906

Heynes, William Munger (Jaguar) 780
Honda, Soichiro (Honda) 711

Issigonis, Alec (Morris) 1074

Jellinek, Emile (Mercedes) 999
Jordan, Edward S. 'Ned' (Jordan) 799

Kaiser, Henry J. (Kaiser) 810
Kelsey, C.W. (Kelsey) 817
Kimber, Cecil (MG) 1029

Lamborghini, Ferruccio (Lamborghini) 855
Lanchester, Frederick (Lanchester) 859
Lord, Leonard (Morris) 1073

Maserati, Alfieri (Maserati) 966
Maserati, Bindo (Maserati) 967
Maserati, Carlo (Maserati) 967
Maserati, Ernesto (Maserati) 967
Maserati, Ettore (Maserati) 967
Maybach, Karl Wilhelm (Maybach) 980
Morris, William (Morris) 1069

Nash, Charles (Nash) 1102
Northup, Amos (Graham-Paige) 643

Olds, Ransom Eli (Oldsmobile) 1141

Rootes, William E. (Humber) 732
Rootes, Reginald C. (Humber) 734

Spring, Frank (Hudson) 729

Thomas, Miles Webster (Morris) 1071
Turnbull, George Henry (Hyundai) 743

Wankel, Felix (NSU) 1126
Winter, Bernard B (Humber) 735
Woollard, Frank G. (Morris) 1072

Alphabetical List of Biographies included in Volume 3

Bache, David (Rover)	1378	Panhard, Adrien (Panhard)	1182
Black, John Paul (Standard)	1495	Panhard, Joseph (Panhard)	1183
		Panhard, Louis (Panhard)	1182
Charles, H.N. (MG)	1025	Piëch, Ferdinand (Volkswagen)	1697
Coatalen, Louis Hervé (Sunbeam)	1543	Pomeroy, Laurence (Vauxhall)	1657
		Porsche, F.A.E. 'Ferry' (Porsche)	1256
Day, Graham (Rover)	1379	Porsche, Ferdinand (Volkswagen)	1690
Edwardes, Michael (Rover)	1379	Renault, Louis (Renault)	1315
Exner, Virgil (Studebaker)	1528	Roesch, Georges Henri (Talbot)	1563
		Röhr, Hans Gustav (Röhr)	1350
Fedden, Roy (Straker-Squire)	1524	Rolls, Charles Stewart (Rolls-Royce)	1355
		Romney, George (Rambler)	1294
Gabrielsson, Assar (Volvo)	1702	Rosengart, Lucien (Rosengart)	1368
Gillbrand, Per S. (Saab)	1398	Royce, Henry (Rolls-Royce)	1357
Gubitz, Werner (Packard)	1170		
		Siddeley, John Davenport (Siddeley)	1448
Hirst, Ivan (Volkswagen)	1693	Sloan, Alfred Pritchard, Jr (Pontiac)	1249
Hives, Ernest Walter (Rolls-Royce)	1358	Stokes, Donald Gresham (Triumph)	1616
Holbrook, Claude Vivian (Triumph)	1614	Stout, William Bushnell (Stout)	1522
Joy, Henry Bourne (Packard)	1175	Teague, Dick (Rambler)	1295
		Toyota, Eiji (Toyota)	1601
King, Charles Spencer 'Spen' (Rover)	1377		
Knudsen, Semon Emil (Pontiac)	1246	Voisin, Gabriel (Voisin)	1686
Larson, Gustaf (Volvo)	1705	Webster, Henry George (Standard)	1496
Ledwinka, Hans (Tatra)	1573	Wilks, Maurice (Rover)	1373
Levassor, Émile (Panhard)	1184	Wilks, Spencer Bernau (Rover)	1372
Loewy, Raymond (Studebaker)	1527	Wills, Childe Harold (Wills Sainte Claire)	1744
		Willys, John North (Willys)	1746
Martin, Karl (Wasp)	1725		
Nordhoff, Heinz (Volkswagen)	1694		

Alphabetical List of Colour Illustrations included in Volume 2

1959	AC Ace-Bristol sports car	Nick Georgano/National Motor Museum
1965	AC Shelby Cobra 7-litre sports car	National Motor Museum
1911	Alco 4-seater	Nicky Wright/National Motor Museum
1931	Alfa Romeo 1750 2-seater sports car	Nicky Wright/National Motor Museum
1938	Alfa Romeo 2900 Superleggera 2-door coupé	National Motor Museum
1974	Alfa Romeo 2000 Spyder	National Motor Museum
1950	Allard J2 2-seater sports car	National Motor Museum
1937	Alvis Speed 25 2-door Sedanca coupé	Nicky Wright/National Motor Museum
1972	AMC AMX 2-door coupé	Nicky Wright/National Motor Museum
1920	Apperson 8 Sportster	Nicky Wright/National Motor Museum
1937	Aston Martin 2-litre Abbott 2-door drop-head coupé	Nick Georgano/National Motor Museum
1964	Aston Martin DB5 drop-head coupé	National Motor Museum
1986	Audi Quattro coupé	National Motor Museum
1935	Auburn 851 speedster	National Motor Museum
1923	Austin 7 2-door 4-seater	National Motor Museum
1935	Austin 7 Ruby 2-door saloon	Nicky Wright/National Motor Museum
1948	Austin 16 saloon	Nick Georgano/National Motor Museum
1952	Austin A90 Atlantic saloon	National Motor Museum
1959	Austin SeVen saloon	National Motor Museum
1982	Austin Metro 1.3S hatchback	Nick Georgano/National Motor Museum
1954	Austin Healey 100 sports car.	Nick Georgano/National Motor Museum
1972	Austin Healey Sprite competition sports car	National Motor Museum
1913	Baker Electric 2-seater	Nicky Wright/National Motor Museum
1923	Bentley 3-litre saloon	National Motor Museum
1934	Bentley 3 1/2-litre drop-head coupé	National Motor Museum
1953	Bentley Continental R coupé	Nicky Wright/National Motor Museum
1996	Bentley Continental R coupé	National Motor Museum
1938	BMW 328 2-seater sports car	National Motor Museum
1958	BMW 507 2-seater sports car	National Motor Museum
1984	BMW 323i cabriolet	National Motor Museum
1999	BMW Z3 M coupé	National Motor Museum
1938	British Salmson 20/90 2-seater sports car	Nick Georgano/National Motor Museum
1927	Bugatti Type 41 Royale coupé de ville	National Motor Museum
1934	Bugatti Type 57 Ventoux coupé	Nicky Wright/National Motor Museum
1939	Buick Special with English convertible Albemarle coachwork by Carlton	Nicky Wright/National Motor Museum
1963	Buick Riviera coupé	Nicky Wright/National Motor Museum
1931	Cadillac 452-A V16 convertible coupé	Nicky Wright/National Motor Museum
1959	Cadillac coupé de ville	Nicky Wright/National Motor Museum
1988	Cadillac Allante 2-door convertible	National Motor Museum
1954	Chevrolet Corvette sports car	Nicky Wright/National Motor Museum
1963	Chevrolet Corvette Stingray coupé	National Motor Museum
1955	Chrysler C300 2-door sedan	Nicky Wright/National Motor Museum
1935	Chrysler Airflow sedan	National Motor Museum
1922	Citroen Type C 5CV 2-seater	National Motor Museum
1952	Citroen Light 15 4-door saloon	National Motor Museum
1959	Citroen 2CV CI 4-door saloon	Nicky Wright/National Motor Museum
1972	Citroen DS21 Pallas 4-door saloon	Nick Georgano/National Motor Museum
1994	Citroen Xantia SX 4-door saloon	National Motor Museum
1936	Cord 810 convertible phaeton	Nicky Wright/National Motor Museum
1974	DAF 44 2-door saloon	Nick Georgano/National Motor Museum

1995	Daimler Double Six saloon	National Motor Museum
1978	Datsun 260Z coupé.	National Motor Museum
1901	De Dion-Bouton vis-à-vis	National Motor Museum
1975	De Tomaso Pantera GTS coupé	National Motor Museum
1937	Delage D8 coupé	National Motor Museum
1947	Delahaye 135 MS 2-door cabriolet	National Motor Museum
1929	Duesenberg Model J convertible roadster	Nicky Wright/National Motor Museum
1988	Excalibur Series VI sedan	Nicky Wright/National Motor Museum
1960	Facel Vega HK500 2-door coupé	National Motor Museum
1950	Ferrari 166 Barchetta sports car	Nicky Wright/National Motor Museum
1960	Ferrari 250GT cabriolet	National Motor Museum
1964	Ferrari 330GT coupé	National Motor Museum
1974	Ferrari Dino 246GT spyder	Nicky Wright/National Motor Museum
1982	Ferrari BB512 coupé	Nicky Wright/National Motor Museum
1985	Ferrari Testa Rossa coupé	National Motor Museum
1996	Ferrari F50 coupé	National Motor Museum
1937	Fiat Topolino 500 saloon	Nicky Wright/National Motor Museum
1977	Fiat 127 hatchback	National Motor Museum
1983	Fiat Uno 55S hatchback	National Motor Museum
1981	Fiat X1/9 targa sports car	National Motor Museum
2000	Fiat Multipla MPV	Fiat SpA
1914	Ford Model T 2-seater	National Motor Museum
1930	Ford Model A phaeton	National Motor Museum
1933	Ford V8 cabriolet	National Motor Museum
1956	Ford Thunderbird 2-door convertible	National Motor Museum
1957	Ford Zodiac Hyline saloon	National Motor Museum
1964	Ford Mustang 2-door convertible	Nicky Wright/National Motor Museum
1978	Ford Capri Ghia 3-litre coupé	Nicky Wright/National Motor Museum
1996	Ford Mondeo GLX saloon	National Motor Museum
1964	Ginetta G4 sports car	National Motor Museum
1965	Gordon Keeble 2-door coupé	National Motor Museum
1950	Healey Silverstone sports car	Nicky Wright/National Motor Museum
1963	Hillman Imp 2-door saloon	National Motor Museum
1912	Hispano-Suiza Alfonso sports car	Nicky Wright/National Motor Museum
1924	Hispano-Suiza Tulip Wood H6C dual phaeton	National Motor Museum
1967	Honda S800 convertible	Nicky Wright/National Motor Museum
1992	Honda NSX coupé	National Motor Museum
1950	Hotchkiss 2-door cabriolet	National Motor Museum
1957	Hudson Hornet 4-door sedan	Nicky Wright/National Motor Museum
1903	Humberette 5hp 2-seater	Nicky Wright/National Motor Museum
1934	Invicta 4-litre S Type Salmons drop-head coupé	National Motor Museum
1937	Jaguar SS100 2-seater sports car	National Motor Museum
1950	Jaguar XK120 2-seater sports car	Nicky Wright/National Motor Museum
1954	Jaguar MkVII saloon	Nick Georgano/National Motor Museum
1962	Jaguar Mk2 3.4 saloon	Nick Georgano/National Motor Museum
1963	Jaguar E Type roadster	National Motor Museum
1985	Jaguar XJ6 saloon	Nick Georgano/National Motor Museum
1997	Jaguar XK8 convertible	National Motor Museum

1974	Jensen Interceptor coupé	Nicky Wright/National Motor Museum
1953	Jowett Javelin saloon	Nick Georgano/National Motor Museum
1938	Lagonda V12 4-door saloon	Nicky Wright/National Motor Museum
1968	Lamborghini Miura P400 coupé	National Motor Museum
1993	Lamborghini Diablo coupé	National Motor Museum
1908	Lanchester 20hp landaulet	National Motor Museum
1928	Lancia Lambda 8th series tourer	National Motor Museum
1937	Lancia Aprilia 4-door saloon	National Motor Museum
1973	Lancia Stratos coupé	National Motor Museum
1941	Lincoln Continental club coupé	National Motor Museum
1962	Lotus Elite 2-seater hard-top	National Motor Museum
1972	Lotus Elan Sprint 2-seater sports car	National Motor Museum
1996	Lotus Elise 2-seater sports car	National Motor Museum
1949	Maserati A6-1500 coupé.	Nicky Wright/National Motor Museum
1973	Maserati Bora coupé.	Nick Georgano/National Motor Museum
1982	Mazda RX7 Elford Turbo coupé.	National Motor Museum
1995	Mazda MX5 2-seater sports car.	National Motor Museum
1907	Mercedes 40/45 Simplex tourer.	National Motor Museum
1929	Mercedes-Benz SS 38/250 tourer.	National Motor Museum
1935	Mercedes -Benz 500K convertible coupé.	National Motor Museum
1957	Mercedes-Benz 300SL Gullwing coupé.	National Motor Museum
1965	Mercedes-Benz 600 limousine.	National Motor Museum
1993	Mercedes-Benz S280 saloon.	National Motor Museum
1955	Messerschmitt KR200 bubblecar.	National Motor Museum
1930	MG M Midget sports car.	National Motor Museum
1933	MG J2 Midget sports car.	Nick Georgano/National Motor Museum
1947	MG TC Midget sports car.	National Motor Museum
1955	MGA 1600 MkI sports car.	National Motor Museum
1971	MGB roadster.	Nicky Wright/National Motor Museum
1995	MGF 1.8i sports car.	Rover Group
1948	Morgan 4/4 sports car.	Nicky Wright/National Motor Museum
1990	Morgan Plus 8 sports car.	National Motor Museum
2000	Morgan Aero 8 sports car.	Morgan Cars
1926	Morris Bullnose saloon.	National Motor Museum
1949	Morris Minor saloon.	Nicky Wright/National Motor Museum
1960	Morris Minor Traveller estate car.	National Motor Museum
1964	Morris Mini Cooper 'S' saloon.	National Motor Museum
1974	NSU Ro80 4-door saloon.	National Motor Museum
1912	Opel 5/14 2-seater.	National Motor Museum
1971	Opel GT coupé.	National Motor Museum
1920	Packard Twin 6 3-35 landaulet.	Nicky Wright/National Motor Museum
1939	Packard 120 Series 1700 convertible.	Nicky Wright/National Motor Museum
1947	Packard Clipper Custom Super 8 sedan.	Nicky Wright/National Motor Museum
1899	Panhard 6hp wagonette.	Nick Georgano/National Motor Museum
1955	Pegaso Z102B coupé.	Nicky Wright/National Motor Museum
1937	Peugeot 402B 4-door saloon.	Nick Georgano/National Motor Museum
1989	Peugeot 205 Gti 1.9 hatchback.	National Motor Museum
1996	Peugeot 306 Gti-6 hatchback.	Peugeot
1913	Pierce Arrow Gentleman's Roadster.	National Motor Museum

1930	Pierce Arrow 7-passenger phaeton.	National Motor Museum
1969	Piper GTT 1.6-litre coupé.	Nick Georgano/National Motor Museum
1970	Plymouth AAR 'Cuda hard top.	Nicky Wright/National Motor Museum
1965	Pontiac GTO coupé.	Nicky Wright/National Motor Museum
1968	Pontiac Firebird convertible.	Nicky Wright/National Motor Museum
1951	Porsche 356 cabriolet.	National Motor Museum
1961	Porsche 356B Super coupé.	Nick Georgano/National Motor Museum
1997	Porsche 911 coupé.	Porsche Cars Great Britain

1911	Renault AX 2-seater.	National Motor Museum
1928	Renault NN-2 tourer.	Nick Georgano/National Motor Museum
1958	Renault 4CV saloon.	Nicky Wright/National Motor Museum
1977	Renault 16TX hatchback.	Nick Georgano/National Motor Museum
1982	Renault 5 Gordini Turbo hatchback.	National Motor Museum
1986	Renault Espace 2000TSE MPV.	National Motor Museum
1937	Riley Sprite 2-seater sports car.	Nicky Wright/National Motor Museum
1911	Rolls-Royce Silver Ghost Holmes torpedo tourer.	National Motor Museum
1936	Rolls-Royce 25/30 Tickford cabriolet.	Nick Georgano/National Motor Museum
1938	Rolls-Royce Phantom III Park Ward saloon.	National Motor Museum
1958	Rolls-Royce Silver Cloud I saloon.	National Motor Museum
1960	Rover 100 P4 saloon.	National Motor Museum
2000	Rover 75 saloon.	Rover Group
1993	Range Rover V8 3.9 estate car.	National Motor Museum
1948	Land Rover pick-up.	National Motor Museum

1966	Saab 96 saloon.	National Motor Museum
1988	Saab 900 turbo 2-door saloon.	National Motor Museum
1927	Salmson VAL 3 tourer.	Nick Georgano/National Motor Museum
1957	Simca Aronde Plein Ciel coupé.	National Motor Museum
1963	Skoda Felicia Super convertible.	Nick Baldwin
1963	Studebaker Avanti coupé.	Nicky Wright/National Motor Museum
1999	Subaru Impreza Turbo RB5 saloon.	Subaru

1987	Toyota MR2 sports car.	National Motor Museum
1955	Triumph TR2 sports car.	National Motor Museum
1973	Triumph Stag convertible.	National Motor Museum
1980	Triumph TR7 convertible.	National Motor Museum
1948	Tucker Torpedo sedan.	Nicky Wright/National Motor Museum
1996	TVR Cerbera coupé.	National Motor Museum

1915	Vauxhall Prince Henry tourer.	National Motor Museum
1920	Vauxhall 30-98 E Type 2-seater.	National Motor Museum
1939	Vauxhall 10hp saloon.	National Motor Museum
1999	Vauxhall Tigra 1.6i 16v coupé.	Vauxhall
1970	Volkswagen Beetle 1500 saloon.	Nick Georgano/National Motor Museum
1985	Volkswagen Golf Gti hatchback.	National Motor Museum
1962	Volvo P1800S coupé.	National Motor Museum

Alphabetical List of Original Manufacturers' Promotional Images included in Volume 1

	Page number	
Alfa Romeo	39	National Motor Museum
Alvis	67	National Motor Museum
Aston Martin	105	National Motor Museum
Bucciali	169	National Motor Museum
Bugatti	185	National Motor Museum
Buick	223	National Motor Museum
Cottereau	243	National Motor Museum
Chrysler	291	National Motor Museum
Citroen	303	National Motor Museum
Crossley	351	National Motor Museum
Daimler	379	National Motor Museum
De Dion-Bouton	401	National Motor Museum
Delaugere	415	National Motor Museum
DeSoto	427	National Motor Museum
DKW	443	National Motor Museum
Essex	501	National Motor Museum
Fiat	545	National Motor Museum
Ford	569	National Motor Museum
Ford	573	National Motor Museum

Alphabetical List of Original Manufacturers' Promotional Images included in Volume 2

	Page number	
Gilburt	623	National Motor Museum
Graham	637	National Motor Museum
Guy	655	National Motor Museum
Hillman	687	National Motor Museum
Hispano Suiza	701	National Motor Museum
Hupmobile	737	National Motor Museum
Itala	771	National Motor Museum
Jaguar	779	National Motor Museum
Kissel-Kar	827	National Motor Museum
Krit	837	National Motor Museum
Lagonda	849	National Motor Museum
Lanchester	861	National Motor Museum
Lea-Francis	883	National Motor Museum
La Buire	911	Nick Baldwin
Lorraine-Dietrich	923	Nick Baldwin
Marmon	957	National Motor Museum
Mathis	973	Nick Baldwin
Metz	1021	Nick Baldwin
MG	1027	National Motor Museum
Moon	1061	National Motor Museum
Morgan	1065	National Motor Museum
Morris	1077	National Motor Museum
Napier	1099	National Motor Museum
Nash	1103	National Motor Museum
Oldsmobile	1139	National Motor Museum
OM	1147	National Motor Museum
Opel	1153	National Motor Museum

Alphabetical List of Original Manufacturers' Promotional Images included in Volume 3

	Page number	
Packard	1173	National Motor Museum
Panhard	1185	National Motor Museum
Peugeot	1215	National Motor Museum
Plymouth	1239	National Motor Museum
Pontiac	1247	National Motor Museum
Renault	1313	National Motor Museum
Riley	1337	National Motor Museum
Rolland Pilain	1353	National Motor Museum
Rolls-Royce	1359	National Motor Museum
Rosengart	1367	National Motor Museum
Rover	1375	National Motor Museum
Royal Enfield	1388	National Motor Museum
Salmson	1407	Nick Baldwin
Sima-Standard	1453	National Motor Museum
Singer	1461	National Motor Museum
SS	1491	National Motor Museum
Standard	1497	National Motor Museum
Steyr	1513	National Motor Museum
Studebaker	1531	National Motor Museum
Sunbeam	1545	National Motor Museum
Talbot	1565	National Motor Museum
Tatra	1575	National Motor Museum
Terraplane	1583	National Motor Museum
Th. Schneider	1591	National Motor Museum
Triumph	1613	National Motor Museum
Trojan	1623	National Motor Museum
Vauxhall	1661	National Motor Museum
Willys-Knight	1749	National Motor Museum
Wolseley	1761	National Motor Museum
Zedel	1783	Nick Baldwin

Foreword
by Lord Montagu of Beaulieu

It has long been a dream of mine that the National Motor Museum at Beaulieu should be closely associated with a major international motoring work of reference. The opportunity came after a meeting at Beaulieu with Rupert Pennant-Rea shortly after he took over as Managing Director of Her Majesty's Stationery Office (HMSO), soon to be privatised and relaunched as The Stationery Office.

The *Beaulieu Encyclopedia of the Automobile* can trace its roots back to a slim volume, published privately in 1932 by George Ralph Doyle entitled *The World's Automobiles*. Keen-eyed readers will notice that this encyclopedia is dedicated to Ralph Doyle. 'Doyle', as this work of reference became known, was just a listing of manufacturers, dates, and addresses – the first ever to be published. Whilst studying at Oxford, Nick Georgano found a copy of Doyle and realised that with fuller facts that he had accumulated from his own researches, he could enlarge on that slim volume. The two enthusiasts met and became firm friends. When he died in 1961, Ralph Doyle left all his research notes to Nick Georgano, and the fourth and last edition of Doyle was put together by Nick for publication. Throughout this time, he had been developing ideas for a much more comprehensive book which would have biographical details of all manufacturers as well as photographs. A chance meeting in 1965 with British motoring historian Tim Nicholson resulted in Nick being introduced to the publishers George Rainbird Ltd, who had been thinking along similar lines. Thus was born the great *Complete Encyclopædia of Motor Cars*, published by Ebury Press in 1968, and this now famous work of reference has sold over 90,000 copies and been translated into five languages. There have been three editions, the last being in 1982, and to quote the words of Michael Lamm, Editor of *Special-Interest Autos* (and a contributor to this encyclopædia), in 1971:

'If an auto historian were sentenced to life in prison and allowed only one book in his cell, that book would have to be Georgano's *The Complete Encyclopædia of Motor Cars, 1885-1968*. I consider it the single most important work ever published in the field of automotive history – the one book about 20th century cars that 25th century historians will still keep handy. The dog-eared copy I bought in 1968 stands in the most accessible spot on my desk.

Even aside from the encyclopedia's reference value, I find myself picking it up constantly and reading it for pure pleasure – or just looking again and again at the 2000-odd photos. Anyone who has even glanced through this book has marvelled at the monumental job it must have been to compile.'

That splendid bible of motoring knowledge has long been out of print and second-hand copies change hands at inflated prices. We all knew that Nick Georgano was capable of great things and I persuaded him to put his name forward again as the editor for a brand new reference work which we were to propose to The Stationery Office. The result is a book of tremendous detail, produced from many years of research by many different people and three years of concentrated effort by Nick Georgano. So many people have helped over the years that it would be invidious of me to single out any one person but I would like to pay tribute to the late Michael Sedgwick, for so long my historical mentor at Beaulieu and the Museum's Director of Research. Sadly, Michael died in October 1983 but his memory lives on in many ways, including much of the background work in these volumes.

I am delighted that the National Motor Museum at Beaulieu was chosen by The Stationery Office to be its partner in this important work. Beaulieu has been connected with motoring from the earliest days. My father, who had a lifelong interest in all forms of transport, purchased his first car in 1898, followed a year later by the first 4-cylinder Daimler to be built in England, which is now owned by the Science Museum but is a prize exhibit on display at the National Motor Museum. Motoring is in the blood here at Beaulieu, in terms of both driving motor cars and recording their history. My father wrote a number of books about driving in the early days and in 1902 became founder editor of the weekly magazine *Car Illustrated*, which he continued to edit until the beginning of World War I. Many years later, in August 1956, I started *Veteran & Vintage* magazine, which ran through until August 1979 and is now incorporated with *Thoroughbred and Classic Cars*.

Palace House opened to the public in April 1952 with just a few old cars on show, and from this grew the Montagu Motor Museum and latterly the National Motor Museum. In 1960

I opened a Library of Motoring at Beaulieu based on my father's collection of books and in 1962 this was supplemented by a Photographic Library and later, in 1979, a Film and Video Archive. These Libraries are now renowned as important research establishments throughout the motoring world and much of the background research for that first encyclopædia was done by Nick Georgano at Beaulieu, whom I first met when he was trawling through the Montagu Motor Museum Library in Palace House for photographs to use in that first edition. I am pleased that the majority of the photographs in this book have come from our own files here at Beaulieu, supplemented from the private collection of Nick Baldwin, who is Chairman of the National Motor Museum's Advisory Council.

There are motoring historians in practically every country in the world, many of whom are members of the Society of Automotive Historians, and I know that much research in the future will start with a look into this encyclopedia. The study of motoring history is not adequately covered by Universities, one reason being because it is a new subject, but even so its impact on design, engineering and social history has been tremendous. The development of motoring has profoundly influenced the landscape around us and the way we live; the motor vehicle has carried goods to help keep the wheels of industry turning and has completely revolutionised personal mobility. We remember with affection not only our first car and those which have given us good service but also all the bad vehicles that stick in our minds.

Whilst there are nearly 1000 motor museums in the world, relatively few can claim to also be academic institutions, as we strive to do at Beaulieu. As competition increases for people's leisure time, motor museums find themselves struggling to stay afloat and have relatively few resources available for future research or publication. I hope we can reverse this trend in the next few years and I am confident that this great work of reference will be a catalyst for future research.

Montagu of Beaulieu

Acknowledgements

My thanks are due, first and foremost, to the contributors who not only delivered their material on time, but also answered the many queries that inevitably arose during preparation of the entries for the publishers.

I would like to thank Lord Montagu of Beaulieu and Michael Ware, former director of the National Motor Museum, for their tireless efforts to revive the encyclopedia over a number of years, culminating in the successful link with The Stationery Office.

Annice Collett, Marie Tieche, and Mike Budd of the National Motor Museum's Reference Library were always painstaking and prompt in replying to my abstruse queries, as was Jonathan Day of the Photographic Library in providing last-minute photos. Caroline Johnson, Library Secretary, was very helpful in rapid delivery of photocopies and information. The bulk of the illustrations have come from the collections of the National Motor Museum or Nick Baldwin, but others who have provided many excellent and rare photos include Mike Worthington-Williams, Bryan K. Goodman, John A. Conde, Keith Marvin, Halwart Schrader and Ernest Schmid, who lent a number of photos used in his excellent book on Swiss cars. Mike has also been very helpful with additional information and picture identification, as have Malcolm Jeal and Peter Heilbron. Gary Axon and Richard Heseltine gave valuable help with small postwar makes. Philip and Sue Hill toiled for many hours preparing a list of *Automobile Quarterly* entries for the further reading sections. Countless other people have provided help in many ways; to name some would be invidious but to name all would be impossible.

On the publishing side I am deeply grateful to Mick Spencer, Editorial Manager at The Stationery Office; always patient with last-minute changes and additions, he has enabled the encyclopedia to be up-to-date to within three months of publication. The layout has been the responsibility of Designer Guy Myles Warren, who has worked wonders fitting some 3500 photos of assorted shapes and sizes and a text of almost 1.5 million words into something under 2000 pages. The complete text was checked by Editor Sallie Moss, and the galley proofs were read by freelance proof reader Lynne Davies.

Finally, I should thank my wife Jenny without whom this book could never have been produced. She has been responsible for dealing with all correspondence, filing, packing and posting proofs, often at very short notice, as well as providing a steady flow of tea, coffee, and, sometimes, stronger beverages.

NICK GEORGANO
Guernsey, May 2000

Introduction

According to the Oxford English Dictionary, an encyclopedia is 'an elaborate and exhaustive reportory of information on all branches of some particular art or department of knowledge, especially one arranged in alphabetical order.'

This seems as good a definition as any for what we have set out to do in this encyclopedia, although some limitations have to be placed on the concept of exhaustiveness. For a name to qualify as a 'make of car', there must be some evidence of an intention to manufacture, even if it was not a success, and resulted in no more than a single prototype. This is clearly not a water-tight definition, for to establish 'intention to manufacture' one would have to read the minds of men long dead. In the early days many people built a car to prove to themsleves that they could do so, and to make some improvements on what had gone before. Their friends might say "That's nice, will you make one for me?" and some sort of production would follow. Louis Renault might never have become a manufacturer had friends not admired his first effort and asked for replicas. Many of his contemporaries took a stand at the Paris Salon on which to show their hastily-assembled prototype, and if no customers came forward they went no further, and never formed a company. These must, nevertheless, be considered as makes.

On the other hand there were countless backyard tinkerers who built a car or two purely for their own amusement, but through lack of capital or interest in business never planned to make cars for sale. They flourished chiefly in the years up to 1914, though some appeared up to World War II, such as Willard L. Morrison of Buchanan, Michigan, who built a Ford V8-powered streamlined sedan in 1935.

Also in this category are the 19th century steam car makers, with the honourable exception of Thomas Rickett, who not only buiilt two 3-wheelers to the order of British aristocrats, but placed an advertisement in *The Engineer* offering replicas for sale. This earns him a place in the encyclopædia, unlike his contemporaries Yarrow & Hilditch or on the Continent, Etienne Lenoir, Gustav Hammel, or Siegfried Markus, whose vehicles were purely experimental.

Other categories not included are the following;

1 Motorcycles are obviously ruled out, though some 2-wheelers with car-like bodywork, such as the Atlantic, Monotrace and Whitwood Monocar, are included. A more difficult problem is posed by the distinction between a tricycle and a 3-wheeled car. Early tricycles, such as the De Dion-Bouton, were no more than motorcycles with a third wheel, but from about 1903 a type of vehicle appeared which used the frame, saddle, engine and final drive of a motorcycle with two wheels in front, and a body, often of wickerwork, for a passenger. Known as tri-cars, they were still of motorcycle descent, but gradually the driver's saddle became a seat and the handlebars were replaced by a steering wheel, giving them the appearance of a tandem car on three wheels. With makes such as Riley it is almost impossible to decide at what point they became cars. The more car-like vehicles, such as the Bat or Rexette are included, while the many makes which never progressed beyond saddle, handlebars and wickerwork, are not.

2 Cars built purely for racing, and not usable on public roads, such as Formula One and Indy cars.

3 A number of makes listed in earlier encyclopedias are absent as research has placed them in the one-off experimental category. Sometimes evidence is lacking that they ever built even one car, despite advertising that they did. An exception is made for the Owen of Comeragh Road, which persisted on paper for 36 years, and is one of the great conundrums of motoring history.

No attempt has been made to describe every model made by any firm, large or small. In 1927 Daimler listed 27 models, and to mention them all would be tedious and wasteful of space. However, we have endeavoured to indicate the range of models, highlighting any unconventional or unexpected designs, and technical features which were unusual for the period. Up to about 1900, when there was great diversity, and engines might be at the front, centre or rear of the frame, vertical or horizontal and cooled by water or air, these features are generally mentioned. With the coming of a relatively standard layout of front-mounted vertical water-cooled engine, driving by a 3- or 4-speed sliding pinion gearbox and propeller shaft to a bevel rear axle, it is only the exceptions which are noted. Front wheel brakes were noteworthy in the early 1920s, but later were noteworthy only by their absence, as on the 1950 Bond Minicar or its contemporary, the Mochet.

The dating of cars, especially in the illustration captions, may cause confusion because of the discrepancy between the model and calendar year. Normally the date represents the year in which the car was made, a practice followed by the Dating Committee of the Veteran Car Club of Great Britain. An exception has to be made for American cars, which were generally announced in September or October of their model year. The Mercury was introduced in November 1938, (hence a starting date of 1938 in our entry) but even the first cars were always thought of as 1939 models. Similarly, Ford Thunderbird enthusiasts will not recognise that there was a 1954 Thunderbird, though quite a number were made in that calendar year.

The nationality of a make is indicated by the letter(s) used on touring plates, and refers to the country where the parent firm was located. An exceptions is EU which is not yet a nation state, but is used for Fords built in various European factories and which are quite international in design. The Fiesta is no more British than it is German, Belgian, or Spanish. Dual nationality may occur in two ways:

- Cars like the Pennington which had factories in two countries at the same time, are indicated by (US/GB).
- Cars whose nationality changed for political reasons, such as Bugatti and Mathis, which were German up to 1918 when the province of Alsace became French, are indicated by (D;F).

The makes are listed in alphabetical order, but the following points should be noted:

- Makes which consist of Christian and surnames are listed under the Christian name e.g., Georges Irat, not Irat, Georges.
- Makes beginning with Mc are listed between MCC and M.C.M., not at the beginning of the letter 'M'.

- Makes beginning with De are listed under the letter 'D'. Thus De Lavaud is found in 'D', not 'L'.
- Makes using initial letters joined by 'and', such as S & M Simplex are treated as if they were spelt S M.
- Chinese names are romanised using the Pinyin system.

We hope that this encyclopedia will be not only readable, but accurate. Some familiar stories have been corrected. For example, it was long held that Ned Jordan started his upward progress by marrying the daughter of his boss, Thomas Jeffery. Not so; recent research has revealed that his bride was Lotta Hanna whose father ran a furniture store in Kenosha, Wisconsin. History is being rewritten all the time, and it would be unrealistic to suppose that production figures and other statistics may not be revised in the future. More generally, one cannot do better than quote the words of the great historian and journalist Laurence Pomeroy Jr. 'It is manifestly desirable that any reference book should be wholly free from error, but this is an ideal which it seems impossible to realise. The author can only plead that he, like others, has found that "sudden fits of inadvertancy will surprise vigilance, slight avocations will seduce attention. and casual eclipses of the mind will darken learning"'.

NICK GEORGANO

Guernsey, May 2000

Further Reading

Readers seeking more detailed information are referred to marque histories or serious historical articles in magazines. For obvious reasons of space, we are not including contemporary magazine announcements or road tests. These can be found in the Reference Library at the National Motor Museum, which offers a photocopying service and is happy to answer queries by post, telephone, fax or e-mail.

The Reference Library, National Motor Museum, Beaulieu, Hampshire SO42 7ZN, tel. 01590 614652; fax. 01590 612655; e-mail motoring.library@beaulieu.co.uk

Photographic enquiries should be made to the Photographic Library at the same address, tel. 01590 614656; fax as above; email motoring.pictures@beaulieu.co.uk.

Again, for space reasons we have not referred under each entry to the many excellent books devoted to the makes of one country or era. Among the more valuable of these are:

Great Britain

A to Z of Cars of the 1920s, Nick Baldwin, Bay View Books, 1994.

A to Z of Cars of the 1930s, Michael Sedgwick and Mark Gillies, Bay View Books, 1989.

A to Z of Cars, 1945-1970, Michael Sedgwick and Mark Gillies, (revised by Jon Pressnell),
  Bay View Books, 1993.

A to Z of Cars of the 1970s, Graham Robson, Bay View Books, 1990.

A to Z of Cars of the 1980s, Martin Lewis, Bay View Books, 1998.

The Complete Catalogue of British Cars, David Culshaw and Peter Horrobin,
  Veloce Publishing, 1997.

Germany

Autos in Deutschland 1885-1920, Hans-Heinrich von Fersen, Motorbuch-Verlag, Stuttgart, 1965.

Autos in Deutschland 1920-1945, Werner Oswald, Motorbuch-Verlag, Stuttgart, 1981.

Autos in Deutschland 1945-1975, Werner Oswald, Motorbuch-Verlag, Stuttgart, 1980.

France

In First Gear. The French Automobile Industry to 1914, James M. Laux, Liverpool University Press, 1976.

French Cars 1920–1925, Pierre Dumont, Frederick Warne, 1978.

Toutes les Voitures Francaise 1935, René Bellu, Herme-Vilo,1984.

Toutes les Voitures Francaise 1939, René Bellu, Edita Vilo, 1982.

Les Voitures Francaise des Annees 50 (actually covers 1945-1959), René Bellu, Editions Delville, 1983.

Switzerland

Automobiles Suisses des Origines à nos Jours, Ernest Schmid, Editions du Chateau de Grandson, 1967.

Schweizer Autos, (expanded version of above, in German) Ernest Schmid, Editions du Chateau de Grandson, 1978.

Netherlands

Autodesign in Nederland, Jan Lammerse, Waanders Uitgevers, Zwolle, 1993.

Belgium

Histoire de l'Automobile Belge, Yvette and Jacques Kupélian and Jacques Sirtaine, Editions Paul Legrain, c.1972.

Austria

Gesichte von Oesterreiche Kraftfahrt, Hans Seper, Oesterreiche Wirtschaft Verlag, 1968.

Spain

El Automovil en Espana, Pablo Gimenez Vallador, RACE, Madrid, 1998.

Historia de l'Automobilisme a Catalunya, Javier del Arco, Planita, 1990.

Italy

Marche Italiane Scomparse, Museo dell' Automobile Carlo Biscaretti di Ruffia, Turin, 1972.

Hungary

A Magyer Auto, Zsuppan Istvan, Zrini Kiado, 1994.

Canada

Cars of Canada, Hugh Durnford and Glenn Baechler, McLelland & Stewart, 1973.

United States

There are many titles, but none can rival the incomparable:

The Standard Catalog of American Cars 1805-1942, Beverly Rae Kimes and
   Henry Austin Clark Jr, Krause Publications, 1996.

For more recent cars, and in the same series:

The Standard Catalog of American Cars 1946-1975, edited by John A. Gunnell,
   Krause Publications, 1982.

Japan

Autos made in Japan, Jan P. Norbye, Heicher Verlag, 1991.

Terms and Abbreviations Used

Throughout the encyclopedia technical and other terms are generally described according to current English usage. For the convenience of American readers a short list of the more frequently-used terms whose meaning differs in American usage is given below.

English	American	English	American
bonnet	hood	paraffin	kerosene
boot	trunk	petrol	gasoline
capacity (of engine)	displacement	saloon	sedan
coupé de ville	town car	sedanca de ville	town car
dickey (seat)	rumble seat	shooting-brake	station wagon
engine	motor	silencer	muffler
epicyclic (gears)	planetary (gears)	track	tread
estate car	station wagon	two-stroke	two-cycle
gearbox	transmission	windscreen	windshield
hood	top	wing	fender
mudguard	fender		

The following have generally been used in the text for frequently-repeated terms.

bhp	brake horse power
cc	cubic centimetres
cr	compression ratio
CV	cheveaux-vapeur (French horsepower rating)
fwd	front-wheel drive
GP	Grand Prix
GT	GranTurismo
hp	horse power
ifs	independent front suspension
in	inch(es)
ioe	inlet over exhaust
km	kilometre(s)
km/h	kilometres per hour
kg	kilogram(s)
lb	pound(s)
LPG	liquid petroleum gas
lwb	long wheelbase
mm	millimetre(s)
mpg	miles per gallon
mph	miles per hour
ohc	overhead camshaft(s)
ohv	overhead valve(s)
PS	Pferdestärke (German horsepower rating)
psi	pounds per square inch
rpm	revolutions per minute
rwd	rear-wheel drive
sv	side valve(s)
swb	short wheelbase
TT	Tourist Trophy

1959 AC Ace-Bristol sports car.
NICK GEORGANO/NATIONAL MOTOR MUSEUM

1965 AC Shelby Cobra 7-litre sports car.
NATIONAL MOTOR MUSEUM

1911 Alco 4-seater
NICKY WRIGHT/NATIONAL MOTOR MUSEUM

1931 Alfa Romeo 1750 2-seater sports car
NICKY WRIGHT/NATIONAL MOTOR MUSEUM

1938 Alfa Romeo 2900 Superleggera 2-door coupé.

1974 Alfa Romeo 2000 Spyder.

1950 Allard J2 2-seater sports car.
NATIONAL MOTOR MUSEUM

1937 Alvis Speed 25 2-door sedanca coupé.
NICKY WRIGHT/NATIONAL MOTOR MUSEUM

1972 AMC AMX 2-door coupé.
NICKY WRIGHT/NATIONAL MOTOR MUSEUM

1920 Apperson 8 Sportster.
NICKY WRIGHT/NATIONAL MOTOR MUSEUM

1937 Aston Martin 2-litre Abbott 2-door drop-head coupé.
NICK GEORGANO/NATIONAL MOTOR MUSEUM

1964 Aston Martin DB5 drop-head coupé.
NATIONAL MOTOR MUSEUM

1986 Audi Quattro coupé.
NATIONAL MOTOR MUSEUM

1935 Auburn 851 speedster.
NATIONAL MOTOR MUSEUM

1923 Austin 7 2-door 4-seater.
NATIONAL MOTOR MUSEUM

1935 Austin 7 Ruby 2-door saloon.
NICKY WRIGHT/NATIONAL MOTOR MUSEUM

1948 Austin 16 saloon.
NICK GEORGANO/NATIONAL MOTOR MUSEUM

1952 Austin A90 Atlantic saloon.
NATIONAL MOTOR MUSEUM

1959 Austin SeVen saloon.

1982 Austin Metro 1.3S hatchback.

1954 Austin Healey 100 sports car.
NICK GEORGANO/NATIONAL MOTOR MUSEUM

1972 Austin Healey Sprite competition sports car.
NATIONAL MOTOR MUSEUM

1913 Baker Electric 2-seater.
NICKY WRIGHT/NATIONAL MOTOR MUSEUM

1923 Bentley 3-litre saloon.
NATIONAL MOTOR MUSEUM

1934 Bentley 3½-litre drop-head coupé.
NATIONAL MOTOR MUSEUM

1953 Bentley Continental R coupé.
NICKY WRIGHT/NATIONAL MOTOR MUSEUM

1996 Bentley Continental R coupé.
NATIONAL MOTOR MUSEUM

1938 BMW 328 2-seater sports car.
NATIONAL MOTOR MUSEUM

1958 BMW 507 2-seater sports car.
NATIONAL MOTOR MUSEUM

1984 BMW 323i cabriolet.
NATIONAL MOTOR MUSEUM

1999 BMW Z3 M coupé.
NATIONAL MOTOR MUSEUM

1938 British Salmson 20/90 2-seater sports car.
NICK GEORGANO/NATIONAL MOTOR MUSEUM

1927 Bugatti Type 41 Royale coupé de ville.
NATIONAL MOTOR MUSEUM

1934 Bugatti Type 57 Ventoux coupé.
NICKY WRIGHT/NATIONAL MOTOR MUSEUM

1939 Buick Special, with English convertible Albemarle coachwork by Carlton.
NICKY WRIGHT/NATIONAL MOTOR MUSEUM

1963 Buick Riviera coupé.
NICKY WRIGHT/NATIONAL MOTOR MUSEUM

1931 Cadillac 452-A V16 convertible coupé.
NICKY WRIGHT/NATIONAL MOTOR MUSEUM

1959 Cadillac coupé de ville.
NICKY WRIGHT/NATIONAL MOTOR MUSEUM

1988 Cadillac Allante 2-door convertible.
NATIONAL MOTOR MUSEUM

1954 Chevrolet Corvette sports car.
NICKY WRIGHT/NATIONAL MOTOR MUSEUM

1963 Chevrolet Corvette Stingray coupé.
NATIONAL MOTOR MUSEUM

1963 Chevrolet Corvette Stingray coupé.
NATIONAL MOTOR MUSEUM

1935 Chrysler Airflow sedan.
NATIONAL MOTOR MUSEUM

1955 Chrysler C300 2-door sedan.
NICKY WRIGHT/NATIONAL MOTOR MUSEUM

1922 Citroen Type C 5CV 2-seater.
NATIONAL MOTOR MUSEUM

1952 Citroen Light 15 4-door saloon.
NATIONAL MOTOR MUSEUM

1959 Citroen 2CV CI 4-door saloon.

1972 Citroen DS21 Pallas 4-door saloon.

1994 Citroen Xantia SX 4-door saloon.
NATIONAL MOTOR MUSEUM

1936 Cord 810 convertible phaeton.
NICKY WRIGHT/NATIONAL MOTOR MUSEUM

1974 DAF 44 2-door saloon.
NICK GEORGANO/NATIONAL MOTOR MUSEUM

1995 Daimler Double Six saloon.
NATIONAL MOTOR MUSEUM

1978 Datsun 260Z coupé.
NATIONAL MOTOR MUSEUM

1901 De Dion-Bouton *vis-à-vis*.
NATIONAL MOTOR MUSEUM

1975 De Tomaso Pantera GTS coupé.
NATIONAL MOTOR MUSEUM

1937 Delage D8 coupé.
NATIONAL MOTOR MUSEUM

1947 Delahaye 135 MS 2-door cabriolet.
NATIONAL MOTOR MUSEUM

1929 Duesenberg Model J convertible roadster.
NICKY WRIGHT/NATIONAL MOTOR MUSEUM

1988 Excalibur Series VI sedan.
NICKY WRIGHT/NATIONAL MOTOR MUSEUM

1960 Facel Vega HK500 2-door coupé.
NATIONAL MOTOR MUSEUM

1950 Ferrari 166 Barchetta sports car.
NICKY WRIGHT/NATIONAL MOTOR MUSEUM

1960 Ferrari 250GT cabriolet.
NATIONAL MOTOR MUSEUM

1964 Ferrari 330GT coupé.
NATIONAL MOTOR MUSEUM

1974 Ferrari Dino 246GT spyder.
NICKY WRIGHT/NATIONAL MOTOR MUSEUM

1982 Ferrari BB512 coupé.
NICKY WRIGHT/NATIONAL MOTOR MUSEUM

1985 Ferrari Testa Rossa coupé.
NATIONAL MOTOR MUSEUM

1996 Ferrari F50 coupé.
NATIONAL MOTOR MUSEUM

1937 Fiat Topolino 500 saloon.
NICKY WRIGHT/NATIONAL MOTOR MUSEUM

1977 Fiat 127 hatchback.
NATIONAL MOTOR MUSEUM

1983 Fiat Uno 55S hatchback.
NATIONAL MOTOR MUSEUM

1981 Fiat X1/9 targa sports car.
NATIONAL MOTOR MUSEUM

2000 Fiat Multipla MPV.
FIAT SPA

1914 Ford Model T 2-seater.
NATIONAL MOTOR MUSEUM

1930 Ford Model A phaeton.
NATIONAL MOTOR MUSEUM

1933 Ford V8 cabriolet.
NATIONAL MOTOR MUSEUM

1956 Ford Thunderbird 2-door convertible.
NATIONAL MOTOR MUSEUM

1957 Ford Zodiac Hyline saloon.
NATIONAL MOTOR MUSEUM

1964 Ford Mustang 2-door convertible.
NICKY WRIGHT/NATIONAL MOTOR MUSEUM

1978 Ford Capri Ghia 3-litre coupé.

1996 Ford Mondeo GLX saloon.

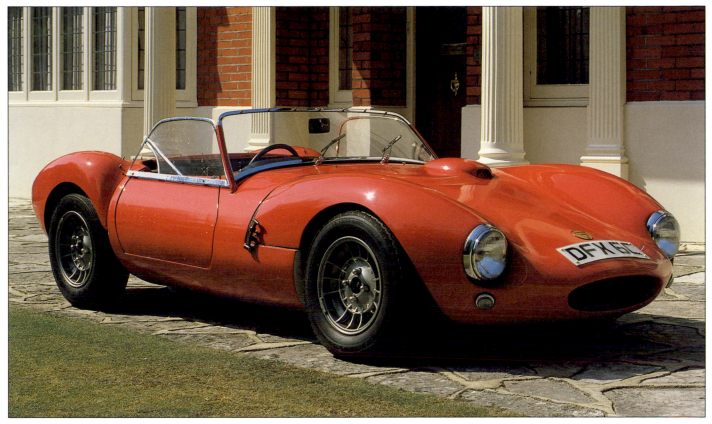

1964 Ginetta G4 sports car.
NATIONAL MOTOR MUSEUM

1965 Gordon Keeble 2-door coupé.
NATIONAL MOTOR MUSEUM

1950 Healey Silverstone sports car.
NICKY WRIGHT/NATIONAL MOTOR MUSEUM

1963 Hillman Imp 2-door saloon.
NATIONAL MOTOR MUSEUM

1912 Hispano-Suiza Alfonso sports car.
NICKY WRIGHT/NATIONAL MOTOR MUSEUM

1924 Hispano-Suiza Tulip Wood H6C dual phaeton.
NATIONAL MOTOR MUSEUM

1967 Honda S800 convertible.
NICKY WRIGHT/NATIONAL MOTOR MUSEUM

1992 Honda NSX coupé.
NATIONAL MOTOR MUSEUM

1950 Hotchkiss 2-door cabriolet.
NATIONAL MOTOR MUSEUM

1957 Hudson Hornet 4-door sedan.
NICKY WRIGHT/NATIONAL MOTOR MUSEUM

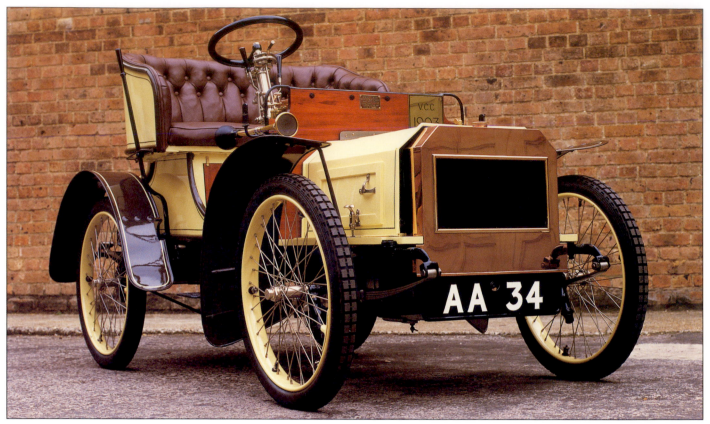

1903 Humberette 5hp 2-seater.
NICKY WRIGHT/NATIONAL MOTOR MUSEUM

1934 Invicta 4½-litre S Type Salmons drop-head coupé.
NATIONAL MOTOR MUSEUM

1937 Jaguar SS100 2-seater sports car.
NATIONAL MOTOR MUSEUM

1950 Jaguar XK120 2-seater sports car.
NICKY WRIGHT/NATIONAL MOTOR MUSEUM

1954 Jaguar MkVII saloon.
NICK GEORGANO/NATIONAL MOTOR MUSEUM

1962 Jaguar Mk2 3.4 saloon.
NICK GEORGANO/NATIONAL MOTOR MUSEUM

1963 Jaguar E Type roadster.
NATIONAL MOTOR MUSEUM

1985 Jaguar XJ6 saloon.
NICK GEORGANO/NATIONAL MOTOR MUSEUM

1997 Jaguar XK8 convertible.
NATIONAL MOTOR MUSEUM

1974 Jensen Interceptor coupé.
NICKY WRIGHT/NATIONAL MOTOR MUSEUM

1953 Jowett Javelin saloon.
NICK GEORGANO/NATIONAL MOTOR MUSEUM

1938 Lagonda V12 4-door saloon.
NICKY WRIGHT/NATIONAL MOTOR MUSEUM

1968 Lamborghini Miura P400 coupé.
NATIONAL MOTOR MUSEUM

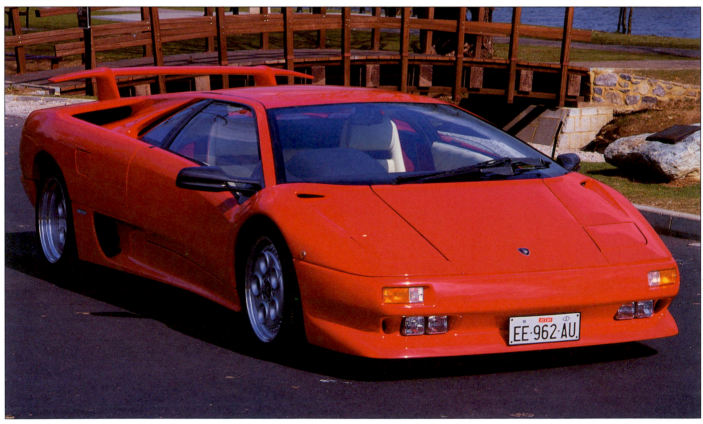

1993 Lamborghini Diablo coupé.
NATIONAL MOTOR MUSEUM

1908 Lanchester 20hp landaulet.
NATIONAL MOTOR MUSEUM

1928 Lancia Lambda 8th series tourer.
NATIONAL MOTOR MUSEUM

1937 Lancia Aprilia 4-door saloon.
NATIONAL MOTOR MUSEUM

1973 Lancia Stratos coupé.
NATIONAL MOTOR MUSEUM

1941 Lincoln Continental club coupé.
NATIONAL MOTOR MUSEUM

1962 Lotus Elite 2-seater hardtop.
NATIONAL MOTOR MUSEUM

1972 Lotus Elan Sprint 2-seater sports car.
NATIONAL MOTOR MUSEUM

1996 Lotus Elise 2-seater sports car.
NATIONAL MOTOR MUSEUM

1949 Maserati A6-1500 coupé.
NICKY WRIGHT/NATIONAL MOTOR MUSEUM

1973 Maserati Bora coupé.
NICK GEORGANO/NATIONAL MOTOR MUSEUM

1982 Mazda RX7 Elford Turbo coupé.
NATIONAL MOTOR MUSEUM

1995 Mazda MX5 2-seater sports car.
NATIONAL MOTOR MUSEUM

1907 Mercedes 40/45 Simplex tourer.
NATIONAL MOTOR MUSEUM

1929 Mercedes-Benz SS 38/250 tourer.
NATIONAL MOTOR MUSEUM

1935 Mercedes -Benz 500K convertible coupé.
NATIONAL MOTOR MUSEUM

1957 Mercedes-Benz 300SL Gullwing coupé.
NATIONAL MOTOR MUSEUM

1965 Mercedes-Benz 600 limousine.
NATIONAL MOTOR MUSEUM

1993 Mercedes-Benz S280 saloon.
NATIONAL MOTOR MUSEUM

1955 Messerschmitt KR200 bubblecar.
NATIONAL MOTOR MUSEUM

1930 MG M Midget sports car.
NATIONAL MOTOR MUSEUM

1933 MG J2 Midget sports car.
NICK GEORGANO/NATIONAL MOTOR MUSEUM

1947 MG TC Midget sports car.
NATIONAL MOTOR MUSEUM

1955 MGA 1600 MkI sports car.
NATIONAL MOTOR MUSEUM

1971 MGB roadster.
NICKY WRIGHT/NATIONAL MOTOR MUSEUM

1995 MGF 1.8i sports car.
ROVER GROUP

1948 Morgan 4/4 sports car.
NICKY WRIGHT/NATIONAL MOTOR MUSEUM

1990 Morgan Plus 8 sports car.
NATIONAL MOTOR MUSEUM

2000 Morgan Aero 8 sports car.
MORGAN CARS

1926 Morris Bullnose saloon.
NATIONAL MOTOR MUSEUM

1949 Morris Minor saloon.
NICKY WRIGHT/NATIONAL MOTOR MUSEUM

1960 Morris Minor Traveller estate car.
NATIONAL MOTOR MUSEUM

1964 Morris Mini Cooper 'S' saloon.
NATIONAL MOTOR MUSEUM

1974 NSU Ro80 4-door saloon.
NATIONAL MOTOR MUSEUM

1912 Opel 5/14 2-seater.
NATIONAL MOTOR MUSEUM

1971 Opel GT coupé.
NATIONAL MOTOR MUSEUM

1920 Packard Twin 6 3-35 landaulet.
NICKY WRIGHT/NATIONAL MOTOR MUSEUM

1939 Packard 120 Series 1700 convertible.
NICKY WRIGHT/NATIONAL MOTOR MUSEUM

1947 Packard Clipper Custom Super 8 sedan.
NICKY WRIGHT/NATIONAL MOTOR MUSEUM

1899 Panhard 6hp wagonette.
NICK GEORGANO/NATIONAL MOTOR MUSEUM

1955 Pegaso Z102B coupé.
NICKY WRIGHT/NATIONAL MOTOR MUSEUM

1937 Peugeot 402B 4-door saloon.
NICK GEORGANO/NATIONAL MOTOR MUSEUM

1989 Peugeot 205 Gti 1.9 hatchback.
NATIONAL MOTOR MUSEUM

1996 Peugeot 306 Gti-6 hatchback.
PEUGEOT

1913 Pierce Arrow Gentleman's Roadster.
NATIONAL MOTOR MUSEUM

1930 Pierce Arrow 7-passenger phaeton.
NATIONAL MOTOR MUSEUM

1969 Piper GTT 1.6-litre coupé.
NICK GEORGANO/NATIONAL MOTOR MUSEUM

1970 Plymouth AAR 'Cuda hard top.
NICKY WRIGHT/NATIONAL MOTOR MUSEUM

1965 Pontiac GTO coupé.
NICKY WRIGHT/NATIONAL MOTOR MUSEUM

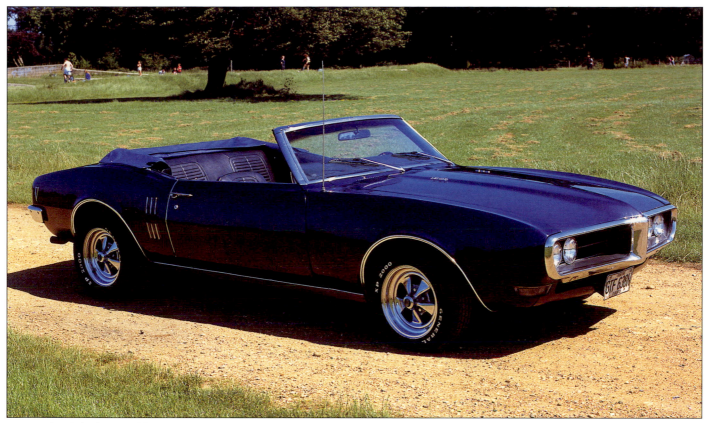

1968 Pontiac Firebird convertible.
NICKY WRIGHT/NATIONAL MOTOR MUSEUM

1951 Porsche 356 cabriolet.
NATIONAL MOTOR MUSEUM

1961 Porsche 356B Super coupé.
NICK GEORGANO/NATIONAL MOTOR MUSEUM

1961 Porsche 356B Super coupé.
NICK GEORGANO/NATIONAL MOTOR MUSEUM

1997 Porsche 911 coupé.
PORSCHE CARS GREAT BRITAIN

1911 Renault AX 2-seater.
NATIONAL MOTOR MUSEUM

1928 Renault NN-2 tourer.
NICK GEORGANO/NATIONAL MOTOR MUSEUM

1958 Renault 4CV saloon.
NICKY WRIGHT/NATIONAL MOTOR MUSEUM

1977 Renault 16TX hatchback.
NICK GEORGANO/NATIONAL MOTOR MUSEUM

1982 Renault 5 Gordini Turbo hatchback.
NATIONAL MOTOR MUSEUM

1986 Renault Espace 2000TSE MPV.
NATIONAL MOTOR MUSEUM

1937 Riley Sprite 2-seater sports car.
NICKY WRIGHT/NATIONAL MOTOR MUSEUM

1911 Rolls-Royce Silver Ghost Holmes torpedo tourer.
NATIONAL MOTOR MUSEUM

1936 Rolls-Royce 25/30 Tickford cabriolet.
NICK GEORGANO/NATIONAL MOTOR MUSEUM

1938 Rolls-Royce Phantom III Park Ward saloon.
NATIONAL MOTOR MUSEUM

1958 Rolls-Royce Silver Cloud I saloon.
NATIONAL MOTOR MUSEUM

1960 Rover 100 P4 saloon.
NATIONAL MOTOR MUSEUM

2000 Rover 75 saloon.
ROVER GROUP

1993 Range Rover V8 3.9 estate car.
NATIONAL MOTOR MUSEUM

1948 Land Rover pick-up.
NATIONAL MOTOR MUSEUM

1966 Saab 96 saloon.
NATIONAL MOTOR MUSEUM

1988 Saab 900 turbo 2-door saloon.
NATIONAL MOTOR MUSEUM

1927 Salmson VAL 3 tourer.
NICK GEORGANO/NATIONAL MOTOR MUSEUM

1957 Simca Aronde Plein Ciel coupé.
NATIONAL MOTOR MUSEUM

1963 Skoda Felicia Super convertible.
NICK BALDWIN

1963 Studebaker Avanti coupé.
NICKY WRIGHT/NATIONAL MOTOR MUSEUM

1999 Subaru Impreza Turbo RB5 saloon.
SUBARU

1987 Toyota MR2 sports car.
NATIONAL MOTOR MUSEUM

1955 Triumph TR2 sports car.
NATIONAL MOTOR MUSEUM

1973 Triumph Stag convertible.
NATIONAL MOTOR MUSEUM

1980 Triumph TR7 convertible.
NATIONAL MOTOR MUSEUM

1948 Tucker Torpedo sedan.
NICKY WRIGHT/NATIONAL MOTOR MUSEUM

1996 TVR Cerbera coupé.
NATIONAL MOTOR MUSEUM

1915 Vauxhall Prince Henry tourer.
NATIONAL MOTOR MUSEUM

1920 Vauxhall 30-98 E Type 2-seater.
NATIONAL MOTOR MUSEUM

1939 Vauxhall 10hp saloon.
NATIONAL MOTOR MUSEUM

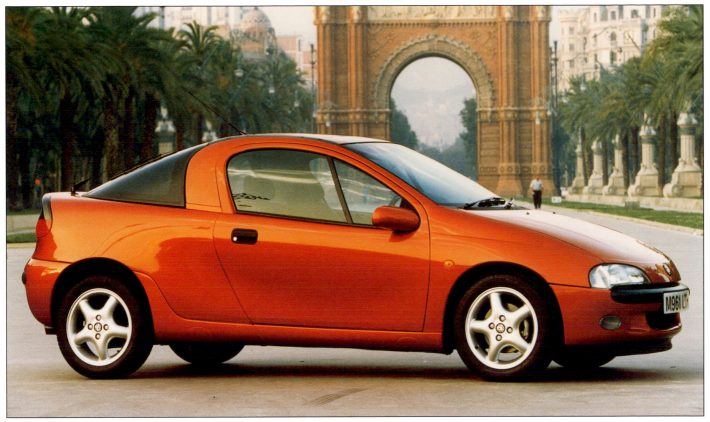

1999 Vauxhall Tigra 1.6i 16v coupé.
VAUXHALL

1970 Volkswagen Beetle 1500 saloon.
NICK GEORGANO/NATIONAL MOTOR MUSEUM

1985 Volkswagen Golf Gti hatchback.
NATIONAL MOTOR MUSEUM

1962 Volvo P1800S coupé.
NATIONAL MOTOR MUSEUM

1985 Volkswagen Golf Gti hatchback.
NATIONAL MOTOR MUSEUM

1962 Volvo P1800S coupé.
NATIONAL MOTOR MUSEUM

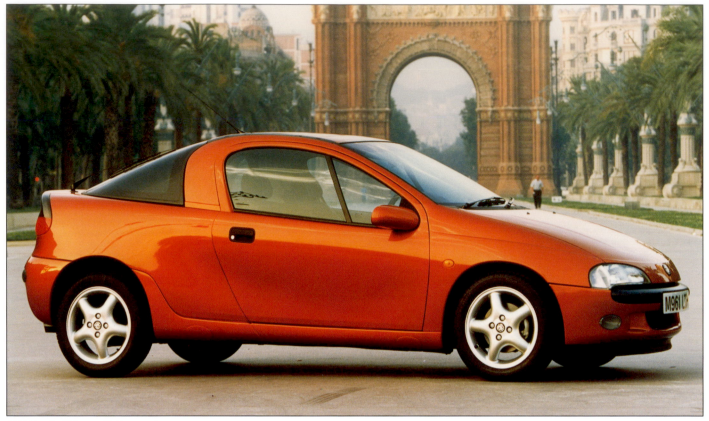

1999 Vauxhall Tigra 1.6i 16v coupé.
VAUXHALL

1970 Volkswagen Beetle 1500 saloon.
NICK GEORGANO/NATIONAL MOTOR MUSEUM

GABRIEL (i) (US) 1910–1912

Gabriel Auto Co., Cleveland, Ohio.

This company grew out of the carriage makers W.H. Gabriel Carriage & Wagon Co., which had been founded in 1851. They announced a 25/30hp 4-cylinder tourer in March 1910, and made a limited number for two years. The introduction of trucks in 1913 proved more profitable, and passenger cars were dropped. Trucks continued to be made up to 1918.

NG

GABRIEL (ii) (F) 1912–1914

Gabriel Campana, Paris.

The Gabriel was a conventional car made in three 4-cylinder models, a 1943cc 9/12CV, 2722cc 13/18CV and 4500cc 20/30CV. All models had 4-speed gearboxes and shaft drive.

NG

GABRY (I) 1963

Aeronautica Macchi SpA, Milan.

The Gabry was a microcar produced by an aeronautical firm. It looked quite modern for 1963, with a smartly-styled plastic body featuring two sliding doors for access. The rear-mounted engine was a 150cc single-cylinder 2-stroke unit developing 6bhp, although later a 250cc 13bhp twin was fitted. The Gabry remained in prototype form.

CR

GADABOUT (US) 1914–1916

1914–1915 Gadabout Motor Corp., Newark, New Jersey.
1915–1916 Gadabout Motor Corp., Detroit, Michigan.

The Gadabout had a conventional chassis and was powered by a 12hp 4-cylinder Sterling engine. Its body was distinctly unconventional, being made of wickerwork, which was lighter than metal and was claimed to give a more comfortable ride. It was also easy to clean; after the seats had been removed, a hose could be turned directly through the body, cleaning it inside and out in a few minutes. Described by the makers as 'the aristocrat of cyclecars', the Gadabout had a 2-speed gearbox and shaft drive. In 1915 the makers moved to Detroit, added 18in (457mm) to the wheelbase and abandoned the wickerwork for steel. In the late summer of 1916 the Gadabout's promoter Philip Heseltine launched a new company at Buffalo to make the HESELTINE light car.

NG

GAETH (US) 1902–1910

Gaeth Motor Car Co., Cleveland, Ohio.

Paul Gaeth (1873–1952) was a German-born immigrant who built two experimental cars, one steam-powered and one with an internal combustion engine, in 1898. The following year he built another, which he sold for $500, then formed the PEOPLE'S Automobile Co. which made buses and cars for two years. In 1902 he set up his own company, financed by local businessmen, and made about 25 examples of a light car with single- or 2-cylinder engine, epicyclic transmission, chain drive and 2- or 4-seater bodies. These were sold under the name Gaethmobile.

In 1904 he brought out a larger car with a 25/30hp 3-cylinder engine mounted horizontally under the seat, also with planetary transmission but now with shaft drive. It was known as the Gaeth Triplex, but by 1906 had given way to a more conventional car with front-mounted vertical engine, and these made up the Gaeth range for the rest of the company's existence. They were made in several sizes, 20/24, 30/34, 50/54hp, ending up with a 40/45hp in 1910. Originally no more expensive than the $2600 Triplex, they grew in price, and the 1910 models ran from $3500 to $4500. Gaeth was no businessman, and his company was taken over by the STUYVESANT Motor Co. in November 1910. A modified version of Gaeth's 4-cylinder car was made as the Stuyvesant Four 40/45. Total production of Gaeths was about 300 cars. Paul later ran a small garage and workshop in Cleveland, driving a Gaeth car into the mid-1920s, and working on cars new and old, but preferably old, until his death at the age of 79.

NG

1908 Gaeth XXI 40/45hp tourer.
NICK BALDWIN

1907 Gaggenau in Circuit des Ardennes.
NATIONAL MOTOR MUSEUM

GAGGENAU (D) 1905–1911

1905–1910 Süddeutsche Automobilfabrik GmbH, Gaggenau.
1910–1911 Benz-Werke Gaggenau GmbH, Gaggenau.

BERGMANN's Industriewerke extended its vehicle activities in 1905. The former LILIPUT was continued and often appeared under the name of Safe. In 1907 the range was enlarged by 18/22PS and 24/36PS versions under the name Gaggenau. The Types 35 (4700cc, 55bhp) and 60 (8830cc, 75bhp) used modern engines with a single overhead camshaft driven by vertical shaft. They ranked among the most advanced designs on the market at that time. The first car to cross Africa from East to West (Dar-es-Salaam to Swakopmund, a distance of 630 miles) was a Gaggenau. In 1907 the factory was taken over by Benz, which concentrated on the production of commercials there, though the Types 35 and 60 were continued for a short time.

HON

GAIA (GB) 1996 to date

1996–1997 Gaia Cars, Dibden Purlieu, Hampshire.
1997 to date Gaia Cars, Parkstone, Dorset.

Described by its manufacturer as 'a fusion of superbike and supercar' and 'Batman meets Stealth bomber' the Gaia Deltoid was a dramatically styled 3-wheeler. A complete motorbike rear section (usually Suzuki) bolted on to a steel tube front half, and the car could even be converted back to a motorbike with little trouble. The centre section of the wild fibreglass bodywork was bonded to the chassis. Early cars were designed with a 'fighter pilot' style sliding canopy but the design was set to be altered to accept gull-wing doors.

CR

GAINSBOROUGH (GB) 1902–1903

Gainsborough Motor Engineering Co. Ltd, Gainsborough, Lincolnshire.

This was a somewhat unusual car with a 16hp horizontal 4-cylinder engine mounted under the floorboards. The complex engine was described by *The Motor Car Journal* as 'having connecting rods outside the cylinder and fixed to a shaft which passes transversely through the cylinder and piston, conveying the power to the crankshaft. At the point where the shaft goes through the cylinder, the latter is slotted, the slots being equal in length to that of the stroke'. The car had chain drive to a 2-speed gearbox, and final drive was also by chain. The body, called the Duchess, was a 4-seater tonneau, the rear part of which could be converted to an aluminium closed brougham.

NG

GAITAN (E) 1953
Construcciones Gaitan SL, Seville.
This was a little 3-wheeler with a motorcycle engine and was produced by a company which specialised in the production of invalid cars.

VCM

GALASSI (I) 1947–1950
Zeno Galassi, Macerata.
One of many stylish microcar hopefuls built in Italy after the war, the Galassi was a doorless 2-seater roadster with aluminium bodywork. A 2-cylinder 2-stroke 250cc engine was mounted in the tail, developing 6.5bhp.

CR

GALBA; HUASCAR (F) 1929–1931
1929–1930 Sté Sylla, Courbevoie, Seine.
1930–1931 Voiturettes Huascar, Courbevoie, Seine.
These two cars, of essentially similar design, were the work of Marcel Violet, the tireless exponent of the 2-stroke engine, who had previously been responsible for the VIOLET BOGEY, MAJOR, MOURRE, SIMA-VIOLET and DEGUINGAND cars. The Galba, named after a Roman emperor, had a 564cc 2-stroke vertical twin engine, a 2-speed gearbox and shaft drive. Front suspension was by transverse leaves, as on Violet's previous efforts. It was very reasonably priced, a 2-seater costing the equivalent of £75. For 1931 Violet offered a similar car, with engine capacity increased to 625cc, under the name Huascar.

NG

GALE (US) 1905–1907
Western Tool Works, Galesburg, Illinois.
The first Gale was a 2-seater runabout powered by an 8hp single-cylinder horizontal engine mounted under the seat. Five of these were made in 1905, but in 1906 more than 100 cars were made in an expanded line which included an 18/20hp 2-cylinder model with tourer or runabout bodies, as well as the single. A feature of the Gale was the tilting body hinged at the rear, so that the whole body could be lifted up when the engine needed attention. By 1907 there were two twins, a 14hp and a 24/26hp, and engines were now mounted at the front. About 600 of the single-cylinder cars and 140 twins were made, and they were exported quite widely, going to Canada, Europe, Australia, New Zealand, and Borneo.

NG

GALE FOUR (US) 1920
Garde Gale, Indianapolis, Indiana.
The Gale Four was introduced at the Indianapolis Automobile Show in 1920 but went no further. Gale was unable to find the necessary financial backing to put the car into production although the car sparked the interest of Lynn McCurdy, an automobile enthusiast and the son of Col. W. H. McCurdy of the Hercules Corp. of Evansville, Indiana. Plans for further development of the Gale Four by Hercules followed. This resulted in changing the four to a six named after McCurdy. The McCurdy Six failed to get into production although several pilot models were completed.

KM

GALILEO (I) 1904
Officine Galileo, Florence.
This company was a small-scale producer of electric cars, some of which were exported to the United States.

NG

GALKAR see RADWAN

GALLET ET ITASSE (F) 1900–1901
Gallet et Itasse, Boulogne-sur-Seine.
Also known as La Gazelle, the Gallet et Itasse voiturette was powered by a 2.5hp De Dion-Bouton engine geared to the rear axle. The front wheels were carried in cycle-type forks, and front suspension was by vertical compressed air plungers. By early 1901 G. Itasse was on his own, and was making a voiturette powered by an Aster engine, with single-chain drive.

NG

GALLIA see REGINA (i)

GALLICA (F) 1920–1924
Made in Bordeaux, the Gallica used a number of Ford Model T components, although a surviving example shows considerable differences. The front suspension has longitudinal semi-elliptic springs instead of the Ford's transverse spring, and the radiator and body are unlike any T. Probably the engine and transmission came from Ford, whose factory at Bordeaux would have been conveniently near for the makers of the Gallica to obtain components. The survivor has a coupé de ville body.

NG

GALLIOT (F) 1908
Sté d'Allumage Électrique et d'Accessoires, Paris.
This was an unusual tandem 2-seater in which the single-cylinder engine was mounted between the front and rear seats. The radiator was behind the engine and formed a dashboard for the rear seat, whose occupant was responsible for the steering. Final drive was by single chain. A more powerful Anzani radial 3-cylinder engine was projected. The company was still listed in 1910 and 1911, but without details of their cars.

NG

GALLOWAY (i) (US) 1908–1911
The William Galloway Co., Waterloo, Iowa.
Founded in 1906, the Galloway company made agricultural equipment and decided to enter the car field in 1908 with a high-wheeler that could double as a load carrier and as a passenger vehicle that could take a large family to church on Sunday. It had a 14hp 2-cylinder engine, chain drive and solid tyres. In 1910 William Galloway persuaded Fred Maytag to move production of the MAYTAG car to Waterloo by investing in Maytag's business. He also made a few 4-cylinder tourers which were simply rebadged Maytags. He was subsequently involved with the Dart Manufacturing Co. which made the successful Dart truck, and in 1917 went in for more badge engineering when he sold a rebadged ARGO light car under the name Arabian.

NG

GALLOWAY (ii) (GB) 1921–1928
1921–1922 Galloway Engineering Co. Ltd, Tongland, Kirkcudbright.
1923–1928 Galloway Engineering Ltd, Heathhall, Dumfries.
The Galloway was a light car made by a subsidiary of ARROL-JOHNSTON, to extend the range into a lower-priced bracket, and also to use up components left over from the disastrous Arrol-Johnston Victory model. It was based on the Fiat 501, and had a 1460cc monobloc side-valve engine with detachable cylinder head and the central ball gearchange from the Victory. This car's other contribution to the Galloway was that its rear axles were melted down to form the Galloway's cylinder blocks. Various body styles were offered, mostly 2- and 4-seater open tourers. The Galloway was designed by T.C. Pullinger, formerly with Sunbeam and Humber, and he put his daughter Dorothée in charge of the former aero engine factory at Tongland, with a largely female workforce.

The Galloway only lasted for two years at Tongland, after which surplus capacity at Arrol-Johnston's factory at Heathhall made it more economic to combine production of both makes under one roof. However, the Galloway company kept its separate identity. For 1925 there was an additional, larger, Galloway, the Twelve, which shared the 1669cc engine of the 12hp Arrol-Johnston. It was dropped from the A-J range in 1926, as was the smaller Galloway. From then until 1928 the 1669cc 12/30 was the only Galloway model, getting ohvs and front wheel brakes. It was, in effect, a small Arrol-Johnston, a fact reinforced by its similar radiator. Closed bodies were offered, coupés and saloons, and artillery wheels replaced the characteristic discs of the earlier Galloways. Production ended in 1928, at the same time as that of Arrol-Johnston.

NG

GALOPIN (GB) 1992
Bonny Days, Ryde, Isle of Wight.
A company run by the man who designed the Frogeye replica produced the Galopin, which was a Vignale Gamine ('Noddy car') replica based on Fiat 126 floorpan. A version with electric power was also developed.

CR

GALT (i) (CDN) 1911–1913
Canadian Motors Ltd, Galt, Ontario.
This company aimed to produce a fully-equipped medium-priced car in which items such as lamps, hood, speedometer and comprehensive tool kit would be included in the price. Before they were able to make such a car themselves, they imported cars from the ALPENA Motor Co. of Alpena, Michigan. The Alpena Model C became the Canada Tourist, and the Model D the Canada Roadster. They were offered with either lhd or rhd and were guaranteed for life. By the spring of 1911 Canadian Motors were assembling cars at Galt; they were still based on the Alpena, and used the same Hazard engines. Bodies were built by the Guelph Carriage Co. For 1912 the Galt was offered with an electric starter, following Cadillac's lead and being the first Canadian car to be so fitted. Unfortunately they chose an unreliable system, and the problems with this did their reputation no good at all. Also, the Model E Special which used the electric starter was expensive at CDN$2350. For 1913 they adopted a different starting system on the Model G, which was the largest Galt, with a 40/45hp engine and a price tag of CDN$2750. The directors of Canadian Motors decided to close the factory before the end of 1913. Not more than 50 Galts were sold in all.

NG

GALT (ii) (CDN) 1913–1914
Galt Motor Co., Galt, Ontario.
Two Galt engineers, Moffat St Claire and Eddy Fleming began experimenting with petrol-electric drive in 1911. When Canadian Motors, makers of the GALT (i), closed down, the partners bought up the remaining components and assembled ten cars which they sold as Galts to raise funds for their petrol-electric car. This emerged in 1914 with a 2-cylinder 2-stroke engine running on a mixture of petrol and paraffin. This drove a Westinghouse generator which recharged the batteries and powered an electric motor to drive the rear wheels. The car could travel 15-20 miles on the batteries alone. It was fitted with a modified Canadian Motors Galt tourer body and used by St Clair until 1927. It was resurrected in 1941 and fitted with an ugly coupé body and undersized wheels. One other Galt petrol-electric car was built in 1914, but soon scrapped.

NG

GALY (F) 1954–1957
Automobiles Galy, Paris.
Launched at the 1954 Salon de Paris, the Galy was a very small 2-seater coupé with pleasing metal bodywork, produced by a forged and cast metalworks. The chassis was tubular and the suspension used rubber. A choice of models with various rear-mounted single-cylinder engines was offered: the Vistand (with an Ydral 175cc 11bhp 2-stroke), and the Vibel and Visport (with an AMC 250cc 15bhp 4-stroke, upgraded in 1955 to 280cc). At the 1955 Salon, a Willys Jeep-style steel body was shown on the basis of a Vistand but this probably did not enter production. Despite competitive pricing, only around 100 cars of all types were sold.

CR

G.A.M. (F) 1930
Éts G.A.M. St Étienne.
This was a cyclecar with two seats in tandem. 1930 was very late for such a design, which harked back to the Bedelia, of 1910–14, and the G.A.M. did not go into production.

NG

1922 Galloway(ii) 10.5hp 2-seater.
NATIONAL MOTOR MUSEUM

1928 Galloway (ii) 12/30hp coupé.
M.J.WORTHINGTON-WILLIAMS

1903 Gamage 6hp 2-seater.
NATIONAL MOTOR MUSEUM

GAMAGE (GB) 1903–1904; 1914–1915
A.W. Gamage Ltd, Holborn, London.
The famous department store had several involvements with car sales, as well as offering a wide variety of accessories. Their first cars were single- and 2-cylinder light cars with De Dion-Bouton or Aster engines, almost certainly built by LACOSTE ET BATTMANN in Paris. They had 3-speed gearboxes and shaft drive. Gamages were also selling De Dion-Boutons and Renaults at this time.

1926 G.A.R. 7CV tourer.
M.J.WORTHINGTON-WILLIAMS

The next Gamage car appeared in 1914, and was a light car powered by a 1½-litre 4-cylinder Chapuis-Dornier engine which could be started from the driver's seat by a cable linkage. It is not known who made this car for Gamages as they certainly had no factory of their own. In 1920 they were selling the German S.B. (Slaby Beringer) single-seater electric cyclecar.

NG

GAMBIER ET DUFLOS (F) 1900–1901

This Paris-based partnership exhibited a car at the 1900 Paris Salon with a single-cylinder horizontal engine which was geared to an intermediate shaft carrying the gear wheels, with belt final drive.

NG

GAMMA (F) 1921–1922

Sté des Automobiles Gamma, Courbevoie, Seine.
The Gamma was a conventional light car powered by either a 1590cc Ballot or 1994cc Altos engine, both 4-cylinder side-valve units. It had a handsome vee-radiator which gave it a certain air of distinction, despite its uninspiring engines.

NG

GANZ see RAPID (iv)

GANZHONG (CHI) 1997

Ganzhong Auto Corp., Yichun City, Jiangxi Province.
The Ganzhong Corp. was a very small auto factory producing 4-wheel drive vehicles of the Cherokee class. The Ganzhong 6300 was a small car made of polyester with a length of 3m.

EVIS

G.A.R. (F) 1922–1934

1922–1929 Cyclecars G.A.R., Clichy, Seine.
1929–1934 Gardahaut et Cie, Asnières, Seine.
The G.A.R. took its name from the first three letters of the surname of its creator, M. Gardahaut. It began as a cyclecar powered by a 2-cylinder engine, but soon grew into a small sports car powered by C.I.M.E., S.C.A.P. or Chapuis-Dornier engines. These were in several sizes, to meet various racing regulations, and varied from 840 to 1095cc. The latter was an ohv Chapuis-Dornier with three valves per cylinder which was used in the G.A.R.s raced at Le Mans. A 1492cc straight-8 S.C.A.P. engine was also offered.

The failure of Chapuis-Dornier in 1928, due largely to the collapse of their best customer, Benjamin, led M. Gardahaut to make his own engines. Launched at the 1929 Paris Salon, one was a 770cc 4-cylinder single-ohc unit, made *en bloc* with a 4-speed gearbox. Like the earlier G.A.R.s, this car had a transverse semi-elliptic front spring. The other engine was a 1375cc straight-8, also with single ohc, though this was driven by a train of gears, instead of the vertical shaft of the smaller engine. Front suspension was by conventional semi-elliptics. Both cars could be had with sports bodies whose two seats were slightly staggered. The catalogue also showed touring bodies on a longer wheelbase, a cabriolet and 2- or 4-door saloons, but these may not have been built. Probably no more than 12 straight-8s were made. After dwindling production, Gardahaut

closed his doors in 1934. Three or four left-over straight-8 engines were bought by J. Pipault who used them in a car he called the J.P.

GARANZINI (I) 1924–1926

Fabbrica Automobili Oreste Garanzini, Milan.
This was a small sports car made by a former motorcycling champion. It had a 1200cc ohv 4-cylinder engine, independent suspension and headlamps which turned with the wheels.

NG

GARBACCIO (CH) 1913

François Garbaccio, Sierre.
Garbaccio was one of the many inventors and tinkerers who believed that automobiles should be driven by a propeller, thus doing away with noisy and complicated gearboxes, chains, differentials and so on. However, he went one step further and created a vehicle that could be driven on the road as well as on the surface of water. Before giving up his experiments he also modified his exotic vehicle to drive on snow. There was no production.

FH

GARBATY (D) 1924–1927

Autowerk Garbaty, Mainz.
This was a small car powered by a 1.2-litre 5PS 4-cylinder engine developing 25bhp. It was made in open and closed versions, and some of the latter were used as taxicabs.

HON

GARCIN see B.G.S.

GARDNER (i) (F) 1898–1900

Frank L. Gardner, Paris.
The American company promoter Frank L. Gardner was best known for his financing of steam car builder Léon Serpollet. Without the support of Gardner, Serpollet would probably never have reached the position of the leading maker of steam cars in France. Before he was involved with Serpollet, Gardner made a few petrol-engined cars in his large premises in the Rue Stendhal in Paris. They were designed by an Englishman, Charles W. James, and had single-cylinder horizontal engines and belt drive. At least one 12hp 2-cylinder car was made, with a streamlined body and claimed top speed of 40mph (65km/h).

NG

GARDNER (ii) (US) 1919–1931

Gardner Motor Co. Inc., St Louis, Missouri.
Like St Louis neighbour MOON, the Gardner automobile had its roots in the carriage industry. The Banner Buggy Co. was organised by Russell E. Gardner in 1882, and rose to become the largest manufacturer of speciality buggies in the USA. In 1913, Russell Gardner and sons Russell Jr and Fred entered the automobile business, building bodies for CHEVROLETs. By 1915 they had formed the Chevrolet Motor Co. of St Louis, and were manufacturing Chevrolets under licence. During World War I, with his sons serving in the US Navy, Russell Gardner sold out to General Motors.

Work on the Gardners' own car had begun by the time the boys returned home in 1919. Prototype cars were ready late that year, and production began early in 1920; 6431 cars were completed by year's end. The Gardner 'Light Four', intended to compete with DODGE, was an assembled car. Power came from a Lycoming 3154cc side-valve engine, with two main bearings and thermosyphon-cooling. Offered in touring, roadster and sedan bodies, all on a 112in (2843mm) wheelbase, the Gardner sold for $1125 (open models) to $2145 (sedan). A recession in 1921 nearly halved production, but better times in 1922 boosted output to over 9000 cars, which would be the firm's high point.

Gardners for 1923 featured Lycoming's new five-main-bearing four, of 3501cc. Despite the new engine, slightly lower prices and an unprecedented one-year warranty, sales stagnated and then declined in 1924. An upmarket 'Radio Special' model, intended to capitalise on the popularity of the new wireless, featured Spanish leather upholstery and lots of nickel-plated trim. It did not actually have a radio, as car radios had not been developed. Despite the catchy name and stylish appointments it failed to spur sales.

1930 Gardner (ii) front-drive sedan.
NATIONAL MOTOR MUSEUM

Heading the 1925 model line was a new 8-cylinder car, the 'Eight-in-Line', featuring a 4526cc Lycoming 2H engine which made 65bhp. The wheelbase for this car was extended to 125in (3172mm); offered as a 4-door tourer or 2-door brougham, it sold for $1995. Additional closed bodies and a roadster and cabriolet were soon added, at prices up to $2495, which put it into competition with BUICK and the LOCOMOBILE Junior Eight. The 4-cylinder Gardner had been kept in production after introduction of the eight, but was soon replaced by a 6-cylinder model, with a 3395cc Lycoming 2S engine, on a 117in (2969mm) wheelbase. Not very successful, the six was replaced during 1927 by a smaller eight of 3700cc. By 1928 there were three sizes of Eight-in-Line, on wheelbases of 122 (3096mm), 125 (3172mm) and 130in (3299mm); they sold for $1195 to $2495. Engines for all cars came from Lycoming, gearboxes from Warner, axles from Columbia, clutches from Borg and Beck and ignition components from Delco. Lockheed hydraulic brakes were new that year. The 1928 Gardner was a high-style automobile; cars had a low stance and distinctive double row of bonnet louvres which were grouped into clusters.

The same model line-up continued in 1929, but sales were disappointing. Production was down to an average of eight cars per working day. The company became more daring at this point, entering negotiations with Archie Andrews regarding production of the RUXTON for New Era Motors, but then suddenly withdrew. Then there were talks with mail-order merchants Sears, Roebuck & Co., then interested in re-entering the auto market (the company had sold the high-wheeled SEARS car earlier in the century). This, too, fizzled out.

The most innovative Gardner was the front-wheel drive car readied for the 1930 New York Auto Show. Forsaking Lycoming, the car had a 6-cylinder Continental engine and rode a 133in (3375mm) wheelbase. It had the long bonnet characteristic of the period's front-wheel drive cars, and was lower than most cars of its day (although taller than either Ruxton or the CORD L29). A streamlined radiator grill was novel for its time; the car's sedan body was by Baker-Raulang. Although noteworthy, the 'Griffin' (named for Gardner's traditional radiator mascot) did not generate any significant business, perhaps because

Cord and Ruxton had already captured and then dissipated the enthusiasm of front-wheel drive proponents.

The 'conventional' 1930 line, in addition to the larger two eights, reintroduced a six on the 122in (3096mm) wheelbase. This mix was carried over for 1931 models, which were very slightly changed from the 1930s. However, they were short-lived. Gardner had been linked with merger discussions involving KISSEL and STUTZ, as well as Moon, perhaps because the firm had, despite mediocre sales, maintained a strong financial base. Nothing came of these talks, however, and the Gardners chose to wind up their company rather than involve themselves in speculative alliances or debt. A line of funeral cars, in association with St Louis Casket Co., was continued into 1932. Then operations ceased. When the Gardner Motor Co. closed its doors, it had over $600,000 in clear assets.

KF

Further Reading
'Assembling Quality: Gardner's Spring, Summer and Fall', Karla A. Rosenbusch, *Automobile Quarterly*, Vol.37, No.1.

GARDNER (iii) (US) c.1950–1953

Vince Gardner, South Bend, Indiana.

Vince Gardner won a styling contest put on by *Motor Trend* and *Ford Times* magazines to design a sports car body to fit a Ford Anglia chassis. The prize was enough money to build his car. It was a stunningly beautiful body, made from aluminium by master metalsmith Emil Diedt. Gardner intended to produce the car with Singer, MG, Ford V8/60 or other suitable engines.

HP

GARDNER-DOUGLAS *see* G.D.

GARDNER-SERPOLLET *see* SERPOLLET

1988 Gateau La Vision microcar.
GATEAU INTERNATIONAL

GAREAU (CDN) 1910
Gareau Motor Car Co., Montreal, Quebec.
Detroit-born Charles Gareau and Willy Davidson designed this Montreal-built car. It was a conventional tourer powered by a 35hp 4-cylinder engine. Its only slightly unusual feature was a worm drive differential, as on the British Daimler, rather than the usual straight or spiral bevel. Only three Gareau 35s were made; two were sold and Charles Gareau drove the third for more than ten years.

NG

GARFORD (US) 1907–1908; 1911–1913
The Garford Co., Elyria, Ohio.
Arthur L. Garford was president of the Federal Manufacturing Co. of Elyria, an important supplier of components to the motor industry. Established in 1903, they soon turned to complete chassis, which they supplied to a number of manufacturers, including ARDSLEY, CLEVELAND (ii), GAETH, RAINIER and STUDEBAKER. The latter became their most important customer; Garford enabled Studebaker to enter the petrol car business in 1904, as they had previously made only electrics, and, of course, the wagons and carriages for which they had been famous for 50 years. Garford began by supplying a 16hp 2-cylinder chassis, followed by 20, 28 and 30hp fours. They were called at first Studebaker-Garfords, then simply Studebakers.

In 1907 Garford launched two cars under his own name, the 30hp Model A and 40hp Model B. These expensive cars ($3500 and $4000 respectively) were only made to the end of the 1908 season, and then for three years Garford's whole output was for Studebaker. When Studebaker took over E.M.F. production in 1909 Garford were free to sell cars under their own name again. They launched a 40hp 4-cylinder car at the New York Automobile Show in January 1911, following it up with a 50hp six in 1912. One of the 1913 sixes, which had full electric lighting and starting, had a single headlamp recessed in the radiator header tank, and was known as the One Eyed Garford. Garford was absorbed by Willys Overland in 1912, and production was discontinued after the 1913 season. The truck division, which remained independent of Willys, stayed in business until 1933.

NG

GARY (US) 1914
Gary Automobile Manufacturing Co., Gary, Indiana.
This company made a 34hp 6-cylinder car offered in two models, a 2-seater speedster and a 6-seater tourer. They shared the same 135in (3426mm) wheelbase and $2300 price. The Gary truck, also made in Gary, Indiana, was unrelated to the car, as was a Gary taxicab made in Chicago in 1909.

NG

GAS-AU-LEC (US) 1905–1906
1905–1906 Vaughn Machine Co., Peabody, Massachusetts.
1906 Corwin Machine Co., Peabody, Massachusetts.
As the name implied, this was a petrol-electric car (gasoline-auxiliary-electric) which combined a large 40/45hp 4-cylinder engine of more than 7-litres capacity

with an electric motor. Unlike some petrol-electric systems, in which the drive to the rear wheels is entirely electric, in the Gas-Au-Lec the electric motor was only used for starting, slow-speed running and reverse. In normal running the petrol engine was connected directly to the propeller shaft and rear axle. The engine's valves were electro-magnetically-operated, doing away with the need for a camshaft or tappets. How well all this worked is not known but no more than four cars were made, possibly only one. In 1906 the company president Hamilton S. Corwin changed the company's name to his own, and renamed the car Gasaulec.

NG

GASHOPPER (US) c.1983
Bolt-on Parts Co., Miami, Florida.
This was a modern interpretation of the 3-wheeled 'city cars' of the 1950s. It had a tiny engine, weighed 200lbs and supposedly delivered 100mpg. It had a fibreglass monocoque hard-top body and chassis with tiller steering, single headlight, bicycle-size wheels and a 2-speed transmission. Although it seated two, it was intended for short commutes and recreational use.

HP

GASI (D) 1921
Gasi Motorradwagen GmbH, Berlin-Dahlem.
This was an unusual 3-wheeler with single front wheel and tandem seating for two, and the driver in the rear seat. It was powered by an air-cooled 2-cylinder engine, with chain drive to an intermediate shaft, and final drive by belts.

HON

GASLIGHT (US) 1960–1961
Gaslight Motors Corp., Detroit, Michigan.
This was a replica of the 1902 Rambler, using a single-cylinder 4hp engine. It was a continuation of an earlier replica called the Rambler.

HP

GASMOBILE (US) 1900–1902
Automobile Co. of America, Marion, New Jersey.
This car was launched as the American Voiturette in 1899, but was renamed a year later. In its original form it had a 3hp single-cylinder engine mounted under the seat and chain drive, but the makers became more ambitious, and offered in 1902 three models of 3-cylinder cars, of 9, 12 and 20hp, a 25hp 4-cylinder and a 35hp six. The latter was exhibited at the New York Automobile Show in January 1902. It was a custom order from millionaire C.V. Brokaw and never marketed. It does, however, deserve credit as the first 6-cylinder car in America, and indeed in the world. Its price was not quoted, but must have been pretty high, as even the 4-cylinder Gasmobile cost $5000. The company had made 140 cars by November 1901, but was in receivership four months later. Clearly their expansion into multi-cylinder engines had proved disastrous. At the sale in August 1902 the machinery was bought by the Pan-American Motor Co. and used for their manufacture of the PANAM car.

NG

GATEAU (F) 1983–1992
Gateau International, St Gilles-Croix-de-Vie.
It was not only this manufacturer's name that had a double meaning ('Gateau' means cake in French) – its first model was the Egzo-7 (pronounced 'exocet'). This was a rather handsome one-box microcar styled by Joël Brétecher. A wide range of engines was offered, from 50cc to 500cc, as well as two electric versions (1.8kW or 2.2 kW), although diesels were the mainstay, the petrol units being quickly abandoned. The Gateau was renamed several times despite being essentially the same model: Egzo-3, Maximini, Break and Grande. A larger Vison model was launched in 1988 with a 325cc diesel engine, then revised with new frontal treatment in 1991 and renamed the Forum.

CR

GATSBY (US) c.1978–1998
Gatsby Coachworks, San Jose, California.
Gatsby built two neoclassic cars, the Gatsby and the Griffin. The Gatsby was similar to the Clenet in concept, with an MG Midget body set on top of a Ford

chassis that had a long bonnet and running boards grafted on. Although they were originally steel bodied, in 1983 they were also offered in fibreglass. Fully assembled Gatsbys were built on new Fords and came with a warranty, and were available in kit form as well. Gatsby Coachworks also sold the Griffin kit car, which was a neoclassic with a more rakish style. It had formerly been known as the Sceptre. It also used the MG cockpit area and windshield and fitted on a Ford chassis. All Griffins had fibreglass bodies. In 1998 Gatsby Coachworks was sold to JPR Cars Ltd in Topping, Virginia.

HP

GATSO (NL) 1948–1950

M. Gatsonides, Heemstede.

The Gatso – sometimes in the beginning known as the Gatford, until that was squashed by the Ford (Matford!) – was a short-lived venture by the international rally driver Maurice Gatsonides (1911–1998). Before World War II he experimented with Ford mechanical components and a Mercury 3.9-litre V8-engine.

The first experimental car, 'Kwik' (= quicksilver), was assembled in 1939 and had a number of successes in rally-sport, and that particular car still exists in Holland.

After World War II Gatsonides built some interesting cars on the French Matford chassis. At the Geneva show in 1948 he displayed one of the first cars with a duralumin-panelled body of aircraft-fuselage type, with a 'bubble' cockpit hood. The car had three headlights, the central one mounted on top of the radiator grill. The catalogue showed several models: Sports Roadster, Aero-Coupé, 4-seater Touring, and Cabriolet. The Mercury engine was tuned up to 120hp, but an ohv-engine of 175hp was in the programme: it had a top speed of 112mph (180 km/h). From a technical point of view it was a very interesting car with a 3-speed gearbox, an overdrive in the rear-axle, Girling hydraulic brakes at the front and mechanical at the rear, four hydraulic shock absorbers, and the option of twin spare wheels and a second petrol tank, giving a total capacity of 150 litres instead of 90 litres. About 11 Gatso cars were built, of which some were exported to Switzerland and South Africa. Because of production problems Gatsonides stopped building cars, although later in 1949 he made one smaller experimental car using Fiat 1500 mechanicals. Officially the Gatso 1500, they called it 'Platje' (plat = flat), because of its very flat shape. It did not go into production, but this particular one-off still exists in Holland.

FBV

Further Reading
The Amazing Gatso – The Never Ending Race, Michael Allen, Gatsometer BV, 1993.
Rallies and Races; Gatsonides' Adventures, William Leonard, Greyhound Press, 1995.

GATTER (CS) 1928–1934

Autopodnik Gatter, Zakupy.

In 1928 the brothers Vilibald and Rudolf Gatter began to produce simple cyclecars in their small workshop. These were first fitted with 2-stroke water-cooled 9bhp 350cc engines, 2-speed gearbox and chain-driven rear wheels with two alongside-mounted leaf springs (weight 290kg, top speed 37mph (60km/h), price 13,800 Kc). An open 2+1-seater body was used also at the bigger type with 448cc 10bhp engine (weight 340kg, price 14,800 Kc). Only some 40 cars were produced before the firm became a repair shop in 1934.

MSH

GATTS (US) 1905

Alfred P. Gatts, Bethel, Ohio.

Alfred Parmer Gatts came from a farming background, but, like Henry Ford, preferred machinery to agriculture. He built five cars in 1905, all high-wheelers powered by a single-cylinder air-cooled engine with a fan integral with the flywheel. Three he sold and the other two he kept for his own use.

NG

GAUDIN (AUS) 1909

Gaudin Motor Exchange, Melbourne, Victoria.

A high-wheeled motor buggy, the Gaudin was the KIBLINGER-cum McINTYRE relabelled and fitted with a 12hp engine. Simply a retail operation, unlike the FRANKLINITE which had local content, it is puzzling how the same vehicle

1989 Gateau Grande diesel microcar.
GATEAU INTERNATIONAL

1948 Gatso 4000 Aero coupé.
NATIONAL MOTOR MUSEUM

1929 Gatter prototype tourer.
NATIONAL MOTOR MUSEUM

could be handled by two competing firms, unless one of them obtained stock form TUDHOPE in Canada.

MG

1902 Gautier 16CV spider.
NICK BALDWIN

1894 Gautier-Wehrlé Paris-Rouen steam car.
NATIONAL MOTOR MUSEUM

1955 Gaylord (ii) Gentleman coupé.
NATIONAL MOTOR MUSEUM

GAUTHIER (F) 1904–1937

1904–1932 Gauthier et Cie, La Garenne-Colombes, Paris.
1932–1937 G. Gauthier, Blois, Loir-et-Cher.

According to his widow, Gauthier was an engineer, innovator and inventor rather than a businessman and every vehicle made was in some sense a one-off rather than part of a production run. Two or three personal prototypes were made before the first vehicles was offered for sale in 1904, this being a De Dion-engined forecar, and most pre–1914 production was of 3-wheelers of various types. Experiments with supple suspension, interconnected fore and aft, led to

the 'Avionette' cyclecar, so named because of the impressive performances achieved over rough terrain when demonstrated to the French army authorities in 1918. However, no military contract was forthcoming. At the end of his life Gauthier claimed that CITROËN's 2CV design infringed his patents but he was unable to muster sufficient resources to mount a proper challenge. During the 1920s a variety of lightweights were made with 2, 3 or 4 wheels, using whatever proprietary engines (usually single-cylinders) might be available and these were often marketed under such names as Auto-Plume 'Cabri' and Auto-Fauteuil. Brochures for the latter were most imaginative, featuring numerous passengers on seats less comfortable than that provided for the centrally positioned driver, or such features as a power take-off for sawing logs or driving farm machinery. Advertising was targetted particularly towards the Church, where simplicity, modesty and low running costs were seen as virtues to be sought after. His widow confirmed the armchair comfort implied in the name, having retained one for her own use into the 1950s, and she estimated overall production at around 350.

DF

GAUTIER (F) 1902–1903

Charles Gautier et Compagnie, Courbevoie, Seine.

Gautier offered a wide range of cars, but it is possible that not all were built. The smallest was a voiturette with 6½hp single-cylinder De Dion-Bouton or Aster engine, larger cars having a 12hp twin or fours of 16, 22 and 30hp, by Aster or Mutel. The smaller cars could be had with shaft or chain drive, while the larger models were all chain-driven. Charles Gautier had formerly been a partner with Wehrle in the GAUTIER-WEHRLE enterprise.

NG

GAUTIER-WEHRLÉ (F) 1894–1900

1894–1897 Rossel, Gautier & Wehrlé, Paris.
1897–1900 Sté Continentale, Paris.

This was a pioneer French make which entered a 4hp steam car in the Paris-Rouen Trial of 1894. Driven by Charles Gautier, it finished sixteenth out of 21 starters. In 1895 an improved car with Serpollet boiler and equal-sized wheels, called La Cigale, was entered in the Paris-Bordeaux Race, but dropped out. In 1896 they turned to petrol-engined cars, advertised as 'chainless and vibrationless', with engines mounted under the seat and final drive by shaft to a gearbox on the rear axle, very advanced for the time. Steam was dropped in 1897, when a new company made petrol cars with front-mounted 8hp horizontal engines. In 1898 they were offering 5 and 12hp single-cylinder engines and a vertical twin, as well as an electric car. They made their own bodies and also supplied coachwork to other firms. Another activity was sub-contract work for SERPOLLET. The 4½hp dogcart of 1899 was the last Gautier-Wehrlé car. Charles Gautier later made cars under his own name. One of the original partners, Rossel, may have been Edouard Rossel, who made a few cars at Lille in 1898–99.

NG

GAYLORD (i) (US) 1910–1913

Gaylord Motor Car Co., Gaylord, Michigan.

The Gaylord was one of a number of cars designed to be convertible from passenger to goods carrying. Built on a conventional chassis with 35hp 4-cylinder engine, the passenger body was a 4-seater tourer, and alternative bodies were a station wagon-type with inward-facing seats for six as well as two at the front, and a flat platform for load carrying. Production of these may have reached 350. For 1912 Gaylord added three models with ohv 4-cylinder engines of 20/25, 28/30hp. These were not available with the convertible utility bodies, being made as tourers or roadsters only.

NG

GAYLORD (ii) (US) 1956–1957

Gaylord Cars Ltd, Chicago, Illinois.

The Gaylord was an ambitious sports car project with a body by renowned stylist Brooks Stevens. It was intended to be a very upscale car with a $17,500 price tag in 1956. The chassis, designed by Ed Gaylord, was a backbone tube frame with A-arm front suspension and a live axle at rear. The all-metal body for the prototype was built by Spohn in Germany, and a Chrysler V8 was used with a 4-speed automatic transmission. This prototype was scrapped and three production chassis, intended for Cadillac V8 power, were built by Zeppelin in Germany. However, only one of these had a body installed before the project was suspended by partners Ed and Jim Gaylord. Some of the many innovations on the Gaylord were a retractable hard-top and variable-assist power steering.

HP

Further Reading
'Gaylord: One Auto-holoc's view on another's Ultimate Car', Alex S. Tremulis, *Automobile Quarterly*, Vol. XII, No. 4.

GAZ (SU) 1932 to date

Gorkovskji Avtomobilnji Zavod, Zavod Imenji Molotova, AO GAZ, Gorki.
The Ford Motor Co. literally put Soviet Russia on wheels, when helping to erect in Nishny Novgorod (from October 1932, known as Gorky) the then largest auto plant in Europe and licensing its first model-A truck called NAZ-AA (later GAZ-AA).

The truck's components were shared with a tourer-bodied GAZ-A, modelled on the lines of the Ford-A, with no Ford involvement. Ambi-Budd in Germany supplied a set of body dies for GAZ-A. Altogether nearly 42,000 open A-models were assembled (including pick-ups GAZ-4), but open cars were basically unsuitable for the Russian climate. A closed GAZ-M1 followed, sporting a 3285cc engine which developed 50bhp against 42 of its predecessor and more than made up for the weight difference. Improved suspension made 'Emka', as it was called, more comfortable over roads rutted by autumn rains. As a new 3.48-litre six of 76bhp was tooled up by the factory, it found its place behind rounded grillwork (in place of the original shovel nose) of the model GAZ-11/73. A number of closed and open models followed, including a 4 × 4 saloon GAZ-61, a phaeton GAZ-11/40 and pick-ups GAZ-11/415 and GAZ-11/415.

Over a ten year period (1943–53) a Russian equivalent to the famous Jeep was manufactured, a 4-cylinder GAZ-67B. Its successor GAZ-69 was made for just over three years, then moved over to Ulyanovsk Auto Works. Two milestone cars were created under chief designer Andrei Lipgart. GAZ-M20 Pobieda (Victory) of 1946 was among the very first mass-produced cars with all enveloping bodywork. The unibodied GAZ-12 (also ZIM – for Zavod Imjeni Molotova named after the then Minister of Foreign Affairs, Vyacheslav Molotov) was rather unusual with its 126in (3200mm) wheelbase and 7-seater capacity. Its heavily modified truck Six gave 90bhp and the luxury model featured such novelties as a fluid coupling and a hypoid final drive. After producing around a quarter of million Pobiedas at Gorky (and even more were made in Poland under the Warszawa badge), a new 'middleweight' model called GAZ-21 Volga replaced it in 1956. It was soon fitted with an aluminium ohv engine of 70–75bhp. Some of these dynamically styled 190in (4800mm) long 5-seaters were furnished with Russia's first-ever automatic transmissions. Tubeless tyres, centralised lubrication system, reclining front seats were other novel features. Various bodystyles joined a saloon: estate car, ambulance, van – but the prototype cabriolet never made it.

The second luxury car from Gorky was indexed GAZ-13 and named Chaika (Seagull). Its 5.53-litre all-aluminium V8 was actually lighter than ZIM's cast iron engine by 13kg. With 190–195bhp available, the car went beyond 99mph (160km/h) and its acceleration times were twice as good as ZIM's. The 3-speed automatic transmission destined initially for the Volga was beefed up for the Chaika, the car was fitted with power-everything: steering, brakes, windows, antenna. A massive X-frame made a phaeton body possible. In 1960 a Chaika cost 17,000 roubles against 5100 which bought a Volga. Gorky's top model was no longer available for the general public, unlike ZIM.

1968 brought the second Volga model, indexed as GAZ-24. The car was just a bit shorter, but lower by 5in (130mm). A 2445cc engine had a cr of 8.2 and developed 95bhp, power brakes got hydrovac, and 15in tyres were replaced by 7.35-14. Production started late in 1970, followed by a taxi version, which ran on low 76 octane petrol and developed 85bhp.

In some ways GAZ and the ZIL works of Moscow were rivals, certainly their engineering and design people were. Thus, in 1977 the second generation Chaika appeared and got closer than ever to ZIL limousines. This was a totally new car on a 136in (3450mm) wheelbase and overall length of 241in (6114mm), just 7.5in (191mm) short of the then-current ZIL-117. Among the novelties were front disc brakes with one vacuum and two hydrovac power brakes, but for extracting 220bhp from the original 5530cc capacity two 4-throat carburettors were employed in place of a domestic fuel injection which never really got off

1932/36 Gaz tourer.
MARGUS H. KUUSE

1936 Gaz M1 saloon.
MARGUS H.KUUSE

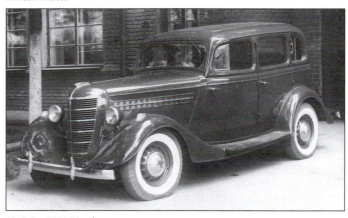

1940 Gaz M11-73 saloon.
NAMI, MOSCOW

the ground. Cylindrical side glass was employed, and jet-type headlamp washers. There were 17 electric motors in all under the squarish bodywork.

Volga moved from one modernisation to another; 1986 brought a GAZ-24-10 (100hp), and a liquid petroleum gas conversion of 85bhp. Since 1981 directors and lower-ranking Party functionaries were seen around in 195in (4960mm) long black GAZ-3102 with square headlamps and rounded bodywork, a car heavier by 50kg. That car's 102bhp engine had a 2-stage mix admission, something like that in the Honda CVCC (GAZ had used the process in its truck engines back in the 1950s). The factory lost money on every GAZ-14 it built and its accountants were rather happy to get rid of the model in December 1988, after 1120 cars were completed. Prestige-wise, it was a great loss, and mourned by engineers and workshop wizards who lost their unique jobs.

1955 Gaz M-72 Pobieda 4x4 saloon.
MARGUS H.KUUSE

c.1964 Gaz 21 Volga saloon.
MARGUS H.KUUSE

1965 Gaz 13 Chaika saloon.
MARGUS H.KUUSE

1969 Gaz M-24 Volga saloon.
NICK BALDWIN

In the 1990s there was just one car left, the evergreen Volga Model 24, modified at every opportunity. 1992 brought a model 31029 instead of model 24-10, elongated by 6in (150mm), to 192in (4885mm). For this model a new 16-valve inline four was developed, one of 2287cc and 150bhp, featuring Bosch fuel injection, but up to 1995 just a couple of thousand cars were so fitted.

As tools for building a 'new Chaika' were destroyed under Gorbachev's economy drive, GAZ had only one way to reinstate itself as a luxury car builder: to create a new, this time sensibly-sized, model like GAZ-3105 Volga, 200in (5050mm) long, with a 113in (5050mm) wheelbase. A 24-valve V6 engine developed the same power (194bhp) as the latest Chaika's V8. A rather good-looking car, it had 4WD, disc brakes all around and ABS.

In 1998 a prototype of a model of the future, the GAZ-3103 was shown, a 6-light saloon with a huge 700-litre luggage space. A front-wheel drive car with double wishbone suspension, a subframe mounted ZMZ-406 engine, rack and pinion steering, four disc brakes, ABS by Bosch, and dual air bags. This and the Model 3104 with 4-wheel drive may materialise by 2003 or 2004. It is immensely cheaper to put the tried and tested mechanicals of a rear-drive model in a modern bodywork and that may happen with the Model 3111 by the end of 1999 or early in 2000. That particular car is built with Volga's 110in (2800mm) wheelbase and is 194in (4940mm) long. A small selection of petrol engines, generally of 150–170bhp range will be offered, along with the Steyr-licensed 2.1-litre diesel of 114bhp. AO GAZ in the town renamed once again Nishny Novgorod, continues to manufacture rather antiquated 3102 and 3110 models, with questionable quality as ever–and in huge quantities. Constantly building 124–125,000 thirsty and unreliable Volgas per annum during the crisis years seems a miracle, supported in real life by high import tolls on similar-size foreign cars.

MHK

G.B. (i) (GB) 1922–1924

George Baets, London.

This was a very light 3-wheeler with tiller steering to the single front wheel. Power came from a 688cc flat-twin Coventry-Victor engine, transmission was by a 2-speed gearbox and final drive by shaft, unexpected in such an otherwise cyclecar type of vehicle. Three models were proposed, De Luxe, Sporting and Camionette, all at 150 guineas (£157.50). It is unlikely that more than a prototype or two were made, as the inventor George Baets (or Baetz) never formed a company. His address at Wilton Mews, Belgravia, may have been his home rather than a workshop, though he also had an address in Clapham where a car might have been made.

NG

G.B. (ii) (GB) 1980s

G.B. Cars Ltd, London.

Although the main product of this company was the Radnor small vintage-style van, it also produced the Raglan, a very small 4-seater tourer in the style of the 1930s. The chassis and mechanicals were taken from the Reliant Fox, including its 40bhp 848cc all-alloy engine. The fibreglass bodywork was by Protoco and the company even contemplated special one-off bodywork to order.

CR

G.B. (iii) (GB) 1986–1988

G.B. Racing Sports, Standish, Wigan, Lancashire.

This was one of the earliest of the 1980s rash of Countach replicas, created by Andrew Grimshaw and Dave Forsyth of KINGFISHER Mouldings. The prototype had Jaguar V12 power but the unsubtle space frame chassis could also accept Renault V6, Rover V8, Audi and Chevrolet V8 engines. There were LP500, 1988-specification and Koenig bodykit styles.

CR

G.C. (F) 1908

Automobiles G.C., H. Guyot et Compagnie, Paris.

This was a light car powered by a 1940cc 4-cylinder Sultan engine.

NG

1977 Gaz 14 Chaika saloon.
MARGUS H.KUUSE

G.C.E. (US) c.1985

G.C.E. Import and Export Corp., Broussard, Louisiana.
This company imported Brazilian-built kit cars into the US and sold them directly or through BREMEN. Among their offerings were the Puma and a Cobra replica.

HP

G.C.S. (GB) 1990 to date

G.C.S. Cars, Orpington, Kent.
Plainly inspired by the Morgan, the G.C.S. Hawke kit car was wider than the Morgan because of its Cortina front subframe and rear axle, but at least that made it a little more spacious and purposeful in appearance. The ladder frame chassis was in steel, the main body tub, wings, nose cone and doors were in fibreglass, and the bonnet could be ordered in fibreglass or aluminium. Multi-link rear suspension was optional, as were a 2+2 version and a chassis designed for Rover V8 engines and Ford Sierra suspension.

CR

G.D. (GB) 1990 to date

Gardner Douglas Sportscars, Bottesford, Nottinghamshire.
Although its heritage can be traced back to the R.W. 427, the Gardner Douglas was not really an A.C. Cobra replica, although its inspiration was the 1966 Cobra Mk III. It was a modern interpretation of the Cobra theme, with such features as a rear-exit exhaust and multi-tubular backbone chassis with semi-monocoque fibreglass bodywork. It used unmodified Jaguar axles and running gear, with a choice of Ford V6, Rover V8 or American V8 engines with power outputs up to and beyond 500bhp. A novel gull-wing hard-top was available. G.D. adopted a high-tech, modernising approach, for example offering a chassis for Ford Cosworth mechanicals.

CR

G.D.X.M. *see* GRIFFIN (i)

G.E.A. (S) 1905

AB Gustav Ericssons Automobilfabrik, Stockholm.
Truck builder Ericsson made a single example of a large car with 6-cylinder engine, almost certainly the first six to be made in Sweden. It was known as the Ormen

1982 Gaz 3102 Volga saloon.
MARGUS H.KUUSE

1998 Gaz 3111 Volga saloon.
V. ARTEV

1905 G.E.A. 6-cylinder roadster.
NATIONAL MOTOR MUSEUM

Lange (Long Serpent), and had a round radiator similar to that of a Delaunay-Belleville.

NG

GEARLESS (i) (US) 1907–1909

1907–1908 Gearless Transmission Co., Rochester, New York.
1908–1909 Gearless Motor Car Co., Rochester, New York.
Friction transmission was common enough on cyclecars in the prewar era, but the Gearless was unusual in combining this transmission with large engines. In their first year they offered 4-cylinder engines of 50, 60 and 75hp with chain final drive and 5- or 7-seater touring bodies. 1908 saw the 75hp Great Six, made in touring or roadster forms. The latter was called the Greyhound and had an exceptionally long bonnet under which lay both engine and gearbox. Prices were as high as $3000. The company was reorganised in March 1908 and turned to smaller and cheaper cars. These had 32/35hp 4-cylinder engines and came in two series, one with friction transmission and the other, called the Olympic, with conventional gearboxes. At $1650, the Olympics were $150 more expensive than the friction drive cars.

NG

GEARLESS (ii) (US) 1920–1923

Gearless Motor Corp., Pittsburgh, Pennsylvania.
The Gearless was one of several steam cars introduced during the years immediately following World War I. President of the corporation was Duncan MacDonald, who was simultaneously operating another enterprise – the MacDonald Steam Automotive Corp. – in Garfield, Ohio. The Gearless featured two separate 2-cylinder double-acting side-valve steam engines, each operating one rear wheel which, it was claimed, avoided the necessity of a rear axle. Both engines were controlled by a single throttle. The Gearless was available as a touring car at $2600 and a roadster at $2650 and wheels could be either wood or wire types. The corporation failed after four of its officials were indicted for conspiracy and mail fraud in the sale of more than $1 million worth of company stock fraudulently, MacDonald being among them. At least five of the cars, and possibly more, were completed but total production is unknown. MacDonald retained an interest in steam car design or conversions for the rest of his life.

KM

GECKO (i) (GB) 1965–1966

Langsett Industries Ltd, Sheffield, Yorkshire.
23-year old Stuart Smith conceived this minute two-seater car that was designed to stand on its end for parking. It hardly needed that facility, as it measured just 66in (1675mm) long. Powered by a 200cc 2-stroke engine, a top speed of 50mph (80km/h) was claimed, while the inventor said that the transparent side sections and roof could be removed from the steel bodywork for 'a real sports car feeling'. An intended production run never materialised.

CR

GECKO (ii) (GB) 1984–1992

1984–1990 Autobarn Fabrications, Tamworth, Staffordshire.
1990–1992 Simmons Design, Lichfield, Staffordshire.
The engaging little Gecko was a sort of modern Mini Moke kit car using Mini subframes and mechanicals, although Autobarn offered a good alternative to rusty rear subframes: a special beam axle with coil spring/dampers. The bodywork was a mixture of fibreglass, plywood and aluminium. Wheelbases varied from 50in (1269mm) to 100in (2538mm), while a 6-wheeled version was also offered.

CR

GEERING (GB) 1899

T. Geering & Son, Rolvenden, Kent.
This company made stationary engines running on heavy oil, and made a prototype car with a rear-mounted 3hp 2-cylinder engine, powered by Tea Rose lamp oil. It had tube ignition ('no electricity, no explosions', said the brochure). A 3-speed gearbox gave speeds of 4, 6 and 12mph (6, 10 and 19km/h), and final drive was by chain. As proof of ease of driving, the brochure said 'It has been driven by a lad aged 15 years.'

NG

GEHA (D) 1910–1923

1910–1917 Elektromobilfabrik Gebhardt & Harhorn, Berlin-Schoneberg.
1917–1923 Elitewerke AG, Zweigniederlassung, Berlin-Schoneberg.
The Geha was an electric 3-wheeler with single front wheel, made in passenger and goods carrying forms. It had a 1.8kW motor mounted in the front wheel hub. Design was by Victor Harhorn who, with his partner Gebhardt, gave his name to the car. He had previously designed the B.E.F., also a front-drive 3-wheeler. In 1917 ELITE (ii) took over the design and carried on production until 1923. Four-wheeled vehicles were marketed under the Elite name.

HON

GELRIA (NL) 1900 – 1906

Gelria Machine- en Motorenfabriek, Arnhem.
The Machine- en Motorenfabriek Gelria was a manufacturer of stationary gas- and oil-engines before they decided to begin the production of automobiles in 1899. They started with a car with a large single-cylinder water-cooled 4hp engine mounted at the front, a 2-speed gearbox, and final drive by chain. There were three body styles: a 4-seater tourer, a *dos-à-dos*, and a Duc 3-seater. At the RAI exhibition of 1902 there was a new 2-cylinder on display with an output of 6hp, but it was never successful. In 1906, after about 30 cars had come from the production line Gelria finally decided to stop production.

FBV

G.E.M. (F) 1907–1909

Sté Générale d'Automobiles Électro-Mécaniques, Puteaux, Seine.
First seen at the 1907 Paris Salon, the G.E.M. was a petrol-electric car designed by Léon Girardot who had been one of the partners in C.G.V. It used a 20hp 4-cylinder engine driving a dynamo, and bodies included an open tourer and a sedanca de ville. When the Daimler-Knight sleeve-valve engine became available in 1909 Girardot adopted this for his power unit. It is possible that these were made under licence from the Belgian AUTO-MIXTE company as the technique was similar and Auto-Mixte also used Daimler engines. The G.E.M. did not sell well, and 1909 was the last year for the make. Girardot turned to selling Daimlers, becoming the concessionaire for the whole of France. In 1912 he built a single example of a car under his own name; it was powered by a sleeve-valve Panhard engine in a Charron chassis.

NG

GEM (i) (US) 1917–1919

Gem Motor Car Co., Grand Rapids, Michigan.
The Gem company, who made a typical assembled car of its time, completed an estimated 85 cars in less than two years of activity. The Gem used a 4-cylinder G. B. & S. engine, its offerings including a 5-seater touring car and a light delivery van.

KM

1903 General (ii) 40hp racing car.
NATIONAL MOTOR MUSEUM

GEM (ii) *see* GRANTURA

GEMINI *see* ELYSEE

GENEER (AUS) 1960–1967

Geneer Enterprises, Burwood, Victoria.

Barry Coutts was both a Volkswagen specialist and racing driver when he developed his Outlaw sports car. Although VW components were used, he built his own large-diameter tube frame in which the engine was mounted ahead of the rear axle. Its wheelbase was 84in (2134mm) and it weighed 463kg. The fibreglass bodywork featured a lift-up rear section for mechanical access. Sold in either track or road forms, a hard-top was available. Geneer, derived from engineer, also built Formula Vee racing cars.

MG

GENERAL (i) (US) 1902–1903

General Automobile & Manufacturing Co., Cleveland, Ohio.

This company succeeded the HANSEN Automobile Co. in September 1902, although Rasmus Hansen remained at the head of it. The single-cylinder 6hp Hansen was uprated to become the 8hp General, and a 12hp twin was added. Hansen wanted to expand production beyond one car per day but was unable to raise the necessary capital, and his company went bankrupt in the summer of 1903. STUDEBAKER bought 25 incomplete 12hp Generals and marketed them as the Model A Studebaker for the 1903–04 season.

NG

GENERAL (ii) (GB) 1902–1905

1902–1903 General Motor Car Co. Ltd, Norbury, London.
1903–1905 General Motor Car Co. Ltd, Mitcham, Surrey.

This company was said to be building a 24hp racing car for the 1902 Bexhill Speed Trials, but it did not appear. However, another racing car, powered by a 40hp 4-cylinder Buchet engine, with chain drive, was announced towards the end of 1902. It was built to the order of W.G.Crombie, who intended to enter it for the Nice Speed Trials. In the cause of aerodynamics it had a pointed nose attached to the front of the bonnet which projected some two feet ahead of the front wheels. It must have been the least pedestrian-friendly car ever made; *The Autocar* observed that 'It would certainly deter any police constable from physical obstruction to the progress of the car'.

1903 General (ii) 4½hp 2-seater.
NATIONAL MOTOR MUSEUM

In 1903 General made a light tradesman's delivery van called the G.M.C., powered by a 4½hp single-cylinder engine, possibly a Bradbury, and later in the year, after they had moved to Mitcham, light cars with 6½hp Aster or 12hp Buchet engines. Vans based on these chassis were among the first motor vehicles supplied to the Post Office. The 1904 light car had a spiral radiator and shaft drive. Some larger cars with 30hp Simms and 40hp Buchet engines were made in 1905.

NG

GENERAL ELECTRIC (i) (US) 1898–1900

General Electric Automobile Co., Manyunck, Pennsylvania.

This company was an offshoot of the J.G. Brill company, well-known makers of tramcars and, later, buses. It was organised by John A. Brill and its most important feature was a light yet long-lasting battery, which weighed 700 pounds compared with over 1000 for the average battery of its time. Various models were offered, including a light runabout, 4-seater *dos à dos*, brougham and delivery van. In July 1900 the company was sold up to pay creditors.

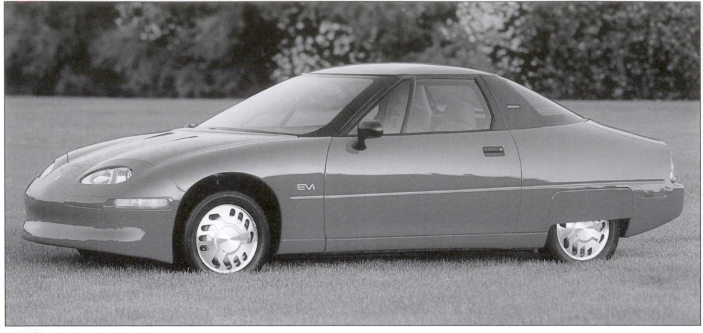

1999 General Motors EV-1 electric coupé.
GENERAL MOTORS

This General Electric had no connection with the better-known General Electric of Lynn, Massachusetts, who made a number of experimental cars between 1894 and 1903. None was intended for sale to the public.

NG

GENERAL ELECTRIC (ii) (US) c.1979
Triad Services, Dearborn, Michigan.
The Centennial Electric was an electric car built to honour GE's 100th anniversary. It was built by Triad to test GE components for use in automobiles and was not intended to be a prototype for production. It used a 24hp GE motor and 18 lead-acid batteries.

HP

GENERAL ENGINES (US) c.1978
General Engines Co., Sewell, New Jersey.
General Engines bought the SEBRING-VANGUARD electric car project in 1978 and sold improved versions of their cars called the Comuta-Car and Comuta-Van. The bumpers were brought into compliance with stricter US regulations, the braking system was improved and the suspension and frame were re-engineered. They also sold an electric neoclassic car based on a CMC Gazelle-style body. Named the Electro-Sport, it was built to order on a limited production basis. Power was from a 72-volt motor with a 4-speed manual transmission. General Engines also made electric trucks, bikes and trikes.

HP

GENERAL MOTORS EV-1 (US) 1996 to date
General Motors Corp., Lansing, Michigan.
The only passenger car to bear the General Motors name, the EV1 was an electric 2-seater coupé derived from a 1990 concept car called the Impact. It had a 3-phase AC motor which developed 137bhp and drove the front wheels. Lead-acid batteries mounted on the aluminium backbone frame gave a range of 70–90 miles. The aerodynamic body, with a Cd of 0.19, was made of composite plastic. Top speed was limited to 80mph (129km/h), and features included dual airbags, anti-lock brakes and cruise control. The first cars were available in California in December 1996, to be leased for $580 per month, or for sale at $33,995. This was in the Buick Park Avenue bracket, and was the main reason for limited sales. Only 289 were sold in the first year of production, 1997, and fewer than 500 by September 1998. The EV1 was distributed through selected SATURN dealers.

NG

GENESTIN (F) 1919–1929
P. Genestin, Fourmies, Nord.
Paul Genestin began by putting back on the road cars that had been left by the retreating German army, and followed this by assembling a few cars using 1¹/₂-litre side-valve Fivet engines in Malicet et Blin chassis. The torpedo bodies were made by Bastien whose premises were next door to Genestin's. After making about 15 of these cars Genestin gave up manufacture for a few years. His interest was rekindled by a visit to Paris where he met M. Poyet, maker of C.I.M.E. engines. In 1925 he launched a range of cars using these engines in three sizes, the 1098cc G7 and 1202cc G6, both pushrod ohv units, and the 1494cc single-ohc G5. The latter powered short-chassis sports cars which competed in the Circuit des Routes Pavées, where Genestin won his class in 1926. Heavy-looking tourers and saloons were also made, using these engines and a 1681cc C.I.M.E. side-valve six. They had slightly pointed radiators until 1927, when Genestin followed fashion with a flat type very similar to that of the Donnet. Some saloons had Pegamoid fabric bodies, a cheaper version of the Weymann design. Genestin used Perrot-Piganeau servo-assisted brakes, modified to his own design. Two chassis lengths were available; Paul Genestin's nephew remembered seeing them arrive at Fourmies station from Firminy where they were made, piled up on railway wagons. Generally the short chassis were used for sports cars and cabriolets, and the long for saloons and tourers for up to eight passengers, and for light trucks. The latter used the smaller engines of 1098 and 1202cc.
In 1927 the 1094cc C.I.M.E. G7 gave way to a 1093cc Chapuis-Dornier, while a lowered sports model was offered with 1098cc S.C.A.P. engine which could be had with supercharger. Genestin hoped to equip this chassis with a 1808cc straight-8 S.C.A.P. engine, but this was probably never built as the company closed down by the end of 1929.

NG

GENESEE (US) 1912
Genesee Motor Co., Batavia, New York.
This huge car had a 148in (3756mm) wheelbase and a 6-cylinder 11.1-litre engine. It featured electric lights and a compressed air starter. The 8-seater tourer was listed at $8000, and the limousine at $10,000.

NG

GENEVA (i) (US) 1901–1904
Geneva Automobile & Manufacturing Co., Geneva, Ohio.
This Geneva was a light steam car with 2-cylinder marine-type engine geared

directly to the differential. Six models were listed in 1901, three types of runabout, a tourer, *dos-à-dos* and light delivery wagon. For 1903 a folding front seat model was offered with the smaller 4/6hp engine, and there was also a tonneau with 10hp engine. This had the appearance of a petrol car, with frontal bonnet, and inclined wheel steering column in place of the vertical tiller of earlier models. Annual production was about 20 to 30 cars.

NG

GENEVA (ii) (US) 1916–1917
The Schoeneck Co., Harvey, Illinois.
This company was formed by George Schoeneck who had been in partnership with John L. Owen in making the OWEN-SCHOENECK, and Forrest Alvin, who also had an unsuccessful car in his past, the NEW ERA (ii). The Geneva was the planned 6-cylinder Owen-Schoeneck, and was an assembled car with 6.8-litre Herschell-Spillman engine, Brown-Lipe gearbox, and Timken rear axle. The body was a sporty-looking roadster with cycle-type wings and two spare wheels mounted flat on the rear deck behind the driver and passenger. Few were made.

NG

GENIE (GB) 1989–1996
Genie Kit Cars, Ancrum, Roxburghshire.
The Scottish-made Genie Wasp was a sort of traditional/fun car cross-over. Two fibreglass body styles were offered: the Mk I with a rounded tail and the Mk II with a longer and very sharply pointed rump. The steel tube ladder chassis was designed for Ford Cortina components, with optional Fiat twin cam power. The manufacturer's remote location and lack of marketing consigned it to the sidelines.

CR

GENTRY (GB) 1973 to date
1973–1989 R.M.B. Motors, Barwell, Leicestershire.
1989 to date S.P. Motors (T.P. Motors), Barwell, Leicestershire.
Roger Blockley's Gentry was the first of many MG TF lookalikes (it was not an exact replica). Blockley used to work on the Triumph Spitfire production line and so based the Gentry on a Triumph Herald/Vitesse chassis. A tubular frame carried plywood inner body panels and aluminium main panels, with a fibreglass scuttle, wings and doors (and curiously a cast replica of the MG Magnette ZA grill). A Spitfire chassis version was offered from 1975, as well as R.M.B.'s own chassis. The Gentry passed to S.P. Motors in 1989, which developed a Ford-based chassis option. Some 2000 examples had been made by 1998. R.M.B. also offered a short-lived Austin-Healey 100 replica in the late 1980s. It used a steel tube chassis cleverly incorporating a complete MGB centre section, including the windscreen, reskinned doors and interior. All the mechanicals also came from the MGB.

CR

GEO (US/J) 1989–1996
Geo/Chevrolet Motor Division, General Motors Corp., Warren, Michigan.
The Geo was the result of a marketing exercise by General Motors to rival imports by firms such as Honda and Nissan. These provided fully-equipped cars whereas the traditional Chevrolet dealer offered a base model with a long list of options. To set up a new dealer network in competition with Chevrolet's nearly 5000 locations was clearly impossible, so GM compromised with a new brand name called Geo. All Chevrolet dealers had the opportunity to add Geo cars to their existing lines. The Chevrolet Sprint (alias Suzuki Swift) became the Geo Metro, and the Chevrolet Nova, a rebadged Toyota Corolla built at Fremont, California, became the Geo Prizm. To reach the light 4x4 market, the Suzuki Samurai was branded the Geo Tracker. Geos were launched in 1988 as 1989 models, later additions being a Metro convertible and the Storm coupé. A competitor for the Honda CRX, this was an Isuzu Impulse with 125bhp 16-valve twin-cam 4-cylinder engine. In 1990 the Metro was the lowest-priced car on the US market, at $5995 undercutting the Ford Festiva by $500, while the Metro convertible was the cheapest convertible on the market.
The Storm was dropped at the end of the 1993 season, and for 1997 the Geo range of Metro, Prizm and Tracker became Chevrolets again. In September 1998 the Metro was hailed as America's most economical car by the American

1927 Georges Irat 2-litre sports car.
NATIONAL MOTOR MUSEUM

1939 Georges Irat 2-litre cabriolet.
NATIONAL MOTOR MUSEUM

Automobile Association, but it was also one of the country's poorest sellers. 'People don't care about fuel efficiency any more', said an AAA spokesman.

NG

GEORGE FITT (GB) c.1946–1950s
George Fitt Motors, Tankerton, Kent.
This company made a conventional invalid tricycle powered by a 197cc single-cylinder engine with a 3-speed gearbox. It differed from some of its contemporaries in having a smaller front wheel similar to that of a scooter. They made 500 of the Continental model in 1950. Frames for this and the TIPPEN tricycles were made by the Co-op Cycle Works.

NG

GEORGES IRAT (F) 1921–1953
1921–1929 Automobiles Georges Irat SA, Chatou, Seine-et-Oise.
1929–1934 Automobiles Georges Irat SA, Neuilly, Seine.
1935–1949 Automobiles Georges Irat SA, Levallois-Perret, Seine.
1950–1953 Sté Chérifienne George Irat, Casablanca, Morocco.
The first appearance of the Irat name was in 1914 when a company called Automobiles Irat was listed at Boulevard Pereire, Paris. There is no record of car production though until 1921, when Georges Irat who also made the MAJOLA in his factory at Chatou, launched a fast tourer powered by his own make of 1990cc ohv 4-cylinder engine, designed by ex-DELAGE engineer Maurice Gaultier. It had Dewandre vacuum servo brakes on all four wheels. The first full year of production was 1922, when 150 cars were made, followed by 100 in 1923 and 200 in 1924. Apart from the bodies, the whole of the car was made in-house. Gaultier returned to Delage in 1928, just after Irat launched a 2985cc six with the same dimensions as the 2-litre four, which remained in production.

1910 Georges Roy 16hp 2-seater.
NATIONAL MOTOR MUSEUM

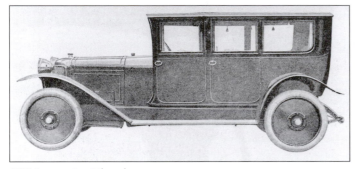

1921 Georges Roy 14hp saloon.
NICK BALDWIN

Output stayed at around 200 per year up to the end of the 1920s, when Irat caught the American engine bug which afflicted a number of his compatriots, including Lucien Bollack and the makers of Delaunay-Belleville. In a new factory at Neuilly he built large cars powered by straight-8 Lycoming engines, of 4350 and 5105cc, in a chassis of 126in (3198mm) wheelbase. The larger engine had a cover to give the impression of ohvs, on which was written Irat Huit. Saloon and 2-door cabriolet bodywork by Saoutchik was offered on these cars, but very few were made. At the same time the Neuilly factory saw production of the 1086cc 4-cylinder car designed by Georges Irat's son, Michel, which had begun life under the name MICHEL IRAT. Poor sales of this and the big straight-8s brought George Irat to the brink of financial collapse, but 1935 saw a revival of his fortunes. Backed by engine makers Godefroy et Levecque, who needed a new customer for their Ruby engines after so many of the small car makers on which they relied had gone out of business, Irat produced a small sports car powered by a 1100cc Ruby engine driving the front wheels. Made only in open 2-seater form the 6CV Georges Irat was more sporting in appearance than in performance, but they became quite popular, and Irat sold about 1500 of them between the end of 1935 and 1939. He also listed a larger car with 2450cc 6-cylinder Lycoming engine in 1935, but very few were sold.

In 1938 he continued the front-drive theme with a new sports car powered by the 1911cc Citroën 11CV engine, with all-round rubber independent suspension. Only about 200 were made before the war interrupted production. The 6CV was continued alongside the larger car, with which it shared styling after 1938. A number of small electric cars were made during World War II, and at the 1946 Paris Salon Irat showed a completely new car, powered by an 1100cc flat-four engine, with a magnesium alloy frame and body. The engine was mounted in a cradle which was an extension at the front of the frame, with the gearbox beneath it driving the front wheels. This never went into production, nor did a 3-headlamp development shown at the 1949 Salon. A new company was formed at Begles-Tartifume, Gironde, to make diesel engines which powered Isobloc buses, Field Farmer tractors and a few Irat-built trucks.

In 1950 Georges Irat struck out in a new direction with the VDB, or Voiture du Bled. Made at Casablanca, it was a light Jeep-type vehicle powered by a rear-mounted Dyna Panhard engine. A 3-seater, it was supplied with a matching 2-wheeled trailer. Production was very limited, and after showing a restyled VDB at the 1953 Salon, Georges Irat bowed out of car production altogether.

NG

GEORGES RICHARD *see* BRASIER

GEORGES ROY (F) 1906–1929
Automobiles Georges Roy, Bordeaux.
Like Barré and Delaugère, the Georges Roy was a regional make never very well known outside its area, which sold in sufficient numbers to keep the company afloat for more than 20 years, only to succumb to competition from the mass producers in the end. In 1906 they offered three models, each with a different number of cylinders. The smallest was an 1100cc single, followed by a twin with the very large capacity of 2.9 litres, and a 4.6-litre four. All had 3-speed gearboxes. 1907 saw a 6-cylinder car of 10.6 litres capacity. The twins were still listed in 1908, together with fours of 2.9, 3.8 and 5.9 litres, and an 8.5-litre six. The two largest models offered the option of chain or shaft drive, but by 1910 only smaller cars were made, a four and a six with the same cylinder dimensions, and capacities of 2.2 and 3.3 litres. By 1912 all Georges Roys had 4-speed gearboxes and shaft drive. Their appearance was characterised by round radiators, and the 1913 models included a light car with 1.5-litre monobloc engine.

The postwar Georges Roy was a very conventional 2940cc four, with fixed cylinder head, 4-speed unit gearbox, disc wheels, and a bull-nose radiator. Known as the OBD it acquired front wheel brakes in 1923, and was made until 1926. A companion smaller car was the 1536cc SBD, made from 1921 to 1929, which was braked on the rear wheels only up to 1928. A year later passenger cars were dropped, although light trucks on the same chassis were continued for a year or two longer.

NG

GEORGES VILLE (F) 1904–c.1909
Sté d'Industrie Mécanique, Paris.
Georges Ville was a designer rather than a manufacturer, and many of his components were made by other firms, notably Morane. His cars were mainly intended for town use, and some had frames dropped at the rear to allow for low-entrance brougham bodies. 1904 models had 15 or 30hp 4-cylinder engines said to be so flexible that only two forward speeds were necessary. Reverse was obtained by a separate epicyclic gear. Georges Ville designed the English CROSVILLE cars.

NG

GEORGIA COMPOSITES (US) c.1998
Georgia Composites, Div. Heidelberg International, Doraville, Georgia.
The Georgia Composites T2 was a prototype for a futuristic 2-seat sports car with tandem seating and a mid-mounted Porsche 911 engine. Constructed of lightweight composites, it weighed only 1800lbs. Estimated price was to be $66,000.

HP

G.E.P. (F) 1913–1914
Automobiles G.E.P., Gennevilliers, Seine.
This company was founded by Emile Godefroy who had been in partnership with Louis Le Metais, maker of the LE METAIS from 1904 to 1910. Godefroy, whose brother Henri joined Leveque in making Ruby engines, took the names of himself and his partners Esmenard and Pons for the G.E.P., a cyclecar which featured friction transmission and chain drive. Three engine options were available, a 664cc 8hp single, 1058cc 10hp twin and 1131cc 10hp four, the latter made by Ballot. 2- or 4-seater torpedo bodies were offered on the 4-cylinder chassis, with 2-seaters on the others. Light vans were also available. There were plans to revive the G.E.P. after World War I, but these never materialised.

NG

GEPARD (PL) 1990 to date
1990–1992 Studio Samochodowe Gepard, Warsaw.
1992–1993 Fabryka Samochodowe Gepard, Mielec.
1995 to date Leopard Automobile, Warsaw.
Design work on Zbyslaw Szwaj's sports car started in 1983, but it was 1990 before the Gepard car was ready. It was powered by a 3.9-litre Rover V8 engine in a steel frame with an aluminium body and all-round independent suspension. Only five had been built before disagreements between the designer and owners of the company put an end to the project. Szwaj then found new partners and prepared a new car called the Leopard, powered by a 3.9- or 4.6-litre Rover V8

1906 Germain 14hp tourer.
NATIONAL MOTOR MUSEUM

or a 6-cylinder BMW engine. It had a steel spaceframe and aluminium body, and was assembled in Sweden.

RP

GERALD (GB) 1920
Gerald Cyclecar Co., Birmingham.
The Gerald cyclecar was powered by an 8hp water-cooled J.A.P. engine modified by its builder D.G. Taylor, mounted lengthways in the frame on two tubular cross members. Transmission was by chain to a countershaft, and thence by belt to the rear axle. It had a 2-seater body and a very long wheelbase for a cyclecar.

NG

GERARD (i) (F) 1927
Automobiles Gerard, Clichy, Seine.
This was a conventional light car which barely passed the prototype stage. It was powered by a 1480cc S.C.A.P. 4-cylinder side-valve engine, and had a 4-speed gearbox.

NG

GERARD (ii) (US) c.1977–1985
Gerard Coach, Kirkland, Washington.
This kit car company was best known for their Jaguar XK-SS replicas. They started as OMNA AUTO, selling a line of VW-based kits. They changed their name to Gerard Coach and sold a version of the Witton Tiger called the Tiger II. It was an open roadster with low lines and running boards based on Ford Pinto or General Motors running gear. They progressed to the Lion, a fibreglass-bodied replica of the XK-SS that used General Motors V6 or V8 running gear.

HP

GERMAIN (B) 1898–1914
SA des Automobiles Germain, Monceau-sur-Sambre.

The Ateliers Germain were founded in 1873 to make railway carriages, and, later, tramcars. In November 1897 they bought from Mme Emile Levassor the rights to the Daimler-Phoenix engine for manufacture in Belgium. With these rights went those for the Panhard-Levassor car, which Louise Levassor had inherited from her husband on his death in 1897. For this reason the first cars made by Germain were called Daimler Belge or Panhard Belge. At the beginning of 1898 a new extension to the factory was completed for the manufacture of cars, with, initially, a workforce of 100. The first car left the factory on 25 June 1898; it and its immediate successors could easily be mistaken for Panhards, with 6hp vertical-twin engines mounted under the bonnet, and double-chain drive. They were soon being made at the rate of ten cars a month, joined towards the end of 1898 by the French ÉLAN voiturette, also made under licence.

A Panhard-derived 12hp 4-cylinder car was added in April 1900, and the 1901 range consisted of the 6 and 8hp twins and 12hp four, more up to date-looking with a longer and lower chassis, and equal-sized wheels. Production was now running at three cars a week. In 1901 Germain acquired another licence, for Renault light cars, which replaced the now defunct Élan. The larger cars continued to be built on Panhard lines until the 1904 season, when a new range called Germain Standards appeared. They came in three sizes, 16/22, 24/32 and 35/40CV, with side-valve engines, chain drive and armoured wood frames. The largest had a capacity of 9847cc, putting it on a level with the Mercedes 60. Germain delivered its 1000th car in the middle of 1905, when the workforce numbered 650, of which about half were working on vehicles, the others on railway equipment. Another activity started at about this time was the manufacture of motor boats in conjunction with the Cockerill steel works.

1906 saw a smaller and more modern car, the Germain Chainless. This had shaft drive, a steel frame and a 2923cc 4-cylinder engine. They could be distinguished from the Mercedes-like Standards by an oval radiator which became round in 1907 and characterised Germains until the end of production. The Chainless range expanded, and although 6-cylinder engines were adopted in 1907 and quickly abandoned, there were several fours by 1909, all with side-valves in a T-head, from the 2923cc 14/20 to a 12,447cc 70/80CV. For

619

1907 Germain 30hp roadster.
NATIONAL MOTOR MUSEUM

some reason, the middle of the range 5878cc 28/35CV could be had with chains, while all the others were shaft-driven. In 1910 came a new model, the 2612cc Type M with L-head side-valves and monobloc casting. Impressed by the success of the sleeve-valve Minerva, the Germain directors added two sleeve valve engines to their range from 1912 to 1914. The engines of the 20 and 26CV were made by Daimler in Coventry.

Car production was not resumed after World War I, though a handful of cars were assembled from existing components, and Germain lingered on some lists until 1922. They continued with railway work, and in 1937 exhibited a 5-ton truck and an agricultural tractor, neither of which went into production. Immediately after World War II a return to car manufacture was considered, and a steam engine was looked at, but nothing came of this idea. Germain remained active until 1967; among their last products were rotary discharge bodies for refuse trucks.

NG

GERMAN-AMERICAN (US) 1902–1903

German-American Automobile Co., New York, New York.
This company announced a 24hp 4-cylinder car which, it was said, 'closely followed the general lines of the Daimler (ie Mercedes), but with some novel features to make the car more suitable for American roads'. These included double strength chassis components and a lever-locking device to prevent stripping of gears. It might have been a reasonable proposition, but internal feuding among the partners led to bankruptcy before many cars could be made.

NG

GERONIMO (US) 1917–1920

Geronimo Motor Co., Enid, Oklahoma.
Named after the famed Apache chief, the Geronimo started its existence as a 4-cylinder touring car powered by a Lycoming engine. The car, open models exclusively, was a typical assembled product, built with proven parts, made by specialists in their fields. In 1918 the Geronimo dropped its 4-cylinder line, replacing its engine with a six which would continue as standard during the three further years of production. Production was limited, largely due to the restriction of material caused by World War I, and during 1918 the Geronimo passenger car models were augmented by a truck. Automotive Historian Beverly Rae Kimes has noted that the Geronimo enjoyed the export market, shipping about 100 cars to France under the 'WING' badge and further states that Geronimo production was 143 units. A fire in August 1920, resulting in a $250,000 loss from which the company could not recover, put the Geronimo out of business.

KM

GEROPA see HUMO

GETE see BOSSAERT

GETTY DESIGN (US) c.1991

Getty Design, Santa Ana, California.
This Porsche speciality shop sold a rebodied 911 upgraded to look like a Porsche 959. There were coupé and convertible versions, sold in both kit and complete form. Owner Arnold Getty also designed and built the ARIA.

HP

GF (E) 1995–1996

Grupo Fiero, Arganda del Rey, Madrid.
Using mechanical parts of the Pontiac Fiero, this group built replicas of Ferrari F50 and Lamborghini Countach with fibreglass bodies.

VCM

G-FORCE (AUS) 1990 to date

G-Force Sports Cars, Kardinya, Western Australia.
Initially intended for shortened Toyota Crown chassis, this Cobra replica builder developed a ladder frame to accept Jaguar suspensions and, additionally, a space frame, with the same running gear, to cope with V8 engines to 7-litre capacity and provide increased interior space.

MG

GHENT (US) 1916–1918

Ghent Motor Co., Ottawa, Illinois.
Prototypes of this car were built in Chicago in late 1916, but no production took place until after the move to Ottawa. The Ghent was a typical assembled car, though the makers showed some uncertainty about what sort of engine it should use. The 1917 range included the Models 4-30, a 23hp four and 8-40, a 22hp V8, made only with tourer bodies, while the 1918 Model 6-60 had a 23.5hp 6-cylinder engine, and was offered in sedan as well as tourer form. Total production was 187 cars.

NG

GIANNINI (I) 1963 to date

Giannini Automobili SpA, Rome.
Attilio Giannini established his company in 1920 and specialised in tuning engines, mainly Fiat. After World War II Giannini went into partnership with Bernardo Taraschi and formed Giaur.

Giannini left the partnership before Giaur faded in 1955 to concentrate on engine design. In 1963 he formed a new company to tune and customise Fiats. Among the firm's initial range was a 1000cc Formula 2 engine, used mainly by Italian entrants, and an 850cc coupé based on Fiat 600 components.

In 1965 this was replaced by another coupé based on Fiat 850 components but with its engine enlarged to 930cc. In 1969 Giannini fitted its 994cc double ohc engine to the Francis Lombardi 850 Grand Prix (aka OTAS Grand Prix) and sold it as the Giannini 1000 Grand Prix. OTAS also used Giannini engines in cars it sold under its own banner.

1972 saw the 'Sirio', a 650cc 2-seat sports car based on Fiat 500 parts. It did not find favour and soon afterwards Giannini concentrated on tuning and modifying Fiat saloons. In 1998 it was making a sporting version of the Fiat Seicento.

MJL

GIAUR (I) 1950–1955

Officina Meccanica Bernardo Taraschi, Teramo.
Giaur was a collaboration between Attilio Giannini, an engine tuner who also made cars under his own name, and Bernardo Taraschi who took over a maker of racing cars called Urania. Most of Giaur's cars were single seaters with small capacity engines, beginning with a 500cc F3 car in 1950. In 1954 Taraschi drove a supercharged 750cc car in the Rome GP – it was unsuccessful, but qualified as a Formula One car.

Giaur also made some basic dual-purpose sports cars, with a simple ladder frame and modified Fiat suspension, and attempted to sell Crosley-engined cars in America. These were uncompetitive because locally-made specials had superior chassis and aerodynamics.

Giaur faded during 1955, but a Giaur monoposto design was revived as the Taraschi Formula Junior car in 1958 and was competitive until Lotus and Cooper built cars for the category in 1960.

MJL

GIBBON (US) 1971 to date

Gibbon Fiberglass Reproductions, Gibbon, Nebraska.
Second Chance Classics, Inc., Gibbon, Nebraska.
Gibbon made replicas of many classic American cars. Their 1934 Ford 3-window coupé, 1928–34 Ford roadster, 1929 Ford sedan delivery, 1937 English Ford Anglia, 1932 Ford 5-window highboy, and 1939 Ford convertible kits were popular starting for hot rodders. Body and chassis kits were available, and the engines were, naturally, V8s. Their most ambitious project was an extremely accurate replica of the 1933-34 Packard coupé/roadster. The moulds were pulled off an original car and the chassis was a special ladder frame with Chrysler torsion-bar suspension. Any V8 engine could be specified. They were only sold in kit form.

HP

GIBBONS (GB) 1917–1929

Gibbons & Moore, Chadwell Heath, Essex.
One of the more unusual cyclecars, the Gibbons was a very basic machine with plywood body and an air-cooled engine mounted on the offside of the body, an unsatisfactory arrangement though one which was used as late as 1954 on the GORDON (iii). A prototype monocar with front-mounted engine and barrel-shaped body on a single-tube chassis was made in 1914, and production commenced in 1917 with a side by side 2-seater powered by a 4hp single-cylinder JAP engine. Three sizes of engine were offered, a 349cc single-cylinder Precision, a 488cc single-cylinder Blackburne, and a 688cc flat-twin Coventry-Victor. The last of these seems to have been the most popular on the few Gibbons sold, hardly surprising as the smaller engines must have given a very poor performance. Two forward speeds were provided with final drive by belts, high gear to the nearside rear wheel and low to the offside. The 1925/6 models had 3-speed Sturmey-Archer gearboxes and chain drive. This model was offered as a 4-seater, and a 988cc V-twin Blackburne engine was used. Braking was by blocks on the belt pulley rims, and steering was by wire and pulley to a centre pivot front axle. On the smallest model the two seats were in tandem, with side by side seating for the larger ones. At one point the Gibbons could be had in kit form, a basic set of plans costing five shillings (25p). An advertisement claimed that over 1000 were being built, but total production was probably considerably less than that. The V-twin Blackburne-engined model was offered to 'special order' as late as 1929, alongside a light aeroplane.

NG

Further Reading
'Plain and Simple, the Gibbons Cyclecar', M. Worthington-Williams, *The Automobile*, November 1999.

GIBSON (US) 1899

C.D.P. Gibson, Jersey City, New Jersey.
Charles Gibson's 2-seater Stanhope was powered by a horizontal 2-cylinder engine which was fuelled by carbonic acid gas stored in batteries which had been tested to 6000 p.s.i. He claimed that this gave his car a top speed of 60mph (97km/h), sufficient to gain the Land Speed Record in the early part of 1899 (Jenatzy's 65.79mph (105.86km/h) was not achieved until April). However, Gibson was never able to demonstrate this speed, nor could he get financial backing to put his remarkable car into production.

NG

GIDEON (DK) 1913–1920

R. Kramper & Jorgensen, Horsens.
Rudolph Kramper began building stationary engines in 1895, and went into car production in partnership with Jorgensen in 1913. The cars used 4-cylinder engines of 9.7hp with separately cast cylinders on an aluminium crankcase. Apart from the Bosch magneto, all components were Danish-made. Gideon trucks and fire engines were also built, with 3.9- and 5.5-litre engines, the latter with ohvs. The firm was liquidated in 1920 after 129 vehicles had been made, but it restarted a few years later, making machine tools.

NG

GIESBERGER (F) 1921

Like the car that Wolseley built for Count Schilovsky, the Giesberger was a gyroscopically-balanced 2-wheeler, with a 4-cylinder engine, 3-speed gearbox

1963 Gilbern GT coupé.
NICK GEORGANO/NATIONAL MOTOR MUSEUM

and double-shaft drive. The radiator had a curious double-vee layout on either side of the front wheel. The inventor took a stand at the 1921 Paris Salon, but his car did not go into production.

NG

GIGLIATO (J) 1989–1998

Gigliato Design Co. Ltd, Fukaya.
Founded in 1987 by ex-Isuzu designer Nobuo Nakamura, Gigliato Design was to be a Japanese equivalent of an Italian carrozzeria. His handsome Aerosa sports coupé was first shown as early as 1989 as a representation of the company's skills but following a favourable reaction it was developed into a production-ready car and launched at the 1993 Frankfurt Motor Show. It used an American-made Ford V6 3-litre engine developing 220bhp, mounted centrally and mated to a 5-speed gearbox. Its chassis was tubular and clothed with aluminium stressed panels and fibreglass bodywork, while the suspension was all-independent by double wishbones. Gigliato first announced its intention to build cars in the UK with an unspecified Formula 1 constructor. That came to nothing but an office was set up in Düsseldorf, Germany and at the 1997 Geneva Motor Show Gigliato announced that Lamborghini had signed a 'letter of intent' to produce the Aerosa. This plan was scuppered by the acquisition of Lamborghini by Audi. The 1997 version had a 4.6-litre 330bhp V8 engine mounted longitudinally, not transversely as before, and a 6-speed gearbox.

CR

GIGNOUX (F) 1907

C. Gignoux, Lyons.
Gignoux was a cycle-maker who built a very small number of 4-cylinder cars, probably fewer than 10.

NG

GILBERN (GB) 1959–1973

Gilbern Sports Cars (Components) Ltd, Llanwitt, Pontypridd, Glamorgan.
Gilbern was one of the few car makers to have been based in Wales and one of the few makers in the 1960s to graduate from kits to turn-key vehicles. The name derived from the founders, GILes Smith, a master butcher, and BERNard Friese, a German engineer. The first Gilbern, the 2+2 GT, was offered in 1959, when there was a minor boom in kit cars.

The Gilbern GT had a multi-tubular frame with Austin A35 front suspension and a BMC live axle suspended on coil springs. Usually, BMC engines were fitted, sometimes supercharged, but the specification was not set in stone and some cars had Coventry Climax engines. The GT found a niche, about 300 were sold, largely because it was well-engineered and finished, and owners spread a positive story.

The GT was followed by the Genie in 1966. It used the GT chassis but with MGB front suspension and rear axle, front disc brakes and, usually, a 3-litre Ford V6 engine. The body was new and inspired by the Alfa Romeo Giulia.

1970 Gilbern Genie coupé.
NATIONAL MOTOR MUSEUM

1972 Gilbern Invader Mk III coupé.
NICK GEORGANO

1923 Gilchrist 11.9hp tourer.
NICK BALDWIN

The Genie could carry four adults at speeds up to 115mph (185km/h), although the ride was crude and the road holding was marginal. About 200 Genies were made, from 1966–1969 when it was replaced by the Invader which retained its broad layout, but which had much-improved trim and suspension while options included overdrive and automatic transmission.

In 1968 Gilbern sought outside capital and was taken over by Ace Capital Holdings Ltd, a Welsh company which was Britain's foremost maker of slot machines. Following the takeover, Giles Smith left Gilbern.

There was then a series of takeovers of the parent company – Gilbern was a minor asset, but making steady progress. The Invader Mk II of 1972 had revised front suspension and could be has as a 'sporting estate'. Work also began on a mid-engined coupé, the T11, which was built around an Austin Maxi drive-train.

The Invader Mk III, which was shown at the 1972 London Motor Show, had a revised box section frame, Ford Cortina front suspension, and back axle, and 140bhp.

The majority of Gilberns were supplied in component form, but the introduction of VAT in 1973 altered the position. Gilbern went into receivership in July 1973 and, despite efforts to save it, expired soon afterwards.
MJL

GILBERT (i) (GB) 1901
Ralph Gilbert & Son, Birmingham.
The Gilbert was powered by a 3½hp single-cylinder horizontal engine, with final drive by chain. The 2-stroke engine was of Gilbert's own design, and could run on either petrol or paraffin.
NG

GILBERT (ii) (US) 1902
C.S. Gilbert, St Joseph, Missouri.
This was a 4-seater with two auxiliary seats ahead of the driver and passenger, as in some models of De Dion-Bouton. It was powered by a 6hp single-cylinder engine with over-square dimensions (139.7 × 114.3mm), mounted under the seat, with final drive by chain. Gilbert hoped to find financial backing to put his car into production, but failed to do so.
NG

GILBURT (GB) 1904–1906
Gilburt Motor Car Co. Ltd, West Kilburn, London.
This company was founded in October 1904, but the first mention of cars came in February 1905 when a light 2-seater was announced. It was powered by a 6hp 2-cylinder Fafnir engine mounted transversely, with chain drive to the gearbox and another chain to the rear axle. An unusual feature was that the differential was located in the offside hub. A 3-seater body was also available.
NG

GILCHRIST (GB) 1920–1923
Gilchrist Cars Ltd, Govan, Glasgow.
This car was designed by Sam Gilchrist who had worked for commercial vehicle builders Caledon before setting up on his own, with finance from his colliery-owning brother. His car was a conventional tourer powered by an ohv version of the 1550cc Hotchkiss engine which was also bought by William Morris. Various body styles were made by Sim & Wilson of Cathcart, Glasgow, mostly 4-seater tourers. About 20 cars had been made when Gilchrist's brother withdrew his aid as the money was needed to support his strike-hit colliery. The car would probably have succumbed in the face of competition from Morris anyway.
NG
Further Reading
'The Gilchrist', Lytton Jarman, *Old Motor*, January 1963.

GILCO (I) 1948–c.1955
Gilberto Colombo built a number of small sports cars, mostly using Fiat components, although Giannini 750cc engines were usually fitted. Larger-engined cars using Fiat, Alfa Romeo and Lancia powerplants were made after 1952, and some even had very high-performance engines from the likes of Maserati, Ferrari and Nardi.
CR

GILCOLT (GB) 1972
Ricketts Ltd, Streatham, London.
No doubt inspired by the Bond Bug, the Gilcolt was an attempt to create a sporting vehicle on a Reliant Regal chassis and was made by a Reliant dealership. Its fibreglass bodywork was rather slab-sided, although it had the exotic appeal of gull-wing doors. Kits were advertised from £250, or Ricketts could also supply complete cars.
CR

GILDA (RYCSA) (RA) 1957
Rosati y Christoforo, Buenos Aires.
Designed by Giovanni Rossi, previously with Fiat, this 6-seater, 2-door saloon was powered by a V4 engine producing 57bhp. Also available as a pick-up, the Gilda had a top speed of 70mph (113km/h).
NG

The Gilburt Light Car.

. . Specification. . .

Seats	... ...	Two or three.
Engine	... ...	6 H.P. Two cylinder vertical.
Bore and Stroke	...	75 m.m. by 80 m.m.
Ignition	... ...	High tension.
No. of Speeds...	...	Three and reverse.
Gearing	... ...	Sliding spur wheels, direct drive on top speed.
Transmission ...	...	By chains.
Cooling	... ...	Pump on cam shaft and radiators.
Frame	... ...	Weldless steel tube.
Brakes	... ...	Two double acting, foot and hand lever.
Wheels	... ...	Artillery, 26-in.
Tyres	... ...	Pneumatic, 2½-in. Palmer.
Wheel base	...	5-ft. 9-in
Weight	... ...	7 cwt.

Upholstered in real leather.

Price	... ...	Two Seats, £125; Three Seats, £130.

1994 Gillet Vertigo sports car.
NICK BALDWIN

1902 Gillet-Forest 7hp 2-seater.
NICK GEORGANO/NATIONAL MOTOR MUSEUM

GILETTE *see* AMPLEX

GILL (GB) 1958–1961
Gill Getabout Cars Ltd, London.
The Gill Getabout microcar was based on the ASTRA utility vehicle, also made by another subsidiary of the British Anzani Co., using the Astra's chassis, all-independent springing, hydraulic brakes and front portion of the alloy-panelled bodywork. However, the rear end of the metal bodywork was revised to become a 2-seater coupé. A 4-seater taxi version was also listed. A rear-mounted 15bhp 322cc Anzani twin engine was used with a 3-speed gearbox. At £500 it was vastly overpriced and did not last long.
CR

GILLET (B) 1991 to date
Gillet Automobiles S.A., Namur.
Former racing driver Tony Gillet was behind the audacious Vertigo, which he described as 'a modern interpretation of the Lotus 7'. The 2-seater sports car had its front lamps initially mounted on stalks but in an evolution version the front wings were enclosed, forming part of the bonnet, and the headlamps were faired into the wings. There were no doors as such, rather removable curved plastic side windows, and the canvas targa roof could be lifted out for open motoring. The advanced monocoque chassis was made of Nomex and carbon fibre and featured double wishbone suspension all round. A 220bhp Ford Cosworth turbocharged 2-litre engine was the standard choice but other units, such as the Alfa Romeo V6, were capable of being fitted and the chassis was claimed to handle a maximum of 550bhp. A Quaife 6-speed sequential gearbox was an optional alternative to Borg Warner or Hewland transmission. 17in alloy wheels were shod with very wide tyres (235 front, 265 rear). The first prototype appeared at the 1991 Brussels Motor Show, although it took until 1993 for production to begin. A significant milestone occurred in 1994 when a Vertigo broke the 0–62mph (0-100km/h) acceleration world record, in a blistering time of 3.266 seconds.
CR

GILLET-FOREST (F) 1900–1907
Sté des Automobiles Gillet-Forest, (Gillet, Forest, Bocande et Cie)
St Cloud, Seine.
The first Gillet-Forest had a 5hp horizontal single-cylinder engine and shaft drive. It was joined in 1902 by a 9/10hp and a 12hp, still with horizontal single-cylinder engines. They all had 3-speed gearboxes and the drive was encased in an aluminium oil bath. They were of distinctive appearance, having large, curved gilled-tube radiators which rather resembled the condenser of a steam car. In fact, it did act as a condenser for the steam given off by the water jacket. It was, perhaps, the only water-cooled car which was designed to boil. The condensed water returned to the cylinder head, while any surplus water went to a tank at the rear of the car. The Gillet-Forest was very economical; in fuel consumption trials held at the end of 1901, one used so little fuel that the judges at first refused to accept the result.
Despite their attractions, by 1905 the horizontal-engined cars were no longer competitive, though the layout was continued on light vans. For passenger cars the company turned to the Belgian MÉTALLURGIQUE whose vertical-engined models they made under licence. These included twins of 8 and 12hp, and fours of 16, 24, 30 and 40hp, with chain drive on the two larger cars.
NG

GILLETT (GB) 1926–1927
British Ensign Motors Ltd, Willesden, London.
The Gillett was one of a group of cars intended to sell at the magic figure of £100, others including the CENTURY (iv), SEATON-PETTER and WAVERLEY. It was designed by E.H. Gillett who had made the BRITISH ENSIGN earlier in the decade, and was a neat little car powered by a 1020cc 4-cylinder ohv engine which, together with the 3-speed gearbox, was made in the British Ensign works. Features included 4-wheel brakes and electric lighting and starting, while the body could seat two adults and two children. The price of £100 went up to £103 if nickel-plated radiator and fittings were required. Sadly, few people were attracted by this bargain, and only 25 Gilletts were made.
NG

GILLYARD (GB) 1912–1916
Barkerend Engineering Co. Ltd, Bradford, Yorkshire.
This was a cyclecar powered by an 8hp Chater-Lea 2-cylinder engine, with chain final drive. In 1920 *The Autocar* announced that manufacture of the CHATER-LEA cyclecar would be taken over by the makers of the Gillyard, and marketed under their own name. This does not seem to have come about, and soon Chater-Lea returned to car manufacture themselves.
NG

GILSON (CDN) 1921–1922
Gilson Manufacturing Co., Guelph, Ontario.
Founded in 1850, the Gilson company was a foundry and machine works which added marine and stationary engines to their output in 1906. Then in 1921 they planned to enter the car market, with a 4-cylinder tourer. Surprisingly for an engine-making firm, they chose Continental to provide their power units, though they made the frames and some other components. They purchased enough parts for six cars, but only made two, plus a partly completed one which was dismantled to provide spares for the other two. Gilson were more successful with their tractors, of which they sold between 50 and 100.
NG

GINETTA (GB) 1957 to date
1957–1962 Walklett Bros, Woodbridge, Suffolk.
1962–1972; 1974–1989 Ginetta Cars Ltd, Witham, Essex.
1972–1974 Ginetta Cars Ltd, Sudbury, Suffolk.
1989 to date Ginetta Cars Ltd, Sheffield, Yorkshire.
In the 1950s the Walklett brothers, Bob, Douglas, Ivor and Trevers, ran an agricultural engineering business. Ivor built a special based on a Wolseley Hornet which, in retrospect, became known as the Ginetta G1.

1907 Gillet-Forest 30hp tourer.
NATIONAL MOTOR MUSEUM

The brothers offered their first car, the G2, built on similar lines to Lotus VI, in 1957. Unlike most kit cars, it was well-engineered and about 100 kits were sold. The G3 was a G2 with a fibreglass coupé body, also sold separately, but the breakthrough came with the G4 of 1961.

A fibreglass body covered a spaceframe, there was coil spring and double wishbone front suspension, a live rear axle located by trailing arms and an A bracket, and a 997cc Ford engine. It was successful in racing, yet was a practical road car.

By 1962, on the back of the G4, Ginetta had grown sufficiently for the brothers to abandon their agricultural business and to move to new premises. The talents of the four men complemented each other: Ivor designed the cars, Trevers styled them, Bob administered the company and Douglas ran the works.

The company essayed a G4 variant, some competition cars, which enjoyed mixed success, and even essayed a stillborn F1 car, but the next major step was the Imp-engined G15.

Introduced at the 1967 London Motor Show, the G15 had a semi-monocoque fibreglass body bolted to a ladder frame. Front suspension was Triumph Herald, while the engine, transaxle and trailing arm irs were from the 55bhp Hillman Imp Sport. Top speed was 93mph (150km/h) with exceptional economy.

Before long there was a Mk II version, with a front-mounted radiator. It was successful as a road or competition car, but the introduction of VAT in 1973, hit Ginetta hard.

The company stayed in business with a series of cars which strengthened Ginetta's reputation for sound engineering and sharp styling. Most notable was the G21, a pretty 2+2 coupé with Rootes Rapier H120 running gear which was sold fully assembled, but only 150 were made from 1971 to 1978. Ginetta survived by being unusually self-sufficient.

When kit cars enjoyed a revival in 1980, however, Ginetta was poised to exploit it. The G4 was revived as the Series IV, which was longer and wider. In 1985 came

1965 Ginetta G.4 sports car.
NATIONAL MOTOR MUSEUM

the G27, an updated version of the G4 with all-independent suspension and a list of optional engines up to the 3.5-litre Rover V8.

By 1989, Ginetta was also making a series of mid-engined coupés and convertibles which used Ford Fiesta XR2 components. The older brothers were ready to retire and they sold their company, with Ivor staying on as a consultant. The new owner had sufficient capital to relocate and undergo Type Approval so that cars could be sold fully assembled.

Ginetta had introduced the G32, a mid-engined coupé which used many Ford Fiesta components, but it begged comparison with the Toyota MR-2. While road testers praised the car's dynamics, they damned its build quality and finish.

1972 Ginetta G.21 coupé.
NATIONAL MOTOR MUSEUM

1990 Ginetta G.32 coupé.
GUERNSEY PRESS

1991 Ginetta G.33 V8 sports car.
GINETTA CARS

1999 Ginetta G.27 sports car.
GINETTA CARS

In 1990 came the G33. In essence, it was a development of the G27 with a new body and a choice of Rover V8 engines. With the most powerful unit, it had a top speed of 128mph (206km/h) (0–62mph (0–100km/h) in 6.7 seconds). The failure of the G32 coupé, however, allied to general economic recession, soon saw the new company in financial difficulties.

To raise capital, it sold design rights of the G4 and the G12, a mid-engined coupé, to its Japanese importer. Ivor Walklett left to found, with brother Trevers, a company called Dare to build the cars.

Ginetta's overseas agents assisted the funding of the G33 to be stretched and re-engineered in Sweden as the G34, with Volvo components. They were made by a company called Gin-1 (in Swedish 1 is 'etta'). This project folded after 16 cars were made.

In 1998, Ginetta announced a G27 with revised styling and either a Ford Pinto or Zetec engine. With the latter unit top speed was 124mph (200km/h) (0–62mph (0–100km/h) in 6.8 seconds) and it was available as a kit or turn-key car.

MJL

Further Reading
Ginetta, the Illustrated History, J. Rose, Bookmarque, 1983.
Ginetta, the Inside Story, Bob Walklett, Bookmarque, 1992.
Ginetta G4, Trevor Pyman, Bookmarque, 1990.

GIRARDOT *see* G.E.M.

GIRINO *see* CIMEM

GIRLING (GB) 1913–1914
Girling Motors Ltd, Bedford.
This was a 3-wheeled cyclecar powered by a 6hp single-cylinder air-cooled engine, with friction transmission and shaft drive to a bevel gear on the rear wheel. It was a 2-seater but there was a third additional seat just ahead of the rear wheel. It had tiller steering, and a spare wheel was included in the price of £110.
NG

GITANE (GB) 1962
George Fowell Plant Ltd, Wolverhampton, Staffordshire.
An ambitious and highly attractive coupé, the Gitane GT was a 2-door 2-seater with a mid-mounted engine. It was planned at one stage to use a Giannini engine but in the end a B.M.C. Mini unit was specified. The manufacturer quoted an output of 84bhp from the 998cc engine, which was enough for a claimed top speed of 130mph (209km/h). The chassis was made of square-section tubes and featured inboard disc brakes on all four wheels. It was too highly-priced to have any true market impact.
CR

GIZMO (US) 1997 to date
Nevco, Eugene, Oregon.
This tiny 3-wheeled Neighborhood Electric Vehicle was powered by a 3hp DC electric motor powering the single rear wheel. The extremely basic bodywork featured a nose section that lifted up for passenger entry. The accelerator, brake and steering were handlebar-operated. Early models had a top speed of 30mph (48km/h) but this was increased to 45mph (72km/h) on later versions.
CR

G.J.G. (US) 1909–1914
G.J.G. Motor Car Co., White Plains, New York.
The G.J.G. derived its name from that of its manufacturer, George John Grossman. It was a conventional car made with two sizes of 4-cylinder engine, the 26hp Junior and 42hp Senior. Both lines were available with runabout, raceabout and touring bodies. The runabout was a straightforward 2-seater tourer, while the raceabout, with a claimed top speed of 65mph (105km/h), was starker and more sporty in appearance. The Senior models carried names such as Pirate Runabout, Scout Tourer and Carryall Tourer. In 1910 Grossman built a near-replica of the Junior for Walter J. Allen to sell as the ALLEN-KINGSTON Junior. Only one model of G.J.G. was made in 1914, the speedster, and very few of them, as Grossman was preparing to close his business, saying that he had never made any money from it.
NG

1902 Gladiator tonneau.
NATIONAL MOTOR MUSEUM

G.J.M (AUS) 1986–1987

G.J. McHattan, Manly, New South Wales.

Exhibited at the 1986 Sydney Motor Show, the G.J.M. Taipan was a Cobra-inspired roadster which differed from many similar kit offerings in being only available as a complete car. Raw performance was the emphasis as the engine was a 7.4-litre V8, with twin Garrett turbochargers, putting out 299bhp. In 1987 the Chevrolet 350 'small block' V8 engine of 5790cc was offered at lower cost.

MG

GLADIATOR (F) 1896–1920

1896–1909 Sté Gladiator, Pré St Gervais, Seine.

1909–1920 Puteaux, Seine.

The Société Gladiator was founded by Paul Aucoq and Alexandre Darracq in 1891 to manufacture bicycles. They were very successful, too successful, in fact, for the British cycle makers who suffered from Gladiator's cost-cutting methods. In 1896 a British syndicate, led by Dunlop boss Harvey Du Cros and company promoter Ernest Hooley, bought out Gladiator, forming a new company called Clement, Gladiator & Humber (France) Ltd. They quickly added motorcycles and light cars to the bicycle range.

The cars were voiturettes powered by 4hp single-cylinder horizontal engines mounted at the rear, with tubular frames and handlebar steering. By 1899 the engines had been moved to the front; they were Aster units of 2½ and 3½hp driving via a 2-speed gearbox and chain drive to the rear axle. They had wheel steering and were among the neatest-looking small cars of their day. They were also sold under the CLEMENT name as Adolphe Clément was on the board until 1903 when he left to make CLEMENT-BAYARD cars. The Clement name continued to be used by Gladiator for several years.

1903 Gladiator 10hp tonneau.
NATIONAL MOTOR MUSEUM

By 1903 the Gladiator works at Pré St Gervais was making more than 1000 cars a year, of which 80 per cent were sold in England. The Clements, which were handled in Britain by E.H. Lancaster and were the ancestors of the TALBOT (i), had shaft drive, while the otherwise similar Gladiators used chain drive and were handled by S.F. Edge until he became too busy with Napiers. In 1905 the range ran from an archaic twin with automatic inlet valves, rear-mounted water tank and a sprag, through a four with 3-litre Aster engine to a 4-litre 28hp four.

1907 Gladiator 25/35hp tourer.
NATIONAL MOTOR MUSEUM

1913 Gladiator 12hp 2-seater.
NATIONAL MOTOR MUSEUM

1961 Glas Goggomobil T300 saloon.
NATIONAL MOTOR MUSEUM

By 1906 the range was a complicated one, though all engines now had mechanically-operated valves. The 4-cylinder 12/14 could be had with either armoured wood or steel frame in the English catalogue, while the French customer was limited to armoured wood. The largest four was the 4.8-litre, but during the year a chain-driven 5.5-litre 38hp made its appearance. In 1908 it was announced that certain Gladiator models would be built by AUSTIN; although it is thought that none were made, the 1908 and 1909 catalogues contained some very Austin–like cars, the 18/24, 40 and 60hp. A more positive British connection was with SWIFT who made Clements from 1908 to 1914 (see CLEMENT (ii)).

In 1909 VINOT ET DEGUINGAND bought up Gladiator, and the following year production was transferred to the Vinot works at Puteaux. From then onwards Gladiators were virtually identical to Vinots, though there were no 6-cylinder cars with Vinot badges. The Pré St Gervais factory was devoted solely to bicycles. The 1912 Type AL Gladiator and Vinot had a 12/14hp monobloc engine and pressure lubrication. 1914 models were all fours, of 1692cc (12/14hp), 2210cc (15.9hp), 2612cc (15/20hp) and 4804cc (25/30hp). The two smaller models were offered again in 1919, but there seemed no point in having two lines of the same car, so the Gladiator name was dropped after 1920. Vinot soldiered on for another six years.

NG

GLAS (D) 1955–1969
Hans Glas GmbH, Isaria Maschinenfabrik, Dingolfing.
This was an agricultural machinery business established in 1883. They entered the motor vehicle field in 1951 with a scooter named the Goggo. In 1955 they launched a minicar called the Goggomobil, a neat-looking little 2-door saloon powered by a rear-mounted 2-cylinder 2-stroke engine in three sizes, 247, 296, and 395cc. Also made in attractive coupé form, it was a great success, and outlived all its later models from the Glas factory, being made up to June 1969, by which time 280,739 had been built, including forward-control vans. From 1962 to 1966 a Spanish factory, Munguia Industrial SA of Bilbao, built Goggomobil cars and vans.

A larger model with 584 or 688cc 4-stroke engines came in 1958. Called the Isar after the river that runs through Dingolfing, it had an American-style wrap-around windscreen and front engines driving the rear wheels. Larger again were the 4-cylinder types 1004 (992cc), 1204 (1189cc), 1304 (1289cc), and 1700 (1682cc). These had overhead camshafts driven by cogged belts rather than chains. The 1700 (1965–67) was a 4-door saloon in the same class as the BMW 1800. There were also two handsome Frua-styled coupés, the 1300GT and 1700GT, and the range was topped by the 2580cc V8 coupé. This seems to have been one step too far, finances became overstretched, and in 1966 BMW bought Glas for DM91 million. The Frua coupés were continued with BMW badging, the V8 with engine enlarged to 2980cc, while the body presses for the 1700 saloon went to South Africa where they were combined with BMW engines and radiator grills as the basis of a locally-made range that lasted until 1975.

The Dingolfing factory became one of BMW's most important plants with plenty of room for expansion. It currently makes 3, 5, and 7 Series models.

HON

GLASCAR (US) 1956
Bob Tucker, Richmond, Indiana.
Bob Tucker started with a 1953–55 Corvette and customised it to make this kit car. He added a pair of rear fins and relocated the headlights into the grill. A tubular chassis was offered, with Ford suspension and Oldsmobile or Ford flathead V8s. Tucker intended to sell completed cars in the $2500 range and kits in any stage of completion.

HP

GLASSIC (US) 1966–1976
Glassic Motor Car Co., Palm Beach, Florida.
This company made replicas of the Ford Model A roadster and phaeton. The first ones were built on International Harvester Scout chassis with a 4-cylinder engine. Bodies were fibreglass and they were only sold in fully assembled form. In 1972 Glassic was sold to Fred Pro, who changed the engine to a Ford V8. In 1975 Glassic added a replica of the 1935 Auburn Speedster called the Romulus. From 1976 to 1980, the Glassic line of cars was produced by REPLICARS in Palm Beach.

HP

GLASSPAR (US) 1951–1958
Glasspar Company, Santa Ana, California.
Glasspar was America's first major producer of fibreglass car bodies. Although their primary business was the construction of a highly successful line of boats, designer and company vice president Bill Tritt took time to style a handsome sportscar on a 1941 Willys chassis for Major Ken Brooks. This car, known as the 'Brooks Boxer', was highly publicised and featured in *Life* magazine, among others. Demand was heavy so the Glasspar G-2 was put into production. It was

a kit body that fitted a 1939–48 Ford or Mercury chassis and running gear. Cadillac and GMC engines were frequently substituted. Glasspar also offered an improved tube frame, built by the Mameco Co., with Ford suspension. Although Glasspar would recommend assemblers, they did not sell completed cars. Glasspar would also build bodies for other companies to sell under their own names. Among these were the WOODILL WILDFIRE, VAUGHN-SINGER, YANKEE CLIPPER and the aborted Volvo P–1900. Tritt also worked with Dutch Darrin on the DARRIN-built roadster with clamshell mudguards and designed to fit on a new chassis with Studebaker running gear. It was to have been sold as a complete car, but the plans fell through and Ascots were sold in kit form instead. Glasspar stopped building cars in 1958 to concentrate on their growing boat business.

HP

GLASS STATION (US) 1998 to date
The Glass Station, Lemon Grove, California.
This kit car company made something truly unique – a VW Beetle replica based on a VW Beetle. The Pro-V started with a Beetle floorpan and added a customised fibreglass Beetle body with a lowered top and other accents. The Pro-V8 model used a tubular frame that accepted a Chevrolet V8 in the front. The body was similar to the Pro-V, except that it had discreet holes in the front for cooling.

HP

GLASTECH (US) 1994 to date
Glastech, Harveysburg, Ohio.
The Glastech Pirana is a rebody kit for the Pontiac Fiero. It used styling cues from the Ferrari Testarossa without being an outright replica.

HP

G. L. CARS (US) c.1994
G. L. Cars and Concepts, Burton, Michigan.
This kit car company sold replicas of the Lamborghini Countach and Ferrari Testarossa based on Pontiac Fiero and Trans Am donor cars.

HP

GLEASON (US) 1909–1914
Kansas City Vehicle Co., Kansas City, Missouri.
This was a late example of a high-wheeler, and was made in the factory which had previously housed the CAPS and KANSAS CITY (i) cars. It was powered by a 20hp flat-twin engine and, unusually for a high-wheeler, had shaft drive. Five body styles were offered and the Gleason was made with little change during its five-year lifespan, though pneumatic tyres were available on later models. After Gleason discontinued production the factory was used for making the short-lived BAUER cyclecar.

NG

GLEN (CDN) 1921–1922
Glen Motors Ltd, Toronto.
The Glen was a rare example of a Canadian cyclecar, also unusual for having a 3-cylinder engine. This was air-cooled and lived behind a Rolls-Royce-type front. Only a limited number were made.

NG

GLENFROME (GB) 1977–1988
1977–1986 Glenfrome Engineering, Bristol.
1986–1988 Elektiar, London.
This company's main business was the transformation of Range Rovers into 6-wheelers and convertibles. Its first original project was the 1975 Delta, a striking 2-door coupé with flying rear buttress styling and a rubber-faced front bumper. It used a mid-mounted Triumph Dolomite Sprint engine but intended production never began. In 1981 the company embarked on a very different project, asking Dennis Adams to design a 'luxury all-terrain sports coupé' called the Facet. The 4 × 4 Facet featured very angular bodywork and a removable roof panel that stowed under the power-operated bonnet. Mechanically the Facet was based on the Middle East specification air-conditioned Range Rover and had an additional roll cage. Some 23 Facets were sold, mostly to Arabian countries, before the model was replaced in 1985 by the mildly restyled Profile.

CR

1961 Glas 1004S coupé.
NATIONAL MOTOR MUSEUM

1965 Glas 2600 V8 coupé.
NATIONAL MOTOR MUSEUM

1975 Glassic phaeton.
ELLIOTT KAHN

GLIDE (US) 1903–1920
The Bartholomew Co., Peoria, Illinois.
'Ride in a Glide, Then Decide' was the slogan of this company which had a remarkably long life for a small firm which never made more than 500 cars in a year, and usually less. It was founded by J.B. Bartholomew who had previously manufactured peanut and coffee roasters, and his experimental cars, dating from 1901, were named after him. His first production car, a tiller-steered 6hp single-cylinder runabout, was called the Glidemobile, and from 1904 simply the Glide. By then it had acquired a steering wheel and power was upped to 8hp. With horizontal engine under the seat, single-chain drive and an optional tonneau body, it was not unlike the Cadillac Model A, and sold for the same prices, $750 for the 2-seater, $850 with tonneau. About 25 were sold in 1903 and 50 in 1904.

GLIDE

1904 Glide 8hp 2-seater.
NATIONAL MOTOR MUSEUM

c.1908 Glide tourer.
NATIONAL MOTOR MUSEUM

1918 Glide Light Six-40 4-seater roadster.
NICK GEORGANO

A 14hp 2-cylinder engine came in 1905 and a 36hp 4-cylinder front-mounted engine in 1906. This was made by Rutenber, Glide using this make in all their 4- and 6-cylinder cars until the end of production. 1906 was the last year for the single- and 2-cylinder Glides, and for 1907 the fours were joined by a 50/60hp 6-cylinder Model H, a large car on a 132in (3350mm) wheelbase selling for $3500. This was only made for two seasons, and from 1909 to 1915 Glides were conventional 4-cylinder cars with 45hp engines, shaft drive and a range of roadster or tourer bodies. They did not offer a closed car until 1916. Production ran at about 200 per year, rising to 500 in 1916, the year in which they returned to six cylinders. The Model 6-40 was smaller than the Model H, with a 40hp engine on a 119in (3020mm) wheelbase, and sold for $1095 for a tourer and $1295 for a sedan. It was made with little change up to 1920. The make's demise seems to have been caused by their unwillingness to expand, though how many more Glides could have been sold is doubtful. It was by all accounts a good car, but faced with competition from makes like Buick and Studebaker, it had nothing special to offer.

NG

GLISENTI (I) 1900
Ditta Glisenti, Brescia.
This well-known ordnance works made a few light cars with 3hp Bernardi engines.
NG

GLOBE (i) **(GB)** 1904–1907
Hitchon Gear & Automobile Co. Ltd, Accrington, Lancashire.
Two types of Globe were made, one with a 9hp single-cylinder engine with variable-lift inlet valve, designed by Alfred Hitchon, and worm drive, the other a tourer with 12hp 4-cylinder White & Poppe engine. Not more than 12 were made of each type. The cars sometimes went under the name Hitchon-Weller, a partner was John Weller who had made the WELLER at West Norwood, and designed the Autocarrier which became the A.C.
NG

GLOBE (ii) **(GB)** 1913–1916
Tuke & Bell Ltd, Tottenham, London.
The Globe cyclecar was designed by J.H. Forster, and made in England by sanitary engineers Tuke & Bell, and in France by F. Terrier as the SPHINX-GLOBE. An 8hp Aster single-cylinder engine was used on the first Globe, with an Anzani single or J.A.P. V-twin on later models. Drive was by flat belt to the 2-speed gearbox and thence by chain to the offside rear wheel. The Globe was sold by Harrods as well as by the firm's London office in Manchester Square. After World War I Forster made a cyclecar under his own name at Richmond, Surrey.
NG

GLOBE (iii) **(US)** 1920–1922
Globe Motors Co., Cleveland, Ohio.
The Globe was a conventional assembled car powered by an 18.2hp 4-cylinder Supreme engine, with a Warren 3-speed gearbox. The choice of engine was hardly surprising, as the Globe's sponsor, Charles H. Davies had been vice-president and general manager of Supreme. Three body styles were offered, tourer, roadster and sport roadster, all on a 115in (2918mm) wheelbase and at the same price of $1800. Though the Globe was made with a number of ingenious features, including an under-bonnet light, and a light on an extension cord for passengers, it did not sell well. Those sold in 1922 were left-over 1921 models.
NG

GLOBE-UNION (US) c.1979
Globe-Union, Milwaukee, Wisconsin.
Batteries were the primary product for this company, but they had a number of experimental electric cars built. The Globe-Union Maxima was a prototype station wagon designed as a test bed. The Endura was a 4-seater sedan with a fibreglass body. It was built by McKEE Engineering and used 20 lead-acid batteries in a special lightweight chassis with a battery tray that slid out for easy maintenance. Power came from a 25hp motor.
HP

630

GLORIETTE; GLORIA (A) 1932–1938

Gloria Automobilfabrik, Brunn.

The Gloriette car with 4/20PS engine and backbone frame was designed by Hans Pitzek. Financial problems prevented its development, but in 1934 a new car which he called Gloria was announced. This seems to have been made in limited numbers up to 1938.

HON

GLOVER (i) (GB) 1912–1913

Glover Bros, Coventry.

This was very small even for a cyclecar, with a 3½ hp Triumph or 4½ hp Precision single-cylinder engine, belt drive, and a wooden frame. Only nine were made.

NG

GLOVER (ii) (US) 1920–1921

Glover Motor Co., New York City, New York.

The Glover was an assembled car with 27hp 4-cylinder Le Roi engine built in America for sale in Great Britain, where it was marketed by Glover's Motors Ltd of Leeds, Yorkshire. Glover had no New York factory, and the cars were made for them by one of the companies that were happy to make cars to be sold under another name. SENECA of Fostoria, Ohio, has been suggested as a possible source. Whittaker and Barron's *Automobiles of the World 1921* states that the American manufacturer made no other car than the 2262cc 4-cylinder Glover, but perhaps they were simply quoting Glover's advertising.

NG

G.M. (F) 1922–1928

Gendron et Compagnie, Paris.

This car's initials stood for Gendron et Michelot, the partners in a company dating back to pre-World War I days, when they were manufacturers of components including gearboxes, rear axles and steering gears. In 1922 they announced a tourer powered by a 2815cc or 3620cc 4-cylinder T-head Janvier engine, but it was not put into production. At most, one may have been made for M. Gendron. More serious production started in 1924 with the GC1, a light car with 1098cc ohv C.I.M.E. engine, 3-speed gearbox and 4/5-seater tourer and saloon bodies. These were of steel construction, but fabric bodies could be had from specialist coachbuilders. Four speeds were available from 1927. For 1928 the GC1 became the GC3, with a slightly larger engine of 1203cc, also by C.I.M.E. The GC2 was made only in 1925 and had a 1494cc single ohc C.I.M.E. engine. and a longer wheelbase than the GC1.

The G.M. had quite an active sporting career, particularly in the Circuit des Routes Pavées and Le Mans, as well as in rallies like the Tour de France. Both the partners Gendron and Michelot drove their cars in these events. Michelot was killed while testing a car at night before the 1926 Le Mans race. This was a special car powered by a 1099cc twin-ohc Robert engine, of which only two were made. The last new model appeared at the 1927 Paris Salon. Called the GC6 or G.M. Six, it had a 1215cc 6-cylinder side-valve C.I.M.E. engine. It was not made in such large numbers as the 4-cylinder models. An unusual feature of the G.M., shared with CHENARD-WALCKER, was that the brakes operated on the front wheels and the transmission, but not on the rear wheels.

A second-hand GC1 was the first of many hundreds of cars owned by the eminent French historian, Serge Pozzoli.

NG

Further Reading

'Les Automobiles G.M.', Serge Pozzoli,
l'Album du Fanatique, November–December 1982.

GM108 *see* OPEL

G.M.F.S.A. (F) 1986–1989

Garantie Mutuelle des Fonctionnaries S.A. (Département Automobiles), Lognes, Torcy.

Launched at the 1986 Paris Salon, the G.M.F.S.A. SL was developed on behalf of a pension fund group with an eye for a niche in the sports car market, and was engineered by Michel Landois of S.O.V.R.A. It used the complete steel centre body section of the Matra Murena in a specially designed steel chassis, which meant that the Matra's novel 3-abreast seating arrangement was retained. The

1904 Globe (i) 9hp chassis.
NATIONAL MOTOR MUSEUM

1913 Globe (ii) cyclecar.
NATIONAL MOTOR MUSEUM

new front and rear bodywork was made in plastic. There were Peugeot/Renault 200bhp 2.5-litre V6 and 165 bhp 2-litre 4-cylinder versions, both with the engine sited amidships and both with 5-speed gearboxes. Three prototypes were built but no production run ensued.

CR

GM PLASTICS (US) c.1989

GM Plastics, Mentor, Ohio.

GM built a Bugatti replica that was intended to be a prototype for a production kit car. It had a typical replica body with exaggerated mudguard fairings, side-mounted spare tyres and wire wheels. However, only one car was built before the project was put up for sale in 1989.

HP

G.M.T. (F) 1980–1983

Générale de Mécanique et de Thermique, Wingles, Nord-Pas de Calais.

The Rivelaine microcar was initially presented with a 47cc Sachs engine and automatic tranmission, though later examples had 49cc Motobécane power. The 4-wheeled 2-seater featured a long sloping tail and the luxury of winding windows.

CR

GMUR (CH) 1914

Gmur et Cie, Schänis.

This company made a few heavy electric cars, using their own motor and chain final drive.

NG

1920 G.N. (i) Touring.
NATIONAL MOTOR MUSEUM

1922 G.N. (i) 2-seater.
NATIONAL MOTOR MUSEUM

G.N. (i) (GB) 1910–1925

1910–1920 G.N. Ltd, Hendon, Middlesex.
1920–1923 G.N. Motors Ltd, Wandsworth, London.
1923–1925 G.N. Ltd, Wandsworth, London.

The G.N. was the first and best-known British cyclecar. It was the work of two young engineers, H.R. Godfrey (1887–1968) and Archibald Frazer Nash (1889–1965) who had both worked at Willans & Robinson (now English Electric) at Rugby. There they built a number of purely experimental cars while still in their teens, and in December 1910 they launched a cyclecar with V-twin engine and belt drive. *Motorcycle* remarked 'All parts except the engines (J.A.P. or Peugeot) and the magneto (Bosch) and minor fittings, are made at the works of Godfrey and Nash'.

For the first six cars, the 'works' were the stables at the Frazer Nash family home, The Elms, Golders Green Road, Hendon, but they soon moved to The Burroughs, Hendon, a series of sheds occupied by several small businesses, what today would be called an industrial estate. In 1911 the partners started making their own V-twin engines, using Peugeot cylinders and valves, and in 1912 they made their own inlet-over-exhaust cylinder heads. The engine was mounted transversely in a simple ash frame. Transmission was by a 2-speed chain and dog clutch system, with final drive by belts. Although the engine gave no more than 12bhp, the light weight of the car (around 400lbs, 181kg on the early models) made for a reasonable performance, with a top speed of about 60mph (100km/h).

In 1913 the engine was repositioned, so that the crankshaft was parallel with the frame, the cylinders projecting from holes in the bonnet's sides. Sporting models were offered, including the Vitesse and Grand Prix, the latter developed from the cars entered in the 1913 French Cyclecar Grand Prix. It had staggered instead of side by side seating, and a top speed of 65mph (105km/h). By the outbreak of war in 1914 the G.N. had been recognised as one of the best British cyclecars, although not more than 200 had been made.

In 1919 the little G.N. company was bought by the British Gregoire Co. for £70,000, and production was transferred to a larger factory at Wandsworth in South West London. The ash frame gave way to a steel one, and chain final drive took over from the belts of prewar days. About 500 men were employed and for the first three years of peace G.N.s sold well. The maximum output was 58 cars a week and during the best month in 1920, 220 cars were built. G.N. appointed two travelling service representatives to inspect owners' cars; the only other company to offer this facility at the time was Rolls-Royce. In 1919 a licence was sold to the French SALMSON company, who built about 1600 cyclecars of G.N. type up to 1922 when they started making their own light cars. Salmson paid G.N. £15,500 in royalties over the three years.

G.N. sales began to fall at the end of 1921 as the postwar car boom ground to a halt, and the introduction of the Austin Seven in 1922 was a further blow. A receiver was appointed and the company was bought by a Mr Black who wanted to go for mass production of touring models, while Godfrey and Frazer Nash preferred to continue with sports cars. A water-cooled 4-cylinder shaft drive G.N. was introduced for 1922, powered by a 1098cc D.F.P. engine. Godfrey and Frazer Nash left in October 1922, and the 4-cylinder car was in production by December. Both partners later made their own cars, Godfrey the GODFREY-PROCTOR and later the H.R.G. and Frazer Nash the well-known sports cars bearing his own name.

The change to shaft-drive touring cars was not a wise decision, for there were a large number of these already on the market, and the traditional G.N. owners preferred the old type. In 1923 G.N. offered a choice of two engines, an air-cooled V-twin G.N. or 4-cylinder Chapuis-Dornier, chosen because they were cheaper than the D.F.P. Production ended in May of that year; Black withdrew and another company was formed by two G.N. employees to provide service and spares for the older cars. A few cars with 4-cylinder Anzani engines and chain drive were assembled in 1924 and 1925. In 1928 an unsuccessful attempt was made to market a 3-wheeled delivery van powered by a single-cylinder engine. The following year G.N. Ltd became a retail outlet for General Motors products, and the Wandsworth factory was taken over by the Clayton Mineral Water Co.
NG

G.N. (ii) (GB) 1912
F.W. Berwick & Co. Ltd, London.

This is a mystery car, said to be of entirely British origin, and sold by F.W. Berwick & Co. who were later involved in the SIZAIRE-BERWICK. The G.N. had a large 4-cylinder engine of 3308cc, front-mounted flywheel, 4-speed gearbox and overhead worm drive. The chassis was fully described in *The Autocar*, but there seems to be no subsequent trace. It may well have been an imported car, possibly the G.N. (iii), though that may not have been made as early as 1912, and the engine sizes do not tie up.
NG

G.N. (iii) (F) c.1914
Gustave Nabot, Étampes.

This ephemeral make was the work of a garage owner who offered touring cars powered by Chapuis-Dornier engines in three sizes, 8CV (1460cc), 11CV (1846cc), and 16CV (2296cc). Seating capacity was two, four, and six passengers respectively. Bosch magnetos and Zenith carburettors were used, and the cars had quite attractive vee-radiators. According to M. Nabot's great grandson, about 15 or 20 cars were made, possibly one or two after World War I, although by 1920 Gustave Nabot had become a Citroën agent.
NG

GNESUTTA (I) 1900
Officine Meccaniche E. Gnesutta, Milan.
The prototype Gnesutta had a 2-cylinder Welleyes engine designed by Aristide

Faccioli, which was virtually identical to that used in the first F.I.A.T. of 1899. The company was backed by Adolfo Schlegel, but the car never went into production.

NG

G.N.L. *see* NEWEY

GNOM (A/CS) 1906, 1922–1936
Gnom, Kleinautowerke - tovarna automobilu - Fritz Huckel, Senov u Noveho Jicina.
Hat-maker F. Huckel and locksmith Otto Kloss built, in 1906, one light passenger car with a 4-cylinder air-cooled 10bhp engine, capable of 14mph (22km/h), very similar to the voiturette of the A type produced by Laurin & Klement. After World War I they returned to car production and from 1922 they assembled about one or two cars per year. No technical data survives.

MSH

GNOME (i) *see* BOYER

GNOME (ii); NOMAD (GB) 1925–1926
1925–1926 Gnome Cars Ltd, London.
1926 Nomad Cars Ltd, London.
This was a late example of a cyclecar, powered by a rear-mounted 343cc Villiers single-cylinder engine, with friction transmission giving four speeds in forward and reverse. There were no springs as the balloon tyres at a pressure of only 6psi were said to give a comfortable ride. The integral body and chassis were of steel and plywood. The original price was £75, but this went up to £100 for the Nomad, which had an electric starter. Despite two names and addresses in as many years, very few of this design were made.

NG

GNOME ET RHONE (F) 1919
Sté des Moteurs Gnome et Rhone, Paris.
Gnome et Rhone were well-known aero engine makers who, along with HISPANO-SUIZA and FARMAN, exhibited a large and expensive 6-cylinder car at the 1919 Paris Salon. The Gnome et Rhone was the largest of the three, with a capacity of 8725cc for its seven-bearing single-ohc engine. It had a 3-speed gearbox, 145in (3680mm) wheelbase and brakes on the rear wheels only. Two cars were shown at the Salon, a chassis and a rather angular 6-light saloon with body made in-house. These, together with one other car, made up the total car production of Gnome et Rhone.

NG

GOBRON-BRILLIÉ; GOBRON (F) 1898–1930
1898–1918 Sté des Moteurs Gobron-Brillié, Boulogne-sur-Seine.
1919–1930 Automobiles Gobron, Levallois-Perret, Seine.
One of the best-known and most individual pioneer French cars, the Gobron-Brillié was made by the partnership of Gustav Gobron and Eugene Brillié. Gobron had achieved some fame when, during the siege of Paris in the Franco-Prussian War, he escaped from the city by balloon to continue the fight. Brillié was an engineer who developed an opposed-piston engine which powered the cars long after he had left the company. Strictly speaking the Gobron-Brillié ended with Brillié's departure in 1903, though the name was quite often used up to World War I. Postwar cars were always Gobrons.

Brillié's design involved cylinders cast in pairs with four pistons per pair, the lower ones direct-coupled by normal connecting rods to a common crankpin, and the upper ones coupled to a crosshead, from each end of which tubular connecting rods gave motion to crank throws opposed at 180 degrees to the rods articulated by the lower pistons. A similar layout was used by ARROL-JOHNSTON, and the layout was revived in the 1950s on the Commer TS3 diesel engine for trucks. The first application in a car was in a vertical 6hp 2-cylinder engine mounted either in the middle or rear of the tubular frame, with chain drive, wheel steering and solid tyres. An ingenious metering device, an ancestor of fuel injection, took the place of a carburettor. The Brillié engine was said to be a multi-fuel unit, performing well in the alcohol fuel trials of 1902. The 1901 catalogue claimed that it would 'perform with equal felicity on whisky, brandy or gin' but there is no evidence that these fuels were tried. At the

1926 Gnome (ii) 343cc 2-seater.
NATIONAL MOTOR MUSEUM

c.1898 Gobron-Brillié 4-seater.
NATIONAL MOTOR MUSEUM

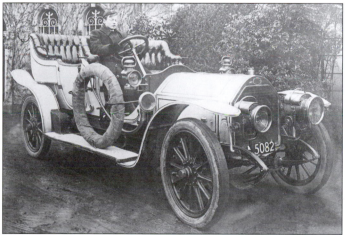
1906 Gobron-Brillié 25 or 35hp tourer.
NATIONAL MOTOR MUSEUM

low prices of spirits at the time, it would not have been so extravagant as it might seem today. A gallon of cheap whisky would have cost a little over one pound. By 1901 some models had front-mounted engines, but the larger cars still kept their engines in the centre of the frame. There were two gear levers, one for forward and reverse, and one for selection of the speeds.

For the first two years the company was located in Paris, but in 1900 they moved to larger premises in Boulogne-sur-Seine, and production rose from 75 to 150 cars per year. They were sold in England by Botwoods of Ipswich under

1907 Gobron-Brillié tourer in Criterium de France.
NATIONAL MOTOR MUSEUM

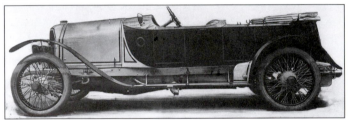

1913 Gobron 20hp sporting tourer by Rothschild.
NATIONAL MOTOR MUSEUM

1929 Godfrey-Proctor 7hp sports car.
NATIONAL MOTOR MUSEUM

the name Teras. Firms to take out a licence included NANCEIENNE in France and NAGANT in Belgium. In 1903 Brillié left to make cars under his own name in conjunction with the Ateliers Schneider. 1903 Gobron-Brilliés were all front-engined and looked quite conventional. 30hp 4-cylinder models were made, and buyers had the choice of magneto, coil or even tube ignition, though how many chose the latter outdated system is not known. It was not listed in 1904, when a 110hp racing Gobron-Brillié became the first car to exceed 100mph (160.93km/h). Other features of the 1904 cars were T-head engines, pressed steel frames, single-lever gear change, spray carburettors (so the metering device

cannot have been all that successful), and Mercedes-type radiators. By 1907 L-head engines had replaced the T-head throughout the range, which ran from a 4523cc 24/35hp to a massive 40/60hp of 7598cc, with twin transmission brakes and chain drive. 1908 saw a smaller car in the form of the 2650cc 15/20, and at the other end of the scale the 11,398cc 6-cylinder 70/90, which cost £1600 for a chassis alone, when a Rolls Royce Silver Ghost chassis retailed for £985.

In 1910 Gobron-Brillié reintroduced a 2-cylinder engine, the 2290cc 12/16 which powered a number of taxicabs as well as private cars. Other models of the final prewar years included the 15/20, now with pressure lubrication and 4-speed gearbox, a 4580cc 20/30 with shaft drive and two large chain-driven fours, the old 40/60 and a 9498cc 50hp with inlet-over-exhaust valves and cylinder dimensions of 110 × 250mm.

After the war the new company, Automobiles Gobron, was set up in new premises at Levallois-Perret. At first the opposed piston models were revived, including the prewar 20/30 and a new 25CV which had the added complications of sleeve-valves. Despite its relatively modest horsepower rating (as it was calculated on cylinder bore only), it had a capacity of 7486cc, larger than rivals such as the Farman or Hispano-Suiza H6, and its wheelbase was 155in (3934mm). It was very solidly built, the rear axle being described as more suitable for a bus. It had a 3-speed gearbox and Perrot 4-wheel brakes. In addition there was an engine brake in which one of the arms controlling the sleeve-valves could be disconnected. A chassis was shown at the 1921 Paris Salon, but the 25CV never went into production.

It was succeeded by a modest family car powered by a 1496cc Chapuis-Dornier engine, known as the Type L, or A2. This was made up to 1925, then capacity was reduced to 1350cc to bring it within the 8CV tax bracket, disc wheels replaced wire and a squarer radiator, very like a Donnet's, was adopted. Still called the A2, it was made up to the end of 1926 or beginning of 1927. Total production was between 100 and 250 cars, including some marketed with STABILIA badges. The final Gobron was an attractive small sports car in the Amilcar mould, powered by a new 1496cc 4-cylinder side-valve engine with Cozette supercharger, which gave 88bhp. The engine was inspired by the Anzani, but apparently made by Gobron. Only two were made, a competition car with cycle-type wings and sloping radiator, and a more touring style with vertical radiator. It has been said that the supercharged Gobron was designed by M. Cuminato, first trombone player with the Opéra de Paris. Although he owned the touring model, there is no evidence that he was involved in its design.
NG

GODET (F) 1919
M. Godet, Paris.
This was a light 3-wheeler powered by a 2-cylinder Anzani engine, with a 3-speed gearbox and chain drive to the single rear wheel.
NG

GODFREY-PROCTOR (GB) 1928–1929
Godfrey-Proctor Ltd, Richmond, Surrey.
This car was made by H.R. Godfrey, the 'G' of G.N. and later of H.R.G., and Stuart Proctor. It had an Austin Seven engine and gearbox combined with the lines of a miniature Aston Martin International. The Austin chassis was lengthened with a double-drop frame, the steering column was raked and suspension was by underslung quarter-elliptic springs at front and rear. The engine was given an aluminium cylinder head and a special Solex carburettor. The occasional 4-seater fabric body was by Newns of Thames Ditton. At least 10 were made, several being sold to Cambridge undergraduates thanks to the connections with the University of Stuart Proctor and sales manager John Rooth.
NG

GODIVA see PAYNE & BATES

GODSAL (GB) 1935
This was a would-be Anglo-American hybrid, using a Ford V8 engine with preselector gearbox, Charles Godsal's own design of ifs and an attractive 2-seater sports body by Corsica. The prototype, which survives today, was assembled by Research Engineers Ltd of London. Lack of finance prevented Charles Godsal from following in the path of Sydney Allard and other makers of Anglo-Americans.
NG

1935 Godsal V8 sports car.
NATIONAL MOTOR MUSEUM

GOFF (US) c.1956

Charles Goff, Texarkana, Texas.
This small company built the Goff in kit or assembled form. It was a fibreglass-bodied 5-seater sportscar based on 1939 Ford running gear. Price in 1956 was $600 for the body or $1500 for a running car. A fibreglass top was optional.

HP

GOGGOMOBIL (i) see GLAS

GOGGOMOBIL (ii) (AUS) 1958–1962

Buckle Motors Pty Ltd, Sydney, New South Wales.
Bill Buckle was building his own fibreglass sports coupé when he replicated the body of the T300 in fibreglass. It was visually similar but its dimensions differed and it was 45.5kg lighter. In 1959 an Australian initiative, the Dart roadster, appeared. Formed as upper and lower tubs, the body was a step-in without doors. It was the lightest model at 380kg and was then the lowest priced sporty type. For 1960 a Farina-like coupé was also produced in fibreglass, and had a larger engine and was designated TS 400. Two further fibreglass bodies were a convertible and the 'Carryall' van. Following the arrival of the Mini, sales fell away and the programme was halted in 1962 after 5000 units (including more than 700 Darts had been produced at a useful profit.

MG

GOGGOMOBIL (iii) (E) 1962–1966

Munguía Industrial SA, Munguía-Bilbao.
Planned to start in the late 1950s, the Spanish Goggomobils finally appeared in 1962. The first version was the T-300 with a 2-cylinder 296cc 14.8bhp engine. This was followed in 1964 by the T-350 and T-400 with 17bhp and 18.5bhp respectively, the first an exclusively Spanish version. Munguia also offered the 400-S with a body 5.9in (150mm) longer, which gave more space for the rear seats 121.5in (3080mm) instead of 117.5in (2930mm) long, a station wagon and a delivery van on the same chassis. These Spanish versions were different from those produced in Germany. About 5000 Spanish Goggomobils were made. The Spanish Goggomobil also took part in several racing events and there was a national racing event using only these small cars.

VCM

GOICATTOLO (AUS) 1986–1989

Goicattolo Motori Pty Ltd, Caloundra, Queensland.
This was the idea of Paul Halstead, of a Sydney exotic car business named The Toy Shop, which had inspired the car's name in Italian. Intended to be ALFA-ROMEO derived, with a 3-litre V6 engine mid-mounted in a Sprint coupé shell, the plan had to be revised when the cost of the Alfa engine became prohibitive.

Holden's Engine Co. offered its 4.9-litre V8 at a realistic price and, as it produced 241bhp, performance of the 1085kg coupé was in the supercar league. Design was by Barry Lock, formerly of McLaren Racing, who devised a totally new rear suspension with cast alloy hub carriers. Cast alloy wheels with very wide tyres required heavily flared wheel arches, which, like other special panels, were of kevlar. Problems with the supply of body shells arose and the project was terminated in 1989. It was suggested that 14 had been made.

MG

GOLD (GB) 1991–1996

1991–1993 Gold Motor Co., Dorking, Surrey.
1993–1996 Scorhill Motor Co., Chertsey, Surrey.
Nick Butler – a renowned tuning and customising specialist – designed his own mid-engined sports car during the 1980s, taking nine years to bring the Gold Cirrus to fruition. The dimensions were similar to a Mazda MX-5, but the Cirrus boasted a mid-mounted Rover V8 engine and Ferguson 4-wheel drive. Novel features included double pop-up headlamps, a targa roof with twin detachable panels and a rear window which could be hinged forward for fresh air motoring. Initially it was offered complete for £45,409 but later the project passed to SCORHILL, which offered kits with the option of Ford XR3 power.

CR

GOLDEN (US) 1915

Golden Motor Car Co., Chicago, Illinois.
This company offered a conventional-looking tourer with wire wheels and a round radiator. It was listed for only one year and mechanical details are not known, though its size would indicate a 4-cylinder engine.

NG

1958 Goliath 1100 coupé.
NATIONAL MOTOR MUSEUM

1948 Gordano prototype sports car.
NATIONAL MOTOR MUSEUM

GOLDEN GATE (US) 1894–1895
A. Schilling & Sons, San Francisco, California.
This company was well known for its Golden Gate gas engines. In 1894 a 3-wheeled, 2-seater car with 2hp engine was sold to a customer in Santa Maria. This was probably the first petrol car built for sale in California.
NG

GOLDEN STATE (US) 1902–1903
Golden State Automobile Co., San Jose, California.
This company succeeded the Christman Motor Carriage Co. in the same premises, and made a 2-seater runabout powered by an 8hp 2-cylinder Brennan engine with two cone-shaped flywheels.
NG

GOLDSCHMIDT-DIRECT see DIRECT

GOLF CAR IMAGES (US) c.1992
Golf Car Images, Newberry Springs, California.
The 1965 Mustang was scaled down to create a kit body that would fit onto a production golf cart and made it into a Mini-Mustang. Options included two trunks, CD player, ice chest, colour TV and wire wheels.
HP

GOLIATH (D) 1931–1963
1931–1933 Hansa-Lloyd und Goliath-Werke Borgward & Tecklenburg, Bremen.
1950–1963 Goliath-Werke GmbH, Bremen.
When Carl Borgward moved from making components to complete cars he chose the name of Goliath. A start was made in 1924 with small 3-wheeled vans, and

in 1931 a derivative was launched under the name Goliath Pionier, with a 2-seater coupé body and 198cc single-cylinder 2-stroke Ilo engine mounted in the rear of a conventional channel section frame. Two adults could sit in the coupé body, with space for two children in the dickey seat. Up to 1933 owners of such cars were exempt from annual tax and from a driving licence, but when these concessions were abolished by Hitler there was no point in the 3-wheelers, and Borgward concentrated on light vans and trucks.

In 1950 the name was revived and again at first light commercials appeared, followed by a 4-wheeled passenger car called the GP700. Made as a saloon and cabriolet (station wagon from 1952) this had a 688cc 2-cylinder 2-stroke engine (886cc from 1956) driving the front wheels. A sports coupé with Rometsch body was made in small numbers in 1951 and 1952. Fuel injection was an option from 1953. 36,270 were made with the smaller engine, and 8071 with the larger.

In 1957 the 2-stroke engines gave way to 4-strokes, and the following year the name was changed to Hansa. The engine was now a flat-4 with capacity of 1093cc developing 40bhp or 55bhp in twin-carburettor form. A few examples of a cross-country version, the Jagdwagen, were made, but the Army chose the D.K.W. Munga instead. The collapse of the Borgward empire in 1961 brought Hansa production to an end in 1961, though 487 were assembled from parts on hand up to 1963. Total production of the 4-cylinder cars to 1961 was 42,659.
HON

G.O.M. see F.I.M.

GOODCHILD (GB) 1914–1915
F.B. Goodchild & Co. Ltd, London.
This company sold light cars powered by 1327cc 10.4hp or 1778cc 10.8hp 4-cylinder engines, with 2-seater bodies and neat, slightly pointed radiators. Goodchild had no factory, and the actual maker of the cars is unknown.
NG

GOODSPEED (US) 1922
Leland F. Goodspeed, Chicago, Illinois.
A former vice-president of the Barley Motor Car Co., builder of the ROAMER, Leland F. Goodspeed joined Commonwealth Motors of Chicago late in 1921 shortly before Commonwealth merged with the Markin Auto Body Corp. of Kalamazoo, Michigan. Goodspeed was ambitious to launch a high-priced quality car named after himself and was able to construct prototypes for the car in the Commonwealth factory. The Goodspeed phaetons were handsome, lithe-looking cars powered by an in-house 6-cylinder engine, equipped with wire wheels and such sporting treatment as individual step plates instead of running boards, and cycle-type bumpers riding on a 124in (3147mm) wheelbase. The Goodspeed was priced at $5400 and drew considerable attention at the New York Automobile Show in January 1922 and later at the automobile show in Chicago. The fusing of the Commonwealth Motors Co. with the Markin Auto Body Corp. had taken place during this time and the amalgamation would become the Checker Motors Corp. to produce the CHECKER CAB. Leland Goodspeed subsequently became chief engineer for Checker, and abandoned his desire to become an automobile manufacturer.
KM

GOODYEAR (GB) 1924
American Auto Agency Ltd, Manchester.
Like the AEROFORD, ALBERFORD, MAIFLOWER and others, the Goodyear was basically a Model T Ford, modified to suit British tastes. Although engine, transmission and axles were pure Ford, the frame was lengthened and lowered, and the body was restyled into a 2-seater sports car. The engine was tuned to give a top speed of 50mph (80km/h).
NG

GORDANO (GB) 1946–1950
Gordano Motor Co. Ltd, Clifton, Bristol.
The name derived from the attractive little Gordano valley, adjacent to Bristol, now overshadowed by the M5 motorway. During World War II a group of enthusiasts planned a radically new sports car, featuring all-round independent suspension and a gearbox in unit with the rear axle. Design details were entrusted to the lateral-thinking specials builder Dick Caesar and engineering

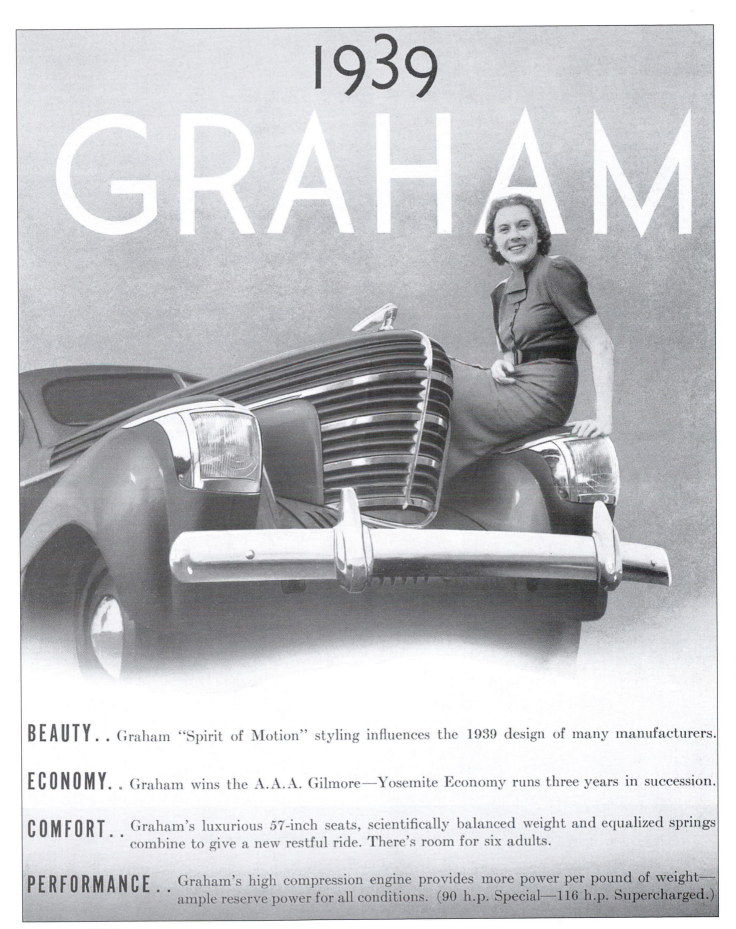

1939 GRAHAM

BEAUTY.. Graham "Spirit of Motion" styling influences the 1939 design of many manufacturers.

ECONOMY.. Graham wins the A.A.A. Gilmore—Yosemite Economy runs three years in succession.

COMFORT.. Graham's luxurious 57-inch seats, scientifically balanced weight and equalized springs combine to give a new restful ride. There's room for six adults.

PERFORMANCE.. Graham's high compression engine provides more power per pound of weight— ample reserve power for all conditions. (90 h.p. Special—116 h.p. Supercharged.)

1904 Gordon (i) Miniature 6hp 2-seater.
NATIONAL MOTOR MUSEUM

1945 Gordon (iii) Diamond sedan.
SPECIAL-INTEREST AUTOS

1956 Gordon (iv) 197cc 3-wheeler.
NICK GEORGANO/NATIONAL MOTOR MUSEUM

facilities were to be provided initially through Edwards Bros, a large motor repairers and undertakers. Finance was promised by the Fry cousins, members of a prominent confectionery-making family. For rigidity with light weight a box-section chassis was featured and despite enormous unforeseen development problems two prototypes were eventually put on the road, with 1548cc MG VA and 1767cc Lea-Francis engines respectively, pending the resolution of teething problems with the 1.5-litre Cross rotary valve engine. In the event these problems were never resolved and the project died after the death of Joe Fry at the wheel of his hill-climb special the 'Freikaiserwagen', also designed by Caesar. Dick Bickerton, a director of Edwards, ran the MG-engined car as his personal transport for many years.

DF

Further Reading
'1948 Gordano prototype', Brian Heath, *The Automobile*, July 1993.

GORDON (i) (GB) 1903–1904

Gordon Cycle & Motor Co. Ltd, London.
Known as the Gordon Miniature this was a light 2-seater powered by a 6hp single-cylinder engine, with 2-speed gearbox and single-chain drive. The makers claimed that the car was made throughout at their works in Seven Sisters Road, which helped keep the price down to 125 guineas (£131.25). Despite their boast, 'At Last – Something Substantial, Something Good, Something Cheap', the Gordon was soon out of production.

NG

GORDON (ii) (GB) 1912–1914

East Riding Engineering Works, Beverley, Yorkshire.
Designed by Gordon Armstrong, this was a cyclecar powered by a rear-mounted 9hp V-twin J.A.P. engine, available in air- or water-cooled form, with chain drive to the gearbox and chain final drive as well. It had unit construction of body and chassis and both 2- and 4-seater bodies were available, the latter very unusual on a cyclecar. One front-engined car was built with 1093cc 10.2hp 4-cylinder engine. It was said that these were intended for export to Australia, but a UK price of £200 was quoted. The outbreak of war prevented further development of this car.

NG

GORDON (iii) (US) 1945–1947

H. Gordon Hansen, San Lorenzo, California.
The Gordon Diamond was a 4-wheeler with a difference. The wheels were arranged in a diamond pattern with one in front, two following at each side and one behind. This gave it a very tight turning circle. The front and rear wheel steered and drive was through the middle wheels. Power came from a Ford V8 truck engine.

HP

GORDON (iv) (GB) 1954–1958

Vernons Industries, Bideston, Cheshire.
Developed after the parent company's experiences producing the ViCar invalid carriage, the Gordon was designed by Erling Poppe of Sunbeam motorcycle fame. This was intended to be a very simple economy 3-wheeler with the lowest possible cost of ownership: indeed it was Britain's cheapest car, costing just over £300. It used a Villiers 197cc single-cylinder engine mounted outside the main bodywork in a little 'pouch' of its own on the offside. This in turn meant that there was only one door to get in by – on the passenger's side. The steel bodywork featured a folding roof and early cars had optional rear hammock seats. Drive was transmitted to only one of the rear wheels by chain.

CR

GORDON KEEBLE (GB) 1960–1961; 1964–1967

1960–1961 Gordon Automobile Co. Ltd, Slough, Buckinghamshire.
1964–1965 Gordon Keeble Ltd, Eastleigh, Hampshire.
1965–1967 Keeble Cars Ltd, Southampton.
John Gordon was associated with the Peerless and Warwick GT projects, while Jim Keeble was a garage owner who had installed a Chevrolet V8 engine in a Peerless.

The car which became the Gordon Keeble GK1 was essentially a Peerless, with its spaceframe construction, De Dion rear axle and 4-wheel disc brakes, which was fitted with a 300bhp 5.4-litre Chevrolet engine and Borg-Warner 4-speed gearbox. It was clothed by a 4-seat Bertone body which was actually the first product of Giorgetto Giugiaro.

The result was displayed in 1960 as the Gordon GT but, though it was well-received by the motoring press, it did not reach production until 1964. By then it had become the Gordon Keeble and the bodywork specialists, Williams and Pritchard, had reworked the body to be made in fibreglass.

The delay probably sealed the car's fate. In 1960 a 140mph (225km/h) 4-seat GT car, with 0-62mph (0-100km/h) acceleration in 7.5 seconds, was sensational but, by 1964, the Gordon Keeble was part of a genre: English chassis, American engine, Italian styling.

At £2798 the Gordon Keeble was priced too low to make money (the Jensen Interceptor found buyers at £5838) and the company failed in 1965. It was revived as Keeble Cars, and the price was raised to £4058, but few were made.

1965 Gordon Keeble GT coupé.
NATIONAL MOTOR MUSEUM

Production ended after 99 cars had been made – some claim 104. In 1968, the project was taken over by another company which attempted to sell it under the name 'DE BRUYNE'.

MJL

GORHAM (J) 1920–1922

Jitsuyo Jidosha Seizo Co., Osaka.

This car was built by the American William R. Gorham who went to Japan in 1918 to manufacture aircraft and engines. Finding little demand for these, he turned to motor vehicles, first an experimental truck built in 1919, and then a light 3-wheeled car which could be used by the disabled. This was originally made for his plant manager, Mr Kusibicki, but in 1920 the Jitsuyo Jidosha company was formed for its manufacture. Powered by an 8hp air-cooled 2-cylinder engine, it had chain drive to the offside rear wheel, tiller steering and seated three, the driver and two passengers behind him. A folding hood gave reasonable weather protection, and a delivery van version was made as well. About 250 3-wheelers had been completed by the end of 1921.

During 1921 a 4-wheeler Gorham was introduced with a 10hp engine and the same body options as the 3-wheeler. For 1923 this was dropped in favour of the LILA, and in 1926 Jitsuyo Jidosha merged with DAT, which later made the DATSUN. William Gorham became technical director of the Tobata Foundry, a company associated with DAT Jidosha Seizo, and which was a pioneer of the diesel engine in Japan. In 1932 he returned to Detroit.

NG

GORICKE (D) 1907–1908

Bielefelder Maschinen- und Fahrradfabrik August Goricke, Bielefeld.

This light 3-wheeler was clearly of motorcycle ancestry, though the two rear wheels were shaft driven and, unusual for such a light vehicle, steering was by wheel.

HON

GORKE (D) 1921–1922

Fritz Gorke Kleinautobau, Leipzig.

This was a 3-wheeeled cyclecar powered by a NSU motorcycle engine and transmission mounted on the side of the car, with chain drive to one rear wheel. It could seat two or three passengers.

HON

GORM (DK) 1917

Karl J. Smidt, Copenhagen.

The short-lived Gorm was powered by a $6^{1}/_{2}$ hp 4-cylinder engine believed to be of foreign origin. It had wire wheels and was made in 2- and 4-seater form. About 20 were built.

NG

GOTTSCHALK (D) 1900–1901

Berliner Motorwagenfabrik Gottschalk & Co. KG, Berlin

This company was mainly known as a maker of commercial vehicles, though a few small passenger cars were built. After 1901 it became known as the Berliner Motorwagenfabrik (BMF) and concentrated on commercials.

HON

GOUJON (F) 1896–1901

E. Goujon, Neuilly-sur-Seine.

The first Goujon was built on Benz lines, with a $3^{1}/_{2}$hp horizontal single-cylinder engine, three forward speeds and belt drive. Unlike the Mannheim product, it had hot tube ignition. His car made its final appearance at the 1901 Paris Salon, and seems to have changed little in five years apart from having four speeds and chain drive to the countershaft and thence to the rear wheels. Output was now quoted as 5hp at 300rpm. *The Autocar* observed somewhat disparagingly 'E. Goujon started manufacturing autocars when it was the practice to put motors at the rear of the carriage, and he shows a vehicle on this system'.

NG

1982 G.P. Madison sports car.
G.P.SPECIALIST VEHICLES

c.1990 G.P. Spyder sports car.
NICK BALDWIN

1924 Grade Type F2 3/16PS 2-seater.
M.J.WORTHINGTON-WILLIAMS

GOVE (US) 1921
Gove Motor Car Co., Detroit, Michigan.
This was a somewhat shadowy car, probably made only in prototype form. These were made in Detroit, or possibly Brighton, Michigan, though the company claimed to have headquarters in Pocatello. Idaho. The prototype tourer had a 45hp Falls 6-cylinder engine and was to have sold for $2150. They also planned to make a 1½-ton truck.
NG

GOZZY (GB/J) 1978–1983
Church Green Engineering, East Knoyle, Dorset; and Italya Co. Ltd, Tokyo.
The Gozzy came about when a Japanese clothing manufacturer, Italya of Tokyo, asked the British restoration and engineering company Church Green Engineering to restore a genuine Mercedes-Benz SSK. The result was so good that replicas

were ordered. Len Terry was called in to toughen up the original-style chassis, which used modified Leyland Sherpa van suspension and a Mercedes 280 power train. The replication was superb, including an aluminium-over-ash body and specially-made spoked wheels. Prices started at £30,000 but the project turned sour and only six were made.
CR

G.P. (GB) 1968 to date
1968–1972 G.P. Speed Shop, Feltham, Middlesex.
1972–1975 G.P. Speed Shop, Isleworth, Middlesex.
1975–1993 G.P. Concessionaires (G.P. Vehicles), Isleworth, Middlesex.
1993–1994 G.P. Developments, Princes Risborough, Buckinghamshire.
1994 to date G.P. Projects, Princes Risborough, Buckinghamshire.
John Jobber and Pierre du Plessis made their mark with Britain's first domestic beach buggy, which remained in consistent production ever since its launch in 1968, selling over 4000 examples. As an insurance policy against the buggy boom bursting, G.P. developed the Centron, Britain's first-ever VW Beetle-based 'exotic' kit car, a genre developed in the USA. The low fibreglass body featured a distinctive forward-hinging canopy. Only 12 were built in one year but a revised Centron II appeared in 1974, swapping the canopy for conventional doors, but it was highly marginal, even after a revival in 1983 by Lalande of St Columb Major, Cornwall and from 1986 to 1987 by M.D.B. Sportscars of Tredegar, which renamed it the Sapphire. G.P. next forged a relationship with designer Neville Trickett, who in 1976 created a fibreglass VW Kubelwagen replica, followed by the Camel, a 'modern' Kubel-inspired car intended for production in developing nations. Neither reached full production, though the Kubel replica was later taken over by a company called GT Mouldings.

Trickett's next project was the Talon of 1979, which resembled a Fiat X1/9 in style. It was a 2+2 coupé based on a VW Beetle floorpan with gull-wing doors that could be removed for open-air motoring. Only 30 were made before a Mk II revamp in 1983, which had a thicker rear pillar. The Talon was made by Talon Sportscars of Christchurch, and subsequently of Leeds, from 1988 into the 1990s. It also developed a spaceframe chassis for mid-mounted Ford Escort Mk III power and added a full convertible body option.

Trickett's own firm, Ground Effect Developments, was set to make his 1980 Madison, a Packard-inspired pastiche, but G.P. produced it in fact. The first ones had a VW Beetle floorpan but a Ford Cortina based chassis became available from 1983. A rare variant was the Madison Coupé, an attractive fixed-head fastback. The project was taken over by the Madison Sportscar Co of West Kingsdown, Kent and manufactured until at least 1993.

G.P. really made its fortune with the Spyder, introduced in 1982, an accurate replica of the 718 RSK Porsche based on a shortened VW chassis. A mid-engined chassis for Porsche was even more authentic, though you could choose VW Golf engines as well. Some 1200 Spyders had been made by 1998.
CR

G.P.A. (RA) 1975
F.A.A.S., Buenes Aires.
This was a replica of the Alfa Romeo 1750 with Fiat 125 engine, gearbox, and final drive, with a body made partly of steel and partly of fibreglass. Only a few were sold.
ACT

G.P.M. (F) 1994–1997
G.P.M. Automobile SA, Roanne.
Created by two ex-Auverland engineers, the Éole was a small buggy-like open car with fibreglass bodywork over a simple square-tube chassis, sold in 2-and 4-seater versions. It relied on Citroën AX mechanicals, including a 1360cc 50bhp diesel engine, permitting it a top speed of 90mph (145km/h). 100 examples were sold in 1995 alone.
CR

GRACIANO (US) 1998 to date
Graciano Design, Corning, California.
The Graciano Venum was a Dodge Viper replica that fitted on 1984 Corvette chassis. It was shorter than a real Viper and the proportions were not authentic.
HP

GRACIELA (RA) 1957–1963

DINFIA (Direccion Nacional de Fabricaciones e Investigaciones Aeronauticas), formerly IAME, Cordoba.

When General Juan Domingo Peron's government was toppled by the military in 1955, IAME was renamed, and sports car and commercial vehicle production stopped. Only what used to be the Justicialista saloon continued in production, but under a different name, which had no connections with Peron's Justicialista political party. This car was the Graciela, which also had a redesigned grill and a 37hp, 3-cylinder East German WARTBURG engine powering the front wheels. Suspension was independent at the front, and by semi-elliptic springs at the rear. Top speed was around 63mph (100km/h). This vehicle was discontinued after 2300 units had been made, and DINFIA started to build the Wartburg 900, under licence, using the Graciela badge. In 1960 Rastrojero commercial vehicle production started, with a few of these fitted with large and clumsy 4-door saloon bodies.

ACT

GRACILE see BOYER

GRADE (D) 1921–1926

1921–1925 Grade Automobilwerk AG, Bork bei Bruck.
1925–1926 Grade Automobil AG, Bork bei Bruck.

Hans Grade (1879–1946) was a well-known aircraft pioneer who looked for new work after World War I when he was no longer allowed to work in this field. He launched a most unusual design of car, with boat-shaped chassisless body made of aluminium, with tandem seating. It was powered by a 808cc 2-cylinder 2-stroke engine of Grade's own design, with friction transmission and chain final drive. The narrow track did not require a differential. Later models were more civilised, offering side-by-side seating and even for four passengers in 1927.

HON

GRÄF & STIFT (A) 1907–1938

1907–1908 Gräf & Stift, Vienna.
1908–1938 Wiener Automobilfabrik AG vorm Gräf & Stift, Vienna.

The Gräf & Stift was the finest car to be made in Austria, and fully deserved its title 'the Austrian Rolls-Royce'. Although they made some smaller cars than the British company, all their products were of the highest quality.

The Gräf brothers Karl, Franz, and Heinrich, were well placed to make cars, for Karl was a bicycle repairer, Franz a coachbuilder and Heinrich a mechanical engineer. During the years 1895/97 they designed and built a light 2-seater car powered by a 3½hp single-cylinder De Dion-Bouton engine driving the front wheels, probably the first light petrol-engined front-drive car ever made. It had no immediate successor, but in 1902 the brothers joined forces with car importer Willy Stift to make cars which were sold by Arnold Spitz under the name SPITZ. Designed by the racing driver Otto Hieronimus, these were Gräf & Stifts in all but name, and when Spitz went into liquidation in 1906 the brothers and Stift sold them under their own names. Models made up to 1914 included four large 4-cylinder cars, of 4240cc (16/22PS), 5880cc (18/32PS), 7320cc (28/45PS) and 7686cc (35/65PS). They all had T-head engines, 4-speed gearboxes and shaft drive. The bodies were made in the firm's own factory at Liesing, and output varied between 250 and 500 cars per year. Gräf & Stifts soon became favourites at the Imperial Court. The Emperor Franz Joseph had several, and his son Karl, the last Emperor went into exile in Switzerland in a Gräf & Stift. More notorious than any of these was the 18/32PS tourer in which the Archduke Franz Ferdinand and his wife were assassinated in Sarajevo in 1914, precipitating World War I. This was not owned by the Archduke but was lent to him by a member of the Court for the visit. It has been on display for many years in the Army Museum in Vienna.

During the war Gräf & Stift made trucks, production of which had begun in 1909. These were continued in the interwar years, gradually assuming more importance than the passenger cars. Nevertheless some fine examples of these were made. The smallest were the 1877cc VK1 (1920–1925) and 1950cc VK2 (1926–1930), the former with side valves, the latter with overhead valves. As might be expected, more were sold of these, about 800, than of the larger Gräf & Stifts. These included the SR series (1921–1928), with 7749cc 6-cylinder engine which received overhead valves on the SR4 in 1926, a smaller six, the 3920cc SP5/6 (1924–1935), and the 5923cc single-ohc straight-8 SP8/9 (1930–1938).

1913 Gräf & Stift 45hp tourer of ex-Emperor Karl of Austria.
NATIONAL MOTOR MUSEUM

1921 Gräf & Stift SR1 8-litre tourer.
NICK GEORGANO

1925 Gräf & Stift S.3 6-litre sports car.
NICK GEORGANO

These carried high-quality coachwork, mostly made in-house. In 1927 Gräf & Stift acquired the Automobilfabrik PERL to increase space for body production. These were mostly tourers, saloons and limousines, though some sports models were made which competed in Austrian and Czechoslovakian events. They had the usual Germanic vee-radiators until 1925, then vertical flat radiators, though a few of the later models had slightly sloping radiators. They all carried a distinctive silver lion mascot. Production of the SP5/6 totalled about 500, and of the SP8/9, about 400, though both dwindled from about 1932 onwards. The last cars of native design were the G35/G36/G8 with 4587cc straight-8 engine which reverted to side valves, of which about 150 were made from 1935 to 1938, and the C12, a 4036cc side-valve V12, built only as a single prototype in 1938.

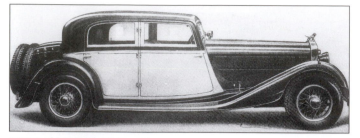

1933 Gräf & Stift SP8 5.9-litre saloon.
HANS-OTTO NEUBAUER

1920 Grahame-White 7hp 2-seater.
NATIONAL MOTOR MUSEUM

Gräf & Stift also built two foreign designs under licence, the Citroën MF6 and the Ford V8, the latter sold under the name Gräfford. About 150 were made of each, the Citroëns between 1934 and 1936, and the Gräffords in 1936 and 1937. After the war a few examples of the Czech AERO MINOR were assembled in 1949 and 1950, but otherwise the Gräf & Stift name was found only on commercial and military vehicles. In 1970 they merged with O.A.F. (formerly AUSTRO-FIAT), which shortly afterwards was taken over by M.A.N. Trucks were dropped in the early 1970s, but the name can still be seen on Viennese buses, either as Gräf & Stift or Gräf Steyr.

NG

GRAHAM see ROYALE

GRAHAM ELECTRIC (US) 1903
Graham Automobile & Launch Co., Chicago, Illinois.
This was a small electric roadster with angle-iron frame and single-chain drive. An 8hp single-cylinder petrol car was promised, but the company failed before it could be made.
NG

GRAHAME-WHITE (GB) 1920–1924
The Grahame-White Co. Ltd, Hendon, Middlesex.
Claude Grahame-White was a pioneer aviator who set up a flying school at Pau in France in 1910. Three years later he started a factory to make biplanes at Hendon, running the 500 acre (120 hectare) aerodrome which was the leading airfield in Britain. Today it is the site of the RAF Museum. After the war he felt the need to diversify, and the products of his company were quoted as aeroplanes, cyclecars, coachwork, bedroom suites, and office furniture. The cyclecars were of two kinds, the G-W Buckboard and the Wonder Car/7hp. The former was on the lines of the BRIGGS & STRATTON, with no suspension apart from the flexing of the frame, though it had a little more bodywork and normal drive to the rear wheels. It was powered by a 3hp single-cylinder air-cooled engine, with 2-speed gearbox and chain drive, and was priced at 95 guineas (£99.75). The

Wonder Car and 7hp were similar in appearance but the former was powered by a 348cc 3.5hp Precision engine and shared the Buckboard's 2-speed gearbox, while the latter had a 685cc 7hp Coventry-Victor flat-twin and friction transmission.

Several hundred of these three models were made, and there was also a proper light car powered by a 1094cc 4-cylinder Dorman engine and shaft drive. Only three of these were made.

After the end of car production under their own name, Grahame-White assembled a number of ANGUS SANDERSONs. They also built, in 1919/20, a few bodies on Rolls-Royce and Daimler chassis.

NG

GRAHAM-FOX see COMPOUND

GRAHAM MOTORETTE (US) 1902–1903
1902–1903 Graham Automobile Co., Brooklyn, New York.
1903 Charles Sefrin & Co., Brooklyn, New York.
This was a small 2-seater with piano-box type frame and 3hp air-cooled single-cylinder engine. It had chain drive, tiller steering and could be started from the seat. When Charles Sefrin bought the company he changed the name to his own and installed a slightly more powerful Thomas engine of 3½hp. In 1904 he added a 9hp tourer to the range, which was renamed SEFRIN.
NG

GRAHAM-PAIGE, GRAHAM (US) 1928–1940
Graham-Paige Motors Corp., Detroit, Michigan.
The Graham brothers, Joseph (1882–1970), Robert (1885–1967) and Ray (1887–1932), began their industrial careers in the glass business. Their inventiveness brought the Lythgoe Bottle Co. of Loogootee, Indiana, later renamed Graham Glass Co., from a craft shop making hand-blown bottles to a major mechanised concern. Having sold their interests to the Libbey-Owens firm, the brothers embarked on an enterprise of building trucks and tractors. The first product, the 'Truck-Builder' conversion for Model T FORD chassis, proved a marked success with farmers and delivery-men; by 1917 conversion units were offered for 30 makes of chassis. The popularity of this unit led to the assembly of complete trucks of Grahams' own design in 1919, using proprietary components and engines from such manufacturers as Continental, Ford and DODGE. An advanced tractor designed during this period was stillborn.

The Graham Brothers Speed Truck, using much Dodge componentry, became so popular that the Dodge Brothers firm took notice, and entered into an agreement for the Grahams to supply complete trucks to be sold through Dodge dealers. In 1926 they sold their interests in the truck firm to Dodge, then owned by bankers Dillon, Read & Co. On 10 June 1927 they purchased the PAIGE-DETROIT Motor Car Co. of Dearborn, Michigan. The firm's name was soon changed to Graham-Paige Motors Corp.

The Grahams continued the existing line of Paige cars for a time. Six months after acquiring the firm, their own Graham-Paige car was ready and debuted at the New York Automobile Show. There were four 6-cylinder cars, Models 610, 614, 619 and 629, on wheelbases of 111 (2817), 114 (2893), 119 (3020), and 129in (3274mm) respectively. Side-valve engines of 2872, 3393 and 4731cc were used, the latter serving both the 619 and 629 series. The single eight, Model 835 on a 135in (3426mm) wheelbase, was of 5279cc displacement. A Warner Gear 4-speed gearbox was standard on the top four series. This unit, which had first been seen on the 1927 Paige eight, had close ratio third and fourth, sometimes referred to as 'twin top'. Styling of the new Graham-Paige, by LeBaron designers R.L. Stickney and Hugo Pfau, was contemporary yet novel. Its radiator shell was reminiscent of HISPANO-SUIZA, and carried the Grahams' new emblem, a profile view of three knights wearing helmets. Sales of over 73,000 set a record for an automotive marque in its introductory year. A new series of 1929 cars appeared in January of that year, featuring two sizes of eights and three sixes; all cars had hydraulic brakes and the upper part of the line had Bijur central chassis lubrication. LeBaron custom bodies were offered on the long-wheelbase 837 chassis.

In 1930, 'Paige' was dropped from the cars, but not from the company name. By now there were four eights and two sixes, but sales were off by a half, in a year reeling from the Wall Street crash of the previous October. A smaller eight, the Special 820, and the low-priced 'Prosperity Six' attempted to lure penny-conscious purchasers for 1931, but sales continued to ebb.

In a bold new stroke, Graham introduced the 'Blue Streak Eight' for 1932. Styled by Amos Northup, with detail work by Raymond Dietrich, the new car abandoned the upright look of its predecessors and adopted a steeply-sloped grill and hidden radiator cap. Skirted wings concealed the car's undercarriage, and were soon copied throughout the industry. A new chassis frame located the rear axle through openings in the side rails. Cannonball Baker set a new record with a stripped down Blue Streak at Mount Washington, New Hampshire, and a Graham-powered racer qualified for the 1932 Indianapolis 500, but retired with a broken crankshaft. The attractive design, however, could not turn the tide against the Depression, and production fell to under 11,000 by 1933, despite Blue Streak styling on the 6-cylinder cars. More power was enlisted for 1934 by supercharging the eight, with a centrifugal unit patterned after that used by Duesenberg. Horsepower of the 'blown' cars was pushed upwards to 135bhp, with an accompanying 20 per cent boost in torque, remarkable for a $1245 car. A supercharged Special Eight was later added, selling for $200 less.

A much less expensive Standard Six led the 1935 line. Priced from $595, it sought to compete with PONTIAC and Hudson's TERRAPLANE, even Ford, CHEVROLET and PLYMOUTH. It had, however, been made less attractive by a narrowing of the grill and an ungraceful fastback shape. Ironically, however, production rose. Economies of production were realised for 1936 by adopting bodies from the REO Flying Cloud. This was the sole result of abortive merger talks with AUBURN, PIERCE-ARROW, HUPP and Reo. Eight-cylinder engines were discontinued, and the supercharger applied to the larger of the two sixes. This Supercharger series sold for even less that the blown Special Eight of the year before. The supercharged Graham chassis was adopted by Lammas Ltd for the Anglo-American LAMMAS-GRAHAM of 1936–38. Exploring ways of raising additional cash, the surviving Graham brothers (Ray had died in 1932, following a nervous breakdown) sold their body dies and engine tooling to

1929 Graham-Paige Model 835 5-seater coupé.
NICK GEORGANO

NISSAN of Japan. A Graham-Bradley tractor, to be sold by mail-order merchandiser Sears-Roebuck, enjoyed an all-too-short production run, and a marine version of the supercharged engine was no more successful.

For 1938, Graham attempted another bold stroke, the Spirit of Motion cars, characterised by a striking grill, sometimes described as 'shark-nose', flanked by bulbous wings bearing square headlamps. A forward-looking touch was the use of high-mounted tail-stoplamps, located at the top of the boot 'bustle'. A single 6-cylinder model of 120in (3045mm) wheelbase was offered, in four stages of trim. Public reception was not good. A Grand Prize at the Paris Concours d'Élégance failed to impress American consumers, and Graham sales fell to a new low of barely 4000 cars.

In a final attempt to make it in the auto business, Joseph Graham made a deal with Norman DEVAUX, who owned the body dies from the discontinued CORD 810. DeVaux had previously entered into an agreement with Hupp, but moribund Hupp had been unable to bring their version of the car to production.

MICHAEL LAMM

NORTHUP, AMOS (1889–1937)

Amos E. Northup was born 23 October, 1889 in Bellevue, Ohio and attended the Cleveland Polytechnic Institute, where he studied design under Henry G. Keller. He began his career in 1908 as a designer of furniture, home interiors and draperies. In 1918, he joined Pierce-Arrow as its truck designer and soon helped select Pierce's paint colors and interior trim. He also created some wonderfully lively, colorful artwork that Pierce used in its advertising.

Northup left Pierce around 1921, opened his own art studio in Buffalo and continued to do ads, illustrations and custom auto designs for, among others, Pierce-Arrow. He also provided artwork to designer/builder Leon Rubay and production body designs to Wills Ste Claire. He's credited, in fact, with designing all 1924 and later Willses.

In 1927, Murray Corp. of America, the independent autobody builder, hired Northup as its chief designer. But he felt Murray wasn't paying him enough, so he left again in March 1928 to join one of Murray's larger customers,

Willys-Overland in Toledo. At Willys, Northup had charge, according to a company news release, of 'all body styles, colour combinations, upholstery, decorative work and appointments'. While in Toledo, Northup styled the 1930 Willys 66B series, including that year's very striking plaidside roadster. He also revised Willy's low-priced Whippet line.

When Northup went to Willys, he hired Jules Andrade as his assistant. Andrade had previously been chief designer for Chandler-Cleveland Motors, which had been absorbed by Hupmobile in 1928. A year or so after Northup left Murray, they wanted him back and offered him more money than Willys-Overland. Northup accepted and was reinstated as chief designer, and he brought Andrade along as his assistant. Andrade stayed with Murray for another year and then moved on to a long career with General Motors, under Harley Earl.

LeBaron's Hugo Pfau said long ago that Northup never followed fashion; he set it. During his decade with Murray, Amos Northup generated designs, complete or partial, for practically all of Murray's customers. He's credited with the 1930 Hudson, several Hupmobiles, the 1930–32 Ford A/B-400 convertible victorias, the compact 1933 Willys 77, the entire Willys line through 1938, plus others. In 1935, Northup designed a luxury ocean liner and a streamlined locomotive. He was developing the 1938 Sharknose Graham when he died.

Northup was a short man, just over five feet tall, and he had an unusually large head. On Saturday morning, 13 February, 1937, he left his home in Pleasant Ridge, Michigan and walked down the street to buy a newspaper. The sidewalk was icy. Northup slipped, fell and cracked his skull. He died two days later in Harper Hospital. At the time of his death, the 1938 Graham, a design he'd begun in 1935, wasn't yet finished. Northup originally meant the Graham's front fenders to be skirted and to flow back into the front doors, like the 1941 Packard Clipper. Someone else–probably Graham-Paige chief body engineer William Nealey, according to Jeff Godshall–finished the Sharknose Graham, adding the square headlamps and the front fender creases. But the overall result was just as original as the rest of Northup's work. Designers called him a designer's designer, and he had more impact on the industry than he's ever been given credit for.

ML

1930 Graham-Paige 66 roadster.
NATIONAL MOTOR MUSEUM

1935 Graham Standard Six coupé.
NATIONAL MOTOR MUSEUM

1938 Graham Custom Supercharger convertible.
NATIONAL MOTOR MUSEUM

A joint manufacturing plan was worked out in 1939, with Graham building Hupp Skylarks under contract and in turn receiving the rights to produce their own Graham Hollywood. These were conventional rear-drive cars, using the companies' respective drive trains. Production was slow to start, and a weary Hupp withdrew after a mere 319 Skylarks had been built. Graham managed slightly under 2000 Hollywoods before production was suspended in September 1940, and their auto plants never reopened.

War work, however, sustained the firm, seeing it into profitability in 1941. Joseph Frazer assumed control in 1944, and his later ties to Henry J. Kaiser associated Graham-Paige with the KAISER-FRAZER automobile venture. In 1947, G-P sold its automotive assets to Kaiser-Frazer, continuing to make farm machinery, eventually becoming an investment corporation which survives today as Madison Square Garden Corp., owner of the sports arena by that name in New York City.

KF

Further Reading
The Graham Legacy: Graham-Paige to 1932, Michael E. Keller, Turner Publishing Co., 1998.
'The Graham Brothers and Their Car', Jeffrey I. Godshall, *Automobile Quarterly*, Vol. 14, No. 1.

GRAMM (CND) 1913
Gramm Motor Truck Co., Walkerville, Ontario.
Mainly known as a truck builder, Gramm made a few cyclecars with 2-cylinder air-cooled engines, tandem seating, and belt drive.

NG

GRAMME (F) 1901
Sté des Accumulateurs Compound, Levallois-Perret, Seine.
This was a light electric 3-wheeler powered by a 3hp motor which drove the single front wheel by belt. It took its name from the make of batteries and motor that drove it.

NG

GRANDE (AUS) c.1925

Grande Motors (Australia) Ltd, Sydney.

This was a shadowy make which was probably no more than a promoters' dream. The catalogue showed side views of six body styles, typical large, American-style bodies of the mid–1920s. The three engines offered were described as 'Double 4 Baby', Double 8 Model' and 'Double 12 Model'. Each cylinder had two pistons, one attached to the crankshaft in the usual manner, the other attached to the opposite throw of the crank. The explosion took place between the pistons which moved in opposite directions, somewhat on the Gobron-Brillié system, though that did not involve two con rods on one crank.

The Grande was described as being 'by the designers of America's first automobile'. This would presumably have been Duryea or Haynes, but there is no record of an Australian involvement by any of the men behind these cars. The address in the Kembla Building, Sydney, was only an office. No mention was made of a factory, which probably never existed.

NG

GRAND ILLUSIONS (US) c.1991

Grand Illusions, Planada, California.

The Cardinelli was a Ferrari Testarossa-inspired kit car design for the Pontiac Fiero chassis. It was sold in coupé or convertible form.

HP

GRANDIN see DALLAS

GRANT (i) (US) 1913–1922

1913 Grant Motor Co., Detroit, Michigan.
1913–1916 Grant Motor Co., Findlay, Ohio.
1916–1922 Grant Motor Corp., Cleveland, Ohio.

The Grant began life as a quality small car powered by a 1563cc 12hp 4-cylinder engine, with two-speed gearbox integral with the rear axle and shaft drive. Its suspension was somewhat unusual, with full elliptics at the front and a transverse semi-elliptic at the rear. Designed by George S. Saltzman, it was made only as a 2-seater, priced at $495. After limited production in Detroit, the company secured new premises at Findlay, Ohio, in the factory of the defunct FINDLAY Motor Co. There they continued to make the 12hp, a total of 3000 being made up to the end of the 1915 season. They were sold in England by Whiting Ltd of Euston Road, London, under the name Whiting-Grant.

Realising that the light car was not a surefire seller in America, Grant brought out a standard-sized car in 1915, which became the only model from 1916 onwards. It had a 2710cc 20hp 6-cylinder engine, enlarged to 2953cc and 22hp in 1916, and was made in tourer, roadster and cabriolet versions, with a sedan joining the range for 1917. A roadster was bought by the Findlay Fire Department in 1916, for the use of the Fire Chief. Also in 1916 the Grant company became a corporation, and moved to much larger premises in Cleveland, though the Findlay plant was retained for munitions manufacture. About 4000 cars were made at Findlay in 1916 and 12,000 in Cleveland in 1917. They bought up the Denneen Motor Co., makers of the Denmo truck, and relaunched it as the Denmo-Grant.

Grant entered the postwar market full of optimism, claiming 21,000 orders for their new Model H, which had a larger engine of 35hp (3253cc). They bought up the H.J. Walker engine-making company, which provided their engines, whereas previously they had used Falls. Unfortunately sales were not up to prewar levels, only 5400 in 1920, and fewer after that. Components continued to arrive, adding to the cash-flow problems. The Walker company was sold in 1921, but Grant went into receivership in October 1922. The cars were dropped at once, though the receivers continued to make trucks up to June 1923.

NG

Further Reading
'A Wonderful Car – the Grant 1913–1922', Alan Sutton,
Veteran Car, April 1997.

GRANT (ii) see EUREKA (viii)

GRANTA (GB) 1906

Granta Motor Co., London.

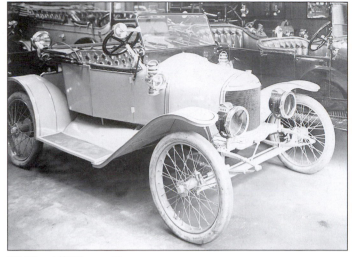

1914 Grant (i) 12hp roadster.
NATIONAL MOTOR MUSEUM

1916 Grant (i) Model V 6-cylinder roadster. The first Fire Chief Vehicle owned by the city of Findlay, Ohio.
R.A.SUTTON

Sold from an address in Horseferry Road, Westminster, the Granta was almost certainly an imported car. It had a 28/34hp 4-cylinder Ballot engine and double-chain drive. The WESTMINSTER was sold from the same address.

NG

GRANTHAM (US) c.1953

Grantham Motors, Hollywood, California.

Bill Grantham built a kit car called the Grantham Stardust that would fit a wide variety of American car chassis. A complete car on a modified Ford chassis was $3750 or the body kit could be purchased for $950 with windscreen and hardware. Wheelbase was 110in (2792mm) and the engine was moved back in the chassis. Weight was 2650lbs.

HP

GRANT SIX (US) 1912–1913

Grant Motor Car Co., Cleveland, Ohio.

This car began life as the ELMER SIX, and was built in Cleveland by a subsidiary of the Grant-Lees Machine Co. Like the Elmer it had a 50hp 6-cylinder engine, but the styling was somewhat modified. The car's uninspiring slogan was 'The Pioneer Semi-Assembled Car'.

NG

GRANTURA (GB) 1968–1973

Grantura Plastics, Blackpool, Lancashire.

This company had connections with T.V.R., and its first product, the Gem, had a definite visual resemblance with contemporary T.V.R.s. Its fibreglass 2-seater coupé bodywork had a more cut-off front end, however. The power unit was a Ford 3-litre V6, suspension was independent all round and there were four disc

1923 Gray (ii) tourer.
NATIONAL MOTOR MUSEUM

1917 Gray-Dort tourer.
GLENN BAECHLER

brakes. Grantura also made fibreglass hard-tops for Mini Mokes and so its next car, offered from 1969, was equally logical: a successor to the Moke called the Yak, which looked very similar. It had a tubular chassis with standard Mini subframes and a one-piece fibreglass body. 150 cars were supplied, mostly in kit form, of which 30 were exported to holiday destinations.

CR

GRAVES & CONGDON see CROWN (iii)

GRAVETTI (GB) 1983–1988

1983–1985 Gravetti Engineering, Staplecross, East Sussex.
1985–1986 Gravetti Engineering, Sandhurst, Kent.
1986–1987 Gravetti Engineering, Mere, Wiltshire.
1987–1988 Gravetti plc, Wincanton, Somerset.
This was a revival of the A.D. Cobra replica, orchestrated by Nigel Gravett. Various Ford components were used and recommended engines included Ford V6, Rover V8 and American V8s. Gravetti launched its 'Cob in a Box' idea, supplying everything the builder needed in kit form, short of a power train. Alongside rare aluminium bodies, there was a more usual fibreglass body with steel inner framework. The Gravetti chassis was later re-engineered by Bob Egginton of A.S.D. to become the C.K. 427.

CR

GRAY (i) (US) 1920

Gray Light Car Corp., Denver, Colorado.
America had virtually abandoned the cyclecar by 1916, so the Gray, introduced four years later, did not stand a chance. Only two prototypes were made, both using Harley-Davidson motorcycle engines, one a single cylinder and the other a twin. Projected prices were $350–450. There were ambitious plans for a large factory at Longmont, Colorado, but these did not come to fruition.

NG

GRAY (ii) (US) 1922–1926

Gray Motor Corp., Detroit, Michigan.
This concern was an offshoot of the Gray Motor Co., engine builders who supplied power units to, among others, KELSEY (ii). The car corporation was staffed by a number of ex-Ford employees including Ford's treasurer Frank L. Klingensmith. The car was aimed directly at the Ford market, having a 2805cc 20hp side-valve engine and an identical 100in (2538mm) wheelbase, but the gearbox was a conventional 3-speed unit, and suspension was by single cantilever springs at the front and double cantilever at the rear. Prices were inevitably higher than Ford's, $490 for a roadster and $520 for a tourer, compared with $364 and $348. Gray predicted sales of 250,000, but by the end of June 1923 only 1772 had been sold. Their response was to move upmarket with a longer wheelbase on the 1925 models and four wheel brakes for 1926. Prices rose too, running from $630 for a tourer to $995 for a sport sedan in 1925, just as Henry was cutting his prices still further. Klingensmith resigned in January 1925, and Gray was out of business 18 months later. Plans to make the British Tilling-Stevens petrol-electric bus under licence came to nothing.

NG

GRAY-DORT (CDN) 1915–1925

Gray-Dort Motors Ltd, Chatham, Ontario.
The Gray-Dort was based on the American DORT, and the Canadian company only went out of business when the American firm closed down. It was one of the most successful Canadian-made cars, and for a while outsold the much cheaper Chevrolet.

Gray-Dort originated in a carriage and sleigh-building concern, William Gray & Sons Co. Ltd of Chatham, established in 1856. By the turn of the century they were making 15,000 wagons, carriages and sleighs a year. A merger with the Manson-Campbell Co. in 1911 led to a change of name to William Gray Sons-Campbell Ltd, and Gray-Dort was an offshoot of this company. The 1915 models were almost all American-built cars with fresh badges and hubcaps, but real production from Canadian-made components began in 1916. While generally similar to the Flint product, Gray-Dorts included some de luxe sports models including the 1918 Special of which 200 were exported to the United States as Flint made nothing so exciting, and the 1922 Special which was said to have the first automatic reversing light as standard equipment. Gray-Dorts were generally more stylish than the Flint variety, some having nickel-plated radiator shells, wheel discs, Spanish leather upholstery and other luxury features. Surprisingly for a Canadian car, the coupé models carried the names of American universities, Harvard and Yale.

Throughout the Gray-Dort's life the 4-cylinder Lycoming engine was used, 2727cc up to 1918, then 3146cc. It was joined by the 3205cc Falls six for 1924, as used in the American Dorts. The closure of Dort at the end of 1924 prompted a hasty search for another American partner. HUDSON and NASH were considered, but nothing was settled. A deal was made to establish a link with the Detroit-GRAY but this company closed before any concrete plans could be made. Gray-Dort continued in business into 1925 to sell off the cars that had been made in 1924. Total production was about 26,000 cars. Bill Gray, grandson of William, formed a new company to make and distribute components, and this continued successfully into the 1940s. He died in 1971.

NG

Further Reading
'Venturing across the border: The Story of the Gray-Dort', Tom LaMarre, *Automobile Quarterly*, Vol. 29, No. 1.

GRAZIOSA (A) 1900–1904

Grazer Fahrradwerke Benedikt Albl & Co., Graz.
This company started with motor tricycles and then progressed to light voiturettes powered by 5PS De Dion-Bouton engines. Various body styles were offered, and the car had some success as it was light and economical.

HON

GREAT EAGLE (US) 1910–1915

United States Carriage Co., Columbus, Ohio.

Appropriately for its name, the Great Eagle was a large car with 40hp 4-cylinder engines and a 126in (3198mm) wheelbase in 1910/11, enlarged by 1913 to a 50hp four on a 135in (3426mm) wheelbase and a 60hp six on a 142in (3604mm) wheelbase. The largest of all was the 1913 60hp 10-seater limousine on a 147in (3731mm) wheelbase, which sounds more like a small bus than a car. Until 1913 the only body styles were a limousine and a landaulette, an unusual situation which was rectified with a 7-seater tourer from 1913 onwards. A 2-seater roadster was listed for 1914/15. The U.S. Carriage Co. was in receivership by February 1915, and although there were rumours in 1918 that production would restart with a revival of the 1915 models, this never came about.

NG

GREAT LAKES (US) c.1984–1989

Great Lakes Motor Cars, Rochester, New York.

The MG TF was replicated by this company that had formerly made Ford Model A restoration parts. The TF–1800 was a high-quality kit that used MGB running gear and trim to give it an authentic feel. Many of their parts would interchange with the originals. In 1986 they added a V6 or V8 Chevrolet powered version called the TF-V8, available in kit or assembled form. They later added a replica of the MG PA Airline coupé called the Phantom. It was designed to take big Chevrolet V8s and was a cross between an MG replica and a hot rod. These MG kits were passed on to NOBLE Motor Works in Penn Yan, New York.

HP

GREAT SMITH see SMITH

GREAT SOUTHERN (US) 1912–1914

Great Southern Automobile Co., Birmingham, Alabama.

Although this company had been formed in October 1909, no cars were produced until January 1912. This makes somewhat hollow the company's claim in 1911 that 'the Great Southern has met with rare success so far'. The cars were conventional machines with a choice of 30 or 45/55hp 4-cylinder engines and open bodywork. In 1914 they were down to one model, the 50hp four which had a sizeable engine of 8.6 litres. No cars were made after 1914, though trucks were continued to 1917 when Great Southern went bankrupt.

NG

GREAT WESTERN (US) 1910–1916

Great Western Automobile Co., Peru, Indiana.

These cars were made by E.A. Myers who had previously made cars under the name STAR (iv) and before that the MODEL. The first Great Westerns were not all that different from the 1909 Star 30, 40 and 50hp, but from 1911 he offered an updated range of bodywork, although the engine remained the 40hp four. Five open models, 2- and 5-seaters were made in 1911/12, with a sedan being added for 1913. Myers sold his Model Gas Engine Works in 1912 to a firm in Pittsburgh, a decision he perhaps regretted later, as in 1916 Great Western's failure was attributed to faulty engines supplied from Pittsburgh. In 1914 they experimented with the Carter piston-valve engine and for 1916 dropped all the fours in favour of a lower-priced small six of 21.6hp. At $1185 it cost less than half a 1915 40hp four, but did not sell well, and Great Western were out of business before the end of the year.

NG

GREELEY (US) 1902–1903

Miller Automobile Co., Greeley, Colorado.

This was a 2-seater runabout powered by an 8hp 2-cylinder engine, with epicyclic transmission and chain drive. A price of $1150 was quoted, but possibly only one car was made. This was the cause of a dispute between Dr W.L. Miller who ordered the car, formed the company and claimed that he had designed it, and machinist E.L. Miller (no relation) who built it and also claimed that he had designed it. He said that Dr Miller could not even drive a car, let alone design one. Though the Automobile Co. was Dr Miller's, it was E.L. Miller who advertised the building of cars to special order, which may have happened for a few years.

NG

1916 Great Western Six tourer.
NICK BALDWIN

GREENLEAF (US) 1902

Greenleaf Cycle Co., Lansing, Michigan.

The Greenleaf was a 4-seater tourer powered by a 10hp flat-twin engine with transverse crankshaft placed under the seat, and 3-speed gearbox. Apart from its side-entrance body it bore a close resemblance to the 1903 Cadillac, but was no bargain at $1750, when the Cadillac cost $850. This is doubtless the reason why only two Greenleafs were made.

NG

GREEN MOTOR WORKS (US) c.1994

Green Motor Works, North Hollywood, California.

This company built a Porsche Speedster replica powered by an electric motor developed by SOLAR ELECTRIC. It sold for $33,200 in 1994.

HP

GRÉGOIRE (i) (F) 1904–1924

1904–1907 Grégoire et Cie, Poissy, Seine-et-Oise.
1907–1918 SA des Automobiles Grégoire, Poissy, Seine-et-Oise.
1919–1924 Forges et Ateliers de la Fournaise, Poissy, Seine-et-Oise.

This company can trace its origins back to 1899, when Soncin was formed, becoming Soncin, Grégoire et Cie two years later. They made engines which they supplied to Émile Ouzou et Cie, makers of the OUZOU voiturette. In 1903 J-P Grégoire left Soncin to form his own company which began to turn out cars in 1904. Three models were offered initially, an 8hp single-cylinder, 12hp twin and 20hp four. In 1905 came an 8/10hp in-line twin which became better known than any of the earlier models. It had a capacity of 1105cc, chain drive and a 2-seater body, though a single spyder seat could be provided behind. They were soon entered in competitions, road events such as the Tour de France as well as the Circuit des Ardennes and Coupe des Voiturettes, though without great success until 1913 when Porporato won the Coupe de la Sarthe. A 7.4-litre 4-cylinder car built for the first Grand Prix in 1906 retired.

The production Grégoires were much smaller, the 1906 range consisting of the 6/8hp twin and two fours, of 12/14 and 16/20hp, all with pair-cast cylinders and shaft drive on the smallest. Sales rights to the Grégoire were held by Xavier Civelli de Bosch who also sold some cars under his own name. *La Vie Automobile* in their report on the 1906 Paris Salon described the CIVELLI DE BOSCH as 'a young make with interesting novelties', without mentioning the link with Grégoire. In fact, the 8/10hp Civelli de Bosch was very similar to its Grégoire counterpart, though slightly more expensive. He also offered a 3052cc 16/20 with pair-cast cylinders which became a monobloc under the Grégoire name in 1908. Civelli de Bosch cars were only offered to the end of 1907 when he went bankrupt.

In 1909 Grégoire introduced a new 2-cylinder car, the 1526cc 10hp, and 1910 saw the 3052cc 16hp which was the first of the make to have a 4-speed gearbox. The 16/24 of 1911 had a smaller bore than the 16, (80mm instead of 90mm), but a very long stroke of 160mm gave a capacity of 3215cc. There was also a 6-cylinder 20hp of 3617cc. These larger chassis carried some very striking closed coachwork in the years up to 1914, including a *berline de voyage* with three coach-like compartments, and some highly streamlined saloons. These attracted several aviators including Hubert Latham and Claude Grahame-White.

1905 Grégoire (i) 2-seater.
NATIONAL MOTOR MUSEUM

1919 Grégoire (i) 12/30hp 2-seater.
NATIONAL MOTOR MUSEUM

Most Grégoires of this period had side-valves in an L-head, but 1914 saw a reversion to a T-head in the 2155cc 11hp Sport, and there was also a brief flirtation with sleeve-valves in 1912/14. Production in 1914 was about 500 cars and a few commercial vehicles.

In 1920 Grégoire returned to the market with a 15hp 4-cylinder car with ohv and Delco lighting and starting. They were now owned by the Forges et Ateliers de la Fournaise who also assembled the 17CV BIGNAN which was sold on the British market as the Grégoire-Campbell. The last Grégoire was a light car with 1098cc C.I.M.E. 4-cylinder engine. This was, in fact, made by HINSTIN but sold in France as a Grégoire and in Britain as a Little Greg. Few were made, and the Grégoire name disappeared after 1923.

NG

GRÉGOIRE (ii) **(F)** 1945–1962
Automobiles Tracta J.A. Grégoire, Asnières, Seine.

Born in Paris in 1899, the multi-talented Jean Albert Grégoire was an engineer, writer, athletic champion, racing driver, inventor, and vehicle builder. He was a front-wheel drive pioneer, with a patented drive-shaft system, proven in his successful Tracta race and road cars during the 1920s. In the 1930s Grégoire turned his attention to lightweight aluminium Alpax chassis applications, first seen in the 1938 AMILCAR Compound, engineered by Grégoire and built by

Hotchkiss. He also developed a number of electric cars during the War. Postwar, Grégoire built an ingenious all-alloy prototype in collaboration with Aluminium Français (A.F.G.). This small saloon boasted a 15bhp 600cc flat-twin engine, hydro-mechanical brakes and all-independent suspension. Like the Amilcar, it used an Alpax aluminium platform chassis and dash (which weighed a mere 100lb). The 1945 A.F.G. served as the inspiration for the subsequent Panhard Dyna X of 1948, along with the ill-fated British KENDALL, the Australian HARTNETT and for Kaiser in the USA. Next, in 1947, Grégoire developed an innovative front-wheel drive, 2.0-litre flat-four 64bhp saloon with all-round independent suspension and a 4-speed overdrive gearbox. This concept was acquired by Hotchkiss and launched as the Hotchkiss-Grégoire in 1951. This was followed by the Socema-Grégoire turbo coupé, a rear-wheel drive, front-engined 100bhp Cematurbo gas turbine concept, claimed to be the world's first gas turbine grand tourer. This exceptionally aerodynamic coupé amazed the crowds at the 1952 Paris Salon, and was claimed to reach 125mph (201km/h) but, ultimately, it amounted to nothing. In 1956 Grégoire announced an attractive grand tourer under his own name, with supercharged 2.2-litre Hotchkiss engines and pleasing coupé and cabriolet sporting bodies, styled and constructed by Henri Chapron of Paris.

Production did not start until 1956, and Gregoire wisely limited himself to an initial batch of 15. In fact, only 10 were ever completed and the last was not sold until 1962.

In 1970 Gregoire was back with an electric car powered by a UNELEC motor driving, as usual, the front wheels. The frame was a cast light alloy structure similar to that of the A.F.G. but more solid in appearance. Only four were made.

NG

GREGORI **(GB)** 1998 to date
Gregori Sportscars, Kidderminster, Worcestershire.

The Gregori GPR was a small 2-seater mid-engined sports coupé offered in kit form. It utilised the engine and running gear of the front-wheel drive Ford Escort, as well as much of its interior. In construction it was a fibreglass monocoque with bolt-on subframes and, as well as the Escort power option, other Ford engines up to 2.5-litre V6 could be fitted. An open-topped Spider version was previewed for 1999.

CR

GREGORY (i) **(US)** 1920–1922
1920–1922 Gregory-Craun Motor Co., Kansas City, Missouri.
1922 Front Drive Motor Co., Kansas City, Missouri.

Ben F. Gregory (1890–1974) was a persistent advocate of front drive, making cars over a period of 42 years, though only intermittently. His devotion to this system was inspired by J. Walter Christie, one of whose racing cars Gregory drove in 1912, and in whose Hoboken, New Jersey factory he worked on army trucks during World War I. He built a front-drive racing car in 1915, and in 1920 formed the Gregory-Craun Motor Co. in partnership with William H. Craun, a fellow inventor of whom little is known. In 1920 he built a tourer based on a Scripps-Booth chassis, with the engine turned round and a De Dion front axle. He also built another racing car, powered by a Curtiss OX-5, and later a Hispano-Suiza V8 aero engine. A roadster was catalogued at $1550 in 1922, and possibly as many as 10 were built, being made for Gregory by the O.E. Szekely Co. of Moline, Illinois.

Gregory next appeared after World War II with the GREGORY (ii).

NG

Further Reading
'L'attraction avant americaine', Griffith Borgeson,
l'Album du Fanatique, May 1981.

GREGORY (ii) **(US)** 1948–1956
1948–1949 Ben F. Gregory, Kansas City, Missouri.
1956 Gregory Front Drive Cars, Kansas City, Missouri.

After an interval of 26 years Ben Gregory returned to car design with a small sedan powered by a 1963cc 4-cylinder air-cooled flat-4 Continental engine, rear-mounted but driving the front wheels. It was possibly the only example of this lay-out, which necessitated a propeller shaft when all other front drive cars avoided it. The Gregory had a 3-speed Borg Warner gearbox. He never formed a company for its manufacture, and only a single prototype was made.

1956 Grégoire (ii) 2.1-litre.
NATIONAL MOTOR MUSEUM

In 1956 he tried again, this time with an aluminium-bodied sports car powered by a 1590cc Porsche flat-4 engine in a modified Porsche chassis. The engine was front-mounted and, of course, drove the front wheels. Unlike with the rear-engined sedan, Gregory did quote a price of $5000 for the sports car, but again, production was precisely one.

NG

GREMLIN see AMERICAN MOTORS

GREPPI (I) c.1973–c.1983
Greppi, Colico, Colorado.
Starting out in the early 1970s making buggies with names such as Drag and Smash and a VW-based utility called the Safari, this company later made off-road vehicles based on the Ford Transit. Two models were offered: the Savana, equipped with a 2.3-litre diesel engine, and the smaller Alpina fitted with a 1.3-litre petrol engine (both from Ford). The transmission included 4-wheel drive.

CR

GREUTER see HOLYOKE

GREYHOUND (i) (US) 1914–1916
1914–1915 Toledo Cyclecar Co., Toledo, Ohio.
1915–1916 States Motor Car Co., Kalamazoo, Michigan.
Although dubbed 'The Aristocrat of Cyclecars', the Greyhound had all the features of a light car, such as a 4-cylinder water-cooled engine of 14/18hp, sliding gearbox and shaft drive. The body was more in the cyclecar vein, though, seating two in tandem with the driver in the rear seat. The makers said that they were ready to deliver 2400 cars in 1914, but when orders failed to materialise, they moved to Kalamazoo. There they operated under the name States Motor Car Co., though the car was still called the Greyhound. It now had a larger engine and was made as a 2-seater roadster with side-by-side seating or as a 5-seater tourer. In 1916 the car's name was changed to STATES.

NG

GREYHOUND (ii) (US) 1919–1920
1919–1920 Greyhound Motors Corp., New York, New York.
1920 Greyhound Motor Car Co., East Warren, Rhode Island.
The Greyhound started life, with headquarters at Five Columbus Circle in New York City, promoting a speedster with a 'Trinka Patent Body', round bonnet louvres and the slogan 'Just as Good as it Looks'. Historian Beverly Rae Kimes states that 'it looked rather like it might have been an attempt to make a sporting vehicle of the Model T Ford'. This is an apt description as numerous companies offered plans for such customising at this time. However, the Greyhound was a serious attempt to produce a car of this type at a 'reasonable' price, which was never announced. It failed before any production began, existing only in prototype form.

KM

GRICE (GB) 1927
G.W.K. Ltd, Maidenhead, Berkshire.
Arthur Grice was the 'G' of G.W.K., and while working for that company he designed a 3-wheeler with single front wheel and powered by a rear-mounted 680cc air-cooled J.A.P. V-twin engine. Surprisingly he did not choose the friction transmission that was a hallmark of G.W.K., but gave his car a conventional 3-speed gearbox. It had coil suspension all round and brakes on all three wheels. A price of £90 was quoted, but the Grice did not go into production.

NG

GRIDI (D) 1923–1924
Gridi Kraftfahrzeugbau GmbH, Saulgau (Wurttemberg).
This was a light car powered by a 565cc 5/15PS single-cylinder engine. Production was very limited.

HON

GRIFFIN (i) (GB) 1975–1985
1975–c.1979 Group Design, Poole, Dorset.
c.1979–c.1983 Nomad Sales, Burnham-on-Crouch, Essex.
c.1983–1985 Balena Cars, Swanage, Dorset.

1964 Griffith GT coupé.
NATIONAL MOTOR MUSEUM

1996 Grinnall Scorpion K1100.
GUERNSEY PRESS

Launched as the G.D.X.M., this kit car was produced by a fibreglass panel company. The car's name was changed to Griffin in 1977. It was a promising idea, with its sharp styling and a clever body concept – you could lift the estate-type hard-top right off for open-topped motoring in fine weather. The choice of donor vehicle was rather odd, though: the Morris Minor van. In place of the rather unsuitable Minor engine, an MG Midget or Rover V8 engine could be installed. Alternatively, from 1978 a VW Beetle floorpan could be used under a longer shell. The designer, Jim Clark, later produced the MANX.

CR

GRIFFIN (ii) (US) c.1980
John Griffith, Los Angeles, California.
This road-worthy racing car was designed by John Griffith, who had been involved with the LeGrand racing car company. The Griffin was a sports car with a semi-monocoque chassis and LeGrand Super Vee racing car suspension with room for a variety of engines in the middle. The prototype used a VW, but optional engines included Ford V6s and the Buick/Oldsmobile 215 V8. Bodywork resembled a 2-seat formula race car with wings on both ends. It could be built from a set of plans or purchased as a rolling chassis for $15,750 in 1980. Completed cars were also available.

HP

GRIFFITH (US) 1963–1965
Jack Griffith, Hicksville, New York.
The success of the Shelby Cobra inspired Ford dealer Jack Griffith to shoehorn a 4700cc Ford V8 into a TVR Grantura Mk3 that had formerly held an MGA 1600cc engine. It was very quick, and he persuaded TVR to build a special model, which was shipped to his dealership where the engine was installed. The first model was the Griffith 200, and it was offered with 195hp and 271hp engines. In 1964 the body was modified with a shorter tail and enlarged rear windows and became the Griffith 400. Approximately 300 of both models were built before Griffith ceased production in 1965. The Griffith later reappeared as the TVR Tuscan. In 1966 Griffith came out with a new car built in Italy by Frank Reisner's INTERMECCANICA. It was an attractive steel-bodied coupé or convertible styled by Bob Cumberford and Franco Scaglione. It was to have a

Ford engine, but supply problems dictated a switch to Chrysler V8s. These engines proved to be too heavy and handling was impaired. About 90 cars were built before the project folded. It was reborn as the OMEGA.

HP

GRIFFON (i) (F) 1906–1910; 1921–1924
SA des Cycles Griffon, Courbevoie, Seine.
This well-known bicycle and motorcycle maker launched a light 2-seater car at the 1906 Paris Salon. It was powered by a 7hp single-cylinder engine and had Truffault suspension. After about four years of manufacture Griffon returned to 2 wheelers, but they were attracted by the 1920s cyclecar boom to offer a typical cyclecar powered by a 984cc V-twin Anzani engine, with chain drive to the gearbox and belt final drive. It lasted only three years. In the mid–1920s Griffon were taken over by Peugeot, but continued to make motorcycles under their own name up to about 1930.

NG

GRIFFON (ii) (GB) 1985–1992
Griffon Motors, Underwood, Nottinghamshire.
The mechanical basis of this traditional-style roadster kit was, unusually for the genre, the Vauxhall Viva/Magnum, with the option of Ford crossflow power if required. A 4-seater Cortina-based version was also planned. The fibreglass body fitted on to a ladder chassis, and the style closely resembled the MERLIN.

CR

GRIGNANI (I) 1950–1953
Fratelli Grignani, Turin.
The Grignani Parva was a very compact microcar with open 2-seater bodywork. Powered by a rear-mounted 125cc 2-stroke 5bhp engine, it could achieve a top speed of 37mph (60km/h).

CR

GRINNALL (GB) 1993 to date
Grinnall Specialist Cars, Bewdley, Worcestershire.
Mark Grinnall's name had become well-known from 1983 for Triumph TR7 conversions, but the Grinnall Scorpion took a radically different approach. A BMW K-series motorcycle rear end provided the basis for this startling high-performance 3-wheeler. It attached to a square steel tube chassis, with Ford front suspension, Cosworth brakes, a BMW rear swinging arm and a single rear coil/spring damper. Engines came from the K75/K100/K1100 (75–120bhp), and the total weight was just 750lbs, which meant 0–60mph (0-97km/h) could be achieved in under 5 seconds. The dramatic roofless fibreglass body was styled by Steve Harper of M.G.A. Developments. An optional electric reverse gear could supplement the BMW 5-speed sequential transmission. Over 150 had been made by 1998, when a lightly restyled version became available and a larger BMW K1200 engine joined the options list. 200 Scorpion's had been made by March 2000.

CR

GRINNELL (US) 1912–1915
Grinnell Electric Automobile Co., Detroit, Michigan.
This brand name followed that of the PHIPPS-GRINNELL made in 1911 and 1912. The cars were conventional electrics made in various types of closed coupé and brougham at prices between $2800 and $3400. By the end of 1915 the Grinnells found that cars were less profitable than their chain of music stores, so they closed production down.

NG

GRISWOLD (US) 1907
Griswold Motor Car Co., Detroit, Michigan.
Designed by J.P. La Vigne, who was also responsible for the LA PETITE and LA VIGNE cyclecars, the Griswold runabout looked conventional enough, with a long bonnet and 2-seater body with a third spyder seat behind. However, under the bonnet there was a 2-cylinder engine stood on end, with the flywheel at the bottom and the crankshaft vertical. Three engine sizes were listed, 10, 15, and 20hp, but very few cars were made. C.H. Blomstrom had faith in the idea, though, for in 1908 he marketed the design under the name GYROSCOPE.

NG

GROFRI (A) 1921–1927
Grofri-Werke AG, Motorfahrzeugfabrik, Atzsgersdorf.
This was a ambitious company who began with a 12/45PS 6-cylinder car, but in 1925 they took out a licence to make the AMILCAR for the Austrian market. They used the 1074cc engine in several models, a 4-seater tourer based on the Amilcar CGS and a 2-seater sports car based on the lowered chassis CGSs. Known as the AG1, the latter could be had in supercharged form increasing power from 20 to 40 or 50bhp. These gained a good number of successes in sporting events.

HON

GRONINGER (NL) 1898–1899
Groninger Motorrijtuigenfabriek, Groningen.
The Groninger Motorrijtuigenfabriek claimed that they built the first real Dutch car, and not EYSINK in 1897, because they had used a foreign engine, the Benz. At the automobile show in Amsterdam visitors could see the first two Groninger cars, with their own-designed water-cooled 2.5hp and 4hp engines. The weight was about 800kg and the top speed of the heaviest one was about 15mph (25km/h). After launching these cars, the firm accepted an order to built two buses for the Hollandsche Automobiel Maatschappij at Delft, but so many financial problems resulted that they built no more cars and closed the factory in 1899.

FBV

GROSE (GB) 1899–1900
Grose Ltd, Northampton.
Joseph Grose (1861–1939) was a bicycle maker who invented a patent-leather chain cover incorporating a lubricating device. This made him enough money to buy the first motorcar in Northampton, an 1897 Coventry Motette. Dissatisfied with this he bought six Benz engines and countershafts, fitted them in his own tubular chassis and with a locally-made dogcart body, selling them as the Grose or Grose-Benz at £180 each. Their appearance was very close to that of the Benz Velo, although *The Autocar* said that they were built on somewhat stronger lines than the regular Benz. After he had completed his batch of six cars Grose did not make any more, but became a successful coachbuilder, making car bodies up to 1939, and commercials for about 20 years longer. Grose Ltd are still in business as dealers.

NG

GROUP FIVE *see* COBRETTE

GROUP SIX (GB) 1972–1977
Group Six Fibres, Clerkenwell, London.
John Mitchell built the first Group Six in 1972, inspired by the Group 6 sports/racing style. Underneath the kit-form glassfibre body lay nothing more exotic than a VW Beetle floorpan. Early cars were all open, but a targa hard-top was available from 1973 and subsequent cars were all enclosed coupés.

CR

GROUSSET (F) 1904–1905
Atelier de Mécanique et d'Automobiles Grousset et Fils, Firminy, Loire.
Paul Grousset and his sons owned a general engineering business, and made about 12 cars for local clients before concentrating on the manufacture of hexagonal screws, which is still the firm's business today.

NG

GROUT (US) 1900–1912
1900–1909 Grout Bros Automobile Co., Orange, Massachusetts.
1909–1912 Grout Automobile Co., Orange, Massachusetts.
The three Grout brothers, Carl, Fred, and C.B., made a few experimental cars, both petrol and steam-powered, between about 1898 and 1900, when they were set up in business by their father William H. Grout. He had made a fortune in the manufacture of sewing machines, originally in partnership with Thomas H. White who moved to Cleveland and also set his sons up in steam car manufacture. The first Grout steamers left the factory in the summer of 1900; they were typical of their kind, with 2-cylinder engines under the seat, single-chain drive, tiller steering and bicycle-type wheels. A more distinctive model was the coupé of 1901, which had a completely enclosed body so tall that it looked like a

1926 Grofri 1074cc sports car.
NATIONAL MOTOR MUSEUM

mobile sentry box. All the early steamers were called New Home, after the name of the Grout sewing machine company.

In 1903 the runabouts were joined by a larger 4-seater tonneau with double chain drive, a bonnet and a large locomotive-type cow catcher which acted as a bumper. This lasted only one or two years, and the 1904/05 Grouts had circular bonnets with a single headlamp mounted in the centre. Weekly output in 1904 was 18 cars, but nevertheless the Grouts felt that steam had had its day, and the 1905 12/18hp side entrance tonneau was the last steamer. The same year they offered a 20hp 4-cylinder petrol car, and followed this up with larger cars of 30/35 and 40/45hp. They were of conventional design with shaft drive, but did not sell as well as the steamers, doubtless because of the enormous competition. In 1907 William Grout, dissatisfied with the way his sons were running the company, took it over from them; they were so angry that they left Orange altogeher. William Grout died in 1908 and the company was reformed as the Grout Automobile Co. Production dwindled from then onwards, ending in 1912.

The earlier steamers were sold in England under the name Weston.

NG

G.R.P. (F) 1924–1928
G. et R. Paul, Paris.
The brothers George and René Paul made a small number of tourers and sports cars powered by a 1690cc ohv 4-cylinder engine, later enlarged to 1890cc. These engines were also used in G.R.P. taxicabs, of which more were made than of the cars.

NG

G.R.S. (GB) 1982–1989
G.R.S. Cars, Witham, Essex.
A new marque was created by GINETTA in 1982 when it created the Tora kit-built estate car. This was unique in using a Hillman Hunter donor, using its doors, windscreen, interior and all the mechanicals. The style followed Matra's Rancho, the chassis was a galvanised steel ladder frame and the bodywork was fibreglass. A 4-door Cortina-based Tora 2 was announced in 1989 but that was the end of the line.

CR

GRUMETT (U) 1968–1976
General Motors de Uruguay, Montevideo.
This was a 2-door car with Australian coupé utility overtones. It used a locally-built tubular chassis and a fibreglass body. Mechanical elements were HA Viva. Grumetts were marketed in Ecuador using the Condor and Gacel badges. One Grumett was exported to the UK where it was tested by GM.

ACT

1965 GT Malzoni coupé.
ALVARO CASAL TATLOCK

GRUNBERG (F) 1960

Rodolphe Grunberg built a very small 2-seater roadster called the RG 125 in 1960. It was powered by a 125cc single-cylinder 2-stroke engine, permitting the 150kg car to attain a top speed of over 40mph (64km/h).

CR

GRX (US) c.1993

Tommy Mouzes, Kenosha, Wisconsin.

The GRX Interceptor was a radical mid-engined prototype with Chevrolet sedan suspension and V8 engine. It was built by Tommy Mouzes, who hoped it would be used in a movie. It was later put up for sale for $1.8 million.

HP

G & S (US) 1998 to date

G & S Motorsports, Buellton, California.

This company bought the BUTLER Cobra replica kit car that had originated with the ARNTZ company. This was a continuation of the first successful Cobra replica that had launched this craze in the American kit car industry. The heavy ladder frame mounted Jaguar rear suspension and fabricated front suspension with mounts for Chevrolet or Ford engines. G & S was also involved with performance engine building.

HP

G.S. (GB) 1975–1980

G.S. Cars, Bristol.

William Towns designed this angular body conversion for the Lotus Europa, which featured on *The Daily Telegraph* stand at the 1975 Earls Court Motor Show. Both the front and rear ends of the Lotus were drastically restyled, and around 15 cars were produced.

CR

G.S.M. (ZA/GB) 1958–1964

1958–1966 Glassport Motor Co. (Pty) Ltd, Cape Town.
1960–1961 G.S.M. Cars Ltd, West Malling, Kent.

Bob van Niekirk was the man behind the G.S.M. Dart sports car, which was designed by Rootes stylist Verster de Wit. It used a ladder chassis with modified Ford 100E running gear using a front transverse leaf spring and coil-sprung rigid rear axle. The Dart was available with a variety of engines, including Ford 105E, Ford 100E, Coventry Climax FWA, and Alfa Romeo Giulietta. The lightweight fibreglass-bodied open 2-seater achieved numerous successes in club racing, both in South Africa and in Britain. This led to the car being manufactured in Great Britain as well as Cape Town, in the UK under the name G.S.M. Delta; however, that operation lasted only one year. A coupé version was also offered with an unusual reverse-angle rear screen (a handful of fastbacks were also made). Back in South Africa, a new model for 1962 was the Flamingo, a redesigned coupé featuring a split-window fastback with a central fin. It was powered by a 1.7-litre Ford Taunus engine (later Cortina 1500) and had Mini rubber springing and twin trailing arms on the right rear side.

CR

GT-40 DEVELOPMENTS (ZA) 1990s

GT-40 Developments, Nancefield, Johannesburg.

This company produced a replica of the Ford GT40 that followed all the conventions of the type.

CR

G.T.D. (i) (GB) 1985 to date

1985–1986 G.T.D. Developments, Manchester.
1986–1996 G.T.D. Developments, Poole, Dorset.
1996 to date G.T.D. Supercars, Poole, Dorset.

Ray Christopher set up G.T.D. to improve on the K.V.A. GT40 replica. A space frame chassis was developed and was soon acknowledged as the class-leader. It was designed to accept a 5.7-litre Ford V8 engine and race-orientated suspension. The fibreglass bodywork was available in Mk I or (from 1990) Mk II GT40 styles, and an optional authentic-style aluminium monocoque costconsiderably more. Over 200 chassis had been supplied by 1989. In 1994 came a Series 2 Mk I replica, with a Le Mans type nose panel and an optional 6-speed transaxle. G.T.D. also produced a painstaking replica of the Lola T70 from 1986 using the same GT40 space frame chassis and engineered the SPECTRE coupé. In 1998 it announced that it would be ending GT40 production with a final run of 40 cars. Other marginal G.T.D. projects were a Ferrari 250 GTO replica using Datsun 240Z/260Z parts and the Sportstar, a 2-seater Ford Fiesta-based sports car.

CR

G.T.D. (ii) (GB) 1993

G.T.D. Sports Cars, Doncaster, Yorkshire.

This operation had nothing to do with the other G.T.D. company; although it, too, produced a replica of the Ferrari 250 GTO using a Datsun 240/260Z as a basis.

CR

GTF see CUSTOM DESIGN ASSOCIATES

G.T.M. (GB) 1966 to date

1966–1968 Cox & Co. (Manchester) Ltd, Hazel Grove, Cheshire.
1968–1971 G.T.M. Kit Cars, Hazel Grove, Cheshire.
1971–1972 Howard Heerey Engineering Ltd, Hazel Grove, Cheshire.
1972–1976 G.T.M. Cars Ltd, Hartlepool, Co. Durham.
1976–1980 K.M.B. Autosports Ltd, Wellingborough, Northamptonshire.
1980–1981 G.T.M. Engineering, Nottingham.
1981 to date G.T.M. Cars, Sutton Bonington, Leicestershire.

This pretty 2-seater kit car began life as the Cox G.T.M. (which stood for Grand Touring Mini) in 1966. Mini front subframes were used front and rear, so that engine was mid-mounted in a semi-monocoque steel structure using fibreglass body panels. The rear suspension and gear linkage were specially made. It lasted just over a year as the Cox, Howard Heerey acquiring it in 1968, refining the concept. Its production life did not really settle until 1980, and it was finally farmed off to Primo Designs of Stoulton, Worcestershire in 1995. The reason was G.T.M.'s expansion into new models, starting with the 1986 Rossa, styled by Richard Oakes. The layout was similar to the G.T.M. but it had a fibreglass monocoque, 2+2 seating and a detachable hard-top. In 1993 the model was superseded by the Rossa K3, a redesigned, stronger, more up-market car using Rover Metro components. G.T.M. also took over the MIDAS Gold and some N.G. models from Pastiche. Further models were launched in the 1990s. First came the Midas 2+2 Coupé, an Oakes-restyled version of the Midas with a front-mounted Metro engine. Then in 1998 came the Libra, a high performance coupé again designed by Richard Oakes, with mid-mounted Rover K-series power. The current range encompasses the 2+2 Coupé, Rossa K3, Midas Gold Convertible, and Libra.

CR

GT MALZONI (BR) 1965–1966

Sociedade de Automoveis Luminari Ltda., São Paulo.

In the early 1960s, Italian-born Rino Malzoni started to make his own cars in Fazenda Chimbo, in Matao. He teamed up with Jorge Lettry who dedicated himself to the mechanicals of the cars, and Anisio Campos, designer. They then formed a group with Luis Alves da Costa and Mario Cesar Camargo, to give birth to the Sociedade de Automoveis Luminari, dedicated to building GT Malzoni sports cars, based on the mechanical elements of the 3-cylinder fwd DKW made under licence by Vemag in Brazil. The success of the GT Malzoni was such that its creators founded a larger enterprise which in 1967 would start to make the even more succesful PUMA GT sports car. The GT Malzoni is also sometimes known as the DKW Malzoni.

ACT

GUANCI (US) c.1978–1990
Guanci Automobiles Inc., Woodstock, Illinois.
The Guanci SJJ-1 was a mid-engined sports car with turbocharged Buick V6 or Chevrolet V8 engines. It was an attractive 2-seat coupé design with European styling.

HP

GUEPARDO see ARTES

GUERRAZ (F) 1900–1902
Voitures Légères Louis Guerraz, Levallois-Perret, Seine.
Guerraz light cars used a variety of single- and 2-cylinder engines, Aster, Bolide, Buchet, and Sonçin, all between 5 and 7hp. They had 3-speed gearboxes, chain drive, and wheel steering. Bodies were mostly 2-seaters, but one was a *vis-à-vis* with single rearward-facing seat.

NG

GUILDFORD (GB) 1920
Griffith's Engineering Works, Guildford, Surrey.
The Guildford cyclecar was more attractive-looking than many, though it followed the usual formula of an 8hp V-twin Blackburne and chain drive. The makers did not have the facilities to manufacture it in quantity, so they advertised the whole project for sale. There were apparently no takers, though it is possible that the car was briefly built under another name.

NG

GUILLICK (F) 1919–1927
G. Guillick et Cie, Maubeuge, Nord.
The Guillick began life as the S.U.P. (Sté des Usines du Paquis), acquiring its later name after World War I. Early models used Fivet engines, followed in 1924 by a 1994cc Altos, all these being side-valve units. In 1925 a slightly smaller Altos (1990cc) was used, now with ohvs. This was known as the Type AL74, after its 74mm bore. More sporting was the AL70, powered by a 1494cc single-ohc C.I.M.E. unit. This gave as much power as the larger Altos.

The Guillick's chassis was generally conventional, apart from very long inverted cantilever rear springs. Bodies were the usual 2-seaters and tourers, though a Weymann fabric saloon was shown at the 1927 Brussels Salon. Guillick sales were mostly confined to Northern France and Belgium.

NG

GUILLIERME (F) 1906–1910
Automobiles Guillierme, Paris.
The Guillierme was a conventional shaft-driven car powered by an 1846cc 10/12hp 4-cylinder Ballot engine. The company also made delivery vans with engine under the seat, using either the 10/12hp engine or a larger one of 15/17hp.

NG

GULDSTRAND (US) c.1965 to date
Guldstrand Specialty Automobiles, Culver City, California.
Dick Guldstrand was a legendary Corvette racer when he started building improved versions of Chevrolet street cars. Most were built to order, but in 1985 he built a Grand Sport 80 package with 355hp and a top speed of 171mph (275km/h). About 4 to 5 a year were sold until they were discontinued in 1990. In 1994 Guldstrand introduced the Grand Sport 90, a heavily modified ZR-1 Corvette coupé with striking, rounded bodywork by Steve Winter. Prices started at $134,500. Two engine types were developed, a 480hp petrol-powered version and one that ran on compressed natural gas and delivered 400hp. The natural gas engine was tested but not installed in a car. Guldstrand radically reworked

1994 Gurgel BR800 saloon.
ALVARO CASAL TATLOCK

the suspension for better handling. About a dozen ZR-1-based GS-90s had been sold as of 1999. A convertible Corvette conversion called the Guldstrand Nassau was offered in 1997, to be built on customer-supplied non-ZR-1 Corvettes.

HP

GULL-WING CAR COMPANY (US) c.1982–1993
Gull-Wing Car Co., Gardena, California.
West Coast Car Sales, Gardena, California.
Not surprisingly, this company made replicas of the Mercedes 300SL Gull-wing sports car. A tubular space frame was powered by either turbocharged Plymouth 6-cylinder or Chevrolet V8 engines. The fibreglass body was virtually identical to an original in shape. Aluminium bodies were optional, as were special turn-key editions with Mercedes 280SE engines and running gear.

HP

GUNDAKER (US) c.1982–1985
Gundaker Fabrication, Metuchen, New Jersey.
Kit car replicas of the MG-TC are pretty rare, with most similar kits based on the MG-TD. Gundaker made a very accurate kit with a simple chassis that accepted MGB running gear and realistic 19in wire wheels. They also sold the Vandetta, a kit to transform a VW Beetle into a minivan.

HP

GURGEL (BR) 1966–1995
1966–1968 Macan Ind e Com Ltda., São Paulo.
1969–1995 Gurgel Veiculos, São Paulo.
The Gurgel was a 4-seater with fibreglass coachwork, suitable for off-road use. There were doorless open versions and also closed 2-door ones. Engines were by Volkswagen with capacities of 1300, 1500, or 1600cc. The company developed the Itapu, a small wedge-shaped electric city car, but this was never volume produced. The Gurgel saw use in Brazil's hinterland and also as a beach car. It was adopted by some police departments, like that of Alagoas State. However, the company got into financial difficulties and after several attempts to continue production, Mr Gurgel closed it down.

ACT

GURIK see G.E.A.

GURLEY (US) 1900–1901
T.W. Gurley, Meyersdale, Pennsylvania.
Tom Gurley was a jeweller and bookseller as well as repairing and selling bicycles. The latter led him into car manufacture, and he launched a 2-seater buggy with single-cylinder engine, tubular reach frame, bicycle wheels, and tiller steering. He thought he could make a profit by selling them at $600, but had to raise the price to $1000, and very few were made.

NG

GUSTAV NABOT see G.N.(iii)

1920 Guy (iii) 20hp V8 tourer.
NATIONAL MOTOR MUSEUM

GUTBROD (D) 1949–1954
Gutbrod Motorenbau GmbH, Plochingen; Calw.
Wilhelm Gutbrod was a motorcycle maker whose first venture with 4-wheelers was the STANDARD (xi). At the end of World War II Wilhelm's son Walter introduced under his own name the Superior 600 which was very advanced in comparison with the competition. It was a small car powered by a 593cc 2-cylinder 2-stroke engine, soon succeeded by a 663cc unit. This was also made with fuel injection, the first time this had been employed in a 2-stroke engine. The body was a 2-seater coupé, with roll-back roof, called a cabrio-limousine; an estate car and a sports roadster were made in small numbers. A 4-seater saloon did not make it beyond a few prototypes. Production ended in April 1954 after 7726 Superiors had been made. From 1975 to 1990 small 4 × 4 farm and municipal vehicles were made by a new Gutbrod company at Bubingen near Saarbrücken.

HON

GUY (i) *see* LE GUI

GUY (ii) (CDN) 1911
Matthew Guy Carriage & Automobile Co., Oshawa, Ontario.
Introduced at the 1911 Toronto Show by a firm that had made heavy carriages and hearses for more than 50 years, this was a conventional 30hp 4-cylinder tourer. It was made in very small numbers, and a projected 1-ton truck probably never got off the ground at all.

NG

GUY (iii) (GB) 1919–1925
Guy Motors Ltd, Wolverhampton, Staffordshire.
Former works manager for SUNBEAM, Sidney Guy (1885–1957) formed Guy Motors to make commercial vehicles in 1914. After the war years spent making Wasp and Dragonfly aero engines, Tylor truck engines and gearboxes for Maudslay,

Guy decided to enter the luxury car market, like other heavy vehicle makers BRITISH ENSIGN and LEYLAND. Designed by R.H. Rose, also ex-Sunbeam, the Guy had a 4072cc V8 engine with horizontal side valves which were said to give the advantages of overhead valves with easier maintenance. It had detachable cylinder heads, aluminium pistons and automatic chassis lubrication which was activated every time the steering was turned to full right lock. Transmission was by a cone clutch, 4-speed gearbox and spiral bevel rear axle. Chassis price was £1275, more than a Daimler Thirty though less than a Rolls-Royce 40/50 or Leyland Eight. It fell to £1095 in 1923, the last year in which the V8 was offered. About 25 were made.

In 1922 Guy offered a companion 4-cylinder car, the 2465cc 16.9hp selling for a chassis price of £550, or £750 complete. This was expensive for an untried product, and in 1924 Guy tried again with the 13/36, which used a 1954cc Coventry-Climax engine. This also had automatic chassis lubrication and a more realistic price of £495 for a complete 4-seater. Sales were about 110 up to 1925, when Guy dropped passenger cars. They became one of the best-known British commercial vehicle makers, being acquired by JAGUAR in 1961 and thus becoming part of the British Leyland empire in 1968. The last complete Guy trucks were made in 1976, though the factory continued to make components up to 1983.

NG

GUYOT SPÉCIALE (F) 1925–1931
Éts Albert Guyot et Cie, Clichy, Seine.
Albert Guyot was a racing driver who began his career with a Minerva in the 1907 Kaiserpreis, and later drove for Delage, Sunbeam, Ballot and Rolland-Pilain. In 1925 he built a car of his own, using a 1984cc Burt McCollum sleeve valve engine in a Rolland-Pilain chassis. These competed without success in several Grands Prix in 1925 and at Indianapolis in 1926. After building two 2-seater racing cars Guyot turned to the manufacture of touring cars. His first, built in 1925, had a 2.5-litre 6-cylinder engine of his own design. Guyot's son

GUY MOTOR CARS

"GUY" 20 H.P. 8-Cylinder TOURING CAR

The only British eight-cylinder car, proved to be one of the outstanding features at the Olympia Motor Exhibition.

SPECIAL POINTS.

Detachable cylinder heads, exposing pistons and valves. Pistons and connecting rods can be withdrawn without dismantling the engine.

Automatic oil distribution to all moving parts, and entire absence of solid lubricants.

Our patented flexible three-point suspension of subframe carrying engine, gear box, clutch and change speed.

Radiator carried by spherical trunnions on the main frame.

Silent spiral bevel axle drive.

Accessibility to all parts for adjustments. 2 years' periodical inspection and advice.

Telephone : 1141 (4 LINES). **GUY MOTORS, LTD.** Telegrams : "GUYMO, WOLVERHAMPTON."

FALLINGS PARK, WOLVERHAMPTON.

Also makers of the celebrated "GUY" 2-TON COMMERCIAL VEHICLE.

1914 G.W.K. 8hp 2-seater.
NATIONAL MOTOR MUSEUM

1921 G.W.K. 10.8hp 2-seater.
NATIONAL MOTOR MUSEUM

André came across this car 40 years later, used as a breakdown truck in Brittany. For production cars Guyot chose Continental engines, for which he was already the agent for Belgium and France. For his GST27, launched in April 1926, he used a 3450cc 6-cylinder side-valve engine with an aluminium valve cover to give the appearance of ohv. The car had a 4-speed gearbox and Lockheed hydraulic brakes. This and its successor of 1929, the GST29, were offered with six different body styles, including a town car for chauffeur drive, 4- and 6-light saloons, and a Weymann fabric saloon.

In 1929 Guyot was persuaded to offer a larger and more expensive car using a 5172cc straight-8 Continental engine. It was the worst possible time to offer a luxury car, and only two were made, a 4-seater cabriolet and a 2-seater roadster.

The Depression hit sales of the 6-cylinder Guyot Spéciale as well, and the last left the factory in 1931. About 70 were made in all. Guyot was more successful as an agent than as a manufacturer, for all the Continental engines used by such firms as ALPHI, BUCCIALI, DELAUNAY-BELLEVILLE, GEORGES IRAT, MATHIS, and ROLLAND-PILAIN were bought through Guyot.

NG

Further Reading
'Les Guyot Spéciales et les Automobiles d'Albert Guyot', Jacques Iuri, *Le Fanauto*, May–September 1983.

GUYSON (GB) 1974–1977

Guyson International, Skipton, North Yorkshire.
The Guyson E12 was an extraordinary body conversion designed by William Towns for Guyson International, a shot-blasting equipment manufacturer. The rebodying exercise took a Jaguar E-Type V12 as its basis and added fibreglass panelling to create a very slab-sided wedge shape – extremely clean according to one school of thought, though one writer described it as a 'trendy sideboard'. The conversion remained available until the late 1970s but the production run ended at the second car.

CR

GUY-VAUGHAN see VAUGHAN

GWALIA (GB) 1922

Stanfield Ltd, Cardiff.
One of the very few cars built in Wales, the Gwalia used a 9hp Alpha engine but all other parts were said to have been made locally. These presumably included the 3-speed gearbox and worm drive rear axle, and the most unusual feature of the design, the suspension by coil springs and bell cranks similar to that of the Citroën 2CV nearly 30 years later. With a 3-seater clover-leaf body, the price was £250, but production did not last out the year of introduction.

NG

1923 Gwynne 8hp sports car, by Compton & Hermon.
NATIONAL MOTOR MUSEUM

G.W.K. (GB) 1911–1931

1911–1912 G.W.K. Ltd, Beckenham, Kent.
1912–1914 G.W.K., Datchet, Buckinghamshire.
1914–1931 G.W.K., Maidenhead, Berkshire.

This car was made by three men, Arthur Grice, J. Talfourd Wood, and C.M. Keiller. Grice had worked for a crane company and both Wood and Keiller were ex-Great Western Railway engineers. The friction drive which characterised the cars was Grice's idea, based on the system he had seen for grinding optical lenses. For power they used a rear-mounted 2-cylinder Coventry-Simplex marine engine in the prototype, together with De Dion-type radiators, Chater-Lea wire wheels and front axle. The rest of the car they made themselves in a stable at Beckenham. A few more cars were made there in 1911, but probably not the 52 sometimes claimed, and in 1912 they moved to Datchet where series production started. The engine was still by Coventry-Simplex, a 1045cc vertical twin, driving through a friction-disc transmission and chain final drive. The 2-seater cost £150 complete, rising to £158 for 1915, when few cars were made anyway because of the switch to war work for the Admiralty. A total of 1069 cars were made before World War I.

G.W.K. moved to new premises at Maidenhead in 1914 and the business was run by Grice during the war, while his partners were in the Army. He had already secured the Maidenhead factory, known as Cordwallis Works, in 1913 to make a rotary engine in conjunction with a Belgian marble merchant, M.A. van Roggen, under the name G. & V.R. Ltd. The link with van Roggen later resulted in plans to build the IMPERIA in the Cordwallis Works, though this never came about. Grice left G.W.K. in 1920 to make the UNIT at nearby Wooburn Green. Wood and Keiller revived the rear-engined design as the Type E, making 82 of them to use up prewar components while they waited for supplies to become available of the 1368cc 4-cylinder Coventry-Simplex engine. This went into the first front-engined G.W.K., the Type F, which still used friction transmission. It proved much less satisfactory than the rear-engined designs, suffering from transmission whip and unpleasant noises from the driven disc. These were largely eliminated in the Type H made from 1921, but the damage had been done, and G.W.K. went into liquidation in 1922. Production of the Type H was resumed without the participation of Wood and Keiller, and continued up to 1926, though on a smaller scale. Total production of the Types F and H between 1919 and 1926 was about 1700. Four wheel brakes were available as a 10 guinea (£10.50) extra from 1924. A small number of Type Js was made in 1922; this was a reversion to the rear-engined layout, though with a frontal bonnet which made it almost indistinguishable from the F and H. Not many

1927 G.W.K. Chummy 4-seater.
NATIONAL MOTOR MUSEUM

were made, and even fewer of the Type G of 1930, which had a 4-cylinder Coventry-Simplex engine mounted at the very back of the frame, driving forward to the axle. The body was a roll-top convertible which gave the car some resemblance to a Thames camping punt on wheels. This was the work of Grice, who had returned to G.W.K. in 1923. Later the Cordwallis Works, famously nicknamed 'The Jam Factory' in Lord Montagu's *Lost Causes of Motoring* because it became the home of St Martin's jam and marmalade, housed the BURNEY and MARENDAZ.

NG

Further Reading
Lost Causes of Motoring, Lord Montagu of Beaulieu, Cassell, 1960.

GWYNNE (GB) 1922–1929

1922–1925 Gwynne Engineering Co. Ltd, Chiswick, London.
1925–1929 Gwynne Cars Ltd, Chiswick, London.

Gwynne Engineering was founded in 1849, and became famous in the early twentieth century for its centrifugal fire pumps. During World War I they made Clerget rotary aero engines as modified by W.O. Bentley and machine tools, and got into the car business by making engines for the ALBERT. In March 1920 Gwynne bought up Albert, transferring production to their Chiswick works, and in 1922 made an enlarged version of the 12hp Albert as the 14hp

GWYNNE

Gwynne-Albert. Meanwhile they started production of a smaller car under the Gwynne name. This was inspired by the Spanish VICTORIA (iv) designed by Arturo Elizalde, the design of which Neville Gwynne bought up. The Gwynne Eight had a 850cc overhead valve 4-cylinder engine whose 24bhp gave a lively performance. Body styles were mostly 2+2-seater chummies or 4-seater tourers, though there were a few saloons and a pointed tail sports model capable of 60mph (97km/h). About 2250 were made up to 1928, the majority before 1923 when a receiver was appointed and after which production dropped to a handful per week. In 1927 a larger model was introduced, the 1247cc Ten with an extra 18in (457mm) of wheelbase, making it more suitable for 4-seater bodies, both open and closed. About 600 were made between 1927 and 1929.

NG

GYROSCOPE (US) 1908–1909

Blomstrom Manufacturing Co., Detroit, Michigan.

C.H. Blomstrom bought up the GRISWOLD design of vertical crankshaft engine, and as he thought it had a gyroscopic effect he renamed the car the Gyroscope. The only design difference was that he increased the track from 55in (1396mm) to a standard 56in (1421mm). He also reduced the price from $1500 to $1250 for the runabout and $1350 for the tourer. Finding sales difficult he dropped the prices still further for 1909, to $750 and $800 respectively, but found very few buyers. He tried to sell the design to the Page company in Adrian, Michigan, and then to the LION company, also of Adrian, but they spurned the Gyroscope in favour of a more conventional car which they launched in 1910.

NG

HA (H) 1928–1929
Andor Hajdu, Budapest.
Among those who tried to build a Hungarian people's car in 1920s was Andor Hajdu. It was powered by a 500cc engine (just like its 'rivals', the SZEKELY, MERAY, and UHERECZKY) and it was entered into local races against Morgans. Plans were announced for a fence-factory to take over the manufacturing rights, but by late 1929 everything was abandoned and Hajdu emigrated to the United States.
PN

HAASE (US) 1902–1904
Northwestern Furniture Co., Milwaukee, Wisconsin.
When this furniture company decided to enter car manufacture they chose the name of their president, Mr Haase. The cars had 2-cylinder engines, 6hp in the Model A and 8hp in the Model B, mounted under the seat, and started by a handle next to the left-hand seat. Speed was controlled by variable lift of the inlet valves. About 15 cars had been sold by the end of 1902; later figures are not known, but they cannot have been very encouraging as prices were slashed in mid–1904. It is thought that the Haase was not built in Milwaukee, but by the H. Brothers of Chicago who later made the H.B. high-wheeler.
NG

HACHE ET LASSOUGADE see LASSOUGADE

HACKER (GB) 1991 to date
Hacker Motor Co., Littlehampton, Sussex.
By the end of the 1980s, DUTTON had abandoned kit car manufacture but its founder Tim Dutton developed a new model, the Hacker Maroc. This was a heavily-modified Ford Fiesta Mk III, given new fibreglass panelling and a convertible roof. Ex-Aston Martin designer Simon Saunders did the design work. Initially it was offered only fully-built but a lack of demand forced the company to offer kit versions from 1993, in which form the car remained available in 1999.
CR

HACKETT (US) 1917–1919
Hackett Motor Car Co., Jackson & Grand Rapids, Michigan.
The Hackett was an assembled car, successor to the earlier ARGO (1914–1917), using a 4-cylinder G. B. & S. engine and priced at $885 for both its roadster and touring version. The production of Hacketts was temporarily halted by World War I and following the Armistice, failed to get into anything near full operation, with an estimated 125 or fewer cars completed when the company went out of business. The factory subsequently became the plant of the LORRAINE car which would have David D. Buick as its president during its three-year existence.
KM

HADFIELD-BEAN see BEAN

HADLEIGH (GB) 1992–1995
I.P.S. Developments, Hadleigh, Suffolk.
Garnered by the long waiting list for a new Morgan, the Hadleigh represented a kit-built lookalike. It first appeared with a backbone chassis, but entered production in 1993 with an aluminium-panelled space frame, plus a fibreglass nose, scuttle and wings. The Ford Sierra supplied most of the mechanical parts. Two models were offered: a 2-seater Sprint and the 2+2. This firm also took on the M.C.A. and the DASH.
CR

HADLEY (US) c.1980
Hadley Engineering Co., Cost Mesa, California.
The Skamp, formerly called the Veep, was a replica of the World War II military-style Jeep. It had a steel body and frame that used Volkswagen Beetle running gear. Assembly time was estimated at 40 hours.
HP

HAGEA-MOTO (D) 1922–1924
Dipl. Ing. O. Bischoff & M. Althoven GmbH, Berlin-Wilmeresdorf.

1991 Hacker 2+2-seater sports car.
NICK BALDWIN

This was a light car powered by a 1017cc 4-cylinder Steudel engine, and used friction transmission.
HON

HAGEN (D) 1903–1908
Kölner Accumulatorenwerke Gottfried Hagen, Cologne.
Hagen was an early maker of electric vehicles who had a better start than many as he made his own batteries. Private and commercial vehicles were made, the vehicles also being known under the names KAW and Urbanus. The challenge of petrol-engined vehicles eventually forced Hagen to close down.
HON

HAG; HAG-GASTELL (D) 1922–1927
1922–1925 Hessische Automobil AG, Darmstatt.
1925–1927 Waggonfabrik Gebrüder Gastell, Mainz-Mombach.
The HAG was a very sound design, and the maker's concentration on one type with steady improvements helped them to stay in business longer than most small firms. The 5/25PS had a 1305cc 4-cylinder engine of HAG's own design, with shaft-driven single overhead camshaft. Open 2- and 4-seaters and a 4-door saloon were made. In 1925 production was taken over by railway wagon manufacturers Gastell Brothers. Under their control a 1.5-litre sports model was made. After World War II the factory at Mainz-Mombach was used for manufacture of bus and coach bodies for Magirus-Deutz (now IVECO).
HON

HAINAN (CHI) 1988 to date
Hainan Auto Works, Haikou City, Hainan Province.
Hainan Island in South China is famous for its test track, where all important Chinese motor vehicles have been tested. In 1990 this works developed a car of the HUAXING type, which was sold as the Hainan HX 7080. The 1970cc Hainan HMC 6470 station wagon was based upon an earlier Mazda 929 design and produced since 1992. A 1.6-litre saloon of the Mazda 323 type was sold as the Hainan HMC 6430. The Mazda MPV was named Hainan HMC 6450, with a V6 3-litre engine. The LWB version was named HMC 6472. The stamping, welding, painting, assembling, testing lines and other equipment were bought from Ford Philippines. Before that the Hainan Auto works was a typical small Chinese car factory. A project to produce a Mercedes-Benz 7-seater MPV was dropped in the late 1990s. By then the factory had become part of the First Auto Works Group.
EVIS

HAINES & GRUT (AUS) 1908–1909
Haines & Grut Motor Buggy Co. Ltd, Melbourne, Victoria.
Designed by Tommy Haines along the lines of the HOLSMAN, this car had a 10hp flat-twin engine which was driven via a 2-speed countershaft and cables. The floating countershaft tensioned the cables for forward drive, while bobbins at each end coming into contact with the solid tyres, gave reverse. Only the US hickory wood for the wheels and a French Longuemare carburettor were imported. Peter Grut was the manager of the company, which made five examples before it failed.
MG

1916 Hal Twelve tourer.
NATIONAL MOTOR MUSEUM

HAINSSELIN *see* H.L.

HAISHEN (CHI) 1993–1995
Beifan Haishen Auto Ltd Corp., Changchun City, Jilin Province.
A very interesting project, this very inexpensive mini car (Y20,000) the Haishen ('Poseidon'), was introduced with the English name Handsome, and was made in closed and convertible version (HS 6250 A/HS 6250 B). Several prototypes were produced, with 2- and 4-cylinder engines. It was 97.6in (2480mm) long. There was no serial production. The basic address of the company was a hotel room, but the company later disappeared.

EVIS

HAIYAN (i) (CHI) 1959–1962
Shanghai Bus Repair Works, Shanghai Municipality.
The Haiyan ('Sea-swallow', a local Shanghai bird) 730 was related to the FEIYUE, as both open mini vehicles were of the same size and model; they were built as contemporary taxis. All Haiyans show a big 'V' on the grill, which probably represents the wings of the sea-swallow. First editions of the Haiyan had no doors, though later a 2-door version was made. A closed car of a different design was also made.

EVIS

HAIYAN (ii) (CHI) 1966–1970
Shanghai Mini-Auto Works, Shanghai Municipality.
The Haiyan SW 710 was one of the successes of the people's republic, as it was shown for years in the Shanghai Industrial Exhibition Hall. In the streets this 300cc rear-engined Goggomobil look-alike was in use as a taxi; several were built. In 1978 a whole batch was still parked in the streets of Shanghai, waiting for destruction.

EVIS

HAL (US) 1916–1918
1916 H.A.Lozier Co., Cleveland, Ohio.
1916–1918 Hal Motor Car Co., Cleveland, Ohio.
Harry A. Lozier resigned from the company bearing his name in 1912, but he was back four years later with a car for which he used his initials, just as Ransom Eli Olds (REO) and Harry C. Stutz (H.C.S.) had done. The Hal was a large car on a 135in (3429mm) wheelbase powered by a 6.4-litre Weidely V12 engine, made initially in tourer and roadster models only, and priced quite modestly at $2100. Production started in the summer of 1916, in a factory that had previously made the ROYAL TOURIST, but in September Lozier left the company, which was reorganised under a new name. By October, 200 Hal Twelves had been made, and production was running at 10 per day. Prices were increased for 1917, to $2385 for a roadster or tourer and to $4250 for a limousine. The entry of America into World War I hampered the supply of components, and by the end of 1917 Hal was in serious trouble. 1918 models were announced, but the company was bankrupt by February. Among the assets auctioned in April were 10 unsold cars, one of which was snapped up by future President, Warren G. Harding.

NG

H.A.L. (IND) 1960–1961
Hindustan Aircraft Ltd, Delhi.
Sometimes known as the Pingle or H.A.L.-Pingle after its designer Pingle Reddy who was a senior executive at the Hindustan Aircraft Co., this was a small but roomy 4-door saloon powered by a 700cc 2-cylinder 2-stroke engine driving the front wheels. It had a fibreglass body on a separate steel chassis, hydraulic brakes and torsion bar suspension on all four wheels. A price of 4600 rupees (about £345 at the prevailing rate of exchange) was fixed, but production never started.

NG

HALCON (U) 1978–1984
Horacio Torrendell SA, Montevideo.
Horacio Torrendell, who used to be Uruguay's Bentley, Rolls-Royce and Rover importer, made this sports car of MG-like appearance to special order. Mechanics were Argentine Ford Falcon, though there was also a Rover power unit. A 4-seater with Chrysler V8 engine was also available. Only four cars were made.

ACT

HALDANE (GB) 1987 to date
1987–1993 Haldane Developments Ltd, Blantyre, Glasgow.
1993–1994 Haldane Developments Ltd, East Kilbride, Glasgow.
1994 to date Haldane Motor Co. (Pilgrim Cars Ltd), Henfield, Sussex.
This was a convincing kit-built Scottish replica of the Austin-Healey 100M. The first ones laboured under a box section chassis and Vauxhall Chevette suspension but the definitive 1991 Mk II gained a steel backbone chassis with a stressed fibreglass bodyshell (in 100 or 3000 styles) and mainly Ford Sierra components, with a choice of Sierra, Pinto or Toyota twin-cam engines. Low Volume Type Approval was gained just prior to PILGRIM taking over production.

CR

HALL (i) (US) 1903–1904
1903 Hall Motor Carriage Co., Dover, New Jersey.
1904 Hall Motor Vehicle Co., Dover, New Jersey.
This car had a 20hp 2-cylinder engine and an aluminium rear-entrance tonneau body. It was priced at $3500 which seems high for what was offered. Maker Hiram P. Hall evidently thought so too, for he dropped the price to $3000 in 1904, but still the buyers did not flock around, so he gave up cars and made traction engines instead.

NG

HALL (ii) (US) 1905
Charles Hall, St Louis, Missouri.
This was an ungainly-looking tourer powered by a flat-twin engine driving the front wheels. Hall was helped by two friends in the building of the prototype, but they could not raise enough finance to put it into production.

NG

HALL (iii) *see* BUFFUM

HALL (iv) (US) 1914–1915
1914 Hall Cyclecar Manufacturing Co., Waco, Texas.
1915 Hall Motor Car Co., Waco, Texas.
The original Hall cyclecar had a V-twin Spacke engine and an underslung frame through which the front axle passed. Seating was in tandem and final drive was by belt. For 1915, as befitted the change of company name, an 18hp 4-cylinder Perkins engine was adopted, seating was side by side and drive was by shaft. A coupé version was built, but production did not last out the year.

NG

HALL (v) (GB) 1918–1919
H.E. Hall & Co., Tonbridge, Kent.
The Hall Flat-8 was an attempt to make a smooth-running car for town use. The prototype had a 20.8hp horizontal 8-cylinder engine specially made in the company's workshops. A number of components from other makes were incorporated,

such as a Talbot radiator and a Studebaker rear axle. With a very short bonnet and a long wheelbase for the 4-door landaulette body, the car was reminiscent of a prewar Lanchester or N.E.C. Probably only one was made, and this survives today.

NG

HALL & MARTIN *see* MARTIN (i)

HALLADAY (US) 1905–1922
1905–1913 Streator Motor Car Co., Streator, Illinois.
1913–1917 Barley Mfg Co., Streator, Illinois.
1917–1919 Halladay Motor Car Co., Attica and Warren, Ohio.
1920–1922 Halladay Motors Corp., Newark, Ohio.

Lou P. Halladay ran the Streator Metal Stamping Works who made pressed-out music stands. In 1905 he designed a large tourer powered by a 35/40hp Rutenber engine, a make which the company would use in various sizes for the rest of its life. Some sources give Oswald as the engine maker up to 1907. It was made only as a tourer for the first three years, joined in 1908 by a runabout and a limousine. It was supplemented in 1909 by a smaller four, with 24hp engine. The Halladay was a reliable car, being the only one to finish without a halt in the 250-mile race at Atlanta in 1910, and was chosen as the press car for the 1911 Glidden Tour. Their best year was 1912, when about 300 cars were made.

In 1913 the company was acquired by Albert Barley, president of Rutenber, to which firm Halladay owed a lot of money. Barley gave his own name to the reorganised company, but in 1916 left to form another business which made the ROAMER. He sold Halladay to a group of businessmen who moved production to Ohio. By now the Halladay used 6-cylinder engines in two sizes, the 30hp Light Six on a 122in (3096mm) wheelbase and the 50hp Big Six on a 134in (3401mm) wheelbase. A sedan was listed for 1920/21, but in 1922 only open models were in the catalogue. A number of different locations in Ohio were mentioned in connection with Halladay manufacture, including Attica, Lexington, Mansfield, Newark and Warren, but it seems that only Attica, Warren and Newark saw serious manufacture, and even then annual output seldom rose into three figures. The constant moving cannot have helped the balance sheet. In January 1922 Halladay showed a companion small car, the FALCON (v) which never saw production, and reported total output from Halladay that year was only six cars.

NG

HALLAMSHIRE (GB) 1901–1906
Durham, Churchill & Co. Ltd, Sheffield, Yorkshire.

This company made communication tubes for ships and the Champion Friction Clutch which they supplied to a number of car makers including NAPIER who used it on their 1901 50hp racing car. They built a car for the 1901 Agricultural Hall Show in London, chiefly to display their clutch, but encouraged by its favourable reception they decided to put it into production. It was powered by a 7hp single-cylinder Simms engine and its design was a mixture of the progressive and the obsolete. The 2-speed gearbox was in constant mesh, with the aid of two Champion clutches, so that gear changing was by actuating either of the clutches rather than sliding the gear wheels. Fibre meshing discs at the sides of the meshing pinions reduced gear whine. Final drive was by chains, and the chassis of armoured wood, neither unusual at the time, but the really antiquated aspect of the design was the centre-pivot steering. In 1902 two engine sizes were offered, 6 and 12hp, but the centre-pivot axle was not replaced until 1903, when the Simms engines gave way to Durham Churchill's own. These were in two sizes, a 2078cc 10hp twin, and a 4156cc 20hp four, the latter using two 10hp blocks on a common crankcase. They were now making the whole chassis themselves, but this must have proved too costly, for the 1905 Hallamshires used 2-cylinder Aster engines (10/12hp) or fours of 12 and 14/18hp by Forman and Aster respectively. Aster 12 and 24hp engines were used in 1906, but this was the last year for passenger car production. Charabancs and trucks were continued under the name Churchill until 1925. Car production was largely to special order and very limited. Not more than 40 were made in five years, and each took two months to complete, though two were often built at the same time. One of the cars' designers was Alliot Verdon Roe, the aircraft pioneer and car builder (AVRO).

NG

1918 Hall (v) 20hp landaulet.
GORDON BROOKS

1905 Hallamshire 14/18hp tourer.
NATIONAL MOTOR MUSEUM

c.1921 Hamilton (iii) 9hp 2-seater.
M.J.WORTHINGTON-WILLIAMS

Further Reading
Cars from Sheffield, Stephen Myers, Sheffield City Libraries, 1986.

HAMARD *see* BUCKINGHAM

HAMILTON (i) *see* COLUMBIA MOTOR BUGGY

HAMILTON (ii) (US) 1917
Hamilton Motors Co., Grand Haven, Michigan.
This was a reorganisation of the Alter Motor Co., and the Hamilton Four was similar to the ALTER, with a 28hp engine and made only as a tourer.

NG

HAMILTON (iii) (GB) 1920–1925
D.J. Smith & Co. Ltd, Wickford, Essex.
The Hamilton could be thought of as a light car or a late model of cyclecar.

1914 Hampton 10hp 2-seater.
NATIONAL MOTOR MUSEUM

1927 Hampton 12hp 2-seater.
NATIONAL MOTOR MUSEUM

It was powered by a 1096cc 9hp air-cooled V-twin Precision engine, with friction transmission and chain final drive. It had a round 'radiator' and 2-seater body. The price dropped steadily from £235 in 1921 to £150 in 1925, its last year of manufacture.

NG

HAMLIN-HOLMES; HAMLIN (US) 1919–1930

1919–1929 Hamlin-Holmes Motor Co., Chicago and Harvey, Illinois.
1930 Hamlin Motor Co., Chicago and Harvey, Illinois.
The Hamlin-Holmes marketing concept was targeted more toward selling an idea rather than a car per se, the idea being a front-wheel drive car priced in the marketplace beside the most popular low-priced cars of various standard makes. The first pilot model resembled the Model T Ford and was powered by a 4-cylinder Lycoming engine, with a wheelbase of 114in (2893mm). Subsequent cars appeared piecemeal, although a company prospectus published in the late 1920s carried photographs illustrating different cars, all ostensibly produced by Hamlin-Holmes and representing each year including the 1919 prototype touring car. These cars all looked like other makes, notably Moon, Cleveland and Nash. This was hardly surprising because, basically, this is exactly what they were, with a badge change to Hamlin-Holmes and the front-wheel drive principle. In 1923, the company announced upcoming production but this never happened and, although presumably a serious plan, substantial financial backing was not forthcoming from any source. A Hamlin-Holmes was entered in the Indianapolis 500 in 1926 but made a poor showing and failed to complete the circuit. By 1929, only test cars had appeared, all of them since 1920 being rebadged cars of other makes. For 1930, the Holmes name was dropped and the lone pilot model was announced in the automotive press, the photograph closely resembling the Gardner front-wheel drive prototype which never went into production. The Hamlin was a 4-door club sedan featuring a slanted radiator and horizontal bonnet louvres. The car never went into production although both the Cord and the Ruxton front-drive cars did appear on the 1930 roster of American automobiles which made it to the marketplace.

KM

HAMMER; HAMMER-SOMMER (US) 1903–1905

1903–1904 Hammer-Sommer Auto Carriage Co., Detroit, Michigan.
1904 Hammer Motor Co., Detroit, Michigan.
The Hammer-Sommer was a light car powered by a 6.7hp single-cylinder or 12hp 2-cylinder engine, mounted under the seat, with epicyclic transmission. In 1904 the partners split up, Henry Hammer making under his own name a larger car with 24hp 4-cylinder engine and 5-seater tourer body. The Sommer brothers also went it alone, with the SOMMER car which was made from 1904 to 1905.

NG

HAMMOND (GB) 1919–1920

Whitworth Engineering Co. Ltd, Finchley, London.
The 11/22hp Hammond was made by several ex-ARROL-JOHNSTON employees. Its cylinder bore of 69mm was shared with many other light cars, whose 100mm stroke gave a capacity of 1496cc. The Hammond, however, had a 150mm stroke, so its capacity was 2242cc, yet the owner paid a tax on only 11.9hp. The specification included a 4-speed gearbox, worm-drive rear axle and cantilever rear springs. The makers took a former aircraft factory on a 50 acre (20.3 hectares) site, and had ambitious plans to make vast numbers of cars. Nothing came of these, and probably no more than a few prototypes were made.

NG

HAMPDEN (US) 1900–1901

Hampden Automobile & Launch Co., Springfield, Massachusetts.
This company was organised by J. Frank Duryea after the break-up of the partnership with his brother Charles. The product was a light 2-seater powered by a 2-cylinder engine which could be started from the seat. Few were made, and in the autumn of 1901 the design was taken up by the Stevens Arms & Tool Co. who put it into production as the STEVENS-DURYEA.

NG

HAMPTON (GB) 1911–1933

1911–1912 Hampton Engineering Co., Hampton-in-Arden, Warwickshire.
1912–1913 Hampton Engineering Co., Kings Norton, Birmingham.
1913–1918 Hampton Engineering Co. Ltd, Kings Norton, Birmingham.
1910–1920 Hampton Engineering Co. Ltd, Dudbridge, Stroud, Gloucestershire.
1920–1924 Hampton Engineering Co. (1920) Ltd, Dudbridge, Stroud, Gloucestershire.
1924–1926 Stroud Motor Manufacturing Co. Ltd, Dudbridge, Stroud, Gloucestershire.
1926–1930 Hampton Cars (London) Ltd, Dudbridge, Stroud, Gloucestershire.
1931–1933 Safety Suspension Car Co., Cainscross, Stroud, Gloucestershire.
The Hampton name derived from Hampton-in-Arden, where William Paddon set up a motor sales business after trade experience with ARROL-JOHNSTON, SINGER and STANDARD. He augmented this business by offering the construction of light cars and motorcycles to order. His enterprise was strengthened by the involvement of Tulloch & Co. (Shippers), but serious production was not undertaken until amalgamation with the receivers of Crowdy Ltd and the consequent transfer to Lifford Mills in Kings Norton. The smaller CROWDY model was developed into the 12/16, announced in November 1912 with an imported 4-cylinder side-valve engine of 1726cc and this (intended to represent a one-model policy) remained the staple product until World War I. The 1914 brochure listed a smart torpedo tourer at £295. Paddon, however, experimented continually with smaller designs, such as a belt-

20 H.P. 8 CYLINDER HAMPTON SPORTSMAN SALOON.

1931 Hampton Sportsman saloon.
TREVOR PICKEN

driven cyclecar announced in February 1913 with a V-twin Precision engine at £115, followed by a water-cooled version with worm drive. In 1914 a 2-cylinder 2-stroke was offered and 4-cylinder cars were also produced with small Ballot or Chapuis-Dornier engines.

Production ceased with the outbreak of war and a receiver was appointed in 1915. The Chairman, Lewis Radmore, was killed in 1916, but Charles Apperly, another prewar director, was involved with the Stroud Metal and Plating Co. Ltd, which had considerably expanded its facilities and activities during the war. When Paddon and Apperly joined forces in 1919 to re-create the Hampton firm, it was expedient to use the Stroud facilities and consequently all future productions emanated from there. Paddon had already used the nearby 1 in 2.5 Nailsworth Ladder hill for promotional activities, foreshadowing Hampton trials and successes throughout the 1920s. The first postwar Hampton used a side-valve Chapuis-Dornier engine of 60 × 120mm (1357cc), and, pending completion of a new factory, the first cars were built at the Dudbridge Iron Works used during the war for the assembly for Salmson radial aero-engines. Production later standardised on ohv engines of 1496 or 1795cc by Dorman of Stafford, with most other parts, including many bodies, manufactured 'in-house'.

The economic recession of 1920 found the company with a promising sales record, including much export interest, but a cashflow problem which could not be resolved without a complete restructuring. The majority shareholding passed to John Daniel from South Wales, where several Hamptons had been sold, and Paddon left for AUTOCRAT of Birmingham. B.S. Marshall, the main London dealer, produced a racing version which achieved success at Brooklands, but price cuts could not offset general trade conditions and sales were disappointing at only 87 for 1921. In 1922 John Dorman defected to Henry Meadows Ltd of Wolverhampton and Hamptons followed suit, most subsequent cars having Meadows engines of either 1247 or 1496cc. The smaller engine (variously 9.8hp, T10, Junior, 9/21, 9hp or 10hp) was the most successful, totalling 386 sales between 1922 and 1930, although none of the five known surviving Hamptons had this engine.

In 1923 the 1920 sales figure of 235 was equalled, William Milward from CHARRON-LAYCOCK of Sheffield succeeded Thomas Joseph as Chief Designer and John Leno, son of the comedian Dan Leno, came in as Sales Manager.

Financial stability was still lacking, however, and Sir John Daniel lost control when the firm again went into receivership the following year. Milward and Leno, with assistance from Gerald Dixon, formed a new company and introduced a larger model, the 14hp with 75 × 120mm Meadows engine, but few of t hese were sold. 4-wheel brakes were standard and prices commenced at £275 for a 10hp 2-seater, but this was too much when a comparable MORRIS or CLYNO was £100 less. In October 1925 the receiver was called in once more, but Milward and Leno persuaded retired businessman John Hatton-Hall to invest in a new company, with a registered office in London. His coat of arms featured on the radiator badge. Limited horizons, simplified designs and later a move to smaller premises nearby at Selsey Hill were commensurate with reduced sales. Another attempt at a larger car, the 1928 model 15/45 side-valve 6-cylinder, was as unsuccessful as the earlier venture. The 1929–30 6-cylinder reverted to Meadows power, the 20hp with ohv 72.5 × 120mm (2973cc) engine, but at £525 for an Empire saloon the effect on sales figures was miniscule. Even more unnoticed were announcements of Meadows 4ED-engined sports models with supercharged or 'Brooklands' specifications, or with adjustable rear suspension derived from the Yorkshire-built HODGSON designs. Some mystery attaches to listings of a short-stroke 12hp in this period (69 × 80mm). This does not tally with any proprietary motor and it is doubtful if Hamptons ever made any such themselves. The connection with Kitson Components Ltd is also unclear. They advertised the Cowburn epicyclic gearbox, featuring tapered steel rollers, available as a Hampton option. Despite no apparent sales, they purchased part of the Hampton works after the demise of 1930.

The final Hampton incarnation was masterminded by Thomas Godman, a receiver with high ambitions and Teutonic connections, the son of a former Mayor of Gloucester, who lived in nearby Cainscross House. 50 ohv straight-8 engines and 100 chassis of advanced design were ordered from RÖHR of Ober-Ramstadt in Germany, but only one or two were delivered. The extra chassis were to be fitted with a side-valve 6-cylinder Continental engine of 2414cc as a cheaper option, also to be available with conventional chassis of Hampton's earlier type. One 18/80 Empire Sportsman saloon was built with H.H. Martyn of Cheltenham body, 2262cc Röhr engine, Warner-Aphon

c.1990 Handcraft Continental Royale.
ELLIOT KAHN

1921 Handley-Knight Model A sedan-coupé.
JOHN A.CONDE

1923 Handley Six sedan.
JOHN A.CONDE

1922 Hands 11/22hp coupé.
NICK BALDWIN

gearbox, platform chassis, double transverse-leaf front suspension and independent cantilever rear. It was rumoured to exist into the 1960s. Later listings with 2.5 or 3.3-litre engines were hopeful rather than actual. The last car constructed, which does still exist, was a Röhr-engined special with conventional chassis, assembled by Milward from parts acquired from various sources after the firm's final demise, and used as his personal transport up to World War II. Total production of all models had been about 1100.

DF

Further Reading
The Story of Hampton Cars, Trevor G. Picken, Hampton Cars, 1997.

HANDCRAFT (US) c.1986–1997

Handcraft Motorcar Co., Bradenton, Florida.
The Handcraft Cormorant was a neoclassic kit car based on 1979–93 Cadillac running gear. It used the Cadillac chassis as well and had a long bonnet and flowing running boards. It was sold in kit or fully assembled form. The Continental Royale was a larger neoclassic on a 156in (3959mm) wheelbase with Lincoln running gear. They were only sold in fully assembled form. The Handcraft GT 2+2 was a rebody kit for 1982–92 Pontiac Firebirds that made them look a bit like a Ferrari Testarossa.

HP

HANDLEY-KNIGHT; HANDLEY (US) 1921–1923

Handley Motors Inc., Kalamazoo, Michigan.
'America's finest Knight-engined Motor Car' sang the advertising copy in late 1920 when production of the new Handley-Knight car commenced at Kalamazoo, the sixth Knight sleeve-valve-engined car to appear on the American automobile roster that year. The new venture was headed by J. I. Handley, formerly associated with both the Marion and Marion-Handley cars. The Handley, available as a touring car, coupé and sedan with prices from $2985 to $3750, used a 4-cylinder engine and had a 125in (3172mm) wheelbase. For 1923, the 4-cylinder Knight engine was dropped and the Handley-Knight was renamed the Handley Six. It was offered in two models, the smaller 6-40 with a 115in (2919mm) wheelbase and powered by a Falls engine and the larger 6-60 by a Midwest engine but retaining the earlier 125in (3172mm) wheelbase. The cars also differed with their radiators – the larger Handley Six with a conventional flat type and a pointed vee-type on the 6-40. Both models shared decorative handles placed on top of their headlamps and a promotional line that a Handley could be identified by the (headlamp) handles, had a false ring to it as the contemporary Reo had simultaneously introduced the same feature in its design. In early 1923 Handley was bought by Checker and it was announced that production of the Handley Six would be continued. It never was. Production of the Handley-Knight as well as both models of the Handley Six was minimal.

KM

HANDS (GB) 1922–1924

G.W. Hands Motor Co. Ltd, Birmingham.
George Hands was the originator of the CALTHORPE light car, and in 1922 he decided to make a car under his own name, using part of the Calthorpe motor cycle factory as his works. Whereas Calthorpe made their own engines, Hands bought his from Dorman in several sizes, 9.5hp (1196cc), 10.5hp (1498cc) and 10/20hp (1246cc). About 150 were made, and in 1924 he announced a 1991cc 14/45hp 6-cylinder car with single-ohc engine. Though the gearbox came from Moss it seems the engine was Hands' own, but very few were made, and at the end of the year he returned to the Calthorpe fold. A few of the sixes may have been made as the Type C 15.7hp Calthorpe, as the engine size and prices were identical with the Hands, but Calthorpe were on their way out at this time.

NG

HANNIBAL (H) 1998

Zoltán Kozma, Dabas.
Kozma proved that Hungary could be a dreamland after all. He completed his dream car before his 18th birthday. The chassis was reworked from a locally made Lotus 7 replica, and power came from a 2-litre Ford Cosworth engine. Its outrageous styling was just a preview of things to come, said the young designer, who soon received foreign orders for similar models.

PN

HANOMAG (D) 1925–1952

1925–1931 Hannoversche Maschinenbau AG, Hannover-Linden.
1932–1935 Hanomag Automobil-und Schlepperbau GmbH.
1932–1952 Hannoversche Maschinenbau AG, Hannover-Linden.

Hanomag was an established name when the company produced its first car in 1925. A contraction of the corporate title, the Hanomag name came into use in 1885, but its roots date back to 6 June 1835, when Georg Egestorff (1802–68) founded the Eisen-Giesserei und Maschinenfabrik Hannover. It was reorganised in 1871, becoming Hannoversche Maschinenbau AG.

Georg Egestorff built a 6hp steam engine in 1836, and soon became a major producer of steam boilers. By 1842 he had 200 workers and was also producing a line of ploughs and other farm implements. His first steam locomotive was built in 1846 for the Hannoverian State Railways, and in 1870 the factory turned out its 500th locomotive.

About 1905 the Kaiser was making plans for more modern military transport, and the army became interested in a steam truck designed by Peter Stoltz. Two procurement contracts went out in 1906, one to Eisenwerke Gaggenau AG, and one to Hanomag.

In 1910 Hanomag's leaders determined that the future of mechanised farming would not lie with steam power. They called in Joseph Vollmer to design two families of petrol-powered tractors, one for ploughing, and the other for hauling trailers on the road. Production began in 1912. In 1920 Vollmer also designed new 20hp and 50hp multi-purpose crawler tractors, following up with 35hp and 80hp wheeled tractors in 1923.

The steam-locomotive market was in a slump, and Hanomag's president, Gustav ter Meer, began looking for an alternative product line. He found it in a letter arriving from Berlin, signed by two engineering students, Carl Pollich and Fidelis Böhler. The letter included drawings and a description of a new kind of small economy car.

The two side by side seats made up the entire passenger compartment and formed a central core for the structure. The remainder was put together with weight the primary concern. The water-cooled single-cylinder engine (and its radiator) were installed behind the seats, while the front end was occupied by the fuel tank and spare wheel.

Built on a 75.6in (1920mm) wheelbase, it was only 109in (2780mm) long overall, and the open car had a dry weight of 370kg. The vehicle was built up on a pressed-steel frame with channel-section side members. Front and rear body sections were bolted up from sheet-metal stampings, while the middle section was a laminate of wood and steel. Front suspension was independent, with upper and lower transverse leaf springs, and the chain-driven rear axle (without a differential) was held by coil springs and radius rods.

Hanomag bought their two prototypes and all rights to the design, and put the students on the payroll. Ten test cars were built and the plant was tooled up as the testing went on. Gustav ter Meer had hired a top production man, Otto Dyckhoff, away from Hansa-Lloyd, and Dyckhoff organised car assembly on a moving line. The car was advertised as the Hanomag 2/10 PS, but its odd looks earned it the nickname Kommissbrot (army loaf).

The base-model 2/10 was priced at RM 2300 at a time when the cheapest mass-produced Opel 4/8 PS Laubfrosch was listed at RM 4000. A closed body was offered in 1926, along with a 750kg (payload) commercial version.

In 1927 and 1928, the Linden plant was humming along, turning out 80 cars a day. When 2/10 production ceased in 1928, Hanomag had built 15,775 cars.

Successful it was, but it did not carry a big profit margin, and Hanomag began running up big losses. Generalkonsul Hans Lerch, head of a prosperous local trading company, provided the collateral for hefty bank loans in return for a seat on the Hanomag board. He also arranged the sale of the locomotives division to Henschel & Sohn of Kassel for RM 5.25 million.

Carl Pollich was named chief engineer of Hanomag, while Fidelis Böhler left. Hans Lerch's management wanted Hanomag to build the same kind of car as Brennabor, Mannesmann, Dixi and Wanderer, and the car Pollich drew up went into production late in 1928 as the 3/16 PS. It was purely conventional, with an L-head 797cc 4-cylinder engine, riding on semi-elliptic springs on the front and splayed quarter-elliptics in the rear end. Otto Dyckhoff completed its tooling and then left to join Wanderer.

Due to good tractor sales (with a new diesel model) Hanomag produced RM 12,000 profit in 1928, and the company was worth RM 36.5 billion. The market turned sour in 1929 and Hanomag lost RM 700,000 that year. Hanomag

1926 Hanomag 2/10PS coupé.
NICK GEORGANO/NATIONAL MOTOR MUSEUM

1929 Hanomag 3/16PS cabriolet, towing a Wanderer 6/30.
NATIONAL MOTOR MUSEUM

1936 Hanomag Rekord saloon.
NICK GEORGANO/NATIONAL MOTOR MUSEUM

entered 1930 with a stockpile of 3250 unsold cars, and was still losing money in 1930, with a turnover of RM 15 million from cars and RM 6 million from tractors.

Carl Pollich developed a proposal for a radically different all-steel saloon with a rear-mounted flat-twin engine, but Lerch turned it down, ordering Pollich to do an enlarged 3/16 instead.

The new 4/23 PS model had a 1094cc L-head engine with an output of 23hp at 3500rpm, giving a top speed of 53mph (85km/h). The wheelbase was stretched to 97in (2450mm) and the car weighed 650 to 950kg, depending on body style. Bodies came from Ambi-Budd in Berlin. Other innovations were hydraulic brakes and dampers. Three body styles were offered: saloon, cabrio-limousine, and cabriolet, priced from RM 2800 to 3000.

Sales picked up, and Hanomag's domestic market share climbed to 14 per cent in 1930, putting it second only to Opel, just ahead of Adler and BMW. In the autumn of 1931, however, the banks refused a new bridge loan and Hanomag stopped payments on 17 December 1931. To that date, Hanomag had produced 9300 cars with 4-cylinder engines in just over two years.

1939 Hanomag 1.3-litre saloon.
HALWART SCHRADER

Accumulated losses stood at RM 3.7 billion. The factory was mortgaged to the City of Hanover and the Vereinigte Stahlwerke of Bochum, a powerful steel trust, and reorganised as Hanomag Automobil-und Schlepperbau GmbH when debts of RM 2.6 billion had been written off. Hans Lerch was dismissed, and his place was taken by Walter Borbet, a steel executive since 1922 and also a member of H. Büssing & Co.'s supervisory board.

In 1931 Hanomag had 25 per cent of the small-car market in Germany (under 1200cc) with DKW at 19.5 per cent and BMW at 17.4 per cent. For 1932, Hanomag concentrated on a single series, the 1.1-litre (ex 4/23) which was renamed Garant when modernised for 1934. The gamble worked, and soon the Linden plant was running on a two-shift basis to satisfy the demand.

Even in 1931, Pollich had been instructed to draw up a bigger car, and the Rekord went into production in 1933 with a 1494cc ohv engine and 4-speed gearbox. The frame was a deep-section steel platform, developed for integration with the Ambi-Budd body structure. Front suspension was independent with a low-mounted transverse leaf spring, while the rear axle was kept on semi-elliptics.

By the end of 1936, Hanomag could celebrate a small milestone: its 65,000th car rolled off the line. By that time, the model range had expanded to include the 6-cylinder Sturm and the smaller Kurier and Garant. All shared the construction principles of the Rekord, with detail variations.

The Kurier was new in 1934, built on a 107in (2725mm) wheelbase, sharing the front and rear suspension assemblies with the Rekord but having the small Garant engine. It was priced alongside the Garant at RM 2975 – about RM 500 less than the Rekord.

The Sturm was competing in a small, select market segment, and Hanomag did not expect to sell a lot of them. But it was a highly visible market segment, where Dr Borbet thought it was important to be present. Hanomag made only a few hundred Sturm cars each year. The best seller was the Rekord – almost 19,000 cars were built from 1934 to 1940. Hanomag's domestic car sales climbed from 4675 in 1933 to 6321 in 1934 and 8171 in 1935.

The Rekord was also Hanomag's first diesel car, exhibited at the Berlin motor show in February 1936, where Mercedes-Benz also unveiled its 260-D.

In 1936 Carl Pollich began working on a new concept for a modern, streamlined, and economical middle-class family car. That led to the launching in January 1939 of the 1.3-litre. (Strangely, this outstanding car never got a real name.)

With Ambi-Budd's assistance, Hanomag now adopted a full unit-construction body, eliminating the conventional frame. The naked body shell weighed only 200kg.

Built on a 98in (2500mm) wheelbase, the roomy car weighed only 970kg. The engine was a 1299cc short-stroke version of the Rekord unit. The 1.3-litre also introduced ifs with rubber blocks. The car's top speed was 72mph (116km/h) and average fuel consumption 8.8l/100km. Hanomag produced 9187 of these cars in 1939. Then the plant converted to produce 4.2-litre 6-cylinder Maybach engines for military vehicles.

After the war, Hanomag's first products were trailers. Slowly, farm-tractor production resumed, and in 1949, a new 1½ ton truck was added.

But Hanomag was operating in a corporate vacuum, since the steel trust had been dissolved in 1945. The problem was solved by Rudolf Hiller, former president and co-owner of the Phänomen truck company, who joined Hanomag in 1950. He talked things over with Dr Wolfgang Linne of Rheinstahl, and full ownership of Hanomag passed to the Rheinstahl group in 1952.

Carl Pollich was still there, and he put a new car on the drawing board in 1947. The first prototype was shown in Frankfurt in April 1951. The Hanomag Partner was a front-wheel drive car with a 3-cylinder 697cc 2-stroke engine carried in the front overhang, rubber-block front suspension, and a dry weight of 730kg. The project was cancelled after a test fleet of 11 cars had been put on the road.

Truck production continued, and in 1964 Rheinstahl took over Henschel & Sohn, which was then merged with Hanomag. The farm-tractor activity was sold to Massey-Ferguson. The truck activity of Hanomag-Henschel was sold to Daimler-Benz AG in 1969, and the Hanover plant concentrated on earth-moving equipment. After an unfortunate affiliation with IBH (International Baumaschinen Holding) which lasted from 1977 to 1984, Hanomag sold its diesel-engine tooling to Volvo. The plant and the earth-moving machinery business were ultimately taken over by Komatsu of Japan.

JPN

Further Reading
'A bit of tin, a stroke of lacquer – the Hanomag', Dieter Korp, *Automobile Quarterly*, Vol. 3, No. 2.
Pulsschlag eines Werkes 160 Jahre Hanomag, Horst Dieter Görg, Mundschenk Verlag, Soltau, 1998.
Hanomag Personwagen von Hannover in die Welt, Horst Dieter Görg and Torsen Hamacher, Mundschenk Verlag, Soltau, 1999.

HANOVER (US) 1921–1927

Hanover Motor Car Co., Hanover, Pennsylvania.

This was a small 2-cylinder air-cooled, wire-wheeled roadster built for export, mostly to Japan. Some 160+ were built.

NG

HANSA (D) 1906–1939

1906–1914 Hansa Automobil-GmbH, Varel; Bielefeld (1913–1914).
1914–1929 Hansa-Lloyd Werke Varel; Bremen (1929–1931).
1931–1937 Hansa-Lloyd und Goliath-Werke Borgward & Tecklenborg, Bremen.
1937–1939 Hansa-Lloyd-Goliath-Werke Carl F.W. Borgward, Bremen.

The Hansa Automobile Gesellschaft was founded at the end of 1905 to build light cars, these being comparatively rare in Germany at the time. The first Hansa car was the 7/9PS, a 2-seater using a single-cylinder De Dion-Bouton engine and based on the French ALCYON. It was sold under the name HAG (not to be confused with the later HAG made at Darmstatt in the 1920s). It was joined by the 5/10PS 2-cylinder and 10/12PS 4-cylinder cars, the latter using a Fafnir engine. From 1907 Hansa made their own engines in larger sizes such as the 1550cc 6/16PS, 2060cc 8/20PS and 1612cc 10/30PS. The latter, made from 1911 to 1914, had overhead valves, as did the largest prewar Hansa, the 3815cc 15/50PS. Several sporting models were made, in particular the Typs B and F (1796 and 2515cc), which had pointed tail 2-seater or 4-seater torpedo bodies, oval radiators and sometimes a single cyclops eye headlamp in the middle. Despite their sporting appearance, Hansas did not feature in the major competitions until 1914 when a Typ F did well in the Alpine Trial.

In 1913 Hansa took over the WESTFALIA works at Bielefeld and built cars there as well as at Varel. The following year they merged with the Norddeutsche Automobil und Motoren AG of Bremen, makers of LLOYD (i) cars and commercial vehicles. This resulted in two parallel ranges of car being made in the 1920s, the small/medium-sized Hansas at Varel and the large, luxurious Hansa-Lloyds at Bremen.

Only one model of Hansa was made from 1921 to 1928. This was the 4-cylinder Typ F with 2090cc side valve engine. In the first series (1921–24) this gave 30bhp, but this was increased to 36bhp on the later models. Appearance followed German fashions of the time, with the vee-radiator of the first series giving way to a flat radiator from 1924 onwards. In 1928 Hansa took a new direction with a series of larger cars powered by Continental engines from America. These included the 3262 and 3489cc 6-cylinder Typ A6 and 3996 and 4324cc straight-8 Typ A8. A smaller 2577cc 6-cylinder Continental engine was used in the Konsul and Matador of 1930/31, although, confusingly, these models could also be had with 2098 or 3252cc 4-cylinder Hansa engines. The American-engined Hansas were much cheaper than the Hansa-Lloyds, even in straight-8 form. In 1929 a Type A8 Hansa 4-door cabriolet cost RM16,000 compared with RM27,500 for a similarly-bodied Hansa-Lloyd Trumpf As.

In 1929 Hansa and Hansa-Lloyd were merged by Carl Borgward, and the Hansa-Lloyd was dropped, though commercials were continued under that name up to 1938. Borgward also made the GOLIATH 3-wheeler in the Bremen factory until the tax concessions for 3-wheelers were abolished by Hitler in 1933. However, Borgward kept up his interest in small cars with the Hansa 400. This was a coupé with rear-mounted 396cc 2-cylinder engine as used in the Goliath delivery van. It had a backbone frame and wood panelled body. In 1934 capacity was upped to 494cc on the Hansa 400. About 500 of these little cars were made, in 1933 and 1934 only.

The Berlin Show of March 1934 saw the appearance of new Hansa models which were more successful than any previous ones. They were the 1100 and 1700, powered by new Hansa-built ohv engines of 1088 4-cylinders and 1634cc 6-cylinders. They were mounted in backbone chassis with the bodies carried on outriggers. Ifs was provided by transverse leaves and brakes were hydraulic.

1924 Hansa Typ P 8/36PS saloon.
NICK GEORGANO/NATIONAL MOTOR MUSEUM

1934 Hansa 400 saloon.
NATIONAL MOTOR MUSEUM

1939 Hansa 1100 cabrio-limousine.
ROBERT STRAUB

The all-steel bodies were also made in the Hansa factory, and came in 2-door saloon and cabriolet styles, together with an attractive 2-seater sports car made by Hebmüller. These two models enabled Hansa to chalk up sales of 5985 units in 1936, not enormous by the standards of Opel or Mercedes-Benz, but encouraging compared with their 1934 figure of less than 1000.

The 1100 was continued up to the outbreak of war, as was the 1700 for the export market, but for home consumption the engine was increased to 1962cc for 1938, when there was a restyled 4-door saloon. This Hansa 2000 lasted for only one season, and for 1939 it was renamed the Borgward 2000. In October 1939 it was joined by the 2247cc Borgward 2300 which was made in small numbers up to 1942. After the war all cars were called Borgwards, although from 1949 to 1958 Hansa was used as a model name. In 1958 the Goliath from the same factory was renamed Hansa.

c.1960 Hansa 1100 saloon.
NICK GEORGANO/NATIONAL MOTOR MUSEUM

1923 Hansa-Lloyd Treff-AS 18/60PS limousine.
NICK BALDWIN

The only other prewar Hansa was the 3500, a 3485cc six with conventional channel frame, of which about 200 4-door saloons and cabrio-saloons were made from 1937 to 1939. By contrast, about 17,000 of the 1100 were made from 1934 to 1940, and 8000 of the 1700/2000.

NG

HANSA-LLOYD (D) 1921–1930

Hansa Lloyd Werke AG, Bremen.
After the merger with Hansa in 1914, the former Lloyd factory made mostly commercial vehicles, but also produced two models of luxury car in the 1920s. These were the Treff As (Ace of Clubs) and Trumpf As (Ace of Trumps), the former with 4-cylinder engines of 4100cc (1920–1922) and 4500cc (1923–1925), and the latter a straight-8 of 4640cc (1926–1927) and 5220cc (1927–1930). The Treff As had side-valve engines, the Trumpf As single ohcs with output up to 100bhp. The prototype Trumpf As appeared in the autumn of 1923, when it was Germany's first straight-8, though it did not go into production until early 1926. They were of higher quality than the equivalent Hansa, and correspondingly more expensive. Coachwork was mostly made by outside firms, including Seegers of Leipzig, Rembrandt of Bremen, Glaser of Dresden and Karmann of Osnabruck. Carl Borgward's take-over of Hansa and Hansa-Lloyd brought the production of Hansa Lloyd cars to an end, though the name was used on commercial vehicles up to 1938.

NG

HANSAN (NL) 1958

This short-lived microcar had a 489cc engine developing 15bhp.

CR

HANSEN (US) 1902

Hansen Automobile Co., Cleveland, Ohio.
Danish-born Rasmus Hansen built a light runabout powered by a 6hp single-cylinder engine mounted under the seat. The steering tiller could be positioned in the centre or at the right-hand side. Although the company bore his name, the cars were sometimes called Cleveland. In September 1902 he reorganised as the General Automobile & Manufacturing Co., and built a larger car called the GENERAL (i).

NG

HANSEN-WHITMAN (US) 1907

Hansen Auto & Machine Works, Pasadena, California.
This company produced a small number of cars powered by 2-cylinder 2-stroke engines, with friction transmission and chain drive. A roadster with solid tyres and wicker back seat was built, as well as a claimed 10 tourers.

NG

HANSON (US) 1917–1925

Hanson Motor Co., Atlanta, Georgia.
The Hanson got off to a slow start due to the US declaration of war against the Central Powers, production being delayed until mid–1918. The car was the result of the conviction of its builder, George W. Hanson, that there would be a viable market for a well-built car manufactured in the South, such as the ANDERSON which had become a successful going concern at Rock Hill, South Carolina. Although operating on a smaller scale, the Hanson was successful on a regional basis. The car was an assembled car like so many others of its time, powered by a Continental 7R engine (succeeded by the 8R from 1923 to the end of production) with a single exception of a smaller series which was built only in 1922 and used the Continental 7U which developed 48bhp at 2600rpm (the 7R's output was slightly higher – 54bhp at 2650rpm). Hansons sold relatively well in the Southern market but with an abundance of corporation cars of the same general size and specifications priced at a similar or even lower figure, national competition was out of the question. Hanson's

production was almost entirely focused on the touring car, although a coupé and sedan were available until 1923 and 1924. Total production is uncertain with estimates ranging from 840 to nearly 1900. If the Hanson did not become a household word on a national scale, it was well known in and around the Atlanta area, where the majority of the cars were sold.

KM

Further Reading
'Deep South', M. Worthington-Williams, *The Automobile*, December 1999.
'Til the Weevil Hit: George Washington Hanson and his Automobile', William D. Hammack, *Automobile Quarterly*, Vol. 14, No. 2.

HANZER (F) 1900–1903
Hanzer Frères, Petit Ivry, Seine.
This company began by making motor tricycles in 1899, following these with a voiturette powered by a front-mounted 3hp De Dion-Bouton engine and 3-speed gearbox. In 1901 Hanzers had Aster engines of 6hp and were available with 4-seater bodies as well as 2 seaters. The 1902/03 range consisted of 5 and 6½hp singles and a 9hp twin. During 1903 they were taken over by DUREY-SOHY who continued the range for at least a year. One Hanzer survives, a 5hp 2-seater of 1902.

NG

HARBRON (GB) 1986–1987
Bill Harbron, Bridport, Dorset.
This was a very basic traditional-style open roadster offered for only £1500 for the full kit.

CR

HARDING (i) (CDN) 1911–1912
Harding Motor Car Co., London, Ontario.
Fred Harding built an attractive 2-seater runabout with a close resemblance to the 20hp Hupmobile, powered by a 20hp G.B. & S. engine. It was priced at CDN $750, the same as the Hupmobile, but despite the slogan 'A Canadian Car for Canadians' it did not sell well, and production ended in 1912.

NG

HARDING (ii) (US) 1915–1916
Harding Motor Car Co., Cleveland, Ohio.
The Harding Twelve was built by two ex-Peerless staff, Frank I. Harding and Nathan Wyeth, having a 5840cc V12 engine made up of two 6-cylinder engine blocks on a common crankshaft. A modest sounding price of $2000 for a 7-seater tourer was announced, but Harding was never able to find a factory or obtain the necessary amount of materials. The prototype tourer was the only Harding Twelve made. Wyeth later took it to Boston and drove it for a number of years, substituting a 6-cylinder engine for the 12.

NG

HARDING (iii) (US) c.1919
Although one Harding still exists, it is a mystery make whose manufacturers are unknown, although the factory is thought to have been in Kenosha, Wisconsin. The surviving car has a 60hp 6-cylinder Wisconsin engine, and probably not more than four or five were made.

NG

HARDING (iv) (GB) 1921–c.1950
R.A. Harding (Bath) Ltd, Bath, Somerset.
This maker of invalid cars was founded by J. Gordon and E. Loxley, but they took the company name R.A. Harding from that of Mr Loxley's wife's maiden name. They made a greater variety of vehicles than any other firm in the invalid car field. These included hand-propelled, petrol and electric cars. In the late 1920s they made a range of eight types, from the Model A 98cc bath chair type 3-wheeler to the 4-wheeled Pultney Model IV and Model VI. The former could be had in single and 2-seater forms, at £66 and £72 respectively. It had cycle-type wheels, tiller steering and a 250cc engine. The Model VI, on the other hand, was a wheel-steered 2-seater resembling an Austin Seven. Powered by a 300cc JAP engine, with Sturmey-Archer 3-speed gearbox, it was the most car-like of any invalid vehicle, and cost £102, more than the utility version of the Morris Minor.

1902 Hanzer 5hp 2-seater.
NATIONAL MOTOR MUSEUM

c.1930 Harding (iv) Pultney Model VI invalid car.
NATIONAL MOTOR MUSEUM

Harding were willing to make one-offs to special order, such as the spinal carriage made in 1932 for a customer who could only drive the car lying on his back. It was powered by a 250cc JAP engine.

After World War II Harding made more modest tricycles, though with some ingenious features. The De Luxe Model B of 1949 had a 147cc 2-stroke engine beneath the seat, to which was attached the petrol tank in order to minimise unsprung weight. Suspension was by tiny coil springs under the back of the seat, and rubber insert front forks. They also made an electric version. Harding received substantial contracts from the Ministry of Health in the late 1940s, but the marque vanished soon afterwards, probably due to competition from AC, who made Ministry specified models from 1949.

Harding had quite a flourishing export market, their cars being sold in South Africa, Canada, Scandinavia and New Zealand.

NG

HARDINGE see PULLMAN (i)

1905 Harper (i) 10hp landaulet.
NATIONAL MOTOR MUSEUM

1923 Harper (iii) Runabout 3-wheeler.
NICK GEORGANO/NATIONAL MOTOR MUSEUM

HARDY MOTORS (US) c.1993–1998
Hardy Motors, Visalia, California.
Hardy Motors Bonita, California.
Hardy Motors, Mooresville, North Carolina.
Neil Hardy started his company by purchasing an Allard J2X replica from
ELITE. Hardy offered it with a steel tube chassis that used a VW front torsion
bar suspension unit with a Chevrolet, Cadillac or Chrysler V8 up front. They
were sold in kit or turn-key form. Hardy also assembled the GTD-40 replica
from England and imported the Guitolar 1930 Mercedes SSK replicas from
Brazil. These were sold only in turn-key form with Mercedes running gear for
$72,500.

HP

HARE ENGINEERING (GB) 1989–1992
Hare Engineering, Bournemouth, Dorset.
The H.E.40 MkIII was a Ford GT40 replica based on K.V.A.'s MkIII bodyshell
and using a space frame chassis. Each car was individually hand-built and was
intended as much for historic replica racing as road use.

CR

HARE ENGINEERING (GB) 1989–c.1992
Hare Engineering, Bournemouth, Dorset.
The H.E.40 Mk III was a Ford GT40 replica based on K.V.A.'s Mk III bodyshell
and using a space frame chassis. Each car was individually hand-built and was
intended as much for historic replica racing as roadgoing use.

CR

HARISCOTT (GB) 1920–1921
Harrison, Scott & Co., Bradford, Yorkshire.
This was an assembled car with 1498cc 4-cylinder side-valve Coventry-Simplex
engine and 4-speed gearbox. A 5-seater tourer and 2-seater sports car were
offered, the latter said to be capable of 60mph. Suspension was by semi-elliptic
springs at the front, quarter-elliptic at the rear, and disc wheels were
standardised. Few were made but according to Gregor Grant, writing in *British
Sports Cars* 'those that were purchased by private owners gave good, reliable
service for many years'.

NG

HARLE see SAUTTER-HARLE

HARMER (US) 1906–1907
Harmer Motor Car Co., Columbus, Ohio.
Frederick S. Harmer had worked for the Oscar Lear Automobile Co., makers
of the FRAYER-MILLER, where he had been attracted by air-cooling. His
prototype car had a 24hp air-cooled engine with overhead valves, a 3-speed
gearbox and shaft drive. He planned to make 40hp tourers and runabouts as
well as a 5-ton truck, but the prototype 2-seater was probably the only Harmer
made. Apparently he took his admiration of the Frayer Miller design too far,
and faced litigation from his former employers.

NG

HARPER (i) (GB) 1905–1906
Harper Motor Co., Aberdeen.
The Harper Motor Co. was a subsidiary of Harper & Co. who operated a
substantial ironworks at Craiginches on the outskirts of Aberdeen. Their car was
an all-weather landalette which used the 10hp Cadillac single-cylinder engine,
but with the gearbox located well forward under the footboard. Transmission
was by epicyclic gears, and final drive by spur gears from a countershaft to the
rear axle. Although *The Car* described the Harper as 'ingenious', it seems that
not many were sold.

NG

HARPER (ii) (US) 1907–1908
Harper Buggy Co., Columbus City, Indiana.
Although this company had announced that they would make a car 'of the auto
buggy type with 4hp engine', when the Harper appeared it was a conventional
2-seater powered by a 2-cylinder 2-stroke engine, with 2-speed epicyclic transmission.
It was priced at £800, but Harper did not last long in the car business, soon returning
to horse-drawn vehicles exclusively.

NG

HARPER (iii) (GB) 1921–1926
A.V. Roe & Co Ltd, Stretford, Manchester.
R.O. Harper had been works manager at Newton & Bennett, makers of the
N.B., and after the war he designed an ingenious little car, described as 'the most
practical of the 3-wheeled cyclecars', though it was even smaller than most of
the breed. Little more than a 3-wheeled scooter, it seated two in tandem (with
the passenger facing rearward) in an integral construction body, mainly of
plywood but with substantial metal castings bolted transversely across the
frame. The engine was a 269cc single-cylinder Villiers 2-stroke driving through
a 3-speed gearbox and chain to the rear wheels which were braked by discs.
Advertisements claimed that it would climb any hill in the country, and that a
top speed of 35mph (56km/h) was guaranteed. Indeed, one reached 42.5mph
(68km/h) at Brooklands. It was a highly original design and clearly met a need,
as about 500 were made up to 1926 certainly, and possibly as late as 1929.
    The Harper Runabout was made in the factory of aircraft manufacturers
A.V. Roe Ltd. At least one of Roe's 2-wheeled AVRO cars used Harper wheels.

NG

Further Reading
'The Harper Runabout', M. Worthington-Williams,
The Automobile, November 1996.

HARPER (iv) (GB) c.1951–1960
Harper Engineering Ltd, Exeter, Devon.

This invalid car maker succeeded the Stanley Engineering Co. which made the ARGSON 3-wheeler. They made a series of 3-wheelers with fibreglass bodies of increasing comfort, powered mostly by 197 or 250cc engines, with 3-speed gearboxes. The Mark VI of 1957 had a form of rubber suspension. In 1959 Harpermatic automatic transmission by variable belt pulley was tried in a prototype, but never produced. The last model had a raised roof-line, and was called the Stanley.

NG

HARRIER (GB) 1991 to date
Harrier Racing Ltd, Camberley, Surrey.
This primarily competition company developed the LR9 sports car for road and track use. It was an open car with a fixed roll-over bar and rear glass section. The chassis was a tubular steel space frame and much use was made of carbon fibre in the construction. The standard powerplant was a tuned Alfa Romeo 164 3-litre V6 mounted amidships that provided a power-to-weight ratio of 320bhp per ton and a top speed of over 150mph (241km/h). A 4-litre Ferrari V12 was installed in at least one car.

CR

HARRIGAN (US) 1922
Harrigan Motors Corp., Jersey City, New Jersey.
Anyone seriously trying to identify exactly what the Harrigan really was during its lone year of 'production' would have been hard put to find a viable answer, although the car was listed on a few contemporary automotive rosters. The car appears to have been built in Cleveland, Ohio, although 'factory' promotion listed both Jersey City and nearby Hoboken (New Jersey) as the centre of 'operations'. Its president and chief engineer, William C. Harrigan, who claimed to have been on the engineering staff of Isotta Fraschini as well as Locomobile and Packard, claimed to have produced 500 cars, 200 of which had been consigned to the export market. What the Harrigan turned out to be – on close investigation – was apparently Mr Harrigan's personal car, a Case Model V-22 with a Continental 9N engine and 126in (3198mm) wheelbase, redesigned with the addition of a high, square radiator and a badge proclaiming the car to be a Harrigan. One wonders what occurred or might have occurred had anyone actually tried to buy a Harrigan Six.

KM

HARRIS (i) (US) 1910
Chicago House Wrecking Co., Chicago, Illinois.
The only car known to have been made by a demolition company, the Harris was a 2-seater runabout powered by a 12hp 2-cylinder engine mounted under the seat, with epicyclic transmission and shaft drive. Pneumatic or solid tyres were offered. With its vertical dashboard and tiller steering it looked very old-fashioned for 1910.

NG

HARRIS (ii) (US) c.1994
Harris Engineering, San Francisco, California.
The Harris SRT 9000 was a Lamborghini Countach replica based on a custom space frame with Corvette or Pontiac Fiero running gear.

HP

HARRIS-LÉON LAISNE see LÉON LAISNE

HARRISON (US) 1906–1907
Harrison Motor Co., Grand Rapids, Michigan.
The Harrison was a large car with 6.3-litre 40hp 4-cylinder ohv engine with the unusual feature of self-starting by injection of a measured mixture of acetylene into the cylinders. It was expensive at $5000, and few were made.

NG

HARRIS SIX (US) 1923
Wisconsin Automotive Corp., Menasha, Wisconsin.
The Harris Six is probably unique in American automotive motordom as being the only automobile produced under court order to help defray bankruptcy proceedings. The car itself was named after G. D. Harris, vice president of the

1960 Harper (iv) Mk VI invalid car.
NATIONAL MOTOR MUSEUM

1906 Harrison 40hp tourer.
NATIONAL MOTOR MUSEUM

US Tractor Co. who was instrumental in adding a line of passenger cars to the existing output of tractors. Plans for this production were outlined late in 1922 when patterns for the design of the recently discontinued WINTHER car were purchased from that car's parent company, the Winther Motor Truck Co. of Kenosha, Wisconsin. The announcement of the Harris Six appeared in the 30 April issue of the *Menasha Record*, in an advertisement including a sketch of the projected Touring Phaeton and a listing of the various models to be built and their corresponding prices. The Harris Six design called for a rather good-looking car with disc wheels and matching side-mounts. Its wheelbase measured 120in (3046mm), and power was by a 6-cylinder Herschell-Spillman Model 40 L-head engine. Prices were set at $1275 to $1675. Its delay of getting into production killed the venture and the US Tractor Co. was re-organised, becoming the Wisconsin Automotive Corp. with bankruptcy proceedings immediately following. The court decided that production of the intended cars was impracticable and decreed that the corporation complete as many cars as possible from existing parts. An estimated nine cars, all disc-wheeled sport phaetons, were thereby completed and sold for what they could bring to local purchasers, the proceeds being used to pay court costs. Thus ended the Harris Six and the US Tractor Co. G. D. Harris moved to Appleton, Wisconsin and became more successful in the manufacture of snowploughs.

KM

HARROUN (US) 1917–1922
Harroun Motor Corp., Wayne, Michigan.
The Harroun was designed by racing great Ray Harroun, winner of the first Indianapolis 500, and was available as a roadster and a touring car at $595 and a sedan at $850. The Harroun used its own 4-cylinder engine and had a wheelbase of 107in (2716mm). Production was suspended in the Spring of 1918 due to the factory's switching to war material and was not resumed until 1921. An estimated 1000 cars were produced in the Harroun's four years of manufacturing.

KM

1951 Hartnett saloon.
NATIONAL MOTOR MUSEUM

1915 Harvard 2-seater.
KEITH MARVIN

HART (GB) 1900–1901

E.W. Hart & Co., Luton, Bedfordshire.

Hart's main business was the importation of Lohner-Porsche electric and petrol-electric cars, and later Austro-Daimler, but he also made a few electric cars on his own account, which he sold under the name Lutonia. This had a 2hp Bergmann motor geared directly to the rear axle. Hart's children, 14-year old Oscar and 11-year old Marguerite, were pioneer juvenile motorists, and before the 1903 Motor Car Act brought in a minimum age of 17, they regularly drove themselves to school in their father's cars.

NG

HARTMAN (US) 1914–1918

George V. Hartman, Red Bluff, California.

George Hartman built a number of light cars powered by 4-cylinder Model engines in unit with 3-speed gearboxes, which he bought at rock bottom prices, as Model were moving their factory from Peru, Indiana, to Pittsburgh. He used two sizes, 3151 and 3205cc, and though he never formed a company, he may have made as many as 20 cars. America's entry into the war, and Hartman's joining the Army, put an end to the project.

NG

HARTNETT (AUS) 1951–1955

Hartnett Motor Co. Ltd, Melbourne, Victoria.

After his resignation from General Motors-Holden, Larry Hartnett was persuaded, by a Government viewing seriously the prospect of a foreign company having a monopoly in the motor industry, to identify a small car suitable for production in Australia. His selection was the front-wheel drive, 600cc flat-twin GRÉGOIRE design which had been taken up, postwar by KENDALL in England and, in a modified form, by PANHARD in France. As the Kendall had failed, its remains were purchased by Hartnett.

Initially bodywork and electrics were required and it was the failure of Commonwealth Engineering to honour its body pressing contract which

brought down the project. The components were assembled, French starter motors obtained and, apart from a few examples with roadster, saloon, and tourer bodies, the approximately 120 produced were completed as the Vanette, a 'woody' station wagon. As Hartnett also held the rights to Grégoire's 2-litre model, it would have followed if the small car had succeeded.

MG

Further Reading
'Australian Pioneer', Gavin Farmer, *The Automobile*, March 2000.

HARVARD (US) 1915–1920

1915–1916 Pioneer Motor Car Co., Troy, New York.
1916–1919 Adironback Motor Car Co., Hudson Falls, New York.
1920 Harvard Motor Car Co., Hyattsville, Maryland.

An open 2-seater with right-hand drive, built for export to New Zealand, the Harvard featured a concealed spare wheel. Initially powered by 4-cylinder Model engines, from 1917 Sterling engines were used.

NG

HASBROUCK (US) 1901–1902

Hasbrouck Motor Works, Piermont, New York.

This company experimented with delivery trucks and buses, but also made a 2-seater phaeton powered by a 6hp single-cylinder engine with chain drive. In March 1902 they reported shipping two to South America, and also that they were ready to build others. At the end of the year they moved to Yonkers, New York, but it appears that no cars were made there.

NG

HASSLER (US) 1917

Hassler Motor Co., Indianapolis, Indiana.

The Hassler was an abortive attempt by Robert H. Hassler, one of the organisers of the Marion Motor Car Co., to enter the automobile business with a car of his own design. Several prototypes of a roadster were completed, with a Buda 4-cylinder engine, various standard components, wire wheels and a 112in (2843mm) wheelbase. These were exhibited in Chicago during the summer, but further development in the production of the car failed and the Hassler went out of business.

KM

HATAZ (D) 1921–1925

Hataz Kleinautofabrik Hans Tautenhahn, Zwickau.

'Small and handy' was the slogan of this make. It used a 927cc 4/12PS 4-cylinder Steudel engine, with an engine tuned to give 16PS in the sports model. In 1925 a new 18PS model was introduced, but financial problems prevented this from going into production.

HON

HATFIELD (i) (US) 1907–1908

Hatfield Motor Vehicle Co., Miamisburg, Ohio.

This was a typical high-wheeler powered by a 12hp 2-cylinder engine with friction transmission, double chain drive and solid tyres. It was made for the Hatfield company by the Kaufman Buggy Co., also of Miamisburg, and when Hatfield went into receivership in the spring of 1908 it was merged with Kaufman. They formed a new company, the Advance Motor Vehicle Co. to make the KAUFMAN car.

NG

HATFIELD (ii) (US) 1916–1924

Cortland Car & Carriage Co., Sydney, New York.

This company was linked with HATFIELD (i) in that, when that make failed, the family returned to New York State, where they made trucks from 1910 to 1914. Two years later they returned to cars. These were conventional cars powered originally by a 23bhp 4-cylinder G.B. & S. engine, followed by a 42bhp Herschell-Spillman four in 1920 and a 55bhp Herschell-Spillman six in their last year, 1924. Probably the Hatfield's greatest contribution to history was their Suburban introduced in 1917. This had an open sided body and could be considered an early form of station wagon, seven years before a similar type was offered by STAR (v). For the last year or two of production Hatfield offered tourer and roadster models in sports versions, with wire wheels and individual step plates. Their best year was 1921, when 237 cars were made. Total output was 1554 cars.

NG

HATHAWAY (US) 1975–1984
Hathaway Motor Co., Santee, California.
The Hathaway Hunter was a kit sports car that looked like a traditional British roadster in the Morgan tradition. It was originally designed for installation on Triumph TR-2 up to TR-6 chassis. In 1982 it was updated with wider mudguards and better weather protection. It was sold in kit form or completely assembled with a 12-month warranty. In 1985 the Hunter project was sold to VINTAGE MOTOR WORKS in Sonoma, California.

HP

HATHORN (US) 1914
C.E. Hathorn, Davenport, Iowa.
This was a typical cyclecar powered by a 9/13hp Spacke V-twin engine and long belt final drive. The body was steel and the seats leather. Although it was praised for its hill climbing and Hathorn promised production, only a prototype or two were made.

NG

HATTON-McEVOY (GB) 1929–1930
Derby Engineering Co. Ltd, Derby.
Although it may have existed only on paper, the Hatton-McEvoy is worth recording as it was an unusual and most ambitious car. It was powered by a long-stroke (110 × 170mm) 9.7-litre 6-cylinder engine with four valves per cylinder but only six pushrods on each side of the block. Output was said to be 260bhp at 3000rpm. The chassis was underslung and two wheelbases were planned, the short (110in/2794mm) for a 2-seater sports, and the long (134in/3401mm) for a 4-seater close-coupled sports saloon. Drawings of the latter closely resembled the low-chassis Double Six Daimler built at about the same time. The specification included a 4-speed gearbox and Lockheed hydraulic brakes all round.

The partners were Fred Hatton who had worked for motorcycle makers New Hudson, and Michael McEvoy who was well-known for his work with Zoller superchargers, and in the 1930s produced tuned and supercharged versions of the Wolseley Hornet and other sports cars. Lavish catalogues were printed and the car was written up in *The Autocar* and *The Motor* with accompanying drawings, but no photographs were published, even of a chassis or engine, let alone of a complete car.

NG

HAUSER (D) 1998 to date
Hauser GmbH, Eichenau.
Designed and built by Luxembourg-born Jean-Claude Hauser, the Hauser H1 was an open 2-seater sports car in the Caterham Seven/Westfield mould, powered by a 6-cylinder BMW engine, the 2793cc in the standard model, with the option of the 3152cc US market M3 or the European specification 3201cc unit used in the M3 Evo and M Roadster. The latter developed 321bhp, and gave the 900kg car a top speed of over 150mph (241km/h).

NG

HAUTIER (F) 1899–1905
Société Hautier, Paris.
This company's first car was an electric hansom cab built in 1899, but at the 1900 Paris Salon they showed a voiturette powered by a Soncin petrol engine, and do not seem to have made any further electrics. By 1902 they were offering a range of three models with single, 2- and 4-cylinder engines. They had identical cylinder sizes, giving capacities of 902, 1804 and 3608cc respectively. Customers were offered a choice of chain or shaft drive on these models.

NG

HAVERS (US) 1911–1914
Havers Motor Car Co., Port Huron, Michigan.
The Havers was a well-built and conventional car, unusual only in that the company never made anything but 6-cylinder models. These started with a 44hp

1917 Hatfield (ii) Suburban.
KEITH MARVIN

1899 Hautier electric cab.
BRYAN K. GOODMAN

1902 Hautier 7hp tonneau.
NATIONAL MOTOR MUSEUM

1911 Havers Six tourer.
NATIONAL MOTOR MUSEUM

1924 Hawa electric coupé.
M.J.WORTHINGTON-WILLIAMS

in roadster and tourer forms, which was continued throughout the company's life. They were joined for 1913 by a 55hp Six-55, and for 1914 by the even larger Six-60. This was made as a 'Speed Car' as well as the roadster and tourer. Havers sold 200 cars in 1912, and seemed set for a successful future, but a disastrous fire in July 1914 destroyed the factory, and they were unable to start up again.

NG

HAWA (D) 1923–1925
Hannoversche Waggonfabrik AG, Hanover.

This railway carriage builder, founded in 1898 as Hannoversche Holzbearbeitungs-und Waggonfabriken, opened a car department in 1923 to make a small electric car. It had a simple chassis and wooden body seating two passengers in tandem. A coupé as well as an open car were made, and the rear seat could be replaced by a box to transform it into a delivery van. It was doubtless even slower than a petrol-engined cyclecar, and demand was limited. Later the company, which was a large concern with more than 2000 workers, made bus bodies and coachwork for APOLLO, HANOMAG and other makes.

HON

HAWK (i) (US) 1914
Hawk Cyclecar Co., Detroit, Michigan.

Mechanically, the Hawk was a typical cyclecar, with 9/13hp Spacke air-cooled V-twin engine and belt final drive. In appearance, though, it was closer to a larger car, with swept-up line from bonnet to scuttle, and rounded rear end, behind the two seats. The frame was of white ash, armoured with steel.

NG

HAWK (ii) (GB) 1991 to date
Hawk Cars (Hawkridge Development Engineering), Frant, Sussex.

In a world dominated by 427 style Cobra replicas, it was refreshing to see Gerry Hawridge of TRANSFORMER produce a range of precursors to the Cobra. The round tube, twin rail chassis made his A.C. 289 replica more accurate than most. It used MGB mechanicals, although a Jaguar-based independent rear end was an option. Triumph straight-6 engines could also be fitted. Body options included the Le Mans (hard-top), the Willment 39 PH (a wide-arch, cut-away door racing replica) and the 2.6 (an A.C. Ace replica). Also on Hawk's price lists was a replica of the Ferrari 275GTB. The chassis was inspired by the original Ferrari and many of the Jaguar XJ donor components required modification; a Ferrari 400 V12 could be fitted if desired. Another Ferrari replica was the 288GTO, based on Ferrari parts. As the Transformer brand faded, Hawk also made its own Lancia Stratos replicas, the HF2000 and HF3000, and produced the Stewart & Ardern, a kit-form fibreglass replica of the Minisprint.

CR

HAWKEYE (US) c.1981

Hawkeye Classics Ltd, Waverly, Iowa.
This company made a replica of the 1957 Ford Thunderbird, complete with removable hard-top.

HP

HAWKINS see XENIA

HAWLEY (US) 1906–1908

1906–1907 Hawley Automobile Co., Constantine, Michigan.
1907–1908 Hawley Automobile Co., Mendon, Michigan.
Designed by R.B. Hawley, this car had a 16hp 2-cylinder 2-stroke engine, with friction transmission and single chain drive. Two models were listed, a 2-seater runabout on an 84in (2132mm) wheelbase at $450 and a 4-seater tourer on a 96in (2437mm) wheelbase at $700. Very few cars were made at either of the addresses.

NG

HAY-BERG (US) 1907–1908

Hay-Berg Motor Car Co., Milwaukee, Wisconsin.
Unlike some car makers, Hay-Berg admitted that they bought in components for their roadster, but stressed that they were the finest of their kind. The engine was a 20hp 4-cylinder air-cooled Carrico, the gearbox came from Brown-Lipe, axles from Timken and frame from A.O. Smith. All were well-known suppliers to the industry. Nevertheless, the company was out of business the year after its introduction, and a projected 40hp tourer was never built.

NG

HAYDEN (ZA) 1998 to date

Dart Engineering, Cape Town.
The Hayden Dart was a modified revival of the G.S.M. Dart produced in South Africa in the 1960s. Changes included widened wheel arches, moulded-in bumpers and a front spoiler.

CR

HAY & HOTCHKISS (US) 1898–1899

Hay & Hotchkiss Co., New Haven, Connecticut.
Walter Hay was the designer and E.M. Hotchkiss the financial backer for this unusual car. The engine was described as an 8-stroke 4-cylinder horizontal unit giving an explosion in each of the four cylinders every fourth turn. It was said to need no oil or water, though 'the engine simply runs a trifle harder when no oil is used'. The car never went into production, although the prototype still exists in the United States.

NG

HAYNES-APPERSON, HAYNES (US) 1897–1925

1897–1898 Riverside Machine Works, Kokomo, Indiana.
1898–1905 Haynes-Apperson Co., Kokomo, Indiana.
1905–1925 Haynes Automobile Co., Kokomo, Indiana.
The early days of Haynes and Apperson are delicately intertwined. Latter-day attempts to cleanly unravel them are often complicated by the acrimonious parting of the principals, after which each sought to obscure the contributions of the other. Elwood Haynes (1857–1925) had a formal engineering education with training in metallurgy. He conceived his idea for a self-propelled vehicle while supervising pipeline installations for the Indiana Gas & Oil Co. Deciding that steam was too dangerous and electric power too limiting, he settled upon a petrol engine for his car and purchased a 1-cylinder, 1hp marine engine from the Sintz Gas Engine Co. of Grand Rapids, Michigan, in the summer of 1893.

After the first experiments in his kitchen proved unsatisfactory, Haynes approached the Riverside Machine Works of Kokomo, Indiana, run by brothers Elmer (1861–1920) and Edgar (1869–1959) Apperson. The Appersons undertook the construction of the car, to Haynes's drawings, on a spare time basis, having it completed by 3 July 1894. Haynes wanted to test it the next

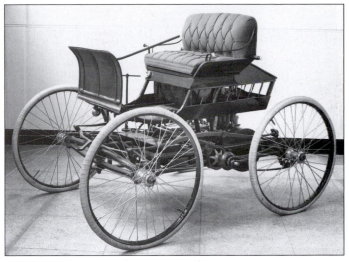

1894 Haynes 2-seater.
NATIONAL MOTOR MUSEUM

1913 Haynes Model 22 tourer.
NATIONAL MOTOR MUSEUM

1923 Haynes Model 57 sports tourer.
NATIONAL MOTOR MUSEUM

morning, but celebrations for American Independence Day had crowded the centre of Kokomo, so Haynes and the Appersons towed the car out to the country behind a horse. A buggy body perched on a chassis frame of square steel tubing, the car had its engine located under the seat. It had two speeds forward, engaged by clutches on a countershaft, chain drive and no brakes. After being pushed to start, the car ran well, although it proved to be somewhat underpowered. This would later be claimed as the first journey of a petrol-powered car in America, which it was not. Both John LAMBERT and the DURYEA brothers had driven their own petrol cars before Haynes and the Appersons took to the road.

Elwood Haynes obtained a more powerful engine from the Sintz firm, a 2hp unit, to power the car he called the Pioneer. Performance was better, but still did not satisfy the inventor. Initially, Haynes merely wished to have an automobile for his own use, but when he heard of the $5000 prize money being proffered by the *Chicago Times-Herald* newspaper for winners of a horseless carriage race, his efforts became more ambitious. Again co-operating with the Appersons, Haynes designed a new car, to be powered by an aluminium 2-cylinder opposed engine, largely the work of Apperson. Standing higher than its predecessor, the car could seat four in *dos-à-dos* fashion. Snowfall on the morning of the race dashed the colleagues' hopes for victory; the car slid into a tramway track and shattered a wheel, effectively putting it out of the contest for no spare was available.

A third vehicle was produced in 1896, making use of Elwood Haynes's metallurgical training in adopting nickel steel in its construction. Exhibited with the other Haynes-Apperson cars at the Ohio State Fair, it was soon leased to the Robinson Circus for use in parades. By 1897 the Riverside Machine Works was delivering a series of surrey-topped self-propelled carriages that could accurately be described as automobile production. The Haynes-Apperson Co. was incorporated in May 1898, and celebrated the completion of a new, 'fireproof' factory with the capacity of one vehicle per day. The cars were powered by a 5hp engine, its 'heavy parts' made of aluminium alloy, and had 3-speed gearboxes with reverse. In 1899, Haynes and Edgar Apperson gained desirable publicity by delivering a car, to the customer's order, by driving it from Kokomo to New York City, a distance of 1050 miles. At an average speed of 14mph (22km/h), their trip was a first in the country.

Edgar Apperson was enamoured of racing, and entered the cars in numerous competitions, winning several. Meanwhile, Elwood Haynes concentrated on refining his design, and conceived a carburettor to replace the simple vaporiser used earlier. By 1901 the cars were giving very good accounts of themselves in all kinds of service, including several endurance runs. Haynes and the Appersons, however, were losing favour with each other, and the brothers withdrew from the partnership to form the Apperson Brothers Automobile Co. at the old Riverside Machine Works. Thereafter, they would manufacture their own APPERSON car. Elwood Haynes finally left the gas company to concentrate on automobile manufacture, continuing to market the cars as Haynes-Appersons. Two lines of cars, both twin-cylinder, would be offered in 1902–03, an 8hp runabout and a 12hp model available either as a phaeton or surrey. In 1904, the engine was moved up front, under a bonnet, and a 4-cylinder model was introduced. That year the Apperson name would be dropped from the cars, and in the next firm would be renamed the Haynes Automobile Co. Fours were standardised in 1906, by which time all cars had shaft drive.

A Haynes entered the 1906 Vanderbilt Cup race, placing third in trials and finishing the contest, though without notable result. This led to a 'Vanderbilt Speedster' model for 1907, a 50bhp model riding a 106in (2690mm) wheelbase. It sold for $3500. The larger Model T, on a 108in (2741mm) wheelbase, topped the line at $3500–4500.

A 6-cylinder car was introduced in 1913, although it was slightly less powerful than the large Model Y 4-cylinder car from the previous year. By this time, Elwood Haynes, who was more fond of research and engineering than management, had let go of his business responsibilities and was deeply engaged in metallurgical research. He had formed the Haynes Stellite Co. in 1912, developing a range of cobalt-based alloys used for machine tools. Even more widely known is his stainless steel alloy, developed and patented in 1915.

The New York Automobile Show of January 1916 introduced a Haynes V-12, powered by a 5842cc ohv unit built, as all Haynes engines had been since the second car, in-house. Put into production that August, the Light Twelve, as it would be called from 1917, was built on a 127in (3223mm) wheelbase, also used by the larger of two sixes, named by this time Light Six-37, as opposed to the Light Six-36, which rode the 121in (3071mm) wheelbase used on all 1915 Haynes cars. The Light Twelve would be carried through into 1922, but not many were sold. Total production is estimated at fewer than 650. The Light Six was the lifeblood of the company, being a well-built, if conservative, car. Prices rose significantly as the war ended; by 1920 Haynes prices started at $2685, almost as much as 1917's most expensive car, and ran all the way to $4950.

The short wheelbase cars were dropped in 1920, when both six and twelve had a 127in (3223mm) wheelbase; the next year it stretched again to 132 (3350mm). The 121in (3071mm) car returned in 1922, as the Model 55, not only smaller

than its immediate predecessors but cheaper to boot: entry-level Haynes cars were back to 1918 pricing, $1785 for a 5-passenger touring car. The 132in (3350mm) 6-cylinder car was continued after the demise of the twelve for just one year. Then for 1924 a Model 60, in five choices of body styles, all under $2000, was the sole offering. All rode the 121in (3071mm) wheelbase. The 5-passenger touring, at $1295, was advertised as the lowest-cost Haynes ever built. It did not, however, find many buyers, and in September of that year creditors petitioned the US District Court to have the firm declared bankrupt. Production halted, then resumed briefly in January 1925 to use up parts on hand. Some 200 cars were built, and then the lines stopped for good. Elwood Haynes died in April 1925, and so did the Haynes automobile.

KF

Further Reading
'Haynes-Apperson: Elwood Builds an Automobile', Stuart W. Wells, *Automobile Quarterly*, Vol. 38, No. 4.

HAZARD (US) 1914–1915

Hazard Motor Manufacturing Co., Rochester, New York.
Chiefly an engine manufacturer, Hazard offered two 4-cylinder models of 24 and 30hp, powered by their own engines.

NG

H-B (H. BROTHERS) (US) 1908

H. Brothers, Chicago, Illinois.
This carriage-building company's first venture into car making was with HAASE cars for the Northwestern Furniture Co. of Milwaukee. That venture lasted only three years, after which the H. Brothers concentrated on carriages until 1908 when, like so many Chicago firms, they were bitten by the high-wheeler bug. Their car was typical of the breed, with 10hp 2-cylinder engine, friction transmission and oak frame. Its price was $500, but production did not last out the year 1908.

NG

H-C (US) 1916

H-C Motor Car Co., Detroit, Michigan.
This company was listed in *Scientific American* as making a 28hp 4-cylinder in roadster and tourer forms, but nothing else is known about the car or company.

NG

H.C.E. (GB) 1912–1913

1912 H.C.E. Cars, London.
1913 Earlcycar Co., Harold Wood, Essex.
The H.C.E.was a low-slung cyclecar powered by a 6/8hp single-cylinder Buckingham engine, with chain drive to a 2-speed countershaft, and belt drive to the rear wheels. The announcement in *The Cyclecar* spoke of several bodies being available, including a 2-seater 'semi racing sociable' and a 4-seater. A friction transmission was promised, and when the 1913 model appeared, made at a new works in Essex, it had the very unusual feature of 4-wheel brakes. The premises covered 30 acres, allowing for a test track with properly banked corners. *The Cyclecar* thought this was the first purpose-built track for testing cyclecars, and said '. . . it is all to the benefit of the purchaser that these developments should be carried out', but sadly it did not seem to be to the benefit of the H.C.E., which did not survive into 1914.

NG

H.C.S. (US) 1920–1924

H.C.S. Motor Car Co., Indianapolis, Indiana.
This company was formed by Harry C. Stutz (1876–1930) after he had resigned from the Stutz Motor Car Co. It was not the first H.C.S. car as that name had been used for a lower-priced model of Stutz in 1914. The H.C.S. company had been formed in the autumn of 1919, and the first cars were delivered to dealers in May 1920. They were good-looking high-quality cars powered by a 3723cc 4-cylinder ohv Weidely MB engine, developing 50bhp, with 3-speed gearbox. Initially only a tourer and a roadster were offered, with quite a sporty appearance thanks to their wire wheels and individual step plates. Prices were quite high, at $2975 and $2925 respectively. In 1922 a coupé and a sedan joined the range, which were continued into 1923 and 1924. New engines appeared in 1923, a

1922 H.C.S. tourers and a 2-seater.
NATIONAL MOTOR MUSEUM

slightly larger Weidely four (3982cc/55bhp) and an 80bhp Midwest six of 4730cc. Harry Stutz capitalised on the renown of the Stutz car in the slogan of the H.C.S., 'The Car Born with a Reputation'. It was never a big seller, the best year being 1923 when 606 found buyers. Useful publicity was gained when Tommy Milton won the 1923 Indianapolis 500 in the H.C.S. Special, though this was in fact a Miller.

In October 1924 Harry Stutz decided that taxicabs were a better bet than passenger cars. He ended production of the H.C.S. car and formed the H.C.S. Cab Mfg Co. which made Waukesha-engined cabs up to 1927. He also ran the Stutz Fire Engine Co. until his death in 1930. As the New Stutz Fire Engine Co., this lasted until 1940.

NG

H.D.S. (GB) 1991 to date
1991–1995 Hooper Design Services, London.
1996 to date Hooper Creative Design Services, London.
This was a kit car influenced in style by the Ferrari 166 Corsa Spyder. It used a lengthened Spitfire/GT6 chassis, adding steel floorpan extensions, outriggers and front bulkhead, then bolting a fibreglass body on top. It was launched with the name Lindy but was soon renamed H.D.S. There was a ladder frame option with a Dolomite rear axle (briefly known as the Defender) or a full spaceframe (called the Warrior). Fiat twin cam-engined cars arrived in 1993.

CR

H.E. (GB) 1919–1931
Herbert Engineering Co. Ltd, Caversham, Reading, Berkshire.
This company was owned by Herbert Merton and during World War I was engaged on repairing damaged aero-engines. In order to find work for his 500 employees, Merton decided to enter car manufacture in 1919 and engaged as a designer Roland J. Sully who had operated a pioneer motor taxi business in Wales. Announced in February 1919, the first H.E. had a 1795cc side-valve monobloc 4-cylinder engine, with 4 speeds in a separate gearbox, and overhead worm drive. It was called the 13/20, but soon the cylinder bore was increased to give 2120cc, in which form it became the 14/20. Open 2-seater plus dickey or 4-seater tourer bodies were made by Morgan of Leighton Buzzard. The sporting character was somewhat spoilt by artillery wheels on the early models, and when H.E. went over to wire wheels they looked much better. All H.E.s wore a pear-shaped radiator not unlike that of a Bugatti.

In 1922 the 14/20 became the 14/40 and was made up to 1927, though in 1926 and 1927 it was the 14/50. A popular body style was the 3-seater sports with rounded tail, nicknamed the 'Dutch Clog'. There was also a smaller four, the 1982cc 13/30 and 13/40, made from 1923 to 1925. Front wheel brakes were introduced in 1923. Herbert Engineering had their own foundry in the mid–1920s, and cylinder blocks, gearbox casings and frames were all made in-house. Only coachwork was still bought in. Maximum production in 1923 was about 14 cars per week. Although sales held up well, the company was often in financial trouble, partly due to an expensive racing programme for which special 16-valve engines were built, and also because their generous guarantee cost a lot in repair work. Few cars were made in 1924 and production was

1921 H.E. 14/20hp 2-seater.
NATIONAL MOTOR MUSEUM

c.1925 H.E. 13/45hp sports tourer.
NATIONAL MOTOR MUSEUM

suspended just before the Motor Show in October. It restarted in the middle of 1925, but on a smaller scale, not more than three a week.

For 1928 a 2290cc 6-cylinder engine replaced the four; with its longer wheelbase this 16/55 was the best-looking H.E., and carried 4-seater tourer or 4-door fabric saloon bodies. An interesting feature was the Chinn Synchrometer, in which the driver could synchronise engine speed with that of the gearbox layshaft by glancing at a dial on the dashboard. In theory at any rate, this enabled gear changes to be made without double declutching. H.E. no longer made their own axles and frames, these being bought in from Moss

1930 H.E. 12/35hp coupé.
NATIONAL MOTOR MUSEUM

1897 Headland electric dogcart.
NATIONAL MOTOR MUSEUM

and Rubery Owen respectively. The last H.E. was a smaller six, the 1419cc 12/35 which could be had with a Cozette supercharger. So far as is known, only one of the 12 small sixes was supercharged, this being at the request of record-breaker George Eyston. Capacity went up to 1622cc for 1931, but the company closed its doors that year. Several hundred of the 4-cylinder models had been made, together with 61 16/55s (16/60 from 1930) and 12 12/35s. The premises were bought by Thornycroft for marine engine work.

NG

Further Reading
'H.E., The Car of Character', M. Worthington-Williams,
The Automobile, September 1983.

HEADLAND (GB) 1897–c.1900

Headland Patent Electric Storage Battery Co. Ltd, Leyton, London.
Although Headland's main business was the manufacture of batteries, they made a few electric vehicles under their own name which were exhibited at various shows. These included a rear-drive *dos-à-dos* dogcart, and a phaeton in which the motor drove the front wheels, the whole unit being centrally pivotted and therefore turning with the steering.

NG

HEALEY (i) (US) c.1905–c.1916

Healey & Co., New York, New York.
Healey & Co. were well-known coachbuilders, in business from the 1890s to 1926. They sold a number of electric town cars under their own name, though exact dates of production are hard to establish. Their first known car was made for its inventor W.H. Douglas of Belleville, New Jersey in 1905, and was unusual in having front-wheel drive. It seems that the running gear was Douglas', with Healey providing the coachwork, and this probably applied to all the other Healey electric cars. At least 20 were registered in New York in 1914. John D. Rockefeller Sr was a loyal customer, owning three, made in 1912, 1914 and 1916. Later, Healey built the first airport bus bodies for Uppercu-Cadillac.

NG

HEALEY (ii) (GB) 1946–1954

Donald Healey Motor Co. Ltd, Warwick.
Donald Healey (1898–1988) was a well-known prewar rally driver whose achievements included winning the 1931 Monte Carlo in an Invicta. He became technical director of Triumph in 1937, and then moved to Humber where he spent the war years working on armoured cars. There he met Ben Bowden and Achille 'Sammy' Sampietro, both of whom were to become vital to the car which was to bear the Healey name. They worked on the design in their spare time, Bowden being concerned with the body and Sampietro the chassis. For an engine Healey chose the 2443cc 4-cylinder Riley with hemispherical head and valves operated by two camshafts set high in the block. The engine was set in an X-braced box section frame, with front suspension by coil springs and trailing arms, and hydraulic brakes. Two body styles were offered initially, a 4-seater sports tourer made by Westland Motors of Hereford, and a 2-door saloon by Elliot of Reading. They were good-looking, aerodynamic and light, the saloon being the fastest 4-seater closed car in the world. It achieved 110mph (177km/h) at Jabbeke in Belgium in 1947.

The first open car was completed in January 1946 at the Benford works in Warwick, and Healey did not move into his own premises at The Cape, Warwick, until later in the year. Production began in the autumn of 1946 with a workforce of 40. The Westland roadsters were made up to 1949, only 64 cars being built, while 101 Elliott saloons were made up to 1950. A number of other coachbuilders worked on the Healey chassis, including Duncan who built 39 bodies altogether, saloons less attractive than the Elliott design, and at least one stark open 2-seater with cycle-type wings called 'The Drone'. An estate car was built in order to avoid Purchase Tax, while among Swiss coachbuilders Beutler and Ramseier used the Healey chassis for coupés and convertibles.

1949 saw a bulkier and wider body called the Sportsmobile, of which only 23 were made. More significant was the Silverstone, an open 2-seater on a shorter frame with front anti-roll bar and cycle-type wings, suitable for road and circuit use. The recessed spare wheel doubled as a rear bumper. It became very popular for club racing, and a total of 104 were made. In 1950 the Elliot saloon and Westland roadster were replaced by heavier bodies, a saloon by Tickford and a convertible by Abbott. These were made up to 1954, 222 saloons and 77 convertibles.

All the foregoing cars used the Riley engine, but other power units were used in different models. In 1950, as a result of a shipboard meeting between Donald Healey and Nash president George Mason, the 3848cc 6-cylinder Nash Ambassador engine was used in a 2-seater sports car called the NASH HEALEY. The first 104 used British-built bodies with Nash grills, but in 1952 a new Pininfarina design was adopted, and with a larger engine of 4138cc a further 402 were made. As American engines were not available on the UK market, a British version using a 2993cc 6-cylinder Alvis TB21 engine and gearbox was made from 1951 to 1953, but only 25 were built. At the 1952 Earls Court Show, Donald Healey exhibited a new design, the Healey 100, which used the 2660cc 4-cylinder engine from the Austin Atlantic in a box-section chassis with coil-and-wishbone ifs and 2-seater sports body by Tickford. Healey enjoyed good relations with Leonard Lord of Austin, and the good reception by press and public of the Healey 100 at the Show encouraged Lord to take over manufacture of the car under the name AUSTIN-HEALEY 100. Healey and his son Geoffrey had obtained costings from suppliers based on an output of ten cars a week, rising to 25 cars which was the maximum that the little factory at The Cape could cope with. Lord found that these figures were as good as he could obtain for a much larger volume. The Austin-Healey 100 went into production at

1946 Healey (ii) 2.4-litre Elliott saloon.
NATIONAL MOTOR MUSEUM

Longbridge in May 1953, with bodies supplied by Jensen, as Tickford could not cope with the volume required by Lord.

NG

Further Reading
The Healey Story, Geoffrey Healey, Haynes, 1996.
Donald Healey, My World of Cars, Peter Garnier with Brian Healey, P.S.L., 1989.
'The Cars of Donald Healey: A colour Portfolio',
Automobile Quarterly, Vol. 24, No. 4.
'Donald Healey: His Own Way', M. Taylor and J.M. Fenster,
Automobile Quarterly, Vol. 24, No. 4.

HEALEY (iii) (GB) 1997 to date

1997–1998 I.P.I. Motors, Cowes, Isle of Wight.
1998 Healey Sprite Motor Co., Maidenhead, Berkshire.
1998 to date Healey Sprite Motor Co., Newport, Isle of Wight.
Announced at the 1997 London Motor Show, I.P.I. (better known for its motor caravan conversions) was the company that developed this Austin-Healey Sprite Mk1 replica. It quickly passed to another company which announced its intention to build 50 examples of the 'Healey' but it immediately ran into problems over the unauthorised use of the Healey name. The replica used fibreglass bodywork, though with a boot lid. The chassis was a modern stainless steel monocoque with all-independent suspension. As first released, the power source was quoted as a 1.8-litre Isuzu, although by 1998 the option of Ford Zetec 1.8-litre power had been added. Two versions were offered, a classic model with leather upholstery and a sports model with bucket seats and a roll-over bar fitted. Another project was the Workhorse, a 4×4 utility vehicle based on the Mercedes-Benz G-Wagen. As production was running at six units per week, the company hoped to set up licensed production in Bulgaria, Israel and the USA.

CR

HEARTLAND GLASSWORKS (US) c.1985–1990

Heartland Glassworks, Bartlesville, Oklahoma.
Heartland briefly built the Manx SR kit car that had originally been introduced by MEYERS. They added some improvements, with rectangular headlights replacing the original round ones. It was sold in kit form for $3495 in 1985.

HP

1950 Healey (ii) 2.4-litre Silverstone sports car.
NATIONAL MOTOR MUSEUM

1951 Healey (ii) 2.4-litre Tickford saloon.
NATIONAL MOTOR MUSEUM

1962 Heinkel (Trojan 200) 3-wheeler.
NICK BALDWIN

HEATHFIELD (GB) 1993–c.1996

Highfield Automotive, Chesterfield, Derbyshire.

Following the trend for kit-form Morgan trike lookalikes, the Heathfield Slingshot was distinguished by its robust, large diameter round-tube space frame chassis. It used Cortina front uprights and double wishbones, Escort Mk II rack and a specially-made hoop-shaped rear arm and Honda motorcycle hub at the rear. The barrel-back fibreglass or aluminium body was much larger than other kit trikes. At the front was a distinctive brass cowl, overlooking a Honda CX Vee-twin unit of either 500cc or 650cc capacity.

CR

HEBE (E) 1920–1921

Fábrica Española de Automóviles Hebe, Barcelona.

These were a cyclecar of 6/8hp and a light delivery van only built in very small numbers. One of the cars participated in the Trofeo Armangué, where normally only Davids started, and finished sixth. The cars had some peculiarities, like a horizontal spare wheel behind the driver. They were extremely small, but had a long wheelbase.

VCM

HEDEA (F) 1913–1914

Accary et Compagnie, Paris.

Accary had been founded in 1894 to make components and later complete chassis for the motor industry. In 1913 they launched a car of their own which they called Hedea, this being the Greek adjective for 'agreeable'. It was available with four different engine sizes, 1460, 2296, 2994 and 3014cc, all 4-cylinder side-valve units by Chapuis-Dornier. A 4-speed gearbox and conventional shaft drive were employed. Three body styles were offered, 2-seater tourer, 4-seater tourer and coupé-de-ville.

NG

HEIJKENSKJOLD (S) 1916

G. Heijkenskjold, Gavle.

Engineer Heijkenskjold built a cyclecar with spacious 4-seater body, a windscreen from a Model T Ford, and a 4-cylinder Henderson motorcycle engine. He hoped to put it into production in Stockholm in 1917, but wartime shortages prevented this from going ahead.

NG

HEIM (D) 1921–1926

Heim & Co., Badische Automobilfabrik, Mannheim.

Franz Heim worked as an engineer for BENZ before deciding to work on his own. In 1921 he introduced a sports car powered by a 2086cc 4-cylinder engine. A more serious sports car had a 2385cc 6-cylinder engine with single overhead camshaft, detachable head and twin carburettors. Heim raced his cars himself with some success, but when financial problems arose as a result of the recession, he had to abandon production.

HON

HEINE-VELOX (US) 1905–1906; 1921–1923

1905–1906 Heine Motor Car Co., San Francisco, California.
1921–1923 Heine-Velox Engineering Co., San Francisco, California.

Gustav Otto Heine (1868–1959) was a German-born piano manufacturer who had emigrated with his family to California when he was five years old. He formed the Heine Motor Car Co. in 1905 and built a prototype with 40/45hp 4-cylinder engine and a tourer body. It was planned to sell at $4000, and he spoke of an 80/85hp car priced at $8200, but this was never built. By February 1906 he had built three cars, now called Heine-Velox, with power quoted as 35/45hp; they were probably the same 5805cc engines as in the prototype Heine. Plans to make 50 cars in 1906 were frustrated by the San Francisco earthquake which wiped out both car and piano factory in April. Though one Heine-Velox was shown at the San Francisco Auto Show in February 1907, none were built after April 1906, and Heine concentrated on his piano business.

He continued to toy with automotive ideas, though, and in 1921, when he was 53 years old and perhaps considering retiring from the piano business in which he had become very prosperous, he launched another car. This was an enormous machine, powered by a 6382cc Weidely V12 engine giving 115bhp on a 148in (3756mm) wheelbase. It had Lockheed hydraulic brakes on all four wheels. The bodies, which were built in his works, were fixed to the side of the frame rather than on top of it, giving a lower roof line. He quoted prices of $17,000 to $25,000, making them the most expensive car in America, yet, curiously, he never sold one. At least one customer, a Hollywood film star, offered to buy one and sent a cheque, but Heine returned it, saying 'We do not accept charity'. Five cars were made, three sedans, a sporting victoria and an unfinished limousine. He kept two for himself and gave the others away. The sporting victoria was part of Harrah's Automobile Collection for many years, while the unfinished limousine and a sedan were still in the hands of the Heine family in the 1980s.

NG

HEINIS (F) c.1925–c.1930
Éts Charles Heinis, Neuilly, Seine.
Charles Heinis was a manufacturer of gears who built a small number of cars using a variety of engines. Some were his own designs with single ohcs, while he also used 4-cylinder S.C.A.P. engines of 1100, 1170 and 1690cc, and the 5-litre straight-8 Lycoming. It is possible that not all these were built. Heinis production was *très confidentielle* and his cars were not listed in many of the better-known magazines.

NG

HEINKEL (D) 1955–1958
Ernst Heinkel AG, Stuttgart-Zuffenhausen.
Heinkel were well-known aircraft manufacturers from 1922 to 1945 who, like Messerschmitt, had to find fresh activities after World War II. They launched the Tourist scooter in 1952, and three years later brought out a 'bubble car' similar in concept to the Isetta. It had a single front door and Heinkel's own make of 175cc single-cylinder 4-stroke engine. At first it was a 3-wheeler, but in 1957 twin rear wheels mounted close together were adopted, and capacity went up to 198cc. About 6000 were made in Germany, then in 1958 the licence was sold to Dundalk Engineering in the Irish Republic. In August 1961 the rights were bought from Dundalk Engineering by the Lambretta-Trojan Organisation, and the car was put into production as the Trojan 200 at the Trojan factory at Croydon, Surrey. To suit British tax laws only the 3-wheeled version was made, though a few 4-wheelers were built for the Dutch market. About 12,000 Trojan 200s were made up to 1965.

HON

HELBÉ (F) 1905–1907
Levêque et Bodenréder, Boulogne-sur-Seine.
This car derived its name from those of its makers (L et B), and was a light assembled car powered by single-cylinder De Dion-Bouton engines of 4½, 6, and 9hp. The first PUCH cars were based on this make. For 1907 a 12hp 4-cylinder model was added to the range. Some Delage components were used in the Helbé.

NG

HELEM (F) 1997 to date
R.J. Racing, Téloche.
After racing with some success at Le Mans and various GT Championship events, the Helem V6 GTR was released in road-going form. It was essentially a GT1 coupé version of the Renault Sport Spider with significantly altered bodywork and an alloy chassis lengthened by 4.7in (120mm) to make room for a larger engine: a Renault V6 turbo derived from the Alpine A610, complete with its transmission. The centrally mounted engine developed 260–280bhp and a top speed of 177mph (285km/h) was claimed. The 2-seater interior of the roadgoing version was luxuriously equipped with leather, air conditioning and an airbag.

CR

HELIAN (GB) 1983
Island Classics, Brynsiencyn, Anglesey.
This was a promising traditional roadster kit with four seats, but ultimately it was extremely short-lived. It had a space frame chassis fitted with a Ford engine, Vauxhall Viva suspension and bodywork in aluminium, steel and fibreglass.

CR

HELIOS (i) (S) 1901–1902
AB Sodertalge Verkstader, Sodertalge.
Agents for Kuhlstein, NAG and Protos, this company also made a few cars of their own. The first was a *vis-à-vis* with single-cylinder engines of 3½ or 5hp mounted under the seat, and chain drive. Three or 4-seater versions were made; the Turistautomobil Typ VIII had a 2-speed gearbox. In 1902 the company began to make the American Northern buggy under licence.

NG

HELIOS (ii) (CH) 1906–1907
Automobiles Helios, J.J. Muggli, Zürich.
Muggli, a trained engineer, chose the prestigious Paris Show in 1906 to launch his 18/24hp car which had a 4-cylinder in-line offset engine in a conventional chassis with shaft drive. A chassis as well as a landaulet were on display. The mechanical components of the cars were made by BRUNAU-WEIDMANN, Zürich. Helios was present again in 1907 but disappeared shortly afterwards.

FH

HELIOS (iii) (D) 1924–1926
Helios-Automobilbau AG, Cologne-Ehrenfeld.
The 2/8PS Helios was another small car of the 1920s which used a 972cc flat-twin 2-stroke engine. It was of only local importance.

HON

HELO (D) 1923
Helo Kraftfahrzeugbau Hermann & Lommatzsch, Berlin.
A 3PS DKW engine drove the single front wheel of this simple cyclecar which made a very limited impact on the market. Small 2-stroke motorcycles were also made.

HON

HELVETIA (F) 1899–1900
Compagnie des Voitures Électrique Helvetia, Combs-la-Ville, Seine et Marne.
Jacques Fischer-Hinnen (1869–1922), a Swiss technician, worked in Paris where he designed a small electric vehicle. Cabs and victorias were built in small numbers. Two were used by Fischer's familiy in Zürich but plans to establish a factory in Switzerland did not materialise. One Helvetia, however, was supplied to Bohemia and Fischer was engaged in 1900 to manage the factory of Frantisek KRIZIK in Prague, which in 1895 had made three prototypes of heavier 4-seater electromobiles. For unknown reasons the intended production of Helvetia electromobiles in Prague was not taken up.

FH

HENDERSON (US) 1912–1914
Henderson Motor Car Co., Indianapolis, Indiana.
Former employees of the Cole Motor Car Co., the Henderson brothers set up on their own in 1912 in time to parade their car before the Indianapolis 500 race. It was a medium-priced 4-cylinder machine, designed by technical writer Chester Ricker, made in four body styles, two roadsters and two tourers, priced between $1385 and $1685. Stutz gearboxes were used. For 1914 they were joined by a 6-cylinder model at $2285–2885, but shortage of working capital brought the company to an end that year. The Hendersons returned to Cole, and Ricker formed a company to make the Bicar cyclecar, which never got off the ground. In 1923–24 he was general manager of Duesenberg. Better known than the cars were the Henderson motorcycles, made by W.G. Henderson, son of one of the brothers, from 1911 to 1931.

NG

1899 Henriod (ii) 4hp duc.
NATIONAL MOTOR MUSEUM

HENNEGIN (US) 1908
Commercial Automobile Co., Chicago, Illinois.
This was one of many high-wheelers made in Chicago, having a 12/14hp 2-cylinder engine and chain drive. Two body styles were offered, a 2-seater Physician's Car and a Family/Utility with load-carrying space as well as two seats.
NG

HENNEY (US) 1920–1931; 1960–1979
Henney Motor Car Co., Freeport, Illinois.
Henney was a highly respected manufacturer of funeral cars which built a handful of sporting-type cars in addition to the usual limousines and large sedans available for funeral directors for the use of pallbearers in funeral processions. The first conventional offering consisted of 50 sports-touring cars, designed by the Don Lee Studios of Los Angeles, California, for West Coast distribution. In 1930 the company again experimented with a design not intended for the funeral trade, a low-slung convertible sedan, resembling the contemporary Cord L-29 to some extent. Two of these were completed in 1930 and another two followed in 1931, all four with a price tag of $5000. Any further development was presumably halted by the Depression and the cars were purchased by funeral directors. In 1960, Henney, using a rebadged Renault Dauphine, completed some experimental cars which it called the Henney-Kilowatt and which had 36 2-volt batteries and a 7.2hp engine. The Henney-Kilowatt was claimed to have a driving range of 50-60 miles on a single charge. R. S. Witkoff of Watkins Glen, New York was advertising the car as late as 1979.
KM

HENOU see S.U.P.

HENRIETTA (US) 1901
Henrietta Motor Co., New York, New York.
This company made a light steam car powered by a 4-cylinder single-acting engine, unusual at a time when most steamers relied on two cylinders. In appearance it was similar to others of its kind, with a short wheelbase, single-chain drive and wire wheels.
NG

HENRIOD (i) (CH) 1893–1898
1893–1896 Fritz Henriod, Bienne.
1896–1898 Henriod Frères, Bienne.
Fritz Henriod built an experimental steam tricycle in 1886. The local police prohibited test runs in town and requested that the noisy and dangerous vehicle must be drawn by horses to the open country. In 1893 he finished his first real motorcar with a single-cylinder petrol engine, 2-speed gearbox and direct drive to the rear wheels. The tiller steering was operated from the rear seat and two passengers sat on the front bench seat. The second model had a horizontal air-cooled single-cylinder engine of 4bhp, 3-speed gearbox plus reverse and chain drive. In 1896 Fritz was joined by his younger brother Charles Edouard and together they produced a few cars with air-cooled, rear-mounted horizontal single or opposed twin-cylinder engines of 4–10bhp. Power transmission was by way of 3-speed gearbox of advanced design, with pinion drive without chains to the differential and rear wheels. They also projected front-wheel driven town cars and a system which would have enabled existing horse-drawn coaches to be motorised but apparently none were produced in quantity. In 1897 Charles Edouard single-handedly drove one of the Henriod cars from Bienne to Paris, which was hailed as a sensation by the French press. One year later the engine was moved to the front and chain drive reinstalled. The two brothers then went their separate ways. While Charles Edouard founded his own factory in Neuilly, Paris, to build motorcars, his brother Fritz in 1903 began to produce air-cooled cars under the name S.N.A. in Boudry near Neuchâtel.
FH

HENRIOD (ii) (F) 1898–1908
Henriod et Cie, Neuilly, Seine.
Charles-Edouard Henriod began car manufacture in France after several years working in Switzerland with his elder brother Fritz. His car of 1898 was claimed to be the first to run on alcohol fuel, and he supported alcohol trials for several years. In 1899 he made a 4hp 2-cylinder light car with vertical tiller steering and chain drive. In 1902 he offered two models, the Simplon 6hp single-cylinder voiturette which looked very like a De Dion-Bouton, and a 12hp 2-cylinder car. He entered three cars in the 1903 Paris–Madrid race, two 12hp models and a new 24hp four which appeared as a production model at the Paris Salon in December that year. He also exhibited a light car powered by a 6/8hp single-cylinder engine. All Henriods from now on had their gearboxes combined with the rear axle. The 6hp single and 12hp 2-cylinder cars were continued into 1905, and in 1906 came a 32hp 4-cylinder air-cooled model which used the same system of cooling by lateral fans as the S.N.A. made by Fritz Henriod in Switzerland. After giving up cars in 1908, C.E. Henriod designed a rotary valve engine which was used by Darracq for a few years.
NG

HENRY (i) (US) 1910–1912
Henry Motor Car Co., Muskegon, Michigan.
This car was named after its designer, David W. Henry, who had 10 years' experience working with the Columbia company in Hartford, Connecticut. The 35hp 4-cylinder Model 35 tourer was the only offering in 1910, but the following year there were two fours, of 24 and 30hp, and a 40hp six, with a wide variety of body styles, tourers with or without front doors, a roadstar (sic), a demi-tonneau and a torpedo-tourist. Without seeing photographs it is difficult to describe the latter two styles, except that they were open bodies. Henry never offered a closed car. David Henry left during 1912 to design the COLBY, and soon afterwards the company closed down. About 600 cars had been made in under three years.
NG

HENRY (ii) (GB) 1920
Oxted Motor Co. Ltd, Oxted, Surrey.
Designed by Geoffrey Henry, this car used a high proportion of American components including a 19.6hp 4-cylinder Lycoming engine, and Borg & Beck clutch. It was sold from Oxted, and possibly built there, or it may have been imported from the USA.
NG

HENRY J (US) 1950–1954
Kaiser-Frazer Corp., Willow Run, Michigan.
Named after Henry J. Kaiser, the Henry J was an early entry into the compact car market. The prototype was built by American Metal Products in Detroit, and it was launched in March 1950 as a 1951 model. It was a 2-door sedan on a 100in (2538mm) wheelbase, with a choice of Willys engines, a 2199cc 68bhp four or 2638cc 80bhp six. The four was the same unit that powered the Jeep, though Kaiser did not reveal this in any of their publicity. The light Henry Js performed well, but were cheaply finished and very basic in amenities. On the original models there was no external access to the luggage boot, though this later became optional and then standard. Some owners also complained of poor workmanship, even of windows breaking if the doors were closed too hard.
    The Henry J's biggest problem was its price. Kaiser had hoped for a sub- $1000 price, but when they appeared the figure was $1363 for the four and $1499 for

the six. These did not seem such bargains when a basic Ford six 2-door coupé cost only $1324, and this was a full-sized car from an established maker. Nevertheless, Kaiser sold 130,322 Henry Js in four years, and in addition built about 15,000 in overseas plants in the Netherlands, Israel and Japan. Kaiser also built 2363 ALLSTATEs for sale through Sears Roebuck outlets.

NG

Further Reading
Last Onslaught on Detroit, Richard M. Langworth,
Automobile Quarterly Publications, 1975.
'Fifties Milestone, the Henry J', Karla A. Rosenbusch,
Automobile Quarterly, Vol. 39, No. 4.

HENSCHEL (D) 1899–1906

Berliner Maschinenfabrik Henschel & Co., Berlin-Charlottenberg.
This make is not to be confused with the better-known firm of the same name from Kassel who were important builders of locomotives and also of trucks and buses. Henschel of Berlin made electric cars, at first by transforming horse-drawn vehicles by adding batteries and electric motors. In 1899 they made the first self-propelled taxicab in Berlin. Power transmission was by flexible shaft which allowed for only very slow speeds. A 2-seater petrol car was not successful, and Henschel concentrated on electrics, making passenger cars up to 1906 and trucks up to 1918.

HON

HENSEN (GB) 1983–1986

1983–1985 Hensen Automotive, Milford Haven, Dyfed.
1985–1986 Eagle Cars Ltd, Worthing, Sussex.
Hugo Hensen was the first person to design a kit car based around Ford Granada parts but this 2+2 coupé was a very ugly device. Its saving grace was a tremendously strong chassis and thick fire-retardant fibreglass body. The M30 was the standard car but the M70 offered a chassis for V8 engines; both were later offered by EAGLE. A Cobra 427 replica was also produced.

CR

HEPING (CHI) 1958–1960

Tianjin Auto Repair Works, Tianjin Municipality.
During the 'Great Leap Forward', when all important Chinese cities showed their first motor cars, Tianjin developed two saloons. Both cars were named Heping ('Peace'). The first one was turned out in June 1958, and it was a perfect copy of the contemporary Toyopet Crown, the technical data (a 1453cc 4-cylinder petrol engine, 3-speed gearbox, independent coil and half elliptic springs, a wheelbase of 100in (2538mm), etc.) were exactly the same. The original Toyopet styling was changed to a more American-influenced one which was also apparent in the oriental glitter. All photos show the same two-tone colour vehicle which had the Beijing-registration 1*10691. The second vehicle, made in 1960 and named Heping No.2, was a much larger limousine. It had styling elements of the American Packard and Russian GAZ-Chaika. At least two of these cars were made and shown in Beijing on Tian'anmen Square, together with three Beijing CB-4 and two Hongqi CA 72s.

EVIS

HÉRALD (F) 1901–1906

Sté Hérald, Levallois-Perret, Seine.
The first Hérald was a voiturette made with the help of Pierre Onfray who also made cars under his own name. It had a 6hp single-cylinder engine, probably of Onfray make. Also in 1901 Hérald made a 14hp 2-cylinder car, and in 1902 offered two 2-cylinder models, of 9 and 12hp. These were continued in 1903, when two 4-cylinder cars were offered as well, of 16 and 20hp. They were rather old-fashioned looking, with gilled-tube radiators and chain drive. In 1905/6 a 10hp twin and two fours, now rated at 16 and 28hp, were made. In 1906 a fleet of 15 Herald hansom cabs plied for hire in London.

NG

HERBERT (GB) 1916–1917

Herbert Light Car Co., London.
This was an assembled car powered by an 11.9hp S.U.P. engine in the prototype, with Sterling providing the 1496cc engines for production cars, such as they

1951 Henry J 2-door sedan.
NATIONAL MOTOR MUSEUM

1905 Hérald 28hp tourer.
NATIONAL MOTOR MUSEUM

1916 Herbert 11.9hp coupé.
NATIONAL MOTOR MUSEUM

were. Axles came from Salisbury and electrical equipment from Smiths. It was named after Herbert Smith who obtained his engines through S. Smith & Sons of Cricklewood, though he was no relation to the well-known electrical suppliers. The first few cars were assembled in a mews off Albany Street, near Regents' Park, with subsequent production taking place at Cricklewood, but 1916 was an unpropitious year to start making cars, and the Herbert did not last long. It was distinguished by a sharply-pointed radiator top. Two-seater bodies were offered, an open model and a drophead coupé.

NG

HERCULES (i) *see* DUCROISET

HERCULES

HERCULES (ii) (US) 1907
James McNaughton Co., Buffalo, New York.
McNaughton was a carriage maker who built electric cars for just one year. Two models were offered, a runabout for two or four passengers, and a 2-seater landaulette. Final drive was by single chain.

NG

HERCULES (iii) (US) 1914–1915
Hercules Motor Car Co., New Albany, Indiana.
This company was a successor to the Crown Motor Car Co., which had made CROWN (iv) cyclecars in Louisville, Kentucky. The Hercules was not a cyclecar, though its $495 price was quite modest, but a full-sized 4-seater light car on a 100in (2538mm) wheelbase, and powered by a 20hp 4-cylinder engine. Only one body style, a tourer, was offered. The designer, R.W. Fishback, was said to have 'brought to perfection the Fishback motor and car in Europe', though no trace of a car under that name has been found. He was, however, involved in a number of suspect stock promotion schemes in the US. The Hercules venture also ended in lawsuits, after about 100 cars had been made.

NG

HERCULES (iv) (D) 1932–1933
Nurnberger Hercules-Werke AG, Nuremberg.
This bicycle maker also built trucks from 1905 to 1928, but only turned to cars after tax reductions were offered for 3-wheelers. Their car was a small 2-seater coupé powered by a 200cc 2-stroke Ilo engine mounted at the rear and driving the single rear wheel by chain. The 2-seater coupé body had a wooden frame covered in leatherette. When the tax advantage disappeared, Hercules gave up their car and returned to 2-wheelers.

HON

HERFF-BROOKS (US) 1915–1916
Herff-Brooks Corp., Indianapolis, Indiana.
The Herff-Brooks Corp. was formed to handle sales of the MARATHON (i), and they also built a few Marathons as well as selling them. When Marathon went bankrupt in the summer of 1914, Herff-Brooks began to make Marathon-like cars in the shape of the 32hp Model 4-40, and added a 38hp 6-cylinder Model 60. They lasted for only two seasons.

NG

HERITAGE (GB) 1995 to date
1995–1998 Heritage Industries Ltd, Doncaster, Yorkshire.
1998 to date Vintage Replicas, Pontefract, Yorkshire.
The main custom for this company came from a range of kit-form commercial vehicles based around the styling of the 1931 Ford Model A. From 1995 it also offered passenger car variants, which were the Skellow (a 2-door saloon), the Burghwallis/Barnsdale (a 4-door saloon), the Bramwith (a long-wheelbase limousine) and the Rycroft (a tourer).

CR

HERITAGE AUTOMOTIVE (US) c.1986 to date
Heritage Automotive & Fiberglass Replicar Bodies Ltd, Posen, Illinois.
Heritage Motor Cars Inc., Miami, Florida.
Heritage Industries, Frazee, Minnesota.
Ferrari replicas were popular with this kit car company. The Heritage Evolution was a Pontiac Fiero-based replica of the F-40, the Heritage Magnum copied the 308 and the Heritage Rossa was a clone of the Testarossa. The Heritage 500K was a replica of the Mercedes 500K and they also sold Cobra, Mercedes 540K and Lamborghini Countach kits. Heritage also carried a line of Duesenberg replicas. Heritage merged with CLASSIC ROADSTERS in 1991, and were closed down in 1994. Heritage reformed under its original management in 1994 and resumed production of the 500K replica.

HP

HERITAGE REPLICAS (GB) 1985 to date
Heritage Cars, Hitchin, Hertfordshire.
This company produced a vast range of replicas, mostly designed for racing

purposes but also for road use. These included a Jaguar C-Type replica, based on Jaguar XJ parts, an SS100 replica, again XJ based, a Lister-Jaguar Knobbly replica (from 1989) and, from 1991, a superb Lola T70 copy, using an aluminium centre hull, steel subframes, fibreglass body panels and Chevrolet or Aston Martin V8 engines that was intended mainly for historic racing. A further limited run of Maserati 450S racer replicas with aluminium bodywork over an original-style Maserati chassis was produced.

CR

HERMES (i) see ACCLES-TURRELL

HERMÈS (ii); H.I.S.A. (B/I) 1906–1909
SA Hermès, Bressoux, Liège.
Hermes Italiana, Naples.
This Belgian/Italian venture made cars in both countries at about the same time, and only in one model. A car with 20/24hp 4-cylinder T-head engine and tourer body by Botiaux was shown at the Paris Salon in December 1906. Production started at Bressoux during 1907 in a factory which had a theoretical capacity of 600 cars per year, though nothing like this number was made. The Italian connection came through the friendship between Baron de Caters, who was backing the Belgian venture, and Alberto Manzi-Fe who had considered buying cars made in Liège by the Société MÉCANIQUE ET MOTEURS for the Italian market. He thought the 12/14hp Belgian car insufficiently powerful and asked for at least a 16/18hp, so clearly the 20/24hp Hermès was more to his liking. Instead of buying them from Belgium he set up a factory in Naples, though probably not many cars were made there. At least two 40hp sporting models with larger engines, Renault-style bonnets and sloping, flush-mounted radiators were built in 1907, and took part in the Coupe de la Commission Sportive, but neither completed the course.

NG

HERMES (iii) (US) 1920
Demos Tsaconas, New York, New York.
This was a car promoted by a Greek for export to his home country, and said to be designed especially with Greek demands in mind. It had a 3800cc 4-cylinder Buda CTU engine, Bosch magneto and other well-known components, and was made in two models of tourer, with five or seven seats. The radiator bore the name Hermes in Greek lettering, with a small statue of the god of speed as a mascot. Two chassis were shipped to Athens in June 1920, but soon afterwards the Greek Government banned the import of foreign cars.

NG

HERMES-SIMPLEX (D) 1904–1906
E.E.C. Mathis, Sté Alsacienne de Construction Mécanique, Graffenstaden.
In 1904 Ettore Bugatti left DE DIETRICH (i) and joined forces with Emile Mathis who was the French agent for the German-made De Dietrich cars. At the 1904 Paris Salon they showed a Bugatti-designed car with a 50hp 7430cc 4-cylinder engine, 4-speed gearbox and chain drive, under the name Hermes-Simplex. The engine had overhead inlet and side exhaust valves, the inlets were operated by rockers and pullrods, in turn operated by a camshaft in the crankcase driven from the crankshaft by fibre gears. Later the range was extended to include a 60hp (8616cc) and a 90hp (12,057cc). Possibly these larger models may have got no further than Mathis' catalogue: Bugatti expert Hugh Conway does not think that more than 15 Hermes-Simplexes were made altogether. The astute publicist Mathis had his name painted on the radiator of at least one car. The contract between the two men came to an end in 1906, and Bugatti joined DEUTZ before setting up on his own in 1909.

HON

HERMON (GB) 1936
Hermon Car Co. Ltd, Orpington, Kent.
The Hermon was a light car based on the BRITISH SALMSON 1½-litre engine and chassis, though it had Andre-Girling coil ifs and semi-elliptic rear suspension, in place of the Salmson's quarter elliptics. Probably only a prototype was made, though it is possible that there was a second car with the 20/90 British Salmson engine.

NG

THE CAR OF THE MODERNS

HILLMAN WIZARD FIVE-SEATER FAMILY SALOON £270

1906 Heron (i) 14hp tourer.
JOHN SPICER

1924 Heron (ii) 8hp tourer.
M.J.WORTHINGTON-WILLIAMS

1962 Heron (iii) Europa GT coupé.
NATIONAL MOTOR MUSEUM

HERO (D) 1934

This was another car built to benefit from tax concessions on 3-wheelers. It had a 584cc 2-cylinder 2-stroke DKW engine driving the rear wheel, and a 2-seater coupé body. A 4-seater body was also available.

HON

HERON (i) (GB) 1904–c.1906

Heron Motor Co., Birmingham.
The Heron name was an anagram of that of its maker J.J. Horne. It was an assembled car powered by 10/12 and 12/14hp 2-cylinder Aster engines, or 4-cylinder units listed in various sizes from 16 to 28hp. The Aster-engined cars had shaft drive and armoured wood chassis made by E.J. West, but the fours were chain-driven and had steel frames made by another manufacturer. The cars were sometimes known as Heron-Aster.

NG

HERON (ii) (GB) 1924–1926

Strode Engineering Works, Herne, Kent.
The Heron was made in the same country-house stables as the WESTCAR, but whereas that car was thoroughly conventional, the Heron was anything but. The integral body/chassis was of Consuta stitched plywood construction, under patents from MARKS MOIR in Australia, and was made by Samuel E. Saunders Ltd of East Cowes, Isle of Wight. They were taken by boat to Southampton, and thence by truck to Kent. The prototype had a 997cc Ruby 4-cylinder engine, mounted behind the seats, and drove the rear wheels by belt, though chains were soon adopted. The first production car appeared at the British Empire Exhibition at Wembley in April 1924 under the name Westcar Colonial model. Its engine, still mid-mounted, was a 11.9hp Dorman. An order for 20 cars was received from India. At the 1924 Olympia Show in October, it was renamed a Heron, and used the Ruby engine. It was very modestly priced, at £135.

The Heron's next, and last, Show appearance was in 1925, when the design was radically changed. The plywood construction was retained, but the engine and transmission were now mounted on a detachable sub-frame at the front. The engine was a 1368cc 10.8hp Coventry-Simplex, and the car looked somewhat like a scaled down Lancia Lambda in appearance. Not many were made, and Major Prescott-Westcar closed his works in 1926, ending production of both Herons and Westcars.

NG

Further Reading
'The Westcar and the Heron', M. Worthington-Williams,
The Automobile, June 1993.

HERON (iii) (GB) 1962–1964

Heron Plastics, Greenwich, London.
Fibreglass specialists Heron made bodyshells for Austin Seven chassis from the 1950s and it was an evolved version of one of these shells that formed the basis of a rather more ambitious exercise, the Europa, first seen in 1962. It had its own backbone chassis with outriggers, a plywood floor and all-round independent suspension. The well-proportioned fibreglass coupé bodywork was bonded on to the chassis. Either Ford Anglia or Ford Cortina 1500 engines could be fitted but the kits sold by the company were too expensive and only 12 cars were made. The Europa formed the basis of the first DIVA and Peter Monteverdi made a licence-built version in Switzerland under the name M.B.M.

CR

HERON (iv) (NZ) 1983–1990

Heron Developments, Rotorua, North Island.
Ross Baker was always keen on performance cars, having built his Mk 1, a Lotus 23-like car with a 1500cc Ford engine, as early as 1965. The Mk 2 was designed to accept Chevrolet Corvair flat-six engine/transaxle units but the two examples made ran with Daimler SP 250 V8 and Ford 289 V8 power. The production MJ 1 emerged in 1983, being a mid-engined 2-seater coupé with a 1600cc twin-ohc Fiat engine which was coupled to a Skoda transaxle. Later the engine size increased to 2-litres and the gearbox was modified to give five speeds. Its structure was an all-fibreglass body-chassis unit to which were attached Skoda independent suspension units, Triumph rack and pinion steering, disc/drum brakes and wide rim wheels. Twenty-four examples had been produced by 1985, when a revised model was developed to accept the engine/transmission unit from the Ford Telstar/Mazda 626. This power pack was retained for the MJ 2 of 1989, which was lengthened to provide 2+2 seating.

MG

HERRESHOFF (US) 1909–1914

1909–1914 Herreshoff Motor Co., Detroit, Michigan.
The Herreshoff boat-building family had several involvements with motor cars, but only one carried their own name. Their Model 20A of 1909 was a conventional 4-cylinder car made as a tourer, roadster and Colonial coupé. Its 24hp engine was uprated to 25hp in 1911, when there was also a larger 30hp Model 30 made in open styles and as a limousine. For 1913 they moved further upmarket with a 40hp six on a 124in (3147mm) wheelbase. The 4-30 and 6-40 were also listed in 1914, which was Herreshoff's last year. Poor quality Lycoming engines were blamed for the bad reputation the cars were getting,

and C.F. Herreshoff left the company that year. In April he announced a new company, the Herreshoff Light Car Co., which would build the HARVARD in Troy, New York. Another family member, Sidney Dewolf Herreshoff later made the NOVARA, and A.G. Herreshoff was the designer of the HERMES (iii).

NG

HERSCHELL-SPILLMAN (US) 1901–1904; 1907

Herschell-Spillman Inc., North Tonawanda, New York.

Herschell-Spillman was one of America's leading suppliers of proprietary engines, enabling at least 40 car makers to get on the road. The company was founded in 1880 as the Armitage Herschell company, makers of merry-go-rounds. Edward Spillman joined the firm around the turn of the century, and suggested that they investigate the motor business. In 1901 they announced that they were ready to build cars to order, but the first evidence of a car came in 1904 when a chain-driven 18hp 4-cylinder tonneau was built. A further car was made in 1907, a 60hp tourer, but after that Herschell-Spillman concentrated on engines, which they made up to 1923. The merry-go-round side of the business lasted up to the 1960s.

NG

HERSOT (F) c.1922

Éts L. Hersot, Limours, Seine-et-Oise.

The Hersot Super Helice Sport was a propeller-driven car made in open and closed models, with the propeller at the rear, unlike the contemporary LEYAT and TRACTION AERIENNE which carried theirs at the front. It had 4-wheel brakes, those at the front being of Hersot patented design. No details were given of the engine, and the catalogue was illustrated only by drawings, so it is possible that no car was built.

NG

HERTEL (US) 1895–1900

Oakman Motor Vehicle Co., Greenfield, Massachusetts.

Max Hertel built his first car in 1895, intending to enter it in the *Chicago Times-Herald* race, but he did not make it to the starting line. He subsequently put his design into production at Greenfield in 1899. It was a very light 2-seater, with two 3½hp engines and the front wheels carried in bicycle forks. Hertel quoted a price of $750, but did not sell many cars. He was also involved with the IMPETUS car made in France, possibly at the same time as he was running the Oakman company.

NG

HERTZ (US) 1925–1927

Yellow Cab Manufacturing Co., Chicago, Illinois.

The Hertz was the first car manufactured for leasing and carrying the badge which would identify it as such. The Hertz was named after John Hertz who had acquired the Ambassador car from the Walden W. Shaw Livery Corp. in early 1921 and who had attempted to market the Ambassador as a luxury automobile. Unsuccessful in this, Hertz redesigned the car to a smaller size which initially carried the name of the Ambassador 'D-1' in late 1924, this being changed to 'Hertz' shortly thereafter. Although the Hertz was basically manufactured for leasing purposes, it was available to the public as a sedan and touring car, each at $1675. Few Hertz open cars were completed, although sales for all Hertz cars were reported at 1672 and 2303 in 1925 and 1926 respectively. After the completion of an estimated 35 cars in 1927, the Hertz ended production. The company went on to become the world's largest car hire organisation with a fleet of more than 400,000 cars.

KM

HERZ & SCHROTER (A) 1929

Herz & Schroter, Vienna.

This company made a small car with 2-cylinder air-cooled engine and a sporty 2-seater body, but had no success, and withdrew from the market within a year.

HON

HESELTINE (US) 1916–1917

Heseltine Motor Corp., Buffalo, New York.

This company succeeded the GADABOUT Motor Corp. of Detroit, whose

1911 Herreshoff Model 25 runabout.
NATIONAL MOTOR MUSEUM

1897 Hertel 2-seater.
NATIONAL MOTOR MUSEUM

president Philip Heseltine gave his name to the new car. It was larger than the Gadabout, with a 27hp 4-cylinder Lycoming engine, and was available only as a 2-seater roadster at $695.

NG

HEWITT (US) 1906–1907

Hewitt Motor Car Co., New York, New York.

Edward Ringwood Hewitt made cars with one, four and eight cylinders, all in the space of two years. His single-cylinder car had an 8hp engine and epicyclic transmission; rather surprisingly for so small a vehicle it was offered as a 4-seater town car and limousine, as well as a 2-seater 'Little Touring Car'. It was made in England as the ADAMS-HEWITT. The 4-cylinder Hewitt was a conventional car with 20/30hp engine, with tourer or limousine bodies. It was replaced in 1907 by a 50/60hp V8 in the same chassis. This was based on the French Antoinette which was also offered in the Adams-Hewitt. Not many V8s were made in either America or England. After 1907 Hewitt concentrated on heavy trucks, merging with Mack and American Saurer in 1912. Edward Hewitt remained on Mack's engineering staff until the 1940s.

NG

HEWITT-LINDSTROM (US) 1900–1902

Hewitt-Lindstrom Motor Co., Chicago, Illinois.

John Hewitt and Charles A. Lindstrom made a variety of electric vehicles, from a 2-seater stanhope to a 20-seater bus, as well as a light delivery van and a 4-seater brake with a range of 40 miles per charge. In December 1901 Charles Lindstrom moved to Buffalo where he made the NIAGARA (i) electric car.

NG

1919 Highlander 6-cylinder tourer.
KEITH MARVIN

HEXE (D) 1905–1907
Achenbach & Co., Hamburg.

This was one of the few attempts by a German company to build American cars under licence. The make chosen was a prestigious one, LOCOMOBILE, but production did not last long. In 1906 Achenbach turned to making the Belgian NAGANT under licence. The range consisted of a 2-cylinder 9/10PS, and 4-cylinder cars of 18/20, 24/30 and 40/45PS, with the later addition of a 6-cylinder 30/35PS. However, these did not find many buyers either, and after 1907 the company imported Nagants from Belgium. The name, Hexe, is German for 'witch'.
HON

HEYBOURN (GB) 1914
A.W. Heybourn & Co., Maidenhead, Berkshire.

The Heybourn cyclecar was powered by a 5hp single-cylinder Stag engine with two flywheels, one at each end of the crankshaft. The front one was provided with vanes which assisted with cooling.
NG

HEYMANN (US) 1898–1907
Heymann Motor Vehicle & Manufacturing Co., Melrose, Massachusetts.

The first Heymann was a 2-seater stanhope on a very short wheelbase of 56in (1421mm), powered by a 3-cylinder 6hp engine, with tiller steering and solid tyres. At the end of 1898 50 were said to be under construction, but little more was heard from Heymann until 1904, when they announced a revolutionary car with 40hp 5-cylinder rotary engine and 'gearless variable speed control' a form of friction transmission which, in theory, offered an infinite number of ratios, though the makers limited the number to 20, which sounds more than enough. A price of $4000 was quoted, and the Heymann Rotary was last seen at the 1907 Boston Automobile Show. Probably only a prototype or two were made.
NG

H.F.G. (GB) 1919–1921
C. Portass & Son Ltd, Sheffield, Yorkshire.

Charles Portass founded his business in 1889, making optical and scientific instruments. He was joined by his son Stanley in 1907, and after the war years spent on aircraft work, they decided to enter the car business. Designed by H.F. Goode, the H.F.G. was a cyclecar with some unconventional features. The 1244cc flat-twin engine was mounted on the nearside, with the crankshaft transverse to the frame, and the flywheel acted directly on a friction disc on the offside, giving three forward speeds. The propeller shaft ran diagonally to the bevel drive rear axle. Front suspension was by inverted quarter-elliptic springs, and the rear springs were cantilever. All the major components were made in the factory, and the price was a not unreasonable £195, but few cars were sold. The company remained in business making bodies for cars, vans and light trucks under the name Heeley Motor & Manufacturing Co. Ltd up to about 1930. After this they made the Portass Lathe until they finally closed down in 1977.
NG

H.H. (HUTTIS & HARDEBECK) (D) 1906–1907
H & H Motorwagenfabrik, Aachen.

This company was better known for commercial vehicles, but passenger cars were offered with 10, 24 or 28PS proprietary engines. The cars were sometimes called Ferna. In 1907 the Swiss BRUNAU took over the designs, and production at Aachen was given up.
HON

HIDIEN (F) 1898–1902
E. Hidien, Chatillon-sur-Indre, Indre.

Emile Hidien had a background in steam engineering and farm machinery from his father's works in Chateauroux, graduating as a mechanical engineer in 1899. He had built his first car a year earlier in the Forge des Lampes at Chatillon, with a 2-cylinder engine fitted horizontally under the seats, 3-speed gears and final drive by chain. Engine, gearbox and axle castings were sourced from different foundries in Tours to Hidien's own designs, and this layout was still used in the Paris Show models of 1900 and 1901. *The Autocar's* comment that the car was 'of excellent construction' was supported by the recollections some 50 years later of the works foreman, M. Tousin, who remembered the care and pride which had gone into the preparation of the Show cars. He recalled two subsequent types before the final design, which resembled the contemporary Renault in using a vertical 2-cylinder engine, dashboard radiator and shaft drive, and confirmed total production as approximately 20. The cars achieved a sound local reputation and at least one remained in use until after World War I. Manufacture ceased when Hidien accepted a post at Le Creusot and in 1913, on the death of his brother Jean-Baptiste, he took over the family firm in Chateauroux.
DF

HIDLEY (US) 1901–1902
Hidley Automobile Co., Troy, New York.

Bicycle dealer J.H. Hidley built a steam car for his own use which attracted so much local attention that he decided to form a company in the autumn of 1901. The cars had 8hp engines and were offered in three forms, a 2-seater runabout at $750, a 4-seater trap at $800 and a delivery wagon at $900. Production does not seem to have lasted beyond 1902.
NG

HIGHGATE (GB) 1903–1904
Highgate Motor Co., Highgate, London.

Sometimes sold under the name H.M.C., the Highgate was an assembled light car of the Lacoste et Battmann variety, powered by a 6½hp single-cylinder Aster or De Dion-Bouton engine, with a gilled-tube radiator. The 1904 models had a more up-to-date honeycomb radiator, and prices were reduced from 170 guineas (£178.50) to 125 guineas (£131.25).
NG

HIGHLAND *see* AUSTRALIS

HIGHLANDER (US) 1919–1922
Midwest Motor Co., Kansas City, Missouri.

The Highlander was first shown at the Kansas City Auto Show in March 1919 but production of the car was delayed due to insufficient funds to start manufacturing and the few cars completed were presumably put together on a one-car-at-a-time fashion. The Highlander (frequently misspelled Hylander in contemporary automobile rosters) was an assembled car of little significance and consisted of an open 5-seater touring car with a Continental 7R engine. Although a roadster was announced, it never arrived and the estimated 25 to 30 Highlander cars completed were limited to touring car models.
KM

HILDEBRAND (D) 1922–1924
Martin Hildebrand Automobilwerke AG, Singen (Hohentwiel).

This was a small 3-wheeler powered by a 5/15PS proprietary engine which also went under the name Hisiho (Hildebrand-Singen-Hohentwiel).
HON

HILL (US) 1904–1908

Hill Motor Car Co., Haverhill, Massachusetts.

The first of George S. Hill's cars was a tourer powered by a 16/18hp 2-cylinder air-cooled engine, followed by a larger 22hp twin in 1905 which was joined by a 35hp four for 1907. Hill's engines, which were built for him by the Upton Machine Co. of Beverly, Massachusetts, who also made cars of their own, featured cooling by aluminium pins, on the lines of the KNOX. Hill made only 10 cars.

NG

HILLCREST (GB) 1980s

Hillcrest Classics, Pontypool.

This was one of dozens of replica makers that proliferated in the 1980s. Among its offerings were AC Cobra and Jaguar V12-powered Ferrari Daytona reproductions.

CR

HILL LOCOMOTOR (US) 1895–1896

C.C. Hill, Chicago, Illinois.

C.C. Hill built a motor carriage powered by a 6hp 2-cylinder engine, and offered replicas for sale at $350 for a 2-seater and $600 for a 4-seater, both with surrey fringe top. A few were completed and sold during 1896, but Hill did not form a company. He tried again with a steam car in 1900, but this never got off the ground.

NG

HILLMAN (GB) 1907–1976

1907–1909 Hillman-Coatalen Motor Car Co. Ltd, Coventry.
1910–1946 Hillman Motor Car Co. Ltd, Coventry.
1946–1970 Hillman Motor Car Co. Ltd, Ryton-on-Dunsmore, Warwickshire.
1963–1970 Hillman Motor Car Co. Ltd, Linwood, Glasgow.
1970–1976 Chrysler UK Ltd, Ryton-on-Dunsmore, Warwickshire.

Like many British car manufacturers, the Hillman Motor Co. had its origins in the bicycle industry. William Hillman (1847–1926) made cycles under various names from the 1870s and in 1907, in partnership with the French designer Louis Coatalen (1879–1962) he formed the Hillman-Coatalen Motor Co. Ltd to make a large touring car powered by a 6432cc 25hp 4-cylinder engine. The cylinders were separately cast and had square dimensions of 127 × 127mm, with side-valves in a T-head. The prototype was driven by Coatalen in the 1907 Tourist Trophy race, but without success. The 25hp went into small scale production in 1907, joined by an enormous 6-cylinder car with the same dimensions, giving a capacity of 9648cc. Very few of these were made.

In 1908 a smaller Hillman-Coatalen appeared, the 2388cc 12/15hp, which was made in slightly larger numbers. Even so, Hillman production did not exceed an average of 50 cars per year up to 1913. Coatalen left in 1909 to join SUNBEAM for which company he did his most famous work. The little Hillman Motor Car Co., as it was renamed, struggled on with the 12/15, which was also offered as a taxicab, and with a 10hp 2-cylinder car. An increase in stroke from 1912 gave the 12/15 a capacity of 2736cc. William Hillman was over sixty and had no sons to take over the firm (one of his six daughters married Louis Coatalen and two others married motor industry men, John Black of Standard and Spencer Wilks of Rover). The Hillman car might have disappeared like so many others but for the arrival in 1913 of a new designer, A.J. Dawson. He scrapped all Coatalen's T-head engines which were pretty old-fashioned by then, and committed Hillman to a one-model policy with an attractive small car, the 1327cc Nine with monobloc 4-cylinder engine and side-valves in an L-head.

Although the Hillman Nine had a number of rivals, such as the Enfield Nimble Nine, Singer Ten and Standard Nine, it sold well. Between its introduction in June 1913 and the end of the year, 65 found customers, followed by 450 in 1914 and 244 in 1915 when the company was already turning over to war work. A few Nines were made up to 1917, by which time capacity had been increased to 1593cc with an RAC rating of 11hp. In June 1918 Dawson left Hillman to make a car under his own name, though this only survived from 1919 to 1921. His place was taken by Hillman's son-in-law, John Black.

Dawson's design was continued after World War I on the Hillman, which was updated with electric lighting, but otherwise not greatly changed until the end of its career in 1925. A sports version was introduced in the spring of 1919,

1907 Hillman-Coatalen 25hp tourer, with designer Louis Coatalen.
NICK BALDWIN

1920 Hillman 10hp Speed Model.
NATIONAL MOTOR MUSEUM

1928 Hillman 14hp Tickford all-weather saloon.
NATIONAL MOTOR MUSEUM

being the first postwar British sports car. Capacity was reduced to 1496cc to enable it to compete in the 1½-litre class, but the tuned engine gave 28bhp compared with 18bhp from the touring engine. Top speed was 60mph (97km/h), and the sports Hillman had a very rakish appearance, with its pointed radiator, polished aluminium body, burnished copper exhaust pipe and disc wheel covers. It was the first competition car of Raymond Mays who later had such a successful career at Brooklands and elsewhere, and was behind the E.R.A. and B.R.M. racing cars. The Hillman Super Sports was expensive for its size, at £680, and not more than 120 were sold between 1919 and 1921. Total sales of the 11hp from 1919 to 1925 were about 4000.

In 1925 John Black took Hillman into a larger class with the Fourteen, a 1954cc 4-cylinder family car in the same class as the Austin Twelve or Humber 14/40. Despite having many rivals, the Hillman Fourteen sold well, production up to 1930 being about 11,000. In 1927 the Rootes brothers, car distributors from Maidstone, Kent, became sole agents for Hillman at home and abroad.

1930 Hillman Straight-Eight saloon.
NATIONAL MOTOR MUSEUM

1936 Hillman Minx saloon.
NICK GEORGANO

1949 Hillman Minx Mk III saloon.
NATIONAL MOTOR MUSEUM

A year later, Hillman merged with Humber and both companies came under the control of the Rootes family. This led to some rationalisation between the ranges, though Hillman generally kept their position as a cheaper car than Humber. Several body styles on the Fourteen included the Safety saloon, Segrave coupé and Husky tourer, a name revived in the 1950s. For 1929 the Fourteen was joined by a 2620cc straight-8 which was similar in appearance apart from a longer wheelbase. Two years later came a hybrid model called the Vortic, which used the straight-8 engine in a Humber chassis and body. The 58bhp engine gave a top speed of 70mph (113km/h), and the straight-8s carried handsome coachwork, but unfortunately they had a very bad reputation for big end failure which was never properly rectified. Nevertheless sales reached 2795 in four years, more than any other British-built straight-8.

Mass Production with the Minx

At the 1931 Olympia Show Hillman launched what was to be their best-known car, the Minx. It was a reasonably-priced family saloon with a 4-door body resembling a small Humber, an 1185cc 30bhp side-valve 4-cylinder engine,

Bendix brakes and better equipment than most rival cars. The Minx quickly became one of Britain's most popular small cars, and pioneered such developments as a radio fitted as standard (the Melody Minx of 1934), and an all-synchromesh gearbox in 1935. Other developments on the pre-World War II Minx included pressed-steel wheels from 1936, in which year running boards were dropped, external access to the luggage compartment in 1938, and integral construction on the 1940 models. The Minx lost its synchronised bottom gear in 1939, as a cost-cutting measure, and did not regain it until 1965. Open bodies, including 4-door tourers and 2-door roadsters, were offered on earlier Minxes, though by 1939 only two body styles were available, a 4-door saloon and a 2-door cabriolet. The estate car on the Minx chassis, made from 1937 onwards, was badged as a Commer, the name of Rootes commercial vehicles. There was also a sporting variant, known as the Aero Minx, made in fairly small numbers from 1933 to 1935. An underslung frame and different styling distinguished it from the regular model, though it was unchanged mechanically. In 1936 the Aero Minx was developed into the TALBOT Ten as the Talbot company had also been absorbed into the Rootes empire. Minx production rose from 16,671 in the 1932/33 season to more than 55,000 in 1938/39, while the total number made up to the outbreak of World War II was more than 152,000.

Alongside the Minx there were larger Hillmans including a 6-cylinder car with 2110 or 2810cc engines, called the Wizard from 1931 to 1933, and the 20/70 in 1934 and 1935. This was succeeded by the 3181cc Hawk which was designed by the American Barney Roos, and incorporated transverse leaf ifs. A long wheelbase version was called the 80, and became official government transport. Prime Minister Neville Chamberlain brought his 'Peace with Honour' sheet which he waved so optimistically at Heston Airport, back to London in a Hillman 80. The last prewar larger Hillman was the Fourteen which was more of a Humber, using an enlarged version (1944cc) of the old Humber Twelve engine in a Humber chassis and body. Only the bonnet and radiator grill were Hillman. After the war this was made as the Humber Hawk. About 14,800 6-cylinder Hillmans of all types were made in the 1930s, and 4600 Fourteens.

The Minx remained in production for the Army and essential civilian users up to 1944, and was quickly back in production in 1945. There was very little change in the design until 1948 when the body received a modernised front end with recessed headlamps, and the chassis was given hydraulic brakes. For 1949 the Minx was completely restyled with full-width bodywork, and there were now coil ifs. The Minx was steadily developed over the next 20 years, with a 1390cc ohv engine in 1955, a new body inspired by that of the Sunbeam Rapier in 1956, optional automatic transmission in 1958, front disc brakes in 1964 and full synchromesh in 1965. Until the advent of the Imp in 1963, the Minx was the only Hillman model, though there were some variants such as the Husky, a short-wheelbase estate car made from 1955 to 1965, and the Super Minx (1962–66) a longer and wider saloon with 1592cc and later, 1725cc engines. Throughout this period, three body styles were offered, 4-door saloon, 2-door cabriolet and estate car. From 1953 to 1966 there was the Californian, an American-style hard-top in two-tone colour schemes. The Minx was made under licence in Japan by ISUZU from 1953 to 1961, and was sold in New Zealand under the Humber nameplate from 1949 to 1967. With the side-valve engine it was the Humber Ten, with ohv from 1955 the Humber 80, and the Super Minx was the Humber 90.

The Imp

In the early 1960s the Rootes Group set up Project Apex to build a completely new small car which would compete with the BMC Mini. A new factory was built at Linwood, near Glasgow, and the car, named the Hillman Imp, began to come off the production lines in May 1963. It was a 2-door saloon with a rear-mounted 875cc 39bhp 4-cylinder single-ohc aluminium engine developed from the Coventry-Climax FWM. This engine was mounted in-line, and canted at an angle of 45 degrees so that it would fit below the luggage floor. The engine designer was Leo Kosmicki, who had been responsible for the Vanwall racing cars, while the rest of the car was largely the work of Mike Parkes, later to become a Formula One driver for Ferrari.

The Imp was a very attractive little car with an excellently designed engine and gearbox, but it suffered from a variety of problems in the engine and transmission which earned it a bad reputation. By 1968 most of these faults had been put right, but the damage had been done. The Imp was made up to 1976, but Rootes' new owners, the Chrysler Corp., showed little interest in it,

1966 Hillman Super Imp saloon.
NATIONAL MOTOR MUSEUM

and hardly had the design faults been put right than quality control began to slip. There were several variants, including the better-trimmed Singer Chamois, an estate car for which the name Husky was revived, and a series of fastback coupés sold under three names, Hillman Imp Californian, Singer Chamois and Sunbeam Stiletto. The latter had a 55bhp engine. Rootes had planned to make 150,000 Imps per year, but after 13 years only 440,032 had been built.

The Imp had a successful career in racing and rallying, with Rosemary Smith's victory in the 1965 Tulip Rally, while Alan Fraser's team of tuned Rallye Imps won the British Saloon Car Championship in 1970, 1971 and 1972.

The Chrysler Era
Development work on the Imp was so costly that Rootes were driven to seek outside aid which came from the Chrysler Corp. They took an initial stake in 1964, and by 1967 had become sole owners. The name was changed to Chrysler (UK) Ltd in 1970. Apart from the Imp the cars built under the Chrysler regime were not very exciting. In 1966 the Super Minx was replaced by the Hunter, which had the same 1725cc engine in a new body shell with Ford-like strut suspension. A cheaper version with 1496cc engine was called the New Minx (1967–70) and was the last car to bear this famous name. From 1967 Hunter components were exported to Iran where they were assembled and sold under the name Peykan. This continued into the 1970s, was interrupted by the Iranian Revolution of 1978, and then resumed in the 1980s.

The last model to bear the Hillman name was the Avenger, a 4-door saloon with coil independent suspension all round and a choice of 1248 or 1798cc engines. It was launched in 1970, became a Chrysler in 1978 and a Talbot in 1979, before being dropped in 1981. There were several high-performance versions of the Avenger, including the 100mph (161km/h) 2-door GT (1973–76) and the 110mph (177km/h) 4-door Tiger (1972–73), a limited production model intended for rallying and racing. A few had 16-valve twin-ohc engines developed by B.R.M., of 2-litres capacity and giving up to 210bhp. The Avenger was sold in America for a few years as the Plymouth Cricket and was badged as a Dodge in other countries. South African-assembled Avengers had Peugeot engines.

From 1977 the Hunter and Avenger were badged as Chryslers, so the Hillman name died. The Hunter was dropped in 1979, apart from the Iranian Peykan

1972 Hillman Avenger GL saloon.
NATIONAL MOTOR MUSEUM

version, but the Avenger carried on for two more years under the Talbot name, being made at Linwood after Imp production there ended. With the demise of the Avenger the Linwood factory closed, ending the manufacture of motor vehicles in Scotland. The Ryton-on-Dunsmore factory is now used for the production of Peugeots.

NG

Further Reading
Apex, the Inside Story of the Hillman Imp, David and Peter Henshaw, Bookmarque, 1990.

HILL & STANIER (GB) 1914
R. Hill, Stanier & Co., Newcastle-upon-Tyne.
This was a cyclecar powered by a 6/7hp air-cooled V-twin engine, with belt drive from the engine to the countershaft, and chain final drive. The frame was of 'specially selected English ash'. The projected price was a modest £85-90, and, when it was announced in May 1914, delivery time was quoted as six weeks. Not many can have been delivered before the outbreak of World War I.

NG

1967 Hindustan Ambassador Mk II saloon.
NATIONAL MOTOR MUSEUM

1965 Hino Contessa saloon.
NATIONAL MOTOR MUSEUM

1921 Hinstin-Sup 10hp 2-seater.
NICK BALDWIN

HILTON (US) 1921

Motor Sales & Service Corp., Philadelphia, Pennsylvania.

The short-lived Hilton was marketed exclusively as a 3-seater wire-wheeled coupé and was produced at Riverton, New Jersey. Designed by Hilton W. Sofield, president of the Motor Sales & Service Corp., the 116in (2944mm) wheelbased coupé was powered by a Herschell-Spillman 7000 4-cylinder L-head engine and was priced at $2375. Production had barely begun when a fire in June 1921 levelled the plant, thus ending the Hilton Four.

KM

HINDE see VAN GINK

HINDUSTAN (IND) 1946 to date

Hindustan Motors Ltd, Uttarpara, West Bengal.

This company was formed by Calcutta industrialists the Birla brothers in 1942, but as this was in the middle of the war, no cars were produced until 1946. Then they went into production with the Hindustan Ten, a saloon very closely based on the contemporary MORRIS Ten Series M. It was followed by two more Morris-based models, the Minor-derived Baby in 803 and 948cc forms, and the Oxford-derived Ambassador, initially with a 1489cc side-valve engine.

Introduced in 1954, this has remained the standard Hindustan model ever since, and the same basic shape was still being made in 1999. The engine gained ohvs in 1959, in which year assembly from imported British-made components was replaced by full manufacture in India. This was possible because BMC sold the dies which they no longer needed as they were making the new Farina-styled saloons. 1959 was also the first year that the Ambassador name was used. A diesel version of the BMC B-type engine was available from 1978, and has assumed increasing importance in Hindustan output. Export versions, however, had an Indian-built Isuzu petrol engine for greater power. Since 1994 these have been exported to England, with some refinements such as catalytic converters and rear seat belts. For many years Ambassadors were available only in cream, but a greater variety of colours was listed from 1998. Ambassador production in 1997 was about 24,000. In 1960 Hindustan's aircraft division developed an economy car called the H.A.L. Pingle, but it never went into production.

Another car produced under the Hindustan badge was the Contessa, a 1970s-styled Vauxhall FE Victor introduced in 1984. Originally it had the same 1496cc engine as the Ambassador, but more recently it has followed the Ambassador in adopting a diesel and the single-ohc Isuzu petrol unit. In 1998 Hindustan Motors also sold the MITSUBISHI Lancer to widen their range with a more modern car, and to rival the Suzuki-based MARUTI, they planned to offer the Mitsubishi Minica as well.

NG

HINES (US) 1908–1910

National Screw & Tack Co., Cleveland, Ohio.

William R. Hines had made a few experimental cars from 1902. He was chief engineer of the National Screw & Tack Co. when he began to offer cars for sale, but as his own factory was unsuitable for anything as large as a motorcar he had them built for him by the Moelhauser Machine Co., also of Cleveland. The cars were conventional-looking 5-seater tourers, but the 4.2-litre 4-cylinder engines were 2-strokes.

NG

HINO (J) 1953–1967

Hino Motors Ltd, Tokyo.

As Hino Heavy Industries Ltd, this company was formed in 1942 as a breakaway from the Tokyo Jidosha Kogyo Co., makers of diesel engines. They concentrated on commercial vehicles until 1953, when they began to make the RENAULT 4CV under licence. This continued until 1961 when Hino brought out their own small car. Obviously influenced by the Renault, the Contessa was a 4-door saloon with rear-mounted 893cc 4-cylinder engine. In 1964 it was restyled by Michelotti when engine capacity was enlarged to 1251cc (60bhp) and the 4-speed gearbox became all-syncromesh. A 70bhp coupé version was also available, but in 1967 Hino was taken over by TOYOTA and passenger car production ended. Hino continued to be major producers of trucks and buses.

NG

HINSTIN (F) 1921–1928

SA des Éts Jacques Hinstin, Maubeuge, Nord.

Jacques Hinstin was a partner of André Citroën in the latter's gear-cutting business which dated back to the turn of the century. It was he who introduced Citroën to Adolph Kegresse, the pioneer of half-track vehicles which Citroën built in some numbers in the 1920s. In 1920 Hinstin decided to enter the cyclecar market, and placed an ambitious order for 700 with the Société des Usines du Paquis who made cars under the S.U.P. name. They were conventional small cars with 1098cc 4-cylinder ohv engines, 3-speed gearboxes and shaft-drive without differential. Front suspension was by a single transverse spring. Only one body style was offered, a simple open 2-seater. They sold well and S.U.P. doubtlessly completed the contract for 700 cars and possibly exceeded it. Three special streamlined Hinstins ran at Le Mans in 1921, and they did well in other competitions. They were sold on the British market under the name Little Greg.

Production ceased at the end of 1923 or early 1924, but some S.U.P. employees led by the Lequeux brothers installed themselves in a small workshop and assembled a few more Hinstins with a lower chassis and pointed-tail body. This lasted until 1928.

NG

1940 Hispano-Argentina saloon.
ALVARO CASAL TATLOCK

H.I.S.A. *see* HERMES (ii)

HISIHO *see* HILDEBRAND

HISPANO-ALEMAN (E) 1970–1976
Automóviles Hispano Alemán SA, Alcobendas, Madrid.
Verne B. Heiderich was the importer of Porsche cars in Spain, when he presented at the Geneva Motor Show 1971 his version of the VW-Porsche 914/6, designed by Pietro Frua, under the name of Hispano-Aleman. At the same time he formed a company at Madrid to build the Mallorca, a Lotus Seven replica with a plastic body and Seat 1430cc engine of 76bhp. He also tried to build the Castilla, a replica of the Lotus Europa, and the Valencia, a Seven with 1300cc engine, but these came to nothing. About 200 Mallorcas were built. After closing the factory in 1976, Heiderich continued with his own car projects. He worked together with the Canadian ASC company, trying to build a convertible Peugeot 205, and he also intended to assemble a RELIANT SS with a Seat engine for the Spanish market.
VCM

HISPANO-ARGENTINA (RA) 1940–1945
Hispano-Argentina Fabrica de Automoviles SA (HAFDASA), Buenos Aires.
From 1925 Ing. Carlos Ballester-Molina was the Argentine Hispano-Suiza importer, and in the 1930s he also was already making some very good quality automatic weapons favoured by the local armed forces. But like Horacio Anasagasti in earlier years, Ballester-Molina dreamed of an Argentine automobile. He started in 1934 by making his Motor Criollo diesel engines in 4- and 6-cylinder versions developing 75, 95 or 150bhp. Hundreds of those engines were made entirely in Argentina, except for the injectors. He then made lorries and buses, fitted with the Motor Criollo engines. They sold well, being bought by the Navy, Army, local national oil industry and private individuals. Then, in 1940, Hispano-Argentina Fabrica de Automoviles SA (HAFDASA) produced their first automobiles, also powered by the Motor Criollo engines. There were two versions, both being large 4-door luxury saloons. One was conservatively styled. The other one was streamlined, with small windows and no running boards. The cars were driven to the Casa Rosada, seat of Argentine

1931 Hispano-Fiat Type 514 saloon.
NICK GEORGANO/NATIONAL MOTOR MUSEUM

government, and were examined by President Ortiz, who was almost blind. Apparently, the revolving-door politics of those days and the military coup of 1943, put an end to Ballester-Molina's dream. During World War II he also made a small open economy car powered by a 2-cylinder, 2-stroke, 550cc engine. It was called the PBT. But production was strangled by the lack of imported components. By 1945 nothing was left of the automobile production side of the Campichuelo industrial plant, although firearms production continued: most Argentine police and army officers used a replica of the Colt automatic pistol, made by Ballester-Molina. Argentina's motor industry would have to wait until 1948 for its take-off, when President Juan Domingo Peron would back the production of the Justicialista.
ACT

HISPANO-GUADALAJARA; HISPANO-FIAT (E) 1916–1932
La Hispano-Guadalajara SA, Guadalajara.
In 1916 Hispano-Suiza founded an independent company at Guadalajara, responding to a whim of King Alphonso XIII. In Guadalajara they built trucks and buses, but also the 8/10CV and 15/20CV car, and there was also a department

c.1907 Hispano-Suiza (i) 60/75hp tourer; King Alfonso XIII at the wheel.
NATIONAL MOTOR MUSEUM

dedicated to aeroplanes. The cars differed in the winged badge carrying only the colour of the Spanish flag, red–yellow–red. In 1923 the factory was declared a branch of Hispano-Suiza, due to financial problems. In 1931 Fiat bought half of the shares and built its 4-cylinder 514 family car as a Hispano-Fiat. Fiat assembled about 300 cars in Spain, which were distinguished by the badge with a woven crown and a capital H on the Spanish colours, but had to abandon this one year later due to the Civil War in Spain.

VCM

HISPANO-SUIZA (i) (E) 1904–1944

1904–1911 La Hispano-Suiza, Fabrica de Automoviles S.A., Barcelona.
1911–1944 La Hispano-Suiza S.A., La Sagrera, Barcelona.

The company was founded on 14 June 1904 to take over J. Castro Sociedad en Comandita, Fabrica Hispano-Suiza de Automoviles, by Don Damian Mateu y Bisa, Marc Birkigt, Francisco Seix, and others. The announced capital stock of 250,000 Pesetas was not fully subscribed, but 162,000 Pesetas was raised by the sale of 324 shares with a par value of 500 Pesetas.

Marc Birkigt became Technical Director. He had designed the Castro cars, and his Swiss nationality was honoured by the 'Suiza' part of the new trademark. Damian Mateu served as Chief Executive and Francisco Seix as Sales Director. The Mateu family had been in the iron and steel industry since 1801.

The proclaimed purpose of the company was to produce automobiles distinguished by their dependability, speed, silence and elegance. It was clear from the outset that Birkigt was not expected to design cars providing basic transport. The company aimed for a high reputation, which meant a wealthy clientele. Yet Birkigt was not given a cost-no-object brief, for the statutes specified a minimum production of three cars per month as a means of moderating the manufacturing costs. The planned model range had five sizes of 4-cylinder chassis: 10hp, 14hp, 20hp, 24hp and 30hp.

The engine blocks were cast in pairs, with equal-size inlet and exhaust valves, drilled crankshaft (for pressure lubrication), honeycomb radiator and gear-driven water pump, progressive cone clutch, 3- or 4-speed gearbox and shaft drive. The rear axle had a differential with eight satellite pinions and was carried by platform springs. Some models had pressed-steel frames; others were made of wood with steel-plate reinforcements.

No more than four chassis were completed in 1904: two 14hp units, and two 10hp units. But over its initial four-year period, the factory turned out 200 cars, or a monthly average of 4.16 cars, comfortably clear of the stipulated minimum.

The engines were redesigned with T-heads for 1905, the first being a 3770cc 20hp model which combined light weight with good power. It was quickly followed by a long-stroke version (up from 120mm to 180mm) of 5655cc for heavier coachwork.

In 1906 Birkigt began experimenting with 6-cylinder engines. The first test unit had equal bore and stroke (115mm) giving 7167cc displacement. The second one had 130mm bore and stroke (10,352cc). The 30/40hp production

NICK GEORGANO

BIRKIGT, MARC (1878 – 1953)

Marc Birkigt was Technical Director of Hispano-Suiza in Spain from 1904, and in France and Spain from 1911, and he was a majority owner of the French Hispano-Suiza company from 1923. He was universally recognised as one of the world's leading creators of fine automobiles and powerful aircraft engines.

Born in Geneva on 6 May 1878, the son of a tailor, he was orphaned at the age of 11. His grandmother took him in, and when he was 17, she enrolled him at the École de Mécanique in Geneva, where he showed a remarkable aptitude for physics and kinetic mechanisms. On graduation, he was awarded a scholarship to the ETH (Eidgenössische Technische Hochschule), the Swiss Federal Polytechnic College in Zurich. He was obliged to turn it down, however, as his grandmother no longer had the means to support him.

He did his military service as a gunsmith in the Swiss Army, and found his first civilian job in a factory which made machine tools for the watch-making industry. At the age of 20, he joined Piccard, Pictet & Cie, a 100-year old firm famous for its water turbines and foundries at Les Charmilles, near Geneva, as an engineer. There he came in contact with a Swiss engineer representing a Spanish entrepreneur. The engineer, Bouvier, offered Birkigt an opportunity to work for his employer, Emilio la Cuadra, who owned an electric power station, and wanted to make electric railway locomotives and highway buses.

After some hesitation, Birkigt accepted and moved to Barcelona in 1899. He was assigned to the development of the electric bus, which he redesigned with a petrol–electric power train, but it was a failure. Nevertheless, at Birkigt's urging, La Cuadra then decided to begin making passenger cars. The first La Cuadra, designed by Birkigt, was a single-cylinder 4.5hp machine with front-mounted engine and chain drive, completed in 1901. A parallel-twin soon followed, but then La Cuadra sold the factory to Jaime Castro, his biggest creditor. Birkigt agreed to stay on, but as a partner. The cars bore the Castro name, but the company title included the magic words model had 7412cc displacement (110 × 130mm) and the 60/75hp had 11,149cc displacement (130 × 140mm).

These models established the *marque* in the luxury and prestige car market, but Birkigt was also looking after the lower end, and drew up a 12hp 2212cc L-head engine for a lightweight chassis offered with a choice of 112 (2843mm) or 118in (2995mm) wheelbase. The rear axle was suspended by ¾-elliptic leaf springs. Launched in 1907, it was produced in considerable numbers up to 1919 when the engine was converted to pushrod-operated ohvs. A long-stroke version of the L-head engine, of 2614cc size, was introduced in 1908 as the 12/14hp model. Also new for 1908 was a 30hp car with a T-head (100 × 130mm) 4084cc engine, which became 30/40hp in 1909, with 150mm stroke and 4712cc displacement.

Yet the real sensation of 1908 was the T.15 with its (80 × 130mm) 2610cc T-head on a chassis based on the 12hp models, robust yet light, with the same choice of wheelbase, plus a short (96in/2436mm) sport model. When King Alfonso XIII took one on a high-speed test trip, he was so pleased that he ordered one. Damian Mateu asked the King for permission to name the car after him, and had his wish granted.

The Alfonso XIII introduced the one-piece 4-cylinder block and suspension by parallel semi-elliptics all round. In 1911, however, the rear springs were changed to ¾-elliptics. From 1908 to 1913 the car had a 3-speed gearbox, then a 4-speed box was fitted from 1913 to 1918.

In 1911 the engine grew to 3620cc (80 × 180mm) with a new crankshaft running in four main bearings (no centre-bearing), iron pistons and tubular steel con-rods, a Hispano-Suiza triple-diffuser carburettor and magneto ignition. The clutch was changed from a multi-plate type to a cone-type. The main pedal-operated brake was a 100mm-wide drum on the propeller shaft, the handbrake operating brakes in rear-wheel drums. The engine put out 64hp at 2300rpm, and even the long-wheelbase chassis weighed no more than 750kg.

The small factory in Calle Floridablanca was not nearly adequate by this time, and in July 1911, Hispano-Suiza moved into spacious premises at La Sagrera on the south side of Barcelona, off the road to Montjuich. Since qualified Spanish personnel for the upper-echelon posts were scarce, Marc Birkigt hired experts

1914 Hispano-Suiza (i) Alfonso XIII sporting tourer.
NATIONAL MOTOR MUSEUM

1914 Hispano-Suiza (i) Type 8/10 1.8-litre sedanca de ville.
NICK GEORGANO

'Hispano-Suiza' for the first time (J. Castro, Sociedad en Commdita, Fabrica Hispano-Suiza De Automoviles). Both 2- and 4-cylinder Castro cars were made to Birkigt's design in 1902–03, but then the Castro firm went into bankruptcy. They were rescued in 1904 by Don Damien Mateu, who decided to call the cars 'Hispano-Suiza'.

In 1905 Birkigt was granted his first patents, and by making licensing agreements, he began making a personal fortune. In 1906 he also designed complete cars for SAG (Société D'Automobiels Á Genève) to be built by Piccard-Pictet under Hispano-Suiza licence.

Birkigt made several trips to France in 1908 and 1909 with the factory racing team, which enjoyed considerable success. Late in 1910 he moved to Paris in order to set up a branch factory, which opened in 1911. He remained in France until 1914, creating new racing cars, experimenting with supercharged engines, and introducing new touring car models. In 1914 the French government of President Raymond Poincaré gave Hispano-Suiza an order to produce Gnome & Rhône aircraft engines, which meant a complete retooling of the French plant, and an end to car production. Birkigt was offended that he had not first been asked to design the engine, if he was going to make one, and returned to Barcelona.

Spain's King, Alfonso XIII, had earlier impressed upon Don Damien Mateu his coming need for aircraft engines, and Birkigt drew up a water-cooled V8 of remarkable simplicity, yet covered by no less than 17 patents. Prototypes were running in 1915, and production began immediately, in Spain. The A8 engine was produced with progressively bigger cylinders, but the layout always remained the same, with a single shaft-driven ohc per bank, in versions from 130 to 308hp. Soon the French government was asking for Hispano-Suiza engines, and the French plant began production of the A8. It was also built (under licence) by Peugeot, Chénard-Walcker, Voisin, Delaunay-Belleville; De Dion-Bouton, Ariés, DFP, SCAP, Ballot, Brasier, Emile Mayen, Fives-Lille, and Leflaive & Cie in France.

Wolseley was licensed to manufacture it in Britain, SCAT, Itala, and Nagliana in Italy, Wright-Martin in the US, The National Arsenal in Russia, and Mitsubishi in Japan. When the World War I came to an end, the total number of A8 engines produced was just shy of 50,000 units. Royalty income made Birkigt a rich man, and in 1923 he bought a 51 per cent interest in the French Hispano-Suiza company. He continued as technical director, naming his lawyer, Pierre Forgeot, president of the company.

When not working on the drawing board, Birkigt was making sketches which were given to the drawing office for detailing. He treated his assistants with patience, always ready to elaborate his explanation of given instructions. He gave a lot of thought to finding the best way to make things, and usually worked out the production methods in his head while sketching out a new device. He was demanding, uncompromising, and anything but lavish with praise, himself working six days a week at the factory. What he did not do a lot of was mathematical calculations. His creative mind would be bored with figuring out the stress loads on critical parts, gear dimensions and tooth spacing, and many other tasks, no matter how indispensable to the final product; he had specialists working in all those areas. He had an instinctive sense of the right size for everything, and often exaggerated the safety margin, in the interest of quality, dependability, and durability.

Birkigt stayed on in Paris when car production stopped in 1937, and a year later, his son Louis was appointed director of aircraft engine production. It was not until 1940 that Marc Birkigt returned to Barcelona, soon to be joined by Maurice Heurteux, husband of his daughter Yvonne. Marc devoted himself to the development of diesel engines for trucks, while Maurice flew to the US and organised American production of Hispano-Suiza aircraft engines.

Birkigt was married and had two children. In 1947 he retired to Versoix on Lake Léman, where he spent his time sailing, fishing, and sketching new precision rifles. He died of cancer on 15 March 1953.

JPN

c.1941 Hispano-Suiza (i) Tipo 60RL saloon.
NATIONAL MOTOR MUSEUM

1922 Hispano-Suiza (ii) H6 limousine by Grosvenor.
NATIONAL MOTOR MUSEUM

1928 Hispano-Suiza (ii) H6B sports car, by Compton.
NATIONAL MOTOR MUSEUM

1929 Hispano-Suiza (ii) H6B coupé by Kellner.
NATIONAL MOTOR MUSEUM

from Switzerland on his visits to Geneva (Olivier as Plant Director, Dufour as Works Manager, and Catherine as Test Engineer).

In 1913 Birkigt converted the 4712cc 30/40hp T-head engine to single-ohc operation, with an offset vertical shaft and rocker arms to splayed valves. The same arrangement was adopted for the 15/35 2614cc (80 × 130mm), 25/50 3817cc (90 × 160mm) and 30/90 5655cc (100 × 180mm) engines.

At the same time, he converted the 4580cc (90 × 180mm) T-head engine from two to four valves per cylinder, but it was made only in 1914–15. He retained the L-head configuration for the lowest-priced models, such as the 8/10hp 4-cylinder (70 × 120mm) 1847cc chassis introduced in 1914.

The King's enthusiasm for cars went hand-in-hand with his desire to develop Spanish industry, and Hispano-Suiza became involved with a scheme for building motor vehicles in the southern province of Guadalajara where unemployment was rampant and the population poor.

By order of King Alfonso XIII La Hispano Fabrica de Automoviles y Material de Guerra was founded in 1916 and plant construction began in 1917 on an 11,000m sq site. See HISPANO-GUADALAJARA.

Marc Birkigt having settled in Paris, Damian Mateu brought in a former schoolmate and industrial engineer to serve as inspector at La Sagrera in 1921, José Gallart Folch, who was named Technical Director and given a seat on the board in 1924.

The T.15 chassis served for a new 4-cylinder (85 × 130mm) 2950cc ohc engine introduced in 1916. It was bored out to 87mm in 1921 (and 3089cc) and the car was renamed T.16.

In 1923 the La Sagrera plant had 1100 workers and was turning out 600 vehicles a year.

So in 1923 Marc Birkigt, who was still a partner in the Spanish company, sent designs for two new models to Barcelona. They had a strong relationship with the Paris-built H6 whose chassis design they followed, with semi-elliptic leaf springs front and rear, and torque-tube drive. They had a similar single-ohc arrangement, with the valves vertically in line with the cylinder axis, aluminium blocks with screwed-in Nitralloy steel liners and detachable heads. Bore and stroke were the same (85 × 110mm) in both, giving 2469cc for the 4-cylinder T.48 and 3746cc for the 6-cylinder T.49. They delivered 60 and 90hp, respectively, at 4000rpm. They went into production in 1924 and were produced until 1933.

Two design engineers were engaged in 1927: François Burdin, a Frenchman who had been working for Steyr in Austria, and Carlo Caneparo, an Italian who left OM for a future in Spain. They were put to work on the T.56, a Spanish edition of the H6C 7969cc model from Paris. It went into production at La Sagrera, but perhaps only 20 chassis were built.

Next they tackled the T.60 which appeared in 1932 with a 6-cylinder 3016cc iron block, iron head, pushrod ohv engine in a chassis featuring lhd and hydraulic brakes. It was bored out to 3405cc for the T.60 RLA of 1934. The T.60 models were produced up to 1944 alongside the T.64 from 1929, a 4581cc 6-cylinder ohc model.

By 1938 Hispano-Suiza was producing 6000 vehicles a year, but only a fraction were passenger cars. Major changes had come about in Spain since 1921, causing big differences in the company's operations. King Alfonso XIII was forced to leave his throne in 1931, leaving the firm without its royal protector. The truck plant at Guadalajara was closed in 1931 (only the aero-engine department continued). Fiat bought a half-stake (minus one share) in the truck plant and prepared to set it up for assembly of the Fiat 514. Approximately 300 cars were made before the government determined that the product must be 100 per cent Spanish, which led to a complete pull-out by Fiat.

Don Damian Mateu had died in 1935 and was succeeded by his son, Miguel Mateu y Pla, but it was José Gallart Folch who kept the business alive during the Civil War, and managed its relationship with the Franco administration afterwards. The Guadalajara works were demolished in 1937, and the aviation department was moved to Alicante, while the rest was given back to wilderness or farming, where possible.

On 25 September 1941 the Government set up its Instituto Nacional de Industria to manage (and add to) the State's industrial holdings. Yet the truck and aero-engine industry was left in private hands until 1946. In the beginning of the year, the State established CETA (Centro de Estudios Tecnicos de Automocion) under the authority of Wilfredo P. Ricart as a design and development group in Madrid.

In October 1946 INI took over the Hispano-Suiza factories, patents and projects. Miguel Mateu had no choice but to 'sell', though he retained all rights

1931 Hispano-Suiza (ii) Junior coupé by Pareja.
NATIONAL MOTOR MUSEUM

to the Hispano-Suiza name. The Hispano-Suiza drawing office was integrated with CETA. The industrial property was given a new identity as ENASA (Empresa Nacional de Autocamiones S.A.) and its products wore a Pegaso badge.

All that was left of Hispano-Suiza was the machine-tool factory at Hostafranchs near Barcelona. A prototype front-wheel drive chassis arrived there in 1947 from Bois-Colombes, and another two identical chassis were built at Hostafranchs. Designed by Rodolphe Hermann, it had all-independent suspension and was intended for a V8 engine which never materialised.

The three chassis were tested with 4-cylinder 1089cc Simca engines. A water-cooled aluminium-block ohv twin-carburettor 80hp 2000cc flat-four was made at Hostafranchs and testing continued on a modest scale until 1955 when the project was abandoned.

During 1956 the plant, now trading as Furgoneta Hispano SA, produced a number of very small vans and pick-up trucks, with Hispano-Villiers two-stroke engines (9hp single-cylinder and 15hp twin).

JPN

HISPANO-SUIZA (ii) (F) 1911–1938

1911–1914 Sté des Automobiles Hispano-Suiza, Levallois-Perret, Seine.
1911–1916 Sté des Automobiles Hispano-Suiza, Bois-Colombes, Seine.
1916–1923 Hispano-Suiza Section Aviation, Bois-Colombes, Seine.
1923–1938 Sté Française Hispano-Suiza, S.A. Bois-Colombes, Seine.

France was the leading export market for the Spanish-built Hispano-Suiza cars. The company began taking a stand at the Paris Salon in 1906 and a distributor was appointed. The Alfonso XIII model was in such demand in France that the management decided to set up a branch factory near Paris. In April 1911 Marc Birkigt found a vacant tram depot at Levallois which seemed suitable, and moved in quickly. The first French-assembled Alfonso XIII was completed in July 1911.

Hispano-Suiza never bought that plant, but occupied the premises on a three-year lease. After a modest beginning with an output of 98 cars in 1911, the Levallois plant turned out 294 cars in 1912 and 377 in 1913. By then it was too small to work efficiently. Hispano-Suiza bought land for a factory site at Bois-Colombes in 1913 and cancelled the lease at Levallois. Construction work was completed in 1913 and the tooling was in place early in 1914.

At the start of World War I Marc Birkigt leased the new plant to the makers of the Gnome air-cooled radial engine and returned to Barcelona. On orders from the Royal House of Spain, he went to work on the design of an aero-engine. He chose a V8 layout with water-cooling and a single-ohc per bank. Though its simplicity was remarkable, it was nevertheless covered by 17 patents. Prototypes ran in 1915, and orders from the Spanish Air Force followed. Later, a test engine was submitted to the French military who extended the test duration five times longer than for engines made by French companies – only to conclude that the Hispano-Suiza was indeed superior. Suddenly France wanted this engine in preference to all others.

The Bois-Colombes plant was taken back from Gnome and retooled for the V8. It was still a fully-owned subsidiary of the Spanish parent firm but took a new name: Hispano-Suiza Section Aviation. Its capacity was totally inadequate, however, and the engine was produced under licence by Peugeot, Chénard-Walcker, Voisin, Delaunay-Belleville, De Dion-Bouton, Ariès, DFP, SCAP, Ballot, Brasier, Emile Mayen, Fives-Lille, and Leflaive & Cie.

Allied forces also wanted the Hispano-Suiza V8, and Wolseley made it in England, SCAT, Itala and Nagliata in Italy, Wright-Martin in the USA, the National Arsenal in Russia, and Mitsubishi in Japan. In France and elsewhere, it was given progressively bigger cylinders and its output went up from an initial 140hp to an ultimate 308hp. At the end of its development, it weighed less than 0.5kg per hp. When the war came to an end, the total number produced was just shy of 50,000 units.

The fame of the Hispano-Suiza name had spread around the world and far beyond the motoring public. The experience convinced Marc Birkigt that the make's return to the automobile market must be made only with a product so outstanding that it would add further lustre to its renown. He was familiar with the prewar Rolls-Royce 40/50 which became a sort of yardstick for dimensions, and a base that should be surpassed in refinement, performance and quality.

That was the brief he set for the H6, which did not go on the drawing board until November 1918, though every detail was already planned in his head. The first test prototype was ready for the road in May 1919. As the most expensive chassis in the world, it had to impress also by its size, and stood on a 145.5in (3693mm) wheelbase, weighing 1450kg. The massive ladder-type steel frame, slightly tapered forward of the bulkhead, was produced by the Acieries d'Imphy in a factory situated near Nevers. This factory also supplied the axles, held by parallel semi-elliptic leaf springs, front and rear. The propeller shaft was enclosed in a torque tube, short and conical, its forward end anchored to a big

1934 Hispano-Suiza (ii) V12 coupé.
NATIONAL MOTOR MUSEUM

ball joint flanged to a frame cross-member. Its rear end was bolted to the axle. The 3-speed gearbox was bolted to the clutch housing, with a short propeller shaft running back to the big ball joint.

The 6594cc (100 × 140mm) in-line six had a one-piece aluminium block with screwed-in Nitralloy steel liners. Vertical valves in a single row were operated by an ohc driven by vertical shaft and bevel gears. The crankshaft, machined from a solid billet of steel, ran in seven bronze-backed main bearings and was drilled for pressure-lubrication to both main and crankpin bearings.

Its relationship to the V8 aero-engine is very close, for a V12 version of the V8 had been designed (and went into production in 1923). The H6 engine represents exactly one bank of that V12. With two spark plugs per cylinder, a single updraft carburettor and a cr of 4.5:1, it delivered 120hp at 2600rpm. And it was beautifully styled, with the block and camshaft cover finished in black stove enamel applied by a high-pressure process, contrasting with the bright aluminium of the crankcase, inlet manifold, and steering gear. Even the large external water pump, curved-blade fan and straight water hoses were styling elements.

Internal refinements abounded. The big-end bearing caps had cooling fins, and the carburettor was flanged to a tower rising from an oil-sump extension, drawing crankcase fumes for recirculation. The carburettor was made by Solex to Birkigt's design. The valves were operated by self-locking carps riding on the cams while being screwed into the hollow valve stems.

One of the patented features of the H6 chassis was the braking system. One patent covered the finned aluminium drums with iron liners; another covered the gearbox-driven power assist, with servo force rising proportionally with the speed. The linkage to the front wheels included a differential to equalize the braking effort. The screw-and-nut steering gear gave only 2½ turns, lock to lock, with quick response and great accuracy.

Soon after presenting this car to the motoring public, Hispano-Suiza received a bad shock from the French Tax Bureau, in the form of a punitive bill for 'war profits' collected by 'aliens' (referring to the Spanish nationality of the parent firm). Hispano-Suiza brought counter-suit, invoking a bilateral treaty between France and Spain from 1862, and the case went before the Supreme Court. A compromise solution was found by registering the French branch as a French corporation. As in the parent firm, the principal shareholders were Damian Mateu and Marc Birkigt, the latter holding a controlling 51 per cent stake. Emile Mayen, one of the many who had produced the V8 aero-engine, was a co-founder. Société Française Hispano-Suiza S.A. came into being on 23 May 1923. Jean Lacoste became Managing Director. Ferdinand Fouré was chief of the drawing office and Edmond Bellinger, head of product development. François Develay was factory manager, and Louis Massuger, chief test engineer. Pierre Forgeot, a lawyer who represented Hispano-Suiza in the tax case, was given a seat on the board of directors. Massuger, who had an engineering diploma from the École des Arts et Métiers and had formerly worked for Delaunay-Belleville, soon reached director's rank also.

The original H6 was supplanted by the H6B in 1921, the latter being supplemented by the H6C in 1924. The H6B engine retained the same cylinder dimensions as the H6. Then came an intermediate Monza competition model with the engine bored out to 102mm, with 6860cc displacement, in 1922–23. André Dubonnet, a prominent client who also raced Hispano-Suiza cars in major events, wanted the engine bored out to 110mm, giving 7982cc displacement. After testing in the Boulogne racing model, it was adopted for the

NATIONAL MOTOR MUSEUM

The Stork in Flight

The unique mascot that adorns the radiator cap of the Hispano-Suiza is a stork in flight, mounted by the wingtips, its neck stretched and legs tucked under the belly for minimum aerodynamic drag. The stork is more than a mascot, for it is held in high esteem as a patriotic symbol as well as a historical emblem.

When the stork first appeared as a radiator ornament on the H6 in 1919, it was widely acclaimed for its artistic beauty. But the connection between a stork and the cars from Bois-Colombes is not readily apparent. Why a stork? The Hispano-Suiza was not generally used as a fleet car for maternity clinics.

The explanation lies in the story of Georges Guynemer, a sergeant in the French Army who became one of the nation's best-known fighter pilots in the war against the Red Baron. He was promoted to the rank of Captain before his SPAD biplane failed to return from a sortie on 9 September 1917. It was powered by a Hispano-Suiza V8.

It all came about when the No. 3 fighter squadron of the 12ème Groupe d'Escadrilles de la Chasse, led by Commandant 'Père' Brocard, was stationed at Vadelaincourt in Lorraine. Brocard called his boys The Black Band (Bande Noire), symbolised by a black ribbon painted on the wings. That was No. 3 Squadron's official badge up to the summer of 1915.

A rigger (member of the ground crew) by the name of Gévaudan, was assigned to the 12ème Groupe, an artist in civilian life. He drew clever caricatures of the pilots, and painted portraits of some of them. While Guynemer was sitting for his portrait, Gévaudan chatted about storks.

Storks, having a habit of spending their summers in Alsace and the Vosges, breeding and giving their offspring basic training in flying, had become a symbol of the freedom of Alsace, annexed by Bismarck after the Franco-Prussian war of 1870–71. Now France was fighting to get Alsace back.

What would a stork look like as an aircraft decoration?, wondered Guynemer. Gévaudan quickly sketched something on a pad. Yes, he wanted the stork on his plane. Soon, all the planes in No. 3 Squadron had the same stork on the sides of the fuselage. The Bande Noire was forgotten. Now Brocard's pilots were Les Cigognes.

At that time, Guynemer's plane was a Nieuport, whose airscrew was turned by an air-cooled radial 7-cylinder Le Rhone engine. The link between the stork and Hispano-Suiza was not forged until the 12ème Groupe was equipped with SPAD aircraft (originally Société pour l'Aviation Deperdussin, later changed to Société pour l'Aviation et ses dérivés) powered by the famous V8.

At Bois-Colombes, the factory gates opened on to the Rue de la Réunion. In 1918 it was renamed Rue du Capitaine Guynemer. Louis Massuger, the test engineer, liked the stork associated with his memory so much that he cobbled up a three-dimensional frame.

He went to see a professional sculptor, François Victor Bazin, who then created the definitive stork, the pride and joy of every Hispano-Suiza driver then and now.

JPN

HISPANO SUIZA

54/220-12 cyl.

30/120-6 cyl.

THE SUPER
CAR OF
1934

SPEED

SAFETY

SILENCE

COMFORT

ELEGANCE

NATIONAL MOTOR MUSEUM

701

1937 Hispano-Suiza (ii) K6 cabriolet.
NATIONAL MOTOR MUSEUM

H6C production model, delivering 180hp at 2500rpm. With the standard 3.37:1 axle ratio, top speeds ranged from 93 to 96mph (150 to 155km/h).

Some of the fame of Hispano-Suiza was due to coachbuilders. The elegance and individuality of the bodywork, expensive construction materials and master-craftmanship, originality of design, and the high level of equipment and finish, attracted celebrities, royalty and nobility, politicians and the wealthiest bourgeoisie to this make of car. Such a clientele selected the most elite, innovative and fashionable coachbuilders, not just in France, but also in Italy, Britain, Switzerland and Belgium.

Among the earliest were Franay, Kelsch, Belvallete, Duvivier, Gallé, Kellner, Gaston Grummer, D'Ieteren, de Villars, M. Proux, Janssen, Pourtout, Henry Binder, Labourdette, and Million-Guiet. Later ones included Letourneur & Marchand, Saoutchik, Freestone & Webb, Henri Chapron, Hermann Graber, Pinin Farina and the Stabilimenti Farina, Lancefield, H.J. Mulliner, and Barker. Most prolific of all was Vanvooren, whose role grew to the point of being semi-official cabriolet-maker for Hispano-Suiza.

By 1927 the Bois-Colombes plant covered 60,000m sq and had a 4000-man workforce. In addition to the machine shops and assembly halls, there were foundries and forges. However, most of the big aluminium castings were supplied by Montupet. Radiators were made by G. Moreux & Cie and Chausson. In all, 2158 chassis of H6, H6B and H6C specifications were produced up to 1933.

In 1929 Hispano-Suiza took over the Ballot company and its factory on Boulevard Brune, Paris. This led to an interesting new car, known by many names including Ballot HS 26 and Hispano Junior. It was powered by the Spanish-built T.64 engine, essentially a scaled-down H6 design with six cylinders (90 × 120mm) 4580cc, and 95hp at 3000rpm. Built on a lighter frame with a 140½in (3566mm) wheelbase, it was priced at two-thirds of an H6B chassis. But it was completely eclipsed by its bigger stablemates, and only 126 Juniors were built from 1930 to 1933.

Marc Birkigt thought that the H6C might itself be overshadowed some day, and he was determined that it should be by another Hispano-Suiza, not a competing make of car. Preparations for the J 12 (or T.68) began in 1929 and production got under way in September 1931.

Compared with the H6C, it had a much lower frame, but the same general chassis composition, with both axles on parallel semi-elliptics, and torque tube drive. The engine was a V12, following the usual material specification, with aluminium cylinder blocks, Nitralloy steel liners, and crankshaft machined from a solid billet. It had a single gear-driven central camshaft with pushrods to ohvs on both banks, the valves being lined up with the cylinder axis. The first series had 100mm bore and stroke, giving 9424cc and 220hp at 3000rpm. The clutch was a twin-plate type and the 3-speed gearbox had constant mesh on second gear. Buyers had a choice of final drive ratio (2.7, 2.89, 3.0 or 3.30:1) and wheelbases (135, 146, 150 or 158in/3426, 3705, 3807, 4013mm).

An optional engine with longer stroke (100 × 110mm) and 11,310cc displacement became available in 1932, delivering 250hp at 3000rpm. This J12 or T.68bis was to rank forever as the ultimate in supercars by Hispano-Suiza. Counting both J 12 models, the production total comes to 114 units (10 test cars, 47 short-chassis, 44 medium and 13 long-wheelbase).

The K 6 went in to production in 1933 as an upgraded replacement for the HS 26 with a 6-cylinder engine derived from the V12 (i.e. pushrod-operated ohvs, parallel and in-line). Its 100 × 110mm bore and stroke gave 5184cc displacement. Designed by Rodolphe Herrmann, a recent recruit to Birkigt's personal design team, it put out 125hp at 3200rpm. The K6 chassis followed the same layout as the J12, but was considerably lighter (1200 to 1250kg depending on wheelbase, compared with 1425 to 1580kg for the J12).

No more than 204 cars of K6 specification were built, for all car production at Colombes ended in 1938.

When Damian Mateu died in 1935, his shares in the French company became the property of his family, but Pierre Forgeot was named President. In 1936 Hispano-Suiza escaped outright nationalisation by Léon Blum's left-wing government because its owners were foreigners, while the State appropriated the entire aircraft and aero-engine industry. But the stay was only temporary, since the government set up an agency called Société d'Exploration du Matériel Hispano-Suiza which had a stranglehold on it by controlling both the order flow and the supplies. This agency even placed other weaponry and ordnance factories in dispersed locations (Tarbes, Jonzac, Saintes, Houilles and Le Havre) under Hispano-Suiza management. During the Nazi occupation, the Bois-Colombes factory made parts for BMW aero-engines and other German engineering companies. From 1943 onwards, it was a regular bombing target for the RAF, and the Germans began removing its machine-tools to plants inside Germany.

In 1945 Rodolphe Herrmann still had hopes of resuming car production. He designed a V8 engine and a front-wheel drive chassis with all-independent suspension. But he could not get it built in the Bois-Colombes factory since it was still under the control of the Société d'Exploitation put in place in 1936. He had it made in a private shop at Asnières and fitted with a body by the Ateliers de Carrosserie de Bécon. But Maurice Heurteux, a board member and husband of Marc Birkigt's daughter Yvonne, told him their only chance was to send it to the Spanish company for development and, perhaps, production, until the French company was freed of its shackles.

As soon as the Bois-Colombes works was sufficiently repaired, it was put to use manufacturing Eco farm tractors, Albaret road rollers, and Poclain agricultural tip-carts. Next, the company began producing Hercules diesel engines under licence, and secured manufacturing rights to the Rolls-Royce 'Nene' turbojet gas turbine.

In 1953 Pierre Forgeot retired and was succeeded by Maurice Heurteux (who died in October 1965). Since the factory worked almost exclusively as a subcontractor to French state-owned enterprises, the government tightened its grip on the still, nominally, private company in 1951. In 1953 Hispano-Suiza purchased the Bugatti company and its remaining assets, proceeding to a full merger in 1966.

In 1968 Hispano-Suiza (including Bugatti) became part of SNECMA (Société Nationale d'Études et de Construction de Moteurs d'Aviation) which had been formed in 1936 to take over the Gnome & Rhone company. The corporate structure was modified to include a Messier-Hispano-Bugatti sub-group, and the Hispano-Suiza trademark survived. At the end of 1977 a new Société Hispano-Suiza was formed, with turbochargers and thrust-reversers as its main product lines.

JPN

Further Reading
The Legendary Hispano-Suiza, Johnnie Green, Dalton Watson, 1977.
Hispano-Suiza, Ernest Schmid d'Andres, Editions d'Art J.P. Barthelemy, 1997.
Hispano-Suiza, Paul Badré, Edijac, Paris, 1990.
Hispano-Suiza/Pegaso, Manuel Lage, Lunwerg Editores, Barcelona, 1992.

HISPANO-VOLPE (E) 1947
Genicar Internacional Auto SL, Madrid.
This was a Spanish minicar built under Italian Volpe licence, and which used an aerodynamic body with boarded rear wheels and a 125cc engine.

VCM

HISPARCO (E) 1923–1928
P. de Arco y Compañía, Madrid.
The agent of French BNC cyclecars in Madrid, Manuel Pérez de Arco, launched in 1923 his own light cars, using French Chapuis-Dornier engines. The cars participated in several competitions, such as the Grand Prix of San Sebastian, and over 150 were sold to private owners. In the Madrid exposition Hisparco shared a stand with BNC and D.F.P.

VCM

1926 Hisparco 750cc sports car.
NATIONAL MOTOR MUSEUM

HITCHCOCK (US) 1907–1908
Hitchcock Motor Car Co., Warren, Ohio.
This car featured a 20hp 2-cylinder 2-stroke Speedwell engine and friction transmission. The company disappeared soon after it was formed, and very few cars were made.

NG

HITCHON-WELLER *see* GLOBE (i)

HI-TECH (i) (US) 1983 to date
Hi-Tech Cobra Inc., Scottsdale, Arizona.
This company made the most accurate Cobra replicas built in the United States. The chassis were nearly identical to the originals and most of the parts would interchange. The standard bodies were fibreglass, but aluminium was optional. They made replicas of all the various Cobra models and would also build an exact copy of a particular car. These were among the most expensive Cobra replicas made and were sold in kit or assembled form.

HP

HI-TECH (ii) (GB) 1986–1990
Hi-Tech Welding Services, Kidderminster, Worcestershire.
This was one of the also-rans of the GT40 replica scene created by a steel fabrication company. The model replicated was the classic Mk I but using a multi-tube space frame chassis intended for Rover V8, American V8 or Renault 30 power. Quality was lacking and the Hi-Tech's major footnote is that at least two cars were built with a targa roof arrangement.

CR

HI-TECH (iii) (CDN) 1987
Collaborating with British and American companies, this was an early plastic-bodied Lamborghini Countach replica powered by a mid-mounted V8 engine.

CR

H.K. (F) 1907
A.S. de Kostka, Paris.
This company made two light cars, one a voiturette with 10hp single-cylinder engine, and the other a 12/16hp 2-cylinder. An example of the 10hp was entered for the 1907 Coupe des Voiturettes but did not reach the starting line.

NG

H.L. (F) 1912–1914
Hainsselin et Langlois, St Cloud, Seine-et-Oise.
This company made cars with large 4-cylinder engines in two sizes, a 10/15 of 2120cc and a 12/18 of 2650cc, the latter being enlarged to 3014cc in 1913. They had coil ifs and 2-speed gearboxes in the rear axle. Body styles included 2-seater and 5-seater tourers and a landaulette, and the cars were fronted by a large rounded radiator not unlike that of the first Morris Oxford. They were described in British advertising as 'Europe's Reply to America'.

c.1984 HM Free-Way 3-wheel coupé.
ELLIOTT KAHN

1923 Hodgson 1½-litre sports car.
BRIAN DEMAUS

There is a solitary reference to a postwar car, now known simply as Hainsselin, with 2402cc engine and still with 2 speeds, listed in 1924.

NG

H.L.B. (GB) 1914

H.L.B. Motors, Islington Green, London.
This company made a most unusual type of vehicle, a steam-powered cyclecar. It had a Stanley-type paraffin-fired boiler, two double-acting cylinders, and an armoured wood frame. The engine was mounted under the floorboards, and drove the rear axle directly by single chain. Front suspension was by an inverted semi-elliptic spring. It is doubtful if such a curious machine would have had much success at any time, but its announcement in June 1914 was unpropitious, to say the least.

NG

H.M.C. (i) (GB) 1913

Hendon Motor Cycle Co., Hendon, Middlesex.
This was a cyclecar powered by an 8hp Chater-Lea, with transmission by a 2-speed gearbox and belt final drive. The name H.M.C. was also used for the HIGHGATE car.

NG

H.M.C. (ii) (GB) 1989 to date

H.M.C. Sportscars Ltd, Stroud, Gloucestershire.
A prototype replica of the Austin-Healey 3000 initially appeared under the name Harrier as early as 1985 and it was developed into a production-ready prospect by 1989. There was a hope that this car could be marketed as a Healey, since Geoffrey Healey – son of Donald – endorsed and collaborated with this modern reinterpretation of the classic Austin-Healey 3000. However trademark problems forced the company to be called H.M.C. The H.M.C. range was launched in two versions, the Mk IV (with luxury trim) and the Silverstone

(a more stripped-out version). Both had a tubular backbone chassis, irs, all-disc brakes and a 190bhp Rover Vitesse V8 engine. Most production went for export to Germany, where a new Lightweight model (weighing only 940kg) was presented in 1995.

CR

H-M FREE-WAY (US) c.1977–1985

High Mileage Vehicles, Burnsville, Minnesota.
The Free-Way was a tiny economy car available with a variety of power packages. The fibreglass coupé bodywork had one headlight and room for a single occupant, although a temporary tandem seat was available for a tiny passenger. It had three wheels arranged with two in front and a mid-mounted engine. The Deluxe Free-Way Electric was powered by a 6hp motor with four 12-volt batteries. The Free-Way II was powered by a 340cc or 450cc single-cylinder petrol engine, or an optional diesel engine. Unlike most electric and high-mileage cars, the Free-Way actually was produced in respectable numbers.

HP

HOBBIE (US) 1908–1909

Hobbie Automobile Co., Hampton, Iowa.
The Hobbies, father and son, were blacksmiths who set up a car dealership early in the century, and ventured into manufacture of their own vehicle in 1908. Known as the Hobbie Accessible, it was a typical high-wheeler with 2-cylinder air-cooled engine, double-chain drive, solid tyres and tiller steering. Although it was made for only three seasons, and was little changed during that time, its bodies carried three names, Road Wagon in 1908, Piano Box Buggy in 1909, when it was a 4-seater, and Runabout in 1910. Leslie Hobbie, the son, later became a dealer for Overland and then Chrysler, and in 1939 took the little Crosley under his wing.

NG

HOBBYCAR (F) 1992–1996

Hobbycar SA, Garancières.
Having finished working with the Renault Formula 1 effort, François Wardavoir presented the extraordinary Hobbycar amphibian at the 1992 Paris Motor Show. In layout, it was a forward-control 4-seater with pivoting seats and was designed to be offered in open, closed and pick-up styles. Either a 1.4-litre 74bhp petrol or 1.8-litre 80bhp diesel engine (later 1.9-litres and 92bhp) from Peugeot could be mounted amidships in the steel-reinforced plastic monocoque body/chassis, and a top speed of 87mph (140km/h) on land and 5 knots on water was claimed. Propulsion in water was by joystick-controlled hydrojets. Among its numerous novel features were an electrically-retractable windscreen, gullwing 4-door hard-top, retractable dashboard and hydropneumatic suspension. Its outrageous price prevented any commercial success for this 'unsinkable' vehicle but this did not dissuade the development of a second model, the Passport, which was designed by Gérard Godfroy. This was a luxury MPV with four electrically-opening sliding doors and five seats. Its lavish specification included a front-mounted Opel 2-litre 4-cylinder turbocharged engine with 204bhp driving all four wheels via a 6-speed gearbox and 'Contractive' all-independent suspension. The Passport never reached production and its high development costs sunk the amphibian along with it.

CR

HODGSON (GB) 1924–1925

Hodgson Motors, Leeds, Yorkshire.
Before World War I Harry Hodgson gave driving lessons and engineering instruction, and planned to make a racing car when the war intervened. In 1922 he built a racing car using an Anzani engine, with which he had a number of successes in speed trials and hill climbs. In 1924 he began to make cars for sale in a very modest factory with a staff of only four men. Like his first car they all had 1496cc Anzani engines and Meadows 4-speed gearboxes. The wheelbase was 108in (2741mm). Several types were made, including a rather staid-looking 2-seater called the 12/25, and sporting 2- and 4-seaters (12/40) with aluminium bodies. Prices were £295 for the 2-seater, £395 for the 2- and 4-seater Super Sports and £550 for the 12/50 supercharged racing car. Production was very limited, only about eight cars being made in all. In 1927 Hodgson patented a dual quarter-elliptic suspension, and in 1929 built five cars under the name

1988 Hofstetter Turbo 2-litre coupé.
TECNODESIGN

British Eagle, still using Anzani engines, but with shorter wheelbases than the Hodgson, 94 (2386mm) and 100in (2538mm).

NG

Further Reading
'Fragments on Forgotten Makes; the Hodgson', W. Boddy,
Motor Sport, March 1969.

HOFFMAN (US) 1901–1904

Hoffman Automobile Manufacturing Co., Cleveland, Ohio.
Louis E. Hoffman was a bicycle manufacturer who built a light steam car in 1901, and formed a company to make it in January 1902. It was a 2-seater with 6hp engine and a boiler wound with piano wire. Final drive was by single chain. In January 1903 a petrol-engined car joined the steamer; it had a 7$\frac{1}{2}$hp single-cylinder engine and a 4-seater tonneau body. The steamer was continued into the 1904 season, but the petrol model was made by a reorganised company as the ROYAL TOURIST.

NG

HOFFMANN (D) 1954–1955

Hoffmann-Werke, Lintorf.
Hoffmann were among the first companies in Germany to take out a licence for making Vespa scooters. Jakob Oswald Hoffmann was intrigued by the ISETTA and decided to make a modified version which had a single door at the side instead of at the front, and his own 298cc flat-twin engine in place of the Isetta's single. He made the mistake of claiming that Iso had copied his design, although it had clearly appeared first, and he was sued by both Iso and BMW who were making the Isetta design. This ended production of the Hoffmann Kabine after about 100 had been made.

HON

HOFFMANN & CZERNY (A) 1907

Continental-Musik-Werke, Automobil-Abteilung, Vienna.
After making various musical instruments, this company began production of a small car powered by a 9PS 2-cylinder engine. Few were made, and the company quickly concentrated on pianos.

HON

HOFLACK (B) 1901

François Hoflack, Ypres.
Hoflack was the Belgian agent for the French-built Lamaudière et Labre motorcycle, and made under his own name a few voiturettes powered by 3$\frac{1}{2}$hp Aster engines, with 2-speed gearboxes.

NG

HOFSTETTER (BR) 1986–1989

Tecnodesign Mecanica Industrial e Comercial Ltda, São Paulo.
In 1980, the Hofstetter family built a prototype sports car, powered by a Ford engine. In 1982, Tecnodesign Mecanica Industrial e Comercial Ltda was founded in order to build this fibreglass sports coupé with gull-wing doors. In 1984, the first vehicle of the final configuration, was shown at the São Paulo Motor Show. By then, the Hofstetter car was powered by a Volkswagen Santana 2000 engine, with Garrett turbocharger. Options included airconditioning, cast-alloy wheels and Blaupunkt stereo/cassette equipment. A top speed of 145mph (230 km/h) was claimed. Production started in October 1986, but the Hofstetter was a commercial failure. Exact production figures were not released, but in 1989, Mario Richard Hofstetter stated that production was by then very low and admitted that in 1988 only four cars were made.

ACT

HOLBORN *see* McLACHLAN

HOLBROW (GB) 1903

E.T. Holbrow, Earlsfield, London.
Holbrow ran the Earlsfield Cycle & Motor Works, and made a small number of light 2-seaters powered by a 4$\frac{1}{2}$hp front-mounted vertical single-cylinder engine, with 2-speed gearbox, and belt drive to a countershaft behind the rear axle, to which the countershaft was geared.

NG

HOLCAR *see* HOLROYD-SMITH

1949 Holden 48-215 sedan.
HOLDEN

1954 Holden FJ sedan.
NATIONAL MOTOR MUSEUM

1965 Holden HD sedan.
NICK BALDWIN

HOLDEN (AUS) 1948 to date

General Motors-Holdens Ltd, Port Melbourne, Victoria.

The Holden was brought into existence against the wishes of the General Motors head office and without funding from it, largely because of a joint effort between its managing director, Laurence Hartnett, and the Australian Prime Minister. It took its name from the body builder which had been absorbed by the General Motors Australia organisation. Based on a prewar US-designed light six prototype, the Holden was technically state-of-the-art and set a benchmark for its load capacity to weight ratio. This resulted in a remarkable performance and economy envelope but its austerity was unusual in a car of its size.

The Type 48/215 had a 2172cc ohv engine giving 60bhp in a roomy 6-seater on a 103in (2616mm) wheelbase, which weighed 1009kg. Built as a sedan and utility (pick-up), with very high local content, and sold through the largest dealer network, it immediately became the top seller. In 1954 first exports to New Zealand were with the updated FJ. The 1956 FE, with a 105in (2667mm) wheelbase, was heavier and performance was maintained by increasing power to 70bhp, but at the expense of economy. A station wagon was added and a freshened FC arrived in 1958.

The new 1960 body shell, with tail fins and dog-leg screen pillars, was longer and heavier with an enlarged 2263cc engine giving 76bhp. Exports of lhd cars commenced and the cosmetic EK of 1961 offered the optional Hydramatic automatic transmission. A lower body marked the 1962 EJ, the first to include the Premier upmarket version. The EH of 1963 had a squared roof line but the major change was a new 7-bearing engine in sizes of 100bhp, 2443cc and 115bhp, 2936cc for automatics. The 1965 HD, on a wheelbase of 106in (2692mm) and weighing 1182kg, had curved side windows and offered a 140bhp performance x2 version. The HR of 1966 had engines enlarged to 2640cc for 115bhp and 3050cc giving 127 or 145bhp and the optional automatic became a 2-speed Powerglide. The Torana of 1967 was a revised Vauxhall Viva HB, which commenced a smaller line and included a Brabham performance version. With the introduction of the HK in 1968, the light six concept was abandoned. The HK had a wheelbase of 111in (2819mm), weighed 1274kg and made the 5053cc Chevrolet V8 available. Belmont, Kingswood and Premier denoted trim levels, a 2-door coupé was named

706

Monaro and the Brougham was a longer, luxury offering. With the arrival of the 1970 HG, locally-made 4200 and 5052cc V8 engines and Trimatic automatic transmissions were fitted. The Torana was a reworked LC with 4in (102mm) extra wheelbase to accommodate the 6-cylinder engines, topping out with the 160bhp GTR-XU1.

When GM Overseas Operations moved into South-East Asia in 1971, Australia became involved in the light utility vehicle programme which used Vauxhall Viva mechanicals. Development and testing were done at the Lang Lang proving ground and the Malaysian plant building the Harimau was managed by Bob Holden. The Torana was built in both the Philippines and South Korea. In 1971 the HQ became a full-sized car weighing 1341kg with the 6-cylinder engines enlarged to 2837 and 3312cc. The 114in (2896mm) wheelbase Statesman was added and its exports to rhd countries were badged Chevrolet. A revised LJ Torana used the enlarged sixes while the fours were 1256cc and the ohc 1600-1760cc Vauxhall units. A wholly new body for the LH Torana debuted in 1974 and was fitted with an 1900cc Opel 4-cylinder, the local six and V8. Top performance was provided by the SLR 5000, while the Viva-based four continued as the TA. The HQ was current for three years, becoming the most numerous type and was followed by revised models which featured reduced emissions. The 2-door was also dropped. The Holden-Isuzu Gemini, GM's first world car, catered to the 4-cylinder needs from 1974, having a high local content, including the Trimatic auto. The Torano LX of 1976 included a hatchback, the A9X high-performance version with disc brakes all round and the four was renamed Sunbird.

An effect of the energy crisis was a downsizing to the Commodore VB in 1978, the second GM world car, on a 105in (2668mm) wheelbase designed in collaboration with Opel. A 4-cylinder variant of the local six became the Sunbird engine, and was also offered as one of five engines on the following Commodore, as was a 5-speed gearbox. The Torana had been phased out and the large car was only available as the Statesman WB series and commercials. In 1981 a new factory, to make the Family 2 engine, came into use producing the 1600cc ohc four to power the Camira JB, a further world car design (Vauxhall Cavalier, Opel Ascona, American J-cars, and the first front-drive Holden). The 1984 Commodore gained a third window, deleted the 4-cylinder engine, fitted electronic fuel injection to the largest six and an electronic instrument to the top-line Calais. The Astra, the result of project co-operation with NISSAN, was the Pulsar design with body panels pressed by Holdens and fitted with the Family 2 engine. The engine was an export-oriented programme and 500,000 had been made by 1985 when the Camira update had 1800cc. A tie-up with SUZUKI at this time resulted in the Swift appearing as the Holden Barina, the Sierra 4-wheel drive as the Drove and the Carry van as the Scurry. A wholly new front-drive Gemini went on sale, as did the Isuzu-sourced Jackeroo 4-wheel drive station wagon.

The VL Commodore no longer used the long-running local six but fitted the 3-litre Nissan Skyline, which also became available with a turbo charger. The V8 substituted a 4.9-litre badge for the 308cu in. The Isuzu Piazza coupé was rebadged as a Holden in 1986. For 1987 a Camira revision used a 1998cc engine and an Astra revision added a saloon with a luggage trunk.

A Holden-Toyota joint venture, United Automotive Industries, was formed in 1988 and an enlarged Commodore VN was released. On a 107in (2731mm) wheelbase, it used the US-derived 3.8-litre V6 engine. Holden Special Vehicles was building high performance versions and a restyled Barina arrived. In 1989 TOYOTA shared models were on sale, and the Nova (Corolla) replaced the Astra and the Apollo (Camry) displaced the Camira. These were balanced by Toyota offering a Commodore-based Lexcen. For 1990 the Statesman reappeared on the Commodore, with a longer wheelbase, fuel-injected engine and irs. The car-based ute (pick-up) was also revived and the Group A competition Commodore had the first 6-speed gearbox in an Australian car. Total Holden production had then reached five million. The 1991 Commodore update offered irs, computer-controlled functions and security system.

The OPEL Calibra was the first German car to be given the Holden label and was the first Holden to have anti-lock brakes, which were extended to the Statesman shortly afterwards. Air bag installations and safety-oriented changes marked 1993, while in 1995 an ECOTEC engine management system, 5-speed manual gearbox and, later, a supercharged version of the V6 engine appeared. The Frontera, a European-sourced 1998cc, 4-cylinder, 4-wheel drive arrived in 1996.

1999 Holden Statesman sedan.
HOLDEN

1990 Holden Commodore sedan.
HOLDEN

The 1997 VT series was the first wholly Australian designed Commodore, being larger on a wheelbase of 109in (2778mm) and fitted with 4-wheel disc brakes. A Spanish-built Barina was introduced while the end of the Toyota alliance saw the European Astra and Vectra models selected to fill the void, the Vectra being included in the local manufacturing programme. For 1998 the large Chevrolet Suburban 4-wheel drive was rebadged as a Holden and the first Holden convertible was offered on the Barina. Three million Family 2 engines had then been produced for fitting to cars in many countries, at one point being the best manufactured item export earner for Australia.

In 1998 Commodore production was 117,021 units, made up of 103,665 VT sedans, 4255 VS long wheelbase sedans, and 9101 VS utilities. These easily exceeded the 87,941 of the Ford Falcon in all its forms. A new high-performance Commodore was announced in the summer of 1999; the HSV had a 335bhp 5.7-litre Chevrolet Corvette engine, giving performance very close to that of the BMW M5. Transmission was by 4-speed automatic or 6-speed manual gearboxes, and an estate version was available in addition to the sedan.

MG

Further Reading
The History of Holden since 1917, Norm Darwin, Eddie Ford Publications, 1983.

HOLDSWORTH (GB) 1903–1904

Light Car & Motor Engineering Co. Ltd, Birmingham.
This company offered light cars powered by a choice of 4¹/₂ , 6 and 6¹/₂hp Aster engines, with final drive by shaft or central chain.
NG

HOLLAND (i) (US) 1898–c.1906

Sam Holland, Park River, North Dakota.
Sam Holland was a blacksmith who built a number of cars for his employees and friends, but never formed a company. His first was a high-built 4-seater steam

1904 Holley 5hp 2-seater.
NICK GEORGANO

1915 Hollier V8 tourer.
NATIONAL MOTOR MUSEUM

car, and this was followed by several petrol-engined tricycles, and a 4-wheeler runabout which survives today in the collection of the State Historical Society of North Dakota. It had a 6hp single-cylinder engine with two radiators, one to cool the cylinder head, the other the block. An 8½hp touring model followed, and then, in 1905, a 12hp 4-cylinder car with air-cooling. Holland considered manufacturing this one, and advertised in the local press for six weeks, but so far as is known, no production followed.

NG

HOLLAND (ii) (US) 1902–1903

Holland Automobile Co., Jersey City, New Jersey.

This company sold components including 6 and 12hp engines, epicyclic transmissions and chain-drive in bare chassis ready to receive bodies. A few complete steam cars were made as well.

NG

HOLLEY (US) 1900–1904

Holley Motor Co., Bradford, Pennsylvania.

George M. Holley built a 3-wheeled car in 1897, with chain drive to the single rear wheel, and two years later he and his brother Earl began to make motorcycle engines and later, complete motorcycles. In 1900 they launched a small car powered by a single-cylinder engine whose power they quoted very precisely as 5.27hp. It had a 2-seater body and a De Dion type bonnet. Not many were made, and the Holley brothers found a much more profitable line in making carburettors, developed after they imported the French Longuemare. They sold the Holley Motor Co. to a group of local businessmen who formed the Bradford Motor Works to sell left-over Holley components in kit form under the name Bradford. The Holley Brothers Co. became a leading carburettor manufacturer, becoming almost the sole supplier to Henry Ford in 1912, and selling their company to him in 1917. They later formed another company which made not only carburettors but also cooling fans, distributors and accelerator pedals, becoming again major suppliers to the motor and aircraft industries.

NG

HOLLIER (US) 1915–1921

Lewis Spring & Axle Co., Jackson and Chelsea, Michigan.

The Hollier car was built by Charles Lewis, formerly president of the Jackson Automobile Co. and, to all intents and purposes, as a sideline to his main undertaking, the Lewis Spring & Axle Co., being manufactured in two of that concern's factories. Initially, the Hollier was fitted with an in-house 40hp V8 engine, this being augmented in 1917 by a Falls 6-cylinder type. In early 1918, due to World War I, the V8 was discontinued due to shortages of material and was not resumed following the Armistice. With the exception of a roadster on the V8 chassis, Hollier production was limited to touring cars and whereas annual production closely approached the 1000 mark on occasion, it was never reached. An estimated 3500 to 4000 units were produced in Hollier's seven year existence.

KM

HOLLY (US) 1913–1915

Holly Motor Co., Mount Holly, New Jersey.

This company succeeded the Otto Gas Engine Co. of Philadelphia which had made the OTTO (called OTTOMOBILE in 1912). They had 4-cylinder engines, but when Holly brought out their own car it was a six, with a big 60hp engine and on a wheelbase of 130in (3299mm). It was initially made as a 5- or 7-seater tourer, but a roadster was added in 1914, when the tourers were listed as 5-, 6- or 7-seaters, all on the same wheelbase and at the same price of $2750. By 1915 the range was down to a single 5-seater tourer and 2-seater roadster.

NG

HOLLYWOOD PLASTIC PRODUCTS (US) c.1956

Hollywood Plastic Products, Hollywood, California.

This company sold fibreglass materials to the growing kit car industry in California in the 1950s. They also sold bodies, including the early BANGERT body shells and an attractive, rounded sports car model.

HP

HOLMAN (US) c.1994

Lee Holman, Charlotte, North Carolina.

This Ford GT-40 Mk II was a continuation of the original Mk II produced at Holman & Moody in the 1960s. Built by the son of Holman & Moody founder, John Holman, they carried consecutive serial numbers that followed the original cars. The chassis were built in England to original specifications and shipped to North Carolina where assembly took place. The engines were period-correct 7000cc Ford V8s. Price was an expensive $750,000 and few were sold.

HP

HOLMES (i) (US) 1906–1907

1906 Charles Holmes Machine Co., Cambridgeport, Massachusetts.
1906–1907 Holmes Motor Vehicle Co., Cambridgeport, Massachusetts.

This company offered 2- and 4-cylinder cars during its short life, both in air- or water-cooled versions. The 2-cylinder engines were horizontally-opposed, and powered 2-seater runabouts, while the fours had conventional vertical cylinders and tourer bodies. The friction transmission was variously described as a Reeves or of Holmes' own design, and it was claimed that the car could be started from the seat. The Holmes Motor Vehicle Co. was the marketing arm of the parent Machine Co.

NG

HOLMES (ii) (US) 1918–1923
Holmes Automobile Co., Canton, Ohio.
The Holmes stands apart from its contemporaries for two specific reasons: first, it was the second most popular air-cooled car in the United States, second only to FRANKLIN; and second, its unbelievable ugliness, due to its false front with herringbone slots. Arthur Holmes, formerly a vice president and chief engineer for the H. H. Franklin Co., introduced the car in 1918. The Holmes had a wheelbase of 126in (3198mm) and its own ohv 6-cylinder engine, offering cars priced from $2950 for the roadster to $4150 for the sedan. Although the company anticipated production of as many as 3000 annually, the actual production figures fell considerably lower than that and for its six year existence, approximately 700 cars per year left the Canton factory. Plans to introduce a 4-cylinder companion car in 1921 failed to materialise and the company went out of business in 1923.

KM

HOLROYD-SMITH; HOLCAR (GB) 1897–1905
M. Holroyd-Smith, Tooting, London.
Michael Holroyd-Smith was an inventor rather than a manufacturer, though he exhibited several cars at motor shows, and quoted a price for the 1903 Holcar. His first design, shown under his own name, had a rear-mounted 6/8hp V-twin engine, and an unusual frame which passed outside the rear wheels. In 1901 he showed another car, also with 6/8hp engine now mounted in the centre of the frame, cone-and-pulley transmission which was claimed to give any speed between 5 and 15mph (8 and 24km/h), and shaft final drive. The body was a 4-seater *dos-à-dos* and the horn was mounted on the steering tiller. Its solid tyres gave it a very old-fashioned appearance. The 1903 Holcar had a front-mounted 20hp V4 engine and shaft drive. It was exhibited at the Agricultural Hall Show in April 1903 when a price of £850 was quoted.

NG

HOLSMAN (US) 1903–1910
Holsman Automobile Co., Chicago, Illinois.
The Holsman was the ancestor of the high-wheeler, a breed of car peculiar to the United States and particularly to the Middle West. It had a horizontally-opposed 2-cylinder engine, initially of 5hp, increased to 7hp for 1904 and 10hp from 1905 to 1909. In 1910 the twin was rated at 12hp and there was also a 26hp 4-cylinder engine. On the first Holsman final drive was by 7/8in manila rope, but this slipped badly in wet weather, so in 1905 it was replaced by a chain braided with manila and steel wire, and later a straightforward chain. The wheels were of 44in diameter and always ran on solid tyres right up to the end of production. Steering was by vertical tiller, and the brakes acted directly on the solid tyres. The body was a simple 2-seater piano-box type, though a 4-seater surrey was added in 1905, and a closed coupé in 1909. The latter was popular with doctors who, with farmers, made up the greater part of Holsman customers. Total sales were 6348 cars, the best year being 1906 when 1473 were sold. The company went into receivership in 1910, and Henry Holsman set up a new company called the Independent Harvester Co. at Plano, Illinois, to make a Holsman look-alike. This lasted only a year.

NG

HOL-TAN (US) 1908
Hol-Tan Co., New York, New York.
This company was named for its partners, E.R. Hollander, G.P. and C.H. Tangeman. They were the earliest importers of Fiats to the United States, and when they lost this business due to Fiat setting up their own agency, they turned to an American product. This was the 25hp MOON which Hol-Tan brought to New York in chassis form and mounted bodies either of standard type or made by leading custom coachbuilders such as Demarest and Quinby. Tourers and roadsters were offered on two wheelbases, 110 (2792mm) and 121in (3071mm), but the venture lasted only a year. From 1909 Hol-Tan returned to selling other people's cars, notably Delaunay-Belleville and Lancia.

NG

1908 Holsman high-wheeler.
NATIONAL MOTOR MUSEUM

HOLTZER-CABOT (US) 1892–1895
Holtzer-Cabot Electric Co., Brookline, Massachusetts.
German-born Charles Holtzer and Bostonian George E. Cabot formed a company in 1875 to make electric equipment. Among their achievements was the first telephone exchange outside Boston, with 14 subscribers. In 1892 they were approached by paper manufacturer Fiske Warren to assemble an electric vehicle, the components of which Warren had bought in London. It was a 4-seater brake with a steering wheel and inclined column, probably the first examples of these features. The batteries and motor were placed under the front seat, but it was found that additional batteries were needed, so the rear seats were given up to this purpose.

In 1895 Fiske Warren ordered another brake from Holtzer-Cabot, this time with all-American components. It was larger, with seats for six or seven passengers, and had a top speed of 15mph (24km/h). Steering was by tiller, though the column was still inclined rather than vertical. In November 1895 Holtzer announced that he would make replicas of the Warren brake, but it is not known how many orders he received.

NG

HOLYOKE (US) 1899–1903
1899–1900 Holyoke Motor Works, Holyoke, Massachusetts.
1900–1903 Holyoke Automobile Co., Holyoke, Massachusetts.
Swiss-born Charles R. Greuter built an experimental car in 1898 and the following year set up the Holyoke Motor Works to make a 4-seater trap powered by a 7hp 2-cylinder engine. He announced that he would build ten cars per month, and on the strength of this a new company was floated in 1900. A few more large cars were built, the engines being unusual in having ohvs. In 1903 Holyoke was bought by the MATHESON Motor Car Co. who began building engines and transmissions at Holyoke, while assembling their cars at Grand Rapids, Michigan. In 1904 they moved the whole operation to Holyoke, only to move again to Wilkes-Barre, Pennsylvania in 1906. Greuter lasted with Matheson until 1908. His most important subsequent work was for STUTZ for whom he designed the Vertical Eight.

NG

1966 Honda S.800 sports car.
NATIONAL MOTOR MUSEUM

HOMER-LAUGHLIN (US) 1916
Homer-Laughlin Engineers Corp., Los Angeles, California.

Homer Laughlin Jr designed an advanced light car powered by a 1954cc V8 engine driving the front wheels via a friction transmission and chain final drive. Rear suspension was by a patented arrangement of twin cantilever springs, and the body was a 2-seater. A price of $1050 was quoted, but only one roadster was made. Two years later the company was selling an auxiliary transmission for Fords.

NG

HOMMELL (F) 1994 to date
Automobiles Michel Hommell, Lohéac.

Michel Hommell was the owner of the French magazine *Échappement* and his Berlinette was a personal conception of the sort of sports car missing from the market. It was presented in prototype form at the 1990 Paris Salon and proved so well received that the car was engineered for production, being presented at the 1994 Geneva Motor Show. This was a closed 2-seater coupé with a fibreglass body, a very stripped-out feel and a low weight of 950kg. It used a mid-mounted 152bhp Peugeot 2-litre engine in train with a 6-speed manual gearbox. The tubular steel chassis used all-independent suspension (front transverse arms, rear MacPherson struts) and ventilated disc brakes all round. A completely open-topped model without a windscreen was also presented under the name Barquette, which was finally productionised in 1998, at the same time as a revised version of the coupé model called the Berlinette RS. This had a more powerful 167bhp Citroën 16V engine and double headlamps.

CR

HONDA (J) 1962 to date
Honda Motor Co. Ltd, Tokyo.

The rise of the Honda Motor Co. is one of the greatest success stories of the postwar motor industry. Soichiro Honda saw his flourishing piston ring company completely destroyed during World War II, and had to build up a new business from scratch. In October 1946 he started with 12 workers and one machine tool in a bomb site shed 3.6 × 5.5m in size, making motor-assisted bicycles. By 1948 he had 34 workers, and ten years later was the first motorcycle maker to sell more than one million machines in a year. By 1962 Honda was the world's largest manufacturer of motorcycles. This position has been maintained, and by 1997 Honda had made 100 million 2-wheelers.

The first 4-wheeled Honda was a light truck powered by a 356cc twin-ohc 4-cylinder engine, which also powered the S360 sports car announced in the autumn of 1962. This was a remarkable little machine whose engine developed 33bhp at the very high speed of 9000rpm. On the early models, the rev counter read up to 14,000rpm. Transmission was by a 5-speed gearbox, very rare in the early 1960s, driving to a differential from which final drive was by chains. This was understandable from a motorcycle maker, but quite unique on a car. A 531cc engine (S500) was offered as an alternative, and in fact very few cars were made with the 356cc unit. Only 1363 S500s were built, and it was followed for 1964 by the 606cc S600 which was the first Honda car to be sold in Europe. By this time the gearbox had only four speeds, and the chain drive had given way to a conventional hypoid rear axle, though it seems that some Japanese market S600 and S800s had chain drive. A coupé was added to the convertible in the S600 range, and this was continued in the final evolution of the series, the 791cc S800. Europeans found it a curiosity rather than a serious sports car, for the high-speed engine (8000rpm on the S800) was rather fragile, and the gearbox had to be used a great deal. It did not offer serious competition to cars like the MG Midget or Triumph Spitfire.

The S800 was discontinued in 1970, after about 11,400 had been made (figures for other models were 1363 S500s and 13,034 S600s). Meanwhile Honda had introduced their first 4-seater saloon, the N360 with 354cc air-cooled vertical twin engine, 4-speed unsynchronised gearbox and front wheel drive. It was also offered with automatic transmission, surely the smallest car ever to be so equipped. The Japanese tax system favoured cars with capacities below 360cc, and the N360 had several rivals, by Daihatsu, Mitsubishi, Suzuki and others, but it was the only one to be exported in serious numbers. For export markets a 598cc engine was offered, and this was sold as the N600. It was made until 1974, being joined in 1971 by the egg-shaped Z coupé, with the same engine options, which was sold in only one colour, a bright orange.

Once Honda was seriously into the export business, they realised that they could not sell in large numbers cars like the S800 and N360/600 which had been developed for Japanese conditions. In May 1969 they brought out the 77 with a 1298cc 4-cylinder air-cooled engine driving the front wheels, and made in saloon or coupé form. It did not sell very well on the home market and was barely exported at all. It was dropped in 1972, but meanwhile Honda had launched the Civic, the car which was to establish their name worldwide and to be an enormous export success.

Smaller than the 77 in both engine and overall dimensions, the Civic was a competitor in the new supermini class which included the Fiat 127, Renault 5 and Volkswagen Golf. It had a 4-cylinder single-ohc engine of 1169cc mounted transversely and driving the front wheels, with an option of 4-speed all-synchromesh gearbox or Hondamatic transmission. Suspension was independent all round, and there were front disc brakes. At first only a 2-door coupé was offered, but a 3-door hatchback soon arrived, and later a 5-door hatchback on the longer wheelbase 1500. Capacity grew to 1238, 1335 and eventually 1488cc before the first generation Civic was discontinued in 1979. From 1974 it was offered with the CVCC (Compound Vortex Controlled Combustion) engine which Honda had developed in 1971 and which gave excellent fuel economy and low pollution. In particular it met the strict standards of the Muskie Clean Air Act in America at a time when US manufacturers were claiming that the standards were impossible to meet. The CVCC 3-valve engine (2 inlet, 1 exhaust) was made only for the US and Japanese markets. The Civic sold very well in America, where the Honda name

1968 Honda N.360 saloon.
NATIONAL MOTOR MUSEUM

was previously known only for motorcycles, and in Europe it was especially popular in Britain, Germany, Belgium and the Netherlands, and later in Scandinavia and Switzerland.

The success of the Civic spurred Honda to consider a larger car that would reach a new sector of the US market, as well as on their home ground. The answer was the Accord which bore family resemblance to the Civic, but was larger all round, with a 1599cc engine. Announced in 1976 as a 3-door hatchback, the Accord gained a 4-door saloon version in 1979, and was made until 1981 when it was succeeded by the second-generation version. All models had 5-speed gearboxes or Hondamatic transmission and all-independent coil suspension.

HONDA

HONDA, SOICHIRO (1906–1991)

Soichiro Honda was born on 17 November 1906, in Komyo, central Japan. His father was a blacksmith, and he was the eldest of nine children. Watching his father in the blacksmith's shop gave him a taste for mechanics, and his interest in cars was sparked when, at the age of eight he saw a Model T Ford, probably the first car he set eyes on. He was apprenticed to a Tokyo garage in the early 1920s, and although it was almost destroyed in the 1923 earthquake, he was asked to stay on. He gained valuable experience repairing fire-damaged cars, and in 1925 his employer encouraged him to build a racing car. This formidable machine was powered by an 8-litre Curtiss-Wright V8 aero engine mounted in a 1916 Mitchell chassis. Soichiro built most of the components, including carving the wooden wheel spokes. He had several successes with this car, and also with smaller cars powered by offset Ford engines for oval track racing. He gave up racing in 1936, after a serious accident.

In 1928 he returned to his home town and started his own garage. Like his Tokyo workshop, this was called Art Trading, with his former employer's approval. In the late 1930s he began to make piston rings, which sold well to the aircraft industry. The flourishing factory was completely destroyed by bombing in 1945, and Honda had to start again from scratch. He worked on the commercial extraction of salt from seawater and on designing a rotary weaving machine. He also acquired 500 Mikuni small army surplus generating engines, with a view to motorising bicycles. In October 1946 he started production of these, with 12 workers in a tiny shed on a bomb site in Hamamatsu. He soon used up his 500 engines, and began to build his own 50cc 2-stroke units, tuned to use raw pine resin fuel, all that was available at the time. In 1948 he was joined by a very valuable partner, Takeo Fujisawa (1907–89). He was particularly concerned with sales and dealer relations, while Honda concentrated on manufacture. The clip-on engine bicycle was developed on to the Model A in which the entire machine, engine and frame, were made in the factory, and from then on the company went from strength to strength. Exports began in 1957, and in 1958 the first Honda motorcycles went to the USA. Honda was the first company in the world to sell more than one million motorcycles in a year. (In the 1990s they were selling more than five million a year.) Soichiro was active in encouraging motorcycle racing from 1954 onwards. He thought that this not only encouraged sales but exercised the engineers' minds and raised morale at Honda factories. From 1959 onwards Honda began winning major international races such as the TT.

Soichiro personally tested all new models of car and motorcycle until he retired from the presidency in 1973. Like so many great car makers such as W.O. Bentley and Henry Royce, he could be very severe on shoddy workmanship. 'Soichiro Honda could be pretty thunderous when upset', remembered Nobuhiko Kawamoto, later president of the company from 1990 to 1998. In his younger days, at any rate, Honda wore colourful clothes and claimed that nonconformity was essential to an artist or innovator.

Soichiro Honda married Sachi in 1935; they had one son and two daughters.
NG

Further reading
Honda 50th Anniversary History, Honda Motor Co., 1998.

1973 Honda Z coupé.
NICK GEORGANO

1978 Honda Civic saloon.
NATIONAL MOTOR MUSEUM

1979 Honda Prelude coupé.
NATIONAL MOTOR MUSEUM

1990 Honda Legend coupé.
HONDA MOTOR CO.

In the late 1970s Honda began to expand their range, offering a Civic estate car and two derivations of the Accord, the Quintet 5-door hatchback and the Prelude coupé. Despite its many luxury features including a gas-strut tailgate, the Quintet was not a great success as it offered less space than the Accord saloon, and it was dropped in 1983. The Prelude sold well in America, where the personal car concept pioneered by the Ford Mustang had a great following, but elsewhere it was criticised for cramped accommodation and the absence of true sports car performance. However, both these matters were put right in the second generation Prelude which appeared in 1983. A new model for 1981 was the Ballade, a slightly enlarged Civic but made only as a notchback 4-door saloon.

International Links

In 1981 Honda opened an American factory at Sidney, Ohio, where Accords were initially made, and another international move involved links with British Leyland. An agreement was signed in 1979 whereby BL would market a Ballade-based saloon under the name Triumph Acclaim. The engines and transmissions were made by Honda, while the bodyshells were built at BL's Pressed Steel factory at Cowley, with final assembly taking place at the old Morris Motors factory, also at Cowley. The Acclaim was made from November 1980 to June 1984, when it was replaced by a new saloon based on the current Honda Ballade, and named the Rover 200. During its lifetime 133,000 Acclaims were made, more than Honda built of the Ballade in the same period. The Rover 200 was made in two models, the 213 which was pure Honda apart from the front end, and the 216 which used the Austin-Rover S-Series engine. They were continued until 1990, being joined in 1986 by the 800 executive saloon. This was developed alongside Honda's Legend with a great deal of shared technology, although the companies designed their own bodywork so that the cars looked quite different. The Legend was powered by a choice of 24-valve V6 engines, 2493cc 145bhp and 2675cc 165bhp; the larger of these powered the top of the range Rover 825i. In addition the Rover Group, as BL became in 1986, made the Legend at Cowley for the European market and Honda made the Rover for the Japanese market. This arrangement lasted until 1988. In 1989 Honda announced a joint manufacturing and engine supply agreement with Rover, in which a new plant at Swindon, Wiltshire, would make engines for Rover. This was extended to cover complete cars, and in October 1992 the first Accord left the production lines at Swindon. It was followed by the 5-door Civic in September 1994 and the Civic Aerodeck in 1998.

The Smaller Honda

Honda did not neglect the small car market, very important in Japan where cars with a sub-550cc (now sub-660cc) capacity have valuable tax and parking advantages. In 1985 came the Today, a low 3-door hatchback with an almost continuous line from windscreen and bonnet down to the front of the car. Originally powered by a 546cc 2-cylinder engine, this was replaced by a 12-valve 3-cylinder unit, also of 546cc, in 1988. In fuel-injected form it gave 44bhp, and was available with three transmissions, 4- or 5-speed manual or 3-speed automatic. In 1990 capacity was increased to 656cc, in line with the K-car regulations, and a 4×4 version was available. It was still made in 1999, joined by the Life which had a similar engine and transmission but a higher body in the style of the Daihatsu Move. Mainly a domestic market car, the Today was not sold in Britain or France, but was available in the Netherlands and the Channel Islands.

Another small Honda, though above the K-car class, was the City, sold in some markets as the Jazz. Introduced in 1981, it had a 67bhp 1232cc 4-cylinder engine and a very high body for its length, with sharply sloping windscreen and short bonnet. In 1983 came a 100bhp turbocharged version which became the most popular turbo car in Japan. A convertible was also available on the non-turbo model. Although the City sold well in Japan its unusual appearance was not always liked in export markets, and it was replaced for 1987 by a new model with more conventional styling closer to that of the Civic, and an all-new aluminium 16-valve 4-cylinder engine of 1237cc.

The Range Expands

As well as the Sidney, Ohio, manufacturing plant, Honda had a design studio in California, and it was there that the new and wider Civic range was styled. Launched in 1984, it was made in four almost unique body styles, sharing only a common front end to retain corporate identity. The four models were the 3-door hatchback, Ballade 4-door saloon, CRX 2-door coupé and Shuttle 4×4 high roof estate car. Engines varied from a 71bhp single ohc 1342cc in the basic hatchback through an 85bhp 1488cc in the Civic GT and Shuttle, to a 125bhp 1590cc unit in the CRX, which had a twin-cam head from 1987. The latter had four valves per cylinder, while the other engines used Honda's long-lived 3-valve layout. The 1488 and 1590cc engines were used in the Integra 5-door hatchback, while next up the range was the Accord, made as a 4-door saloon or, from 1989, as the Aerodeck 3-door sporting estate. The 1989 Inspire and Vigor versions of the Accord had 1996cc 5-cylinder engines. The Prelude coupé was powered by a 1958cc twin-cam 16-valve engine. The 1987 third generation Prelude was the world's first production car with 4-wheel steering. The original mechanical system was replaced by a sophisticated electronic system in 1991.

After the demise of the S800, Honda kept away from sports cars for some time, but in 1984 they began work on a new model which went into production in 1990. This was the NS-X (New Sports eXperimental), a mid-engined coupé to compete in the Ferrari and Porsche market, yet easier to drive than either, with a clutch and gearbox as simple as a Civic. It was powered by a 2972cc 24-valve V6 derived from that used in the Legend, but with improvements such as twin camshafts to each bank of cylinders. The 250bhp unit was mounted transversely behind the driver and drove through a 5-speed manual or 4-speed automatic transmission. Among its sophisticated features was a traction control system which reduced power to the rear wheels as soon as the brakes' anti-lock sensors detected variable slip. At the 1996 Detroit Show the NS-XT had a new semi-automatic transmission controlled from buttons on the steering wheel. A convertible was offered, and for 1996 engine capacity went up to 3179cc (294bhp) and the manual transmission came with six speeds. The NS-X was made in a dedicated small factory at Tochigi. By early 1998 sales were so slow that the cars were virtually made to order. Although a V12 development of the NS-X was planned, its immediate companion at Tochigi was a conventional front-engined 2-seater, the S2000 roadster, powered by a 2-litre 4-cylinder engine, and with 6-speed manual gearbox.

During the 1990s the regular Honda models, Civic, Accord, Prelude and Legend evolved, and there were numerous niche cars aimed at specific markets. June 1995 saw the ten millionth Civic, and in September came the sixth generation of this popular model, made as a 2-door coupé in the USA, 3- and 4-door models in Japan and a 5-door hatchback in England, as well as the Japanese-built CRX Targa top sports car. The Swindon-built Aerodeck estate appeared in 1997. Four 4-cylinder engines were available, from 1396 to 1595cc. The fifth generation Accord came in 1993 and the third generation Legend in 1996. The Accord saloon was made in England and the coupé and estate car in America, with four engines from 1850 to 2156cc, including a 1994cc turbo diesel. The coupé had a 2997cc V6 engine, of the same family as the Legend's, though smaller. The Legend had a 3474cc V6 and was available only as a 4-door saloon. The sixth generation Accord was released in two stages, and in different models according to nationality; the US and Japanese models came in September 1997, and the European in October 1998. This followed Honda's philosophy of catering for local tastes even with a mass-produced car, summed up by *The European*, 'Americans want cup holders and a cushy ride, Japanese demand satellite navigation systems and other sophisticated electronics, and Europeans want speed'. Honda no longer attempted to persuade buyers that the car it sold in Nebraska had much in common with the one it sold in Nagasaki or Nantes, though underneath the sheet metal they had much in common. Thus the American-built coupé used the same platform as the European saloon, and shared its wheelbase but had the same width as the American saloon.

Among more specialised models were the 1973cc CR-V 4×4 introduced in 1997, and its smaller sister, the 1590cc HR-V launched in October 1998, and Honda's entry in the MPV market, the 6- or 7-seater Shuttle with transverse 2253cc engine driving the front wheels. In America and Japan it was called the Odyssey, and there was a companion model called the Stepwgn, pronounced Stepwagon. In May 1991 came the Beat, a small 2-seater sports car with mid-mounted turbocharged 660cc 3-cylinder engine, made until 1995.

In 1996 Honda launched the EV Plus, an electric 3-door hatchback with a range of 125 miles per charge. Aimed at the Californian market, it was not for sale, but could be hired for about $30,000 for three years. Like the General Motors EV1, it did not find a very enthusiastic reception. More promising was the VV hybrid with a 995cc 3-cylinder lean-burn engine combined with a battery-fed electric motor in the flywheel that gave the engine a boost under hard acceleration. The batteries were recharged through regenerative braking. Shown at the Detroit Show in January 1999, it went into production at Tochigi

1993 Honda Civic VTi saloon.
NATIONAL MOTOR MUSEUM

1993 Honda NSX coupé.
NATIONAL MOTOR MUSEUM

1998 Honda Accord 2.3 VTEC saloon.
HONDA MOTOR CO.

1999 Honda HR-V 4x4 estate car.
HONDA MOTOR CO.

c.1973 Hongqi CA-770 limousine.
ERIK VAN INGEN SCHENAU

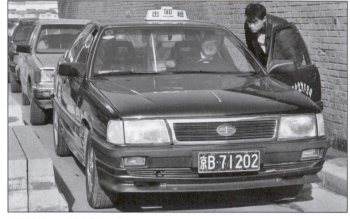

c.1994 Hongqi 2.2-litre saloon.
ERIK VAN INGEN SCHENAU

later in the year. Renamed the Insight, it reached European markets in the spring of 2000.

In 1998 Honda had 95 production facilities throughout the world. Important developments included a greatly expanded Swindon plant to raise annual output from 150,000 to 250,000 cars, a joint venture with the Dongfeng Motor Corp. in China to make 30,000 Accords in 1999, and new plants in Turkey, India and Brazil. The South African plant, owned by Daimler-Chrysler SA, built European-type Civics. Brazilian-built Civics were designed to run on alcohol fuel. The American factories, now at Marysville and East Liberty, Ohio, (also in Canada at Alliston, Ontario) made 694,760 cars in 1998, with hoped-for expansion to 1.13 million by 2003. A third US factory, at Lincoln, Alabama, was announced in the summer of 1999, to concentrate on Sports Utility Vehicles and engines. In 1986 the American Honda Motor Co. created a new brand-name, Acura, for the more upmarket models such as the Legend and NS-X. This was to distance them from the mid-market cars like the Civic, in the same way that Nissan created Infiniti and Toyota, Lexus. The Isuzu Trooper 5-door 4×4 estate was also sold under the Acura badge as the SLX.

NG

HONGQI (CHI) 1958 to date
First Auto Works, Changchun City, Jilin Province.
China's most important motor car range of the 20th century was the Hongqi ('Red Flag') series. It was not China's first motor car, as this was the DONGFENG, built by the First Auto Works. But soon after the introduction of the Dongfeng CA 71, a 4-door, 5-seater prestige limousine appeared, named Hongqi CA 72IE. In the same year (1958) a convertible version was introduced. Both vehicles were powered by V8 engines and they could do 118mph (180km/h). Doors and windows were all electrically controlled. The dashboard was made of scented mahogany, which gave the car, together with a Chinese rug on its floor, a special Chinese flavour. Several prototypes appeared between 1960 and 1964.

The first serial batch of 30 vehicles of the Hongqi CA 72 appeared in 1959. One made its appearance in Europe when it was shown at the Leipziger Messe in

1960. This car had a 2-speed hydraulic transmission and a 200hp V8 engine. In 1966, with the first batch of 20 units, the most produced Hongqi limousine version, the Hongqi CA 770 started its career. It was a 7- to 8-seater, 230in (5830mm) long. The wheelbase was 107in (2730mm). The 5650cc V8 engine, taking 20 litres per 100km, powered the vehicle with 220bhp (164 kWh). In 1983 production was stopped, following a State Council circular saying the car used too much fuel and supported by a formal decision made by the Party Central Committee in the same year. But in 1989 the car was back on the road: the State asked for production to be resumed that year. By 1991 the basic CA 770 version was still in the programme, about 1520 units were made in total by then. Other versions were known: CA 771 (1967), a smaller 4-door, 6-seater version (two rows of seats), length 210in (5330mm); CA 772 T (1972), a safety protected limousine; CA 773 (1968), a 16in (400mm) shorter type (length 217in/5500mm); CA 774 (1972), with two rows of seats, a smaller rectangular type; CA 770 JG, a convertible of 1970; CA 774-5E (1979) with modernised body; a CA 770 W ambulance (station wagon); CA 770 TJ (1984), a state-limousine cabrio-coach version in use by Deng Xiaoping during the 35 years' celebration of the People's Republic; CA 770 D (1988) model, also named CA 775, was a bit longer (238in/6060mm) and had a modernised square grill, with rectangular headlights. The final version of the CA 770 limousine was the CA 7560 LH (1992), even longer (243in/6180mm) than the original one, the vehicle finally vanished in 1998.

Since the mid–1980s First Auto Works has looked for foreign partners. In 1984 two smaller Hongqi prototypes were shown: the CA 750 and CA 760. Both were based upon a Dodge 600 design, the CA 750 with two rows of seats and a 2163cc 4-cylinder engine and the CA 760 with three rows of seats and a 3244cc 6-cylinder engine. These were a result of a short flirtation with Chrysler USA. First Auto Works also bought in this period a complete Chrysler engine line; the line was the basis for the Chinese CA 488 engines assembled in the CA 7220 series.

The next partner was Mercedes-Benz, but this project comprised local assembly (1987–88) of completely knocked-down cars, the Types 200 and 230E LWB of the W123 series. 818 units were made.

The third and most important partner was the Volkswagen-Audi A.G. Co-operation with Audi started in 1988. The Audi 100 (C3 series) assembly was transferred from Shanghai-Volkswagen to First Auto Works' Hongqi factory in Changchun. The basic type used a 4-cylinder (1781cc) engine, the 100 2.2 E and the 200 a 5-cylinder (2226cc) engine. The C3 type was followed in 1993 by the Audi 100 C4V6, but then the complete Audi production moved again, this time to the new First Auto Works-Volkswagen factory. There the Audi production was resumed with the restyled Audi 200, again a C3 type. Two versions were made: a 1.8T and a 2.4 model. In 1999 it was replaced by the Chinese equivalent of the Audi A6 (a C5 type), which was a little longer (13.5in/90mm) than the German version. In 1994 the Audi V8 Lang (4.2-litre) was also assembled in Changchun for a short period.

The Audi C3 was the basis of a smaller Hongqi type. The first variant was seen in Beijing in 1989, the CA 7225 LH long wheelbase version made with help from Lorenz and Rankl, body builders from Germany. But it lasted till 1993 before a whole range of new 'Small' Hongqi cars was introduced. First came three models: the CA 7221 saloon, CA 1021 U3 pick-up, and CA 7221 L LWB type, all with 2.2-litre CA488 engine. In the nineties a complete range of different versions was developed. The (Chrysler) engines ranged from 1779cc (CA 7180), 1996cc (CA 7200), 2194cc (CA 7220, the standard model), 2.4-litre (CA 7240), up to 2.6-litre (CA 7260). There were about six different lengths. There was a great variety in accessories. Even open versions, short wheelbase CA 7220 EA2 and long wheelbase CA 7220 EL2A2 were developed. The yearly production was about 20,000 units. An interesting version was the CA 7300 with a Japanese Nissan VG30S V6 engine, developing 141bhp.

First Auto Works started a joint venture with Volkswagen in 1990. Smaller cars were built here. This works' main product was the FAW-VW Jetta CL, for a short period accompanied by the City-Golf (a rebadged Seat Cordoba). In 1997 the Jetta was face-lifted. Independently, F.A.W. developed in 1993 a small 5-seater named Hongqi CA 7080. The 462 engine (792cc) developed 35bhp/5500rpm. After the introduction of the prototype, nothing more was heard of this 'people's car'. Another small prototype was seen in 1997, a Jetta equipped with the 2194cc engine. To house the engine, the nose was lengthened. It was marketed as the FAW 2.2.

In 1998 foreign partner number four showed up: Ford of USA. A new 'Big' Hongqi, named CA 7460, based upon a Lincoln, rolled off the production line. It was equipped with electronic fuel injection 4.7-litre V8 engine, a luxurious interior, electronic 4-speed transmission, traction control system, automatic cruise control and a monitoring system, as well as air conditioning with automatic temperature control.

EVIS

HONGYUZHUAN (CHI) 1958–1959

Tianjin University, Tianjin Municipality.

Two prototype passenger cars named Hongyuzhuan ('Red and Expert') were developed by the Tianjin University. Both cars were of the same size, one a saloon and the other a convertible. The saloon was a clear twin of the first Heping motor car.

EVIS

HOOD (US) 1899–1901

Simplex Motor Vehicle Co., Danvers, Massachusetts.

Ralph Otho Hood built a steam car in 1899, and the following year formed the Simplex Motor Vehicle Co. to produce it. Sometimes known as the Simplex or the Electronomic, it looked like many other steamers externally, but the engine was unusual in having four cylinders cast *en bloc* with the steam chest. The inlet valves were electro-magnetically operated by three small batteries. A simple 2-seater body was provided and the price was $1000, quite expensive compared with a Locomobile at $750. Only two steamers were made, both of which survive today in the hands of the Hood family. In 1908 Ralph Hood started to build a 4-cylinder tourer; it was not completed until 1910 and was never offered for sale.

NG

HOOSIER SCOUT (US) 1914

Hoosier Cyclecar Co., Indianapolis, Indiana.

Named after the nickname for the State of Indiana, the Hoosier Scout was a cyclecar with striking streamlined body culminating in a pointed tail. It was based on that of the Blitzen Benz racing car. The passengers sat in tandem, and the car was powered by a 9/13hp Spacke V-twin engine, with transmission by friction disc and final drive by belts. It was reasonably priced at $375.

NG

HOOVER (US) 1913–1914

H.H. Hoover, St Louis, Missouri.

Hoover's cyclecar was exceptionally light with a 5hp single-cylinder air-cooled engine, tandem seating, chain drive and an underslung chassis. He planned to sell it for $375, but could not raise enough money to form a company, let alone find a factory.

NG

HOPE see WHISPER

HOPESTAR (J) 1960–1962

Hope Jidosha Co., Tokyo.

The Hope company, founded in 1952, mainly produced 3-wheeled delivery wagons of the type so popular in Japan during the 1950s. In 1960 it launched production of the Unicar, a very small estate car conforming to Japanese microcar size laws. It was powered by a 356cc 2-cylinder engine developing 17bhp but was very short-lived, despite the introduction of a 4×4 version.

CR

HO-PING see HE-PING

HOPPENSTAND (US) 1949–1950

Hoppenstand Motors Inc., Greenville, Pennsylvania.

This small economy car had a 2-cylinder engine with a hydraulic transmission. It was sold in coupé, runabout and convertible forms. Top speed was 50mph (80km/h).

HP

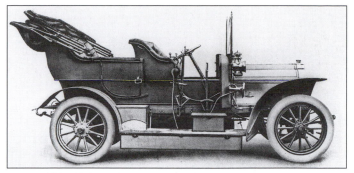

1907 Horbick 15/20hp tourer.
NATIONAL MOTOR MUSEUM

1904 Horch 16/20PS tonneau.
NICK BALDWIN

HORBICK (GB) 1902–1909

Horsfall & Bickham Ltd, Pendleton, Manchester.

This company was a large-scale maker of textile machinery, and cars were never more than a sideline. Managing director H. Worthington and his brother-in-law George Kennedy built a prototype in 1900, powered by a 6hp M.M.C. engine, and two years later put on the market a similar light car. Although the engine was a 6hp M.M.C. *The Motor Car Journal* observed '…otherwise the makers have mostly fallen back on their own resources'. It had a 3-speed gearbox, shaft drive and wheel steering, while the body was a 4-seater tonneau. For 1903 the Horbick had a 12hp 2-cylinder Forman engine, and for 1904 they went shopping to Johnston, Hurley & Martin for a 2-cylinder power unit for the Horbick Minor. In 1905 they changed engine suppliers again, turning to White & Poppe which powered some of their best-known cars. These included the Minor, now with a 10/12hp 3-cylinder engine, the Major with 4-cylinder 15/20hp engine and the 18/24hp six of 1907. Their largest six, the 45/60hp of 1907 had an engine made by Horsfall & Bickham themselves. Some of these large Horbicks were reputedly sold to Indian potentates including the Nizam of Hyderabad.

Horbick also made taxicabs and it was an order for 2000 of these for London which, ironically, brought about the end of car making. Faced with the choice of expanding cars to the detriment of textile machinery, the directors decided to stick to the business they knew best. They declined the taxi order 'with thanks' and closed the car division. They remained in the textile business at least into the mid–1950s.

NG

HORCH (D) 1900–1939

1900–1902 A. Horch & Co., Cologne-Ehrenfeld.
1902–1904 A. Horch & Co., Reichenbach/Vogtland.
1904–1939 A. Horch & Co., Motorwagenwerke AG, Zwickau.

August Horch (1868–1951) began his working life in his father's blacksmith's workshop, followed by a spell with a railway company building a new line from

1906 Horch 11/22PS tourer, winner of the Herkomer Trophy.
Dr Rudolf Stöss at the wheel.
NATIONAL MOTOR MUSEUM

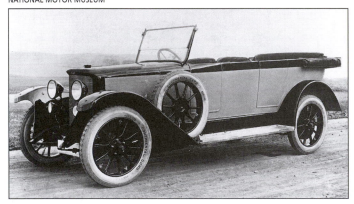

1923 Horch 10/35PS tourer, by Voll & Ruhrbeck.
HALWART SCHRADER

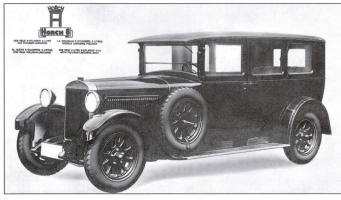

1927 Horch Typ 303 12/60PS saloon.
NATIONAL MOTOR MUSEUM

Serbia to Bulgaria, but he gained his experience of the motor industry as manager of the Benz factory at Mannheim, from 1896 to 1899. In the spring of 1899 he left Benz to form his own company, setting up in a small workshop at Ehrenfeld near Cologne. His first car was ready the following year, a 4-seater with front-mounted horizontal 2-cylinder engine, belt-drive to a 2-speed constant-mesh gearbox which was in unit with the rear axle. It was heavy and expensive to make, but his next design was a great improvement with a 10/12PS vertical 2-cylinder engine, sliding gearbox and shaft-drive. It had a light 2-seater body and wire wheels. Although the prototypes were made at Cologne, Horch did not start production until he moved to a former spinning mill at Reichenbach in Saxony. A few cars were made there, after which Horch made his second, and final, move to Zwickau, where the company was to remain until car production ended, long after August had left. The 10/12PS was joined by a 4-cylinder of 16/20PS, and output soon reached 50-60 cars per year. The

10/12PS was continued until 1907, but the 16/20PS was replaced in 1904 by a larger four, the 2385cc 18/22PS with overhead inlet and side exhaust valves, followed in 1905 by a 5800cc 23/40PS with the same valve layout. One of the 18/22PS cars was entered in the 1906 Herkomer Tour, a long-distance (500 mile/800km) trial with hill climbs and speed events as well as the road section. The Horch, driven by Zwickau lawyer Dr Rudolph Stoss, won the event against strong opposition from more powerful and expensive cars by Benz and Mercedes.

Encouraged by this success, Horch prepared a team of cars for the 1908 Prince Henry Trial. They had 2785cc 11/22PS engines, and striking bodies styled by Horch and built by Kathe of Halle. The front and rear seat passengers sat in separate compartments with cowled bodywork between them, as in the American dual-cowl phaetons fashionable 20 years later. The sketchy wings were horizontal and resembled surf boards. Horch finished seventh and Stoss eighth. The 8-litre cars entered in the 1907 Kaiserpreis did not shine either, and this led Horch's directors to question the value of entering cars in competitions. Horch left the company he had founded and promptly started another one, also in Zwickau. He was prevented from using his own name so he chose the Latin word, Audi, which has the same meaning, 'hark' or 'listen' as the German Horch. His new company flourished alongside the old one, and eventually both firms became part of the Auto Union group. The Audi name was dropped after 1939, but revived in 1965 to become one of the most respected among quality cars today. The post of chief designer at Horch went to Georg Paulmann.

Most Horchs of the 1909–1914 era were touring cars ranging from the 1588cc 6/18PS to the 6395cc 25/60PS. They had L-head side-valve engines in place of August Horch's overhead inlet layout. In 1914 there was a very large 33/80PS model, with a capacity of 8494cc, of which only 46 were made. Sleeve-valve engines of Knight design were considered in a range of three models, 10/28, 13/36 and 19/50PS, but the World War I put an end to the project. Just before the war a new small car, the 1300cc 5/14PS Pony was announced, but never went into production. Total Horch production up to the war was about 3500.

During the war Horch made Argus aero engines, and in 1920 Argus owner Dr Moritz Strauss became the majority shareholder in Horch. Swiss-born Arnold Zoller, later to achieve fame with his superchargers, moved from Argus to Horch and designed three new 4-cylinder side-valve engines, the 2612cc 10/35PS, 3560cc 14/40PS and 4710cc 18/50PS. These did not go into production straightaway, as several prewar designs were revived up to 1922. Zoller also designed two single-ohc engines, a four and a six, but these did not see production, although the four powered a racing car which competed in the first event at Berlin's AVUS track.

In 1923 Paul Daimler, son of pioneer Gottlieb, left the Daimler Motoren Gesellschaft to join Horch. He redesigned Zoller's 10/35PS with a shaft-driven ohc, increasing output from 35 to 50bhp. He also lengthened the wheelbase and added 4-wheel brakes. The typical Germanic pointed radiator, worn by Horchs since 1914, gave way to a flat shape not unlike a Fiat 503. In 1926 Daimler made his most important contribution to Horch in the shape of a twin-ohc straight-8 engine which, over the next five years, was made in three sizes, 3132cc (12/60PS), 3378cc (13/65PS) and 3950cc (16/80PS). The camshafts were driven by a vertical shaft which also actuated the fan, distributor, oil and water pumps. The stroke remained the same at 118mm, but the bore was gradually increased from 65 to 67.5 and 73mm. The twin-ohc layout was very rare at the time, being confined mostly to racing and sports cars such as the Grand Prix Alfa Romeo and Fiat, or 3-litre Sunbeam. The Horch was the first touring twin-ohc straight-8, and it is all the more remarkable that they sold nearly 6800 between 1926 and 1931. Among their other features were servo-assisted four-wheel brakes and semaphore-type direction indicators, both firsts for the German motor industry. The engines were made in the Argus factory in Berlin, and the rest of the cars at Zwickau. The success of these straight-8s enabled Horch to increase their workforce from 1500 to 2500, and daily output to rise from eight to sixteen cars.

Paul Daimler left Horch in 1929, but his designs were continued for two years. He was replaced by Fritz Fiedler, who came from Stoewer, and Hans Schleicher who had been in charge of BMW's motorcycle sport division. They developed a new range of straight-8s, this time with single ohcs, made in four sizes, 3009, 4014, 4517 and 4944cc. Bodies were lowered and fronted by a slightly sloping radiator. Though very elegant, these Horchs were deliberately priced below the

1938 Horch Typ 855 roadster, by Erdmann & Rossi.
NATIONAL MOTOR MUSEUM

equivalent Mercedes-Benz straight-8s and sold in larger numbers, about 2200 compared with 891 of the big straight-8s from Stuttgart. ZF-Aphon 4-speed synchromesh gearboxes were available on the larger models. Suspension was semi-elliptic up to 1935, then independent by transverse leaf springs, with all-round independent suspension on the 850 and subsequent series from 1936 onwards. They were heavy cars, and the 2600kg weight of the 853 cabriolet limited speed to 84mph (135km/h). An extra 6mph (10km/h) was available from the 855 2-seater roadster, but this was much more expensive at RM22,000 compared with RM14,900 for the 4-seater cabriolet. It is not surprising that only seven 855s were made, against 1027 of the 853/853A.

The other Horchs of the 1930s had vee-engines, a short-lived V12 and a series of V8s. The V12 was launched at the 1931 Paris Salon and had a 6021cc side-valve engine developing 120bhp. Two wheelbases were available, 136in (3450mm) for 2- or 4-door cabriolets and 147.6in (3750mm) for the Pullman-Limousine and Pullman-Cabriolet. Only 80 were made in three seasons. The V8s were also side-valve designs, and came in several engine sizes beginning with the 2984cc Typ 830 of 1933/34 and finishing with the 3823cc Typ 930V of 1938/40. Like the straight-8s they gained all-round independent suspension in 1936, and the Typ 930s had 5-speed gearboxes of which top was an overdrive. Styling was on the same lines as the straight-8s, though the engine was mounted further forwards, giving a less classic appearance. At the 1939 Berlin Show appeared a 930 with aerodynamic saloon body for autobahn cruising, which might have gone into production had not the war intervened. Horch had become part of the Auto Union combine in 1932, and the V8s were designed to fill the gap between the 6-cylinder Audi and the straight-8s. They did this very well; of a total Horch production in the 1930s of about 18,000 cars, more than 11,700 were V8s. The 3.8-litre V8 engine was also used in a 4×4 Army command car, of which Horch made 4200 up to 1941. Later examples of these command cars were made by Ford, with their own V8 engines.

After the war the Zwickau factory was in East German territory and car production was not resumed, though six or seven Typ 930 V8s were built from existing parts for officers of the Soviet Army. The factory was used exclusively for truck production until 1956 when a saloon with 2407cc 6-cylinder engine went into production under the name Sachsenring. The first examples wore the old crowned H badge carried by prewar Horchs. Only 1382 of these cars were made. The former Auto Union group is now owned by Volkswagen, and there have been rumours that the Horch name might be revived for a luxury VW. It would not be out of place since Mercedes-Benz are reviving the name of Maybach, one of Horch's rivals between the wars.

NG

Further Reading
Horch – Prestige und Perfektion, Peter Kirchberg, Schrader Verlag, 1994.
'Horch, the August Motor Car', Hans-Otto Neubauer,
Automobile Quarterly, Vol.33, No.2.

1939 Horch Typ 930 saloon.
NATIONAL MOTOR MUSEUM

1988 Horlacher electric coupé.
NICK GEORGANO

HORLACHER (CH) 1988 to date
Horlacher AG, Basle.

This company specialised in light electric vehicles, the first of which was a tandem-seated 3-wheeled coupé with a range of 75 miles per charge and a top speed of 50mph. It is still in regular use by a hotel in Interlaken, taking its charge from solar panels on the hotel's roof. Later Horlachers have included several 4-wheelers, including a coupé, a pickup used at a US Air Force base, and the Taxi-Kurier for four passengers plus the driver and an overall length of 90in (2284mm).

NG

1906 Horley 9hp 2-seater.
NICK BALDWIN

1921 Horstman kick-starter.
NATIONAL MOTOR MUSEUM

1921 Horstman 10.5hp tourer.
NATIONAL MOTOR MUSEUM

HORLEY (GB) 1904–1909

Horley Motor & Engineering Co., Horley, Surrey.

The first car made by this small engineering works was a light shaft-driven 2-seater powered by an 8hp single-cylinder M.M.C. engine, and priced at 100 guineas (£105). For some reason this car was also called the No Name. By 1906 the engine was quoted as a 9hp, though it may have been the same unit. It gave way after 1907 to an 8½hp 2-cylinder White & Poppe. Aster engines were also used in 1908, when light vans were listed as well as cars. Horley were agents for Lacoste et Battmann chassis components, and doubtless used many of these in their cars.

NG

HORMIGUER (E) 1904

Victoriano Alvargonzalez, Gijon, Asturias.

This was a 12hp car with a Delahaye marine engine, the first car ever built in Asturias.

VCM

HORNET (i) (GB) 1905–1907

Horner & Sons, London.

The Hornet was a light car powered by a 9hp 2-cylinder engine under the seat, driving through an epicyclic gearbox and single chain to the rear axle. It had a dummy bonnet and 2-seater body. An 18hp 4-cylinder was also listed. The car is said to have been made for Horner & Sons by the Lenox Autocar Co., though this company cannot be traced as a British manufacturer. In 1908 a second-hand Hornet with 10hp 2-cylinder Stevens engine and Vincent body was advertised.

NG

HORNET (ii) see AMERICAN MOTORS

HORNSTED see MOLL

HORSE SHOE (F) c.1908

This name was given to a French car sold in England around 1908. Two models were listed, an 8hp single-cylinder 2-seater, and a 12hp 2-cylinder 4-seater. Both had shaft drive, and carried a horse shoe surround to the radiator, complete with nails.

NG

HORSTMAN(N) (GB) 1914–1929

Horstman(n) Cars Ltd, Bath, Somerset.

The Horstmann Gear Co. was founded in 1904 by Sidney Horstmann (1881–1962) whose father Gustav was a German immigrant who had set up a clock making business in Bath in 1854. In 1912 Sidney began work on a light car which went into production two years later in a former cinema and skating rink. It had a 995cc 4-cylinder engine of Horstmann's own design and manufacture, though some parts were supplied by Listers of Dursley. Among its unusual features were a detachable head and horizontal ohvs working by vertical rockers operated positively by the camshaft. There were no chassis members forward of the flywheel; the crankcase was extended to form the front of the frame and an undershield. The 3-speed gearbox was housed in the rear axle. The engine was started by a pedal-actuated Archimedes screw on the propeller shaft. A small number of 2-seaters were sold before the war intervened. During the conflict Horstmann made precision equipment, particularly screw thread gauges which were very important in munitions manufacture. For his efforts Sidney Horstmann was awarded the MBE.

Some time during the war he anglicised his surname to Horstman, and when cars appeared in 1919 they, too, had lost their second 'n'. The prewar design was revived briefly, but most cars were fitted with a 1498cc Coventry Simplex engine, though sports and racing models used a 1496cc Anzani. According to Fletcher's *Motor Car Index*, Anzani engines were standardised from 1923, though a 1246cc Coventry Climax four was also listed up to 1929. A saloon was listed in 1921, but most Horstmans had open bodies, 2- or 4- seaters, and there was a rakish Super Sports model with polished aluminium body, external exhaust pipe and pointed tail. Racing models competed at Brooklands, one finishing fifth in the 1923 200 Mile Race, and Horstman also experimented with supercharging. Two British 'firsts' attributed to the make are Lockheed hydraulic 4-wheel brakes in late 1924, and cellulose spray painting in 1925. The hydraulic brake claim might be disputed by Triumph enthusiasts, although both they and Horstman exhibited them at the 1924 Olympia Show.

The cars sold well at the start of the 1920s, but by 1924 there were serious financial problems; the original company was wound up and a new one, Horstman Ltd, was formed with a handful of former employees who did not mind a rather erratic pay packet. Production to the end of 1924 has been estimated as high as 500, but after that very much fewer were made, though the make was listed up to 1929. A 2-door saloon called the Pulteney, powered by the Coventry-Climax engine, was announced in March 1928, and later in the year a special car called the Silver Car was built, with a saloon body finished in aluminium cellulose, and with coil springs all round. It was driven for 250,000 miles, but had no successors.

After car production ended, Sidney Horstman made camshafts, gears and gauges, and curious sidelines such as electric hair clippers. The company passed into the hands of Simms Motor & Electronic Corp. and then to Lucas, still making components under the name Horstman Camshafts Ltd. The parent company, Horstman Gears Ltd, also survives, both firms still in Bath.

NG

HOSKINS (AUS/US) 1919
G.J. Hoskins, Burwood, New South Wales.

Following his retirement from Hoskins Iron & Steel, prominent engineer and industrialist George John Hoskins, applied himself to his long-cherished ideal of driving cars from the front. Aware that the cross-type Hooke's joint was deficient in the steering application, he invented an early type of constant velocity joint, patented in 1915 as the 'co-ordinated spherical radial gear'. A 1912 Standard 15hp car was modified to accept a front-drive axle, with much testing and modification being carried out until 1919, when Hoskins went to the United States, and where a car was specially built in Los Angeles using a 6-cylinder Beaver engine. It was driven on the Lincoln Highway to the East, where attempts were made to interest the industry in producing it. No such interest was forthcoming, and the car was then taken to England where a similar negative response was encountered. Following the failure of Hoskins' health, the project lapsed.

MG

HOSTACO (NL) 1955–1957
N.V. Alweco, Veghel.

The Hostaco Bambino was a licence-built version of the aluminium-bodied FULDAMOBIL microcar, powered by a 200cc Ilo 9bhp engine and similar in all major respects to the German car. A novelty unique to the Dutch market was the Bambino Sport, a convertible version of the Fuldamobil, with no doors and a fibreglass body.

CR

HOTCHKISS (F) 1903–1955
1903–1954 S.A. des Anciens Établissements Hotchkiss et Cie, Saint-Denis.
1954–1955 S.A. Hotchkiss-Delahaye, Saint-Denis.

The name came from an American family of English extraction, and the French connection was made when Benjamin Berkeley Hotchkiss (1826–1885) set up an arms factory at Vivierz in the Aveyron at the invitation of Louis Bonaparte Napoleon III in 1867.

With plants in New England and the New York Arsenal, Hotchkiss had been a major supplier of arms and munitions to the Union Army in the Civil War. He patented the Hotchkiss revolving cannon in 1872 and set up a factory at the Route de Gonesse, Saint-Denis, in 1875. He died suddenly on 14 February 1885, and the company was reorganised by his business partners as Favarger, Koerner, Latouche & Cie, Ancienne Maison Hotchkiss & Cie.

In 1887 it was recapitalised by British investors, becoming S.A. des Anciens Établissements Hotchkiss et Cie, Saint-Denis, a subsidiary of the newly formed Hotchkiss Ordnance Co. Ltd of London.

Due to its experience in the treatment of special steels, high-precision methods and machinery, and skilled machinists, it was inevitable that the burgeoning auto industry should come to Hotchkiss, and the Saint-Denis factory accepted orders for crankshafts, pistons, con-rods, gears and valves from customers whose ranks included Panhard & Levassor, De Dion-Bouton, CGV, De Dietrich, and others. By 1903 Hotchkiss was also making complete engines for Clayette Fils.

About two years earlier, John James Mann of Mann & Overton, London, had begun enticing Laurence Vincent Benet, managing director of Hotchkiss et Cie, into building complete cars, offering to buy their total production. Thus the Hotchkiss car came into being, but Mann was allocated about one-third of the output, while two-thirds went to Henri Fournier (1871–1919) and his Paris-based sales organisation.

Benet purchased a 40hp 1902 Mercedes Simplex for his engineers to examine. The engine of the 1904 Hotchkiss Type C was a close copy, except for the ubiquitous use of ball bearings rather than plain ones. This car was mainly

c.1912 Hotchkiss tourer.
NICK BALDWIN

1924 Hotchkiss AM2 all-weather tourer.
NICK GEORGANO

c.1927 Hotchkiss AM2 saloon.
NICK BALDWIN

designed by weapons engineers, led by the young son of Henri Mercie, tireless inventor of mechanical devices, who had been with B.B. Hotchkiss since the Vivierz days.

Benet then succeeded in luring Georges Terrasse away from Mors to design a full range of Hotchkiss cars. Under him were also Maurice Sainturat, Robert Delvoye, and the young Henry M. Ainsworth, nephew of J.J. Mann. In 1904 Benet became chairman and Charles Duplomb was to serve as managing director for the next five years.

1930 Hotchkiss AM80 coupé.
BRYAN K. GOODMAN

Type D was a derivative of Type C, but in 1905 came Type F, a 4728cc 4-cylinder 17CV model, followed by the J and JJ in 1906, with the same engine enlarged to 4986cc. The L, M, O, R, and T went into production in 1907, replacing all earlier models. L and O were six-cylinder, 30 and 35CV respectively, continuing the T-head and an all ball bearing tradition. The T was the smallest, with a 3119cc 16CV four, but it was not a big seller, as only 100 were built in its best year, 1908.

Types U and V of 1908 were 4- and 6-cylinder T-head versions of the same design, 6333 and 9499cc respectively, but marked the end of the ball bearing era and the adoption of counterweighted crankshafts running in plain bearings. The cost-conscious Ainsworth was gaining influence in the drawing office, being named chief engineer in 1910, as Terrasse was moved over on the production side.

For the 30CV Type X and subsequent engines, L-heads were adopted. With the announcement of the 12CV 2212cc 4-cylinder Type Z in 1910, Hotchkiss took a step downmarket, pricing it exactly opposite the 15CV chassis from Peugeot and Panhard. The 30CV Type AC.6 of 1912, however, was a rival for De Dietrich, Delaunay-Belleville, and Rochet-Schneider.

In 1911 the Hotchkiss Ordnance Co. was merged into Hotchkiss et Cie, and for the first time, Hotchkiss shares were traded on the Bourse in Paris. In August 1914, Ainsworth, a British officer, reported for duty, but after about six months at the Front, he was detached to set up a Hotchkiss factory for producing machine guns in Coventry. The Saint-Denis plant was, for the most part, retooled for war material production, and a vast tract of land was acquired for plant construction at La Plaine Saint-Denis, fronting on boulevard Ornano. In 1920, the arms department was moved out of Saint-Denis and installed in the former Clerget-Blin factory at Levallois-Perret.

The Coventry plant, now without military orders, was converted to engine production, some of own origin, others made under licence from Continental Motors in Detroit, and supplied power units to Morris, BSA, Gilchrist, and Autocrat.

Throughout, Laurence V. Benet led the French company, with the title of vice-president. In 1922, H.E. Boyer, former director of the Crédit Commercial de France, took over the presidency from F. Manant.

Car production resumed at Saint-Denis in 1919 with a range of four prewar models (AF, AD, AD.6, and AG). The following year the AF was replaced by the 3969cc 4-cylinder 20CV Type AH, designed mainly by Robert Delvoye. Maurice Sainturat, who had spent the war years designing aircraft engines for Delaunay-Belleville, returned to Hotchkiss and was briefed to create a luxury car. That resulted in the superbly advanced AK, which was abandoned after two prototype chassis had been built. Among its outstanding features were 4-wheel servo brakes, deep-section X-braced frame, and a 6-cylinder 6597cc 32CV engine with single-ohc.

After finishing the AL (20CV 3969cc with pushrod-operated ohvs), produced from 1922 to 1924, Sainturat left Hotchkiss for Delage.

The arrival of the AM in 1923 signalled the institution of a one-model policy at Hotchkiss. This car had been designed in Coventry by H.M. Ainsworth and A.H. Wilde. After selling Hotchkiss's Coventry plant to Morris, Ainsworth returned to Saint-Denis in April 1923, and was attached to L.V. Benet's office. Wilde joined him at the end of the year, and in 1925, with Ainsworth named general manager of the car division, Wilde became chief engineer, accompanied by H.E. Taylor as works director.

In 1926 the plant construction in boulevard Ornano was completed and engine production was transferred there from Route de Gonesse. At the same time, Hotchkiss bought a stamping plant at Clichy and began making its own bodies at Saint-Denis. The AM was a car in the tradition of the low end of the prewar range, with influence from Continental in the engine (one-piece block, detachable head). The 4-cylinder 2413cc L-head engine put out 38hp at 2400 rpm and gave it a top speed of 56mph (90km/h). It was a middle-class car, advertised as 'Le Juste Milieu'. While it was not produced in great numbers (barely 3000 units in 3 years) it helped cut costs by being the sole model. It evolved into the AM.2 in 1926, the engine redesigned with pushrod-operated ohvs, and the propeller shaft enclosed in a torque tube.

Before the end of 1926, Wilde decided, primarily for family reasons, to return to England. Ainsworth took about a year to settle on the right man to replace him, and Vincent Bertarione came to Saint-Denis as chief engineer on 1 January 1928.

By mid-summer, he had the AM.2 bis Sport ready, with the engine enlarged to 2957cc. At this time, Ainsworth determined to give up the one-model policy, and Bertarione was briefed to develop a 6-cylinder companion model for the AM.2.

First came the AM.73 in 1929, with a 2511cc short-stroke engine, joined within months by the AM.80 3016cc version, notable for its 7-main-bearing crankshaft and Lanchester-type vibration damper. The AM.80S of 1931 had the same engine, bored out to 3485cc, raising output from 65hp at 3300rpm to 80hp at 3400 rpm, and top speed from 71.4 to 76mph (114.8 to 122km/h).

Mare Brosset, manager of the body plant, began styling the cars in 1929, as J.H. Jacobsen's sales department invented names for the body styles, taken from seaside resorts, health spas and wintersports venues. The basic Cabourg was a coach, Deauville and Monaco were saloons, Hossegor was a roadster, Basque a coupé, Biarritz a cabriolet, Vichy and Chantilly limousines.

After 1933, Alphonse Constant and his assistant, Jean Dhuit, were in charge of styling, continually egged on by Alex Kow, the illustrator, who worked with the advertising departments of several auto companies.

In 1933 the AM.2 was replaced by the 411 (11CV, 4-cylinders, 2000cc) and the 413 (13CV, 4-cylinders, 2312cc). The AM.80 gave way to the 615 and 617, while the AM.80S evolved into a 620.

These were good years for Hotchkiss, and production topped 7000 cars in 1934. The 480 (4-cylinder, 80mm bore) replaced the 411 in 1936, supplemented by the 486, replacing the 413. The 480 became 480 A in 1937, and a 1995cc 484 (with 90mm stroke) was added in 1939.

1938 Hotchkiss 686 GS roadster.
NICK BALDWIN

1949 Hotchkiss 864 13CV saloon.
NICK GEORGANO

1950 Hotchkiss-Grégoire saloon.
NATIONAL MOTOR MUSEUM

NICK BALDWIN

AINSWORTH, HENRY M. (1884–1971)

Born into a well-to-do family at Buxton, Derbyshire in August 1884, Henry Ainsworth was educated at Parkhurst School in Buxton and studied engineering at Manchester School of Technology. He went to work in the Hotchkiss drawing office at St Denis in 1904, becoming a test engineer, and serving as chief engineer from 1910 to 1914.

He spent six months as a lieutenant in the Royal Army Intelligence Corps from August 1914, but was discharged to run a machine-gun factory for Hotchkiss in Coventry. He turned it into an engine plant in 1919 and sold it to Morris in 1923. Returning to Saint-Denis, he was general manager for Hotchkiss automobile department from 1925. In 1940 the British Army assigned him to the Ministry of Supply, and from 1942 to 1944 he served as technical advisor to the Department of Munitions and Supply in Ottawa, Canada. Late in 1944 he returned to Paris and in 1945 was reinstated in his Hotchkiss office.

He retired in 1950, living in an apartment at 30 Avenue Marceau in Paris. He died on 24 January 1971.

JPN

The 686 arrived in 1936, replacing the 620. High-performance versions, 686 Grand Sport and 686 Paris-Nice, with high-compression heads and twin carburettors, appeared in 1937. They became highly successful competition cars, winning the Monte Carlo rally in 1932, 1933, 1934, 1939 (joint first with Delahaye), 1949, and 1950.

It was a blow to Hotchkiss when Léon Blum's 'Front Populaire' government expropriated the arms factories at Levallois-Perret and the stamping plant at Clichy for a paltry 71.5 million Francs.

V. Benet retired shortly after celebrating his fiftieth anniversary as a Hotchkiss executive in March 1935, and Hotchkiss, with its arms amputated, was de facto run by H.M. Ainsworth, although H.E. Boyer still had the title of president. Hotchkiss took control of Amilcar in 1937 and made an alliance with Laffly for the production of military vehicles, as well as developing its own light tank, the H.35. Ainsworth made his way to London before the Germans occupied Paris in 1940, and the factories at Saint-Denis became repair shops for tanks and other military vehicles.

Automobiles Peugeot acquired majority control of Hotchkiss in 1942. Two years later, the Peugeot family installed Maurice de Gary, their accounting chief,

1904 Howard (ii) 24hp tourer.
KEITH MARVIN

as president of Hotchkiss, replacing H.E. Boyer who was dismissed, later to be tried and imprisoned for collaboration with the Germans. H.M. Ainsworth returned to Paris in 1944, and resumed his responsibilities at Hotchkiss in 1945.

V. Bertarione still headed the engineering staff, and the product line consisted of prewar cars, plus a new PL.20 light truck and the H.45 crawler-tractor. In 1948 the board of directors voted to buy a front-wheel drive car design from J.A. Grégoire. It was powered by a horizontally opposed 2188cc 4-cylinder engine mounted in the front overhang and had a modern body, scale models of which had shown aerodynamic drag coefficients down to 0.20 in the Société Rateau wind tunnel.

For 1950, the bodies for the traditional Hotchkiss models were modernised, the 864 being renamed 1350 and the 686, 2050. Only one body style, the Anjou 4-door saloon was offered. The Anthéor cabriolet was added in 1952, in both 1350 and 2050 form.

Production of the Hotchkiss-Grégoire got under way in June 1951, but it was priced 20 per cent higher than the Anjou 2050 and sales were slow. Anjou sales were falling, too, with less than 4000 built in 1951.

The Peugeot family sold its Hotchkiss shares, Ainsworth retired in 1950, and Paul Richard succeeded M. de Gary in 1951. Richard authorised production of coupé and cabriolet versions of the Hotchkiss-Grégoire by Henri Chapron, but by November 1952, he decided to stop all Hotchkiss-Grégoire production.

Only 247 Hotchkiss-Grégoire cars were produced. The litigation that followed depleted the Hotchkiss coffers, and Paul Richard began searching for a business partner. In 1954 Hotchkiss and Delahaye merged, pooling their assets, but early in 1955, all car production discontinued. However, the long-planned production of Jeeps, under Willys-Overland licence, finally began.

In 1956, the company was absorbed by Brandt, makers of electric household appliances, becoming Hotchkiss-Brandt and continuing to produce Jeeps and trucks. In 1966 Hotchkiss-Brandt was taken over by Thomson-Houston, a heavy-industry giant and big defence contractor. Hotchkiss began making military vehicles in 1967 but made its last trucks in 1971.

JPN

Further Reading
Hotchkiss, Petit Dictionnaire du Juste Millieu, Daniel Tard, Editions Massin, Paris, 1994.
'The Golden Mean: The Hotchkiss History', Michael Sedgwick, *Automobile Quarterly*, Vol. 10, No. 4.
Hotchkiss, l'Age Classique 1935–1955, Marc-Antoine Colin, E.T.A.I., 1996.

HOTZENBLITZ (D) 1996 to date
1996 Hotzenblitz Mobile GmbH & Co. LG, Ibach; Suhl.
1998 to date Fahrzeuge und Technologien GmbH & Co. KG, Ibach.
The Hotzenblitz EL Sport was a 4-seater electric car with fibreglass body on a tubular steel frame, made in the former Simson motorcycle factory where SIMSON SUPRA cars had been made in the 1920s. It was too expensive to be a commercial success, and production ended after about 150 cars were made, though not all were sold. In 1998 a new attempt was made with an electric and also a hybrid car.

HON

HOUGHTON (US) 1900–1901
Houghton Automobile Co., West Newton, Massachusetts.
The Houghton steam carriage featured a 2-cylinder car, typical of the steamers of the time and was equipped with a boiler heated by either petrol or paraffin. It featured wood artillery spoke wheels and was available as a surrey or a stanhope with prices in the $750 to $850 range. Although plans were made for expansion of its factory and its choice of body styles, the Houghton operation went out of business after an existence of a few months.

KM

HOULBERG (DK) c.1913–1921
C. Houlberg, Odense.
The Houlberg was a light car powered by a 5/12hp 4-cylinder Ballot engine, though smaller engines possibly came from Eysink. Magnetos were by Bosch and carburettors by Zenith. They were 2-seater roadsters or 4-seater tourers with a radiator of Bugatti shape. About 30 cars were made in the home town of Hans Christian Andersen.

NG

HOUPT; HOUPT-ROCKWELL (US) 1909–1910
1909–1910 Harry S. Houpt Manufacturing Co., New Britain, Connecticut.
1910 New Departure Manufacturing Co., New Britain, Connecticut.
Harry Houpt was the New York agent for Thomas and Herreshoff cars, and in mid–1909 he announced a car of his own, to be built for him by Albert F. Rockwell who made ball bearings under the name New Departure, and also built some cars for Allen-Kingston. The Houpt was a large car made in two models, a 60hp four and a 90hp six, the latter with a wheelbase of 140in (3553mm) and prices from $6000 to $7500. By the end of 1909 they were called Houpt-Rockwells, and in April 1910 Houpt's company was absorbed by New Departure. Car production ended six months later, after about 100 cars had been made. Harry Houpt then became sales manager for Alco.

NG

HOWARD (i) (US) 1900–1903
Howard Automobile Co., Trenton, New Jersey.
William L. Howard built a number of experimental cars from as early as 1893, including a large 9-seater 'gasoline carryall' powered by two 3hp Wing engines in 1895. It was used for public transport around the Trenton Fair grounds. He built at least one steam car before forming his company to make steamers commercially. They were typical of their kind, with 2-cylinder vertical engines, single-chain drive, tubular frames, wire wheels and tiller steering. Later he built a heavier-looking car with artillery wheels.

NG

HOWARD (ii) (US) 1901–1904
1901–1903 Trojan Launch & Automobile Works, Troy, New York.
1903–1904 Howard Automobile Co., Yonkers, New York.
William S. Howard built an experimental car in 1895, but the first cars manufactured for sale under his name were built for him by the Grant-Ferris company of Troy. Their speciality was marine engines, and when Howard set up his Trojan company it seems that he made more of these than of cars, though a few single-cylinder runabouts were built, also a larger car which he sold under the name TROJAN. In 1903 he set up a new company in Yonkers which made cars with 2-, 3- and 4-cylinder engines, of 8 and 12hp for the twins, 12hp for the three and 24hp for the four. In November 1904 he sold his company to Charles L. Seabury who built the 4-cylinder Howard under the SEABURY name. Howard later built engines for the COLT in Yonkers, and in 1908 offered a Colt-like six in kit form or complete. In 1909 he built 30 6-cylinder cars for Charles Munch who later made the cars himself in DuBois, Pennsylvania, under the name KEYSTONE. In 1910 Munch returned to build the Keystone in Yonkers, probably again using Howard's factory. A complicated story which seems to have resulted in very few cars.

NG

HOWARD (iii) (GB) 1913
Howard Motor Works, Sutton, Surrey.

'The Howard appears to be very substantially constructed throughout', said *The Cyclecar*. It was a fairly typical cyclecar, with 8hp water-cooled V-twin J.A.P. engine, driving through a friction transmission and long chain final drive. An unusual feature was the canvas case protecting the chain. It had a pointed radiator and, with roomy 2-seater body, cost £110.

NG

HOWARD (iv) (US) 1913–1914
Central Car Co., Connersville, Indiana.
The Howard was a large car powered by a 6.9-litre 60hp 6-cylinder Continental engine. The wheelbase was 132in (3350mm) and it was made as a 5-seater tourer. Its most interesting feature was an early example of a dual exhaust system. It was marketed by the Howard Motor Car Co. of Chicago, and made by the E.W. Ansted Co. which had recently acquired the LEXINGTON Motor Car Co., also of Connersville. Howards were built alongside Lexingtons, but the marketing company did not renew their order so the Howard was discontinued.

NG

HOWARD (v) (US) 1916–1917; 1919
Howard Co., Galion, Ohio.
The first Galion-built Howard was announced in 1911 by Adam Howard who had been making carriages for 25 years. However it never got off the ground, and it was not until 1916 that a car appeared. This was a 50hp six made only as a 5-seater tourer at $1800, and it lasted little more than a year. In 1919 one further car was made, a 50hp sport-touring destined for the New York Automobile Show. This car is still in existence.

NG

HOWARD (vi) (US) 1928–1930
Howard Motor International Corp., New York, New York.
The Howard, despite grandiose plans for an export car, turned out to be a matter of 'much ado about almost nothing' in its final reckoning. Plans for the car entailed two different 6-cylinder chassis and two eights on wheelbases from 103 (2614mm) to 134in (3401mm) with a variety of both open and closed bodies. The basic concept of this ambitious undertaking which included such model designations as the 'Silver Dawn', 'Silver Morn' and 'New Day' was hatched by John Howard Rees who had attempted to market the unsuccessful Rees car in 1921. Rees' idea was to produce a widely varied line of cars economically viable with international demand and targeted to various overseas markets. To emphasise this, no Howard car, regardless of its power or size, would exceed a $2500 cut-off figure, with prices as low as $600. The ambitious John Howard Rees also planned to include a series of trucks to augment the passenger car offerings. Apart from the basic specifications including Continental engines, the Howard operations were vague, as were the intended overseas markets. According to historian Beverly Rae Kimes, an estimate listed 23 completed Howard cars, all of which were marketed in Canada.

KM

HOWETT (GB) 1912–1913
Fowler's Garage, Hockley Brook, Birmingham.
The Howett cyclecar was powered by a 10hp V-twin Blumfield engine, with friction transmission giving eight forward speeds, and belt final drive. At 46in (1041mm) the track was wider than on many cyclecars. £100 was quoted for the air-cooled model, £105 for water-cooling.

NG

HOWEY (US) 1907–1908
Howey Motor Car Co., Kansas City, Missouri.
This was a typical high-wheeler powered by a 10hp 2-cylinder engine, with chain drive, solid tyres and tiller steering.

NG

HOWLAND (US) c.1984
Howland Roadster, Wakefields, Maine.
This neoclassic-inspired kit car had a long bonnet and flowing mudguards typical of the category. It could be ordered with steel or fibreglass body panels and to fit a modified Chevrolet or Ford chassis. Like the CLENET, it

1927 H.P. (ii) 3-wheeler.
NICK BALDWIN

used MG Midget doors, cowl and windscreen. It was offered with a full complement of luxury features.

HP

H.P. (i) (F) 1913
This was a French-built cyclecar, maker unknown, offered on the British market for £125. It had a 703cc 6hp single-cylinder engine.

NG

H.P. (ii) (GB) 1926–1928
Hilton-Peacey Motors, Woking, Surrey.
This was a very light 3-wheeler made by Hilton Skinner and Bob Peacey. Skinner had planned to make a 3-wheeler at Letchworth called the Pixie 3, and a drastically modified version of this became the H.P. It had a laminated ash frame and BLERIOT-WHIPPET front axle; many components were acquired from this company which had just closed down. Front suspension was by quarter-elliptic springs, while the rear wheel was not sprung at all. Most H.P.s had a 500cc single-cylinder J.A.P. engine, though one had a 600cc J.A.P., two had 500cc Dunelt 2-strokes and three, 500cc British Vulpine ohv units. Transmission was by chain to a 3-speed Sturmey-Archer gearbox, and by long chain to the rear wheel. The fabric-covered plywood bodies were made at the Woking factory by an ex-Hooper coachbuilder.

The cars were assembled by a staff of four, including Skinner and Peacey, and about 40 were made over an 18 month period. The price was only £65, less than half that of an Austin Seven.

NG

Further Reading
'Fragments on Forgotten Makes; the H.P.3-wheeler', W. Boddy, *Motor Sport*, October 1966.

H.R.G. (GB) 1936–1956
H.R.G. Engineering Co. Ltd, Tolworth, Surrey.
This company took its name from the three partners, Ted Halford who had designed the VALE Special, Guy H. Robins who was in the design department of TROJAN, and H.R. Godfrey who had been the 'G' in G.N. and a partner in the GODFREY-PROCTOR company. Their car was a traditionally-styled 2-seater sports powered by a 1496cc ohv Meadows 4ED engine, driving through a Moss 4-speed gearbox and E.N.V. spiral bevel rear axle. Many of the other components were bought out as well, such as the Marles steering gear and Rubery Owen chassis members. The prototype's simple aluminium body on an ash frame was made in the works, but production bodies were by Alban Croft of South Croydon.

The prototype H.R.G. was built in 1935 at the Mid Surrey Gear Co.'s premises at Norbiton, Surrey, and the company was registered on 1 January 1936, soon moving into their own premises at Tolworth. Only five cars were completed in 1936 and 11 in 1937. Ten of these had the original A chassis and one the W chassis, which was 3in (76mm) wider. The eight cars made in 1938 and one in 1939 all had the W chassis. By 1938 the Meadows engine was at the end of its production run, and a replacement was found in the 12hp single-ohc Singer, with reduced stroke to bring it within the 1½-litre class for competition

1936 H.R.G. 1½-litre sports car.
NATIONAL MOTOR MUSEUM

1947 H.R.G. 1500 aerodynamic sports car.
NATIONAL MOTOR MUSEUM

1952 H.R.G. 1500 sports car.
NATIONAL MOTOR MUSEUM

purposes. Only two cars were made with this engine before the war, but H.R.G. also used the 1074cc Singer engine, in a shorter chassis, of which eight were made up to 1939. Bodies were nearly all the traditional slab-tank 2-seater, by

Croft on the 1500 and Reall on the 1100, though a pointed-tail car with cycle-type wings was built for Le Mans in 1938, and there was one fastback coupé with 1½-litre Triumph engine.

During the World War II H.R.G. was engaged on sub-contracting to aircraft companies Vickers, Bristol and Armstrong-Whitworth. One car was completed in 1940, the prototype of the postwar aerodynamic 2-seater, using prewar running gear. Production restarted before the end of 1945, the Aerodynamic model being made alongside the conventional cars. The Aerodynamic bodies were made by Fox & Nicholl, who had run Lagonda and Talbot racing teams before the war. They were not coachbuilders but undertook the necessary sheet metalwork. The arrangement was not entirely satisfactory, and when Fox & Nicholl terminated the contract in 1947, the Aerodynamic was withdrawn after 31 cars had been made.

Meanwhile, the conventional cars were continued almost unchanged, with 1074 or 1496cc Singer engines. Other power units were considered, including Riley, Rover, Jowett Javelin and Lea-Francis, but the first two were too heavy and the Javelin insufficiently powerful. Although increasingly old-fashioned by postwar standards, the classic H.R.G.s had a loyal following, and more were sold than in prewar days. Between 1946 and 1956 sales of the 1500 totalled 111, and of the 1100 (up to 1950), 41. Among many competition successes were class and team wins in the 1948 Alpine Rally, and first and second in class in the 1951 RAC Rally. A team of cars with special lightweight bodies swept the board in their class in the 1949 Spa 24 Hour Race.

The last 12 1500s had the slightly larger engine as used in Singer's SM1500 saloon. Before the last was delivered a completely new H.R.G. had been announced. This was the Twin Cam which used the SM engine fitted with H.R.G.'s own twin-cam head, and with a twin-tube chassis, all-round independent suspension and disc brakes, and a full-width aluminium body. Only four were made, one being quickly dismantled and reassembled at a much later date. The company remained in business, engaged in cylinder head conversions and light engineering. One final car was made in 1965, with a tubular spaceframe and a Vauxhall VX4/90 engine. H.R.G. went into voluntary liquidation in April 1966. A total of 241 cars were made, of which about 225 survive today.

NG

Further Reading
H.R.G., The Sportsman's Ideal, Ian Dussek, Motor Racing Publications, 1985.

HRUBON (F) 1980–1988

1980–1981 Sté Hrubon, Neuilly-sur-Seine.
1981–1983 Automobiles Schmitt, Guebwiller.
1984–1988 Charlatte, Migennes.
Jean-Claude Hrubon built racing cars in the late 1960s and turned his attention, in 1980, to the construction of a miniature Mini Moke replica. It used a welded steel punt frame and Mini subframes complete with suspension and brakes. A 998cc Mini engine could be fitted or, alternatively, a 125cc Sachs single-cylinder unit. Later examples could also be bought with a 50cc Polymécanique engine and automatic transmission to qualify under the *sans permis* regulations. A 6-wheeled version was also available.

CR

H&S (US) c.1988

H&S Engineering, Ventura, California.
This company built a kit car that looked like a Lotus Super 7 called the H&S Seven. It was based on the Ford Pinto and used its running gear attached to a spaceframe chassis. Most used the 2000cc Ford single-ohc 4-cylinder engine in stock or modified form. They also built a special version with a turbocharged 525hp Oldsmobile Quad 4 engine and a rigid space frame that weighed 1400lbs.

HP

HS ENGINEERING (US) c.1988

HS Engineering, Ventura, California.
HS took over production of the HATHAWAY sportscar. This had classic roadster styling and was originally designed to fit a Triumph chassis. HS added a custom tube frame with Ford Pinto or Capri running gear.

HP

H.S.M. (GB) 1913–1918

H.S.M. Motors, New Cross, London.

The H.S.M. was an unusual cyclecar whose layout resembled that of the SEAL, with a 2-seater sidecar attached to a motorcycle but steered from the sidecar by a steering wheel. The engine was an 8hp J.A.P. and transmission was by chain to a 3-speed Chater-Lea gearbox, and thence by another chain to the rear wheel. An improved model with one-piece sidecar chassis integral with the motorcycle frame was announced in 1918 by its maker, F. Hellens, who planned to put it into production after the war under the name Hellenson.

The letters H.S.M. were also used for the Triumph Dolomite straight-8s which were sold by High Speed Motors in 1938.

NG

H.T. (D) 1925

Hans Thiele Fahrzeugbau, Berlin-Friedenau.

This tandem 2-seater cyclecar was powered by a 2/8PS BMW flat-twin engine mounted on the offside running board.

HON

HUANDU (CHI) 1994 to date

First Auto Works – Chengdu Auto Works, Chengdu City, Sichuan Province.

In 1994 the Chengdu works bought the production line of the MORRIS Ital. Planned production was an estate car and a pick-up, and in 1998 the Huandu CAC 6430 5-door estate car was introduced, the Chinese copy of the Ital.

EVIS

HUASCAR see GALBA

HUAXING (CHI) 1990 to date

Guizhou Aviation Industry Corp. (Yunma Aircraft Works), Anshun City, Guizhou Province.

Hainan Auto Works, Haikou City, Hainan Province.

Huaxing Automobile Group Corp., Beijing Muncipality.

The Huaxing was made in several factories, under several names and designations, but the Huaxing YM 6390, made in the Yunma factory was the main type. This 152in (3870mm) long Toyota Starlet copy was also sold as YUNMA YM 6390 and YUNQUE GHK 7080. The engine was the Jilin JL462Q 4-cylinder 797cc petrol type. Another factory producing this car was the Hainan Auto Works, they named the car Huaxing HXJ 7080 but this one was also sold as HAINAN HX 7080. The Beijing Group sold it as Huaxing RK 5010X; it was made by the Army Xima Auto Refit Works and also named XIMA XM5020.

EVIS

HUB (i) (US) 1899–1900

Hub Motor Co., Chicago, Illinois.

This was an electric car which derived its name from the hub-mounted motors, one to each wheel which gave 4-wheel drive. It had tiller steering and was made in 2- or 4-seater surrey models. A contributor to the design was Joseph Ledwinka, later famous for his work with Budd bodies.

NG

HUB (ii) (US) 1907

Hub Motor Car Exchange, Boston, Massachusetts.

This company bought the factory in Dorchester that had made the CRESTMOBILE and its successor, the DORCHESTER. Realising that the primitive Dorchester would not sell, they came up with a more up-to-date design with 10hp single-cylinder air-cooled engine, epicyclic transmission and shaft drive. It fared no better than the Dorchester.

NG

HUBBARD (GB) 1904–1905

Hubbard's Motor & Engineering Co. Ltd, Coventry.

The Hubbard was best-known as a tricar with inclined 4hp single-cylinder engine and handlebar steering. In 1905 they announced a shaft-driven car powered by a 16/20hp 4-cylinder engine, but it did not go into production.

NG

1901 Hudlass 9hp light car.
NATIONAL MOTOR MUSEUM

HUDLASS (GB) 1897–1902

Phoenix Motor Works, Southport, Lancashire.

When Felix Hudlass (1874–1965) inherited some money from his father he invested it in a small workshop at Southport where he built a prototype car. It had a vertical twin engine mounted at the front, very unusual for its date, which has been variously quoted as 1894 or 1896. Final drive was by belt. Apart from the coachwork Hudlass built the car entirely himself, so it took a long time to be completed. This possibly explains the discrepancy over dates. Over the next seven years he built and sold about 12 cars. Some were of Benz layout, with large horizontal single-cylinder engines at the rear; one of these had an early example of an enclosed doctor's coupé body. By 1902 four models were offered, single-cylinder 6 and 10hp, and twins of 12 and 20hp, their engines being front-mounted under a bonnet. The larger of the singles, sometimes quoted as a 9hp, had square dimensions of 156 × 156mm, giving a capacity of 2980cc. Hudlass moved to London in about 1903 and made a few cars powered by Villiers 2-stroke engines. In 1904 he joined the RAC as their only engineer, and remained with them until 1947, when he retired as Chief Engineer. In the early 1920s he took a few years off to make some 3-wheelers at Mitcham, Surrey. His son Leonard made two specials in the 1920s, a 3-wheeler and a 4-wheeler, but these were not production cars.

NG

Further Reading

'The Real Story of the Hudlass Specials', W. Boddy, *Motor Sport*, September 1996.

HUDSON (i) (US) 1901–1902

Bean-Chamberlain Manufacturing Co., Hudson, Michigan.

No relation to the famous HUDSON (ii), this was a light steam car of conventional layout, with vertical 2-cylinder engine, single-chain drive and tiller steering. In the spring of 1903 Roscoe Bean formed the Hudson Motor Vehicle Co. to make steam cars and motorcycles, and in 1904 it became the Hudson Auto Vehicle Co. to make petrol cars and motorcycles. Nothing came of either of these ventures.

NG

HUDSON (ii) (US) 1909–1957

1909–54 Hudson Motor Car Co., Detroit, Michigan.

1954–57 American Motors Corp., Detroit, Michigan.

The Hudson was named not for any of the founders of the company, but for the man who put up the money: Joseph L. Hudson, a prosperous Detroit merchant. Hudson's niece was married to Roscoe Jackson, treasurer of the new firm; the other principals were Roy Chapin (1880–1936), Howard Coffin (1873–1937), and Frederick Bezner. All four had worked at OLDSMOBILE, and Chapin, Coffin and Bezner had spent a few years at THOMAS-DETROIT and CHALMERS-DETROIT. Initially allied with Chalmers-Detroit, Hudson soon broke into independence and introduced its first car, the Model 20, a 4-cylinder roadster designed by engineer George Dunham. Attractively priced

1909 Hudson (ii) 20 roadster.
NATIONAL MOTOR MUSEUM

engine. The first of the sixes to seriously enter the mid-priced field, the Model 54 soon earned Hudson the right to bill itself as the 'World's Largest Builder of Six-Cylinder Cars'. In 1916 came the 4378cc Super Six engine, designed by Charles Vincent and the first engine built in-house by Hudson, which featured a counterbalanced crankshaft. Racing driver Ralph Mulford set a record for North American transcontinental auto travel in the Super Six.

As World War I waged, Roy Chapin devised a plan for a lower-priced line of cars, ultimately consummated as the ESSEX, first of the so-called companion makes, after hostilities ceased. Swift sales of Essex bolstered the fortunes of parent Hudson in the 1920s, and the simple low cost 'coach' bodies devised for the companion car were fitted to Hudson models as well. Thus the firm started a trend in bringing the price of closed cars below that of open models. A stylish brougham close-coupled saloon introduced in mid–1925 proved similarly popular, and would remain a significant part of the line through the end of the decade. The Super Six was converted to inlet-over-exhaust configuration for 1927, which resulted in 92bhp. Rising fortunes culminated in fourth place nationally for the company in 1929, and best showing of an 'independent' manufacturer. By this time Hudsons were being built on two wheelbases, 122.5 (3109mm) and 139in (3528mm), and a line of semi-custom Murphy-designed bodies was being supplied by tied coachbuilder Biddle and Smart.

Hudsons were downsized for 1930, and given a new 3505cc 8-cylinder engine, essentially an elongated version of Essex's lightweight six. Despite being

at $900, the new Hudson proved popular, and put the company at 11th place nationally in the fledgling industry. The Model 20 was soon joined by a touring version.

In 1911 the firm adopted an oil-filled cork clutch, which would be a hallmark for most of the marque's life. In July 1912, Hudson entered the 6-cylinder market with the Model 54, after its horsepower rating, with a 6902cc side-valve

NICK BALDWIN

CHAPIN, ROY DIKEMAN (1880–1936)

Roy Dikeman Chapin was born in Detroit on 23 February 1880. He attended the University of Michigan but broke off his studies to go to work. He began his career as a photographer, but found a job at the Olds Motor Works in 1899. One of his first tasks was to file transmission gears, but his competence and ambition soon brought him more challenging work. He turned out to be a first-class mechanic, and became part of the team that stayed on after hours and finished the day's production.

He also demonstrated considerable skill as a driver, and by 1901 he was named chief tester. That year he drove an Oldsmobile from Detroit to New York in 7½ days, an exploit that opened the Atlantic states as a market for Oldsmobile. In 1904 he was named sales manager of Oldsmobile.

He formed a close friendship with Oldsmobile's chief engineer, Howard Coffin, and in 1906 they both left Oldsmobile and approached Erwin Ross Thomas (1850–1936) of Buffalo, New York, with a plan to build light cars of a sporting nature, selling at a reasonable price, in Detroit.

Thomas agreed to finance the venture, along with Frederick O. Bezner (1879–1951) and James J. Brady (both formerly of Oldsmobile) and Coffin

designed the car, which was put on the market as the Thomas-Detroit. In the first year of operations, they built and sold more than 500 cars at a retail price of $750.

The company came close to bankruptcy, however, in the financial crisis of 1907, and E.R. Thomas suggested putting it into receivership, Chapin disagreed, but understood that they needed help. He started looking for a live-wire salesman with executive experience and a thorough grasp of money matters. He found him in the person of Hugh Chalmers, the 27-year old vice president of the National Cash Register Co., where he was making $72,000 a year.

Chapin talked enough to stir Chalmer's interest and clinched the deal by offering him the title of president and a generous stock option in the company. E.R. Thomas sold his shares. Hugh Chalmers (1880–1932) saved the company, but changed the name of the car to Chalmers New Detroit in 1908. He also did not like Coffin's planned new models and began consulting outside engineers. Then he reorganised the company as Chalmers-Detroit Motor Co.

Chapin and Coffin organised the Hudson Motor Car Co. as a subsidiary of Chalmers-Detroit, with financial support from Joseph Lowthian Hudson (1846–1912), owner of Detroit's biggest department store. Hudson's nephew, Roscoe B. Jackson, was a college classmate of Chapin's who had also worked at Olds Motor Works and became a shareholder and executive of the Thomas-Detroit Motor Co.

In December 1909, Chapin, Coffin, and Bezner exchanged their Chalmers-Detroit stock, plus a cash bonus, for Hugh Chalmers' shares of Hudson Motor Car Co., achieving a complete split between the two firms. Chapin took over the former Aerocar factory and moved Hudson production there. The Hudson car succeeded, while the Chalmers-Detroit began to falter.

Roy D. Chapin headed the Highway Transport Committee of the Council of National Defense in World War I, served as president of Hudson from 1920 to 1923, and from then on, as chairman. US president Herbert Clark Hoover (1874–1964), inaugurated in 1928, prevailed on Chapin to serve as Secretary of Commerce, and he ran his department with customary dedication and skill.

Hudson Motor Car Co. lost $2 million in 1931 and $5 million in 1932, leading Chapin to resume the presidency in May 1933. It took him two years to bring in the $6 million that Hudson needed to stay in business. But the stress had taken its toll on his health. Early in 1936 he caught pneumonia, and died in the Henry Ford Hospital in Detroit on 16 February 1936.

He married Inez Tiedeman. They had a son, Roy Jr, and a daughter.
JPN

shorter, lighter and less expensive than the previous year's cars, they sold poorly as a result of the recent Wall Street crash, which curtailed all car sales. Prices started out at $1050 to $1650, some 5 per cent below 1929; at mid year they were slashed by another 15 per cent, but sales were hardly more than half those of a year earlier. The following year they were worse, and did not start to recover until 1934, by which time the Hudson adopted most features of the new TERRAPLANE companion car, which had replaced the Essex. Now Hudson had Terraplane's tapered, lightweight cruciform chassis frame, bolted rigidly to the body. All-new bodies for the whole corporate line, from Hudson style engineer Frank Spring, featured flowing and skirted wings. A complete redesign two years later was characterised by a fencer's mask grill of debatable beauty.

Baker Axleflex, a primitive form of ifs, became optional in 1934, and Electric Hand remote gear change a year later. Hudson adopted hydraulic brakes, by then common in the industry, in 1936, but backed them up with a Duo-automatic arrangement that automatically applied the parking brakes should the hydraulics fail. This was at the insistence of chief engineer Stuart Baits, whose continued refinements had evolved the old Essex 6-cylinder engine into a refined engine for all Hudson products, albeit with splash lubrication, to which Baits was thoroughly dedicated. From 1934, Hudson sixes had displaced 3475cc, the eights 4164cc, and made, in top tune, some 100 and 124bhp respectively. By 1938 the Hudson and Terraplane had become so much alike that the latter was absorbed into the parent marque as a Hudson-Terraplane.

1918 Hudson (ii) Super Six touring limousine.
JOHN A. CONDE

Terraplane's place as an entry-level car competing with Ford, Chevrolet and Plymouth was taken by a new lightweight model, the Hudson 112, named for the inch dimension of its wheelbase. The 112 sold for $694 to $891, some 12 per cent less than the cheapest Hudson-Terraplane, these prices made possible by small size, basic trim, and a short-stroke 2869cc engine.

NATIONAL MOTOR MUSEUM

CHAPIN, ROY D. Jr (born 1915)

Roy D. Chapin Jr seemed to have everything in his favour, with a wealthy father, the head of a thriving auto maker, an exclusive education, ample private means, and a harmonious family life. Nevertheless, it was his destiny to preside over the decline and dismantling of the industrial enterprise he was called upon to lead. American Motors was eventually brought down by its inadequacies in an age when corporate gigantism prevailed.

He was born at Grosse Pointe, Michigan, on 21 September 1915, as the son of Roy Dikeman Chapin. He studied business administration at Yale University and graduated with honours in June 1937. Early in 1938 he went to work for the Hudson Motor Car Co. as an experimental engineer. He was given all possible qualifications for one day becoming the chief executive, by working in production planning, accounting, car distribution, sales administration, and manufacturing.

In 1945 he was a district manager in Hudson's sales department, rising through the stages of regional manager, zone manager, and special sales representative, before being named assistant sales manager of Hudson in 1952. When Hudson and Nash merged in 1954 to form American Motors, Chapin became assistant treasurer and director. In 1955 he was promoted to treasurer and a year later he was elected a vice president.

In these positions he carried lots of responsibility, but had little opportunity for exercising leadership. That changed in 1956 when he was appointed Executive Vice President and General Manager of the Automotive Division. However, in December 1960 he was sidelined, with the title of Vice President, AMC International Operations. He did well enough to be called back to Detroit in September 1966, in his former position as Executive Vice President and General Manager of the Automotive Division.

He announced that American Motors would henceforth concentrate on niche markets and avoid building cars which competed head-to-head with products from General Motors, Ford Motor Co., and the Chrysler Corp. However, it did not quite work out that way, for some models (Ambassador, Rebel, Matador) never found a niche of their own, and others (Gremlin and Pacer), though full of originality, had little appeal. The merger with Kaiser Jeep and the establishment of AM General (for buses and military trucks) promised to stabilise the business on a broader footing, but for years the Jeep products suffered from total stagnation at the technical level. In 1968 Chapin improved AMC's cash position by selling Kelvinator Division (inherited from Nash) to White Consolidated Industries, Inc.

On 9 January 1967, Chapin was elected chairman of AMC, while Roy Abernethy took over as chief executive officer. In 1972 Chapin began taking a back seat, watching younger talent competing for the succession, and he finally retired in1978 (though remaining a management consultant to AMC). It was Chapin who initiated an industrial relationship between AMC and Renault, by making a deal for Rambler assembly at Renault's Haren plant in Belgium in 1965, but he had no part of the AMC sell-out to Renault, beginning in 1979-80. And he, least of all, could foresee Renault's failure and eventual resale to Chrysler.

In October 1937 he married Ruth Mary Ruxton. They had three sons: Roy D. Chapin III, Christopher King Chapin, and William Ruxton Chapin, and one daughter, Cicely Penny.

JPN

1929 Hudson (ii) Super Six convertible sedan.
NATIONAL MOTOR MUSEUM

1935 Hudson (ii) Custom Eight sedan.
NATIONAL MOTOR MUSEUM

1936 Hudson (ii) showroom display.
NATIONAL MOTOR MUSEUM

1939 Hudson (ii) Six touring sedan.
NICK GEORGANO

Hudson was a major exporter of automobiles in the inter-war period, and maintained assembly plants in several overseas locations, principal among them the United Kingdom. One of the most popular American cars sold in Britain, Hudson also supplied chassis for both the RAILTON and BROUGH SUPERIOR Anglo-American hybrid cars. Hudson offered small bore 6-cylinder engines for those countries where the standard engine was at a tax disadvantage.

Ifs was introduced on 1940 cars, at which time a new Traveler series became the lowest-priced Hudson. The appearance of the cars was updated with new front end sheet metal on the old bodies; the following year a new body with Symphonic Styling was adopted. A short run of 1942 cars ended in February of that year, as all US industrial capacity was diverted to war work. Hudson had been working on armaments contracts since early in 1941, and would build guns, aeroplane components, and marine engines for the duration of World War II.

Postwar production at Hudson began in August 1945. Cars were very modestly updated versions of the 1942 models, although catalogue offerings were curtailed to two series, Super or Commodore, with either 6- or 8-cylinder engines, all on a 121in (3071mm) wheelbase (prewar, there had been as many as four wheelbases in some years). Prices had been driven up by inflation, such that the cheapest Hudson now sold for $1481, well above the low-priced range. Pent-up demand meant that the cars sold well, production being limited by materials allocations.

Hudson was among the first of American manufacturers to field an all-new postwar car, the innovative step-down design of 1948. Begun as a radical teardrop design initiative during the war, the step-down featured a truss-type chassis frame that enveloped the passenger compartment, and placed frame rails outside the rear wheels. Its name derived from the fact that the floor was even with the bottom of the rails, allowing the passengers to actually step down into the car. Extremely strong, the step-down structure was exceedingly roomy inside. A new 6-cylinder engine was introduced at the same time, a 4295cc unit, the largest displacement of any American six, producing 121bhp. Notable in this engine was the use of full pressure lubrication, the first on any Hudson; it was still, however, a side-valve design. Eight-cylinder models continued to use the splash-lubricated 4164cc unit carried over from prewar days. The new models proved very popular, and sales rose to levels not seen since the late 1920s.

The Hudson model range was broadened with the addition of the lower-priced Pacemaker in 1950. The Pacemaker featured a shorter, 119in (3020mm) wheelbase and smaller engine (3803cc, 112bhp), although the larger six could be purchased in a Pacemaker Deluxe. That year would see Hudson sales peak at over 143,000, which was a feat never to be repeated. The next year was notable for the debut of the legendary Hudson Hornet, with a 5049cc version of the 6-cylinder engine. The Hornet, when equipped with twin dual-throat carburetion (Twin H-Power) quickly became popular in NASCAR stock car racing. The 8-cylinder cars, with engines virtually unchanged since the 1930s, were discontinued after 1952.

1939 Hudson (ii) Six 3.4-litre coupé.
AMERICAN MOTORS CORPORATION

MICHAEL LAMM

SPRING, FRANK (1893–1959)

Frank S. Spring belonged to a wealthy California family that at one time owned most of what's now the Silicon Valley. At age 12, his mother sent Frank to Paris with a private tutor. Together they toured Europe. Spring attended the Paris Polytechnic and graduated just before World War I, taking a degree in aeronautical engineering.

At the outbreak of war, he joined the U.S. Signal Corps and became involved with aircraft production in Detroit. It was here that he learned to fly. Frank also kept up an interest in motorcycles and enjoyed driving and tinkering with fast, mostly European sports cars.

In 1919, Spring took a job designing engines for Paige-Detroit. Then in 1921, he laid out an entire car for the Standard Steel Car Co., including its overhead-cam Straight Eight powerplant. After a short stint as chief engineer of the Courier Motor Co. in Ohio, he returned to California and joined the Walter M. Murphy Co. in Pasadena. He started with Murphy as a consulting engineer in 1923 but soon became general manager and subsequently married Walter Murphy's sister.

Spring was never a creative body designer--couldn't sketch or model clay-- but he did oversee Murphy's excellent styling staff, which at that time included Frank Hershey, Phil Wright, George McQuerry Jr. and W.E. Miller. Spring effectively acted as Murphy's director of design as well as general manager.

Murphy's dealings with the Hudson Motor Car Co. allowed Spring to meet the company's top executives. In April 1929, William J. McAneeny became Hudson's new president, and Murphy built him a custom 1931 Hudson convertible sedan. McAneeny, seeing fledgling styling departments at General Motors, Chrysler, Briggs, Murray and others, decided that Hudson needed one too, so in 1930 he offered Spring a position as Hudson's "style engineer." By 1931, things weren't going well at Murphy, so Spring accepted and arrived at Hudson that September.

The higher-ups at Hudson viewed Spring as an educated, cultured man of taste, but with an added insight: He understood how machines worked. That knowledge impressed Hudson's engineers. Spring admired European automobile design and soon built himself a rakish 1932 Essex-Terraplane personal/show roadster with cutdown doors.

Spring studied oriental philosophy, practiced yoga and slept on the floor. He and his second wife, Clara, believed in health foods and physical fitness long before those beliefs became trendy. In good weather, Spring rode to work on his BMW motorcycle or in one of his many sports cars, always impeccably dressed. He flew a Beechcraft Staggerwing and an AT-6 and was among the first in Michigan to own an Autogiro.

Spring's always small department hired stylists as needed for new models and facelifts and let them go again after they'd finished. The pace at Hudson was said to be so slow that designers usually left out of boredom. But in 1934, Spring hired an assistant, Arthur H. (Kib) Kibiger, from Auburn. Among the first cars they worked on together were the 1936 Hudson and Terraplane. Both cars shared the same body, which Spring and Kibiger had to keep restyling through 1947. The best of those revisions were the 1939–42 models.

Spring oversaw Hudson design, but Kibiger kept projects on track, made all the less important decisions and managed the designers. Not that Hudson ever had many designers to manage. Strother MacMinn arrived from GM in 1938 and, at that time, Hudson's styling staff numbered seven, including Spring and Kibiger. There were MacMinn, John B. Foster, John Aldrich, Holden Koto and Earl Hovey. Later Ted Pietch, Betty Thatcher, Arthur M. Fitzpatrick and Robert M. Thomas arrived. Betty Thatcher might have been the first woman designer ever employed by an automobile manufacturer.

Frank Spring deserves considerable credit for Hudson's final production design, the 1948 model. This car pioneered and popularized the "stepdown" concept and integral construction. Two other men who played important roles in the stepdown's creation were body engineer Carl W. Cenzer and stylist Robert F. (Bob) Andrews. Andrews, who also occasionally worked for Raymond Loewy, designed the 1948 Hudson body, and Cenzer engineered it.

One problem with unitized and semi-unitized construction is that it's difficult and expensive to change. For that reason, Hudson stayed with the 1948 body through the 1954 model year, with only one major facelift for 1954.

Hudson ran into money problems after it introduced the unsuccessful Jet compact for 1953. Frank Spring loathed the car because he'd been forced to base its styling on the 1952 Ford. The limited-production 1954 Hudson Italia coupé was also less than successful.

Spring stayed on after Hudson merged with Nash in 1954 to form American Motors Corp. but retired in 1955 at age 62. In July 1959, Frank and Clara were driving their Nash Metropolitan from California to Detroit and, as they approached Ardmore, Oklahoma, a Ford station wagon crossed the median and crashed head-on into them. Frank Spring died on August 8, 1959. Clara was severely injured but survived.

ML

HUDSON

1952 Hudson (ii) Wasp sedan.
NICK GEORGANO/NATIONAL MOTOR MUSEUM

1905 Hugot 2-seater.
NATIONAL MOTOR MUSEUM

Hudson attempted to enter the compact car market typified by NASH's Rambler, in 1953. The new Jet was styled by Frank Spring, but executive decisions rendered the car taller than Spring had intended, and it looked rather ungainly compared to the competition. A short, 105in (2665mm) wheelbase was used, and construction was similar to the big step-down cars. Power came from a downsized (3311cc) version of the side-valve six, and a Jet version of Twin H-Power was also offered, with twin single-choke carburettors. Jet sales were disappointing from the beginning, despite an attempt to bolster them with an upscale, leather-trimmed model called the Jet Liner. By 1954, the step-down design was quite dated, but there was little development money, as most remaining funds had been spent on the Jet. Moreover, because of the Step-down's integrated design, any significant change would have been expensive. A low-budget re-skin was carried out for 1954, the result being a car that was more contemporary-looking, but still dated, as the competition had ohv V8s and Hudson clung to the large, long-stroke side-valve six. However, change was not long in coming, as long-simmering talks with other independent automakers finally produced an agreement to merge Hudson with Nash Motors to form the new American Motors Corp., which came into being on 1 May 1954. Nash president George Mason was in charge; Hudson's president A.E. Barit was pushed aside into consultantcy. Changes to the cars, however, were held in abeyance until the 1955 model year.

A final gasp at independence had taken place earlier in 1954 when Hudson placed an order with Carrozeria Touring of Milan for construction of the limited production Italia sports coupé on a modified Jet chassis. Styling, by

Frank Spring, was striking but controversial. Promotion and sales were both low-key, perhaps because of the impending merger. In the end, only 26 Italias were built, the last being sold as 1955 models. A single sedan version, called X-161, was built on a Hornet chassis, perhaps as a prototype for a new full-size Hudson, but the concept went nowhere.

All 1955 American Motors cars took on a corporate shell, based on Nash's Airflyte unibody design and built in Nash's Kenosha, Wisconsin, plants, though corporate headquarters were maintained in Detroit. Drive trains were adapted from the parent companies' lines, Hudson Hornet and Jet engines were used in the Hudson versions, and, because a V8 was now obligatory in the market, the small PACKARD unit was bought in for a Hornet V8 (and a version of the Nash Ambassador). Badge-engineered versions of Nash's Rambler and Metropolitan were also created, to be sold by Hudson dealers; the former was the best-selling Hudson of 1955.

The big Hudsons were restyled for 1956, and an AMC-developed ohv 4098cc V8 joined the line, in the mid-year Hornet Special. Rebadged Metropolitans continued, and that year's all-new Rambler also had a Hudson version. For 1957, only V8 Hornets were built (now 5360cc), and a few sixes were exported. In the 1958 model year, AMC discontinued both the Hudson and Nash badges, as the firm concentrated on compact cars under the Rambler label. A few Ramblers were badged as Hudsons in some export markets, though, as late as 1959.

KF

Further Reading
History of Hudson, Don Butler,
Motorbooks International Crestline series, 1992.
'Hudson, the Car Named for Jackson's Wife's Uncle', Maurice D. Hendry, *Automobile Quarterly*, Vol. 9, No. 4.

HUDSON (iii) **(GB)** 1990 to date
Hudson Component Cars, Norwich, Norfolk.
Roy Webb's Free Spirit trike was unusual in many ways. First there was the narrow-bodied styling. Then there was the fact that you only had one seat. Under it sat a simple twin rail chassis with a steel cage enclosing the cockpit. Renault 5 parts were used throughout, including a reversed rear suspension arm. A stretched tandem 2-seater called the Kindred Spirit proved to be the more popular model, but an abortive 4-wheeled version called the Mystic received no orders at all. In 1994 the company also developed a tiny traditional-style tourer called the Rose.
CR

HUFFIT (F) 1914
Huffit Cyclecar Co., Paris.
This was a light car powered by a 1206cc 9/11hp 2-cylinder Clement-Bayard engine. Possibly the only thing that Huffit had in common with Hispano-Suiza was that both listed bodies called 'Alfonso XIII' named after the Spanish king. With this body, the Huffit sold for 90 guineas (£94.50) on the British market.
NG

HUFFMAN (US) 1920–1925
Huffman Bros Motor Co., Elkhart, Indiana.
The Huffman Bros Motor Co. had been building trucks for several months when it decided to branch into passenger car production. Introduced during 1920, it proved to be a conventional assembled car with a 6-cylinder Continental 7R engine and a wheelbase of 120in (3046mm). Its most popular model was a 5-seater touring car at $1250 and little change was made in its design until 1923 when a Continental 8R engine supplanted the earlier 7R, and the touring car price increased to $1395. The Huffman's 1925 line would be its last, the 1925 models featuring 4-wheel hydraulic brakes and disc wheels. The Huffman truck continued until mid–1926 when it was taken over by the Valley Motor Truck Co. which continued the Huffman truck under its own name until the end of the calendar year. Huffman also built some cars on contract for Bush.
KM

HUGHES & ATKIN (US) 1899–1904
Rhode Island Auto Carriage Co., Olneyville, Rhode Island.
This was a light steam car made by William Hughes and Joseph Atkin, with 2-cylinder double-acting engine, and tiller steering. 2- and 4-seaters were made,

as well as a delivery wagon. In 1901 the partners bought up the J.H. Hill Co. of Knightsville, Rhode Island, and made some cars there. Only 18 cars were made altogether before the partnership ended in 1904. Hughes later moved to England where he sold Reos.

NG

HUGOT (F) 1897–1905
C. Hugot, Paris.

The first Hugot was a light voiturette powered by a 2¼hp De Dion-Bouton engine, mounted at the rear and driving through a 2-speed gearbox on the rear axle. On at least one car the body and mudguards were made entirely of cane. In 1899 these cars were to be sold in England under the name Paris. There was a hiatus of a few years after 1901, but in 1905 a number of 2-seaters powered by front-mounted 697cc single-cylinder engines with belt drive were sold under the name Hugot et Pecto. One of these took part in the six-day reliability trial organised by *l'Auto* in November 1905.

NG

HUMBEE SURREY (J) 1947–1962
Mitsui Precision Machinery & Engineering Co. Ltd, Tokyo.

Founded in 1928, Mitsui had specialised in machinery and tools, but decided to venture into vehicle manufacture in 1947 with a range of 3-wheeled commercial vehicles. The company's first passenger model was the Humbee EFII Surrey, a 3-wheeler with a motorcycle-type front end, including handlebars, and plastic bodywork. Two rear passengers perched high up, rickshaw-style, behind the single driver's seat and could be protected from the elements by a 'Surrey' top. The engine was a 285cc single-cylinder air-cooled 11.5bhp unit mounted in the rear, driving the rear wheels by chain. Mitsui joined forces with HINO in 1961 and the Humbee was marketed as a Hino from 1962.

CR

HUMBER (GB) 1896–1976
1896–1946 Humber Ltd, Coventry.
1903–1908 Humber Ltd, Beeston, Nottinghamshire.
1946–1970 Humber Ltd, Ryton-on-Dunsmore, Warwickshire.
1970–1976 Chrysler UK Ltd, Ryton-on-Dunsmore, Warwickshire.

Humber was one of the oldest names in Britain's cycle industry, for Thomas Humber (1841–1910) began making copies of the French Michaux velocipede in Nottingham in about 1870, moving to nearby Beeston in 1878. He later acquired factories in Coventry and Wolverhampton where he made large numbers of the new Safety Bicycle from 1886 onwards, and also tricycles.

Humber's entry into powered vehicles came about through their plans to make the LÉON BOLLÉE 3-wheeler in their Coventry factory. This was destroyed by fire in July 1896 before manufacture could begin so Humber were given space in part of the Motor Mills, where DAIMLER and M.M.C. cars were later built. It is not certain exactly when manufacture began. *The Autocar* reported in September 1896 that 'Mr. Crowden (works manager) hopes to have his first British-built Bollée on the road this week'. Hopes are not always realised, but by November *The Autocar* was able to report that nine Coventry Motettes were shown at the Stanley Cycle Show in London. The names Coventry Bollée and Coventry Motette were both used for these vehicles. How many were made in 1896 is not certain, but even if there were no more than the nine seen at the Stanley Show one could claim that manufacture had started that year. This gives Humber the honour of being the first maker of series-production cars in England, albeit they were 3-wheelers and of foreign design. They were made up to 1899, some having side by side seating and going under the name Humber Motor Sociable. In 1900 Humber began to make motorcycles, 3-wheeled forecars and quadricycles. The motorcycles were made up to 1930, and had an excellent reputation for quality. Humber were among the few firms (with SUNBEAM) to make bicycles, motorcycles and cars at the same time for a considerable period.

Though a production Humber car did not appear before 1901 there were a number of prototypes before then. In 1896 Christopher Shacklock, manager of the Humber bicycle factory at Wolverhampton, made a 4-seater car with 2-cylinder horizontal engine and epicyclic gearbox, though apparently this did not carry the Humber name. It was only in his obituary in 1934 that a local paper called his machine 'the first Humber'. In 1899 a light 2-seater called the

1903 Humberette 5hp 2-seater.
NATIONAL MOTOR MUSEUM

Humber Phaeton emerged from the Coventry factory. It had a front-mounted horizontal air-cooled engine ('fully exposed to all the winds that blow', said *The Autocar*) and belt drive. It was advertised with engines of 3, 3½, and 5hp, though it is not certain that all of these were made. In November 1899 a curious vehicle called the MD Voiturette was shown at the Stanley Show. It had front-wheel drive and rear-wheel steering and was started by lifting the steering wheel and giving it a sharp turn, which actuated a system of bevels, cross-shafts and chains. It is hardly surprising that it never went into production, but for 1901 a more conventional car was built and catalogued at £275 for the standard model and 300 guineas (£315) for the de luxe. It was powered by a 4½hp De Dion-Bouton engine and had shaft-drive and a rear-entrance tonneau body. It had a single-spoked steering wheel which was a feature of Humbers until 1910. Larger cars with 4-cylinder engines of 12 and 20hp appeared in 1902 and 1903, and there was also a 9hp 3-cylinder model which did not go into production. These were designed by Louis Coatalen who joined Humber in 1901 and remained with them for six years before going to Hillman and later to Sunbeam.

In 1903 came the most important early Humber, and the car which established the firm's reputation. The Humberette was a light 2-seater with a 613cc single-cylinder De Dion-Bouton engine, 2-speed gearbox controlled by levers on the steering column, a tubular frame and shaft drive. An improved model (the Royal Humberette) with three speeds and 773cc 7½hp engine came in 1904. It was the first Humber to be built at both the Coventry and Beeston factories, and set the tradition whereby the Beeston cars were better finished. The Humberettes from Beeston had bucket seats and side doors, and were more expensive, at £147 compared with £125 for the Coventry product. In the first six months of Humberette production, 500 were made, of which 190 came from Beeston. In 1906 Humber added to their manufacturing capacity by taking over the premises in Coventry of the defunct CORONET company.

The Humberette was made up to the end of 1905, when the single-cylinder car was out of date. Coatalen replaced it with a small four of 1885cc (8/10hp), which was developed in 1906 into the 2365cc 10/12hp. Together with a larger 15hp they were the staple products of the Coventry factory for the next few years. Beeston made altogether larger and more expensive cars, the 3544cc 16/20 and 4942cc 30hp. They also made 14 examples of a large 6-cylinder car, rated at 30/40hp and with a capacity of 5652 or 6838cc according to different sources. This had a different radiator from other Humbers, a round shape similar to that of a Delaunay-Belleville or Hotchkiss. The 30hp Beeston had four speeds and a gate change, while the 15hp Coventry had only three speeds and the more old-fashioned quadrant change. The 10/12hp from Coventry had a tubular frame, while all Beeston-built cars after the Humberette had pressed-steel channel section frames.

By the end of 1906 Humber was one of Britain's largest car makers, with a weekly output of 75 vehicles, 50 from Coventry and 25 from Beeston. In 1908 a new factory was built at Stoke on the outskirts of Coventry. It employed 5000 men and had a potential to make 150 cars and 1500 bicycles per week. Unfortunately, 1908 saw a serious slump in the motor industry all over Europe, and Humber could not afford to run two large factories. As Stoke was more modern they concentrated production there, and closed Beeston. New models

c.1910 Humber 28hp limousine.
NATIONAL MOTOR MUSEUM

1923 Humber 8/18 coupé by A.D.Matthews.
NATIONAL MOTOR MUSEUM

were added at both ends of the range, a 1527cc 8/10hp vertical twin at the lower and a 5589cc six at the top, the first 6-cylinder Humber to be made in any numbers. These cars had T-head engines, but in 1911 new L-head designs were introduced which were carried on until the 1920s. The last T-head was the 4849cc 28hp, made up to 1914.

In 1913 the Humberette name was revived for a 2-seater with 998cc air-cooled V-twin engine. Because it weighed less than 700lbs it was classed as a cyclecar, but it was a much more satisfactory design than most of its kind, with a conventional 3-speed gearbox and shaft drive. A water-cooled engine was offered as an alternative on 1914 Humberettes. In May 1913 *The Cyclecar* reported that 70 Humberettes were being turned out every week, and more than 2000 had been made by the outbreak of war. At £125 or £135 it was appreciably cheaper than the rest of the Humber range, which started at £255 for a 10hp 2-seater. This 10hp was a real harbinger of the future, with 1593cc monobloc engine including a detachable head, and unit construction of engine and gearbox; it was the basis of a range that continued until 1923.

Humber has never been considered as a sporting make, though they competed in the Tourist Trophy races in 1906 and 1907. They built an important car for the 1914 TT, which was for racing cars, not the tourers that had contested earlier events. The Humber had a 3.3-litre twin-ohc engine with four valves per cylinder, very similar to that of the Grand Prix Peugeots. It was designed by Frank Burgess who joined BENTLEY after the war, and the 3-litre Bentley owed quite a lot to the Humber.

Humber had opened an aircraft department in 1909, so they were well placed to contribute to the war effort, with BR-2 engines designed by W.O. Bentley, as well as complete Avro 504 aircraft. The first postwar Humbers were revivals of the 1914 10 and 14hp models, the latter enlarged to a 15.9hp (2813cc). Like the later 1920s cars they were reliable and well-built, and were noted for their excellent all-weather equipment. They were conservative in appearance and unexciting in performance, but the little 985cc 8/18 which joined the range in 1923 was a more lively car. It had a new engine design incorporating inlet over

exhaust valves, a layout which was extended to the larger Humbers. In 1925 the range consisted of three models, the 8/18, the 1794cc 12/25 and the 2815cc 15/40. The latter was the first Humber to have front wheel brakes, as an option for 1925. Two years later they had spread across the whole range. The 8/18 grew up into the 1057cc 9/20 in 1926, and the following year two new models appeared, the 2016cc 14/40 and the 3075cc 20/55, the latter Humber's first six since before the war. It was available with a chauffeur's division and appealed to these who aspired to Rolls-Royce ownership, but couldn't afford one. In 1928 this was given Dewandre servo brakes.

NICK BALDWIN

ROOTES, SIR WILLIAM EDWARD (1894–1964)

William Edward Rootes was renowned as a super-salesman of unbridled and infectious enthusiasm, who did not know the meaning of the words shyness, reserve, or reticence. A man of limited schooling, he could on occasion appear strangely naïve and even ignorant, but his personality was anything but one-dimensional, and his business methods were adapted to the situation: sometimes brusque, sometimes diplomatically persuasive, with an underlying shrewdness and an obvious tinge of recklessness.

Son of a small-time general engineering shop owner and bicycle manufacturer, he was born on 17 August 1894, at Goudhurst, Kent. He was unhappy in school, but very happy in the family shops, and took an early liking to motor cars. He was only ten when he took his first joyride, 'borrowing' his father's New Orleans, with his little brother Reg as a passenger.

By 1898 his father was operating a motor car agency at Hawkhurst, Kent, selling cars such as Star, Clement, Swift, Argyll, Darracq, and Panhard, later adding Humber, Napier, and Vauxhall.

Young Billy was sent to Cranbrook School, but dropped out at 15 and went into chicken-farming, later also breeding cattle and sheep. After a year of profitable farming, he was apprenticed to Singer in Coventry, where he proved a fast learner and an even faster amateur racing motorcyclist. But he broke off his apprenticeship a year early, leaving Coventry with an order for 50 Singer Ten cars which he sold in Kent as soon as they were delivered. This was done without any connection with his father's agency, but in 1914 father and son set up a partnership with an agency in Maidstone.

He was registered with the Royal Navy Voluntary Reserve, and served as a sub-lieutenant with the Royal Naval Air Force in World War I. He was aghast at the way damaged engines were simply scrapped, and filed a plan for an engine reconditioning plant to salvage and re-use serviceable parts. That resulted in a contract which enabled him to establish Rootes Maidstone in 1917 as a rebuilding factory for aircraft engines, motor

Humbers remained conservative throughout the 1920s, though steady improvements were made. Low-pressure tyres were used from 1927, and wire wheels were optional on all models by 1929, apart from the 14/40. Fabric bodies were available from 1928 to 1932. Production rose steadily, from 1750 in 1920 to about 3000 per year in the middle of the decade, and 5618 in 1930. In 1928 Humber bought up their Coventry neighbours, Hillman, and four years later they were acquired by the Rootes Group. Rationalisation between Hillman and Humber had started before then, with the Hillman Vortic which used that company's straight-8 engine in a Humber chassis and body. Under Rootes

1929 Humber 20/65 coupé.
NATIONAL MOTOR MUSEUM

vehicles, and agricultural machinery. It grew into the Lea Engineering Works when he took over the old tannery in Mill Street, Maidstone.

His brother Reginald joined the business in 1919, and their father contributed £10,000 to set up Rootes Ltd to take over the surviving dealer contracts. Billy visited the US in 1920 to get first-hand knowledge of the motor industry and trade in America. They prospered in the Kentish market, and in 1923 set up a branch in London's Long Acre. In 1924 they tackled the British Dominions and other far-flung export markets, setting up a shipping depot on the river Thames at Chiswick. In 1925 they joined forces with Thrupp & Maberly, London coachbuilders.

In 1926 the brothers acquired Devonshire House in Piccadilly and moved their headquarters there. By 1928 Rootes Ltd were the biggest car distributors in Britain, and a leading exporter, having taken over and united the export departments of Hillman, Humber and Commer Cars Ltd in 1927. Gradually, Rootes Ltd bought control of the manufacturing companies, financed by the Prudential Assurance Co.

Rootes Securities Ltd was formed in 1932 as a holding for Humber, Hillman, and Commer, adding Karrier in 1934, Clement Talbot Ltd in 1935, British Light Steel Pressings Ltd in 1937, and Sunbeam in 1938.

In 1940 William Rootes was elected chairman of the joint aero-engine committee, the governing body of the six 'shadow factories', operated by the motor industry. Rootes built a 'shadow' factory on Speke Road, Liverpool, for bomber plane assembly, and a second one at Ryton-on-Dunsmore, Coventry, for making aircraft engines. During World War II he held office with the Ministry of Supply, Air Ministry, and the Board of Trade.

He spearheaded Britain's postwar export drive to the US and the Commonwealth. In 1950 he arranged the takeover of Tilling-Stevens, which held control of Vulcan Motors. At the end of 1950 the Rootes Group was converted into a joint stock corporation, Rootes Motors Ltd. He did not stop with that, but acquired Singer Motors Ltd in 1955 and Tempair Ltd of Dorking in 1956.

The downfall of Rootes Motors Ltd began with a strike at the British Steel Pressings plant at Acton in September 1961. Its position was further weakened by the heavy investments at Linwood in Lanarkshire to make the Hillman Imp, and its thunderous failure in the marketplace. Sir William Rootes was quite receptive to Chrysler representatives in 1964, when they came to assess the property of Rootes Motors Ltd and began buying into it. By 1967, Chrysler held 100 per cent control, but Sir William did not live to see that.

In the summer of 1964 he chartered a yacht and was cruising in the Mediterranean when he slipped and fell, sustaining severe head injuries. That did not stop him from hosting a new-model presentation in London in September, or attending the Paris Salon in October. Back in London he was diagnosed as having cancer of the liver, and he died on 12 December 1964.

He married Nora Press in 1916 and they had two sons, Geoffrey (1917–1992) and Brian (1919–1971), both of whom figured prominently in the annals of the Rootes Group. He was divorced in 1951, but remained on friendly terms. Before the end of the year, he was remarried, to the twice-widowed Lady Ann Peek.

JPN

Further Reading
The Rootes Brothers - Story of a Motoring Empire, John Ballock, Patrick Stephens, 1993.

ownership Humber moved upmarket in the 1930s, as the lower end was catered for by the Hillman Minx. The little 9/28 was dropped after 1930, and the smallest subsequent Humber was the 1669cc Twelve, made from 1933 to 1937. Although saloons and tourers were made on the Twelve, it was best known for the Vogue pillarless 2-door saloons said to have been designed by couturier Captain Molyneux. Production of the Twelve totalled 8486 cars. More typical of Humber were the Snipe, Super Snipe and Pullman. The Snipe appeared in 1930, and combined the chassis and body styles of the 2110cc 16/50 with a 3498cc 6-cylinder engine. Although a much better performer, the Snipe did not sell so well as the 16/50 (4994 compared with 6828 in 1930–32) as it came into a higher tax bracket. A long-wheelbase limousine version of the Snipe was called the Pullman, a name which was to be associated with formal Humbers up to the 1950s. In 1925 Rootes had bought up the old-established London coachbuilders, Thrupp & Maberly, who became responsible for Pullman bodywork.

For 1933 Rootes brought Humber into line with Hillman by abandoning the inlet-over-exhaust valves in favour of side-valves. The 16/50 became the 16/60 (2276cc), while the Snipe and Pullman kept the same engine size of 3498cc. Synchromesh gearboxes came in 1934, together with sloping radiators, built-in jacks and, for 1935, the option of a De Normanville semi-automatic transmission. The Snipe was revised for 1936 with more curvaceous coachwork and transverse ifs designed by American Barney Roos who had devised it during his time at Studebaker. Capacity went up to 4086cc, giving 100bhp, and this engine was used in Snipes and Pullmans until the 1950s, as well as powering the wartime 4×4 Heavy Utility, armoured cars, scout cars and several models of Commer commercial vehicle. For 1938 the Snipe name was given to a saloon which shared a body and a wheelbase with the Hillman Fourteen, though engines were larger and still Humber-designed; the Snipe used a 3183cc six, while the same car with a 2576cc engine was called the Sixteen. The previous Snipe with 4086cc engine was called the Snipe Imperial, and for 1938 was offered with a new razor-edged 4-light sports saloon body, as well as 6-light saloon and a drop-head coupé. 1939 Snipe Imperials had hydraulic brakes, as did the smaller Sixteen and Snipe. The Pullman, despite its weight, did not get hydraulics until 1940, by which time customers were mostly the military top brass. Pullmans were also popular with Cabinet ministers and with the Royal Family.

A new model for 1939, which had a better performance than any other prewar Humber, was the Super Snipe. This followed the formula of a powerful engine in a relatively light body, in this case the 4086cc six in the Sixteen/Snipe bodies, especially the 4-light sports saloon. This had a top speed of 85mph (137km/h).

The Super Snipe was one of the most familiar army staff cars during World War II, being made as an open tourer and estate car as well as a saloon. The open tourers by Thrupp & Maberly were made especially for desert work, two of these being used by Field Marshal Montgomery throughout his Eighth Army campaigns in North Africa and Italy. The 4×4 Heavy Utility was an impressive vehicle, combining saloon car comfort (though its body was of estate car shape) with cross country ability associated with the Jeep. In concept it was a forerunner of the Range Rover or Toyota Land Cruiser type of vehicle, but Rootes dropped it immediately the war ended. A curious hybrid that appeared at the end of the war was a 15cwt truck fitted with a Karmann saloon body. These were made in small numbers for the British forces in Germany in 1945/46.

Four models made up the postwar Humber range, the 1944cc 4-cylinder Hawk

733

1937 Humber Pullman limousine.
NATIONAL MOTOR MUSEUM

which was a Hillman Fourteen with hydraulic brakes and Humber styling, the 2731cc Snipe which was derived from the prewar Humber 18, and the 4086cc Super Snipe and its long-wheelbase limousine version, the Pullman. In 1948 steering column gearchange reached all Humbers, while the Super Snipe and Pullman were mildly restyled with recessed headlamps and narrow grills. The Hawk was more drastically restyled for 1949, with a completely new 4-light saloon body, while it also had coil ifs and a hypoid rear axle. Hawks were made only as saloons, as were the majority of Super Snipes, though Tickford built a few handsome 2-door cabriolets in 1949/50. From 1950 the Pullman could be had without the chauffeur's division, this model being the Imperial. At least one 4-light Pullman was built, and kept for the use of the Duke of Windsor when he visited London.

Humbers sold well in the postwar years, 1951 production was around 13,200, made up of 8000 Hawks, 4400 Super Snipes and 800 Pullman/Imperials. In 1953 the Super Snipe received a new body in the style of the Hawk, together with a 4138cc ohv engine shared with Commer trucks. The Pullman also had this engine, but was not restyled, and disappeared from the range after 1954. The Hawk also had an ohv engine from 1954, in this case the 2267cc unit shared with the Sunbeam Talbot 90.

The Hawk and Super Snipe were made with little change apart from mild restyling until 1957, when a new range of unitary construction saloons appeared which were the last individual Humbers. They had American full-width styling and 4-speed gearboxes with steering column change, or the option of an automatic transmission. From 1961 there were disc brakes on the front wheels. The Hawk and Super Snipe names were still used, the Hawk having the old 4-cylinder 2267cc engine and the Super Snipe a 2655cc six (2965cc from 1963). For 1961 the Super Snipe gained four headlamps, the first British car to adopt this fashion. The Hawk was dropped in 1964, the Super Snipe in 1967, by which time there was also a luxury version with black leatherette roof covering, called the Imperial.

The Rootes Group was fully acquired by Chrysler in 1967, and the place of the Humber at the top of the range was supposed to be taken by the Australian-built Chrysler Valiant, though few were actually sold in Britain. An American Chrysler V8 was tried in the Super Snipe, but the idea was abandoned after a few prototypes had been made. The French-built Chrysler 180 might have carried the Humber name, but this was thought to be insufficiently known on the international scene. There was a small Humber called the Sceptre, which had been in production since 1963. It had a Hillman Super Minx body, although

NICK BALDWIN

ROOTES, SIR REGINALD CLAUD (1896–1977)

Younger brother of Sir William, Reginald too was born at Goudhurst, Kent, on 20 October 1896, and was educated at Cranbrook School.

He began his career by joining the Admiralty in 1914 as a civil servant, leaving his office in 1919 to join his father and brother in the motor business at Maidstone. While Billy was out selling cars or lining up new franchises, Reggie stayed in the office, handling administrative duties, accounting, and other tasks.

As the Rootes Group grew, so did his executive capacity and responsibilities, and his titles became more and more important, from managing director to vice chairman in 1950, and chairman from 1965 until his retirement in 1969. He died in December 1977.

JPN

Further reading
The Rootes Brothers - Story of a Motoring Empire, John Bullock, Patrick Stephens, 1993.

1949 Humber Pullman limousine.
NATIONAL MOTOR MUSEUM

NATIONAL MOTOR MUSEUM

WINTER, BERNARD B. (born 1894)

Bernard B. Winter served as technical director of the Rootes Group from 1938 to 1959. He did not design cars but was creative in another sense, for it was his responsibility to concoct a coherent model range that could be manufactured economically while maintaining a certain amount of individuality among the group's makes. He accomplished this task with steadfast competence, erring perhaps in favour of economy at the expense of individuality, under ever-increasing pressure from top management.

In 1946 he was a member of an SMMT delegation to Wolfsburg, where the Volkswagen was offered to the British Motor Industry. He quickly saw that it was not the kind of product that the Rootes Group was equipped to make, nor to sell in its home or export markets, and turned it down. Hidebound he was not, but realistic, yes. He had a clear grasp of the facts and always avoided starry-eyed schemes to change them.

He had a general and technical education, but reaching the age of 20 in 1914 he was called up for military service. After the war, he gained valuable experience in the motor repair trade. He joined the Rootes enterprise in 1923 as chief service executive, when it was strictly a retail organisation.

In 1929 he was delegated to Humber as a service engineer, where his efficiency singled him out for promotion. In 1934 he was named executive manager of the Humber-Hillman engineering department, with the additional task of integrating Talbot and Sunbeam into a programme that put a premium on sharing components. The Talbot Ten, type BE, introduced in October 1935, was based on the Hillman Minx, and the Talbot 3-litre, introduced in October 1937, shared the Humber Snipe chassis and body shell.

In 1938 he became a member of the Rootes Group board of directors and within 18 months was given responsibility for the group's military vehicles, from the Hillman Utility pick-up and the Humber Super Snipe staff car, through the 4-wheel drive 'Box Humber' and 15cwt Commer and Karrier trucks, to components for bigger vehicles assembled by other makers.

After World War II, he co-ordinated a revised model range with all assembly operations concentrated in the former shadow factory at Ryton-on-Dunsmore, including Sunbeam-Talbot. He streamlined the engine programme to just two sizes of 4-cylinder and two sizes of 6-cylinder units, and the body shells down to a mere four. A fifth body was added in the takeover of Singer and shared with the Hillman Hunter until 1963, when the Humber Sceptre replaced the Hawk and the Hunter came to share the Sceptre body.

He retired in 1959.

JPN

1959 Humber Hawk saloon.
NATIONAL MOTOR MUSEUM

with different roof, windscreen and rear wing treatment, Sunbeam Rapier radiator grill and the quad headlamps from the Super Snipe. The engine was the Minx's 1592cc but with alloy head and twin-choke Stromberg carburettor as used in the Singer Vogue and Sunbeam Rapier. This was made up to 1967 when it was replaced by an even more badge-engineered car, also called the Sceptre. This was a quad headlamp, twin carburettor variant of the Hillman Hunter, though with better trim which cost an additional £277. Engine capacity was now 1725cc, as it had been on the 1965/67 Sceptres. It had a long life with little change, 43,951 being made up to 1976.

In New Zealand the Humber name was used for the Hillman Minx for a number of years. From 1949 to 1954 it was the Humber Ten, then with the arrival of ohvs it became the Humber 80, and in the 1960s it became the Humber 90.

In 1987 former marketing manager at Chrysler's Linwood plant, Andrew Boulton, formed a new company, The Humber Motor Co. Ltd. His ambitious plans envisaged a 2.7-litre 6-cylinder executive car and a 5.4-litre V12 luxury car, but with an estimated £500 million needed to set up a factory and get the project running, it was a complete non-starter.

NG

Further Reading
The Humber Story 1868–1932, A.B. Demaus and J.C. Tarring, Alan Sutton Publishing, 1989.
The Humber, an Illustrated History 1868–1976, Tony Freeman, Academy Books Ltd, 1991.
The Humber, Nick Georgano, Shire Publications, 1990.

HUMBER and HILLMAN (AUS) 1956–1972

Rootes (Australia) Ltd, Port Melbourne, Victoria.
Chrysler Australia Ltd, Port Melbourne, Victoria.

A Rootes assembly operation began in 1946 in a wartime aircraft plant and there was a plan for increased local content. A site was purchased at Clayton but this was not built on.

In the mid–1950s the Hillman Minx-based Commer pick-up was joined by a car-type utility on the latter Mark models. In 1962, when the SINGER name

1912 Hupmobile Model 32 tourer.
NATIONAL MOTOR MUSEUM

plate was discontinued in Australia, the Gazelle, wearing a Hillman grill, became the Series 3C Australian DeLuxe. When the Vogue arrived in 1963, it was sold under the Humber label. From 1964 a Vogue Sports was listed at a price more competitive against the FORD Cortina GT than was the imported Humber Sceptre. It was lowered and had the 2-carburettor engine. In final 6-window form it carried the Chrysler Pentastar because assembly continued after the 1965 Chrysler takeover. The Gazelle Series 6, with a 1725cc engine, also reappeared as a Hillman in 1966.

MG

HUMBLE (AUS) 1904

Humble & Sons Pty Ltd, Geelong, Victoria.
Makers of all manner of machinery for agriculture, mining and refrigeration, Humble & Sons entered motor construction with a contract to build two motor buses in 1903. This was followed by a 4-passenger car powered by a single-cylinder De Dion-Bouton engine and fitted with a rear-entrance tonneau body. It was exhibited at the Melbourne Show but failed to attract a buyer, and was retained for family use. Further buses, however, were made.

MG

HUMMBUG (US) 1997 to date

Hummbug Kit Cars, Vancouver, Washington.
The Hummbug was a VW-based kit car that looked like a half-size AMG Humvee. The kit included a steel subframe for reinforcing the VW Beetle floorpan.

HP

HUMMER (US) 1904–1905

Hummer Motor Car Co., Kansas City, Missouri.
The Hummer was a short-lived air-cooled car, production being limited to runabouts and a touring car prototype. The car featured a 2-cylinder opposed engine driving through a planetary transmission and single-chain drive.
For a more recent use of the Hummer name, see AMG.

KM

HUMPHRIS (GB) 1908–1909

Humphris Gear & Engineering Co. Ltd, Eastleigh, Hampshire.
The Humphris car was built to demonstrate the Humphris gear system, in which the crown wheel on the rear axle was replaced by a vertical disc with concentric rows of holes; a pinion from the propeller shaft engaged with different rows of holes for each speed, the disc sliding back laterally so that the pinion could move from one row of holes to another. The system had been tried on a Darracq before any Humphris cars were made. Although various engines were listed as being available in the Humphris, including a 10/12, 12/14, 15/17 and 25/30hp, it is likely that these were all experimental vehicles. Few were sold, though one went to a hotel owner at nearby Gosport.

NG

HUNGERFORD ROCKET (US) 1929

Daniel D. & Floyd D. Hungerford, Elmira, New York.
The Hungerford Rocket was one of America's most unusual but potentially viable automotive ventures, built by two clairvoyant brothers who were expert aircraft repairmen and rocket propulsion enthusiasts. Their car, a teardrop design constructed of a light wooden frame and thick cardboard skin, was mounted on a 1921 Chevrolet chassis equipped with a rocket motor built to their specifications by the Gould Pump Co., of Seneca Falls, New York. It was a dual-powered affair, capable of being operated as a conventional automobile or at speed by a rear-mounted rocket in the car's tail. The Hungerford Rocket was also the first, and presumably only, rocket car in the country to be legally licensed for highway operation. That further manufactured rocket cars by the Hungerfords failed was due to the brothers' inability to secure sufficient financial backing, although the car was widely promoted and exhibited in rocket form throughout the United States in the early and mid–1930s.

The Hungerford brothers kept a sharp interest in the experiments in rocketry by such European pioneers as Max Valier and Fritz von Opel in Germany, and furthered their own experiments in such related fields as the construction of a rocket lawnmower. The brothers came to the attention of countless thousands of children in 1934 through a radio broadcast of 'Buck Rogers in the 25th Century', a programme based on the comic-strip syndicated in numerous newspapers in which rocket travel in the future was the basic theme. Daniel Hungerford had written to the sponsor of the programme explaining the rocket car he and his brother were promoting and parts of the letter were subsequently read during one of the Buck Rogers programmes in January 1934.

In 1964, the Hungerford Rocket was brought to the Capital District (Albany-Troy-Schenectady Area) of New York State, completely restored, and for many years exhibited at automobile shows, as a participant in parades and other similar events. Shortly before his death, the last owner of the Hungerford Rocket presented the car to the New York State Museum at Albany.

KM

HUNTER see J. & S.

HUNTINGBURG (US) 1901–1903

Huntingburg Wagon Works, Huntingburg, Indiana.
This company motorised a small number of the horse-drawn buggies, using a single-cylinder engine located under the seat. Standard equipment included a leather whip for chasing dogs, and a heavy anchor to supplement the brakes.

NG

HUOBAN (CHI) 1998

Jaixing Taisun Engine Research & Development Corp. Ltd, Jaixing City, Zhejiang Province.
Designed as a taxi-concept car, the Huoban ('Buddy') was developed by the Taisun Shipyard Co. of Singapore. This car had remarkable dimensions: with a length of 167in (4250mm), its width was 75in (1920mm). The back seat had sufficient room for three (large) passengers, while the front passenger seat could be folded to make space for luggage. The frame was made from stainless steel tube, the body of fibreglass-reinforced plastic. The fuel system was an integrated dual-fuel system of LPG or CNG and petrol. The engine was the CA 488 2.2-litre 4-cylinder, developing 87bhp.

EVIS

HUPMOBILE (US) 1908–1940

Hupp Motor Car Corp. Detroit, Michigan.
The Hupp Motor Car Co. was founded in November 1908 by Robert Craig Hupp (1876–1931), who had gained experience with Oldsmobile, Ford and Regal before building his own light car. This was a 2-seater on a short wheelbase 83.5in (2184mm), powered by a 2.8-litre 4-cylinder engine. In conception and appearance it was not unlike the first Hudson which appeared six months later, though at $750 it was $150 cheaper. It was unusual in having a 2-speed gearbox; these were common enough in epicyclic systems such as Ford's, but sliding pinion gearboxes usually had three or four speeds.

Known as the Model 20, the little car was introduced to the public at the Detroit Auto Show in February 1909, and production began in March. By December an encouraging 1608 had been sold, rising to 5340 in 1910 and

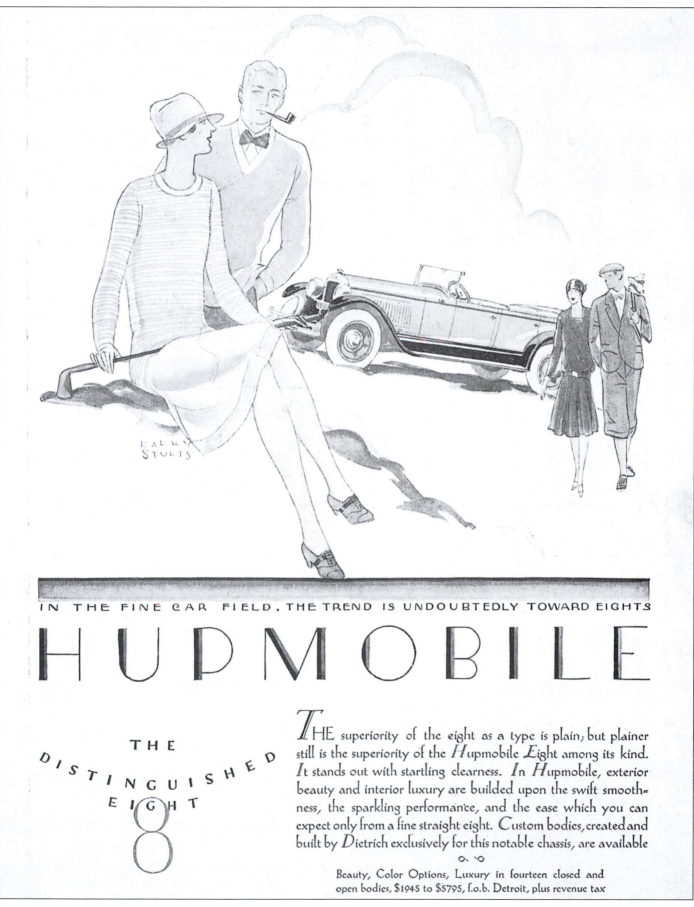

LARRY STULTS
IN THE FINE CAR FIELD, THE TREND IS UNDOUBTEDLY TOWARD EIGHTS
HUPMOBILE
THE DISTINGUISHED EIGHT
8
THE superiority of the eight as a type is plain; but plainer still is the superiority of the Hupmobile Eight among its kind. It stands out with startling clearness. In Hupmobile, exterior beauty and interior luxury are builded upon the swift smoothness, the sparkling performance, and the ease which you can expect only from a fine straight eight. Custom bodies, created and built by Dietrich exclusively for this notable chassis, are available
Beauty, Color Options, Luxury in fourteen closed and open bodies, $1945 to $5795, f.o.b. Detroit, plus revenue tax

NATIONAL MOTOR MUSEUM

c.1920 Hupmobile 35hp tourer.
NICK BALDWIN

1929 Hupmobile Century Six sedan.
NATIONAL MOTOR MUSEUM

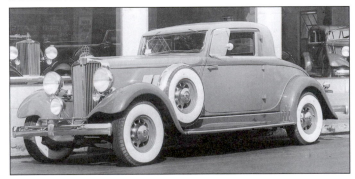

1932 Hupmobile Series 226 cabriolet-roadster.
NATIONAL MOTOR MUSEUM

1911 Hupp-Yeats electric coupé.
NATIONAL MOTOR MUSEUM

6079 in 1911, when a 4-seater tourer on a 100in (2540mm) wheelbase joined the 2-seater. This was now made in three models, the original roadster with exposed bolster fuel tank behind the seats, a torpedo in which the tank was concealed under a streamlined tail, and a closed coupé. The Model 20 was made up to 1913, and Hupmobile's sales prospects were further helped by the appearance for the 1912 season of the Model 32. This had a larger 2980cc engine rated at 32hp, hence its name, and a 106in (2692mm) wheelbase capable of carrying a more spacious 5-seater tourer body. This extended the appeal of the Hupmobile, which sold 7640 cars in 1912 and 12,543 in 1913. Robert Hupp had left the company by this time, to set up the R.C.H. Corporation which made HUPP-YEATS electric cars and a small petrol car called the R.C.H.

The Model 32 had a somewhat unusual appearance, with large headlamps mounted on a horizontal bar running across the front of the radiator, so that the lamps stood higher than the bonnet top. In 1912 Frank E. Watts became chief engineer, a post which he would hold for the next 26 years, and for 1915 he designed a new car of much more conventional appearance. This was the Model K with 3-litre engine, a more rounded radiator, bonnet faired into the cowl in the modern manner, and normally-placed headlamps. It was also the first Hupmobile to have left-hand drive. The Model 32 was continued alongside the K in 1915, but for 1916 both were replaced by a larger car, the 4-litre Model N, which featured electric lighting and starting. Body styles included a 2-door sedan with the doors placed halfway down each side, and there was also a longer wheelbase 134in (3404mm) chassis which carried 7-seater tourer or limousine coachwork. The latter was a really luxurious body, with speaking tube and call buzzer, toilet case, smoking set and flower vase. It cost $2365, $1000 more than the sedan, and few were made.

Although the Model N sold well, 27,514 in two seasons, Hupmobile decided to return to a concept closer to their original idea of a compact yet roomy car. For 1918 they replaced the N with the R, a 3-litre car on a 112in (2845mm) wheelbase, and at first available as a 2-seater roadster or 5-seater tourer. A sedan and a coupé were added in 1919, and the Model R was made with little change until 1925. More than 124,000 were built, making Hupmobile one of America's more important manufacturers. During the 1920s they varied between 7th and 13th places in the production league. Bodies were made mostly by the H & M Body Co. of Racine, Wisconsin, a company formed by Hupp and Mitchell in 1919. After Mitchell closed down in 1923 H & M built solely for Hupp. In 1923 they were bought by the larger Murray Body Co. who proved Hupmobile bodies well into the 1930s.

Up to 1925 no Hupmobile had more than four cylinders, but they then followed the prevailing fashion by offering a straight-8 in January 1925. The 4042cc 60bhp Model E had 4-wheel hydraulic brakes by Lockheed, and came in four body styles which were not particularly exciting to look at. This was rectified on later models which included a line styled by Ray Dietrich and called the Distinguished Eight. At prices up to $2595 these were expensive, nearly twice the price of the sixes, and in 1927 only 16 per cent of Hupmobile sales were of the straight-8s.

Styling of all Hupmobiles was greatly improved on the 1928 models, which were the work of Amos Northup. A variety of attractive colours was used, often in dual-tone schemes, and the bumpers, lights and luggage racks were chrome-plated. Though wood-spoked artillery wheels were standard, wire or disc wheels were optional. Northup played an important part in the design of later Hupmobiles, included the 1934 models, as well as being responsible for such striking cars as the Willys-Knight Great Six, Reo Royale, and Graham Blue Streak.

The Hupp Motor Co. had a record year in 1928, with deliveries of 65,862 cars and profits of more than $8 million. In November they bought the Chandler-Cleveland Co. of Cleveland, Ohio, who were making cars in roughly the same class as Hupp. For six months they continued the Chandler line, then started making the 6-cylinder Hupmobile in the Chandler factory and bodies in the Cleveland factory. This continued for three years, but the Depression hit Hupp so badly that they could barely keep the Detroit factory going, and the former Chandler factory was sold. The Cleveland plant was retained for body building until 1934.

The 1932 Hupmobile Eights were strikingly restyled by Raymond Loewy who began his long automotive career on these cars. The radiator had a slightly vee-shaped grill topped by a large open ring with the letter H inside. The wings followed the contour of the wheels instead of flowing down to the running

boards as on most cars, and chrome plated discs could be had to cover the wire wheels at only five dollars a set. The engines were 4108 and 4560cc straight 8s, and there was also a 3703cc six which did not have Loewy's wings and mascot. In a prosperous year these Hupmobiles might have found many buyers, but 1932 was the worst year of the Depression, and Hupp's sales were only 10,076 cars. 1933 models were slightly changed, with sloping grills, and sold even fewer, 7316, but 1934 saw some advanced-looking aerodynamic sedans. Styled by Loewy and Northup, they had headlamps faired into the bonnet sides, curious three-piece windscreens and streamlined backs with the spare wheel mounted in the boot lid. Mechanical improvments included an anti-roll bar at the rear and a hypoid rear axle. Engines were a 4020cc six and a 4977cc eight. Like Chrylser, Hupp hedged their bets with a conventionally styled 3665cc six, which was a wise decision as only 3218 aerodynamic cars were sold, out of a total of 9420 for the 1934 season.

Hupmobiles were little changed for 1935, but the year was a disaster for the company because of the activities of its new president, Archie M. Andrews. He had ambitious plans for a front-drive car and a merger with Willys which would have led to a compact Hupmobile based on the Willys 77. Nothing came of this, and Andrews' bad reputation in the industry (see RUXTON) scared off investors who might have provided some much needed capital. Charlie Nash in particular refused to have anything to do with Hupmobile, knowing that it was headed by Andrews. By December 1935 Hupp had debts of over a million dollars and no credit. Only 74 1936 models were made before production was suspended.

The factory remained closed until July 1937, when it opened to assemble 238 more of the 1936 models, and to prepare for the new 1938 line which was launched in September. These were more conventional, looking not unlike 1938 Hudsons. The only body style was a 4-door sedan, powered by either the 4020cc six or 4977cc eight. These cars were made sporadically during 1938 and up to May 1939, by which time 3483 had been made. Only 397 of these had the straight-8 engine.

Hupp's final fling paralleled that of Graham, both companies making use of the Cord 810 body dies. Hupp planned to build the new car themselves, and announced it with fanfares of publicity in September 1938. However they could not afford to put it into production, and were forced to buy the bodies and chassis from Graham; the only Hupmobile part of it was the old 6-cylinder engine and the name, Skylark. These did not reach the market until May 1940, 20 months after the initial announcement. Only 319 Skylarks were made, production ending on 12th July 1940. Some were not sold until early 1941, and were marketed as 1941 models.

NG

Further reading
'1934–35 Aerodynamic Hupmobile', Mike Covello,
Automobile Quarterly, Vol. 39, No. 3.

HUPP-YEATS (US) 1911–1919

1911–1914 R.C.H. Corp., Detroit, Michigan.
1914–1919 Hupp-Yeats Electric Car Co., Detroit, Michigan.
This was an electric car made by the corporation which Robert C. Hupp had founded after he left HUPMOBILE. It made R.C.H. petrol cars and Hupp-Yeats electrics. The first of these was a 3-seater landaulette, but for 1912 they branched out into a wide range of styles, with grand names such as the Patrician coupé and torpedo, Regent coupé and Regina roadster. They had Westinghouse motors and five forward speeds, with a range of 75 to 90 miles. In 1913 Robert Hupp left to try his luck with the MONARCH Motor Car Co. About 1000 cars had been made, and a further 20 were assembled in 1914. The R.C.H. Corp. was bought by a group of businessmen who discontinued the R.C.H. but continued with the electric. Waning demand meant that far fewer were sold than during Robert Hupp's regime, and production ended in 1919.

NG

HURACAN (E) 1958

Huracán Motors SA, Barcelona.
This was one of the numerous Spanish minicars using a 197cc Hispano-Villiers engine. Owing to its high price the car had no chance of competing with the Seat 600.

VCM

1907 Hurmid 40hp tourer.
NATIONAL MOTOR MUSEUM

HURLINCAR (GB) 1913–1916

Hurlin & Co. Ltd, Hackney, London.
This was a light car whose first model was powered by an 8/10hp V-twin J.A.P. engine, with chain final drive. For 1915 it became a more substantial car, with 8/10hp 4-cylinder Ballot engine and shaft drive. The Hurlin company also sold the ultra-light AVIETTE cyclecar.

NG

HURN (GB) 1990 to date

1990–c.1994 Hurn Ltd (Mk14 Components), Loddon, Norfolk.
c.1994 to date Mk14 Components, Swindon, Wiltshire.
The classic 1957 Lotus Elite was an obvious choice for replication and this was easily the best on offer because it used a fibreglass monocoque, as per the original. As the company's main business was restoring genuine Elites, every item was painstakingly reproduced, although modern composite techniques were used. Original Coventry Climax FWE engines were used and most cars were bought for historic racing.

CR

HURST; HURMID (GB) 1900–1907

1900–1906 G. Hurst, Holloway, London.
1906–1907 Hurst & Middleton Ltd, Holloway, London.
In 1900 George Hurst's partnership with Lewis Lloyd (see below) ended, and he set up on his own in Holloway. The cars were on Panhard lines, with 12hp 2-cylinder and 24hp 4-cylinder engines and chain or shaft drive. Output was sporadic and very small, though a 20hp was sold in 1902 to the Member of Parliament for Aberdeen. The first appearance at a Motor Show was in 1903 when George Hurst exhibited his 12hp 2-cylinder and 24hp 4-cylinder cars. They had 3-speed gearboxes with direct drive on top. *The Automotor Journal* said the cars were 'of very taking appearance', but *The Car* qualified their general praise by saying that the Hursts were in a very unfinished state, and there were several details which would need radical alteration. In 1906 he was joined by R.E. Middleton and listed three models, a 10hp twin, 15/18hp four and 30/40hp six. The latter had a capacity of 5880cc and was reasonably priced at under £500 complete with 5-seater tourer body. In June 1906 the name of the cars was changed to Hurmid. It is possible that only the 6-cylinder car was marketed under this name.

NG

HURST & LLOYD (GB) 1897–1900

1897–1898 Hurst & Lloyd, Holborn, London.
1898–1900 Hurst & Lloyd, Wood Green, London.
George Hurst was a model maker working at 293 High Holborn who began his partnership with Lewis A. Lloyd in making engines. In 1897 they built a car with 2-cylinder horizontal engine under the floorboards and final drive by flat belt. In 1898 they acquired a small workshop in Wood Green. This was only large enough to hold 10 cars and to employ 30 men. They made a few more cars there. Hurst left in 1900 to make cars under his own name at Holloway, while Lloyd was joined by W.E. Plaister. Six cars in the course of construction were named LLOYD & PLAISTER, as were all subsequent cars.

NG

c.1898 Hurtu dogcart.
NATIONAL MOTOR MUSEUM

1913 Hurtu 14hp 2-seater.
NATIONAL MOTOR MUSEUM

1914 Hurtu Model F landaulet.
NICK BALDWIN

HURTAN (E) 1998
Talleres J. Hurtado SL, Maracena-Granada.
Long experience building prototypes for other companies helped Juan Hurtado to prepare a small series of his own cars with classic design elements. The Hurtan

had a fibreglass body and a purpose-built chassis, but used mechanical parts and engines from Renault, the 4-cylinder 1100cc with 75bhp or the 1400cc with 100bhp. The 2-seater convertible weighed only 1477lb (670kg).
VCM

HURTU (F) 1896–1930
1896–1899 Diligeon et Cie, Albert, Somme.
1899–1930 Compagnie des Autos et Cycles Hurtu, Albert, Somme; Neuilly, Seine; Rueil, Seine et Oise.
This company had its origins in Messrs Hurtu, Hautin et Diligeon, founded in 1880 at Albert to manufacture sewing machines. They soon branched out into machine tools, grinders and bicycles, sold under the name Hurtu. In 1895 E. Diligeon bought out his partners to form the Sté Diligeon et Cie, but he still called the products Hurtu. With some 500 employees the company was one of the largest metal-working businesses in France. In 1896 they became car manufacturers when they undertook licence production of the LÉON BOLLÉE tricar; more of these were made by Diligeon than by Bollée who had originated the design. In 1897 they launched the first Hurtu car, a close copy of the BENZ Velo, for which they sold a licence to Marshall of Manchester, who made it as the Marshall-Benz, ancestor of the BELSIZE. In 1899 Diligeon et Cie was reorganised as the Compagnie des Automobiles Cycle Hurtu. They made the Benz-based cars up to 1900 when a more modern design appeared. This was not very original, following the pattern of front-mounted 3½hp single-cylinder De Dion-Bouton engine, shaft drive and 2- or 4-seater bodies, the latter a rear-entrance tonneau. They also used Aster engines with one, two or four cylinders. 1907 models included an 8hp single and fours of 14 and 24hp, and the single was still listed in 1912. They adopted the Renault-type dashboard radiator in 1907, and continued this until 1920, when most other manufacturers apart from Renault had abandoned it.

In 1913, when about 600 Hurtus were made, there were two 4-cylinder models, the 1692cc 10hp and 2120cc 14hp. They had monobloc engines and unit construction of engine and gearbox. Both were listed to 1916, though doubtless few were made in the last year because of the war. Cars were only a small part of Hurtu's business, which also included bicycles and metalwork of all kinds. For 1920 the radiator was moved forward to a conventional position, and had a slight vee-shape. The engine was a 2358cc side-valve four, replaced in 1922 by a smaller Altos ohv unit of 2 litres. This had front-wheel brakes and was sold on the UK market with British-built bodies. It was offered on its home market with semi-sporting 4-seater bodywork, though Hurtu were one of the few French firms never to have engaged in sporting events. In 1925 it was joined by a smaller car, the 8CV with 1328cc side-valve Altos engine. It had a 4-speed gearbox and was fitted with 4/5-seater tourer, cabriolet and saloon bodies. This and the 2-litre were made up to 1930, together with light trucks on the same chassis. In 1930 *La Vie Automobile* wrote eulogistically about the company's success over the years, that they had never suffered from the problems that affected so many car makers, even the grave crisis of the past twelve months. Alas, they wrote too soon, for Hurtu dropped cars at the end of 1930.
NG

HUSELTON (US) 1911–1914
Huselton Automobile Co., Butler, Pennsylvania.
The first car dealer in Butler County, Edgar Huselton entered manufacture with a large and impressive car powered by a 6.7-litre 40hp 4-cylinder engine, with 4-speed gearbox and shaft drive. He started building it in 1909, but it was September 1911 before he formed his company and offered the car for sale. Tourers and roadsters were listed, but only 13 cars were completed, one of which survives today, owned by Edgar Huselton's grandson.
NG

HUSQVARNA (S) 1943
Husqvarna Vapenfabriks AB, Husqvarna.
Sweden's most celebrated motorcycle manufacturer, in business from 1903, built a prototype 3-wheeler powered by a 500cc air-cooled 2-stroke engine, with chain drive to the single rear wheel. It was intended for production after the war, but Husqvarna decided to concentrate on motorcycles.
NG

HUSSEY (US) 1903
Hussey Automobile & Supply Co., Detroit, Michigan.
Hussey's main business was the manufacture of a patent tilting steering wheel. They built a runabout with single-cylinder 7hp engine to demonstrate the wheel, and offered a few for sale, both complete and without power. This side of the business lasted barely six months.
NG

HUSTLER see INTERSTYL

HUTSON (GB) 1986 to date
Hutson Motor Co., Bradford, Yorkshire.
Restoration specialists Hutson took over the NAYLOR, an M.G. TF replica, in 1986. As well as fully-built cars, a kit-form version was marketed under the name Mahcon TF.
CR

HUTTON (GB) 1900–1905; 1908
1900–1902 J.E. Hutton Ltd, Northallerton, Yorkshire.
1903–1905 J.E. Hutton Ltd, Thames Ditton, Surrey.
1908 D. Napier & Sons Ltd, Acton, London.
The first Hutton was a voiturette powered by M.M.C., De Dion-Bouton or Aster engines of 5 or 6hp, rear-mounted and driving through a 2-speed belt transmission, with a *vis-à-vis* body. These were made in small numbers in Yorkshire, and the Hutton next surfaced in Surrey as a larger car with 4-cylinder pair-cast engines of 12 and 20hp, and shaft drive. These engines were designed by T.W. Barber and built by Willans & Robinson of Derby. Barber was also responsible for the transmission, incorporated in the rear axle, and for the radiator and carburettor. The transmission, which combined the functions of clutch, change-speed gear and differential, involved an eccentric whose degree of eccentricity could be varied by the action of an oil pump. This system was not used on the 12hp 2-seater, which had a conventional 3-speed gearbox close to the engine. J. Ernest Hutton also sold Panhard and Mercedes cars, which may have brought him more reward than his own cars, and built engines for motor launches.
In 1908 Hutton's name appeared on three 4-cylinder cars built by NAPIER for the Four Inch Race. They were pure Napier in design, but as S.F. Edge had promoted 6-cylinder cars so energetically he did not want the Napier name to be associated with a four. Hutton was quoted as a nominal sponsor, and he drove one of them in the race, which was won by another Hutton. Shortly afterwards he joined WOLSELEY.
NG

HYDRO-CAR see RAMBLER

HYDROCAR (US) 1917–1918
1917–1918 Monnot-Sacher Auto Co., Canton, Ohio.
1918 Hydro Motor Car Co., Canton, Ohio.
George Monnot was a car dealer who designed an amphibious car powered by a 12hp Hercules engine, which ran forward on the road and backwards when in the water. For this reason the propeller was mounted at the front, under the radiator. Two steering wheels were provided, one at each end of the vehicle. Two prototypes were built and tested in a local lake, where speeds of 8–9mph (13–15km/h) were reached, with 25mph (40km/h) being the modest maximum on land. Monnot formed a company in 1918, and hoped to interest the Army. For once, failure was blamed not on the war but on the coming of peace, for after the Armistice in November 1918 the Army showed no further interest.
NG

HYDROMETER (US) 1914–1917
Automobile Boat Manufacturing Co., Seattle, Washington.
This was another amphibious car contemporary with the Hydrocar, but unlike it the Hydrometer travelled in the same direction whether on land or water. The prototype was powered by a Haynes engine, but production models were intended to use Continental. It had a streamlined body more boat-like than the Hydrocar, with the rudder mounted at the rear just behind the propeller. Top speeds of 60mph (97km/h) on land and 25mph (40km/h) in the water were

1930 Hurtu 8CV saloon.
NATIONAL MOTOR MUSEUM

1982 Hyundai Pony 1400 GLS.
NATIONAL MOTOR MUSEUM

claimed, and the Hydrometer was offered in roadster, tourer, limousine and light delivery models, at $2000–3000, though it is unlikely that all these were made. In 1916 it was promoted briefly as the Delia, and in 1917 the factory was said to be ready for production, but nothing further was heard.
NG

HYDROMOBIL (D) 1903–1907
Pittler Motorwagen-Gesellschaft, Berlin-Reinickendorf.
W. von Pittler invented a hydraulic transmission, and his cars were built to test and demonstrate this system. Although he worked for more than four years, little, if any, production resulted. He also built several prototypes using his own design of friction drive.
HON

HYLANDER see HIGHLANDER

HYSLOP (US) 1915
Hyslop & Clark, Toledo, Ohio.
A cyclecar with semi-elliptic springs all round, a 4-cylinder water-cooled engine, and a vee-shaped radiator.
NG

HYTHE see NEW CENTURY (i)

HYUNDAI (KO) 1975 to date
Hyundai Motor Co. Ltd, Seoul.
Hyundai was the largest industrial corporation in Korea, with interests in shipbuilding and civil engineering. In 1968, at their factory at Ulsan, they began to assemble British Ford cars and trucks, and in the early 1970s they considered manufacture. Much of the support for this was British, finance coming from Barclays Bank and City of London financial houses, while the man in charge of the car project was George Turnbull, formerly deputy chairman of Standard-Triumph and at the time of his appointment to Hyundai,

1989 Hyundai Sonata 2.4i GLS saloon.
HYUNDAI (UK)

1992 Hyundai X2 1.5GSi hatchback.
HYUNDAI (UK)

1998 Hyundai Atoz hatchback.
HYUNDAI (UK)

1998 Hyundai Sorrento 2.0L estate car.
HYUNDAI (UK)

managing director of the Austin-Morris Division of British Leyland. Most of the dies for the Hyundai Pony came from British Leyland, though it was styled by Giugiaro in Turin. It was powered by a 1238cc single-ohc 4-cylinder Mitsubishi Saturn engine, with gearbox, rear axle and suspension also sourced from Mitsubishi. The 4-door saloon was first seen at the Turin Show in October 1974, and went into production about a year later. Although of conventional rear-drive layout, the Pony sold well, especially in Canada where, within two years of its arrival, it was the best-selling import. A Canadian factory was opened in 1989.

By 1979 Hyundai was making 103,000 cars per year, as well as a wide range of heavy commercial vehicles. A slightly modified Pony appeared in 1982, with an optional 1439cc engine, but the first big change came in 1985 when the Pony was given a transverse engine and front-wheel drive, and was made in hatchback as well as saloon forms. The previous year they moved into a larger bracket with the Cortina-sized 1597cc rear-drive Stellar, and for 1989 they introduced the front-drive Sonata with 4-cylinder engines of 1796cc, 1997cc or 2351cc, and a 3-litre V6. The Sonata was a competitor in the Ford Sierra class, but at a lower price and very well-equipped. A 2-door 2+2 coupé joined it for 1990. All engines were of Mitsubishi design, the Japanese company having a 10 per cent stake in Hyundai.

Hyundai production rose rapidly, from 91,000 in 1982 to 226,000 in 1985, and 1,037,706 in 1996. In 1987 they launched the Grandeur, a locally-built version of the Mitsubishi Debonair, for which Hyundai made all the bodies for the Japanese market as well as Korean cars. The Pony, called Excel on some markets, was restyled along Sonata lines in 1989, and there was a coupé version called the S Coupé, or more familiarly the Scoupé. It was the first individual Hyundai model, as opposed to a Mitsubishi-derived design. This was made up to 1997 when it was replaced by a new model called simply the Coupé (Tiburon in the United States). For 1999 this was given a 2½-litre V6 engine in addition to the 1.6- and 2-litre units already offered. The Pony was sold on the US market under the name Mitsubishi Precis. For 1991 came the Lantra, a saloon falling between the Pony and Sonata in size, with 4-cylinder engines of 1500cc single-ohc or 1600cc twin-ohc, the latter with 16 valves.

A new Grandeur appeared in 1992, again derived from the Mitsubishi Debonair, and other Mitsubishi clones, not exported, were the Shogun-based Hyundai Galloper and Space Wagon-based M-2. On the other hand, the 1995 Accent, the Pony's successor, was entirely Korean-designed, with no input from Mitsubishi. It had one engine, a 1341cc single-ohc 4-cylinder, and three body styles, 2-door coupé, 4-door saloon and 5-door hatchback. The Lantra gained a diesel engine and an estate car version in 1997, and an important new model in 1998 was the Atoz, a high-roof 5-door hatchback taller than it was wide, powered by a 999cc 4-cylinder single-ohc engine. The Accent was the best-selling car in 1998 in Australia. The Lantra and Sonata were continued, both available with twin-ohc in their largest 4-cylinder engines, while September 1998 saw a new 2493cc 160bhp V6 in the Sonata. A step up in size and luxury from the Sonata was the XG launched at the 1998 Paris Salon. This was built on the Sonata platform, and was offered with the Sonata's 160bhp V6 or a 182bhp 3-litre version. Both engines were coupled to a 5-speed automatic transmission, whereas the Sonata's had four speeds. For the Korean market only there were three large models, the Grandeur and Dynasty, still Mitsubishi Debonair-derived, and the Marcia which was based on the Sonata but had a Mazda engine. In 1999 they moved still further upmarket with the 4½-litre V8 Equus, a 4-door saloon larger than the BMW 7 Series, which was also made in stretch limousine form. The Shuttle MPV was based on the Mitsubishi Space Gear.

For 2000 Hyundai planned two 4x4 models, a rival to the Range Rover Freelander called the Highland with 3- or 3½-litre V6 petrol engines or a 2½-litre 4-cylinder intercooled turbo diesel, and an estate car which was built on the platform of a new Lantra range. Also new in 2000 were the Amica, a 5-door hatchback based on the Atoz platform but with more rounded lines and with a 1.4in (35mm) lower roofline, and a full-size MPV with 2-litre 4, or 2.7-litre V6 engines, called the Trajet.

In 1998 Hyundai had assembly plants in Thailand, the Phillipines, Taiwan, Venezuela, Botswana, Zimbabwe, Egypt, Turkey, the Czech Republic and Holland, and a factory in India where a slightly modified Atoz, called the Santro, was built. In October 1998 Hyundai took over two Korean rival vehicle makers, Kia and Asia Motors.

NG

1999 Hyundai Sante Fe 4×4.
HYUNDAI (UK)

NICK BALDWIN

TURNBULL, GEORGE HENRY (1926–1992)

Reputedly one of the best brains in Britain's motor industry, he seemed destined to hold jobs where he was forever fighting against the odds. His whole career, which seemed so full of promise at the beginning, turned into a sequence of no-win propositions.

Born on 17 October 1926, he was educated at King Henry VIII School in Coventry and won a scholarship to Birmingham University, where he earned an honours degree in engineering.

He joined the Standard Motor Co., in 1950 and advanced through a series of appointments in engineering and production. He was deputy chairman of Standard-Triumph International when it was taken over by Leyland Motors in 1961. The following six years were perhaps the most fruitful of his career. Sir Henry Spurrier, and later, Donald Stokes, gave him a lot of leeway to run the Triumph operations with a comfortable budget. He did so well that they rewarded him with an appointment to be managing director of Austin-Morris in 1968.

He was also deputy managing director of British Leyland Motor Corp. from 1968 to 1973 and his career assumed a guilty-by-association aspect throughout a long period of mismanagement. The board thought well of him and he was widely regarded as the heir to Lord Stokes's office. He was named managing director of BLMC in 1973, serving concurrently as chairman of the BL truck and bus division. It could not last. His disagreement with senior management on policy, personnel, planning, and other matters, grew to conflict proportions, which he solved by leaving in September 1973.

In 1974 he moved to Korea with a three-year contract and a vice presidency with Hyundai Motor Co. to set up a £36m factory to turn out the Pony car (basically a Mitsubishi). He brought with him a team of British engineers who were also frustrated with life in England. Many Pony components were supplied from British sources. When that contract expired, he signed up with the Iran National Motor Co. of Teheran as a consultant and deputy managing director, where he ran the plant that assembled the Paykan (Hillman Hunter).

When he returned to the UK in 1979, he became chairman of Chrysler UK, then in the throes of being sold to Peugeot SA. The company was reorganised as Talbot UK, and he stayed on as chairman and managing director. He increased production at the Ryton-on-Dunsmore plant, retooled it for assembling rhd Peugeot models, and closed the loss-making Linwood plant in Scotland in 1981. Yet he remained an outsider in the Peugeot organisation, with no further promotion in sight.

In 1984 he joined Inchcape, worldwide motor distributors and a trading company of considerable scale, being named chairman in 1986.

He retired due to ill health in 1991 and died in December 1992.

George Turnbull married Marion Wing in 1950. They had one son and two daughters.

JPN

HYUNDAI

1999 Hyundai XG saloon.
HYUNDAI (UK)

2000 Hyundai Accent 1.3 GSi hatchback.
HYUNDAI (UK)

2000 Hyundai Trajet MPV.
HYUNDAI (UK)

IATO (I) 1988–c.1995

Iato SpA, Nusco (AV).

This 4 × 4 estate resembled a Mitsubishi Pajero but, being Italian, was fitted with Fiat or Lancia engines from 1.6- to 2.0-litres capacity, or a 1.9-litre turbodiesel. The bodywork was realised in fibreglass.

CR

IBANA (FIN) 1996

Helsinki Institute of Technology, Helsinki.

Appearing at the 1996 Paris Salon was the Ibana city car from Finland. It was a very small enclosed 2-seater that looked like a 3-wheeler, but the rear 'single' wheel was in fact two very narrow-set wheels claimed to overcome stability problems. The prototype had a 547cc 2-cylinder petrol engine driving the front wheels via a semi-automatic transmission, but intended future examples were to have serial hybrid power for low-emissions reasons. However, nothing further was heard.

CR

IBERIA (E) 1907–1908

M. Vehil, Madrid.

Little is known about this company that presented two cars, a sedan and an open tourer, at the Madrid Fair in 1907. No technical data are known.

VCM

IBEX (US) c.1996 to date

Ibex Automotive Design & Engineering, San Antonio, Texas.

The Ibex Meridian was a small sport/utility vehicle that was designed for long life in marine environments. It looked like a wildly styled mini pick-up truck with no doors. It had a special fibreglass body and used running gear from Daihatsu Charade or Ford 1100cc vehicles. A 4-wheel drive version was offered with turbocharging. They were sold in kit or fully assembled form in the US and the Caribbean.

HP

IBEX *see* FOERS

IBIS (F) 1907

Automobiles Ibis, Levallois-Perret, Seine.

Two models of Ibis were made, an 8/10hp 2-cylinder and a 12/14hp 4-cylinder. Both were shaft-driven.

NG

I. C. M. (US) c.1996

I. C. M. Industries, Burbank, California.

This kit car company built replicas of the Porsche Speedster based on VW floorpans. They made a standard body and a modified one with wheel flares for wider tyres.

HP

IDEAL (i) (US) 1902–1903

B & P Co., Milwaukee, Wisconsin.

This company made a light runabout powered by a 5hp single-cylinder horizontal engine with 3-speed gearbox, in an angle-iron frame. The 2-seater body tilted for easy access to the engine. The company also made petrol and steam engines for other firms.

NG

IDEAL (ii) (US) 1907

Ideal Runabout Manufacturing Co., Buffalo, New York.

This was a very simple 2-seater runabout powered by a 5hp single-cylinder engine, with chain drive. Its tiller steering and absence of any mudguards was distinctly old-fashioned for 1907. The price was $400.

NG

IDEAL (iii) (US) 1910–1911

Ideal Electric Vehicle Co., Chicago, Illinois.

This was a conventional chain-driven electric brougham priced at $1875 in 1910

1916 Ideal (v) cyclecar.
NATIONAL MOTOR MUSEUM

and $2200 in 1911. In 1912 Bruce Borland acquired the design and marketed it as the BORLAND.

NG

IDEAL (iv) (US) 1914

The Ideal Shop, Buffalo, New York.

The second Buffalo car to bear the name Ideal, this was a cyclecar powered, like so many of its kind, by a 9/13hp V-twin Spacke engine, with 2-speed epicyclic transmission and belt drive. Three seating arrangements were available, a single-seater, tandem 2-seater and side by side 2-seater.

NG

IDEAL (v) (E) 1915–1918

Talleres Hereter SA, Barcelona.

Founded in 1905, as stove-fitters, Talleres Hereter (T.H.) soon expanded business to automotive components. In 1915 the company presented a little cyclecar called the Ideal with a 4-cylinder, 1099cc, 6/8hp (20bhp) engine and aluminium T-head. This car was almost entirely made in the T.H. factory. The Ideal was entered into a lot of races, always in competition with the DAVID cyclecars. A company named Robert Soyer prepared several Ideals, which began to defeat works-entered models in racing. The technician behind them, Sebastian Nadal, was made chief engineer of T.H.

VCM

IDEAL (vi) (US) 1920

Bethlehem Motor Truck Corp., Allentown, Pennsylvania.

This was an export-only car planned by a well-known truck maker, using a 40hp 4-cylinder engine of the company's own make. A small number of sports tourers were built. Truck production continued until 1926.

NG

IDEN (GB) 1904–1907

Iden Motor Car Co., Coventry.

This company was formed by George Iden, formerly works manager of M.M.C. The first models of 1904 had 4-cylinder engines of 12 and 18hp, with shaft drive and 5-seater tourer bodies. They were continued up to 1907, and a 25hp four was announced for 1905, but only made for one season. In 1907 a front-wheel drive car was announced, with 12hp V-twin engine under the seat, and drive via a 3-speed gearbox. It had a landaulette body and was intended for taxi work as well as a private car. Few were made.

NG

I.E.N.A. (I) 1922–1925

Industria Economica Nazionale Automobili di Tommasi & Rizzi, Lodi.

This was a conventional light car powered by 750 or 1100cc 4-cylinder Chapuis-Dornier engines. The latter was an ohv unit used in the Tipo Spinto sports model. About 150 I.E.N.A.s were made.

NG

1905 Iden 12hp or 18hp town car.
NATIONAL MOTOR MUSEUM

IFA (DDR) 1948–1956
Industrie-Vereinigung Volkseigener Fahrzeugwerke, Zwickau; Eisenach.
This was not a brand name but it covered a variety of designs made by a nationalised combine in East Germany. The firms which made up the IFA were the former Audi, DKW, Horch, Wanderer and Phänomen, as well as some tractor makers and coachbuilders. However, the IFA badge was used on motorcycles and also cars of prewar DKW design, the 684cc 2-cylinder and 804cc 3-cylinder, the latter not going into production because of the war. The 2-cylinder cars (F8) had prewar style bodies, some of wooden construction, and were thus very old-fashioned by 1955, though some had bodies with more modern styling by IFA Karosseriefabrik Dresden (formerly Glaser), and in West Germany, by Baur of Stuttgart. The 3-cylinder cars (F9) had more streamlined bodies whose styling was shared with the West German DKW Meisterklasse of the early 1950s. The IFAs were made in considerable numbers, 26,270 F8s between 1949 and 1955, and about 30,000 F9s between 1950 and 1956. The F8 was the basis of the ZWICKAU made from 1956 to 1959, and the F9 was rebodied to become the WARTBURG. The F8s were made at Zwickau, the F9 began at Zwickau but was later transferred to Eisenach.
HON

I. F. G. see WARLOCK

I.H.C. (US) 1910–1911
Independent Harvester Co., Plano, Illinois.
This car was built by Henry Holsman after he had left the Chicago company which bore his name, and which was probably the best-known maker of high-wheelers in America. Advertised as 'The Farmer's Favorite' it differed little from the Holsman in design. The initials Holsman chose for his car were also

used by INTERNATIONAL (iii) who were making much the same sort of car. This was a source of confusion, possibly intentional on Holsman's part, but the days of the high-wheeler were over, and the I.H.C. lasted for less than two years.
NG

IHLE (D) 1947
Gebr. Ihle, Bruchsal.
The coachbuilders Ihle Brothers were best-known for the sports bodies they built on the 1930 BMW 3/15PS, which pioneered the 'double kidney' radiator grill pattern, which has been used by BMW ever since. In 1947 they brought out a tiny roadster somewhat resembling a fairground scooter. It was powered by a rear-mounted 125cc DKW or 150cc Ilo engine which drove by chain to the right rear wheel only. Only a few were made as it was too small even for the car-starved market of the day.
HON

I.J.F. see SAXAN

I.K.A. see KAISER CARABELA and TORINO

IKENGA (GB) 1968–1969
David Gittens, London.
American-born David Gittens designed the Ikenga on a McLaren M6 Can-Am chassis supplied by Ken Sheppard. The extraordinary coupé bodywork, built in aluminium by Williams & Pritchard, was initially presented as a rather block-like form with a forward-hinging central canopy. The bodywork was revised by coachbuilders Radford with a smoother front end that hinged up as a piece. A mid-mounted 325bhp Chevrolet Camaro Z-28 engine and ZF 5-speed transmission

were used. The car was claimed to reach 162mph (261km/h) and 0–60mph (97km/h) in 5.0 seconds. Curious features included fluid-filled instruments, a distance proximity sensor, rear-view TV camera and Perspex boot lid that doubled up as an air brake. Gittens announced his intention to make up to 150 cars at £9000 each but he joined Radford and the Ikenga remained a one-off.

CR

ILFORD (GB) 1902–1903
Ilford Motor Car & Cycle Co., Ilford, Essex.
This was a short-lived light car powered by a 5hp single-cylinder M.M.C. engine mounted at the front and driving through a 3-speed gearbox and shaft to the rear wheels. It had a 4-seater *vis-à-vis* body. The company's motorcycles, called Regina, were more successful, being made up to 1915.

NG

ILINGA (AUS) 1973–1975
Ilinga Pty Ltd, Port Melbourne, Victoria.
A prestige high-performance coupé conceived by Daryl Davies and Tony Farrell, the Ilinga (aboriginal for 'the far distance') AF2 was built on a combined chassis and structure incorporating roll bars, to which alloy panels were attached. A Leyland Australia 4.4-litre V8 had Weber carburettors and modifications to raise power to 221bhp and was coupled to a Borg-Warner 35 automatic. Built on a wheelbase of 103in (2625mm), it weighed 1250kg and had all-coil suspension, rack and pinion steering, 4-wheel ventilated disc brakes and Globe alloy wheels.

The transmission was declared unsuitable after two cars had been made, and the supplier declined to offer a guarantee. The unit was designed for 4-cylinder 2-litre engines and was used with the Rover V8 and the enlarged Australian engine but the uprated output took it beyond its limits. As the cost of re-engineering for another unit had not been budgeted for, finances were depleted and the project was liquidated in 1975.

MG

Further Reading
'Hostile Horizons: The Short Life of Australia's Ilinga', Gavin Farmer, *Automobile Quarterly*, Vol. 33, No. 2.

ILLINOIS (i) (US) 1907
Moline Pump Co., Moline, Illinois.
This company, better known for engines, announced two models of car in February 1907. Called the Illinois, these were a 12hp runabout at $650 and a 20hp runabout at $850, both naturally using Moline Pump's engines. Production did not last out the year.

NG

ILLINOIS (ii) (US) 1909–1912
The Overholt Co., Galesburg, Illinois.
Designed and built by Ed Overholt, the first cars by this company went under the Overholt name. They were 4-seater doorless runabouts powered by a 12hp 2-cylinder air-cooled engine with chain drive. Bodies for these and the later Illinois were by a local coachbuilder, A.L.Nelson. Ten Overholts were made in 1909, but the cars were renamed Illinois for 1910, when they became larger, with 30hp 4-cylinder Reeves engines, still air-cooled, and 5-seater tourer bodies. For 1911 he used a 35/40hp water-cooled Waukesha engine in a larger car still, on a 120in (3046mm) wheelbase. This was continued in 1912, along with a smaller four of 25.6hp. The 1912 35/40 was offered with two closed body styles, a coupé and a limousine, as well as three open models. Production was never large, 15 cars in 1910 and about 50 in 1911/12. Overholt later bought the rights to the Reeves engine and all of that company's assets. He made engines as well as accessories for the Model T Ford from 1912 to 1914 when his factory burnt down.

NG

IMFAP (E) 1955–1956
Talleres Soto, Madrid.
In 1955 the co-technician of NACIONAL-G, Natalio Horcajo, developed a motorcycle for the Soto workshop, sold under the name of Raid. Using this single-cylinder 2-stroke engine he developed several small cars, which worked very well. The workshop soon decided to build a larger car with a new 2-cylinder,

1950 IFA F8 saloon, by Baur.
NICK GEORGANO/NATIONAL MOTOR MUSEUM

2-stroke 700cc engine. This car looked good and had excellent mechanical components, but the omnipresent Ministry of Industry forbade the project; only some prototypes were finally built.

VCM

IMMERMOBIL (D) 1905–1907
Max Eisenmann & Co., Hamburg.
This company made two models, both on French lines and using French engines. The 8hp had a single-cylinder De Dion-Bouton engine and the 10/12hp a 4-cylinder Reyrol. Both had 2-seater bodies. The name Immermobil means 'Ever Ready'.

HON

IMMISCH (GB) 1887–c.1897
Acme & Immisch Electrical Works Ltd, Chalk Farm, London.
Acme & Immisch were important electrical contractors who built a few cars, mostly to special order. They provided the motors and running gear for the electric cars made by Magnus VOLK, including the two he supplied to the Sultan of Turkey. There was insufficient demand to justify anything that one could call production of cars.

NG

IMOLA (i) (GB) 1990s
Under this name, an A.C. Cobra replica was marketed from 1991 onwards. Aluminium was used for the bodyshells and subframes, which fitted on to customer-supplied chassis.

CR

IMOLA (ii) (GB) 1994
Imola, Salford Priors, Evesham, Worcestershire.
This was a highly promising mid-engined car designed by Peter Rawlinson, a Jaguar employee. It was an extremely attractive open 2-seater sports car with a mid-mounted engine (MG Montego in the prototype but Rover/Honda engines up to V6 could be fitted). There was a stainless steel monocoque with MacPherson strut rear suspension in a separate subframe and double wishbone/rocker arm/inboard coil spring front suspension. The main bodyshell was in fibreglass, with an intention to produce a carbonfibre option. The project finally foundered when Rawlinson joined Lotus, after only a handful of bodyshells, but no chassis, had been supplied.

CR

I.M.P. (A/I) 1960–1961
Intermeccanica Puch, Turin.
The result of a collaboration between STEYR-PUCH and INTERMECCANICA, the I.M.P. 700GT was an Austro-Italian equivalent of the Abarth 500 coupé. Using the rear-engined Steyr-Puch 500 as a basis, a pretty aluminum 2-seater coupé was developed. Its 40bhp 645cc engine enabled a top speed of 100mph (161km/h). It was fully approved by Steyr and between 11 and 21 examples were produced, including racing versions, of which one won the 500cc class at the Nürburgring.

CR

1914 Imp (i) cyclecar.
M.J.WORTHINGTON-WILLIAMS

IMP (i) (US) 1913–1914

Imp Cycle Car Co., Auburn, Indiana.

The Imp Cyclecar Co. was a subsidiary of the W.H. McIntyre Co., which had made the McINTYRE high-wheeler. Seeing that the day of the high-wheeler was over, they latched onto the latest fashion, the cyclecar, and had more success with it than many other firms. The Imp was generally typical of its kind, with 15hp V-twin air-cooled engine, friction transmission and belt drive. Seating was either in tandem or staggered side by side. Among its unusual features were the absence of axles as the wheels were mounted on the ends of transverse springs, and starting by inserting a crank into the centre of the steering column.

Imp production began at ten per month, and by July 1914 had reached 50 per month. By then the V-twin was joined by a 4-cylinder model on a longer wheelbase. 'Imp cyclecars are produced in larger quantities probably, than any other manufacturer in the same line', said *Automobile Trade Journal* in July 1914. However, the good times did not last for long, as all cyclecars, even the good ones, faded from popularity. The Imp's designer, William B. Stout, who was responsible for the streamlined SCARAB in the 1930s, estimated that total production of Imps was several hundred.

NG

IMP (ii) (US) 1949–1951

International Motor Products, Glendale, California.

This early commuter car was designed for short hops around town. It was a small, open car with a single-cylinder 7½hp engine. Mileage was reputed to be about 60mpg.

HP

IMPALA *see* FOULKES

IMPERATOR (D) 1905–1906

Michaelis & Ebner Automobilwerke, Berlin.

The firm started by importing American LOCOMOBILE steam cars, and in 1905 they put on the market their own steamer. It was not a success and in the same year they turned to petrol power. A 2-cylinder 10PS and 4-cylinder 16PS were made, but not in large numbers. The 4-cylinder car found some interest among Berlin taxi operators.

HON

IMPERIA (i) (B) 1906–1949

1906–1920 Automobiles Imperia, Liège; Nessonvaux.
1920–1929 Automobiles Imperia SA Mathieu van Roggen, Nessonvaux.
1929–1935 SA des Automobiles Imperia-Excelsior, Nessonvaux.
1935–1949 Minerva-Imperia SA, Nessonvaux.

Automobiles Imperia was established by Adrien Piedboeuf who had made a few motorcycles under his own name since 1904. He chose as his badge the crown of the Emperor Charlemagne (hence the name Imperia), and in various forms this remained the company's trademark up to the end of car production. The first Imperia was a conventional 4-cylinder car with pair-cast cylinders, and shaft or chain drive. Rated at 24/30CV, it was made in very small numbers, and sold mostly to Piedboeuf's family and friends.

In 1908 he expanded with the purchase of the PIEPER factory at Nessonvaux, outside Liège, and engaged a German chief engineer, Paul Henze, who later became famous as the designer of STEIGER and SIMSON SUPRA cars in the 1920s. Henze added to the 4.9-litre 24/30 a smaller 3-litre car with shaft drive and a larger chain-driven model, the 9.9-litre 50/60. In 1909 he joined the fashion for small monobloc fours, with the 1764cc 12CV, which was made up to 1914. The last of the chain-drive 50/60s was made in 1911, and by the outbreak of war Imperia was making a range of conventional L-head 4-cylinder cars in 1764cc (12CV), 1846cc (12/14CV) and 2612cc (14/16CV) sizes. In 1912 Imperia merged with Automobiles SPRINGUEL, a small Liège firm which had been making 4-cylinder cars since 1907. Its proprietor, Jules Springuel, became managing director of Imperia, and some cars were sold under the name Springuel-Imperia. The largest in the range, the 5024cc 28/35CV, was a Springuel design, with pair-cast cylinders and inlet-over-exhaust valves. In sporting form it had wire wheels and a handsome vee-radiator which was adopted on all Imperias after the war.

Also sold under the Imperia name were two sporting models, the 3014cc 15/22CV and 3617cc 20/26CV. These engines were T-head designs by the Spaniard Francisco Abadal, and it seems that he ordered the components to be made in Belgium for assembly in Barcelona where he sold them under the name ABADAL. Some were also marketed in Belgium as Imperias, and, to complicate matters further, a French dealer sold them in Paris as French cars! The 20/26CV engine had the same dimensions (80 × 180mm) as the Hispano-Suiza Alfonso, and seems to have been a pretty close copy of that car, though disguised in appearance by its vee-radiator.

In 1920 Imperia was bought by a young businessman, Mathieu Van Roggen, who continued the Abadal designs for a few years. These included the 15/22 and 20/26, as well as two models with ohcs, the single-ohc 5630cc luxury chassis, and a twin-ohc sports car with the same dimensions (80 × 149mm) as the contemporary 3-litre Bentley. The luxury car had a seven-bearing crankshaft straight-8 engine in unit with a 4-speed gearbox, ignition by double Scintilla magnetos and Perrot four-wheel brakes. It was one of the most advanced luxury cars of its day, but at 55,000 francs for the chassis alone, it was more expensive than a Minerva or Excelsior, and only three or four prototypes were made.

The sports car was also an advanced design, with four valves per cylinder, four-wheel brakes and a top speed of 87mph (140km/h). Three were entered in the 1922 Belgian Grand Prix, that of Baron de Tornaco winning at an average of 55mph (89km/h). It is possible that a few cars were made in addition to the team cars, but production was very small. Indeed, not more than 200 cars left the Imperia factory between 1919 and 1923. Unlike the prewar cars they were called Imperia-Abadals, apart from a pedestrian 2120cc 12CV which was mainly seen as a taxicab.

In 1923 Van Roggen decided that the expensive Abadal designs must go, to be replaced by a cheaper car which could be sold in much larger quantities. He engaged as chief engineer Arnold Couchard who had been in the motor industry since 1899, spending most of his time with F.N. Couchard produced a small 4-cylinder engine with slide valves, in which sliding sleeves were located on either side of the cylinder wall, moving vertically covering and uncovering double ports. Although expensive to repair, this engine had a high speed for the period, up to 4000rpm, and had a good power output for its size. This was originally 994cc, increased in 1924 to 1094cc (6CV) when it gave 27bhp. The engine rotated anti-clockwise, and another unusual aspect of the car's design lay in the braking, foot brake by servo on the transmission and hand brake on the rear wheels. Front-wheel brakes were optional for 1926, and by 1932 the 6CV Imperia had coupled hydraulic brakes on all four wheels. Top speed with four passengers in an open torpedo body was 50mph (80km/h), and Van Roggen entered the cars in a variety of events from the 1923 Brooklands 200 Mile Race to the 1925 Belgian 24 Hour Race and Monte Carlo Rally. They took first three places in their class in both events, Van Roggen driving the winning car in the Monte.

The new design enabled Imperia production to rise, though not dramatically. In 1925 250 cars were made, in 1926, 420 and in 1927, 504. Two attempts were made at foreign production, by VOISIN in France and in the G.W.K. factory in England. Neither came to anything, apart from a few Imperias being fitted with Voisin bodies in exchange for Van Roggen buying a considerable quantity of

Voisin stock. In 1927 a 1650cc 6-cylinder model was added to the range, capacity going up to 1794cc in 1929. This gave 47bhp and a speed of over 60mph (97km/h) was possible, even with a 4-seater saloon body.

Despite a number of sporting successes, including winning the Coupe du Roi in the 1930 Belgian 24 Hour Race, Imperia's sales dropped in the early 1930s. The slide-valve cars were increasingly old-fashioned looking, not helped by the square bodies and artillery wheels, and anyway all Belgian manufacturers were increasingly threatened by cheaper imports. To broaden his base Van Roggen bought up four other Belgian firms in 1929, EXCELSIOR, MÉTALLURGIQUE, NAGANT and the coachbuilders Mathys et Osy. However, none of the cars was the answer to American imports. Van Roggen needed a new design, but could not afford to develop one, so he turned to the German ADLER company which had recently introduced a new small front-wheel drive car, the Trumpf. He imported the 1645cc engine from Germany, and made the chassis, suspension and bodies in Belgium.

The new Imperia came on the market early in 1934, under the name TA-9. Although made in Belgium, the bodies followed Adler lines fairly closely, and included a 2-seater sports car. A smaller car, based on the Adler Trumpf Junior and called the TA-7, appeared later in 1934, and four years later came the 1910cc Imperia Jupiter (TA-11) based on the Adler *Zweiliter*. In 1934 a car of TA-7 appearance but using a 1900cc slide-valve engine, called the TA-4SS, was announced but it did not go into production.

In 1935 Van Roggen bought up the MINERVA company and founded the Minerva-Imperia group. The only significant result for Imperia was that some TA-9s and TA-11s were sold on the French market with Minerva badges. Van Roggen revived his links with Voisin, and some of the French market cars were assembled in the Voisin factory. Towards the end of the 1930s it became increasingly difficult to deal with the Nazi regime in Germany in the normal commercial way, and to obtain his engines Van Roggen had to barter Belgian textiles. This put him in debt to the Gerard-Hauzeur textile company, who took control of Imperia in 1940. Van Roggen retained the Minerva side of the business, though no cars were made after 1938. The front-drive Imperias were made up to the middle of 1940, and even after the German invasion Belgians could buy new Imperias against the appropriate authorisation and a promise that they would run their cars on either gazogene (charcoal fuel) or bottled gas.

In 1945 Imperia obtained the Belgian concession for STANDARD and TRIUMPH cars, and later assembled them at Nessonvaux. These included a convertible Standard Vanguard which was never made in Britain. In 1950 they were assembling 300 Vanguards a month. The postwar Imperia car appeared in 1947. It was another front-wheel drive design of foreign origin, this time the 1340cc Hotchkiss-built Amilcar Compound, clothed in Belgian-designed bodywork, a 2-door saloon, cabriolet and roadster. The all-round independent suspension was inherited from the prewar Adler designs. It performed well, with a top speed of 70mph (112km/h), but the engine and drive train were fragile and gave many problems. About 1000 were made up to 1949, and Imperia thereafter concentrated on Vanguard assembly, followed by that of Adler scooters, Alfa Romeo cars and Büssing trucks. Standard ended its agreement withImperia in 1958, and the company was liquidated soon afterwards.

NG

IMPERIA (ii) (D) 1935
Imperia-Werk AG, Bad Godesberg.

This well-known motorcycle manufacturer, in business from 1924 to 1935, made their first attempt at a 4-wheeler in 1924, but it was not successful. In 1935 they tried again, with an ambitious streamlined coupé powered by a 3-cylinder radial 2-stroke engine of 750cc designed by Dr Ing Rolf Schroedter. It had independent suspension all round. Unfortunately Imperia over-stretched themselves on this car and expensive motorcycle designs such as an opposed piston single-cylinder supercharged 2-stroke, and they were out of business by the end of 1935.

HON

IMPERIAL (i) (US) 1900–1901
Philadelphia Motor Vehicle Co., Philadelphia, Pennsylvania.

This was a 2-seater runabout powered by a 4hp single-cylinder engine with a tiller which served not only for steering, but also for starting and stopping the engine. Its artillery wheels gave it a more substantial appearance than many contemporary runabouts.

NG

1914 Imperia (i) 15.9hp landaulet.
NATIONAL MOTOR MUSEUM

1927 Imperia (i) 11/26hp saloon.
NATIONAL MOTOR MUSEUM

1948 Imperia (i) TA8 saloon.
NICK GEORGANO

IMPERIAL (ii) (GB) 1901–c.1906
Imperial Autocar Manufacturing Co. Ltd, Manchester.

Imperial offered two contrasting designs to start with, a *vis-à-vis* with 3.5hp single-cylinder engine under the seat, and a 4-seater rear-entrance tonneau with front-mounted 6hp 2-cylinder engine. This had shaft drive, while the rear-engined car was driven by bevel gearing from the gearbox. Later cars sold under the Imperial name were French-built, of the LACOSTE ET BATTMANN type, with English-built bodies. A 20hp 4-cylinder double phaeton was made in 1906.

NG

1904 Imperial (ii) tourer.
NATIONAL MOTOR MUSEUM

1956 Imperial (ix) C-73 Southampton 4-door sedan.
NATIONAL MOTOR MUSEUM

1964 Imperial (ix) Crown 4-door hard-top.
NATIONAL MOTOR MUSEUM

1974 Imperial (ix) Le Baron 4-door hard-top.
NATIONAL MOTOR MUSEUM

IMPERIAL (iii) (US) 1903–1904

Rodgers & Co., Columbus, Ohio.

Made by a carriage-building company, the Imperial was a light 2-seater powered by an 8hp flat-twin engine, with shaft drive. Two passenger models were made, an open car and a 'physician's coupé', and there was also a light delivery van. The car also went under the names Columbus or Rodgers.

NG

IMPERIAL (iv) (US) 1903–1904

Imperial Automobile Co., Detroit, Michigan.

This company made one model, a light electric 2-seater runabout suspended on C-springs, which sold for $950.

NG

IMPERIAL (v) (GB) 1904–1905

The Anti-Vibrator Co. Ltd, Croydon, Surrey.

Anti-Vibrator was probably a good name for this company as its cars were electrically powered by two 3hp motors mounted in the rear wheels. It was unusual in having integral construction of body and chassis, and its build was lower than most electric cars of the period.

NG

IMPERIAL (vi) (US) 1906–1907

Imperial Motor Car Co. Williamsport, Pennsylvania.

This Imperial was a roadster with a low centre of gravity thanks to its double-dropped frame, one of the first in America. It was powered by a 35hp 4-cylinder Milwaukee engine, and was available only as a 2-seater, or 4-seater with two passengers in a dickey seat. 'The Imperial roadster is strictly a gentleman's machine', gushed the local *Williamsport Gazette & Bulletin*, inspired perhaps, by the Stanley Gentleman's Speedy Roadster of the same era, but not enough gentlemen came forward with the necessary $2500, and the company closed within two years. Not more than 50 cars were made.

NG

IMPERIAL (vii) (US) 1908–1916

1908–1909 Jackson Carriage Co., Jackson, Michigan.
1909–1916 Imperial Automobile Co., Jackson, Michigan.

This former carriage company made very conventional tourers powered by 4-cylinder engines of 30hp, rising to 45hp in 1911. They were joined by the 6-cylinder Models 44 and 54 (33.7 and 40.9 rated horsepower) in 1914, by which time, as the original factory had burnt down, they were being made in the former Buick truck plant in Jackson. In 1915 the Campbell brothers who owned the company merged it with MARION of Indianapolis to form the Mutual Motors Corp. This then moved to Jackson to make the MARION-HANDLEY, while the Campbells joined with Robert C. Hupp to make the EMERSON.

NG

IMPERIAL (viii) (GB) 1914

Implitico Ltd, London.

This was a cyclecar powered by an 8hp V-twin Precision engine, with seven forward speeds (but no reverse) provided by a belt-and-pulley system and a movable rear axle. Prices varied from £95 for the Model B Type S without hood and screen to £110 for the Model A Type SR with both these items *and* a reverse gear. The makers were lighting engineers who specialised in theatre lighting and also lit the Olympia Motor Shows. Unfortunately, 1914 was a bad time to launch a new car, and not more than 12 Imperials were made, three of which were exported to Spain.

NG

Further Reading

'Fragments on Forgotten Makes – the Imperial', W. Boddy,
Motor Sport, May 1964.

IMPERIAL (ix) (US) 1955–1975

Chrysler Corp., Detroit, Michigan.

Chrysler used the name Imperial for their top line of cars from 1926, but it was not until the 1955 season that it became a completely autonomous division, in

1999 Imza 700 hatchback.
JETPA

the same way that De Soto, Dodge and Plymouth were. The object of this move was to give the Chrysler Corp. a prestige marque that would rival Cadillac and Lincoln. The first Imperials were quite distinctive in appearance, with a divided grill shared only with the Chrysler 300, and, from 1961 to 1963, free-standing headlamps. The engines were the largest in Chrysler's range, a 5424cc V8 in 1955, 5800cc in 1956, and rising to a peak of 7210cc from 1966 to 1975. From the mid–1960s onwards Imperials followed Chrysler styling more closely than before, although while other Chrysler models adopted unitary construction in 1960, Imperials kept separate chassis until 1967. This enabled the Italian coachbuilder Ghia to build a small number of limousines on an extended wheelbase. Known as the Crown Imperial Ghia Limousine, they cost more than $16,000, compared with $6400 for a standard Imperial. A total of 132 were made between 1957 and 1966. An important US first for Imperial was the introduction of anti-lock brakes on the 1973 models. The energy crisis hit the Imperial Division badly as they had no smaller car, and Chrysler closed it down on 12 June 1975.

Chrysler revived the name, though not the separate division, in 1981 for a personal-luxury coupé using fresh styling on the 1980 Cordoba coupé shell, with a 5211cc V8 engine. Made at Chrysler's Windsor, Ontario, factory, production was limited to 25,000 for 1981, but they sold only 7225, and even less in 1982 and 1983. The Imperial name went into abeyance for a second time, to be revived for 1990 on a luxury version of the front-drive V6-engined New Yorker. This sold scarcely any better than its predecessor, and lasted only to the end of the 1993 season.

NG

IMPERIAL (x) *see* ROYALE (ii)

IMPETUS (F) 1899–1903
Max Hertel, Automobiles Impetus, Pornichet, Loire-Inférieure.
Impetus cars were designed by American Max Hertel who had made cars under his own name at Greenfield, Massachusetts. They were elegant light vehicles powered by 3 or 4hp single-cylinder De Dion-Bouton engines, suspended at the rear on large C-springs. By 1902 they had bigger 2-cylinder engines of 9hp. The small seaside resort of Pornichet was an unusual location for a car factory.

NG

IMPULS (S) 1977
The Impuls 77 was a very small electric car prototype.
CR

IMZA (TK) 1999 to date
Jetpa, Istanbul.
Jetpa was founded in 1989 by Fadil Akgunduz as a driving school, and expanded rapidly to include construction and property development. In 1997 they began to sell Proton cars, with CKD assembly beginning in 2000. In October 1999 they launched their own car, the Imza 700 (Imza = signature, and the date was the 700th anniversary of the founding of the Ottoman Empire). The car was a 5-door hatchback with steeply-raked windscreen and bonnet in the style of the A Series Mercedes-Benz. At 94.5in (2400mm) the wheelbase was shorter than the Mercedes or other rivals such as the VW Golf, Opel Astra, or Ford Focus. The prototypes were powered by 1.2-litre Australian Orbital engines, but other engines in the 1.2- to 1.6-litre range were planned for production cars. A factory was built at Siirt in Anatolia, with cars coming off the production line from mid-2002.

Among the team working on the Imza was Erich Bitter who had made his own cars in Germany, and ex-Volvo engineer Jan-Erik Jannson, who had worked with Bitter and also with AC on the Ace and Aceca.

NG

INAUCO (RA) 1960
Inauco SA, Cordoba.
Industrias de Automotores y Construcciones SA (INAUCO) was created on 23 May 1960. The production of the Inauco automobile was announced shortly thereafter. This was a 2-door, 6-seater saloon with boxy lines, powered by a rear-mounted flat-4 engine of 1490cc and developing 55bhp. Another version would be fitted with a flat-eight 2400cc, 85bhp engine. All around independent suspension was included and a top speed of 87mph (140km/h) was claimed for the 8-cylinder version. Unfortunately, production never started.

ACT

1997 Indigo 3000 sports car.
JOSSE CAR AB

INCAMP (E) 1952

This was a short-lived minicar built in Bilbao.

VCM

INDESTOR (I) 1974–1975

Indestor, Turin.

The miniature 'torpedo' (open fun car), launched at the 1974 Geneva Motor Show, was baptised the Croisette and used Fiat 126 mechanicals, including its rear-mounted 594cc engine.

CR

INDIAN (US) 1927–1929

Indian Motorcycle Co., Springfield, Massachusetts.

Whether commercial production of the minute Indian car was intended is a moot point. Four were built under the direction of Jack Bauer, the son of Indian's president, two roadsters, a coupé and one other type. One of the cars was fitted with a 2-cylinder Indian motorcycle engine; the other three with a 4-cylinder Continental. The four cars shared a wheelbase of 84in (2132mm), wire wheels and 19×4.75 tyres. Two of the cars were fitted with bodies by Merrimac, one by LeBaron and the fourth 'in-house'. Any further production was curtailed in 1929 when the company was reorganised.

KM

INDIANA (U) 1974–1975

General Motors de Uruguay, Montevideo.

Built along Vauxhall Viva lines, the Indiana's 2-door hatchback body was moulded in fibreglass. The engine was a 4-cylinder Opel 1100cc unit. Sixty per cent of the car was made in Uruguay, but the contemporary Grumett, also made by General Motors, proved more popular, and the Indiana was short-lived.

ACT

INDIGO (S) c.1997 to date

Josse Car AB, Arvika.

The Indigo 3000 was a traditional sports car powered by a front-mounted Volvo 3-litre 24-valve 6-cylinder engine giving 204bhp and a top speed of 155mph (250km/h). The body was of spaceframe construction with composite body panels bolted to the frame. The transverse-leaf rear suspension came from Volvo, but at the front the double-wishbone aluminium and transverse composite leaf spring was the maker's own design.

NG

INDIO (U) 1969–1977

Horacio Torrendell, SA, Montevideo.

Horacio Torrendell designed and built the Indio, which came in three versions: station wagon, pick-up truck and jeep-style vehicle. They all used the same basic body panels and had a conventional 2-wheel drive transmission. Power came via Bedford petrol or diesel engines. A smaller version was introduced later on,

powered by an Opel engine. A total of 2200 Indios were made at Torrendell's plant on Cuareim Street. Indios were the best-selling Uruguayan motor vehicles of their day. Many are still seen in daily use in Uruguay, earning their keep the hard way. Mr Torrendell still supplies all the spare parts necessary to keep them running.

ACT

INDRA (US/I) 1969–1975

Automobili Intermeccanica, Turin, Italy and Santa Ana, California.

Frank Reisner owned Automobili Intermeccanica and had built the APOLLO, OMEGA, SQUIRE and MURENA sports cars in Italy for American backers to sell in the United States. The Indra was a Chevrolet V8-powered sports car built for Opel dealers to sell in Europe. The mechanicals were similar to the Omega, as were the windscreen and some other parts. The sleek, droop-nose body was by master stylist Franco Scaglione and the De Dion rear suspension, engine and transmission were from the Opel Diplomat. Although the body was widely praised, the handling was not developed and production was slow. About 125 coupé and convertible models were built before Opel cancelled the contract and switched their allegiance to former Indra distributor Erich Bitter. Reisner moved Intermeccanica to the United States in 1975, hoping to resume Indra production with Ford engines. However, money troubles intervened and his 16 unfinished Indras were sold at auction. Reisner reformed AUTOMOBILE INTERMECCANICA in California and began production of fibreglass-bodied Porsche Speedster replicas.

HP

INDUCO (F) 1922–1925

Automobiles Induco, Puteaux, Seine.

Induco was one of a group of makes all emanating from the same factory, which included MADOU, MARGUERITE, M.S. and the Spanish HISPARCO. Whereas the former were all sporting cars, the Induco was strictly a tourer, made mostly with open 4-seater or Weymann fabric saloon bodies and using Chapuis-Dornier engines of 1095 or 1498cc. It seems that Induco ordered their chassis from Marguerite and mounted the bodies themselves. Only about 20 were made.

NG

INDUHAG (D) 1922

Industrie- und Handelsgesellschaft mbH, Düsseldorf.

This was a very small 3-wheeler for one or two passengers. It could be had with an electric motor or 2/4PS single-cylinder petrol engine. The single wheel was at the front, and drive was to the two rear wheels.

HON

INDUSTRIAL DESIGN RESEARCH (US) c.1985 to date

Industrial Design Research, Laguna Beach, California.

This company was primarily involved in the construction of concept vehicles for the automotive industry. Designer David Stollery has been with GM and Toyota, and produced the FIRE AERO and TRIHAWK kit cars. He also designed the AREX (American Roadster Experimental) in 1993, which was to have been put into production with a Corvette LT-1 V8 engine in the middle. It was a radical looking car, but does not appear to have made it into production.

HP

INDY EXOTICS (US) c.1994 to date

Indy Exotics, Indianapolis, Indiana.

This company carried an extensive line of kits that they built under licence from ELEGANT MOTORS. The Magna was a Lamborghini Countach replica based on Fiero running gear, while the IEX Turbo was a modified Porsche 935-inspired shell that fitted on Fiero, VW or Porsche running gear. They also made replicas of the Bill Thomas Cheetah, Porsche 911, Mercedes 500K, Auburn, 1934 Ford coupé and the 427 Cobra. The LaGrande was a Duesenberg-like kit based on Ford or Chevrolet running gear.

HP

INFINITI (J) 1989 to date

Nissan Motor Co. Ltd, Yokohama.

1966 Innocenti C sports car.
NATIONAL MOTOR MUSEUM

Like Toyota's LEXUS, the Infiniti was an up-market model of Nissan set up to distance the marque from the bread-and-butter cars generally associated with the Nissan name, especially in the United States. The first Infiniti was a luxury saloon developed from the CUE-X (Concept for Urban Executive) concept car of 1985. Launched in 1989, the Infiniti Q45 was powered by a 284bhp 4498cc V8 engine which was also used in Nissan's home-market President. As well as the usual luxury features, it was offered from 1990 with 4-wheel steering and hydraulically-controlled active suspension. Slightly longer than a BMW 7 Series, the Q45 was competitively priced. As with the Lexus, it was marketed by a completely separate organisation from Nissan. A smaller Infiniti, the 3-litre V6 M30 coupé and convertible joined the Q45 soon after it was introduced, and in January 1992 came a saloon version, the J30 based on the Nissan Leopard. In 1995 came another saloon, also 3-litre V6-powered, the more simply-appointed J30 based on the Nissan Maxima QX. The J30 was dropped in 1997, and the 1999 range consisted of the Nissan Primera-based G20, the I30 and Q45, the latter a new design with a slightly smaller V8 of 4130cc. There was also a large 4 × 4, the QX4, which was an Infiniti-badged Nissan Terrano exclusively for the US market.

NG

INGRAM-HATCH (US) 1917

Ingram-Hatch Motor Corp., Staten Island, New York.

This was a most unconventional car promoted by what it lacked compared with ordinary cars, such items as clutch, gearbox, radiator, magneto, water system, central (propeller) shaft, carburettor or fan. The absence of radiator and water system was because it was air-cooled, which many other more successful cars were as well, while there was no need for gearbox or clutch as it had friction drive. However, the boasted 'no central shaft' was pretty hollow, for it had two shafts, one for each half-shaft on the rear axle. They might have added that it had no spokes, for in their place were springs, with compressed air cushions to help absorb shocks as the tyres were made of leather and steel. 'It is not necessary to discard a whole tyre because one little spot becomes badly worn or damaged; that particular section can be discarded and a new one inserted in less time than it takes to tell about it.' The Ingram-Hatch was powered by a 40hp 4-cylinder

single-ohc engine running on paraffin. One chassis was shown at the Brooklyn Automobile Show in January 1917; it was probably the only car made by Joseph Ingram and William Hatch who soon returned to making engines for stationary or marine use.

NG

INNES (i) (AUS) 1905–1906

George Innes & Co., Sydney, New South Wales.

This cycle building business quickly involved itself with motors by acquiring the Gladiator motor-tricycle which had been demonstrated by Mlle Serpollet in 1897. By 1905 Innes cars were being marketed, of unidentified French origin with De Dion-Bouton engines. There was a 9hp 2-cylinder of 1885cc, weighing 763kg and a 19hp 4-cylinder of 3770cc which weighed 1155kg, both 3-speed and with magneto ignition.

MG

INNES (ii) (US) 1921

American Motors Export Co., Jacksonville, Florida.

The short-lived Innes was an attempted revival of the SIMMS made in Atlanta, Georgia, the previous year. Simms' production manager Henry L. Innes moved to Florida where he announced a light car powered by an 18.2hp 4-cylinder Supreme engine, with Grant-Lees gearbox and Columbia axles. No more than six pilot models had been made when Innes died suddenly at the age of 46, and his company died with him. As the company name implies, the Innes was intended mainly for export.

NG

INNOCENTI (I) 1961–1996

1961–1975 Stà Generale per l'Industria Metalurgica e Meccanica, Milan.
1976–1996 Nuova Innocenti SpA, Milan.

Ferdinando Innocenti was a major manufacturer of steel tubing before the war, and in 1946 he turned to scooters, making the Lambretta which, together with the Vespa, became the best-known of its kind. They also made heavy presses for the motor industry, supplying Fiat, Alfa Romeo, Ford, Lancia and Volkswagen.

1975 Innocenti Mini 120 saloon.
NATIONAL MOTOR MUSEUM

1975 Innocenti Regent 1300 De Luxe saloon.
NATIONAL MOTOR MUSEUM

1902 International (i) Armstrong tonneau.
NATIONAL MOTOR MUSEUM

In 1961 they decided to enter car manufacture, not making their own designs but building under licence the Austin A40 hatchback. They soon added an Austin Healey Sprite with Ghia body, and in 1963 began to make the BMC 1100 series under the name Innocenti IM3. In 1965 they added the Mini, which became the best-known of Innocenti's cars. Despite costing considerably more than a Fiat 850, the Innocenti Mini acquired cult status among young Italians, and sold very well. Total Innocenti car sales exceeded 150,000 by the end of 1966.

The Sprite was dropped in 1971 and the following year Innocenti's car division was taken over by British Leyland. They launched the Allegro-based Regent in 1974, and a completely restyled New Mini with Bertone body for 1975. This was a 3-door hatchback with 998 or 1275cc engines. In December 1975 British Leyland pulled out of Innocenti which was bought by Alessandro de Tomaso. He dropped the Regent and the old-style Mini, but continued with the Bertone version, replacing the original engines with a 993 3-cylinder Daihatsu

unit in 1982. The basic shape was continued through the 1980s with little change, though a longer wheelbase was added in 1986. In 1990 two sizes of Daihatsu engine were available, a 548cc twin and 993cc three, the latter in petrol or diesel forms, with an optional turbocharger. By 1993 the twin had been dropped and replaced by a 31bhp 659cc 3-cylinder unit. The larger, still of 993cc, gave 53bhp. They were the last individual Innocentis, as Fiat, who had bought the company from de Tomaso in 1990, closed the factory in March 1993. The Innocenti name survived, but only on imported cars, the YUGO 45 and the Brazilian-built Elba 3- and 5-door estate based on the Fiat Uno. For a few years the Piaggio-built Daihatsu minivan was sold as the Innocenti Porter. Even these activities came to an end in 1996.
NG

INNOVATIONS (US) c.1992–1996
Innovations in Fiberglass, Phoenix, Arizona.
The Innovations 930-Vee was a special body kit for a VW Beetle floorpan. It resembled a wildly customised Beetle with wheel flares, scoops and a dropped nose. They were sold in coupé and convertible versions and in kit or turn-key form. Engine choices included VW, Porsche, V6 and Mazda rotary.
HP

INTEGRITY COACH WORKS (US) 1992–1997
Integrity Coach Works, Stuart, Florida.
Integrity made their own replica of the 427 Cobra, with Corvette or Jaguar suspension. They also sold an improved version of the British-built KVA Ford GT-40 replica, which they later bought from KVA and developed with Corvette suspension. They sold replicas of the GT-40 coupé, roadster and Mk III road car. In 1997 they were sold to SABRE AUTOMOTIVE.
HP

INTER (F) 1953–1956
Sté Nationale de Construction Aéronautique du Nord, Lyon.
Conceived by les Ateliers Électromagnétiques de la Seine and produced by the S.N.C.A.N. aircraft company, the Inter could be summed up as a French equivalent of the Messerschmitt. The aircraft connections were equally apparent in the styling, which resembled a plane's fuselage, and even the method of entry – by a tilting canopy – was the same as the Messerschmitt. One distinctive feature was that the front wheels folded up to reduce the overall width of the car by some 18in (45cm), down to only 36in (90cm). A single-cylinder Ydral 175cc developing 8bhp was mounted in the tail, driving the single rear wheel by chain via a 3-speed gearbox. Two passengers sat in tandem in the very narrow body and there was a single central headlamp.
CR

INTER-CONTINENTAL CARRIAGE (US) c.1989–1993
Inter-Continental Carriage, West Plains, Missouri.
The Pegasus Cabriolet was an unusual car with sculptured sides, triple vents and a rectangular radiator grill inset into a steeply raked nose. They were sold in turn-key form for $49,600 or as a kit for $5000.
HP

INTERMECCANICA see AUTOMOBILI INTERMECCANICA

INTERNATIONAL (i) (GB) 1898–1904
International Motor Car Co. (Ltd from 1900), London.
This company never built a car, although a few were assembled in their showrooms in Great Portland Street, and some work was undertaken at their service depot in Kilburn. However, a number of cars were sold under the International name, starting with the International-Benz, in fact a French-built ROGER which was not selling well in its own country. International probably thought that less sophisticated English buyers would snap it up, although they did add a few improvements such as a reverse gear and locally made bodywork. Single and 2-cylinder variations on the Benz theme were made up to 1901, later cars being bought from Germany when Emile Roger's business closed down.

In 1899 International offered a 'light 2-seater racing car' with wheel steering, a Benz-based 12hp with wheel-steering, pneumatic tyres and double phaeton coachwork at £800, and a 9hp 'vibrationless' flat twin which was not of Benz

1907 International (iii) 4-seater high-wheeler.
NATIONAL MOTOR MUSEUM

origin. They became a limited liability company in 1900 when they approached two Coventry firms, ALLARD (i) and PAYNE & BATES, to make designs for them. The Payne & Bates was unsatisfactory but the Allard-built International Charette, introduced in November 1900, sold in some numbers. It was a belt-driven light car with front-mounted vertical engine of 823cc, of De Dion-Bouton type, designed to run at only 1000rpm, a coal shovel-shaped bonnet and rack-and-pinion steering. It sold for £165. Early cars were rated at 5hp, later increased to 6hp, and both 2- and 3-speed models were offered. All Charette chassis were driven from Coventry to London under their own power. The Charette was dropped after 1903, and apart from the Mountaineer motorcycle, the later cars sold by International were of French origin. The Armstrong of 1902 had a 1100cc single-cylinder engine and Renault-type shaft drive, while the Portland (1903–04) used Aster engines in a variety of sizes from a 6hp single to a 24hp four. The smallest Portland was still available in 1904, but by this time International were mainly concerned with importing the DIAMANT. By 1905 they were no longer in business.

NG

INTERNATIONAL (ii) (US) 1900

International Motor Carriage Co., Stamford, Connecticut.
This was a light 2-seater stanhope powered by a 5hp 2-cylinder engine and selling for $1200. It was made in the factory of Percy Klock, and more cars were probably sold under the Klock name than as Internationals.

NG

1910 International (iii) Model J 26/30hp tourer.
JOHN A. CONDE

INTERNATIONAL (iii); I.H.C. (US) 1907–1911; 1956–1980

1907 International Harvester Co., Chicago, Illinois.
1907–1911 International Harvester Co., Akron, Ohio.
1956–1980 International Harvester Co., Akron, Ohio.
The International Harvester Co. was founded in 1902 as an amalgamation of five leading agricultural equipment companies. Tractor production began in 1906,

757

1965 International (iii) Travelall station wagon.
NICK GEORGANO/NATIONAL MOTOR MUSEUM

1971 International (iii) Travelall station wagon.
NATIONAL MOTOR MUSEUM

1914 Inter-State Model 45 tourer.
NATIONAL MOTOR MUSEUM

and in the same year E.A. Johnston designed a high-wheeler using one of the company's engines in a buggy-type vehicle. The prototype ran in October 1906, and production cars were built in the Chicago factory of McCormick, one of the companies which had been merged in 1902. They had 14/16hp flat-twin engines, with a 2-speed friction transmission and chain drive. Solid tyres were used. After 100 had been made in Chicago, production was transferred to Akron, Ohio, in October 1907. Body styles included 2- and 4-seaters and delivery trucks. In 1910, when the title I.H.C was adopted, water-cooled engines made by British-American, of 2- or 4-cylinders, were used, and they made two conventional cars with standard size wheels and pneumatic tyres, a 18/20hp roadster and a 26/30hp tourer. These did not sell so well as the high-wheelers, of which about 4500 were made.

After 1911 International concentrated on trucks, at first developments of the high-wheeler, then from 1915 conventional vehicles. By the 1930s they were making a wide range, from ¹/₂-ton pickups to a 10-ton 6-wheeler. A few passenger cars and station wagons were built on the pick-up chassis, including taxis bodied in Norway, around 1935 to 1937, but there were no catalogued passenger vehicles from International until 1956, when they launched the Travelall, a station wagon on the Model S ¹/₂-ton truck chassis. This was joined in 1961 by the Scout as a competitor for the Jeep. It was powered by a 2488cc 4-cylinder engine, with a 4677cc V8 option, and was made in 4 × 2 or 4 × 4 forms with a hard-top body. The rear seats could be removed for load carrying. The Scout sold very well, being more popular with women than the Jeep, and by the summer of 1964 sales reached the 100,000 mark. More luxuriously trimmed models appeared, such as the 'Red Carpet' with full carpeting and stainless steel wheel covers. The Travelall was also offered with 2- or 4-wheel drive and a choice of 6-cylinder or V8 engines. In 1971, facing competition from Ford's Bronco and Chevrolet's Blazer, International brought out the Scout 11, longer and better fitted, with a choice of engines from a 3211cc four to a 4982cc V8. A Nissan diesel option came in 1976, and in 1978, models included the SS 11 Scout, a high-performance model with anti-roll bar and fuel tank skid plate. However, International were in serious financial difficulties at the end of the '70s, and there was no money available to develop a new Scout, although at least one full-size clay model of the Scout III was made in February 1980. They decided to pull out of the small vehicle market altogether (the pick-ups had been dropped in 1975, as had the Travelall). The last Scout was built on 21 October 1980.
NG
Further Reading
International Trucks, Fred Crismon, Crestline Publishing, 1995.

INTERNATIONALE (NL) 1942
Internationale Automobiel Mij, The Hague.
This was a very light electric 3-wheeler built to combat the wartime absence of petrol.
NG

INTERNATIONAL MOTORS CARS *see* E3D

INTER-STATE (US) 1909–1918
1909–1914 Inter-State Automobile Co., Muncie, Indiana.
1914–1918 Inter-State Motor Co., Muncie, Indiana.
'The best automobile made in America, even though everyone doesn't know it', proclaimed the makers of the Inter-State. In fact it was a conventional car with nothing much to distinguish it from many others made at the time. Early models had 35/40hp 4-cylinder engines on a 122in (3096mm) wheelbase, with touring or runabout bodies, joined by a 3-seater roadster in 1910. A 38.4hp six was made in 1913/14, but the Inter-State Automobile Co. was bankrupt at the end of 1913, and was reformed in February 1914 by F.C. Ball, a manufacturer of jam jars, as the Inter-State Motor Co. The six cost $2750, and in order to reach a wider market Ball brought out a $1000 car powered by a 19.4hp 4-cylinder Beaver engine. This brought about improved sales, with 1238 in 1916 and 1413 in 1917. The small car was built up to 1918, and was made as a sedan and coupé, as well as open models. The war brought production to an end in May 1918 after 876 cars had been made that year. Although Ball promised a resumption of car making in February 1919, this never came about. Instead, he sold the factory to General Motors for production of the SHERIDAN. This lasted only from 1920 to 1921, after which the factory was bought by William C. Durant for the manufacture of the 6-cylinder DURANT.
NG

INTERSTATE (SWAZ/ZA) 1978–c.1985
1978–1980 Interstate International, Mbabane, Swaziland.
1980–c.1985 Interstate Motor Vehicle Co., Pretoria.
Originating in the tiny enclave of Swaziland, the Interstate Trax was an original all-terrain vehicle with squarish bodywork. It was unusual in that its engine was mounted transversely, and a wide variety of engines was offered, including 4-cylinder petrol engines from Ford, GM and Peugeot, 6-cylinders from Chrysler, Datsun, Ford, GM and Mercedes-Benz, and a Mercedes-Benz diesel. The transmission was automatic and the suspension was by torsion bars at the

front and leaf springs at the rear. Two wheelbase lengths were available and there were four model variations: Utility, Ranch Master, Ranch Cruiser Executive and Multiwagon, plus a new up-market Vista Wagon from 1979. The operation moved to Pretoria in 1980.

CR

INTERSTYL (GB) 1979–1989

Interstyl, Compton Verney, Warwickshire.

Having just seen his Lagonda design for Aston Martin reach fruition, William Towns constructed the amazing Hustler for Jensen Special Products in 1978. When it backed out, Towns' own company, Interstyl, entered production. The design was very simple: a steel tube chassis/frame on to which were hung a fibreglass main tub, bonnet and side/end panels. The upper 'body' was effectively all flat glass, the front panes acting as sliding doors. The Mini mechanical basis made the concept highly adaptable: as many as 72 different versions were offered, with four or six wheels, closed or convertible rear sections, a Holiday 'one-box' body style, Sprint and Sport lowered sports versions, a Hellcat pickup, an all-wooden version and Force 4 models with proper opening doors. There was even an enlarged 6-wheeled Jaguar V12-powered Hustler called the Highlander.

From 1986 Interstyl also marketed the Tracer, a mid-engined sports car with Mini subframes and any A-series engine up to the Metro Turbo. Quad headlamps were activated by dropping down a panel just under the windscreen. One Tracer went to Switzerland and was fitted with a Fiat Uno Turbo engine, while another had Norton rotary power. There were also plans to market the Black Prince, a Reliant Kitten-based teardrop-winged traditional roadster, but these came to nought.

CR

INTERURBAN (US) 1905

F.A. Woods Auto Co., Chicago, Illinois.

Francis Woods designed a most unusual car which combined the advanced feature of integral construction with the outmoded one of centre-pivot steering. Drive was to the front-wheels, and the pivoting axle incorporated an electric motor which could be replaced by an 8hp 2-cylinder petrol engine in 10 minutes, Woods claimed. The body was a single-seater. Probably no more than a single example of the Interurban was made. Woods had more luck later with the WOODS MOBILETTE cyclecar.

NG

INTHELCO (GR) 1985–c.1990

Inthelco was a company based in Munich, Germany, which collaborated with NAMCO of Greece to make the Citroën 2CV-based Pony. In 1985 it set up a new company, Desta (being a contraction of Deutsche Standard Technologie). It totally re-engineered the Pony to accept Ford Fiesta mechanicals and restyled the open utility bodywork. This was sold under the name Desta ATV, Pony or Kondogouris.

CR

INTREPID see ROTARY

INVACAR (GB) 1947–1977

Invacar Ltd, Westcliff-on-Sea, Essex.

One of the most prolific of Britain's postwar invalid cars, the Invacar was made by Derry Preston-Cobb and Bert Greeves, who later achieved fame as a maker of trials motorcycles. It was a major advance on trike design, with a tiller which incorporated depression braking, twist-grip throttle and a short gearchange lever on top of the gearbox. This was eventually developed to provide gear changing by raising and lowering the tiller, thus giving total one-hand control. The Invacar Mark 1 had a 125cc B.S.A. Bantam engine and was based on a sidecar outfit with the front wheel centralised and a comfortable seat slung between the back wheels. It cost £215. Some early Invacars were made under licence by Samuel Elliot of Reading and Vernon Industries of Bidston, Cheshire.

In 1948 came the New Era which had a widened frame with hand-operated lift-up ramp at the rear and a load platform onto which a purpose-built wheelchair could be bolted down by the driver. The Mark 8 (Ministry of Health Model 42) of 1952 had better weather protection, an electric starter and rubber sprung forks, while the Mark 8a had a body 2in (51mm) wider, and a hand

c.1980 Interstyl Hustler H4.
NICK BALDWIN

1958 Invacar Mark 10 197cc 3-wheeler.
NICK GEORGANO/NATIONAL MOTOR MUSEUM

1977 Invacar P70 3-wheeler.
NICK GEORGANO

starter mounted on the dashboard. 1957 saw a greatly improved Invacar Mark 10 (MOH Model 56) with steel-panelled body with a canvas top and wheel steering. The engine was a 197cc Villiers, with 4-speed gearbox and Siba Dynastart electric starter. This was developed into the Mark 12 of the early 1960s, with two-tone fibreglass body. The final Invacar was the DHSS Model 70, made from 1972 onwards, whose design and production was shared with AC. Powered by a 500cc Steyr-Puch flat-twin engine, it had stepless automatic transmission by infinitely variable single-belt drive. Handlebar steering was standard with the option of steering wheel or tiller. Power-assisted braking was standard.

NG

INVADER (US) c.1970–1980

Autokit Invader, Alameda, California.

Bruce Weeks was a young entrepreneur who set out to build his own kit cars while he was still in college. Invaders were low sports cars with clear plexiglass gull-wing doors. There were four models, culminating in the GT-IV, and they were built in California and Spain. The Invader bolted to a Volkswagen Beetle chassis and was a popular kit. Production of the Invader passed to KAYLOR Energy Products.

HP

1926 Invicta (iv) 2½-litre 2-seater by May & Jacob.
NATIONAL MOTOR MUSEUM

1930 Invicta (iv) 4½-litre A Series saloon.
NATIONAL MOTOR MUSEUM

1931 Invicta (iv) 4½-litre S Series, showing the name on the dashboard mounting.
NICK GEORGANO

1933 Invicta (iv) 4½-litre S Series coupé.
NATIONAL MOTOR MUSEUM

INVICTA (i) **(GB)** c.1900

H.E. Richardson, Finchley, London.

The Invicta name was carried on bicycles, motorcycles and a voiturette of which few details are known. Both the motorcycle and car were said to be powered by engines of Richardson's own manufacture, although Erwin Tragatsch credits the 2-wheelers with Minerva or Kelecom engines in his *The World's Motorcycles 1894–1963*.

NG

INVICTA (ii) **(I)** 1906

Stabilimento Meccanico Carlo Mantovani & Compagnia, Turin.

Formerly technical director of Bender & Martiny who made PERFECTA cars, Mantovani built a few cars under the Invicta name in the Bender & Martiny factory. They had 6/8hp 2-cylinder or 10/12hp 4-cylinder engines, with chain drive on both models.

NG

INVICTA (iii) **(GB)** 1913–1914

Clark's Engineering Works, Leamington Spa, Warwickshire.

This Invicta was a cyclecar powered by an 8hp water-cooled V-twin J.A.P. engine, with 3-speed gearbox and chain final drive.

NG

INVICTA (iv) **(GB)** 1925–1950

1925–1933 Invicta Cars, Cobham, Surrey.

1933–1938 Invicta Cars, Chelsea, London.

1946–1950 Invicta Car Development Co. Ltd, Virginia Water, Surrey.

Although the Invicta became one of Britain's classic sports cars, it was not conceived as such. The aim of its creator, Noel Campbell Macklin, was to build a car in which gear changing would be virtually unnecessary. It is said that he was inspired in this aim by his friend and financial supporter Philip Lyle, whose wife could not cope with pre-synchromesh gearboxes. Macklin imported a Doble steam car chassis for examination, but found it too complicated and expensive to manufacture, so he chose a 2-litre 6-cylinder Coventry-Simplex engine as his power unit. He installed this, together with a 4-speed gearbox also by Coventry Simplex, in a Bayliss-Thomas chassis. Six prototypes were made, and performed very satisfactorily, including starting from rest in top gear on the steep Guildford High Street. Unfortunately, all six engines were ruined when they were left without anti-freeze during a cold spell, and Macklin had to start all over again.

This time he chose a larger engine, a 2692cc ohv six made by Henry Meadows of Wolverhampton, the company which was to provide most of Invicta's engines for the rest of the car's life. Macklin's little factory at Cobham did not make much of the car, apart from the brakedrums and cast aluminium dashboards. The gearboxes came from E.N.V. or Moss, the front axle from Alford & Alder, the chassis frame from Thompson. Most of the bodies on the early cars were made by Gordon England. It was a handsome car, characterised by a square-cut radiator and rivets down the bonnet sides. The 2½-litre Invicta went on sale in early 1925, and soon fulfilled its maker's ambition of outstanding top gear performance. The driver could engage top at walking speed, or even at a standstill, and then accelerate smoothly up to the maximum of 62mph (100km/h). One owner, who had run out of petrol, managed to cover two miles by engaging top gear and using the battery and starter motor.

In order to improve top speed, Macklin ordered a new engine from Meadows after about 147 2½-litres had been made. The 75bhp 2973cc Meadows six was designed, like the later 4½-litre, with Invicta in mind, though one or two other manufacturers used it as well. With the 3-litre engine, which was introduced for the 1926 season, top speed went up to more than 70mph (112km/h), and the cars looked faster too. Wire wheels were used on most 3-litres as opposed to the artilleries of the 2½-litre. In 1926 Macklin's young sister-in-law 25-year old Violet Cordery started her series of long-distance journeys which did more than anything else to bring the name of Invicta before the general public. She first led a team to Monza where they captured world records for 10,000 and 15,000 miles, then covered 5000 miles at Brooklands at an average speed of more than 70mph (112km/h). This won for Invicta the Dewar Trophy presented by the Royal Automobile Club, and in 1929 Violet won this again, with a Brooklands run of 30,000 miles in 30,000 minutes. She also drove a 3-litre Invicta round

1947 Invicta (iv) Black Prince Wentworth saloon.
BRYAN K. GOODMAN

the world at an average speed of 24.6mph (39.58km/h) carrying a collapsible tent and a great deal of extra weight, and in a 4½-litre car in 1930 she drove more than 100 miles round central London in top gear, from London to Monte Carlo in third gear, and from London to Edinburgh and back in bottom gear. The latter might seem a rather pointless exercise for a car whose top gear flexibility was among its greatest assets, but at least it proved the reliability and good cooling of the Meadows engine.

In the summer of 1928 Macklin added a still larger engine to the Invicta range, the 4467cc Meadows which was used exclusively by Invicta until the end of 1933, when LAGONDA took it up. By then, Invicta production had practically ceased. The 4½-litre was made in three models, the NLC (1928–30), the A (1930–34) and the S (1931–35). The first two have come to be known as the high-chassis models, and differed mainly in cheaper components being used in the A, in order to cut the chassis price from £1050 to £650. The S-type was the most famous Invicta of all, having a frame underslung at the rear and swept up over the front axle, shorter wheelbase and lower radiator. This carried a winged motif exclusive to the S-type, in place of the usual rectangular badge. The engine gave 115bhp, increased to 140bhp on later models, and with light bodywork the later S-type was capable of around 100mph (161km/h). In 1936, after Invicta production had ended, some of the Meadows engines were modified to Sanction 111 standards, with improvements made by W.O. Bentley and Harry Weslake to the engines used by Lagonda. With these modifications, the S-type could easily exceed 100mph (161km/h), with nearly 80mph (129km/h) possible in third gear.

While many of the high-chassis cars carried 4-door saloon or tourer coachwork, by Cadogan, Gordon England and Mulliner mostly, the S-type was invariably seen in 2-door form. The standard body was an open close-coupled 4-seater, but there were some handsome coupés, fixed and dropheads by Corsica, Freestone & Webb, Grose and other manufacturers.

The S-type was Invicta's first true sports car, and earned its makers a number of rally successes. Donald Healey won the 1931 Monte Carlo, only the second time a British car and driver had won this event (the first was the Hon. Victor Bruce in an A.C. in 1926), and they finished second in 1932. There were also several successes in the Alpine Rally. They were less successful in racing, and 'Sammy' Davis had a bad crash at the 1931 Brooklands Easter Meeting, which damaged not only himself and the car, but also the S-type's reputation. In fact, sales were disappointing from the start, largely because the Depression was the wrong time to launch an expensive sports car. Estimates of the number of S-types made have varied a lot, but the most reliable figure, agreed by Invicta expert Derek Green, is 75, of which a remarkable 68 are known to survive. 64 S-types were made at Cobham, and a further 11 at Invicta's service depot in Flood Street, Chelsea, where all production was transferred after production at Cobham ceased during the summer of 1933. The stock of parts was bought by Earl Fitzwilliam who had been one of the Macklin's original backers; about

nine A-types were assembled at Flood Street as well. Some chassis for the 4½-litre had been made for Invicta by Lenaerts & Dolphens, formerly makers of the BEVERLEY-BARNES.

Before the end, Macklin had tried to enter a cheaper market with a smaller car. This had a 1498cc 45bhp single-ohc 6-cylinder Blackburne engine in a scaled-down 4½-litre frame. It was underpowered and overpriced for its size, and the addition of a supercharger on the 12/90 model only increased the cost and shortened the bearing life, while top speed was still barely 70mph (113km/h). About 60 1½-litre cars were made, mostly with 4-door tourer or saloon bodies by Carbodies. A proposed twin-ohc 1½-litre car got no further than the Olympia Motor Show, while a 4.9-litre twin-ohc version of the S-type was not even displayed to the public, though it is believed that one or two were built.

There were two attempted revivals of the Invicta. The first came in 1937 when it was announced that Invicta Cars of Chelsea would build a range 'based on a well-known Continental make'. This turned out to be the French TALBOT (ii), and there were plans to make 2½-, 3-, and 4-litre cars. In the event, only one car ever saw the light of day; it was a 2½-litre Talbot with an Invicta radiator.

The second revival was a little more substantial, producing 16 cars over a three year period. In 1946 a new company was formed called the Invicta Car Development Co. Ltd. Macklin had just died, but a well-known Invicta engineer, William G. Watson, who had been with the company from 1925 to 1933 before having a spell with Lagonda, was invited back. For his new design Watson turned to Meadows again for a power unit, a 2998cc twin-ohc six with dual ignition and three SU carburettors, which developed 120bhp. Transmission was fully automatic by a Brockhouse Turbo Transmitter, a complicated system which absorbed a lot of power and was reluctant to engage reverse. The proposed body builders were Charlesworth who offered a saloon and a drophead, but they went out of business after two prototypes had been made. Subsequent bodies, all dropheads, were made by Airflow Streamlines and Jensen. The chassis were made in a small factory at Virginia Water, Surrey, but the change of coachbuilder necessitated a large price increase, from £2940 to £3820. Such prices were quite unrealistic when a Mk V Jaguar could be had for £1263, and even a standard steel Mk VI Bentley at £4038 cost only a little more than the Invicta. The company was wound up in February 1950, and the assets acquired by A.F.N., makers of the Frazer Nash. They sold the three complete cars which came with the stock, but the large quantity of spares were put into store and scrapped many years later. However, they had a supply of nuts, bolts and spring washers for many years to come.

NG

Further Reading
'Invicta: Too Good to Last', David Owen, *Automobile Quarterly*, Vol. 15, No. 3.
The 4.5-litre S-type Invicta, J.R. Buckley, Profile Publications, 1966.
'British Beef on the Bone', Douglas Blain, *The Automobile*, April 1998.

1905 Iris 25hp tourer.
NICK BALDWIN

c.1907 Iris 40hp tourer.
NATIONAL MOTOR MUSEUM

1912 Iris 15.9hp tourer.
M.J.WORTHINGTON-WILLIAMS

INVICTA (v) (GB) 1982–1984

Invicta Cars, Plymouth, Devon.

The first model offered by Invicta was the Tourer, a Jaguar XJ-based traditional-style tourer. The later Tredecim was an abortive and rather ill-proportioned replica of Jaguar's one-off V12-powered XJ13 racer, again based on Jaguar XJ running gear. The XJ13 replica was acquired by CHALLENGER but no production run ever materialised.

CR

INVICTA REPLICAS (GB) 1985

Invicta Replicas, Hawkhurst, Kent.

This A.C. Cobra 427 copy was fitted with a Ford V6 engine, but only two cars were ever built.

CR

IOTA (GB) 1951–1952

Iota was an off-shoot of the Bristol Aircraft Motor Club and offered a range of parts, up to a complete car, to encourage the growth of 500cc single-seater racing, later Formula 3.

Iota made 22 chassis, but most owners gave their cars individual names. None achieved much success. In 1951, some of those who had been associated with both the Iota 500cc movement and the Gordano sports car project, showed the world's first sports car with monocoque construction. Low and slippery, it had a mid-mounted 350cc Douglas flat-twin engine, and the all-independent suspension – sliding pillar front, swing axle rear with radius arms and a transverse leaf spring – was mounted on tubular subframes.

It was followed in 1952 by a revised model with a 350cc vertical-twin Royal Enfield engine, while the swing axle rear suspension was replaced by fixed-length drive shafts and small coil springs mounted in tension. It was intended for production, but only one was made.

MJL

IPAM-LEEDS (RA) 1961

Industrias Platenses Automotrices, La Plata, Buenos Aires.

Guillermo Leeds worked for four years on the prototype of his amphibious car. This vehicle was completed in 1959 and tested extensively, covering 50,000 miles (80,000 kilometres). The bubble-car with 2-doors and 4-seat capacity was powered by a rear-mounted Villiers 2-cylinder 2-stroke 325cc engine. In order to travel on water, a propeller had to be fitted and the acceptable load, which over land was 740kg, had to be reduced to 250kg. Although a production of 200 vehicles was claimed, this could not be confirmed.

ACT

IPE (D) 1919–1921

Ipe Auto-Gesellschaft mbH, Berlin.

This light car had been designed during the last days of the war, and was one of the first on the market after the end of hostilities. It had a 1181cc 4/12PS 4-cylinder engine, 2-speed gearbox and shaft drive, and was available with 2-seater or express delivery van bodies. Few were made because of the uncertain economic conditions, though it was still listed by *Automobiles of the World* in 1921.

HON

I.P.I. *see* HEALEY

I.P.S *see* HADLEIGH

IRADAM (PL) 1925–1939

The engineer Adam Gluchowski was obsessed with small cars and in 1921 he designed, and four years later built, his first car. It had a narrow frame with drilled side members, independent suspension all round, and engine and gearbox placed at the rear. The engine was a 495cc JAP (later replaced by a 600cc unit), and the designer planned to install a V-twin.

In 1927 Silesia's steel mills showed an interest in Gluchowski's work, and ordered two light car prototypes. Probably only one was made, in 1928, before the steel mills withdrew their support. It had a central box frame, ifs, like its predecessor, and a proprietary engine. In the mid-1930s the design was reworked, with a tubular frame replacing the box section one, a 1-litre 2-cylinder 2-stroke engine of Gluchowski's own design, direct fuel injection, and a torque converter. Sadly, this was never built.

In 1937 Suchedniowska Huta Ludwikow (SHL) decided to enter motorcycle and car production. They bought the latest version of Gluchowski's project. Air cooling for the rear engine was taken in at the front and mated to a continually variable transmission. All dials were placed in the steering wheel hub (a patent of Gluchowski's). The project was abandoned at the outbreak of World War II.

RP

IRIS (GB) 1905–1915

1905–1907 Legros & Knowles Ltd, Willesden, London.
1907–1909 Iris Cars Ltd, Willesden, London.
1909–1915 Iris Cars Ltd, Aylesbury, Buckinghamshire.

Legros & Knowles was formed in 1904 by Lucien Alphonse Legros and Guy Knowles, initially specialising in gear cutting and repairs. The first two cars they made were called Legros & Knowles, and were exhibited as such at the 1904 Olympia Show. With 20hp 4-cylinder engines they were clumsy and slow, and earned from those who worked on them the epithet 'The Old Buggerinas'. Knowles invited his school friend Ivon de Havilland (elder brother of Geoffrey who started the family aircraft business) to design a new car to be called the Iris, and the result appeared at Olympia in November 1905. Two cars were shown, a 25 and 35hp 4-cylinder shaft-drive chassis with the first of the diamond-shaped radiators which were to characterise all Iris cars. The name was taken from Greek mythology, Iris being the speedy messenger of the Gods, though at least one advertisement carried the slogan 'It Runs In Silence', which some people thought was the origin of the name.

In 1906 came a 7320cc 6-cylinder Iris; like the fours it had pair-cast cylinders, but in place of the drip feed lubrication it had a gear-driven force feed system. The six was short-lived, probably suffering from the crankshaft vibration which afflicted so many of the early 6-cylinder engines, but the fours, the 4871cc 25hp and 6735cc 35hp, were continued up to 1915. Their design was modified by Frank Burgess, who later went to HUMBER for whom he designed the 1914 TT racing cars, and then joined the fledgling BENTLEY company in 1919. A smaller car appeared in 1910 in the shape of the 2290cc 15hp four, which made up the bulk of production thereafter.

Iris Cars Ltd had originally been a sales company for cars made by Legros & Knowles, but in 1908 it collapsed, and a new Iris Cars Ltd was formed in 1909 to acquire both businesses. It was backed by American-born George Augustus Mower who owned a number of companies, one of which, the Bifurcated & Tubular Rivet Co., had a factory at Aylesbury. The Willesden premises were retained to manufacture components which were assembled at Aylesbury. This arrangement lasted until 1913 when the Willesden works were sold. Cars were made at Aylesbury until shortly after the outbreak of World War I. Iris was allocated a stand at the 1919 Olympia Show, but they never took this up. One car was completed, assembled from prewar parts, but that was all, despite the make's presence in various Buyers' Guides up to 1925.

NG

Further Reading
'The Story of the Iris', M. Worthington-Williams,
The Automobile, January 1984.

IRM (US) c.1987 to date
International Research Motorsports Inc., Gaithersburg, Maryland.
This company made a full line of performance parts for the Pontiac Fiero, including several distinctively styled body packages. These resembled racing Fieros that IRM had built for SCCA and IMSA GTU racing.
HP

IRONSMITH (US) c.1984–1997
The Ironsmith, Forest Lake, Minnesota.
This Bugatti T35 replica was a better car than most of the VW-based versions that were once popular in the US kit car industry. It had a ladder frame that mounted Ford 4 or V6 engines, or a Chevrolet V6, in the front with Mustang II suspension. They were sold in kit or completed form.
HP

IROQUOIS (US) 1903–1907
1903–1904 J.S. Leggett Manufacturing Co., Syracuse, New York.
1905–1907 Iroquois Motor Car Co., Seneca Falls, New York.
Carriage and car body builder J.S. Leggett built a few examples of a 15hp 4-cylinder with runabout or tonneau bodies, but during 1904 production came to an end, with only one mechanic at the factory 'to finish up a few machines'. In December 1904 he obtained more financial support and founded the Iroquois Motor Car Co. in Seneca Falls. Here he built a larger four of 20hp, followed by 25/30 and 40hp models in 1906–07. This venture failed at the end of 1907, and an attempt to form yet another company in Syracuse never got off the ground.
NG

IRWIN (US) c.1951–1953
Eric Irwin, Costa Mesa, California.

1986 Isdera Imperator 108i coupé.
NICK GEORGANO

The Irwin Lancer was one of the first high-quality fibreglass bodies built in the US. It was a handsome car that fitted large American sedan chassis. The first Lancer was built on a modified 1932 Graham chassis with a Studebaker V8 engine. A revised Lancer came out in 1952 and had a more squared-off grill. Irwin also advertised a hard-top and a custom chassis. Actors Nick Adams and Natalie Wood had an Irwin-bodied custom with a more rounded grill. Although Lancers were never produced in large quantities, at least seven had been completed by 1953 on a variety of chassis.
HP

ISABELITA (RA) 1960
DURA Sociedad en Comandita, Cordoba.
Werne Dura announced production of what he defined as a 100 per cent Argentine electric 3-wheeler, powered by a rear-mounted 50 Volt electric motor. He claimed that the diminutive 4-seater saloon could top 30mph (50km/h). Mr Dura said he planned to make 100 cars in the first year of production and 500 in the following year. He also said he had numerous orders. No production figures were ever released and nothing else was heard about the Isabelita after 1960.
ACT

ISARD (RA) 1958 – 1965
Isard Argentina saicf, Buenos Aires.
Isard Argentina started out in 1958, making, under licence, the German GLAS cars. The Isard T300, TS-400 and Royal T700 were nothing more than Glas creations with the Argentine badge. In 1963 Isard acquired Los Cedros SA which was making Studebaker trucks. These continued to be produced by Isard, alongside the Glas inspired minicars. In 1964, the Isard 1204 was announced with 4-cylinder 1189cc, 53bhp engine and 4-seat 2-door saloon body. Only 550 of these were made. At the same time Isard announced that an agreement had been reached with Nissan to produce, in Buenos Aires, a Datsun with a 1200cc engine. However, no Datsuns were produced and that was the end of Isard.
ACT

ISDERA (D) 1983 to date
Ingenieurgesellschaft für Styling, Design, und Racing mbH, Leonberg.
Making its first appearance at the 1983 Geneva Show, the Isdera was an aerodynamic sports car using mid-mounted Mercedes-Benz engines. The first was the Spyder 033i with 3.2- or 3.6-litre 6-cylinder engine. In 1984 came the Imperator 108i coupé using 5-, 5.6- or 6-litre V8 engines. Top speed with the 5.6-litre engine was 180mph (290km/h) and the price DM290,000. In 1993 came the Commendatore 112i with 6-litre V12 engine, also available with tuned 6.9-litre engine giving 620bhp. These cars are built to order. Research and development work for other car makers keep the company going, as they could not be profitable from their cars alone.
HON

1954 Isetta bubble car.
NATIONAL MOTOR MUSEUM

1977 ISH-21251 estate car.
MARGUS H.KUUSE

ISETTA (E) 1954–1958
Iso España SA, Carabanchel, Madrid.
The Isetta bubble car was also built in Spain by Iso España, which had a licence from the Italian Iso company. They also offered the Isettacarro, a small delivery van with the familiar Isetta front.

VCM

ISH (SU) 1966 to date
Ishmash, Ishevsk.
From December 1966, a huge armaments works in the Ural mountains called Ishmash had a new sideline product in the shape of a locally assembled small saloon Moskvitch-408. It was really a rehearsal model, since from the next year the new 75hp Moskvich-412 replaced it on one production line, and from 1971 on two lines. The first original model from the factory was a van called Ish-2715 in 1972 and the next year brought a real surprise – the first 5-door hatchback of Soviet origin, numbered as Ish-2125, also known as Ish-Kombi. Thanks to

reinforcements, the body was actually stronger than that of a saloon – despite a sizeable rear opening. The 6-window body differed also in square headlamps, turn indicators and the rear lights layout. Reaching 122,000 units in 1973, the output did not change much over the two following decades. Two thirds of the cars produced were Ish-412 saloons, and about one third Ish-Kombis. There were also a few hundred Ish-2175 vans. The first totally original model Ish-2126 Orbita was planned long before the demise of the USSR, but as the economy slowed down everywhere, including the military industry, there just was no surplus money for finishing the car. Between 1990 and 1991 about 500 Model 2126 were assembled. It retained, unlike the new Moskvich generation, rear-wheel drive. Only 160in (4068mm) long, the car stood on a 97in (2470mm) wheelbase. The base engine was the evergreen 1479cc unit, to which later on was added a new UZAM-3320 engine by Ufa Motor Works, developing 91bhp from its 1945cc capacity. In that case curb weight rose to 1040kg, but zero to 62.1mph (100km/h) equalled 12.6 seconds and the car achieved 101.8mph (163.8km/h). By 1995 the output rose to 12,858 units, but slipped in 1997 – to 8020 cars and 4586 bodies. In 1998 some 8000 workmen assembled 10,454 cars, or just 1.3 per person. The situation at the works was clearly out of control. The experimental model ISH-21261 Orbita with a hybrid drive seemed an out of place joke and a pure waste of money during the Udmurtian auto industry's fight for life. Talks with Skoda may result in the assembling of Felicias and Octavias sometime in the future.

MHK

ISHIKAWAJIMA (J) 1916–1927
Ishikawajima Dockyard & Engineering Co. Ltd, Tokyo.
This company made several experimental cars from 1916 to 1918, when they obtained a licence to manufacture WOLSELEY cars and trucks for sale throughout Asia. This lasted until 1927, after which Ishikawajima made military trucks. In 1933 they combined with DAT to form Jidosha Kogyo and started to make SUMIDA cars.

NG

ISIGO (I/USA) 1998 to date
Rivolta Group, Sarasota, Florida.

With the Isigo Piero Rivolta created a spiritual successor to a previous family jewel, the Isetta bubble car. Aimed at the youth market, this was a fibreglass-bodied open 2-seater with a choice of hard- or soft-tops. 500cc petrol or diesel engines were offered, the 'sports' version having 20bhp and a top speed of 53mph (85km/h). The tubular chassis was in stainless steel and had coil independent suspension all round. A production rate of 4000 cars per year was planned from a brand new factory at Foligno, Italy, at a price of $9000 each. A new model presented at the 1998 Bologna Show was the Iso City, which had a 'bubble' rear hatch section.

CR

ISIS (CS) 1923–1928
Karel Krcil, Praha.

Nobody knows why Frantisek Beutelschmidt chose for his first car the name of a goddess of health and life Isis. What is known is only that as a young electrical engineer Beutelschmidt worked for F. Krizik and later he produced switchboards together with workshop owner Karel Krcil.

The first Isis was built during only 3 months in 1923 and was powered by a 2-cylinder slide-valve 2-stroke 770cc 16bhp engine of the Baer system (aluminium stepwise pistons, lubricated by a pressure oil pump). The car with 2-seater open body was capable of 43.5mph (70km/h). Later cars were fitted with 4-cylinder 1093cc 19bhp Chapuis-Dornier ohv engines with detachable cylinder head, aluminium pistons and thermo-siphon cooling. Cone clutch and worm-type steering were other features of the cars capable of 56mph (90km/h) and priced at 56,000 Kc.

More powerful 1481cc 30bhp-engined cars had 4-wheel brakes, Rudge-Whitworth wire wheels and 65.2mph (105km/h) top speed. About 20 passenger and sports cars were built.

MSH

ISO (I) 1953–1955; 1962 – 1979; 1997 to date
1953–1955; 1962–1976; 1997 to date Iso SpA, Bresso, Milan.
1976–1979 Ennezeta sdf. Milan.

Iso was a motor cycle maker which, in 1953, started the bubble car craze with its ISETTA which was made under licence in Germany (BMW), France (VELAM), Spain (Borgward-Iso), and Brazil (Iso-Romi). In 1955 Iso sold the rights of the Isetta to BMW.

Iso made no cars between 1955 and 1962, when it introduced the Rivolta, a 140mph (225km/h) 4-seat GT car with a 5.4-litre Chevrolet engine in a platform chassis designed by Giotto Bizzarrini. The style resembled the Gordon Keeble (both were by Bertone) and 797 were built, from 1962 to 1970.

The 2-seat Grifo coupé of 1965 was built on a shortened Rivolta chassis, again with a body by Bertone. The base model had a 300bhp Chevrolet engine, but one could buy a 365bhp version (158mph (254km/h), 0–62mph (–100km/h) in 7 seconds) or even a 7-litre 400bhp model which could touch 177mph (285km/h). During 1965 to 1974, 504 Grifos were made and a lightweight version, the Strada 5300, was made by Bizzarrini with Iso's approval.

Two new models arrived in 1969. The Fidia had a long wheelbase version of the Rivolta chassis and the body, by Ghia, bore the influence of the Jaguar XJ6. It was launched with a 300bhp Chevrolet engine, but 5.8-litre Ford units were fitted after 1973. Production ended in 1979 when 192 examples had been built.

The other 1969 arrival, the Lele, was intended to replace the Rivolta, and shared its chassis. The models overlapped for two years and Ford engines were used from 1973. Iso also made a special edition of the car called the 'Marlboro' after the Iso-Marlboro F1 car, one of Frank Williams' early efforts.

A mid-engined GT car designed by Bizzarrini, the Varedo, was shown in 1972 but did not reach production. Iso was hit by the 1973 OPEC oil crisis, but there were also financial and labour problems which had the effect of narrowing the price gap between Iso and makes such as Ferrari and Maserati.

When Iso's founder, Renzo Rivolta, died the firm was taken over by his son, but it folded in 1975. Iso was sold to an American refrigerator manufacturer who formed another company, Ennezeta. Between 1976 and 1979 a small number of Lele and Fidia models were made.

In 1997 Piero Rivolta, the founder's son, started to make the ISIGO, a inexpensive 505cc 20bhp 2-seat runabout with a stainless steel chassis, front disc brakes and all-independent suspension. The following year, Rivolta announced plans to build

c.1965 Iso Rivolta saloon.
NICK GEORGANO

1968 Iso Grifo coupé.
NICK BALDWIN

1974 Iso Lele saloon.
NICK GEORGANO

a limited edition of a new Grifo with a composite body styled by Zagato and a supercharged 4.6-litre Ford V8 engine.

MJL

ISOTTA-FRASCHINI (i) (I) 1900–1948
1900–1904 Stà Milanese d'Automobili Isotta, Fraschini & Cia, Milan.
1904–1948 Fabbrica Automobili Isotta-Fraschini, Milan.

Italy's most famous make of luxury car began through the partnership of lawyer Cesare Isotta and car enthusiast Vincenzo Fraschini who set up a business in 1898 to import Renault and De Dion-Bouton cars and Aster engines into Italy. Two years later they built a car carrying their names. It was a light 2-seater voiturette similar in concept to the Renault and powered by a 5hp Aster engine. It was joined by a 12hp twin in 1902, and in 1903 Isotta-Fraschini moved upmarket with a range of 4-cylinder cars on Mercedes lines, with engines of 12/18, 16/24 and 24/34hp. These were made only for a short time as in 1905 the company acquired as its chief designer Giustino Cattaneo (1891–1973) who brought out a new range, and was to be responsible for all Isotta-Fraschinis up to 1933.

1907 Isotta-Fraschini 16/22hp tourer.
NATIONAL MOTOR MUSEUM

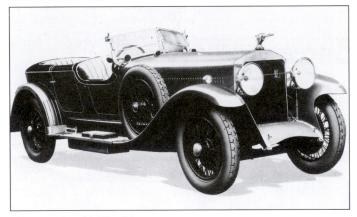

1925 Isotta-Fraschini Tipo 8A sports tourer.
NATIONAL MOTOR MUSEUM

1935 Isotta-Fraschini Tipo 8B saloon, by Hooper.
NATIONAL MOTOR MUSEUM

Within the next three years Cattaneo brought out nine new models, from a 2-litre light car to a 17-litre racing car of which only two were made. All had 4-cylinder engines with pair-cast cylinders, and some of the larger models from 1907 onwards had compressed air starters. The company prospered, building 300 cars in 1906 which put them in second place among Italian car makers, though a long way behind Fiat's 1800. The Depression of 1907–08 hit Isotta-Fraschini as it did all Italian car makers, and they sold 50 per cent of their shares to LORRAINE-DIETRICH. The arrangement did not last long, due to personality clashes. In particular, Cattaneo resented the French firm's unwarranted claim for the success of his racing cars. One result of the partnership was Isotta's first 6-cylinder car, which Lorraine suggested would be good for the French market. They also persuaded Cattaneo to change from chain to shaft drive on

most models, though two chain-driven monsters were made as late as 1914. In 1909 Isotta sold a licence to PRAGA, but the Austrian firm did not make many cars on Isotta patterns as they soon developed their own designs.

An advanced little car marketed from 1909 to 1911 was developed from the 1327cc Coupe des Voiturettes entrants of 1908. These had single-ohc engines and were said to rev up to 3500rpm. They did not, in fact, do very well in the race, their best position being Buzio's eighth, but they had a number of successes in private hands. A few came to Britain, and Lionel Martin used the chassis of one for his ASTON MARTIN Special of 1914.

In 1910 Cattaneo and Vincenzo Fraschini's brother Oreste devised a front-wheel braking system in which longitudinal brake rods pulled universally-joined transverse shafts which in turn activated the expanding shoes inside the brake drums. This was exhibited on some of the cars at the 1910 Paris Salon, and offered on production cars for the following season. By 1914 front-wheel brakes were standard on the larger Isottas, making the company the world's first to make a commercial success of a system that was still distrusted by many experts. Isotta-Fraschini made a wide variety of cars up to 1914, with several different engine designs. The small fours, a 2296cc 12/15hp and 2950cc 16/20hp, had monobloc engines with side-valves in an L-head, while the old-fashioned T-head layout persisted on some of the larger models. In addition there were two sporting cars with 16-valve single-ohc engines, a layout which Cattaneo had pioneered on racing cars as early as 1905. These were the 6235cc TM and 10,618cc KM, both with chain drive. The KM had dual magneto ignition and could be had either with a pear-shaped radiator or a sharply-pointed Mercedes type. They were made in small numbers, twenty TMs and fifty KMs. Total production of Isotta-Fraschini in 1914 was 125 cars.

The Tipo 8
Between 1905 and 1914 Isotta-Fraschini marketed about fifty different models. In complete contrast they decided on a postwar policy of one model only, and it was to be a luxury car competitive with the best that Britain, France or America could offer. This time Cattaneo came up with another first, a straight-8 engine with alloy cylinder block and 3-speed gearbox in unit with the engine. Capacity was 5880cc and power output 80bhp, quite a low figure compared with the 135bhp developed by the 6-cylinder Hispano-Suiza. However they were aimed at a rather different market, for while Marc Birkigt must have had sporting ambitions in mind when he designed the Hispano, Cattaneo's main concern was to produce a car which would meet the highest standards of luxury and silence. For this reason he did not use an ohc, choosing instead a straightforward pushrod ohv layout. The alloy block was a single casting, but the fixed cylinder heads were in two blocks of four. The brakes operated on four wheels, of course, and were now coupled so that either the hand or footbrake operated all four. They also had mechanical servo assistance.

Introduced in 1919, the Tipo 8 was supplied as a chassis only. Coachbuilders included Italy's best, such as Castagna and Sala, and many of the most celebrated firms in Europe and America. The Tipo 8 did particularly well on the American market, with about 450 being sold there between 1919 and 1932, out of a total production of 1380. Buyers included many Hollywood stars such as Rudolph Valentino and Clara Bow, while boxer Jack Dempsey and newspaper tycoon William Randolph Hearst were also Tipo 8 owners. Elsewhere buyers included the Queen of Rumania, the King of Egypt, the Aga Khan, several Indian princes, Pope Pius XI, Benito Mussolini, and the Swedish millionaire Erik Akerlund.

In 1924 Cattaneo increased the size and power of his engine, in order to counter criticism that an Isotta was easily outperformed by a Hispano-Suiza. The Tipo 8A had a capacity of 7370cc giving 110bhp, and 135bhp in the Tipo Spinto 8AS. The latter was the nearest that Isotta came to making a sports car in the 1920s, and one was driven into first place in the 1925 and 1926 Targa Abruzzo races by the Duke Pio Arate di San Pietro.

During the 1920s Isotta-Fraschini became increasingly involved with aero-engines which they supplied in large numbers for commercial and military use. By 1928 the management clearly favoured this side of the business, and the best engineering talent was diverted away from the cars. Production of the Tipo A declined after 1928, and the Depression hit Isotta particularly badly, virtually killing off their valuable American market. For 1931 they brought out the Tipo B which had the same size engine but with numerous improvements. The cylinder block, pistons and connecting rods were of nickel steel, the valve gear was lighter and there were two completely separate exhaust manifolds. The result was an increase in power to 160bhp. Other up-to-date features included

1947 Isotta-Fraschini Tipo 8C Monterosa saloon, by Zagato.
NATIONAL MOTOR MUSEUM

coil ignition in place of magneto and a synchromesh gearbox, with the option of a Wilson self-changing box. The chassis was considerably strengthened, with much deeper side members.

Magnificent though it was, the Tipo 8B came at quite the wrong time, and only thirty were sold. Manufacture of components ended in 1931, but a handful of cars were assembled from existing parts over the next four years. In June 1932 there were 19 unsold cars, 8As as well as 8Bs, 52 new 8B chassis and components for assembling 48 more. The last 8B was completed in 1935, and most of the chassis and components were scrapped. Cattaneo, who had become managing director, retired at this point, and devoted the rest of his life to marine engineering.

Isotta-Fraschini came under new ownership and concentrated on trucks and aero-engines. During World War II their new owner Count Caproni de Taliedo bought up several other concerns in the fields of marine engines, ordnance and aluminium manufacture. In 1942 they turned their attention to cars once more, and engineer Fabio Rapi began work on the car which was to emerge in 1946 as the Tipo 8C Monterosa. Named after the street where Isotta's car factory was located, the Monterosa was a total break with any previous Isotta-Fraschini. It had a rear-mounted V8 engine with hemispherical combustion chambers and a single camshaft for each bank of cylinders. The chassis was a platform steel frame, and suspension was independent all round by rubber cushions controlled by hydraulic shock absorbers. Several different sizes of engine were tried; the catalogue mentioned a 3378cc unit, but the car exhibited at the 1947 Paris Salon had a 'square' engine of 2980cc, and production cars were planned to be of 2544cc. Six Monterosas were built but only four received bodies, the others being the original test chassis and a chassis for display at the 1948 Geneva Show. The four, which were also show cars and not sold to the public, had saloon bodies by Touring (1), Zagato (2) and a convertible by Boneschi. Monterosa production never started because Isotta-Fraschini, starved of funds by an unsympathetic government, was liquidated in September 1948. Under new ownership they made a few trucks, buses and trolley buses in the 1950s. The factory in the via Monterosa was acquired by Siemens of Italy and later demolished.

In 1993 the Isotta-Fraschini name was revived by coachbuilders Fissore.
NG

Further Reading
The Isotta-Fraschini Tipo 8, T.R. Nicholson, Profile Publications, 1965.
Isotta Fraschini, Angelo Tito Anselmi, Interauto, 1977.
'The fabulous Isotta Fraschini: Majesty in Motion', Gianni Rogliatti, *Automobile Quarterly*, Vol 12, No. 1.

ISOTTA-FRASCHINI (ii) (I) 1996 to date
Isotta-Fraschini Fabbrica Automobili Spa, Cervere.
In 1993 the rights to the Isotta-Fraschini name were purchased from Finmeccanica by Fissore. Its intention was to relaunch the marque with an all-new convertible grand touring car, to be made at a new factory built with government aid at San Ferdinando in the deprived southern Italian region of Calabria. The original T8 with Audi, the drive-train from the Audi A8 quattro was used – namely its 300bhp V8 engine, suspension and 4-wheel drive. The bodywork was in aluminium with

an electric soft-top or removable hard-top. The final production version of the T8 was shown at the 1998 Paris Show alongside a new 4-seater fixed-head coupé model known as the T12. This shared the same platform as the T8 but had all-new bodywork designed by Tom Tjaarda and a 400bhp V12 engine.
CR

ISPANO-FRANCIA (F) 1913–c.1920
V.P. Pelladeux, Biarritz.
The Ispano-Francia was appropriately named as it was made a few miles from the Franco-Spanish border. One model was listed in 1913, a 2-seater voiturette powered by an 8hp single-cylinder engine. The postwar range included two models, an 8/10hp, possibly the prewar 8hp revived, and a 16/20hp 4-cylinder car. The company also made motorcycles and marine engines.
NG

I.S.S. *see* KESTREL (iii)

I.S.S.I. (I) 1952–1954
Istituto Scientifico Sperimentale Industriale SpA, Milan.
The I.S.S.I. Microbo was an extremely short 86.6in (2200cm) but tall enclosed microcar. Unusual features included a single door on the right-hand side, integral construction and a transparent Plexiglas roof. A 125cc single-cylinder 2-stroke Idroflex 5.5bhp engine was mounted in the tail driving the single rear wheel.
CR

ISUZU (J) 1953 to date
Isuzu Motors Ltd, Tokyo.
The origins of Isuzu Motors Ltd date back to the earliest days of the Japanese motor industry. A predecessor company, the Tokyo Ishakawajima Shipbuilding & Engineering Co. built WOLSELEY cars under licence from 1918 to 1927, following these in the 1930s by American-inspired SUMIDA cars and trucks, after they had merged with DAT. The first vehicle to bear the name Isuzu (a sacred river) was a 2-ton truck made in 1933, and commercial vehicles were the only Isuzus until 1953. By then the company had separated from DAT, which had become NISSAN, and had been set up as Isuzu Motors in 1949.

In 1953 Isuzu began to make the HILLMAN Minx under licence. The first cars had a 70 per cent local content, and by 1955 they were 100 per cent Japanese made, although similar in styling to the British product. The bodies were made by Mitsubishi, using dies bought from Pressed Steel. Minxes in various models were made up to 1965, but in 1961 came the first Isuzu designed car, the Bellel. It had unitary construction and a choice of three engines, the Minx's 1494cc unit, and a 1991cc Isuzu engine which could be had in 93bhp petrol or 55bhp diesel form. In 1962 30 per cent of all Bellels were sold with the diesel engine, remarkable at a time when the diesel for passenger cars was in its infancy. An unusual feature of the 1962 Bellel de Luxe was light-sensitive automatic headlamp dipping.

1966 Isuzu Bellett 1600GT coupé and saloon.
NATIONAL MOTOR MUSEUM

1968 Isuzu 117 coupé.
NATIONAL MOTOR MUSEUM

1988 Isuzu Piazza coupé.
ISUZU (UK)

2000 Isuzu Trooper 3.0 diesel estate car.
ISUZU (UK)

By 1961 Minx production was running at 1000 per month. The Bellel began at 600 per month, rising to a monthly total for all Isuzu passenger vehicles of 7000 by the mid–1960s. The Bellel was joined in 1966 by the smaller Bellett which replaced the Minx. It had a 1471cc engine available in several degrees of tune up to a 90bhp twin-carburettor GT which gave the 2-door coupé a top speed of 100mph (161km/h). A year later came the Bellel's replacement, the Florian with 1584cc single-ohc engine and the option of an automatic transmission.

The Florian, Bellett and 117 coupé made up the Isuzu range for nearly ten years. The Florian and 117 used either a 1584cc 120bhp petrol engine or a 2238cc 73bhp diesel. In 1971 General Motors acquired a 34.6 per cent stake in Isuzu, and this led to the LUV (Light Utility Vehicle) pick-up being marketed in the United States as a Chevrolet, and in 1974 to the Gemini. This was Isuzu's version of the international T-car, made in Britain as the Vauxhall Chevette and in Germany as the Opel Kadett. It was later sold in Australia as the Holden Gemini and in Korea as the Daewoo Maepsi-Na. In November 1984 it was replaced by a new front-wheel drive Gemini with 1471cc petrol or 1488cc diesel engine. This also became a Holden Gemini, and was sold in America as the Chevrolet Spectrum and, from 1989, as the Geo Spectrum.

Isuzu's other 'world car' was the Aska, with transverse 1818 or 1995cc engine driving the front wheels. It was Isuzu's version of the General Motors J-car, made elsewhere as the Chevrolet Cavalier/Vauxhall Cavalier/Opel Ascona/Holden Camira. Launched in 1981, the Aska was a 4-door saloon with four engine options, from a 66bhp diesel to a 150bhp 1995cc turbo.

A more individual car was the Piazza coupé. This originated in 1979 as a Giugiaro-styled prototype on the 117 chassis, and went into production two years later. It had a 1950cc 4-cylinder engine available in single- or twin-ohc versions, and in 1985 came a turbocharged version of the latter, with 180bhp and a top speed of 130mph (210km/h). At the end of 1985 a convertible joined the Piazza range which was made up to 1990, when it was replaced by the Impulse, a front-drive or 4 × 4 coupé with 1588cc engine, sold in America as the Geo Storm. Isuzu dropped their regular cars in 1993 to concentrate on 4 × 4s, but the names Gemini and Aska survived as badged-engineered Honda Domanis and Accords.

In 1981 Isuzu entered a new field with the 4 × 4 Trooper, a competitor in the Mitsubishi Shogun class. It was made with open or closed bodywork on two wheelbases with a variety of petrol or diesel engines up to 2.8 litres. It was assembled in Australia by Holden who sold it under the name Kangaroo and was made throughout the 1990s without great change. By 1999 it was available with two engines, a 3-litre turbo diesel and a 3.5-litre petrol unit. In 1989 Isuzu brought out a new off-roader, called the MU (Mysterious Utility) in Japan and the Amigo or Frontera-Sport everywhere else. It was a 'fun utility' using engines, transmissions and many other components from the Trooper in a smaller vehicle coming in size between the Suzuki Vitara and the short-wheelbase Trooper. Amigos for the European market were assembled at the former Bedford truck plant at Luton, Bedfordshire. This plant also assembled the Trooper which was sold in Europe under the names Vauxhall or Opel Frontera. They had smaller engines than the Japanese-built Troopers. The Amigo was dropped in 1998, its place being taken by the Vehi-Cross whose unusual styling was the work of Briton Simon Cox.

NG

I.T. *see* ITALMECCANICA

ITALA (I) 1904–1935
Itala SA Fabbrica Automobili, Turin.
After importing PANHARD et LEVASSOR and CLEMENT cars from France and producing a few voiturettes under the marque WELLEYES together with his elder brother, Matteo Ceirano formed in 1904 the Itala company in Turin, with the help of Guido Bigio, a talented engineer, and a financial group based in Genoa.

The first Itala, a 24hp model with a T-head 4-cylinder in-line engine of 4562cc, technically followed closely the trendsetting new Mercedes of the German DAIMLER company. The cylinders were cast in pairs and the engine generated 35bhp at 1200rpm. Ignition was by low tension magneto and cooling through a honeycomb radiator, a pump and a fan. Power was transmitted via a separate 4-speed gearbox and the more advanced shaft drive to the differential of the rear axle. A lighter 18hp and a heavier 50hp touring car on similar lines were also offered.

1998 Isuzu Vehi-Cross 4x4 estate car.
ISUZU (UK)

In 1905 Alberto Balloco was hired and appointed technical director, a position he held until 1919. In the same year, Itala presented the first of a range of giant racing cars, the 100hp with a 4-cylinder engine of 14,759cc, which was driven to victory in the Coppa Florio by G.B. Raggio. In 1906 A. Cagno won the first Targa Florio in Sicily in a new 35/45hp model with a 7433cc engine and Italas also claimed second, fourth and fifth places. This model soon became available commercially and Count Scipione Borghese chose it to compete in the famous Peking-Paris trial of 1907, which he won in 60 days. Among sportsmen, this was an excellent publicity boost for the young marque. Two new touring models of 14/20hp with a 4-cylinder engine of 2610cc and a big 60hp with the first 6-cylinder engine of 11,148cc were launched. The former was dropped one year later, but the 35/45hp and the six remained available until 1915. New racing cars with engines of up to 16,666cc capacity were entered with more or less success in various races.

From 1908 to 1915, several touring models on the conventional lines of their earlier types were introduced. The 4-cylinder programme included the 20/30hp of 5401cc, the 50/65hp of 10,604cc, the 16/20hp of 2799cc, the new 50/65hp of 9236cc and the 18/24hp of 3308cc. An enlarged 6-cylinder, the 75hp of 12,930cc was produced. The big models obtained either sporting, long-distance or heavy, luxurious town bodies in the best coachbuilding tradition. In 1910 a more advanced small 12/16hp model with monobloc 4-cylinder engine with side-valves and L-head of 1944cc was launched. With increased bore and 2235cc, it became the 14/18hp and remained in production until 1916. It was supplemented in 1913 by the 18/30hp of 3308cc. Alberto Balloco created a totally new engine with variable stroke, hoping to eliminate the noisy and expensive gearbox. A 40hp chassis with this revolutionary engine was exhibited at Turin and Paris in 1912. It was unsuccessful and was quietly dropped. Another approach to improve car engines was the elimination of the poppet-valves. Knight and others proposed sleeve-valves of various designs. Balloco again introduced a completely new type of engine with rotary-valves. The Itala Avalve engine had vertically arranged rotary-valves, one serving two cylinders, and the first Avalve models,

1913 Itala 25hp valveless saloon.
NATIONAL MOTOR MUSEUM

the 25hp with 3308cc and the 35hp with 5195cc were first seen in 1912. One year later a heavy 50hp model of 8496cc was introduced and Itala bravely chose the rotary-valve system for their 1913 GP cars of 8345cc. Their drivers, however, did not complete the race owing to mechanical failures – none of which, however, concerned the valves. These cars were sold to England after that race.

In 1915 a large order, for 3000 HISPANO-SUIZA V8 200hp aeroplane engines, was obtained from the Italian Government. When Itala, after much delay and many changes, was in a position to start volume production in early 1918, the armistice was just a few weeks away. Itala, like many other companies, had to rely on prewar designs, when commercial production was resumed. The Tipo 50 25/35hp was a conventional 4-cylinder side-valve model of 2813cc. It was also available again in 1919, was replaced by the Tipo 55 Avalve with a somewhat

c.1912 Itala 18/24hp tourer.
NICK BALDWIN

1926 Itala Tipo 61 drophead coupé.
NICK GEORGANO/NATIONAL MOTOR MUSEUM

smaller 4-cylinder engine of 4426cc offering 80bhp. By 1922–23 Itala was struggling heavily to increase production and sales. The Tipo 54 Taxi and Tipo 56 15/20hp, both with a 4-cylinder engine of 1954cc, were introduced but did not meet with much success. In 1924 the Istituto Finanziario Italiano di Liquidazioni, a government-controlled financing organisation, took control of the sick company. It appointed Giulio Cesare Cappa, a gifted engineer, late of FIAT, as technical consultant and soon after he became general manager. He immediately set to work on a new model in an effort to regain the market popularity and prestige of Itala. At the Paris Salon of 1924, the new Tipo 61 was unveiled. It was a complete breakaway from earlier designs. Its 6-cylinder alloy engine of 1995cc had pushrod operated ohvs and offered 60bhp at 3500rpm. The conventional chassis had wire-spoke

wheels and 4-wheel brakes. The Itala Tipo 61 was well received even if its performance and top speed were not always quite up to expectations. By early 1926 regular production was underway and the Tipo 61 took part in various sports events.

Cappa then tried to realise his great ambition, which was for Itala to be put back on the map of international and national motor racing. He developed Tipo 11, a racing voiturette of 1049cc with a very exciting, expensive and complex V12 engine with ohc and supercharger. It was one of the early front-wheel drive cars of modern design and all wheels were independently suspended. The body was a single-seater of very clean lines. A slightly larger engine of 1450cc would have made this jewel of engineering suitable for the formula GP from 1927 onwards. Before the car was completely tuned and developed, the whole project was stopped due to the excessive costs involved. The prototype survived and is on display at the Biscaretti Museum in Turin.

In 1928 two Itala Tipo 61Ss took part in the Le Mans 24-hour race. They were specially prepared and their engines had twin-ohcs. Robert Benoit and Christian Dauvergne won the 2-litre class. Soon the Tipo 65 Sports, a development on the Le Mans cars, with double ohc and 70bhp at 4000rpm with a top speed of 84mph (135km/h) was offered. It remained available until 1932 and about 150 examples were delivered.

In 1929 financial difficulties became overwhelming and the company was sold to Officine Metallurgiche di Tartona, which up to then had been manufacturers of truck trailers. Remaining parts for the Tipo 61 and 65 were assembled and a limited number of cars sold. In 1932 the Tipo 75, with basically the former Tipo 61 engine enlarged to 2310cc and 65bhp in the standard F-version, or 70bhp in the mildly tuned V-version, was introduced. This, too, was a handsome medium-sized car, offered with various Italian style bodies, but could not turn the wheel around and by 1935 the dwindling production and deliveries ceased. The remains of the once proud marque were taken over by FIAT.

FH

Further Reading
'Itala', Ferdinand Hediger, *Automobile Quarterly*, Vol. 38, No. 1.

The 2-Seater *ITALA* Sports Body de Luxe

The clean-cut lines of this very beautiful English-built two-seater body will emphatically commend themselves to the connoisseur.

A low and comfortable dickey seat at the rear affords accommodation to one extra passenger, and the super quality of the fittings and finish effectively sets off what is not only a very sporting but also a very luxurious car.

Upholstered and painted to choice.

PRICES of CAR

With 17/30 h.p. Standard Chassis, - £745
With 17/30 h.p. Super-Sports Chassis, £795

1900 Ivel 8hp landaulet.
NATIONAL MOTOR MUSEUM

ITALIAN IMAGE (US) c.1991–1993

Italian Image, Lake Park, Florida.

Ferrari Testarossa replicas on Pontiac Fiero chassis were the products of this kit car company. They had two versions for standard length or lengthened Fiero chassis.

HP

ITALMECCANICA (I) 1950

Italmeccanica, Turin.

Also known as the I.T., this was a prestige coupé displayed at the 1950 Turin motor show. Its full-width Stabilimenti Farina coachwork was handsome and its mechanical specification of a Mercury 3.9-litre 165bhp V8 engine, plus torsion bar suspension, showed promise for its intended American market. However, a production run did not occur.

CR

ITALYA see GOZZY

IVANHOE (i) (CDN) 1903–1905

Canada Cycle & Motor Co., Toronto, Ontario.

The Ivanhoe was a light electric runabout made by a successor company to CANADIAN MOTORS Ltd, and designed by Hiram Percy Maxim. It was one of the first electric cars to have the batteries divided into two groups, some under a small bonnet, the others at the rear, giving a better weight distribution. Solid or pneumatic tyres could be had, and top speed was 14mph (22km/h), with a range of about 40 miles. The makers turned to petrol power in 1905, making one of Canada's most successful early cars, the RUSSELL.

NG

IVANHOE (ii) (GB) 1905–c.1906

Ivanhoe Motor Co., Cricklewood, London.

This company exhibited two 24hp 4-cylinder cars under the name Mercury at the February 1905 Olympia Show. They were of conventional design, and the 111in (2817mm) wheelbase was said to be large enough to allow for a large body with side entrance. One of the cars shown had a tonneau with three rows of seats, and a Cape Cart hood. *The Autocar* remarked that it was not often that a new maker arrived on the scene through the large car direct, without attempting something smaller first. The same two cars were shown in November 1905, this time with no mention of the Mercury name. See also MERCURY (ii). Ivanhoe were also agents for the friction-drive DOUGILL cars.

NG

IVEL (GB) 1899–c.1906

Dan Albone, Biggleswade, Bedfordshire.

Dan Albone (1860–1906) began making bicycles in the 1880s, naming them after a local river. He started work on an agricultural tractor in 1897, and became more famous for these than for his cars, the first of which appeared in 1899. It had a 3hp Benz engine, but mounted in the opposite position to those in Benz cars, i.e., with the combustion chamber at the rear. It had two speeds and chain drive. Albone made a point of passenger comfort; the chassis was suspended on coil springs, and the body was supported on the chassis by C-springs. The first Ivel had a 4-seater *vis-à-vis* body, and in 1900 Albone exhibited a landaulet with 8hp 2-cylinder engine. It is not certain how many of these, or any later Ivel cars, were made, though the make has been quoted as late as 1906, the year of Albone's death. It is quite possible that the *vis-à-vis* and the landaulet were the only Ivel cars made. Tractors were made until 1921.

NG

Further Reading
A Thoroughly Good Fellow, The Story of Dan Albone,, Kathy Hindle and Lee Irvine, Bedfordshire County Council, 1990.

IVERNIA (GB) 1920

Very few references to the Ivernia exist, and it is not certain that any cars were built. Published specifications show it to have been a large car on a 144in (3655mm) wheelbase with 'underhung suspension'. The engine was a large 4-cylinder unit of 4576cc, with the unusual dimensions of 89 × 184mm.

NG

IVOR (GB) 1911–1916

Ivor Motors Ltd, London.

Named after one of the company's directors, Ivor Henry Miller, the Ivor had a 12/14hp Ballot engine (a 15/20 and a 20/30 were also mentioned), Malicet et Blin gearbox, rear axle and steering, and what was described as a shell-shaped body with sliding doors. The company existed from May 1911 to November 1916, but it is not certain if cars were made throughout this period. Published references to the Ivor are few, and the factory location is not known. The agents were Barimar Ltd, of whom it was said in July 1912 that they were interesting themselves in the sale of this car in England. This would indicate that it was of foreign origin, probably French because of the use of French engine and other components.

NG

IVRY (F) 1906–1913

Compagnie Générale d'Électricité d'Ivry, Ivry, Seine.

This company began by making a tricar with a cone-shaped bonnet, followed by a light 4-wheeler with 6hp single-cylinder engine, chain drive and a 2-seater body. Later Ivrys, from about 1911, were conventional-looking tourers powered by 12 or 16hp pair-cast 4-cylinder engines. In 1913 the factory was sold to Charron, or possibly Grégoire.

NG

IZARO (E) 1920

Construcciones de Automóviles Izaro Srl, Madrid.

Made by D.J. Azqueta, this car used 3-cylinder 2-stroke and 4-cylinder 4-stroke engines of 600cc and 750cc.

NG

IZZER (US) 1911

Model Gas Engine Co., Peru, Indiana.

This car owed its name to the man who ordered the first one, a Dr H.H. Bissell of Watseka, Illinois. He wanted an up-to-date car, an 'is-er' not a 'was-er'. It was built to order by E.A. Myers of the Model Gas Engine Co., and used, naturally, a Model 4-cylinder engine, with some components coming from GREAT WESTERN, another Peru-built car. The body was a neat 3-seater roadster. Having completed Dr Bissell's car, Myers then built two more, one for himself and the other for his office manager. The Bissell car still exists.

NG

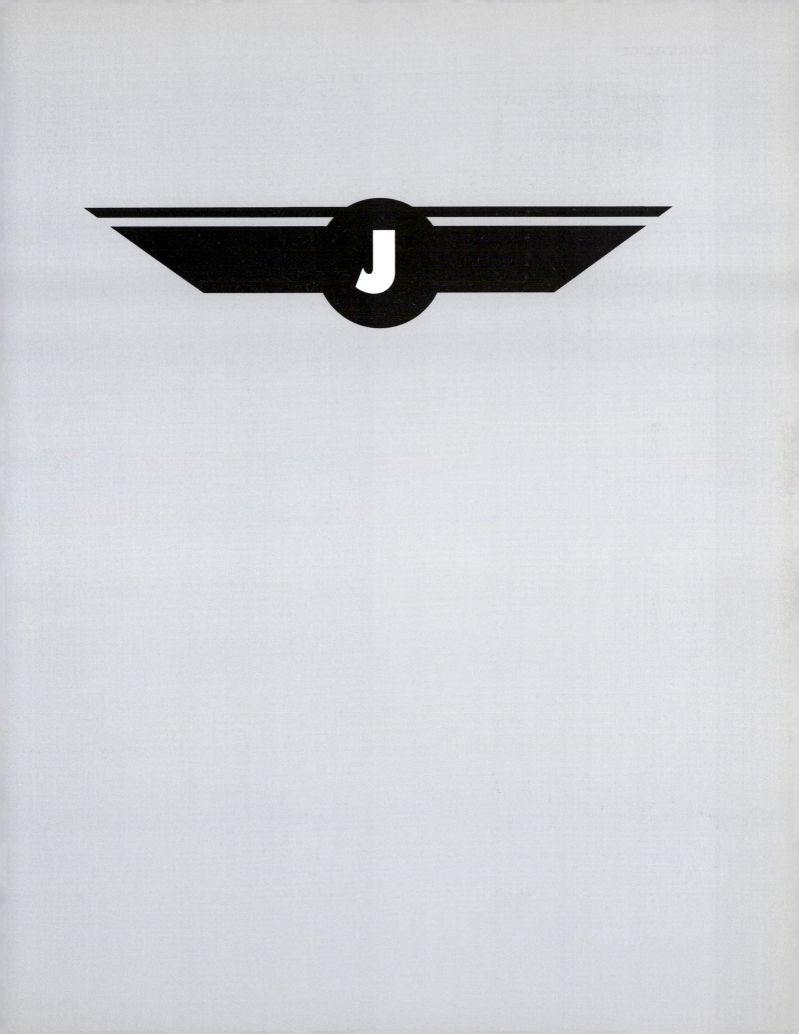

J. A. C (US) c.1993–1994
J. A. C. Milwaukee Ltd, Milwaukee, Wisconsin.
This company made a stretched Cobra replica with more room for passengers. They were only sold in turn-key form for $48,814 in 1993.
HP

JACK ENDERS (F) 1914–1920
Enders Jack et Cie, Asnières, Seine.
This was a light car made in touring or sports models, powered by a 900cc twin or an 1100cc 4-cylinder engine.
NG

JACK FROST (US) 1903
Kammann Manufacturing Co., Chicago, Illinois.
This was an open electric car with three rows of seats carrying six passengers. The tyres were solid on tubular steel wheels, but pneumatic cushions were provided for the seats to give a more comfortable ride than would otherwise have been possible.
NG

JACKSON (i) (GB) 1899–1915
1899–1900 Yorkshire Motorcar Manufacturing Co. Ltd, Bradford, Yorkshire.
1903–1915 Reynold-Jackson & Co. Ltd, Notting Hill, London.
R. Reynold Jackson's first car had an imported single-cylinder engine, probably a De Dion-Bouton, but the few production cars made in Bradford had 4hp horizontal-twin Mytholm engines. These were made by Brown & Buckton, makers of engines at Hipperholme, a Bradford suburb, who were taken over in 1900 by the Yorkshire Motorcar Manufacturing Co. The latter made a few cars under the MYTHOLM name up to 1902, but Reynold Jackson left Yorkshire in 1900 to try his luck in London. For three years he sold American cars, notably the Buckmobile, Century and Covert before offering cars under his own name in 1903. These were of Lacoste et Battmann type, therefore probably also largely imported, with 6 or 9hp De Dion-Bouton engines. The cars were originally *dos-à-dos* dogcarts, though later more conventional seating was adopted.

In 1905 Jackson contracted to make cars for TRACKSON Bros of Brisbane, though it is not certain if he delivered any. He used De Dion-Bouton engines for a number of years, including some with exceptionally long strokes. The biggest of these was used in the 1909 Black Demon racer which had a slipper-shaped bonnet coming to a sharp point. Its dimensions of 104 x 213mm gave a capacity of 1808cc, and the bonnet was so tall that the driver had almost to peer round rather than look over it. Six months after it was announced in November 1909 Jackson advertised that 'orders can now be taken for early delivery of the Black Demon', but probably not many orders were received for this freakish machine. More conventional Jacksons of 1909/10 included a 3-seater with a 9hp Aster engine and a 4/5-seater tourer powered by a 12/15hp 4-cylinder Chapuis-Dornier. By 1913 this had a Métallurgique-type pointed radiator. In 1909 Jackson made a very early example of an estate car, and in 1913 he was offering a 3-wheeled cyclecar powered by a 1350cc V-twin J.A.P. engine.
NG

JACKSON (ii) (US) 1903–1923
Jackson Automobile Co., Jackson, Michigan.
The Jackson was made by two businessmen, George A. Matthews and English-born Charles Lewis, and engineer Byron F. Carter who had designed a steam stanhope in 1901, which was built under the name MICHIGAN (i) at Grand Rapids. In 1902 he invented a 6hp 3-cylinder steam engine, and in 1903 formed the Jackson Automobile Co. to make a car using this engine and called the Jaxon. It had chain drive and a folding front seat. The name was also used for one year for a single-cylinder petrol-engined car which resembled the Curved Dash Oldsmobile. The steamer did not survive into 1904, and neither did the name Jaxon, most subsequent cars being called Jacksons. The exception was the ORLO, a 16hp 2-cylinder car made in 1904 only. This was renamed the Model B Jackson for 1905, when there was also the 6hp single-cylinder Model A and the 18hp 2-cylinder Model C. The single-cylinder car was dropped for 1906, and a 40/45hp four added at the top of the range. Thereafter the Jackson followed a conventional pattern, although a 20hp twin was still made in 1911, and a real curiosity was the DUCK of 1913, also known as the Jackson Back Seat Steer, in

1909 Jackson (i) Black Demon racer.
NATIONAL MOTOR MUSEUM

1910 Jackson (i) 6hp Special 2-seater.
JOHN FASAL

1910 Jackson (i) No. 8 roadster.
NICK BALDWIN

which two passengers sat in front and the driver with another passenger in the rear seats. Familiar in some cyclecars, this arrangement was unique in a full-sized car like the Jackson.

Jackson's first six, the Sultanic of 1913, used a 40hp Northway engine, and from 1916 to 1918 one model was powered by a 28.8hp Ferro V8 engine. This was the sole model in 1917 and 1918, though in the latter year it was made with six body styles. 1915 was Jackson's best year, with 2138 cars delivered. By then two of the three partners had left; Carter went early on, to make the CARTERCAR, while Lewis, who already owned the Lewis Spring & Axle Co.

1914 Jackson (i) 3-wheeler.
NATIONAL MOTOR MUSEUM

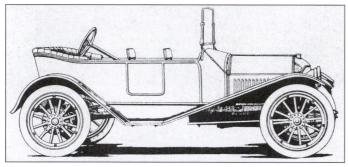

1913 Jackson (ii) Duck tourer.
KEITH MARVIN

c.1920 Jackson (ii) Model 6-38 tourer.
NATIONAL MOTOR MUSEUM

left to make the HOLLIER from 1915 to 1921. No Jacksons were made in 1919, when the company was struggling to get back to normal after war work. Only one model was offered from 1920 to 1923, the 6-cylinder 6-38, made in 1920 as an ordinary-looking tourer and sedan, and a rather smart sport 4-seater, with disc wheels and step plates. Despite a greater variety of bodies for 1921, including the Broadway Special Sports, Princess Coupé and Hollywood Sedan, production dwindled and in 1923 Jackson merged with DIXIE FLYER and NATIONAL (i) to form Associated Motor Industries. The 1923 Jacksons, of which only 24 were made, were sold as the National 6-51.

NG

JACQUEMONT (F) c.1922–1925
Automobiles Jacquemont, Paris.
The Jacquemont was a cyclecar unusual for its date in having a single-cylinder engine, and a large one at that, with capacity of 1057cc. It had a spidery chassis

with very narrow track, and final drive was by twin belts. The designer was Robert Bourbeau, better known as one of the original partners in making the BÉDÉLIA, a much more successful cyclecar.

NG

JACQUES MULLER (F) 1920–1922
Jacques Muller, La Garenne-Colombes, Seine.
This cyclecar was powered either by a 995cc Train V-twin with air- or water cooling, or a water-cooled 894cc S.C.A.P. 4-cylinder engine. It had a 2-speed gearbox, quarter-elliptic springing and no differential. In 1922 Muller sold out to B.N.C. who made a car based on the 4-cylinder Jacques Muller, though with a 3-speed gearbox and different engines.

NG

JACQUET FLYER (US) 1920
Jacquet Motor Corp. of America, Belding, Michigan.
The Jacquet Flyer was a relatively high-priced sporting car which never got completely off the ground productionwise, primarily because of the infighting of corporation officials and lack of sufficient funds. The car, from existing factory sketches, was one of striking design – a long, rangy sporting 2-seater roadster, its aluminium body mounted on a wheelbase of 130in (3299mm). The car had a 4-cylinder engine developing 80bhp and sported wire wheels. Its price was listed at $4000. Only a single car was completed before the company went out of business.

KM

JAEGER (US) 1932–1933
Jaeger Motor Car Co., Belleville, Michigan.
The Jaeger was one of the few would-be low-priced automobiles that received considerable attention from the national automotive press in the lean days of the Great Depression, when such other new short-lived attempts were being introduced in the interest of motoring economy. Thus, while such cars as Studebaker's Rockne and the Continental Flyer and Beacon had a brief active run in the marketplace, the independently produced Jaeger, without the necessary financial backing, did not. The car was built by Charles F. Jaeger and differed from conventional cars by the substitution of coil springs for semi-elliptic ones. The car resembled most other cars of its time and was fitted with a 70hp Continental engine. Its wheelbase was 113in (2868mm) and its price was to have been in the $550 to $600 range. The Jaeger Company limped into the 1933 calendar year having produced five convertible sport coupés.

KM

J.A.G. (GB) 1950–1952, 1954–1956.
1950–1952 J.A.G. Cars, Thames Ditton.
1954–1956 R.G.S. Automotive Components Ltd, Windsor.
John A. Griffiths first made a 2-seater with a 3622cc Ford V8 engine, followed by a model with a smaller Ford 1172cc engine. A version using an MG engine achieved some competition success. Altogether some 50 J.A.G.s were sold.

DF

JAGO (GB) 1965–1997
1965–1979 Geoff Jago Custom Automotive, Chichester, Sussex.
1979–1994 Jago Automotive, Chichester, Sussex.
1994–1997 Jago Developments, Chichester, Sussex.
Geoff Jago's first offerings, as early as 1965, were street rod kits but he branched out in 1971 to create the Geep kit car. The fibreglass body was moulded directly off a genuine wartime Willys Jeep and mounted on a simple ladder chassis designed for Ford Anglia 105E parts. A Morris Minor-based version arrived in 1974 and the definitive Ford Escort Mk I/2 based version in 1976. The Geep name was dropped in 1991 because Chrysler wanted to sell Jeeps in the UK, and was therefore renamed the Sandero. This name had previously been used for a 1983 sports utility prototype but this never reached production. The Samuri, also first seen in 1983, did make production, as a curious Ford-based sports buggy with a spacious 4-seater interior, permanently fixed T-bar roof, lift-out roof panels, lift-off solid half-doors and a removable rear hard top. A Suzuki 4 × 4-based Sandero was added in 1994 but by then Jago's products were very outdated and the company ceased offering kits.

CR

1914 Jackson (ii) tourer.
NICK BALDWIN

JAGUAR (GB) 1945 to date

Jaguar Cars Ltd, Coventry.

The Jaguar name first appeared on a model of S.S.(ii), the 2½-litre saloon which debuted at the 1935 Olympia Motor Show. It became a make name in March 1945 with the formation of Jaguar Cars Ltd. Up to 1948 Jaguars were of prewar design; the 1767cc 4-cylinder engine was still made by Standard, but machinery for the larger engines, the 2664cc 2½-litre and 3485cc 3½-litre, had been moved into Jaguar's factory before the end of the war. All three engines had pushrod ohv, and the specification included 4-speed syncromesh gearboxes, mechanical brakes and beam axles. The first cars left the production line in October 1945, and were made with little change until the autumn of 1948, when they gave way to the Mark V, made in saloon and drop-head coupé versions, with 2664 or 3485cc engines. The body was restyled, with spatted rear wheels and better forward vision, though it was still clearly recognisable as a Jaguar. Innovations included independent front suspension and hydraulic brakes.

The Mark V, of which 10,466 were made up to 1951, was overshadowed by a dramatically-styled and very high performance sports car launched at the same Earls Court Show. This was the XK120, named for its claimed top speed of 120mph (193km/h), though in fact it could exceed this, an early production model reaching 124.5mph (200km/h) in a road test by *The Motor*. It had a 3442cc twin-ohc engine which developed 160bhp, whose origins dated back to the war years. While on fire-watch duty, William Lyons, Bill Heynes and Claude Baily discussed the design, which was originally to have been made in 2-litre 4-cylinder XK100 and 3½-litre 6-cylinder XK120 forms. Most of the testing was done on the 4-cylinder engine, which got as far as the original catalogue, but never went into production. Indeed the whole XK120 project was conceived as a testbed and publicity vehicle for the new saloon which was to emerge in 1950 as the Mark VII. Before the roadster went into production, Lyons did not envisage that more than 200 would be made, but the car proved so popular that production continued up to 1954, by which time just over 12,000 had been made, of which 92% went for export. The first 200 had light alloy bodies, replaced by steel on subsequent cars. Most were open roadsters with detachable sidescreens, but two alternative bodies joined the range, a fixed-head coupé in 1951 and a convertible in 1953. From 1952 the XK120 was available with a

1947 Jaguar 2½-litre saloon.
NATIONAL MOTOR MUSEUM

Special Equipment package which included high-lift camshafts, lightened flywheel, twin exhausts and centre-lock wire wheels. The engine modifications boosted power to 180bhp.

Lyons launched the car for which the twin-cam engine had been designed, the Mark VII saloon, at the 1950 Earls' Court Show. It was the biggest and heaviest Jaguar yet made, with a full-width 6-seater body and unladen weight of 3862lbs. More than 30,000 of the Mark VII and improved VIIM were made up to 1957, when it was succeeded by the Mark VIII with one-piece windscreen and overdrive or optional automatic transmissions. For many years both options were available on touring Jaguars. The Mark VII won the 1956 Monte Carlo Rally, inaugurating a series of Jaguar successes in saloon racing which lasted up to the mid-60s.

The Jaguar competition tradition, established with the prewar S.S.100, was revived in 1951, when the disc-braked C-type won the Le Mans 24-hour race, repeating the success in 1953. In 1955, 1956 and 1957 the unitary construction D-type took the flag at Le Mans, with much support from Jaguar, while the official entry was by the Écurie Écosse. Jaguar was now represented in almost every category of motoring competition, apart from Formula One, which would not come until the 2000 season. Their major successes included wins

1951 Jaguar XK120 roadster.
NATIONAL MOTOR MUSEUM

NICK BALDWIN

LYONS, SIR WILLIAM (1901–1985)

Sir William Lyons is forever associated with Jaguar and the styling achievements, first of SS cars, and then a succession of Jaguar roadsters, saloons, and coupés. He also shared the glory of Jaguar's racing successes, notably at Le Mans. Much less known is his role as a captain of industry: he invested Jaguar's profits in other automotive companies, forming a more-or-less coherent group, with the acquisition of Daimler and Lanchester in 1960, along with their coachbuilding affiliates, Barker & Co. and Hooper & Co. He bought Guy Motors in October 1961 and Coventry Climax in 1963, following up with the purchase of Henry Meadows Ltd in 1964.

He was born in Blackpool on 4 September 1901, son of William Lyons, musician, conductor and music-shop owner from Ireland, and his wife Minnie, née Barcroft. After Poulton-Le-Fylde Grammar School, he attended Arnold House School in Blackpool. He joined Crossley Motors as a trainee, taking engineering classes at night at Manchester Technical College.

In 1919 he joined Brown & Mallalieu, Sunbeam agents, as a junior salesman. In 1921 William Walmsley moved in next door to the Sunbeam showrooms, exercising the business of buying war-surplus motorcycles and fixing them up for resale, with a sideline in making very stylish sidecars. In 1923 Lyons and Walmsley founded the Swallow Sidecar Co. with shops on Bloomfield Road in Blackpool.

In 1925 he bought an Austin Seven but disliked its style and began to draw special bodies for it. In 1926 he hired a skilled designer and coachbuilder, Cyril Holland, who had been an apprentice with Lanchester and held positions with Austin and Morris. They arrived at a production model, Austin Seven Swallow, that was put on the market at a very attractive price (£175 in 1927).

When Henley's placed an order for 500 cars, Lyons began to search for a larger factory, and in 1928 leased an idle shell-filling plant in Lockhurst Lane, Coventry. Here they also built a number of bodies on the Fiat 509 and Swift Ten before creating an aluminium-panelled four-light saloon on the Standard Nine chassis. This car impressed John Black of the Standard Motor Co. so much that he signed a contract with Lyons for special bodies, making special 6-cylinder chassis for the Standard Swallow cars. Thus was born the SS badge and the low-built cars with their modern-style radiator shell.

Cyril Holland had stayed in Blackpool when the Swallow Sidecar Co. moved to Coventry, and went to work for Burlingham (later Duple), but in 1929 Lyons sent for him to set up a new body engineering and production facility in Coventry. Walmsley left in November 1934, and Swallow Sidecar Co. was absorbed by the newly founded SS Cars Ltd.

Before the end of World War II Lyons decided that Jaguar should make its own engines, telling his engine specialists that he wanted 120hp from a 3500cc six. That led to the engine which powered the XK120 and the Mk VII. Cyril Holland left Jaguar in 1945, and W.C.E. 'Ted' Orr was promoted to works manager.

Lyons personally drew the styling themes and main visual features of the Jaguar production car bodies, while the competition cars were designed by Malcolm Sayer; an aerodynamicist recruited from Bristol Aeroplane Co., John Silver, replaced Orr in 1965.

In July 1966, Jaguar Cars Ltd was sold to the British Motor Corp. At the end of 1967 Lyons gave up the duties of managing director but remained Chairman of Jaguar Cars Ltd in a relationship with Sir Donald Stokes that grew steadily uneasier. Lyons finally retired on 8 February 1972. He was knighted in 1956.

He died at his home in Warwickshire on 8 February 1985.

He married Greta Brown, a schoolmaster's daughter, on 15 September 1924. They had one son, John Michael, born 1930, who was killed in a traffic accident driving a production-model Jaguar on his way to Le Mans for the race in June 1955, and two daughters, Patricia and Mary. Lady Lyons died on Easter Monday, 1986.

JPN

S. S. JAGUAR

"THE AUTOCAR" SAYS

"A credit to the British Automobile Industry"

1960 Jaguar MkIX saloon.
NATIONAL MOTOR MUSEUM

1962 Jaguar MkII 3.4 saloon.
NATIONAL MOTOR MUSEUM

on the 1950 and 1951 Tourist Trophy, the Sebring 12 Hour Race, and Ian Appleyard's Alpine Gold Cup for three successive unpenalised runs in his XK120, co-piloted by his wife Patricia (nee Lyons) in the International Alpine Rally.

The XK120 was succeeded buy the XK140 (1955–1957) and XK150 (1957–1961). The same three body styles were available, but the coupé and convertible had two small additional seats 'for little children or legless dwarves' according to some members of the press. Power went as high as 250bhp on the 150S with 3781cc engine. An important improvement on the XK140 was rack-and-pinion steering in place of the XK120's recirculating ball. The 3.8-litre engine was also used in the Mark IX saloon (1958–1961), a Mark VIII development with power steering and all-disc brakes, which was the last of the separate chassis saloons.

In 1956 came a new generation of smaller unitary-construction saloons. The first was the 2.4-litre (2483cc), whose engine was a short-stroke edition of the XK unit. A year later the full-size 3442cc engine was inserted in the 2.4's hull, while in 1958 the 3781cc engine was also available in the disc-braked Mark II, as well as the smaller engines. A new big saloon came in 1961 in the shape of the Mark X. This had a completely restyled unitary construction body, coil front suspension, the E-type's independent rear suspension, and power steering as standard. In 1964 it received a 4235cc engine, and in 1966 became the 420 with new front end, also badged as the Daimler Sovereign.

In 1956 plans were laid for a new sports car which would take over from the D-type in competitions and eventually replace the XK road cars. The production sports car was announced in March 1961 as the E-type. It had a 265bhp 3781cc engine, disc brakes and independent suspension all round, a novelty for Jaguar. It had a monocoque aerodynamic open 2-seater or coupé body with headlamps faired into the nose. It offered 150mph (241km/h) for less than £2100, while the Aston Martin DB4 with comparable performance cost £3755. From 1966 onwards it was available with a 2+2 seater coupé body, offered also with automatic transmission, mainly for the USA, still Jaguar's most important export market. The E-type in slightly modified and lightweight forms competed in many sports events, including Le Mans in 1962, when Briggs Cunningham and Roy Salvadori finished a highly creditable fourth.

The production E-type became heavier and power was reduced in the US market cars because of emission regulations, so to restore performance a completely new engine was introduced in 1971. It was a 5343cc V12, the first quantity production 12-cylinder engine since the demise of the Lincoln Continental in 1948, and was based on the experimental mid-engined XJ-13, of which only one was made in 1966. This had two camshafts per bank of cylinders, but the production engine made do with one. Even so, it developed 272bhp, which restored the E-type's performance while still meeting emissions regulations.

NICK BALDWIN

HEYNES, WILLIAM MUNGER (1904–1989)

William Heynes was the man who created the engineering reality behind the Jaguar name, winning the Dewar Trophy in 1951 for outstanding engineering achievements, and the James Clayton Prize in 1958.

Born on 31 December 1903, at Leamington Spa, he was educated at Warwick School from 1914 to 1921. During that time he had thoughts of becoming a surgeon, but the practical side of his mind told him to study automobile engineering. He joined Humber Ltd in Coventry as a trainee in 1922. In his trainee period, he designed a motorcycle engine with hemispherical combustion chambers and twin-ohcs.

He stayed on with Humber, holding a position in the drawing office from 1925 to 1930, and being head of the drawing office from 1930 to 1935. He worked under E.G. 'Ted' Grinham, J.S. Irving, and Norman Wishart, and was responsible for the detail work on the original Snipe. He also came in for a big share of the preparations for integrating the Humber and Hillman model ranges.

However, he saw his future clouded by the Rootes way of doing things, and the B.B. Winter way of directing an engineering department. He left Humber in 1935 and joined SS Cars Ltd. It became his task to modernise the SS and Jaguar chassis, and to modify the Standard engines for higher performance.

In 1945 he convinced Sir William Lyons that Jaguar should make its own engines, dusted off his motorcycle drawings from 1924, and delivered the design for the XK engine which Claude Baily executed in brilliant detail. It went into the XK120, while Heynes developed the interim saloon (Mk V) and the competition cars, the C-Type (1951-53) and D-Type (1954-56). He also supervised the limited-production SS project, and masterminded the Mk VII, E-Type, and Mk X.

He retired in 1969 and died in September 1989.

JPN

Distinguished by its cross-hatch radiator grill, the V12 E-type was available as a roadster or 2+2 coupé, with power steering as standard equipment, and automatic transmission and air conditioning in the coupé. A total of 15,287 Series IIIs were made before the model was dropped early in 1975.

A new saloon, the XJ6, came for 1969, powered initially by the familiar 4235cc six and a new 2790cc six for the economy-minded. The latter suffered from overheating and piston failures, and was quietly dropped in 1973. Meanwhile the V12 engine was installed in the XJ6 body shell, to make the XJ12. The XJ series set new standards of refinement and comfort. Daimler versions were produced, which remained technically identical, and in appearance differed only in the traditional Daimler fluted grill. For the V12 Daimler, the old name Double Six was revived. A 2-door coupé version was the XJC, made with 6- and 12-cylinder engines. A more distinctive 2-door coupé was the XJ-S, a 2-seater with freshly styled body and also made with both engines. A full cabriolet version arrived in 1988, and this model remained in production until 1996. The XJ-S HE (High Efficiency) was capable of 155mph (249km/h) and returned 27mpg.

There were many corporate changes for Jaguar between the 1960s and 1989. William Lyons acquired Daimler in 1960, followed by Guy, a commercial vehicle maker since 1914, and proprietary engine firms Meadows and Coventry Climax. In 1966 he merged Jaguar with the British Motor Corporation, making him a partner in a massive organisation which also made Austin, Morris, Wolseley and Riley cars. The new group was called British Motor (Holdings) Ltd, but it was short-lived, for two years later it merged with the Leyland Group to form the massive and unwieldy British Leyland. Lyons remained as chairman until 1972, when he was succeeded by F.R.W. (Lofty) England, who had been Jaguar's competition manager in the 1950s. He retired himself in 1974, and the chairmanship passed to Geoffrey Robinson, who left after a short time in protest against Leyland's increasing rationalisation. The later 1970s were unhappy years for Jaguar who lost their independence for a while, becoming part of Leyland Cars from 1975 to 1978, then part of the newly-formed Jaguar-Rover-Triumph Ltd, which was created to separate the quality makes from the mass-produced Austin and Morris. Quality control slipped badly, resulting in particularly bad damage to Jaguar's reputation on the American market. Then, under Sir Michael

1967 Jaguar E-Type 2+2 coupé.
NATIONAL MOTOR MUSEUM

1989 Jaguar Sovereign 3.6 saloon.
JAGUAR CARS

NICK BALDWIN

EGAN, JOHN LEOPOLD (born 1939)
Without John Leopold Egan, Jaguar would have failed. When he took over, in April 1980, sales were so slow that production was throttled to 35 per cent of capacity, far below break-even point, the products had terrible quality problems, and the company was losing £2m a month.

He was educated at Bablake School, Coventry, and attended London University, graduating with a BSc in petroleum engineering. He collected a master's degree in Business Studies from the London Business School, and went to work for General Motors as manager of replacement parts for the UK market. Leaving GM for British Leyland, he was named director of Unipart, and next headed the parts organisation of Massey-Ferguson.

Sir Michael Edwardes brought him to Jaguar with a five-year contract and the title of chairman, succeeding Percy Plant who was reassigned to cleaning up BL's other car programmes. His first task was to settle a strike, which he accomplished by putting the bare facts before the 80 shop stewards, who then got the rank-and-file workers to pick up their tools. He arranged Jaguar's take-over of the former Pressed Steel Fisher plant at Castle Bromwich and put in a highly automated engine line for the XJ6 at the Radford works. He ordered studies, which revealed that 60 per cent of the defects in Jaguar cars were found in parts purchased from outside suppliers, and simultaneously raised the productivity level in the Browns Lane factory. In 1980 Jaguar produced 1.2 cars per worker. Within three years, he had raised the figure to 3.5 cars per worker.

In 1984 he organised the separation of Jaguar from state-owned BL, putting it back in private ownership. At the end of 1985, Jaguar bought the ex-Chrysler technical centre at Whitley, with a five-year £400m investment plan to give the 600 engineering staff complete and up-to-date facilities. Jaguar became profitable, and production climbed from 14,577 cars in 1981 to 38,500 in 1985.

He launched the new XJ6 in 1986, but ran into quality problems again. As sales increased to 52,000 cars in 1988, the 8250 manual workers demanded wage rises of up to 20 per cent, which the company could not afford. Profits actually shrank from £159 million in 1987 to £97million in 1988.

In November 1989, the government put its remaining stake in Jaguar on the stock market. Egan worked hard to organise a take-over by General Motors, but in the end, it was Ford who won, paying £1.56 billion for 100 per cent control of Jaguar. Egan resigned in June 1990 and became managing director of British Airports Authority, which he led with great competence until he abruptly stepped down on 1 October 1999.
JPN

1999 Jaguar S-Type saloon.
JAGUAR CARS

1989 Jaguar XJ-S V12 convertible.
JAGUAR CARS

1996 Jaguar XK8 coupé.
JAGUAR CARS

Edwardes, Leyland began to value corporate identity more than rationalisation, and Jaguar resumed its old title of Jaguar Cars Ltd in 1980. The post of full-time chairman was resurrected, and went to John Egan, who began a successful revival of the company's reputation for quality. Under the Thatcher Government's policy of selling-off publicly-owned companies wherever possible, Jaguar was privatised in August 1984. The shares were over-subscribed by about eight times, putting a value of £300 million on the company, and suggesting a high degree of confidence in its future. The Egan regime saw a great increase in output, from

about 14,000 cars in 1980 to 41,437 in 1986. This was made up of 32,385 saloons and 9052 XJ-S sports models.

Like Rolls-Royce and other firms, Jaguar tend to introduce new engines and bodies at intervals, rather than bringing out an all-new car all at once. Thus the important dates in the 1980s were October 1983, when the AJ6 engine was announced, and October 1986 which saw the arrival of the new XJ6 saloon powered by this engine. The AJ6 was a 3590cc single-ohc six with four valves per cylinder, electronic ignition and fuel injection. Developing 225bhp, it was used first in the XJ-S coupé, with a 5-speed Getrag manual gearbox replacing the automatic. The XJ6 looked similar to its predecessors, but was greatly changed under the skin. Apart from the new engines, 2.9-litre 12-valve and 3.6-litre 24-valve versions of the AJ6, it was 1.2in (30mm) longer, and had more accommodation for passengers and luggage, as well as new rear suspension and Bosch-system anti-lock braking. A new 5993cc 318bhp V12 engine became available in 1992. The six was available in supercharged form, giving 320bhp. In 1997 the saloon became the XJ8, retaining similar lines to its predecessors but with a V8 engine in 3253 or 3996cc versions. The latter could be had in supercharged XJR form, giving 363bhp. The V8 engine had made its debut one year earlier in Jaguar's first new sports car since the E-type. Known as the XK8 or XKR in supercharged form (from March 1998), it was made in coupé and convertible models.

In November 1989 Jaguar was taken over by the Ford Motor Company, which provided massive funding for new models and an improvement in quality control. Away from the mainstream of Jaguar design was the XJ220, a mid-engined supercar developed by TWR and built in their factory at Bloxham. As announced at the Birmingham Motor Show in October 1988, it had a 6222cc 48-valve V12 engine developing more than 500bhp, with drive to all four wheels via a 5-speed gearbox and viscous differential. Only one was built in this form, and when it went on sale the engine was a 3.5-litre twin-turbo V6 driving the rear wheels. It was priced at £332,000, and production was limited to 280, but they sold slowly and were available at a substantial discount several years later. In contrast a successful new model funded by Ford investment was the S-type which appeared at the 1998 Birmingham Show. Reviving the Mark II concept of a smaller Jaguar saloon, the S-type was powered by a brand-new 2967cc 24-valve

V6 or the familiar 3996cc 32-valve V8, and was a direct competitor to the Mercedes-Benz E-class or BMW 5-series saloons. An even smaller saloon with 4-wheel drive, provisionally named the X400 or T-type, and an obvious challenger to the BMW 3-Series, was planned for introduction in 2001.

The S-type did not appear on the market until the second quarter of 1999, but had sold 38,801 by the end of the year. This contributed to record Jaguar sales of 75,312 for the year, 50 per cent higher than the previous year, which was also a record, and more than five times the 1980 figure.

HS/NG

Further Reading
Jaguar, Lord Montagu of Beaulieu, Quiller Press, 1990.
Jaguar XK Series, the Complete History, Jeremy Boyce, Crowood Press, 1996.
The Classic Jaguar saloons, Chris Harvey, Motor Racing Publications, 1981.
Jaguar XJ6 and 12, and XJ-S, Chris Harvey, Osprey, 1982.
Jaguar Project XJ40, Philip Porter, Haynes, 1987.
Jaguar E-type, the Definitive History, Philip Porter, Haynes, 1989.
Jaguar XJ-S, the Complete Story, Graham Robson, Crowood Press, 1997.

JAIDECAR (US) c. 1984
Jaidecar, Long Beach, California.
The Jaidecar Mearas was a restyled body kit for the Porsche 914 chassis. It was an attractive coupé with fibreglass body panels. Jaidecar also made kits to install V6 or V8 engines into the 914.

HP

JAMES (US) 1909–1911
J & M Motor Car Co., Lawrenceburg, Indiana.
This was a high-wheeler powered by a 14/16hp 2-cylinder air-cooled flat-twin engine, with epicyclic transmission and chain drive. It was very close to the DE TAMBLE in design, and was possibly bought from that company when they gave up high-wheelers, and simply rebadged as a James. Very few were made, but in 1911 James made, or sold, a 35hp 4-cylinder car called the Dearborn.

NG

JAMES AUCLAIR (US) c.1994
James Auclair, Warwick, Rhode Island.
The James Auclair Denaro was a Pontiac Fiero rebody kit car that resembled a Ferrari Testarossa.

HP

JAMES & BROWNE (GB) 1901–1910
1901–1902 Martineau & Browne, Hammersmith, London.
1902–1910 James & Browne Ltd, Hammersmith, London.
The original partners in this company were Francis Leigh Martineau, who had been with the Premier and New Beeston cycle companies, and Tom Bousquet Browne, former branch manager of the electrical engineers New & Mayne. Martineau designed the early cars, which had mid-mounted horizontal engines, originally a 9hp twin with transverse crankshaft and the flywheel between the cylinders. It had a 4-speed gearbox and chain final drive. James & Browne was registered in January 1902 'to carry on the business of automobile, flying machine and submarine manufacturers' – there is no evidence that they ever went in for the two latter activities. James seems to have been a sleeping partner and no one in the Browne family can remember anything about him.

An 18hp 4-cylinder car followed, and both this and the 9hp had conventional bonnets though the engine still lived under the front seats, and quite a number of bonnetless town cars were made. Even the little 9hp twin was made with landaulet body. In 1905 Martineau left to join the Pilgrims Way Motor Co. to make the PILGRIM (i), also a horizontal-engined car. James & Browne then turned to a conventional car with 4-cylinder vertical engines mounted at the front. Logically called Vertex, these were made in four models, with 20 or 35hp 4-cylinder, and 30 or 45hp 6-cylinder engines, available with shaft or chain drive. The 45hp was an enormous engine of 10,581cc. As with other firms such as Ader and Gillet-Forest, this switch to vertical engines did not pay dividends, for there were too many good conventional cars already, and few Vertexes were sold. In 1906 petrol-engined cars were banned from using Hyde Park, and this damaged sales of the smaller underfloor-engined town cars. Production dwindled from then onwards, though in 1909 they obtained some useful work making the

1998 Jaguar XJR 4.0 V8 supercharged saloon.
JAGUAR CARS

c.1902 James & Browne 9hp tonneau.
NATIONAL MOTOR MUSEUM

1904 James & Browne 9hp 2-seater.
NICK GEORGANO

chassis for the Railless, Britain's first trolleybus. Unfortunately, the order for production chassis went to Alldays & Onions. In December 1910 James & Browne sold their premises in Hammersmith, and their spare parts went to Rawlings Bros who took on some J & B staff.

Tom Browne had a distinguished career in the Royal Army Service Corp. during the war, and later he founded a very successful advertising agency. He died in 1965 at the age of 92.

NG

1906 James & Browne Vertex 45hp limousine, by Lacre.
NATIONAL MOTOR MUSEUM

JAMES HERITAGE CARS (US) c.1992–1993

James Heritage Cars, West Patterson, New Jersey.
This kit car company built a replica of a Ferrari 308 that fitted on a Chevrolet Camaro or Pontiac Firebird body called the Cavalo. They were sold in kit or assembled form.

HP

JAMIESON (US) 1902

M.W Jamieson & Co., Warren, Pennsylvania.
Only a few of these light, tiller-steered, 2-seaters with 7hp 2-cylinder engines and single-chain drive were made, but one survives today.

NG

JAMOS (A) 1964

Rudolf Moser, Vienna.
The Jamos 650GT was a pretty fibreglass-bodied coupé using a Steyr-Puch 650 TR chassis with its 643cc 2-cylinder 46bhp engine. The coachwork was by Jauerning and the car was prepared by Rudolf Moser. Only a handful were built.

CR

JAN (DK) 1915–1918

Jan Hagemeister, Copenhagen.
The Jan was an all-Danish car powered by a 1328cc 4-cylinder engine, with 3-speed gearbox and shaft drive. It had a pointed radiator of hammered steel, and was made mainly in open 2- and 4-seater form, though there were some saloons, and a limousine supplied to the Danish Royal Family. About 50 cars were made before Hagemeister went bankrupt in 1918, despite support from the Landsmansbanken. He then merged with two other Danish car makers, ANGLO-DANE and THRIGE, to form De Forenede Automobilfabriker AS, who made Triangel commercial vehicles up to 1950.

NG

JANÉMIAN (F) 1920–1923

M. Janémian, Bièvres, Seine-et-Oise.

The Janémian was a rear-engined cyclecar powered originally by a flat-twin engine of 1100 or 1400cc, which by 1922 had given way to a 1095cc V-twin. The crankshaft was mounted transversely and the radiator faced sideways, just behind the driver. Final drive was by single chain, and the rear wheels were set close together. Front suspension was by a single transverse spring.

NG

JANSEN (NL) 1900–1901

B.A. Jansen, 's-Hertogenbosch.
As an importer of Sparkbrook bicycles from 1883, Jansen began to build bicycles of his own, too. He sold them under the name Yankee-Style. But he experimented in building motorcycles or tricycles. The result was a small production of tricycles with a front-mounted single-cylinder 3.5hp De Dion-Bouton engine. However, he began importing Cambier and De Dion-Bouton cars from France and discontinued the production of his own De Toerist voiturettes.

FBV

JANSSENS (B) c.1903–c.1907

Ateliers A. Janssens, St Nicholas.
This company made an *avant train* unit with 2 or 4 cylinders, which could be attached to a horse-drawn vehicle. The first examples were sold at the end of 1903 or beginning of 1904, and after a while complete vehicles were made. Production was on a very small scale.

NG

JANVIER (i) (F) 1903–1904

V. Janvier, Paris.
This was a rare example of a 6-wheeled car, with three equally spaced axles. The front two axles steered, the wheels being slightly smaller than the rear driving wheels. The car had a 4-cylinder engine and a wide 4-seater tourer body. It was shown at the 1903 Paris Salon, but production must have been very limited, if it took place at all. Janvier later made a 7-ton truck on the same principles.

NG

JANVIER (ii) **(F)** 1926–1928

Janvier, Sabin et Cie, Châtillon-sous-Bagneux, Seine.

Janvier were well-known makers of proprietary engines, but from 1926 to 1928 they listed two complete cars, powered by their 1994 or 2983cc 4-cylinder T-head engines. There was also a Picker-Janvier sports car which ran in the Grand Prix de France at Le Mans in 1912.

NG

JARRETT *see* VOITURE ÉLECTRONIQUE

JARVIS-HUNTINGTON (US) 1912

Jarvis-Huntington Automobile Co., Huntington, West Virginia.

This was a large and powerful car with a choice of 45hp or 60hp 6-cylinder engines, on 128in (3248mm) and 142in (3604mm) wheelbases respectively. The six had a capacity of 9.4 litres and was made with 8-seater tourer or limousine bodies. Final drive by double chains was very old-fashioned for 1912. The Jarvis-Huntington did not last out the year of its announcement, and production must have been very limited.

NG

JAVELIN *see* AMERICAN MOTORS

JAWA (CS) 1934–1945

Zbrojovka Ing. F. Janecek, a.s., Praha-Nusle, and Tynec nad Sazavou.

Czech arms manufacturer Franisek Janecek (1878–1941) decided, after the decline of the armament industry in 1929, to start the production of motorcycles. There was no time to develop a motor of his own so he decided to make a foreign design under licence. Not only did he get the licence to produce Wanderer motorcycles (because of the collapse of German motor industry, Wanderer had already stopped production), but also the complete production set-up with many completed parts. The trademark 'Jawa' (derived from the first two letters of Janecek and Wanderer) was patented in August 1929. During the years, motorcycle production was growing well and in the mid–1930s Jawa also went into car building.

In 1934, a foreign licence was bought again – now by the DKW F4 Meisterklasse – and the new front-wheel drive car was called Jawa 700. It had a 2-stroke 2-cylinder 692cc 20bhp engine placed in front of a backbone pressed frame, with independently suspended wheels all round. Two-door wooden bodies, first covered by leatherette, later by tin plates, either with removable top or as closed 'hatchback' were delivered. Engines were produced in Prague, the bodies assembled and the cars completed in Tynec nad Sazavou (not far from Prague). The car was capable of 56mph (90km/h) and its fuel consumption was 7 litres of 25:1 mixture for 100 km. From May to December 1934 203 cars were sold being priced at 22,900 Kc.

The Jawa cars with tuned 750cc 27bhp engine were capable of 68mph (109 km/h) and with Jaray-type streamlined body took part in the 1935 '1000 Miles of Czechoslovakia' races. Another was bodied as an open roadster and started in races until 1937.

At the same time, Jawa worked on their own construction of a light car. In 1935 an aircraft engineer Zdenek Pilat (born 1910) came from Walter to Jawa and designed a car with an engine placed in front of the front axle, outside the axis (25 years before being used in Issigonis' Austin/Morris Mini). Another designer, Rudolf Vykoukal, who came from Praga, projected a car with an engine behind the front axle, which later came into production as the Jawa Minor, being introduced in autumn 1937.

Jawa Minor had a backbone frame of square section with swinging axles, and a 2-stroke 2-cylinder 615cc 20bhp water-cooled engine. The bodies (2- and 4-seater cabriolets, roadsters and sedans) were built at the Kvasiny Works again, and the cars were completed in Tynec nad Sazavou. Until 1939, when car assembly was stopped and war production started, there were 1990 Jawa Minors manufactured, and the simplest version cost 16,000 Kc.

Some parts and components survived until the war's end, and in July 1945 the last Jawa Minor cars – a series of 710 units – were sold for 35,500 Kcs.

A whole new car, first called Jawa Minor II, launched in January 1947, but renamed Aero Minor, was assembled in three or four diverse automobile works.

MSH

Further Reading
Spremo, Milan: Jawa, Jan Kralik, Brno: Auto Album Archiv, 1989.

1938 Jawa Minor I roadster.
NATIONAL MOTOR MUSEUM

JAXON *see* JACKSON (ii)

JAYA (IND) 1994

This company had been making diesel engines since 1980, but in 1994 it presented two passenger car prototypes named after a legendary Indian princess, Mayura. Designed by B. Jayachandran, the M-11 was a compact 5-door hatchback fitted with an in-house 1339cc 38bhp diesel engine. The M–18 was a larger 4-door saloon with a 1.8-litre 50bhp diesel engine developed in Germany by Elsbett. Petrol-engined versions were anticipated.

CR

JAYE (GB) 1980–c. 1983

Peter Jaye, Wooton, Bedfordshire.

A classic car restorer made a 1952 Jaguar C-Type replica and customers soon placed orders for more. Jaguar XK components were used in a triangulated steel frame.

CR

J & B (US) c.1996

J & B Snakes, Christiansburg, Virginia.

The Cobra Warrior was a Shelby replica with a non-removable fastback hard-top. It had roll-up windows, vent windows, outside door handles and air conditioning. It was mounted on a tubular frame with Ford Mustang suspension and a V8 engine. A conventional roadster was available as well.

HP

J.B. (i) **(GB)** 1926

Jones, Burton & Co. Ltd, Liverpool.

Most ephemeral makes were light cars or cyclecars, but the J.B. was a medium-sized family car powered by a 2121cc 13.9hp 4-cylinder Meadows engine. A price of £400 was quoted for a complete car, but it never progressed beyond the prototype stage.

NG

J.B. (ii) **(AUS)** 1949

The Automotive Co. of Australia, Northgate, Queensland.

Manufactured by Jeffress Bros, the J.B. Minor was a feature of the Queensland Industries Fair. In line with the then current fad for miniature cars, it was a 3-wheeled 2-seater having, unusually, front-drive and rear steering. The engine was a 5hp 2-stroke twin and the body was by bus builder Athol Hedges. Production depended on a new foundry coming into use, but this did not materialise.

MG

J.B.A. (GB) 1982 to date

JBA Engineering, Standish, Wigan, Lancashire.

J.B.A. managed to overcome the poor reputation of British kit cars by creating high-quality, well-engineered products. Its first model was the Falcon whose tourer bodywork was upright and traditional in style, and initially made of

1923 J.B.R. 750cc 2-seater.
NATIONAL MOTOR MUSEUM

1915 J.B.S. 10hp 2-seater.
M.J.WORTHINGTON-WILLIAMS

individual steel panels, though that changed to aluminium with fibreglass wings fairly quickly. (All-fibreglass bodywork followed in due course.) The Ford Cortina donated its components, though other options included a Rover V8 engine or Ford Sierra mechanicals. Larger 2 + 2 and Tourer models were popular, as well as a lower-slung Sports model from 1989. Less successful was the 1985–89 Javelin, basically a restyled convertible fibreglass Ford Capri with a steel chassis. The bonnet echoed Lagonda themes, while the roof featured a fixed targa bar and fold-down rear section.

CR

J.B.F. (GB) 1992
John B. Fernley, Manchester.
The J.B.F. Boxer was a Citroën 2CV-based plywood-fibreglass-and-aluminium barrel-back bodied trike. It was scheduled for production, but only one was ever made.

CR

J.B.M. (GB) 1947–1950
James Boothby Motors Ltd, Horley; Crawley.
Assembled from reconditioned parts, so that no purchase tax was payable, the J.B.M. was a very light 2-seater powered by a modified Ford V8 engine giving 120bhp.

J.B.R. (E) 1921–1923; 1947
Cyclecars Josep Boniquet Riera, Barcelona.
Boniquet Riera was a famous dentist who prepared his first cyclecar in 1920

using a 2-cylinder MAG engine. He entered this car in several races, competing himself as driver with the David cars. Later he used Ruby engines with 14–20bhp, like other cyclecar-builders, and prepared several bodies, such as torpedo, closed sedan and a 2-seater racing car. Success in a lot of races helped to sell the cars, but in 1924 financial problems pushed Boniquet to build the STORM, more sophisticated and luxurious, but on the same base. This attempt failed. In 1947 Boniquet introduced a small 3-wheeler with the third wheel at the rear, one front light, and a motorcycle engine. The body was made of papier-mâché using the famous newspaper LA VANGUARDIA and paste.

VCM

J.B.S. (GB) 1913–1915
J.Bagshaw & Sons Ltd, Batley, Yorkshire.
The first J.B.S. was a cyclecar powered by an 8hp V-twin J.A.P. engine, though more civilised than many in that it had shaft drive. For 1915 an 8hp V-twin Blumfield and a 10hp 4-cylinder Dorman engine were offered. So far as is known the J.B.S. was not revived after World War I, though a note in *Fletcher's Motor Car Index* stated 'Manufacture may be resumed in the near future'.

NG

J.C. (GB) 1984 to date
1984–1987 J.C. Autopatterns, Sheffield, Yorkshire.
1987–1989 J.C. Sportscars, Sheffield, Yorkshire.
1989–1992 T&J Sportscars, Rotherham, Yorkshire.
1992–1994 R.L.T. Developments, Sheffield, Yorkshire.
1994 to date White Rose Vehicles, Gillingham, Kent.
Following his successful MOSS range of cars, John Cowperthwaite turned his attention to making plans-built cars. The first was the Midge, a very compact traditional style roadster of very basic construction. The body was all-wooden with aluminium engine side panels, a cast grill shell and a fibreglass double scuttle. It was intended for a Triumph Herald/Vitesse chassis, although a chassis was offered for Ford Escort parts. The Midge went to T&J in 1989, but it returned to R.L.T. by 1993, and then went to White Rose. The next plans-built car was the Locust of 1986, which brought to mind the Lotus 7. The plywood bodywork was skinned in aluminium or Medite, though an all-fibreglass body was shown in 1993. Ford basis was usual, or a Triumph Herald/Vitesse or Viva chassis could be ordered specially. Next (in 1991) came the Husky, a Ford Escort based jeep-style car made from medium-density fibreboard (MDF). This was later produced by White Rose.

CR

JCF (US) c.1994
John's Custom Fabrication, Coos Bay, Oregon.
The JCF 289 was a replica of the 289 Cobra street car, while the JCF 427SC replicated the Cobra 427SC. These were inexpensive kits with simple frames and Mustang II suspension.

HP

J.D.M. (F) 1981 to date
S.A. Simpa J.D.M., Avrille.
J.D.M. arrived on the French microcar scene as the market was burgeoning and cut a niche for itself producing a range of conventional designs. It started out in 1981 making the monobox 2-seater 49SL and 125, which were powered by engines ranging from 49cc petrol to 325cc diesel. In 1984 came the Parthenon, a larger 2-box design and a year later the even larger, more rounded Nueva arrived. A new Furio model was launched in 1987 with squarish bodywork resembling a Fiat Panda, although it was only 96in (2440mm) long. It was even offered in GTI form with a twin-cylinder Ruggerini 654cc diesel engine. The following year came the X5 offered in 2-seater (Honda 317cc diesel-powered) and 4-seater (654cc Ruggerini-powered) forms. The range coalesced in 1994 around the Orane, of which 1000 examples were built in 1995 (ranking it as France's fourth largest microcar constructor). The Orane was available with Honda 317cc as well as Lombardini 502cc engines. A convertible version with an electric roof was offered under the name Madeira from 1995. A new Titane model in 1997 slotted in at the top of the microcar range and, along with its sister models, was powered by a Yanmar 523cc diesel twin.

CR

JEAN BART (F) 1907

Automobiles Jean Bart, Nanterre, Seine.
These cars had previously been sold under the PROSPER LAMBERT name. Three models were offered, a 9hp single-cylinder, and two fours of 16/20 and 40hp.
NG

JEAN GRAS (F) 1924–1930

SA des Automobiles Jean Gras, Lyons.
Jean Gras owned two garages in the Lyons area, and showed his cars for the first time at the 1924 Paris Salon. Two models were offered, the Type A with 1494cc single-ohc C.I.M.E. engine and the Type B with 1200cc pushrod ohv engine, also by C.I.M.E. The chassis was of conventional design, with Perrot 4-wheel brakes. Although the catalogue showed a handsome coupé de ville and torpedo tourer, the actual body was a rather heavy-looking 6-light saloon. A 1557cc 6-cylinder Jean Gras, which carried better-looking low-slung saloon bodies, was announced in 1927, made at Dijon by the Constructions Électriques et Mécaniques de Dijon. Gras' Lyons factory is believed to have been the former PHILOS works.
NG

JEANNIN (US) 1908

Jeannin Automobile Manufacturing Co., St. Louis, Missouri.
Designed and built by H.W. Jeannin, this was a high-wheeler with 10/12hp 2-cylinder air-cooled engine with shaft drive. This was distinctly unusual on a high-wheeler, most of which used chain, or even rope, drive. It was made as a runabout, Doctor's Car (presumably a closed coupé), and open or closed delivery truck. Jeannin claimed that nothing under his car would ever require any attention, but his company lasted less than a year.
NG

JEANPERRIN (F) c.1899–1904

Jeanperrin Frères, Glay, Doubs.
Louis Jeanperrin (1856–1905) started his business in the mid–1880s, making components for the clock and watch industries, and also gear wheels. Bicycle wheels followed, and complete bicycles in 1888. Jeanperrin's son claimed that motorcycles were introduced in 1890 and cars from 1892, but these dates seem very early. Nothing is known about the cars before about 1899, when a light *vis-à-vis* similar in appearance to a De Dion-Bouton was made. It used a single-cylinder engine of Jeanperrin's own design and manufacture, water-cooled and with hot tube ignition. It had wire wheels and a vertical steering column, but a later version had artillery wheels and a sloping column. By 1903 he was making a 4-seater tonneau with front-mounted vertical 2-cylinder engine.

While visiting the Paris Salon in December 1904, Jeanperrin caught an infection from which he died in January 1905 at the age of 48. No more cars were made, though motorcycles were continued for one year longer, and the company closed down in 1910.
NG

JEANTAUD (F) 1893–1906

C. Jeantaud, Paris.
Charles Jeantaud (1843–1906) built an experimental car in 1881, but did not start commercial production until 1893. Even then he was the first to make electric vehicles in any numbers for commercial sale. He built a large carriage for the 1895 Paris-Bordeaux-Paris Race with seating for six, two speeds and chain drive. Production cars had motors mounted under the driving seat, wheel steering, double-chain drive and pneumatic tyres. Within a few years Jeantaud was making a wide variety of vehicles for town use, coupés, open landaus, and cabs including a hansom variety with the driver perched behind the passengers. In this the batteries were under a short bonnet, so the motor was relocated close to the rear axle. Jeantaud was the instigator of the Paris Motor Cab Trials held in June 1898. Perhaps it is no coincidence that his cab won the event.

In December 1898 a 2-seater Jeantaud driven by the Comte de Chasseloup-Laubat covered a flying kilometre at 39.24mph (63.15km/h). In response the Belgian Camille JENATZY drove one of his electric cars at 41.4mph (66.62km/h), and thus began the quest for what became known as the World Land Speed Record. The 1898 record Jeantaud was a standard 2-seater, at any rate in appearance, but in response to Jenatzy's reply the Count built a vee-fronted wind-cheating body with which he achieved 57.6mph (92.69km/h) in March 1899. Final

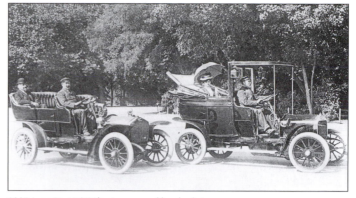

1907 Jean Bart 16/20hp tourer and landaulet.
NATIONAL MOTOR MUSEUM

1908 Jeannin 10/12hp 2-seater.
KEITH MARVIN

1900 Jeanperrin 3hp *vis-à-vis*.
NATIONAL MOTOR MUSEUM

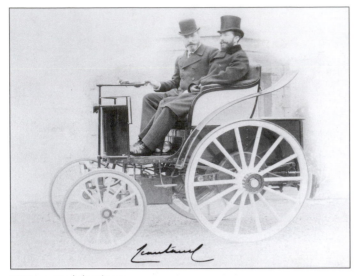

1894 Jeantaud electric car.
NATIONAL MOTOR MUSEUM

1976 Jeep Wagoneer station wagon.
ELLIOTT KAHN

1990 Jeep Wrangler Laredo.
JEEP CORPORATION

victory went to Jenatzy (see entry), after which Jeantauds were seen no longer in competitions.

The 1901 Jeantauds had front-mounted batteries and rear-mounted Postel-Vinay bi-polar motors, with five speeds forward and reverse and an electrically assisted brake. Top speed was 12½mph (20.11 km/h) and range 38 miles, though the latter figure was doubled by 1903. In that year Jeantaud broke with tradition by offering petrol cars, with 12hp 2-cylinder, 18hp 3-cylinder and 24hp 4-cylinder engines. They lasted for only two seasons. 1905–06 Jeantauds had front-wheel drive, but *le Patron's* suicide in 1906 put an end to the business.

NG

JEECY-VÉA (B) 1926
Motos Jeecy-Véa, Brussels.
This name was better known in connection with motorcycles than with cars. Jean Watelet and Jacques Vergote de Lantsheere built 2-wheelers from 1923 to 1927, and in 1926 announced a light car powered by a 750cc flat-twin Coventry-Victor engine. Tourer and coupé bodies were offered, but very few were made as the competition from the many French light cars was too great.
NG

JEEP (US) 1963 to date
1963–1970 Kaiser-Jeep Corp., Toledo, Ohio.
1970–1987 Jeep Corp (American Motors Corp.), Detroit, Michigan.
1987 to date Jeep-Eagle-Division, Chrysler Corp., Detroit, Michigan.
Although the Jeep first appeared during World War II, it has been regarded as a make in its own right only since the formation of Kaiser-Jeep in 1963. Before that it was a model of WILLYS-OVERLAND. The Jeep range in 1963 consisted of 2- and 4-wheel drive Wagoneer station wagons with 3770cc single-ohc 6-cylinder engines, and updated versions of the original wartime Jeep with 2199cc 4-cylinder or a 3707cc side-valve six as well as the ohc version. For 1965 the Wagoneer could be had with an optional 5354cc Rambler V8 engine, while the Jeep Universal CJ-5 (descendant of the original Jeep) could be had with a 3687cc Buick V6 from 1966.

In February 1970 Kaiser-Jeep was bought by American Motors, but the range continued unchanged for that year. For 1971 the CJ-5's 4-cylinder engine was dropped, and in its place came AMC-built sixes and V8s, the largest of the latter being a 5899cc 195bhp unit. In 1973 Wagoneers had AMC's new Quadra-Trac full-time 4x4 drive whereby each wheel could spin at its own speed, making 2-wheel drive unnecessary. By 1974 power-assisted front disc brakes were generally available; they were standard on all but the basic CJ range by 1978. Also new for 1974 was the Cherokee, a 3-door sports-utility station wagon which became the junior partner to the 5-door Wagoneer.

The AMC take-over resulted in a great increase in output, from 45,805 in 1970 to 140,431 in 1979. In 1981 4-cylinder engines returned with the lightweight 2474cc Hurricane and its new 4-speed gearbox, available in both the CJ-5 and Cherokee ranges. In 1983 two smaller station wagons were announced, the 3-door Cherokee and 5-door Wagoneer. They had integral construction and a choice of 2458cc AMC-built 4-cylinder or 2834cc General Motors V6 engines, supplemented by a 2.1-litre Renault 4-cylinder diesel. The former large Wagoneer with V8 engine was renamed the Grand Wagoneer. In mid-1986 came the totally revised Universal, now called the Wrangler. It was slightly wider though no longer, had a restyled bonnet and grill, with square headlamps, and came with a fuel-injected 2458cc four or optional 4228cc six.

In 1987 Chrysler bought American Motors from Renault who had owned it since 1978, so Jeep became a division of the Chrysler Corp., but the Toledo factory was retained, and the Wrangler and Cherokee continued to be made there. The Grand Wagoneer was dropped at the beginning of 1991, its place taken by the Grand Cherokee with 3960cc six or 5216cc V8 engines. The smaller Cherokee, now with 5 doors and 2068cc turbo or 2464cc single-ohc engines was continued as well. For 1994 a 2499cc turbo diesel was available in the Cherokee. This engine also went into the Grand Cherokee for 1996. The Wrangler continued without great change, though a return to round headlamps was seen on the 1997 models. A new Grand Cherokee for 1999 had revised styling, a new 230bhp 4.7-litre V8 which replaced the former 212bhp 5216cc unit, and a new 5-speed automatic transmission. Engine options included a 4-litre six and (for Europe only) a 3.1-litre 5-cylinder turbo diesel. European models were built at Chrysler's plant at Graz, Austria, from January 1999. In America the Grand Cherokee was made in Detroit, the Cherokee and Wrangler in Toledo. 1997 production was 81,956 Wranglers, 130,041 Cherokees and 260,875 Grand Cherokees.

Jeeps have been made in various guises in many countries including Spain, Turkey, Iran, India (see MAHINDRA) and China (see BEIJING).
NG

Further Reading
Jeep, from Bantam to Wrangler, Bill Munro, Crowood Autoclassics, 2000.
'Jeep', Patrick R. Foster, *Automobile Quarterly*, Vol. 39, No. 3.

1997 Jeep Grand Cherokee station wagon.
CHRYSLER JEEP

JEEPIE *see* E3D

JEFE (RA) 1956
Casa Fehling, Buenos Aires.
This company made a limited number of coupés and station wagons powered by 700cc 2-stroke DKW engines.

JEFFERY (US) 1914–1917
Thomas B. Jeffery Co., Kenosha, Wisconsin.
Thomas Jeffery, whose company had made the RAMBLER, died in 1910, and his son Charles decided to rename the cars after him when he introduced new models in 1914. They had side-valve monobloc engines, a 40hp four and a 48hp six, joined by a smaller four of 27hp. The latter lasted only a season, but the larger cars were made up to 1917. Charles Jeffery, apparently traumatised by spending four hours in icy water after the sinking of the *Lusitania*, had sold his company to Charles W. Nash in July 1916, and for the 1918 season they were renamed NASH.
NG

Further Reading
'A family in Kenosha: The story of the Rambler and the Jeffery', Beverly Rae Kimes, *Automobile Quarterly*, Vol. 16, No. 2.

2000 Jeep Grand Cherokee 3.1 Turbo Diesel station wagon.
CHRYSLER JEEP

JEFFREY (GB) 1971–1975
1971 Jeffrey Racing Cars, Minster Lovell, Oxfordshire.
1971–1972 Jeffrey Racing Cars, Shilton, Oxfordshire.
1972–1974 Jeffrey Automotive Ltd, Little Clanfield, Oxfordshire.
1974–1975 Emba Cars, Cowley, Oxfordshire.
This company built various Formula 750 racers from 1968 before relenting to customer demands for road cars in 1971. George Jeffrey built the J4 with a near racing-specification space frame chassis, Ford engines, a Morris Minor or Ford Cortina rear axle and Formula 750 suspension. The main body was aluminium with fibreglass wings, nose and bonnet. It weighed only 1120lb (509kg), so performance potential was substantial, even if it was a crude road machine. After making 30 cars, a new model called the J5 was launched in 1972. This had a strengthened J4 chassis, softer suspension and Triumph Herald steering. The bodywork was much more curvaceous, at first using aluminium-and-fibreglass bodywork, though from 1973 an all-fibreglass body was employed. Thirty-two examples of the J5 (also known as the JS5) were made.
CR

1914 Jeffery tourer.
NICK GEORGANO/NATIONAL MOTOR MUSEUM

1974 Jeffrey J5 sports car.
NATIONAL MOTOR MUSEUM

1991 Jehle Artemis coupé.
FERDINAND HEDIGER

1955 Jenard Jabeka sports car.
NATIONAL MOTOR MUSEUM

JEG (BR) 1979–c.1980s
Dacunha GT SA Engenhuvia Industria e Comercio, São Bernardo do Campo.
Based on the VW Beetle, this was a jeep-type vehicle available in open and closed form, with either 2- or 4-wheel drive and 1600cc engine.
NG

JEHLE (FL) 1978–c.1992
AR-Studio Xavier Jehle, Schaan.
The tiny Alpine principality of Liechtenstein's main industries are postage stamps and false teeth, but it has had a motor industry as well. The DIAVOLINO was built there and Audi had a competition wing based there also. Xavier Jehle was the country's greatest car proponent, however. Apart from beach buggies, his first project was the MX Safari, a Citroën Méhari style leisure vehicle based on 2CV/Dyane parts, derived from the Greek NAMCO Pony. Jehle was also a

formidable tuner of the De Tomaso Pantera. His first all-original project was the extraordinary Saphier, an uncompromisingly wedge-shaped car that featured a large canopy that swung upwards for entry for three passengers sitting abreast, and side windows that pivoted open and which could be used for emergency exits. The basic car was designed for a VW Beetle chassis and had a Golf 1500cc engine, although a monocoque model was also offered with a bored-out 200bhp 2-litre Golf engine, while there was a mid-engined Ford V8-powered version with a claimed 500bhp. The last model from Jehle was the Artemis of 1991, a super-coupé with a mid-mounted 6.5-litre V12 engine. Jehle claimed its power output could be anywhere between 500 and 1000bhp, and that the top speed of the most powerful version was no less than 248mph (399 km/h).
CR

JENARD (GB) 1956
G.A. Elsmore, Yeovil, Somerset.
A 2-seater sports car with a tubular chassis intended for Austin A40 or Coventry-Climax 1100cc engines, the Jenard Jabeka used Austin front suspension, gearbox, and back axle, linked to Woodhead-Monroe suspension units.
NG

JENATZY (B/F) 1898–1903
1898–1903 Camille Jenatzy, Brussels.
1899–1901 Compagnie Internationale des Transports Automobiles, Boulogne-sur-Seine.
The son of Belgium's first manufacturer of rubberised fabric, Camille Jenatzy (1868–1913) trained as a civil engineer, and built his first car at the end of 1897. It was a chain-driven electric car with 4-seater *dos-à-dos* body, and the following year he began to make electric cabs in a factory at Boulogne-sur-Seine. This resulted from an order for 30 cabs from a Paris cab company. He drove one of his cars to victory in the Chanteloup hill climb in November 1898, and this encouraged him to challenge the Comte de Chasseloup-Laubat to a speed contest, after the latter had reached 39.3mph (63.15km/h) in his JEANTAUD electric car. After the record had changed hands several times, Jenatzy built a special car with torpedo-shaped body made of partinium, an early aluminium alloy, and built by Rheims & Auscher. He called it *La Jamais Contente* (Never Satisfied), and with it took the record at 65.75mph (105.8km/h) in April 1899. It was the first time that any road vehicle had exceeded 100km/h.
Jenatzy's French company, which became the Compagnie Internationale des Transports Automobiles in 1899, made cabs and light delivery vans up to 1901, but Jenatzy himself became more interested in the petrol-electric system. In January 1901 he exhibited a 4-seater tonneau at the Paris Salon using a 6hp Mors engine combined with the Pieper petrol-electric drive, and in the same year he built an enormous car in conjunction with F.N. which had an output of 100hp. This and the Mors-powered car were one-offs, but in 1903 he did make a few Jenatzy-Martini cars using 12/15 and 20/28hp 4-cylinder engines. They were built at the Liège factory of the Swiss armaments company, who also made cars, though their design had no connection with the Jenatzy-Martini.
His father's death in 1904 caused Jenatzy to devote much more time to the family business, and he made no more cars. He had a successful racing career, capped by victory in the 1903 Gordon Bennett Race in a 60hp Mercedes. He used to say that he would die in a Mercedes, and his prophecy came true though not on a racing circuit. While shooting wild boar in the Ardennes in 1913, Jenatzy, who was a great practical joker, hid in the undergrowth and imitated the sound of a boar. One of his companions opened fire and Jenatzy, mortally wounded, was carried to his Mercedes where he died.
NG

JENKINS (i) (US) 1907–1912
Jenkins Motor Car Co., Rochester, New York.
J. William Jenkins moved from the manufacture of shoes to motorcars in 1907, making one model of conventional tourer powered by a 40/45hp 4-cylinder engine. In 1908 he added a town car to the range, though it lasted only for one year. The Jenkins was little changed for the rest of its life, apart from annual increases in wheelbase. The 1912 model was described as a 38hp, but in July of that year Jenkins sold the company to his chief engineer who took on the agency for Cole cars.
NG

JENKINS (ii) (GB) 1914

P.W. Jenkins, Ponders End, Middlesex.

Jenkins was a coachbuilder who assembled a few light cars powered by an air-cooled engine. This may have been an 8hp J.A.P., as this was also used by Hurlin & Co., from whom Jenkins bought his chassis components, in their HURLINCAR.

NG

JENMARTI (US) c.1994

Jenmarti Motor Works, Orlando, Florida.

The Jenmarti Roadster was a neoclassic car that was sold in fully assembled form. It used Ford running gear and had a long bonnet with sweeping running boards.

HP

JENNINGS (GB) 1913–1915

Jennings Chalmers Light Car Co., Birmingham.

The Jennings light car was made with two sizes of Dorman engine, a 1085cc 7.9hp flat twin in 1913 and a 1093cc 10.2hp vertical four in 1914/15. Both had shaft drive.

NG

JENNIS (US) 1903–1905

Peter Jennis, Chestnut Hill, Pennsylvania.

Peter Jennis of Chestnut Hill, a suburb of Philadelphia, Pennsylvania, built at least three, and perhaps as many as six, cars in a period of two-and-a-half years, with plans to form a company to continue manufacture. The surviving car exemplifies Jennis' plans to target sales to the market of the affluent. It is a large car with a 48hp engine, a 5-seater touring car body with coachwork by Quinby and a 3-speed transmission with double-chain drive. The surviving Jennis car participated on the American Glidden Tour revival of 1957.

KM

JENSEN, JENSEN-HEALEY (GB) 1936–1976; 1983–1992; 1999 to date

1936–1976; 1983–1984 Jensen Motors Ltd, West Bromwich, Staffordshire.
1984–1992 Jensen Cars Ltd, West Bromwich, Staffordshire.
1999 to date Jensen Motors Ltd, West Bromwich, Staffordshire.

The first cars built by the Jensen brothers, Alan (1906–1993) and Richard (1909–1976), were not badged with their name. In 1928 they built up an AUSTIN Seven special, and later another on a STANDARD chassis. During 1931 they were in business with J.A. Patrick of Selly Oak, Birmingham, as Patrick Jensen Motors Ltd, but the firm was dissolved at the end of that year.

The brothers then joined a West Bromwich coachbuilder, W.J. Smith & Son, at the behest of a customer and part-owner of the firm, grocer George Mason. They were able to improve Smith's production of commercial bodies, and soon began dabbling in sports bodies for cars. By 1933, their bodies were being offered on MORRIS, SINGER, Standard and WOLSELEY chassis, and FORD had catalogued their 'Mistral' bodies on the 8hp chassis, offered through the Birmingham dealer, Bristol Street Motors. The next year the name of the Smith firm was changed to Jensen Motors Ltd.

A series of Model 40 Ford V8s was bodied and outfitted for the 1934 Tourist Trophy race at Ards in Northern Ireland, although the cars did not make a notable showing. But that autumn a Jensen Special Ford V8, with lowered sports tourer body, was shown at Ford's 'alternative' motor show at the Royal Albert Hall. Fewer than 30 replicas were built over the next three years, on Ford Models 40, 48 and 68 chassis, and a few were shipped to the USA, including one ordered by screen idol Clark Gable, who ultimately decided not to consummate his purchase.

The Jensen 3½ Litre appeared in the motoring press in October 1936. Built on modified Ford chassis supplied through M.B.K. Motors, an enterprise of Lt Col J.T.C. Moore-Brabazon and Harold Kahn, the cars featured an extended wheelbase and dropped suspension, both patterned after a design of Ford designer E.T. Gregorie. Offered in saloon, tourer and drophead models, the cars have been retroactively designated S-Types, after their chassis serial numbers. Styling was in the classic English fashion, and the bodies carefully coachbuilt by the Jensens' craftsmen. The cars sold for from £645 to £765, depending on body style. Some 50 3½-litre cars were built, the last one finished in 1941. Two or three were fitted with Ford's small 2227cc 60hp engine, but were found to have unsatisfactory performance.

1913 Jenkins (ii) cyclecar.
NICK BALDWIN

1914 Jennings 10hp 2-seater.
NATIONAL MOTOR MUSEUM

1938 Jensen 4½litre saloon (foreground) and 3½-litre saloon (behind).
NATIONAL MOTOR MUSEUM

A more powerful 4¼-litre model was introduced at the 1938 Earls Court Motor Show. Powered by a NASH twin-ignition ohv 4279cc straight-8, the cars continued to use Ford chassis, modified for the heavier engine. Some 15 cars were built, one or two fitted with LINCOLN Zephyr V12 engines. During this period, Jensen Motors was kept afloat mostly on the strength of its commercial body business.

1958 Jensen 541-R coupé.
NATIONAL MOTOR MUSEUM

1967 Jensen Interceptor coupé.
NATIONAL MOTOR MUSEUM

1973 Jensen-Healey sports car.
NATIONAL MOTOR MUSEUM

1992 Jensen Interceptor S4 EFI convertible.
JENSEN CARS

After the war, a Jensen straight-eight 6-seater saloon was announced, and was to use a newly-developed Meadows 3860cc engine. However, the Meadows unit proved to have annoying high-speed vibrations, which the engineers were unable to cure. A few were built with leftover Nash engines and then a 3993cc six from the Austin Sheerline was substituted. Fewer than 20 of these PW (for postwar) models seem to have been built between 1946 and 1952.

The Austin alliance paved the way for sharing of resources for a sports tourer, and this resulted in the supply of Austin A70 chassis for a new Jensen Interceptor and Jensen-supplied bodies for a smaller sibling Austin A40 Sports. Cabriolet and saloon (actually a 2-door hard-top coupé) models of the Interceptor were built, clothed with smoothly rounded aluminium bodies. Introduced in 1949, the Interceptor sold for £2257, considerably more than the contemporary JAGUAR; 88 were built before production was halted in 1957.

Discussions with Leonard Lord of Austin led to the building of a proposed new sports car based on Austin mechanicals. The Jensen car was not ready for the 1952 Earls Court event, however, and instead Donald Healey's Hundred stole the show. Jensens, however, were well-placed to manufacture the bodies for this new AUSTIN-HEALEY, when coachbuilders Tickfords were found to have insufficient capacity. The big Austin-Healeys were built at West Bromwich, alongside the contemporary Jensen models, to the end of Healey production in 1968. This was, in fact, the most profitable part of Jensen's business, and other contract work was sought and secured, including outfitting of the VOLVO 1800 coupé and conversion of SUNBEAM Alpines into Ford-engined Tigers for Rootes.

In 1953 Richard Jensen had the idea for a high-performance grand tourer, something lighter than the Interceptor. Chief body designer Eric Neale suggested glass-reinforced plastic for the body, and worked up drawings for a prototype. A new chassis was designed, with tubular side members, and fitted with the 3993cc Austin engine. Designated 541, it was later joined by a Deluxe version with Dunlop 4-wheel disc brakes, twin exhaust and Laycock de Normanville overdrive. This was the 541R. Final iteration of the 541 was the 541S, a somewhat restyled car introduced at the 1960 motor show. New on the 541S was a General Motors Hydra-Matic gearbox, with the manual unit offered as an option.

The luxury touring market now demanded more power than the Austin engine could supply, so Jensen looked at alternative units. Chosen was the American CHRYSLER V8 of 5910cc, which developed a healthy 330bhp. Beefing up the 541's chassis made it stronger, but considerably heavier overall. Body was again fibreglass, with doors skinned in aluminium; a novel slant-eyed headlamp arrangement gave the car an aggressive look. It was designated C-V8; the first car was completed in November 1962. A Mk II version came out in October 1963, and its engine was upgraded to Chrysler's 6276cc V8 a few months later. The final C-V8 was the Mk III of 1965–66, which had considerable changes to its frontal appearance.

Jensens had made an agreement with Harry Ferguson Research to use the Ferguson 4-wheel drive system, together with Dunlop Maxaret anti-lock braking, in a car, but the idea was not fully developed until 1965. The car, christened FF for Ferguson Formula, was based on an elongated C-V8.

With the phase-out of the Austin-Healey, Jensen decided to attempt a volume produced sports car of their own, and again went to Chrysler for power. The name Interceptor was revived for a lightweight prototype designed to sell for considerably less than the C-V8. However, Jensens had come under financial control of the Norcros Group in the late 1950s, and the Norcros interests felt that an Italian design on a C-V8 chassis was a better proposition, and had a prototype built up by Vignale. This 1966 initiative deepened a rift within the company, and Alan and Richard Jensen resigned. The new C-V8 based, Italian-styled Interceptor entered production in September. An FF model was made ready at about the same time. Three versions of Interceptors (Mk I, II and III) were made through to December 1976, all with the Chrysler 6276cc V8. Three versions of FFs were also offered, with similar dates, although the last FF appeared in December 1971.

The Jensen-Healey owed its start to Jensen's role in Austin-Healey production. British Leyland declined to renew Donald Healey's contract and took the name Healey off the remaining A-H cars, the Sprites, in 1972. An American distributor of British sports cars, Kjell Qvale of San Francisco, became concerned, and through discussions with Donald Healey learned of Jensen's role in Austin-Healey. It also happened that Jensen's bankers were looking for additional capital in the firm,

2000 Jensen S-V8 roadster.
JENSEN MOTORS

and a deal was arranged for Qvale to become the majority shareholder and Donald Healey the new Jensen chairman. A new car, to be called Jensen-Healey would be designed and marketed, targeted at the USA. Its concept was more in the Austin-Healey idiom than any current Jensen, a William Towns-styled roadster body being placed on a unibody platform of 92in (2335mm) wheelbase. A VAUXHALL engine was contemplated, and a BMW unit also considered. The final car used a LOTUS dohc 4-cylinder engine of 1973cc and suspension of the Vauxhall Firenza. Intended to sell at around $5000, the car did not appear in US showrooms until late in 1972. Early models were troublesome, and a Mk II version was introduced in August 1973. A Getrag 5-speed gearbox followed in 1974, the year also that Federal impact-resistant bumpers required for the US market were added. A GT coupé-estate version was the final incarnation of the Jensen-Healey introduced in mid–1975 but surviving for a mere 509 units. The last Mk II Jensen-Healey, of production barely topping 10,000, was produced in August of that year.

Jensen Motors Ltd entered receivership a few months later; in May 1976 the firm closed, though two new companies, Jensen Special Products and Jensen Parts & Service Ltd, were spun off and sold. The latter catered to owners and dealers of the surviving cars. It evolved into a distributorship for SUBARU.

A reprise for Jensen occurred in 1983, when Ian Orford, who had joined Jensens in 1968, bought Jensen Parts & Service. Orford's first act was to put the Interceptor, now designated Series 4, back into production as a coupé and convertible. This used the Chrysler 5910cc engine. Renamed Jensen Cars Ltd, the new company struggled along until 1988, only producing 11 cars. Orford sold out to Unicorn Holdings of Stockport, and new chairman Hugh Wainwright commissioned designs for a new Series 5. The Series 5 was stillborn, but a few more Series 4s were built, the last in 1992.

A revived Jensen Motors Ltd appeared in the autumn of 1998. Announcing plans for a completely new Jensen, the new owners, Creative Design Ltd, showed a prototype S-V8 model, with a Howard Guy/Gary Doy-designed 2-door, 2-seater roadster body in aluminium and 4.6-litre Ford quad-cam 32-valve V8. It had a 5-speed Borg Warner manual gearbox and suspension by coils and double unequal-length wishbones all round. Production of the £39,650 car began in 1999.

KF

Further Reading
Jensen & Jensen-Healey, Keith Anderson, Sutton Publishing Limited, 1998.
'Jensen - Gems for the Gentry', David Owen,
Automobile Quarterly, Vol. 32, No. 2.
'Edsel's English Enigma - How the Ford Special Sports Became A Jensen',
Kit Foster, *Automobile Quarterly*, Vol. 36, No. 2.

JET (E) 1951

This was a short-lived minicar made in Madrid. It was fitted with a 197cc Hispano-Villiers engine.

VCM

JEWEL (i); **JEWELL (US)** 1906–1909

Forest City Motor Co., Massilon, Ohio; Jewel Motor Car Co., Massilon, Ohio.

The cars made by these two companies underwent a complicated change of name. The prototype high-wheeler was built in Cleveland (the Forest City), and called the Jewel, but before production began the sponsors moved to Massilon, about 60 miles to the south, and renamed the car the Jewell. It had a single-cylinder engine, originally of 8hp but increased to 10hp for 1908, and rope drive. It did not sell well, and later in 1908 the makers replaced it by a full-sized conventional car, powered by a 40hp 4-cylinder Rutenber engine and reverting to the name Jewel. Late in 1909 Herbert Croxton, who was a substantial investor in the company, was joined by Forrest M. Keeton, and together they formed the CROXTON-KEETON Motor Car Co. The Rutenber-engined Jewel was continued as the 'German type' Croxton-Keeton.

NG

JEWEL (ii) **(GB)** 1919 –c.1938

John E. Wood, Bradford, Yorkshire.

The Jewel started out as a cyclecar powered by a 10hp air-cooled V-twin Precision engine, with 4-speed friction transmission and chain drive. There was nothing unusual about that, but John Wood continued to make its successors for nearly twenty years, yet never formed a company. The first car had disc wheels and a

1906 Jewel (i) 8hp 2-seater.
ELLIOTT KAHN

1923 Jewel (ii) 9.8hp 2-seater.
M.J.WORTHINGTON-WILLIAMS

1925 Jewett Six tourer.
NATIONAL MOTOR MUSEUM

bullnose radiator, but the latter had been replaced by a flat design in 1922 when a 1088cc 4-cylinder Alpha engine was used. Wood's premises were very small, on the ground floor of a building above which there was a firm of luggage makers for whom Wood made steel case frames. He also built all the bodywork for his cars. Jewel cars were made in very small numbers, and exact figures are not known.

By 1925 he was using a 1247cc 4-cylinder Meadows engine, and had abandoned the friction transmission and chain drive for a conventional 3- or 4-speed gearbox and Moss spiral bevel rear axle. It was quite a large car, offered in 2- or 4-seater tourer forms at £245 and as a 3-door saloon at £295. A 1496cc Meadows could be had for only £4.50 extra, and this would seem to have been a worthwhile expenditure considering the substantial size of the Jewel, especially the saloon. Very few cars were made after 1930, although there was a one-off with a high-powered 6-cylinder engine, and a 4-door fabric saloon with 1247cc Meadows engine was described and illustrated in *The Autocar* in 1935. This 9/21hp and the 12/40hp which used the larger 1496cc Meadows were listed by Stone & Cox *Motor Specifications and Prices* up to 1938, though there is no evidence that they were made as late as this. Prices were quoted for both chassis and complete cars, £190 and £230 for the 9/21, £210 and £250 for the 12/40, being lower by £10 from 1936 to 1938. Wood clearly did not make a living from car manufacture, and he also did contract machining for Jowett, assembled tracks for Bristol tractors and engaged in general garage work. After the war he made caravans to special order, building the complete caravan including plumbing for hot and cold water. In 1962 he sold the business to the Yorkshire and England cricketer, Herbert Sutcliffe.

NG

Further Reading
'Built in Bradford –the Jewel', M. Worthington-Williams, *The Automobile*, December 1990.

JEWETT (US) 1922–1927

Paige-Detroit Motor Car Co., Detroit, Michigan.
Organised in December 1921, Jewett Motors, Inc. was set up by the Paige-Detroit Motor Car Co. to produce a smaller, less expensive companion car to the Paige, named after Paige president Harry M. Jewett. With an in-house L-head engine of $3^{1}/_{4} \times 5$in bore and stroke and a price range of less than $1000 for its open models, the Jewett was an instant success on America's burgeoning 1922 automobile market with production slightly under 10,000 cars completed. The Jewett, with its pleasing appearance, would continue its healthy annual production, peaking with more than 28,000 for the 1925 calendar year, offering a complete line of body types – three of these open and four closed. In 1926, Jewett announced its 'New Day' series, a restyled car with a Continental 9U 6-cylinder L-head engine of $2^{3}/_{4} \times 4^{3}/_{4}$in bore and stroke, shorter wheelbase and lighter in overall weight. The 'New Day' would be the swan-song of the make, and after January 1927, subsequent and final production would be rebadged and sold as the Model 6-45, the smallest Paige – which itself would cease production that year. More than 100,000 Jewetts were produced during its six years of manufacture.

KM

J.G. (F) 1922

J. Goupy, Paris.
This was a sporting cyclecar powered by a 970cc 4-cylinder Ruby engine, with 6-speed friction transmission and chain final drive. Front suspension was independent by transverse spring in the style of the Sizaire-Naudin. The oval-topped radiator was similar to that of the Bugatti Brescia. Only three J.G. cyclecars were made.

NG

JIANGNAN (CHI) 1988 to date

State Operated Jiangnan Machinery Works, Xiangtan City, Hunan Province.
This army ordnance works was erected in 1952 by the Beifan (North) Corp. Car production started in 1988 with the limited production of the mini-car Jiangnan HN 710, later renamed JNJ 7050. Jiangnan means 'South of the River'. The engine was a single cylinder with a displacement of 530cc. The design was remarkably influenced by the French AIXAM models. Production in 1991 was 100 units. In that year Suzuki Alto (model 1985–1990) licence-

production replaced these mini-cars. This 4-door car was named Jiangnan JNJ 7080 and was powered by the Jiangling 796cc 3-cylinder engine. In 1994 the yearly Alto production was 2500 units. Two other products, both from 1995, followed: a bigger Jiangnan JNJ 7110 with a length of 147in (3729mm) and a smaller Jiangnan JNJ 7050A 2-door, 4-seater 'monospace' with a length of 107in (2730mm).

EVIS

JIANHUA (CHI) 1989 to date
Jianhua Auto Refit Works, Wangcheng County, Hunan Province.
'Classic' cars based on the Beijing 4 × 2 jeep chassis, mostly powered by the Beijing 2445cc 4-cylinder engine, were made in Hunan Province. A complete range of open and closed versions were marketed and indicated as 'grandfather vehicles'.

EVIS

JIDÉ (F) 1969–1974; 1977–1981
1969–1974 Jacques Durand, Châtillon-sur-Thouet, Deux Sèvres.
1977–1978 Sté des Automobiles Jidé, Cherves-de-Cognac.
1978–1979 Club Jidé France, Bergerac.
1980–1981 Club Jidé France, La Force.
The Jidé name was formed by the initials of the marque's creator, Jacques Durand, who had previously made the A.T.L.A., SERA and SOVAM. The Jidé was a 2-door coupé with a monocoque polyester and fibreglass body with steel strengthening. It was powered by a mid-engined Renault 8, 8s or 8 Gordini engine or, with an auxiliary subframe, a Renault 12 or 16 engine, and it featured all-independent suspension and 4-wheel disc braking. Some competition success was achieved with a fuel-injected 1600 Gordini-engined car and road cars were sold in kit form or complete. Having made fewer than 100 examples, in 1974 Jacques Durand stopped the Jidé marque and created SCORA but, after a gap, the Jidé 1600S was revived again, first by Société des Automobiles Jidé and subsequently the Club Jidé, newly formed by Jacques Herment, who was affiliated with a company called ARC Industrie based in Talence. Alternative engines were the 1300 Gordini or Renault 20 2-litre unit. In 1981, Club Jidé proposed to productionise a second model, the Narval, an extraordinary arrow-shaped coupé design exercise by Michel Fauré that had originally appeared in 1968.

CR

JILI (CHI) 1998 to date
Sichuan Geely Motor Co. Ltd., Deyang City, Sichuan Province.
The Geely (Chinese name: Jili) Group Corp. Ltd. from Taizhou City, Zhejiang Province, was a large business corporation producing motorcycles, engines, scooters and vehicles, but also trading as an import-export trade company, real estate, hotel and travelling service company. A motor car works was erected together with Deyang Auto Works. Products were the Jili CJB 6360 4-door saloon, the CJB 6410 5-door station car, the CJB 1010 2-door pick-up and the CJB 1010 S 4-door (crew cab) pick-up truck. These vehicles were based on the XIALI TJ 7300 and used plastic bodies.

EVIS

JILIN (CHI) 1987
First Auto Works Jilin Small Auto Works, Jilin City, Jilin Province.
This mini auto factory started in 1980 to produce minivans, minibuses and mini pick-ups, based on Suzuki models. In 1987 a licence-made Suzuki Alto (first generation) was introduced as the Jilin JL 730, but it was never mass-produced.

EVIS

JIMENEZ NOVIA (F) 1994 to date
Jimenez Motors, Monteux.
Ramon Jimenez was a Grand Prix motorcyclist in the 1970s and ran Yamaha motorbike dealerships in the Avignon area. His Novia was a supercar inspired by Group C racing cars of the 1970s. Its most notable feature was a 4-litre engine with 16 cylinders, composed of four banks of four cylinders arranged in a 'W' pattern around a common crankshaft and fitted with Yamaha FZR1000 superbike cylinder heads. It had five valves per cylinder and an output of 550bhp at 10,000rpm – later boosted as high as 609bhp – and was mated to a Hewland 6-speed

1995 Jimenez Novia W16 coupé.
JIMENEZ MOTORS

transmission. The engine formed part of the car's structure and the bodywork was made of carbon fibre and aluminium honeycomb. Its weight being only 820kg, a maximum speed of over 217mph (349km/h) was claimed. The company planned a Le Mans entry, a half-size 2-litre 8-cylinder engine and the development of a W16-engined 4x4 off-roader.

CR

JIMI JIMP (GB) 1981–1984
P.K. Engineering, Sandbach, Cheshire.
Conceived to fill spare capacity by a car restorer, the Jimi Jimp was a utility-type kit car styled by Steve Kirk. It had all-flat panels and used a Reliant Kitten van chassis and box section steel supporting frame. The steel inner body (clothed in aluminium panels) was simply riveted in place. Not many were sold, and those that were tended to go to Africa and the Caribbean in C.K.D. form.

CR

JIMINI (GB) 1973 to date
1973–1981 Vanspear Ltd, Peterborough, Cambridgeshire.
1984–c.1986 Highlander Cars, Curbridge, Hampshire.
1990–1993 Jimini Automobiles, Botley, Hampshire.
1993 to date The Scamp Motor Co., Rowfant, West Sussex.
The first Jimini in 1973 not only looked very like the Mini Moke, which by then had left production in Britain, it was also unique among kit-form substitutes in having an all-steel body. In 1976 the front end was distinctively restyled around square headlamps and a sloping bonnet. The Jimini's body switched in 1983 to a glassfibre monocoque, whereupon it was known as the Jimini 2 (and also briefly as the Highlander). There were some gaps in production, but the Jimini was determinedly revived in the early 1990s.

CR

JINGGANGSHAN (CHI) 1958–1960
Beijing Auto Works, Beijing Municipality.
On the morning of 20 June 1958, the first trial run of the Jinggangshan took place. In the evening the car was inspected by Chairman Mao Zedong. The motor car and tractor department of the Qinghua University assisted in the design of this rear-engined vehicle. Its name was based on the Revolutionary base in Jiangxi Province, where Mao Zedong and the Red Army retreated to in 1927. The white-painted 2-door prototype bore the registration 1*05895. After 40 years this first model still exists. Small production of a 4-door version took place in the Beijing factory. A decision was made to produce 10,000 units of these cars each year for use as taxis in the larger Chinese cities, but, as the economic situation worsened, only a few were made. In 1968 the car disappeared from the Beijing streets. A number of defects and lack of raw material were the main reasons. Technically, the Jinggangshan was based on the monocoque Volkswagen Beetle.

EVIS

1920 J.L. (i) Light Ten sports car.
NICK BALDWIN

1935 J.M.B. 3-wheeler.
M.J.WORTHINGTON-WILLIAMS

JINGUI (CHI) 1995
Hainan Industry New Technology Research Institute, Haikou City,
Hainan Province.
The egg shaped 4-wheel 'scootmobile' Xiao Jingui MC 2 ('Small Tortoise') was
99.5in (2528mm) long and powered by a 570cc engine. Though shown at several
national exhibitions, there was no serial production.
EVIS

JINLEI (CHI) late 1990s
Golden Thunder Classic Motors Company, Beijing.
A Chinese company signed a deal with an American replica maker based in
Wisconsin to produce an Austin-Healey 3000 copy with the name Jinlei Golden
Thunder 5000. This had a Ford V8 engine (either a 4.9-litre unit with 245bhp or
a 5.7-litre one with 260bhp).
CR

JINMA (CHI) 1996 to date
Jinma Auto Refit Works, Qingdao City, Shandong Province.
Like the JIANHUA, the Jinma (Golden Horse) QJM 5020 series were 'classical
cars', imitations of the 1930s, known in China as 'grandfathers' vehicles'. Many
versions were known, long wheelbase and short wheelbase, open and closed. These
cars were favourites as background cars on wedding pictures.
EVIS

JIOTTO (J) 1989–1992
Dome Co. Ltd, Kyoto.
Curiously the major funder for this Japanese supercar project was an underwear
manufacturer called Wacoal. The Group C-style Jiotto Caspita made its debut at
the 1989 Tokyo Motor Show and was engineered by the DOME racing car
constructor. Initial plans called for a modified 3.5-litre flat-12 450bhp Formula 1
racing engine developed jointly by Motori Moderni of Italy and Subaru of
Japan. However by 1991 the company intended to use a Nissan Infiniti 32-valve
V8 engine and in 1992 that had changed again to a Judd 3.5-litre V10 engine.
The Caspita was to use a 6-speed transmission, active suspension and, possibly,
4-wheel drive, and a top speed of over 200mph (320km/h) was claimed. It was
intended to be built in Italy at an extremely high price ($650,000), but production
never began.
CR

JIUZHOU (CHI) 1992–1993
Shuyang Bus Works, Shuyang City, Jiangsu Province.
This small bus factory produced Suzuki-based minivans and pick-ups. A very
ugly square-off home-designed mini saloon (4-doors, 4-seater), named Jiuzhou
SYC 1014 was also made. The 797cc Jiangling engine was the power unit.
EVIS

J.L. (i) (GB) 1920
A.E.Creese, East Dulwich, London.
The J.L. Light Ten was a sports car powered by a 1½-litre 4-cylinder Decolange
engine, with a pointed-tail 2-seater body made of plywood.
NG

J.L. (ii) (F) 1980–c.1982
Éts J. Lelièvre, Foix.
With lines vaguely inspired by the MG TF, Jean Lelièvre's fibreglass-bodied J.L.
roadster languished on a VW Beetle platform. Kits were offered from 45,000
francs.
CR

J.M. (CH) 1913
Jaquemot et Marlier, Geneva.
This small company was the first to produce a popular voiturette in Geneva. It
had a MOSER proprietary twin-cylinder engine of 5bhp, a 2-speed gearbox and
a very pleasant 2-seater body. It weighed less than 350kg and was offered complete
with windshield and hood for just SFr3000. Nevertheless, only a handful of J.M.
cars were made before production ceased.
FH

J.M.B. (GB) 1933–1935
J.M.B. Motors Ltd, Ringwood, Hampshire.
A small Hampshire market town was an unusual location for a car factory, and
the J.M.B. was an unusual car in that it was a late example of a 3-wheeled
cyclecar, somewhat resembling a B.S.A. in appearance. It was less powerful as it
used a 497cc single-cylinder J.A.P. engine, mounted behind the seat and driving
the single rear wheel by chain. This was available in side-valve form in the
Gazelle standard model (£75.50), and with ohv in the Mustang sports model
(£91.35), which also boasted a close-ratio gearbox, clock, speedometer and
other luxuries. The frame was of ash, and on the 1933/34 models the bodies
were in fabric, but for 1935 steel panelling was used. The J.M.B. was designed,
so the catalogue said, for 'Jack and Jill, The New Motorist, The Sidecarist, The
Motor Cyclist, The Sports Girl, The Lady Motorist, and the Commercial
Representative', yet fewer than 100 were sold. A prototype 4-wheeler of 1935
with 350cc Villiers 2-stroke engine never went into production. The initials
stood for the makers, G.H. Jones, R.W. Mason and C.S. Barrow.
NG
Further Reading
'Fragments on Forgotten Makes – the J.M.B', W. Boddy,
Motor Sport, January 1964.

JM CARS (US) c.1985
JM Cars, Pompano Beach, Florida.
The JM Elegant Opera Coupé was a customised 1976–1979 Cadillac Seville.
The cockpit area was shortened to only two seats and the bonnet lengthened
to make up the room. Spare tyres were mounted in housings on both sides, and
a vertical grill with a bonnet bulge was added. They were sold in kit and completed
form.
HP

JOEL (GB) 1899–c.1902

National Motor Carriage Syndicate Ltd, London.

Joel electric cars used two motors of 2hp each, driving by chains to each rear wheel. Closed and open models were made; among the latter was the Brighton 2-seater, so called because it made the journey from London to Brighton (57 miles) on a single charge. The name came from the designer, Henry M Joel.

NG

JOHNEX (CDN) 1990s

Johnex Cobras, Brampton, Ontario.

This company made A.C. Cobra replicas with a full roll cage and what was described as a 'race-designed chassis'. The fibreglass bodywork could be bought as part of a kit or ready-mounted in turn-key form.

CR

JOHN O'GAUNT (GB) 1902–1904

William Atkinson & Sons, Lancaster.

Named after the celebrated fourteenth century Duke of Lancaster, this was a light car with 4 or 6hp single-cylinder engines and 2- or 4-seater bodies. Production did not exceed 12 cars.

NG

JOHNSON (i) (US) 1905–1912

Johnson Service Co., Milwaukee, Wisconsin.

Warren S. Johnson was a professor of natural science who invented the electric thermostat in the 1880s. He formed a company to make this and other items such as gigantic tower clocks, church chandeliers, beer carbonators and push-button toilets. They built a 1-ton steam truck in 1901, and four years later made their first car, also a steamer, a limousine powered by a 30hp 4-cylinder engine. Its amenities included an arrangement by which the passengers could cook their meals on the boiler.

Twenty steamers were made up to the end of 1907, ten open tourers and ten limousines, and in 1908 Johnson turned to petrol cars made in three sizes, 25, 35 and 50hp. These were made in small numbers up to 1912, many being to special order. Bodies were built in-house and were renowned for their fine interiors. Commercial vehicles of all kinds were also made, including mail vans, hearses and tower wagons. These accounted for two thirds of the 15 vehicles per month delivered by Johnson. Warren Johnson died in 1911, and this brought vehicle production to an end the following year. The company then concentrated on automatic temperature control systems, in which field, as Johnson Controls, it is still active today.

NG

JOHNSON (ii) (US) c.1985

R. M. Johnson Co., Annandale, Minnesota.

This company made a replica of the 1932 Packard roadster powered by a V8 engine.

HP

JOHNSONMOBILE (US) 1959

Horton Johnson, Inc., Highland Park, Illinois.

The Johnsonmobile was a plywood-bodied replica of an early 1900s horseless carriage. It was powered by a 3hp Clinton engine.

HP

JOHNSON MOTOR CARS (US) c.1982

Johnson Motor Cars Ltd, Fort Lauderdale, Florida.

The Rumbleseat Roadster was a neoclassic speciality car based on Cadillac running gear. It had a long bonnet and running boards in the CLENET manner, with MG Midget doors and windscreen.

HP

JOLLY (I) 1984

This was a short-lived and very small 3-wheel saloon of mediocre styling success, powered by a small diesel engine.

CR

1900 Joel electric car.
NATIONAL MOTOR MUSEUM

1911 Johnson (i) Silent Four limousine.
KEITH MARVIN

JOMAR (US) 1954–1959

Saidel Sports-Racing Cars, Manchester, New Hampshire.

Although Jomar was perhaps best known for their small-displacement sports-racing cars, they also had a strong influence on the success of English car builder TVR. After a pair of Dellow-based racing cars proved unsuccessful, Jomar owner Ray Saidel turned to the TVR chassis as the basis for his specials. The first was completed in 1956 using a Coventry-Climax engine and an aluminium body built by Jomar. Jomar did much of the development that lead to the first TVR fibreglass-bodied street coupés, which were sold as Jomars in the US. In addition to the fastback coupés, there were notchback coupés and a roadster as well. Jomar terminated their contract with TVR in 1959.

HP

Further Reading

'Jomar, The British Sports Car from New Hampshire', Jonathan A. Stein, *Automobile Quarterly*, Vol. 35, No. 2.

JONES (US) 1914–1920

Jones Motor Car Co., Wichita, Kansas.

John J. Jones began his automotive career by selling Model T Fords, and in 1914 he launched a car of his own. The Jones Six was a very conventional assembled tourer powered by a Continental Red Seal engine. It was the only model until 1917, when a roadster and a sedan were added to the range. Jones cars sold quite well, output peaking at 1025 cars in 1918. In 1919 he brought out the Oil Field Special, a combined roadster and pick-up truck with a rack for drilling bits on the rear deck. The company seemed to have a bright future until a fire in February 1920 destroyed nearly half the factory, 14 complete cars and 50 bodies. They went into receivership in August that year. Nearly 4000 Jones cars had been made.

NG

1925 Jordan Line Eight sedan.
NATIONAL MOTOR MUSEUM

JONES-CORBIN (US) 1903–1907

1903 Jones-Corbin Co., Philadelphia, Pennsylvania.

1903–1907 Jones-Corbin Automobile Co., Philadelphia. Pennsylvania.

George Jones and E.O. Corbin Jr built a car closely based on European designs, with an 8hp single-cylinder 'genuine De Dion-Bouton' engine and a Mercedes-type radiator. It was a 2-seater runabout priced at $1000. Before the year was out the company was reorganised, and for 1904 a 24hp 2-cylinder car, also with De Dion-Bouton engine, was announced. Neither sold very well, and in 1906 they went drastically upmarket with a 45hp 4-cylinder car costing $4500 for a tourer and $5000 for a limousine. Late in 1907 they sold out to the Matthews Motor Co. of Camden, New Jersey, who launched a 40hp car called the SOVEREIGN. This may have been the Jones-Corbin renamed.

NG

JONSSON (S) 1921

Alfred Jonssons Motorfabrik, Lidköping.

This marine engine company made two attempts at car manufacture. A prototype with 2-cylinder paraffin engine was made in 1902, and in 1921 they announced production of a tourer powered by a 2212cc 4-cylinder side-valve engine, a 3-speed gearbox and an aluminium body. The engine and all components apart from the Bosch magneto were made in the Jonsson factory. At least ten cars were ordered but only one was built. This still exists today.

NG

JONZ (US) 1909–1912

1909–1910 Jonz Automobile Co., Beatrice, Nebraska.

1910–1912 American Automobile Manufacturing Co., New Albany, Indiana.

The Jonz company was set up by Chester Charles Jones and his brother Ellsworth, and they claimed to have a car ready for the 1909 Chicago Automobile Show. It had a 30/35hp 3-cylinder engine which, like that of the Ingram-Hatch, lacked many components thought necessary for most engines, such as valves, cams, gears, rocker arms, pumps, radiator and water. It could have been an air-cooled 2-stroke, and was said to be 'vapour-cooled'. The brothers were unable to find the necessary finance in Beatrice, and formed a new company in New Albany, Indiana. They issued one of the most lavish prospectuses ever seen in the industry. A range of 2-, 3- and 4-cylinder cars was listed, with engines of 20, 30 and 40hp, and a variety of body styles including a taxicab and a delivery truck. An impressive factory was pictured (a drawing not a photograph) and a lot of stock was sold, but how many cars were made is unknown. It was said that Continental engines were brought in to replace the unsatisfactory Jonz engine.

NG

Further Reading

'Fact or Fiction? Jonz Motor Cars', Frank T. Snyder Jr,
Antique Automobile, November–December 1970.

JORDAN (US) 1916–1931

Jordan Motor Car Co., Inc., Cleveland, Ohio.

The Jordan was remarkable not for its construction but for its advertising. A well-built assembled car of moderate price, it was the beneficiary of some of the most imaginative advertisement copy of its time.

Edward S. Ned Jordan (1882–1958) was a born salesman with a gift for words. Working his way through university as a newspaper reporter, he became a salesman for National Cash Register Co. before joining the auto industry at the Thomas B. JEFFERY Co. in Kenosha, Wisconsin. Jordan founded the Jordan Motor Car Co. in January 1916, before he had an actual car or a place to build it. He did, however, have words to woo investors: 'Comfort and convenience, power in reserve, durable service, quality in construction', all would be virtues of his product.

The Jordan 60, designed by chief engineer Russell Begg and some assistants, emerged from a factory in Cleveland that July. Available as a roadster or two sizes of touring car, the new Jordan sold for $1650, $1750 for the tourer with wire wheels. Power came from a 4918cc Continental side-valve six, set in a chassis of 'finest universally approved mechanical units' from a myriad of manufacturers – all on a 127in (3223mm) wheelbase. Its price was at the high end of the range covered by BUICK and OLDSMOBILE. Jordan called on imagery and flattery in naming his colour choices: 'Venetian green', 'Liberty blue', 'Briarcliff green', or 'Mercedes red'. Sales were good for a newcomer to the industry, and a line of closed cars, limousine, town car, brougham and sedan, was introduced in 1917. From then the model names gained imagery too, the stylish Model C Sport Marine tourer appearing late in 1918 and wearing all-aluminium bodywork. In April 1919 came the Silhouette touring cars and the Playboy roadster, a name that would become almost synonymous with Jordan for all time. The Playboy was a fairly ordinary roadster, initially on a chassis common to other Jordans, called Model F. Later that year came the smaller, lighter (120in (3046mm) wheelbase) chassis for the Playboy and Silhouette, designated Model M, for which a smaller, 3639cc six was sufficient. But it was around the Playboy that the most lyrical lines were woven: 'It is the unexpected car in America today – chic, long, low, racy – and smartly continental' wrote Jordan, who also embellished the bliss of newlyweds with 'a Jordan Playboy, the blue sky overhead, the green turf flying by and a thousand miles of open road'. The classic of Jordan advertising is the Playboy piece of 1923 which begins 'Somewhere west of Laramie', inspired by Ned Jordan's fascination with a young woman on horseback. Writing of the girl he had seen from a train in Wyoming, Jordan told the nation's readers his car was 'built for the lass whose face is brown with the sun when the day is done of revel and romp and race. She loves the cross of the wild and the tame. The Playboy was built for her'.

An 8-cylinder Jordan debuted in 1925, the Line Eight with a Jordan-designed, Continental-built side-valve unit of 4403cc capacity. All Jordans now had Lockheed 4-wheel hydraulic brakes. Production peaked at over 11,000 cars in 1926, by which time the sixes had been dropped and a smaller eight, still called Line Eight, became the entry-level car. The old eight was continued with a new name, Great Line Eight. A new Little Custom car came in mid–1927, a short, 107in (2746mm) wheelbase car with a 3262cc Continental six. Bodies offered included the Blueboy tourer, Sport Salon sedan with leather upholstery, and a Tomboy roadster. A 116in (2444mm) wheelbase Air Line Eight was its companion, its light weight and increased power yielding excellent performance. The Little Custom, however, sold poorly, and Jordan's fortunes took a bad turn. A less expensive Cross Country Six for 1928 did not help, and Ned Jordan's poor health left something of a leadership vacuum at the company. Only 8-cylinder cars were built in 1929, the top of the line Ninety including a dual-cowl Speedboy phaeton, convertible, sport sedan, tourer, limousine and another Playboy roadster, all priced under $3000.

The final and most magnificent Jordans were the Model Z Speedway Ace roadster and Sportsman sedan of 1930–31. Sporting Coburn custom aluminium bodies on a 145in (3680mm) wheelbase, the Ace and Sportsman were sleek and powerful, courtesy of a 5213cc straight-8 of 125bhp. A 4-speed gearbox was usual for American prestige cars of the time; the Speedway models would do 100mph (160kph), but cost a hefty $5500. The rest of the Jordan line continued to be offered, but few of any model sold. Jordan Motor Car Co. entered receivership in May 1931, and full liquidation followed the next year.

KF

Further Reading

'Ned Jordan, the Cars He Built', Richard M. Langworth,
Automobile Quarterly, Vol. 13, No. 2.

'Ned Jordan, the Spell He Wove', Tim Howley,
Automobile Quarterly, Vol. 13, No. 2.

1929 Jordan Model 6RE sedan.
NATIONAL MOTOR MUSEUM

NIATIONAL MOTOR MUSEUM

JORDAN, NED (1882–1958)

It is not unfair to say that Ned Jordan will be remembered more for his advertising than for his cars, for while the latter were assembled products, they were enhanced by his lyrical prose, some of the finest ever written with the aim of selling automobiles.

Edward S. Jordan was born in the lumber town of Merrill, Wisconsin, the only boy in a family of five daughters. His mother was described as 'a spare, snappy little woman who couldn't get along with anybody'. Ambitious from the start, Ned worked his way through the University of Wisconsin as a newspaper reporter, then joined the National Cash Register Co., whose president, John Patterson, taught him some useful lessons, of which perhaps the most important was 'Remember; a man is only half sold until his wife is sold'.

In 1906 he became advertising manager for the Thomas Jeffery Co., maker of the Rambler car. He soon rose to become company secretary, remaining with Jeffery until 1916 when he organised the Jordan Motor Co.. For three years they made unremarkable cars, but in 1920 came the Playboy roadster, and to accompany it, the first of Ned Jordan's lyrical prose ads. An early example took its inspiration from the Bible: 'What shall it profit a car to gain complete mechanical excellence if it must sulk under a drab and sombre body?' It was followed by classics such as The Port of Missing Men ('Somewhere far beyond the place where men and motors race through the canyons of the town – there lies the Port of Missing Men. Go there in November when the logs are blazing in the grate. Go there in a Jordan Playboy if you love the spirit of youth, and spend an hour in Eldorado).

In 1922 came the most famous of all, 'Somewhere West of Laramie, there's a bronco-busting, steer-roping girl who knows what I'm talking about. She can tell what a sassy pony, that's a cross between greased lightning and the place where it hits, can do with eleven hundred pounds of steel and action when he's going high, wide and handsome. The truth is, the Playboy was built for her'.

Some have questioned whether Jordan himself wrote all the stirring ads, which graced the pages of the *Saturday Evening Post* between 1919 and about 1926. There is no evidence that he didn't, though from 1924 onwards the quality of copy was varied, as if he was farming out some of the writing. In the late 1920s things began to go wrong for Ned Jordan; an unwise attempt to make a quality smaller car, the Little Custom, failed to please the market; hundreds remained unsold, Jordan stock slumped, and his marriage collapsed. In the 1930s he worked in New York for advertising agencies Young & Rubicam and Campbell-Ewald, but his blunt speaking lost him both jobs. During World War II he worked for McArthur Aircraft Corp., makers of aluminium aircraft seats, and later wrote a regular column for *Automotive News*, 'Ned Jordan Speaks'. He was in demand as a speaker at dealer conventions until shortly before his death in December 1958.

Ned Jordan married Lotta Hanna, daughter of the owner of a furniture store in Kenosha. They had two daughters and a son. One of the daughters, Jane, was said to have been the inspiration for the girl in 'Somewhere West of Laramie', though he took the idea from a girl who rode alongside his train as it rumbled across the Wyoming plains. The marriage was dissolved in about 1929. He married again in about 1940 and had another daughter.

NG

Further Reading
'Ned Jordan; The Spell he Wove', Tim Howley,
Automobile Quarterly, Vol.13, No.2.

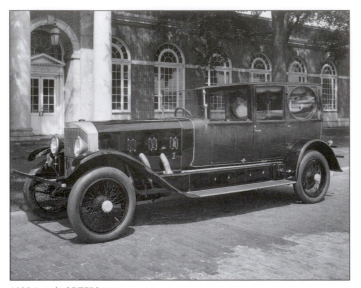

1922 Joswin 25/75PS town car.
NATIONAL MOTOR MUSEUM

JÖSSE *see* INDIGO

JOSWIN (D) 1920–1923

Josef Winsch, Joswin Motorenfabrik, Berlin-Halensee.
This car took its name from the abbreviations of the name of the founder, Josef Winsch. His cars used Mercedes engines of 6370ccc (25/75PS) and 7290cc (28/95PS). The radiator was a typical Germanic vee shape. They carried high-quality bodies by Szawe, resulting in an exclusive car which was inevitably very expensive. Production was limited, but one Joswin survives, in the Henry Ford Museum at Dearborn, Michigan.

HON

JOU (F) 1913–1924

Automobiles A. Jou, Suresnes, Seine.
The Jou was a light car powered by a 1540cc side-valve engine, with a 3-speed gearbox and shaft drive. It was introduced in 1913 and continued until 1924 with very little change, apart from electric lighting and starting from 1920 onwards, when the quoted maximum speed rose from 37 to 53mph (60 to 85km/h), though the engine size and design remained unchanged. In 1925 Automobiles Jou were said to be making spare parts only.

NG

JOUFFRET (F) 1920–1928

H. Demeester, Colombes, Seine.
Demeester had made voiturettes under his own name before World War I, and in 1920 he launched the Jouffret, a solid-looking tourer powered by a 1590cc side-valve Ballot engine. Later cars used 1200 or 1598cc C.I.M.E or 1170cc S.C.A.P. engines, in unit with 4-speed gearboxes. Suspension was conventional, with semi-elliptic springs all round, but the front ones tapered towards the forward ends. Perrot 4-wheel brakes were used on the later models.

NG

JOURDAIN (F) 1920

Automobiles Jourdain, Tours.
The Jourdain was a cyclecar with 2-cylinder engine. One was entered in the 1920 Coupes des Voiturettes, but did not feature in any race reports, and may not have reached the starting line.

NG

JOUSSET (F) 1923–1926

Louis Jousset, Bellac, Haute-Vienne.
The Jousset was a regional make, far from the traditional centres of car manufacture such as the Seine basin or Lyons, and was made in very small numbers. Ruby and C.I.M.E. engines were used, and Jousset entered cars at Le Mans in 1925 and 1926. The former carried a remarkable streamlined saloon body, while the latter was a tourer. Neither completed the course. Only about 12 Jousset cars were made, after which Louis Jousset turned to the manufacture and marketing of hair-restoring lotion, apparently with no more success than with his cars.

NG

JOUVE (F) 1913

Jouve et Cie, Paris.
The Jouve was a cyclecar powered by an air-cooled 8hp J.A.P. engine, with belt drive. The company also sold the CARDEN Monocar under the name Le Sylphe.

NG

JOVI (US) c.1994 to date

Jovi Ltd, Fort Lauderdale, Florida.
Ice Cars, Fort Lauderdale, Florida.
Jovi was the first to build a replica of the Mercedes 500SL convertible based on Chrysler LeBaron running gear. It was called the Autobahn Cruiser. They followed that with a second version based on Ford Mustang 5.0 donor cars. Both of these kits proved to be popular and a host of imitators sprang up. Jovi also sold a Lamborghini Diablo replica based on the Pontiac Fiero chassis. Called the Jovi VT, it required that the chassis be stretched to a 104in (2639mm) wheelbase and power choices included the Cadillac Northstar V8. All Jovi models were sold in kit and fully assembled form.

HP

JOWETT (GB) 1906–1954

1906–1919 Jowett Motor Manufacturing Co. Ltd, Bradford, Yorkshire.
1919–1954 Jowett Cars Ltd, Bradford, Yorkshire.
The Jowett had an unusual history in that it began as a strictly utilitarian small car, most of which were sold in the North of England, while its last models were sporting saloons more advanced than any British contemporaries, and which found buyers all over Europe.

The company was founded by the brothers Benjamin (1877–1963) and William (1880–1955) Jowett. Their father Wilfred had a blacksmiths and small engineering works, and the boys joined him as soon as they left school at the age of thirteen. Their first involvement with motor vehicles came in 1897 when they fitted one of their father's engines to a chassis built by the Yorkshire Motor Car Co. at Mytholm Mills. It was not a success, though a few cars were subsequently made under the name MYTHOLM, while the company secretary, R. Reynold Jackson, achieved some fame as the maker of JACKSON (i) cars in London. In 1901 the brothers set up the Jowett Motor Manufacturing Co. with a capital of £90, to make bicycles and V-twin engines of their own design, some of which were installed in cars as replacements for Aster or De Dion-Bouton units. In 1905 they turned to a horizontal flat-twin engine which became their stock in trade; all Jowett cars and light vans were powered by this design up to 1936, and it was still being used in the Bradford van in 1953.

The flat twin went into the first Jowett car, made in 1906. This was a light 2-seater, modern in its worm drive rear axle but old-fashioned in its steering which was by side tiller. Experiments occupied the next four years, during which time the brothers made a few engines for Alfred Angas Scott's motorcycles, and it was not until 1910 that the Jowett light car was put on the market. The worm drive was replaced by bevel, but the tiller steering was retained on the first 24 cars made in 1910–11. The 2-seater aluminium-panelled bodies were made by Ryder, but when the original flat radiator was replaced by a slightly curved one in 1912, the brothers turned to another Bradford coachbuilder, Humbouldt. A further batch of 36 cars was made from 1912 to 1916, wheel steering being adopted in 1914.

In October 1916 cars gave way to war work, in particular fuse components, and car production did not restart until April 1920, now in a much larger factory at Idle, on the northern outskirts of Bradford. They were to remain on this site until car making ended in 1954.

There was little change in the early postwar models, but later in 1921 engine capacity went up from 815 to 907cc, at which it remained until 1936. The Jowett engine earned an excellent reputation for reliability and delivery of power at low speeds. Company advertising, which was in the hands of Gladney Haigh from 1927 to 1938, stressed this with whimsical slogans such as 'The pull of an elephant with the appetite of a canary and the docility of a lamb' and 'With spurs, would climb trees'.

Coil ignition replaced the magneto in 1923, when the first 4-seater appeared on a 102in (2540mm) wheelbase. A 4-door saloon arrived on this chassis in 1926, when both open and closed bodies were offered on both wheelbases. Jowetts had become distinctly old-fashioned by the late 1920s, with their fixed cylinder heads and 2-wheel brakes. However, production rose encouragingly, from about 110 in 1920 to 2223 in 1925 and peaking at 3474 in 1927. Sales gradually spread southward as more people heard about this extraordinarily tough little car from Yorkshire. The first one-make club in the world was the Jowett Light Car & Social Club, formed in Bradford in May 1922. A Southern Jowett Car Club was founded in Mitcham, Surrey, in 1923, and other clubs followed around Britain.

After the collapse of Humbouldt in 1920 Jowett began to make more and more of the bodywork themselves, and indeed few components of any kind were bought in, apart from oil pumps, gearboxes, back axles, and tyres.

In 1928 a sports 2-seater was announced, with the engine set back in the frame, and a very light doorless aluminium body. Only 15 were sold, but a stripped version was driven at Brooklands for 12 hours at an average speed of 54.85mph (88.28km/h), creditable when compared with the touring Jowett's top speed of about 43mph (70km/h). A different kind of achievement was the crossing of Africa in April 1926 from Lagos to Massawa (3800 miles/6115kms) by two 2-seaters named 'Wait' and 'See', towing trailers.

No great changes were made to Jowetts in the early 1930s apart from fabric bodies on the saloons, and a stiffer and wider frame from 1931. Four-wheel brakes had finally arrived in 1929. A variety of body styles was offered in 1932, including 2-door fabric or coachbuilt saloons on the short wheelbase, and 2- and 4-seater tourers and both types of saloon on the long wheelbase. Names for body styles first appeared in 1930, the De Luxe saloons being called Black Prince, Grey Knight and Silverdale. By 1934 there was the Kestrel sports saloon, Simba tourer and Weasel sports tourer, the latter with twin carburettor engine. A 4-speed gearbox arrived on the 1934 models, though there was no synchromesh. The Jowett brothers said "Personally we experience a feeling of well-being in handling a gearbox with skill, that we do not experience when an automatic change is fitted". By automatic they meant synchromesh which did eventually arrive on the 1940 models.

The Jowett was almost unique among 4-wheeled British cars in having only two cylinders. Two prototypes, called La Roche, with a 1½-litre vertical four were built in 1934, but production never went ahead. In 1935 a 1146cc flat four with side-valves and an aluminium crankcase was introduced. A comparatively large 6-light saloon body was used, named Jupiter or Jason according to interior trim. The Jason was £8 more expensive, at £205. The styling, with sharply sloping radiator, proved unpopular, and after 299 had been made, Jowett hastily replaced them with the Plover, which had a body similar to that of the 2-cylinder saloons.

From 1937 to 1940 both 2- and 4-cylinder Jowetts shared the same saloon body, and the open cars were dropped. The flat-twin engine was enlarged to 946cc for 1937. The twins averaged £30 less than the fours, and sold 2088 units between 1937 and 1940, while 1582 fours found buyers. Jowett Cars Ltd went public in 1935, and the brothers soon withdrew from the firm. William became managing director of Bristol Tractors Ltd, makers of small crawler tractors which used the Jowett flat-twin engine. Benjamin retired and concentrated on gardening and golf. Jowett sales and profits declined in the late 1930s, and only 1661 vehicles, including vans, were delivered in 1939.

Javelin and Jupiter

As with most manufacturers, the war gave a great boost to Jowett; the workforce rose from about 600 to more than 2000 who worked as many as three shifts making a variety of weapons including field guns, bullets, shells and capstan lathes. Alongside this, work began on a postwar car which was to take the company in a completely new direction. The Javelin was designed by Gerald Palmer, who had been brought in from MG to finalise the design of the Bradford utility before starting work on the all-new Javelin. The Bradford was essentially an update of the prewar 8hp van, though its bodies (estate car, van and truck) came from Briggs who also supplied Javelin bodies.

The Javelin was totally new, though its horizontally-opposed engine was in the long-standing Jowett tradition. It was a flat-4 1486cc unit with ohvs and vertically-split aluminium crankcase. Other features of this advanced car included rack-and-pinion steering, torsion bar suspension all round and an integral construction streamlined saloon body with a sloping back reminiscent of the

1915 Jowett 8hp 2-seater.
NATIONAL MOTOR MUSEUM

1922 Jowett 8hp 2-seater.
NATIONAL MOTOR MUSEUM

1938 Jowett 10/4 saloon.
NICK GEORGANO/NATIONAL MOTOR MUSEUM

1951 Jowett Javelin saloon.
NATIONAL MOTOR MUSEUM

1952 Jowett Jupiter sports car.
NATIONAL MOTOR MUSEUM

prewar Lincoln Zephyr. The Javelin was a complete change of direction for Jowett, from the slowest family car on the market to the fastest in its class, with well above average roadholding as well. A pre-production model reached 76mph (123km/h) when tested by *The Motor*, and later Javelins easily exceeded 80mph (128km/h). This compared very favourably with the 70mph (112km/h) of the Morris Oxford which had the same capacity engine. Because the factory at Idle was not equipped for making the unitary construction bodies these were contracted out to the Doncaster factory of Briggs Motor Bodies.

The Javelin was slow to get into production, and although the first examples were shown to the public in July 1946, they were still a rare sight on Britain's roads two years later. However they were popular in export markets, and the name Jowett suddenly became familiar in Portugal, Switzerland, the Scandinavian

countries and as far afield as New Zealand. It is worth remembering that Jowett were not complete strangers to exporting cars. Examples of the original 2-seater were sold to Greece, New Zealand, India and Burma in 1911.

Publicity and advertising in the early postwar years were in the hands of John Baldwin (father of Nick Baldwin who provided many of the photos for this Encyclopaedia), who managed Jowett's first London showroom, opened in Albemarle Street in 1946. Javelins did well in rallying for several years, winning their class in the 1949 Monte Carlo, and finishing 1st, 2nd and 4th in 1951. In 1953 the Graaf van Zuylen won the Tulip Rally outright. Javelins also went racing, winning the 2-litre Touring Car class in the 1949 Belgian 24 Hour Race.

Having established themselves in motor sport, Jowett decided to enter the sports car field. They engaged the ex-Auto Union engineer, Eberan von Eberhorst, who designed a tubular space-frame chassis which was to be made by the racing car firm E.R.A., and to be sold under the name E.R.A.-Javelin. However the London-built stubby coupé body was not liked when it was displayed at Albemarle Street, and the E.R.A. connection was dropped after they had supplied five chassis. A completely new body was designed in-house by Jowett's chief bodywork designer Reg Korner, to be made by Jowett themselves. Called the Jupiter, it was an open roadster which seated three abreast, thanks to the steering column gearchange. This and the opulent curves of the body were aimed at the American market. The Jupiter was raced with some success, winning its class at Le Mans in 1950, 1951 and 1952, finishing 1st and 2nd in the 1951 Tourist Trophy and winning outright the 1951 Bremgarten Sports Car Race in Switzerland. However it did not sell well, only 899 in four years, compared with around 23,000 Javelins.

Javelin sales were falling by the end of 1952, partly caused by problems with the Jowett-built gearbox which replaced a Meadows box in 1951. In December there were more than 1000 in stock and the Jowett factory could not keep up with the supply of bodies from Briggs, which were piling up all around Bradford, even on the town's football ground. They asked the bodybuilders to suspend deliveries for a few months, and only 600 were delivered thereafter. It has been said that the end of the association between Briggs and Jowett was due to pressure from Ford, but they did not acquire Briggs until February 1953, before which it was clear to Briggs that they could not profitably continue as Jowett's suppliers. Indeed about half their labour force was made redundant in

December 1952 as a result of Jowett's request for delayed delivery. Javelin output ended in September 1953. The Jupiter was continued into 1954, the last one leaving the factory in November. There were plans for a new Jupiter, the fibreglass-bodied R4, but only three were made. Jowett also hoped to save the day with new models of the Bradford. This had done much to keep Jowett afloat during the Javelin's development period, and 40,000 had been made by Spring 1953. New models, using the same 1005cc flat-twin engine with up-to-date bodies to be made by Briggs were built in prototype form, a 4-door saloon, van and pick-up, but this CD Bradford never went into production.

The Idle factory was acquired by International Harvester for tractor manufacture, and was demolished in 1983. Four years later a large supermarket opened on the site.

NG

Further Reading
The Complete Jowett History, Paul Clark and Edmund Nankivell, Foulis/Haynes, 1991.

JOYMOBILE (B) 1953–1954
Washmobile Holland Co., Amsterdam.
First displayed at the 1953 Paris Salon, this ambitious project was for a 4-door 6-seater car, featuring a wrap-around rear screen and turbine-style air intake. The Joymobile Turbomatic used a 45bhp 1.8-litre Delettrez diesel 4-cylinder engine and a liquid-operated turbine to transmit the power to the rear wheels (the liquid being stored in tanks in the tubular frame). Production did not begin.
CR

J.P. (i) (F) 1905
J. Prunello et Cie, Puteaux, Seine.
Named after J. Prunello who marketed the car, the J.P. was made in the PRUNEL factory where BOYER, GNOME and GRACILE cars as well as Prunels were built. It was listed in three models, a 10/12hp 2-cylinder, a 16/20hp four and a 24/30hp four. The largest model had chain drive. Gnome engines were used, and it is difficult to sort out how close the J.P. was to the Gnome and the Gracile; possibly it was a case of badge engineering for different dealers. They were sold in London by the J.P. Motor Co., of Mortimer Market, London.
NG

J.P. (ii) (F) c.1934
Automobiles J.P.
After the failure of the G.A.R., J. Pipault acquired some components including three or four of the 1375cc straight-8 engines, and assembled them for sale under the name J.P. They had low bodies by Bellon Frères.
NG

J.P.B. (P) 1985–c.1992
Presented by Armando da Costa, this was a Citroën 2CV-based open car inspired by the British LOMAX, but boasting a Bugatti-style horseshoe grill. Cars were sold both complete and in kit form but by 1991 the company was making bodies only to special order.
CR

JPL *see* LA VIGNE

JPR (GB) 1984–1996
JPR Cars, Goodwood, Chichester, Sussex.
JPR, named after its founder, John Randall, built the 'Wildcat', a kit car evocation of the Jaguar E-type. It had a tubular backbone chassis, based on a TVR frame, and although the moulds for the fibreglass body were taken from an early E-type, it was widened by 8in (203mm). It was designed to be built using Ford Cortina suspension and the Cortina's rear axle dictated the width. Most owners fitted Ford V6 engines.

Later, a version using Sierra irs was offered, as was a coupé body which recalled the one-off aerodynamic coupé (reg. CUT 7) which Jaguar built for racing.

Wildcats were built in the Super Shell building at the Goodwood circuit and were well-made, engineered, and finished. Though few more than 100 were made, their owners paid the car the accolade of forming an enthusiastic Owners' Club.
MJL

J.P. WIMILLE *see* WIMILLE

JRP CARS (US) 1998 to date
JPR Cars Ltd, Topping, Virginia.
This company purchased GATSBY COACHWORKS and moved it to Virginia.
HP

J. & S. (AUS) 1957–1985
J. & S. Fibreglass Pty Ltd, Haberfield, New South Wales.
John Jennens' and Jeff Simmonds' first body was a one-off on a Ford V8 but commercial activity began with a sports body, the Reno Spyder, designed by Len Moir, for fitting to a Renault 750 or Dauphine base; 20 were sold. The Hunter coupé, also a Moir design, was built on a specially built chassis to accept Holden mechanicals and held out the promise of being profitable but it was badly impacted by the 1961 'credit squeeze' and only about 20 were produced. The BUCHANAN after-market body had been taken over in 1959; a variety of hard-tops and the BUCHANAN Cobra body later kept automotive interest alive during a time when boats and industrial work were a priority.

When VW-based beach, dune and street buggies became popular in the 1960s, Jeff Simmonds was a major supplier. A later design, with a sports car emphasis, the Trail Buggy, was introduced, but tight regulations governing shortened floorpans caused so many problems that J. & S. leased the moulds to APOLLO. The final effort, of 1985, was a revised Trail Buggy for the normal wheelbase but the buggy market had diminished and so ended a long involvement with fibreglass bodywork.
MG

J.S.A. (AUS) 1980–1982
James Smith Automotive, Melbourne, Victoria.
Representing Lotus in Victoria, this firm had imported the Lotus 7 made by Steel Bros in New Zealand. As it was a track rather than road vehicle, Jim Smith took the view that a clubman car could be developed with more comforts and without detracting from its sporting ability. His 95 had such amenities and also met the design rules with approved door locks and side anti-intrusion bars. Built on a backbone frame, it used a 1600cc Ford Escort engine and transmission and, with a fibreglass body, weighed 550kg.
MG

JUHO (D) 1922
Julius Höflich AG, Nuremberg.
This was a simple cyclecar powered by a 2/4PS single-cylinder proprietary engine. Very few were made.
HON

JULES (CDN) 1911
Jules Motor Car Co. Ltd, Guelph, Ontario.
This was a low-slung 5-seater tourer powered by a 3705cc 30hp 4-cylinder engine. Its most unusual feature was a horn button in the centre of the brake pedal. It was developed for C.M. Preston of Toronto who sold the project to the Jules Motor Co. Only two cars were made, plus one roadster body.
NG

JULIAN (US) 1925
Julian Brown Development Co., Syracuse, New York.
Julian Brown was a wealthy Syracuse resident who was interested in automotive design, and who had formed a short-lived automobile engine company. In 1918, he unsuccessfully attempted to market a car of his own unconventional design. A man of independent means, Brown experimented with several automotive designs over several years and in 1925 had a luxurious closed coupé built to his own design which was replete with numerous mechanical ideas, this Julian car being in variance with otherwise accepted automotive design.

His Julian coupé featured a radial 6-cylinder air-cooled engine which developed 60bhp at 2500rpm. The 5-seater coupé body was built by Fleetwood and featured the driver's seat in the centre of the car, flanked by two front seats, one at either side, plus two more seats in the rear. The wheelbase was 125in (3172mm) and disc wheels were fitted with sidemounts mounted flush with the rear wheels on the running boards. The coupé weighed 3450lb and carried a projected price of $2500.

1925 Julian coupé.
NICK BALDWIN

Despite its coverage in the automotive journals of the day, plus other promotion, the Julian failed in its designer's attempts to get it into production. The car survives, an apt reminder of the Julian's failure to reach the marketplace, a good deal of which was presumably due to its unconventional design.

KM

JULIEN (i) (F) 1925–1926

G. Julien, Blois, Loire-et-Cher.

This was a tiny single-seater cyclecar powered by a 174cc single-cylinder engine, with 2-speed gearbox.

NG

JULIEN (ii) (F) 1946–1950

Société des Études Automobiles M.A. Julien, Paris.

Maurice Julien was one of the creators of the Citroën Traction Avant, and during the war he built two small car prototypes. At the 1946 Salon de Paris, his 2-seater open car was presented, with a rear-mounted air-cooled 310cc engine. With some modifications the definite MM5 production version appeared in 1947 with a 325cc single-cylinder engine driving the rear wheels by a single chain. The entire rear body lifted up for access to the mechanicals. A monobox estate body was displayed at the 1948 Paris Salon. The following year a new 2-seater open model with a larger 368cc engine was shown, called the MM7. Unfortunately it was more or less a direct copy of the rival Rovin D3 and a production run did not ensue.

CR

JUNIOR (i); F.J.T.A. (I) 1905–1910

1904–1905 Giovanni Ceirano Junior, Turin.
1905–1910 Fabbrica Junior Torinese d'Automobili, Turin.

This was one of the makes organised by Giovanni Ceirano who had previously been with S.T.A.R. He called the cars Junior to distinguish them and himself from his elder brother, also Giovanni, or Giovanni Battista (John the Baptist) who had made Ceirano cars a few years earlier. The company was founded in 1904, but changed to F.J.T.A. before any cars were built. They were made in three models, a 9½hp single-cylinder voiturette, a 12/14hp twin and a 16/20hp four. The latter was on Mercedes lines, with pair-cast cylinders, side-valves in a T-head and chain drive. Ceirano did not stay long with the company, leaving in 1906 to start another Turin business, S.C.A.T.

NG

JUNIOR (ii) (E) 1955–1956

Junior SL, Barcelona.

This was a 3-wheeler with single rear wheel and a 197cc Hispano-Villiers engine.

VCM

JUNIOR SPORTS (GB) 1920–1921

Aluminium & General Foundry Co., London.

This was a 2- or 3-seater sports car powered by a Peters 4-cylinder engine, with Moss gearbox and shaft drive. The axles were from the Model T Ford.

NG

JURASSIC TRUCK (US) 1998 to date

Jurassic Truck Corp., Arlington, Texas.

The AMG Humvee military vehicle was made famous in the US during the highly televised Gulf War with Iraq. AMG capitalised on this by going into production with the civilian Hummer, which was both slow and expensive. Jurassic Truck was one of several companies that produced similar vehicles in kit form. The Jurassic T-Rex was based on a Chevrolet Suburban 4-wheel drive chassis, and could be finished out for much less than a Hummer. It was also more practical and much faster. All body panels were steel and it was simple to assemble.

HP

JUSSY (F) 1898–1900

SA des Automobiles Jussy, St Étienne, Loire.

Jussy was one of the first car makers in St Étienne, building a small number of light cars with single-cylinder engines and hot-tube ignition. Production ended in 1900, and in 1906 the company became the SA des Ateliers du Furan, makers of the S.A.F. 3-wheeler.

NG

JUSTICIALISTA (RA) 1953–1955

IAME (Industrias Aeronauticas y Mecanicas del Estado), Cordoba.

IAME was created in 1952 during General Juan Domingo Peron's strongly nationalist presidency. One of Peron's and IAME's objectives was to produce genuinely Argentine sports and touring automobiles. The Justicialista was named after Peron's political party. There were saloon, pick-up and station wagon versions, powered by 2-stroke engines. The saloon's design was based on the 1951 Chevrolet, and had a 4-cylinder 800cc 2-stroke engine.

1954 Justicialista Sport.
NATIONAL MOTOR MUSEUM

The Justicialista sports car was powered by a front-mounted Porsche 1500cc engine. The hard-top coupé body was moulded in fibreglass. Only a few open prototypes were made. A couple of these were fitted with V8 engines. About 250 Justicialista sports cars were made and were amply publicized. President Peron was photographed driving around in an open Justicialista and Juan Manuel Fangio demonstrated the car in the Autodrome of Buenos Aires, where a race exclusively for Justicialistas was held.

In 1955 a military coup toppled the Peron government and the sports car production line, along with 50 unfinished vehicles, was sold to TERAM, who continued production under the Puntero name. However, this was a highly modified version of the Justicialista. About 100 Teram sports cars were made. Of the 2-stroke engined vehicles, only the saloon survived, under the GRACIELA name. The new regime did not want to hear anything about the Justicialista name.

ACT

JUWEL (B) 1922–1928

1922–1927 Sté des Automobiles Juwel, Herstal; Waremme.
1927–1928 Usines Juwel, Construction des Automobiles SA, Herstal.
Introduced at the Brussels Salon in December 1922, the Juwel was a light car powered by a 1131cc 4-cylinder side-valve engine, and offered in two models, the 6/8CV voiturette and the 8/10CV voiture, though the same engine was used in both. They had vee-radiators and a variety of bodies was offered, open 2- and 4-seaters, 3-seater sports, 2-door saloon and delivery van. An initial run of 800 cars was proposed, but financial problems intervened before anything like that number had been made.

At the 1924 Salon, with fresh capital, a new range was offered with the same size of engine but now with ohvs. The radiator was now flat and there were brakes on the front wheels and the transmission. Few of these were made, and in September 1927 a new company was formed. Their car appeared at the Salon in December 1928, a low-slung coupé called the TA-4, with the same 1131cc ohv engine, now driving the front wheels with a design closely based on Jean Grégoire's TRACTA. It was not made under the Juwel name, but by a new company set up in 1929, the Société Astra Motors SA operating in the Juwel factory. The car was made as the ASTRA, though this venture lasted only two years.

NG

1962 J.W.F. Milano GT coupé.
NICK BALDWIN

JVA (RA) 1998 to date

JVA Automoviles Especiales SA, Buenos Aires.
The JVA Spyder 550 Replica was a copy of the Porsche Spyder with fibreglass body and modern chassis and suspension. It was powered by an 1800cc Audi engine and had a claimed top speed of 120mph (193km/h).

ACT

J.W.F. (AUS) 1959–1969

J.W.F. Fibreglass Industries, Brookvale, New South Wales.
This firm grew out of a friendship of boyhood model makers, being founded by Ian Johnson, Jeff Williams and Grant Furzer. The first car body produced was the Milano 750 for the Austin 7 and it was modified to give eight variations of length and width for other chassis. Its final development was the Milano GT and a team of Holden-powered cars had a successful competition career during 1964–67. In 1960 the Italia was revealed to suit larger cars of 96in (2430mm) wheelbase. Mounted on a NOTA space frame and using HOLDEN mechanicals, it was offered as a complete car. In 1969 the monocoque GT2 was built for competition use.

MG

1995 J.Z.R. 3-wheeler.

J.Z.R. (GB) 1989–1998
John Ziemba Restorations, Darwen, Lancashire.
Morgan fanatic John Ziemba's J.Z.R. was a successful Morgan-style 3-wheeler sold principally in kit form. It was based on the Honda CX motorbike, from which the rear end was taken complete and mated to a square tube chassis with stressed steel inner panels; the engine sat exposed at the front. Fibreglass upper body panels were added, with a long cockpit option for taller drivers and a barrel back as an alternative to the standard rounded rump. Other engine options included Moto Guzzi (up to 95bhp), Honda Pan European V4 (105bhp) and 1340cc Harley Davidson. From the mid-1990s, licensed production took place in Spain under the name Bandido.

CR

K.A.C. (DK) 1914

A. Jacobsen, Københavns Automobil Central, Copenhagen.
The short-lived K.A.C. had a 6/16hp 4-cylinder engine of unknown make. Body styles included 2-seater roadsters and 4-seater tourers.

NG

KAHA (D) 1921–1922

Elektromobilwerke Kaha GmbH, Wasseralfingen.
One of a number of electric cyclecars made in Germany in the 1920s, the Kaha was very modest, with a single-seater body.

HON

KAIG (GB) 1998 to date

Kaig Motors, Mansfield Woodhouse, Nottinghamshire.
Kaig (pronounced 'cage') was a branch of ROBIN HOOD, formed to manufacture and market a rather different product to the company's Lotus 7- style roadsters. The Kaig was a very basic and very compact car based on Austin Metro components. It had a tubular steel chassis/roll-over cage fitted with mild steel body panels.

CR

KAINZ (A) 1900–1901

Josef Kainz, Vienna.
The Kainz was a voiturette powered by a 3¹⁄₂hp vertical single-cylinder engine mounted at the front under a bonnet. It had three speeds and drive by spur gear to the rear axle.

NG

KAISER (i) (D) 1911–1913

Justus Christian Braun-Premier Werke AG, Nuremberg.
The J.C. Braun company was better-known for commercial vehicles, especially fire engines, than for passenger cars, but they made some under the name Kaiser, a 6/18PS petrol car and electrics. In 1913 they made the PREMIER (iv) light car, also built in the company's Austrian factory at Eger (Bohemia) and sold under the Omega name.

HON

KAISER (ii) (D) 1935

Kaiser Fahrzeugbau, Oschersleben.
This was a highly streamlined single-seater 3-wheeler with the front wheels enclosed in aircraft-type spats, and the rear wheel driven by a motorcycle engine. Various models could be had, from 200 to 600cc, made by NSU and Columbus-Horex. With the most powerful, a top speed of 75mph (120km/h) was possible. However, the high price and the limited appeal of a single-seater car meant that very few Kaisers were sold.

HON

KAISER (iii) (US) 1946–1955

1946–1953 Kaiser-Frazer Corp., Willow Run, Michigan.
1955 Kaiser-Willys Sales Corp., Toledo, Ohio.
By the 1940s it was generally assumed that no newcomer could successfully challenge the established Detroit car makers for a significant slice of the popular car market. Then the Kaiser-Frazer Corp. appeared and, while they failed in the end, they had several successful years and made nearly three quarters of a million cars. Their success was due to the car-hungry postwar market, and also to the experience and drive of the two men behind the project.

Henry J. Kaiser (1882–1967) became famous for his shipbuilding work during World War II, while Joseph W. Frazer (1892–1971) had been vice-president of Chrysler and president of Willys Overland and Graham-Paige. They rented, and later bought, the Willow Run factory from Henry Ford, the world's largest bomber factory where Liberators had been made.

The cars were to be built in two series, both powered by a 100bhp 3706cc 6-cylinder Continental engine, the front-drive Kaiser and the more expensive rear-drive Frazer. The Kaiser was also to have integral construction and torsion bar suspension, but because of engineering problems the front-drive and other advanced features never got beyond the prototype stage, and when production began in June 1946 the two cars were generally similar, with rear drive through a hypoid axle, box-section frames and slab-sided 4-door sedan bodies designed

1935 Kaiser (ii) 3-wheeler.
M.J.WORTHINGTON-WILLIAMS

1946 Kaiser (iii) Special sedan (prototype, with front-wheel drive).
NATIONAL MOTOR MUSEUM

1948 Frazer (Kaiser (iii)) Manhattan sedan.
NICK GEORGANO

by Howard 'Dutch' Darrin and much revised by Robert Cadwallader. Their full-width coachwork with wing line running unbroken from front to rear was more modern than any rivals from GM or Ford, which still had prewar styling. Only Studebaker had all-new styling, and that was not as smooth as Kaiser-Frazer's. Kaiser prices ran from $1868 to $2301, while the better-equipped Frazer cost from $2053 to $2550. These figures put them well above the low-priced three, Chevrolet, Ford and Plymouth, and on a level with the Buick Roadmaster and Chrysler Saratoga, both of which had straight-8 engines. Thus the cars from Willow Run were over-priced from the start, although they sold well in their first few years, 144,490 in 1947 and 181,316 in 1948. These figures put them in eighth place in the US production league, above the other independents such as Studebaker, Nash and Hudson. In 1947 the K-F Corp. made a profit of nearly $20 million, but this only just compensated for a $19 million loss during the set-up year, 1946. Profits in 1948 were $10 million.

1951 Frazer (Kaiser (iii)) 4-door sedan, and Vagabond.
NICK GEORGANO

For 1949 all American car makers brought out genuine postwar models, so that the full-width styling of Kaiser and Frazer no longer seemed particularly advanced. They were mildly restyled, and the range included three significant new models. One was a hatchback sedan which gave the loading space of a station wagon without the expense of new body dies. Sold as the Kaiser Traveler or Vagabond, they had heavy-duty springs and shock absorbers to cope with the heavier loads, and the nearside rear door was welded shut. The other new styles were the Frazer Manhattan/Kaiser De Luxe 4-door convertibles, the first postwar American cars of this design, and the Kaiser Virginian 4-door hard-top. Unfortunately none of these pioneering designs sold very well, as the convertibles and hard-top were too expensive. The 1949 Frazer Manhattan convertible cost $3295, compared with $3442 for a Cadillac Series 62 convertible. They sold only 62 convertibles in the 1949/50 season, against 9690 Manhattan sedans, and 15,169 of the cheaper Standard sedans.

Total sales for the group in 1949 were 57,995, and they dropped to seventeenth place in the league; only Lincoln, Willys and Crosley sold fewer cars. New models were desperately needed, but Kaiser-Frazer did not have the money, and had to borrow $69 million from the Government-backed Reconstruction Finance Corp. Much of this went towards a new compact car, the HENRY J, which was announced in September 1950. There was also a new full-size Kaiser for 1951, and a slightly modified Frazer. The latter name was dropped at the end of 1951. Joe Frazer had stepped down from executive responsibility in 1949, although he retained the title of Board Vice Chairman

NATIONAL MOTOR MUSEUM

KAISER, HENRY J. (1882–1967)

Unlike many car makers, Henry J. Kaiser came to auto-making late in life; he was 64 before the first Kaiser car rolled out of the enormous Willow Run factory. He was born on 9 May 1882 in Springbrook, New York, of German immigrant parents, and left school at the age of 13. While working in a dry goods store he became interested in photography, became a travelling photographer and soon bought his own shop in Lake Placid, New York. Two more shops in Florida followed, but he tired of the work because, as he later said, 'I couldn't do what people wanted in portrait photography. They all wanted to look like actors or actresses, not like themselves'.

In 1906 he moved to the West Coast, took a job in a hardware store and then, in 1909, entered what was to become a lifelong career in the construction business. By 1914 he had his own pavement contracting business, and was soon building roads up and down the coast, moving from site to site, and sometimes living in his car, together with his family. He built the first paved roads in Vancouver, British Columbia. Although he made little money at first because of inflation fed by the war, by the early 1920s he was able to set up his own rock crushing plant, and also to make his own machinery. Some of these were innovations for the industry, including a 3-wheeled powered dumper, the ancestor of the site dumper so widespread today, tractor-pulled road scrapers and diesel engines for power shovels, cranes and tractors. In 1921 they built a road from Red Bluff to Redding, California, establishing a record for laying one mile every week, double the speed of other contractors. In 1927 the Kaiser Co. built 750 miles of road in Cuba, and from 1931 to 1936 they were one of nine companies involved in building the Hoover Dam on the Colorado River. Kaiser and his partner company, the W.A. Bechtel Corp. were now among the top construction firms in the country, and went on to be involved in such major projects as the Bonneville and Grand Coulee Dams, the San Francisco-Oakland Bridge, subways in Chicago, dry docks in Pearl Harbor and a set of locks on the Panama Canal.

In 1940 Kaiser turned to the new field of shipbuilding. The Six Services Inc. group of which Kaiser Co. was one, bought shipyards at Richmond, California and Portland, Oregon, later opening seven more, of which three were owned solely by the Kaiser Co. By the end of the war they had built 811 of the well-known Liberty ships, 219 Victory cargo ships, 50 small aircraft carriers and 360 other vessels. They reduced time for keel laying to launching of a Liberty ship to 4 days, 15 hours and 20 minutes, achieved with only one vessel, but which was a world record for ship construction.

Even while his company was working flat out on shipbuilding, Henry Kaiser was thinking about making a low-priced people's car. He had advanced ideas including front-wheel drive, torsion bar suspension and nylon mesh bodywork. Apparently when Joe Frazer first heard about these, he dismissed them as 'half baked', but the two men were brought together by Amedeo Giannini, founder and president of the Bank of America, and first met in July 1945. The Kaiser-Frazer Corp. was formed a month later, and the first cars were delivered in June 1946.

Unlike Joe Frazer, whose interests were almost entirely concentrated on the K-F Corp., Henry Kaiser continued to be involved in other activities including shipbuilding, aluminium, cement, bauxite and gypsum. One of his few unsuccessful ventures was the Spruce Goose, the enormous wooden-bodied seaplane he built with Howard Hughes, which made only one flight, and then merely skimmed the surface of the water. In 1954 he bought a house in Hawaii for personal use, then built the Hawaiian Village Complex, with accommodation for several hundred guests in two 14-storey blocks as well as cottages. Always concerned about the health of his employees, he started a health care plan in the 1930s, and in the 1960s built 19 hospitals in the western states. He was still working and planning new ideas when he died at the age of 85. He was then chairman of the worldwide business, Kaiser Industries Corp., with assets of $2.7 billion and factories in 33 countries.

Henry Kaiser married Bess Fosburgh in 1905. They had three sons, of whom Edgar (1908–1981) worked for many years in the Kaiser construction business, and became general manager of the Kaiser-Frazer Corp. in 1945.

NG

Further reading
'The Many Lives of Henry J. Kaiser', Karla A. Rosenbusch,
Automobile Quarterly, Vol. 36, No. 1.

for appearances' sake. However, the main reason was that the more expensive Frazers were not selling well.

The 1951 Kaisers were very distinctive cars, with a lower belt line than any other American car until 1956, and more glass area than any of their rivals. The styling was again by Dutch Darrin, with help on later models by Buzz Grisinger. The engine was still the old Continental six, uprated to 115bhp. Only the first engines were purchased from Continental. Thereafter they were made by Kaiser-Frazer in a former Hudson engine factory. Sales initially improved to 146,911 for 1950 (the 1951 models were launched in February 1950), but the lack of a V8 engine became increasingly serious to Kaiser, as more and more of their rivals began to offer powerful ohv V8s. Sales dropped steadily from 1951 onwards, and there were no major changes apart from the offering of a McCullough supercharger on the 1954 Manhattans, which increased power to 140bhp. Some models had particularly fancy trim; the most expensive was the $4400 Dragon of 1953, with gold-plated interior accessories, a gold plaque on the glovebox lid inscribed with the owner's name, and gold-plated script outside. Only 1277 were sold, out of total 1953 sales of 21,686. The following year they were down to 7039, while 1955's figure was only 100. The Willow Run factory was sold to General Motors in 1954, when Kaiser merged with Willys Overland, and production was transferred to the Willys factory in Toledo, Ohio. The last Toledo-built Kaiser cars were delivered in March 1955, but the design had a further seven years of life when Willys signed an agreement with the Argentine Government to make Jeeps and Kaiser sedans in Buenos Aires. During its heyday Kaiser had assembly plants in Holland, Israel, India and Japan.

A departure from the usual sedans was the Kaiser-Darrin 161 sports car, which was announced in September 1952 and finally went on sale in January 1954. It had a fibreglass 2-seater body on a Henry J chassis; the doors slid forwards instead of opening outwards in the usual way. The engine was a 2638cc Willys six whose capacity in Imperial measurement (161 cubic inches) gave the car its

1954 Kaiser (iii) Darrin DKF-161 sports car.
NATIONAL MOTOR MUSEUM

name. It was striking to look at, but with only 90bhp it was hardly a sparkling performer. Only 435 were made by Kaiser, in their special products factory at Jackson, Michigan, but afterwards Dutch Darrin bought 50 bodies and chassis and fitted them with Cadillac V8 engines. These developed 270bhp in 1955, and 335bhp by 1958, when Darrin's supply of chassis had been used up. They were very fast, with top speeds of up to 135mph (220km/h). Built in California, they were known simply as Darrins.

NG

Further Reading
Last Onslaught on Detroit, Richard M. Langworth,
Automobile Quarterly Publications, 1975.

KAISER (iv) (RA) 1956–1962

1956–1959 Industrias Kaiser Argentina (IKA), Cordoba.
1959–1962 IKA Renault S.A., Cordoba.

IKA was established in January 1955. It was a joint-venture involving KAISER, IAME and a bank loan. At first, only Jeeps were produced. The first one left the

NATIONAL MOTOR MUSEUM

FRAZER, JOE (1892–1971)

Unlike Henry Kaiser, Joseph Washington Frazer had been an automobile man all his life. He was born in Nashville, Tennessee on 4 March 1892, to James S. Frazer and the former Mary Washington, whose family was descended from an uncle of George Washington. He was educated at the prestigious Hotchkiss School and Yale University's Sheffield Scientific School, after which it seems something of an anti-climax that in 1912 he joined Packard, working as a mechanic for 16 cents an hour. He soon moved to Packard's New York agency and found his true métier in selling cars rather than making them. In 1919 he joined the export division of General Motors, and became assistant treasurer of the GM Acceptance Corp., where he played a key part in instalment financing (hire purchase). He spent a year as general manager with the Pierce-Arrow Finance Corp., then in 1924 joined Walter Chrysler in the Maxwell-Chalmers Motor Co. He was to remain with Chrysler

for 15 years, being responsible for co-ordinating sales of the newly-launched DeSoto and Plymouth marques from 1928. He became assistant sales manager for the whole Chrysler Corp. in 1936.

Presumably frustrated at rising no higher in the Chrysler hierarchy, he left in 1939 and joined the ailing Willys-Overland Corp. as president and general manager. Together with some Chrysler colleagues who had gone with him, he revamped the Willys' styling for 1940, and was rewarded with a modest increase in sales, but his main achievement was in obtaining part of the massive contract for manufacture of the Jeep. However he did not get on with Willys' chairman Ward Canaday, and in September 1943 resigned to become chairman and president of Graham-Paige Motors Corp. This company had made the last of their cars two years earlier, but were busy with the production of naval ordnance at the time that Frazer joined them. No sooner had he settled into his office than he announced that Graham-Paige would return to car making after the war. He commissioned William B. Stout and Howard Darrin as designers; the rear-engined Stout design was too radical and would have cost $10,000, but Darrin's slab-sided 4-door sedan was the basis for the production car. By then Frazer had formed a partnership with Henry Kaiser, essential if large-scale production was to come, as Graham-Paige did not have the necessary resources. In essence one could say that Kaiser had the money but Frazer knew the market. Out went Kaiser's front-drive and torsion bar suspension, to be replaced by rear-drive from a conventional 6-cylinder Continental engine and coil ifs. Frazer's name went on the upmarket cars, while the Kaiser was around $200-300 cheaper. Joe Frazer was president of the company until 1949, when he gave way to Edgar F. Kaiser. He remained a vice-chairman until 1954, and subsequently headed a series of ventures which included the Sterling Engine Co., Standard Uranium Co., and Frazer-Walker Aircraft Corp.

Joe Frazer was a great contrast to Henry Kaiser. Coming from a patrician background, he was a more persuasive speaker and a better dresser (someone said that one would not be surprised if a little gravel rolled out of Henry Kaiser's trouser turn-up), but was a perfect foil to Kaiser's dynamism and home-spun speech making. He married Lucille Frost.

NG

production line in April 1956, and only about 40 per cent of its components were made in Argentina. When Kaiser ceased manufacture of the Manhattan sedan in the USA, the dies were shipped to Argentina. Many trucks were needed to carry to Cordoba the 9,000 tons of industrial equipment which reached the Port of Buenos Aires. The Kaiser Manhattan became the Kaiser Carabela.

Slightly over 1000 complete cars were exported from the USA to Argentina, but then the Argentine version took over. It was slightly different from the former Willow Run machines. Although powered by the same 6-cylinder 3.7-litre engine, they had beefed-up suspension to cope with Argentine road conditions. Some exterior and interior modifications were also included. Leather upholstery was introduced. Only 4-door sedans were catalogued in Argentina. The Carabela was discontinued in 1962 and the Ramblers were introduced. From 1960, under an agreement with Renault of France, Renault Dauphine saloons were also produced.

ACT

KAISER JEEP *see* JEEP

KALAMAZOO *see* WOLVERINE (i)

KALITA *see* APOLLO

KALMAR (S) 1970s
Kalmar Verkstads, Kalmar.
Having been produced for several years as a postal van, the Kalmar was launched in 1972 in passenger guise, with five seats. Its boxy plastic bodywork featured sliding doors and hid Daf 44 mechanicals.

CR

KAMALA *see* D.J.

KAMINARI (US) c.1979 to date
Kaminari, Brea, California.

Kaminari started by making spoilers and trim parts for Datsuns and other sports cars. In 1988 they hired Pete Brock, who had styled the AC Cobra Daytona Coupé. He designed a body kit for the 1984 to 1989 Corvette with a resculpted nose and pronounced mudguard vents. The tail was lengthened and a raised 'ring' spoiler was added. The prototype had a supercharged engine and custom seats. They were sold in kit form.

HP

KÄMPER (D) 1905–1906
Heinrich Kämper Motorenfabrik, Mariendorf, Berlin.
Kämper was a well-known maker of proprietary engines, and in 1905 they decided to make complete cars. Most of their production, which did not last more than a year, was sold to the taxi trade.

HON

KAN (A) 1911–1914
Kralovehradecka tovarna automobilu Alois Nejedly, Kukleny.
The KAN (for Kukleny, Alois Nejedly) light cars were introduced as a single-cylinder 4-stroke 731cc 7bhp SV-engined type A with torpedo body, shown for the first time at the 1912 Prague motor exhibition. These 2-seaters had a top speed of 37mph (60km/h), and soon the 1206cc twin-cylinder 9/11hp engines for 2-seater torpedo or 4-seater phaetons were made. With this car Frantisek Czernil won the endurance run organised by the Vienna Automobile Club on the 460km long route.

In 1913, KAN started to produce bigger cars of type LC with 4-cylinder 1330cc 18/20hp SV engines. Bodied as 5-seater phaetons, these cars were capable of 43.5mph (70km/h). About 80 units were built in 1913 and a few in 1914 when the war stopped further development. Car production in Kukleny was revived in 1919 when Frantisek Petrasek began assembling his cars, named START.

MSH

KANE-PENNINGTON *see* PENNINGTON

NICK GEORGANO

DARRIN, HOWARD 'DUTCH' (1897–1982)
Howard Addison (Dutch) Darrin was born in Cranford, New Jersey in 1897. He entered the Army Air Corps in World War I, learned engineering and became a pilot. In 1919, he started Aero Ltd., one of America's first scheduled airlines.

When that failed, he went to New York and dealt in used European luxury cars. This brought him to the LeBaron offices in Manhattan, where he met one of the partners, Tom Hibbard. When Hibbard went to Paris to set up a LeBaron branch there, he ran into Darrin and, together, they established Hibbard & Darrin. The two Americans rented a showroom across the Champs Elysees from Kellner et Freres and took on the Minerva franchise. Many of their cars and designs were sold to wealthy North and South Americans traveling through Paris.

After a few years, however, Minerva's fortunes faltered, so H&D opened a huge custom body shop in the industrial Paris suburb of Puteaux, employing some 200 panel beaters. Here they created many custom bodies for wealthy patrons, won several important concours and were highly esteemed by the Europeans.

They created the 'arrow' hood moulding (later adopted by Packard) and also developed a way of casting thin aluminum body panels in a process called Sylentlyte. After Harley Earl joined General Motors, Hibbard & Darrin did some concept cars for GM, and Hibbard eventually went to work for Earl.

Darrin, however, stayed in Paris and, in 1931, teamed with a partner named Fernandez. Fernandez & Darrin again built custom bodies on luxury chassis. This relationship lasted until the mid 1930s, when the Depression finally did them in.

In 1937, Dutch Darrin returned to the US and settled in California. Here he built his Packard-Darrin series, which Packard eventually adopted as their own. Darrin also contributed to the design of the trendsetting 1941 Packard Clipper.

After World War II, he freelanced for Kaiser-Frazer. The 1947 Kaiser and Frazer were basically Darrin designs. Dutch received a 75 cent royalty for every 1947–50 Kaiser and Frazer built. The handsome 1951 Kaiser was also his, as was the 1954 Kaiser-Darrin sliding-door fiberglass roadster. Darrin himself bought and sold the last 50 Kaiser-Darrins, putting Cadillac V8s into some of them.

Darrin also consulted for Willys-Overland and several European automakers. He brought out a line of fiberglass nosepieces for GM's early 1960s Buick Special/Oldsmobile F-85 and was working on a custom Rolls-Royce when he passed away at his home in Santa Monica, California on 3 January 1982.

ML

KANGO see FIBREGLASS DESIGNS

KANKAKEE (US) 1916
Kankakee Automobile Co., Kankakee, Illinois.
Prototypes were built of a 6-cylinder tourer, and it was announced that the company 'were corresponding with manufacturers of engines and other components to cover a good-sized output', but the Kankakee never went on sale.
NG

KANSAS CITY (US) 1906–1909
1906–1908 Kansas City Motor Car Co., Kansas City, Missouri.
1909 Wonder Motor Car Co., Kansas City, Missouri.
This company took over the factory vacated by the CAPS brothers, J.C. Caps remaining behind the design of the cars marketed under the Kansas City name for 1906. These were 20 and 25hp 2-cylinder cars and a 4-cylinder tourer. In September a new designer arrived, L.M. De Dieterich. He had no connection with the famous French De Dietrich, but he and the Kansas City Motor Car Co. were happy to let people think there was a connection. His cars were large tourers with 4-cylinder engines of 60 or 75hp, the latter of 10-litres capacity and selling for $4300 for a tourer. They evidently did not sell very well because the company was in receivership by December 1907.

Kansas City was reorganised to make an 18hp 4-cylinder motor buggy, but this did not succeed, and early in 1909 it was renamed as the Wonder Motor Car Co. to make a 16hp 2-cylinder buggy called the Kansas City Wonder. This lasted less than a year, and in late 1909 the factory was taken over by another company to make the GLEASON.
NG

KANSAS CITY HUMMER (US) 1904–1905
Hummer Motor Co., Kansas City, Kansas.
This company made a motor buggy powered by a front-mounted flat-twin engine with epicyclic transmission and chain drive.
NG

KANZLER (US) c.1979
Newport Coachworks, Santa Ana, California.
The Kanzler Coupé was a neoclassic car based on a Mercury Cougar chassis with an Opel GT body mounted at the rear. The nose was removed and a customary long nose with sculpted mudguards added on. A 5700cc Mercury engine was used and the price of a new Kanzler was $60,000 in 1979.
HP

KAPI (E) 1950–1956
Automóviles y Autoscooter Kapi (Federico Saldaña), Barcelona.
Captain Federico Saldaña had published several of his designs of minicars in car magazines before he started small-scale production in 1950. Prototypes were made in Bilbao, but the company eventually produced them at Barcelona. The first Kapi was a 2-door coupé with a 125cc Montesa engine and single motion front wheel. Others were the Kapiscooter which was fitted with an Hispano-Villiers engine, the JIP, which resembled an American Jeep but had a 197cc engine, the Chiqui, with a single wheel at the rear and the Platillo Volante, a closed 4-wheel coupé. Kapi also offered the M190, a minicar with a Mercedes 190 SL body. The company offered Hispano-Villiers 2-stroke engines of 125cc, 150cc and 197cc, and FITA-AMC single-cylinder 4-stroke engines with aluminium cylinder head. They may also have used 2-cylinder engines as well.
VCM

KAPPO (J) 1998 to date
Japan Electric Vehicle Association, Tokyo.
This was a very small single-seater electric prototype developed jointly by the University of Tokyo and model builder Sivax. It had open-sided bodywork, handlebar steering, irs and a joystick controlling acceleration and braking. Wheelchairs could be used instead of the seat. The power output was limited to 0.8bhp by law. Production was targeted with a proposed price of 400,000 yen.
CR

KARENJY (MAD) 1985–c.1988
Karenjy, Tananarive.
This Madagascan company presented the Mazana off-roader in 1985. It used a 2068cc Renault diesel engine and 4x4 transmission with a 5-speed gearbox. The Iraka was a second model, resembling a Volkswagen Beetle in appearance. It used a 1397cc Renault petrol engine and had only two driven wheels. The project manager, Rabearivelo Andriamalagasy, planned to make 500 cars per year and sell complete production lines to other African nations but this plan was apparently not fruitful. Neither was a new Citroën BX diesel-based model called the Tily, which in 1987 was under development in collaboration with the French company TEILHOL.
CR

KARMA COACHWORKS (US) c.1972–1979
Karma bought the rights to build the Manx SR from MEYERS and produced it until the late 1970s. Their version was called the Max SR-2. They made a number of improvements to the doors and also offered a tube frame option for those wishing to take part in autocross competitions.
HP

KAT (GB) 1989–1992
KAT Designs, North Perrott, Somerset.
Ex-General Motors, Aston Martin and Tickford stylist Simon Saunders founded KAT Designs in 1983 to make styling bodykits for production saloons such as the Mini and Ford Escort. The MPV marked a change of direction, being a multi-purpose vehicle with interchangeable bodywork: you could flip between a basic jeep, convertible, targa, van and estate – ten different styles in all. The basis was a strengthened new Ford Escort Mk III/4 floorpan complete with its original bulkheads, inner wings and cross-members, fitted with fibreglass body panels.
CR

KATO (US) 1907–c.1913
Four-Traction Auto Co., Mankato, Minnesota.
This was a 4-wheel drive car designed and built by Ernest Rosenberger. It used a 24hp 2-cylinder 2-stroke Brennan engine, and five were built by early 1908 when the company was formed. These early cars were called Four Traction, and later ones Kato or Mankato. By the end of that year 25 vehicles had been completed, though a number of these were trucks. Production is believed to have continued to about 1913, when Four Traction sold up. About 12 cars and perhaps as many as 30 trucks were made between 1909 and 1913.
NG

KAUFMAN (US) 1909–1912
Advance Motor Vehicle Co., Miamisburg, Ohio.
This company was formed by the merger of the Kaufman Buggy Co. and the Hatfield Motor Vehicle Co. who had made the HATFIELD high-wheeler. In contrast to this, the Kaufman was a conventional car with normal-sized wheels, powered by a 20hp 4-cylinder air-cooled engine.
NG

KAUFMANN (CH) 1896–1905
Eugen Kaufmann, Tägerwilen TG.
After completing his engineering studies in Winterthur, Eugen Kaufmann worked for some time with Carl Benz in Mannheim. In 1896 he established a small company in Tägerwilen to manufacture automobiles. The first model had a 3-cylinder engine and belt transmission. Within a few months about 20 workers were employed and some chassis were delivered to Seitz brothers, coachbuilders in Emmishofen. Later models with a 12hp engine had either friction or chain drive and some buses were made. In 1905 the strained financial situation forced the closure of the factory. However, in 1906 Kaufmann founded the MILLOT Automobile factory in Zurich.
FH

KAUZ see ANSBACH

1916 Kearns Model L 12hp 2-seater.
KEITH MARVIN

1914 Keeton Model 4-35 tourer.
GLENN BAECHLER

KAVAN (US) 1905

Kavan Manufacturing Co., Chicago, Illinois.

The Kavan was a light runabout powered by a single-cylinder engine under the bench seat, with friction transmission and chain drive. It was to have sold at the very low price of $200, or £40 at the prevailing rate of exchange, but the company's life was very short, and probably only a prototype was made.

NG

K.A.W. see HAGEN

KAYLOR (US) c.1980 to date

Kaylor Energy Products, Redwood City, California.

Kaylor made electric and electric-hybrid conversions for a variety of cars. They also sold two Volkswagen-based kit cars. One was a Ferrari Dino 246 replica similar to the MAGNUM. Their most popular kit was the INVADER GTE, which they had purchased from Autokit. Their version kept the VW suspension, but substituted a 30hp electric motor coupled to a small petrol or diesel engine that could recharge the batteries when needed. It was also available as a straight electric vehicle.

HP

KAYSER see PRIMUS

K-D (US) 1912–1913

K-D Motor Co., Brookline, Massachusetts.

The K-D was designed by Margaret E. Knight, who had 87 patents to her name, not all in the motoring field, aided by Mrs Beatrice Davidson. The engine was a remarkable design, having crescent-shaped slide valves which formed an almost complete sleeve, with only 1/16in between the two halves. It had six cylinders and 4.9-litres capacity, developing 90bhp. The only body style offered was a tourer with very sleek lines for its period. It appeared at the 1913 Boston Automobile Show with a very high price tag of $6000 (contemporary Model 38 Locomobile prices ran from $4300 to $5650), and apparently the ladies did not find any customers. In all probability the show car was the only K-D built.

NG

K.D. (GB) 1991–c.1996

K.D. Kit Cars, Wakefield, Yorkshire.

This was a budget kit-form AC Cobra 289 replica using Ford Cortina suspension, Ford Escort rear axle, multi-tube steel backbone chassis and Ford 4-cylinder twin cam or V6 (or even Fiat double-ohc) engines. A much revised spaceframe chassis was developed during 1994–95 to accept Ford Sierra running gear, including the Sierra's independent rear end, and larger engines could be fitted (up to V8s).

CR

KEARNS (US) 1909–1916

1909–1912 Kearns Motor Buggy Co., Beavertown, Pennsylvania.
1912–1916 Kearns Motor Truck Co., Beavertown, Pennsylvania.

The Kearns company followed on from the EUREKA (vi) after Maxwell Kearns took over the company. At first similar machines were made, motor buggies with 12/14hp 2-cylinder, or 20hp 3-cylinder engines, but a 32hp 4-cylinder was made in 1912 only. Although they were typical high-wheelers with solid tyres and chain drive, they differed from most in having round bonnets which gave them something of the looks of a conventional car. Only the 3-cylinder, now rated at 26.4hp, was listed for 1913, and the following year saw something completely different. The Lu-Lu was a cyclecar made in roadster or speedster form, with 12hp 4-cylinder Farmer engine, 3-speed gearbox and shaft drive. By November 1914 Lu-Lu output had reached 25 cars per week, and it was continued into 1915. Then for 1916 Kearns brought out the Trio, a light car with 12hp 4-cylinder engine, probably the same that had powered the Lu-Lu. Its name came from the three interchangeable bodies, runabout, tourer or light delivery truck, any of which could be attached to the rear deck by four bolts. Kearns made only trucks after 1916, carrying on this business until 1928.

NG

KEEN (US) 1948–1968

Keen Manufacturing Corp., Madison, Wisconsin.

Charles Keen built two steam-powered prototypes. The first was built in 1948, and was based on a shortened 1946 Plymouth convertible. A V4 steam engine was mounted at the rear, with the boiler at the front. In 1955 he built a second car with a fibreglass VICTRESS S-4 body. This car was tested by the United States Senate Commerce as part of their anti-smog investigations in 1968. There was no connection between this car and the visually similar car built by WILLIAMS.

HP

KEENELET (GB) 1904

Keene's Automobile Works, London.

The Keenelet steam car had a 12hp vertical single-cylinder engine, a semi-flash boiler and friction cone transmission, the latter unusual in a steamer which normally had such low-speed torque as to render any kind of gearing unnecessary. Although it received glowing tributes in such varied magazines as *Automobil Welt* and *The Tatler*, the makers were bankrupt by September 1904.

NG

KEENE STEAMOBILE see STEAMOBILE

KEETON (US) 1912–1914

Keeton Motor Co., Detroit, Michigan.

Forrest M. Keeton had been in partnership with Herbert A. Croxton in making the CROXTON-KEETON in Massilon, Ohio. In 1912 they parted company and Keeton set up on his own in Detroit to make a car which was similar to the 'French' Croxton-Keeton, with dashboard radiator and Renault-type bonnet. This was made in 22hp 4-cylinder and 38hp 6-cylinder models, the latter

1999 Keinath GTR sports car.
NICK GEORGANO

available in three body styles, increased to six for 1914. In January of that year Keeton was absorbed by the American Voiturette Co., makers of the CAR NATION cyclecar, but nine months later American Voiturette was in liquidation. The liquidators sold off 600 Car Nations at $350 each, and 100 Keetons at $1000 each. The latter were bargains as the list prices ran from $3250 to $3975.

NG

KEINATH (D) 1996 to date
Horst Keinath Automobilbau GmbH, Dettingen.
Keinath's name had been familiar for some time for his cabriolet conversions of the Opel Ascona, when in 1996 he brought out his own car, the Keinath GTR. This name harked back to the Opel GT coupé as Keinath saw his car as a new version of this popular small coupé of the 1970s. He used 4- and 6-cylinder Opel engines of up to 3 litres and 210bhp, in a spaceframe structure with composite fibre body. This was a 2-seater with a roof which automatically folded into the back.

HON

KELLER (US) 1948–1950
Keller Motors Corp., Huntsville, Alabama.
The Keller was a renamed BOBBI-KAR, built by a company that had moved to Alabama after running foul of California stock regulations. The company was taken over by George D. Keller, who had been with Studebaker. He restyled the car and named it the Keller. There was a convertible model with rear-mounted 4-cylinder 2180cc or 1650cc engines, and a front-engined station wagon. With a 92in (2335mm) wheelbase, the Keller was poised to compete with Crosley for smaller car buyers. Unfortunately, George Keller died in 1949 and the company fell apart after building only 18 cars.

HP

KELLER KAR (US) 1914
Keller Cyclecar Corp., Chicago, Illinois.
The Keller was a tandem-seated belt-driven cyclecar no different from many others, except that as originally planned it was to have a miniature version of the

1948 Keller roadster.
NICK BALDWIN

Knight sleeve-valve engine. It was never built as such, and the power unit eventually chosen was a 10hp air-cooled 2-cylinder Wilson. It was priced at $375, but few were sold before the company closed at the end of 1914.

NG

KELLISON (US) c.1959–1972
Kellison Engineering and Manufacturing, Folsom, California.
Kellison Inc., Lincoln, California.
Grand Prix Sports and Racing, Lincoln, California.
Jim Kellison founded the Kellison kit car company in 1959, and introduced an attractive fastback coupé that stood only 39in (990mm) tall. Called the J-4, it was designed to fit chassis with a 98in (2487mm) wheelbase. The J-2 roadster that followed fitted full-length American car chassis. A shorter series, the K-2 roadster and K-3 coupé, fitted VW and MG chassis. These bodies proved to be very popular and made Kellison one of the largest US kit car manufacturers. Kellison offered two tube chassis, the first designed by Chuck Manning, a successful race car builder. It was a simple ladder frame with live axles front and rear. A later replacement would accept Corvette or Chevrolet sedan suspension.

c.1980 Kelmark coupé.
ELLIOTT KAHN

1921 Kelsey (i) tourer.
KEITH MARVIN

1924 Kelsey (i) sedan and tourer.
KEITH MARVIN

Over the years the Kellison coupés received minor trim changes, most apparent a move to dual headlights. In the 1960s the J-series was renamed the Panther. In 1965 ASTRA took over production of most of the Kellison coupé line. Kellison expanded into other fibreglass projects, selling dune buggy bodies and a street version of a Huffaker racing car. The Kellison Can-Am was a wide, low sports-racer body developed for a one-off racing car, and the Dagger was a dune-buggy sized coupé that fitted shortened VW chassis. Kellison also developed one of the first Ford GT-40 replicas, which was available with a semi-monocoque chassis for V8 engines and transaxles, although most were sold to fit on a VW pan. Kellison sold replica bodies for the Jaguar D-Type, XKE, Lotus Elite and Corvette Stingray. They also bought the moulds for the BYERS SR-100. In addition to kit bodies, Kellison sold hot rod kits, racing cars, and performance accessories. Jim Kellison left in the late 1960s to start KELMARK and later built the STALLION Cobra replica.

HP

KELLY (US) c.1989

Michael Kelly, Arlington, Texas.
Former AVANTI company president Michael Kelly purchased a limousine conversion company in Arlington, Texas after selling his shares in the financially ailing South Bend firm. In 1989 he announced a new car, the Legado, which was to be built in his Arlington limo plant using sub-assemblies from Brazil. It was to have been a sporty $40,000 convertible with understated lines and an aluminium body. There was room up front for a 5.7-litre V8, said to be patterned after NASCAR engines. 4-speed automatic and 6-speed manual transmissions were to be offered, Kelly was waiting for his prototypes to be completed before soliciting backers, but no finished cars appear to have been built.

HP

KELLY PYTHON see AKA

KELMARK (US) 1969–1994

Kelmark Cars, Okemos, Michigan.
The Kelmark GT resembled a Ferrari Dino 246 GT. It was designed around the Volkswagen floorpan, but many Kelmarks were built on custom frames supplied by Mid-Engineering. These would accept a number of GM engines, but the most popular selection was the Oldsmobile Toronado V8. One Kelmark was built with a 737hp Chevrolet V8 and was timed at 202.70mph (326.14km/h). Kelmark offered stock VW, turbo VW Porsche, and Mazda rotary engines in mid- or rear-mounted configurations. Kelmarks sold well and were one of the most common kit cars of their era. The Kelmark body was imitated by MAGNUM.

HP

KELSEY (i) (US) 1897–1902; 1921–1924

1897–1899 Autotri Co., Chestnut Hill, Pennsylvania.
1900–1902 C.W. Kelsey.
1921–1924 Kelsey Motor Co., Newark and Belleville, New Jersey.
Cadwallader Washburn Kelsey built his first automobile in 1897 and later teamed up with an acquaintance, to form the Autotri Co. with the intention of manufacturing a single-cylinder chain-driven 3-wheeled car. The first Autotri proved to be the last although the two promoted their company throughout 1899, using their pilot model and working on a second 3-wheeler which never reached completion. This car was given to the Smithsonian Institution in Washington, D.C. in 1923. Carl Kelsey completed a larger 4-cylinder prototype car in 1902 in an unsuccessful attempt to again get into automobile manufacturing.

The first Kelseys of 1921 were widely promoted. There were friction drive and a Falls 6-cylinder engine was used. The car was available as a runabout, touring car and sedan, and rode on a chassis with a 116in (2944mm) wheelbase. The Kelsey resembled most contemporary designs except for a spare friction drive wheel located within the spare tyre at the rear. For 1922 the 6-cylinder line was continued but with a Walker engine and the wheelbase increased to 118½in (3008mm). The 6-cylinder car was augmented by a new 4-cylinder series, powered by a Gray engine, with a wheelbase of 112in (2843mm). Production was low and sales were ample for both the six and the four. In mid-year, the six was relegated to the 112in (2843mm) wheelbase, similar to the four.

The 6-cylinder series was dropped for 1923 and the friction drive car was continued unchanged. Demand for a friction drive car had dropped considerably and, to boost sales, a car with a conventional transmission was introduced, the series physically identical to the friction drive model but powered by a Lycoming CF 4-cylinder engine. As sales increased immeasurably with this new series, Carl Kelsey dropped the friction drive series toward the end of the year, simultaneously adding a taxicab to the existing line which consisted of a touring car and a sedan.

Kelsey production had been good and the company entered 1924 with a backlog of orders for both the sedan and touring car plus a considerable number for the new taxicab which was interesting several franchised taxicab fleet operators.

Operations ground to a halt in June 1924 when the Kelsey Motor Co. was illegally forced into backruptcy and went out of business. Remaining cars and a number of taxicabs were sold at cost.

KM

KELSEY (ii) (US) 1913–1914

Kelsey Car Corp., Connersville, Indiana.
This was a moderately-priced conventional 6-cylinder car which had no connection with the other Kelsey cars.

NG

KELSEY MOTORETTE see MOTORETTE

KELVEDON (GB) 1987

Kelvedon Motors, Spalding, Lincolnshire.
Offered by a Lotus dealer and restorer was a replica of the Lotus Type 47 (in other words, a wide-arch Lotus Europa). Bodies were offered and there were plans to make full kits using original Europa components but this never occurred.

CR

KELVIN (GB) 1904–1906

Bergius Car & Engine Co., Glasgow.
The Kelvin had a 3052cc 16hp 4-cylinder engine and shaft drive. It was available with solid, 'semi-solid' or pneumatic tyres, and was equipped originally with a rear-entrance tonneau body, later with a side entrance. All components, including the bodywork, were made in a factory formerly occupied by Albion. Although only 14 Kelvins were made, the company had an eye on the export market, and published a catalogue in Spanish. The engine was later developed into a marine unit, running on petrol or paraffin – they were installed in many fishing boats. As a marine engine manufacturer Bergius were active at least up to the late 1960s.

NG

C.W. Kelsey, standing, filling the petrol tank in a Maxwell.
NICK BALDWIN

KELSEY, C.W. (1880–1969)

Cadwallader Washburn Kelsey was born in Clarens, Switzerland, to socially prominent American parents, and was educated at Haverford College, Pennsylvania. With a Haverford classmate, I. Sheldon Tilney, he built a 3-wheeled car which they called the Autotri, powered by a single-cylinder 5hp Buffalo engine. They planned to build replicas for sale, and printed company stationery but the venture went no further.

After graduation Kelsey became manager of the sub-agency for Autocar in Philadelphia, and then in a similar capacity for Locomobile. In 1904 he began running a servicing and repair garage, then took time off to visit Europe, where he studied car factories and taxi-cab operation. On his return he sold his garage, which had become very successful, and took on the agency for Maxwell-Briscoe, a make which was to sell far more cars than Autocar or Locomobile. He went in for many 'stunt' demonstrations in Philadelphia, including climbing the steps of prominent buildings. As he pointed out later, it did not matter very much if he was arrested during his climbing exploits, because newspaper coverage of the incidents gave more publicity for Maxwell. An important 'first' was the making of films to promote the cars, thanks to a friend who was now a minor executive of a Long Island film company. The first film was made as a private venture, but Maxwell company officers were so impressed that they commissioned a number of films. From 1905 to 1909 Kelsey was sales manager for Maxwell, and in 1906 he won the Deming Trophy as a participant in the Glidden Tour. In 1909 he was responsible for a major promotion when he suggested that 22-year old Alice Huyer Ramsay, wife of a Congressman from New Jersey, should drive a car across the American Continent. She successfully completed the journey from Hackensack, New Jersey, to the start point in New York City, and then on to San Francisco, in 59 days, accompanied by her husband's two sisters and a friend. It was the first crossing from East to West, and the fact that it was achieved by an all-women crew gave added publicity to Maxwell, who presented Mrs Ramsay with a new car at the end of the trip.

Later in 1909 Kelsey parted company with Maxwell, chiefly because he disagreed with Benjamin Briscoe's empire building in which he tried to emulate General Motors. Kelsey built a 4-cylinder tourer which was to be called the Pilgrim of Providence, at Briscoe's Providence, Rhode Island factory, but was not completed until he became manager of the Columbia Motor Co. at Hartford, Connecticut. It was renamed the Spartan, but was never put into production. From 1911 to 1914 he made the Motorette 3-wheeler in Hartford, and during the war he left the motor industry for banking and public relations, followed by work perfecting the design of a gun for the US Navy powered by a buoy, and attached to a submarine.

In 1920 he purchased a factory in Belleville, New Jersey, and formed the Kelsey Motor Co., with the intention of producing a friction-drive car. Kelsey reasoned that there were enough friction-drive enthusiasts to make the car a success, together with maintaining source facilities for such other friction-drive cars as Cartercar and the Metz, of which a good number were in use.

Friction-drive Kelsey cars were made until 1924, the last models having conventional gearboxes, but production ended when he became the victim of a fraud by 'the Bankruptcy Gang' who forced a number of companies into bankruptcy so that they could 'reorganise' the firm. The perpetrators, as well as Kelsey's sales manager who was the inside man, went to prison, but Kelsey was not able to salvage his company. He was by no means finished with business, though, as after a spell in banking in Philadelphia, he became the American manager of the German Frazen company which made garden machinery. In 1932 he separated the American branch from its parent, and reorganised it as Rototiller, with a factory at Long Island City. In 1936 they moved to Troy, New York, where it subsequently became Garden Way, and continues today under the name Troy-Bilt. Kelsey managed the firm until his retirement at the age of 80 in 1960.

Towards the end of his life he designed a flying car which could be used for crop dusting. He was perfecting this at the time of his death, nine weeks before his 90th birthday.

Kelsey married Marion Ticknor and had a son and two daughters.

KM

Further Reading
'Kelsey, the Man and his Car', Keith Marvin,
The Horseless Carriage Gazette, March-April 1960.

1905 Kelvin 14/16hp tourer.
M.J.WORTHINGTON-WILLIAMS

1945 Kendall (ii) saloon.
MICHAEL POINTER COLLECTION

1946 Kendall (ii) Grégoire 6hp saloon.
GILES CHAPMAN

KEMPTEN (D) 1900–1901

Süddeutsche Fahrzeugfabrik, Kempten.

This company offered a voiturette powered by a 3PS proprietary engine, but despite its impressive name the business was a small one, and few cars were made.

HON

KENDALL (i) (GB) 1912–1913

Kendall Motors Ltd, Sparkhill, Birmingham.

The Kendall was one of many cyclecars which made their appearance at the 1912 Olympia Show. It was made in two models, a typical belt-driven cyclecar powered by an 8hp air-cooled V-twin J.A.P. or 7/9hp Peugeot engine, and a more car-like model which used the same J.A.P. engine and 2-speed epicyclic gearbox but with underslung worm final drive, the latter an unusual sophistication on a cyclecar. The frame was of ash and the price complete with hood, windscreen and lamps was a not unreasonable £89–£95 for the belt-driven model and £130 for the worm drive, but the make did not last long.

NG

KENDALL (ii) (GB) 1945–1946

Grantham Productions Ltd, Grantham, Lincolnshire.

Britain's first postwar 'people's car', the Kendall was the work of William Denis Kendall (1903–1995), the Independent MP for Grantham from 1942 to 1950. With the laudable aim of providing large-scale employment for Grantham people, he announced a revolutionary small car in November 1944, which would be made in numbers up to 10,000 per year. He already had the factory as he was managing director of the British Manufacture & Research Co., makers of aircraft cannon and shells.

The first Kendall was a rather angular 2-door saloon powered by a rear-mounted 700cc 3-cylinder radial engine designed by Horace Beaumont. According to an engineer who worked for Kendall 'it was so fundamentally flawed from a technical standpoint that it amounted to a fraud.' In August 1945 Kendall was to have driven it from Grantham to London to demonstrate it to fellow MPs, but it almost certainly went on a trailer. The engineer doubted that it could even have travelled the one mile down Whitehall to Parliament Square! The car also lacked an electric starter and synchromesh, and had only one headlamp. Beaumont was fired (he was later jailed for fraud in connection with an electric car), and a completely new car was built, with full-width body and a redesigned 3-cylinder engine. This did not perform much better, and the engine was quickly replaced by a Volkswagen unit which Kendall managed to obtain from Germany. This car made a number of successful journeys and was shown to the public, though always with the boot firmly locked.

Tiring of home-grown designs, Kendall next turned to the Aluminium-Française-Grégoire, which Jean Grégoire had designed and tested during the war. This had a 594cc air-cooled flat twin engine driving the front wheels, and in Grégoire form, a 2-door saloon body with roll-back canvas roof. Kendall built about five of these at Grantham, and at least one open roadster, but his creditors withdrew their support in November 1946. This was at least partly because Kendall proposed to bypass the Society of Motor Manufacturers & Traders, and sell his cars through the Co-operative Wholesale Society. He returned to America where he had worked before the war, and was involved in outboard motor manufacture, followed by electronic devices used to treat arthritis.

The Grégoire design was made in small numbers in Australia as the HARTNETT, and more successfully in France as the DYNA PANHARD.

NG

KENDRICK (US) c.1983–1985

Kendrick Industries, Wheat Ridge, Colorado.

The Kendrick Mondrea was an attractive roadster inspired by the 1955 Ferrari Mondial. The KS500 version fitted onto a Volkswagen Beetle chassis, while the KS501 used a special tube frame for front-mounted V6 or V8 engines. KS501 chassis used Ford front suspension with Corvette irs.

HP

KENLEY (GB) 1986

The Kenley TT was a squarish open roadster kit based on a Triumph Herald chassis.

CR

KENMORE (US) 1910–1912

Kenmore Manufacturing Co., Chicago, Illinois.

The Kenmore was first seen as a 2-seater runabout or 3-seater roadster powered by 14 or 18hp flat-twin engines, with epicyclic transmission. Though it had standard-sized wheels and pneumatic tyres, it had something of the motor buggy about its appearance. The 2-cylinder models were continued through 1912, joined for 1911 by a 30hp 4-cylinder 5-seater tourer. In 1912 Kenmore was acquired by Sears Roebuck. They had just given up marketing their SEARS Motor Buggy, and did not want to continue in the car business, but they adopted the Kenmore name for a line of household appliances which is still made today.

NG

KENNEDY (i) (US) 1898–1903

C.W. Kennedy, Philadelphia, Pennsylvania.

This was a light 2-seater electric carriage with drive to the front wheels and a centre pivot front axle. Though no company was formed, it seems that the Kennedy was sold quietly for five years.

NG

KENNEDY (ii) **(GB)** 1907–1910

Hugh Kennedy & Co., Glasgow.

The Kennedy was a conventional car powered by a 15/20hp 4-cylinder engine. It was also known as the Ailsa, though it had no connection with the Ailsa Craig, which was another name for the Craig Dorwald. After the war Hugh Kennedy had a second go at car manufacture, with the ROB ROY.

NG

KENNEDY (iii) **(CDN)** 1909–1910

Kennedy Manufacturing Co., Preston, Ontario.

Named after its promoter, buggy salesman William Kennedy, this was a high-wheeler made for him by the Clare brothers who were stove manufacturers. The engine was an 18hp flat-twin mounted under a bonnet, with epicyclic transmission and shaft drive. The engine and some other components were bought from DE TAMBLE. About 75 were built in 1909, but Kennedy then left for the West Coast, and control of the company passed to the chief engineer Herb Hambrecht. He reduced the size of the wheels and fitted pneumatic tyres, but otherwise the 1910 Kennedy was similar to the 1909. However it was increasingly difficult to sell 2-cylinder cars and Hambrecht was unwilling to use his own capital to finance work on a 4-cylinder engine, so production ended after about 100 of the 1910 models had been made.

NG

KENNEDY (iv) **(GB)** 1914–1916

Kennedy-Skipton & Co. Ltd, Leicester.

This was a 2-seater light car powered by an 11.9hp 4-cylinder Salmons engine. The first model used friction transmission and belt drive, but these gave way to a 3-speed gearbox and overhead worm final drive.

NG

KENNEDY (v) **(US)** 1915–1917

G.L. Kennedy, Los Angeles, California.

This was a light car with 4-cylinder engine, dashboard radiator and Renault-type bonnet. It was built only as a coupé and this combined with its short wheelbase gave it the appearance of an electric car. Few were made as wartime demands interrupted the supply of components. It was also known as the Petite.

NG

KENSINGTON (US) 1899–1904

1899–1902 Kensington Bicycle Co., Buffalo, New York.
1902–1904 Kensington Automobile Co., Buffalo, New York.

This company announced their 'Small Electric Stanhope' in August 1899, and soon afterwards dropped bicycles to concentrate on cars. A steam car of similar appearance to the electric was added in 1901, having a 4hp 2-cylinder engine and single-chain drive. For 1902 Kensington offered three motive powers at the same time, for a tonneau with 12hp 2-cylinder Belgian-built Kelecom engine joined the range. For 1903 and 1904 it was the only model, but it was not very satisfactory; one owner returned his to the factory saying that it was 'worthless'.

NG

KENT (US) 1916–1917

Kent Motors Corp., Belleville, New Jersey.

The Kent was a conventional car powered by a 3.6-litre 4-cylinder Continental engine and made as a 4-seater Club Roadster or 5-seater tourer. Both models were priced at $985, which included a robe carrier, foot rail and 8-day clock. The promoters had plans to build a car factory in Cuba, but some company officials were indicted for fraud in July 1917, which put an end to the Cuban plans and the Kent car.

NG

KENTER (D) 1924–1925

C. Kenter Automobilbau AG, Berlin-Charlottenburg; Leipzig.

This was a continuation of the KOMET (ii), a small car made in two models, with 4/14PS Steudel and 5/18PS Atos engines. It had no more success under the new name than the old, and did not last out the year 1925.

NG

1910 Kennedy (iii) tourer.
GLENN BAECHLER

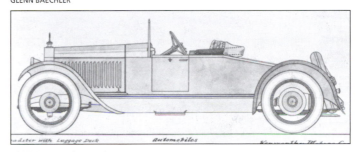

1920 Kenworthy roadster.
KEITH MARVIN

KENT'S PACEMAKER (US) 1899–1901

Colonial Automobile Co., Boston, Massachusetts.

Named after its designer, A.W. Kent, this was an unusual steam car with a single front wheel and three rear wheels, of which only the central one transmitted power to the road. The other two could be raised when sufficient speed had been reached, enabling the car to ride, bicycle-like, on two wheels. Surprisingly, a few were actually sold.

NG

KENWILL (US) c.1912–1914

Nothing is known about where, or by whom, these cars were built, but 1912–14 registration lists for Connecticut carry seven Kenwill cars, of 32, 36 and 40hp. They were probably made in Connecticut as all the owners were from that state.

NG

KENWORTHY (US) 1920–1921

Kenworthy Motors Corp., Mishawaka, Indiana.

The Kenworthy was a high-class and expensive car made by Cloyd Kenworthy, who had previously been vice-president of ROAMER. Two models were announced in January 1920, a four powered by a Rochester-Duesenberg engine and a Continental-powered six. The former had a 4-speed gearbox, the latter a 3-speed. Only one body style was listed, a sporty-looking 5-seater tourer with cycle-type wings, disc wheels and step plates instead of a running board. Styling of this was by Karl H. Martin who also designed the WASP. The four cost $5000 and the six $3900. More expensive than either was the Line-O-Eight announced for 1921 at $5550. This had a straight-8 engine of Kenworthy's own design, and 4-wheel hydraulic brakes. Claims have been made for Kenworthy as a pioneer of the hydraulic-braked straight-8, but it seems that Duesenberg beat them by about a month, and anyway the Duesenberg was made in much larger numbers. While 143 Kenworthys were made in 1920, and 71 in 1921, the Line-O-Eight accounted for only a handful. It was similar in appearance to the other Kenworthys, apart from having wire wheels in place of discs.

NG

1992 Kewet El-Jet electric coupé.
KEWET

KERMATH (US) 1907
Kermath Motor Car Co., Detroit, Michigan.
The Kermath was a 3-seater roadster powered by a 26hp 4-cylinder engine, with shaft drive. Its most distinctive feature was a radiator in the shape of a heraldic shield. One car was exhibited at the Detroit Automobile Show in February 1907, but the company failed before proper manufacturing premises could be found. The show car was probably the only Kermath made.

NG

KERSTING (D) 1949–1950
Gebr. Kersting, Waging, Oberbayern.
The three Kersting brothers built an attractive small coupé powered by a 123cc DKW engine, with chain drive to the rear axle. A more powerful 200cc Ilo engine was used later, in a new model with all four wheels enclosed. There was no series production.

NG

KESLING (US) c.1979
H. D. Kesling, Westville, Indiana.
The Kesling Yare was a streamlined 4-wheeled electric vehicle. It looked like an elongated egg and had its wheels arranged in a diamond pattern with one each in front and back, and two more on the outside edges of the middle. As it steered, the vehicle tilted to one side. Top speed was 55mph (89km/h) with a 12hp motor and a 72-volt battery pack. The Yare was a prototype built at a cost of $60,000.

HP

KESSLER (US) 1920–1921
Kessler Motor Co., Detroit, Michigan.
Martin C. Kessler, a Detroit engineer, formed the Kessler Motor Co. in January 1920, the Kessler car being introduced at the Detroit Automobile Show with production following that summer, the first cars being completed as pilot models. The Kessler was powered by a supercharged 2-litre 4-cylinder engine of Kessler's own design, with a 3¾ × 3¾ inch bore and stroke developing 70bhp at 3000rpm. Any sales of cars built in 1920 are doubtful although perhaps 20 cars produced the following year presumably reached the marketplace, the only model built – a 5-seater touring car – carrying a list price of $1995. Except for its in-house engine, the Kessler used standard parts throughout. With a 117in (2970mm) wheelbase, the car was of typical appearance with wood artillery wheels and its spare tyre mounted aft. During the latter part of 1921, Martin Kessler and the company's vice-president, W. H. Radford, were developing a new 8-cylinder engine which they planned to use in the upcoming models. Toward this end, it was decided to market the projected series as an entirely different car to divorce its identity from the Kessler 4-cylinder line, and Kess-Line Motors was formed, actually another company within the Kessler umbrella

(see KESS-LINE). Thus, to all intents and purposes, the Kessler Motor Car Co. as an active organisation was phased out for further activity and attention entirely focused on the Kess-Line.

KM

KESS-LINE (US) 1922
Kess-Line Motors, Detroit, Michigan.
The Kess-Line was the lineal descendent of the Kessler, presumably the pragmatic approach toward a more powerful automobile than its predecessor on the part of its designers. Equipped with a new in-house supercharged ohc straight 8-cylinder engine of 2½ × 3¼ inch bore and stroke developing 100bhp at 3500rpm, the Kess-Line appeared at the 1922 Detroit Automobile Show as a 5-seater touring car priced at $2150. It rode on a 119in (3020mm) wheelbase with wire wheels as standard equipment. Production, however, failed to exceed 15 completed cars and ceased before the end of the year. A modified Kess-Line engine was later used by the short-lived Balboa Motors Corp. of Fullerton, California in one of its three prototype automobiles of 1924.

KM

KESTREL (i) (GB) 1914
Bristol Road Motor Garage Co., Gloucester.
The owner of this firm also ran a leather-working company in Gloucester and was impressed by the possibilities of extending this business by improving on the materials hitherto in general use for friction-drive transmission linings. A 4-cylinder proprietary engine of 60 x 100mm was used and most chassis parts were 'bought in', although the bodies were reputed to have been built on the premises. Leather was used to face the clutch, the main countershaft which gave four 'gear' positions, and the differential, whilst final drive was by chain. It was claimed that only World War I impeded production, after some 15 cars had been assembled, but an ex-employee, speaking in the 1960s, recalled some problems with the complex systems used to maintain the requisite pressures on the various friction contacts. Sadly, the executors failed to make available the records and documentation which the owner's daughters had retained until their deaths in the 1990s.

DF

KESTREL (ii) (GB) 1984–1985
1984 Dovetail Plastics, Woodlands, Berkshire.
1984–1985 Kestrel Cars, Chesterfield, Derbyshire.
The Kestrel Scorpion was a revival of the Tom Killeen-designed SCORPION. The old car's rear-engined Imp basis was changed to a mid-mounted Alfasud engine in a new spaceframe chassis with suspension which, it was claimed, had been developed in conjunction with Lotus. The fibreglass shell was much as before, now reinforced with Kevlar, and the problematic gull-wing doors remained. Very few were built.

CR

KESTREL (iii) (GB) 1984–1989
1984–1988 Protoflight (I.S.S. Car Co.), Gillingham, Dorset.
1988–1989 F.E.S., Scotland.
The Kestrel kit car had many points in its favour: it was well designed with handsome lines and was made to high quality standards by a company better known for its work in the aircraft industry. Its one problem was its chassis – a VW Beetle floorpan and rear-mounted air-cooled engine. The project passed in 1988 to a Scottish firm, which renamed the car the Briton.

CR

KÉVAH (F) 1920–1924
Éts Kévah, La Garenne-Colombes, Seine.
This was a cyclecar made in two models, an 1100cc twin and a 1057cc 4-cylinder Ruby-engined car. Both used shaft drive.

NG

KEWET (DK) 1992 to date
Kewet Industri, Hadsund.
A small electric 2-seater, the Kewet El-Jet (later known as the Citi-Jet) achieved better commercial success than most battery-powered cars, largely due to the tax

advantages offered to electric vehicles in the Danish market. It had a monobox plastic body over a tubular steel chassis, with all-independent suspension and all-round disc brakes. A rear-mounted 5.4kW (7bhp) or 7.5kW (10bhp) electric motor was powered by four 12-volt batteries, giving a top speed of 43–50mph (69–80km/h) and a range of 45 miles. Some 500 cars were made in the first year of production.

CR

KEYSTONE (i) (US) 1899–1900

Keystone Match & Machine Co., Lebanon, Pennsylvania.

This company took two years off from match manufacture to make an unusual steam car powered by a 3-cylinder engine in each rear wheel hub, fed by steam from a tubular boiler mounted in the body. How the steam was fed to cylinders revolving at speed was not explained. The company planned to make light cars and heavy trucks using this system.

NG

KEYSTONE (ii) (US) 1900

Keystone Motor Co., Philadelphia, Pennsylvania.

This was a light 2-seater with 5hp single-cylinder engine mounted vertically behind the seats. In November 1900 rights were acquired by the SEARCHMONT Motor Co. who put it into production under their own name.

NG

KEYSTONE (iii) (US) 1909–1910

1909 Munch-Allen Motor Car Co., Du Bois, Pennsylvania.
1910 Munch Motor Car Co., Yonkers, New York.

The partners in the first company were C.P. Munch and R.M. Allen. Although the factory was at Du Bois, the first 30 cars were made for Munch by W.S. Howard of Yonkers, who had just ceased making cars under his own name. The Keystone Big Sixes were large, powerful cars with 60hp 6-cylinder engines made only in open styles, 2-seater roadster, 4-seater baby tonneau and 5-seater tourer. For 1910 a smaller Light Six was made, but production in Du Bois was unsatisfactory and Munch moved back to Yonkers, without Allen, and formed a new company. It is possible that the 1910 Keystones were again made in the Howard factory.

NG

KEYSTONE (iv) (US) 1914–1915

H. Cook & Brothers, Pittsburgh, Pennsylvania.

This was a conventional car powered by a 55hp 6-cylinder Rutenber engine, with 4-speed gearbox and electric lighting and starting. Nothing was heard about it after the initial announcement in October 1914.

NG

KEYSTONE (v) (US) c.1993

Keystone Metal Engineering, Lawrence, Kansas.

The Keystone SC 427 was a Cobra replica based on a simple ladder frame with Ford, Jaguar or Corvette suspension packages. It was sold in kit or assembled form.

HP

KIA (KO) 1985 to date

KIA Motors, Seoul.

This company was set up jointly by Mazda and Ford to make a small 3-door hatchback with 1138 or 1324cc transverse 4-cylinder engines and front-wheel drive. Called the Kia Pride, it was sold on the US and other markets as the Ford Festiva. A similar model was made by Mazda and sold on Japanese and European markets as the Mazda 121. Kia also made a Mazda 626-based medium-sized 4-door saloon called the Capital. In 1992 the Capital was replaced by the Sephia, a Mazda 323-based 3-door hatchback or 2-door cabriolet powered by a 1500cc engine developing 92bhp in single-cam form or 105bhp in its twin-cam 16-valve version and the Sportage, a 4x4 estate using the Mazda 121 floorpan and a twin-cam 2-litre engine. For the domestic market they also made two larger cars, the Concord derived from a former Mazda 626 and the Mazda 929-based Potentia with 2.2-litre four or 3-litre V6 engines.

1910 Keystone (iii) Six-Sixty baby tonneau.
NICK BALDWIN

1989 Kia Pride hatchback.
FORD MOTOR CO.

1994 Kia Mentor saloon.
KIA CARS (UK)

1995 Kia Pride Pzazz hatchback.
KIA CARS (UK)

1998 Kia sports car (ex-Lotus Elan).
KIA MOTORS

1999 Kia Clarus saloon.
KIA MOTORS

In 1994 there appeared a Pride replacement, the Avella with 3- or 5-door hatchback body sold in the US as the Ford Aspire and on some other markets as the Ford Festiva. Production of the Pride was taken over by Asia Motors, to be made under licence in the Phillipines, Vietnam, Turkey, Iran, and Venezuela. In 1996 came two British links with Kia; the Lotus Elan was made with a redesigned body, and the Mazda 626-derived Credos was available with a 2¹/₂-litre Rover V6 engine as well as a 2-litre 4-cylinder Mazda. In 1997 and 1998 a slightly modified Sephia was made in Indonesia under the name Timor.

The economic crisis which hit several Far Eastern countries forced Kia into liquidation in April 1998, and in October they were taken over by Hyundai. For 1999 the Sephia (Mentor in the UK) was replaced by the Shuma, a completely restyled 5-door hatchback, and the Mentor 11 4-door saloon, both powered by 1498 or 1793cc engines. They also launched the Clarus, a Mondeo-sized saloon with 1798 or 1998cc engines based on the former Mazda 626. The Sportage was continued, in 3- and 5-door forms, with the choice of two petrol engines, single- and twin-ohc 1998cc units, and a turbo diesel, also of 1998cc. Two MPVs were announced for 2000, the Shuma-based Carens in 5-, 6-, and 7-seater versions, and the larger Sedona 7-seater, with 2496cc V6 petrol or 2902cc 4-cylinder diesel engines.

NG

KIBLINGER (US) 1907–1909

W.H. Kiblinger Co., Auburn, Indiana.

This company launched a wide range of high-wheelers in 1907, six models with three engine sizes, 4, 6 and 10hp. The 4hp Model A was exceptionally cheap at $250, and even the top Model F cost only $450. The 4 and 6hp models had single-cylinder engines, unusual among high-wheelers which mostly had horizontally-opposed twins, which the 10hp Kiblinger did. Bodies were 2- and 4-seaters, and steering was by tiller. Kiblinger advertising boasted that they made 'the only gasoline automobiles that any woman, or even a boy, can feel safe to drive'.

In 1909 the makers of the SUCCESS motor buggy claimed patent infringement against Kiblinger, whose factory manager W.H. McIntyre bought out the directors and renamed the car the MCINTYRE. A total of 613 Kiblingers had been made, although some of the 1909 figure of 264 were McIntyres.

NG

KICO (D) 1924

Kieling & Co., Frankfurt am Main.

This small manufacturer was unusual in making their own engines, and in four sizes, 4/12, 5/15, 6/18 and 7/32PS. It was probably too ambitious for a small company, which failed to survive Germany's economic crisis.

HON

KIDDER (US) 1900–1901

Kidder Motor Vehicle Co., New Haven, Connecticut.

The Kidder was a steam car which used two separate cylinders of 3hp each, mounted horizontally on each side of the boiler. Drive was direct to the rear axle. Two models were made, a 2-seater runabout at $1000 and a delivery van at $1600. Both had tiller steering. Production figures for the Kidder are not known, though in November 1900 it was reported that 35 were under construction. After the company closed in 1903 Wellington P. Kidder made about half a dozen more cars, but only for his friends.

NG

KIDDY (F) 1921–1922

Ateliers Lecourbe, Paris.

The Kiddy was one of the smaller-engined French cyclecars, with a flat-twin of only 397cc. However it was more refined than most as well, with a conventional 2-speed gearbox and shaft drive. It was suspended by a single transverse leaf spring at the front, and quarter-elliptics at the rear. Maximum speed was less than 30mph (48km/h).

NG

KIEFT (GB) 1954–1955

Kieft Cars Ltd, Wolverhampton, Staffordshire.

Cyril Kieft was a senior manager in the steel industry but, when it was nationalised in 1947, he left and sought his challenges in motor racing. Kieft designed a ladder frame 500cc Formula Three car with Metalastic bushes as the springing medium. A 2-seat version with a 650cc BSA engine and cycle mudguards was built to commission in 1951, and it was offered to the public, but there were no takers.

A bought-in F3 design achieved huge success in the hands of Stirling Moss and Don Parker, but Kieft's next sports car was a batch of eight central-seaters, half with Bristol engines, half with MG units. They were intended for racing, but were taxed for the road. One won the 2-litre class in the 1954 Sebring 12-hours.

In 1954 Kieft made a conventional sports car with all-independent suspension, a ladder frame and the world's first one-piece fibreglass body. At Le Mans one ran with a Coventry Climax FW (Feather Weight) engine – it was the first time this unit had been used in a car. The FW would become the FWA (Feather Weight Automotive).

One of these cars won its class in the Tourist Trophy and that (plus the class win at Sebring) was enough for Kieft to be offered a stand at the 1954 London Motor Show. The car was crude, impractical and expensive, but six were made in all.

During 1954 the steel industry was privatised, Cyril Kieft returned to it and he sold Kieft Cars to fellow-Welshman, Berwyn Baxter. By the end of 1956, Kieft Cars had become a race preparation shop.

MJL

KIELEY (USA) c.1992–1995

Kieley Engineering, Inc., Grafton, North Dakota.

The Kieley Audacia was a rebody and performance upgrade kit for the Pontiac Fiero chassis. Owner Lee Kieley designed the $1,500 body kit that included wider rear mudguards and a recontoured nose clip with a deep nose spoiler. It was a clean and original design. He also sold a kit for installing an Oldsmobile Quad-4 16-valve engine and transaxle. His most interesting conversion, the Audacia 2MV8, used a longitudinally mounted Chevrolet, V8 and a Porsche 914 transaxle. This was almost unique among the many transverse-mounted V8s installed into Fiero kit cars.

HP

KIENER (F) 1957

Christian Kiener presented his engaging 4-door saloon at the 1957 Salon de Paris. It was notable for its very wide (176cm) bodywork, which could therefore seat six passengers. Elements of Citroën's front-wheel drive system were incorporated together with a front-mounted Volkswagen 1200cc engine, while the suspension was by torsion bars all round. The Kiener remained a prototype.

CR

KIKOS (F) 1980–1983

Société Française Kikos, Antibes.

This was one of the most basic of the rash of microcars that appeared in France around 1980. Two single-seater styles were offered: an open step-in model and an enclosed version; both had plastic bodywork. Both were 3-wheelers with a rear-mounted engine (either 50cc air-cooled Motobecane or 125cc water-cooled Zündapp), with drive by automatic transmission to the left rear wheel. Other features included all-drum brakes (later discs at the rear) and handlebar steering.

CR

KILLEEN see SCORPION

2000 Kia Sedona MPV.
KIA MOTORS

2000 Kia Sportage 4×4 estate car.
KIA MOTORS

1953 Kieft sports car.
NATIONAL MOTOR MUSEUM

KILO (GB) 1983–1986

1983–1984 The Thousand Workshop, Bodmin, Cornwall.
1984–1986 B&S Horton, Tintagel, Cornwall.

The Kilo Sports marked a most unusual approach to the traditional-style kit roadster idiom. The mechanical basis was the Morris Minor 1000, doubtless chosen because its creator was a Morris Minor specialist. The very basic, angular doorless fibreglass body sat on a steel ladder chassis. More performance could be achieved by fitting a 1275cc MG Midget engine.

CR

KIM (SU) 1930–1947

Zavod imjeni Kommunisticheskogo Internatsionala Molodjeshi, Moscow.

Nearly 20 years before the first Moskvitch 'people's cars' appeared on the streets of Moscow, an auto assembly works was built in the capital city and named after International Communist Youth (abbreviation KIM in Russian). During 1930 to 1932 it really assembled Ford's A and AA models, a kind of rehearsal site before full production of clones of these got underway at the huge Nishny

1941 Kim-10 saloon.
MARGUS H.KUUSE

1912 King (ii) Model A tourer.
NICK BALDWIN

1922 King (ii) Model J tourer.
NATIONAL MOTOR MUSEUM

Novgorod plant. Later on the KIM works was associated with the first unlucky attempt at launching an affordable closed automobile in the USSR. There was a 2-door KIM-10-50, a cabrio version called KIM-10-51 and a number of prototypes KIM-10-52, fitted with 4-door bodywork. The bodywork was modelled after the Ford Prefect and dies – some say bodies – were acquired from Ambi-Budd of Germany. The 4-seater was just 156in (3960mm) long and weighed 1850lb (840kg). KIM's 1172cc engine was rated at 26bhp and top speed equalled 56mph (90km/h). Between 1940 and 1941 supposedly about 500 cars were completed, but the information is controversial and inexact. In 1941 the equipment and tools were dismantled and sent to the Urals where various military equipment was made. After the war the tools and most of the

workers returned, and the factory was set up again under the name MZMA, making the Moskvitch.

MHK

KIMBALL (US) 1910–1912
C.P. Kimball & Co., Chicago, Illinois.
The C.P. Kimball company were well-known piano manufacturers who began making electric cars to special order, possibly as early as 1900, although standard production models did not appear until 1910. They also set up a coachbuilding department, specialising in converting rear-entrance tonneaus to side entrance. Their electric cars of 1910–1912 were made in two lengths, a runabout and coupé on a 72in (1827mm) wheelbase, and a 4-seater landaulet on a wheelbase of 100in (2539mm). For 1912 they offered what they called a George IV Phaeton on an 82in (2081mm) wheelbase. In May 1912 they announced that cars would once again be made to special order only; this may have continued for a few years.

NG

KING (i) (GB) 1904–1905
King & Co. Leicester.
This short-lived car was powered by a 12hp vertical twin engine with single-chain drive. The radiator bore some resemblance to that of the Daimler.

NG

KING (ii) (US) 1911–1924
1911–1923 King Motor Car Co., Detroit, Michigan.
1923–1924 King Motor Car Co., Buffalo, New York.
Charles Brady King (1869–1957) completed his first car in the early part of 1896, several months before Henry Ford finished his quadricycle. King's first drive, on Detroit streets on 6 March, is regarded as the first journey by a petrol-powered automobile in that city. Henry Ford reportedly followed the new car on a bicycle. King had intended to enter his car in the 1895 *Chicago Times-Herald* race, but had been unable to have it ready in time. The King automobile, a 4-cylinder, tiller-steered runabout, came to the attention of Detroit's business community, but the times were harsh. Discouraged by the weak economy of 1896, Charles King dismantled his car, selling the chassis to Byron Carter, who was later to build the CARTERCAR. King then concentrated on marine engines, eventually selling his business to OLDS Motor Works.

In 1902, King became chief engineer of Northern Manufacturing Co., makers of the NORTHERN automobile, whose principals included Jonathan MAXWELL and W.E. Metzger, later the 'M' of E-M-F. King left Northern in 1908, when its precarious condition led to acquisition by E-M-F.

The King Motor Car Co. was incorporated at Detroit in February 1911. The company's first product was the King Silent 36, a 4-cylinder car with a unique gravity lubrication system in which the flywheel served as a form of oil pump. The Silent 36 sold for $1350 in basic form, $1565 when fully-equipped with windscreen, hood and gas lamps. But by the end of the year, King Motor Car Co. was in receivership. It was rescued by chewing gum manufacturer Artemas Ward, whose son, Artemas Junior, was delegated to run it. Ward's plans included new products – a V8 car was introduced in December 1914. Using a 3893cc side-valve V8 of in-house manufacture, the King Model D sold for $1350 and claimed to be the 'World's First Popular-Priced V8'. The 4-cylinder cars were discontinued after 1915. In announcing the 1918 models, King touted the 'same reliable chassis, with minor improvements', and called it the 'Car of No Regrets'. However, the King Motor Car Co. fell victim to the postwar doldrums of 1919–20. The Wards sought to dissolve the firm, and a court-ordered sale in December 1920 was consummated by Charles Finnegan and associates of Buffalo, New York. Retirement of debt resulted in lifting of the receivership in 1922.

The new owners moved the firm to their home city in 1923. By that time, the company's only product was the 124in (3147mm) wheelbase Model L, whose styles included a 3-passenger Road King roadster with all-aluminium body, Foursome 4-door tourer, a 5-passenger sedanette, and a pair of 7-passenger models, a sedan and a touring car. Prices were now in the $1795 to $2550 range. After building 240 cars, however, King Motor Car Co. filed for bankruptcy, although some cars continued to be sold into the following year, and as late as 1925 in England.

Charles Brady King, however, had accumulated wealth and renown, and was fêted at auto industry events, including the 1946 Golden Jubilee in Detroit, to the end of his life.

KF

Further Reading
'Following the Mystery Ride - The Life and Cars of Charles B. King', L.M. Thomas, *Automobile Quarterly*, Vol. 30, No. 3.

KING (iii) (GB) 1970–1971
Mike King Racing, Liss, Hampshire.
Mike King made a number of specials to order (notably Bugatti Type 35s and a Renault 4-engined trike), but also offered the King Thing, a very weird Ford-engined single-seater hot rod tub, in 1970–71.

CR

KING (iv) (GB) 1985–1987
Libra Cars, Wrexham, Clwyd.
The King Cobra 427 was born to fill a perceived gap in the market for a cheap, high quality replica. The box section steel ladder chassis was normal enough, but the use of Ford Cortina Mk III/IV parts was fairly innovative; only the steering link needed modification. Rover V8 engines were optional but for larger units, a kit for Jaguar axles was also marketed. A 289 body style was also offered.

CR

KING & BIRD (GB) c.1903
King & Bird, Mansfield, Nottinghamshire.
Little is known about this car, of which a number were registered in the Nottingham area in 1903. It was a dogcart powered by a 3½hp De Dion-Bouton engine.

NG

KINGFISHER (GB) 1982–1985
1982–1983 Kingfisher Motors, Rothbury, Northumberland.
1984–1985 Vortex Developments, Morpeth, Northumberland.
Roger King's Kingfisher Sprint was an over-ambitious attempt to reinvent the MINIJEM as a Porsche rival. The Minijem was substantially redesigned to become 6in longer, 2in taller, and it gained large front and rear spoilers. Underneath the fibreglass bodywork were Mini parts, and King even offered a 125bhp 1480cc Super Sports engine with a Rajay turbocharger. Complete cars as well as kits were sold, latterly under the name Vortex.

CR

KINGFISHER KUSTOMS (GB) 1983 to date
Kingfisher Kustoms, Smethwick, West Midlands.
The American sand-rail off-road racer idea achieved some success in Britain, mainly as a motorsport idea but many cars were used in roadgoing trim. Kingfisher's Kommando sand-rail was one of the better efforts, with a very tough steel tube space frame housing VW suspension and a Beetle engine or optional V6/V8 engines. Other models included the Kombat beach buggy and the Kango, an angular Beetle-based sports buggy of South African origin, with a fixed roll-over bar and interchangeable rear coupé bodywork.

CR

KINGFISHER MOULDINGS (GB) 1982–1986
Kingfisher Mouldings (Countess Cars), Wigan, Lancashire.
There was not very much commendable about the Countess, whose only claim to fame was that it was the very first attempt to offer something that looked like a Lamborghini Countach, though it was so vague and ugly that extremely willing suspension of disbelief had to be employed. The standard kit came on a Beetle floorpan, although a multi-tube chassis was also designed, accepting Austin Maxi mechanicals. A more accurate but equally poor-quality true Countach replica later resurfaced under the name G.B. There were two other listed models: the Vulcan (a Morris Marina based Bugatti Type 57 replica) and a rather poor Jaguar E-Type Series 2 coupé replica based on Ford parts and using any Ford or Rover V8 engine.

CR

1982 Kingfisher coupé.
KINGFISHER

1951 King Midget 8½hp 2-seater.
ELLIOTT KAHN

1965 King Midget 9¼hp 2-seater.
NATIONAL MOTOR MUSEUM

KING MIDGET (USA) 1947–1969
Midget Motors Manufacturing, Athens, Georgia.
This tiny micro-car was designed and built by aeroplane pilots Claude Dry and Dale Orcutt and was one of the most successful cars of its type. The first single-seat model came out in 1947 and resembled Midget racing cars that were popular at that time. It used a single-cylinder Wisconsin engine with 6hp and was sold in kit form for $270. A 3-speed manual or single-speed automatic was offered. Total weight was 350lbs. In 1951 the second series Midget was introduced. It had a more practical 2-seat roadster body and more powerful 8½hp engines were offered. The bodies were metal and they could be bought in

1921 Kingsbury Junior 2-seater.
NATIONAL MOTOR MUSEUM

1909 Kissel Model 6-60 speedster.
NATIONAL MOTOR MUSEUM

1925 Kissel Model 75 brougham sedan.
NATIONAL MOTOR MUSEUM

kit or turn-key form. The third series King Midget came out in 1958, with more angular styling but similar mechanicals. For the first time, doors were optional. This model was very successful and helped total Midget sales climb to over 5000 cars. A bodyless version was also available for driver training classes, as was a special model with controls for the handicapped. In 1967 a 12hp Kohler engine was installed but sales had started to decline with the introduction of practical economy cars like the VW Beetle. In 1969 a fire destroyed the moulds for a dune buggy-like replacement with a fibreglass body, and King Midget closed its doors.

HP

KING-REMICK (US) 1910

Autoparts Manufacturing Co., Detroit, Michigan.
The King-Remick was a 2-seater runabout powered by a 6.6-litre 6-cylinder engine, with bolster fuel tank behind the driver and passenger, in the manner of the Mercer Type 35 Raceabout, though it was higher and less elegant than the Mercer. It was made for Messrs King and Remick by A.O. Dunk who was famous for buying up defunct car companies, so it probably contained

components intended for other cars The prototype had a 115in (2929mm) wheelbase, but this was planned to be increased to 123in (3122mm) on production models. Few, if any, of these were made.

NG

KINGSBURGH (GB) 1901–1902

Kingsburgh Motor Construction Co., Granton, Edinburgh.
This company was founded in 1900 to take over the works and business of the makers of the MADELVIC electric car. A small number of 12hp 2-cylinder petrol cars were made in 1901, one of which took part in that year's Scottish Automobile Club Run. This was described as a 14-seater, making it a bus rather than a car. In 1902 the works were taken over by STIRLING.

NG

KINGSBURY JUNIOR (GB) 1919–1922

Kingsbury Engineering Co. Ltd, Kingsbury, London.
This company had made Le Rhone aero engines during the war, and turned to car manufacture to keep their workforce employed, though it is highly unlikely that the 800 workers on the payroll in 1918 were all employed on the Kingsbury Junior. It was a typical light car unusual only in the origin of its engine. The 1021cc flat-twin unit was a Koh-i-Noor made in Scotland by the Kennedy Motor Co. who also built the ROB ROY car. The gearbox, pedals and levers came from the same source. Final drive was by shaft to a bevel rear axle. Kingsbury went into liquidation in May 1921, but stock continued to be sold into 1922. The following year the factory became the home of Vanden Plas coachworks.

NG

KINMONT see PUCKRIDGE

KIRKHAM (US) 1996 to date

Kirkham Motorsports, Provo, Utah.
Although this Cobra replica was a painstaking reproduction of the original car, its origins were anything but Anglo-American. They were built in a former MiG fighter plane factory in Poland. Each part on these cars would fit onto an original Cobra without modification, but Kirkham replicas were made to a much higher standard of fabrication and assembly. The bodies were aluminium.

HP

KIRKSEL (US) 1907

Dr James Selkirk, Aurora, Illinois.
Dr Selkirk was part owner of the AURORA Motor Works, and decided to make a car of his own, reversing the syllables of his surname. A 50hp 4-cylinder 4-seater tourer, it was made for him by the C.C. Hinckley Machine Co. of Aurora. Two cars were made, one for himself and the other for the man who supplied the upholstery for the cars. Selkirk planned to make more, to sell for $3000 each, but his Kirksel Motor Co. never got off the ground, and he returned to his medical practice.

NG

KISSEL KAR, KISSEL (US) 1906–1931

Kissel Motor Car Co., Hartford, Wisconsin.
Hartford, Wisconsin was the domain of the Kissel family, who had emigrated from Germany in the mid-nineteenth century. Starting out as farmers, they had become grocers, builders and manufacturers of farm equipment. Included in the latter category were stationary engines for agricultural use, so it was a natural progression for brothers William and George Kissel to form the Kissel Motor Car Co. to build automobiles in 1906. Their first car, an experimental 4-cylinder shaft-drive vehicle, had been built the year before. The first production KisselKars, as the early units were called, used a Beaver engine and bodies built by a sleigh manufacturer in neighbouring Waupun, Wisconsin. An order for 100 cars, from a Chicago merchant then distributing the STODDARD-DAYTON line, established Kissels as an auto manufacturer in earnest. A German-educated engineer, Herman Palmer, joined the company as head of chassis engineering, and was instrumental in the firm's success, receiving patents on several lubrication and suspension features. By 1908, the company often spaced the name to appear Kissel Kar, but surviving documents are inconsistent.

KisselKar *EVERY INCH A CAR*

The ALL-YEAR Car

Kissel's original idea that changed the motoring habits of a nation.

KisselKars will be displayed at all the important Automobile Show

The Car for All Purposes, In All Seasons and All Weather

For every social function or business use the ALL-YEAR Car is supreme 365 days in the year.

The ALL-YEAR Top is BUILT-IN, not on. It is *completely removable.*

See the ALL-YEAR Cars at the Chicago Show, Coliseum, that created big enthusiasm among New York's critical car buyers.

Inspect the HUNDRED POINT SIX—the car of a Hundred Quality Features. Prices f. o. b. factory—ALL-YEAR Models, $1635 to $2100. Open cars $1195 to $1750.

KISSEL MOTOR CAR CO.
Hartford, Wis., U. S. A.

1929 Kissel White Eagle Eight brougham sedan.
NATIONAL MOTOR MUSEUM

1926 Kissel 8-75 Gold Bug speedster.
NICK BALDWIN

Some commercial bodies were now being mounted on Kissel chassis. Friedrich Werner, a body engineer who had worked for OPEL in Germany, arrived that same year.

The 1909 line of Kissel Kars appeared on three wheelbases from 107 (2715mm) to 128in (3248mm) at prices of $1350 to $3000. Two sizes of in-house 4-cylinder engines, both cast in pairs, were offered, 3954 and 4693cc. A Big Six of 7040cc was devised by adding a third pair of cylinders from the larger Regular four. A Mercedes-style radiator was adopted in 1910, with a distinctive button emblem on its left, a feature that would remain with the marque for two decades. A double drop chassis frame appeared in 1911, and electrification of the cars proceeded in stages; by 1914 the company boasted the first indirect instrument illumination in the industry. A winter top, a removable fixed roof, was devised by Fritz Werner, a style that was adopted by other manufacturers in time.

A 6-cylinder *en bloc* engine of 4732cc was developed by Palmer in 1916; the Hundred Point Six (The Car with a Hundred Quality Features) developed 52bhp and stayed in production for five years, its engine continuing with few changes until 1928. It claimed the first use of the Stewart vacuum fuel feed system, an Autovac competitor. For 1917, Kissel adopted the Weidely ohv V12 engine, also used by PATHFINDER and others, for a Double Six model that would last but two seasons. To this time, Kissel Kars had been good, reliable performers but not overly stylish. In mid–1917, the New York distributor, Mr Conover T. Silver, induced the Kissels to apply some European styling concepts to their cars, and a 4-passenger 2-door tourster was built to his order and shown at the 1918 New York show (another appearing on the chassis of APPERSON, the other car for which Silver had a franchise). Hit of the show, however, was a Kissel Silver Special Speedster, painted a brilliant yellow. Silver would drop his franchise in 1919, by which time the marque name had been shortened to Kissel (Kissel Kar sounding too German for the times); his speedster would endure, however, as the renowned Kissel Gold Bug. The name Gold Bug came about as the result of a contest run by newspaperman W.W. Brownie Rowland, auto editor of the *Milwaukee Journal*. Having borrowed one of the yellow speedsters for a tour of Wisconsin highways, Rowland offered $5 to the reader suggesting the best name for the car. Gold Bug was never an official designation applied by Kissel, but the nickname has lasted to this day. Built on the 6-45 chassis, the Gold Bug had smooth lines and a graceful sloping tail. From the side one could slide an occasional seat out of a drawer, where a daring passenger could perch for a hair-raising ride. A similar arrangement was later used on the PAIGE Daytona and some models of MARMON.

Razor-edged closed bodies and a number of new open models led the 1921 model announcements. Speedsters and toursters offered cycle wings and aluminium step plates in place of running boards. So popular was this style that it was adopted for all open models the next year, though the step plates were later replaced with three-quarter length aluminium boards. An 8-cylinder car , the Custom Built Eight, entered the Kissel line as a 1925 model. Lycoming supplied 5086cc engine blocks, which were fitted with Kissel aluminium heads and oversized cast sumps. Automatic lubrication was standard, as were 4-wheel hydraulic brakes. Three wheelbases of eights and two of sixes were offered, at prices up to $3585. Production, which had bottomed out at 748 cars in 1924, rebounded a bit to 2122 cars in 1925. Talks were held with Wisconsin neighbour NASH regarding a possible merger, but nothing permanent resulted. A smaller, 3831cc eight became part of the 1927 line, using a Lycoming engine shared with AUBURN, ELCAR and GARDNER. Also a New Smaller Kissel appeared on a 117in (2969mm) wheelbase, with a 6-cylinder version of the same engine.

New, higher bodies were introduced for 1928. A top-of-the-line White Eagle Deluxe, with an overbored Lycoming 8, headed the catalogue, luxuriously trimmed. But overall sales were really in the doldrums, barely over 1000 units. A Hispano-like high radiator design was adopted, and sweeping wings led to reintroduced full-length running boards. Herman Palmer's old six was dropped; now all Kissel engines were Lycoming-derived. A line of funeral cars, to be marketed by National Casket Co., was devised, and the firm entered the taxi market with Bradfield and New Yorker cabs, but neither deal produced the desired success.

Early in 1930, Archie Andrews approached the Kissel brothers in search of production facilities for his RUXTON car. For Andrews' promise of $250,000 in financing, the Kissels were to manufacture 1500 Ruxtons a year. A killer clause in the contract, however, provided that if the Kissels were unable to fulfil the orders then Andrews would gain control of their company. But Andrews put forward only $100,000, and the Kissels, unwilling to lose their company for an incomplete contract, filed for voluntary receivership in September 1930. After selling off the parts and service business, a reconstituted Kissel Industries struggled on for some years with various enterprises, including an abortive return to automaking in 1934. Kissel Industries sold out to West Bend Aluminum Co. in 1944.

KF

Further Reading
The Classic Kissel Automobile, Val V. Quandt, Kissel Graph Press, 1990.
'The Kissel Kaper', Gene Husting, *Automobile Quarterly*, Vol. 9, No. 3.

KIT CAR CENTRE (ZA) 1982 to date
Kit Car Centre Pty, Boksburg.
This company offered probably the largest range of kit-built products ever seen in South Africa. It started off with the Salamander buggy, of which nearly 2000 were built, but very soon after came a VW-based Porsche 718 RSK replica, of which around 1200 were made between 1982 and 1991. Another Porsche copy was a 356 Speedster replica based on Beetle mechanicals; an alternatively styled model was the 356 Speedster Sebring, with wide arches and more modern trim. Air-cooled VW engines were the norm but VW Golf, Toyota and Mazda rotary engines were also popular. Another Porsche replica – the 550 Spyder – was launched in 1998. Since 1984 an AC Cobra replica had also been produced, with a ladder type chassis using Jaguar XJ6 suspension components, and Chevrolet or Ford V8 power. Several hundred kits and some complete cars were supplied. In 1986 came the Lynx, a neo-classic roadster using Ford Cortina parts. Also that year arrived a Ford GT40 replica using Ford Granada suspension components, Ford or Chevrolet V8 engines and Audi ZF 5-speed manual transmissions. Two body styles were offered, the Mk 1 and the Mk 3. A completely in-house design was the 1995 Razzo, a front-wheel drive sports car based on the VW Golf Mk1. It used a semi-space frame type chassis and was offered in screen-less Barchetta and Sports forms. It acquired the Veep from FIBREGLASS DESIGNS in 1996, offering it in two wheelbase lengths. Another rugged design was the 1991 Mantis, with a tube frame chassis using Ford Cortina suspension and drive train. The company's latest product was the Freeranger, with styling inspired by the Jeep CJ7 Wrangler. The body could be placed on existing Jeeps as well as other 4x2 or 4x4 vehicles, while a special chassis for Ford Cortina pickup or Toyota Hilux parts was also offered.

CR

KIT CAR WORLD *see* CLASSIC SPORTS CARS

KLASSIC KARS (US) c.1981
Klassic Kars, Las Vegas, Nevada.
The Lynx kit car was a pseudo-replica of a Mercedes SSK. Actually, it resembled the CMC Gazelle kit. The Lynx used a custom chassis with Ford Pinto running gear and bobbed running boards.

HP

KLAUS (F) 1894–1899
Th. Klaus, Boulogne-sur-Seine.

1929 Kleiber straight-eight sedan.
KEITH MARVIN

The first Klaus car was a 3-wheeler powered by a 2hp single-cylinder engine, with tiller steering to the single front wheel. A 4-wheeler of 1897 used the same engine. The 1898 Klaus was more ambitious, with two 2½hp horizontal engines, one at each side of the car, just inside the frame. The barrels were air-cooled and their heads water-jacketed. One of these cars took part in the Paris-Rambouillet-Paris voiturette race of October 1899. Klaus' vehicles were mainly experimental, but they were exhibited at shows, and he sold a few to his friends.

NG

KLEIBER (US) 1924–1929
Kleiber Motor Truck Co., Los Angeles, California and San Francisco, California.
In 1923, the Kleiber Motor Truck Co., a prominent and highly respected West Coast manufacturer of commercial vehicles, decided to augment its production with the introduction of a line of passenger cars. These would be marketed in the Pacific Coast states of California, Oregon and Washington, plus the Canadian Province of British Columbia. The car was launched early in 1924, a typical assembled car not unlike so many others of the period falling into the $1885 to $2350 price range for its line of four open and closed models. With a 6-cylinder Continental 8R engine and a wheelbase of 128in (3244mm), an estimated 75 units were produced in the initial year of manufacture. For 1925 the wheelbase was reduced by 6in (152mm) and the angular body lines were modified to give the Kleiber lines more in keeping with the period. Sales, though not large, were consistent. The Kleiber's promotion was minimal with an annual production never exceeding 225 units. Additional body types, both open and closed, were added to the existing models for 1926, prices increasing to $2675 for the sedan. For 1929, the 6-cylinder line was continued despite a lack of modernisation in design, and augmented by a straight-8 powered by a Continental 15S engine. The eight only reached the prototype state with two cars completed. Production dropped off severely in 1929, probably because of the 6's out-of-style design, unchanged since 1926, and the stock market crash in October that terminated further manufacture of the Kleiber passenger car. Less than 1000 Kleiber cars were completed in six years of production, but the company continued its complete line of ½- to 9-ton trucks until 1937.

KM

KLEINSCHNITTGER (D) 1950–1957
Kleinschnittger-Werk, Arnsberg.
The Kleinschnittger was relatively successful among German microcars, though it provided pretty basic transportation, with an open 2-seater body and a single-cylinder ILO engine of only 125cc driving the front wheels. About 3000 were made up to 1957, and it was marketed in Belgium under the name Kleinstwagen. In 1954 Paul Kleinschnittger tried to made a coupé with 250cc 2-cylinder ILO engine, but it did not go into production.

HON

1955 Kleinschnittger F-250 coupé.
HANS OTTO NEUBAUER

KLEINSTWAGEN (B) 1952

This was a licence-built version of the KLEINSCHNITTGER first presented at the 1952 Brussels Salon. The company announced it would be making convertible, sports and coupé models, all powered by single-cylinder 175cc Ilo engines.

CR

KLIEMT (D) 1899–1900

C. Kliemt Wagenfabrik, Berlin.
This coachbuilding firm made a few electric vehicles, for passenger use as well as delivery vans, the latter being made up to 1903. The first motorised vehicles for the German Post Office were made by Kliemt.

HON

KLINE KAR (US) 1910–1924

1910–1911 B.C.K. Motor Co., York, Pennsylvania.
1911–1912 Kline Motor Car Corp., York, Pennsylvania.
1912–1923 Kline Motor Car Corp., Richmond, Virginia.
The Kline Kar was named for James A. Kline, a Pennsylvania machinist and bicycle dealer. Kline built his first car in 1900, and took on a LOCOMOBILE franchise that same year. He later had agencies for OLDSMOBILE and FRANKLIN. He was hired by Samuel E. Baily to redesign the YORK car, which would later become the PULLMAN. After leaving Pullman he went into partnership with Baily and a Joseph Carrell in the B.C.K. Motor Co., the name taken from the initials of the principals.

Kline Kars of four and six cylinders were introduced for 1910, the former on a 110in (2792mm) wheelbase and the latter on 123in (3122mm). The cars, which listed for $1575 to $3750, sold fairly well, and also established a respectable reputation in competition. A group of investors from Richmond, Virginia bought the firm, reorganised it as Kline Motor Car Corp. and moved the factory to their home town in 1912. Engines, which were built to Kline's design, were supplied by the Kirkham Machine Co. of Bath, New York. Sales of Kline Kars were reported as around 1000 per year, which was remarkable for a small firm producing quality cars. The prosperity was not to last. The firm went into receivership in 1915, but emerged and produced 1399 vehicles for 1917. Then the postwar recession took its toll, and the Kline Kar, formerly built to James Kline's designs, became an assembled car. From 1920, Continental 7R engines of 3672cc were used, on a 121in (3071mm) wheelbase. Prices ranged from $1865 to $2790. A 3959cc Continental 8R engine was adopted in 1923, but the firm wound up operations early the next year.

KF

KLINK (US) 1907–1910

Klink Motor Car Manufacturing Co., Dansville, New York.
John F. Klink (1869–1940) was a photographer who made a number of assembled cars, using Continental 4-cylinder engines, Brown-Lipe gearboxes and bodies made in Buffalo. Three cars were exhibited at the New York Automobile Show in October 1907. The 1908 range consisted of the original 30hp and a 40hp, but production was very small. Klink closed his factory in

September 1909 after an estimated 20 cars had been made, including possibly a few 35hp sixes. In 1910 he started to assemble two sixes from parts on hand, but could not find any buyers. The incomplete cars were stored behind his photographic studio until 1934 when they were junked. Klink continued to live and work in Dansville for the rest of his life, which ended in November 1940 when he was knocked down by a car.

NG

KLOCK see INTERNATIONAL (ii)

KLONDIKE (US) 1916–1920

Fred Kohlmeyer & Sons, Logansville, Wisconsin.
Powered by a 65hp 6-cylinder Wisconsin engine, the Klondike was made in very small numbers, just seven tourers and one 4-door sedan. Like the Ford Model T they were made only in black, and cost $1650. Kohlmeyer made trucks up to 1929, but again output was small, only 25 vehicles in nine years.

NG

K & M (US) 1905

Kreider Machine Co., Lancaster, Pennsylvania.
Designed by Enos Kreider, the K & M was a fairly typical high-wheeler with 18hp 2-cylinder engine mounted in the centre of the frame, 2-speed gearbox and chain drive. It was a 4-seater, but the rear seats could be removed to make a delivery truck, and there was a power take-off from the engine by which a belt was driven to power farm machinery such as a saw, water pump, corn grinder and even a washing machine. It seems a good idea, and has been widely used in light trucks in recent years, but perhaps the car itself was unsatisfactory, because Kreider's company was in business for less than a year.

NG

KNAP (B/F) 1898–c.1909

1898–1900 Sté de Construction Liégoise d'Automobile, Liège, Belgium.
1904–c.1909 SA des Moteurs Knap, Troyes, Aube, France.
Georgia Knap was a native of Troyes who built a 3-wheeler not unlike the Léon Bollée voiturette, though even in 1896 it had electric ignition while Bollée used the hot-tube system. The Knap had two forward speeds in place of the Bollée's three, and belt drive. It was put into production by a manufacturer of bicycle components in Liège. A run of 50 was planned, and certainly quite a number were built. One had more generous bodywork. The makers even organised races especially for Knap cars. They were marketed in England under the name The Tourist, for 125 guineas (£131.25).

After 1899 the 3-wheelers were too old-fashioned to sell, and Knap returned to Troyes where he made motorcycles and experimented with various engines from one to six cylinders. In 1904 he started to make a light car with single-cylinder engine and shaft drive, which was built until about 1909.

NG

KNEELAND (US) c.1988

Kneeland Motor Cars, Shelton, Washington.
This company picked up the old MANTA Mirage and Montage kits, as well as a Lamborghini Countach replica built on a custom tube frame with V8 engine and Z-F 5-speed transaxle.

HP

KNICKERBOCKER (US) 1901–1903

Ward Leonard Electrical Co., Bronxville, New York.
Ward Leonard announced the 3½hp De Dion-Bouton powered CENTURY Tourist in 1901, following it with a similar-looking car powered by a 5hp engine, also by De Dion-Bouton, called the Knickerbocker. They closely resembled contemporary Renaults, and may have been imported from France. By 1903 Knickerbockers had single- or 2-cylinder De Dion-Bouton engines, or a 24hp 4-cylinder Buchet. Ward Leonard also marketed a larger car under their own name.

NG

KNIGHT (i) (US)) 1901–1902

F.D. Knight & Son, Hudson, Massachusetts.

This was a typical light steam car powered by a 2-cylinder engine, with tiller steering and single-chain drive. They were priced at $800, and only eight were made.

NG

KNIGHT (ii) *see* SILENT KNIGHT

KNIGHT OF THE ROAD (i) (GB) c.1902

This name was given to a light car sold by the Motor Carriage & Chassis Co. It had a 5hp Aster engine and was designed for commercial travellers. Another car sold by the same company was the Esculapius intended, appropriately, for doctors. This had a 5hp Ader engine, and may have been built by Ader.

NG

KNIGHT OF THE ROAD (ii) (GB) 1913–1914

Knight Brothers, Chelmsford, Essex.
Knight of the Road and Knight Junior were two cars made by Knight Brothers for sale by Friswell & Co., the well-known London dealers. They both had 4-cylinder engines, the former a 15.9hp of 2412cc with a 5-seater tourer body and the latter a 1742cc 11.8hp 2-seater. Both had distinctive vee-radiators.

NG

KNIGHT SPECIAL (US) 1917

Watson & Stoeckle, New York, New York.
The Knight Special was a sporty-looking 4-seater tourer with wire wheels, cycle-type wings and a long step plate rather than individual ones as many such cars had. It was powered by a 4-cylinder Moline-Knight sleeve-valve engine, with Entz electro-magnetic transmission and shaft drive to a worm rear axle. The planned price was $4000. One car was completed in January 1917, and the makers said 'plans are going ahead for modest production this year' but this never took place because of America's entry into the war.

NG

KNIGHTT (US) c.1993

Knightt Industries, Covington, Louisiana.
The Knightt GTO was a kit car replica of the Ferrari 308 GTB with a few 288 GTO touches thrown in. It was based on the Pontiac Firebird chassis and running gear and was sold in kit and assembled form.

HP

KNOLLNER (D) 1924

Karl Knollner Automobilefabrik, Ravensbrück bei Furstenberg.
This company offered two small cars, the Carolette 3-wheeler with 2PS Helios engine, and the Carolus 4-wheeler with 5/12PS engine, also by Helios. Production lasted less than a year.

HON

KNOX (US) 1900–1914

Knox Automobile Co., Springfield, Massachusetts.
The Knox was one of the more successful air-cooled cars made in America, although its lifespan was much shorter than that of the Franklin. Henry A. Knox (1875–1957) had his first automotive experience with the Overman Wheel Co., where he built three experimental cars in 1898. His employer A.H. Overman favoured the steam car, while Knox was all for internal combustion, so he left and, in partnership with his former employer Elihu H. Cutler, set up the Knox Automobile Co. in 1900. His first product was a light 3-wheeler powered by a 1562cc 5hp horizontal single-cylinder engine driving the rear axle by a single chain. With a wheelbase of only 60in (1523mm) and a turning circle of 108in (2741mm), the makers did not bother to fit a reverse gear. The air-cooling was unusual in that in place of the usual fins to catch the cooling air, Knox used steel rods 7/8in in diameter and 2in long which were screwed into the cylinder. He claimed that these gave four and a half times the cooling surface provided by fins. The rods sticking out from the cylinder led to the car's nickname 'Old Porcupine'. To keep the engine cool when the car was stationary or running slowly in towns, Knox used a fan driven off the crankshaft.

In 1900 the company made only 15 3-wheelers, but the next year output rose to 100, and in 1902 to 250. By then a delivery van was available on the 3-wheeler,

1900 Knox 3-wheeler.
NATIONAL MOTOR MUSEUM

1904 Knox 16/18hp surrey.
NATIONAL MOTOR MUSEUM

1910 Knox Model R 40hp double raceabout.
NICK BALDWIN

and a 4-wheeled 2-seater was made with the same 5hp engine. In 1903 this could be had with a folding front seat for a third passenger, and 1904 saw the first 2-cylinder Knox engine, of 16/18hp. Only 4-wheelers were made from 1903 onwards, and these grew in size, to a 35/40hp in 1906 selling for $4000 or $5000 according to body.

1899 Koch 6hp phaeton.
NATIONAL MOTOR MUSEUM

1922 Koco 4/16PS 2-seater.
HANS OTTO NEUBAUER

Harry Knox left his company in 1904 because of a disagreement with Cutler over policy, and set up a rival concern in the same town, which he called the Knox Motor Truck Co. He later changed the name to the Atlas Motor Truck Co., which remained in business up to 1913.

Apart from their air-cooling, Knox followed the usual progress of contemporary American cars. The engine was moved to the front under a bonnet in 1905, and shaft drive replaced chains two years later. In 1908 came the first water-cooled Knox, the 30hp 4-cylinder Model L. This used the same engine design as the air-cooled Model H, with separately-cast cylinders each with its own water jacket. The 1908 range consisted of the Models H and L, and a larger air-cooled car, the 40hp Model G. The advantage of offering air-cooled cars which were otherwise identical to the water-cooled ones was that if a customer was dissatisfied with his choice he could go back to the factory to have a new engine fitted, at a much lower cost than if he were to buy a new car. The water-cooled Model L sold for exactly $100 more than the air-cooled H, right across the range of seven body styles.

The Knox directors soon bowed to the popular preference for water-cooling. Out of four 1909 models, only the H was still air-cooled, and from 1910 onwards all Knoxes were water-cooled. They were now conventional large, expensive cars, prices running from $3200 for a 40hp 4-cylinder runabout to $6400 for a 60hp 6-cylinder limousine. Cylinder dimensions of the fours and sixes were similar, which enabled common pistons and connecting rods to be used, while the same machinery could be used for casting the pairs of cylinders. Dimensions were either oversquare (127 × 120.65mm) or undersquare (127 × 139.7mm), giving the 4-cylinder Model R capacities of 6110 or 7075cc, and the 6-cylinder Model S capacities of 9165 or 10,612cc. The latter was one of the largest engines of any American passenger car of the time, though not up to the 13½-litre Pierce-Arrow 66.

The big Knoxes were undoubtedly very well made, but their fame was largely local, and they were competing with such formidable, and better-known, cars as the Locomobile, Peerless and Pierce-Arrow. Their peak year was 1910, with 1412 cars sold, but by 1912 business was so bad that a receiver was called in, and

in February 1913 the Knox Automobile Co. was declared bankrupt. A much reduced range of cars was announced for 1914, but only 383 were made. However, the company had an alternative in the form of the 3-wheeled tractors designed by Charles Hay Martin, which they had been making since 1909. After reorganisation as Knox Motors Corp., the cars were dropped, but the tractors were continued, with 4-wheelers taking over in 1915. They were made in large numbers for the American and French armies, and a few for the British during the war, production continuing until 1924.
NG

Further Reading
'Knox – "The Perfect Car"', John J. Keebler III,
Automobile Quarterly, Vol. 20, No.2.

KNUDSEN (US) c.1992
Knudsen Automotive, Inc., Omaha, Nebraska.
Knudsen made two kit cars based on the Chevrolet Camaro and Pontiac Firebird. The Trojan kit added a lengthened, pointed nose and wider wheel flares to the basic shape. The Carralo also had widened wheel flares and was more rounded than the angular Trojan. Both were offered in kit and turn-key form. Knudsen also made restyling kits for GMC trucks and Suburbans. These kits were also sold by MARPLE.
HP

KOBOLD (D) 1920
Kobold Kleinauto GmbH, Berlin-Charlottenburg.
This was a small car in production for only a few months. Technical details are not known.
HON

KOBUSCH (US) 1906
Kobusch Automobile Co., St Louis, Missouri.
This company was really the automobile department of the St Louis Car Co., who were mainly builders of railway carriages. They had launched the ST LOUIS light runabout in 1905 but it had not been a success, so they moved upmarket by making three 4-cylinder cars closely based on the French MORS, of 20, 35 and 50hp. They were not successful, and later in 1906 St Louis took out a licence to manufacture a genuine Mors, this being sold as the American Mors.
NG

KOCH (F) 1898–1901
Sté des Automobiles Koch, Neuilly, Seine.
The Koch was based on the first SAURER car, and used the same 3140cc 6hp horizontal opposed-piston single-cylinder engine, mounted at the rear and driving the rear axle by chains. It ran on heavy oil fuel. Most were sold outside Europe, to the British and Dutch East Indies, Persia, Turkey, and Egypt. The first car in Madagascar was a Koch, one of six delivered to the island in 1900. Total Koch production was about 25 cars.
NG

KOCO (D) 1921–1926
1921–1922 Kleinauto- und Motorenwerke Koch & Co., Erfurt.
1922–1926 Koco-Werke GmbH, Erfurter Kleinauto- und Motorenbau, Erfurt.
The Koco lasted longer than many of the ephemeral German small cars, thanks to superior reliability. The first was a 3-seater powered by a 4/16PS or 5/25PS flat-twin engine, available with air- or water-cooling. In 1925 came a 4-seater with 1540cc 6/30PS 4-cylinder engine.
HON

KOEB-THOMSON (US) 1910
Koeb-Thomson Motor Co., Leipsig, Ohio.
Emil Koeb and Ralph M. Thomson had built an experimental car with 2-stroke engine and chain drive in 1902, and followed it with a 40hp racing car. In 1910 their company was set up, backed by the American Foundry Co. Their car was a 5-seater tourer powered by their 4-cylinder 2-stroke engine, and it had their patent platform rear suspension. It is unlikely that many were made.
NG

1911 Koechlin 3-litre racing car.

KOECHLIN (F) 1911–1914

S. Gerster & Cie, Courbevoie, Seine.

The Koechlin name first appeared on a racing car with 2-stroke engine which was entered for the 1911 Coupe des Voiturettes, though it did not start. For 1912 and 1913 two production cars were listed, a 2995cc four and a 3000cc six, with monobloc engines, 4-speed gearboxes and three wheelbases.

NG

KOEHLER (US) 1910–1912

H.J. Koehler Co., Bloomfield, New Jersey.

The H.J. Koehler Sporting Goods Co. of New York had been selling cars since 1898, and in 1910 they decided to manufacture them as well. The Koehler 40 was a conventional 4.6-litre 4-cylinder 5-seater tourer selling for $1650. They also made trucks, and these were evidently more profitable for they were continued until 1923, while the cars lasted barely three seasons.

NG

KOENIGSEGG (S) 1997 to date

Koenigsegg Automobile AB.

Created by Christian Koenigsegg and Michael Bergfelt, the Koenigsegg CC was a fearsome supercar. The prototype used a 4-litre Audi V8 engine but the production version was powered by a detuned Formula 1 engine. With 500bhp available from the Motori Moderni flat-12 3.8-litre engine, a top speed of 220mph (354km/h) and a 0–60mph (97km/h) time of 3.1 seconds was claimed. Technically it featured a 7-speed gearbox, double wishbone suspension all round and race-derived carbon-fibre ventilated disc brakes. The dramatic bodywork, with its detachable roof, was made of carbon-Kevlar honeycomb and incorporated competition-derived twin Venturis for aerodynamic performance.

CR

KOHL (US) 1900–1902

1900–1902 Kohl & Gates Motor Co., Cleveland, Ohio.
1902 Kohl Automobile Co., Whitney Point, New York.

Edward Kohl built at least 12 cars in Cleveland, with 6hp single-cylinder engines and 2-speed gearboxes. He announced a new car after his move to New York State, but no production took place.

NG

KOHOUT (A) 1905–1906

První moravska tovarna motorovych kol a vozu, Petr Kohout a spol., Brno.

At the 1905 Prague International automobile, motorcycle and cycle exhibition, motorcycle producer Petr Kohout introduced his two voiturettes: one with air-cooled 4bhp engine for one passenger, and a 2-seater with water-cooled 8bhp engine, with Bosch ignition and belt drive. Both were designed for practical purposes only (for physicians, postmasters, etc.) and were capable of about 16mph (26km/h). In 1906 at the Kohout's works 65 workers were employed and some cars were exported also to Russia.

MSH

KOLLER (RA) 1960

Assembled in Argentina, the Koller used a 3-cylinder 2-stroke Wartburg engine and had a fibreglass saloon body with a wrap-around windscreen.

NG

KOLOWRAT (CS) c.1920

Count Alexander Kolowrat (see LAURIN-KLEMENT) produced a light car with a flat-twin 1100cc engine, plate clutch, three forward speeds, shaft drive, and no differential.

KOMET (i) *see* STERLING (i)

KOMET (ii) (D) 1922–1924

Komet Autofabrik Buchmann & Co., Leisnig.

This was a small car powered by a 4/14PS 4-cylinder Steudel engine. From 1924 to 1925 it was made by another company under the name KENTER.

HON

KOMNICK (D) 1907–1927

1907–1922 F. Komnick Autofabrik, Elbing.
1922–1927 Automobilfabrik Komnick AG, Elbing.

The Elbinger Maschinenfabrik was already well established when its founder Franz Komnick extended their activities to car production in 1907. The first cars had 4-cylinder T-head engines of 1520cc (K10), 3052cc (K20) and 5536cc (K30), 3- or 4-speed gearboxes, shaft drive and dashboard radiators. Later models had inlet-over-exhaust valve engines. Komnick's company had extensive

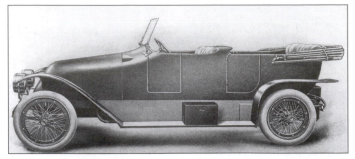

1913 Komnick 17/50PS tourer.
HANS OTTO NEUBAUER

1925 Komnick Typ C2 8/40PS saloon.
HANS OTTO NEUBAUER

1903 Korte 12/14hp tonneau.
NATIONAL MOTOR MUSEUM

connections in Eastern Europe, especially Russia, and the bulk of car production was exported, or sold in the eastern part of Germany. The factory was the most easterly car plant in Germany. Elbing is now in Poland, and has been renamed Elblag.

After World War I Komnick concentrated on a single model, the 2064cc 8/30PS C2. The 4-cylinder engine had a shaft-driven ohc. The prewar dashboard radiator was replaced by a front-mounted vee-radiator. Open tourers and saloons were made. In 1925 power was increased to 8/40PS and front-wheel brakes were provided. Two years later Komnick abandoned passenger cars to concentrate on commercial vehicles and motor ploughs which had become an important part of their business. In 1930 they were taken over by Büssing.

HON

KONDOR (D) 1900–1902
Kondor Fahrradwerke AG, vorm. Liepe & Breest, Brandenberg.
This bicycle maker built a small number of light cars powered by 5hp single-cylinder engines.

HON

KONINGS (NL) 1901–1906
P. Konings' Machinefabrich, Swalmen, Limberg.
In 1901 Konings started with the production of six cars designed by Ferdinand L.A.H. Anderheggen of Amsterdam. They were sold until 1906.

NG

KOOBLE KAR (US) 1997 to date
Kooble Kar by Skunkwerkes, Albuquerque, New Mexico.
The Kooble Kar was a replica of the 1940 Porsche-designed Kubelwagen military vehicle. Like the original, it was based on VW running gear but, with a steel body and subframe to reinforce the chassis, it was very rigid. Options included jerrycans, a shovel, gun mounts, searchlight, soft-top, side curtains, and a camouflage paint job. They were sold in kit and assembled form.

HP

KOPPEL (B) 1901
Compagnie Belge de Vélocipèdes, Liège.
This bicycle maker built a small number of 4-seater rear-entrance tonneaus powered by a rear-mounted vertical single-cylinder engine geared to the rear axle. The engine could be started from the seat by a lever. Access to the engine was by lifting the bodywork. Although made for only a year, the Koppel was exported to Germany and England.

NG

KOPPIN see FENTON

KORN ET LATIL (F) 1901–1902
A. Korn et Latil, Paris.
A native of Marseilles, Latil designed an *avant train* attachment which could be fitted to any horse-drawn vehicle. It had a vertical single-cylinder Aster engine of 3½ or 5hp mounted ahead of the axle and driving, via a friction clutch, a series of spur gears which meshed with pinions on the axle giving three forward speeds. Pedal-operated brakes on all four wheels were provided, a very early example of 4-wheel braking. The standard body, which could be provided with the power unit, was a 3-seater voiturette, one passenger facing the others in *vis-à-vis* style. Few of these voiturettes were made, but Latil became famous as a maker of commercial vehicles, starting in 1903.

NG

KORSER (F) 1998 to date
Korser Sarl, Malestroit.
Two young Breton engineers conceived the KS420 as a lightweight, inexpensive sports car. It used a centrally-mounted 132bhp Ford 2-litre engine and featured wedge-shaped open bodywork offered in two guises: a stark Spider and a more comfortable Berlinette.

CR

KORTE (GB) 1903–c.1905
Rice & Co. (Leeds) Ltd, Leeds, Yorkshire.
As Korte, Atkinson & Co., this firm had made motor tricycles and quadricycles of De Dion-Bouton type since 1900, and in 1903 a new company launched the Korte car. It had a 12/14hp 2-cylinder engine mounted transversely at the front of the car, with a 4-speed gearbox and double-chain drive. 4- or 6-seater tonneau bodies could be provided. A distinguishing feature was a large acetylene headlamp which projected way ahead of the front of the car.

NG

KÖRTING (D) 1922–1924
Wilhelm Körting Automobilwerk, Wülfrath.
Körting was originally a maker of engines, and as such came into conflict with N.A. Otto over patents for the 4-stroke engine. In the 1920s a branch of the company went into car production with a light car. Curiously, these did not use Körting engines but Selve power units in 6/20 and 8/32PS versions.

HON

KOUGAR (GB) 1977 to date

1977–1979 Kougar Cars Ltd (Starcourt Wells Ltd), Crowborough, Sussex.
1979–1982 Kougar Cars Ltd, Mark Cross, East Sussex.
1982–1990 Kougar Cars Ltd, Uckfield, East Sussex.
1990–1994 Kougar Cars 1990 Ltd, Trent, Sherborne, Dorset.
1994 to date Kougar Cars, Warwick, Warwickshire.

Not a replica, but an impressive stand-alone design, the Kougar Sports embodied elements of Frazer Nash in its stark doorless roadster design. Unusually for this type of car, it used Jaguar S-Type components in a space frame chassis, and could be supplied as an up-market conversion or in kit form. The roll-over bar, windscreen and weather gear were all optional. In time, a Rover V8 power option became available. A second, equally impressive model was the Monza, first seen in 1980. Inspired vaguely by 1950s Ferraris, it incongruously used Ford Cortina mechanicals, but subsequent models had Rover V8, Jaguar or American V8 engines. Most Kougars were exported to the USA.

CR

KOVER see LIVRY

KOVER CAPILLA (E) 1953

Talleres José Capilla Hurtado, Valencia.

Alejandro Kover and Jose Capilla Hurtado presented in 1953 three different minicars; a 4-wheeler with normal track, another with the rear wheels close together, and a motorcycle with front box. These vehicles were not related to Kover of France.

VCM

KRAL (A) 1921–1923

Felix Kral, Vienna.

This car used a 750cc 2-cylinder 2-stroke engine, with friction transmission. Kral appeared frequently in national sporting events, but this did not help him to sell many cars.

HON

KRASTIN (US) 1902–1904

Krastin Automobile Manufacturing Co., Cleveland, Ohio.

Designed by Latvian-born August Krastin, this car was conventional enough in its 10hp 2-cylinder engine and single-chain drive, but its steering column was unusually versatile. Instead of turning the wheel, the driver tilted the column to left or right for steering purposes. A turn of the wheel to the right disengaged the clutch, while further turns engaged low, and then high, gear. Turning it to the left engaged reverse. The patent carburettor was said to be smokeless and the silencer noiseless. The standard body was a 2-seater, but a tonneau for an additional two or four passengers could be provided, all for $2500. It is thought that not more than four Krastins were built before a fire destroyed the factory, which was uninsured. One survives today.

NG

K.R.C. (GB) 1922–1924

White, Holmes & Co. Ltd, Hammersmith, London.

Named after its designers, Kingston, Richardson and Crutchley, this was a light car powered originally by a 10hp V-twin Blackburne engine, in side-valve or ohv forms, with a non-differential Wrigley rear axle. For 1923 4-cylinder engines were adopted, either a 1246cc 8.9hp Coventry Climax in the touring model, or a 1092cc 7.5hp Janvier in the sports. These cars had Meadows 4-speed gearboxes. The predecessor company to White, Holmes was the National Cab Co. which had run a fleet of Unic cabs in London before the war, and as the cars were not selling very well they decided to offer the Coventry Climax engined chassis with a 2-passenger cab body. Announced in May 1925 they never ran in London as the 2-seater cab was not licensed for the capital, but a few K.R.C. taxis were operated in Harrogate.

NG

KREIBICK (CS) 1949

This was an experimental 3-wheeler with a 2-cylinder air-cooled engine and single rear wheel, with all-enveloping 2-seater body.

NG

1922 Körting 6/25PS tourer.
M.J.WORTHINGTON-WILLIAMS

c.1990 Kougar sports car.
NICK BALDWIN

1922 K.R.C. sports car at Brooklands.
NICK BALDWIN

KRIÉGER (F) 1897–1908

1897–1900 Sté des Voitures Électriques (Système Kriéger),
Courbevoie, Seine.
1900–1907 Compagnie Parisienne des Voitures Électriques (procédés Kriéger),
Courbevoie, Seine.
1907–1908 Compagnie Parisienne des Voitures Électriques, Colombes, Seine.

The Kriéger was the best-known and most widespread French electric car, being used for taxi work as well as a private car. Louis Antoine Kriéger (1868–1951) was an electrical engineer who formed his company in 1897, backed by a wealthy Cuban-born friend, Severiano de Heredia. His first car was an *avant train* attachment for horse-drawn vehicles, with a separate electric motor in each of the two wheels. This gave not only power steering but also 4-wheel braking, since there were already brakes on the rear wheels, albeit pretty crude ones, acting directly on the solid tyres. The cab won the prize for 4-seaters in the 1897 Paris Motor Cab Trials. By 1898 Kriéger was making complete vehicles and

c.1902 Kriéger electric coupé.
NATIONAL MOTOR MUSEUM

1907 Kriéger 12/14hp petrol-electric landaulet.
NATIONAL MOTOR MUSEUM

c.1914 Krit Model L tourer.
NICK BALDWIN

payload must have been taken up with batteries. The typical Kriéger was a town car, coupé or landaulet, but there was a voiturette called the Electrolette in 1902. The 2-seater body was light, and 60 per cent of the overall weight was accounted for by the batteries. By 1904 some Kriéger had dummy bonnets, but were still driven by hub-mounted motors.

Kriéger began experiments with petrol-electric drive as early as 1902, when he made a light car powered by a 4hp De Dion-Bouton engine. This actually used alcohol fuel. In 1903 he used a 24hp Richard Brasier engine to generate power for an electric motor which drove each rear wheel by spur gear. These went on sale, in England as well as in France, but cannot have been very successful as in 1906 the factory was still concentrating almost entirely on electrics. Kriéger moved to smaller premises at Colombes in 1907, and his last cars were taxicabs in which a 15hp 4-cylinder Brasier engine generated power for electric motors in the front wheels. These were made up to 1908, after which Kriéger devoted himself to general electrical engineering work. His name cropped up again during World War II in association with another famous name among electric vehicles, MILDE. The Milde-Kriégers were battery electric conversions of La Licorne cars and Chenard-Walcker light vans.

NG

KRIM-GHIA (US) c.1966
Krim Car Import Co., Detroit, Michigan.
Krim imported Ghia-bodied conversions for the Fiat 1500 and Plymouth Barracuda. The 1500 coupé was an attractive shape with a fastback top. The Ghia 450S was a Plymouth Baracuda with a sleek roadster body. Price for the 450S was to have been $7000 to $8000 in 1966. Few of either were sold.

HP

KRIT (US) 1910–1915
Krit Motor Car Co., Detroit, Michigan.
Named after its designer Kenneth Crittenden, the Krit company was formed in 1909, but its first cars were marketed as 1910 models. Known as the K.R.I.T. in its early years, the Krit was a conventional 4-cylinder car rated at 22.5hp, made originally as a runabout, roadster and surrey for 2, 3 and 4 passengers respectively. An underslung runabout joined the range for 1911, being considerably more expensive at $1200 than other models, which were priced at $800–850. The Krit used the same 4-cylinder engine throughout its lifetime, though in 1913 there was a short-lived 36hp six which was sold under the name M.C.C. In 1911 they moved from their first factory, which had been the home of the BLOMSTROM to one just vacated by the makers of the OWEN (ii).

Krit sales were severely damaged by the outbreak of war in Europe as they had relied heavily on the export market. They were bankrupt in January 1915; a rescue plan failed and the assets were sold off. A few cars were assembled from parts on hand in the spring. The Krit used a swastika as a badge 'to assure the favour of auspicious gods', long before it had acquired Nazi connotations.

NG

KRIZIK (A) 1895–1908
Fr. Krizik, elektrotechnicky závod, Praha-Karlin.
Frantisek Krizik (1847–1941), famous Czech electrical inventor, built his first electric vehicle (according to his memoirs) in 1895, with a 3.7kW motor placed at the rear axle, and with a light, open 2-seater body. It is more probable that this car was constructed by the Swiss Jakob Fischer-Hinnen (1900–1902 director at Krizik's works) in Paris in 1899 and named Helvetia. In 1901 the second car, with a 4-seater phaeton body and a motor placed under the floor between axles, was built. Rear wheels were driven by chains. The third electromobile had two 2.2kW motors, an elegant 4-seater landaulet body and wheels with tyres. In 1908 Krizik rebuilt the Laurin & Klement 24/28hp type E as a petrol-electric car on which all commands were operated by a simple lever or combined controller.

MSH

KROBOTH (i) (CS) 1931–1932
Gustav Kroboth, stavba motoru a vozidel 'Favorit', Sternberk.
Gustav Kroboth (1903–1985) belonged among those constructors who hoped to be successful with simple 2-seater cars. His 'Favorit' had a single-cylinder 2-stroke 567cc water-cooled 10bhp engine mounted in front of the central tube

soon sold foreign licences, to the British Electromobile Co., who sold Kriéger with English bodies under the name Powerful, to NAMAG (Lloyd) in Germany and S.T.A.E. in Italy, who made some Kriéger-like electrics in 1905.

Design changed little until around 1905. Kriégers retained front-wheel drive by a Postel-Vinay motor in each wheel. They drove the wheel through a small pinion engaging the large fixed gear on the hub. Each had a power of 3kW. The controller gave six forward speeds and two coasting gears in which the motors were used as generators to recharge the batteries. The range was about 45 miles to a charge, but in 1901 a Kriéger covered 192 miles on a charge. Most of the

K-R-I-T

The K-R-I-T is sold at a price that will enable any man with a moderate income to own one. It is a light, elegantly-finished, perfectly reliable runabout; without doubt the greatest value ever offered in Australia in a car of this type. The K-R-I-T 4-cylinder, 22½ A.L.A.M. horse-power Runabout, seating two persons, complete with adjustable hood, folding wind screen, 2 side lamps, tail lamp, number board, pump, tool kit, jack, and tyre repair outfit complete, ready for the road—Price, £265.

Come in early and examine a K-R-I-T. We will give you a practical demonstration of its goodness.

Body Building and Car Repair Department.

We have special facilities and competent tradesmen for the building of car bodies and the repairing of cars. These enable us to guarantee prompt, satisfactory work at prices which are the lowest possible on a quality basis.

THE MEA High-tension MAGNETO.

The MEA has bell-shaped magnets placed horizontally instead of the customary horse-shoe type, which are mounted vertically. This innovation makes practical the simultaneous advance and retard of magnets and timer, so that the spark is always generated in the strongest part of the field. A range of timing may be obtained many times that possible with a stationary field such as used in the horse-shoe type. The MEA High-tension Magneto is most efficient in shape and execution, excellent in principle and construction, admittedly unrivalled in results and reliability.

We are Sole Agents for N.S.W.

GARRATTS Ltd.

173-5 ELIZABETH ST., 148-50 CASTLEREAGH ST., SYDNEY.

ALICK McNEIL, General Manager.

1954 Kroboth (ii) 250cc microcar.
AUTOMUSEUM, STORY

1899 Kühlstein-Vollmer avant train cab.
HANS OTTO NEUBAUER

frame (diameter 127mm) with independent leaf spring suspension all round, and rear-wheel band brakes. The project was financed by the thread factory owner K. Grohmann, and about 150 cars with roadster body (priced 14,950 Kc) or as a hard-top (19,000 Kc) were sold.

Kroboth moved to Bavaria (Germany) after 1945 where in 1954–1955 his three-wheeled, all-weather scooters were produced.
MSH

KROBOTH (ii) (D) 1954–1955
Fahrzeug- und Maschinenbau Gustav Kroboth, Seestall über Landsberg.
Gustav Kroboth's second period of car-making came in the 1950s when he introduced a small 3-wheeler powered by a mid-mounted 197cc single-cylinder Ilo engine driving the single rear wheel. Later a 4-wheeler with 174cc Sachs engine was made. Total output from Kroboth's little factory was about 55 cars.
HON

KRONOS (A) 1905–1907
Ludwig Schick, Bruck.
The Kronos was made in three models, an 8PS single-cylinder, 12/16PS twin and 15/20PS four. All had friction transmission using two vertical discs and one horizontal, giving a very smooth operation.
HON

KRUEGER (i) (US) c.1947
Krueger, Beverley Hills, California.
The Krueger was one of the most improbable combinations of running gear ever. A Marmon V16 engine with 225hp was installed into a shortened Duesenberg chassis and topped with a low, rakish roadster body with a 1930s look. Price for the Krueger Speedster was to have been $15,000. Only one is thought to have been built.
HP

KRUEGER (ii) see ECLIPSE (iv)

KRUGER see ELEKTRA

KRUPKAR see MORRISON (ii)

KRUSE (D) 1899–1901
Gebr. Kruse, Hamburg.
This company was a maker of horse-drawn carriages who decided to enter the car market with vehicles powered by petrol, steam or electricity. They were unique among German firms in offering all three motive powers, but hardly any cars were made. They quickly took up building bodies for other car makers, a business which lasted until the 1930s.
HON

KÜBELWAGEN (GB) 1981–1982
Steve Smith, Robertsbridge, Sussex.
This Beetle-based replica of a VW Kübelwagen was offered in kit form and, unusually, had an all-steel body.
CR

KUDOS (GB) 1992–1995
Square One Developments, Swadlincote, Derbyshire.
PELLAND's Sports coupé came under new ownership in 1992 and was renamed Kudos. The package was redesigned around Alfasud/Alfa 33 parts, including a centrally-mounted engine. A convertible model supplemented the coupé but there were only a handful of sales.
CR

KÜHLSTEIN (D) 1898–1902
Kühlstein Wagenbau, Berlin-Charlottenberg.
Kühlstein were well-known horse-drawn carriage makers who took up motor vehicles in 1898. At first they were electric *avant trains*, soon joined by petrol-powered ones. These were designed by Josef Vollmer, and were generally called Kühlstein-Vollmers in his honour. In 1900 the Automobile Fore Carriage Co. was formed in New York to exploit Kühlstein-Vollmer patents in the United States, but only two demonstrators were built. Kühlstein also made JEANTAUD cabs under licence, and in 1900 they made a small 2-seater petrol car with 6hp engine. In 1902 Kühlstein car production was taken over by the electric concern AEG as their way into car manufacture. Josef Vollmer joined AEG at the same time. Kühlstein continued as a coachbuilder for other makes up to 1926.
HON

KÜHN (D) 1927–1929
Otto Kühn, Halle/Saale.
Kühn was a body builder who worked particularly for Opel. In 1927 he announced a car under his own name, using a 1018cc 4/16PS Opel engine in a lengthened wheelbase with Opel gearbox and rear axle, and Kühn-built body. A later model had the 1916cc 6-cylinder 8/40PS Opel engine. Most bodies were saloons or landaulets, and were used as taxicabs as well as for private use.
HON

KUNZ (US) 1902–1905
1902–1903; 1904–1905 J.L. Kunz Machinery Co., Milwaukee, Wisconsin.
1903–1904 Speedwell Automobile Co., Milwaukee, Wisconsin.
John Kunz built his first car in his home town of Appleton, Wisconsin, in 1897, and formed his company in Milwaukee in late 1901. His first production car was a 2-seater runabout powered by a 4½hp single-cylinder engine and 3-speed transmission by what was called the 'sliding wedge system'. During 1902 he changed the name of his company and car to Speedwell. The Speedwell for 1903 was identical to the 1902 Kunz apart from a more powerful engine of 8hp, and epicyclic transmission. Selling for $1000 this was made through the 1904 season as well, then in November he changed company and car name back to Kunz. The 1905 Kunz had the same engine in a slightly longer wheelbase, with a small bonnet in front, though the engine remained under the seat. Kunz said that he had made only 12 cars in 1904, but planned to make 100 in 1905. This figure was probably never reached, and the Kunz car was no more by the end of

1949 Kurtis (i) sports car.
NATIONAL MOTOR MUSEUM

1905. He continued his machinery company, and later made resilient sheet steel wheels.

NG

KUROGANE (J) 1935–1962

1935–1959 Nippon Nainenki Seiko Co. Ltd, Tokyo.
1959–1962 Toyku Kurogane Kogyo Co. Ltd, Toyko.
This company began life as New Era in 1928 making commercial-bodied 3-wheelers of the typical Japanese fashion – a motorcycle-type front end and rear box. The name changed in 1937 to Kurogane, two years after the company had begun making a small 1.3-litre 4x4 vehicle that was mainly used as a military scout car. About 4800 were made up until 1940. Postwar production centred mostly around 3-wheeled trucks but, after the company purchased OHTA in 1957, it launched a range of 4-wheelers. Among these was a model called the Baby, which had fold-down canvas sides and top, and was intended for use as a camping car. Its engine was a 356cc 2-cylinder 4-stroke air-cooled unit sited in the rear and developing 18bhp.

CR

KURTIS (i) (US) 1932–1963

Kurtis-Kraft Inc., Los Angeles, California.
Kurtis Sports Car Corp., Los Angeles, California.
Although Frank Kurtis was primarily known for his exceptional Indianapolis roadsters and Championship cars, he also built a number of sports cars for street or racing. Before he started building racing cars in 1932, he had rebodied several old Fords and Buicks with 'street roadster' coachwork and sold them to make extra money. In the 1930s and 1940s he made a number of special bodied cars for wealthy customers. He also built the prototype for the DAVIS 3-wheeler. In the late 1940s Kurtis built 38 sports cars with sleek, rounded lines and Ford 'flathead' V8s. Earl 'Madman' Muntz bought the project from Kurtis, stretched it out to 4 seats, substituted Lincoln or Cadillac V8s and renamed it the MUNTZ Jet. In 1952 Kurtis decided to cash in on the popularity of kit cars by selling the 500KK, a sports car version of his K500 Indy car chassis. It had torsion-bar suspension and live axles at both ends and could be ordered in a variety of lengths to fit various kit bodies. He then made an assembled version called the 500S with a slender aluminium and fibreglass body mounting cycle mudguards and the buyers' choice of engines. Approximately 35 to 40 were built.

1937 Kurogane Type 95 4x4 2-seater.
NATIONAL MOTOR MUSEUM

The next Kurtis street car was the 500M of 1955. Using the same basic Kurtis chassis, it had a full-width fibreglass body with a wide grill and side indentations. Various engines were fitted. In order to finance production, Kurtis sold his company to a group of businessmen who drove it into bankruptcy after about 25 cars had been built. Kurtis went back to his first love, racing cars, and no more Kurtis street cars were built.

HP

Further Reading
'The reign of Frank Kurtis – Sometimes it's difficult being a king',
Allan Girdler, *Automobile Quarterly*, Vol. 11, No. 4.

KURTIS (ii) (US) c.1992 to date

Frank Kurtis Co., Bakersfield, California.
When Frank Kurtis died in 1987 his son Arlen took over the business. In addition to building racing boats and other projects, Arlen made a run of replica chassis for the 1952 Kurtis 500S racing car. Jon Ward Racing in California built some of the first completed replicas, which finished 1-2 in the 1991 La Carrera

1924 Kurtz Automatic sedan.
KEITH MARVIN

1984 K.V.A. Mk I Replica Ford GT40.
NATIONAL MOTOR MUSEUM

1903 Kyma 3-wheeler.
NATIONAL MOTOR MUSEUM

Panamericana open-road race. Ward updated the cars with modern running gear and intended to sell them for street or track use. Few were sold and he put the project up for sale. Arlen Kurtis continued to build and sell street versions of these cars with Chevrolet V8 engines for around $85,000.

HP

KURTZ AUTOMATIC (US) 1920–1925

Kurtz Motor Car Co., Cleveland, Ohio.

The Kurtz Automatic was built by Cyrus B. Kurtz who had invented a preselector gearshift he was convinced would be a major asset in automobile development. If it had the advantages claimed for it, the Kurtz Automatic never achieved the production Cyrus Kurtz had predicted. The car was attractively designed, powered by a Herschell-Spillman 11000 engine developing 57bhp at 2100rpm, and rode on a wheelbase of 122in (3096mm). Closed and open models

were offered in the $2000 to $2750 range and although the car was favourably received by the automotive press, it failed to catch on to any degree. For 1923, a more powerful Herschell-Spillman engine – the 90 – was substituted increasing the power to 75bhp at 2200rpm. During 1924, the 1925 line of cars was promoted, the projected new model using a Lycoming 8-cylinder engine, 4-wheel brakes and an increased wheelbase of 139in (3528mm). The car probably did not go any further than the pilot models which were completed and exhibited. Production was about 165 to 170 cars per year before Kurtz ended production of the car. The pre-selector gearshift was available optionally, however, on both Apperson and Haynes cars. In his book, *Golden Wheels*, covering cars built in Cleveland and its immediate vicinity, Richard Wager reported that 48 Kurtz Automatic cars were still registered within Cleveland in 1929.

KM

KUSTOM KRAFT (USA) c.1997 to date

Kustom Kraft Kit Kars, Payallup, Washington.

This kit car company built four models, all replicas of European cars. The Fiero-based CT 2000 was a Lamborghini Countach clone, while the Testosterone replicated the Ferrari Testarossa. The Kustom Kraft Classic was a Ferrari Daytona replica on a Corvette chassis, while the VW-based 959 Speedster resembled a cross between a 1958 Porsche Speedster and a Porsche 959. The bodies were available in an assortment of fibreglass types and composites, and could be ordered as kits or in fully assembled form.

HP

KUSTOM MOTORCARS (US) c.1991

Kustom Motorcars, Hereford, Texas.

This very high-end Lamborghini Countach replica had a sophisticated space frame with a new Chevrolet Corvette V8 engine and a Porsche transaxle. The suspension was Corvette-based with adjustable shock absorbers and disc brakes. The KMC 5000Gt was sold in kit and assembled form.

HP

K.V.A. (GB) 1982–1992

K.V.A. Cars Ltd, Tycoch, Swansea, Glamorgan.

Ken Atwell can be attributed as starting the GT40 replica craze, and he was perfectly placed to do so: employed by Ford, he was allowed to take a mould off a genuine Mk III GT40 kept at Swansea. Kit production followed using a non-original type tubular steel space frame chassis for Ford Cortina Mk III/IV suspension and steering, a VW gearbox and engines ranging from Ford CVH to Rover V8. The long-nose Mk III shell was never as popular as the racing-style Mk I, launched in 1984. K.V.A.'s kits were notoriously challenging to build, and other firms used K.V.A. shells to much better effect, notably D.J. and G.T.D. K.V.A. also tried offering various other replicas, including Jaguar XKSS, D-Type, Ferrari Daytona, and Lamborghini Countach 5000S.

CR

K.V.S. (F) 1976–c.1984

SA K.V.S., Lyon-Chassieu.

Made by the successor to the New-Map motorcycle firm that had also made 3-wheeled commercial vehicles and the ROLUX, the K.V.S. featured all-independent suspension by coils, automatic transmission, belt-drive to the rear wheels and mechanical brakes. Two unusual factors were that K.V.S. made its own 49cc and 125cc engines, and that the bodywork (in saloon, estate and convertible forms) was in metal rather than the industry norm of plastic. The 50cc version was called Gad'Jet and the 125cc was called the Mini 125. As many as 150 per year were produced.

CR

KYMA (GB) 1903–1905

New Kyma Motor Car Co. Ltd, Nunhead, London.

The first Kyma was a light 3-wheeler with single front wheel and a 2¾ or 4hp single-cylinder engine driving the rear wheels by belts. The 2-seater body was of basket work. The layout was changed for 1905, with a 6hp 2-cylinder engine and chain drive to a single rear wheel. The body was still of basket work, and a 4-wheeler was also available.

NG

LA BENJAMINE (F) c.1902

L'Éclair, Paris (factory at Suresnes, Seine).

L'Éclair were the selling agents for this unusual car; the manufacturer's name is unknown. It was a 2-seater voiturette with a streamlined prow which could contain clothing or, for a commercial traveller, samples of his merchandise. The engine was a 6½hp water-cooled Buchet located behind the seats and ahead of a large radiator. It had a constant-mesh gearbox and final drive by short chain. The catalogue stressed that this car replaced the 12hp, with which it had no resemblance whatever, being stronger and as easy to maintain as a bicycle.

KB

LABOR (F) 1907–1912

Weyher et Richemond, Pantin, Seine.

The Labor was built by Weyher & Richemond to the designs of De Clèves Chevalier who were the selling agents. It was a conventional car with 15/20 and 20/30hp 4-cylinder engines and shaft drive. They had Hotchkiss-type round radiators. Weyher et Richemond also made steam and petrol cars under their own name.

NG

LABOURIER (F) c.1970

Labourier et Cie, Mouchard, Jura.

Best known for their 4×4 forestry tractors, agricultural tractors and snow ploughs, Labourier made a small number of 4×4 Land Rover-type vehicles powered by 2-litre Peugeot-Indénor diesel engines. One was used by a member of the family for an African expedition in 1971.

NG

LA BUIRE (F) 1904–1930

1904–1905 Chantiers de la Buire, Lyons.
1905–1909 Sté des Automobiles La Buire, Lyons.
1910–1930 Sté Nouvelle de la Buire Automobiles, Lyons.

One of the best-known and most respected of Lyons makes, the La Buire was made by a department of an old-established engineering firm, the Chantiers de la Buire, which had been founded in 1847. They had experience of road vehicles early on, when they built engines for Léon Serpollet's steam cars in 1889, which were marketed by Peugeot. They also made the steam-powered road tractors sold by Scotte between 1897 and about 1910.

In 1903 La Buire was listed as a maker of electric vehicles, but nothing is known of these. The first La Buire car appeared in 1904. It was a conventional 4-cylinder T-head design, made in 16 and 30hp sizes, with 4-speed gearboxes and chain drive. The following year a new company was formed dedicated to car manufacture. The commercial director was Maurice Audibert, who had made AUDIBERT-LAVIROTTE cars until he was bought out by Berliet in 1901. By 1906 La Buire was making three 4-cylinder models, of 4.9, 7.5 and 13.6 litres, the last being one of the largest touring car engines ever made. One was used by Joseph Higginson in English hill climbs for several years. It was to replace this that Higginson asked Vauxhall to make a more powerful Prince Henry, the result being the celebrated 30/98. Shaft drive appeared on the smaller La Buires in 1907, and L-head monobloc engines in 1910.

In September 1909 La Buire went bankrupt, and was taken over by the technical director, Michel Berthier. He remodelled the cars slightly, helped by the engineer Barron, who was later associated with Antoine Vialle in making the BARRON VIALLE. For one year, 1910, he offered three 4-cylinder cars, of 10, 15 and 24hp, and an 18hp six, under the name Berthier. Then, in the autumn of 1910 he was backed by a group of industrialists in forming the Société Nouvelle de la Buire Automobiles, and the former name was revived for the cars. Several of the 1910–14 models were characterised by their long stroke, such as the 80×160mm 3215cc 15hp. By 1912 unit gearboxes and transmission brakes on the differential had appeared, as well as a rounded radiator which was seen throughout the range in 1914. The 1913 15hp had a mechanical starter. The 1914 range consisted of four 4-cylinder cars, the 1724cc 10hp, 2307cc 12hp, 3215cc 15hp and 4070cc 20hp, and two sixes, the 4764cc 24hp and 5341cc 30hp. Production was quite modest, running at around 200 cars per year, as well as commercial vehicles up to 4 tons capacity.

La Buire had little of interest to offer in the 1920s. They made only one model immediately after the war, a 2650cc 12/14CV with fixed-head side-valve engine.

1907 Labor 20/30hp tourer.
NATIONAL MOTOR MUSEUM

1905 La Buire tourer at Coupe du Salon.
NATIONAL MOTOR MUSEUM

1909 La Buire 28hp tourer.
NICK BALDWIN

1914 La Buire 10hp 3-seater.
NICK BALDWIN

1922 La Buire 12/14CV tourer.
FOUNDATION DE L'AUTOMOBILE M.BERLIET

1905 Cupelle (Lacoste et Battmann) 2-seater.
NATIONAL MOTOR MUSEUM

It acquired front-wheel brakes in 1922 and ohvs in 1923, when a Speed Model was offered on the British market. This chassis was used for a team of streamlined saloons which ran in the 1924 French Touring Car Grand Prix, though without success. In the mid–1920s some smaller models were made, including the 1847cc 10CV and 2651cc 12CV, both with ohv engines. Front-wheel brakes were extra on the 10CV until 1925. Production dwindled in the late 1920s; after 1927 La Buires were no longer sold on the British market. Their British agent was the Hollingdrake Automobile Co. of Stockport, Cheshire, who had supplied Higginson with his giant car in 1906. After car production ended in 1930, the La Buire factory was used as a spare parts depot by the French Army.

NG

Further Reading
'Made in Lyon: La Buire', M. Worthington-Williams',
The Automobile, October 1993.

LACKAWANNA (US) 1904

Lackawanna Motor Co., Buffalo, New York.

This company took over from the CONRAD Motor Carriage Co., but whereas Conrad had made both steam and petrol cars, only the latter was offered under the Lackawanna name, and not for long. A runabout/surrey with 2-cylinder engine was shown at the New York Automobile Show in January 1904, but how many were made is not known. They were out of business by November 1904.

NG

LACONIA (US) 1914

H.H. Buffum, Laconia, New Hampshire.

Buffum had made cars under his own name at Abington, Massachusetts from 1901 to 1907, and in 1914 he was back in the field with a cyclecar, powered by a 7hp air-cooled V-twin engine with friction transmission. It had staggered seating for two in an aluminium body on an ash frame, and cost $450. Buffum planned to make 100 cars in 1914 and substantially more in 1915, but this never came about. The Laconia was advertised as 'New Hampshire's first cyclecar', and it was also its last.

NG

LACOSTE ET BATTMANN (F) 1897–1913

1897–1901 J. Lacoste et Cie, Paris.
1901–1905 Lacoste et Battmann, Paris.
1905–1913 Lacoste et Battmann Ltd, Paris.

This company was better known as a supplier of cars, sometimes in chassis form, at other times complete, to other manufacturers to offer under their own names. These included Achilles, Anglian, Cupelle, Gamage, Horse-Shoe, Lacoba, Napoléon, Regal, Speedwell and Simplicia. Some models of Jackson (i) around 1906 used Lacoste et Battmann chassis.

Jacques Lacoste built his first car in 1897, a quadricycle with 4hp engine and electric ignition. Battmann joined the company in 1901, and in 1905 they became British-owned, hence the 'Ltd' added to their name. By then they were selling cars under their own name, as well as supplying others. They offered single-cylinder voiturettes on De Dion-Bouton lines, probably with De Dion or Aster engines, larger 2-cylinder cars which resembled Panhards although they were De Dion-powered, and in 1903 a larger car still with 24hp 4-cylinder Mutel engine. There was little consistency in design; some cars had armoured wood frames, some steel, and although pair-cast cylinders were seen on some of the 4-cylinder engines, the 12/16hp Lacoba of 1906 had its four cylinders cast separately. During the 1905–07 period L et B were offering a 10hp 2-litre twin, a fairly small L-head 2½-litre four, and two larger fours of 3.3 and 4.9 litres. Light electric cars were also said to be available, but whether these were made by L et B or bought from another manufacturer is uncertain.

In 1908 they went into liquidation but were re-formed, now back in French ownership. The only model made from 1909 to 1913 was the Simplicia, with 1.8-litre monobloc 4-cylinder Aster engine in a tubular backbone chassis with transverse front suspension and central gearchange.

NG

LACOUR (F) 1912–1914

Lacour et Cie, Paris.

The Lacour was a cyclecar powered by a 9hp V-twin engine with friction transmission giving six forward speeds, and belt final drive. It had links with LURQUIN-COUDERT, though the evidence is conflicting. *Omnia* reported in 1912 that the Lacour was the successor to the Lurquin-Coudert, but *La Vie Automobile* said in 1913 that M. Lacour had sold his works to Lurquin-Coudert. As L-C were still in business in 1914, it seems that the second report is more probable.

NG

LACRE (GB) 1904–1905

Lacre Motor Car Co., London.

This company derived its name from Long Acre, the London street where it was first in business. They were well-known coachbuilders, both for passenger cars and commercial vehicles, as well as makers of complete commercials. The only model of private car which could be considered as their own make was an electric brougham with two 4hp motors mounted on the rear axle. In 1906 they were selling Albion, James & Browne and other makes. In 1910 they moved out of London to Letchworth Garden City, Hertfordshire where production of commercial vehicles continued. The name survived on Bedford-Lacre sweeping and street-cleansing vehicles up to the 1960s.

NG

LA CROSSE *see* AUTOMOBILI INTERMECCANICA

LA CUADRA (E) 1899–1901

Compañía General Española de Coches Automóviles
Emilio de la Cuadra SC, Barcelona.

After a visit to the Paris Motor Show in 1898 Emilio de la Cuadra sold his electric company to build cars. Together with Marc Birkigt (later technical director of Hispano-Suiza) and other young Swiss engineers he decided to build several electric and hybrid cars. He also took over representation of BENZ cars. After the failure of electric cars – in spite of serious attempts with new light batteries and a petrol engine as supplement to guarantee good ranges – de la Cuadra built petrol cars together with Birkigt. The Swiss developed two different cars called Centauro, first with a single-cylinder engine and 4.5hp, the other 2-cylinder and 7.5hp, with automatic intake valves and a cone clutch. A single chain drove a three-forward-speed gearbox. Birkigt worked on six cars, but only finished two, licensed in 1903. The larger one still exists. De la Cuadra was forced to sell the company due to lack of money, being taken over by a group of creditors who formed J. Castro SC, Fábrica Hispano-Suiza de Automóviles.

VCM

L.A.D. (GB) 1913–1926

1913–1914 Oakleigh Motor Co., West Dulwich, London.
1923–1926 L.A.D. Productions Ltd, Farnham, Surrey.

The L.A.D. was one of the lightest and simplest of the cyclecars, mainly sold as a monocar though a 2-seater was available to special order. It was powered by a 5½hp single-cylinder Stag engine driving the rear axle by a short chain. No gearbox was need as there was only one forward speed and no reverse. The pencil-like body resembled that of the Carden Monocar. It was priced at only £60 in 1913, and when it was revived in 1923 the price had risen to only £75, a considerable bargain in the postwar world. However, most people preferred to save up to buy an Austin Seven at £165, or a second-hand larger car. The 5.7hp 2-cylinder L.A.D. of 1923 was no more appealing, and sales of both models must have been very small.

NG

LADA see VAZ

LADAS see BOWEN (i)

LA DAWRI (US) c.1957–1969

La Dawri Coachcraft, Long Beach, California.
La Dawri Coachcraft, Los Alamitos, California.

Founded by Canadian Les Dawes, La Dawri was one of the largest American kit car companies of the early 1960s. In 1957 they introduced the Conquest. It was a large 2-seat sports car with rounded lines and two small grills in the front. In 1958 they added a smaller version, the Quest GT, to fit VW or other import chassis. The Daytona was a Conquest variant with a full-width front grill to replace the two small ones, and it had a smaller sibling in the Sebring. An even smaller version, the Del Mar, was intended for specials using Crosley and similar chassis. In 1961 La Dawri bought all the moulds from the VICTRESS company and renamed them. The Castilian was a 2-seat coupé that had been the Victress C-3, and the Sicilian was a smaller version. The Cavalier was a large 2-seat convertible with vaguely Aston-Martin lines that had been the Victress S-4. The Vixen was the old Victress S-1a, an attractive sports car with Ferrari-like styling, and the Cheetah had been the shorter S-5 version. The Firestar Mk II was a body kit for small sports-racing cars and they also carried bodies for dragsters and hot rods. The Centurion 21 was a wild 4-seat roadster with Batmobile-like styling and a retracting hard-top that had been acquired from SAVAGE. They also inherited the BYERS SR-100 and CR-90 body moulds from Victress. The last La Dawri was the Formula Libre, which was introduced in 1965. It was a modern coupé that had been designed for the PBS racing car. La Dawri offered to adapt it to front or mid-engined chassis and would make it fit whatever running gear the buyer wanted. But few were sold and La Dawri disappeared in the late 1960s.

HP

LA DIVA (F) 1902

Jules Zimmermann et Cie, Paris.
The La Diva 2-seater voiturette was powered by a 3½ or 4½hp De Dion-Bouton single-cylinder engine, and had a Renault-style bonnet.

NG

1913 L.A.D. 5 1/2hp monocar.
NICK BALDWIN

LAD'S CAR (US) 1912–1914

Niagara Motor Car Corp., Niagara Falls, New York.
Aimed at the juvenile market, this was a 2-seater powered by a 4hp air-cooled single-cylinder engine, with belt drive. Customers had the choice of an American-style or Renault bonnet. The price was $160 with flat belt or $170 with vee-belt, and buyers who wanted to build the car themselves were given a discount of $20 off these prices.

NG

LA DURANCE (F) 1908–c.1910

L. Conchy, Sisteron, Basses-Alpes.
Sisteron, in the mountainous country near Digne, was an unusual site for car manufacture. The Durance was a light 3-wheeler powered by an 8hp single-cylinder engine, with drive to the single rear wheel. The body was a side by side 2-seater.

NG

LADY (GB) 1899–1900

Henry Cave, Coventry.
The Lady was a 2-seater voiturette powered by a 2½hp single-cylinder De Dion-Bouton engine, with drive by flexible propeller shaft to the rear axle. When it was announced in December 1899 Mr Cave said he was about to put it on the market, but it seems that he did not do so.

NG

LA EXOTICS (US) c.1994–1998

LA Exotics, Buena Park, California.
This kit car company made fibreglass-bodied replicas of the 427 Cobra, the Ford GT-40 and the 1934 Ford coupé hot rod. The Cobra and Ford coupé kit were known for being affordable and used simple, inexpensive running gear. Both used Ford Mustang II suspension, but the Cobra used a Ford engine while the coupé was intended for a Chevrolet V8. The GT-40 was a more involved kit with a Ford V8 and Porsche or Z-F transaxles. They were sold in kit and turn-key form.

HP

LA FAUVETTE (F) 1904

La Locomotion Moderne, Paris.
This was a light car powered by a 6½hp De Dion-Bouton engine and shaft drive, and very similar to the contemporary De Dion in appearance. Body styles were open 2- and 4-seaters.

NG

LAFAYETTE (i) (US) 1920–1924

1920–1923 Lafayette Motors Co., Mars Hill, Indiana.
1923–1924 Lafayette Motors Corp., Milwaukee, Wisconsin.
The LaFayette was a luxury car designed by ex-Cadillac engineer D. McCall White, and promoted by Charles W. Nash who wanted a top-class make to complement his Nash range. As well as White he attracted a number of other personnel from Cadillac, including his sales manager and advertising manager. The car had a 5710cc V8 engine developing 90bhp in its original form, upped to 100bhp on the 1923 models. The wheelbase was 132in (3350mm), and five body styles were offered initially, from a tourer at $5025 to a limousine at $7500. These were substantial prices, $1500–2000 above Cadillac's and only a little lower than those of the Packard Twin Six.

1924 Lafayette Model 134 tourer.
NATIONAL MOTOR MUSEUM

c.1976 Lafer MP sports car.
NATIONAL MOTOR MUSEUM

1926 Lafitte 7hp 3-4-seater.
NICK BALDWIN

Production began in a former government hand grenade factory in August 1920, and by the end of 1921 only 685 cars had been made. Charles Nash admitted 'There have been far better times to introduce a motorcar' than in the middle of the postwar depression. For 1922 prices were reduced by between $175 and $750, but still only 349 cars were sold. In 1923 LaFayette was reorganised with closer links to Nash Motors, which became the biggest stockholder. The factory was moved to Milwaukee, to be closer to the main Nash plant at Kenosha. McCall White left and was replaced by ex-Packard engineer Earl G. Gunn, but he had little to do as the design remained virtually unchanged, apart from the slight increase in power. Seven body styles were offered in 1923 and 1924. In August 1923 Nash advised stockholders to agree the sale of Lafayette to the Ajax Motors Co. Though they did not know it at the time, this was a Nash subsidiary set up to make a car cheaper than the regular Nash, and therefore at the opposite

end of the scale from the LaFayette. The last of 1859 LaFayettes was made in early 1924. Ten years later the name was revived for a low-price Nash six which was promoted as a separate make for two years.

NG

Further Reading
'The Strong Lafayette', Beverly Rae Kimes,
Automobile Quarterly, Vol. 39, No. 4.

LAFAYETTE (ii) (US) c.1975–1985
Lafayette Bay Company, Inc, Wayzata, Minnesota.
The Bugatti T35 was loosely replicated by this kit car company. It was available in front- or rear-engined models for Ford Pinto or Volkswagen drive train.

HP

LAFER (BR) 1974 to date
Lafer SA Ind. E Com., São Paulo.
This was a replica of the MG TD which could easily be mistaken for the real thing from a few metres away. Made by a furniture firm, the first MP Lafers were built on stock Brazilian Volkswagen Beetle floorpans. The first 40 cars had 1500cc engines, soon replaced by the 1600. The car was exported to 17 countries, Italy apparently being the best customer. In Brazil a shortage of sports cars meant that the Lafer, with its low-volume production, was still in demand in 1999, particularly in coastal cities such as Bahia and Rio de Janeiro.

ACT

LAFITTE (F) 1923–1928
SA de Construction de Voiturettes Th. Lafitte, Gennevilliers, Seine.
The Lafitte was an unconventional light car powered by a 3-cylinder side-valve radial engine of 736cc. It had a curious form of friction drive in which the whole engine swivelled to give the four forward speeds. When the friction discs met face to face they formed a clutch which gave direct drive. The driven disc was made of compressed paper. Final drive to the rear axle was by shaft. Front suspension was by enclosed coil springs. The body was a fabric 2-seater, but for 1928 a new more sporty Lafitte was announced, with longer wheelbase, frame dropped by about 6in (152mm), cycle-type wings and pointed tail. Performance was improved by an increase in engine size to 895cc. This had a top speed of about 60mph (96km/h). The touring model, which sold for only £100 in England, was continued alongside the sports, but the Lafitte did not survive beyond 1928.

NG

LA FLÈCHE (F) 1912–1913
Guders Jack, Asnières, Seine.
This was a cyclecar powered by an 8hp single-cylinder Buchet engine. It had friction transmission and chain final drive. The body seated two in tandem, the rear seats being convertible into a compartment for luggage or samples. The design featured a hand starter outside the body, which the driver could operate from his seat. It was announced in December 1912 that 300 would be made in 1913, but it is not known whether this figure was achieved.

NG

LA FLEURANTINE (F) 1906
J. Lagarde et Cie, Fleurance, Gers.
The attractively named La Fleurantine was a 2-seater 3-wheeler powered by a 2-cylinder engine and with chain drive to the single rear wheel.

NG

LA FRANÇAISE *see* DIAMANT

LAFRANCE (US) 1903–1905
1903 International Fire Engine Co., Elmira, New York.
1903–1905 American LaFrance Fire Engine Co., Elmira, New York.
This company, which later became one of America's best-known fire engine manufacturers, built about 15 4-seater tonneaus with Renault-style bonnets and radiators slung between the dumb irons. They had 4-cylinder engines and chain drive. One shaft-driven roadster of 1905 is believed to have carried the LaFrance name, but from 1907 to 1914 some cars were sold under the AMERICAN LAFRANCE name.

NG

LA GAULOISE (F) 1907

Sté des Voiturettes La Gauloise, Issy-les-Moulineaux, Seine.
Two models of the La Gauloise were made, one with a 6.2hp single-cylinder engine, and the other with a larger 4-cylinder engine.

NG

LA GAZELLE (i) (F) 1913–1920

M. Tzaut, Neuilly, Seine.
Former Clément-Bayard employee, Tzaut introduced his own light car at the 1913 Paris Salon. It had an 8hp 4-cylinder Chapuis-Dornier engine and shaft drive. Production is believed to have been revived for a short time after the war.

NG

LA GAZELLE (ii) (F) 1920

Poignard, Brin-sur-Sauldre, Cher.
This had no connection with the Neuilly-built Gazelle. Though it was a light car of about the same size, it was less conventional, having a 4-cylinder 6/8hp air-cooled engine and a complex transmission involving two friction discs operating on a conical-shaped stepped drum, and two propeller shafts taking power to a double crown wheel and pinion.

NG

LAGONDA (GB) 1906–1989

1906–1913 Lagonda Motor Co., Staines, Middlesex.
1913–1935 Lagonda Ltd, Staines, Middlesex.
1935–1937 L.G. Motors (Staines) Ltd, Staines, Middlesex.
1937–1947 Lagonda Motors Ltd, Staines, Middlesex.
1947–1957 Lagonda Motors Ltd, Feltham, Middlesex.
1958–1975 Aston Martin Lagonda Ltd, Newport Pagnell, Buckinghamshire.
1975–1989 Aston Martin Lagonda (1975) Ltd, Newport Pagnell, Buckinghamshire.

The Lagonda was the most English of cars throughout its life, yet it began as the product of an American-born opera singer, and was named after a creek running through Springfield, Ohio. The Shawnee Indian name for this was Ough Okonda (buck's horns), which French settlers rendered as La Okonda, then Lagonda. Springfield was the birthplace of Wilbur Gunn (1859–1920) who came to England in his late thirties, and failing to establish a career as a singer, began to make motorcycles, at first assembling them in the greenhouse of his small property at Staines.

In 1904 Gunn formed the Lagonda Motor Cycle Co. Ltd, and added tricars to his two-wheelers. These had single-cylinder engines at first, then twins. Practically the whole machine, including the engine, was made by Gunn and his partner Alf Cranmer, who was to remain with Lagonda until his retirement in 1935. Motorcycles were dropped after 1905 and the tricars, like most of their contemporaries, gradually became more car-like, steering wheels taking over from handlebars in 1906. Sales depended greatly on the seasons, and dwindled to practically nothing in the winter months. This led Gunn to discontinue the tricars in 1908, after 69 had been made, and the next Lagonda was a proper 4-wheeled car with V-twin engine. Probably no more than one of these was made, but it was followed by a small series of cars powered by 4-cylinder Coventry-Simplex engines of 14/16 and 16/18hp. For some reason Gunn decided that Russia would provide a suitable market for his cars, and he established dealerships in St Petersburg, Moscow and several other cities. In July 1910 he and Bert Hammond won the Russian Reliability Trial in a 16/18hp tourer. A number of sales followed, though production of these early Lagondas must have been very small. They were virtually unknown in England, though one ran at Brooklands in 1909, and the Lagonda Club does not know of any survivors.

In 1911 Gunn decided to try for the British market, and brought out two models with Lagonda-built engines, a 3052cc four and a 4578cc six with the same cylinder dimensions of 90 × 120mm. The bore was limited to 90mm by the machinery at the Lagonda factory – the largest of the V-twin tricar engines also had a 90mm bore. These new models were hardly better known than the Coventry-Simplex-powered ones, though *The Autocar* gave one a favourable road test report in December 1911. There were many other cars in the same price bracket (£525–725), and Gunn soon decided that he must make a more popularly-priced car.

1913 Lagonda 11.1hp 2-seater.
NICK BALDWIN

1924 Lagonda 12/24hp saloon.
NICK BALDWIN

1928 Lagonda 2-litre High Chassis Speed Model tourer.
NICK BALDWIN

This appeared in 1913 after he had expanded his factory with the help of Henry Tollemache of the wealthy brewing family. It was an unconventional light car powered by a 1099cc monobloc 4-cylinder engine rated at 11.1hp with inlet-over-exhaust valves and transverse leaf suspension in the style of the Ford Model T. There was an anti-roll bar and the earliest known example of a fly-off handbrake. The steel body helped to provide stiffness to the chassis in a rudimentary form of unitary construction. The only wood used was in the windscreen frame and the hood. At first only a 2-seater was offered, but a 4-seater and a delivery van joined it in 1914. Production did not end immediately with the outbreak of World War I, and one could still buy a new Lagonda in 1916. About 500 were made, and a further 270 in 1919–20. During the war the Lagonda factory made shells, and expanded from the conglomeration of sheds which had grown up

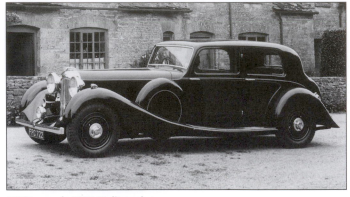

1937 Lagonda LG45 4½-litre saloon.
NICK BALDWIN

1938 Lagonda LG6 4½-litre drophead coupé.
NICK BALDWIN

1954 Lagonda 3-litre saloon.
NICK BALDWIN

1962 Lagonda Rapide 4-litre saloon.
NICK BALDWIN

around the greenhouse where Gunn's first motorcycle had been made. They also acquired separate premises for an office and sales department at 195 Hammersmith Road, West London, which was later to become the home of RAPIER Cars Ltd.

The 11.1hp was revived after the war and soon replaced by the generally similar 11.9hp, whose larger bore gave a capacity of 1421cc. The rounded vertical tube radiator of the 11.1 gave way to a flat honeycomb type on the 11.9. This in turn gave way to the 12/24 for 1924, a heavier and more conventional car using the same engine but with a separate chassis and, from mid-season, front-wheel brakes. This was a sturdy little car, and like its predecessors, did well in long-distance reliability trials. However, few of the original owners would have thought of driving one from London to Cape Town, which is what vintage car enthusiast Hamish Moffatt did in 1954.

A Change of Direction
Wilbur Gunn died in 1920, worn out by his ceaseless work contributing to the war effort of his adopted country. He was succeeded by three directors headed by Colin Parbury, who was a substantial shareholder. Although the 11.9 and 12/24 sold reasonably well, about 6600 between them, Parbury realised that Lagonda could never compete with Morris, who were building 54,000 cars a year by the mid–1920s, and that the best hope of survival lay in a move upmarket.

In 1925 Arthur Davidson was commissioned to design a new car which was launched for the 1926 season as the 14/60. In appearance it was not unlike a later 12/24, but the engine was a brand-new design, with twin camshafts mounted high in the block operating ohvs in fully-machined hemispherical combustion chambers. Capacity of the 4-cylinder unit was 1954cc, and output was 60bhp. Very powerful Rubury 4-wheel brakes were fitted, and it was available with tourer or saloon bodywork. The artillery wheels gave it an unfortunately heavy appearance, but when fitted with wire wheels, as was the norm from about 1927 onwards, it was a handsome car.

The 14/60 cost nearly double the price of the 12/24, at £570 for a tourer and £720 for a saloon compared with £295 and £370 respectively. Because they were catering for a more exclusive market, Lagonda's sales dropped from around 700 per year to 400 after the introduction of the 14/60 (the 12/24 was made alongside it for the 1926 season only), but profits held up. The 14/60 was renamed the 2-litre for 1928, and there was a Speed Model with twin carburettors and a raised cr. With a light 4-seater open body this was capable of 75mph (120km/h). It was a classic vintage sports car, sometimes called 'the poor man's Bentley' as it had much the same appearance as the 3-litre from Cricklewood, at a little over half the price. For 1930 the chassis was lowered, the front brake rods passing through the axle rather than attached to its underside. This low-chassis 2-litre was normally seen with cycle-type wings, whereas the high chassis had normal wings. Top speed was now 80mph (128km/h), or 90mph (145km/h) with a Cozette supercharger. Total production of the 14/60 and 2 litre (1926–1933) was around 1350 cars, of which 170 were supercharged. The 1932 models were called Continentals, and had sloping radiators and bigger brakes.

The other famous Lagonda of the vintage era was the 3-litre, a 6-cylinder version of the 2-litre but with pushrod ohv engine. This began as the 2389cc 16/55 of 1927, but was under-powered, so capacity went up to 2931cc for 1929. It was a substantial car, with the long-wheelbase model 18in (457mm) longer than the 2-litre, at 138in (3502mm). Tourer and saloon bodies were offered by the factory, some being fabric saloons made under Weymann patents, but outside coachbuilders were increasingly exercising their art on Lagonda chassis.

Although it was a good car generally, the 3-litre had a difficult gearbox, and to improve the situation Alf Cranmer adopted the Maybach vacuum-operated pre-selector gearbox known as the *Doppelschnellgang* (double fast speed). This provided two sets of four forward speeds and, if desired, four reverse ratios. Thus equipped, the 3-litre was known as the Selector Special, but it was not a success. The chassis had to be strengthened to carry the large and heavy gearbox, which reduced performance. Lagonda charged £75 extra for the Maybach gearbox, which they assembled at Staines, but with heavy import duties they made no profit at this price. Not more than 30 Selector Specials were made, out of a total of 580 3-litres.

For 1933 a new 2-litre was introduced; the Davidson-designed twin-camshaft engine was dropped and in its place came the first proprietary engine since the Coventry-Simplex of 1909. This was a 1991cc Crossley six which was completely dismantled and re-assembled at Staines. An ENV pre-selector gearbox was optional, and standardised for 1934. The 16/80, as it was called, carried the same coachwork

The Touring Model "LC"

An Ideal Touring Model. The neat, all-weather, fabric hood in conjunction with the latest type celluloid windows, affords complete protection under all conditions, and the whole equipment can be placed in position in a few moments. The four doors are 28 inches in width, and each side window, when not in use, folds into a compartment in its respective door. As in the "S" Model, the front seat is adjustable. The back seat, to which a rear wind-screen is fitted, is 43 inches wide and will seat three passengers. The adjustable wind-screen is raked at an angle of $19\frac{1}{2}°$. The coachwork is fawn, and the upholstery is covered in leather material to match.

Price - £320

Extra for supplying and fitting Triplex Safety Glass Wind-Screen - - - £5 12s. 6d.

Method of storing side curtains. Note the extra wide door and front seat adjustment

1987 Lagonda 5.3-litre saloon.
ASTON MARTIN LAGONDA

styles as the 2-litre and 3-litre, though most of its bodies were metal-panelled rather than fabric. Not more than 260 were made in three years, as Lagonda were badly hit by the Depression. Annual output at this time was about 180 cars, of all models.

For 1934 two new cars were introduced, one smaller than any since the 11.1hp, the other the largest Lagonda yet made. The small car was the Rapier, which used a completely new 1104cc engine designed by Tim Ashcroft. Though made at first by Lagonda, it later became an independent make, and is described under its own entry. The larger car was the 4½-litre, a large sports tourer in the idiom of the old 4½-litre Bentley. For its engine Lagonda again went to an outside firm, this time Henry Meadows who had just lost Invicta as a customer for the 4467cc ohv six, and were very happy to sell some to Lagonda. The gearbox, too, was by Meadows, a 4-speed non-synchromesh unit with right-hand change. In its first version the 4½-litre Lagonda was far from an up-to-date design, but it was fast (95mph (152km/h)for the tourer, 90mph (145km/h) for the saloon) and reasonably priced at £825 to £950. In 1935 it was joined by the M45R (Rapide) which had a more powerful engine (119bhp) mounted further forward in a shorter wheelbase. Tourers and saloons were made, and a lightweight car prepared by Fox & Nicholl won at Le Mans in June 1935. It was ironical that the month of the Le Mans victory, the only one by a British car between the Bentley era of the 1920s and the Jaguar era of the 1950s, saw the future of Lagonda very much in doubt. They had a large stock of unsold cars, particularly Rapiers, and the consequent cash flow problems forced them into receivership. In late June the receiver put up Lagonda for sale, and it was bought by a young lawyer named Alan Good, whose offer was just above that of Rolls-Royce. Good had just persuaded W.O. Bentley to leave Rolls-Royce where he had never been happy since the takeover of his own company.

Bentley set about redesigning the 4½-litre Lagonda to make it more of a refined luxury car. If the original M45 could be described as Lagonda's version of a Bentley, then the new LG45 was more Bentley's version of a Lagonda. Twin Scintilla Vertex magnetos replaced the magneto and coil in the Sanction Two version of the Meadows engine. The gearbox gained synchromesh on the upper three ratios, and other improvements were grouped chassis lubrication and built-in jacks. The Sanction Three engine had an improved cross-flow inlet

manifold and a lightened flywheel. The very similar Sanction Four went into a new car, the LG6, which had torsion bar ifs, hydraulic brakes and a hypoid rear axle. The factory bodies were beautifully styled by Frank Feeley, but outside coachwork was built on the LG6 as well, as befitted one of Britain's finest luxury cars.

As used in the LG6 the Sanction Four engine now gave 140bhp. Bentley also designed a brand new V12 engine to go in the new chassis, launched at the 1936 Olympia Motor Show. It was Britain's only V12 apart from the Rolls-Royce Phantom 111 (the venerable sleeve-valve Double Six Daimler had just come to the end of its run), and had a capacity only slightly larger than the LG6, at 4480cc, though it developed 180bhp. Three wheelbases were offered, which together with two for the LG6, gave the purchaser a choice of five, from 124 (3147mm) to 138in (3502mm). Chassis prices ran from £875 for the shortest LG6 to £1250 for the longest V12. The same factory bodies were offered with both engines, and externally the cars were virtually identical. The main identifying feature was that the exposed horns of the LG6 were concealed on the V12. Although announced in October 1936 these cars did not go into production until 12 months later. Then they took over from the LG45, and were the sole Lagondas made up to the outbreak of war. Production of the LG6 was 85 (64 + 3 prototypes on the short wheelbase and 18 on the long wheelbase), and of the V12, 189 (113 + 4 prototypes on the short wheelbase, 60 on the medium and just 12 on the long wheelbase).

The David Brown Era

W.O. Bentley was certain that the postwar climate would not be favourable to a car as expensive as the V12, so towards the end of the war he set about designing a new 2580cc 6-cylinder engine with twin ohcs. This was placed in a cruciform frame with all-independent suspension and inboard rear brakes. Bentley originally planned to use a Cotal electric gearbox, but when the car was announced in September 1945 it had a conventional 4-speed synchromesh box. The Lagonda 2.6-litre did not go into production until 1949, and then under new ownership. Alan Good had lost interest in cars, and faced with acute difficulties in obtaining supplies he was looking for a buyer. He found one in the tractor manufacturer David Brown who had recently bought Aston Martin, and was attracted by Bentley's engine as a power unit for a new Aston, which would appear as the DB2. In 1947 he bought Lagonda for £52,000 and formed a new company, Aston Martin Lagonda Ltd, as a subsidiary of David Brown & Sons Ltd. The Staines factory was sold, and the new Lagonda was made alongside the Aston Martins at Feltham, only a few miles from Staines. This was to be the home of both makes until 1958, when they moved to Newport Pagnell.

The 2.6-litre Lagonda was made as a 4-door saloon and 2-door drophead until 1953, production totalling 511 plus 9 prototypes. It was succeeded by the 3-litre, a better looking car, though fewer were made, only 266. The body styles were a 2-door saloon and drophead, with a 4-door saloon replacing the 2-door in 1955. The Duke of Edinburgh ran a 3-litre drophead for a while, and was honorary president of the Lagonda Club for many years. The 3-litre was dropped in 1958, and it looked as if the Lagonda name would disappear, but three years later David Brown brought out the Rapide. This was a large 4-door saloon powered by an Aston Martin DB4 engine enlarged to 3995cc which would later be used in the DB5. The Rapide had a lengthened DB4 chassis with dual-circuit servo disc brakes and a De Dion rear axle. The aluminium-panelled body was styled by Superleggera Touring. The Rapide was aimed at the Rolls-Royce/Bentley market, but despite being more than £1000 cheaper than a Bentley S.3, it did not attract many buyers, and only 55 were made in three years, from 1961 to 1964.

Again it seemed as if Lagonda would join the ranks of the lost causes, but in 1974 the name was revived for a long-wheelbase 4-door version of the Aston Martin DB6. Only seven of these were made, but in 1976 came a striking new car which gave Lagonda a further 13 years of life. It used the Aston Martin 5340cc V8 engine in a striking wedge-shaped 4-door saloon body styled by William Towns. A futuristic dashboard contained electronically controlled instruments incorporating graphic and digital displays, but these did not function very well, and were replaced by more conventional American-made instruments in the production cars. These did not reach customers until the summer of 1978, and were made with little change, apart from a softening of body lines and larger wheels in 1987, until production ended in 1989. Its lifetime spanned the years of massive inflation, prices rising from £24,570 on its introduction to more than £85,000 in 1986. There was also a lengthened version with luxury interior including bar and walnut picnic tables, television and video, which sold for more than £100,000. It was prepared by Tickford, in whose original premises Aston Martins and Lagondas were made, though by the 1980s Tickford operated from a separate factory at Milton Keynes. Although saloon production ended in 1989, with about 600 cars made, three remained unsold in dealers' hands in 1996. By then there was yet another Lagonda revival, another 4-door saloon styled by Vignale. Aston Martin's new owners, Ford, decided against putting it into production, and so, for the moment, the name is in abeyance. But considering the number of times it has arisen in the past, who knows what the 21st century holds for the name from Lagonda Creek?

NG

Further Reading
Lagonda, Arnold Davey, David & Charles, 1978.

LAGO-TALBOT see TALBOT (ii)

LA GRACIEUSE (B) 1899
Les Grands Ateliers de Curaghem-Électricité-Mécanique-Automobiles, Brussels.
Displayed in Brussels in March 1899, this short-lived car had a 6hp horizontal engine, described as having two concentric cylinders, one inside the other, with air-cooling by hollow radial aluminium discs. It had coil ignition with auxiliary hot-tube ignition in case the battery became exhausted. Transmission was by friction discs, the frame was tubular steel and the aluminium body had a curved front. The rear wheels were considerably larger than those at the front. An electric model was also offered at a higher price than the petrol one. The makers also listed among their activities dynamos, electric equipment, gas and petrol engines, and spare parts.

NG

LAIGLE (F) 1902–1903
Laigle, Pacquet et Cie, Amiens.
This was a conventional car powered by a 10/12hp 2-cylinder engine or a 14/16hp four, with 4-seater tonneau body and wire wheels.

NG

1914 La Licorne 6CV Type BV 2-seater.
NATIONAL MOTOR MUSEUM

1931 La Licorne 5CV saloon.
NATIONAL MOTOR MUSEUM

LAIR-ROUILLON (F) c.1941–1942
Office de Tous Modes de Traction, Paris.
This was one of the many electric cars made in France during World War II. It used Peugeot components 'adapted for electric traction', and was powered by a 3hp compound motor with 48 volt battery. Top speed was a modest 22mph (35km/h) and range 50 miles (80km). The body was of the wood-panelled estate car type, and it was also available as a delivery van.

NG

LA JOYEUSE (F) 1907–1908
Voitures Légères Taine, Paris.
This was a 4-cylinder light car best known for its appearance in the 1908 Coupe des Voiturettes, when it achieved sixth place, though it is thought that production models were sold in small numbers.

NG

LAKESIDE see BELARO and SPM

LAKSMI (IND) 1990s
Indian racing driver S. Karivardhan sought to productionise an Indian version of the DAX Rush sports car, but was killed in an air crash. The car was brought to production as the Laksmi Kari 65.

CR

LALANDE see GP

LA LICORNE (F) 1901–1950
Sté Française des Automobiles Corre, Courbevoie, Seine.
For the first seven years of this make's life, the cars were known as Corre after their maker, J. Corre, but the name La Licorne (unicorn) was adopted in 1907 and used almost exclusively thereafter. They were little known outside France, but were made in reasonable numbers and were not uncommon sights on French roads up to the mid–1950s, though serious production ended in 1939.

c.1932 La Licorne 8CV saloon.
BRYAN K. GOODMAN

1934 La Licorne 8CV saloon.
NICK BALDWIN

1938 La Licorne 11CV saloon.
NATIONAL MOTOR MUSEUM

J. Corre was a successful racing cyclist who set up as a manufacturer in 1895, and four years later began to make tricycles and quadricycles powered by De Dion-Bouton engines. He used this make as a source of engines for some time, and in 1901 launched a voiturette with single-cylinder engine and a Renault-like bonnet. It had a 3-speed gearbox, shaft drive and a tubular frame. In 1904 he

offered an 8hp single and 10hp twin, both De Dion-powered, and a larger car powered by a 3163cc 4-cylinder Aster engine. In 1905 Corre offered more 4-cylinder cars with De Dion or Mutel engines, and adopted the Renault-type dashboard radiator in place of lateral ones. Unlike Renault they followed this fashion for only three years, after which their radiators were moved to the conventional position at the front of the bonnet. It was also in 1908 that J. Corre left the company he founded to set up on his own at Rueil where he made cars on generally similar lines, which he sold under the names Le Cor or J.C. or even just Corre as his original company had adopted the name La Licorne.

In 1910 La Licornes were offered in a wide variety of models, thanks to the extensive range of engines available from De Dion-Bouton, on whom Automobiles Corre relied. They ran from three single-cylinder models of 763, 1021 and 1257cc, through a big four of 4.9 litres to a 35CV V8, though it is not certain that any of the latter reached the public. The single-cylinder models, which in 1909 included a freakish long-stroke unit of 100 × 300mm, were dropped at the end of the 1912 season, and in the last three years of peace La Licorne turned to Chapuis-Dornier as the supplier of medium-sized monobloc 4-cylinder engines from 1244 to 2650cc. The 2-litre Model DX was said to have an engine of La Licorne's own manufacture.

The postwar La Licornes were solid touring cars in the small to medium-sized class, powered by Ballot, Chapuis-Dornier or S.C.A.P. engines from 1327 to 2292cc. Most were side-valve units, though there was a sports model with 1614cc ohv S.C.A.P. engine. In the early 1920s they had vee-radiators and disc wheels, and retained acetylene lighting and hand starting until 1921. As late as 1925 the cheapest model lacked electric lighting or starting. There were also some competition models, including a 1390cc 16-valve engine designed by Nemorin Causan, with hemispherical combustion chambers and twin camshafts in the crankcase. This was used in a few racing voiturettes from 1920 to 1923, though without great success. La Licornes also competed at Le Mans from 1923 to 1926. A 1500cc single-ohc 6-cylinder engine was used in a 1925 Tour de France entry, but this did not go into production.

These competition engines were built by La Licorne, and by the end of the decade they turned to making engines for touring models as well, as their traditional suppliers such as Ballot and Chapuis-Dornier were going out of business. The 1927 Paris Salon saw the debut of an important new model, the 905cc 5CV with 2-bearing side-valve engine. This was in the same class as the Triumph Super Seven, a small car of superior quality and elegant appearance. At first the engine gave only 15bhp, but with higher compression ratios this figure was raised to 20 or 21bhp. A variety of bodies was offered on the 5CV, made by various small Paris carrossiers of which Duval was the best known. They included a 2-door saloon, coupé and cabriolet, and for the first time the name of La Licorne began to figure in Concours d'Élégance. The cabriolet was called the Fémina and several were driven by women in the Tour de France and Rallye Féminin Paris-St Raphael. A 5CV tourer won the 1930 Monte Carlo Rally, being the smallest engined car ever to win this prestigious event.

By 1930 the 5CV, known also as the Type HO2, was available with 4-door saloon bodywork, and a pillarless saloon was made in 1932. A larger version, the 1125cc 6/8CV (Type LO4) came in 1931, and the 5CV disappeared after 1932. There was also a 1461cc 8CV (L760) and 2.2-litre DR4. The engines were made entirely in the works, which were considerably enlarged to accommodate the engine branch, and could turn out 8 units per day. At this time La Licorne was owned by the Lestienne brothers, one of whom, Waldemar, had a hand in the design of the LO4. The years 1930–1935 saw production running at over 2000 cars per year, compared with 1200 at the beginning of the 1920s. In 1934 came a replacement for the 5CV, the 935cc L610, while larger models for 1935 included the 1450cc Type 415, 1814cc Type 418, 1995cc Type MIR and 2000cc Type 420. These all had ifs by transverse leaves, and synchromesh gearboxes. The bodies were quite stylish, with sloping radiators and Vutotal pillarless windscreens on some of the cabriolets. La Licorne did not forget the utilitarian side, and, unusually, offered a 2-wheel luggage trailer and even a trailer for farm animals.

In 1936 came a larger and more powerful La Licorne, the 2438cc pushrod ohv 14CV Type 424, which gave 80bhp and a top speed of 85mph (136km/h). Like all previous La Licornes, it had rhd, though lhd became available from 1938. Bodies were a handsome 4-door saloon, the Longchamp, pillarless Opéra saloon or Weekend cabriolet. In 1938/39 a 6-light limousine by Labourdette was listed, but few were made. The smaller La Licornes lost their individuality from 1937, when Citroën bodies were adopted, as were the 1628cc 9CV and 1911cc 11CV Citroën engines, though turned round to drive the rear wheels. To complicate matters, the Citroën bodies were also available with La Licorne engines of 1450 or 1814cc. A new model appeared for 1939, the 6CV 2-door saloon with 1125cc side-valve engine, forked backbone frame and ifs by two superimposed semi-cantilever springs. It could also be had with 1628cc Citroën engine as the 7CV, and some were made during the war with electric motors under the names Aéric or Milde-Krieger. About 150 were built between March 1941 and July 1942, when the licence to make cars was withdrawn by the German authorities.

The 6CV was revived briefly when production restarted in October 1944, with a 1450cc engine and an external access luggage boot, but only about 30 were made up to the end of 1946. La Licorne also made a forward-control light van with the same engine. At the 1948 Salon there was a 14CV with the prewar 2438cc engine, clothed in a 2-door cabriolet body in the contemporary all-enveloping style, but only one prototype was made. The final La Licorne design was a coupé to be powered by the 1½-litre Bugatti Type 73 engine developed in the La Licorne factory which Ettore Bugatti had bought in 1942. It never saw the light of day, and in December 1949 the factory was sold to Renault. 345 vans had been made that year, but far fewer cars.

NG

Further Reading
'La 5CV et 6CV La Licorne', Serge Pozzoli,
Le Fanauto, November–December 1984.

LA LORRAINE (F) 1899–1902

Charles Schmid et Feuillette, Bar-le-Duc, Meuse.
This company was founded in November 1897 to make cars and lighting systems by acetylene or gas. The cars had horizontal single-cylinder engines with variable belt drive. Body styles included a 4-seater *vis-à-vis* and a landaulet. Car production does not seem to have lasted more than three years, though the company remained in business until 1909.

NG

LA MARNE (i) (US) 1919–1920

La Marne Motor Car Co., Cleveland, Ohio.
The La Marne, designed by French automobile pioneer François Richard, was essentially a continuation of the Richard car, a few of which had been produced since 1916, but completely redesigned and reasonably priced – a contrast to the $8000 RIchard. The La Marne featured one of America's first straight-engines with a 3¼in × 5½in bore and stroke developing 85bhp, and a weight of 2900lbs for a touring car – its only model. The car was advertised at $1485, at the same time claiming a 'Real Value $3000' and its body style as a 'Semi Enclosed Car', which it was not. The La Marne body was designed in a style which would be termed three decades later as a 'hard-top convertible', with a fixed top and with glass side windows on its third quarter position, a design which would be used in 1925 on the 'Duplex Phaeton' by Studebaker.

Despite its unique body design and other novelties such as disappearing headlights, the La Marne – advertised as 'The Great Sensation of 1920' failed to survive that year. After his factory had closed down Francois Richard continued to design cars for several other automobile companies.

KM

LA MARNE (ii) (F) 1920

Brun et Forest, Châlons, Marne.
This was a short-lived touring car powered by a 12/15hp 4-cylinder engine.
NG

LAMBERT (i) (US) 1891; 1906–1917

The Buckeye Manufacturing Co., Anderson, Indiana.
John William Lambert made a 3-wheeled car at Ohio City in 1891, which is generally considered to be the first petrol-engined car made in the United States. It received little publicity, since, when Elwood Haynes wanted to promote his car in 1894 as 'America's First Car', he extracted a promise from John Lambert that he would not challenge the Haynes claim. Lambert agreed as at that time he was not interested in car manufacture. His Buckeye Manufacturing Co. made stationary engines, and though he made a car in 1898 he did not get into production until 1902, when he called his car the UNION (i). This was assembled

1910 Lambert (i) Model 35 tourer.
NICK BALDWIN

1902 Lambert (ii) Type G 5CV 2-seater.
JAN NORBYE

in Union City, Indiana, from components made in Anderson, and in 1905 production moved to Anderson, where it gave way to new models carrying Lambert's own name for 1906. A wide range of chain-driven cars were sold, from the 16hp single-cylinder 2-seater Model A, through two twins to the 34hp 4-cylinder Models 7 and 8. Like the Unions they had friction transmission, to which system Lambert remained faithful throughout car production. Although the Model A had a bonnet, the engine was under the seat, but the larger Lamberts were front-engined. Shaft drive appeared on the larger models in 1907, and from 1910 onwards all Lamberts had 4-cylinder engines supplied by a variety of manufacturers including Buda, Continental, Davis, Rutenber and Trebert. Car production was not large, averaging about 200 per year, with only 50 delivered in 1917. By then the range was down to one model, a 35hp four made only as a 5-seater tourer. Lambert also made trucks, these outlasting the passenger cars by a year. In view of John Lambert's meeting with Elwood Haynes in 1894, it is interesting that he and his family seemed to prefer Haynes cars to Lamberts. Another family member drove an Apperson.

NG

LAMBERT (ii) (F) 1902–c.1906

A. Lambert et Cie, Paris.
This company began by offering a range of three cars, with 8hp single-cylinder De Dion-Bouton, or 10hp and 12hp 2-cylinder engines by Abeille or Aster. They had shaft drive, artillery wheels and 2- or 4-seater bodies. The 1905 9hp De Dion-powered car was described by *The Motor* as having 'rather a long chassis for a little car', but this was thought to be no bad thing as it afforded ample comfort for rear seat passengers. Lambert also offered larger chassis for 1905, of 14, 16 and 24hp, the latter with 4 cylinders and a side-entrance tourer body.

NG

1911 Lambert (iii) 8hp 3-wheeler.
PETER CARD

1934 Lambert (iv) Sans Choc coupé.
NICK BALDWIN

1940 Lambert (iv) electric 2-seater.
NICK BALDWIN

LAMBERT (iii) (GB) 1911–1912

Lambert's Carriage, Cycle & Motor Works, Thetford, Norfolk.

This was a 3-wheeler with front-mounted 8hp air-cooled V-twin J.A.P. engine, driving by chain to a 3-speed gearbox and thence by another chain to the single rear wheel. The 2-seater body was painted in green and grey stripes. Described as 'The Smartest Car on 3 Wheels', the Lambert was priced at 105 guineas (£110.25). As well as the carriages and cycles mentioned in their name, Lambert made an ash-framed sidecar for light motorcycles.

NG

LAMBERT (iv) (F) 1926–1953

1926–1929 Automobiles Lambert, Mâcon.
1929–1936; 1940–1945 Automobiles Lambert, Rheims.
1948–1953 Automobiles Lambert, Giromagny, Belfort.

Germain Lambert (1904–1983) was a persistent inventor over a period of 27 years, yet he made relatively few cars. Following service in the French Air Force in Morocco and a spell working at the La Buire factory, he set up on his own at Mâcon to make a small sports car powered by a Ruby engine with all-round independent suspension by transverse leaves. He gave it the name 'Sans Choc' because of the smooth ride provided by the suspension. Very few were made. In 1929 he moved to Rheims where he built another design with similar suspension, but driving on the front wheels from a Ruby or Chapuis-Dornier engine. These were also called 'Sans Choc'. In a catalogue issued in 1931 Lambert said that his cars were not, and never would be, made in large numbers. 'We do not sell our car to M. Tout-le-Monde.' This was an understatement, for probably hardly any were sold at all. At least one low-slung coupé was built, and the catalogue showed two other body styles, a racer and a streamlined coupé. In 1935 *The Light Car* reported that Lambert had decided to put his car into production, after several years of experiments, yet in 1936 after advertising a 'Baby Sans Choc' with single-cylinder 350cc Chaise engine and rear-wheel drive, he closed his doors.

In 1940 Lambert joined the ranks of those making small electric cars, producing a few examples of the Baby Sans Choc with electric motors. He also made a mill for flour and grain, a precision vice and a multi-spindle drilling machine. Profits from these inventions enabled him to continue with his first love, cars. After the war he moved again, to Giromagny in Belfort, and began his most productive era of car making, although his workforce numbered only eight men. His 6CV Sport, shown at the 1948 Paris Salon, had an 1100cc 4-cylinder engine which he described as a Lambert-Ruby. He claimed to have obtained the manufacturing rights to the Ruby engine, but it is more likely that they represented the stock that he had acquired in the hope of going into production before the war. His prewar originality had given way to a conventional beam front axle with semi-elliptic springs, and rear-wheel drive. The show car, almost certainly a one-off, had an unusual coupé body in which the voluminous front wings lifted with the bonnet, but the 'production' cars from 1949 onwards were open 2-seater sports cars. These came in stark cycle-type wing form as the CS Grand Sport, or with more flowing lines as the Simplicia. Lambert also made one or two racing cars with which he competed in the Bol d'Or from 1951 to 1953. He also made a miniature 'wall of death' racer for fairground use. The last new Lambert design, though not the last car to be built, was a coupé called the Torino with Italianate lines which looked like a miniature Ferrari, built by Schmitt of Colmar in 1951. It was too expensive to sell and, like so many other Lambert designs, remained a one-off. In 1953 Lambert sold off all his assets at auction, apart from a few cars which he kept in a small museum adjacent to the café at Petit Arran, Parly, about 100 miles (160km) south east of Paris, which he ran until his death.

NG

Further Reading
'Automobiles Lambert Cars', Andrew Nahum,
Thoroughbred & Classic Cars, September 1979.
Franche Comte-Berceau de l'Automobile, Raymond Dornier,
Éditions l'Est Républicain, 1987.

LAMBERT (v) *see* OPUS

LAMBERT-HERBERT (GB) 1913

This light car was powered by an 8.9hp 4-cylinder engine. It was sponsored by racing driver Percy Lambert, the first man to drive 100 miles in one hour. His death at Brooklands in October 1913 put an end to the Lambert-Herbert car.

NG

LAMBERT & WEST *see* WARREN-LAMBERT

LAMB-KAR (GB) 1950

Lamb-Kar Co., Fordham, Ely, Cambridgeshire.

The oddly-named Lamb-Kar was designed to compete with the Bond Minicar. It looked very similar and used a 9bhp 250cc 2-stroke twin engine with a 4-speed gearbox in unit and roller chain drive to the single front wheel. A coil spring was used to suspend the front end and a rubber-suspended torsion bar at the rear; the brakes were rod-operated and on the rear wheels only. The body was a stressed aluminium skin that obviated the need for a conventional chassis.

CR

LAMBORGHINI (I) 1963 to date

1963–1980 Automobili Ferruccio Lamborghini SpA, S. Agata Bolognese.
1980 to date Nuova Automobili Ferruccio Lamborghini SpA, S. Agata Bolognese.

Ferruccio Lamborghini, a manufacturer of air conditioning and tractors, bought a Ferrari and found it wanting. When his complaints were dismissed, he vowed to make a better car. So runs the legend, but Lamborghini had once built Fiat specials so the desire to make his own cars was not new. He chose as his logo a fighting bull, begging a direct comparison with the prancing horse of Ferrari.

The first Lamborghini, the 350GTV was shown in 1963, but received such a poor reception that it was not seen again. The following year, Lamborghini launched the 350GT, which had a tubular frame with all-independent suspension by coil springs and double wishbones. The 3.5-litre 'quad cam' V12 was designed by Giotto Bizzarrini, late of Ferrari, while the styling was by Franco Scaglione. Between 1964 and 1967, 120 350GTs and 23 4-litre versions were made.

Sales improved with the 400GT, which sold 250 examples, from 1966 to 1968. It was similar to the 350GT, but Touring re-worked the body and no two panels were common. Mechanically similar to the 4-litre 350, the 400 was available as a 2+2 GT or as an open 2-seater.

Also in 1966, came the Miura, now regarded as the world's first supercar. Suspension was as before, but the 4-litre engine was set transversely amidships in a fabricated platform chassis. The body, by Marcello Gandini, was a masterpiece of styling although, when the 174mph (280km/h) top speed was approached, the front end lifted.

The Miura S had 375bhp and could almost reach 180mph (290km/h) while the SV, with 385bhp and wider track, could just do it. The Miura made Ferrari look passé and 765 were made, from 1966 to 1972. The Miura lent glamour to all Lamborghinis, but practical GT cars remained the company's staple product. The Islero of 1968 to 1970 (250 made) was a refinement of the 350GT/400GT,

1969 Lamborghini Miura coupé.
NATIONAL MOTOR MUSEUM

1988 Lamborghini Countach LP500 coupé.
NATIONAL MOTOR MUSEUM

NICK BALDWIN

LAMBORGHINI, FERRUCCIO (1916–1993)

Ferruccio Lamborghini bought Ferrari cars from the day he could afford them, and set his mind on proving that he could do better.

He was born into a farming family at Renazzo di Cento, not far from Ferrara, on 28 April 1916. But farming was secondary to mechanics for him. He set up a primitive machine shop on his father's farm, and later went to Bologna to attend classes at an industrial school.

During World War II he served in the Italian air force and was stationed for some time on the Isle of Rhodes. Returning to civilian life in 1945, his primary aim was to build a tractor for his father, and he assembled one from parts found in the junkyard: Morris-Commercial 6-cylinder engine, Ford transmission, GM rear axle.

It was not hard to find engineers in that part of Italy, and in 1949 he opened a factory in Cento to produce farm tractors with small diesel engines. The business prospered, but he began to develop visions of an industrial conglomerate. In 1959 he set up a factory to produce oil-burners (for central heating systems) and added a branch for making air-conditioning equipment in 1960.

He had owned a Mercedes-Benz 300 SL gullwing coupé for a year or two, and a number of Alfa Romeo cars, before he graduated to Maserati and Ferrari. Some time in 1961 or 1962 he decided to make a car that would be better than both. He hired Giotto Bizzarrini to design a V12 engine, Gianpaolo Dallara for chassis engineering, and Franco Scaglione for body styling. He bought land at Sant'Agata Bolognese and built a factory before the first prototype was finished. Road testing began early in 1963.

The GT 350 earned universal respect, but it was the Miura of 1966 that first made international headlines for Lamborghini. Suddenly he had his name on the hottest car on the road. The cars that followed were often spectacular, but Lamborghini's engineering was going stale. Perhaps the cars no longer held the same fascination for him, but industrial diversification certainly did. He set up Oleodinamica Lamborghini, a precision-engineering firm to make tools and instruments for the petroleum and petro-chemical industries.

But in 1969 Italy's economical resurgence had run out of steam, being replaced by social unrest and industrial bankruptcies. Lamborghini sold the tractor factory to SAME of Treviglio and began looking for a buyer to take over the car company. He wanted–at 55–to retire to his estate on Lake Trasimeno, where he cultivated substantial areas of vineyards, and where he later added a museum filled with Lamborghini tractors and cars.

In 1971 he sold a 51 per cent stake in Automobili Lamborghini to Henri-Georges Rossetti of Neuchatel, Switzerland, for SFr10 million. Later, he sold the remaining 49 per cent to René Leimer, another Swiss businessman.

He was married three times and had two children, a son, Tonino and a daughter, Patricia. He died from a heart attack at Perugia on 20 February 1993.

JPN

1988 Lamborghini Jalpa coupé.
NATIONAL MOTOR MUSEUM

1988 Lamborghini LM002 4x4.
NATIONAL MOTOR MUSEUM

with a body by Marazzi and the specification included air conditioning and power steering and windows. The base model had 320bhp, while the 'S' had 340bhp and could just nudge 124mph (200km/h) (0–62mph (0-100km/h) in 7.5 seconds).

With the Espada, from 1969 to 1978, Lamborghini made a full 4-seat GT car, with a body styled by Bertone. Running gear was from the Islero, with 325bhp (350bhp in the Series II of 1970; 365bhp in the 1972 Series III) in a platform chassis, In its ultimate form, it was good for 124mph (200km/h) and 1217 examples were made.

By 1970, Lamborghini was ready for its second generation of cars. Gianpaolo Dallara, who had guided the company through its first stage, left and was replaced by Paolo Stanzani. The last front-engined Lamborghini, the Jarama, was a short wheelbase Espada (with its fabricated chassis) which had similar dimensions to the Islero.

The Jarama was heavier than the Islero, but could match it in performance thanks to 350bhp from the regular 4-litre engine (177 made) or 365bhp in the 'S' model (150 made). Like the Espada, automatic transmission was an option. The Jarama was a strong performer even if the Bertone body lacked charisma.

Also in 1970, Ferruccio Lamborghini suffered a downturn in his agricultural business and he sold the car company to a Swiss, Georges-Henri Rosetti, whose family business was clock making. Unfortunately, Swiss horology was hit by new products from Japan. Rosetti soon sold part of his holding to a property developer. Lamborghini himself died in 1993, aged 77.

Despite Signor Lamborghini's problems, the marque was riding high and it next chose to compete with the Ferrari Dino. The Urraco of 1970 was the Miura's little sister although the front and rear suspension was by MacPherson struts and lower wishbones, and the transversely mounted engine was a 220bhp single-ohc V8 of 2463cc.

The Urraco P250, a 2+2 GT, was more powerful than the Dino, and could outpace it, but Lamborghini miscalculated the problem of catering for a wider

market. The Urraco took two years to reach production and was launched before it was ready. The P300 had a double-ohc 3-litre engine and 265bhp but had no clear place in the market while the 2-litre 182bhp single-ohc P200 was a 'tax bracket' car for the Italian market.

The Urraco range added a further 776 cars to Lamborghini's sales and, a year after it was launched, Lamborghini showed a concept car which would become the Countach, which is Milanese slang for 'that's it'.

First shown in 1971, the Countach LP was a sensation with its aggressive styling and 'butterfly' doors. The mid-mounted 4-litre engine was fitted in-line ('LP' stands for Longitudinale Posteriore) in a tubular frame and the 5-speed gearbox was forward of the engine with the driveshaft passing back through the sump. With 375bhp, the Countach was good for 168+mph (270+km/h).

The 'S' model of 1978 had wider tyres, modified suspension and, as an option, a high-mounted rear wing, while the 2S of 1980 had an improved cockpit and instrumentation.

In 1976 Lamborghini introduced the Silhouette, a re-vamped, 2-seat, Urraco P300 with better cockpit ergonomics and a Targa-top. Indifferent build quality and suspect reliability were against it – industrial unrest was rife in Italy – and it could not be sold in America.

Lamborghini's owners had explored collaborations, notably with BMW, but then these fell through, they sold the company to two Germans: Hubert Hahne, a former racing driver, and a Dr Neumann. Hahne and Neumann sold the company on to an American, Zoltan Reti, who discovered that the company was bankrupt and, in 1981, he auctioned it. It was bought by Patrick Mimram, a 25-year-old whose family leased the factory.

The Jalpa of 1981 was a lightly reworked Silhouette with a 3.5-litre engine modified by the former Maserati engineer, Giulio Alfieri, who mainly improved the torque. Sales were slow, however, and by the mid–1980s, Lamborghini was selling only versions of the Countach. Although the Countach was the ultimate in male jewellery, sales were slow because the American market was out of bounds. That was rectified with the 5167cc LP500. Output remained at 375bhp (325bhp with US emission controls), but torque was improved. In 1985 came the 4-valve-per-cylinder 'Quattrovalvole' which delivered 455bhp (425bhp in America) and was good for 186mph (299km/h) (0–62mph (0-100km/h) in 4.9 seconds).

In 1982 Lamborghini introduced the LM002, a 4-wheel drive off-road vehicle with a 7-litre V12 engine. The company also made marine engines and sold watches and accessories. In 1987, the Mimram family sold the company to Chrysler.

Late in 1989 came the Diablo, a logical development of the Countach with a body styled by Marcello Gandini. The Diablo's technical specification was similar to the Countach on paper, but it had carbonfibre reinforcements and a 492bhp 5729cc engine. Lamborghini claimed a top speed of 202mph (325km/h) with 0–62mph (0-100km/h) in 4.1 seconds.

Soon after its launch, economic recession, coupled with the collapse of the classic car market, caused Lamborghini to cease production as it tried to shift its back-log.

Lamborghini, which had always shunned motor racing, built a V12 engine for Formula One in the early 1990s – it was essentially a Chrysler project. The engine was too long, the block flexed, and it never produced competitive power.

In 1992, came the Diablo VT (Viscous Traction) with permanent 4-wheel drive, power-assisted steering and adaptive damping. In 1995 the limited-edition Diablo SE30 Jota was offered with 590bhp and a claimed top speed of 208mph (335km/h). An open-top Diablo was also offered in 1995. The 1996 Sprint Veloce, also available in open form, had electronic valve timing and a claimed top speed of 208mph (335km/h) with 0–62mph (0-100km/h) in 3.9 seconds. By then, control the company had passed to a consortium of Indonesian entrepreneurs who sold Lamborghini to Volkswagen in 1998. A further development of the Diablo appeared in September 1999. The GT engine was increased to 5992cc, giving 0–60mph (0-96km/h) in 3.5 seconds, with top speeds ranging from 190 to 208mph (305 to 335km/h) according to the gearing. Production was limited to 80 cars, but a Diablo replacement was expected in early 2001.

MJL

Further Reading

Lamborghini, the Legend, David Hodges, Paragon, 1998.
The Complete Book of Lamborghini, Pete Lyons, Foulis, 1988.
Lamborghini Urraco and the V8s, Jean-François Marchet, Osprey, 1983.
Lamborghini Countach, Peter Dron, Crowood Auto Classics, 1995.

1991 Lamborghini Diablo coupé.
BERTONE

LAMBRETTA *see* WILLAM

LAMBRO (I) 1952
A Milanese company produced the very small Lambro 3-wheeler. The 2-seater was powered by a 125cc twin-stroke engine driving the single rear wheel.
CR

LAMINAR CONCEPTS (US) 1986 to date
Laminar Concepts, Media, Pennsylvania.
Laminar began as a race preparation shop for Renault R-5 Turbos. In 1994 they began a programme of upgrading and improving the Lotus Europa which they called the Evolution Europa. The third generation Mazda twin turbo rotary engine was tuned to 300hp and installed in place of the Lotus Twincam. The chassis was re-engineered with larger brakes, improved suspension and better body aerodynamics. A fully appointed interior was added with air conditioning and improved sound deadening and 'wide body' moulds were obtained from stylist Clark Lincoln. In 1996 they purchased the rights to the VIKING kit car from Bob Erickson. This was a Lotus 7-type car with a Toyota engine. Laminar Concepts substituted Mazda engines and expanded the Viking line into three models. The Viking Sport Roadster used the Mazda MX-5 4-cylinder engine and running gear. The Viking BE was a low-cost model similar to the original Viking powered by a first-generation Mazda RX-7 engine and running gear. The Viking TT used the twin-turbo Mazda RX-7 rotary engine with advanced pushrod suspension incorporating RX-7 suspension parts. Engines up to 450hp were offered.
HP

LA MINERVE (F) 1901–1906
Sté la Minerve, Billancourt, Seine.
There seems to have been no connection between the French La Minerve and much better-known Belgian Minerva cars, both named after the goddess of wisdom. The first La Minerve was a voiturette powered by a 3½hp single-cylinder engine, with chain drive. It was followed in 1902 by a 6hp single (sold in England under the name Vesta), 8 and 10hp twins, and a 16hp four, all with shaft drive. A 3-cylinder engine was offered in 1903, and in 1905 the largest models were an 18 and a 24hp four. The company also made stationary engines for agricultural and industrial purposes.
NG

LAMMAS-GRAHAM (GB) 1936–1938
Lammas Ltd, Sunbury-on-Thames, Middlesex.
This was a lesser-known Anglo-American hybrid, which used a 3562cc supercharged

1938 Lammas-Graham drophead coupé.
NICK BALDWIN

6-cylinder Graham engine instead of the more usual Ford V8 or Hudson units adopted by Allard, Brough Superior and Railton. The engine had a special alloy head and SU downdraught carburettor, giving an output of 128bhp. The chassis was a slightly modified Graham, with the usual anglicisations such as Luvax shock absorbers and 12-volt electrical equipment. The bodies were very English in style, a saloon by Carlton, drophead coupé by Abbott and sports tourer by Bertelli. The Lammas-Graham was in the same class as the 3½-litre SS Jaguar, bur considerably more expensive, at £620 to £695. This was probably the main reason why the Lammas failed to attract more than about 30 customers. It changed little in the three years that it was on the market, though more angular Bertelli bodies were used for the 1938 saloons. Production ended in the middle of that year.
NG

LAMMERS (US) c.1993
Lammers' Engineering, Seattle, Washington.
This kit company made a Lamborghini Countach replica called the Aggressor that was based on a custom tube chassis or Pontiac Fiero running gear. Twin-turbocharged engines were optional as was a V8 engine. Lammers also offered a Cobra replica.
HP

LA MOUCHE *see* TESTE ET MORET

1902 Lanchester 10hp air-cooled tonneau (left) with a c.1900 Serpollet 6–8hp steam car (right).
NATIONAL MOTOR MUSEUM

c.1903 Lanchester 16hp water-cooled tonneau.
NATIONAL MOTOR MUSEUM

c.1907 Lanchester 28hp landaulet.
NATIONAL MOTOR MUSEUM

LA MOUETTE (F) 1909

Joanny Fauré, Lyons.

This was a rakish-looking 4-seater runabout with 4-cylinder engine, dashboard radiator and, unusually for the period, front-wheel drive. Very few were made.

NG

LAMY (F) 1903–1904

J. Lamy, Paris.

Lamy exhibited two small cars at the Paris Salon in December 1903. One was a single-seater powered by a 3hp single-cylinder engine mounted under the seat and driving through a Bozier gearbox giving two forward speeds. 'A reverse considered unnecessary because of the light weight of the car' said *The Motor*. The other was a 2-seater powered by a 4hp engine. Both had wooden frames and wire wheels. The single-seater was priced at 1950 francs (nearly £80.00) and the 2-seater at 2750 francs.

NG

LA NATIONALE (F) 1899

Sté La Nationale, Paris.

This small car was powered by a front-mounted 4hp V-twin engine geared to a countershaft, with belt drive to the rear axle. Petrol or paraffin fuel could be used.

NG

LANCAMOBILE (US) 1900–1901

James H. Lancaster Co. Inc, New York City, New York.

The Lancamobile was a light car powered by a 7hp 2-cylinder engine located under the seat, with chain final drive. It had a *vis-à-vis* body and tiller steering. Its most remarkable feature was the starting by 'an independent air motor which starts the gas motor, when the latter is running, the air motor becomes a compressor and stores air in the tubular frame of the vehicle'. Ingenious though it may have been, this system did not give the Lancamobile more than two years of life.

NG

LANCASTER (GB) 1902–1903

E.H. Lancaster & Co. Ltd, Sunderland, Co. Durham.

The Lancaster was one of many 'makes' of car which relied on the products of LACOSTE ET BATTMANN, using their chassis and 6 or 8hp De Dion-Bouton engines. Most Lancasters were shaft driven, but a few had chain drive. E.H. Lancaster later sold Gladiator-built Clement (ii) cars.

NG

LANCHESTER (GB) 1895–1956

1895–1904 Lanchester Engine Co. Ltd, Birmingham.
1904–1931 Lanchester Motor Co. Ltd, Birmingham.
1931–1956 Lanchester Motor Co. Ltd, Coventry.

The Lanchester was unique among early British cars in that it owed nothing to foreign designs such as Benz or Panhard, but was planned from first principles by one of the most original minds of his age, Frederick William Lanchester.

From an early age he manufactured gas engines (see biography), and in 1895 started work on his first car, which made its first road trials in February or March 1896. It was powered by a single-cylinder horizontal engine of $4^{3}/_{4} \times 4^{1}/_{2}$in (120.65 × 114.3mm) giving a capacity of 1306cc, with two overhanging balanced cranks, each with its own flywheel and connecting rod. The cranks revolved in opposite directions, giving a smoothness of running unknown to Lanchester's contemporaries. Other features of this remarkable car included an epicyclic gearchange, tubular frame and full-width body. The car was built in a

NATIONAL MOTOR MUSEUM

LANCHESTER, FREDERICK (1868–1946)

Frederick William Lanchester was one of the cleverest engineers and most original thinkers of his generation. He never accepted the received ideas of others but always worked from first principles, the results of which can be clearly seen in his cars.

He was born on 23 October 1868, in Lewisham, South London, one of eight children of an architect, Henry Jones Lanchester, and a teacher of Latin and mathematics, the former Octavia Ward. The family soon moved to Brighton, where Frederick was educated at a small private school. He left at 14 and attended the Hartley Institute in Southampton from where he won a scholarship to the Normal School of Science (now the Royal College of Science) in Kensington. He also gained practical workshop experience from night classes at the Finsbury Technical School, and started work at the rate of 6d (2½p) an hour as a draughtsman's assistant. In 1888 he joined the Forward Gas Engine Co. of Saltley, near Birmingham, where he was paid only £1 a week, a low wage for a qualified engineer, even then. However, he patented a pendulum inertia governor (the second of 426 patents which he would file during his long life) which earned him a ten shilling (50p) royalty on each engine fitted with it, and became works manager and chief designer.

In 1889 he took on his 15-year-old brother George as an apprentice, and four years later George took his place as works manager, leaving Fred free to set up his own experimental workshop in a small shed. Here he made his first small petrol engines, including one fitted in the first English-built motor boat, and invented a flame starter for stationary engines, an important improvement when all such engines, even the largest, had to be started by pulling on the flywheel. His starter was taken up by Crossleys, one of Britain's most important gas engine makers, who paid him a royalty of £3 per engine. He made about £2000 from Crossley over the next two years, good money in the 1890s, which enabled him to finance experiments which brought in no money at all. These included the motor launch (which was in use for more than 20 years) and a number of gliders which he catapulted from his bedroom window. These experiments were conducted with his brothers Frank (1870–1960) and George (1874–1970) who were known as the 'Unholy Trinity' because much of their work was carried out on Sundays. In 1895 Fred began work on his first car, Britain's first 4-wheeled petrol car of wholly native design, which ran successfully in early 1896. The Lanchester Engine Co. was formed to manufacture cars in December 1899, but this required a board of directors who came into conflict with Fred almost straightaway. They insisted on a coachbuilt body on the third car made, which was entered in the Thousand Miles Trial of 1900, as they considered Fred's light, tubular-framed body on the second car too unorthodox. The coachbuilt body, by Mulliners, broke in two during the Trial, symbolic of the lack of harmony between Lanchester and the directors. At about this time Fred replaced the Whitworth thread, commonly used in the infant motor industry, with various sizes of his own thread, which he called the Lanchester 'M' thread, These were used on all Lanchester cars until after World War I.

The production 10 and 12hp Lanchesters were entirely the work of Fred Lanchester in every detail, down to the fitted drawers for tools and folding picnic table, while the organisation of production, testing and training apprentices were George's work. Frank was responsible for the business side and for sales. The company was under-capitalised from the start, and financial problems meant constant friction between Fred and his directors, who wanted to cut corners and go for conventional and 'safe' designs. The company was in receivership for a year from March 1904, and when it was reorganised Fred's salary was cut from £450 to £250 per annum. However, he was allowed to take on outside work, which enabled him to become a consultant for the Daimler company in 1909. His most important work for the Coventry firm was the crankshaft vibration damper. By making a crankshaft of much greater stiffness than was customary, and placing the flywheel at the front, Lanchester overcame the vibration problem which plagued 6-cylinder engines. It was taken up not only by Daimler but by other firms, providing its inventor with a reasonable income. He also invented the harmonic balancer for 4-cylinder engines, which was used by Vauxhall and Willys as well as by Lanchester and Daimler.

After 1912 Fred had no connection with the company which bore his name, design passing to George. He became a consultant to Wolseley in 1924, and remained a consultant to Daimler until 1927, and in the earlier years at any rate he found the work congenial. 'In all my life', he said, 'I have never been associated with such a harmonious group of men'. In 1918 he designed a very advanced car with all-round independent suspension by hydraulic units at each corner, and a single spoke steering wheel, but Daimler did not take it up. In 1925 he formed a joint company with Daimler called Lanchester Laboratories Ltd, to exploit some of his inventions. However, financial problems led to the association being wound up in 1929; Lanchester used his own capital to buy out Daimler's interest, and set up as a manufacturer of loud-speakers and transformers. This continued in an unprofitable way until 1934, when illness forced him to retire. He had become 'Dr Fred' in 1919 when he received an Honorary Doctorate from Birmingham University. Though recognised as the Grand Old Man of automobile engineering, he was too poor to run a car. However, he continued to produce a variety of papers on a range of subjects such as relativity, jet propulsion, airships, colour photography, and music, as well as writing poetry under the pen name Paul Netherton-Herries. He died in March 1946, and there was a suggestion that London's new airport, then being built, might be called Lanchester Airport. However, this was not taken up and it was called Heathrow instead.

Frederick married Dorothea Cooper in 1919. They had no children.

NG

Further Reading
F.W. Lanchester, P.W. Kingford, London, 1960.
Great Designers and their Work, ed. By Ronald Barker and Anthony Harding, David & Charles, 1970.

1924 Lanchester 40hp limousine.
NATIONAL MOTOR MUSEUM

1925 Lanchester 21hp coupé.
NATIONAL MOTOR MUSEUM

workshop rented from the Forward Gas Engine Co., for which Lanchester had worked, but Lanchester and some associates soon took larger premises where they gathered a staff of ten skilled men. A new 2-cylinder engine of 3459cc was fitted to the car in 1897, in which year Fred Lanchester and his brother Frank were joined by their third brother George. A second complete car was built in the same year.

Experimental work, financed by Fred's royalties from the Clerk-Lanchester gas engine starter, occupied the next two years, and it was not until December 1899 that the Lanchester Engine Co. was formed. Fred was general manager and chief designer, George his assistant and Frank company secretary with particular responsibility for publicity and seeking financial backing. Despite Frank's charm, shortage of capital was always a problem, and after a new factory at Sparkbrook, Birmingham, had been bought and equipped, there was little money left for production.

Six cars were completed during 1900, all being set aside as directors' and demonstration vehicles, so no revenue came to the company until 1901. The cars were similar to the second prototype of 1897, with mid-mounted horizontally-opposed 2-cylinder engines, slightly larger than the prototype at 4033cc, driving through a 3-speed epicyclic gearbox and worm final drive. Steering was by side tiller, or lever as Lanchester preferred to call it, which was still available in 1911, long after all other car manufacturers had gone over to wheel steering. In the autumn of 1901 Max Lawrence joined the firm as works manager. His sisters were the founders of Roedean girls' public school, and it was through them that the Lanchesters found their first celebrated customer, Rudyard Kipling, who owned a number of the cars. Another literary owner in later years was George Bernard Shaw.

At the insistence of the directors, the early Lanchesters had bodies by outside firms, but Fred was dissatisfied as they were not interchangeable, and involved expensive chassis alterations, so in 1903 he was given permission to set up his own body department. In 1906 a new factory was erected next to the main works, which accommodated the coachbuilding, upholstery and paint sections. Four

models of 2-cylinder car were offered up to 1904. The 10 and 12hp engines were of the same size (4033cc), but the former was air-cooled, and it was reckoned that the fans absorbed 2hp at maximum speed, hence the difference in quoted power. There were also two larger models, the 4426cc 16hp and 4838cc 18hp, but these were made in very small numbers, 20 of the former and six of the latter. By 1904 customers were expecting four cylinders for engines of this size, and Fred was in the process of designing a four when the company ran out of cash. Even though they had a full order book, the directors decided to liquidate the firm. Later in 1904 it was reorganised as the Lanchester Motor Co. Ltd, and run by a receiver for nearly a year.

The first 4-cylinder Lanchester, the 2470cc 20hp, appeared at the end of 1904. The engine was now front-mounted and vertical, but the bonnetless appearance was retained by locating the engine between the driver and front passenger. This layout was followed on all production Lanchesters made up to 1914. Engine, clutch and epicyclic gearbox were made in one unit, and Lanchester was a pioneer of pressure lubrication, at 30lb/sq.in. One lever was used to operate the clutch, gear selection and main brake. In 1906 the 4-cylinder 20hp was joined by a six with the same cylinder dimensions and a capacity of 3705cc. This had optional wheel steering from 1908 and the 20hp from 1909, though the lever was still available for those who wanted it up to 1911. These models were made up to 1910 when the 6-cylinder engine was enlarged to 4853cc, being known as the 38hp. A year later the four adopted the same dimensions (101 × 101mm), giving 3235cc. These Lanchesters looked like no other cars on the road, with their almost bonnetless appearance and very long wheelbase, which gave an exceptionally comfortable ride. Customers included several Indian princes, the most loyal being Prince Ranjitsinhji, the Jam Sahib of Nawanagar, usually known as Ranji in England where he was a renowned cricketer, who bought his first Lanchester in 1902 and his last in 1947.

Such innovations as were made between 1911 and 1914 were mostly the work of George rather than Fred, who became increasingly disillusioned with the company, and resigned in 1913. Frank was in the London sales office, where his tact and charm were of immense value. The next design was entirely George's work. Known as the Sporting Forty, it was much more conventional with a 5514cc side-valve 6-cylinder engine mounted under a long bonnet, semi-elliptic springs and a bevel rear axle This design was forced on George by the directors. Although a better car than he would admit, it never pleased him and he was relieved that the outbreak of war prevented more than half a dozen being made.

In the early years of World War I the Lanchester factory made shells, but Frank was able to secure a contract for armoured cars and searchlight tenders which were built on the 38hp 6-cylinder chassis. A total of 42 armoured cars were supplied to the Royal Naval Air Service, and did invaluable work in Russia. Lanchester also made RAF 1 and Sunbeam Arab aero engines, and the Constantinesco interrupter mechanism for synchronised firing a machine gun through the propeller arc of a fighter plane.

For their postwar car the Lanchester directors decided on a single model, the Forty. This had a 6178cc single-ohc engine in a chassis based on that of the prewar Sporting Forty and consequently still using the epicyclic gearbox. It was a luxury car with a chassis price in 1920 of £2200, or £100 more than the Rolls-Royce Silver Ghost. Like the Rolls it soon acquired a smaller sister in the shape of the 2988cc 21hp, which was the first Lanchester to have a detachable cylinder head, and also the first to have a conventional gearbox and 4-wheel brakes. The Forty did not get these until 1924. A total of 392 Fortys were made between 1920 and 1929. Quite a number were sold in America, and among Royal customers were the Duke of York, later King George VI. The first public appearance of the present Queen, at the age of six weeks, was in a Lanchester Forty. As before the war, they found favour in princely India. The Jam Sahib of Nawanagar bought several, and other customers included the Maharajahs of Rewa and Alwar. The latter had an extraordinary state landau, whose passenger compartment was separately suspended on the chassis by C-springs. This was made by Lanchester themselves, like most coachwork on the Forty and 21 chassis. Indeed Lanchester's coachbuilding department did some work on other firms' chassis, such as Austin, Daimler, Rolls-Royce and Sunbeam. Lanchester claimed to be among the first users of cellulose paints, in 1925.

The Forty's engine was used in the second series of Lanchester armoured cars, of which 39 were made between 1927 and 1931, being supplied to the 11th Hussars and 12th Lancers. They were 6-wheelers with steering columns at each end.

1929 Lanchester 21hp fabric sports saloon.
NATIONAL MOTOR MUSEUM

1935 Lanchester Ten saloon.
NATIONAL MOTOR MUSEUM

1951 Lanchester Fourteen saloon.
NATIONAL MOTOR MUSEUM

In 1928 came George Lanchester's last design for his own firm, the 30hp Straight-Eight. This had an 82bhp 4446cc monobloc engine which shared many components with the 21, or 23 as it had become in 1926 when capacity went up to 3327cc. The Straight-Eight was probably the finest Lanchester ever, but the Depression shortened its life, and only 126 were made.

In January 1931 the bank called in Lanchester's overdraft, although it was not exceptionally high at £38,000, and gave the directors an ultimatum to amalgamate or go bankrupt. They chose amalgamation with Daimler, which was looking for the opportunity to expand into a cheaper market, also happy to acquire a modern poppet-valve engine to replace their ageing sleeve-valve units. Daimler was owned by BSA, which transferred Lanchester production to the Daimler works at Coventry and moved one of its subsidiaries, the Burton Griffiths Machine Tool Co., into the Lanchester works. Frank Lanchester became sales director for the new Lanchester division of Daimler, and George a senior member of the design staff. The Straight-Eight was continued in small numbers up to 1932, and was joined by a 2504cc six known as the 15/18. This was a compromise design bridging the two eras of Lanchester, as it had been planned by George but was cheapened at Daimler's insistence, and the original ohc engine was replaced by a pushrod unit. A modern feature was the fluid flywheel in conjunction with a Wilson pre-selector gearbox, used on contemporary Daimlers. Just over 2000 were made until 1935, latterly with a shorter stroke engine of 2390cc, while from 1936 to 1939 the name Lanchester Eighteen was carried by a variant of the Daimler Light Twenty. A very small number of Lanchester Straight-Eights were made in the mid-30s. These were, in fact, 4624cc Daimler Straight-Eights with Lanchester radiators. King George VI had four of these, with Hooper limousine or landaulet bodies, and at least three went to India, two to the Sahib of Nawanagar.

Other Lanchesters of the 1930s were badge-engineered variants of either BSA or Daimler designs. The 1203cc Lanchester Ten was jointly designed by George Lanchester and Daimler's Laurence Pomeroy, and shared bodies, though not engines, with the BSA Ten. The 1378cc Lanchester Light Six was almost identical with the BSA of the same name, apart from the radiator, and shared the same six body styles. These bodies were made by Carbodies, Holbrook and other Coventry firms. The 1938/39 Lanchester Fourteen Roadrider De Luxe was essentially a Daimler DB17/18, though with Bendix brakes in place of the

Daimler's Girlings, and a spiral bevel rear axle instead of the Daimler's underslung worm. At £525 it was £75 cheaper than the DB18. Over 22,000 Lanchesters were made in the 1930s, far more than in any previous decade. Of these, the Ten accounted for about 12,250.

After the war Lanchester made only a single model, the 1287cc 4-cylinder LD Ten with fluid flywheel and coil ifs. The 6-light all-steel saloon was made by Briggs, and gave way in 1949 to an aluminium-panelled 4-light saloon by Barker. Only 579 of the latter were made, out of a total of 3003 Tens. They were joined for 1950 by the Fourteen, essentially a Daimler Conquest with a 1968cc 4-cylinder engine and a Lanchester grill. Like the Conquest it was made in saloon and drophead forms, and lasted up to 1954. The 1953 Earls Court Show saw the Lanchester Dauphin, a luxury 2-door saloon with Hooper razor-edge body and a 2433cc Daimler Conquest engine. It was quite unrealistically priced at £4010 (a Fourteen cost £1144) and only the two show cars, one with lhd, the other with rhd, were built. The last Lanchester was the Sprite, a unitary-construction saloon with 1622cc 4-cylinder engine and Hobbs automatic transmission. It would have required annual sales of 5000 to be viable, and the new Edward Turner regime at Daimler decided that this would never be reached. The Sprite was dropped after 13 cars had been made, and the once great, and always respected name of Lanchester died.

NG

Further Reading
Lanchester Motor Cars, Anthony Bird and Francis Hutton-Stott, Cassell, 1965.
The Lanchester Legacy 1895–1931, C. S. Clark, Coventry University, 1995.

LANCIA (I) 1906 to date
Fabbrica Automobili Lancia & Cia, Turin.

Vincenzo Lancia (1881–1937) was the youngest child of a wealthy Turin soup manufacturer. In 1898 he joined Ceirano as bookkeeper, though he spent most of his time as an unofficial apprentice to Aristide Faccioli, Ceirano's designer. When Ceirano was bought out by F.I.A.T. in 1899, Lancia became chief inspector and test driver for that company. In July 1900 he had his first race victory at Padua. Between then and 1908 he had a number of competition successes, including winning the 1904 Coppa Florio, though he did nothing like as well as his team mate Felice Nazzaro. When it came to making cars, though, the tables were turned, for Nazzaro was a manufacturer for only a few years, whereas Lancia is a household name today.

Friends had suggested to Lancia as early as 1902 that he should become a car manufacturer, but he felt that he lacked experience, and it was not until November 1906 that he formed his own company with the backing of several friends including one of the founders of Fiat, Count Carlo Biscaretti di Ruffia. He bought a factory from Itala, and hired 20 employees. His first car was ready for trials in February 1907, but before it had left the workshop a fire destroyed the car, tools and all the drawings. Lancia had to start again from scratch, but seven months later he had another car ready. It was of conventional layout with a 4-cylinder F-head engine of 2543cc developing 24bhp. The cylinders were pair-cast and the carburettor was an interesting 2-stage design, with a primary stage covering up to 200rpm, after which a secondary stage took over for engine speeds up to 1800rpm. The 4-speed gearbox was bolted directly to the engine, and final drive was by shaft.

Sixteen cars were built in 1907, and about 120 in 1908, when body styles included a double phaeton, limousine and landaulet. The first Lancia was known simply as the 12hp, but the second model with a slightly larger engine of 3120cc was christened the Beta, starting the company's long association with letters of the Greek alphabet. The 12hp was retrospectively called the Alfa, though this name was not used when the car was new. There was also a 3815cc 6-cylinder Di-Alfa, of which only 23 were made in 1907/08. Lancia was not to make another six for 42 years. The Beta had a monobloc engine and was succeeded by the 3460cc Gamma in 1910 and the 4080cc Delta in 1911. These were much the same in design, but new trends were seen in the Epsilon introduced in 1912. This had the same engine dimensions as the Delta, but a modified and enlarged water jacket and a new dry multi-plate clutch. To accommodate the new cooling system the radiator was higher, and this characterised the Epsilon and its successors the Theta and Kappa.

Lancia bought a new factory site in 1911, though he retained the original works for coachbuilding. As well as in-house bodies, Lancia cars were often fitted with outside coachwork by Locati e Torretta, Farina and Garavini, while in England

1914 Lancia 20/30 coupé.
NICK BALDWIN

1925 Lancia Lambda 5th Series detachable top saloon.
NATIONAL MOTOR MUSEUM

1931 Lancia Dilambda coupé.
NICK BALDWIN

a number of handsome bodies were built by Maythorn. Exports began in the first year of production, initially to Britain and the USA, but later special models with higher ground clearance were made for the Italian and British colonies, Russia and Argentina. Although Lancia was not a major name in motor sport at this time, they competed successfully at Brooklands and won two races in America, the Savannah Light Car race in 1908 and the Tiedemann Trophy in 1910.

Other pre-World War I Lancias included the 2628cc Zeta with transaxle gearbox and the 5-litre Eta, which was the only prewar Lancia to have an ohc engine. More important in terms of numbers and technical trends was the Theta, of which 1696 were made from 1913 to 1918. This was developed from the Delta, but a longer stroke gave it a capacity of 4940cc. This engine was, in fact, developed for use in an armoured car before it was put into the Theta. The most interesting aspect of the Theta was its electrical equipment; this was an American-made Rushmore system which provided a starting and complete lighting set, the first offering of such equipment on a European car. Lancia was

1938 Lancia Astura saloon, by Pinin Farina.
NATIONAL MOTOR MUSEUM

1939 Lancia Aprilia saloon.
NATIONAL MOTOR MUSEUM

holes were cut in non-stressed areas. The seat squabs acted as cross members of the frame, contributing to the Lambda's exceptional torsional stiffness. Front suspension was also unusual, by sliding pillars and vertical coil springs. Although the prototype Lambda had rear-wheel brakes only, all production cars had front-wheel brakes as well.

The Lambda went into production in 1923. At first the only factory body style was an open torpedo tourer. However, two styles of hard-top were available, one to make a comfortable saloon, the other a coupé de ville. Because of its unusual construction, the Lambda was not an ideal basis for custom coachwork, but a few *carrozzerie* had a go, including Alessio with a coupé de ville, and Casaro who made about 30 2-seater sports cars. In 1926, on the 7th Series, a separate chassis

NATIONAL MOTOR MUSEUM

FESSIA, ANTONIO (1901–1968)

Born in Turin on 27 November 1901, he studied at the Turin Polytechnic and graduated in mechanical and industrial engineering in July 1923.

He joined Fiat in February 1925 and soon became vice-director of the car and truck design offices. In 1930 he was transferred to the aero-engine branch.

His place in the organisation plan did not separate him from the car projects. At his level, Fiat's top executives and engineers would meet after office hours, and Fessia was not only informed of all projects, but his opinions were eagerly invited. It was Giovanni Agnelli himself who asked Fessia in 1935 to make a proposal for a very small and low-priced economy car.

His thinking on cars evolved towards front-wheel drive. His original concept for what became the Fiat 500 of 1936 had front-wheel drive (but not the production model). In 1936 he was appointed manager of the central technical office for the entire Fiat organisation, holding that title until 1946.

On leaving Fiat, he went to work for a Caproni subsidiary, CEMSA at Saronno, and designed a front-wheel drive car with a flat-four, water-cooled engine. It appeared in prototype form in 1947 but never got into production.

From 1945 to 1950 he lectured at the University of Bologna and from 1950 to 1952 he was technical consultant to Ducati motorcycles in Bologna. He became consulting engineer to Pirelli in Milano in 1953, lecturing at the Milan Polytechnic until 1955. During this period he also worked on experimental cars for Deutsche Fiat.

He joined Lancia as technical director on 2 April 1955, and modernised his Caproni design, which emerged in 1960 as the Lancia Flavia. On his design team were Romanini, Cav. Gillio and Francesco Di Virilio. He led the design of the Fulvia and was given a seat on the Lancia board in 1964.

He died at Borgmasino near Turin in 1968.

JPN

so sure of his electric starter that the Theta carried no handle at the front of the car, though there was one in the tool kit, just in case. Rushmore electrics were standard on the Theta and optional on the Epsilon. About 400 Thetas were made each year up to 1917, but only 35 in 1918 because of war work.

In 1919 came the Kappa which was an updated Theta with a detachable cylinder head and central gearchange. Only 188 of these were made in 1919, but the following year Lancia broke all previous records, with 1059 Kappas being made. It was now the only model, but was joined in 1921 by the Dikappa with full ohvs, and in 1922 by the Trikappa. This broke completely new ground with a narrow-angle (22 degrees) V8 engine of 4594cc. Whereas the Theta developed 70bhp and the Dikappa 87bhp, the output of the smaller Trikappa engine was 98bhp. Vincenzo Lancia had been interested in the vee-engine layout for some time, and its is possible that his interest had been kindled as far back as 1907 when he must have seen the monstrous V-4 Christie racing car at the French Grand Prix. The Christie also featured ifs by sliding pillars which Lancia adopted on his Lambda of 1922. Lancia had built two V12 aero engines during the war, and in 1919 he created a 6032cc V12 which was installed in a car. This was considered to be too expensive to be put into production, but it was the ancestor of a long line of narrow-angle ohc vee-engines that went into the Lambda, Dilambda, Astura, Artena, Augusta and Aprilia.

The Lambda

The Trikappa was continued until 1925, but three years earlier there appeared a car which was arguably the most famous Lancia model ever made, and one of the world's most important designs between the wars. The Lambda engine was a V4, but with an angle between the cylinders of only 13 degrees, compared with 90 degrees for the average vee-engine. Viewed from above, the cylinders seemed staggered rather than in separate banks, and they were cast in one aluminium block and crankcase. The single-ohc was driven by a vertical shaft. The capacity of the original Lambda engine was 2120cc, giving 49bhp at 3000rpm.

Even more innovative than the engine was the Lambda's monocoque construction. This took the form of a pressed-steel skeleton which made up the chassis and lower half of the body, the highest point of the skeleton being at the scuttle and between the front and rear doors. In order to keep the weight down

1954 Lancia Aurelia B.20 coupé.
NICK GEORGANO

was an option, and on the 8th and 9th Series it was standard. Custom coachbuilders now had a better opportunity to work on the Lambda than before, but the car lost something of its individuality. Lambdas were made in nine series from 1923 to 1931. The biggest changes came with the 7th Series which had a larger engine of 2370cc and two wheelbases, as well as the separate chassis. 4-speed gearboxes were standardised from the 5th Series (1925) onwards. In 1927 six Casaro-bodied 2-seaters finished fourth and fifth in the Mille Miglia. This led to a number of Lambda entries in sports car races, though they were not particularly successful.

The 9th Series Lambda was launched in January 1931, and for the first time no open models were offered, only two saloons on the short and long wheelbases. The other major change was that coil ignition replaced the magneto. 500 9th Series Lambdas were made, production ending in November 1931, but they took more than a year to sell. Total Lambda production was 13,501.

Dilambda, Artena, and Astura

The origins of the Dilambda date back to 1926 when Vincenzo Lancia was approached by an American named Flocker, who suggested that an American subsidiary company should be set up, with American finance. All components, apart from the engine and gearbox, would be American-made. The market needed a larger car than the Lambda, so Lancia set about designing a 4-litre V8 engine, and, at Flocker's request, built ten prototypes which were shipped to New York at the end of 1927. Lancia, who went with them, soon found out that Lancia Motors of America Inc was a stock promotion scheme, with no intention of serious manufacture. He was never paid for his ten prototypes, but at least he was able to bring them back to Italy where they formed the basis of his new luxury car, the Dilambda.

Introduced in January 1929, the Dilambda's V8 engine had a capacity of 3960cc and developed 100bhp. The cylinders were at an angle of 22 degrees, and the engine was effectively two Lambda units on a common crankcase. As on the later Lambdas, the frame was separate from the body and was an electrically-welded box section structure. There were three wheelbases and Lambda-like ifs. Although the factory offered two body styles, a saloon and a tourer, the Dilambda was often seen with custom coachwork. Pinin Farina, who set up in business in 1930, built a number of beautiful bodies on the Dilambda, as did Castagna and

Viotti in Italy, and several of the best-known firms in France, Britain and the USA. Dilambdas were frequent winners at Concours d'Élégance. They were made until 1937, total production being 1884.

The Dilambda was a luxury car, and Lancia obviously needed something to replace the Lambda in a lower price bracket. He chose to offer two cars with similar chassis and bodies, one with a 1924cc V4 engine, the other a 2604cc V8. They were named Artena and Astura after old towns and castles, marking a break from the Greek alphabet which was not revived until the Beta in 1972. They followed tradition in having narrow-angle vee-engines, box section frames and sliding pillar front suspension. The Astura's wheelbase was 7.36in (187mm) longer, at 125in (3177mm), to accommodate the larger engine. The bodies at first resembled scaled-down Dilambdas, but as the 1930s passed they followed fashion with sloping radiators and curvacious lines. By 1939 the Artena had been relegated to an army staff car or light van chassis, but the Astura, in its 4th Series form (1937–1940) with platform frame and hydraulic brakes, carried a variety of handsome and advanced coachwork. The coupés and cabriolets by Pinin Farina and Touring were as streamlined as any prewar European coachwork, with elaborate chrome radiator grills, flowing lines and enclosed rear wheels. For the formal market Farina built a number of limousines and landaulettes which were the favoured transport of the Italian government. Few were exported, and those that survived the war mostly ended their days as taxicabs.

The Astura's character could be described as more show than go, for even in its 4th Series with engine enlarged to 2972cc it gave only 82bhp, and the sleek Pinin Farina coupés could not exceed 80mph (128km/h). The Astura was seldom seen in competitions, though after the war Franco Cortese had some success with a special-bodied 2-seater powered by an experimental V8 engine. Total Astura production was 2946, of which 421 were the 4th Series. Artena production was greater, at 5072.

A Move into the Popular Market

In about 1930 Lancia began to think about a mass-produced family car, a completely new field for him. His thoughts became reality at the Paris Salon in October 1932 with a 4-door saloon named the Augusta. This had a steel platform chassis with side members to which was welded a pillarless body. The engine was

1958 Lancia Flaminia coupé, by Pinin Farina.
NICK BALDWIN

1966 Lancia Fulvia coupé.
NICK BALDWIN

1967 Lancia Flavia coupé, by Zagato.
NICK BALDWIN

1978 Lancia Beta 2000ES hatchback.
NICK BALDWIN

an 1194cc V4 with single-ohc, as in previous Lancias, developing 35bhp at 4000rpm. At first only the saloon was made, but Lancia could not resist the temptation to offer a chassis for special coachwork, and from 1934 onwards a number of custom offerings appeared. These included a Pinin Farina drophead coupé, later followed by a similar design made by Lancia themselves, a Stabilimente Farina 2-door saloon with power-operated folding roof, and, in Britain, an open 4-seater sports tourer called the March Special, made by Whittingham & Mitchel for sale by Kevill-Davies & March. The Augusta became popular with several racing drivers, including Tazio Nuvolari, Achille Varzi and Luigi Fagioli. Just over 14,000 were made when they were replaced by the even more famous Aprilia.

From 1933 to 1937 Augustas were assembled in France to avoid import duty. They came from a purpose-built factory at Bonneuil-sur-Marne and were known as Belnas. About 2500 were made, and they were followed by the Ardennes which was an Aprilia imported complete from Turin.

The Aprilia has been described as the most advanced European car built in the 1930s. Citroën enthusiasts might dispute this, but there is no doubt that the Aprilia was a great step forward for Lancia, spreading the marque's popularity wider than ever before. It was Vincenzo's last design, and indeed he acted more as a supervisor to his engineer Giuseppe Baggi and body designer Battisto Falchetto. The Aprilia's engine was a 1352cc V4 with hemispherical combustion chambers which developed 47.8bhp at 4300rpm. This represented 35.35bhp per litre, compared with 29.31bhp from the Augusta. The body was a fastback 4-door saloon, and handling was excellent thanks to independent suspension at the rear as well as at the front. Top speed was just over 80mph (128km/h), but on twisty roads it could outperform faster cars thanks to its light weight, efficient brakes and very controllable road-holding.

Vincenzo Lancia drove prototype Aprilias, but never saw the car in production as he died of a heart attack in February 1937. Although it had been introduced at the Paris and London Shows in the previous autumn, the Aprilia did not begin to come off the production lines until a few weeks after Lancia's death. Detail improvements and a larger engine (1486cc) were made for 1939, but otherwise the Aprilia continued without change until it was dropped in October 1949.

As with the Lambda and Augusta, the Aprilia was available with a separate chassis for those who wanted special coachwork. This was 4in longer than the saloon, and could carry a wide variety of bodies. Before the war Pinin Farina built a number of specials, some of very advanced aerodynamics, and between 1945 and 1949 he made a small series of saloons and drophead coupés which, although heavier and more expensive than the regular saloons, attracted a number of customers. There was also a 6-light taxicab on the separate chassis, and numerous specials by other Italian coachbuilders such as Bertone, Castagna, Ghia, Viotti and Zagato.

The Aprilia had a creditable sporting record, winning its class in the 1937 Spa 24 Hour Race, the 1947 and 1948 Alpine Rallies, and the 1948 Lisbon and 1950 Sestrières Rallies. They finished eighth and ninth overall in the 1938 Monte Carlo Rally, and took five of the six top places in the small car class.

The Aprilia sold better than any previous Lancia, with 14,704 being made up to the outbreak of World War II, and total production being 27,642. However, the new management under Manlio Gracco felt that there was a market for a still smaller car, hence the arrival in 1939 of the Ardea. This was very similar in appearance to the Aprilia, with the same short bonnet and rounded tail, but its engine was a 903cc 29bhp V4, and there was no irs. There was also no external access to the luggage boot, but this was rectified on postwar models. Not many Ardeas left the factory before the war, but they were made up to 1952, with trucks and light vans lasting a year longer. Ardea production was over 22,000.

The Jano Era
In 1937, shortly after Vincenzo's death, Lancia acquired the services of the great Alfa Romeo designer Vittorio Jano, who had been responsible for such masterpieces as the 1750, 2300 and Grand Prix cars, as well as commercial vehicles and aero engines. Ironically, Alfa Romeo decided that, at 46, Jano was too old to provide them with any more successful designs, so he moved on to Lancia. Although he worked on the 3rd series Ardea, the first design which really bore the Jano stamp was the Aurelia, launched in April 1950. The conception was due to Vincenzo's son Gianni Lancia, and the V6 engine was the work of Jano's assistant Francesco de Virgilio, but Jano oversaw all the work, and was particularly responsible for the rear-mounted gearbox.

The Aurelia was the logical replacement for the Aprilia, but was a larger car with an engine that began at 1754cc, and grew to 2541cc before the end of the run. The engine was a V6, and was no longer a narrow vee, for the angle between the cylinders was 60 degrees. With such a wide angle a single-ohc was no longer possible, so the camshaft was located in the neck of the vee operating the valves by pushrods as in an American V8. The 4-speed gearbox, with synchromesh on the three upper ratios, was located on the rear axle. This was not quite a novelty for Lancia, for it had been seen on the 1912 Zeta; more significantly it was a feature of Jano's last design for Alfa Romeo, the 1936 V12 Grand Prix car. The Aurelia's body bore a family resemblance to the Aprilia, but was longer, with more flowing lines. Unfortunately, it was also heavier, and was hardly any faster than an Aprilia.

The original Aurelia saloon, known as the B.10, was not a very exciting car, but in 1951 an enlarged engine of 1991cc went into the saloon, which became the B.21, and into a new coupé, the B.20. This became one of the classic sports cars of the 1950s, and is highly prized by collectors today. Lancia supplied a platform frame to Pinin Farina and the coachbuilder used more than 100 hand-beaten panels welded together to create a monocoque fastback coupé. In 1953 a larger engine of 2451cc, followed a year later by the best-performing of all Aurelias, the 4th Series B.20 which had a De Dion rear axle. This was the first Lancia to have lhd, for previous models, in common with pre–1950 Alfa Romeos and several quality French cars of the 1930s, had rhd regardless of the fact that their countries had always driven on the right.

The B.20 shared the saloon's steering column gearchange, but a floor change was available from Nardi, who would also supply a hotter camshaft which raised output to 145bhp. The 4th Series represented the peak of B.20 development, for the 5th and 6th Series were milder cars with lower performance though greater comfort. B.20 production ended in June 1958, after 2568 had been made. It had a very fine competition record, both in rallying and racing. In 1951 Bracco and Maglioli finished second in the Mille Miglia, being beaten only by a much more expensive Ferrari, while in the same year Bracco and Lurani won their class at Le Mans. In the 1952 Targa Florio B.20s finished first, second and third. The winner, Felice Bonetto, ran out of petrol and crossed the finishing line using the car's battery and starter motor. From 1953 the B.20s were largely replaced in racing by the sports/racing D.20, D.23 and D.24, but rallying successes continued, including victories in the 1952, 1954 and 1955 Sestrières, 1953 Liège-Rome-Liège and 1954 Monte Carlo. The success of the B.20 encouraged Lancia to set up a competition department which produced the remarkable D.20/23/24 sports-racing cars and the D.50 Formula 1 cars which are beyond the scope of this book.

New Ownership and New Designs

In June 1955 Gianni Lancia and his mother sold their company to cement millionaire Carlo Pesenti. He began a big programme of modernisation and expansion, replacing Jano as chief engineer by Antonio Fessia who had been responsible for the Fiat Topolino and the front-drive Cemsa-Caproni. The first product of the new regime was the Flaminia, a 4-door saloon with wide, all-enveloping 6-light body styled by Pininfarina, a 2458cc V6 engine and De Dion transaxle. The traditional sliding pillar front suspension was abandoned after 35 years, to be replaced by a conventional coil-and-wishbone layout. The engine size rose to 2775cc in 1962, and there were several coupé versions of the Flaminia. One of these, the Pininfarina coupé, sold more than the saloon it was derived from, 5282 as against 3424. The others were a coupé and convertible by Touring on a shorter wheelbase (2748 sold) and a coupé by Zagato (525 sold). The standard saloon sold well at first, 2600 in four years, but thereafter sales dropped to around 300 per year, and it took seven years, 1964 to 1970, to sell the last 599 Flaminias made.

Apart from serious rust problems, the trouble with the Flaminia was that it was starved of research and development funds, which were devoted to Lancia's volume-selling small cars, the flat-4 Flavia and V4 Fulvia. The Ardea had been replaced in 1953 by the Appia which was essentially a smaller Aurelia with 1089cc V4 engine and non-irs. It was made in three series up to 1963, and was joined in 1960 by the Flavia. This was basically a 13-year old design, for it had appeared in 1947 as the Cemsa-Caproni. It never saw production under this name, but Fessia kept it up his sleeve, and with a larger, twin-cam engine and completely restyled body it was launched as the Lancia Flavia. The 1488cc flat-4 engine drove the front wheels and gave 78bhp, compared with the Cemsa's 40bhp. An advanced feature for a popular saloon was all-round disc

1982 Lancia Trevi 2000 saloon.
LANCIA & CIA

1990 Lancia Thema 8.32 saloon.
LANCIA & CIA

1991 Lancia Dedra 2000 Turbo saloon.
NICK BALDWIN

braking. Flavia production began in June 1961, and a year later its manufacture was moved from Turin to a new body and assembly factory at Chivasso. Capacity went up to 1800cc in 1963 and to 1991cc in the Flavia 2000 of 1970. Total production of Flavias was 108,175 including 19,293 short-chassis coupés by Pininfarina, and a much smaller number of coupés and convertibles by Zagato and Vignale.

The Flavia marked Lancia's entry into the mass-production field, but it was outnumbered by the smaller V4 Fulvia, of which more than 300,000 were made from 1963 to 1976. This shared many features with the Flavia, apart from the 1091cc 58bhp V4 engine which was the last of Lancia's V4s. The standard body was a 4-door saloon not unlike the Flavia in appearance, and as with other Lancias there were several coupés. Zagato made a number of fastbacks, but the best-known coupé was Lancia's own, originally with 1216cc engine, but later available in larger sizes up to 1584cc and 115bhp. Competition models were known as HF, and came in 1216, 1298, 1320, 1401 and 1584cc sizes. HF stood for High Fidelity, after a club of Lancia enthusiasts who entered competition

1993 Lancia Delta HF Integrale hatchback.
NICK BALDWIN

with factory support. The HF was a very successful rally car, winning for Lancia the World Rally Championship in 1972 and 1974, though in the latter year the Fulvia shared points with the Beta coupé and Stratos. The Fulvia HF won almost every major rally at some time during its life.

Part of the Fiat Empire
In the late 1960s Lancia's sales dropped alarmingly, from a peak of 43,000 in 1967 to 37,000 in 1968 and still fewer in 1969. Carlo Pesenti was losing interest in Lancia, and was happy to arrange a sale to Fiat who paid a nominal one lire per share, though they also took over Lancia's massive debts. The sale took place in October 1969, and there was no immediate effect on the Lancia range of cars, though their heavy commercial vehicles were dropped as they were directly competitive with Fiat's. The Flavia was renamed the 2000, and the Fulvia was reduced in price which brought a satisfying increase in sales.

The first result of Fiat ownership was seen at the 1971 Turin Show in the shape of the Lancia Beta. This was a fastback 4-door saloon designed by Lancia but powered by transversely-mounted Fiat engines of 1438, 1596 or 1756cc. They were derived from the well-known twin-ohc engines with toothed belt camshaft drive which powered the Fiat 124 Sport, 125 and 132 saloons, though they were modified to give more power and smoother running. Thus the 1600 engine gave 105bhp in the Fiat 132 and 110bhp in the Beta. The engines drove the front wheels via a 5-speed gearbox. The Beta was a promising car and sold well at first, but its reputation was damaged by serious, and widely publicised, rust problems which did a great deal of harm to Lancia's name. Nevertheless, 194,916 Beta saloons were made between 1972 and 1981. Later models had a 1995cc engine.

Several sporting developments of the Beta were made, the coupé, HPE estate and Monte Carlo coupé. The coupé was made in closed form or open, Targa-top form as the Beta Spider. It stayed in production after the saloons had been withdrawn. For one season, 1974, they were used in Lancia's rally team. The HPE (High Performance Estate) was in the same class as the Reliant Scimitar GTE, while the Monte Carlo was a more specialised sports car in which the 1756 or 1995cc engines were mounted behind the driver and powered the rear wheels. Designed by Fiat and originally code named X1/20, it was badged as a Lancia because of their greater sporting reputation. Like the HPE and the

coupé, the Monte Carlo survived the Beta saloon, and was made until 1984. In America it was sold as the Scorpion, as Chevrolet held the rights to the name Monte Carlo. A total of 7595 were made, a reasonable figure for such a specialised car, but small compared with the 71,258 HPEs and 121,191 coupés in hard-top and open forms.

In 1976 Lancia brought out the Gamma, a luxury saloon which took the place of the Fiat 130. It was powered by a flat-4 engine of 1998 or 2484cc (the smaller engine was available only on the home market). Handsome and luxurious though it was, the Gamma was not powerful enough to compete with the larger BMW, Mercedes-Benz or Rover 3500, and it was withdrawn in 1984, after 15,296 had been made. Like the Fiat 130, the Gamma had its coupé version (6789 made) which was made in carburettor or fuel injection models.

Lancia's most successful rally car, the Stratos, began life as a concept car by Bertone at the 1970 Turin Show. Deciding that it had competition potential, Lancia's directors had the design completely revamped during 1971. The original Fulvia 1600 engine was replaced by a 2418cc Ferrari Dino V6 giving 190bhp. The body was restyled to give better forward vision, and Lancia set about building enough for the Stratos to be homologated in the Group 4 Special GT category. For this, 500 had to be built in one year, but it is thought that no more than 250 were actually completed, for the combination of higher taxes in Italy on cars of over 2 litres capacity and the international oil crisis made the 1970s a bad time for a car like the Stratos. Nevertheless it proved itself unbeatable in rallies, with an engine tuned to give 230bhp and, from 1974, 240bhp in 24-valve form. With Sandro Munari at the wheel it won the Monte Carlo Rally three times in a row, in 1975, 1976 and 1977, and Lancia took the World Rally Championship in 1974, 1975 and 1976, thanks largely to the Stratos, though in 1974 the Beta coupé and Fulvia HF contributed to the points total.

Lancia's replacement for the Stratos was the Rally Coupé of 1980, which bore a superficial resemblance to the Monte Carlo, but apart from the centre section was a completely different car. The engine was mounted longitudinally instead of transversely, and gave 325bhp in works tuned form, from 1995cc. The Rally Coupé was strictly a homologation special, and once the mandatory 500 had been completed, by mid 1982, no more were made. Its first major success was gained by Walter Röhrl in the 1983 Monte Carlo, and the team went on to win the World Rally Championship that year. Rally Coupés sold to the public cost nearly 44 million lire, compared with 18 million for the Monte Carlo coupé.

The first small Lancia conceived under Fiat ownership was the Delta which appeared in 1978. It was based on the Fiat Ritmo, being a 5-door hatchback powered by 1302 or 1499cc Fiat engines, though its styling was distinctively Lancia, and interior equipment more luxurious. It was, however, made entirely on Fiat's assembly lines. From 1982 it was available with the 1585cc twin cam engine, later to be upgraded with fuel injection and also available in turbocharged form. In 1986 a 1995cc turbocharged 4mult;4 model became the basis for a range of increasingly potent Deltas, all known as Integrales, which were campaigned successfully in Group A form in international rallies. The Group B rally car, called the S4, won the 1985 Monte Carlo and was second in the 1986 World Championship for makes.

The Delta had a notchback version called the Prisma, while another notchback was the Trevi. This was a Beta replacement, made from 1980 to 1984, with engine options of 1585 or 1995cc and a supercharger on the Volumex model from 1983. This was unusual on modern cars, having the blower driven from the engine instead of by the exhaust gases as in a turbocharged engine. The supercharger was also available briefly on the HPE and the Beta coupé.

Two other cars were introduced in the 1980s. The Y10 was the smallest Lancia ever made, a 4-seater saloon with an overall length of only 133.5in (3390mm), and was powered either by the 999cc FIRE engine used in the Fiat Uno, or a 1049cc engine in normally aspirated or turbocharged form. It was badged as an Autobianchi in some markets. Launched in 1985, it was available in 4 × 4 form from 1986, and was upgraded with 1.1 and 1.3-litre engines in 1989. The 1.1-litre was also available with electronic continuously variable automatic transmission (ECVT).

At the other end of the range was the Thema, a luxury saloon powered by a choice of five engines, a 1995cc four with or without turbocharger, a 2445cc 4-cylinder diesel, an 1849cc V6 and a 2927cc V8. The latter, known as the 8.32 (8 cylinders, 32 valves) was a Ferrari engine previously used in the 308GTB. The Thema was one of the Type Four models, also made as the Fiat Chroma, Alfa Romeo 164 and Saab 9000.

A new medium-sized car, the Dedra, appeared in 1989. It used the same floorpan as the Fiat Tipo and had 1.6-, 1.8- and 2-litre fuel-injected engines, the two larger with twin ohcs with contra-rotating balance shafts. A turbocharged 2-litre model was added in 1990 in 4 × 2 and 4 × 4 forms, with an estate car in 1994. In 1993 the Delta was replaced by a new model, also called Delta, which shared the floorpan and suspension of the Dedra, Alfa Romeo 155 and Fiat Tipo/Tempra. The 4 × 4 Integrale version of the earlier Delta remained in production for a further year. The new Delta had 1581, 1747 and 1995cc engines, the larger units having twin ohc with the 1995cc having 16 valves and available with a turbocharger. In 1995 an HPE version of the Delta was introduced with the 1995cc engine. The Thema was replaced in late 1994 by the Kappa, reviving a name from the early 1920s. It was a large saloon using 5-cylinder engines of 1998 or 2446cc in addition to a 2959cc V6. The saloon was joined in 1996 by an estate car, and in 1997 by a coupé of in-house design.

In 1994 Lancia launched their first MPV under the name Zeta. Closely related to the Fiat Ulysse, Citroën Évasion and Peugeot 806, it had a 1998cc 16-valve 4-cylinder engine. In January 1998 the Y10 was succeeded by the Y or Ypsilon, marketed only as a Lancia, the Autobianchi name having been dropped. With 1108 and 1242cc engines, the Ypsilon came with a 5-speed gearbox, although a 6-speed manual and ECVT automatic transmission were available with the larger engine. An unusual feature was the choice of 112 body colours. The Delta, Dedra, Kappa, and Zeta completed the 1999 Lancia range, but the summer of 1999 saw a Dedra replacement, the Lybra 4-door saloon with luxury equipment such as climate control, four airbags, satellite navigation and mobile phone. It was offered with three sizes of petrol engine, 1.6, 1.8 and 2 litres, and two diesels of 1.9 and 2.4 litres.

NG

Further Reading

La Lancia – 70 Years of Excellence, Wim H.J. Oude Weernink, Motor Racing Publications, 1979.

Fiat and Lancia Twin-Cams, a Collector's Guide, Phil Ward, Motor Racing Publications, 1992.

Lancia Fulvia and Flavia, a Collector's Guide, Wim H.J. Oude Weernink, Motor Racing Publications, 1984.

Lancia Beta, a Collector's Guide, Brian Long, Motor Racing Publications, 1991.

1999 Lancia Y hatchback.
LANCIA & CIA

2000 Lancia Lybra saloon.
LANCIA & CIA

LANDA (E) 1919–1931

1919–1922 Talleres Landa, Madrid.
1922–1931 Sociedad Española de Automóviles Landa, Madrid.
Juan A. de Landaluce started in 1916 with the production of motorcycles, but added his first car in 1919, with a 2-cylinder 1200cc engine and 20bhp. This was a 2-stroke engine, using splash lubrication. In 1922 the Marquees of Aldama contributed funds to increase production, with a new 4-cylinder engine with double shaft transmission. These cars sold well, but production capacity was always very low.

VCM

LANDGREBE (D) 1921–1924

C.O. Landgrebe, Dresden.
Like the Cyclonette and Phanomobil, the Landgrebe was a 3-wheeler with single front wheel driven by an engine mounted directly over the wheel. Shaft drive was employed. 2- and 4-seater models were available, but the Landgrebe did not have as long a life as its rivals.

HON

LANDINI (I) 1919–1921

SA Industria de l'Automobile de Novara, Cameri.
This unusual car was made by a flying instructor, and was a cyclecar steered by the feet, with a rudder bar replacing the steering wheel. The gearchange and accelerator were controlled by moving the knees sideways. The engine was a 992cc 8hp V-twin Stucchi mounted on the offside running board, and driving the rear wheels via a 2-speed gear and chain. The first Landinis had tandem seating for two, but later models had four seats and conventional wheel steering. Signor Landini intended to mass produce these cars at Cameri, but nothing came of this project.

NG

1950 Land Rover estate car.
NICK BALDWIN

1987 Range Rover Vogue.
ROVER GROUP

LAND ROVER (GB) 1948 to date

1948–1973 The Rover Co. Ltd, Solihull, Warwickshire.
1973–1975 Rover, British Leyland UK Ltd, Solihull, Warwickshire.
1975 to date Land Rover Ltd, Solihull, Warwickshire.

One of the greatest success stories of the postwar British motor industry, the Land Rover is said to have come about because Rover's head of engineering, Maurice Wilks, wanted a replacement for the Jeep he was using on his Welsh estate, and was piqued that there was no British-built vehicle available. This may have sparked off Land Rover development, but Rover was looking for a means of increasing their exports, as they had never been an export-orientated company. The success of the Ferguson tractor turned them towards an agricultural product. They decided to build something on the lines of the Jeep, which could be used as a road vehicle or as a tractor. They did not envisage a long production run, so there was little money available for tooling, and standard Rover components were used wherever possible. The prototype was completed in the summer of 1947, using a 1389cc Rover Ten engine and gearbox in a Jeep chassis with a specially-designed two-range transfer box and 4-wheel drive. To simplify production for home and export markets, the steering wheel was located in the centre of the dashboard.

Spencer Wilks was sufficiently impressed with the prototype to sanction the building of 25 pilot vehicles, later increased to 50. These were completed in the latter part of 1947, and differed in several ways from the prototype. The 10hp engine was found to be insufficiently powerful, and was replaced by the 1595cc inlet-over-exhaust unit from the Rover 60 car, and the centre steering was abandoned as impractical. The chassis was a Rover-built simple box section, whose frame members were strips of flat sheet steel welded up in a jig. 48 pilot models were made, of which 16 survive today.

The Land Rover went into production in July 1948, and within three months the handbook listed dealers in 68 countries. Its appeal quickly extended beyond the farming community for which it had originally been planned, and customers included builders, industrial users and private buyers who valued cross-country mobility. Demand greatly exceeded supply at first, and production had to be increased, so that from 8000 in 1948/49, it had risen to 17,360 two years later, or double the output of Rover cars. Its sales exceeded those of cars right up to the introduction of the 2000 saloon in 1963.

Various special models were offered early on, including mobile compressor and welding vehicles, a fire engine, and an estate car. None of these sold very well, and Rover soon farmed out production of the special vehicles. The estate car, introduced for the 1948 Earls Court Commercial Vehicle Show, was dropped after only 641 had been made, though the design was later revived on long wheelbase Land Rovers.

The Land Rover gradually evolved in the 1950s, with a larger engine of 1997cc arriving in 1952, and in 1954 the wheelbase was extended from the original 80in (2032mm) to 86in (2184mm). At the same time a new long wheelbase model (107in/2718mm) was introduced. Two years later the wheelbases were extended again, to 88 and 109in (2235 and 2768mm), these being continued until 1985 when they were replaced by the 92.9 and 110in (2358 and 2792mm) chassis, these being known as the Defender Ninety and One Ten. The extensions were in the engine bay rather than in the load area, the reason becoming clear in 1957 when a 2052cc ohv diesel engine was offered as an option. In 1961 came the Series 11 with 2286cc ohv petrol engine, this being used up to 1984 when it was replaced by a 2494cc unit, also made in turbocharged diesel form. An alternative, available from 1979, was the 3528cc V8 also used in the Range Rover and SD1 cars. An important change in the Defender models was the adoption of the Range Rover's coil suspension in place of the traditional semi-elliptics. For 1999 the Defender was available with the 2496cc 5-cylinder turbo diesel also used in the Discovery and Freelander, as well as a 3947cc V8.

The Land Rover's production record was phenomenal, regularly exceeding that of passenger cars. The 100,000th was delivered in Autumn 1954, the 500,000th in April 1966 and the millionth in June 1976. By the spring of 1999, well over 1.5 million had been made. Land Rovers were also made abroad, about 10,000 by Minerva in Belgium between 1953 and 1956, and some by Tempo in Germany at about the same period. In Spain Land Rover Santana made a wide variety of vehicles, normal and forward control, some with locally designed bodywork, from 1956.

The Range Rover

The idea of a more 'civilised' version of the Land Rover had been around since the early 1950s, and prototype Road Rovers were built in 1952 and 1956. The concept was revived in 1966 when the success of upmarket Jeep Wagoneers convinced Rover that there would be a good market for such a machine. Spen King was in charge of the project, aided by Gordon Bashford, and they decided that they would start with a clean sheet, borrowing nothing from the Land Rover. An all-independent chassis with self-levelling rear suspension was chosen, and the prototype was powered by the 3-litre P5 engine. The arrival of the V8 was a boon to the project, giving the extra power needed to propel a substantial estate car at motorway speeds. The body was designed by King, although he was an engineer rather than a stylist, but when styling under David Bache took over the design to prepare it for production they made very few changes. The 4-wheel drive was permanently engaged, unlike the Land Rover whose front wheels could be disengaged, and there were disc brakes all round.

The project was enthusiastically welcomed by Leyland when they took over, and under the name Range Rover it went on the market in June 1970. As with the Land Rover, demand exceeded supply and the 250 cars made per week in the 1970s were quickly snapped up. In the 1980s weekly production rose to around 450. In 1987 Range Rover sales exceeded those of Land Rover for the first time. The design did not change greatly in the first 18 years of its life. An important development was the 4-door model which was introduced for 1982. This had been planned in 1972, but the financial problems of British Leyland delayed its introduction by nine years. In fact, the Swiss specialist Monteverdi had a 4-door Range Rover for sale in 1980. Automatic transmission came in 1982, and the manual box acquired five speeds in 1983. In 1986 a 2393cc VM turbo diesel was available. At the end of that year the 2-door model was dropped in rhd form as there was very little demand for it in Britain; 1986 sales were only 20 cars. In October 1992 came the LSE with 4.2-litre V8 engine and longer wheelbase, and the styling was revised in 1994. The 1999 range consisted of a single body style, the 4-door estate, with three engine options, a 2496cc 5-cylinder turbo diesel,

c.1990 Land Rover Defender 109 estate car.
NICK GEORGANO

and petrol V8s of 3947 and 4552cc. An all-new Range Rover is planned for 2001, with fresh styling and a range of BMW engines, a 4-litre diesel, 3.5 to 4.5-litre V8 and a new V12 with capacity in the region of 5.8 to 6 litres. The price of the latter is expected to be around £100,000, nearly double the most expensive 1999 V8.

A wide variety of special versions of the Range Rover have been made, including long-wheelbase models and 6-wheelers by Glenfrome, the extraordinary Glenfrome Facet, a 2-seater roadster for desert use introduced at the Riyadh Motor Show in 1983, and the luxurious Sheer Rovers by Wood & Pickett. The Range Rover has also been used as an ambulance and as a 6-wheeled fire engine.

Discovery and Freelander

In 1989 Land Rover brought out a new model to fill the gap between the basic Defender and the increasingly expensive Range Rover. Called the Discovery, it offered almost Range Rover comfort (Terence Conran-designed interior) at a lower price. Originally made in 2-door form only, it was joined by a 4-door version in 1990, and from 1998 only the 4-door was offered. Engine options were a 3528cc V8 and a 2495cc 4-cylinder turbo diesel, with automatic transmission available from 1992. It was facelifted in 1994 and again in 1998. Engine options for 1999 were a 2496cc 5-cylinder turbo diesel and a 3947cc petrol V8.

In 1997 Land Rover responded to the challenge of the Far Eastern 'lifestyle' 4 × 4s with the Freelander, a lighter and smaller vehicle than others in the range, made in 2- and 4-door models with the 2-door available in convertible form. They were powered by transversely-mounted 4-cylinder engines, a 1795cc 16-valve petrol or 1994cc turbo diesel. Like the Discovery, Range Rover, and Defender, they had permanent 4-wheel drive.

In March 2000 BMW sold the Land Rover Division to Ford.

NG

Further Reading
The Land Rover, a Collector's Guide, James Taylor,
Motor Racing Publications, 1988.
The Range Rover, James Taylor and Nick Dimbleby,
Crowood Auto Classics, 1996.

LANDRY ET BEYROUX *see* M.L.B.

1998 Land Rover Freelander Xei.
ROVER GROUP

1998 Land Rover Discovery ES.
ROVER GROUP

1905 Lane Steam tourer.
NICK BALDWIN

1906 La Nef 3-wheeler.
AUTOWORLD, BRUSSSELS

c.1955 Lansing Bagnall prototype saloon.
MICHAEL WORTHINGTON-WILLIAMS

LANE (US) 1900–1911

Lane Motor Vehicle Co., Poughkeepsie, New York.

The first steamer was built by the Lane brothers before they incorporated their company. It was a typical light steam car with 2-cylinder engine and chain final drive, but slightly unusual in that it offered seating for four. Fifteen were built in 1900 and 25 in 1901, when the company was formed. Whereas a single model had been offered in 1900, 1901 saw a range of five, from the No.0 Light Steam Runabout to the No.4 Steam Surrey. The 4-seaters had folding front seats, and all had tiller steering. Whereas many makers of steam cars gave up around 1904 or, like Locomobile, turned to petrol, Lane carried on with larger cars having frontal bonnets, wheel steering and 5-seater tourer bodies. By 1909 the largest had a 126in wheelbase and cost $3000. They were made in small numbers, annual production being mostly in two figures, though in 1909 they

turned out 150 cars. They retained single-chain drive to the end. In 1911 they were down to one model, the 20hp Model 25, of which 63 were made. After that the Lane brothers turned to the manufacture of barn door rollers.
NG

LA NEF (F) c.1901–1914

Lacroix et de Laville, Agen, Lot-et-Garonne.

This was the best known of three unconventional 3-wheelers made in Agen at about the same time, the others being the LASSOUGADE and the LA VA BON TRAIN. Joseph Lacroix (1861–c.1940) built his prototype La Nef in 1898. Like the later production models, it had a wooden frame consisting of two long pieces of ash that curved upwards and inwards towards the front, like the prow of a boat, to form the steering pivot point for the front-wheel. When stood on end it looked like a gothic arch, which possibly gave rise to the name, as 'nef' is French for a nave, although an older meaning of 'nef' is 'ship', which also fits well with the shape of the front of the car. The prototype was powered by a 2¼hp De Dion-Bouton engine, and as larger engines of 6 and 8hp became available these were fitted. Transmission was direct by belt to the rear axle, though most surviving La Nefs have a 2-speed Bozier epicyclic 'gearbox' which gave the action of a clutch. Steering was by a tubular steel tiller about 5ft long, and a La Nef could be had with 2- or 4-seater bodywork.

The design seems to have changed very little, and though it was archaic by 1914, the cars no doubt served their purposes for the mostly local customers who bought them. Production was about 200, an average of 14-15 per year, though probably more were made in the 1905–1910 period. At least three replicas were made in the 1960s, 'to use up the spare 8hp De Dion-Bouton engines I had about the place', said their builder Jackie Pichon. It is possible that production did not start until after 1903, as they are not listed as 'constructeurs' in the 1903 Michelin Guide. It is a shadowy make and although there are a surprising number of survivors, not all may be genuine. As historian Malcolm Jeal said 'They are such a simple machine that anybody could make them'.

After ending car production, the versatile Lacroix invented an improved cinematic projection system, followed by medical work which included locating shrapnel fragments in wounded soldiers, and analysis of blood. In his retirement he made electric clocks and carillons.
NG

Further Reading
'Unorthodoxy in Triplicate', Malcolm Jeal, *The Automobile*, April 1992.

LANPHER (US) 1906-c.1912

Lanpher Motor Buggy Co., Carthage, Missouri.

Formerly the Lanpher Brothers Carriage Works, this company made a small number of typical high-wheelers. They were powered by 12/14hp 2-cylinder engines, with epicyclic transmission, double-chain drive and solid tyres. The price was a modest $550. The Lanphers never advertised, even locally, and production was probably strictly limited.
NG

LANSDEN (US) 1906–1908

Lansden Co., Newark, New Jersey.

John M. Lansden formed the Birmingham Electric Manufacturing Co. in Birmingham, Alabama, in 1901, to make electric vehicles, but probably none were made there. By 1904 he had moved to Newark where he started production of electric trucks. In 1906 he added a light electric roadster called the Electrette which had a long bonnet housing the batteries. He also made a limousine which, unusually, had a shorter wheelbase (88in/2233mm) than the roadster (90in/2284mm). For 1907 and 1908 the Electrette and the limousine were continued, together with a longer limousine on a 108in (2741mm) wheelbase. Although Lansden said that they would build pleasure cars to order in succeeding years, their main product was electric trucks, which they continued to make until 1928.
NG

LANSING BAGNALL (GB) c.1956

Shay's Ltd, Basingstoke, Hampshire.

The well-known makers of fork-lift trucks built prototypes of two cars in the works of their parent company, Shay's. One was a 4-seater saloon powered by a 5hp transversely mounted vertical-twin engine driving the front wheels. The 3-speed gearbox was mounted below the engine, Mini style. The doors slid rather than opened in the usual way. The 2-seater sports car had a similar engine and power train, though not the sliding doors. The bodies were of fibreglass. Although both were extensively tested, they did not go into production. They were the last designs of Granville Bradshaw, better known for the A.B.C. in the 1920s.

NG

LANZA (I) 1895–1903

1895–1898 Stà Automobili Michele Lanza, Turin.
1898–1903 Fabbrica Automobili Lanza, Turin.
Michele Lanza owned a candle factory, but his interest in mechanics led him to build a car in 1895 which was the first petrol-engined 4-wheeler to be made entirely in Italy. It had a 2-cylinder horizontal engine mounted at the rear, with hot-tube ignition. The car had three forward speeds but no reverse, and final drive was by chains. The brakes operated directly on the iron tyres, in horse-drawn vehicle style, and steering was by a vertical column. Lanza subsequently made about a dozen cars, one ran in the 1000 mile Giro d'Italia of 1901. Giovanni Agnelli of F.I.A.T. was not impressed: 'Thank God you make candles in your factory. You'd go bankrupt if you manufactured only motorcars'.

NG

LA PERLE (F) 1913–1927

Louis Lefèvre, Boulogne-sur-Seine.
Louis Lefèvre launched his first car towards the end of 1913. It was a cyclecar with a choice of engines, 1060cc 2-cylinder and 1420cc 4-cylinder, friction disc transmission and belt drive. The radiator was sharply vee-shaped. Lefèvre had some sporting successes in 1914, and in 1919 reintroduced his cyclecar with the same transmission and a a V-twin Train engine. In 1921 he was joined by his younger brother Frantz and, becoming more ambitious, they bought five 1390cc 4-cylinder T-head engines from Bignan. Installed in Malicet et Blin chassis, they had a number of sporting successes in 1921, and this led the Lefèvres to begin production in 1922. They made their own engines, closely based on the Bignan design, though larger at 1498cc. The bodies were mostly open 3/4-seaters with pointed tails. For 1923 the engines gained pushrod-operated ohvs. The Lefèvres exhibited at the Paris Salon for the first time in 1924, when a new 1500cc six was shown. Like the other La Perle engines, this shaft-driven single-ohc unit was designed by Nemorin Causan who had been responsible for the T-head Bignan. The six carried similar bodies to the four, the pointed-tail sports model or a pedestrian-looking tourer.

There was no Salon in 1925, and by 1926 the firm's finances did not run to taking a stand, though they still had successes on the race track. Frantz was now the driver as Louis' health was failing, and in 1927 he committed suicide. In later years Frantz claimed that the company had made 300 4-cylinder cars and 75 sixes. Serge Pozzoli thought that these figures were based on orders received at the 1924 Salon, and not on cars actually delivered. His estimate of La Perle production was 75 fours and 10 sixes. A final 6-cylinder racing car was built in 1930, and two roadsters, one of which may have been the racer converted for road use. From 1930 onwards Frantz Lefèvre and his wife ran a garage outside Nice.

NG

Further Reading
'Les Automobiles La Perle', Serge Pozzoli,
Le Fanauto, November 1986 –January 1987.

LA PETITE (US) 1905

Detroit Automobile Manufacturing Co., Detroit, Michigan.
This car was well-named for it was very small, with a 5hp single-cylinder engine mounted under a tiny bonnet, 3-speed epicyclic transmission and shaft drive. The wheelbase was only 65in (1650mm). That it was only offered for one year its inventor J.P. Lavigne blamed on the poor quality of the engines that he bought. The makers offered another car called the PARAGON (i), in 1906, while Lavigne departed, later to make the GRISWOLD and J.P.L. cars.

NG

LA PLATA (GB) 1903–1906

Burgon & Ball Ltd, Malin Bridge, Sheffield, Yorkshire.

c.1925 La Perle 11/2-litre sports car.
NATIONAL MOTOR MUSEUM

1913 La Ponette 8/12hp 2-seater.
NICK BALDWIN

Burgon & Ball was founded in 1866 to make a patent sheep-shearing machine designed by James Ball. It became a limited company in 1898, and by then the works were called La Plata, possibly because of the Latin American market for the sheep-shearing machines. In 1903 they began to offer cars, the first having a 6hp De Dion-Bouton engine and Mercedes-type radiator, and being bought by a director of the company. Three more were registered in 1903, and during 1904 and 1905 a further 11 were sold. They were of 6, 9 and 12hp, the latter having an Aster engine, and the chassis at any rate came from France, the places of origin being Paris, Boulogne and Niort. The latter would indicate manufacture by BARRÉ, and the Paris cars could well have been by those well-known suppliers, LACOSTE ET BATTMANN. In 1905 there was also a La Plata Midget Tricar with 3hp engine, whose origin is unknown. Only one La Plata is known to have been registered in 1906, with a 'movable body by Laycock'. The motor business was a brief episode in the history of Burgon & Ball, who are still active today, their products including garden spades.

NG

Further Reading
Cars from Sheffield, Stephen Myers, Sheffield City Libraries, 1986.

LA PLUS SIMPLE *see* LEGROS

LA PONETTE (F) 1909–1925

1909–c.1920 Sté des Automobiles La Ponette, Chevreuse, Seine-et-Oise.
c.1920–1925 SA des Automobiles La Ponette, Clichy, Seine.
La Ponette (Pony) cars were designed and built by G. Granvaud, who began with a light car powered by an 827cc 8hp single-cylinder engine, with a 2-speed epicyclic transmission and shaft drive. It had a Renault-like bonnet with dashboard radiator, and a doorless 2-seater body with no weather protection. In 1912 these simple cars were replaced by more substantial machines with 1460cc 4-cylinder Ballot engines. Englishman John Averies was said to have had a hand in the design. He was certainly involved in the Rolling chassis made by Paul DUPRESSOIR in Maubeuge. The Rolling was made in England as the AVERIES.

After the war a series of conventional cars emerged from new premises at Clichy. They used Balllot or S.C.A.P. 4-cylinder engines, the largest having a capacity of 2890cc. In 1923 chassis numbers had reached 700, but it is not certain that this represented actual production.

NG

LA RAPIDE (GB) 1920

La Rapide Cyclecar Co., London.

Despite its French-sounding name, the La Rapide was apparently an all-British car. It was powered by an 8hp air-cooled J.A.P. engine bolted to outriggers on the offside of the frame. This drove by chain to a 3-speed Sturmey-Archer gearbox, and thence by belt to one rear wheel.

NG

L'ARDENNAISE (F) 1901

H. Lessieux et Cie, Rethel, Ardennes.

This was a shaft-driven light car powered by a 5hp single-cylinder engine. This could run on alcohol as an alternative to petrol, a feature of a number of cars made in North Eastern France, where the sugar beet industry produced large quantities of raw alcohol as a by-product. 2- or 4-seater bodies were listed.

NG

LARMAR (GB) 1946–1951

Larmar Engineering Co. Ltd, Ingatestone, Essex.

The reason why the Larmar was one of the narrowest cars in history – measuring just 28½in wide – was that it was designed primarily for invalids and the car was sold on its ability to fit through a doorway. A crude-looking single-seater, it was however a significant step up from invalid carriages of the time. It had such refinements as a cyclops headlamp, folding hood and a windscreen. Its 249cc BSA single-cylinder engine sat in the rear and drove only one of the rear wheels by chain to a top speed of 35mph (56km/h). Unusual features included sliding pillar front suspension, irs by torque rods and leaf springs and chain steering giving a turning circle of 15 feet. A slightly improved version, offered with a 350cc engine, was also made up until 1951, when the Larmar's slender appeal had been well and truly overtaken by the times.

CR

LAROS (I) 1932

S.A. Fratelli Pellegatti, Milan.

Pellagatti brothers were makers of outboard motors who planned to make a small 4-cylinder car. Prototypes were made and production was planned to start in the Spring of 1932, but Fiat bought up the designs to avoid competition.

NG

LA ROULETTE (F) 1912–1913

Cyclecars La Roulette, Courbevoie, Seine.

This was a tandem-seated cyclecar powered by an 8/10hp air-cooled V-twin Anzani engine with automatic inlet valves. Drive was by chain to a countershaft,

NICK GEORGANO

EARL, HARLEY (1893–1968)

Harley Jefferson Earl was by far the most important and influential automobile designer in America; perhaps in the world. He was born in 1893 in Hollywood, California, five miles from the Los Angeles shop where his father, J.W. Earl, built horsedrawn carriages. In 1908, J.W. began building automobile bodies and accessories like windshields and bumpers, whereupon the Earl Carriage Works became the Earl Automobile Works. In addition to custom bodies, J.W. began fabricating 'prop' vehicles for the movie industry.

As a teenager, Harley worked for his father and fell in love with motorcars. He learned to drive J.W. Earl's 1911 Mercer and raced it surreptitiously until J.W. found out when a customer congratulated him on his son's victory the previous Sunday. Harley stopped racing, but his fascination with fast cars continued for the rest of his life.

In 1918, the West Coast Cadillac distributor, Don Lee, bought the Earl Carriage Works and made it his coachbuilding bodyshop. Earle C. Anthony had just started a similar operation for his Packard franchise, and Walter M. Murphy would soon establish a similar coachbuilding adjunct to his Lincoln distributorship. Don Lee kept the younger Earl on as manager and chief designer of Don Lee Coachworks.

By this time, Hollywood had become a burgeoning movie colony, and Los Angeles had also produced a number of wealthy film stars, oil barons, land developers and citrus ranchers. Custom cars were in high demand. Earl designed and supervised the construction of special bodies for, among others, movie actors Roscoe 'Fatty' Arbuckle, Mary Pickford, Douglas Fairbanks, Tom Mix, Mary Miles Minter, film director Henry Lehrman and oil tycoon E.L. Doheny Jr.

In late 1925, through his own and Don Lee's Cadillac connections, Harley Earl was given a three-month leave of absence so he could go to Detroit to design Cadillac's forthcoming companion car, the 1927 LaSalle. While in Detroit, he greatly impressed Larry Fisher, the head of Cadillac, and GM president Alfred P. Sloan, Jr. The 1927 LaSalle proved so successful, both economically and stylistically, that Sloan offered Earl a permanent position designing all lines of General Motors vehicles.

Earl initially took part in styling the 1928–29 Cadillacs, the 1929 Chevrolet and the 1929 Buick. The 1929 Buick design became one of the few gaffes in Earl's career. This particular model had a rolled beltline--a puffed-out section that encircled the body below the side windows and around the back of the car. When Walter Chrysler saw the 1929 Buick, he remarked that it looked 'pregnant'. The press published Chrysler's comment, 'pregnant Buick' became a national joke, and the division's 1929 sales fell by some 56,000 cars.

The early Art & Colour Section was generally held in contempt by GM's old-guard Fisher Body Division engineers, but Earl persisted and soon won them over. Throughout the Depression, there was no doubt that Earl's styling group helped boost GM's car sales. When GM threatened to discontinue the 1933 Pontiac and the 1934 LaSalle due to red ink, Earl gave both marques daring new body designs and, in essence, saved them.

Earl had to make up his own job description. He pioneered the use of clay as a modeling medium, established styling competitions among his designers, set up separate studios for the various makes of cars and, in the late 1930s, even founded a school for young stylists. Harley Earl stood an imposing 6ft 4in, dressed like a movie star and sometimes had a short temper. Although he spoke in a soft voice, he soon earned a reputation for dismissing staff members who gave him only 99 per cent. He also occasionally fired people for no reason at all, and his younger designers lived in fear of his darker moods.

The name Art & Colour, which Earl never liked, was changed in 1937 to GM Styling. Earl himself, who by this time ruled over a small but powerful empire within GM, became a corporate vice president in 1940--the first with final drive by variable pulleys and double belts. The driver had 'a small side door fitted for his convenience', said *The Cyclecar*, but the rear seat passenger had to scramble over the side of the body.

NG

LA SAETTA (US) c.1952–1956

Testaguzza Body Co., Ogden, Michigan.
La Saetta was the name of a fibreglass body built by the Testaguzza brothers Gino and Cesare, who had styled cars for various Detroit car companies. It was a long 2-seat convertible based on a stock-length Chevrolet or Ford chassis. The body sold for about $1000, with a complete car going for $1800. They sold about 15 complete cars and an unknown number of shells. A special La Saetta was built for Gene Casaroll on a Dodge chassis, but he was disappointed with it and went to Ghia to produce the DUAL GHIA. La Saetta bodies were also used on the proposed ELECTRONIC electric cars.

HP

LA SALLE (US) 1927–1940

Cadillac Motor Car Co., Detroit, Michigan.
Like its parent make, Cadillac, the La Salle was named after a French explorer, René Robert de la Salle, who claimed Louisiana for his king, Louis X1V, in 1682.

1927 La Salle Series 303 saloon.
NATIONAL MOTOR MUSEUM

designer to hold that title in any major US car company. His vice presidency strengthened his and Styling's position in his rivalry with Fisher Body and GM's engineering staff.

In 1935, Earl had hired the 23-year-old William L. (Bill) Mitchell, a former advertising illustrator and fellow racing enthusiast. Earl soon made Mitchell head of the Cadillac studio, where Mitchell created the 1938 Cadillac 60-Special, a daring design that grafted a coupé trunk onto a sedan body. The 60-Special's window surrounds consisted of thin chrome frames, and Mitchell did away with traditional runningboards. The 60-Special appealed strongly to younger Cadillac owners and promptly became a tremendous sales success.

Earl also introduced the Buick Y-Job in 1938. This was a futuristic boattail convertible based on Buick mechanicals. Earl drove it as his personal car until 1949. Among the Y-Job's nuances were a hidden power top, hidden headlamps, a horizontal grill that anticipated Buick's postwar front ends, pushbutton door handles, 13-inch wheels, full rear skirts and much more.

During World War II, many of Earl's stylists left to serve in the armed forces. Those who remained designed camouflage and military vehicles, including a tank destroyer and at least one airplane. Earl also kept his people busy designing futuristic automobiles, and some of their ideas led to the shapes and styles of GM's postwar cars.

Cadillac's 1948 tailfins, for example, were inspired by those on the Lockheed P-38 Lightning airplane, as were the bullet-shaped 'dagmar' bumper guards. By 1949, each GM car division (except Chevrolet) received stylistic identifiers: Buick's portholes, Pontiac's silver streak, Oldsmobile's rocket and Cadillac's fins. Chevrolets were considered so plentiful that they needed no formal identifier.

Earl was also instrumental in setting up the yearly dreamcar exhibits known as General Motors Motoramas. These were free-admission shows that were trucked from city to city in huge caravans. They consisted of Broadway-like stage revues, displays of future household items like microwave ovens and video telephones, GM's latest production cars plus forward-looking concept vehicles. Harley Earl's second personal car, the 1951 LeSabre, became perhaps the most influential of Motorama dreamcars. Motorama exhibitions continued from 1953 through 1961 and attracted some 10.5 million spectators.

Earl used feedback from Motoramas to reinforce his own notions about how production cars ought to look. GM didn't hold product clinics or focus groups per se, and Earl pretty much knew intuitively what the American public wanted. Motoramas allowed him to extend feelers into the future. GM's wraparound windshields of 1953–55 came directly from his Motorama experience, as did the 1953 Chevrolet Corvette, the 1955 Nomad station wagon and the 1957–60 Cadillac Eldorado Brougham. Many lesser bits and pieces of everyday General Motors cars also originated with Motorama dream machines.

The years 1954–55 stood out as two of Earl's best, perhaps the best, both in terms of aesthetics and the number of GM cars sold. The 1954 Buicks and Oldsmobiles were among the industry's most refined–very carefully wrought, clean and totally appropriate to their markets. So was the 1955 Chevrolet, with its Italianate grill and new V8 engine. Earl peaked in those two seasons, and then, sadly, his Midas touch got mired in chrome.

By 1957, Harley Earl seemed to be groping, and by 1958 he'd lost his way. Good as he'd always been, he couldn't stop adding more chrome and ornamentation. He ordered one designer, Stan Parker, to put 100 pounds of chrome trim on the 1958 Buick. Parker balked but did as he was told. The next time Earl came into the studio, he raged, 'I said 100 pounds; that's only 80!' He wasn't joking.

The 1958 Buick and Oldsmobile became dinosaurs and sold poorly. Not that it was totally Earl's fault: The US economy was in recession that year. But the word was out that Earl was losing it. Lots of designers get stuck in an era, and Earl's had passed.

GM's 1959 models, which represented a total break with Earl's philosophy of rounder/fatter/chromier, resulted from a subtle but definite rebellion on the part of GM's studio chiefs. Several had managed to see Virgil Exner's new 1957 Plymouths and Chryslers in August 1956. Exner's 2-door hardtops, particularly the Plymouth, had delicate, shallow roofs, low, clean beltlines, lots of glass, nicely proportioned fins and a great lack of ornamentation, all of which shocked GM's designers. They immediately recognized a major threat to GM's styling leadership, and they realized Earl's chromed locomotives were headed in totally the wrong direction.

So the design chiefs, led by Earl's second-in-command, Bill Mitchell, went back to their studios. Then, with Earl away at the European motorshows, they developed their own lower, slimmer, more sharply defined models. When Earl returned and recognized the insurrection, he walked from studio to studio but didn't utter a word for three days. Finally, he approved the new design direction. Thus began a 19-month crash program to put the revised 1959 cars into production. With the tight schedule, Fisher Body lobbied to build all five GM nameplates on one basic platform, and that's the way they came out. All shared the same floorpan, roofs, front doors and cowl.

Alfred P. Sloan Jr., whose vision had shaped General Motors and who'd been Harley Earl's patron and ally for 31 years, retired in 1956. Two years later, on 1 December 1958, GM's mandatory retirement age required Earl to leave, too. As a going-away gift, GM designed and built one final Motorama-like roadster for Harley and his wife, Sue, so they could drive into the Florida sunset together. They retired to Palm Beach. Ten years later, Harley Earl suffered a massive stroke. He passed away on 10 April 1968, aged 75.

ML

1940 La Salle Series 40-50 convertible coupé.
NATIONAL MOTOR MUSEUM

1934 La Salle Series 50 convertible coupé.
NATIONAL MOTOR MUSEUM

A car to fill the gap between Buick and Cadillac had been thought of in the early 1920s by Alfred P. Sloan, but it was Lawrence Fisher, Cadillac's president from 1924, who set the programme in motion, and it was he who made the important decision to hire Harley Earl as the stylist for the new car. Earl moved to Detroit in January 1926, and produced the new designs in three months. He openly admitted that he took his inspiration from the Hispano-Suiza, a car he admired above all others. From the French car came the La Salle's strong peaked radiator shape with its winged emblem, the big bowl headlamps with badge tie-bar between them, and the graceful front wings. The 2-tone colour schemes were Earl's own.

The La Salle was powered by a 4965cc V8 engine of the same family as the Cadillac's, but with a smaller stroke/bore ratio, 1.58:1, compared with 1.64:1 for the larger Cadillac unit. The La Salle's was more efficient, giving 80bhp, or 16.1bhp/litre, against 12.71bhp/litre for the Cadillac. The right cylinder bank was 1in forward of the left, making it possible to fit the rods side by side on the crankpins. This layout was adopted on the Cadillac engine for 1928.

The La Salle was launched to great acclaim in March 1927, in eleven body styles, all with dual colour schemes, eight of them on a 125in (3172mm) wheelbase, and three on a 134in (3401mm). Prices ran from $2495 for a short-wheelbase phaeton to $2875 for a 7-seater Imperial sedan on the long wheelbase. In addition, there were four styles made by Fleetwood on the short wheelbase, at considerably higher prices, $4275-4700.

In the years 1927 and 1928, La Salle accounted for more than half of the Cadillac Division's registrations, 26,807 out of 47,136. The La Salle's success earned Harley Earl a permanent appointment with General Motors, heading a newly-created department, the Art & Colour Section, which became GM Styling in 1937. He remained there until his retirement in 1959.

Nearly 60,000 La Salles were sold in the next three years. For 1929 it shared with Cadillac the major improvement of a synchromesh gearbox. American cars were already favoured the world over by drivers who disliked gear changing, as in most of them one could do much of one's driving in top gear, but now came a system which finally banished the crunching of gears for ever. Cadillac had tested ten different kinds of synchromesh over 1½ million miles before putting it on the market. Safety glass was another 1929 innovation, and in this final pre-Depression year the division sold 36,698 cars, of which 20,290 were La Salles. From 1931 La Salle and Cadillac shared the same 115bhp 5784cc V8 engine. This lasted until 1933 when La Salle was dropped half way through the season, to be revived for 1934 as a completely new car, with a 3937cc straight-8 engine. This had the same dimensions as the contemporary Oldsmobile Eight, though Cadillac's publicity claimed that it was developed by Cadillac engineers and built in their factory. Probably it was basically an Oldsmobile engine, but assembled by Cadillac to their standards.

The new La Salle was $1000 cheaper than the lowest-priced Cadillac, and was quite different in styling, with a tall, narrow radiator grill flanked by teardrop headlamps which were mounted on the bonnet sides. It was styled by Jules Agramonte, working under Harley Earl's direction. Sales were more than double the 1933 figures, at 7218 for the model year. There were no major changes on the 1935 and 1936 La Salles, though Fisher all-steel 'turret top' bodies were introduced for 1935, together with a slightly larger engine of 4063cc.

The next major change for La Salle came with the 1937 models, which reverted to a V8 engine, a Cadillac-built unit of 5278cc, in new bodies which were shared with Oldsmobile and the more expensive Buicks. Sales jumped from 13,000 to just over 32,000 in the 1937 model year. This was the best annual figure ever for La Salle, but it was still way behind the Packard 120 which was seen as the La Salle's main rival, and which sold over 50,000 over the same period. Sales dropped to 15,500 in 1938, which was a bad season for the US motor industry generally, and although they picked up somewhat in 1939, the La Salle name was dropped at the end of the 1940 season. By then Cadillac had lowered their prices, and with a difference of only $300 between them, there was not much incentive to buy a La Salle, whose name never had the prestige of Cadillac. For 1941 the position occupied by La Salle was taken by the new Series 61 Cadillac.

NG

Further Reading
Cadillac and La Salle, Walter McCall, Crestline Publications, 1982.

LA SALLE-NIAGARA (US) 1905–1906

La Salle-Niagara Automobile Co., Niagara Falls, New York.
This car was made in two models, the Model A with 26/30hp 4-cylinder engine and shaft drive, and the Model B with 16/18hp 2-cylinder engine and chain drive. This reversed the usual practice at the time of using chain drive for higher-powered cars. The car was occasionally called the Niagara, the name born by a smaller car made in Wilson, New York, which was built by a predecessor company of La Salle-Niagara.

NG

LASER *see* UVA

LA SIRÈNE (F) 1900–1902

Fernandez et Cie, Paris.
Compagnie La Sirène, Paris.
This was a light car powered by a 5hp air-cooled V-twin engine, with 3-speed gearbox and shaft drive. In 1900 it was marketed under the name Fernandez It had a tubular frame and wire wheels. The body was a 2-seater, but there was space at the rear for a luggage carrier or another seat. A V-twin which was claimed to develop 24hp was entered for the 1901 Paris-Berlin Race.

NG

LASSOUGADE (F) c.1904

Hache et Lassougade, Agen, Lot-et-Garonne.
This was another of the odd 3-wheelers made at Agen, and less is known of it than of its rivals, the LA NEF and the LA VA BON TRAIN. Like the latter it had a tubular steel frame and wheel steering, and a surviving example has an Aster engine, whereas the La Nef seems always to have relied on De Dion Bouton power. The maker has been variously rendered as Hache et Lassougade, Ache, or Ache Frères. Since Ache is the French rendering of the letter 'H', it may have been H. Lassougade. In 1907 the De Dion-Bouton agent in Agen was a firm called Lassoujade, which may have been the same. Two, or possibly three, survive out of a claimed production run of 15-20 cars.

NG

LATHAM (GB) 1983–1990

1983-c.1988 Latham Sportscars, Penzance, Cornwall.
c.1988–1990 Latham Sportscars, Bicester, Oxfordshire.
The first Latham prototype appeared at the Stoneleigh kit car show in 1983, as a one-off XKSS lookalike on Triumph TR4 parts. The production version used Triumph Dolomite parts, and the complicated central fibreglass monocoque was supplemented by front and rear steel subframes, steel-reinforced sills and honeycomb floor and bulkheads. It no longer resembled an XKSS but had a curvaceous 1960s-style shape in its own right. 26 Latham Super Sports were built in total.

CR

LA TORPILLE (i) (B) 1900–1902

Sté l'Automobile, Vleurgat-lez-Bruxelles.
Three models of car were advertised under the name La Torpille, of 4, 6.8 and 12hp. The latter had four cylinders and was chain driven, but the two smaller cars, with single-cylinder engines, had shaft drive. Engines were by De Dion-Bouton or Kelecom. The Société l'Automobile, run by J. Matthys, were also body builders, and in 1899 they exhibited an English Daimler with one of their wagonette bodies.

NG

c.1904 Lassougade 3-wheeler.
MALCOLM JEAL

LA TORPILLE (ii) (F) 1907–1923

Léonce et Camille Bobrie, Saumur, Maine-et-Loire.
The Bobrie brothers were bicycle makers and Berliet agents who made a limited number of cars, starting with a tandem-seated cyclecar which they christened La Torpille. It had a 4-cylinder Ballot engine of 6 or 8hp and an Arbel chassis. The front axle was made by the Bobries themselves, as were the bodies. The 2-speed gearbox gave direct drive on top. Not more than 12 were made up to 1914, and perhaps the same number after the war. These had either tandem or side-by-side seating and Ballot engines, though the last two or three were powered by a 6/8hp 4-cylinder Fivet engine. The brothers went their separate ways in 1923; Léonce started a general engineering business at Saintes, while Camille made a final car powered by a 12hp S.C.A.P. engine with a Malicet et Blin chassis. Léonce's family preserved a Torpille for many years; it is possibly still in existence.

NG

LA TORPILLE (iii) (F) 1912–1913

Perrin et Cie, Annonay, Ardèche.
This was a tandem-seated 3-wheeled cyclecar with a very long body, and chain drive to the single rear wheel. This had double tyres in the manner of a heavy truck, to accommodate the weight of the long car. Either a single- or 4-cylinder engine could be provided, driving through a 3-speed gearbox which drove by shaft to the clutch casing. This contained a bevel drive from the cross-shaft, from which final drive was taken by chain. The front of the car resembled an Alda, with coal-scuttle bonnet and dashboard radiator.

NG

LA TROTTEUSE (F) 1913–1914

St Remy, Seine-et-Oise.
Two models were made of this light car, a single-cylinder of 640cc and a 4-cylinder of 1327cc. Both were 2-seaters and had shaft drive.

NG

LAUER (D) 1922

Automobilwerke Lauer GmbH, Merseburg.
The central German town of Merseburg was an unlikely location for a car factory, and the Lauer was the only car made there. It was a small car with a 5/15PS 4-cylinder engine.

HON

LAUGHLIN (US) 1961

Gary B. Laughlin, Fort Worth, Texas.
Gary Laughlin, a Texas car dealer and racing driver, had Italian stylist Scaglietti rebody three new Corvette chassis with bodywork similar to the Ferrari 250 Tour de France berlinettas. Laughlin got one of them, with Jim Hall and Carroll Shelby ordering the other two. Although Laughlin estimated delivery times at about nine months and prices at about half that of a comparable Ferrari, only the first three were completed.

HP

1920 Laurence-Jackson 8-10hp 2-seater.
NICK BALDWIN

1905 Laurin-Klement 8/9hp 2-seater, Vaclav Laurin at the wheel.
NATIONAL MOTOR MUSEUM

c.1910 Laurin-Klement 14/16hp 2-seater.
NICK BALDWIN

LAUNCESTON (GB) 1920

Launceston Engineering Co. Ltd, Willesden Junction, London.
The Launceston had quite a substantial-looking 4-seater tourer body, considering that it was powered by a 12/20hp flat twin engine. Its appearance was enhanced by Michelin disc wheels, but very few were made.

NG

LAUREL (US) 1916–1920

Laurel Motors Corp., Richmond and Anderson, Indiana.
The Laurel began its life in Richmond, Indiana, operations being transferred in late 1917. It was a low-priced car with prices from $850 for the 5-seater touring model to $895 for its 4-seater roadster. Prices would escalate in the company's final days. Laurel cars were powered by a 4-cylinder G. B. & S. engine and were distinguished by the car's name which appeared in script above the louvres on both sides of the bonnet. Wheelbase was 115in (2919mm) and total production failed to exceed 300 cars.

KM

LAURENCE-JACKSON (GB) 1919–1920

Laurence-Jackson Ltd, Wolverhampton, Staffordshire.
This was a light 2-seater powered by a 976cc 8/10hp V-twin J.A.P. engine, with friction transmission giving four forward speeds, and duplex chain drive to a differential-less rear axle. It was priced originally at £200, but this had risen to £295 by 1920. It was also know as the L.J.

NG

LAURENT (i) (F) 1901

Laurent et Cie, Vierzon, Cher.
The Laurent voiturette was powered by a 5hp 2-cylinder engine. Transmission was by a 4-speed constant-mesh gearbox, and it had shaft drive.

NG

LAURENT (ii) (F) 1907–1908

Laurent et Cie, St Étienne, Loire.
This company made a number of steam trucks, and were reported to have produced a few 4-cylinder petrol-engined cars, but further details are not known.

NG

LAURIN & KLEMENT (A/CS) 1905–1926

1895–1905 Laurin & Klement, tovarna velocipedu, motocyklu a automobilu, Mlada Boleslav.
1905–1907 Laurin & Klement, tovarna motorovych kol a vozu, Mlada Boleslav.
1907–1925 Laurin & Klement, a.s., tovarna automobilu, Mlada Boleslav.
In 1895, Vaclav Laurin (mechanic, 1865–1930) and Vaclav Klement (bookseller, 1868–1938) founded a small bicycle repair shop in Mlada Boleslav, Bohemia, which was then part of the Austro-Hungarian Empire. Laurin & Klement began to design and build their own bicycles and were employing 28 people by 1897. In 1898 they moved to larger premises in Mlada Boleslav. On a visit to Paris, Klement was inspired by the designs of motor-driven bicycles and tricycles. His efforts to improve on these designs led to the development of the motor cycle, and production commenced in a newly completed plant where 40 people were employed. The production of bicycles was stopped in 1905, in the same year that the 4-cylinder in-line engined motor cycle was introduced and the automobile era at L&K began. That year two prototypes of a light car were exhibited in Vienna. These were of the model A Voiturette which had its 1005cc 2-cylinder 7hp V-unit positioned in front of the driver and could be ordered to seat either two or four. About 44 cars were sold up to 1907.

The following year the Type A was joined by the type B powered by a 1399cc 2-cylinder 8-9hp engine (250 cars were made), and the type C (2042cc, 2-cylinder of 10-12hp, 14 cars) and later the C2 (2281cc, 12-14hp, 49 cars). In the year 1907, six different types appeared: the D with 3402cc 4-cylinder 18hp engine (2 cars), the E with 4562cc 28hp engine (15 cars), the B2 (1907–1908) with 1595cc V-twin 10-12hp (10 cars), the F (1907–1909) with 2438cc 4-cylinder 14-16 hp engine (350 cars), the FF as open 6-seater with 4847cc 8-cylinder in-line 40hp engine, and finally the BS (1907–1908) fitted with a 2-cylinder 1399 engine. The type FF was the only 8-cylinder vehicle to be built by L&K in the prewar era. The first agency for the importation of L&K cars into Great Britain was set up in 1907, and at least one type B2 was exported to Japan that year.

In 1907 the company went public and an extra 4000 square metres of floor-space was added to the premises. In 1908 L&K products entered an endurance event from St Petersburg to Moscow, took first nine places, and this established them firmly in Russia and led to orders that amounted to 35 per cent of their total exports.

A wide range of models, all 4-cylinder vehicles, was offered right up to the advent of World War I: the types FN, GDV and RC (1909–1913) with 2660cc 18-24hp engines of which about 366 were built, bodied as a taxicab, phaeton, limousine, landaulet, 2- or 4-seater sports car and torpedo; while of the G type (1908–1911, 1555cc, 10-12hp, later 1767cc, 12-14hp) there were 308 made.

The L&K cars of the K and L ranges were manufactured also as light vans. The passenger cars L and O (1909–1911, 212 cars) had a 3686cc 20-25hp engine, the K and Kb (1911–1915, 214 cars) a 4253cc 28-32hp engine, and the LK (1911–1912, only 2 cars for Baron Liebieg) a 4084cc Knight engine.

In 1913 the RAF car works based in Reichenberg (Liberec), and its Knight sleeve-valve engine licence, became part of the L&K. That year the M-series appeared:

1905 L'Automotrice tourer in Coupe du Salon.
NATIONAL MOTOR MUSEUM

the M, Mb (1913–1915, 90 cars) with 3817cc 15-40hp SV engines; the Md, Me, Mf, Mg, Mh, Mi (1917–1923, 657 cars) with 4713cc 18-50hp engines; the MK, 400 (1913–1924, 105 cars) with 3308cc 13-40hp Knight engines (the first 8 cars were produced at the RAF works). The RK (1912–1916) was fitted with a 4713cc 18-50hp Knight engine and a few of them were bodied as a sports phaeton, others were ambulances and light delivery vans. The O-series included the basic O-type (1913–1915; 1919, 100 cars) with 2614cc 11-30hp SV engine, and the OK (1914–1916, 25 cars) had a 2413cc 10-30hp engine, formerly built at the RAF factory.

The S-range started in 1911 and was in production until 1925 when L&K merged with Skoda. The S°; and Sa types (1911–1916, 106 cars produced) had a 1771cc 12-14hp SV engines with an L-head, while the Sb and Sc types (1912–1915, 212 cars) had a 12-16hp output from the same engine. The bigger Sd, Se, Sg and Sk types (1913–1917, 361 cars) were fitted with a 1847cc 7-20hp engine.

In the war years the Sh and Sk models (1914–1917, 161 cars) with 2065cc 8-24hp were produced, as well as the Si, Sl, Sm, So, 200 and 250 types (1916–1924, 840 cars) with 2413cc 9-25hp engines. The light T and Ta types (1914–1921, 102 cars) had 1199cc 5-12hp engines.

In October 1918, Bohemia became a part of the newly formed independent state of Czechoslovakia. After 1918, L&K found themselves faced with a difficult situation. Exports were curtailed, and some traditional markets, notably Russia, were lost.

An improved version of the old S-type of 1911, the Sp (1923–1925, 324 cars) came, fitted with a 2413cc 9-30hp engine. Among the last Laurin & Klement cars belong the models of the A and 100 (1922–1924, 106 cars) with a 1791cc 7-20hp engines, and the type 105 (1923–1925, 277 cars) powered by the same engine.

A disastrous fire in 1924 was a serious set-back and when Skoda acquired Laurin & Klement in 1925, and Vaclav Klement became manager of the new venture, extensive reconstruction work began and a new mechanised assembly plant, a coach-building shop, research laboratories, and a development department were built.

After 1925, the cars were called Laurin & Klement-Skoda. The models 110 (first and second series, 1925–1927, 435 cars made) were fitted with a 1791cc 7-20hp engine, or (third to tenth series, 1926–1929, 2550 cars) had a more powerful 1944cc 7-25hp engine, as also the type 120 had, being made from 1925 to 1928.

The first series of the type 115 (1925–1926, 100 cars) had the 1791cc engine, the second series (1926–1927, 101 cars) and the type 125 (1927–1929, 1650 cars) were equipped with the 7-25hp 1944cc engines.

The other L&Ks were more luxury cars: the L&K-Skoda 350 with 14-50hp 3498cc Knight engine (1925–1927, 50 cars), and the type 360 (1926–1927, 27 cars) with 3970cc OHV 16-55hp engine.

Until a new range was introduced by Skoda in 1927, the cars were still Laurin & Klement, one of the major European makers in the pre-1914 days.

MSH

Further Reading
Laurin & Klement – Skoda, Peter Kosisek and Jan Kralik, Motorpress, Prague, 1995.

LAUTH-JUERGENS (US) 1907–1909
Lauth-Juergens Co., Chicago, Illinois.
Jacob Lauth built two experimental cars in 1905, both with 4-cylinder engines, one having side-valves in a T-head, and the other ohvs. After two years he obtained financial support from Theodore Juergens; together they formed a company to manufacture a large touring car powered by a 40hp engine. This was displayed at the Chicago Automobile Show in December 1907, and another model of 50hp was listed in 1908/09, but few were sold. The partners had more success with trucks, which they made at Fremont, Ohio up to 1915. Their chief engineer was Magnus Hendrickson, who in 1913 set up his own truck-making company which survived into the 1990s, latterly as HMC.
NG

L'AUTOMOBILE (BR) 1978–1980s
The first car of this make was a replica of a 1931 Alfa Romeo Monza, on a VW Beetle floorpan. There was also a streamlined 2+2 coupé called the Ventura.
NG

L'AUTOMOTRICE (F) 1901–1907
1901–1903 Sté l'Automobile, Bergerac, Dordogne.
1904–1907 Sté l'Automotrice, Bergerac, Dordogne.
Despite the change of company name, the cars were called L'Automotrice from the start. They began with a voiturette powered by a 5hp single-cylinder Aster engine, with single-chain drive. By 1904 they were making large 4-cylinder cars

c.1904 La Va Bon Train 6hp 3-wheeler.
MALCOLM JEAL

in several engine sizes from 18/22 to 40/45hp, with honeycomb radiators and double-chain drive. These cars were sometimes known as Radia in 1904 and 1905, and Baudouin-Radia from 1905 to 1907.

NG

L'AUTO VAPEUR (F) 1905–1906

Sté l'Auto Vapeur, Paris.

The Auto Vapeur was one of a crop of short-lived steam cars which appeared in France in 1905. It had a Serpollet-type horizontal 4-cylinder engine under the floor, and a vertical multi-tube boiler under the bonnet. The latter gave it the appearance of a petrol-engined car.

NG

LA VA BON TRAIN (F) 1904–c.1910

Larroumet et Lagarde, Agen, Lot-et-Garonne.

This was one of the trio of odd 3-wheelers made in Agen, (others were the LASSOUGADE and the LA NEF). Messieurs Larroumet and Lagarde founded their business in 1891 as bicycle makers and general engineers, and gained Type Approval for their car in April 1904. It had a similar layout to the La Nef, though there were two important differences, wheel steering instead of La Nef's long tiller, and a steel frame in place of wood. Whereas La Nef was offered in 4-seater form, it appears that La Va Bon Train was made only as a 2-seater. The engine was a single-cylinder of their own make, though they stressed that the cylinders were made in a foundry in the Ardennes. For an extra 250 francs a genuine 6hp De Dion-Bouton engine could be supplied. The price of 2000 francs included two lessons in operating the car. The original model had a Bozier 2-speed epicyclic 'gearbox', but later ones had a conventional sliding pinion gearbox, also giving two forward speeds. Final drive was by belt or chain, according to the customer's choice, and a differential was provided from 1907. Though some lists carry the car up to 1914, a local who owned a surviving example doubted that any were made after 1910. He also quoted a total production figure of 42 cars. The name, La Va Bon Train translates loosely as 'Goes like blazes' or as the charmingly old-fashioned Ralph Doyle said in *The World's Automobiles* 'Goes like Billy-oh'. During the years of car production Larroumet and Lagarde continued to make bicycles, including a special model with stronger tyres for postmen, and one for ladies and priests.

NG

LA VALKYRIE (F) 1905–1907

Sté Parisienne de Construction d'Automobiles La Valkyrie, Montrouge, Seine.

This was a conventional car made in two models, a 1728cc 10hp 2-cylinder and a 2270cc 14/16hp 4-cylinder. Both were shaft-driven.

NG

LAVERDA (I) 1991

Moto Laverda SpA, Vincenza.

Having created a 4×4 vehicle in the Steyr-Puch Pinzgauer mode in 1984, the famous motorcycle manufacturer Laverda nearly became a supercar manufacturer with the 1991 Laverda A-00946. At the behest of the Shinken Corp., an import-export company based in Tokyo, this was effectively a roadgoing version of a Nissan Group C racing car and was to use a modified version of the Nissan 300ZX 3-litre V6 engine. The Laverda was one of several such projects quashed in the general economic downturn of the early 1990s.

CR

LAVIE (F) c.1904

A. Lavie, Paris.

Little is known about this car, which was apparently made in the Avenue de Choisy in Paris. A surviving example is dated 1904, though from its appearance it could be several years younger. It is powered by a 6hp vertical-twin engine and has a 3-speed gearbox and 2-seater body.

NG

LA VIGNE see J.P.L.

LA VIOLETTE (F) 1910–1914

Franc et Cie, Levallois-Perret, Seine.

This make began as a cyclecar powered by a large single-cylinder engine of 700cc, with friction transmission and final drive by long chain to the nearside rear wheel. In 1913 they offered a similar design with 2-cylinder engine, and a light car with 10hp 4-cylinder engine, shaft drive and a 4-seater body.

NG

LAVOIE (CDN) 1923

Lavoie Automobile Devices Ltd, Montreal, Quebec.

The Lavoie was a 'car of the future', designed by Alphonse Joseph Lavoie of Montreal, which failed to exceed its lone prototype, a 4-door sedan. The car, launched at the Montreal Automobile Show in January 1923, featured unitary construction of chassis and body plus 4-wheel brakes and a 4-cylinder engine of Lavoie's own design. The car was built for the then-existing roads of Canada in general and the Province of Quebec in particular. Lavoie, however, was not able to raise sufficient capital to continue his plans for the car's manufacture and its boxy design failed to interest either the public or possible financial backers. After working for several years in automobile plants in the United States, Lavoie returned to Montreal where he designed and completed a prototype of a bus in 1940 which he was planning to promote when he died in early 1941.

KM

LAW (US) 1905–1907

Law Auto Manufacturing Co., Bristol, Connecticut.

The Law was a 4-cylinder car, designed by Frederick A. Law, a Hartford, Connecticut engineer and designer who had designed a petrol-powered car as early as 1902. The car was marketed as a 5-seater touring type priced in the $2000 to $2500 range. Production was small and the company ceased to exist in mid-1907.

KM

LAWIL (I) 1967–1986

Lawil SpA Costruzioni Meccaniche e Automobilistiche, Varzi, Pavia.

Italy's principal microcar constructor during the 1970s was perhaps better known in France, where various models were sold under the name WILLAM (LaWIL LAMbretta); they were also sold in Britain (through Crayford Auto Development) as the William. Lawil really restarted the microcar industry with a tiny, boxy hard-top model called the City. It had a steel square tube chassis with wishbone ifs and bodywork made of steel and fibreglass. A front-mounted 123cc single-cylinder scooter engine drove the rear wheels via a 4-speed manual gearbox; later examples gained a more powerful 246cc 2-cylinder engine. The single-cylinder engine produced 5.6bhp, while the twin-cylinder had 12bhp. A convertible model was also produced under the name Varzina and eventually long-wheelbase estate and pickup versions were marketed. At the 1972 Paris Motor Show, Paolo Pasquini's Log was presented. This fixed-roof plastic-bodied 2-seater had bumpers running all the way around the car. A further model was

1922 Leach (ii) Six Californian Top tourer.
NATIONAL MOTOR MUSEUM

the 3-wheeled Berlina A4, presented in 1984, which resembled certain other Italian microcars of the period.

CR

LAWSON MOTOR WHEEL *see* DOUGILL

LAWTER (US) 1909
Safety Shredder Co., New Castle, Indiana.
Benjamin Lawton designed two cars with 16 or 20hp 2-cylinder engines, 3-speed epicyclic transmission and double-chain drive. He contracted manufacture to the Safety Shredder Co. until he could find his own works, but his money ran out before he could do so. A small number of his cars were built by the Safety Shredder Co.

NG

L.B. (F) 1925
Lucien Borel, Villefranche de Lauraguais, Haute-Garonne.
This was a 2-cylinder cyclecar with front-wheel drive, made in very small numbers.
NG

LCC ROCKET *see* LIGHT CAR COMPANY

L.C.E. (US) 1915–1916
L.C. Erbes, St Paul, Minnesota; Waterloo, Iowa.
Louis C. Erbes built a cyclecar called the Baby Moose, and planned to make a larger car called the Bull Moose. Before it went into production he changed the name to his own initials. At St Paul he was the landlord for the Duesenberg brothers, and built one or two racing cars for Bob Burman. Pilot models of the L.C.E. were made in the former Cutting factory in Jackson, Michigan, but it went into production late in 1914 as a 1915 model from the former Mason plant in Waterloo, Iowa. It was a conventional 4-cylinder car made in tourer, roadster and Gentleman's Speedster form. Shortage of materials prevented many from being made.

NG

L. & E. (US) 1922–1932
Lundelius & Eccleston, Los Angeles, California.
The L. & E. was initially announced during 1922 although it appears that no prototype was forthcoming for another two years. The 'axleless' L. & E. principle incorporated four transverse springs located at both front and rear to support the wheels. The basic promotion was no different from that of any other car, although it is likely from the start that the company was trying to market the idea rather than the car. In 1924 a Franklin, with a wheelbase stretched from 115in (2919mm) to 132in (3350mm), served as the L. & E. prototype. Subsequent L. & E. cars which appeared over the years, presumably changed to update automotive design, were all standard brand cars, suitably rebadged, re-hubbed and changed in other ways, not so much to disguise them as to create an individuality. L. & E. ceased promoting its axleless concept in 1932 although cars were reportedly built in 1933 and 1934 when the company stopped trying to promote the idea and went into other lines of endeavour.

KM

LEACH (i) (US) 1899–1901
Leach Motor Vehicle Co., Everett, Massachusetts.
Like many other car makers, John M. Leach started in business as a cycle maker before building a steam car in 1899. It was typical of its kind, with a 6hp vertical 2-cylinder engine, single-chain drive, tubular frame and tiller steering. 2- or 4-seater bodies were offered. The makers admitted that it was 'intended only for good roads'. John Leach closed his works in January 1901.

NG

LEACH-BILTWELL; LEACH (ii) (US) 1919–1923
Leach Motor Car Co., Los Angeles, California.
The first of these large and expensive cars were sold as Leach-Biltwells, the latter half of the name dropped a year or so after production began. They were large and popular with stars of the silent screen. The Leach was available in a number of models, the most popular of which used the 'California top', a hard-top with sliding windows on the side, which allowed the cars to be used either as sedans or touring-cars. Although they appeared in national trade publications, the Leach cars were basically focused on California buyers who had the $6500 asking price. The cars were impressive, powered by a 6-cylinder Continental engine and during the four years of production, few visual changes were made, if at all, with the exception of switching from wire to disteel in 1921. With a wheelbase of 134in (3401mm), the cars were sold exclusively by two distributors who sold the cars directly to the purchaser. Leach promotional literature made much of movie star ownership, including in their brochures such box office attractions as cowboy Tom Mix and a good many of those who posed for Leach actually owned the cars. In 1921 Harry A. Miller became a member of the Leach board of directors. His new 'Power Plus' 6-cylinder engine, called the 999, which could exceed 100bhp, became the standard power plant for the car, but was not

1905 Leader (ii) 14hp hansom.
NATIONAL MOTOR MUSEUM

1925 Lea-Francis 12/22 tourer.
NICK BALDWIN

1939 Lea-Francis 14hp drophead coupé by New Avon.
NICK BALDWIN

a success and many Leach cars were returned to the factory in 1922 and early 1923 to have Continental engines replace the Miller design. By late 1922, sales were dropping and, to remain in business, the company dropped its price by $1000, making all Leach models available for $5500. It also developed a small 4-cylinder companion car called the California which was displayed in early 1923 and which may have been the only prototype, since before the end of the

year Leach went out of business. Probably several hundred Leach cars found buyers, 1923 production having dropped to from 100 to 50.

KM

LEADER (i) (NL) 1904–1905
Bosch, Zilstra & Rupp, Arnhem.
This was an assembled car made up of mostly imported components, including engines by Aster or De Dion-Bouton. Production was limited.

NG

LEADER (ii) (GB) 1905–1909
1905–1906 Charles Binks Ltd, Apsley, Nottingham.
1906–1909 New Leader Cars Ltd, Apsley, Nottingham.
Charles Binks set up as a bicycle maker in 1901, and was also well-known for his carburettors. His cars were less familiar, though they were well made and popular in their neighbourhood. The first was a 10/12hp with four separately cast cylinders, shaft drive and 2- or 4-seater bodies. At the Cordingley Show in March 1905 he also exhibited a 14hp tourer on similar lines, and a 14hp hansom. He must have had quite a large stand, for in addition to the 14hp cars he showed five examples of the 10hp 'varying slightly in colour and style and upholstering' as well as 'a collection of parts from which these cars are made'.

A serious factory fire in August 1905 forced Binks to move to new premises, and in 1906 he changed the name of his company to New Leader Cars Ltd, and offered two 4-cylinder cars of 10/20 and 20/30hp, and two monstrous straight-8s, quoted as 60 and 120hp. With the dimensions given, even the 60hp had a capacity of 15,497cc. The advertisement spoke of 'Eight separate cylinders, almost as elastic as steam' and a top speed of 80mph (128km/h) and all ordinary hills taken in top. These were almost certainly never built, though a drawing was published showing a tourer with bonnet as long as the rest of the car. A more modest 14/16hp 4-cylinder car was made in 1908 and 1909.

NG

LEADER (iii) (US) 1905–1912
1905–1906 Columbia Electric Co., McCordsville, Indiana.
1907–1912 Leader Manufacturing Co., Knightstown, Indiana.
Despite the company name, the Leader was never anything but a petrol-engined car; the name came from the manufacture of telephones in which Columbia Electric was also engaged. The first Leader was a light 2-seater powered by a 16hp 2-cylinder engine, but from 1906 to 1910 they made larger twins of 18 and 20hp which could accommodate 4-seater tourer bodies, and in 1910 they added a 30/35hp four with 5-seater body. In 1911 and 1912 a 40hp was made as well. The end of car making seems to have been the result of the ill-health of Luther Frost who had been the moving spirit behind car manufacture in the first place.

NG

LEA-FRANCIS (GB) 1903–1906; 1920–1935; 1937–1952; 1960;
1980 to date
1903–1906 Lea & Francis Motor Syndicate Ltd, Coventry.
1919–1935 Lea & Francis Ltd, Coventry.
1937–1960 Lea-Francis Cars Ltd, Coventry.
1980–1998 Lea-Francis Cars Ltd, Studley, Warwickshire.
1998 to date Lea-Francis Ltd, Exhall, Coventry.
Like many Coventry firms, Lea-Francis emerged as car makers from the bicycle industry. Richard H.Lea and Graham I. Francis built their first bicycle in 1895, and later made hub gears and reflectors for other firms. In 1903 they decided to join the ranks of Coventry's car makers, and formed a separate company in order to protect the cycle business should cars prove unsuccessful. This was a wise decision as it turned out. The Lea & Francis Motor Syndicate Ltd hired the designer Alexander Craig who was also doing work for STANDARD and MAUDSLAY. The car he designed for Lea & Francis was a most unusual one, with a horizontal 3-cylinder engine of 3860cc mounted transversely under the floor. The connecting rods were exceptionally long, at 32in, and there were two massive flywheels at each end of the crankshaft. Each flywheel contained a friction clutch, and an extension shaft carried a chain sprocket whence drive was taken directly to the rear wheels. The sprockets were of different sizes which gave the two speeds. Unfortunately this meant that only one chain at a time was

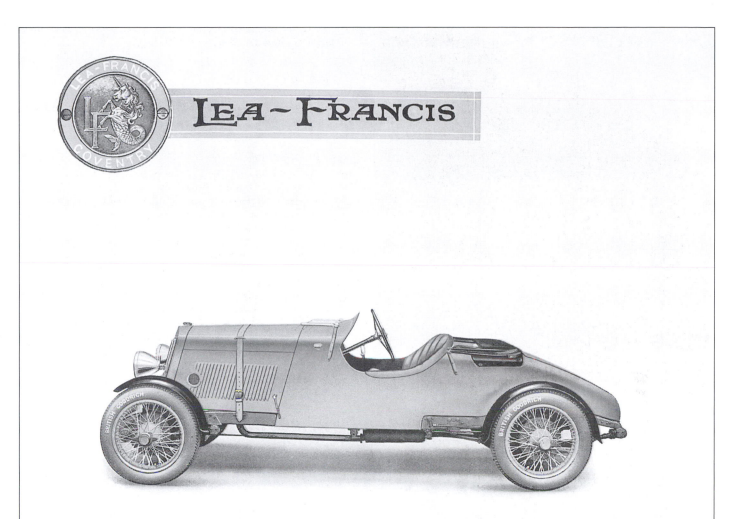

LEA~FRANCIS

1½ Litre Two Seater T.T Model

BODY.—Provides accommodation for driver and passenger. The rear part of the body has a hinged lid inside which is accommodated the spare wheel. The body has no doors but the sides are swept away to provide easy ingress. With the exception of the Armoured Plywood Dashboard, the body shell is constructed throughout from high grade medium hard aluminium, reinforced where necessary with duralumin angle sections. Detachable wind cowls are provided for use when the screen is folded down. The bonnet is provided with the regulation Safety Straps. The seats are bucket shaped and fitted with air cushions.

TRIMMING.—The body squabs and quarters are trimmed in leather to match the paintwork. Loose carpets are fitted over the floor boards.

PAINTWORK.—The body is finished in Cellulose Lacquer. Standard colours :—Blue, Green, Mauve. Special colours extra.

FITTINGS.—The screen is the single panel type, and capable of being folded down flat on the scuttle. The hood is of the two stick pattern, easily folded down and covered with a neat hood envelope. The hood material is of Black Ioco, the hood envelope matching the colour of the body. The wings are of the light cycle type, mounted integral with the brake drums.

Price - £495

The Company reserves the right to alter design, specification or price without notice.

1946 Lea-Francis 14hp saloon.
NATIONAL MOTOR MUSEUM

1949 Lea-Francis 14hp sports car.
NICK BALDWIN

1960 Lea-Francis Lynx roadster.
NICK BALDWIN

1988 Lea-Francis Ace of Spades coupé.
NICK BALDWIN

taking the drive. While single-chain drive was common on light American cars, especially steamers, the Lea & Francis was a pretty heavy machine. Although they were listed up to 1906, only three 3-cylinder cars were made, and only two were sold. However, Lea & Francis salvaged some of their investment by selling the licence to the Craig design to SINGER who made a few 2-cylinder cars of the same layout.

The Alexander Craig episode was the first of five car-making ventures involving the name Lea-Francis. The second began in 1919 when the company, which had made motorcycles since 1911, announced a conventional 4-cylinder car of 1944cc. Only 23 of these were made, and in 1922 Lea-Francis merged with VULCAN of Southport which had made cars and commercial vehicles since 1903. C.B. Wardman, who headed the Vulcan company, became chairman of Lea-Francis as well, and over the next few years there was considerable common use of components between the two companies. Lea-Francis made extensive use of Meadows engines, although Vulcan used mostly their own or Dormans, while gearboxes and steering columns for Vulcan cars were made by Lea-Francis.

At the 1922 Olympia Show Lea Francis exhibited three different models, one of the old 11.9hp fours, a light car powered by a Belsize Bradshaw oil-cooled flat-twin engine and another light car powered by an 8.9hp 4-cylinder Coventry-Simplex engine. Little more was heard of the first two, but the last became the first Lea-Francis to be made in any quantity, and the ancestor of a line of light cars made up to 1928. It was redesigned by Charles Van Eugen who joined Lea-Francis in 1922, and after the first 91 C type cars had been made the Coventry-Simplex engine was replaced by a 1247cc ohv Meadows unit, and this was then the D type. Both types had mainly 2-seater or occasional 4-seater Chummy bodies, plus a few closed coupés and a cabriolet, on the D type. Lea-Francis did not make their own bodies, buying them from Cross & Ellis and Robinsons of Coventry or Avon of Warwick. Later some fabric saloons by Gordon England were used. In 1924 a special aluminium sports 2-seater was fitted with a new 4-speed gearbox, and this was standard on the new and longer 10hp E and 12hp I types for 1925, though three speeds were still available on the cheapest models up to 1928.

In 1925, when Lea-Francis made 750 cars, four chassis were fitted with the famous 1496cc Meadows 4ED engine, and this was introduced on the L and M types for 1926, the first 12/40s. The range still included the strictly touring 10hp K type and 12/22 J type alongside the more sporting 12/40s, of which the L type could be had in twin-carburettor form capable of 70mph (112km/h). Until 1927 all models had quarter-elliptics at the rear end and a weak back axle, which could not cope with 4ED power, so from late 1927 all models were built on a new, longer (111in/2817mm)), and wider chassis with a stronger back axle. They now included the supercharged Hyper Sports, which could exceed 90mph (114km/h), made not only as a 2-seater sports but also as a 4-seater and a fixed-head Sportsman's Coupé, all fabric-covered, apart from some later 2-seaters. The Hyper was distinguished by its sloping radiator, though these were later seen on the 12/40 V-type as well. The first supercharged cars of 1926 were racing single-seaters prepared for Brooklands, which used a Berk blower, but the production Hypers of 1928 onwards had the better-known Cozette unit. Lea-Francis entered five cars in the 1928 Tourist Trophy race, with special roller bearing engines which gave 79bhp compared with 61 from the production engine. Kaye Don won the race by a very small margin over Léon Cushman's Alvis.

Lea-Francis experimented with a 2.2-litre 6-cylinder engine in 1926, but did not put it into production. The following year they announced a smaller six, a twin-ohc unit of 1696cc called the LFS 14/40. Designed by A.O. Lord and built by Vulcan, this was an exciting and promising engine on paper, but it proved very unreliable, and was particularly notorious for bearing failures. At £550 for a saloon it was the most expensive Lea-Francis yet, and it is surprising that the company managed to sell 350 of them in three years. The engine was also used in the 14hp Vulcan, and it seems that Vulcan persuaded Lea-Francis to invest £20,000 in its development. A larger 2-litre 16/60 version was introduced in 1928, but although much improved it was too expensive and suffered from the poor reputation of the earlier car, and in any case, Vulcan gave up car production later the year.

The expense of the LFS programme combined with the company's sporting activities brought about a loss of £17,200 for the year to mid–1928, and the same year Wardman and two other Vulcan directors resigned. Lea-Francis were now on their own, and after floundering for three years they called in a receiver in March 1931. Richard Lea resigned, breaking the link between the company

1999 Lea-Francis 30/230 sports car.
LEA FRANCIS

and its founders, for Francis had departed in 1924 to work for the Swedish Skefco Bearing Co. The 12/40 continued in small scale production under receivership, and there was a new 6-cylinder car, a 1991cc single-ohc design from the pen of Charles Van Eugen. This was nicknamed the Ace of Spades because the front view of the engine resembled the playing card. Production was down to a trickle in the early 1930s; only 29 cars were delivered in 1932, 12 in 1933 and three in 1934, when Van Eugen left in order to design the Riley-built AUTOVIA V8. In 1935 five cars were sold, but 12 remained unsold, and nine of these found customers in 1936, when there was no manufacture at all.

The factory was sold and it looked as if Lea-Francis was at an end, but two former Riley men, general manager George Leek and designer Hugh Rose, formed a new company in July 1937, acquired a factory from Triumph and announced a new Lea-Francis for the 1938 season. This was a Rose design, with the camshafts mounted high in the block but not overhead, an improvement on the layout seen on Rileys for many years. Two sizes of engine were offered, a 12hp of 1496cc and a 14hp of 1629cc. The saloon, drophead and tourer bodies were typical of British quality cars of the period, being not unlike those of two other Coventry car makers, Alvis and Triumph. They were made by Charlesworth and New Avon. There were also a few 2-seater sports cars with tuned 14hp engines and Corsica bodies. A total of 83 of the Rose-designed cars were made before World War II halted production at the beginning of 1940.

As with many engineering firms, the war brought greater profits to Lea-Francis than most of their prewar car making. They were kept busy on sub-contracting work for BSA and other companies. With a substantial profit in hand they launched their postwar cars in January 1946. These had similar engines to the 1938/40 cars, but the 14hp was slightly larger at 1767cc. Most of the bodies were 4-light saloons made by A.P. Aircraft Ltd, but there were a few coupés by Westland and a number of estate cars by various coachbuilders, to take advantage of the fact that an estate car was classed as a commercial vehicle, and carried no purchase tax. Most Lea-Francis cars used the 14hp engine, and a total of 3062 saloons and estate cars were made from 1946 to 1954. Changes included torsion-bar ifs which replaced leaf springs in 1949, together with hydraulic brakes at the front only, and on the 1951 models the headlamps were faired into the wings. There were also two sports models, a 14hp (1947–1949) with twin-carburettor 85bhp engine, and a 2496cc 18hp (1949–1953) whose engine developed 105bhp, giving a top speed of over 100mph (160km/h). From 1949 there was also a 6-light saloon with full-width styling, powered by either the

1767 or later by the 2496cc engine. It was intended originally for export, and was bodied by Charlesworth whose factory Lea-Francis bought in 1948. Between 1949 and 1952 231 of these saloons were made, but production fell off sharply after 1951. The imposition of purchase tax on estate cars undoubtedly harmed Lea-Francis, but the main problem was that with small production runs they could not offer the value of rivals such as Jaguar and Riley. The last chassis was assembled in 1952, though cars were sold up to 1954, and the company kept busy with a variety of sub-contracting jobs.

Lord Montagu devoted a chapter to Lea-Francis in his book, *Lost Causes of Motoring*, published in 1960, ending it with the words 'Here is a Lost Cause which will surely find itself again'. In fact, it has found itself three times since 1960. The first revival took place that year when the Lynx or Leaf-Lynx appeared at the Earls Court Show in October. It had a 2553cc Ford Zephyr engine in a tubular frame, clothed in an extraordinary bulbous 2+2 body. The show car was finished in mauve with gold-plated fittings, which could hardly have helped its appeal, and in fact no orders were taken, either at the Show or later. Only three Lynxes were built, and the whole exercise was a disaster, costing Lea-Francis £35,000. In 1962 they hoped to launch an upmarket saloon called the Crusader, and the following year Trevor Fiore submitted some designs for a saloon, coupé and sports car called the Francesca, but no complete cars resulted from either project.

In November 1962 the assets and name of Lea-Francis were bought by components manufacturers Quinton Hazell, and the rights to the car business by Barrie Price of A.B. Price Ltd. He handled spares and service from Studley, Warwickshire. Quinton Hazell ceased to use the Lea-Francis name on their products in 1972, and a few years later Barrie Price began to consider reviving it on the bonnet of a car. This appeared in 1980 when Price and his partner Peter Engelbach, son of 1920s Austin engineer Carl Engelbach, launched their Jaguar-powered sports car. This was traditionally styled, using a cruciform-braced frame, torsion bar ifs and disc brakes on the front wheels. The engine was a 3442cc Jaguar XJ6. The prototype had a 2-door sports body with cut-away doors, and subsequent cars, for which Price revived the name Ace of Spades, had 2-door saloon bodies. Only six of these were built, though they were still available to special order in 1996, for anyone willing to pay the £68,000 price. At the same time Lea-Francis were planning to make a 7-seater limousine to take over the role vacated by the Daimler DS420, with body by the Park Sheet Metal Co. This plan went on hold so that work could be devoted to a completely

1975 Leata sedan.
NATIONAL MOTOR MUSEUM

1899 Le Blon 4hp voiturette.
NATIONAL MOTOR MUSEUM

1912 L.E.C. 8/10hp cyclecar.
NICK BALDWIN

new Lea-Francis which made its bow at the 1998 Birmingham Show. Called the 30/230 (3.0 litres/230km/h), its box tube and sheet aluminium chassis and all-independent suspension were designed by ex-Jaguar engineer Jim Randle, with bonded aluminium 2-seater sports body by Park Sheet Metal. The show car was a non-runner, but the chosen power unit was an uprated version of the 2962cc 24-valve V6 as used in the Opel/Vauxhall Omega. Deliveries were planned to start in the Spring of 2001, at a price of £40,000.

NG

Further Reading
The Lea-Francis Story, Barrie Price, Veloce Books, 1996.

LEAPING CATS *see* VIKING

LEATA (US) 1975–c.1978
Stinebaugh Manufacturing Inc., Post Falls, Idaho.
Made by Donald Stinebaugh and named after his wife, the Leata was an extraordinary-looking little car, in retro style before retro became fashionable. A boxy 2-door sedan, it was powered by a 50bhp 4-cylinder Continental engine which gave a top speed of 70mph (112km/h) and a claimed 39-55mpg fuel consumption. The price was $2895, and Stinebaugh claimed to have made 20 by March 1975. He had 15 workers, and aimed at an annual production of 1000 to 1500 cars. In 1977 he launched a more modern-looking vehicle called the Leata Caballero, made in sedan and pick-up form, and powered by a 4-cylinder General Motors LY-5 engine.

NG

LEBLANC (CH) 1998 to date
1998 to date Leblanc Automotive Engineering, Wetzikon, Zürich.
This company was formed to realise the personal dream of its founder, Rolf Wyss, born in 1967. This was a 2-seater sports racing coupé with a Ford Cosworth supercharged 2-litre 4-cylinder engine of 512bhp. Weighing only 735kg, it had remarkable acceleration, and would accelerate from 0 to 62mph (100km/h) in 2.7 seconds and 0 to 124mph (200km/h) in just 7.2 seconds. The monocoque frame and body were constructed from carbon fibre, magnesium and titanium. Despite its racing pedigree, the car was licenced to run on Swiss roads, and it was intended to produce a short run of vehicles at a price of around SFr1.5m.

FH

LE BLON (F) 1898–c.1900
Le Blon Frères, Paris.
This was a light car powered by a 4hp V-twin engine and with belt final drive. Chassis could be supplied for any type of body, so the makers claimed. Le Blon cars were sold on the English market under the name Le Lynx.

NG

LE BRUN (F) 1898–c.1900
Automobiles Le Brun, Montrouge, Seine.
The Le Brun was powered by a rear-mounted V-twin engine of Daimler type, made in 6, 8 or 10hp forms. Transmission was by 3-speed gearbox and double-chain drive. Steering was by tiller, and the car was available with various bodies typical of the period, including a 2-seater Duc and 4-seater *vis-à-vis*.

NG

L.E.C. (GB) 1912–1913
London Engine Co., Southall, Middlesex.
The L.E.C. cyclecar was powered by an 8/10hp 2-cylinder water-cooled engine of 1080cc, possibly of the firms's own make as no proprietary maker was quoted in *The Cyclecar* list. It had a 3-speed gearbox and chain final drive. The radiator was similar to that of the Daimler.

NG

LE CABRI (F) 1924–1925
Automobiles Le Cabri, Asnières, Seine.
Two small cars with 2-cylinder engines of 5 and 7hp were made by this company. The name, slang for 'the kid', was also used for models of Gauthier and Salomon.

NG

LE CHAT (GB) 1985

Before companies produced proper Lamborghini Countach replicas, disastrous attempts like the Le Chat were allowed to see the light of day. This abysmal 'lookalike' was seen at the Stoneleigh kit car show but never again.

CR

LECOY (GB) 1921–1922

Lambert Engineering Co. Ltd, Harrow, Middlesex.

The Lecoy was a cyclecar powered by an 8hp V-twin Blackburne engine, though a J.A.P. was an alternative, with friction transmission and chain drive. It had coil front springs, and cantilever at the rear. It was of primitive appearance, with the engine fully exposed to the air. Luggage could be carried in a small well above the rear axle.

NG

LEDA (F) 1908

Thorand, Theim et Cie, Paris.

Although apparently only active for one year, this company listed four models, an 8/9hp single-cylinder, 6/9hp 2-cylinder and two fours of 8/10 and 10/12hp.

NG

LE DAUPHIN (F) 1941–1942

André L. Dauphin, Paris.

This was one of several cars built in response to the acute shortage of petrol in wartime France. The first example was a pedal-driven tandem 2-seater, with provision for a 100 or 175cc 2-stroke Zürcher engine for those lucky enough to obtain a special allocation of fuel. Later it was supplied with a small electric motor. In the original model the driver sat at the front, but in the electric car steering was from the rear, as in the Bédélia or Automobilette made 30 years earlier. Bodies were made by Kellner who, in happier times, had clothed such cars as Delage and Hispano-Suiza.

NG

LEDL (A) 1973–c.1989

Ledl GmbH, Tattendorf.

Numerous models were offered by this company, including three different buggies (called Siva, Europa 2001 and Jagd), two VW Beetle-based hot rod-style kits called the Gold Bug and Replica T, and VW-based replicas of the Bugatti Type 35 and Mercedes SSK. New for 1978 was the Tanga, a coupé obviously derived from the British NOVA, but with a separate chassis designed for Ford Fiesta/Escort components, including mid-mounted engines of 1.3- or 1.6-litres. The model was revised and restyled in 1981 and renamed the AS, and a 1.6 turbo engine was launched in 1986. As many as 150 cars per year were produced.

CR

LEDOUX (CDN) 1914

Ledoux Carriage Co. Ltd, Montreal, Quebec.

This was a well-known carriage builder dating back to 1852. Around 1905 they turned to making car bodies, especially tourers and limousines interchangeable for summer or winter use. In 1912 they commissioned Henri Bourassa, who would later make cars of his own, to design two large cars, a 4-cylinder with monobloc casting, and a pair-cast six. Both had aluminium tourer bodies. The war prevented further production, and after the conflict Ledoux merged with the Jennings carriage and truck-making company. Charles Ledoux was one of the earliest collectors of historic cars, dating back to the 1890s. Sadly, they were all destroyed in a fire in 1923.

NG

LEEDS see IPAM-LEEDS

LEESDORFER (A) 1898–1901

Leesdorfer Automobilwerke AG, Baden bei Wien.

This company began by importing Amedée Bollée chassis and fitting their own bodies, the Petit Duc and Grand Duc. The chassis were of 6 and 9hp, and used Bollée's complex transmission with belt drive to the gearbox which was located behind the rear axle. The rear wheels were driven by bevel gears plus a short

1981 Ledl 1.3-litre coupé.
HALWART SCHRADER

cardan shaft. When Leesdorfer began chassis production themselves, this system was replaced by conventional chain drive. A few cars of Leesdorfer design were made in Belgium by the Société Métallurgique of Antwerp (no connection with the well-known Métallurgique cars made at Marchienne-au-Pont).

HON

LEFERT (B) 1898–1902

J. Lefert, Ghent.

Lefert was a coachbuilder who made six electric cars as well as a bus for the Grand Hotel in Liège.

NG

LEGEND (GB) 1998 to date

The Legend Motor Co., Hanbury, Worcestershire.

This operation marketed kit-form replicas of the Porsche 356 Speedster, 356 Convertible D, California 356, Volkswagen Karmann-Ghia and space frame-chassis Porsche 550 Spyder. It was also involved in the development of a French A.C. Cobra replica and manufactured it for the UK with different suspension consisting of standard coils and springs.

CR

LEGENDARY (GB) 1994 to date

1994–1998 Legendary Sportscars, Ashbourne, Derbyshire.
1998 to date Legendary Sportscars, Middleton, Manchester, Lancashire.

As originally launched, the Legendary 427 qualified as the most expensive kit-form A.C. Cobra replica in Britain at £30,000, and was also sold fully-built. The engine was a fuel-injected Ford 302 V8 (alternatively Chevrolet or Rover V8), the transmission was a Borg Warner 5-speed with limited slip differential, all housed in space frame chassis (multi-tube or round-tube forms) with wishbone suspension.

CR

LEGENDARY AUTOS (US) c.1991

Legendary Autos Inc., Longwood, Florida.

The L.A. Cobra was a Cobra replica based on Ford Mustang II running gear. It was sold in kit and turn-key form.

HP

LEGENDARY MOTORCARS (US) c.1988–1994

Legendary Motorcars Inc., Worthington, Ohio.

The 1932 Ford Model A Woody wagon, Woody pick-up and Woody sedan delivery were replicated by this kit car company. The bodies were actually about 8/10 the size of the original, but were designed to be powered by the Chevrolet Chevette 4-cylinder engine. A tubular chassis was included which mounted the Chevette running gear. The body was fibreglass, with yellow oak woodwork for the back. Kits sold for about $9000, with turn-key cars going for $12,000 to $16,000.

HP

LEGENDARY MOTORWORKS (US) c.1992

Legendary Motorworks, Canonsburg, Pennsylvania.

The Legendary '57C was a kit replica of the 1957 Corvette. It was based on a General Motors' sedan chassis and running gear. They were sold in kit and fully assembled form.

HP

1936 Leidart V8 sports car.
NATIONAL MOTOR MUSEUM

LÉGIA (B) 1900

Usines Deprez-Joassart, Herstal.

This was a light *avant train* voiturette designed by D.D. Sklin and built in the cycle works of Deprez-Joassart. It was powered by either De Dion-Bouton or Aster engines, mounted above, and driving, the single front wheel. It had a 2-speed gearbox.

NG

LEGNANO see F.I.A.L.

LEGRAND (i) (F) 1901

This was a light car powered by two 3hp De Dion-Bouton engines geared together and mounted under the seat. Final drive was by single chain.

NG

LEGRAND (ii) (F) 1913

Albert Legrand, Paris.

Shown at the 1913 Paris Salon, the Legrand had a conventional 4-cylinder monobloc engine and 3-speed gearbox, but a most unusual transmission. The propeller shaft was flexible, being made of coiled wire. To keep this clean the car had a huge undertray which surrounded the whole chassis. This must have added considerably to the weight. It is unlikely that it went into production.

NG

LEGROS (F) 1900–1913

René Legros, Fécamp, Seine-Inférieure.

René Legros (1872–1954) had his first motoring experiences with a Roger-Benz in 1894, and began work on his first prototype in 1897. By 1900 he was ready with his first car, which was shown at the Universal Exhibition of 1900, and also at the Paris Salon in December that year. Called La Plus Simple, it had a front-mounted 3hp single-cylinder engine, 2-speed gearbox and belt drive. He also made a larger car with 5hp engine and seating for four, and an electric car developed by his partner Albert Meynier, sold as the Meynier-Legros. This was a heavy-looking vehicle with unequal-sized artillery wheels and a Panhard-like bonnet under which the batteries were kept. In 1904 Legros introduced a range of cars with 2-stroke engines, an 8hp single, 10 and 12hp twins and 15 and 18hp 3-cylinders. Some of the latter were used in motor boats which Legros also made. By 1907 he had added 4-cylinder engines of 16/20 and 20/25hp. These and a 9hp twin were made up to 1913 with little change. Legros exhibited at the Salon each year, his larger cars being in the mid-priced range, competitive with Brasier, Delahaye and Charron. Engines and chassis were made at Legros' Fécamp factory, but all coachbuilding was by outside firms. He did not revive car production after the war, but he continued to be active in other fields, and was a pioneer of Radio Normandie in the 1930s.

NG

LEGROS & KNOWLES see IRIS

LE GUI see GUY (i)

LEICHTAUTO (D) 1924

Leichtauto Gesellschaft mbH, Berlin.

As its name implies, this was a very light car which used a tubular spaceframe covered with canvas. It was powered by rear-mounted DKW or Columbus engines.

HON

LEIDART (GB) 1936–1938

Leidart Cars Ltd, Pontefract, Yorkshire.

Named after its makers, Leith and Huddart, this was a short-lived Anglo-American hybrid which used a Ford V8 engine and gearbox in an English chassis with Bugatti-type rear suspension. The bodies were simple open 2- and 4-seater sports, and the car had the appearance of a scaled-up Morgan 4-4. A saloon was listed in 1938, but it is not certain that any were made, any more than the smaller Leidart with supercharged Ford 10 engine. It is possible only one Leidart was built, the 2-seater sports which featured in press announcements.

NG

LEITCH (NZ) 1986 to date

Leitch Industries, Invercargill, South Island.

Barry Leitch built the first clubman-style car for his own use but was soon receiving requests to accept orders from prospective buyers. The production Super Sprint had a spaceframe and an aluminium and fibreglass body with power by 1600cc Ford or Toyota engines. By 1996 carbon fibre mudguards were available as was an optional irs with pushrod actuated coil springs. Exports were made to Australia and Japan, and production had amounted to more than 50 units by then. An additional model, a replica of the Brabham BT 21, was also introduced at that time.

MG

LEITNER (SU) c.1911

Leitner and Co., Riga.

The Leitner private car was contemporary with the RUSSO-BALTIQUE, also produced in Riga.

NG

L'ÉLÉGANTE (F) 1903–c.1907

J.B. Mercier, Paris.

This was a light 2-seater very similar to a De Dion-Bouton in appearance. The first examples had single-cylinder De Dion engines of 6 or 8hp, and possibly came from the emporium of LACOSTE ET BATTMANN. Later models had larger engines of 9, 12 and 16hp.

NG

LEMAÎTRE ET GÉRARD (F) 1923–1925

Lemaître et Gérard, Levallois, Seine.

This company made small 4-cylinder engines of 750cc, which were supplied to several manufacturers including Benjamin (before they turned to 2-strokes), Dalila, Tom Pouce and Zevaco. They also made rear axles complete with brake drums which they supplied to a number of cyclecar manufacturers. In 1923 they brought out a complete cyclecar of their own, using, of course, their own engine and rear axle. It was neat-looking little machine, with a slightly veed radiator, but very few were made under their own name. It is possible that the design was taken up by another manufacturer.

NG

LE MANS (i) (GB) 1980s–1990s

Le Mans Sports Cars, Stoke-on-Trent.

This company was one of many Jaguar replica makers of the late 1980s and early 1990s. It specialised in C-Type, D-Type and XKSS reproductions.

CR

LE MANS (ii) **(GB)** 1990 to date
1990–1993 Stardust Sports Cars, Whitton, Middlesex.
1993–1996 Le Mans Sports Car Co., Westbury, Wiltshire.
1996–1998 Auto Milan, Pewsey, Wiltshire.
1998 to date D.C. Mouldings, Llanwrst, Conwy.
Beginning life with the name Stardust, this vague Jaguar D-Type replica kit used Ford Escort/Cortina parts to keep things cheap. The replica was thankfully reproportioned and improved in 1993 and also became available with Jaguar or Triumph 6-cylinder engines; it was renamed Le Mans at the same time, just as the P.A.C.E. Quadriga was acquired. This Ferrari Dino lookalike was overhauled and relaunched as the Le Mans Milan, now with Ford Escort Mk3 components instead of Lancia mechanicals.
CR

LE MARNE *see* LA MARNE

LE MARQUIS (GB) 1987 to date
Robert Jankel Design Ltd, Weybridge, Surrey.
After his PANTHER marque was taken over by Young C. Kim, founder Robert Jankel moved on to coachbuilding, specialising in stretch limousines and coupé or estate car conversions of luxury cars. He also built two unique new models under the Le Marquis name. The first was the 1987 Gold Label, a 2-door convertible based on Bentley Turbo R mechanicals – indeed this was reputedly the only outside company to which Rolls-Royce was happy to supply brand-new engines. It carried a huge £250,000 price tag. Another model was the Tempest, a very high performance sports car based on the Chevrolet Corvette. Its specification included a 535bhp 6.7-litre V8 engine and heavily revised open Kevlar bodywork. This, said Jankel, beat the world record for 0–60mph (97km/h) acceleration in 1992 with a time of 3.89 seconds. After 1995, Jankel confined himself to converting existing cars.
CR

LEMAZONE *see* SN1, BEAUJANGLE, and AMPLAS

LE MÉHARI (F) 1927
F. Reynaud, Nouzonville, Ardennes.
This was a cyclecar, unusual in its place of manufacture, far from the Paris suburbs where most cyclecars were made, and in its date, which was distinctly late for such a light machine. It also differed from the norm in having two engines, single-cylinder Train units of 344cc each, which drove the rear axle via long rubber belts. As well as the touring 2-seater, there was a sports model with tuned engine and front-wheel brakes.
NG

LE MÉTAIS (F) 1904–1910
Voiturettes Le Métais, Levallois-Perret, Seine.
These cars were made by Louis Le Métais, and were light vehicles powered initially by single-cylinder De Dion-Bouton engines, though one 9hp unit was claimed to be of Le Métais' own manufacture. They had friction drive. From 1907 some larger cars were made, with 2- or 4-cylinder Gnome engines. Le Métais was helped by his brothers-in-law, Henri and Émile Godefroy, and when his own production ended in 1910 they both continued in the motor business. Henri joined M. Lévêque in making Ruby engines, which powered so many light French cars in the 1920s, while Émile made the G.E.P. cyclecar. This used the same friction drive as the Le Métais.
NG

LEMS (GB) 1903
London Electromobile Syndicate, London.
This was a very light 2-seater electric car with tiller steering. Maximum speed was only 12mph (19km/h), and the range per battery charge was 40 miles. The company were still advertising in 1905, but their activities were probably limited to servicing and repairs.
NG

LENAWEE (US) 1904
Church Manufacturing Co., Adrian, Michigan.

1904 Le Métais 2-seater.
NATIONAL MOTOR MUSEUM

1904 Lenawee tonneau.
NATIONAL MOTOR MUSEUM

A successor to the MURRAY (i), the Lenawee was a 5-seater tonneau powered by a single-cylinder engine located under the front seat. Final drive was by shaft. Unusually for its date, it had lhd. Not more than 15 were made, of which one survives today.
NG

LENDE (US) 1902–1909
1902–1907 Olaus Lende, Granite Falls, Minnesota.
1907–1909 Lende Automobile Manufacturing Co., Granite Falls, Minnesota.
German-born Lende built a number of cars to individual order with 2-, and later, 4-cylinder engines and chain drive. In 1907 he formed a company to make a 30hp 4-cylinder car with epicyclic transmission and shaft drive. Total Lende production was 17 cars, more built to special order than by his company.
NG

LENHAM (GB) 1968–c.1984
Lenham Motor Co., Harrietsham, Kent.
Lenham was a famous fibreglass panel and hard-top maker which presented a roadgoing GT version of its racing prototype design at the January 1969 Racing Car Show. This Group 6 car could also be used on the road, and featured a semi-monocoque chassis, fully adjustable suspension and all-round disc brakes.

1911 Lenox Four roadster.
NATIONAL MOTOR MUSEUM

1897 Léon Bollée voiturette (Coventry-built).
NATIONAL MOTOR MUSEUM

The plastic bodywork featured gullwing doors and an integral roll-over bar. The mid-mounted engine was either a BMW 2-litre unit or a Lotus-Ford. Only a couple of road cars were ever built. Lenham turned its attention, in 1977, to making a stark sports car out of an Austin-Healey. In style it echoed the great Healey Silverstone of 1949–51. The idea was to bring in your rusty old 'big' Healey and have it converted by the factory. The Lenham was an undoubted brute: it was 5cwt lighter than the Austin-Healey, thanks to its fibreglass bodywork and aluminium bonnet, and many cars took to the track. It was still theoretically available as late as 1984, although by then the days when Healeys had not yet become truly collectible had long since passed.

CR

LENNOX (GB) 1920–1921

This was a light 3-wheeler made in Northumberland, of which at least eight had been delivered by February 1921.

NG

LENOX (i) see MAXIM-GOODRIDGE

LENOX (ii) (US) 1911–1917

1911–1915 Lenox Motor Car Co., Jamaica Plain, Massachusetts.
1911–1912 Boston, Massachusetts.
1912–1915 Hyde Park, Massachusetts.
1915–1917 Lawrence, Massachusetts.
Designed by Chester T. Bates, previously responsible for the MORSE (i), the Lenox began life as a 27hp 4-cylinder car made in five body styles, 2- and 4-seater roadster,

5-seater tourer, 2-seater speedster and limousine. For 1913 these gave way to a 40hp four and 60hp six, the latter a sizeable car on a 130in (3299mm) wheelbase selling for up to $4050. These were made in both Jamaica Plain and Hyde Park, the Boston plant being used mainly as a service depot. In 1915 the company moved into the field of trucks and tractors, which was the reason for the move to Lawrence. The 40 and 60hp cars were powered by Buda engines and continued into 1917, and a 1918 model was announced, but it seems that tooling up for truck production had used all the company's capital, and no vehicles at all were made in 1918. An attempted revival under the name Ajax Motors Corp. of Boston in 1920 came to nothing.

NG

LENTZ (I) 1906–1908

Stà Italiana Automobili Lentz, Milan.
This was a conventional car with 4-cylinder engines of 14/16 and 20/24hp, with shaft drive. It was also known as the Oria.

NG

LÉO (i) (F) 1897–1898

This car took its name from that of its designer, Léon Lefèbvre, who later made the BOLIDE. Like the early Bolide, it had a Pygmée horizontal twin engine of 3 or 6hp, with belt final drive. Two Léos were entered in the 1896 Paris-Marseilles-Paris race, but did not start.

NG

LEO (ii) (GB) 1913

The Leo cyclecar was powered by an 8hp V-twin J.A.P. engine, and sold for £105. It was sold by the department store Derry & Toms, but the factory location is not known.

NG

LEONARD (GB) 1904–c.1906

J.J. Leonard & Co., Crofton Park, London.
The Leonard was made in two models, one with a 6hp single-cylinder De Dion-Bouton engine, and armoured wood chassis, the other with a 10/12hp 2-cylinder Tony Huber engine and steel chassis. The latter was called the Medici, and was said to be particularly suitable for doctors.

NG

LÉON BOLLÉE; MORRIS-LÉON BOLLÉE (F) 1895–1933

1895–1924 Automobiles Léon Bollée, Le Mans.
1925–1931 Morris Motors Ltd, Usines Léon Bollée, Le Mans.
1931–1933 Sté Nouvelle Léon Bollée, Le Mans.
The Bollée family were bell founders, their business at Le Mans dating back to 1839. By the 1880s their foundry was one of the best-known in France, and their bells hung in cathedrals as far afield as Bangkok, Saigon, Canton and Yokohama. The founder's eldest son, Amédée (1844–1917) built a number of steam carriages of advanced design from 1873 onwards, while two of his sons, Amédée *fils* (1867–1926) and Léon (1870–1913) each had their own car manufacturing businesses.

Léon Bollée, with his father and brother, took part in the Paris-Bordeaux-Paris Race of 1895 in their steam carriage *La Nouvelle*, which was already 15 years old. Young Léon was fired with enthusiasm for motor vehicles, and before the year was out he had patented and built a prototype of a light 3-wheeler to which he gave the name voiturette. This seated two passengers in tandem, and was powered by a horizontal single-cylinder engine mounted on the nearside of the frame. The cylinder was air-cooled, and ignition was by the hot tube system. The car had three speeds and belt final drive.

The Bollée engine was made in three sizes, nominally 2, 2½, and 3hp, with dimensions of 75×145mm (640cc), 78×145mm (692cc) and 85×145mm (822cc). The engine and belt drive transmission were temperamental, but when they consented to run they ran well, thanks to their light weight of only 353 pounds (160kg). Speeds of 38mph (60km/h) were reached, while a formidable twin-engined Bollée achieved 47mph (76km/h) in 1898. Had this been officially timed it would have set a new Land Speed Record, which stood at 39.24mph (62km/h) at the time. All Bollées were noisy, but the twin-engined model was said to be so vociferous that when one was started up in Le Mans, mothers in Tours (40 miles/64km) away would strive to soothe their terrified children!

Despite their idiosyncrasies the Bollée tricars became very popular, most being made for Léon by Hurtu & Diligeon of Albert, Somme. Only the prototypes and competition models were made at Le Mans. In May 1896 the British rights were acquired by H.J. Lawson of the British Motor Syndicate, and plans were made for Bollée voiturettes to be built in the Humber bicycle factory in Coventry. However, this was destroyed by fire in July, and when Bollée manufacture was eventually established, it took place in part of Coventry's Motor Mills, where Daimler and MMC were also made. A few were completed before the end of 1896, and manufacture continued up to 1898, latterly under the names Coventry Bollée or Coventry Motette, and in a different factory after Lawson had lost control.

Several hundred Bollée voiturettes were made up to the middle of 1899, including commercial versions in which a box replaced the front seat. Léon then turned his attention to 4-wheelers, building a light car with horizontal single-cylinder engine, independent front suspension by transverse leaves, and belt drive. The licence for this was sold to Darracq who planned to make a series of 500, although it is not certain that that number were actually built.

In 1900 Bollée moved out of the family bell foundry and built a new factory. Here production began in 1903 of a conventional front-engined 4-cylinder car, the 4½-litre 24/30. Chain-driven at first, it received shaft drive in 1908 and was made up to 1913. Other models followed, including the 3920cc 18/24hp, the 7360cc 35/45hp, and the 8580cc 40/50hp, all with 4-cylinder engines, and the enormous 75hp 6-cylinder, with a capacity of 11,940cc. With these cars Léon was in direct competition with his brother Amédée, breaking an agreement they had made earlier that Léon would cater to the popular market with his voiturette, while Amédée would build more expensive cars. While Amédée's production was very limited, seldom exceeding 25-30 cars per year, Léon's output rose from 300 chassis in 1903 to 500 in 1908, and an average of 600 per year from 1911 to 1914. However, Amédée had other interests, including the manufacture of engines for De Dietrich and pistons rings for many manufacturers, for which the company is still famous today, so there were not necessarily any hard feelings between the brothers.

Léon Bollée cars were popular in several foreign countries including Great Britain and the United States, where their distribution was backed by Vanderbilt money. Like many other European firms, Léon Bollée added smaller cars to their range in the years before 1914. At the 1910 Paris Salon, six models were shown, three fours from the 2380cc 12hp to the 4500cc 24/30hp, and three sixes, from the 3570cc 18hp to the 11,940cc 75hp. The larger chassis all had 4-speed gearboxes, with three or four speeds being optional on the smaller cars.

In addition to cars, Léon Bollée was very interested in aviation, and made his factory available to the Wright brothers when they were making their historic flights in the Le Mans region. In 1911 Léon had a serious accident in an aeroplane, which aggravated an existing heart condition. He became a virtual invalid and died two years later, aged only 43. His widow carried on the business, aided by two of the staff, general manager Henri Péan and works manager Faivre. During World War I the Bollée factory made shells, cartridges and machine guns, but also turned out about 300 cars for the French and British armies.

The postwar Léon Bollées were conventional machines and no longer aspired to the heights of luxury and prestige exemplified by the 11.9-litre 75hp. The standard model was the 2612cc 4-cylinder Type H, and this was joined in 1922 by a six with the same cylinder dimensions and a capacity of 3918cc. The six had Perrot front-wheel brakes, but in general the Léon Bollée was old-fashioned and had little to offer a market already overcrowded with undistinguished regional marques. The business was in decline when, in November 1924, William Morris bought the Léon Bollée factory. His plan was to circumvent the French tariffs which made it uneconomic to sell Morris cars in France. Although the Morris-Léon Bollée was to be entirely French-built, any profits from the business would go to Morris. The first, and best-known, model was the 12hp Type MLB which was powered by a 2402cc 4-cylinder ohv Hotchkiss engine, and came with factory-built tourer and saloon coachwork, though it could be supplied as a chassis as well. Among coachbuilders who worked on the MLB chassis was Carel of Le Mans. About 1250 MLBs were made between early 1925 and the end of 1927, and an unknown number from then until the end of 1930. There was also a 6-cylinder of which only 25 were made up to 1930, and a straight-8 powered by a 3072cc single-ohc engine based on that used in the Wolseley 21/60. (The Wolseley company had been bought by William Morris in 1927.) Only six straight-8s were made, hardly surprising at a chassis price of 71,300 francs, compared with 26,000 francs for the MLB chassis.

c.1912 Léon Bollée 18hp coupé.
NICK BALDWIN

c.1928 Morris - Léon Bollée Type MLB coach.
BRYAN K. GOODMAN

1932 Léon Bollée ELB saloon.
NATIONAL MOTOR MUSEUM

The Depression damaged car sales in both Britain and France, and production had been halted some time in 1930 to enable existing stocks to be sold. William Morris cut his losses by disposing of the Le Mans factory to a French syndicate who formed the Société Nouvelle Léon Bollée, The name of the cars became Léon Bollée once more, and a new, smaller engine of 1997cc was launched for the Model ELB. This brought it into the 11hp taxation class, but few were sold, and probably none of the 6- and 8-cylinder cars which were listed up to 1933.

NG

Further Reading

L'Invention de l'Automobile, Jean-Pierre Delaperrelle, Éditions Cénomane, 1986.

1922 Léon Laisne Type B tourer.
M.J.WORTHINGTON-WILLIAMS

1931 Harris - Léon Laisne Model V saloon.
M.J.WORTHINGTON-WILLIAMS

1924 Léon Paulet roadster.
NICK BALDWIN

LÉON DUSSEK (F) 1906–c.1907

The factory location of the Léon Dussek is unknown, but three models of 4-cylinder were listed, of 16/20, 24/30 and 35/45hp. The cylinders were separately cast and the cars had 4-speed gearboxes and chain drive. According to the British agents, Motoria Ltd, shaft drive was also available.

NG

LEONE (I) 1949–1950

Officine Electromeccaniche Vincenzo Leone, Turin.

This was a small sports car with a tubular frame and ifs, based on Fiat mechanical elements. Tuned 1100cc or 1200cc engines were available.

NG

LÉON LAISNE; HARRIS LÉON LAISNE (F) 1913–1937

1913–1926 L. Laisne et Cie, Douai (1913–1914); Nantes (1919–1926).
1926–1931 Automobiles Harris-Léon Laisne, Nantes.
1931–1937 SA des Anciens Établissements Léon Laisne, Nantes.

The cars of Léon Laisne (1880–c.1946) were better known for their advanced design than for their commercial success. He began work in a bronze foundry at the age of 13, then worked for Hurtu and Léon Bollée before setting up a small machine tool works at Douai. Here he made one or two experimental cars with ifs, and in 1913 started to build cars to special order, with Chapuis-Dornier engines and tubular chassis.

Douai was soon invaded at the start of World War I, and Laisne joined the air force, from which he was invalided in 1916. He then returned to machine tool work, taking larger premises at Nantes, where he was kept very busy making shells. In 1919, he began to make cars commercially; they had 4-cylinder Ballot or Chapuis-Dornier engines, and all-round independent suspension by vertical coils. They were made in small numbers, always as a sideline to the machine tool business, and different engines were used from time to time, including Decolange and S.C.A.P.

In the mid–1920s the total workforce was about 100, of which fewer than half worked on the cars. In 1926 Laisne obtained additional capital from an Englishman, Murray Harris, the elder brother of Sir Arthur 'Bomber' Harris who earned somewhat controversial fame during World War II. Harris' intervention enabled a new design to be put into production, This had a tubular frame in which were mounted coil springs which provided the suspension, and sliding pistons which acted as shock absorbers. During a road test *The Motor* found that 'the wheels were leaping up and down through a distance of about 6ins, but the chassis remained absolutely horizontal and rigid'. Low-slung saloon and tourer bodies were used, somewhat reminiscent of the Lancia Lambda, and all seating was within the wheelbase. The underslung worm drive was supplied by David Brown of Huddersfield. A variety of engines was available, to the customer's choice – these included 1170 and 1390cc 4-cylinder S.C.A.P., 1215 and 1491cc 6-cylinder C.I.M.E. and 1492 or 1808cc straight-8s by S.C.A.P. By 1930, when rubber suspension units had replaced the coil springs, larger engines were available, including 3-litre 6-cylinder Hotchkiss and Continental units. These Type V chassis carried some handsome 2-door saloons by Million-Guiet.. About 150 Harris-Léon Laisne cars were made between 1928 and 1932, of which more than half were acquired by the experimental departments of manufacturers at home and abroad. At least one Model A Ford was fitted with Harris-Léon Laisne rubber suspension.

Harris and Laisne parted in 1931, the Englishman later making a single example of a front-wheel drive car with Laisne suspension and Standard 12 engine, which he called the Harris Six. Production of Léon Laisne cars dwindled in the 1930s, and finances were probably not helped by some experimental cars which were never sold to the public. These included a 1.2-litre front-drive saloon made in 1930, and Type V chassis powered by a 4-litre Delage D8 engine (1934) and 3.6-litre Ford V8 engine (1935). The smaller cars were listed up to 1937, and Laisne retired three years later to run a garage in Toulouse. He died in about 1946.

NG

Further Reading
'The Harris-Léon Laisne', M. Worthington Williams,
The Automobile, June 1996.

LÉON MAX (F) 1928

Léon Max, Paris.

In 1928 Léon Max took over the stock of components held by the C.G.V.P. (Compagnie Général de Voitures à Paris), makers of cars and taxicabs under the names CELTIC and CLASSIC. He assembled a few of the latter and sold them under his own name.

NG

LÉON PAULET (F) 1922–1925

Sté Mécanique du Rhône, Marseilles.

The Léon Paulet was a high-quality car powered by a seven-bearing single-ohc 6-cylinder engine with dual ignition. Capacity was 3446cc, soon enlarged to 3904cc. This was designed by the former Delage engineer Michelat, who apparently took more inspiration from Hispano-Suiza than that company was happy about. They took Léon Paulet to court, and he was forbidden to make any more of

Michelat's engines. Rather than turn to another power unit, he discontinued production. He had planned to make at least 100, but it is thought that not more than 20 were actually built. Three survive today.

NG

LÉON RAMBERT (F) 1934–1935

Built in Clermont-Ferrand, the Léon Rambert was a very small car made in single- or 2-seater forms, powered by a 175 or 150cc single-cylinder 2-stroke engine mounted at the rear and driving one rear wheel by chain. About the same size as the English Rytecraft, it weighed 600lbs. About 60 were made.

NG

LÉON RUBAY (US) 1922–1923

The Rubay Co., Cleveland, Ohio.

French-born Léon Rubay came to America in about 1902, and in 1916 set up a coachbuilding business in Cleveland. His bodies were built on local HAL and White chassis, and also on Roamer, Duesenberg, Locomobile and other high-grade chassis. In 1922 he decided to turn car maker, and employed the Belgian Paul Bastien, later famous for his work on the Stutz Vertical Eight, to design an engine for him. Based on a design Bastien had produced for Métallurgique, it was an advanced unit, small by American standards at 2043cc, with a single-ohc. Rubay had no facilities for engine making, and he probably turned to Ferro for this job. The chassis incorporated front-wheel brakes, and five body styles were offered. It was by all accounts a beautiful little car, but vastly overpriced at $5100–5300. For that price buyers expected something much larger both in power and wheelbase, and probably fewer than 12 Rubays were sold. Léon himself suffered a nervous breakdown when disaster loomed; his directors sold off the company to the Raulang Body Co., and its founder, hospitalised in Paris at the time, subsequently took up chicken farming.

NG

Further Reading
'Voitures de Ville – Léon Rubay and his cars', Karl A. Zahm,
Automobile Quarterly, Vol. 37, No.4.

LEONTINA see PETTENELLA

LEOPARD see MIRACH

LEOPARD CRAFT (GB) 1991–1994

This vintage style roadster employed a Triumph Herald chassis. The simple pointy-tailed fibreglass tub was topped off with an aluminium bonnet and sides and fibreglass bullet-shaped wings, the styling influences cited including the Alfa Romeo P3 and Bugatti Type 35.

CR

LEPAPE (F) c.1896–1906

Hippolyte Lepape, Puteaux, Seine.

The first of Hippolyte Lepape's designs was an extraordinary vehicle with six wheels, of which the front pair were driven by the 6hp 3-cylinder radial engine. Needless to say this did not go into production, and it seems that Lepape sold very few of his cars, being, like Émile Claveau of a later generation, too interested in constant improvement to get anything onto the market. At the 1901 Paris Salon he showed a light car powered by a 5hp single-cylinder engine cooled simply by the thickness of the metal forming the cylinder, and also a 3-wheeler with more conventional air-cooling by ribs surrounding the cylinder. This was made as a side by side 2-seater, or a single-seater parcel carrier in which the load area occupied the place of the other seat. In 1906 he offered a spidery little 4-seater tonneau with front-mounted engine and belt drive.

NG

LE PIAF see LIVRY

LEPOIX (D) 1972–1977

Lepoix System GmbH, Baden-Baden.
Also known as the Urbanix or Lepoix Shopi, this was a tiny electric runabout or shopping car closely resembling a golf cart. The front wheels were mounted close together, and the tiller steering was centrally mounted so that the car could be

driven from either side. The 1.5kW motor drove the rear wheels. On the Ding model, the driver sat above and behind the passengers, hansom cab fashion.

NG

LEPRECHAN see AUTOGEAR (ii) and STANHOPE

LERINI (US) c.1985

Lerini Coach Corp., North Hollywood, California.
The Lerini Armaretta was a luxury coupé based on a General Motors chassis featuring 1930s styling. It looked like a Cord 812 brought up-to-date. They were built to customer specification.

HP

LE ROITELET (F) 1921–1923

The Roitelet cyclecar was powered by a 749cc 2-cylinder engine driving the front wheels. Front suspension was by superimposed transverse leaf springs which were centrally pivoted, turning with the steering in the manner of the more primitive vehicles of 1900. It was made in Paris.

NG

LE ROLL (F) 1922

Delaune, Berge et Boudène, Paris.
This was a light car powered by a 900cc Chapuis-Dornier engine driving the rear wheels through a conventional 3-speed gearbox and propeller shaft.

NG

LEROY (CDN) 1899–1904

LeRoy Manufacturing Co., Berlin (now Kitchener) Ontario.
The brothers Milton and Nelson Good built their first car in 1899. It was powered by a single-cylinder engine of their own design and manufacture, installed at the rear of a crude carriage built by Jacob Kaufman. In 1901 they converted an American-built Mobile steamer to petrol propulsion, and in 1902 actually went into production with a single-cylinder 2-seater based on the Curved Dash Oldsmobile. It was somewhat different in appearance, with a wavy front as the Kaufmans said it would be very difficult to make the curved shape of the Olds. The Leroy, whose name came from the LeRoy Motorcycle Co. founded by the Goods' nephew I.G. Neuber, was unusual in having no brakes operating on the wheels. To stop the car, the driver used the reverse pedal of the epicyclic transmission. The brothers lacked the capital to make more modern designs, and by the end of 1904 some of the 30 cars laid down were still uncompleted. They continued in business for a few years selling engines for stationary use.

NG

LESCINA (US) 1916

Lescina Automobile Co., Newark, New Jersey.
The Lescina was a superb example of grandiose promotion followed by minuscule result. Introduced in January 1916 at New York City's Grand Central Palace, several of the cars were exhibited with the announcement that the Lescina would comprise three different chassis at varying prices and no less than 10 body styles. The company had a plant at Newark, with other assembling facilities scheduled for completion in Chicago. The basic plan outlined for Lescina production called for all of its cars to be fitted with standard proven components from specialists in various components or, in automotive parlance, 'assembled cars'. Projected series included two 4-cylinder lines with 106in (2690mm) and 112in (2842mm) wheelbases and a six which would have a wheelbase of 125in (3172mm), and a host of body styles including touring cars, standard and cloverleaf roadsters, and a cabriolet as well as a panel delivery truck, the latter of which probably never reached the prototype stage. Prices ranged from $555 to $1288. The Lescina failed in less than a year with minimal production at best.

KM

LE SPHINX see PODVIN

LESPINASSE (F) 1909

Automobiles et Moteurs L. Lespinasse, Cauderan, Gironde.
This company advertised a range of five models in one year only, and it is not certain how many of them were actually built. They ranged from a small 7hp

1951 Lester-MG sports car.
NATIONAL MOTOR MUSEUM

1907 Lessner limousine.
NATIONAL MOTOR MUSEUM

4-cylinder car to a 20hp six with 5-seater touring body. In all models, the cylinders were cast separately.

NG

LESSHAFT (D) 1925–1926
Lesshaft & Co., Berlin.
This was a light 3-wheeler with single front-wheel. A 3.5hp 2-stroke Rinne engine drove the rear wheels.

HON

LESSNER (RUS) 1904–1909
G.A. Lessner, St Petersburg.
The firm was quoted as the first Russian manufacturer of a significant range of modern automobiles, both cars and commercial vehicles–and even received an award as such. Boris Lutskji, (spelt Loutsky in Western Europe) a Russian engineer employed by Daimler in Germany, helped with the initial designs.

Lessner's variety of 8-, 12-, 22-, 32- and even 90bhp (6-cylinder) models was stunning, considering that the overall number of its cars, trucks and buses remained by most estimates only between 70 and 100 units. Not surprisingly an enterprise with such ambitions and scarce means was unviable and in 1910 the firm discontinued its automobile aspiriations.

MHK

LESTER (GB) 1913
Lester Engineering Co., Shepherds Bush, London.
The Lester was fairly unusual among cyclecars in having only a single seat, set in a very narrow body, although a staggered 2-seater was said to be available. It was powered by an 8hp J.A.P. or Precision V-twin air-cooled engine, with friction transmission and final drive by rubber belts. It had an exceptionally long wheelbase, with the dummy vee-radiator set well back from the front axle, and the rear of the body ahead of the rear axle.

NG

LESTER-MG (GB) 1949–1955
1949 Harry Lester, Knebworth, Hertfordshire.
1949–1951 Harry Lester, Thatcham, Berkshire.
1951–1954 Lester Cars (1951) Ltd, Thatcham, Berkshire.
1954–1955 The Monkey Stable, London.
Harry Lester's MG specials were mainly intended for club racing, though they could be used on the road. They had twin-tube ladder frames of Lester's own design, and lightweight 2-seater bodies. The MG engines were considerably modified from their 1250cc capacity, linered down to 1087cc for the 1100cc class, and bored out to 1467cc for the 1.5-litre class. They had many successes, of which the best was first and second places in the 1952 British Empire Trophy Race in the Isle of Man. In 1955 there were plans for a fibreglass-bodied coupé and a car powered by a 1100cc Coventry-Climax engine, but these were abandoned following the deaths of two of the make's main sponsors, Mike Keen and Jim Mayers. Only seven of these new models had been laid down when the decision was taken to stop production. About 20 of Harry Lester's cars were made altogether.

NG

LETA (GB) 1921
Light Car & Motorcycle Engineering Co., Brixton, London.
The Leta cyclecar was powered by an 8hp V-twin J.A.P. engine mounted just ahead of the rear axle, which it drove via a Sturmey-Archer gearbox and single chain. It could be supplied in kit form, or complete for 160 guineas (£168.00).
NG

LETHIMONNIER *see* SULTANE

LE TIGRE (F) 1920–1923
R. Merville, Asnières, Seine.
Although powered by a 1323cc 4-cylinder Fivet engine which developed at the most 30bhp, Le Tigre had one thing in common with the McLaren F1 – a central driving position with a passenger on each side. The open body could be converted to a saloon with the addition of a hard-top.
NG

LEVENN (F) 1900
Ernst et Cie, Paris.
The Levenn was powered by an air-cooled vertical-twin engine, and had an early example of friction disc transmission. The body was a 2-seater.
NG

LEVER *see* ELCAR and KISSEL

LE VICTOME (CDN) 1977–1980
Le Victome Classic Coachbuilders Inc, St Sauveur des Monts, Québec.
The Le Victome Renaissance neo-classic was unusual in that it did not use the centre section of an MG Midget, as most did. The steel bodywork was an original style 4-seater convertible that evoked the Duesenberg. The substantial (144in/3655mm wheelbase) chassis was a modified Ford van offering with coil sprung ifs. A Ford 6.6-litre V8 engine was installed, along with either automatic or manual transmission.
CR

LEWIS (i) (US) 1894–1895; 1899–1900
1894–1895 George W. Lewis, Chicago, Illinois.
1899–1900 Lewis Motor Vehicle Co., Philadelphia, Pennsylvania.
George Lewis built his first car primarily to demonstrate his friction disc transmission. This differed from most later versions in that the driving disc was the flywheel rather than a separate disc. The car was a heavy-looking 4-seater *dos-à-dos* with chain final drive. In 1895 he built a 2-seater with water and fuel tanks both mounted on the dashboard, one above the other. He entered this in the *Chicago Times Herald* Race and was awarded a $200 prize for the friction transmission.
For the next three years Lewis concentrated on engine manufacture, making single-cylinder units that he marketed to a number of car makers, including the one-off Brown Touring Cart. In 1899 he announced a 3hp single-cylinder runabout which he planned to make in Philadelphia. He obtained enough capital to form the Lewis Motor Vehicle Co., but few cars were made, and the company was dissolved at the end of 1900.
NG

LEWIS (ii) (AUS) 1900–c.1907
Lewis Cycles Works, Adelaide, South Australia.
The Lewis, the first car to be made in South Australia, used a 4½hp single-cylinder engine, belt drive, and wheel steering. Although mainly cycle and motorcycle makers, at least eight cars were made in the years up to about 1907, including 8/10, 10/12, and 14hp models. Some of these had tubular frames and shaft drive. Motorcycles were made up to 1914, and the company remained in business, latterly making invalid chairs, up to 1975.
MG

LEWIS (iii) (US) 1914–1916
L.P.C. Motor Car Co., Racine, Wisconsin.
The initials of this company stood for the three partners, William Mitchell Lewis, René M. Pétard and James M. Cram. All had worked for the Mitchell-

1923 Lewis (iv) 10hp 2-seater.
M.J.WORTHINGTON-WILLIAMS

Lewis Motor Co., makers of the better-known MITCHELL, but, like many before them, they left as they had plans to make a better car. Engine design was by French-born René Pétard, and its chief feature was a longer stroke than was usual, 152mm, with a bore of 89mm, giving a capacity of 5670cc. The 6-cylinder engine developed 60bhp, and the good-looking tourer was priced at $1600. A roadster was added to the range for 1915, even better looking with its wire wheels, but Lewis had lost the service of Pétard who had been recalled to France at the outbreak of war. He was unwilling to continue without his engineer, and the company was wound up in 1916.
NG

LEWIS (iv) (GB) 1923–1924
Abbey Industries Ltd, Abbey Wood, London.
The Lewis light car was available in 2- or 4-cylinder forms. The twin was a 1092cc MAG unit, the four a side-valve Coventry Climax. An Opperman 3-speed gearbox was used and final drive was by shaft. The polished aluminium 2-seater was priced at £195 for the twin and £225 for the four. The market for this size of car was very competitive, and few were made before production ended in April 1924. Apart from the company name, there is no evidence for a link with the Westminster-built ABBEY.
NG

LEWIS AIROMOBILE (US) 1937
Lewis-American Airways Inc, Syracuse, New York.
Designed by Paul M. Lewis, this was a streamlined 3-wheeled coupé powered by a 60bhp 2-litre flat-four engine designed by former Franklin engineers Carl Doman and Ed Marks. Drive was to the front wheels. Top speed was 80mph (128km/h) and the planned price a reasonable $300, less than half that of the cheapest Ford V8. Only one prototype was made, which still exists, but four others were under construction when Lewis realised that a 3-wheeled car was not a marketable proposition in the deeply conservative America of the time. The engine design, however, was used after the war in a number of light aircraft such as the Aeronca, Piper and Taylorcraft.
NG

LEXINGTON (US) 1908–1927
1908–1910 Lexington Motor Co., Lexington, Kentucky.
1911–1913 Lexington Motor Co., Connersville, Indiana.
1914–1927 Lexington-Howard Co., Connversville, Indiana.
1918–1927 Lexington Motor Co., Connersville, Indiana.
The Lexington Motor Co. formed in 1908, started production in 1909, operations moving a year later to Connersville, Indiana where it was acquired by E.W. Ansted, a manufacturer of automobile parts, who continued the car augmented by a companion series, the HOWARD, a 4-cylinder line through 1914. For 1915, the Lexington Four and the Howard were discontinued, all subsequent Lexingtons being 6-cylinder cars. The company was re-organised in 1918. The Lexington offered a wide variety of models and body types, production reaching its zenith in 1920 when more than 6000 cars found buyers. Using the American Revolution and its Battle of Lexington-Concord as its theme, Lexington and Concord models

c.1910 Lexington Model C roadster.
NATIONAL MOTOR MUSEUM

1990 Lexus LS400 saloon.
TOYOTA MOTOR CO.

1998 Lexus GS300 saloon.
TOYOTA MOTOR CO.

2000 Lexus RX300 4×4.
TOYOTA MOTOR CO.

were featured over a period of years enjoying considerable popularity. By the same token, its 'Minute Man Six' models were among Lexington's most successful series. Among the more curious cars produced by Lexington was its ANSTED Six – a sport roadster offered in 1921 which, although actually a sporting model of its 'T Series' line of cars, was sold with its own high 'cathedral type' radiator, badge and other nomenclature, purporting to be a car of its own make. Like the other cars in the 'Series T' line, the Ansted used the same Ansted 6-cylinder engine. Unlike them, however, it was considerably higher in price. Lexington went into receivership in the early 1920s and although it managed to remain in business until 1927, the company was plagued with numerous fiscal difficulties. In 1927, Lexington went out of business, its factory being acquired by E.L. Cord, recently named president of Auburn. The last Lexington cars sold through the Chicago distributor carried the Ansted badge on their radiators.

KM

LEXUS (J) 1988 to date
Toyota Motor Co. Ltd, Toyota City.

When Toyota moved upmarket into BMW/Mercedes-Benz territory, they chose a new brand name, Lexus, the cars being marketed by a separate dealer network in the United States, though not in Europe. The first Lexus LS400 was a 4-door saloon powered by a 250bhp 32-valve V8 of 3969cc, with four ohcs. Suspension was by coils and double wishbones all round, with the option of electronically-controlled air suspension. In 1993 it was joined by the smaller GS300 saloon with 212bhp 2997cc V6 engine and styling by Italdesign. The GS300 and the LS400 were known in Japan as the Toyota Aristo and Celsior respectively, and were still made in 1999, the LS400's output raised to 294bhp. From 1998 this engine was available in the GS300 in addition to the six. In 2000 the LS400 gave way to the LS430 with 4.3-litre V8 engine and a redesigned saloon body with greater head and leg room, and a very low drag co-efficient of 0.255 Cd.

A new model for 1998 was the IS200, a 4-door saloon with 1998cc twin-ohc 6-cylinder engine aimed at the BMW 3 Series market. Lexus was thus marking BMW in three market segments, with the GS300 challenging the 5 Series, and the LS400 the 7 Series. In addition, there was the SC300/400 2-door coupé for the American market only, derived from the Toyota Soarer and made with the 6-cylinder or V8 engines, and the Toyota Camry-derived ES300 V6 saloon, also for the American market only. In 1998 came two 4×4s, also Toyota-derived. These were the RX300 with V6 engine and permanent 4-wheel drive, and the LX470 with 4664cc V8 engine and the option of 2- or 4-wheel drive.

NG

LEY see LORELEY

LEYAT (F) 1919–1927
Marcel Leyat, Paris.

Born in 1885, Marcel Leyat was fascinated by aviation as a young man, and is said to have built and flown an aeroplane of his own design in 1910. Three years later he built a 3-wheeled car with propeller propulsion, and in 1919 announced production of a 4-wheeler. This had an A.B.C. flat-twin motorcycle engine driving a 4-blade propeller at the front of the car, surrounded by a wire mesh grill to protect passers-by. Obviously no gearbox or transmission were needed, and the brakes were on the front wheels only. Steering was on the rear wheels, and the integral construction body seated two in tandem. The first body was open, but in 1921 came a 'saloon', also with two seats in tandem, and the 2-cylinder A.B.C. or a 3-cylinder Anzani engine. A Matchless engine was also available. 600 orders were said to have been taken at the 1921 Paris Salon, but it is thought that not more than about 30 Leyats were made in all, mostly between 1921 and 1923. They also went under the name Hélica.

In 1927 Leyat showed his last car, more of an aeroplane without wings than a car with a propeller. It was a very long and low 3-wheeler with an unprotected 2-blade propeller. It was demonstrated at Montlhéry, but is unlikely to have been used on the road.

NG
Further Reading
Les Automobiles à Hélice, Gustave Courau, Éditions Automobiles Paul Couty, 1969.

1923 Leyat saloon.
M.J.WORTHINGTON-WILLIAMS

LEYLAND (i) (GB) 1920–1923

Leyland Motors Ltd, Leyland, Lancashire.

Leyland was a pioneering British commercial vehicle constructor, making their first steam van in 1896 and their first petrol lorry in 1904. It was during World War I that the company decided to enter the luxury car market, and during 1917/18 their chief engineer J.G. Parry Thomas, aided by Reid Railton, worked on a car which the directors planned to be the finest on the market. Both men were to become well-known in motor sport, Thomas taking the Land Speed Record before his death in another attempt in 1927, while Railton gave his name to the Anglo-American sports cars of the 1930s, and was responsible for the Railton Mobil Special, with which John Cobb took the LSR in 1938, 1939 and 1947.

The Leyland Eight was launched at the 1920 Olympia Show, where it was described as 'The Lion of Olympia'. It had a 6967cc (later enlarged to 7266cc) straight-8 engine with single ohc, and leaf springs to close each pair of valves. This gave 90bhp, and 145bhp in twin-carburettor form. The 4-speed gearbox was cushioned on leather, and there were vacuum servo brakes on the rear wheels. It is rather surprising that it lacked front-wheel brakes; admittedly its rival, the Rolls-Royce Silver Ghost, did not get these until 1924, but it was a prewar design. Other brand-new luxury cars such as the Hispano-Suiza H6 and Duesenberg Model A both had front-wheel brakes, the former with mechanical servo assistance, the latter hydraulic.

The Leyland Eight was offered with rather plain open 2- or 5-seater bodies, and also as a chassis for coachbuilders. Among those who built a custom body on the Eight chassis was Grose, who made a limousine for Mrs Sears, mother of the well-known veteran car collector, Stanley Sears. Another Leyland owner was the Maharajah of Patiala, who had two, while IRA leader Michael Collins was riding in one when he was killed in Cork in 1922. At £2500 for a chassis it was

1920 Leyland (i) Eight tourer.
NICK BALDWIN

the most expensive British-made car, and though prices were progressively reduced each year, reaching £1825 in 1923, customers were hard to find. Probably Leyland's reputation for trucks and buses, excellent though it was, did not help sales in a very class-conscious market. An estimated 18 cars were made, and Parry Thomas built three racing cars after he had left Leyland, which may have been additional to the 18. The last, and only Leyland Eight known to survive, was a 2-seater sports car built up from parts by Thomson & Taylor in 1927.

NG

Further Reading
The Leyland Eight, Hugo Tours, Profile Publications, 1966.

1973 Leyland (ii) P76 Super sedan.
NATIONAL MOTOR MUSEUM

1912 Le Zébre Type A 2-seater.
NICK GEORGANO/NATIONAL MOTOR MUSEUM

1921 Le Zébre Type D 2-seater.
NICK GEORGANO/NATIONAL MOTOR MUSEUM

LEYLAND (ii) (AUS) 1973–1982

Leyland Motor Corp. Australia Ltd, Waterloo, New South Wales.
Succeeding an array of British firms with Australian operations, such as BMC, Rover and the commercial makers gathered into the fold; this name began appearing early when Land-Rover became a Leyland model. The Mini-based Moke, then made only in Australia, was the Leyland Moke and a 4-wheel drive prototype was made for evaluation. The Mini became a Leyland in 1973 while the Marina, always with the Leyland 'wheel' badge, was a MORRIS only at release. Differing from home models by having 1500 and 1750cc E-series ohc

engines, the later Big Red had the 2623cc 6-cylinder version shoe-horned in, to conform with an industry fancy for fitting such local engines in smaller cars.

A wholly Australian model was the full-sized P76, derived from a ROVER study for a P5 replacement, powered either by the E-series six or a 4416cc alloy V8. A creditable design with no more panels to press than a Mini and of notably low weight, it was fitted with many components produced for similarly sized cars but rack and pinion steering and a lightweight V8 set it apart. Released in 1973 it was met with enthusiasm, particularly for the V8, but the breakdown of V8 production, which restricted supply of the desired model, was a setback and the onset of the energy crisis finally drove buyers to 4-cylinder cars. A P76 ran in the World Cup Rally, in which a win on the Targa Florio section spurred a special edition. A station wagon and a Force 7 coupé were ready when the factory closed in 1975. P76 production totalled 19,017, including 650 assembled in New Zealand. The Mini and Moke continued, with imported parts at the Pressed Metal Corp. subsidiary until 1978 for the Mini and 1982 for the Moke.

MG

Further Reading
'Leyland P76: Last Gasp Down Under', Gavin Farmer,
Automobile Quarterly, Vol. 38, No. 1.

LE ZÈBRE (F) 1909–1931

SA le Zèbre, Puteaux, Seine.
The Le Zèbre was a light single-cylinder car designed by Jules Salomon, an employee of Georges Richard, maker of the UNIC car, and financed by Jacques Bizet, a car dealer and son of composer Georges Bizet. The first, the Type A, had a 602cc vertical engine, with 2-speed gearbox and shaft drive. The first batch of about 50 were made in the Unic factory. The engines and chassis were bought from S.U.P. The name Le Zèbre came, not from a horse as has been suggested, but was the nickname of an office boy at Unic, according to the historian of the marque Philippe Schram.

The Société le Zèbre was founded in October 1909, and the partners set up their own factory soon afterwards. The Type A was made up to 1917, with an increase in engine capacity to 645cc for 1912, and was joined at the 1912 Paris Salon by two new models. The Type B had a 1742cc monobloc 4-cylinder engine and was suitable for 2- or 4-seater coachwork, while the Type C had a tiny 4-cylinder engine of 785cc, and a wheelbase only 8in (203mm) longer than that of the Type A. Both these models received a vee-radiator for the 1914 season, and were made up to 1917. According to chassis numbering, 1772 Type As were made, 579 Type Bs and 3712 Type Cs. The Type A was distinguished from the other models by its 'military' type squared off wings, as well as by the flat radiator.

During the war Salomon designed a 4-cylinder car for André Citroën which became the Type A. He left Le Zèbre, and after a short period working for Charron, he joined Citroën in July 1917. The prewar Le Zèbres were not revived in 1919. Instead there was the Type D, with 997cc 4-cylinder engine. It was essentially a modernised Type C but with several important improvements, including unit engine and gearbox and electric lighting and starting. The radiator was rounded rather than a vee, and in conjunction with wire wheels, gave the car a very pleasing appearance. It was made in 2-seater, 4-seater and saloon forms, the bodies coming from Clément-Bayard and Minet. In 1920, in response to public demand, Le Zèbre revived the single-cylinder engine in the Type Monocylindrique. This had a 4hp engine in a chassis very similar to the prewar Type C, and was available in one body style, an open 2-seater. It was listed to 1923, but few were made. The Type D, now with flat radiator, was made up to the end of 1923, and there were two new models in 1923, both short-lived. The Type E was a sports model of the D, sold in chassis form only, and the 10hp was a Type E AMILCAR made under licence, with only minor differences such as a 3-speed gearbox in place of the Amilcar's four. There were strong links between Le Zèbre and Amilcar, as two major Le Zèbre shareholders, Joseph Lamy and Émile Akar, had founded Amilcar. Le Zèbre were now desperately looking for a car to revive their fortunes, and announced two new models for 1924. The Type C/Armée harked back to prewar days in having a Type C chassis with the same 785cc engine in the body used for the Monocylindrique. Such a car, devoid of electric lighting or starting, could hardly be expected to sell in the face of competition from the Citroën 5CV, and the other new model from Le Zèbre was a better bet. This was the Type Z, which had a 1973cc 4-cylinder engine designed by Harry Ricardo with his patent hemispherical combustion chambers, pistons and carburettor. His contract also included the designs of the chassis and body. The former was made for Le Zèbre by the Ateliers de la Fournaise. Four roomy body styles were offered, a 5-seater tourer, 4-seater sports tourer, 4-seater saloon and coupé de ville. Although it was well received by the press, the Type Z did not sell particularly well, about 550 finding customers between 1924 and 1930. An attempt in 1924 to produce a cheaper model, the 8/10CV, with 1100cc engine in a shortened Z chassis with the same body styles, ended with the completion of one prototype. This was sold for £50 to a Ricardo employee, who ran it until 1937. The final Le Zèbre had a single-cylinder opposed-piston 2-stroke diesel engine by C.L.M. It got no further than the stand at the 1931 Paris Salon.

NG

Further Reading
L'Épopée de la Société Le Zèbre, Philippe Schram, Published privately, 1997.

L.F. (F) 1985–c.1989
L.F. Import, Suresnes.
This company imported, then constructed, an A.C. Cobra 427 replica. Power usually came from a Rover V8 engine, although a Ford 7-litre V8, Chevrolet 7.4-litre V8 and various European 6-cylinder engines could be fitted.

CR

LIBELLE (i) (D) 1920–1922
Kleinautofabrik GmbH, Sindelfingen.
This was a light, simple open car powered by a 4/10PS V-twin engine. It was relatively highly priced, and few were sold.

HON

LIBELLE (ii) (A) 1952–1955
Extremely characterful styling distinguished this tiny 3-wheeler microcar, which reflected its name, for Libelle means dragonfly in German. Hence the two passengers sat up front in an open compartment with a single round tube arching up from the nose to the back of the seat, while the rear deck looked like the tail of the dragonfly. A 199cc Rotax 8.5bhp 2-stroke single-cylinder engine sat in the tail and had to be kick-started. The official name of the car was Libelle Allwetter-Autoroller. Plans for it to be made in Italy with a 160cc Mondial engine, under the name Libellula, came to nothing.

CR

LIBÉRIA (F) 1900–1902
G. Dupont, Plessis-Trévise, Seine-et-Oise.
The Libéria was made in two models, with 6½ and 12hp engines, both by Aster. The cars were campaigned in several long-distance races, drivers including the manufacturer M. Dupont himself. These included Berlin-Aachen in 1900, Paris-Bordeaux and Paris-Berlin in 1901 and Paris-Vienna in 1902.

NG

LIBERTA *see* MEAN

LIBERTY (i) (US) 1914
Liberty Motor Co., New York City, New York.
Designed by Joseph A. Anglada, the Liberty cyclecar had an air-cooled V-twin engine, friction transmission and double belt final drive. A price of $375 was fixed, but the company was out of business in less than a year, and probably very few Libertys were made. Anglada later moved south, to Rock Hill, South Carolina, where he designed a 6-cylinder engine for ANDERSON (ii).

NG

LIBERTY (ii) (US) 1916–1923
Liberty Motor Car Co., Detroit, Michigan.
Backed by a number of prominent Detroit industry men, including former Saxon vice-president Percy Owen and other personnel from Saxon, the Liberty was a conventional medium-sized car powered initially by a 3730cc 6-cylinder Continental engine, though they changed to a 3770cc six of their own manufacture in 1921. The usual range of open and closed body styles was offered, and from 1921 if not earlier, wire wheels were an alternative to the more common artillery type. The 1923 models had disc wheels and step plates instead of running boards. The Liberty sold well for a while, the peak year being 1921 when 11,217

1923 Liberty (ii) Model 10-D sports coupé.
JOHN A.CONDE

found customers. Encouraged by this they moved to larger premises, but this brought financial trouble and they went into receivership in January 1923. In September they were acquired by the COLUMBIA (iv) Motor Car Co., who announced that they would continue the Liberty, but any 1924 models were left-over 1923s assembled from parts on hand. Total production of Libertys was nearly 37,000 cars.

NG

LIBERTY CLASSICS (US) c.1985
Liberty Classics, Minneapolis, Minnesota.
The Esquire was an inexpensive neoclassic kit car loosely based on 1930s Mercedes styling. There were two versions, one based on VW running gear, the other with Ford Pinto or Mustang II parts.

HP

LIBERTY SLR *see* FIBERFAB (i)

LIBRA (i) *see* KING (iv)

LIBRA (ii) (ZA) 1990s
Libra Cars, Jeppestown, Johannesburg.
The Libra Aqua Sport was a fibreglass body conversion for a shortened VW Beetle platform chassis. Styled by Mario Nardini, it was a curvaceous, doorless targa-topped design. A rear-mounted VW Golf engine was the intended powerplant.

CR

LIDKÖPING (S) 1923
Lidköping Mekaniska Verkstad, Lidköping.
The Lidköping was an attractive-looking light car with 4-cylinder C.I.M.E. engine and 3-speed gearbox, and a 3-seater cloverleaf body. Only three prototypes were made.

NG

LIÈGE (GB) 1995 to date
1995–1998 Liège Motor Co., Bidford-on-Avon, Warwickshire.
1998 to date Liège Motor Co., Fladbury, Worcesterhsire.
This tiny traditional-style sports car was conceived mainly with trialling in mind. As such, it was a very simple, very lightweight (406kg) car with high ground clearance and 18in wire wheels. The simple chassis used front swing axles, a live rear axle and a Reliant Robin engine with optional supercharging. Complete cars with all-new parts cost £10,000, while kits were also available.

CR

LIFU (GB) 1899–1902
The Steam Car Co. (House's System) Ltd, London.
Henry Alonzo House was a pioneer of steam in America, having built, with his brother Joseph, a steam carriage at Bridgeport, Connecticut in 1866. He later crossed the Atlantic and in 1898 was the manager of the Liquid Fuel Engineering Co. Ltd (Lifu) of Cowes, Isle of Wight, as well as United States Vice-Consul

1901 Lifu steam car.
NATIONAL MOTOR MUSEUM

c.1995 Light Car Co. Rocket 2-seater.
CHRIS REES

at Southampton. Lifu made steam vans and buses, as well as marine engines, but so far as is known, no passenger cars. These were made under House's patents by various sub-contracting firms for sale by the Steam Car Co. Ltd. They had 2-cylinder compound engines driving the rear wheels by spur gear. Some were bonneted with a front-mounted condenser, others had forward control and resembled the contemporary Serpollet. The only known survivor is a 10hp 4-seater made in 1901 by Thomas Noakes & Sons of London. The Lifu company closed their Cowes works in 1900, moving the marine engine business to Hamworthy, Dorset, where they were active in 1908, and possibly later.

NG

LIGHT (US) 1913–1914

Light Motor Car Co., Detroit, Michigan.

This was a very conventional car powered by a 30hp 6-cylinder engine with pair-cast cylinders, a 3-speed gearbox and shaft drive. Three body styles were offered, roadster, demi-tonneau and touring. Light may have been the name of a company official, as it was not a particularly light car.

NG

LIGHTBURN (AUS) 1962–1965

Lightburn Vehicles Ltd, Novar Gardens, South Australia.

As makers of a wide range of items ranging from tools to washing machines, Lightburn & Co. had kept the economy car in view for some while, making one with a Jawa engine and fibreglass bodywork in the late 1950s. The rights to the former British Anzani-built ASTRA were obtained and a fibreglass body was

designed for its own version, named Zeta. A Villiers 324cc 2-stroke twin drove via a 4-speed gearbox to the front wheels. Independently sprung all round, its wheelbase was 74in (1880mm) and the weight was 960lbs (436kg). Although it had a body of station wagon form, there was no rear door and loading was facilitated by easily removed seats and doors which opened to almost 180 degrees. A utility (pick-up) was also made. The 1964 Zeta Sport was a reversal of form, with a rear engine. Based on the former FRISKY Sprint, it was powered by a Fitchel & Sachs 2-cylinder 2-stroke 498cc engine, wheelbase was 70in (1784mm) and it weighed 895lb (407kg). The fibreglass body lacked both doors and bumpers, which made the low-set headlamps vulnerable. As the Mini had, by then, made minicars redundant, only 315 cars and 48 step-in roadsters were made.

MG

LIGHT CAR COMPANY (GB) 1991 to date

Light Car Co. Ltd, St Neots, Cambridgeshire.

The unassuming name of this company belied the exotic nature of its product. Conceived by McLaren's Gordon Murray and racer Chris Craft, the Rocket was an extraordinary motor car. Designed according to lofty engineering principles, it was perhaps the closest thing to a Formula racing car that you could drive on the road. Under the narrow, cigar-shaped doorless body sat a tubular chassis that used its engine as a stressed member, just like a racer. That engine was a Yamaha FZR1000 motorcycle engine with its restrictors removed for an output of 143bhp, in which case a top speed of 143mph (230km/h) was claimed. A tuned 165bhp version was also available, allied to a 6-speed gearbox rather than the standard 5-speed unit. This was unusual in that it was allied to a purpose-built twin-speed rear axle with limited slip differential, effectively giving ten forward speeds and five reverse speeds! The very high price did not dissuade a fanatical following of owners, many of whom were celebrities. The company also pursued a radical V8 engine project intended for the LIGHTNING (ii) road car.

CR

LIGHTNING (i) (GB) 1984–1985

Lightning Sportscars, Stafford, Staffordshire.

It is not surprising that this Chevrolet Corvette lookalike should have failed: it was an imperfect reproduction, quality was lacking and the simple chassis used humble Ford Cortina parts. Delays in production sealed its fate and it quickly disappeared.

CR

LIGHTNING (ii) (GB) 1996

LIGHT CAR Rocket creator Chris Craft and Tony Hart (brother of F1 engine specialist Brian Hart) developed a V8 engine consisting of two Yamaha 1-litre 4-cylinder engines joined together on a common crank. With an almost unbelievable output of 305bhp from just 2-litres, it needed a car to fit into, so Craft asked Peter Stevens to design a sports car body for it. Based on a tubular space frame chassis with all-round double wishbone suspension, the prototype Lightning had an aluminium open body, though production cars were stated to have fibreglass. However, full production never began.

CR

LIGHTSPEED see MAGENTA

LIGIER (F) 1971 to date

1971–1977 Automobiles Ligier, Vichy, Allier.
1980–1983 Seudem, Paris.
1983 to date, Automobiles Ligier, Abrest, Vichy.

Having made his fortune, been a successful racing driver and played rugby for France, in 1970 Guy Ligier – later to found his own Formula 1 racing team – built his own sports car. Named after his friend Jo Schlesser, who was killed in a racing accident in 1968, the Ligier JS was first seen at the Paris Salon in 1970. Then this sports coupé had mid-mounted Ford Cortina power but JS2 production cars, from 1971, had a Citroën SM/Maserati engine turned through 180 degrees in a backbone chassis. The specification also included all-independent suspension by wishbones, 4-wheel disc brakes, plastic bodywork and optional limited slip differential. Citroën acquired Ligier in 1974 to use the factory for SM production, but Peugeot's take-over a year later brought this to a close. The

1972 Ligier JS2 coupé.
LUCIEN LOREILLE

JS2 continued to be made until 1977, when Guy Ligier at first turned his attention to a double-cab pick-up prototype. For three years there was no production.

In stark contrast to its sports and racing cars, in 1980 came the JS4, a very squarish 2-seater microcar powered by a 50cc Motobécane engine and automatic transmission. Unusually it had an all-metal body with quad headlamps and all-independent suspension. It quickly became the best-selling microcar in France (almost 7000 sold in 1981). The 125cc JS8 joined the range in 1982 but diesel engines supplanted petrol ones in 1985. With the 1987 Séries 7, Ligier switched to more conventional fibreglass bodywork. This was powered by a 327cc Lombardini diesel engine. The 1989 Optima included luxury options such as tinted glass and leather upholstery and there was an estate version called the Optimax, as well as a 617cc 3-cylinder model (the Optima 4). Electric power was offered from 1992. Ligier grew ever more sophisticated with models like the 162, launched in 1995, an extremely pretty 2-seater again powered by a 505cc diesel twin engine. A 161 version with a single-cylinder engine was also available. With the Ambra that entered production in 1997, Ligier became ever more the sophisticated microcar constructor, and this theme was followed in the 505cc Dué of 1999.

CR

LILA (J) 1923–1927
Jitsuyo Jidosha Kaisha Co., Osaka.
The Lila was the successor to the GORHAM, and was a more advanced 4-wheeler powered by a 10hp 4-cylinder engine with a 4-door saloon body. 200 were made in the first year, and J.J.K. merged with the Kwaishin Sha Motor Works in 1926, changing the company name to DAT Jidosha Seizo Co Ltd. This made the Datson (later DATSUN) from 1931. It is not certain when production of the Lila ended, probably no later than 1927 as DAT concentrated on trucks until the arrival of the Datson.

NG

LILIPUT (D) 1904–1907
1904–1905 Bergmann's Industriewerke, Gaggenau.
1905–1907 Süddeutsche Automobilfabrik GmbH, Gaggenau.
Bergmann had made the old-fashioned ORIENT EXPRESS from 1895 to 1903, and then turned at last to a more up-to-date design in the Liliput. Designed by Willy Seck, this was a light 2-seater powered by a front-mounted 567cc single-cylinder engine driving the rear wheels via friction transmission and single chain. At 2500 marks it was probably the cheapest car on the German market. However windscreen, hood and lamps were extras.

The car division of Bergmann's Industriewerke became independent in 1905, using the name Süddeutsche Automobilfabrik, but production of Liliput cars was continued. The 4PS single-cylinder was joined by a 9PS twin and a 14/16PS

1985 Ligier Series 7 diesel microcar.
NICK BALDWIN

1999 Ligier Dué microcar.
LIGIER

c.1905 Liliput 4PS tonneau.
NICK GEORGANO

1920 Lincoln (v) Pioneer Six tourer.
M.J.WORTHINGTON-WILLIAMS

four with a 4-seater body, though the smaller cars were sometimes laden with 4-seater coachwork as well. The 12/16 was marketed under the name Libelle, and the smaller cars were made under licence by SCHILLING in Suhl.

HON

LIMA (US) 1915

Lima Light Car Co., Lima, Ohio.
This company was formed to make a light car powered by an 18hp 4-cylinder engine in three models, roadster, speedster and light delivery. The cars were priced at $500, and prototypes were on the road in May 1915, but it is not certain if production followed. Certainly the company was out of business by the end of the year.

NG

LIMING (CHI) 1996–1999

Yizheng Auto Works, Yizheng City, Jiangsu Province.
One of the 60 factories offering jeep-based pick-ups and estate cars, the Yizheng factory started to develop motor car-like vehicles after 1993, starting with a good-looking estate car still using the Beijing Jeep 4 × 2 chassis. In 1996 the factory assembled South-Korean Kia automobiles under its own name: Liming YQC 6420N. In 1998 the Yizheng Works became a subsidiary of the Shanghai Auto Industry Corp. A year later, Yizheng developed a mini-car of their own, using domestic parts and components. It had a maximum speed of 62mph (100km/h). The price was around $3500.

EVIS

LINCK (US) c.1985

Linck Motor Co., Fullerton, California.
The Linck Stealth X-1 was a mid-engined kit car with highly original styling. A tubular space frame mounted front-wheel drive drivetrains from Honda, Subaru, Renault or Chrysler. Designed by James Linck, it featured a composite body with a very low drag co-efficient.

HP

LINCOLN (i) (US) 1900

Lincoln Electric Co., Cleveland, Ohio.
This was a 2-seater electric runabout powered by a 2½ hp motor with Willard batteries. A poorly-explained 'Lincoln Controller' was said to give an increase in range of between 10 and 25 per cent.

NG

LINCOLN (ii) (US) 1908–1909

Lincoln Automobile Co., Lincoln, Illinois.
This was a high-wheeler powered by a 10/12 or 16/18hp flat-twin engine, driving though an epicyclic transmission. Final drive was by chain or shaft, the latter seldom seen on high-wheelers. Prices ran from $550 for the 72in (1827mm) wheelbase 10/12hp Model A to $800 for the 82in (2081mm) 16/18hp Model C.

NG

LINCOLN (iii) (US) 1912–1913

Lincoln Motor Car Works, Chicago, Illinois.
This company made cars for Sears Roebuck to sell as the Sears Motor Buggy, and when the mail-order house discontinued their buggy, Lincoln made virtually the same car under the name Lincoln Model 24 runabout. It had an air-cooled flat-twin engine, friction transmission and double-chain drive. They also made a more expensive light touring model which owed less to the Sears design.

NG

LINCOLN (iv) (US) 1914

Lincoln Motor Car Co., Detroit, Michigan.
Also known as the Lincoln Highway, this was a light car with 4-cylinder engine, 2-speed gearbox and shaft drive. The radiator lived behind a bonnet very similar to the Renault's. Priced at $500, the prototype was tested in February 1914, and limited production started soon afterwards.

NG

LINCOLN (v) (AUS) 1919–1926

Lincoln Motor Co., Sydney, New South Wales.
Charles Innes decided that he would assemble cars from imported US components rather than import them in assembled form, and so he visited the United States to make arrangements. He was so pleased with the reception he was accorded that he chose the Lincoln name for his car, being unaware that the name would be similarly applied in the US. The engine was a 6-cylinder Continental.

MG

LINCOLN (vi) (GB) 1920

Field & Slater Ltd, Liverpool.
This was a 3-wheeled cyclecar powered by an 8hp air-cooled Blackburne engine, with 3-speed gearbox and chain drive. It was announced in August 1920, and the makers said that it had been tested over a two-year period. An alternative address was Lancaster Gardens, Ealing in West London.

NG

LINCOLN (vii) (US) 1920 to date

Lincoln Motor Co., Detroit, Michigan.
Since 1922 the Lincoln has been the prestige marque of the Ford empire, but ironically it started life under the guidance of a General Motors man, Henry M. Leland (1843–1932). Leland had supplied engines to Oldsmobile at the turn of the 20th century, and had left a strong partnership with Ford in 1902 to found the Cadillac Motor Co. In 1917 he left Cadillac and set up the Lincoln Motor Co., which made 6500 Liberty aero engines. Doubtless Leland planned to build a Lincoln car from the moment he left Cadillac, and possibly before.

In 1919, with his war contracts completed he and his son Wilfrid began work on their car. Two prototypes were running before the end of the year, and production began in September 1920.

The first Lincoln was very much the same kind of car as the Cadillac, with a 5863cc V8 engine developing 81bhp. The angle between the cylinder banks was 60 degrees, compared with the Cadillac's 90 degrees. It had full-pressure lubrication at a time when many contemporaries made do with the splash system, and the world's first thermostatically-operated radiator shutters. Fifteen body styles were offered in the first year, at prices at least $1000 more than the equivalent Cadillac. The prices might not have been too serious a handicap, but the styling of the bodies was old-fashioned and uninspiring. Neither Henry nor Wilfrid were stylists, being much too busy with engineering, and body design was left to Henry's son-in-law who was not artistically gifted. A number of orders were cancelled when the cars reached the showrooms, and the Lelands hastily contacted two well-known coachbuilders, Brunn and Judkins, to redesign their bodies. Only 3407 cars were made up to February 1922, way below the target of 6000 in the first 12 months. A heavy tax bill put Lincoln in the hands of the receivers, and the fledgling make might well have disappeared like so many others, but for the intervention of Henry Ford

There were several reasons why Ford was interested in Lincoln – he liked the idea of a luxury car to complement his very basic Model T, and to buy out the Lelands was a kind of revenge for Henry Leland's breaking the 1902 partnership and taking the successful Cadillac design with him.

The first Lincolns made under Ford ownership were the 1922 models, which differed little from the previous cars except that aluminium pistons replaced the cast-iron ones. Prices were drastically cut, so that a 5-seater tourer cost $3300, compared with $4600 under the Leland regime. Ford had invited the Lelands to stay with the company, but there was not room for two strong-minded Henrys in one firm, and in June 1922 they left. Henry M. Leland was now 79 years old, but he continued to be active in local affairs until his death ten years later.

Under Ford control the Lincoln Motor Co. flourished, and between March and December 1922 sales were 5512, or an average of 550 per month. This compared well with the 255 made in the two months before Ford took over. In 1923 Lincoln sold 7875 cars and made a profit for the first time. That year was notable also for the purchase of a Lincoln by President Calvin Coolidge; ever since then Lincoln has been the preferred transport for US Presidents. Lincolns were widely used by police forces and gangsters in the 1920s. The police versions had tuned engines and front-wheel brakes from 1924, which were not available to the general public until three years later. When they did arrive, they were called the 'six-brake system', referring to the handbrake control over the rear brakes and the pedal operating on front and rear brakes.

Few changes were made to the V8 engine during the 1920s, apart from an increase in capacity to 6306cc for 1928. Edsel Ford became president of the company on the Lelands' departure, and his interest in styling led to important developments. Lincoln had their own body department for the standard tourers, but Edsel contracted with several well-known coachbuilders to make batches of popular designs which could be sold at a lower price than a one-off custom body. Among the coachbuilders who supplied Lincoln in this way were Brunn, Fleetwood, Holbrook, Judkins, Lebaron and Locke. Some of these bodies were made in quite large numbers; for example Brunn supplied 829 sedans and 689 phaetons in 1925 alone. In 1926 Lincoln offered 32 body styles.

Up to 1931 the only Lincoln was the Model L (for Leland), but in that year it was replaced by the Model K. This had the same 6306cc engine, now giving 120bhp, installed in a lower and longer frame, and a handsome new radiator with a slight vee. The K was continued for 1932 under the name KA, but the important news for that year was a 150bhp 7340cc V12. This was installed in the KA chassis, the model being designated KB. The 3-speed gearbox now had synchromesh on the two upper ratios. As before, a wide range of standard and semi-customs bodies was available on the KA and KB chassis. Because of the Depression, sales were lower than for the Model L; which had reached 8858 in 1926. In 1932 Lincoln sold only 3388 cars, 1765 KAs and 1623 KBs.

The V8 engine was dropped for 1933, but there were two sizes of V12, the 6255cc KA and 7340cc KB. Lincoln made only 12-cylinder cars for the next sixteen years. A new 6784cc V12 with aluminium cylinder heads was the sole model for 1934 and 1935, but then a completely new Lincoln appeared, taking them into the medium-priced field for the first time.

1923 Lincoln (vii) Model L sedan.
NICK BALDWIN

1932 Lincoln (vii) KB coupé , by Dietrich.
NICK BALDWIN

1936 Lincoln (vii) Zephyr sedan.
NICK BALDWIN

1939 Lincoln (vii) touring cabriolet, by Brunn.
NICK BALDWIN

1941 Lincoln (vii) Continental coupé.
NATIONAL MOTOR MUSEUM

NATIONAL MOTOR MUSEUM

FORD, EDSEL (1893–1943)

Edsel Bryant Ford probably didn't think of himself as a stylist. And yet he did become the ultimate decision-maker and arbiter of Ford styling throughout most of his career.

His father, Henry Ford, made Edsel company president on 31 December 1918, yet Edsel had no real duties. Henry kept a tight grip on virtually every aspect of Ford Motor Co., from engineering through advertising and labour relations.

The one automotive area Henry cared nothing about was styling, which was fortunate for Edsel, because Edsel did have a flair for art. He was interested in painting, photography, architecture, interior and furniture design. Almost by default, then, Edsel transformed those interests into a concern for what

Ford motorcars looked like. Styling duly became the only area in which Henry fully trusted Edsel's judgment.

Edsel Ford was born on 6 November 1893, and by the time he was 10, his father had given him a bright-red 1903 Ford runabout, which Edsel promptly learned to drive. He loved to draw cars and filled a scrapbook with pictures of the latest, most elegant European salon models. As a teenager, he became quite a good mechanic and hot rodded a Model T. And at age 19, he bought himself a chic French Renault.

Edsel attended and excelled at a private high school, Detroit University School, and could have gone to any college in the world. But when he graduated in 1912, his father decided he should join Ford Motor Company. Two years later, Henry gave Edsel $1 million in gold for his 21st birthday and, in 1915, made him company secretary, then president in 1918. He married Eleanor Clay in 1916, and they had four children: Henry II (1917 – 1987), Benson (1919 – 1978), Josephine Clay (b. 1923), and William Clay (b. 1925).

In 1922, Henry bought the ailing Lincoln Motor Car Company and turned it over to Edsel to manage. Some called Lincoln 'Edsel's plaything'; just another toy. But Edsel quickly became determined to make Lincoln nothing less than America's most respected and prestigious luxury motorcar. He realized it wouldn't be easy, especially against such established rivals as Packard, Pierce-Arrow, Locomobile, Peerless and Cadillac. Lincoln was very much the new car on the block.

Lincoln was already quite advanced mechanically, so Edsel decided to concentrate on styling. He contracted with some of the nation's leading coachbuilders to provide both custom and production designs: Brunn, Judkins, LeBaron, Willoughby and Dietrich.

When any of these coachbuilders proposed a new design, Edsel inspected the blueprints in minute detail. He made suggestions and asked questions, and while he might not have realized it, this period formed the basis of his styling education. It taught him the nuances of body design, both in an aesthetic sense and in terms of economics.

Edsel also took an interest in the evolving body styles of the Model T and probably contributed to its many facelifts. Records are scant, but it's certain that he influenced the 1911 'torpedo' body, refined the 1915 sedan and coupelet with curved rather than flat fenders, contributed the 1917 'new look' and lowered the 1923 and 1926–27 Model T bodies.

The Zephyr

Poor sales of the big Lincolns in the early 1930s had led Ford's Charles Sorensen to consider closing down the Lincoln Division. This alarmed the Briggs Body Co. who did a lot of work for Lincoln in finishing and trimming bodies. They therefore planned a new medium-priced Lincoln, and worked on the design in secret until it was ready to show to Ford management as a completed project. For the design of the body they hired Dutch-born Tom Tjaarda who had been working for some time on a streamlined integral-construction rear-engined sedan. He called this the Sterkenberg after his full family name, Tjaarda van Sterkenberg.

At quite an early stage Tjaarda's designs were shown to Edsel Ford who was enthusiastic, but nobody dared to tell Sorensen or the ultra-conservative Henry Ford. However, they need not have worried, for the two were very pleased when they saw a full-size mock-up in mid–1932. At first a rear-mounted Ford V8 engine was considered, but it was thought to be too radical a step, and considering the tail-heaviness of other large rear-engined cars like the Tatra, it was probably a blessing that the original design was not adopted. Edsel felt that the V8 engine would not be powerful enough, so he ordered a V12 which used a number of components from the V8, and shared its stroke of 95.25mm. The 4380cc engine developed 110bhp and gave the 6-seater sedan a top speed of 90mph (145km/h). Suspension was the time-honoured Ford system of transverse leaves front and rear.

Christened the Lincoln Zephyr, the new car was launched in November 1935, and attracted a lot of attention. The American public was only just getting over the shock of the Chrysler Airflow, but the streamlining of the Zephyr was more acceptable, thanks to its vee grill which seemed to cleave the air in a more satisfactory way than Chrysler's waterfall. The Zephyr was reasonably priced, at

1950 Lincoln (vii) 7-seater convertible for the White House.
NICK BALDWIN

1956 Lincoln (vii) Premiere sedan.
NATIONAL MOTOR MUSEUM

It was largely through Edsel's insistence that Henry Ford finally agreed to give up the T and produce the 1928 Model A. Edsel oversaw the Model A's body design and made sure that it had the look of a baby Lincoln. The Model A's appearance had a great deal to do with its tremendous success.

Throughout the 1910s and 1920s, Ford Motor Co. lacked any semblance of a styling department, and didn't have so much as a delineator when Henry Ford bought Lincoln. Soon after Ford's purchase of Lincoln and for the next 20 years, Briggs and Murray built most Ford bodies. By 1927, both body suppliers had professional designers on their staffs: Ralph Roberts at Briggs and Amos Northup at Murray. These men and their fledgling styling staffs generated a steady stream of ideas to Briggs and Murray customers, and particularly to Ford. The Model A, as an illustration of how closely Briggs and Ford worked, was styled primarily inside the Briggs design department.

However, in 1931, Lincoln's chief engineer, Henry Crecelius, hired Ford Motor Company's first and, at the time, only body designer, the 23-year-old Bob Gregorie. Gregorie consulted with Edsel Ford, and the two forged a close business relationship almost immediately. Gregorie designed the British 1932 Ford Model Y, which was 'blown up' to become the 1933–34 American Ford.

The Depression had put a terrible financial strain on Lincoln, and it seemed inevitable that the division would die without a smaller, less expensive model. That model became the 1936 Zephyr, which was based on a radical mid-engined prototype developed at Briggs by engineer/designer John Tjaarda.

Edsel very much liked Tjaarda's overall package but decided to make two major changes. First, the engine would go up front and would be a V12 derived from the Ford V8. Second, the prototype's sloping, VW Beetle-like front would give way to a veed prow grill designed by Bob Gregorie. That's how the Zephyr went into production, and it basically saved Lincoln.

It was in 1935, during the Zephyr's development, that Edsel asked Gregorie to put together a formal styling department within Ford Motor Co. He set aside several large rooms at one end of Ford's engineering complex, and Gregorie immediately began to assemble a staff. Meanwhile, Briggs continued to contribute designs to Ford, and the 1935 and 1936 Fords were essentially done--with Edsel's approval--at Briggs. And so, of course, was the 1936 Lincoln Zephyr.

But all Ford Motor Co. products from 1937 through the 1948 model were all done by Gregorie's staff within his department. Briggs slowly phased out its own design operation, although it did continue to make proposals to its other large customers, notably Chrysler, Hudson and Packard.

The 1938 Lincoln Zephyr caused something of a panic within the design community when it arrived with a low, horizontal grill. Harley Earl was still espousing tall, upright vertical grills and was quite distressed that Ford had beaten him to a new trend.

Gregorie's tiny staff--one-tenth the size of GM's--next created the first Mercury, the 1939 model. This was again Edsel's idea, its purpose being to fill the gap between the common Ford and the Lincoln Zephyr. Edsel visited Gregorie's department every day, and the two might discuss a design or the philosophy of design for anywhere from 10 minutes to several hours. Edsel's interest in the styling of Ford products never waned, and there's now no doubt that if styling had been left strictly to the elder Ford, the company might have been overwhelmed by Harley Earl's juggernaut sometime during the 1930s.

The most spectacular and enduring testament to Edsel Ford's taste in auto design is and will always be the 1939–40 Lincoln Continental. Gregorie simply made sketches over the profile drawing of a Zephyr. By lowering the body, dropping the hood, squaring off the convertible top, stretching the fenders and adding an exposed spare tire to the abbreviated trunk, the Continental was born.

It was initially conceived as a one-off cabriolet for Edsel's personal use. That first Continental was built in the idled Lincoln Model K plant, and Gregorie shipped it to Edsel's winter home in Florida in March 1939. When it arrived, so many people admired it that Edsel talked his father into letting him put the Continental into limited production.

With the outbreak of World War II, Edsel turned his attention to building the huge Willow Run bomber plant. Senility was creeping up on Henry Ford, and his lieutenants, notably production wizard Charles Sorensen and security chief Harry Bennett, began jockeying for position within the company. The stabilizing force was Edsel, but not for long.

In January 1942, Edsel underwent surgery for a stomach ulcer. The surgeons found cancer but didn't tell him about it. He was readmitted late in 1942 and treated for undulant fever. He remained bedridden and passed away on 26 May 1943. Edsel's death plus Henry's senility dealt a severe blow to the order of Ford Motor Company, and it would take an entirely new cast of characters to compensate for early postwar losses.

ML

1958 Lincoln(vii) Continental sedan.
NICK BALDWIN

1970 Lincoln (vii) Continental sedan.
NICK BALDWIN

1972 Lincoln (vii) Continental Mk IV coupé.
NICK BALDWIN

$1275 for a 2-door sedan, and $1320 for a 4-door. Prices of the Model K ran from $4200 to more than $8000. In the calendar year 1936 Lincoln sold 13,635 Zephyrs, compared with 1523 of the Model K. The following year the contrast was even greater, 28,333 Zephyrs and only 960 Model Ks.

Few changes were made to the 1937 models, apart from the addition of a 3-seater coupé at $1165, and the 4-door sedan price was reduced by $55. For 1938 the Zephyr received much-needed hydraulic brakes, and styling was modernised. A new model for that year was a 4-door convertible sedan at $1790, of which only 461 were sold. The engine was enlarged to 4785cc and 120bhp for 1940, when the gear lever was moved from the dashboard to the steering column.

Production of the Model K was gradually run down, with only 426 being made in 1938 and 120 in 1939, a few of which were sold off as 1940 models. However, no sooner had the big prestige Lincolns left the market than a new model appeared, derived from the Zephyr yet with very much a cachet of its own.

Edsel's Classic Continental

In 1939 Edsel Ford ordered a special version of the Zephyr with convertible body styled by E.T. 'Bob' Gregorie, a former yacht designer whom Edsel had taken onto the Lincoln staff. The front end was strictly 1939 Zephyr, as were the engine and transmission, but the rear of the body was quite distinctive, with the European feature of an exposed spare wheel cover. This earned the car its name of Continental Coupé. Edsel used this car during a vacation in Florida in the Spring of 1939, and it was so favourably received that 200 orders were placed for a car which was not yet a production model. Two replicas were built for Edsel's sons Henry II and Benson, and these generated just as much enthusiasm, so a decision was taken to build a limited series of Continentals for the 1940 season. Two models were made, a convertible and a 2-door coupé. They were virtually hand-built, which could justify the claim made in later years that Lincoln never made a cent of profit on any of the Continentals. As with the prototypes, the components all came from the Zephyr, including the 120bhp engine. The enamelled instrument panel came from the Zephyr Town Limousine, and the best available materials were used throughout.

The Continental was not a great performer, but the American public was not greatly interested in performance at that time. Top speed was around 86mph (138km/h) and handling was not helped by Ford's antiquated transverse springing. The Continentals had a long, low look which set them apart from their contemporaries, and they sold reasonably well for a speciality product, 404

HENRY FORD MUSEUM AND GREENFIELD VILLAGE

GREGORIE, BOB (born 1908)

Eugene Turenne (Bob) Gregorie was born on 12 October 1908 and grew up on Long Island, New York, in a well-to-do family. Bob's father owned a succession of European cars--Mercedes, Delage, Amilcar, etc., which got Bob interested in automobiles. Bob attended private schools but never graduated. As a teenager, since he also loved boats, he learned drafting and ship-hull design at a New Jersey yacht manufacturer.

In 1928, he took a job with Brewster, the coachbuilder but left again the next year to look for work with an automaker. After several attempts, he was hired in 1931 by Ford Motor Co.

One of Gregorie's first assignments was to style the small 1932 British Ford Model Y. Gregorie's sketches were submitted to Edsel Ford, who accepted them and sent them to the Ford plant in England. The 1932 Model Y appeared a year later very much as Gregorie had designed it.

Edsel Ford and Bob Gregorie found that they had many common interests, among them art, boats, cars and auto design. Gregorie also had the type of personality Edsel liked: congenial, outgoing, good-humored. Despite the difference in their ages (Edsel was 38 in 1931; Gregorie only 23) both men developed a deep and friendly regard for one another.

in the 1940 model year, and 1241 for the 1941 models. These differed very little from the previous year's, but an immediate recognition point was the use of push buttons in place of door handles on the '41s. Prices that year were $2778 for the convertible and $2727 for the coupé, compared with $1478–1858 for the regular Zephyrs, and $2836 for the Custom Limousines. The 1942 Continentals shared the heavier, more ornate grill of the Zephyr, and lost the clean good looks of their predecessors.

Return of the V8

The Continental and Zephyr models were revived after the war, though instead of the Zephyr name the regular Lincolns were known simply by their body styles: Lincoln sedan, club coupé etc. In March 1948 they were replaced by an all-new car with 5517cc 152bhp V8 engine and a new, all-enveloping body. The old transverse-leaf suspension gave way to coil ifs, as on the 1949 model Fords and Mercurys. The new Lincolns came in two series, the regular models which shared body styling (sedan, coupé and convertible) with the Mercury, and the up-market Cosmopolitan which came only as a notchback or fastback 6-seater sedan. There was no Continental in this new range, though the name would be revived in the mid-fifties. The Lincoln V8s evolved gradually over the next few years, with automatic transmission standardised in 1951, and a new 205bhp ohv engine arriving for 1953. Styling was changed in 1952, bringing the Lincoln closer in appearance to the cheaper Fords and Mercurys. There was a short-lived involvement in sport in 1952–54, when Lincolns ran in the Mexican

1987 Lincoln (vii) Town Car.
LINCOLN-MERCURY

1987 Lincoln (vii) Mk VII LSC coupé.
LINCOLN-MERCURY

Carrera Panamericana Race. In 1952 the three works entries finished 1–2–3 in the touring car class, and in 1953 they took the first four in the class, Chuck Stevenson finishing seventh overall.

For 1956 engine capacity went up to 6030cc, the largest American engine at the time, with a power output of 300bhp. This went into the new Premiere and Capri, and also into the revived Continental Mark II (see separate entry). The Lincolns of 1958–60 were among the largest postwar American cars, with 375bhp 7046cc engines, overall length of 230in (5837mm) and unladen weights up to 5450lbs. They were also the first Lincolns to have full unitary construction, for which a new factory was built at Wixom, Michigan. These large Lincolns did not sell well, as criticism of over-large cars was just beginning to surface in America. Sales dropped from 56,323 in 1956 to only 20,683 in 1960, and for 1961 Lincoln brought out a completely restyled car which they advertised as 'America's only compact luxury car'. By any standards other than Lincoln's own it was hardly a compact, but the overall length was reduced by 15in (380mm). The same 7046cc engine was used, and body styles included a 4-door convertible, the only one on the American market at that time. This style was part of the Lincoln range until 1968.

Engine capacity went up to 7570cc on the 1966 models, but the bodies were not so large or heavy as the 1958–60 ones had been. In 1968 there was a partial return to the idea of a separate prestige car, this time bearing the name Continental Mk III. Advertising stressed its heritage in the Mks I and II, though its styling was not so distinctive, and it was not made by a separate division. Like the Mk II it was a 4-seater close-coupled coupé with an external spare wheel cover. Unlike other Lincolns, the Mk III had a separate chassis, which was adopted throughout the range for 1970. The Mk III sold 21,432 in 1970, out of a total for Lincoln of 53,127.

The Continental Mk III became the Mk IV in 1972, and the theme of a personal coupé was carried on to the Mk VIII made from 1993 to 1998. Somewhat confusingly, the 4-door sedans were given the name Continental and Town Car, while the coupés were called simply Lincoln Mk VIII, dropping the Continental name. As with all American cars, Lincolns were downsized from the late 1970s, the big 7½-litre engine giving way to a 4950 or 5752cc V8 in the 1980 models, which were also shorter and lighter. In 1982 came the smallest

The 1932 British Model Y proved successful, so Edsel asked that the same basic design be 'blown up' to become the 1933–34 Ford. This car was also highly successful and, in 1935, Edsel invited Gregorie to create Ford's first-ever styling department.

Gregorie noted that, 'The setting up of a styling department at Ford coincided with Mr. Edsel Ford's overseeing the development of the 1936 Lincoln Zephyr.' Gregorie's contribution to the Zephyr was everything from the cowl forward, including the prow grill. The rest of the car had been designed by John Tjaarda at Briggs Manufacturing Co. The Zephyr saved Lincoln, which would otherwise have gone under during the Depression.

Bob Gregorie wasted no time setting up Ford's new design center. He quickly assembled a small but skilled staff and became responsible, along with Edsel, for all late 1930s and early 1940s Ford Motor Co. products. Gregorie developed the horizontal-grilled 1938 Lincoln Zephyr and was instrumental in styling the new-for-1939 Mercury and the 1939–40 Lincoln Continental. He introduced the styling bridge to Ford, and by 1939–40, his staff numbered about 50 people.

Considering the size of Gregorie's department, a tenth that of GM's styling staff, the sheer volume of work that Gregorie and Edsel turned out was mind-boggling. They created all yearly styling changes in all body styles for the standard and deluxe Ford cars, the Mercury, the Lincoln, Ford trucks, Ford tractors and buses, all interiors and some dealer accessories. To produce so much consistently good work gives testament to Gregorie's and Edsel's abilities both as designers and administrators.

Pearl Harbor and then Edsel's death transformed everything at Ford. Gregorie's staff was cut to 25. Like Earl at GM, Gregorie sandwiched work on postwar cars between wartime assignments. In September 1943, due to internal politics, Gregorie found himself fired from Ford. After the war, though, Henry Ford II rehired Gregorie, but it wasn't the same.

Ford Motor Co. was losing money at a tremendous clip, and the only way to save it hinged on the success of the 1949 Ford. Gregorie did proposals for this car, but Ford management thought they were too large and expensive to build. They brought in George Walker, the industrial designer, who became Gregorie's rival. When Walker's model won the internal competition for the 1949 Ford, Gregorie's proposals became the 1949 Mercury and Lincoln. But with pressure from Walker and a new regime, Gregorie left the company for good in December 1946, but on amicable terms.

He moved to Florida and took up yacht design, a field in which he still dabbles – at age 90 – occasionally.

ML

1998 Lincoln (vii) stretch limousine.
NICK GEORGANO

2000 Lincoln (vii) Continental sedan.
FORD MOTOR CO.

2000 Lincoln (vii) Navigator 4x4 station wagon.
FORD MOTOR CO.

engine yet, a 3.8-litre V6, but this lasted for only one season, and for the rest of the '80s the standard engine was the 4950cc V8. Because of emission controls, this gave only 152bhp in regular form, and 225bhp in the Mk VII LSC coupé. The Continental and Town Car of the late 1980s were quite distinctive in appearance, the former having rounded lines similar to those of the Mk VII coupé, while the Town Car was more traditional, with vertical grill and headlamps. It was a favourite base for stretched limousines, converted by various specialists, with wheelbases up to 160in (4061mm) and overall length of 261in (6624mm). The 1988 Continental was an all-new car, with 3802cc V6 engine mounted transversely and driving the front wheels. The V6 engine was dropped after 1994, and later Lincolns relied on a 4604cc V8 giving 210bhp in single-ohc form for the Town Car, and 260 or 280bhp in the twin-ohc engine used in the Continental and Mk VIII. The Town Car was restyled for 1995, though it still remained more conservative than the other Lincolns, which came closer in styling, though still distinguished in that the Continental was a 4-door sedan and the Mk V a 2-door coupé. The 1998 Town Car was a new design, almost 4in shorter than its predecessor, and its bonnet was made of aluminium to cut weight. The Continental was also lighter with a bonnet of SMC (Sheet Moulded Compound). In 1997 the Lincoln name went on a 5-door 4 × 4 station wagon, the Navigator. This was essentially a Ford Expedition with more luxurious interior and a Lincoln grill, but it signalled a move into the 4 × 4 market by the top quality marques, to be followed by Cadillac.

1998 was the last year for the Mk VIII, but the New York Show in April saw a new Lincoln to challenge BMW, Mercedes-Benz and Lexus in the mid-sized market. This was the LS 4-door sedan powered by a 190bhp 2997cc V6 or 245bhp 3950cc V8 engine. Both had twin-ohcs and four valves per cylinder, and unlike the Continental, drove on the rear wheels.

NG

Further Reading
The Cars of Lincoln and Mercury, George Dammann and James K. Wagner, Crestline Publishing, 1987.

LINCOLN INDUSTRIES (US) c.1960–1968

Lincoln Industries, Lincoln, California.

This company built a fibreglass dune buggy called the Sandpiper and a buggy-like sports car called the Shark. They were associated with KELLISON and later turned over their direct sales to them.

HP

LINDBERG (US) c.1974–1990

Lindberg Engineering, Tollhouse, California.

Lindberg made an extensive line of replicas of classic cars of the 1930s scaled down to fit the Volkswagen Beetle chassis. These included the 1936 Auburn Speedster, Mercedes 500K and the 1911 Ford delivery van. They also built a replica of the Bugatti Royale Coupé de Ville based on a ladder frame powered by Cadillac or Chevrolet V8 engines. Unlike the VW-based kits, the Bugatti replica was only available in fully assembled form at a price of around $80,000 in 1983. They also sold a replica of the Mercedes 500K with a ladder frame and a diesel engine.

HP

LINDCAR (D) 1922–1925

Lindcar Auto AG, Berlin-Lichtenrade.

This small car used Atos or Steudel engines, but stood out by reason of its optional ZF-Soden preselector gearbox, more usually seen in larger cars.

HON

LINDSAY (i) (US) 1902–1903

T.J. Lindsay Automobile Parts Co., Indianapolis, Indiana.

This company offered kits for the assembly of petrol or electric cars, and also built up a few light runabouts which they sold complete. The head of the engine department was Harry C. Stutz, whose name was to become a household word within ten years.

NG

LINDSAY (ii) (GB) 1906–1908

Lindsay Motor Car Co. Ltd, Woodbridge, Suffolk.

This company had made tricars for several years before they announced their first car in 1906. It was a light car, really a cyclecar before they became fashionable, with 6hp J.A.P. engine in a tubular frame with Lowes variable gear transmission. Later they made two larger cars with 4-cylinder engines and shaft drive. One used a 12hp Fafnir and the other a 28hp Antoine engine. Their last car, of 1907/08, had a short-stroke 4-cylinder engine (80×90mm), which gave a capacity of 1808cc, though the horsepower rating was 15.9.

NG

LINDSLEY (US) 1908–1909

1908 J.V. Lindsley Auto Chassis Co., Dowagiac, Michigan.
1909 Dowagiac Motor Car Co., Dowagiac, Michigan.

J. Victor Lindsley's plan was to offer a high-wheeler chassis for only $250, to which the customer could fit his own body. This idea found few buyers, and he next offered a complete high-wheeler, with 10hp flat-twin engine under the seat, epicyclic transmission and chain drive, for $475. He did not seem to be able to organise production, which involved two weeks in the making of one car. He left town and his father reorganised the company under the Dowagiac name to complete the 15 cars on hand. These cars were sold as Dowagiacs.

NG

LINDY see HDS

LINETT (A) 1921–1928

Linett Automobilfabriks-GmbH, Vienna.

This company was mainly concerned with selling cars, but they made a small number under their own name. Technical details are not known.

HON

LINGKONG (CHI) 1991–1995

People's Liberation Army Works No. 5408, Luoyang City, Henan Province.

Lots of P.L.A. factories changed their production from military into civilian

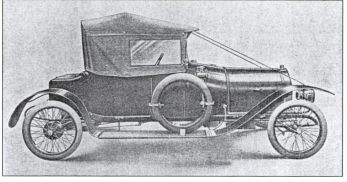

1912 Linon 8CV 2-seater.
NICK BALDWIN

consumption goods. Due to the end of the Cold War, the Chinese army also diminished. A way to make money from other sources was car production. This factory had produced small trucks and mini buses since 1970. A 797cc hatchback and a saloon were made, named Lingkong KJ 6380. Lingkong means 'high up in the air'. The vehicle was also sold as the Tianma KJ 5010. At least 10 were produced. The Lingkong had a very ugly body in Daihatsu styling, it had a length of 150in (3800mm) and used small 12in (305mm) wheels.

EVIS

LINGTON (GB) 1920

Lington Engineering Co. Ltd, Bedford.

This was a light car powered by a 10hp V-twin engine and using shaft drive. Starting was by a floor-mounted pedal.

NG

LINGYANG (CHI) 1993–1994

Jiangling Machinery Works, Chongqing Municipality.

The Jiangling Works was an army factory producing small motor vehicle engines, since 1984. In 1993 they made 64,200 units of the JL 462Q engine. They produced a mini-car in squared-off styling, popular in the early–1990s, made of duplicate material. It was named the Lingyang ('Antelope') JLJ 1010. The vehicle weight was 900kg, length of the body 171in (4350mm) and was a 4-door sedan.

EVIS

LINON (B) 1900–1914

Ateliers Linon, Ensival-Verviers.

Louis and André Linon, father and son, set up as bicycle makers in Ensival, near Verviers, in 1895, and two years later began their involvement with cars by selling the French-built GAUTHIER-WEHRLÉ. At the end of 1898 they took out a licence to build these cars, and made a few, powered by rear-mounted 6hp engines, with a 3-speed gearbox mounted on the rear axle. Body styles included a phaeton, dogcart and wagonette. A 10hp was added in 1899, but at the 1900 Brussels Show, in addition to the Gauthier-Wehrle designs, the Linons showed two cars of their own design, one powered by a front-mounted 3hp De Dion-Bouton engine with 2-speed gearbox, the other with 5hp 2-cylinder Abeille engine and 3-speeds. Both cars were sold in England under the name Mayfair.

From 1901 onwards the Linons made a variety of cars, including 2-seater voiturettes with front-mounted 3½ or 4½hp De Dion engines or 4 or 5hp Linon engines, some with rear-mounted Linon engines including a 4-seater with two such engines coupled together. By 1903 they were making larger cars of up to 20hp with 4- or 6-seater bodies. At the 1904 Brussels Show they exhibited an 8/12hp 2-cylinder and 24hp 4-cylinder car, as well as belt-driven motorcycles. They had steady, if unspectacular, sales up to 1914, and a number were exported. The 1909 range consisted of a 1608cc 10/12hp, a 2110cc 10/15hp and a 3400cc 16/20hp, all with 3-speed gearboxes and shaft drive.

By 1914 there were larger Linons, the range running from the 1130cc 8hp Type AL to the 3815cc 22hp Type H, the latter with monobloc engine. As well as their own engines, Linon bought from Fafnir, Fondu and Vautour, with Ballot predominating from about 1914 onwards. About 2000 Linon cars were made up to 1914. Possibly a handful were assembled from parts on hand after the war.

c.1910 Lion 40 tourer.
BRYAN K.GOODMAN

1910 Lion-Peugeot 2 seater.
NATIONAL MOTOR MUSEUM

In about 1920 the firm was bought by Louis Lambert, who announced that he would make bicycles, motorcycles and cars. However he does not seem to have done so, and soon sold the works to a company operating Citroën taxis. The Linon brothers both lived until 1955.

NG

LINSER (A) 1906–1908
Christian Linser, Liberec.
Christian Linser founded a small foundry in Liberec at the end of the 19th century, and in 1902 started motorcycle production (under the name 'Zeus'). His first voiturette was introduced in March 1906 at the Vienna automobile exhibition. A water-cooled 4-cylinder 1640cc 12bhp engine drove the rear wheels through a cone clutch, 3-speed gearbox and either chain or propeller shaft. Both front and rear rigid axles with semi-eliptic leaf springs were mounted on the pressed steel frame. These cars were bodied as 2-, 3- and 4-seater open voiturettes but some coupés were also built. Production was very limited and after 1908 Linser began to deliver parts for the RAF Works. Linser cars and motorcycles were exported to Germany, Italy and Russia.

MSH

LION (US) 1910–1912
Lion Motor Car Co., Adrian, Michigan.
This company was organised in September 1909 and planned originally to make cars with 'gyroscope' engines such as had been used in the GYROSCOPE car. However this idea was abandoned and the Lion appeared as a conventional car powered by a 40hp 4-cylinder engine. Runabout and tourer models were made,

and the car was advertised as 'The Lion Forty runs like a Sixty'. For 1911 five body styles were offered, all open models, and a slightly longer wheelbase was made for 1912. The company seemed to be doing well, until a disastrous fire burnt the factory to the ground in June 1912, destroying more than 150 cars including the prototype of a new Thirty they planned to introduced for 1913. The factory was seriously under-insured, and the Lion Motor Car Co. never recovered.

NG

LIONHEART (GB) 1991
This was a BMW M1 replica with Jaguar V12 engine, but it is uncertain if any were actually built.

CR

LION-PEUGEOT (F) 1905–1915
1905–1915 Les Fils des Peugeot Frères, Beaulieu and Valentigney (Doubs).
In 1896 Eugène Peugeot signed an agreement with Armand Peugeot (head of Société des Automobiles Peugeot) that he would not produce cars. Eugène's three sons, Jules, Pierre and Robert, who started motorcycle production in 1903, dreamed of nothing better than to build cars. They paid Armand Peugeot a flat fee to avoid litigation, and launched the Lion-Peugeot car in 1905. The lion had been Peugeot's registered trademark since November 1858. Two engineers, Michaux and Kuntz, left Armand Peugeot to work for the young sons of Eugène (who died in 1907).

The first Lion-Peugeot, Type VA, was a *voiturette* powered by a single-cylinder 785cc engine, sold as a 2-seater, phaeton and rear-entrance tonneau. The chassis was quite up-to-date, with the engine mounted just behind the front axle, with a cone clutch, 3-speed gearbox, and chain drive to the rear wheels. Approximately 1000 Type VA cars were made from 1905 to 1908.

It was joined by the Type VC in 1906, essentially the same car with five inches added to the wheelbase and a bigger (1045cc) single-cylinder engine. Over a 2½ year period approximately 1000 VC units were made.

The Type VY was a sports model with a lower frame and an 1841cc single-cylinder engine, built only as a roadster with a barrel-type fuel tank behind the seats. Depending on the gearing, it could reach speeds of 25 to 31mph (40 to 50km/h). Only 142 VY-specification cars were made in 1908–1909.

The VC was renamed VC 1 for 1909, and continued practically without change. The VC 2 had restyled bodied and a longer wheelbase, but the same 1045cc engine. Produced only in 1909 and 1910, the total came to 1175 units. The same engine also went into the VC 3 of 1911, which adopted shaft drive. It was offered with a richer variety of body styles, but only 135 VC 3 cars were made.

An engine designer named Lucien Verdet had prepared a 1325cc V-twin for the 1910 Type V2 C2, sharing the chain drive and the VC 2 chassis. Body styles included landaulet and limousine, phaeton, coupé-cab, and sport roadster. Only 680 units of this model were produced, however.

The 1910 V2 Y2 was the same car with a bigger (1702cc) V-twin, built in a series of 300 units.

For the 1911 V2 C3, shaft drive was standard, but the engine was unchanged from V2 C2 specifications, and the overall dimensions were the same also. The Beaulieu plant put out 520 of them in one year. Similarly, the V2 Y3 replaced the V2 Y2, the big change being the adoption of shaft drive. No more than 215 V2 Y3 cars were built.

Lucien Verdet designed a V4 1725cc engine which was mounted in the 1912-13 V4 C3. It was a narrow-angle L-head design with integral cylinder head, very light, compact, and running up to 1800rpm. In a two-year period, the Beaulieu plant produced 653 of them.

In 1913 the V4 engine was bored out to 1888cc and combined with a 4-speed gearbox for installation in the VD and V4D models, which had a longer wheelbase (88.6in/2249mm) and bigger brakes. A total of 1500 VD and V4D cars were made, with torpedo, landaulet, limousine, and delivery-van bodies.

The 1888cc engine and 4-speed gearbox were also mounted in the 1915 VDZ, 480 of which were produced, on a 91in (2310mm) wheelbase, and geared for a top speed of 37mph (60km/h).

When the automobile branch of Les Fils des Peugeot Frères merged with the Société des Automobiles Peugeot in 1912, and factory expansion began at Sochaux, the Lion-Peugeot brand was phased out. As an interesting postscript, the Bébé Peugeot, made under Bugatti licence, was produced at the Beaulieu factory and not at Sochaux, from 1913 to 1916.

JPN

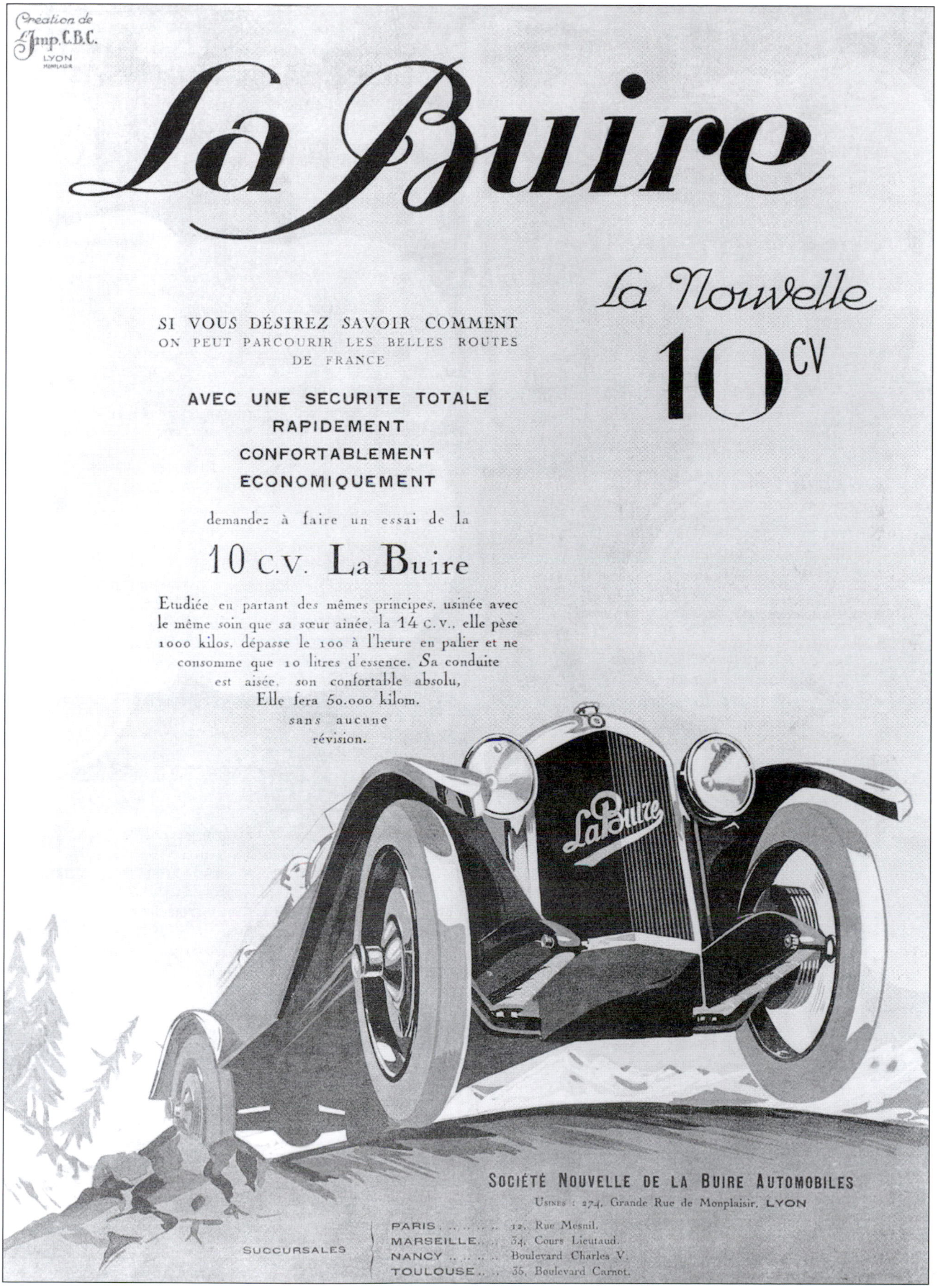

Création de
L'Imp. C.B.C.
LYON
La Buire
La Nouvelle
10 CV
SI VOUS DÉSIREZ SAVOIR COMMENT
ON PEUT PARCOURIR LES BELLES ROUTES
DE FRANCE
AVEC UNE SECURITE TOTALE
RAPIDEMENT
CONFORTABLEMENT
ECONOMIQUEMENT
demandez à faire un essai de la
10 C.V. La Buire
Etudiée en partant des mêmes principes, usinée avec le même soin que sa sœur ainée, la 14 C.V., elle pèse 1000 kilos, dépasse le 100 à l'heure en palier et ne consomme que 10 litres d'essence. Sa conduite est aisée, son confortable absolu, Elle fera 50.000 kilom. sans aucune révision.
La Buire
SOCIÉTÉ NOUVELLE DE LA BUIRE AUTOMOBILES
Usines : 274, Grande Rue de Monplaisir, LYON
SUCCURSALES
PARIS .... 12, Rue Mesnil.
MARSEILLE.... 34, Cours Lieutaud.
NANCY .... Boulevard Charles V.
TOULOUSE .... 35, Boulevard Carnot.

NICK BALDWIN

LIPSCOMB (GB) 1903–1905
English Motor Car Co., London.
The Lipscomb was one of many assembled cars using Aster or De Dion-Bouton engines. It was sold from premises in Euston Road, as was the Bayley, a larger car with 20hp 4-cylinder engine which was built by CRAIG-DORWALD. Both cars were named after the director of the English Motor Car Co., Arthur Lipscomb Bayley

NG

LIPSIA (D) 1922–1924
Lipsia Automobilfabrik GmbH, Schleussig bei Leipzig.
This company offered two models of 4-cylinder car, a 6/20PS and a 6/30PS. The make of the engines and other technical details are not known.

HON

LIQUID AIR (US) 1899–1900
Liquid Air Power & Automobile Co., Cambridge, Massachusetts.
This company was capitalised, so it was said, at $1.5 million, and grandiose claims were made about liquid air being the motive power of the future. The technical descriptions in the press made little engineering sense, but it seems that the idea was to employ a tank of liquid air under high pressure, whose expansion would drive a single-cylinder engine in the same way that steam would. However the efficiency of this system has been estimated at no more than 4 per cent, and it is unlikely to have propelled the car for any distance, if at all. One car was made, with the appearance of a typical New England steam buggy. The organisation had offices in Boston and New York, and the factory was said to be in Cambridge, though its exact location was not divulged. The company went into receivership in 1901, with assets of just $7500.

NG

LISTAIR see DASH

LISTER (GB) 1954–1959; 1986 to date
1954–1959 George Lister & Sons, Cambridge.
1986 to date Lister Cars Ltd, Leatherhead, Surrey.
In the early 1950s, Brian Lister raced a Cooper-MG and an 1100cc Tojeiro-JAP. He was impressed by the skill of Archie Scott Brown, a driver born with a withered right arm which ended in a vestigial palm and a thumb, and they became a team. In 1954, Lister designed a car with a ladder frame, coil spring and wishbone front suspension and a De Dion rear axle. Scott Brown was successful with both MG- and Bristol-powered versions and 16 would be made. A spare chassis became the basis of the Phoenix sports racing car. A slightly larger chassis was built to accommodate a Jaguar engine in 1957. The Lister-Jaguar (and the Lister-Chevrolet) was one of the last of the front-engined sports cars and, thanks to Scott Brown's driving, among the most charismatic. Lister withdrew in 1959 having made 34 Jaguar/Chevrolet cars.

In 1986, however, the name was revived by Laurence Pearce with Brian Lister's blessing. Lister Cars modified some 90 Jaguar XJS coupés, with the 5.3-litre V12 engine enlarged from 6- to 7-litres, with appropriate uprating of suspension and brakes, and built ten replica Lister-Jaguars.

In 1993, the company announced the Lister Storm, a front-engined, 4-seat, luxurious, GT car with a monocoque chassis made from aluminium honeycomb and a carbonfibre body. The 7-litre Jaguar V12 engine delivered 594bhp via a 6-speed Getrag gearbox. By mid–1998 17 cars had been made, 14 for road use, three for racing.

MJL

Further Reading
Archie and the Listers, Robert Edwards, Haynes, 1995.

LISTER NORTH AMERICA (US) c.1994
Lister North America, Tulsa, Oklahoma.
The Lister-Corvette was an original design by Dave Stollery of INDUSTRIAL DESIGN RESEARCH. Although Lister North America had been importing restyled Jaguar XJS body panels from the English Lister company, by 1994 when the Lister-Corvette was introduced they were no longer involved. The body was a radical revamping of the Corvette, and could be purchased as a body kit or an assembled car. The assembled cars had supercharged engines with 435hp and cost about $60,000. The suspension was heavily modified by Dick Guldstrand, and the body panels were made by Chuck Beck.

HP

LITTLE (US) 1912–1913
Little Motor Car Co., Flint, Michigan.
This car was named after William H. Little, former general manager of Buick whom William C. Durant put in charge of the Flint Wagon Works, where the WHITING had been made from 1910 to 1912. Two models of Little were made; the first was a light car with 20hp 4-cylinder engine, made only as a 2-seater roadster and selling for $690. This went into production in the summer of 1912. The second was a 30hp six which Durant ordered because the first Chevrolet turned out to be too expensive. The Little Six cost $1285, the Chevrolet Six $2150. He combined the best features of both in the 1914 Chevrolet Light Six, and the Little Six became surplus to his requirements. It was dropped in May 1913, along with the Four, after about 3500 Littles had been made in both models.

NG

LITTLE DETROIT see DETROIT (iv)

LITTLE GREG see HINSTIN

LITTLEMAC (US) 1930–1932
Thompson Motor Corp., Muscatine, Iowa.
The Littlemac was an unsuccessful attempt by two brothers – Herbert and Ralph Thompson of Muscatine, Iowa – to enter the small-car market with the introduction of a light, low-priced car, its promotion, such as it was, targeted to economical motoring which, in theory, might have been a selling point in the Depression year of 1930 in which the Littlemac was to have been launched. Production, however, was delayed and the first Littlemac was not completed until the spring of 1931. Production was set for an annual output of 100 cars and light panel trucks. The Thompson Motor Corp. failed to obtain badly needed financial backing and the final Littlemacs were built by September – concluding a meagre production of less than 20 cars, several of which were exported.

The Littlemac was powered by a 4-cylinder engine originally used by the Star. Wheelbase length was a meagre 80in (2-3-mm) and 2-wheel mechanical brakes were fitted. Wheels were wood-spoked and the listed prices were $350 for the coupé and $500 for the panel delivery truck.

KM

LITTLE PRINCESS (US) 1913–1914
Princess Cyclecar Co., Detroit, Michigan.
Despite the maker's name (which was soon changed), this was more of a light car than a cyclecar, having a 14/16p 4-cylinder engine, epicyclic transmission and shaft drive. It was distinguished by a dashboard radiator behind a Renault-style bonnet, and the 2-seater cost $395. In 1914 the company changed their name to the Princess Motor Car Co., and the car became the Princess too. It was made up to 1915, then gave way to a larger, more conventional looking car which lasted until 1918.

NG

LITTLE SCOTSMAN see SCOTSMAN (ii)

LITTON see CORSE

LIVER (GB) 1900–1901
William Lea Motor Co. Ltd, Liverpool.
William Lea was the Merseyside agent for Benz engines, and had depots at the entrance to Birkenhead Park, and in Berry Street, Liverpool. In 1900 he decided to build his own cars, using Benz engines and British body components, many of which were made at Birkenhead. The engines were of 3½hp and 6hp, and the cars closely resembled the Benz, though they had a rounded front reminiscent of the Benz-based Hurtu, made in Manchester as the Marshall at the same time as the Liver. Not many Livers were made, but a 3½hp survives today.

NG

LIVRY (F) 1949–1952

Sté Industrielle de Livry, Paris.

The first of three microcar models to be distributed by S.I. de Livry on behalf of DURIEZ was the Atlas Coccinelle of 1949. It was a miniature doorless open 2-seater only 109in (2770mm) long that was powered by a rear-mounted AMC engine of 125cc, 150cc, 175cc or 200cc capacity. The Piaf ('sparrow') launched in 1951 used the same chassis as the Atlas, and could be fitted with the same choice of engines. It was an extremely basic model that somewhat resembled Voisin's Biscuter in that it was a doorless car of very simple aluminium construction. The Kover, built 1951–52, was a doorless convertible 2-seater microcar of more substantial and conventional appearance. A choice of 125cc, 175cc or 200cc 2-stroke engines could be fitted in the 180kg car, driving through a 4-speed gearbox.

CR

L.J. see LAURENCE-JACKSON

LLOYD (i) (D) 1906–1914; 1950–1963

1906–1914 Norddeutsche Automobil- und Motoren AG, Bremen.
1950–1963 Lloyd Motoren-Werke AG, Bremen.

The Norddeutsche Automobil- und Motorenfabrik AG (NAMAG) was founded as a branch of the shipping company Norddeutsche Lloyd by one of the directors of the latter, Heinrich Wiegand. In 1906 they signed an agreement with KRIÉGER, and towards the end of that year production began in Bremen of Kriéger-type cars, trucks and buses, which were sold under the name Lloyd.

In 1908 Jospeh Vollmer joined the company and designed for them their first petrol-engined car. This 15/35PS was a conventional 4-cylinder machine with a side-valve 3685cc engine, 4-speed gearbox and shaft drive. Vollmer himself drove one in the 1908 Prince Henry Trials, where its successful performance brought welcome publicity to the little-known firm from Bremen. The 15/35PS remained in production up to 1914, and was joined by two other models, the 2612cc 10/25PS and the 5520cc 22/50PS. Production was never large; the 1911 figure of 164 cars was probably not exceeded in any year up to 1914, when NAMAG merged with HANSA. After the war cars were marketed under the name HANSA-LLOYD.

In 1929 Hansa-Lloyd was taken over by Carl Borgward, and the expensive cars they were making were discontinued. The cheaper Hansa cars were continued, being re-named Borgward in 1939. After World War II Borgward wanted to expand his range beyond the medium-priced cars he was making, and for his new low-priced car he revived the Lloyd name. Introduced in 1950, the Lloyd LP300 was a simple car. The engine was a 293cc vertical-twin 2-stroke which developed only 10bhp. It drove the front wheels by an unsynchronised 3-speed gearbox. The chassis had a backbone frame and transverse leaf ifs, while the body was a leatherette covered wooden frame with metal corners to allow some curves. Four styles were offered, a 4-seater saloon, 4-seater estate (Kombi), 2-seater coupé and delivery van. At DM3334 the saloon was by far the lowest-priced 4-seater German car of its day, undercutting the VW Beetle by DM1466. The only cheaper cars were open 2-seaters such as the Champion and Kleinschnittger, which were not serious competitors.

By the end of 1952 sales of the LP300 had reached 18,087 and, for 1953, engine size was enlarged to 386ccc (LP400). Hydraulic brakes were available from March 1953, and the price went up to DM3780, still very good value. An increasingly affluent public demanded more power and refinements, but the basic vertical-twin Lloyd lasted until 1961. Capacity went up to 593cc (19bhp) on the LP600 of 1955–61, and a 4-speed synchromesh gearbox came with the Alexander of 1957–61. By then the body was of all-steel construction. The 600 and Alexander had a 4-stroke engine with chain-driven single-ohc, from which 25bhp was extracted in the Alexander TS of 1958–61. Prices were up to DM4060 for the Alexander and DM4330 for the TS. In order to keep a really cheap car in his range, Carl Borgward offered in 1956–7 the very utilitarian LP250 at only DM2980, but it was not popular, and only 3768 were sold. Total production of all 2-cylinder Lloyds was 308,257, getting on for double the figure for the Borgward Isabella, though this was much better known on international markets.

In August 1959 came the first and only 4-cylinder Lloyd, the 897cc Arabella. The 2-door saloon body was more attractive than that of the Alexander, which never managed to shake off the boxy appearance of the original LP300, but it appeared too late and, at DM5250, was more expensive than a VW Beetle 1200. Nevertheless 45,549 were sold between August 1959 and July 1961, with a

1958 Lloyd (i) 600 Standard saloon.
NATIONAL MOTOR MUSEUM

1961 Lloyd (i) Arabella saloon.
NATIONAL MOTOR MUSEUM

further 1493 being sold with Borgward badges up to 1963. The collapse of the Borgward empire brought Lloyd production to an end.

HON

LLOYD (ii) (GB) 1936–1950

Lloyd Cars Ltd, Grimsby, Lincolnshire.

The Lloyd was the only car made in the fishing port of Grimsby, and was unusual in other ways too. The first, the 350 made from 1936 to 1939, was a cyclecar built well past the time when such cars were popular, and almost all the components of the postwar 650 were made in the small factory.

Roland Lloyd was the son of a car salesman who had handled, among other makes, Arrol-Johnston, Crossley, Riley and Willys-Overland. The 350 was a diminutive open 2-seater powered by a 347cc Villiers 2-stroke engine mounted behind the seats, with single-chain drive to the nearside rear wheel. It had backbone chassis and independent suspension all round. Starting was by hand and the windscreen wiper was also hand operated. The price was a very modest £75 and top speed an equally modest 44mph (70km/h). It has been said that production reached 250, but this may be on the high side. However, Lloyd sold a 'fleet' of ten cars to the Gas Light & Coke Co. for its inspectors, and some cars were exported to the Netherlands and South Africa.

The 650 was announced in 1946 and used a 654cc vertical twin 2-stroke engine, front-mounted this time, and driving the front wheels through a 4-speed gearbox in which all speeds, including reverse, had synchromesh. Other features included a double backbone frame, rack-and-pinion steering and all-coil independent suspension. The body was a 2-door 4-seater tourer made partly of steel, partly of aluminium. For such a small firm it is remarkable that not only the body, chassis and engine were made in-house, but the brake components and wheels were made too. Apart from the electrical equipment and tyres, practically nothing was bought in. The 650 had two weaknesses, a top speed of only 46mph (74km/h) and a price of £480 in 1948, when a 4-seater Ford Anglia saloon could be had for only £293. Admittedly there was a longer waiting list for the Ford,

1937 Lloyd (ii) 350 2-seater.
NATIONAL MOTOR MUSEUM

1946 Lloyd (ii) 650 chassis.
NATIONAL MOTOR MUSEUM

1920 L.M. (i) 8hp 2-seater.
NICK BALDWIN

and this factor helped Lloyd sales for a while, but they gave up the struggle in May 1950, after about 350 to 400 had been made. Saloon and van versions never passed the prototype stage, but the tourers were exported to Belgium, Denmark, India and Australia.

The name Lloyd Cars Ltd was retained by the company, which continued with precision engineering work for such firms as Gardner, Perkins, Rolls-Royce, Aston Martin and Lotus until 1983. The company was then wound up and the premises sold to Bird's Eye-Walls, who were already established next door.

NG

LLOYD & PLAISTER (GB) 1900–1911

1900–1909 Lloyd & Plaister, Wood Green, London.
1919–1911 Lloyd & Plaister Ltd, Wood Green, London.
The partnership of Lewis A. Lloyd (1877–1923) and W.E. Plaister began in 1900 after George Hurst left Lloyd, with whom he had made HURST & LLOYD cars. Six Hurst & Lloyds in the course of construction were completed and sold under the Lloyd & Plaister name. They had horizontal underfloor engines, but when Lloyd & Plaister began to make their own cars these had front-mounted vertical engines, and were offered in several sizes, 10, 16, 20 and 40hp. The latter was a sizeable car with capacity of 7718cc and chain drive. Only six of these were made, out of about 50 Lloyd & Plaister cars built over an 11-year period. The works were very small, only large enough to employ 30 men and to hold 10 cars. At least one model, the 16hp of 1908, was fitted with Allen-Liversidge 4-wheel brakes.

Lloyd & Plaister also made petrol-engined rail inspection cars, and a few fire engines from 1908 to 1911. They also supplied engines and some other components for the DOLPHIN car. After they ceased making L & P cars, they made the VOX cyclecar up to 1915. Lloyd died in 1923 at the early age of 46. Plaister's dates are not known, but he was still alive in 1948, when he corresponded with the motoring historian John Pollitt.

NG

Further Reading
'A Man Who Loved Cars', The Rev Mark Rudall, *The Automobile*, April 1993.

L.M. (i) (GB) 1905–1922

1905–1919 William Cunningham, Clitheroe, Lancashire.
1919–1920 Little Midland Light Car Co. Ltd, Blackburn. Lancashire.
1920–1922 Little Midland Light Car Co. (1920) Ltd, Preston, Lancashire.
L.M. stood for Little Midland, though why William Cunningham should have chosen this name for a car built in Northern Lancashire is not known. His first car was a light 2-seater powered by a 7¹/₂hp single-cylinder engine 'of De Dion-Bouton type'. It was made for a few years, joined in 1907 by a larger car with 9hp engine and a substantial 5-seater tourer body, registered as a Midland Special. As the L.M., the make surfaced again in 1911 as a cyclecar with a 7hp air-cooled V-twin J.A.P. engine, 2-speed gearbox and single-chain drive. Appearing at least a year before the cyclecar boom, it weighed only 448lbs in its original form. In 1914 a water-cooled J.A.P. was available as an alternative.

The L.M. was revived in 1919, under different ownership and made in Blackburn. Another reorganisation brought the car to Preston, but it was still the same design, though by 1921 disc wheels had replaced wire, and a dickey seat was provided.

NG

L.M. (ii) (F) 1913

Charles M. Lawrence and Andrew Moulton, Paris.
This car was built by two young Americans living in Paris, who had previously made the B.L.M. (Breeze, Lawrence & Moulton) in Brooklyn, New York. It had a pair-cast 4-cylinder ohv engine of their own design, with peculiar auxiliary ported exhausts as in a 2-stroke engine, controlled by a rotary valve. Only two cars were built, at a reputed cost of $30,000 each, and both were said to be capable of high speeds with good acceleration.

NG

L.M. (iii) *see* S.O.V.R.A.

L.M.B. (GB) 1960–1962

L.M.B. Components Ltd, Guildford, Surrey.
Catching the tail end of the fibreglass special body era (whose multitude of products cannot be covered in this Encyclopedia), Leslie Ballamy's L.M.B. was different to the norm in that it offered its own tubular steel chassis instead of the usual Ford 10 or Austin 7. He was well qualified as a member of the original Allard team and a celebrated modifier of Ford chassis. Either BMC B-series or Ford side-valve engines could be fitted to L.M.B. chassis and there was one complete model, the Debonair, which used an E.B. (Edwards Brothers) fibreglass coupé shell on an L.M.B. chassis.

CR

L.M.X. (I) 1968–1974

1968–1973 L.M.X. Automobile srl, Turin.
1973–1974 Samas di Charlie Fratelli, Ricca d'Alba.

Michele Liprandi and Giovanni Mandelli's coachbuilding concern was responsible for the bodies of the Abarth OT 1300, De Tomaso Vallelunga and A.S.A. before branching out into car production under its own name. Unusually for an Italian car, the bodywork (reputedly designed by Franco Scaglione) was made of fibreglass, only the doors being made of steel. It was available in coupé and convertible forms and covered a forked backbone chassis, Ford Taunus 20M front suspension and Ford Zodiac MkIV rear suspension. The 2.3-litre Ford V6 engine was available in various states of tune from 108bhp up to 210bhp with a turbocharger. Only 43 cars were built in all, including some built in 1973–74 as the Sirex LMS.

CR

LOCKWOOD (GB) 1921–1922

Lockwood's Garage, Eastbourne, Sussex.

This was a miniature car primarily intended for children and advertised as 'the smallest car in the world'. It was possibly the American CUSTER Cootie made, or sold, by Lockwood.

NG

LOCOMOBILE (US) 1899–1929

1899–1900 Locomobile Co. of America, Watertown, Massachusetts.
1900–1929 Locomobile Co. of America, Bridgeport, Connecticut.

The Locomobile, sold as 'The Best Built Car in America', began life as a steam runabout and departed as a high-quality but conventional assembled car. In between it occupied a unique market niche as a large, expensive but very conservative luxury car, the glimmer of which William 'Billy' Durant hoped to capture for the jewel of his automotive empire.

The initial Locomobile was actually a STANLEY. John Brisben Walker, a magazine publisher, badgered F.E. and F.O. Stanley into selling their fledgling steam car business in 1899. Walker enlisted a wealthy merchant of asphalt paving materials, Amzi Lorenzo Barber, to bankroll the purchase, which included the Stanleys' Massachusetts factory, cars, and patents. Walker and Barber chose Locomobile Co. of America as the name of their new firm, as their first choice, Automobile Co. of America was already in use. Barber and Walker soon split, Walker departing to Tarrytown, New York to build the MOBILE steamer, also using Stanley patents and consultation of the brothers themselves. Barber's Locomobile was a 400lb (180kg) runabout selling for $600. Barber consolidated production, which had been accomplished in plants dotted throughout Massachusetts, at Bridgeport, Connecticut, where a new facility was completed shortly after the March 1900 move.

Early Locomobiles had myriad problems with reliability, so the line was made sturdier and heavier by 1902. At that time, Locomobile brought suits for patent infringement against steam competitor WHITE Sewing Machine Co. and against the Stanleys themselves, who had gone back into business in their old Massachusetts factory. The Stanleys promptly changed their design. The sales of Locomobiles were declining, however, and Barber's firm began investigating petrol-powered cars. They hired engineer Andrew Riker (1868–1930), whose principal credits, ironically, had been earned in the design of electric cars, although he also had a string of petrol achievements dating from an 1886 patent for an engine.

Riker began his work surreptitiously, at the Chicopee, Massachusetts plant of the Overman Automobile Co., builders of the VICTOR steam car. He worked fast. The prototype petrol Locomobile was running in May 1902; on 2 November the first production model was delivered to a customer. It had a large 4120cc front-mounted 4-cylinder engine, its integral T-head cylinders cast in pairs. Water-cooled, its coal-scuttle bonnet faired to an aluminium tourer body, selling, fully equipped, for $4000. A wood-bodied Locomobile was available for $300 less. 'Easily the best built car in America' read the advertising. Improvements came swiftly, including longer wheelbase, larger wheels and tyres, and a Mercedes-style upright radiator. A less-expensive 2-cylinder model was introduced in 1903, but lasted only into the next year. By 1905 there were four lines of 4-cylinder cars, from 20 to 45hp on wheelbases of from 92 to 110in (2335–2792mm). Production of steam cars had declined to a small number in 1904, so they were discontinued the following year.

The petrol Locomobiles continued to grow in size and stature, and also in price. By 1907, there were five series of cars on four wheelbases as long as 123in (3122mm),

1961 L.M.B. Debonair GT coupé.
NICK BALDWIN

1902 Locomobile 4-seater steam car.
NATIONAL MOTOR MUSEUM

1911 Locomobile 30 limousine.
NICK BALDWIN

selling for nearly $5000. Perhaps the most famous Locomobiles date from this era. Two cars were built especially for the 1906 Vanderbilt Cup race. Speedsters of 120in (3046mm) wheelbase, they had huge 16.9-litre ohv engines. Both cars were beset with tyre failures, but one of them returned for the 1908 event, where, driven by George Robertson, it won the cup, leading the next-place ISOTTA by one minute and 48 seconds. This car survives, and is known today as Old 16 from its racing number.

In 1911, Locomobile introduced the 6-cylinder Model M, also known as the 48 from its rated horsepower. Its T-head engine was developed from the Model L 30 introduced the year before, and was exactly, at 7033cc, 1½ times its size. Cylinders

1925 Locomobile 48 opera coupé.
NICK BALDWIN

1925 Locomobile Junior Eight sedan.
NATIONAL MOTOR MUSEUM

were cast in pairs, and fitted to a bronze crankcase. A 4-speed gearbox, itself cast of manganese bronze, transmitted power to a full-floating rear axle. Powerful and durable, the 48 would remain in the catalogue almost to the end. The 4-cylinder car was dropped in 1914, the previous year having seen the debut of a smaller 38hp six. For a while both lhd and rhd drive cars were offered, the lhd configuration having a curiously longer wheelbase than rhd models.

Style came to Locomobile in the person of J. Frank de Causse. Hired away from the Parisian coachbuilding house of Kellner et ses Fils, de Causse established Locomobile's Custom Body Department at Bridgeport. The de Causse style came to embody large, flat panels, bordered by a double coachline, usually of gold, cream or black. Raised beads around the doors and on the wings were also a de Causse hallmark. Construction of the de Causse-designed bodies was contracted to the custom houses, like Holbrook, Healey, Locke and Demarest,

although Locomobile policy usually dictated that the coachbuilers' own labels should not be applied. Most standard bodies during this period were the work of nearby Bridgeport Body Co. and Blue Ribbon Body Co.

In 1919, control of the Locomobile Co. of America was taken by a corporation called Hare's Motors, headed by Emlen S. Hare. Other marques swept up by Hare's Motors were MERCER and SIMPLEX. Hare's Motors was crumbling by 1921, and Locomobile gained independence, but precariously so. Production, which had been halted, was restarted at four cars a day. Receivership followed, in February 1922. Riding to Locomobile's rescue, however, was the charismatic and free-wheeling William Crapo DURANT. 'Billy' Durant had been building a new automotive empire, following his second ousting from General Motors. Seeing Locomobile as the prestige badge for his conglomerate, Durant bid for the company at the July 1922 receiver's sale – with no opposition. A new Locomobile Co. of America, Inc acquired the assets of the old firm, and was itself under the control of Durant Motors. Locomobile became parent to a Flint Motor Division, later Flint Motor Co., which built the mid-priced FLINT car. Locomobile's rightful place, though, was at the top of the Durant empire. At this time however, the Locomobile product line consisted only of the 48, a very stale design. In quest of some lighter and more lively new products, Billy Durant looked to engineer Delmar 'Barney' Roos, who had rejoined the firm in 1922 after a sabbatical at Timken Axle and Pierce-Arrow. Roos updated the 48, called in 1923 the Series VIII. A new Delco battery ignition replaced the old magneto, new timing gears and camshafts gave quieter operation, and 4-wheel brakes became an option. The next year the 8606cc six was given higher compression and full-pressure lubrication. Prices now soared to over $11,000 for some models.

Frank de Causse had left Locomobile at the time of the receivership, when the Custom Body Department was closed down. To fill the void, Durant engaged the LeBaron firm to design new bodies for the 48 in 1923. These cars, with higher beltlines, more rounded roofs and slanted windscreens, would stay in production for the remaining lifetime of the model. Bridgeport Body continued to build the bodies, eventually merging with LeBaron to form the full-service LeBaron Inc. design and bodybuilding firm.

A pair of new, smaller Locomobiles headlined the 1925 New York auto show. The Junior Six and Junior Eight were identical cars, except for their wheelbases and engines. The Six, with a 3207cc side-valve engine developing 49bhp, rode a 115in (2919mm) wheelbase. The Eight had an ohv engine of 2975cc and 63bhp; it was built on a 124in (3147mm) wheelbase. The Junior Six, however, was a phenomenon only of the auto show; only the Eight entered production in April 1925, by which time it had 3259cc displacement and made 70bhp. A new upscale series, the 90, was introduced in November. In some ways a further modernisation of the 48, the 90 had a large side-valve six (of 6090cc) and a new light 3-speed gearbox. Wheelbase was 138in (3502mm). Bodies for the 90 were quite conservative, mimicking many of the cues of the old 48, a few of which were still being built for those who wanted them. The outlook at Locomobile was quite promising, as the company turned out over 3000 cars in 1926, the most ever, mostly on the strength of the Junior Eight. But trouble was afoot at parent Durant Motors, as Billy Durant withdrew from active management in order to manage his investments. Things soon started to go downhill; the return of Durant rallied operations a little, but by 1928 only the Locomobile, two lines of Durants and the Rugby truck remained in production. Another new eight, the 8-80 with a 4893cc Lycoming side-valve engine and 130in (3299mm) or 140in (3553mm) wheelbase, was announced in January 1927, selling for $1000 more than the Junior Eight. In June, it was joined by the 8-70, a replacement for the Junior Eight, later called the 8-66. This car had a 4044cc side-valve eight, of 70bhp. It is usually attributed to Continental. But production was off only about 1000 cars annually, and the competition, CADILLAC, PACKARD and the new CHRYSLER Imperial, had more modern and less costly cars. A new 8-88 model appeared in January 1929, with engine basically the same as that of the 8-80. Bodies were new, built by Central Manufacturing Co., an Auburn subsidiary, in Connersville, Indiana. These were the most modern-looking Locomobiles yet, priced from just $2650 to $7500. At this point, however, the business affairs of Locomobile came personally under Mr Durant, who purchased the company out from under Durant Motors in association with Ally S. Freed, president of Paramount Cab Manufacturing Co. A temporary suspension of production in March, 'pending reorganization of the company and designing new lines', proved to be the end of Locomobile. A mere 328 were sold in 1929.

KF

Further Reading
'Locomobile – Bridgeport's Beautiful Beast', Jeffrey I. Godshall,
Automobile Quarterly, Vol. 22, No. 4 and Vol. 23, No. 2.
'Hare's today, gone tomorrow: Emlen Hare's failed empire', Tony Muldoon,
Automobile Quarterly, Vol. 35, No. 3.
The Geneology of the Locomobile Steam Carriage, Donald A. Ball,
Stanley Museum, 1994.

LOCOMOTOR *see* BALDWIN

LOCOMOTRICE *see* NAGANT

LOCOST (GB) 1995 to date
Ron Champion, Oundle, Northamptonshire.
This was an unusual project in many ways. Ron Champion wrote a book called *Build Your Own Sports Car for £250*, showing how to create a Lotus 7 lookalike completely from scratch for the self-builder. It was so successful that a demand grew for pre-manufactured chassis and STUART TAYLOR began making many parts for the car, which became known as the Locost.

CR

LOEB *see* LUC

LOGAN (i) (US) 1904–1908
Logan Construction Co., Chillicothe, Ohio.
The Logan was designed by Benjamin A. Gramm, who was also responsible for the GRAMM and BUCKEYE. In 1904 a 10hp twin was offered, in air- or water-cooled form, with detachable rear-entrance tonneau body and engine under the seat. The 1905 Logan had a 20hp 2-cylinder engine, still under the seat, though there was now a frontal bonnet. The body was now a side-entrance tourer. Front-engined fours of 20 and 30hp came in 1906, though the 10hp 2-cylinder runabout was still listed. In 1907/08 they made a roadster called the Blue Streak Semi-Racer Runabout, with 20/24hp 4-cylinder engine which they said 'could feed its dust to most anything on wheels'. This performance notwithstanding, the Logan company was bankrupt by mid–1908. Gramm's

c.1900 Lohner - Porsche 2-seater victoria.
NATIONAL MOTOR MUSEUM

career was far from over, though, for he moved to Bowling Green, Ohio, where he made Gramm-Logan trucks until 1910, then other trucks under the names Gramm-Bernstein, Gramm-Kincaid, and plain Gramm, the latter lasting up to 1942.

NG

LOGAN (ii) (US) 1914
Northwestern Motorcycle Works, Chicago, Illinois.
This was a cyclecar powered by a 9/13hp air-cooled V-twin Spacke engine, with friction transmission and final drive by vee belt. It had an underslung steel frame.

NG

LOGICAR (DK) 1983–1987
Logicar AS, Viborg.
This company's effort was displayed at the 1983 Frankfurt Motor Show. Designed by Jakob Jensen, it was intended as a 5-seater passenger car that could be converted into a pick-up in a matter of minutes: the rear windows slid into the roof, the roof itself lowered on telescopic springs and the rear window rolled forward to form a watertight seal against the cabin. The one-box shape was very squared off, was made in fibreglass, and hid a Volkswagen Beetle engine in a steel chassis.

CR

LOHNER (A) 1896–1906
Jacob Lohner & Co., Vienna.
Jacob Lohner was a well-established Viennese coachbuilder, the company dating back to 1832, whose son Ludwig became interested in mechanical transport. After attempted collaboration with Benz and Daimler, he made his own car in 1896, using a French 6hp Pygmée engine. He soon turned to electric power, building one or two cars in 1898 with components by Bela Egger Elektrizitäts-AG, under the name Egger-Lohner. In 1899 a young engineer named Ferdinand Porsche joined Lohner; his great contribution was the 'Radnabenmotor' in which the electric motor was incorporated in the wheelhub. This avoided a complicated transmission and drive shaft, and enabled 4-wheel drive to be employed without too much difficulty, though most Lohner-Porsche cars drove on the front wheels. He used the same system in the 'mixte' or petrol-electric drive, in which electricity was generated by a petrol engine to drive the wheel-mounted motors. These were generally at the rear, while the engines were by Mercedes or Panhard. They proved expensive to make, and in 1906 the patents were sold to Emil Jellinek who began production in the AUSTRO-DAIMLER factory, selling the products as Mercedes-Mixte. Meanwhile Porsche had left Lohner in 1905 to become managing director of Austro-Daimler. Lohner concentrated on commercial vehicles, particularly the Lohner-Stoll trolleybuses. From 1950 to 1958 a new company, Lohner-Werke GmbH, made scooters.

HON

1993 Lomax Supa Vee 3-wheeler.
CHRIS REES

1928 Lombard AL3 sports car.
NATIONAL MOTOR MUSEUM

LOHR see ELMER SIX

LOIDIS (GB) 1898–1904

A. Dougill & Co. Ltd, Leeds, Yorkshire.

Caer Loidis was the Celtic name for Leeds, and the name was applied to a number of vehicles imported or made by Dougill, who also built cars under the names DOUGILL and FRICK. The German LUX (i) friction-drive car was imported and sold as Loidis, also probably the MAURER UNION, and a few cars were assembled using 6hp De Dion-Bouton or 9hp Aster engines, with Fafnir gearboxes and shaft drive.

NG

LOMAR (I) 1985–c.1988

Lomar Srl, Parma.

The Lomar Honey was an originally-styled 2-seater 3-wheeler fitting into the microcar category, even though it was fairly large at 142in (3600mm) long. A rear-mounted Cagiva 125cc motorcycle engine drove the single rear wheel via a 6-speed gearbox. The gullwing doors could be removed for hot-weather motoring.

CR

LOMAX (GB) 1983 to date

1983 Lomax Motor Co., Willoughton, Gainsborough, Lincolnshire.
1984 Lomax Motor Co., Snowhill, Birmingham.
1984–1986 Lomax Motor Co., Nailsworth, Gloucestershire.
1986–1992 Lomax Motor Co., Bewdley, Worcestershire.
1992 to date Lomax Motor Co., Halesowen, West Midlands.

Fibreglass specialist Nigel Whall created one of the most ingenious and best-selling kit cars of all time with the 2CV-based Lomax. It was brilliantly simple: on top of an unmodified Citroën 2CV/Dyane floorpan (or Lomax's own steel tube chassis) sat a very simple double-scuttle open body in a Morganesque style. The engine sat semi-exposed at the front. Several models were offered: the 224 (4-wheeler), 223 (3-wheeler with a single reversed Citroën rear trailing arm) and the 424 (with a Citroën Ami flat-4-cylinder engine). In 1989 a rather different model was launched, again based on a 2CV floorpan. The Déjà Vu was a utility vehicle with adaptable bodywork (it could transform into a doorless buggy, estate, pick-up, hard-/soft-top, or even a flat bed truck). After failing to productionise the Supa Vee, a trike with a space frame chassis and 1.5-litre American-made V-twin engine, in 1993 the Lambda was launched as a more up-market 223-style Lomax. It featured a new and much more rigid ladder frame chassis with adjustable inboard coil spring/damper suspension, and boasted more flowing bodywork and more interior space. In 1998 a new Super Touring model was launched.

CR

LOMBARD (F) 1927–1929

1927 E. Brault, Courbevoie, Seine.
1928–1929 Les Fils de E. Salmson, Billancourt, Seine.

André Lombard was competition manager and a successful driver for SALMSON, but left the firm in 1923. Four years later he realised his ambition to make a car under his own name. It was a beautiful little sports car with 1093cc twin-ohc 4-cylinder engine which developed 49bhp, or 70bhp with supercharger. It was designed by Edmond Vareille and built by E. Brault, who also made the prototype twin-ohc RALLY engines. The Lombard AL1 was a prototype, the AL2 was a tank-bodied sports-racing car of which two were built and ran at Montlhéry. The production model was the AL3, which was shown in coupé and open 2-seater forms at the 1927 Paris Salon. The bodies were made by Duval, who supplied Amilcar and other car makers. Only the show models of the AL3 were made by Brault, and when deliveries began in the summer of 1928, the cars were made by Les Fils de E. Salmson, the sons of Émile Salmson, who was making SALMSON cars at the same time.

The AL3 had a number of sporting successes, finishing fourth in the 1928 Spanish GP, and winning the 1929 Bol d'Or. About two-thirds of the 94 made were sold in France, but they were also exported to England, Germany, Italy and Belgium. In the spring of 1929 there was a rumour that the Fils de E. Salmson were going to make a larger engine, and that Lombard manufacture would revert to Brault. In fact, neither happened. A number of parts and unfinished cars were bought by Charles de Ricou of B.N.C. and sold under the B.N.C. name; one of the B.N.C.s raced at Le Mans in 1929 was, in fact, a Lombard. In 1930 André Lombard formed another company to make a luxury car with 3-litre single-ohc straight-8 engine, but only one chassis was completed.

NG

LOMBARDA see ESPERIA

LOMBARDI (I) 1969–1974

Francis Lombardi S.a.s., Vercelli.

Francis Lombardi founded his coachbuilding company in 1947 and specialised in transforming small Fiats and some Lancia models. Only two models could properly be called production cars as such. The first was the 1969 Grand Prix,

1990 Lomax 224 sports car.
LOMAX

based on Fiat 850 components. It had handsome shark-nosed coupé styling that could seat two passengers, and was regarded as suitably sporting for several other manufacturers to fit their own engines and badges: Abarth (calling it the Scorpione), Giannini and O.T.A.S. Lombardi's second sports car, the FL-1, launched in 1972, was a wedge-shaped 2-seater coupé with a mid-mounted Lancia engine (initially Flavia, then Beta 2000). Lombardi closed its doors in 1974.

CR

LONDONIA *see* OWEN (i)

LONDON-PULLMAN *see* PULLMAN

LONDON SIX (CDN) 1921–1924
London Motors Ltd, London, Ontario.
The London Six was one of the more successful all-Canadian cars of its time, offering a variety of open and closed models priced from $2600 for the 5-seater touring car to $3700 for the sedan. Designed by William R. Stansell, who headed the company, the London Six was a heavy car featuring wooden disc wheels and a pointed windshield on the closed models. Its engine was a 6-cylinder Herschell-Spillman generally used for fire apparatus. The London Six was a highly respected make of car and was used on the occasion of an official visit to London by Viscount Julian George Byng, Governor-General of Canada, and Lady Byng, when London owners of London Six cars lent them for use for ceremonies by the

city. In their four years of production, a total of 98 London Six cars were completed and sold.

KM

LONE STAR (i) **(US)** 1920–1922
Lone Star Motor Truck & Tractor Corp., San Antonio, Texas.
The Lone Star started its existence as a badge-engineered product. The cars and trucks were built by Piedmont of Lynchburg, Virginia, and differing little – if at all – from the Piedmont, Bush, the export Alsace, and the last Norwalk cars, although the few tractors completed were ostensibly assembled in San Antonio. The Lone Star line of cars included a touring car, a 'Beauty Top' touring model and a sedan, plus a pick-up truck powered either by a Lycoming 4-cylinder K L-head engine or a six using a Herschell-Spillman 11000. By 1922, a factory had been completed and the actual production of Lone Stars commenced in San Antonio with regional sales being targeted plus an export division for sales in Mexico. The Lone Star failed later in 1922, a victim of the Depression of that time which affected many smaller automobile companies.

KM

LONE STAR (ii) **(US)** c.1992 to date
Lone Star Classics, Inc., Fort Worth, Texas.
Lone Star built a line of replicas that were sold as kits and as assembled cars. They made replicas of the 1955 Corvette and 427 Cobra that fitted on ladder

1924 Loreley M8 8/36PS saloon by Hebmüller.
HALWART SCHRADER

frames with V8 engines. The LS-40 was a GT-40 Ford replica with a sturdy space frame and a Ford V8 with a Porsche transaxle. The LS 300 was a replica of a Mercedes 300SL prototype that used Ford or Chevrolet V8 engines. The LS32 was a 1932 Ford hot rod kit, while the Growler was a modern hot rod with styling hints from the Dodge Prowler.
HP

LONG & NEWMAN (US) c.1984
Long & Newman, San Marcos, California.
The De Tomaso Pantera had not been out of Ford showrooms for long when this company brought out a convincing replica. It used a fibreglass body and tube chassis, and could be equipped with a Chevrolet Citation V6 or an original-type 5700cc Ford V8 with a ZF transaxle. Suspension was fabricated and weight was 500lbs less than an original. In addition to the street version, Long & Newman also sold a replica of the Group V racing Pantera with flared mudguards and wings.
HP

LONG DISTANCE see U.S. LONG DISTANCE

LONGTIN (B) 1901–1904
Longtin et le Hardy de Beaulieu, Jette St Pierre.
These cars were made by Honoré Longtin, who was one of the founders of the PIPE company, and Charles Le Hardy de Beaulieu, who represented the French C.G.V. car in Belgium. They bought a small factory at Jette St Pierre where they made a light car powered by front-mounted single- or 2-cylinder engines, with shaft drive and tubular frame. In 1902 they offered a wider range, with engines of 8, 10, 12, and 20hp. The last had 4-cylinders and chain drive. The gilled tube radiator between the dumb irons was soon replaced by a honeycomb. The company also made trucks and petrol and steam marine engines, and continued the C.G.V. agency during their period of car manufacture, which ended in 1904.
NG

LONSDALE (GB) 1900
Monk & Lonsdale, Brighton, Sussex.
This short-lived car was designed by Albert Lambourne, who later made the OLD MILL car. It was a very light 2-seater, powered by a 2½hp single-cylinder engine of Lambourne's own construction, and had belt drive.
NG

LOOMIS (US) 1900–1904
1900–1903 Loomis Automobile Co., Westfield, Massachusetts.
1903–1904 Loomis Auto Car Co., Westfield, Massachusetts.
Gilbert Loomis built a steam car in 1896, but did not put it into production. He formed his company in 1900, and up to 1903 made rather spidery and old-fashioned-looking cars with 5hp 2-cylinder engines mounted close to the rear axle. Somewhat unusually he offered different tracks, 40in (1015mm) for urban use and 48½in (1231mm) for country roads or streetcar tracks (there were many inter-urban streetcars in America at that time). The first was called the

Model 1 Gas Park Wagon, the second the Model 2 Gas Road Wagon, and there was also a Model 3 Gas Delivery. In 1903 Loomis made the Bluebird tonneau, with front-mounted engine under a De Dion-Bouton type bonnet and single-chain drive. The 1904 model was larger still, with an 18hp 3-cylinder engine and rear-entrance 4-seater tonneau body. Business cannot have been very good, for Loomis sold his factory in 1904 and later worked as a designer for Payne-Modern, Pope Tribune and Speedwell.
NG

LORD BALTIMORE (US) 1913
Lord Baltimore Motor Car Co., Baltimore, Maryland.
This company was set up in April 1911 to make a 3-ton truck, and only offered a passenger car for a few months, from February to May 1913. It was a conventional 4-cylinder car, made as a 35hp tourer or 40hp raceabout, both apparently with the same size engine of 5.1 litres. It had electric lighting and a compressed air starter. Lord Baltimore trucks were made up to 1915.
NG

LORELEY (D) 1906–1928
Rudolf Ley AG, Arnstadt.
The Maschinenfabrik Rudolf Ley was founded in 1856 and made, among other items, shoemaking machinery. In 1905 Albert Ley, brother of founder Rudolf, began to build a prototype car, and this went on the market in 1905 as the 6/10PS. It had a 1559cc 4-cylinder engine, 3-speed gearbox and shaft drive. It was soon joined by a smaller four of 1232cc, the 4/10PS, which was the first car to bear the name Loreley (from the famous rock on the Rhine), soon adopted for all models. In 1907 came the 2599cc 10/25PS 6-cylinder car, possibly the first six to be made in Germany. Between then and World War I a variety of different 4- and 6-cylinder cars were made, the smallest being the 1132cc 5/12PS of 1909–11, and the largest the 2599cc K6 10/28PS of 1912 to 1914. One of these was the first car owned by the composer Sergei Rachmaninoff. The Type 6A of 1912 had an exceptionally small capacity for a six, at 1550cc.
After the war Ley continued with their range of relatively small cars, the 1540cc 4-cylinder 6/20PS made from 1920 to 1925 and a larger four of 3091cc, the 12/32, later 12/36 and 12/45PS, made from 1921 to 1927. They all had side-valve engines and 4-speed gearboxes, apart from the TO sports model of 1924, with 1498cc single-ohc engine. The last model was the V12, not a 12 cylinder, but a 3180cc six with 3-speed gearbox. Only ten of these were made, out of an estimated production between 1920 and 1928 of 2250 cars. In the early 1920s Ley chassis were among those used by Paul Jaray for his streamlined saloon bodies.
HON

LORENC (B) 1903–1904
Transmission Lorenc, Brussels.
This was a most unusual car powered by two single-cylinder De Dion-Bouton engines, each driving a front wheel by chain. The body was a 4-seater tonneau. It was shown at the Paris Salon in December 1903 and then at the Brussels Salon in January 1904.
NG

LORRAINE (i) (US) 1907–1908
Lorraine Automobile Manufacturing Co., Chicago, Illinois.
This was a conventional large tourer made in two models, the 25/30hp Model M on a 110in (2792mm) wheelbase, and the 50/55hp Model L on a 124in (3147mm) wheelbase. The latter was made only as a 7-seater tourer, but the Model M could be had with 5-seater tourer, 5-seater limousine or 2-seater gentleman's roadster bodies. Both models had a Hobbs-Renault compressed air starter, the tank storing enough air for 15 to 20 starts. The pressurised air could also be used to inflate the tyres.
NG

LORRAINE (ii) (US) 1920–1921
1917–1920 Hackett Motor Co., Grand Rapids, Michigan.
1920–1921 Lorraine Motors Corp., Grand Rapids, Michigan.
The Lorraine was the continuation of the Hackett, a low-volume assembled car, which, like its predecessor, continued production with an undistinguished 4-cylinder model, available in 1920 only in touring car form. Listed as the Model 20-A, the

Lorraine was powered by a Herschell-Spillman 7000 L-head engine, featured a 114in (2893mm) wheelbase and was priced at $1695. In 1921, David Dunbar Buick, founder of the Buick Motor Car Co., became president of Lorraine. The new model designation was, not surprisingly, the 21-T and Lorraine added a roadster, coupé and sedan to its touring car, but to no avail. Apart from the addition of the three new body styles, plus the substitution of a Johnson carburettor in place of the Zenith used in 1920 and Westinghouse ignition supplanting the Connecticut featured on the 1920 cars, the cars were unchanged. The Lorraine failed during 1921 and David Buick would subsequently surface in Walden, New York, promoting the ill-favoured Dunbar automobile.

KM

LORRAINE (iii) (US) 1921–1923

1920–1921 Lorraine Car Co., Richmond, Indiana.
1921–1923 Pilot Motor Car Co., Richmond, Indiana.

The Lorraine – not to be confused with the contemporary car of the same name built in Grand Rapids and Detroit, Michigan – was a large passenger car built primarily for funeral purposes by a manufacturer of funeral cars which added the limousines and large sedans to expand the line. In 1921, the Lorraine Car Co. was acquired by the Pilot Motor Car Co. and the Lorraine became a funeral car division of that company with a limited number of the large sedans available on special order. All of these were powered by a 6-cylinder Continental 7R engine, with a wheelbase of 112in (2843mm). Price was $2295. The Lorraine division of Pilot was closed down in 1923, a year before Pilot went out of business.

KM

LORRAINE (iv) (US) c.1985–1995

Lorraine Motor Research, Downers Grove, Illinois.
This Bugatti T-59 replica was only available as a turn-key car. It used a fibreglass body made from blueprints of the original car. The engine was a Ford 2000cc 4-cylinder with performance cam and carburettion.

HP

LORRAINE-DIETRICH; LORRAINE (v) (F) 1905–1934

Sté Lorraine des Anciens Établissements de Dietrich et Cie,
Luneville, Lorraine; Argenteuil, Seine et Oise.

Adrien de Turckheim parted company with Eugene de Dietrich in 1905, formed a new firm and henceforth the cars were called Lorraine-Dietrich rather than de Dietrich, to emphasise their French pedigree. A new factory was acquired at Argenteuil, in the north-western suburbs of Paris, and this soon became a model for up-to-date manufacturing techniques, praised by American as well as European observers. T-head engines gave way to L-heads for 1906, and sales rose to 650 in that year, from only 253 four years earlier. Demand for Lorraine-Dietrich cars was so high that they contracted Émile Mathis' Société Alsacienne des Constructions Mécaniques of Graffenstaden, in German Alsace, who had made the Bugatti-designed HERMÉS-SIMPLEX, to make about 40 chassis for them, and also probably had some chassis made by TURCAT-MÉRY in Marseilles. They also formed a separate company for the promotion of commercial vehicle sales. In 1907 Lorraine-Dietrich acquired two foreign firms, ISOTTA-FRASCHINI in Italy and ARIEL (i) in England. Neither venture prospered; the union with Isotta was ended in 1909 and few, if any, Lorraine-Dietrichs were made in England, despite the French company's purchase of an Ariel factory at Selly Oak, Birmingham. By 1910 this venture had ended as well, both ventures being sold off to raise capital to offset Lorraine-Dietrich's serious debts. Some models, such as the enormous 12.4-litre 60 were uneconomic to produce and probably found hardly any buyers. From 1910 Lorraine wisely introduced smaller models, with monobloc engines and shaft drive, such as the 2121cc 4-cylinder 12/15hp. Under the influence of their new designer, de Grouillard, these modern designs spread up the range, with a similar 3052cc 15/20hp coming in 1911 and a 5700cc 28hp in 1912. There were still some pretty large cars in the range, though, the biggest in the immediate prewar years being the 8340cc 40/75hp made from 1913 to 1916. This had pair-cast cylinders. In 1913 about 800 cars were made. Marius Barbarou (ex Benz and Delaunay-Belleville) joined the firm in 1912, but his influence on design was not felt until after the war.

Aero engines were produced during the war, and remained an important product in the 1920s and 1930s, and in 1919 came Barbarou's 6.1-litre side-valve six. Few of these were made, and a companion V12 never went into production.

1907 Lorraine-Dietrich tourer in Critérium de la France.
NATIONAL MOTOR MUSEUM

1907 Lorraine-Dietrich 24/30hp tourer.
NICK BALDWIN

1929 Lorraine-Dietrich 20/70hp saloon.
NATIONAL MOTOR MUSEUM

The staple postwar product was a 3445cc ohv six, called in France the 15CV and in England the 20.9hp (20/60 from 1925) or the Silken Six. It had a number of American features such as coil ignition, a 3-speed gearbox and central gear change. It acquired a 4-speed gearbox and front-wheel brakes in 1924, and in 1927 the formerly exposed pushrods were enclosed. A sports model, the 20/70, won the Le Mans 24 Hour Race in 1925 and 1926. Between 1923 and 1929 there was a companion 4-cylinder car, the 2296cc 12CV which was not sold on the British market. Several thousand 15CVs were made up to 1932 when it gave way to a 4086cc 20CV six, which reverted to side-valves but had hydraulic brakes. This more expensive and luxurious car was not the best model to launch in the Depression, and relatively few were made before all car production ended in 1934. The cars were known as Lorraines from 1928. Tatra cross-country vehicles and aero engines were made up to World War II at Argenteuil, and

1925 Lorraine-Dietrich 20/70hp saloon by James Young.
NATIONAL MOTOR MUSEUM

1911 Lotis 20/24hp landaulette.
NICK BALDWIN

railway wagons and equipment at Lunéville. These were continued after the war, but the only motor vehicles made were some tractors for rail and dockyard use.
NG

LORYC (E) 1921–1925
Lacy, Ouvrard, Ribas y Cía, Palma de Mallorca.
The representative of DE DION-BOUTON, this company built the first car to be made in the Balearic Islands under a French E.H.P. licence. These cars were first assembled with foreign components, but later on only the engines were French, and the body and all the other mechanical parts were built at Palma de Mallorca. Three different engines were offered on the same chassis: E.H.P., Rugby, and SCAP, and some cars were equipped with racing-car bodies, participating in several racing events. Over 100 cars were built.
VCM

LOS ANGELES (US) 1913–1914
Los Angeles Cyclecar Co., Compton, California; Buffalo, New York.
This cyclecar was originally to have been sold as the California, but after a reorganisation the name of company and car was changed to Los Angeles. Two models were offered: a 10hp 2-cylinder and a 12/15hp four, both with friction transmission and vee-belt drive. The main factory was at Compton, but to supply the East Coast trade they leased a plant from the E.R. Thomas Co. at Buffalo. In fact few cars were made at either place, possibly none at all at Buffalo. In early 1914 an 18hp four was said to be replacing the smaller-engined cars.
NG

LOST CAUSE (US) 1963–1964
Lost Cause Motors, Louisville, Kentucky.
Lost Cause Motors was formed by Charles Peasley Farnsley, a former Louisville distiller of 'Rebel Yell' brand whisky and later mayor of that city. Farnsley's concept of a luxury car was based on his conviction that there was a viable space in the marketplace for a customised car which would offer the buyer a car with an outstanding appearance, equipped with an array of features unavailable in a factory-produced car of that time. Toward that goal he introduced the curiously named Lost Cause, a customised Chevrolet Corvair Monza sedan on a lengthened wheelbase with customising by Enos Derham of the Derham Custom Body Works. The Lost Cause was devoid of a nameplate and featured a leather-covered top and leather-covered seats, walnut panelling, special lap robes and a stop watch plus a tachometer, altimeters, compasses, matching luggage and car rugs, picnic hampers, and – in true Kentucky tradition – mint julep cups of vermeil. The car was, according to the announcement held in conjunction with its introduction at the Coliseum in New York City, to be made on a one-car-per-month basis at prices of $12,000 and, depending on further extras, as high as $23,000. Lost Cause Motors was short-lived.
KM

LOTHIAN (GB) 1920
W.J.M. Auto Engineers Ltd, London.
Specifications were published of this car, showing it to be made in two 4-cylinder models, of 10 and 11.9hp. However no press descriptions or road tests were ever published, and it may never have got off the drawing board. An alternative address was in Callow Street, London, in which street the MAGNETIC was made from 1921 to 1926. There was no connection with the Scottish commercial vehicle of the same name, made from 1913 to 1924.
NG

LOTIS (GB) 1908–1912
Sturmey Motors Ltd, Coventry.
Henry Sturmey founded Britain's first motoring magazine, *The Autocar*, in 1895, and in 1900 built a single example of a light car powered by a 2.75hp M.M.C.

LORRAINE - DIETRICH

1953 Lotus (i) Mark 6 sports car with Colin Chapman at the wheel.
NATIONAL MOTOR MUSEUM

1962 Lotus (i) Elite coupé.
NICK BALDWIN

1965 Lotus (i)Elan coupé.
NICK BALDWIN

motorcycle engine, which he hoped to sell for £100. He never put it into production (though the sole example still exists), and from 1902 to 1906 he made the British Duryea under licence from the American company. When this venture came to an end he used the same factory for the manufacture of Napier-Parsons delivery vans and, from 1908, cars he called the Lotis. They had 10/12 or 12/18hp V-twin Riley engines mounted under the seat, but for 1909 the engines were located under a Renault-type bonnet. There was also a short-lived 8hp single-cylinder model listed in 1908. The twins were made as taxicabs, being supplied to several foreign cities including Warsaw and Rio de Janeiro. From 1910 4-cylinder White & Poppe engines were used, of 18/21, 20/24 and 25/32hp, the last having a capacity of 4082cc. They had worm drive whereas the commercial vehicles had bevel drive.

NG

LOTUS (i) (GB) 1951 to date

1951–1959 Lotus Engineering Co., Hornsey, London.
1959–1966 Lotus Cars Ltd, Cheshunt, Hertfordshire.
1966 to date Lotus Cars Ltd, Hethel, Norfolk.

Lotus was the creation of Anthony Colin Bruce Chapman (his initials are on the badge) and, more than any other modern manufacturer, its history reflects its founder. Like Ferrari and Porsche, Lotus was linked to motor racing and, while Chapman was alive, it became easily the most successful team in Formula One. Chapman was born in 1928 and studied Civil Engineering at the University of London. When not studying, he and a friend bought and sold cars in Warren Street, London's notorious used car street market.

He built an Austin Seven special while still a student and it showed signs of rare ingenuity with a stiffened chassis and tuned engine. It was not registered as an Austin, as most A7 specials were, but as Lotus. According to Yoshio Nakamura, a former Competition Manager for Honda, the name came from Chapman's passing interest in Buddhism. A second car, based on a Ford Ten, was constructed while Chapman was spending his National Service in the RAF, and it was used in trials, races, rallies, hill climbs and autotests.

The Lotus Mk III (three made) was an Austin Seven special designed as a road/race car for the then new 750 Formula and was notable for Chapman's ingenious reading of the rules. In Chapman's hands, the Lotus Mk III was the quickest car in the formula but, while it caused the rule-makers to redefine their terms, it did not win the 750 Championship.

The Mk IV was a trials car built for a customer and was exceptionally successful. The Mk V did not get beyond the design stage, but the Lotus Mk VI which, in November 1951, was launched by the new Lotus Engineering Co., was the largest single step that Chapman took in his career. It was one of the first cars with a spaceframe and was a clever amalgam between advanced design and the mundane mechanical components which were then available. Front suspension was a Ford split axle on coil springs and the live rear axle was suspended on coils. It was also the world's first component car. It was light, quick and versatile and about 100 were sold, all as kits. It also had the first series-built body undertaken by the fledgling Williams & Pritchard, one of many outfits which prospered through the Lotus connection.

Chapman was assisted by outstanding engineers such as Peter Ross, 'Mac' MacKintosh, Keith Duckworth and Frank and Mike Costin and they, and others, were the unsung heroes of Lotus' early days. Len Pritchard, of Williams & Pritchard, recalls: 'They arrived from nowhere and made cars. Lotus had that effect on people'.

It was Chapman, however, who took the credit and none of the volunteers was treated with unforced generosity. The VII was an ERA-engined Formula Two car which was converted into a sports car, the Clairmonte-Connaught, which left the Lotus Seven designation available.

Chapman's next project was an aerodynamic sports racer and Frank Costin, who headed the aerodynamic retrification section of de Havilland Aircraft, was persuaded to design the body. There followed a series of cars – Chapman chassis, Costin body – which put Lotus on the map. By the end of 1957 Lotus had taken international speed records and won the Index of Performance at Le Mans. With the Eleven of 1956, Lotus dominated the important 1100cc sports racing class, which was the category for the serious young driver.

The Eleven was the last Lotus which was primarily designed for racing, yet which could be used on the road. The name of every subsequent road-going Lotus has begun with an 'E'. In a two-year period of astonishing activity, 1955 to 1957, Chapman designed the Eleven, a new chassis for Vanwall, the first British car to win a World Championship race (Frank Costin designed the body) and turned the BRM P25 from a dangerous car into a race winner. Chapman, a driver of Formula One standard, retired from racing in 1957.

In that same period came Lotus' first road cars: the Seven and the Elite GT, both in 1957. The Seven had the chassis of the Lotus Eleven Sports, with Ford or BMC engines and a slipper body with cycle mudguards. The Elite had fibreglass unitary construction and, when production problems were partially overcome, it dominated its class in racing for five or six years.

The Elite was primarily a road car, but the cockpit was noisy and ventilation was poor. Power came from a 1216cc Coventry Climax FWE engine with various power options. Front suspension was by coil springs and double wishbones, and the independent rear was by 'Chapman struts', a modified MacPherson strut; disc brakes were fitted all round, inboard at the rear. When sold fully-assembled,

1965 Lotus (i) Cortina Mk1 at Brands Hatch, with Jim Clark at the wheel.
NATIONAL MOTOR MUSEUM

however, it cost more than a Jaguar XK150, but most Elites were sold as kits – and Lotus lost money on every one.

By the end of 1958 the Elite had begun production in a new factory in Cheshunt and Lotus had entered Formula One, but with a front-engined car because Chapman was afraid of being accused of copying Cooper.

Most of the volunteers had left by 1958, disillusioned with Chapman's way with money. On the other hand, some were inspired to set up on their own account. These included Mike Costin and Keith Duckworth who set up Cosworth Engineering, while Frank Costin became the 'cos' of MARCOS. One of Chapman's greatest achievements was to inspire the foundation of a web of subcontractors which became the British motor racing industry.

Lotus had also lost the 1100cc sports racing market to Lola. This was partly due to the excellence of the Lola Mk 1 and partly to Chapman's insistence that his answer had to be smaller than the Lola – the Seventeen was so small that it compromised the suspension movement. With the Elite proving difficult to productionise, the formula cars being fragile failures and the Seventeen having inherent problems, Lotus was in crisis.

Then, in 1960, small constructors from all over the world met for the first time on a level playing field in Formula Junior. There were more than 150 makes, but Lotus, with its Cosworth-tuned Ford 105E engines, together with Cooper and its BMC connections, wiped most of the little companies out and, with them, their attendant support industries.

Lotus dominated Formula Junior with the mid-engined Lotus 18 single-seater which also won in Formula Two and Formula One, even if the 18 added to Lotus' already unenviable reputation for fragility.

There were two milestones in 1962. One was the Lotus 25 which introduced monocoque construction to Formula One. With the 25 and its successor, the 33, Jim Clark and Lotus dominated Formula One from 1962 to 1965. The other milestone was the Elan with its sheet steel backbone chassis. Each end was like a tuning fork, the front fork cradled the engine, the rear fork, the final drive, and both carried the suspension, which was similar to the Elite. The fibreglass shell was first made as a convertible, but a hard-top was soon available.

1968 Lotus (i) Elan +2 coupé.
LOTUS

1970 Lotus (i) Europa S2 coupé.
NATIONAL MOTOR MUSEUM

1970 Lotus (i) Super Seven Series IV sports car.
NICK BALDWIN

1981 Lotus (i) Eclat Series 2.2 4-seater coupé.
NICK BALDWIN

1985 Lotus (i) Esprit coupé.
NATIONAL MOTOR MUSEUM

1989 Lotus (i) Elan SE sports car.
LOTUS

Lotus made its own engine, the 1588cc 'Twin-Cam', on a Ford block and this initially gave 105bhp, with later versions producing up to 130bhp. The Elan was intended for road use only, but pressure from customers saw it revised to make it suitable for competition, in which it was superb.

The Elite was phased out in 1963 having officially sold 998 examples, but some cars were not accounted for. That year also saw the introduction of the Ford Lotus-Cortina, a Cortina Mk 1 with revised suspension and the Lotus 'Twin-Cam' engine. The Lotus-Cortina heralded a fulfilling relationship between the two companies and a Mk II Lotus-Cortina was made from 1967 to 1970.

By 1966, Lotus had won more World Championship events than any other constructor, and had also become the first British marque to win the Indianapolis 500.

Chapman had long desired to build a mid-engined GT car, but was thwarted by the lack of a suitable powertrain until the front-wheel drive Renault 16 arrived. In the Europa of 1966, Lotus used 78bhp versions of the 1470cc Renault engine with the front-wheel drive transaxle turned through 180 degrees. The

NATIONAL MOTOR MUSEUM

CHAPMAN, ANTHONY COLIN BRUCE (1928–1982)

Colin Chapman is synonymous with Lotus, and associated with hundreds of motor racing victories, but Lotus, of course, also produced road cars. He was born in Richmond, Surrey, on 19 May 1928. After elementary school he went to University College, and at 17 enrolled at London University to study engineering, while learning to fly in the University Air Squadron. He was lucky to be called up for military service in the Royal Air Force, as he was determined to become a fighter pilot, and continued his training, privately, on Harvard planes. He was not selected for fighter-pilot training, however, but spent a lot of time reading motor-racing magazines in the RAF mess, re-focussing on a career in motor racing.

He found employment with the British Aluminium Co. as a development engineer, while his fiancée, Hazel Williams, arranged for the use of a row of small, lock-up garages behind her parents' home, where he could store and rebuild his cars. In 1947 he began turning a 1930 Austin Seven into a trials special. He bought another old Austin chassis and mounted a Ford L-head 1172cc engine in it.

In 1950 he formed a partnership with Michael and Nigel Allen, who had a spacious garage at Muswell Hill, North London, where the Lotus Mk III came into being. In 1952 he could afford to rent factory space at 7 Tottenham Lane, Hornsey, London, where the Lotus VI, the first production model, was created, followed by the Lotus VII, and the Elite coupé. In 1953 he founded the Lotus Engineering Co. Ltd.

One of his talents, which assured much fame for Lotus cars, was an ability to pick collaborators who could make major contributions. Among

backbone chassis was similar to the Elan, but rear suspension was by lower wishbones and transverse top links.

The 108mph (174km/h) top speed and 0–62mph (0–100km/h) in 10.7 seconds were not outstanding, the cockpit was claustrophobic, rearward vision was poor, the interior was cramped, there was little luggage space and the windows did not open but, against that, handling was to Lotus' usual standards and that was enough for many.

In 1967 Lotus unveiled the Lotus 49 Formula One car, the first machine to use the fabulously successful Cosworth DFV engine and the first F1 car to use the engine and gearbox to carry the rear suspension. Until the early 1970s, Lotus' range consisted of the Seven; the Elan, together with, from 1967, the stretched, and widened, 4-seat Elan +2; and the Europa, which became available in Britain in 1969 and, in 1971, was fitted with the 'Twin Cam' engine.

By the end of 1973, Lotus had stopped making production racing cars. The Seven had reached the Series Four and was made by Lotus Components, which made Lotus production racing cars. When Lotus Components was closed

them were Frank Costin, who designed the bodies for the Lotus IX and XI, his brother Mike Costin, engine and chassis engineer (and later the 'cos' in Cosworth, with Keith Duckworth), Peter Kirwan-Taylor (an accountant who drew the basic sketches for the Lotus Elite), and Ron Hickman, the plastics expert.

In 1959 he moved Lotus from Hornsey to Delamere Road, Cheshunt in Herfordshire, where the Lotus Elan was produced alongside the finishing line for the Lotus-Cortina. When Chapman found out how much money he was losing on the Elite, he stopped building it.

By 1965 the Cheshunt factory was bursting at the seams, and Chapman moved into a brand-new building on the site of the former Hethel airfield near Wymondham, south of Norwich, which became the home of the Lotus Europa, the Renault-powered coupé. He also bought an interest in the Moonraker boat-building company and talked about starting production of light aeroplanes.

In 1968 he organised the Lotus Group as a public stock corporation with three main subsidiaries: Lotus Cars Ltd for the road cars and kit cars, Lotus Components Ltd for building clients' racing cars, and Team Lotus Ltd for the group's own racing activities.

By 1970 Lotus Cars Ltd was turning out 3000 cars a year, and Chapman decided to make his own engines. About £7.5 million were spent on setting up an engine factory at Hethel. Chapman learned of Kjell Qvale's plans to build a Jensen-Healey sports car and offered to supply the engine, and secured a contract in 1971. In 1976 he bought Ketteringham Hall, near Hethel, where he installed an experimental design office.

It was easy for Chapman and Lotus to make headlines, but he had no magic wand for turning headlines into financial gain. In 1977 he turned to American Express for a credit line, and in 1978 he signed up to handle development work and redesign of the DeLorean sports car. In 1981 a technical co-operation scheme between Lotus and Toyota was announced, which ended up in Toyota Motor Co. buying a 15 per cent stake in Lotus Cars Ltd.

The market for Lotus road and racing cars, however, was in decline, and in 1980 the DeLorean contract brought in 55per cent of the Lotus Group's £14.3m turnover.

Most of the DeLorean payments were channelled through a Panama-registered company with a letter-drop address in Switzerland. This may have bought Chapman some time, but did not bring lasting solvency. By the end of 1981, the Lotus Group declared a loss of £109,000 and debts of £388,000. The credit line from American Express was due to expire in September 1982.

A press release from Lotus Cars Ltd dated 16 December 1982, stated that Colin Chapman had 'suffered a heart attack at home in the early hours of this morning' and was dead.

He married Hazel Williams in 1954. They had two daughters, Jane born in 1956 and Sarah born in 1957, and one son, Clive, born in 1962.

JPN

in 1973, the manufacture of the Seven was taken over by CATERHAM Cars, a Lotus agent.

The Elan bowed out in 1974 having been made in four distinct base versions, plus special editions. A works-approved version with a BRM-tuned engine was made by works Lotus and BRM driver, Mike Spence, and was sold through his garage.

In the meantime, Lotus was diversifying and was winning a reputation as an engineering consultant. The company produced its own 5-speed gearbox and a new '4-valve' engine which was first used in the Jensen-Healey. The introduction of VAT in 1973 closed the tax loophole which caused most Lotus cars sold in Britain to be kits. Lotus decided to move up-market, selling only fully assembled cars, although the company was still dogged by a reputation for poor quality and reliability.

The Elan +2 was phased out in 1973, with 5200 made; the Elan in 1974 (7895 made) and the Europa (9230 made) followed in 1975.

In 1974 came the Elite, offered in four levels of trim, with a fibreglass 4-seat estate-style body, a backbone chassis, coil spring and double wishbone front suspension and irs by coil springs, fixed drive shafts, lower wishbones and radius rods. It was powered by Lotus' new double-ohc 16-valve, 2-litre, 4-cylinder engine which delivered its 160bhp via a 5-speed gearbox.

Lotus' second 'new generation' car, the Eclat, was a 2+2 fastback version of the Elite, also offered in four levels of trim. It was about 100lbs lighter and would reach 122mph (196km/h) (0–62mph/0–100km/h in 7.9 seconds). There was also an economy model, the Eclat 520, which had a skimpy interior, 4-speed Ford gearbox, and steel wheels. In America the Eclat was sold as the Lotus 'Sprint' while, in the UK from 1977, there was an Eclat Sprint special edition.

In 1972, Lotus showed a prototype with a body by Giugiaro on a Europa chassis and, by 1975, this had become the Esprit which shared its engine and suspension with the Elite/Eclat although it had a new backbone chassis with inboard rear brakes and a 5-speed Citroën transaxle.

The Esprit S1 sold 994 examples from 1976 to 1978, despite disappointing performance (123mph/198km/h top speed, 0–62mph/0–100km/h in 8.4 seconds) and problems with engine vibration and cooling. These problems were solved on the 1978 S2 with a new camshaft, wider wheels, revised interior, and improved cooling. Performance improved to 134mph (216km/h) top speed and 0–62mph/0–100km/h in 8.0 seconds.

During the S2's life, 1978 to 1980, 980 were made and it became the 2.2 in 1980 when it received the larger, and more torquey, 2174cc Type 912 engine. Only 88 examples of the 2.2 were made, largely because Lotus had launched the Esprit Turbo. It was anyway soon replaced by the normally aspirated S3.

The Esprit Turbo had a re-worked 210bhp engine and it set new performance standards for its class: 147mph (237km/h), 0–62mph (0–100km/h) in 6.1 seconds. The Turbo had a stiffer chassis, bigger bumpers, a new front spoiler, improved brakes, and larger wheels. The first 100 cars (of 1658, 1980 to 1987) were finished in the colours of the sponsor of the Lotus Formula One team, Essex Petroleum.

In 1980, Lotus' de facto consultancy work was formalised with the establishment of Lotus Engineering. Much of the company's work has been confidential, but its client list is long. Lotus Engineering has specialised in suspension work, but other projects have included the Sinclair C5 runabout and bicycles for both competition and road use.

In December 1982, Colin Chapman died of a heart attack and he died with his legend intact – he would otherwise have ended his days in disgrace since he had been involved in a fraud, siphoning money from the British government for engineering work undertaken for DeLorean. The judge who sentenced Lotus accountant, Fred Bushell, to prison said that Chapman would have received at least ten years.

Chapman's cars had won 72 World Championship races, six drivers' championships and seven Constructors' Cups. Lotus had introduced monocoque construction to Formula, the use of the engine/transmission as an integral element of the structure, ground effect aerodynamics, carbonfibre construction (concurrent with McLaren) and active suspension.

At the same time as Chapman, and others, were creaming money for themselves, Group Lotus was in debt to its bank and was desperate to raise money to finance a 'new Elan' which was then running in prototype form.

In 1983, British Car Auctions became the major share-holder, in a holding operation, and Toyota took a 20 per cent stake. Toyota's original MR-2 sports car was a Lotus design and Toyota was interested in buying Lotus. Prototype

1999 Lotus (i) Elise 111S sports car.
LOTUS

1999 Lotus (i) Elise 340R sports car.
LOTUS

'replacement Elans' had Toyota mechanicals, but the British government discouraged the move and Lotus was bought by General Motors in 1985.

Lotus also sketched a high speed armour-protected saloon, the 'Eminence', and progressed some way with the 'Etna', a mid-engined coupé. Both were designed to use a 4-litre V8 engine which was essentially two double-ohc 'fours' in harmony. Neither of these projects reached fruition.

In 1985, the Esprit received a revised chassis and front suspension and, by then, top speed had risen to 151mph (243km/h) (0–62mph/0–100km/h in 5.5 seconds). The normally aspirated S3 (767 made, 1981 to 1987) had most of the improvements of the Turbo model and also a new rear suspension layout with lower wishbones, semi-trailing arms, and upper links which were incorporated into the Turbo and later adopted by the Excel when it replaced the Eclat. This model was capable of 133mph (214km/h) and 0–62mph (0–100km/h) in 6.7 seconds.

As the Esprit received the 2.2-litre engine in 1980, so did the Elite although

the model was considered dated and only 133 S2.2 models were made, 1980 to 1983, despite the new engine and a 5-speed Getrag gearbox.

The Eclat was also sold as a S2.2 from 1980, it had all the improvements of the Elite, but it also suffered the same indifference from the public. Just 223 were sold, 1980 to 1985, when it was replaced by the Excel. The Excel was the successor to the Eclat, but was extensively re-engineered with softer body styling, a Toyota 5-speed gearbox and Toyota brake components. The rear suspension was revised along the lines of the Esprit S3; top speed was 133mph (214km/h) and 0–62mph (0–100km/h) was in 7.0 seconds. In October 1985 came the high compression 180bhp SE model and, in 1986, came the SA with a 4-speed ZF automatic transmission.

In 1987, Giugiaro's body for the Esprit was replaced by an in-house design by Peter Stevens. The 172bhp engine, mated to a Renault GTA transaxle, propelled the Esprit S4 to 137mph (220km/h) (0–62mph (0–100km/h) in 6.5 seconds). There was also a Turbo version whose 229bhp meant 149mph (240km/h) (0–62mph (0–100km/h) in 5.3 seconds). In 1989, came the Turbo SE whose 264bhp translated to 161mph (259km/h) (0–62mph (0–100km/h) in 4.7 seconds).

Meanwhile, the connection with General Motors produced the 5.7-litre V8 LT5 engine which was used in the Chevrolet Corvette ZR-1 (and also by Mercury Marine) and the Vauxhall-Lotus Carlton, a twin-turbo saloon capable of 168mph+ (270km/h+). By the end of 1987, Lotus was a spent force in Formula One although it took a few more years for that to become clear. Team Lotus (a subsidiary company of Group Lotus) did not race after 1994, although it exists as a service operation.

In 1989, Lotus finally made a new Elan with front-wheel drive. This was almost heresy, but Lotus broke the mould by using patented interactive wishbone suspension on a floating front subframe and it received enthusiastic reviews. The chassis was a backbone affair, and the body was of composites (in 1982, Lotus asked writers to use 'composites', not 'fibreglass'). The transversely mounted 1588cc engine was badged 'Isuzu Lotus' – Lotus had helped design the unit. The double-ohc 4-valve 4-cylinder engine produced 130bhp when fuel injected, 165bhp when turbocharged. In normally aspirated form, top speed was 120mph (193km/h) (0–62mph (0–100km/h) in 8.2 seconds), but the turbocharged SE model could top 135mph (217km/h) (0–62mph (0–100km/h) in 6.5 seconds).

The Excel was phased out during 1992, when Lotus abruptly dropped the Elan. Although well received by the press, it was too expensive to sell strongly–the Mazda MX-5, which was inspired by the original Elan, was a much cheaper alternative–and Lotus made no money on the car. That left only the Esprit.

The following year, Lotus was bought by Bugatti but, by the time that Bugatti went into receivership in 1995, most of the Elan production line had been sold to the Korean company, Kia, which has since marketed a revised version, the 'Sports'.

Before Bugatti's collapse, Lotus unveiled the Elise, a mid-engined sports car with a 1.7-litre Rover K-series engine and a revolutionary form of chassis construction where aluminium components were glued together – the chassis weighed a mere 70 kg. The driver's seat was to the fore of the passenger's, in order to optimise weight distribution and it was the world's first production car to use aluminium composite brakes. Top speed was 124mph (200km/h) (0–62 (0–100km/h) in 5.9 seconds) and roadholding was hailed as outstanding. At the 1996 Geneva Motor Show, Lotus showed a new 3.5-litre V8 engine. Shortly afterwards the company was bought by the Malaysian company, Proton.

The Elise found a ready audience, and it was widely felt that Lotus had found its soul once more. The Esprit, now in S4 spec., with such features as ABS and air conditioning, was available with either the 240bhp 4-cylinder turbo engine (163mph (262km/h), 0–62mph (0–100km/h) in 5.2 seconds – remarkable figures for so small an engine) or with the new V8.

The twin-turbo V8 produced 350bhp and could power the Esprit to 175mph (282km/h) (0–62mph (0–100km/h) in 4.6 seconds) and the cars were distinguished by a high rear aerofoil. As with the 4-cylinder Esprit, there were also versions for GT racing.

Late in 1998 Lotus announced a wide package of detail improvements on all Esprit models and the range was GT3 (2-litre), V8-GT (a 'softer' car limited to 170mph/274km/h), V8-SE (175mph/282km/h) and the limited edition Sport 350 which incorporated parts from the competition cars. It also exhibited the 340R – so-called because power/weight ratio was 340bhp per tonne. It was a stripped-down Elise with a one-piece, doorless, removable body made from carbon composites and cycle mudguards. A special 170bhp version of the K-series engine was promised. At the 1999 Frankfurt Show, Lotus launched a concept coupé, provisionally called the M250. It had a mid-mounted 250bhp 3-litre V6 engine, driving through a 6-speed gearbox, and a bonded aluminium and carbon fibre structure. Production was planned to start early in 2001. Lotus at last appeared to be returning to the spirit, and excitement, of the Colin Chapman days, but without the quality control problems and financial instability.

MJL

Further Reading
Lotus – the First Ten Years, Ian H. Smith, Motor Racing Publications, 1958.
The Story of Lotus 1961–1971, Doug Nye, Motor Racing Publications, 1972.
Colin Chapmann's Lotus, Robin Head, Haynes, 1989.
Lotus Seven, a Collector's Guide, Jeremy Coulter,
Motor Racing Publications, 1995.
Lotus Elan and Europa, a Collector's Guide, John Bolster,
Motor Racing Publications, 1980.
Lotus Esprit, the Complete Story, Jeremy Walton, Crowood AutoClassics, 1997.
Lotus Elise, John Tipler, Crowood AutoClassics, 1999.

LOTUS (ii) (NZ) 1973–1975
Steel Brothers (Addington) Ltd, Christchurch, South Island.
The rights, jigs and moulds for the Lotus 7 S4 were purchased when production ceased in England. For New Zealand, the frame was strengthened at the expense of an added 9kg. The engine was the 1558cc Lotus-Ford twin-ohc unit and 100 cars were built before it ceased to be available. The Vauxhall-Lotus 907 unit was adopted and the Super 907 was being readied for production when legislative changes killed it.

MG

LOUBIÈRE; ARBEL (F) 1951–1958
1951–1953 Compagnie Normande d'Études, Paris.
1958 Sté François Arbel, Paris.
Also known as the Symétric, Casimir Loubière's design used petrol-electric drive from a 1100cc Simca engine via a generator to electric motors in each wheel.

1903 Louet 9hp tonneau.

It had an all-plastic body, the panels for the bonnet and front wings being used in reverse for the luggage boot and rear wings, hence the name Symétric. The doors slid under the car when opened, with the windows rotating into the roof. It never went into production, but the design re-appeared in 1958 under the name Arbel, with a completely re-styled body and a choice of rotary petrol engine, or one fuelled by the residue from nuclear power plants!

NG

LOUET (F) 1902–1908
1902–1904 Sté des Automobiles Louet, Paris.
1904–1908 E. Louet et Badin, Auxerre, Yonne.
Louet entered the market with a chain-driven car powered by an 18hp 3-cylinder engine. In 1904 a full range of cars was offered including a 6hp single-cylinder, 9hp twin and 12hp 3-cylinder. They also made 40, 70 and 120hp 6-cylinder engines for marine or aircraft use and listed cars with the 40 and 70hp engines. At least one was built, and shown at the 1904 Paris Salon in a shaft-drive chassis with a wheelbase of 147½in (3744mm). In 1905 a new 24/30hp 4-cylinder shaft-drive car was introduced, though the chain-driven 2- and 3-cylinder models were still made.

NG

LOUIS CHÉNARD (F) 1920–c.1932
Automobiles Louis Chénard, Colombes, Seine.
The Louis Chénard was a light car powered by proprietary engines, mainly Chapuis-Dornier, at first a 1095cc 7/9CV with 3-speed gearbox, joined by a 1494cc 10CV with 4 speeds. These two models were still listed in 1926 with quite a wide range of bodies including 2-, 3- and 4-seater tourers, saloons for four or six passengers and two types of commercial vehicle. Some lists carry the make to 1935, but production cannot be substantiated as late as that. They were certainly still active in 1931, when their agent showed three cars at the Lille Salon. There is no known connection with the Chenard family who made the Chenard-Walcker.

NG

LOUISELL (US) c.1989–1995
Louisell Enterprises, Mount Pleasant, Michigan.
An American TV programme called Knight Rider featured a high-tech version of the Pontiac Firebird named 'Kitt' that was loaded with crime-fighting electronics. Louisell made a custom interior and exterior kit for Firebirds that replicated the TV car. The interior package included two television monitors, an overhead console with keypad and switches, and an array of lights and readouts. The nose had a sequential scanner and other TV-correct trim. Louisell later added a kit replica of the Pontiac Banshee show car that was installed on Firebirds and Camaros. They were sold in kit form or Louisell would install the parts on the customer's car.

HP

LOUIS RENARD (F) 1940–1942
Automobiles Électriques Louis Renard, Lyons.
One of many small electric cars made in France during World War II, the Louis Renard differed from most in being a 3-wheeler, with drive to the single rear

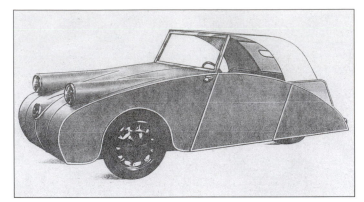

c.1942 Louis Renard electric 3-wheeler.
NICK GEORGANO

1911 Lozier (i) Type 46 Lakewood Torpedo.
NICK BALDWIN

wheel. Top speed was 25mph (40km/h), and range up to 50 miles (80km). M. Renard announced that he would deliver 500 cars by June 1941, but output was probably much less. He planned to restrict sales to a radius of about 150km around Lyons; for places further afield such as Paris, Marseilles and Bordeaux, he would sell licences to other manufacturers. A 4-wheeled taxi was also promised, but may never have been made.

NG

LOUTZKY (D) 1899–1900

Gesellschaft für Automobilewagenbau, Berlin.

Russian-born Boris Loutsky was a capable engineer who was better known for his designs for other car makers. However he made a few small cars with $3\frac{1}{2}$ hp 2-cylinder engines, bicycle-type front forks and handlebar steering. He also made a postal delivery van with front-mounted box and driver's seat at the rear, powered by a 5hp engine below the driver's seat.

NG

LOUVET (F) 1908–1914

E. Louvet, Courbevoie, Seine.

Apart from a listing that cars were made from 1908 to 1914, the only evidence for this make are a surviving car and a faded photograph dating from 1910, which turned out to be of the survivor. This is a 2-seater with concealed dickey seat, powered by a 4-cylinder Chapuis-Dornier engine.

NG

LOVEL (B) 1995 to date

Lovel Sports Cars, Zandstraat, Bruges.

The superbike-engined 3-wheeler was a phenomenon of the 1990s and the Lovel F20 was a Belgian/Dutch project in this vein, created by a Dutch engineer who built numerous one-off prototypes for friends in the 1980s. In 1996 he gained Dutch type approval for the Lovel F20, and the production vehicle was then made by the Van der Starre brothers. Its chassis was a tubular aluminium frame with an alloy-panelled centre section and specially-made suspension consisting of double wishbones up front and a steel swinging arm at the rear. A wide variety of Japanese 4-cylinder motorbike engines could be fitted centrally, but as a good example, the 153bhp Suzuki GSX-R1100 engine provided a

power-to-weight ratio of 450bhp per ton. The open fibreglass/ carbonfibre bodywork was unstressed and featured twin head fairings and no doors. Both complete and kit-form versions were marketed.

CR

LOWELL (US) 1908–1909

Lowell-American Automobile Co., Lowell, Massachusetts.

The Lowell Motor Co. had been building engines for the motor trade since the turn of the century, and in 1908 organised a subsidiary company to make complete cars. These were said to be of 4, 6, or 8-cylinder models, but it seems that only a 16/20hp four was built, and in a single style, a 2-seater runabout. Few of these were made, and the Lowell did not survive 1909.

NG

LOYD-LORD (GB) 1922–1924

Loyd-Lord Ltd, Chiswick, London.

Designed by A.O. Lord who was responsible for the engine of the ALBERT, in partnership with Mr Loyd, later associated with Carden-Loyd tracked military vehicles, the Loyd-Lord started out as a conventional car with 1795 or 2120cc 4-cylinder ohv Meadows engines, Meadows 4-speed gearboxes and a substantial tourer body. With the smaller engine it was the 12/30hp, with the larger, the 14/30 or 14/40hp. After 38 cars had been made, Lord turned to the 2-stroke engine, building his own designs of air-cooled engines with separately-cast cylinders of 1082cc 2-cylinder (11hp) or 2009cc 4-cylinder (18/60hp). They were supercharged by rotary blowers. They still used Meadows gearboxes, of 3- or 4-speeds, and the 18/60 had front-wheel brakes, but the unconventional engines scared buyers away, and very few of the 2-strokes were made.

NG

LOZIER (i) (US) 1905–1918

1905–1915 Lozier Motor Co., Plattsburgh, New York.
1910–1918 Lozier Motor Co., Detroit, Michigan.

Henry Abram Lozier made a fortune from sewing machines and bicycles, selling his Toledo-based cycle factories to the American Bicycle Co. for $4 million in 1897. He invested this in the Lozier Motor Co. which made marine engines at Plattsburgh, New York, from 1900. In their first year they made 200 engines which powered many expensive cabin cruisers and racing boats, acquiring a good reputation among the moneyed clientele who would be buying their cars a few years later. A 2-seater steam runabout was built in 1901, and a petrol car at about the same time. In 1902 Lozier sent one of the company engineers, J.M. Whitbeck, to Europe to study the best in car design, and the following year another engineer, John G. Perrin, studied closely all the high-class imported cars there were to be seen in New York. Together they came up with their ideal of an expensive car, and the result made its appearance at the New York Automobile Show in January 1905. It had a 30/35hp 4-cylinder T-head engine, 4-speed gearbox and chain drive. The show car was made by the Ball Manufacturing Co. of Stanford, Connecticut, in a factory which became Perrin's experimental department, once production got under way at Plattsburgh early in 1905. Only one body style was offered in the first year, an aluminium 5-seater tourer priced at $4500, which put it in competition with Locomobile and top-class imports such as Mercedes, C.G.V. and Fiat.

H.A. Lozier had died in 1903, but he was succeeded by his son Harry A. Lozier, who was enthusiastic about the car-building programme. Only 25 cars were sold in 1905, but the following year, when larger engines of 40 and 60hp were available as well as the 35, Lozier sold 56 cars, some landaulets and limousines as well as the tourers. Perrin spent a year with the Pope-Waverly electric car company in Indianapolis, but returned to Lozier to design the 1907 models, which included the Model E 60hp tourer at $7000 and limousine at $8000. These had water-cooled brakes. The 1908 models had shaft drive and included Lozier's first six, the 50hp Type I. From 1909 models began to be named after exclusive country clubs and hotels, such as Briarcliff, Lakewood, Meadowbrook and Riverside. The head of the sales department was Frederick Chandler, who had looked after the old company's bicycle business in Germany, and would later be a successful car maker himself.

In 1910 the Plattsburgh factory turned out 528 cars, close to the maximum capacity of 600, and Harry Lozier was persuaded to build an additional factory in Detroit. Costing more than $1 million and occupying a 65-acre site, it was designed by Albert Kahn who was responsible for Ford's Highland Park and River Rouge plants, and would later build the Ford-backed GAZ factory at Gorki in Russia. Its capacity was double that of Plattsburgh, and the plan was to build a cheaper car selling for about $3500 there, and leave Plattsburgh to concentrate on the luxury cars. The 6-cylinder Type 77 was not announced until September 1912, by which time Harry Lozier had been eased out of his company by the Detroit investors. He later made the H.A.L. at Cleveland. Lozier's new president Harry M. Jewett, claimed that 450 Type 77s had been sold before the first one left the factory in December 1912. This may have been true, but the staff lacked confidence in the new management, and in January 1913 five leading officials, including Frederick Chandler, left to form the CHANDLER Motor Car Co. This was the beginning of the end for Lozier. For the 1914 season Perrin was asked to design an even lower-priced car, the 28hp 4-cylinder Type 84 to sell for $2100. There were plenty of cars in this price range, including Cadillac who would soon offer a V8 at that price. Sales in 1914, from both factories, were not more than 250, and by the end of the year Lozier was in receivership. The Plattsburgh plant was sold in March 1915 and so was the large Detroit plant. Under new management Lozier moved to a small factory, also in Detroit, and production of the Type 84 four and Type 82 six limped on into mid–1918, but only 62 cars were made that year. There was a revival of the name in 1922 (see LOZIER (ii)), but the connection with the older firm cannot be established.

NG

Further Reading
'Lozier: the big one got away', Beverley Rae Kimes,
Automobile Quarterly, Vol. 7, No. 4.

LOZIER (ii) (US) 1922

Lozier Motor Co. of New York, New York.

There is an aura of mystery surrounding the 1922 Lozier, of which comparatively little is known today. The car was cited, if not advertised, in one or two trade publications of the period as available, in touring car form, at $8500 and as a limousine for $10,000. One theory on its existence believes that it might have been a survival of the earlier Lozier company of Plattsburgh, New York and Detroit, Michigan which had at least begun re-organisation in 1918, although its size and price range would not give credence to this. One photograph is known to exist which shows the touring car, the radiator shape of which is in contrast to the earlier Loziers. The 1922 car was termed the Model 92. It was listed as having a 6-cylinder engine of its own manufacture with a $4^3/_4 \times 5^1/_2$in bore and stroke developing 110bhp, featured disc wheels plus two side-mounted spares and a chassis of 142in (3604mm). The touring car was reported as having weighed 4600lb.

KM

L.P.C. *see* LEWIS (iii)

L&R (GB) 1993 to date

L&R Roadsters, Bobbington, West Midlands.

There was a sudden rash of Triumph TR3 kit-form replicas in the early 1990s, and the L&R 3 was novel in that its intention was to create a very accurate looking replica, while underneath offering modern engineering. This consisted of a robust steel space frame chassis and Ford mechanical components.

CR

L-S *see* POLSKI-FIAT

L.S.D. (GB) 1920–1924

1920–1923 Sykes & Sugden Ltd, Huddersfield, Yorkshire.
1923–1924 L.S.D. Motor Co. Ltd, Mirfield, Yorkshire.

The L.S.D. 3-wheeler was a Yorkshire product through and through, being designed by a Mr Longbottom and made by Messrs Sykes and Sugden. Only the engines came from further afield, being V-twins by MAG or J.A.P. of 964cc driving through a 2-speed gearbox and chain to the single rear wheel. Unlike many 3-wheelers, the L.S.D. was fitted with a reverse gear. Suspension was unusual, being independent by horizontal coils at the front, and quarter-elliptic at the rear. The Huddersfield factory, which employed no more than 50 men and also produced domestic gaslight fittings, made several hundred cars, total production in both factories being 640. After the L.S.D. operation at Mirfield

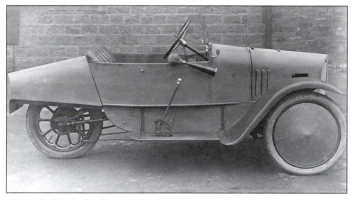

1919/20 L.S.D. 3-wheeler.
NICK BALDWIN

1924 L.S.D. 3-wheeler.
NICK BALDWIN

closed down, Ivor Blakey acquired the remaining components and made about 30 more. It is said that parts to build several more still exist in Norfolk.

NG

L.S.R. (I) 1954

Laboratorio Studi Resine, Castellanza.

First seen in January 1954, the L.S.R. was the first-ever Italian fibreglass-bodied car. It had a doorless sports 2-seater body with a Plexiglass half-windscreen.

CR

L.T. (S) 1923

Anders Rudolf Lindström, Torsby.

This was a neat-looking small car with a vee 'radiator' even though the 20bhp engine was air-cooled, a 3-speed gearbox and front-wheel drive. The engine was made by Solbergs Mekaniska Verkstad at Forshaga. Lindström planned to make at least 50 cars, but only three were completed, of which one was exported to Norway. Lack of capital and a factory fire prevented more being made.

NG

LuAZ (SU) 1967–1998

Lutskji Avtomobilnji Zavod, Lutsk, Ukraine.

LuMZ, a factory in the Ukrainin town of Lutsk, built special bodywork (including refrigerated) on various types of car and truck chassis. A chance to become an automobile manufacturer was accepted enthusiastically and late in 1967 the works was renamed LuAZ – Lutskji Avtomobilnji Zavod. Two models were first developed at Zaporoshje, ZAZ-969 V with front-wheel drive and a 4×4 named ZAZ-969. Both used a 30bhp air-cooled engine. The Soviet Union's first front-wheel drive car had a curb weight of 820kg, rear wheel drive added 50kg. A reduction ratio of 1.2 and a locking rear differential were useful for off-road work. Wheel reduction (1.785) brought ground clearance up to remarkable 284mm. LuAZ showed its benefits as an excellent all-terrain vehicle in deep mud and snow, taking 30 degrees slopes and nearly half-metre deep fords.

1901 Luc Court 8hp 2-seater.
NATIONAL MOTOR MUSEUM

1914 Luc Court H4S tourer.
NICK BALDWIN

Wheelbase was only 71in (1800mm) and overall length 129in (3270mm). The cars were capable of taking four people and 100kg of luggage (or two people and 250kg of luggage). Top speed was a low 46.6mph (75km/h).

In 1975 an interim model LuAZ-969A received a 40bhp (1197cc) engine and wheel reduction of 1.294. Real change came with the LuAZ-969M of 1979, by which time over 54,000 first generation cars had been made. The new car was about 4in (100mm) longer and 1.5in (40mm) wider, with more rounded bodywork. The bodies of these cars were self-supporting, with a simple ladder frame welded directly to the body. The rear seats were foldable to the sides and a 1.4m² of cargo space could be created this way. In ten years (1979–1989) nearly 127,000 969M models were built.

Mechanically these cars were dependent on advances at Melitopol Motor Works and Zaporozhje Automobile Works. When a 1091cc water-cooled engine of 53bhp for the Tavria became available, it was also used in the LuAZ-1302. Larger 135in (3430mm) length and with closed bodywork, the new model became much heavier – 970kg. A few cars also featured a 3-cylinder turbodiesel of 1206cc (60bhp) which reduced unsatisfactory fuel consumption of 10–15l/100 km by 2 to 3 litres. The model LuAZ-1301 with a Tavria engine, a permanent 4WD and a central differential had a 86in (2190mm) wheelbase with a steel stress-bearing structure and plastic exterior panels.

In 1994 only about 2500 cars were assembled, and from there the firm gradually ceased automobile manufacture: in 1997 just 55 cars were made and in 1998 only 4 units. By then AvtoZAZ was the sole remaining Ukrainian auto works.

MHK

LUC (D) 1909–1914
Loeb & Co. GmbH, Berlin.
After acting as agents for various well-known makes, such as Benz, Fiat and Panhard, the Loeb company started to make their own cars in 1909. Their first

was the 3-litre 12/36PS, and from 1911 they turned to sleeve-valve engines, importing English Daimler chassis and fitting them with German bodies. Sold as Luc-Knights, these were the 2025cc 8/22PS and the 4084cc 16/40PS. At the same time two models were offered with conventional side-valve engines, the 2612cc 10/30PS and the 3052cc 12/36PS. The 10/30PS had a complex rear suspension with double semi-elliptic springs and auxiliary coil springs. Aero engines and trucks were made during the war, and Loeb did not return to car manufacture. In 1920 the factory was taken over by Dinos.

NG

LUCANIA see OPPERMAN

LUCAR (GB) 1914
Lucar Ltd, Brixton, London.
This was a light car powered by a 1093cc 10hp 4-cylinder Aster engine, with a 2-seater body and shaft drive. Fully equipped with electric lighting and starting, it was priced at 190 guineas (£199.50).

NG

LUCCIOLA (I) 1948–1949
An engineer called G.B. Pennacchio created the streamlined Lucciola 3-wheeled coupé. Its full-width body looked pleasingly modern but only measured 118in (3000mm) long. The rear-mounted 250cc single-cylinder engine was a Condor-Guidetti 4-stroke usually seen in stationary machinery. Both the brakes and gearbox were hydraulically operated. Lucciola means firefly in Italian and, after a 1948 Milan show appearance, the life of this car was more like the mayfly.

CR

LUC COURT (F) 1899–1936
Sté des Anciens Établissements Luc Court et Cie, Lyons.
Luc Court (1862–1942) was born at Rives, Isère and became an electrical engineer, setting up his own business in Lyons in 1892. Seven years later he became interested in cars ('saisi par le démon automobile', as a French historian wrote), and built a light car powered by a horizontal 2-cylinder engine with 5-speed gearbox (very unusual for the time) and double-chain drive. It was followed by a 10hp twin, and in 1902 a 4-cylinder Luc Court was third in the Mont Ventoux hill climb. A 20/24hp four was made in 1904, and small-scale production of 4-cylinder cars continued over the next few years. In 1906 these were of 12/16, 18/24 and 30/40hp, all with chain drive, though the 10/14hp twin had shaft drive. In 1907 they acquired the patent for the Lacoin detachable chassis. In this the whole chassis behind the engine section could be removed and replaced with another carrying a different body. It was an alternative to the more common system whereby alternative bodies, especially an open summer one and a closed winter one, were mounted on the same chassis. The Lacoin system had the additional advantage that a different countershaft ratio could be used, a lower ratio for the heavier body.

In 1909 Luc Court introduced two engines with the same long-stroke dimensions of 70 × 140mm, the 2154cc H4 and 3230cc H6. These were very long lived, the H4 continuing until the end of passenger car production in 1936. Both chassis were chain-driven until 1915. Although Luc Court extended his works, they were never large, and as cars and trucks had to share the premises and workforce with stationary engines and generators for lighting systems, and also electric cranes, winches, hoists and windlasses, output was never more than two or three vehicles per week. The 1920 Luc Court catalogue ran to 48 pages, of which only one was devoted to road vehicles!

The H4 was revived after the war, joined by the 4.7-litre HR which was made from 1920 to 1925. They were mostly solid touring cars, though there was an H4S with single-ohc engine and sporting bodywork with vee-windscreen and pointed tail, made from 1924 to 1926. Commercial vehicles became increasingly important from the mid-1920s, as passenger car production declined. The H4 was the only model, and by the early 1930s they were said to be available to special order only. The only body style was the classic *conduite intérieure avec malle* (saloon with luggage boot), unchanged from 1932 to 1935, but for 1936 the company produced a modernised version looking not unlike the contemporary Peugeot 301. It is surprising that Luc Court went to the trouble of bringing out a new model (though still with the ancient H4 engine) when sales were minimal. Perhaps they hoped to revive car production, but in fact none were made after

1936. Commercial vehicles, some powered by diesel engines made in-house, were built until 1952.

NG

Further Reading
'Centre Court', M. Worthington-Williams, *The Automobile*, July 1997.

LUCERNA (CH) 1907–c.1909

A.H. Grivel, Lucerne.

Grivel was the Swiss importer of ASTER engines. Four different passenger car models with chassis from the French company Malicet et Blin, all with shaft drive, were offered for sale in 1908. The 4-cylinder engines of 10/14hp, 14/18hp and 20/24hp as well as an in-line six 20/24hp came from ASTER. There were also two commercial vehicles with chain drive. The marque disappeared about 1909 after only a few cars had been made.

FH

LUCERTOLA *see* FERMI

LUCIA (CH) 1903–1908

1903–1904 Lucien Picker, Geneva.
1904–1908 Sté des Établissements L. Picker, Moccand & Cie, Geneva.

After building a 2-cylinder boat engine and stationary engines, Lucien Picker in 1903 presented his first motorcar with an advanced L-head 4-cylinder in-line engine with five bearings of 16bhp of his own construction. It was a good looking tonneau with 3-speed gearbox and chain drive. Its buyer, Charles Moccand, was so pleased with the car that he offered a partnership and the newly formed company moved into larger premises to start production in small series. Only a few of the small 12/16hp type with vertical twin engine were made, but the larger 24/30hp with a 4-cylinder separately cast engine with hemispherical chambers of 4396cc enjoyed much better demand.

The Lucia chamber preceded the Ricardo-head by 18 years but Picker never thought of applying for a patent. The company had a staff of 50 workers and the majority of the approximately 100 chassis made between 1904 and 1908 were sold to France. In 1908 the last Lucia model with a new 24/30hp 4-cylinder engine of 5315cc and chain drive was launched. Owing to financial problems, the company was liquidated shortly after and the factory sold to SIGMA. Lucien Picker was offered a post with FIAT but he preferred to stay in Geneva and became director of the Mégevet company, which produced stationary engines.

FH

LUCIEN BOLLACK (F) 1929–1930

Lucien Bollack, Paris.

Lucien Bollack was one of the founders of B.N.C., and after he left that firm he set up a business importing Lycoming engines into France. There was a vogue for using these or Continental engines in French chassis and bodies, to make a relatively inexpensive luxury car. Among practitioners of this art were Delaunay-Belleville, Georges Irat, Guyot and Rolland-Pilain, and in 1929 Bollack joined their ranks. Naturally he used Lycoming engines, in 4350 or 5105cc sizes, completing the American theme with Warner gearboxes, Gemmer steering and Columbia rear axles. He was helped by the Auburn-Cord-Duesenberg group, who also owned Lycoming, and hoped to sell the Bollack car in America. The prototype had an attractive 2-door saloon body somewhat resembling the D8 Delage. Unfortunately the Wall Street Crash of October 1929 put an end to American support for Lucien Bollack, and it is likely that the coupé, which had been shown in chassis form at the 1929 Paris Salon, was the only Lucien Bollack car made.

NG

LUCK UTILITY (US) 1911–1914

Cleburne Auto Car Manufacturing Co., Cleburne, Texas.

The Rev. Harry Eugene Luck was a Texas preacher who wanted a car capable of travelling 'where there are no piked roads to run on'. To this end the Luck Utility which he built had solid tyres, though it was otherwise conventional, with a 25/30hp 4-cylinder engine and a roadster body which could be converted to a light delivery vehicle. The price was $950, but only about 20 cars were made, plus one heavier Luck Truck.

NG

1923 Luc Court H4 tourer.
FONDATION DE L'AUTOMOBILE M.BERLIET

LUDGATE *see* FLEETBRIDGE

LUFBÉRY (F) 1898–1902

C.E. Lufbéry, Chaunay, Aisne.

This pioneer French make used Daimler-type 2-cylinder engines and a combination of belt and epicyclic gearing which gave five forward speeds and three reverse. Final drive was by double chains, and the forward-control car had tiller steering. From 1900 Lufbéry used a 6hp 2-cylinder engine of his own design, still with the unconventional transmission. The cars were made for Lufbéry by Broquelin et Dupré, engineers in the same town of Chaunay.

NG

LUGLY (F) 1921

Sté des Automobiles Lugly, Courbevoie, Seine.

Apart from its curious and unappealing name, there was nothing to distinguish the Lugly from many other assembled cars of the time. It was powered by a 1590cc 4-cylinder side-valve Ballot engine and made with tourer body.

NG

LUKA DESIGN (F) 1998 to date

Luka Design, Suresnes.

Youthful designer Lucas Bignon presented his Silver Bee sports car at the 1998 Salon du Cabriolet. Its modern, avant garde design owed something to the spirit of the Lotus 7 and it was a real lightweight, tipping the scales at only 390kg. A mid-mounted Alfa Romeo 1.7-litre engine with 125bhp was fitted. It seemed however unlikely that the Silver Bee would enter production at an intended 300,000 francs.

CR

LU-LU *see* KEARNS

LUNA BUG (GB) 1970–1971

Self-Fit Ltd, Portsmouth, Hampshire.

This was a little-modified copy of the STIMSON Mini Bug, offered by the man who built the Mini Bug chassis.

CR

LUNANT (F) 1900–1914

Sté des Constructions de Cycles et Automobiles Lunant, Lyons.

J. Lunant was a cycle maker who built a few cars intermittently over a 14-year period. In 1900 he was listed as a maker of electric vehicles, and in 1902, less specifically, as a 'constructeur'. In 1906 he offered several models, of 8 and 10hp with single-cylinder engines, and fours of 16, 24 and 40hp, these larger models built to order only. In 1908 there were an 8/10hp single and a 16/20hp four. Prices

1897 (right) Lutzmann Arrow 0 light hunting car; (centre) Lutzmann Arrow 1 4-seater; (left) Kuhlstein electric car.
LUTZMANN ARCHIV MANFRED RIEDEL

1895 Lutzmann Arrow 1 3hp 2-seater.
LUTZMANN ARCHIV MANFRED RIEDEL

for these, 3900 and 7500 francs, were quoted for chassis only, but by 1913 Lunant was offering a 10/12hp monobloc 4-cylinder with shaft drive, complete with 4-seater body, for 7500 francs.

NG

LUNKENHEIMER (US) 1902

Lunkenheimer Motor Vehicle Co., Cincinnati, Ohio.

The Lunkenheimer company was a manufacturer of industrial valves which considered entering the automobile business. Toward this, two cars were built, one small with a 2-cylinder opposed engine housed under the front seat – the other a touring car on more conventional lines. Commercial production did not begin and the company returned to its original speciality.

KM

LURASTORE see REPLICAR

LURQUIN-COUDERT (F) 1906–1914

Lurquin et Coudert, Paris.

This company made tricars from 1906, and in 1911 brought out an early example of a cyclecar, powered by a V-twin Train engine with belt final drive. From 1912 they used chain drive.

NG

LUST (US) c.1985

Lust Cobra Inc., Ventura, California.

The low-cost Lust Cobra replica kit used a complete Ford Mustang II as the donor car. The Mustang body was cut away from the frame and reinforcements were added before the body was installed.

HP

LUTÈCE (F) 1906

G. Cochot, Colombes, Seine.

Cochot had made voiturettes under his own name in 1900, and in 1906 launched a conventional shaft-driven car with 12/14hp 4-cylinder engine under the name Lutèce (Lutecia was an ancient name for Paris). There were plans for it to be sold in England by Teste & Lassen, but they did not materialise. The make was still listed in the *Annuaire Générale de l'Automobile* in 1920, but there is no evidence that cars were being made as late as this. Cochot did, however, make a shaft-driven Lutèce motorcycle from 1921 to 1924.

NG

LUTONIA see HART

LUTZMANN (D) 1893–1898

F. Lutzmann, Dessau.

Friedrich Lutzmann was a pioneer German car maker, being anticipated only by Benz and Daimler in starting manufacture. He was a wheelwright and coachbuilder by appointment to the Grand Duke of Saxe-Anhalt, and in 1893 built a light car on Benz lines, called the Pfeil 0 (Arrow 0) with 3hp horizontal single-cylinder engine and chain drive and steering. In 1894 he produced a larger car with 2-litre engine, the Pfeil 1, followed in 1896 by a 2540cc engine, still a single-cylinder unit developing 5bhp at 300rpm; this was an even slower speed than that of the Benz Viktoria, which turned at 470rpm. Transmission was by belts and final drive by double chains. The standard body was a 2-seater victoria, but there was also a 4-seater *vis-à-vis*, a delivery van and a large, closed limousine featured in the catalogue. A Lutzmann was one of the first cars to be imported into Great Britain, in 1894, and several others followed. They exhibited two cars at the first German motor show, in 1897.

The following year Lutzmann sold his patents and designs to OPEL, who made them from 1899 as the Opel, system Lutzmann.

HON

LUVERNE (US) 1904–1918
1904–1906 Leicher Brothers, Luverne, Minnesota.
1906–1917 Luverne Automobile Co., Luverne, Minnesota.
Minnesota's most distinguished car began in a very modest way, when the brothers Fenton and Ed Leicher assembled a car from a kit of parts bought from A.L. DYKE of St Louis. In 1904 they built four high-wheelers of their own design but using Buick engines. In 1905 they started to make a conventional tourer powered by a 20hp 2-cylinder engine, which lasted until 1909 when it was joined by a 40hp four. This set the pattern for increasingly large touring cars made over the next eight years, culminating in the 60hp 6-cylinder ''Big Brown Luverne' made from 1913 to 1917. This impressive car, with German silver radiator and many coats of Luverne Brown paint, was made as a 7-seater tourer or 2-seater roadster. It had a 130in wheelbase, and sold for the relatively modest price of $2250–2500.

Luverne production was never high, averaging about 25 per year from 1906 to 1908, and 50 per year between 1909 and 1916. The engines came mostly from Rutenber. They built their first fire engine in 1912, followed by trucks which took over in importance from passenger cars. Only 25 of these, all Big Brown Luvernes, were made in 1917, and just one in 1918. Trucks were made until 1923, and fire equipment on other chassis has been made up to the present day by the Luverne Fire Equipment Co. The Leicher family remained in control until 1970.

NG

LUWO (D) 1922–1923
Kleinautobau Ludwig von Wolzogen, Munich.
Little is known about this short-lived car except that it had a 4/12PS Steudel 4-cylinder engine.

HON

LUX (i) (D) 1897–1902
1897–1898 Lux-Werke, Ludwigshafen.
1898–1902 Lux'sche Industriewerke AG, Ludwigshafen.
This company built gas lighting equipment, but with the coming of electricity this business declined, so they turned to cars. Their first model was a 4-seater *vis-à-vis* with 6hp horizontally-opposed 2-cylinder engine placed under the seat. It was somewhat similar to a Benz in appearance, and by 1900 was distinctly old-fashioned. The 1901–02 models were more modern, with front-mounted engines of 10/12hp, and a 4-seater tonneau body. An electric car was also offered by Lux, as well as light commercials with both petrol and electric power.

HON

LUX (ii) (I) 1905–1907
Fabbrica di Automobili e Cicli Lux, Turin.
Eugenio Paschetta was a bicycle maker who built cars for a short time. The first models had 10hp 2-cylinder engines, and later, 16hp 4-cylinder engines made under licence from DECAUVILLE.

NG

LUXIOR (F) 1912–1914
Berthaud et Moreau, Vincennes, Seine.
This was a conventional car powered by 4-cylinder engines in two sizes, 1779 or 2257cc. Both models had 3-speed gearboxes and shaft drive, and were distinguished by vee-radiators.

NG

L.W.C. (US) 1915–1917
Columbia Taxicab Co., St Louis, Missouri.

1903 Luverne 2-cylinder tonneau.
JOHN A. CONDE

1905 Luverne 20hp tourer.
JOHN A. CONDE

1897 Lux (i) 6hp *vis-à-vis*.
NATIONAL MOTOR MUSEUM

This taxicab-operating company, which ran a fleet of 100 cabs in St Louis, decided to make their own, and produced a design with 27hp 4-cylinder engine, said to have 'more the appearance of a high-price family car than a taxicab'. With this in mind, they offered them for sale to the general public at $3500 each. After 1917 they returned to buying cabs from other firms.

NG

1900 Lux (i) 6hp tonneau.
NATIONAL MOTOR MUSEUM

LYMAN (US) 1904

C.F. Lyman, Boston, Massachusetts.
C. Frederick Lyman built an expensive car powered by a 30/35hp 4-cylinder engine with 3-speed gearbox and shaft drive. It had a rear-entrance tonneau body with a detachable limousine top, and cost the high price of $6250. At the same time Lyman was offering a cheaper car in conjunction with J.A. Burnham, called the LYMAN & BURNHAM, with an office in the same street in Boston.
NG

LYMAN & BURNHAM (US) 1903–1905

Lyman & Burnham, Boston, Massachusetts.
The partners in this venture were C. Frederick Lyman who also made the Lyman car at the same time, and John Appleton Burnham who had been concerned with the BINNEY & BURNHAM steam car. The Lyman & Burnham was petrol-powered and offered four models with 2-cylinder engines, 10, 12, 15 and 24/26hp, with 2-speed gearbox and shaft drive. The frames were of angle steel and the bodies of wood with aluminium panels. It is not certain that all the larger-engined models were built, and production of all cars was pretty small. At least five were made, as they showed up in Massachusetts registrations for 1905. The address in Kirby Street, Boston, was an office only, as the cars were made for Lyman & Burnham by the Fore River Ship & Engine Co. of Quincy, Massachusetts.
NG

LYNCAR (GB) 1994

Lyncar Engineering, Slough, Berkshire.
With a background in racing car construction, Lyncar was well placed to make a roadgoing supercar. Designed by Martin Slater, it resembled a Jaguar XJ220 and featured scissor-type opening doors. The central monocoque was made of steel and aluminium, while tubular subframes carried wishbones suspension. The prototype used a mid-mounted Jaguar V12 engine driving the rear wheels via a transaxle. Despite appearances at various car shows over several years from 1994, no production cars were ever built.
CR

LYNX (i) (GB) 1975 to date

1975–1976 Lynx Engineering, Staplehurst, Kent.
1976–1980 Lynx Engineering, Northiam, Sussex.
1980 to date Lynx Motors International, St Leonards, Sussex.
Jaguar specialists Guy Black and Roger Ludgate created a Jaguar D-Type replica that would eventually become recognised as the very best. D-Type construction methods were followed, but no panels were interchangeable. The aluminium bodywork was initially by Williams & Pritchard, and the space frame front and rear ends accepted E-Type suspension and 3.8 or 4.2-litre XK engines. Long-nose, short-nose and XKSS versions were sold, mostly fully-built but some in kit form. A Lightweight E-Type replica was also produced and Lynx also made the Eventer, an estate body conversion of the Jaguar XJS; but its main business was either restoring or reproducing classic Jaguars.
CR

LYNX (ii) (GB) 1983–1984

Home-Builts, Stoke-on-Trent, Staffordshire.
The Lynx was a jeep-style car designed for a complete Mini van or estate floorpan. Using a set of plans retailing at only £5, the customer would fabricate all the sheet steel bodywork himself.
CR

LYNX (iii) (GB) 1985–1986

Lynx Kit Cars, Westcliffe-on-Sea, Essex.
The Lynx Bobtail was a rare example of a kit car designed specifically for Ford Capri donor parts. It was an open-topped utility design with a painted fibreglass body, cheap prices, and a solid chassis design. A pair of doors, weather gear and a hard-top were optional.
CR

LYNX (iv) (F) 1986–1987; 1993–1998

Lynx Automobiles SA, Boissise-le-Roi.
An extremely unpromising beginning marked Angelo Toma's Lynx marque, when it began importing and improving on the products of CHEETAH in Britain. These included a poor A.C. Cobra replica and a GT40 replica, both V8 powered. After six inactive years, in 1993 the marque returned with three replicas: an aluminium-bodied A.C. 289 with a 285bhp Ford V8; a GT40, again with aluminium bodywork and a Ford 5-litre V8; and the 7, a car inspired by the eponymous Lotus and fitted with a 220bhp Ford Cosworth engine. The GT40 was finally commercialised in 1996 at rather high prices.
CR

LYON (US) c.1982

Russ Lyon, Ramona, California.
The Lyon Mk V roadster was a superb 1930s style sports car built entirely by hand. It used steel body panels, a ladder-style chassis and a supercharged 375hp Jaguar 6-cylinder engine. The wire wheels were 19in in diameter, the interior was done in leather and ignition was by a cam-driven magneto mounted on the firewall. All casting patterns and the exquisite fabrication was done by Russ Lyon, a 29-year-old engineer. One was built and two more were offered for sale at $150,000 each. The Lyon Mk VI was a drophead coupé version with supercharged Jaguar 6 or V12 engines.
HP

LYONS (US) 1920

This was an export car sold in England by the London & Midland Motors Co. Its American maker is unknown. It was powered by a 35hp Herschell-Spillman 4-cylinder engine, and had a 5-seater tourer body and a radiator somewhat like that of a Rolls-Royce. The price was £725.
NG

LYONS-ATLAS; LYONS-KNIGHT (US) 1913–1915

Lyons-Atlas Co., Indianapolis, Indiana.
This company was formed by three Lyons brothers who bought out the Atlas Engine Works. This company had made 2-stroke engines and had recently started making Knight sleeve-valve engines. Doubtless this was the reason for the Lyons' interest, as a fashion for sleeve-valves was sweeping the industry. The car they put into production as the Lyons-Knight was designed by Harry A. Knox, and was generally similar to the ATLAS-KNIGHT he had been making in Springfield, Massachusetts. It had a 50hp 4-cylinder engine and was made in tourer and sedan models, with a 7-seater limousine added for 1915. For 1914 only there was a 6-cylinder model. Knox resigned in August 1915, and at the same time Lyons-Knight ended car production.
NG

MABON (GB) c.1924–1926

Mabon Motor Works, Tottenham, London.

This company supplied transmission units for the construction of 3-wheeled cyclecars, comprising clutch, enclosed shaft, 2-speed gearbox, crown and bevel wheel, hub fitted with two brakes and controls. They also apparently made some complete 3-wheelers, using their own engines. Their premises consisted of a row of lock-up garages, with a workshop at each end. The garages provided a useful income to supplement whatever they made from their engines, transmissions and cars. There was also a Mabon motorcycle made in Clerkenwell Road, London, before World War I, which may have been by the same family.

NG

MACDONALD (US) 1921–1924

MacDonald Steam Automotive Corp., Garfield, Ohio.

Duncan MacDonald had grandiose plans which would include a complete line of automobiles, trucks, buses and tractors, but it appears that this is all the idea became – plans. By 1923, without having a car to bear the MacDonald badge, a roadster to be called the 'MacDonald Bobcat' was announced. This, it was advertised, would be powered by a 3-cylinder steam engine of MacDonald's own design and, although the car was widely advertised by a rather poor sketch and abridged specifications, it is more than likely that the Bobcat never reached the prototype stage. One MacDonald sedan is known to have been completed in 1924 and this appears to have been the only car produced by Duncan MacDonald, despite his ambitious plans of 1921.

KM

MACH 1 (US) c.1967

Machline Corp., Bridgeville, Pennsylvania.

John Salathe was an engineer with Alcoa who had been involved with the YENKO Stinger project. He decided to build a mid-engined V8 sports car on his own, and enlisted the help of Bob McKee, who had been building the McKEE line of racing cars. He designed a simple backbone frame using a Chevrolet V8, fabricated race-style suspension and a McKee transaxle. Salathe styled an aggressive, if bulbous body that emphasised the mid-engined design. Production cars were to sell for about $8000, with distribution to be handled by Don Yenko. This would have been America's first mid-engined street sports car had it made it into production. The second car was to be bodied in Italy, but it is doubtful that more than these two were made.

HP

MACHIAVELLI (US) c.1985–1988

Machiavelli Motors, Key Biscayne, Florida.

This highly-publicised kit car was a rebody for the Pontiac Firebird and Chevrolet Camaro. The new body for the Machiavelli 305 GTS 2+2, also known as the Max, resembled an oversized Ferrari 308 GTS. The Machiavelli T-Max Testarudo was a Ferrari Testarossa-like kit for the same chassis. Initially, Machiavelli cars were only sold in fully assembled form, but later kits were offered as well.

HP

MACINTORSH see ADT

MACKLE-THOMPSON (US) 1903

Mackle-Thompson Automobile Co., Elizabeth, New Jersey.

The partners in this firm were Frederick Mackle and Andrew Thompson who ran an Oldsmobile agency and in 1903 announced their own car. It was a light 2-seater runabout powered by a single-cylinder engine of 3½ or 5hp, with 2-speed gearbox and shaft drive. Prices were $500 or $600 according to engine size. Thompson had previously made the THOMPSON (i) electric car which had lasted no longer than the Mackle-Thompson.

NG

MACOMBER (US) 1916

Macomber Motors Co., Los Angeles, California.

The Macomber was a transition model by Walter G. Macomber bridging the gap between the earlier Eagle (vii) cyclecar and the projected Eagle-Macomber which was to be built in a newly acquired factory in Sandusky, Ohio. It featured an unusual 5-cylinder air-cooled engine and never proceeded further than the

1924 MacDonald steam car.
KEITH MARVIN

prototype stage, consisting of only roadster and touring car models. The Macomber served as both Macomber's personal car and a promotion vehicle for the projected Eagle-Macomber.

KM

MACON (US) 1915–1917

1915–1916 All-Steel Motor Car Co., Macon, Missouri.
1916–1917 Macon Motor Car Co., Macon, Missouri.

This was an unusual car with platform backbone frame in which the gearbox and propeller shaft were enclosed. The body was electrically welded and attached to the frame at only three points. The engine was conventional enough, a 2-litre 4-cylinder Sterling, and two body styles were proposed, a roadster and a tourer, to sell at the modest prices of $350–400. The company claimed that their factory was to be the largest automobile factory in the world, and also the most sanitary and comfortable for the workers. Two problems arose; the company was accused of irregularity in financial conduct and, in May 1917, the factory burnt to the ground. No more than a prototype or two were ever made. The Macon was sometimes listed as the Alstel or All-Steel.

NG

MACQUE (AUS) 1913

Allan Macqueen, South Melbourne, Victoria.

Made by an engine manufacturer, this cyclecar had the distinction of being fitted with a dedicated engine, which could be had with either air- or water-cooling. It was a 10hp flat-twin of 1137cc with transmission through friction drive and belts to the rear wheels, on a wheelbase of 104in (2650mm). It was entered in a cyclecar race, perhaps to enhance its profile, but soon faded from view. Marine engines and propellers then became the major line of business for Allan Macqueen.

MG

MAC'S AUTO BODY (US) c.1994–1996

Mac's Auto Body, Sarasota, Florida.

The Pontiac Fiero was in for a facelift from this kit car company in the form of fibreglass replica bodies of the Lamborghini Countach and Ferrari 328. They were sold in kit and turn-key form.

HP

MADA (D) 1947–1949

Maschinenfabrik G. Danger GmbH, Säckingen.

This company's first car was a tiny 3-wheeler with 125cc Ilo engine mounted over the front axle, and a doorless body which hinged forward to give access to the single seat. In 1949 they built a 4-wheeler, the Libelle 250, powered by a 250cc Ilo engine, with a closed body similar in profile to the VW Beetle.

NG

MADELVIC (GB) 1898–1900

Madelvic Carriage Co. Ltd, Granton, Edinburgh.

This company was formed by William Peck, who was Scotland's Astronomer Royal. The car consisted of an electric forecarriage with three wheels, two full-size

1899 Madelvic electric brougham.
NATIONAL MOTOR MUSEUM

1916 Madison (i) 7-seater tourer.
KEITH MARVIN

c.1911 M.A.F. 8/10PS 2-seater.
NATIONAL MOTOR MUSEUM

ones which carried the weight, and a much smaller one which delivered power to the road. This power pack could be attached to any horse-drawn vehicle. The company was acquired by the KINGSBURGH Motor Co. in 1900, and a few cars were made with direct drive to the front wheels.

NG

MADISON (i) (US) 1915–1919

Madison Motors Co., Anderson, Indiana.
The Madison company was formed in 1915 to produce a low-priced car which could be ordered either as a roadster or a touring car. The Madison was undistinguished in appearance and was powered by a Rutenber 6-cylinder engine. Production had exceeded about 350 cars by mid–1917 when financial difficulties intervened in continued manufacturing and the company continued by servicing existing Madisons, most of which had been sold locally, and building a few additional cars, in an on-and-off schedule, from existing parts. The Madison car design of 1915 continued unchanged until the company failed in 1919, after a total production of perhaps 400 units.

KM

MADISON (ii) see G.P.

MADOU (F) 1922–1925

Automobiles Madou, Paris.
The Madou was a small car made with a variety of proprietary engines, probably because their credit ran out with one firm and forced them to approach another. Power units included a 900cc Chapuis-Dornier, 985 and 1094cc Ruby, 1170cc S.C.A.P. and 1494cc C.I.M.E. Most had side-valves or pushrod-operated ohv, but the C.I.M.E. had a single-ohc. Madou bought five Model BOs from MARGUERITE and fitted them with their own badges. The car was given its name by a wealthy banker and admirer of the actress Cora Madou.

NG

MAELSTROM (GB) 1986; 1990–1994; 1998 to date

1986 Maelstrom Cars, Preston, Lancashire.
1990–1992 P.A.C.E., Lancaster, Lancashire.
1993–1994 Evans Hunter Sports Cars, Barnsley, Yorkshire.
1998 to date White Rose Vehicles, Gillingham, Kent.
This extraordinary bare-boned roadster was designed by Preston-based Mike Eydman. Under its unique aluminium-and-fibreglass body sat a space frame chassis with steel sheet floorpan. The choice of donor vehicle was either Ford Cortina MkIII/IV or Sierra, giving a choice of live rear axle or irs. There were options of a wrap-around racing screen or laminated screen and surround, plus weather gear. Production did not really begin until the project was taken up by P.A.C.E., who added a hammerhead front. The Maelstrom was revived twice, in 1993 and 1998, reverting to the old pointed front.

CR

M.A.F. (D) 1908–1921

1908–1911 Markranstadter Automobil-Fabrik Hugo Ruppe, Markranstadt.
1911–1921 Markranstadter Automobil-Fabrik vorm. Hugo Ruppe GmbH, Markranstadt.
Hugo Ruppe was the son of Arthur Ruppe, maker of PICCOLO cars, and when he set up on his own at Markranstadt near Leipzig, he followed his father's example in using air-cooling. He made several models with 4-cylinder engines, including the 1192cc 4/12PS, 1375cc 5/14PS, 1620cc 6/16PS and 1800cc 7/21PS. They had 3- or 4-speed gearboxes and shaft drive, and most were sold in 2-seater form.

After the war the 1620cc model was revived under the designation 618PS, later 6/24PS, and there were plans to make a 3400cc 14/38PS with single-ohc engine, but this never went into production. In 1921 the business failed and the factory was sold to APOLLO.

HON

MÁG (H) 1912–1931

Magyar Általános Gépgyár, Budapest.
This company previously produced the PHONIX cars, but its main focus was agricultural machinery. However, as more and more emphasis was put on cars the company was renamed and reorganized under the financial direction of the Hungarian General Loan Bank, and soon developed its own car. It was the work of Jenö Fejes, who previously worked at MARTA and who later established his own car-making workshop.

Two Fejes-designed models were introduced in 1912: a 25bhp passenger car and a 2-ton lorry. For various reasons MÁG decided to slowly phase out its other activities (agricultural machines and so on) and concentrate on car production. As World War I approached they relied on Army orders, and the post office used MÁG cars. Taxi owners were also forced to use local-made cars.

Passenger cars were a sideline, commercial vehicles and buses were made in bigger quantities. However, the MÁG 25bhp was not ignored, winning local races, exhibition prizes, and so on.

Fejes simplified the manufacturing process, and the 25bhp model became the backbone of car production. The chassis looked like any other in Europe, the engine was a water-cooled 3-litre side-valve unit. Wire wheels were options, wooden rims were standard. The car was 4 metres long, with a 3-metre wheelbase.

During World War I aircraft and trucks were made in the cramped factory.

In 1917 Vilmos Heisler, one of the founders retired. The new management was able to resume car production in 1920. During the war they worked together with Austro-Daimler and established a joint showroom in the heart of Budapest, where AUSTRO-DAIMLER, MÁG and PUCH cars and motorcycles were on offer.

MÁG also introduced a new, 10bhp model; in fact it was a ten-year-old construction. Hungarian automobile pioneer, János Csonka designed it for the post office, which was why it had only one door. Luckily, Hungarian coachbuilders offered more elegant bodies as well.

The small MÁG didn't stand a chance against the Austro Daimlers it shared exhibition space with, but for MÁG it was the only chance to market its other products.

By 1923 roughly 100 MÁG cars were in use throughout the country, and a new model was desperately needed; it was completed in a very short time. The 20/25bhp Magomobil became the biggest-selling Hungarian-made car of the prewar years. It was used as a taxi, as a postal van and so on. It followed German patterns, but it was cheap, fairly reliable, and subsidised by the Hungarian government.

Magomobils were offered in many guises, from elegant limousines, to sporty 2-seaters. They were raced frequently in Hungary and sometimes in Austria. But a proper series of Magomobils was never realized. Generally, a shift meant 20-30 similar cars, but lack of funds, shortage of expert workers, and other conditions prevented Magomobil achieving the fame it deserved. Meanwhile, behind the scenes, a few directors complained about the path the company was following and insisted on a new, bigger model. So while Magomobil production lines were installed, development started on a bigger car. In 1926 a 6-cylinder bigger MÁG, the Magosix, was debuted. At the same time the contract with Austro-Daimler was abandoned and MÁG established their own sales network with the help of other automotive dealers.

At the end of 1927 894 MÁGs were registered giving them third place in the market. But confused management, and permanent lack of funds meant that MÁG only survived when successful. And when success ran out in 1928 the company was doomed. A new car, called the Supermagosix was not enough to save it and in 1931 automotive production stopped. What bigger players realized, MÁG failed to notice: Hungary is a small market for an independent carmaker.

PN

MAGALI (F) 1905–1906
Gayon et Cie, Levallois-Perret, Seine.
Like many car makers on both sides of the Channel, Magali made liberal use of Lacoste et Battmann components in the few cars they produced. These came in 10 and 30hp models, and there was also a Magali motorcycle.

NG

MAGENTA (GB) 1972–1986
Lightspeed Panels, Lealholm, North Yorkshire.
The Magenta was a uniquely British fun kit car that used BMC 1100 or 1300 components in a tubular steel chassis – and that even included an MG 1100 front grill. In style it was midway between a traditional roadster and beach buggy, and could seat four. One gullwing hard-top Magenta took part in the 1977 London-Sydney Marathon. The LSR of 1979 was a smoother-nosed Escort-based 2-seater, while the 1980 Sprint was a Mini-based version. Over 500 Magentas were sold over the years. A different approach marked the Tarragon. This glass-hatchback coupé was based on the Ford Escort Mk I/II. An improved TXR model with an extended rear end and Ford Capri parts arrived in 1985, but it was even uglier.

CR

1928 MÁG Magotax 6-cylinder taxicab.
TRANSPORT MUSEUM, BUDAPEST

1977 Magenta 1100 sports car.
NATIONAL MOTOR MUSEUM

MAGGIORA (I) 1905
Automobili Maggiora, Padua.
This company used Austrian-built Laurin & Klement engines of 4 and 8hp, but the business lasted less than 12 months.

NG

MAGNET (i) (AUS) 1907
Edgar Tozer, Melbourne, Victoria.
This cycle builder became interested in the new form of power from the first appearance of the Otto gas engine and was an early constructor of motor-cycles with Automotor and Clement engines. After an unsuccessful venture which included the building of motor buses, he returned to motor-cycles and also made some tricars. A motorcar, with a De Dion-Bouton 8hp engine, was built in 1907.

MG

MAGNET (ii) (D) 1907–1926
Motorenfabrik Magnet GmbH, Berlin-Weissensee.
This company began making motorcycles in 1903, and four years later launched a 3-wheeled car which had more motorcycle parentage than most. Like the later British-built SEAL, it was essentially a motorcycle and sidecar, but the 'rider' and passengers were seated in the sidecar. 2- and 3-seater models were made, and the engine was an 830cc V-twin. The 3-wheeler was made up to the outbreak of war, and a 4-wheeler was introduced in 1922, with 800cc 4/14PS engine.

HON

MAGNETIC (GB) 1921–1926
Magnetic Car Co. Ltd, Chelsea, London.
Like the OWEN MAGNETIC and CROWN MAGNETIC, this car used the Entz magnetic transmission, but with smaller engines. Two models were listed for 1922, both with Burt-McCollum sleeve-valve units, a 2624cc four and a

1924 Magnetic 2-door saloon.
NICK BALDWIN

1990 Mahindra CJ Classic.
NATIONAL MOTOR MUSEUM

1905 Mahoning 9hp side-entrance tonneau.
NICK GEORGANO/NATIONAL MOTOR MUSEUM

5228cc straight-8. The smaller was shown at Olympia in 1921, but not the larger which may never have been built. Its capacity indicates that it was two of the fours, and could easily have been dreamt up as a possible car if anyone ordered one. A chassis price of £1200 was quoted. Even the smaller Magnetics were not cheap, ranging from £750 for a chassis to £1100 for a 2-door saloon. Magnetics were shown regularly at Olympia until 1925, but they did not make much impact on the market, though at least one was offered secondhand. In 1924 a new model with 2888cc 6-cylinder ohv engine was announced, this being continued in 1925 with capacity increased to 3296cc.

NG

MAGNOLIA (US) 1903
Magnolia Automobile Co., Riverside, California.

This was a single-cylinder 2-seater runabout named after the trees which lined the boulevards of Riverside. It was designed by Watt Moreland, formerly with Winton, and later to be involved in the Tourist and Durocar before he began building trucks under his own name, which were much more successful than any of his cars. A price of $750 was fixed for the Magnolia, but only one was made.

NG

MAGNUM (i) (US) c.1983–1989
Custom Classics, Bellflower, California.
Custom Classics, Madison, South Dakota.

The Ferrari Dino 246 was the inspiration for the KELMARK GT, which in turn inspired the Magnum GT. It was basically the Kelmark GT with a boot added in the front and improved doors. It was first built in California under the name of Karma 1, but that was changed to Magnum when Custom Classics was bought by Lyle Mader and moved to South Dakota. The Magnum was well made and most were based on VW Beetle floorpans with Mazda rotary engines. Some were built on a custom steel chassis with 4-wheel disc brakes and mid-mounted Mazda or V6 engine.

HP

MAGNUM (ii) see RAYTON FISSORE

MAGNUM (iii) (GB) 1987–1997
1987–1992 Fieldbay, Daventry, Northamptonshire.
1993–1997 Magnum Engineering, Leamington Spa, Warwickshire.

The Magnum was developed by Auto Power Services and produced and marketed by a company called Fieldbay. Its unique selling point was a bias towards high performance and competition work. Hence the space frame chassis with stressed aluminium inner panels was fitted with double wishbone suspension or Rose joints, and typically sat much lower than standard. Jaguar uprights, hubs and discs, Scorpio diff and drive shaft were used. Fieldbay went bust in 1992 but the Magnum was revived in 1993, the new set-up offering a semi-monocoque (SM) option alongside the space frame (SF). Also a Kevlar body option.

CR

MAGYAR ACELARUGYAR (H) 1928
Magyar Acélárugyár Rt, Budapest.

The Hungarian Steel Wares Factory was established in the 19th century and produced various accessories for railways. In 1925 they obtained the MÉRAY Motorcycle company and opened a division to produce motorbikes in bigger quantities. In 1928 they designed a touring car with headlamps turning with the steering wheel. Further studies revealed that series production would not be profitable so they cancelled all plans. Their MÉRAY arm continued with its own efforts.

PN

MAHCON see HUTSON

MAHDEEN (GB) 1991–1992
This was a very cheap plans-built Lotus 7 style car with a space frame chassis that had to be welded up by the builder.

CR

MAHINDRA (IND) c.1975 to date
Mahindra & Mahindra Ltd, Bombay.

Mahindra specialised in 4×4 vehicles of which the basic model was very similar to the Jeep CJ in appearance. They also made a longer wheelbase full 4-seater with open sided body, and the Armada which was a 5-door estate in the Suzuki Vitara class. The 2199cc licence-built Jeep engine gave way to Peugeot diesel units in three sizes, 2112, 2498 and 2523cc. Transmission was by optional 4-wheel drive, and some models had front disc brakes. In 1997 Mahindra began licence production of the Ford Escort, followed by the Fiesta in 1998. These were made by a separate company, Mahindra Ford India, in a new factory at Chennai in south-west India.

NG

1956 Maico saloon.
NATIONAL MOTOR MUSEUM

MAHONING (US) 1904–1905

Mahoning Motor Car Co., Youngstown, Ohio.

The Mahoning was made originally as a 9hp single-cylinder car with three body styles, side-entrance tonneau, stanhope and delivery car. A larger car with 24/28hp 4-cylinder engine was also made, but it lacked power and very few were sold.

NG

MAHOUT (F) 1905–1907

This was a voiturette powered by a single-cylinder engine with transverse crankshaft and belt drive. The maker is not known, but one was displayed at the Exposition des Petites Inventeurs in Paris in 1905, and it was later written up in *Omnia*.

NG

MAIBOHM (US) 1916–1922

1916–1919 Maibohm Motors Co., Racine, Wisconsin.
1919–1922 Maibohm Motors Co., Sandusky, Ohio.

An assembled car which used a 4-cylinder engine and, from 1918, a Falls Six, the four being phased out in 1919. Open and closed models were available. In 1922 the Maibohm became the COURIER (iv).

KM

MAICO (D) 1955–1958

Maico GmbH, Pfaffingen; Herrenberg.

Maico were well-known for their motorcycles from 1932, and postwar production included scooters such as the Maicoletta. In 1955 they acquired the designs of the CHAMPION (iv) and continued production of the 400 2-seater and 500G estate car. Under Maico ownership, 783 400s and 21 500Gs were made. From 1956 to 1958 they made the Maico 500 4-seater 2-door saloon with 452cc vertical twin 2-stroke Heinkel engine, and in 1957 announced an attractive little sports car with the same engine and a body by the Swiss coachbuilder Beutler. Only about 10 of these were built, but production of the 500 saloon reached 6301 before cars were discontinued in 1958 and Maico returned to motorcycles exclusively.

HON

1921 Maiflower coupé.
NICK BALDWIN

MAIFLOWER (GB) 1919–1921

Maiflower Motor Co. Ltd, Gloucester.

This company was one of many 'improvers' of the Model T FORD who supposed that a market existed for a more expensive car utilising the trusted Ford mechanicals. It is believed that, nevertheless, the post-Armistice euphoria and demand for cars led to some sales success before the first postwar recession began to bite. The name derived from the progenitors, M. Price and A.I. Flower, ex-Army captains with gratuities to use in setting up a business. 4-seater, 2-seater and coupé bodies were listed but the firm were more than bodybuilders. The chassis was lowered and modified, with a revised rear end commissioned from Rubery Owen, a handsome replacement radiator and other modifications. The introduction of the RAC horsepower tax in 1921 killed off sales of large-engined American or American-derived cars and Maiflower deemed that there was insufficient interest, capital or sales to justify diversification.

DF

1908 Maja (i) 28/35PS limousine.
NICK BALDWIN

1921 Majola 12/20 tourer.
NICK BALDWIN

MAILLARD (F) 1900–c.1903

M. Maillard, Incheville, Seine Inférieure.

First shown at the 1900 Paris Salon, the Maillard was made in two models, of 6 and 10hp, power being upped to 8 and 12hp respectively the following year. The Maillard was made under licence in Belgium by the Société Générale de Constructions Aquila.

NG

MAINELY CLASSICS (US) c.1993

Mainely Classics, Biddeford, Maine.

The MC 427 was a replica of the 427 Cobra with a fibreglass body and Ford Mustang II running gear.

HP

MAINSTREAM CLASSICS (US) c.1997

Mainstream Classics, Boca Raton, Florida.

The Group XTC was an attractive Fiero rebody kit with an original design. Although the basic body lines were European in style, they were not a replica of any specific car.

HP

M.A.J. see JULIEN (ii)

MAJA (i) (A) 1907–1908

Österreichische Daimler Motoren AG, Wiener-Neustadt.

The Maja was built by Austro-Daimler to the designs of Ferdinand Porsche, and was named after the younger daughter of Emil Jellinek, as the Mercedes had been named after the elder daughter. It was a conventional car made in a single 4-cylinder model of 24/28PS with chain drive and a 5-seater tourer body. American advertising proclaimed it to be about 750lb less than the corresponding Mercedes, because of the use of vanadium steel 'and to improved design'. 'The makers guarantee Maja for ever' they said, but the car was not a success, and was withdrawn after less than two years on the market.

NG

MAJA (ii) (D) 1923–1924

Maja-Werk für Vierrad-Bau AG, Munich.

This was one of several makes of car to use the 500cc flat-twin BMW motorcycle engine, others including the BZ, Mauser Einspurwagen and Wesnigk, but it was made only in small numbers.

HON

MAJESTIC (i) (US) 1917

Majestic Motor Co., New York City, New York.

Originally called the Monitor Motor Co., the name was changed to Majestic before any cars were made. They had 4.6-litre V8 engines, Fiat-like radiators and came in four body styles, from a tourer at $1650 which was a reasonable price for a V8, to $3500 for a 'convertible touring sedan', which was a high price to pay, even if it included such luxuries as a folding table, lunch boxes and a vacuum ice box.

NG

MAJESTIC (ii) (GB) c.1920

F.J. Wraight & Co., Ramsgate, Kent.

This car was to be assembled in Britain using American mechanical components and British bodies. Engines listed were 15.9, 18/22 and 30hp. F.J. Wraight was part of the WHITEHEAD-THANET scheme, and quite probably no more Majestics were built than Whitehead-Thanets.

NG

MAJESTIC (iii) (US) 1925–1927

Larrabee-Deyo Motor Truck Co., Binghamton, New York.

This was the closest to a passenger car that this well-known truck maker got, but it was a taxicab destined for New York City, though it is possible, as with other taxicabs, that a few were sold for private use.

NG

MAJESTIC (iv) (F) 1926–1930

Automobiles Majestic, Paris.

The Majestic was a conventional car powered by a 3-litre 6-cylinder engine in which the valves were inclined to give a compact combustion chamber. In 1930 a straight-8 was listed; if it was built it probably had an American engine, a Continental or Lycoming.

NG

MAJOLA (F) 1911–1928

J. Majola, St Denis, Seine.

The Majola company was founded in 1908 to make engines, and did not deliver a complete car until 1911. This was designed by F. Doutré and had a 1327cc single-ohc 4-cylinder engine. This was the Type A, and in 1914 it was joined by the 984cc Type B. The main difference in design was that the Type A's camshaft was driven by helical gearing, while the Type B used chain drive. The A had a 3- or 4-speed gearbox, but the B came only in 3-speed form. Otherwise they were conventional machines made with open 2- or 4-seater bodies.

In 1920 Majola was taken over by GEORGES IRAT, though they remained at the St Denis factory. The Type B was revived and joined by the 1393cc Type DT. Four cars took part in the 1921 Coupe des Voiturettes, one finishing fourth behind two Bignans and a Bugatti. In 1922 a Type B won the Grand Prix des Petites Voitures at Boulogne-sur-Mer. These models, together with a 1086cc Type F made up the Majola range up to 1928. A variety of open and closed bodywork was fitted, and the Type F could be had with a pointed tail sports body which looked very like a Type CGS Amilcar.

In 1926 the Majola name went on a completely different car which had begun life as the BELL cyclecar. This had a 1094cc flat-4 engine designed by Vaslin (also responsible for the ALMA), with quarter-elliptic springs all round, with superimposed pairs in front. In Majola guise it was called the Type GV and was made in doorless 2-seater sports form. It lacked front-wheel brakes. Georges Irat took over the Majola factory in 1928, and ended production of all models.

NG

Further Reading
'Le Majola "Alexis"', *La Vie de l'Auto*, 27 February 1986.
'Le Cyclecar Bell devenu la voiturette Majola', Serge Pozzoli, *l'Album du Fanatique*, January 1979.

MAJOR (F) 1920–1923; 1932

Cyclecars Major, Paris.

The Major was one of the many ventures of Marcel Violet, who also made the VIOLET-BOGEY, MOURRE, SIMA-VIOLET, BERNADET and the almost identical GALBA and HUASCAR which became the 4CV DONNET. The first Major had a 1058cc vertical-twin 2-stroke engine in which the two cylinders had a common combustion chamber, the inlet port being in one cylinder and the exhaust port in the other. The pistons moved together. Transmission was by friction discs, and final drive was by chain. The first phase of the Major ended in about 1923, though the Mourre used the same engine. Violet busied himself with other designs, but at the 1932 Paris Salon he was back with a light car powered by a 592cc single-cylinder Staub engine, in a conventional chassis with 3-speed gearbox and shaft drive. Front suspension was by a transverse semi-elliptic spring. It was available in two wheelbases, the 88in (2233mm) MAC and a longer chassis for commercial bodies. Both chassis, as well as a cabriolet and a coupé were on the stand at the show, but no production followed.

NG

MALCOLM (US) 1914–1915

1913–1914 Malcolm Jones Cyclecar Co., Detroit, Michigan.
1914–1915 Malcolm Motor Co., Detroit, Michigan.

This make began as a $395 cyclecar with a V-twin engine and tandem seating for two, though a third passenger could be squeezed in. An unusual feature was a single headlamp above the radiator. For 1915 the cyclecar was replaced by a larger car with 18hp 4-cylinder engine, two headlamps and shaft drive in place of the cyclecar's belts. It was priced at $425, but sold no better than the cyclecar.

NG

MALDEN (US) 1898–1902

Malden Automobile Co., Malden, Massachusetts.

The first Malden was a light steam car with an automatic boiler and vertical 2-cylinder engine. The prototype was built in 1898, but it does not seem to have gone into production until 1902, and then very few were made. They could be had with side- or centrally-mounted tillers, and a folding front seat to increase passenger capacity to four.

NG

MALEVEZ & MICHOTTE (B) 1903–1904

Malevez et Michotte, Namur.

The works of Jules and Adolphe Malevez were founded in 1894 and specialised in ice-making machinery. In 1898 they began to import, or possibly assemble under licence, Lifu steam vans and buses from England which continued nominally until 1909, though Lifus were not made as late as that. Michotte was an old-established coachbuilder with works at Ghent and Namur, and in 1903 the two companies combined to make a car with 10CV 2-cylinder Mutel engine, and also a 12/14CV four and two larger fours of 18/22 and 30CV. They were shown at the 1904 Brussels Salon, but did not sell well. Both companies soon returned to the trades they knew best.

NG

MALIBU (GB) 1990–1993

E-Zee Automotive, Exeter, Devon.

An attempt to recreate the spirit of the Renault 4 Plein Air, the Malibu RV4 was an open jeep-style car using some fibreglass parts and keeping some original Renault 4 metal. Kits were sold at very cheap prices.

CR

1932 Major 3CV chassis.
NATIONAL MOTOR MUSEUM

1897 Malicet et Blin 4hp *vis-à-vis*.
JAKOB DRACH

c.1980 Mallalieu Mercia roadster.
NICK GEORGANO

MALICET ET BLIN (F) 1897–c.1903

Éts Malicet et Blin, Aubervilliers, Seine.

Paul Malicet and Eugène Blin set up their partnership in 1890 to make a chainless bicycle, but soon turned to supplying components to other cycle builders. The coming of the motor car was an incentive to extend their activities, which they did to a great extent, becoming one of France's major suppliers of chassis, steering gears and most components apart from engines. They also made a few complete cars; a surviving example of 1897 has a 4hp horizontal single-cylinder engine, chain drive and a 4-seater *vis-à-vis* body, and another dated 1903 has a vertical 8hp single-cylinder engine and tonneau body.

NG

MALLALIEU (GB) 1974–1981

Mallalieu Engineering Ltd, Abingdon, Oxfordshire.

This company's main business was rebodying old Bentley MkVI chassis in various sports and touring styles, with the names Mercia, Barchetta and Oxford.

1929 Mannesmann Type 8Mb saloon.
HANS-OTTO NEUBAUER

It also ventured into alternative territory when it considered making William Towns' MICRODOT microcar and the extraordinary X600 sports car of John WEITZ.

CR

MALLIARY (F) 1901
G. Malliary, Puteaux, Seine.
Malliary's voiturette had a 5½hp vertical single-cylinder engine, and shaft drive. It had a tubular frame and wire wheels.

NG

MALONE (GB) 1998 to date
Malone Designs, West Putford, Devon.
Details of the Malone S1 and SS1 trikes were released in 1998, though the production model (named Skunk) was not to emerge until the following year. The basis was a space frame chassis with a front-mounted Yamaha motor cycle engine of 650, 750 or 900cc capacity. Drive to the single rear wheel was by shaft and chain and the front suspension was by double wishbones and coil springs. The very simple doorless open bodywork was in fibreglass.

CR

MALTBY (US) 1900–1902
Maltby Automobile & Motor Co., Brooklyn, New York (1900–1901); Matawan, New Jersey (1902).
Frank D. Maltby was a trick cyclist who moved into bicycle manufacture and then, like so many others, tried his hand at cars. The Maltby runabout was a very light machine with 4hp 2-cylinder engine, single-chain drive and bicycle-type wheels. Full-elliptic springs were used all round, transversely-mounted at the front. Maltby offered his engine for sale to other car manufacturers, and would also build any type of vehicle if the customer supplied the drawings. In 1902 he moved to Matawan and completed a few cars there, before becoming a dealer.

NG

MALVERNIA see SANTLER

MANCHESTER (GB) 1904–1905
Bennett & Carlisle Ltd, Manchester.
Bennett & Carlisle were well-known retailers who assembled a few cars using Aster engines and chain drive. Models listed were of 8, 10, 14, 20 and 30hp, but it is not certain that all these were actually built. Building cars was always a sideline to selling them. The cars were sometimes known as Manch-Aster, in reference to their power units. The company later became Newton & Bennett, and sold the Italian-built N.B. cars.

NG

MANEXALL (US) 1920
Manufacturers' & Exporters' Alliance, Inc., New York, New York.
The Manexall was, in fact, a Cyclomobile, manufactured by the Cyclomobile Manufacturing Co. of Toledo, Ohio, although frequently judged as a make of its own. Cyclomobile joined with the Automotive Corp. of Toledo, Ohio, manufacturer of the short-lived Sun. (See CYCLOMOBILE and SUN.)

KM

MANIC (CDN) 1969–1971
1969–1971 Les Automobiles Manic, Terrebonne, Québec.
1971 Les Automobiles Manic, Granby, Québec.
A handsome Canadian coupé, the Manic GT was created by Jacques About. It had a fibreglass body mounted on a Renault 8-1300 platform, and Renault Canada supported the venture by installing the mechanical elements officially. Later examples gained Renault 12 power (60–105bhp).

CR

MANLIUS (US) 1910
Manlius Motor Co., Manlius, New York.
The Manlius was made in two models, a 12hp 2-cylinder and a 28hp 4-cylinder, with epicyclic transmission and shaft drive, and both offered only with 2-seater roadster bodies. The cars were occasionally known by the company's initials, M.M.C.

NG

MANNESMANN (D) 1923–1929
1923–1926 Mannesmann Motorenwerke & Co., Remscheid.
1927–1929 Mannesmann Automobil-Werke AG, Remscheid.
Mannesmann Motorenwerke was a subsidiary of a major engineering concern acquired by Carl Mannesmann in 1911, and which also made Mannesmann-Mulag trucks in another factory. The first Mannesmanns were light cars powered by 4/15 or 5/20PS engines, the latter of 1305cc. Touring and sports models were made, some of the latter having Zoller superchargers. After serious financial problems the company was reorganised in 1927 and moved upmarket with a series of straight-8s, the 2343cc Typ 8M (Modell 60), 2418cc Typ 8Ma (Modell 70) and 5210cc Typ 8Mb (Modell 100). At RM 10,950, even the cheapest of the eights was nearly double the price of the most expensive of the previous 4-cylinder cars, and it does not seem to have been a very wise move. About 2000 of the fours were made, but only 200 eights. Most coachwork on Mannesmanns was by Karmann.

HON

MANOCAR (F) 1953
Éts Manom, Saint-Ouen.
This was an extremely compact (89in/225cm long) microcar with three wheels. Its doorless convertible body could accommodate two passengers. Powered by a 4bhp, 125cc single-cylinder engine driving the left-hand rear wheel by chain, it could achieve a top speed of 34mph (55kmh). It never passed the prototype stage.

CR

MANON (F) 1903–c.1905
H. Chaigneau, Paris.
The Manon was a light car powered by either De Dion Bouton or Aster engines of 6 or 9hp. It was sold in England as the Mohawk-Manon by the Mohawk Motor & Cycle Co. of Chalk Farm, London.

NG

MANS (B) 1899–1901
Léon Mans et Cie, Brussels.
Mans was a bicycle maker who showed at the 1899 Brussels Salon a 3-wheeler very similar to the Léon Bollée, except that final drive was by gears in place of the Bollée's belts. He also showed De Dion-Bouton-powered tricycles. In 1901 he made a voiturette with front-mounted engine and wheel steering.

NG

MANTA (US) 1973–1991
Manta Cars Inc, Santa Ana, California.
After experience working on Can-Am racing cars in the early 1970s, brothers Brad and Tim LoVette began building one of the most popular kit cars of all time. The Manta was a sports car that looked like a Can-Am car for the street. It was based on a steel tube chassis with Volkswagen front suspension and a mid-mounted Chevrolet V8, although a few were built with Ford or Buick engines. The Chevrolet Corvair transaxle was modified to fit. Despite the exotic looks, it was simple to build and over 750 were sold. In 1976 Brad LoVette was

killed in a racing accident and Tim and Craig Shirey took over. They added a second model, the Montage. It was a 1969 McLaren M6GT replica designed to fit on VW chassis. They later added a Montage T with a steel frame and mounts for a GM V6 or VW Scirocco engine. A few special Mantas and Montages were built by Manta dealer Crosby Metal Products, who added longitudinally mounted V8s with Z-F transaxles to a race-style fabricated chassis. The last Manta product was a 1955 Corvette replica with V6 or V8 engines. Although Manta closed down in 1991, the Manta and Montage returned to production in 1994 with WARP FIVE Engineering.

HP

MANTA RAY (US) 1953

Hire and Antoine, Whittier, California.

This futuristic custom car was designed to be produced by Glen Hire and Vernon Antoine. It was built on a 1951 Studebaker chassis and used a fibreglass body with a large, round 'jet-engine' intake in the centre of the bonnet capped by a huge chrome spinner. There were three massive vertical tail lights and the wheels were fully enclosed.

HP

MANTIS (US) 1965–1979

1965–1972 Loring Design and Manufacturing Co., Sausalito, California.
1972–1979 Loring Design and Manufacturing Co., Port Orford, Oregon.
Built on a rear-engined Volkswagen platform, this was a glassfibre coupé not unlike the Adams PROBE. An open version was also available.

NG

MANX (i) (GB) 1991 to date

1991–1998 Manx Cars, Riseley, Berkshire.
1998 to date Ayrspeed-Manx, Reading, Berkshire.
Although first seen in 1991, the definitive spec of the Manx 2- or 4-seater took some time to mature. The man behind it was an experienced race car designer called Jim Clark, who conceived the Manx as a cheap-to-run sports/fun car. In its original form it had high sills and shallow doors that could be removed completely; though later versions had low sills and deeper doors. The basis was a Citroën 2CV floorpan, which did the smart sports car styling little justice. A hard-top was offered from 1993.

CR

MANX (ii) (GBM) 1993

Roger Munk, Isle of Man.
In 1993 details emerged of a new supercar called the Manx 201, designed and built by airship designer Roger Munk. The mid-engined 2+2 coupé used a very lightweight honeycomb chassis and carbon-Kevlar bodywork to keep weight down to only 975kg. An ambitious plan to make a flat-8 3.3-litre engine with a revolutionary 'scotch yolk' crankshaft did not come to fruition; it was claimed that, in twin-turbo form, it would produce 340bhp and power the Manx to a top speed of 180mph (290km/h). Despite announcing plans to make 70 cars per year, the necessary finance never materialised.

CR

MANX MOTORS (US) c.1992

Manx Motors, Columbia, Maryland.
This company built the Meyers Manx SR sports car after MEYERS went out of business.

HP

MAPLEBAY (US) 1907

Maplebay-Windstacker Co., Crookstown, Minnesota.
This company made farm implements and in 1908 announced a 2-seater runabout powered by a 22hp 4-cylinder air-cooled Reeves engine. A price of $1400 was quoted, but it is possible that only one Maplebay was made.

NG

MARAL (TK) 1999 to date

Sports Car Ltd, Istanbul.

1953 Marathon (ii) Corsaire coupé.
NATIONAL MOTOR MUSEUM

This was a close replica of the Morgan 4/4 powered by a 1.6-litre Fiat Regata engine. So close was the resemblance that Morgan was considering taking action to prevent patent infringement.

NG

MARATHON (i) (US) 1907–1914

1907–1910 Southern Motor Works, Jackson, Tennessee.
1910–1914 Marathon Motor Works, Nashville, Tennessee.
The Marathon was a conventional car powered by 4-cylinder engines in various sizes from 20 to 45hp, and mostly with open bodies, tourers, roadsters and speedsters, though a coupé was listed in 1913 and 1914, and there was a solitary limousine in 1912. Production expanded with the move to Nashville, and the Marathon was the best-selling car in the Nashville area for a year or two. However, mismanagement damaged the company, and in 1914 it ceased production, though it is not certain if it actually declared bankruptcy. Sales manager H.H. Brooks joined the Herff brothers in Indianapolis, who had been marketing the Marathon. The machinery was moved to Indianapolis, and the cars were made under the name of HERFF-BROOKS up to 1916.

NG

Further Reading
'Marathon: It almost went the distance', Bill Pryor,
Automobile Quarterly, Vol. 31, No. 2.

MARATHON (ii) (F) 1953–1955

Sté Industrielle de l'Ouest Parisien (Automobiles Marathon SA), Paris.
Taking up a rear-engined SK10 coupé design of Hans Trippel's, French rally driver Bernard Denis produced the Marathon Corsaire in a factory where Rosengart bodies were made. Changes over the Trippel included built-in spotlamps, higher headlamps and different glass. As well as the 3-abreast Corsaire, a more sporting and lightweight 2-seater version called the Pirate was produced. The fibreglass bodywork was extremely light, resulting in excellent performance from the rear-mounted 42bhp twin-carburettor Panhard 850cc engine. A convertible version arrived at the 1953 Paris Salon. Only 17 Marathons were produced.

CR

MARATHON (iii) (CDN) 1976–1981

Marathon Electric Vehicles, Montreal, Québec.
Like so many manufacturers of electric golf carts (an activity this company had carried out since 1969), Marathon produced a roadgoing model. But the C-300 was different to most in having original jeep-style open-topped 2-seater bodywork in either steel or fibreglass, mounted on a tubular steel frame. Power came from an 8hp DC motor and twelve 6V batteries stored behind the passenger compartment, plus a 4-speed gearbox. A 6-wheeled electric van was also produced.

CR

1951 Marauder (i) A-100 sports car.
NATIONAL MOTOR MUSEUM

1903 Marble-Swift 16hp 2-seater.
NICK GEORGANO

MARAUDER (i) (GB) 1950–1952

1950–1951 Wilks, Mackie and Co. Ltd, Dorridge, Warwickshire.
1951–1952 Marauder Car Co., Kenilworth, Warwickshire.
In 1950, two Rover engineers, Peter Wilks (the chairman's nephew), and George Mackie, set up Wilks, Mackie & Co. Ltd and this company, better known as 'Marauder' (which has echoes of Rover's Viking longship badge) operated with the co-operation of Rover, which supplied components.

Based on the Rover 75, the A had a lightly modified (80bhp) 2103cc engine while the 100, which was soon dropped, had a big-bore 2392cc 3-carburettor unit which gave 105bhp. Both engines were fitted in a cut-and-shut Rover 75 chassis, which had slightly different rear suspension and a specially designed overdrive made by H. & A. Engineering. Described as a sports car, because it had a rag top, the buying public perceived it as a touring version of the staid, respectable, Rover 75. The last model made was a coupé but by then the price had risen to £2000, which represented poor value for a sports car with no sporting pedigree. The venture folded in 1952 after only 15 cars had been made.
MJL

MARAUDER (ii) (RSA) 1970–1974

This was a maker of a basic sports car, in the Lotus 7 idiom, which was built on a spaceframe and used Ford Escort Mk I/II running gear.
MJL

MARAUDER (iii) (US) c.1980 to date

Marauder & Co., Potomac, Illinois.
Replicas of famous cars are not unusual in the American kit car industry, but Marauder managed to clone some of the most desirable cars with exceptional accuracy. The Lola T-70 Mk III coupé and McLaren M6B GT were their first models, with Specialized Mouldings in England providing the moulds just as they had done for the originals. Marauder also made a believable replica of the Ferrari 512M. These kits were available with a variety of mid-engine V8 chassis to suit several price ranges. Suspension options ranged from VW front ends to fabricated A-arms. They made a replica of the Chevron B16 coupé with a more basic chassis mounting VW, Porsche, Mazda or transverse V8 engines. In 1982 they added DeTomaso Pantera and Lamborghini Countach replicas to their line, which was later expanded with the BR-X, a replica of a Ferrari Testarossa with Koenig bodywork. In addition to this mid-engined line-up, Marauder sold a Ferrari 250 GTO replica with fibreglass or aluminium bodywork and a front-engined Chevrolet or Ford V8. It was sold in partially assembled form. The DI NAPOLI, a neoclassic kit, was added later. The latest additions to their line were replicas of the Corvette IMSA GTP prototype and the Nissan IMSA GTP championship-winning car.
HP

MARAUDER (iv) (AUS) 1985–1991

Exotic Automobile Manufacturers, Cheltenham, Victoria.
Marauder Sports Cars, Beverley, South Australia.
Inspired by the lines of the Ferrari Dino 246 Ken Knolder intended the Marauder for the VW Type 3 floorpan, with a subframe incorporating a roll cage and side anti-intrusion bars. Power units could range from the original, through a variety of 4-cylinder types, to a Mazda 13 rotor engine for ultimate performance and the fibreglass coupé was offered in either kit or complete drive-away form.
MG

MARBAIS ET LASNIER (F) 1906

This company assembled a few cars varying from an 8hp single-cylinder voiturette to a 30hp 4-cylinder tourer with chain drive.
NG

MARBLE-SWIFT (US) 1903–1905

Marble-Swift Automobile Co., Chicago, Illinois.
This car was made by George W. Marble and George P. Swift, and incorporated a patent friction transmission that they had invented. The 1903/04 car was a 2-seater powered by a 16hp 2-cylinder engine, of which 100 were said to be under construction in July 1903. The radiator was surmounted by a particularly fine brass shell. For 1905 an 18/22hp 4-cylinder engine was used in a longer wheelbase carrying a 5-seater tourer body. In August 1905 the Marble-Swift company was succeeded by the Windsor Automobile Co., although the WINDSOR (i) car was made in Evansville, Indiana.
NG

MARCADIER (F) 1963–1983

1963–1967 Fournier et Marcadier, Lyons.
1967–1969 Fournier et Marcadier, Mions, Rhône.
1969–c.1983 Automobiles Marcadier, Mions, Rhône.
After making karts, André Marcadier and Marcel Fournier began their car manufacturing career in 1963 with the construction of 90 Fournier-Marcadier racing cars. The partners moved into road car production in 1967 with the Barzoï, but by 1969 Marcadier was in sole charge of the company. The Barzoï was a fixed-head gullwing coupé with a tubular chassis, a mid-mounted Renault 1300 Gordini engine and, as an option, Aral Formula France race suspension. The model was sold mostly in kit form and racing cars remained available. The 1977 Barzoï II featured a backbone chassis, coil spring independent suspension and Simca 1000 Rallye rear-mounted 1.3-litre engines of between 60bhp and 103bhp.
CR

MARCA-TRE-SPADE (I) 1908

Fratelli Bertoldo, Turin.
Made by a well-known bicycle manufacturer, the Marca-Tre-Spade was a conventional car powered by an 18/24hp 4-cylinder engine, with 4-speed gearbox and double-chain drive. The radiator was similar to that of the Fiat. At least one came to England, but the marque's life was too short to permit a serious number of imports.
NG

MARCELLO (US) c.1996 to date

Marcello Italia Sports Car Design, Van Nuys, California.

Marcello Ferrari shared more than his name with that famous Italian sports car builder, he also replicated one of his cars. The Marcello Koenig Competition was heavily inspired by a Koenig-modified Testarossa and was built on a Pontiac Fiero chassis. Two versions were offered, the least expensive being a basic rebody kit for a stretched Fiero chassis. A more advanced version used a Fiero cockpit section with front and rear subframes welded on. A 500hp Chevrolet V8 was mounted longitudinally to a Porsche 911 transaxle and the suspension was modified Fiero with racing disc brakes. Price for a completely assembled model was about $49,000 in 1996.

HP

MARCH (GB) 1989

March, Bicester, Oxfordshire.

The famous racing car constructor March was set to ride a wave of interest in roadgoing supercar projects, although ultimately the collapse of this market dissuaded it from going ahead. The March Scar project team included Ken Greenley, Lester Allan and Frank Costin. The company's experience in building the Oldsmobile Aerotech record breaker suggested that an Oldsmobile Quad 4 engine would be fitted, though a Subaru flat-12 and an all-new engine were also mooted possibilities. A scale model was shown and production was due to begin in 1991, but this never in fact happened.

CR

MARCHAND (I) 1898–1909

1898–1900 Orio e Marchand, Piacenza.
1900–1905 Fratelli Marchand, Piacenza.
1905–1906 Stà Anonima Marchand, Piacenza.
1906–1909 Marchand e Dufaux, Piacenza.

Orio e Marchand was a manufacturer of bicycles and sewing machines run by Stefano Orio and the Marchand brothers, Lesne and Paul. They made a small number of cars under their name, under licence from DECAUVILLE, though with some modifications by Giuseppe Merosi who became famous later as the designer of the RL series of Alfa Romeos. Stefano Orio died in 1899, and the Marchand brothers continued on their own. By 1902 all cars were front-engined, in several sizes, including 8, 10, 12, 16 and 20hp, with 2- or 4-cylinders and chain drive. Some motorcycles were built at this time, but in 1906 the Stà Anonima Marchand was in liquidation, and was taken over by the Dufaux brothers who were making DUFAUX cars in Geneva. There were plans to make the Swiss cars in Piacenza, but these do not seem to have materialised, and the Marchands made from 1906 onwards were their own T-head fours of 10/14, 18/22 and 28/35hp. A 50/60hp six was also listed, but may never have been built.

NG

MARCOS (GB) 1959–2001

1959–1961 Speedex Castings and Accessories Ltd, Luton, Bedfordshire.
1961 Monocoque Chassis & Body Co Ltd, Luton, Bedfordshire.
1962–1963 Marcos Cars Ltd, Luton, Bedfordshire.
1964–1969 Marcos Cars Ltd, Bradford-on-Avon, Wiltshire.
1970–1974 Marcos Cars Ltd, Westbury, Wiltshire.
1975–1981 D&H Fibreglass Techniques Ltd, Oldham, Lancashire.
1981–1982 Jem Marsh Performance Cars, Westbury, Wiltshire.
1982–2001 Marcos Sales Ltd, Westbury, Wiltshire.

Marcos was a collaboration in 1959 between Jem Marsh, then best-known for his exploits in the 750 Formula and the parts he sold under the name Speedex Accessories, and Frank Costin, who had just left the de Havilland Aircraft company to become a freelance designer. The first car, officially a Marcos GT, but also called 'Zylon', had gullwing doors and a monocoque constructed from plywood. Front suspension was by Triumph Herald coil springs and double wishbones, the live rear axle was sprung on coil springs and located by parallel leading arms and a Panhard rod. The prototype used a Ford 100E engine, but production models used the new generation of Ford engines and were enormously successful on the circuits.

After six cars had been made, Costin left. The style was gradually modified, a few open cars were made and, in 1963, Dennis Adams designed a new body which

1960 Marcos GT coupé.
NATIONAL MOTOR MUSEUM

1971 Marcos Mantis coupé.
NICK BALDWIN

1982 Marcos GT coupé.
NICK BALDWIN

has remained Marcos' signature. Engines from Ford, Volvo and Triumph were used, and most sold in the UK were kits. When Marcos took on the American market, in 1968, it abandoned the wooden monocoque because of customer resistance and used a steel multi-tubular frame.

From 1965, Marcos also made the Mini-Marcos, a coupé with Mini running gear and a fibreglass body and monocoque. It was based on a design by Paul Emery and was sold as a kit.

Production of the GT had reached about ten cars a week when Marcos folded. It had moved to larger premises, and then had shipped cars to the States which could not be sold due to new emission laws. Marcos lost money and abandoned Ford engines, which had become usual, and used the straight-six Volvo unit. This made the car too expensive (and nose-heavy) to sell well and, stretched by the expansion programme and the introduction of the Mantis 4-seat coupé, the company went into liquidation.

The Mantis, styled by Dennis Adams, used 6-cylinder Triumph components. Marcos made 32 examples of the Mantis and a kit car based on it was made in the 1980s.

1990 Marcos Mantula 2-litre sports car.
NICK BALDWIN

1992 Marcos Mantara 450 sports car.
NICK BALDWIN

c.1979 Marden 49 microcar.
NICK BALDWIN

After Marcos folded in 1971, Rob Walker took over production of the Mini-Marcos and the project was sold to D & H Fibreglass Developments after a total of about 700 cars had been made. D & H made a further 500 cars before taking the broad concept and turning it into the Midas. During 1991 to 1995, Marcos made a further 64 cars.

After Marcos was liquidated, Jem Marsh operated a business which serviced existing owners then, in 1981, he resumed production of the Marcos offering kits, from basic up to nearly fully assembled. At first Ford engines were used, but in 1983 came the Mantula with the 3.5-litre Rover V8 engine and a revised nose treatment to eliminate high-speed lift.

In 1986 Marcos introduced the Spyder, a convertible. 1989 saw extensive revisions which included irs by coil springs and double wishbones, inboard rear disc brakes, and wider rear wheels. By this time, the only engine available was the 3.9-litre fuel injected Rover V8 and top speed was 149mph (240km/h). Since 1990 Marcos has used a variety of engines – a 2-litre fuel injected Ford unit was available from 1990.

By 1999, Marcos was offering a range of engines, including an American Ford 4.6-litre 'quad cam' unit developing 506bhp. Convertible and GT models were made and the Mantis was capable of 168mph (270km/h). The LM 400 and LM 500 were related to a car designed for GT racing. Despite modifications, and variations, all were recognisably the descendents of Denis Adams' 1963 design.

Sadly, after dwindling sales, Marcos closed its doors in April 2001.

MJL

Further Reading
Marcos, the Story of a Great British Sports Car, David Michael Barber, Cedar, 1995.

MARCUS (GB) 1919–1920

L. Marcus, Golders Green, London.
Originally known as the Challenge, the Marcus was a belt-driven cyclecar powered by a front-mounted transverse air-cooled engine driving by a short chain to the gearbox, and thence by a single belt to the rear axle. It was planned to sell at £100, but few were made.

NG

MARDEN (F) 1975–1992

1975–1979 Automobiles Marden, Neuilly, Seine.
1979–1992 Sté d'Exploitation Marden-Automobile (Marden SA), Offranville, Seine.
The name Espace was invented not by Renault but by Marden for its tiny 82in (2081mm) microcar. Open or closed bodywork was available. It was quite

sophisticated for the time, having all-independent suspension, hydraulic brakes and automatic transmission. There was a choice of a Unelec electric motor or a Sachs Wankel-type rotary engine developing 23bhp. More conventional 123cc Sachs or Citroën 2CV engines followed, although commercial pressure to conform with French microcar legislation led to 50cc Sachs or Motobécane engines by 1979. 1981 models used Fiat 126 suspension and all-disc brakes; sales were running at 1000 per year at this stage. New for 1983 was the Fetta, now with a front-mounted engine, four disc brakes and the option of diesel power. The 1987 Channel and 1988 Alizé were more smoothly-styled models. The Marden was also marketed under the name Eufradif.

CR

MARENDAZ (GB) 1926–1936

1926–1932 D.M.K.Marendaz Ltd, Brixton, London.
1932–1936 Marendaz Special Cars Ltd, Maidenhead, Berkshire.

Captain Donald Marendaz had been a partner in MARSEAL Motors Ltd, and soon after this company closed he began to make cars under his own name in premises at the Camberwell end of Brixton Road, which he shared with the London General Cab Co. and Bugatti's London depot. The Marendaz Specials, as the early cars were known, were assembled machines with Anzani engines, mostly of 1496cc, though a few were linered down to 1097cc. They were sporty looking cars with vee-windscreens, flared wings and radiators very similar to those of Bentley. His facilities were limited, being on the first floor of the building, and most of his income came from selling exotic cars. However, in addition to the fours, he made one 1495cc straight-8 engine with overhead inlet and side exhaust valves, which was catalogued as a sports car at £600 for a chassis, and in 1931 offered the 13/70. This had a 1869cc side-valve 6-cylinder engine assembled by Marendaz with Birmid block, and crankshafts and camshafts coming from Continental. This led to a rumour that the complete engines were left over from the Studebaker-built ERSKINE, but Erskine's Continental engine was larger, at 2623cc.

Because of the cramped quarters, not more than 20-25 cars were made at Brixton, and in 1932 Marendaz moved out of town to Maidenhead, where he was again sharing premises. This was the famous 'Jam Factory' where the Burney Streamline and the last G.W.K.s were also made. Here he made about 60 sports cars in three models, the 13/70, the 2469cc 17/97, both with Marendaz-assembled engines, and the final model, the 15/90 with 1991cc 6-cylinder Coventry-Climax engine. Few of these were made, and it was said that the Climax engines came from crashed Triumph Glorias bought from a breaker's yard half a mile from the Jam Factory! The bodies were nearly all open 2- or 4-seaters, though there was at least one closed coupé, and they did well in rallies. One of the leading exponents was Aileen Moss, mother of Stirling, who had a special short-chassis 15/90 built for her. Most models could be had with superchargers. Marendaz Special Cars was wound up in July 1936, and the Captain turned to making light aircraft in Bedfordshire, though the war intervened before many were made. In the 1950s he was making stationary diesel engines in South Africa.

NG

Further Reading
Lost Causes of Motoring, Lord Montagu of Beaulieu, Cassell, 1960.

MARENGO (I) 1907–1909

S.A. Automobili Marengo, Genoa.

This company began by making light cars with single- or 2-cylinder engines and shaft drive. In 1909 they announced a 1326cc 12/12hp four, but very few were made.

NG

MARGUERITE (F) 1922–1928

A. Marguerite, Courbevoie, Seine.

The Marguerite was an interesting make, as the company made numerous cars for sale by other manufacturers under their own names. The first Marguerite, the Type A, was a cyclecar powered by a 995cc Train V-twin engine, of which only about 12 were made. All subsequent Marguerites had 4-cylinder engines, mostly by Chapuis-Dornier. The Type B had a 900cc side-valve unit, but the cars which really made Marguerite's reputation were the BO, BO5 and BO7. The BO and BO5 were touring models with 1093cc engines, side-valve in the

1933 Marendaz 13/70 sports car.
NATIONAL MOTOR MUSEUM

BO and ohv in the BO5, while the BO7 had a longer wheelbase and was fitted at first with a 1495cc engine, but as this proved unsatisfactory it was replaced by the ohv 1093cc. A wide range of bodies was fitted to all these Marguerites, from staid saloons and tourers to sports and racing cars. The Marguerite's swan song was the BO2 (why it had an earlier number than its predecessors is not known), which had a lower chassis with Perrot-Piganeau front-wheel brakes and a 12-valve twin-carburettor version of Chapuis-Dornier's 1095cc engine. It had the racy lines of a Lombard or Rally, and a top speed of 84mph (134 km/h). Two cars were fitted with S.C.A.P. T11 engines and had a top speed of 88mph (141 km/h). A few of the last BO2s were called Morano-Marguerite after a financier Zamorano de Biedema, but he lost his fortune at the Deauville Casino and all Marguerite production came to an end. About 30 BO2s were made, of which five were Morano-Marguerites. Total output of Marguerites was about 450 cars, but 200 of these were sold to other firms, INDUCO, MADOU and M.S. in France, and HISPARCO in Spain.

NG

MARIAH (US) c.1994

Mariah Motorsports/Design Energy Inc., Santa Barbara, California.

The Mode Six Mariah was a radically converted Mazda RX-7 with a 425hp turbocharged engine. It included an extensively modified body with wheel flares, spoilers and ground effect panels. The suspension was reworked and a 540hp racing engine was optional. The price of $89,664 in 1994 included a new RX-7, or the individual components could be bought separately.

HP

MARIE (F) 1907

The Marie was a very small car built at Bayeux, powered by a 1¾hp De Dion-Bouton engine, with belt drive. The body was a single-seater, and it may have been a child's car.

NG

MARIENFELDE *see* M.M.B.

MARINO (I) 1923–1927

Stà Automobili Marino, Padua.

Luigi Marino made small sports cars in the idiom of French makes such as Amilcar, B.N.C. and Salmson. The first models had a 1½-litre 4-cylinder single-ohc engine and 4-speed gearbox, followed in 1924 by a smaller pushrod ohv C.I.M.E. engine of 1100cc, offered in three forms, 21bhp Normale, 32bhp Tipo Sport and 45bhp supercharged Gran Sport capable of 77mph (124km/h). All had 3-speed gearboxes. Car production ended in 1927 though the company survived until 1930, and in 1952 Luigi Marino made an experimental sports car with 750cc twin-ohc engine and rubber suspension.

NG

MARION (US) 1904–1915

Marion Motor Car Co., Indianapolis, Indiana.

The first Marion was a distinctive-looking car powered by a 16hp 4-cylinder air-cooled Reeves engine mounted transversely and fully exposed to the air. In

1911 Marion Model 40 coupé.
JOHN A. CONDE

c.1911 Marion Model A 30hp roadster.
NICK BALDWIN

1917 Marion-Handley 6-cylinder tourer.
NICK BALDWIN

layout and appearance it closely resembled another Indianapolis car, the PREMIER, and also the FRANKLIN. It had a 5-seater tourer body and chain drive. The design was changed for 1906 with a longitudinal engine under a conventional bonnet. The 16hp engine was joined by one of 28hp, also by Reeves, but these soon gave way to water-cooled units by Continental and other firms. Shaft drive replaced chains for 1907, when a roadster was available in addition to the tourer. These Marions were on the expensive side, at $2000-3000, but sales were encouraging, rising from 127 in 1904 to a high of 1437 in 1911. The most distinctive Marion, in name if not in style, was the Bobcat roadster of 1913 with 30/40hp 4-cylinder engine, named in response to Stutz' Bearcat. It only went under that name for one year, although a 2-seater roadster featured in the Marion range from 1907 to 1915. A 33.7hp six appeared in 1915, but later that

year J.I. Handley, who had been president of Marion since 1912 and was also president of American Motors Corp., makers of the AMERICAN UNDERSLUNG, moved production to Jackson, Michigan, where the IMPERIAL (vii) was also made. From 1916 to 1918 the cars were sold under the name Marion-Handley.
NG

MARION-HANDLEY (US) 1916–1918

Mutual Motors Co., Jackson, Michigan.
The Marion-Handley was the lineal successor to the earlier Marion, being one of two cars built under the direction of J.I. Handley, former president of the Marion Motor Car Co. of Indianapolis, Indiana, who had left that post to form the Mutual Motors Co. Handley had moved his operations to Jackson, Michigan after acquiring the Imperial Automobile Co. of Jackson and for several months produced both the Marion and Jackson lines. The Jackson was discontinued at the end of 1915 and Handley concentrated on Marion-Handley production exclusively.

The Marion-Handley was a typical assembled car of the period, body types limited to roadsters and touring cars, selling in a price range of from $1090 to $1575. The car was built into early 1918 when the company failed. An estimated 2000 Marion-Handleys were produced.
KM

MARITIME SIX (CDN) 1913–1914

Maritime Motors Ltd, St John, New Brunswick.
One of only two car makers from Canada's Atlantic provinces (the other was the McKAY), Maritime Motors began by announcing their own 6-cylinder car with Gray & Davis electric lighting and starting system, but they lacked the facilities for manufacture, so made an agreement with PALMER-SINGER of New York to assemble cars from Palmer Singer parts and sell them as the Maritime Singer Six. The first were rather staid artillery-wheeled tourers, but in late 1913 Palmer-Singer announced their 1915 models, with vee-radiators and wire wheels. However, they were expensive at $3295, and few were sold. Maritime's problems were not helped when Palmer-Singer went bankrupt in March 1914. Only two of the original Maritime Sixes were made, and estimates of Maritime Singer production vary between six and 24.
NG

MARKETOUR (US) 1964

Marketour Electric Cars, Long Beach, California.
The Marketour was a shopping car for short trips to the store. It had three wheels with the lone wheel in front. A removable top kept out the weather and two small lights provided safety after dark.
HP

MARK'S CUSTOM KITS (US) c.1997 to date

Mark's Custom Kits, Poinciana, Florida.
Like LOUISELLE, Mark's Custom Kits made the parts to transform a Pontiac Firebird or Chevrolet Camaro into a replica of Kitt the talking car from the *Knight Rider* TV show. These kits included digital instruments and pulsating LED lights for the nose. Kits could be ordered for home assembly or installed at their factory.
HP

MARK SEVEN (CDN) 1980s

This was a fairly close copy of the Lotus/Caterham Seven, fitted with a Toyota twin-cam engine.
CR

MARKS-MOIR (GB/AUS) 1923–1928

Marks-Moir Motors Ltd, Sydney, New South Wales.
The Consuta System of wood veneers, glued by waterproof caseinate and stitched with copper wire, as developed by boat builder Samuel Saunders in England, was adopted by W. A. Moir, patentee of a unitary construction method. The first example appeared in England with a mid-mounted Ford T engine and a novel limited action differential. A car with a Wolseley 10hp engine followed but further development in the UK was by HERON. In 1925 a coupé, with a 12hp Coventry-Climax engine, was exhibited by Sciennes Engineering at the Sydney

Motor Show while a tourer and delivery van were then reported to be in progress. However, in 1928 a roadster was made by Dewick of Strathfield with a Continental Red Seal engine and Ford T axles. The project was backed by Dr Arthur Marks, a pioneer motorist and principal of a Sydney motor firm, whose son was, coincidentally, later involved with the SOUTHERN CROSS.

MG

MARLAND (F) 1969–1982

Marland sarl, Issy-les-Moulineaux.

This competition car constructor first made the BSH sports coupé, with assistance from ex-ARISTA engineer Max Saint-Hilaire, from 1969. It had a tubular chassis designed for Renault 8 Gordini power and about 200 were sold exclusively in kit form (at 9840 francs). The Jorgia, first seen at the 1971 Salon de Paris, was a simple roadster inspired by the 1937 Georges Irat and designed by Philippe Charbonneaux. It was offered in kit form for basis on a Citroën 2CV chassis. Marland also produced the Riboud microcar for VITREX and planned to enter much larger-scale production with a Renault 4-based utility called the Plus (which came to naught). Increasingly Marland specialised in the production of beach buggies before turning to maritime industries in 1982.

CR

MARLBORO (US) 1900–1902

Marlboro Automobile & Carriage Co., Marlboro, Massachusetts.

In most respects the Marlboro was typical of New England steamer practice, apart from the 5hp Mason engine being horizontal rather than vertical. It had a tubular frame, full-elliptic springs and single-chain drive. 2- or 4- seater bodies were offered, and prices ran from $700 to $1000. By January 1901 30 had been sold, and this encouraged the company's president Orrin P. Walker to expand production. By July 1902 he found himself overstocked with cars which he could not sell, and production was closed down.

NG

MARLBOROUGH (i) (F/GB) 1906–1926

1906–1924 Éts Malicet et Blin, Aubervilliers, Seine.
1909–1926 T.B. André & Co. Ltd, London.

Although it bore an English name, the Marlborough was a wholly French car to start with, being made by components suppliers Malicet et Blin for sale on the UK market. The name first appeared on a 7hp single-cylinder light car exhibited at the 1906 Olympia Show, exhibited by the Chassis Construction Co. of Taunton, who also made their own C.C.C. cars. In 1909 T.B. André, best-known for their shock absorbers, took over the agency and began to sell conventional medium-sized cars powered by pair-cast 4-cylinder engines, 3-speed gearboxes and shaft drive. Models included the 4-cylinder 2210cc 15.9hp, 3052cc 20.1hp, and 6-cylinder 3062cc 26.9hp and 3617cc 23.8hp. In 1912 they brought out a light car powered by a 1130cc 8/10hp 4-cylinder engine with rounded radiator and shaft drive. For 1915 the engine was enlarged to 1207cc and artillery wheels replaced wire, giving the car a more solid appearance.

The first postwar Marlboroughs were still largely French, still with round radiators, but for 1921 there was a flat-radiatored 10/20hp with 1496cc British Anzani engine. The 1922 Roadspeed model was guaranteed to reach 60mph (97km/h), but for 1923 it had given way to a smaller car with 1100cc C.I.M.E ohv engine and no differential. This was listed up to 1926, joined by a sports car with 1991cc ohv 6-cylinder Coventry-Climax engine and 4-wheel brakes which never went into production.

NG

MARLBOROUGH (ii) (NZ) 1919–1922

John North Birch, Blenheim, South Island.

John North Birch, also known as George or 'Old Bill', made the Perks & Birch motor-wheel (taken up by SINGER in 1901) and had made the George Eliot motorcycle at Nuneaton before becoming a resident of New Zealand in 1905. He carried on with motor work while drawing up plans to produce his own car. A 4-cylinder fixed-head engine of 5823cc was designed, patterns made and the castings he made himself at a foundry which considered the task too complex. A batch of engines, named after the local region, were made. Some were used in boats, but there was only slow progress towards completing a car by 1919, due to wartime restrictions. He had made the radiator, cut the gears and built the body

1923 Marks-Moir prototype 2-seater.
NICK BALDWIN

1921 Marlborough (i) 10/20hp 2-seater.
NICK BALDWIN

and when completed it tended to be dated but it found a buyer who obtained good service from it as a taxi. Birch also made stationary engines and a large marine engine which became the subject of litigation, and the adverse outcome of this caused him to move to Gisborne in 1922.

Further work was carried on with cars, by then named CARLTON and fitted with coach-built bodies. A project for a small car, prompted by the success of the Austin 7, was commenced but this came to nought when his enterprise was destroyed by fire in 1929. Possessed of undoubted personal ability and having developed a car which was probably the closest New Zealand came to having an indigenous type, Birch's original optimism regarding the development of manufacturing industry in New Zealand went unrealised.

MG

MARLBOROUGH (iii) (GB) 1985–1986

Marlborough Cars, Verwood, Dorset.

This was one of very few cars to use the Morris Marina as a donor vehicle. The Marlborough SR had few other remarkable points, but one was its use of sheet steel for the main body structure and doors (the wings and other curved parts being in fibreglass). The chassis was a conventional affair, and incorporated a steel tube superstructure on to which the steel body parts were mounted.

CR

MARLBOROUGH-THOMAS (GB) 1923–1924

T.B. Andre & Co. Ltd, Weybridge, Surrey.

This was a joint venture between André and J.G. Parry Thomas, and was an advanced sports car powered by a 1493cc 4-cylinder engine with leaf-spring valve gear as used on the Leyland Eight, operated by single or twin-ohcs, according to different accounts. It had quarter-elliptic or torsion bar suspension, 4-wheel brakes and a streamlined body with flared wings. Priced at £575, very few were made, probably no more than five or six. They were built in a shed at Brooklands.

NG

1995 Marlin sports car.
MARLIN

1910 Marmon Model 32 tourer.
NICK BALDWIN

MARLIN (GB) 1979 to date

1979–1993 Marlin Engineering, Plymouth, Devon.
1993 to date Marlin Engineering, Crediton, Devon.
Paul Moorhouse produced one of the most successful of all British kits with the Marlin, having sold well in excess of 1500 cars to date. Neatly styled, its compact bodywork combined aluminium and fibreglass panels over a tubular chassis. This was first offered for Triumph Herald/Vitesse mechanicals, but in 1981 a Marina live axle was adopted, as a prelude to the Marina becoming the standard donor vehicle, and doors were standardised. Alfa Romeo, Fiat, Ford and Rover V8 engines were also commonly fitted. A larger Berlinetta 2+2 model was launched in 1984, boasting four seats and aluminium doors. Its single donor was the Ford Cortina, from which most major components were taken (Sierra and Fiat engined versions followed). Marlin sold the Roadster and Berlinetta to Y.K.C. in 1992, to concentrate on a new if similarly-styled car, the Cabrio, which used a Ford Sierra donor. A stripped-out development of this model was the Sportster, designed for BMW or V8 power. Increasingly Marlin moved away from kits with models like the Hunter, which usually used a BMW engine.

CR

MARMON (US) 1902–1933

1902–1926 Nordyke and Marmon Co., Indianapolis, Indiana.
1926–1933 Marmon Motor Car Co., Indianapolis, Indiana.
Nordyke and Marmon Co. was a prosperous manufacturer of milling machinery. Howard C. Marmon (1876–1943) studied engineering at the University of California, Berkeley, and joined his father's firm in 1899. Three years later, at age 23, he was appointed vice-president and chief engineer. The younger Marmon had conceived a car of his own design in 1898, and set about building it in a corner of the family plant. Frequent design changes and continual testing delayed its completion until 1902.

This first Marmon had an air-cooled, ohv V-twin engine of 1468cc, mounted longitudinally. Remarkable for its day was the use of pressure lubrication, using a drilled crankshaft and gear-type pump. A multiple-disc clutch and 3-speed selective gearbox drove the rear axle through a rigid drive shaft, without universal joints. Marmon's solution to the problem of axle movement was to mount the whole power package on a suspended subframe. Body design was also novel for the time, his side-entrance tonneau credited as the first use of the concept in the USA.

Marmon's second car built from the success of the first, using a V4 this time, still air-cooled with ohvs. Pressure lubrication was now extended to the piston pins, and a planetary gearbox was used. The subframe suspension continued, but with a single pivot point at the front. Marmon's body construction began the use, soon to be extensive, of aluminium castings. During 1904, Howard Marmon built and sold six cars, of design virtually identical to his own, to local citizens. The next year, a successor model on a longer 90in (2284mm) wheelbase was built in 25 copies. A V6 was tested by Marmon, but was not placed on the market. Marmons of this era, with a screen-fronted, u-shaped bonnet, somewhat resembled the contemporary FRANKLIN, although the air-cooled competitor used a transverse engine mounting.

An air-cooled V8 was exhibited at the December 1906 auto show in New York. Designated Model M-37, it had a 7416cc displacement and developed 65bhp. The double three point suspension was featured, and its 7-passenger touring body was all aluminium. A price tag of $5000, however, was probably instrumental in discouraging orders, so the car never reached production. At this point Marmon ceded the air-cooled market to Franklin, and introduced a line of much more conventional cars for 1909, using water-cooled in-line T-head 4-cylinder engines and abandoning the subframe suspension. The Model H lasted but one year, but the Model 32 would stay in production for seven seasons. A Marmon 32, given the name Wasp, was taken to the nearby speedway; it won the inaugural Indianapolis 500 race in 1911, driven by Ray HARROUN, who would later build his own car by that name.

In 1913, a 6-cylinder version of the Wasp was introduced, the Model 48, priced at a heady $5000 to $6250. A smaller, more moderately-priced six, the Model 41, was added the following year, but Howard Marmon became consumed with the design of an all-new car. For this venture he was joined by Fred Moscovics, later to make his name at STUTZ, and Alanson Brush, designer of the BRUSH car which had been a casualty of the U.S. Motor Co. collapse. Marmon went fully into aluminium for his new car. Engine block and crankcase were formed in a single casting of the light alloy, and nearly all other parts, except the crankshaft and valves, were aluminium as well, even the pushrods. The only cast iron used was for cylinder sleeves and head. A Z-shaped chassis frame combined splash aprons and running boards and eliminated the body sills, combining with the extensive use of alloy to reduce the weight of the car by one fourth, compared to competitive vehicles. Its big (5574cc) six developed 74bhp, which gave it excellent performance. Called the Model 34, for its rated horsepower, the car was introduced in December 1915.

For all its sophistication, the new Marmon did not find great success in the market. Despite his engineering expertise, Howard Marmon was not adept at production or promotion, and his advanced designs were considered a bit far-out by some potential purchasers, who opted for CADILLACs or PACKARDs instead. The alloy-block engine also had some problems with creeping cylinder liners, although a cure was found in boiling the castings before machining.

The 34 was redesigned for 1920, entering a more conventional phase. Now its six was constructed of two 3-cylinder cast iron castings, placed on an aluminium crankcase. Pistons were an aluminium-iron composite, and this seems to have been a trouble-free design, for it stayed in production for eight years with few changes.

Although its cars were good, the Nordyke and Marmon firm was not healthy financially. Losses were continual from the beginning of the 1920s. In 1924, George M. Williams of Buffalo Wire Wheel Corp. came on board as president, and Howard Marmon's brother Walter was elevated from that office to chairman of the board. Williams set out to reform the product line, first by adopting the HUDSON tactic of low-priced closed cars. This was somewhat successful, and sales rose by two thirds from 1924 to 1925. However, Williams envisioned further changes to the product line, including the advent of a low-priced 8-cylinder car. Enlisting engineer Delmar 'Barney' Roos from LOCOMOBILE, he initiated work on what would become the 1927 Little Marmon, a 3115cc ohv eight selling for $1795 to $1895. Despite noteworthy performance, the Little Marmon was not a commercial success, and Roos soon departed for STUDEBAKER, and was succeeded by Thomas Litle, whose job was to engineer an all-8-cylinder Marmon line. Nordyke and Marmon had spun off its automotive division as Marmon Motor Car Co. in 1926.

The 6-cylinder Model 34 had been updated as the 74 in 1925, on a longer 136in (3452mm) wheelbase. This car became the 75, big brother to the Little Marmon, in 1927, and continued for one more year, when it was joined by the first two series of Williams' new eights. These, the 68 and 78, were also smaller than the 6-cylinder cars, and sold for, in some cases, less than half the price. The 78, on a 120in (3046mm) wheelbase, used the engine from the Little Marmon, bored out to 3554cc. The smaller 68, introduced a month later, at the January 1928 New York auto show, was on a 114in (2893mm) wheelbase chassis and was powered by a newly-designed side-valve straight-8 of 3298cc. The 78 sold in the Little Marmon's price range; the 68 for $1395 to $1495. For 1929, only 8-cylinder cars were listed, the 68 and 78 being joined by an under-$1000 model called the ROOSEVELT, after the 26th American president. Initially considered a companion make in its own right, the Roosevelt was officially christened Marmon-Roosevelt for 1930, and was fully absorbed into the Marmon line as the Model 70 in 1931. The lower-priced strategy was producing some results, however; production rose steadily to over 22,000 in 1929, but declined, with the fortunes of the times, thereafter.

A Big Eight was readied for 1930, basically signalling a return to the luxury market. Set on a 135in (3426mm) wheelbase, it used a 5164cc side-valve eight developing 125bhp. A Warner 4-speed gearbox was standard. The car was advertised

1921 Marmon Model 34 tourer.
NICK BALDWIN

1926 Marmon Model 74 sedan by Fleetwood.
NICK BALDWIN

1931 Marmon Sixteen convertible coupé.
NATIONAL MOTOR MUSEUM

for $3300, but this rose to $3800 when fully equipped. The Big Eight was carried into 1931, accompanied by replacements for the 68 and 78, the 8-69 and 8-79 respectively. The latter two were new cars, modelled on the Big Eight. Evolutions of all these models continued to 1932, but sales continued to erode. 1932 was the last year of the 8-cylinder Marmons.

Howard Marmon had saved his best for last. Although it was pretty clear that independent luxury car-makers would be unlikely to survive the Depression, Marmon made a valiant attempt. He had started work on his masterpiece in 1926, under the cloak of the Midwest Aviation Co. The heart of the Marmon Sixteen was a compact even-firing 45-degree engine of 8046cc. Its 6.0:1 cr resulted in 200bhp at 3400rpm, and Marmon's aluminium construction meant that the engine weighed 930lbs (425kg) complete, the block and crankcase accounting for but an eighth of that. Valves were overhead, pushrod-operated, and experience with the Model 34 had led Marmon, finally, to use of wet cylinder liners. Built on a 145in (3680mm) wheelbase, the Marmon Sixteen's contemporary styling was by New York industrial designer Walter Dorwin Teague. The actual sketching and drawing was done by Teague's son, Walter Junior, then working

1932 Marmon Model 8-125 convertible coupé.
ELLIOTT KAHN

1900 Marot-Gardon 4¹/₂hp voiturette.
NATIONAL MOTOR MUSEUM

with his father's firm. Described by Teague Senior, as 'a projectile moving in a straight line forward', the Sixteen was low and sleek, though somewhat angular at the edges, its veed radiator shell set off with heavy horizontal louvres.

The 4800lbs (2180kg) car was shown in December 1930, but production did not start until March 1931. Its price was set at $5200. By that time, the luxury car market was on a steep downward slide, and Marmon had the disadvantage of being scooped by Cadillac, whose own 16-cylinder car, while slightly more expensive and nowhere near as stylish, had it to market by over a year. Only 390 Marmon Sixteens were built before the company went into receivership in May 1933. A 12-cylinder model was contemplated, and a single example, with odd wing-mounted headlamps, was built with Howard Marmon's own money, but the concept went no further.

Harry Miller and Preston Tucker attempted to revive the Marmon car operation in 1934, as the American Automotive Corp., to produce the Sixteen, but the effort came to naught. The Marmon name, however, did survive, as Howard's brother, Walter Marmon had teamed with Arthur Herrrington to produced all-wheel drive trucks and truck conversions. These were produced, often on Ford commercial chassis, until 1963. After Herrington's retirement, the Marmon name and some unfinished trucks were sold, and a new Marmon Motor Co. built heavy trucks in Texas until 1997.

KF

Further Reading
The Marmon Heritage, George P. and Stacey P. Hanley, Doyle Hyk Publishing Co., 1985.
'Marmon: A Quest for Perfection', Maurice D. Hendry, *Automobile Quarterly*, Vol. 7, No. 2.

MAROCCHI (I) 1900–1901
Fratelli Marocchi, Milan.
The Marocchi was a very small 2-seater 3-wheeler, not unlike a motorised bath chair in appearance, powered by two 1¹/₂hp single-cylinder engines, one on each side of the front wheel, which they drove. It had tiller steering.
NG

MAROT-GARDON (F) 1899–c.1902
Ph. Marot, Gardon et Cie, Corbie, Somme.
This company began making motor tricycles and quads in 1898, and the following year they brought out a voiturette powered by a 3hp single-cylinder engine, with a 3-speed gearbox. For 1900 power was increased to 4¹/₂hp, and for 1901 two models were offered, a 2-seater with front-mounted horizontal 6hp engine and chain drive, and a racing voiturette with a rear-mounted 7hp Sonçin vertical engine geared directly to the rear axle.
NG

MAROT-GINTRAC (F) 1905
Sté des Moteurs et Automobiles Marot-Gintrac, Bordeaux.
Mainly makers of stationary and marine engines, Marot-Gintrac also built a few cars powered by 35/40hp 4-cylinder engines.
NG

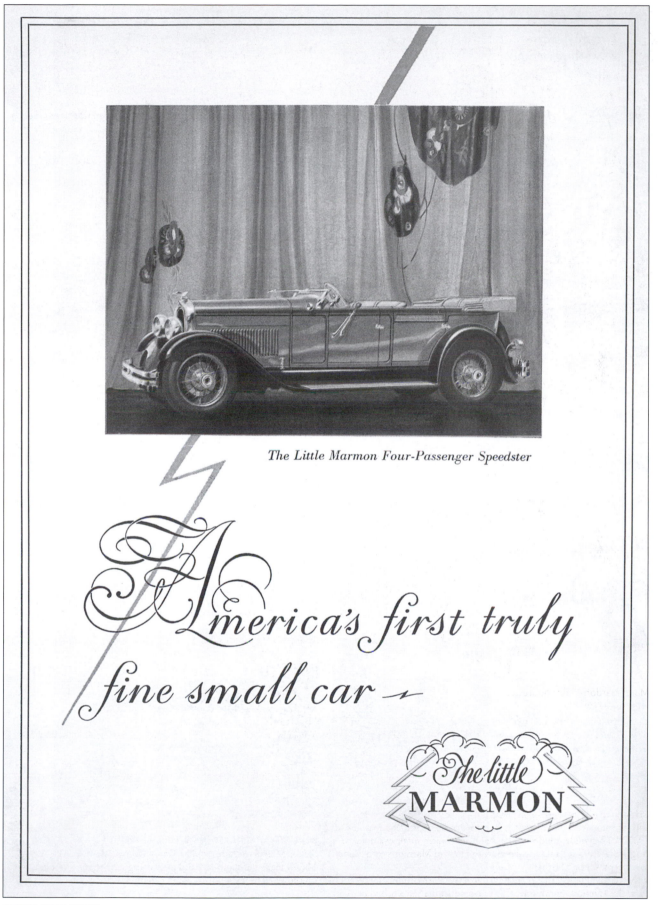

The Little Marmon Four-Passenger Speedster

America's first truly fine small car

The little
MARMON

1930 Marquette (ii) Series 30 coupé.
NICK GEORGANO

1930 Marquette (ii) Series 30 coupé by Grose.
ALAN BURMAN

MARPLE (US) c.1994–1996

Marple Automotive Group, Shelbyville, Tennessee.
Custom Classics, Madison, South Dakota.
The Tojan was a body conversion kit for the Pontiac Firebird that gave it a cleaner, more aggressive shape. The Carralo was a kit for the Chevrolet Camaro that made it look more exotic. Both kits were also sold by KNUDSEN. They were sold in kit and assembled form.

HP

MARQUES PEREIRA (P) 1970s

Marques Pereira e Teles, Cascais.
This company produced the Minitara beach buggy and also a rigidly squared-off open jeep-type vehicle called the Jiptara. Both used a VW Beetle floorpan.

CR

MARQUETTE (i) (US) 1912

Marquette Motor Co., Saginaw, Michigan.
Peninsular Motor Co., Saginaw, Michigan.
The Marquette Motor Co. was set up in 1909 by William C. Durant to continue production of two marques he had bought, RAINIER and WELCH-DETROIT. The factory made complete Rainiers up to 1911, and parts for the Welch-Detroit, also to 1911. The car which emerged under the Marquette name was described as a composite of these two makes. It had a 4-cylinder T-head engine in two sizes, 40 and 45hp, and on two wheelbases, 119 (3020mm) and 122in (3096mm), with the more powerful engine in the shorter wheelbase. The usual body styles were offered, 2-seater runabout, 4-, 5- and 7-seater tourers. At the end of February 1912 the company changed its name to Peninsular, and it seems that some of the cars carried the Peninsular name as well. The marque was discontinued in September 1912.

NG

MARQUETTE (ii) (US) 1930

Buick Motor Co., Flint, Michigan.
General Motors introduced the Marquette in May 1929 as a lower-priced companion car by Buick, production – billed as a 1930 model – starting a month later. The Marquette name had been used previously by William C. Durant when, as president of General Motors, he planned to enter the racing-car milieu and renamed the Buick racer with a different badge in order to follow racing regulations at the time. The 1930 Marquette, unlike Buick, used an L-head 6-cylinder engine and a wheelbase of 114in (2893mm), the car identifiable by its unique herringbone radiator pattern. The price range began with a business coupé at $995 – the price presumably set at this figure to allow an 'under $1000' claim – and peaking with the sedan at $1060. Like the recently introduced Viking by GM, the Marquette was a victim of poor timing and the stock market crash. Production ceased immediately following that debacle after a production run of 35,000 units.

KM

MARQUEZ (i) (F) 1930

Automobiles L.F. Marquez, Paris.
Argentine-born Marquez designed a striking-looking sports car powered by a 2340cc straight-8 S.C.A.P. engine turned round and driving the front wheels via a 4-speed gearbox. This necessitated a very long bonnet and a wheelbase of 110in (2792mm). Front suspension was by four transverse leaf springs. The body was an all-enveloping 'tank' style by Guillaume Busson. The car was built for Marquez by the engineer Hermann who later worked for Hispano-Suiza. Soon after its completion Marquez took it back to Argentina.

NG

MARQUEZ (ii) (BR) 1978–c.1980

Marquez Industria e Comercio Ltda, Cubateo.
The Volkswagen Brasilia 1600 in twin-carburettor form was the basis for this car, made in coupé and cabriolet forms.

NG

MARR (US) 1903–1904

Marr Auto Car Co., Detroit, Michigan.
Walter L. Marr built a light car powered by a 6½hp single-cylinder engine mounted under the seat and driving by single chain. He did not have a factory and contracted with the Fauber Manufacturing Co. of Elgin, Illinois to build 100 cars for him while he looked for suitable premises. The 100 were probably never completed as the Fauber factory was burnt down in August 1904 with the loss of 14 Marr runabouts. Walter Marr returned to working for David Dunbar Buick. He continued to serve as a consulting engineer, and in 1914 designed and built a tandem-seated 4-cylinder cyclecar, but Buick decided against producing it.

NG

MARRIOTT (AUS) 1904

W.J. Marriott, Fairfield, Victoria.
Art-metal worker, James Marriott, whose output included the lamp stands for Victoria's Parliament House, built a rear-entrance tonneau-bodied steam car with the assistance of his son, Clarence, in 1904. Its boiler was a kerosene burning 'flash' type, the engine was imported from England and a large condenser dominated its frontal aspect. If there had been an eye to commercial possibilities they may have been disappointed, and the vehicle was used privately for some years. Later, the business, run by Clarence, introduced Hecla electrical appliances.

MG

MARS (i) (D) 1906–1908

Mars-Werke AG, Nuremberg.
Nuremberg was a leading centre of bicycle manufacture in Germany, and one of these firms, Mars, turned to motorcycles and then to cars. These were a single-cylinder 6/7hp and a 2-cylinder 8/10hp, both with Maurer-type friction drive. After two years Mars returned to 2-wheelers which they made until 1957.

HON

MARS (ii) (A) 1912–1913
Slatinanske tovarny automobilu R.A. Smekal, Slatinany.
Before World War I, the Smekal Works, famous for their fire engine production, built under licence a limited number of light cars, although the contemporary advertisements described them as pure Czech products. The mechanical components of Mars cars were probably of German extraction, with a 4-cylinder 1943cc 16bhp water-cooled engine. Only the 4-seater open bodies and wooden wheels were manufactured at the Slatinany factory.

MSH

MARS II *see* EFP

MARSEEL; MARSEAL (GB) 1920–1925
1920–1923 Marseel Motors Ltd, Coventry.
1923–1925 Marseal Motors Ltd, Coventry.
This was a conventional light car made by Captain Donald Marendaz and Seelhaft, both of whom had worked at Siddeley-Deasy. It was powered by a 1246cc Coventry-Simplex 4-cylinder side-valve engine, and had little to distinguish it from many rivals, apart from the rather up-market worm final drive. The tall vee-radiator gave way to a lower flat profile one, and other sizes of Coventry-Simplex engine were used, including 1368 and 1496cc. A 1018cc oil-cooled four and a small six never saw production. In 1923 Seelhaft left, and Marendaz changed the name of his company and car to Marseal. The 2- and 4-seater bodies were mostly made by Lawson and Hancock & Warman, the latter a Coventry firm who subsequently did a lot of work for Riley. After about 1200 cars had been made, Marendaz closed his company down. Two years later he launched the Marendaz Special in London. A few motorcycles and scooters were made by Marseel in 1920/21.

NG

MARSH (i) (US) 1905
American Motor Co., Brockton, Massachusetts.
The Marsh brothers built three experimental steam cars between 1899 and about 1901, then made motorcycles which lasted up to about 1916. In 1905 they brought out a 2-seater runabout powered by a front-mounted 10hp 2-cylinder air-cooled engine. It had a single acetylene cyclops headlamp ahead of the radiator. It was only made as a Marsh for one year, after which the brothers sold their business to Charles H. Metz. The motorcycles were sold as Marsh-Metz and Metz brought out his own car in 1909.

The Marsh brothers had several subsequent involvements with cars, including the EASTERN, VULCAN (ii), STERLING (iii) and in Cleveland, another car called the MARSH.

NG

MARSH (ii) (US) 1920–1923
Marsh Motors Co., Cleveland, Ohio.
This company was formed by the four Marsh brothers who had begun their automotive careers in Brockton, Massachusetts, then became involved with various makes (see MARSH (i)) before coming together again after World War I. They planned to make a bigger and better Model T Ford, and brought some equipment from the factory at Brockton where they had made the STERLING (iii). The second Marsh used 4- and 6-cylinder engines, both by Continental, but only four were made with the 4-cylinder engine and two with the six. All but one had sedan bodies. This was the last of the Marshs' automotive ventures.

NG

MARSHALL (i) *see* BELSIZE

MARSHALL (ii) (US) 1919–1922
Marshall Manufacturing Co., Chicago, Illinois.
With the colourful if not poetic slogan 'Built on a Promise That's Right Clear Thru. Sold on a Guarantee That Our Promise is True', the Marshall was actually a Norwalk which carried the name of the Chicago Norwalk distributor on its badge. And, like the Norwalk, the Marshall used a Lycoming K 4-cylinder engine with a 116in (2944mm) wheelbase. Unlike the Norwalk, its price was $1295, an increase of $160 above that of its West Virginia parent which we might assume was the cost of shipping. The 5-seater touring car was the only body available.

KM

1923 Marseal 9/26hp 2-seater.
NICK BALDWIN

MARSHALL (iii) (GB) 1919–1920
P.F.E. Marshall, Gainsborough, Lincolnshire.
An obscure car which never made national lists or magazines, let alone motor shows, but a small number were made using side-valve Coventry-Climax F type engines. Although made in the same town, there was no connection with the well-known Marshall Son & Co. Ltd, makers of traction engines, agricultural tractors and steam-rollers.

NG

MARSHALL-ARTER (GB) 1912–1915
1912–1913 Marshall, Arter & Co., Hammersmith, London.
1913–1915 Marshall-Arter Ltd, Hammersmith, London.
Originally known as the Q.E.D., this was a light car powered by an 8hp V-twin J.A.P. engine, with an unusual drive. Instead of a propeller shaft, there was a long flat spring revolving in a casing, which was said to absorb all sudden jerks. This led to a 2-speed gearbox incorporated in the rear axle. The frame was of ash. For 1914 the company adopted 4-cylinder engines by Chapuis-Dorner, of 1096 and 1244cc.

NG

MARSONETTO (F) 1957–1959; 1965–1972
Ateliers Marsonetto, Lyon, Rhône.
Mario Marsonetto founded his company in Lyon as early as 1946. The Luciole coupé was produced in the years 1957–59. This was a handsome coupé using a Dyna Panhard engine (or alternatively Renault 4CV), and around 15 examples were made. At the end of 1965, Marsonetto returned with the Mars 1, a 4-seater coupé using a Renault 8 engine mounted up front and driving the front wheels. The specification included 4-wheel disc brakes, all-independent suspension, a tubular steel chassis and plastic bodywork. A much-revised model appeared in 1968, incorporating a transparent fastback and a Renault 16TS engine. A top speed of 140mph (225km/h) was claimed.

CR

MARTA (H) 1908–1922
1908–1912 Magyar Automobil Részvénytársaság Westinghouse Rendszer, Arad.
1912–1922 Magyar Automobil Részvénytársaság, Arad.
The Hungarian Automobile Rt Arad was established in 1908 and it was the first company in Hungary which was specially formed to manufacture automobiles.

Courtesy of Jenö Böszörményi, a Hungarian-born engineer who worked at the French Westinghouse company, Westinghouse granted a licence for its cars. The new company received free land from the city of Arad – so the company had a jolly good start.

It was set up to make various vehicles, not just cars, and their accessories as well. The management consisted of Hungarian noblemen, and staff from S.A. Westinghouse the local railway company.

In addition to automobiles, trucks and railway-engines were the first products of the Marta company. They organised the first Hungarian bus lines too. These first models were basically Westinghouses assembled in Hungary. But the company suffered trading problems and a lack of funds. In the end, the sole Hungarian tyre-maker, Magyar Ruggantaárugyár took a controlling interest, bringing fresh contacts and orders. The Hungarian Post showed great interest and promptly ordered 175 buses. Three small Marta cars were entered in a 1912 race in Hungary, and they won! The newly established Budapest Taxi Co. ordered 200 taxis.

A year later Marta gained a licence to produce the British Knight-engined DAIMLER cars, but it was a short-lived venture as World War I broke out. During the War the German BENZ Co. took over the company and made Benz cars, various buses and aero-engines there.

After the War the Rumanian government nationalised the company, renamed it Astra, and focused its activities on railway products. As Arad (Oradea) now belongs to Rumania, claims exist that Marta was the first Rumanian-built car.

PN

MARTIN (i) (GB) 1904–1906
Hall & Martin, Croydon, Surrey.
Harry Martin was a dealer in cars and motorcycles, new and second hand, who made a few cars for sale. These included one with a 6½hp De Dion-Bouton engine offered in 1904, and a larger tonneau powered by a 10/12hp 2-cylinder Aster engine in 1905/06. He shared premises with his father who manufactured sewing machines and musical instruments, and never formed a company. In 1912 he built a one-off racing tricycle for a Mr Axford, for use at Brooklands.

NG

MARTIN (ii) (US) 1921–1922
Martin Motor Co., Springfield, Massachusetts.
This was an ultra-light 3-wheeler with two wheels in line, as in the Scott Sociable, powered by a 616cc air-cooled V-twin engine, with a wheelbase of only 60in (1523mm). It was designed by Charles H. Martin, who was better known for his Martin Rocking Fifth Wheel Co. which made Knox articulated tractor/trailer units. Another claim to fame was that its sponsor was Charles Glidden who had organised the Glidden tours in the early years of the century. The first two Martin prototypes had aluminium bodies and the third a steel body. These may have been the only Martins built, as the venture had failed by the end of 1922. During its trials it was sometimes referred to as the Scootmobile, Scootamobile or Scoutmobile.

NG

MARTIN (iii) & (iv) (US) 1927–1932
Martin Aeroplane Factory, Garden City, Long Island, New York.
The Martin – promoted under the names Martin, Dart and Martin-Dart, was a midget car, which was more of an idea than an actuality and, despite vigorous promotion, never went beyond three prototypes. The concept for the Dart was that of James V. Martin who believed that the future of motoring might be better served by an economical miniature car rather than conventional ones. His basic idea was placed in the hands of a Long Island neighbour, Miles Harold Carpenter who had previously manufactured the luxurious PHIANNA from 1919 into 1922. Carpenter completed three of the small cars during 1927 (and possibly a fourth one later). The cars weighed 600lbs, had wheelbases of 60in (1523mm), were powered by 29bhp Cleveland motorcycle engines and guaranteed to 'cruise comfortably' at 40 to 50mph (64 to 80km/h) with a top speed of 60mph (97km/h). Gasoline consumption was advertised at 40 to 50mpg and the wooden crates in which they were to be delivered were suggested as ideal garages for them.

Vigorous promotion of the Darts was done in numerous ways from 1928 through to late 1930 while the Dart personnel tried – unsuccessfully as it turned out – to get financial backing for production. Two expensive catalogues were printed and generous coverage was given by the automotive press as well as exhibitions in various locations and well-advertised road testing.

Martin Motors, Inc. of Garden City, Long Island was formed and plans were outlined for production of a Martin truck, a prototype of which was built in 1929 and an attempt at entering the export market was considered, to no avail. In 1929, an announcement was made that the $200 to $250 Martin-Dart would be assembled by the M. P. Möller Motor Car Co. of Hagerstown, Maryland, which had formerly built the Dagmar automobile and was still actively producing motor vehicles, including the Elysee truck and several different makes of taxicabs. These plans fell through and in a last minute attempt to gain more publicity the Dart underwent two name changes, first as the Martin Midget and then as the Victory, to no avail. By the end of 1931, promotion ceased and further building plans were abandoned as further interest petered out. The Dart, Martin, whatever, was dead.

But not the end of novel automobile design by James V. Martin, who exhibited two rear-engined cars at the National Automobile Show in New York City in 1932. Both of these featured designs ahead of their time with engines in the rear and a teardrop streamlining at the rear, similar to what would become known as a 'fastback' 25 years later. These projected Martins were generously chronicled in the automotive press and elsewhere but failed to arouse public interest and James Martin ceased trying for a while.

He briefly surfaced following World War II with a new design that included prototypes for a Martinette and a Stationette, both of which failed to capture any interest in financial centres. These were Martin's last attempts to invade the automotive milieu and he died in 1956.

KM

Further Reading
'1928 Martin, Plainly Aerodynamic', Bud Juneau,
Special-Interest Autos, SIA, May–June, 1998.

MARTIN (v) (US) c.1950–1954
Commonwealth Research Corp., New York, New York.
Small 3-wheeled cars were the sole interest of James Vernon Martin, who built a series of prototypes over a 22-year period. He also pioneered an automatic transmission that used magnetism to lock up the engine and driveshaft. His first vehicle was called the Martinette, and it was an aluminium-bodied vehicle with a single wheel at the back. The Stationette that followed in 1950 had an attractive wood-panelled body. However, Martin was unable to interest anyone in producing his designs.

HP

MARTIN (vi) (F) 1986–1996
Martin Automobiles, Olonne-sur-Mer.
Although the Lotus Seven never carried quite the same mythology in France as it did in other parts of the world, the Martin TTM (also called the Gmo) was certainly inspired by it. It used a tubular steel chassis and bodywork consisting of aluminium sections fixed by glue and rivets, plus plastic panels. This was mated to Ford components, including a choice of 1.6, 1.6 RS, 1.8 and 2.0 engines. From 1995 it relied on Ford Zetec power. An A.C. Cobra replica (later called the Matou) entered into production in 1990, with Ford Sierra running gear and Ford V6 power; it apparently claimed the right to be called an A.C. Martin took over the TILBURY from 1990. The company's next model was a Ford GT40 replica called the GTA 40, first offered in 1994, and rather disappointingly it had a mere Ford V6 engine mounted amidships.

CR

MARTINDALE & MILLIKAN see CONTINENTAL (iii)

MARTIN ET LETHIMONNIER see SULTANE

MARTINETTE (D) 1921
Volta-Werke, Berlin-Weidmannslust.
Designed and built by the engineer F.A.E. Martin, this was a light sports car powered by a 2-cylinder 2-stroke engine of motorcycle origin. They must have looked distinctive as the standard paintwork consisted of zebra stripes. About 100 were made.

HON

MARTINI (CH) 1897–1933
1897–1903 Martini & Cie, Frauenfeld.
1903–1905 Martini & Cie, St Blaise, Neuchâtel.
1905–1906 Martini Automobiles & Co. Ltd, St Blaise, Neuchâtel.
1906–1908 Hills-Martini Ltd, St Blaise, Neuchâtel.
1908–1911 Sté Nouvelle des Automobiles Martini, St Blaise, Neuchâtel.
1911–1933 Neue Martini Automobilgesellschaft, St Blaise, Neuchâtel.
In 1864 Friedrich Ritter von Martini (1833–1897) took over a small machine factory. He developed the Martini rifle action which was adopted by the British army for its service rifle. In addition to textile machines, Martini also produced his rifle in Frauenfeld. In 1883 he launched the first industrial gas engine which was followed by stationary petrol engines in 1888. Friedrich's eldest son, Adolf von Martini (1865–1926), graduated at the Technical University of Zürich and

was inspired by the Benz Motorwagen to build his own prototype motorcar also in 1888. It was not successful and his father disapproved. With the latter's death in 1897, Adolf took over management of the company and re-started the development of a motorcar. In 1898–99 two prototypes with rear-mounted twin opposed-cylinder engines, designed by Paul Haenlein (who later was with Maybach Zeppelin Motorenfabrik), with low tension magneto ignition, were completed. Not satisfied with these vehicles, Martini engaged Alfred Zürcher to design a car on the lines of the more advanced Panhard system with the same engine placed in the front.

Zürcher left in 1900 to form, together with Huber, the ORION factory in Zürich, where a very similar car was built. Martini still made most of the turnover of the factory with production of book-binding and textile machines and employed about 450 workers.

In 1901 a new 10hp car and the first commercial vehicle were launched. One year later they offered four models with V4 engines of 8, 10, 12 and 16hp but apparently the first production batch of 30 cars comprised only 10hp and 16hp models. These were sold at SFr1000 per 1hp! Shortly afterwards a contract was signed with the French company ROCHET-SCHNEIDER of Lyon. Martini was granted the right to build under licence the French cars, which were strongly influenced by the advanced Daimler design, and he was able to make use of Daimler's distribution network.

Thinking big, Martini built a new factory in St Blaise near Neuchâtel, where the first small series of 14/18hp touring cars with 4-cylinder in-line T-head engines of 4084cc were produced in 1903. The engines and commercial vehicles were still made in Frauenfeld and this continued for some time. Charles Dardel, son-in-law of Friedrich von Martini, was appointed commercial director in St Blaise and Max von Martini, the youngest brother of Adolf, was instructor and works driver. At about this time Captain H.H.P. Deasy of London became responsible for all exportation of Martini cars. In the British 1000 miles reliability trial, Martini won a gold medal. Deasy thought of a special performance to catch the headlines of the motoring press and drove one of the new 14/18hp double phaetons on the railroad bed to the top of the Rochers de Naye mountain (6727ft) in Switzerland.

At the first National Automobile Show in Geneva in 1905, Martini displayed one chassis and two coach-built tourers of 16/20hp. Various models of 16–70hp of similar design with 4-cylinder T-head engines of 3054cc to 7893cc capacity, 4-speed gearboxes, chain drive and often fine coachwork by Geissberger, Zürich were produced from 1905 until 1910. Prices ranged from SFr9000 to SFr24,000. Apart from selling on the home market, Martini was represented in Paris by Farman Frères, in New York, Germany, Austria and exported to many other countries. Rapidly increasing production required more capital than was available and a British investment group took over, renaming the company Martini Automobiles & Co. Ltd and it also took over the Frauenfeld motor vehicle branch in 1906. Shortly afterwards, Captain Deasy formed his own company and Martini was sold again and named for a short time Hill-Martini Ltd. In the 1907 Kaiserpreis competition in Germany, both Martini 40/50hp tourers finished and were placed 12th and 14th in a field which included the best racing drivers in Mercedes, Fiat, Itala, Opel and others. At the Paris Show of 1907, Martini presented the new 12/16hp model with its 4-cylinder monobloc inlet over exhaust engine of 2213cc with 3-, later 4-speed gearbox and shaft drive.

The financial problems persisted and after arrangements with the creditors, a new company with Swiss capital was formed in 1908. It took over both factories, at St Blaise and Frauenfeld and was named Société Nouvelle des Automobiles Martini. Despite dark clouds on the economic sky, Martini hired Charles Baehni, a young and talented engineer who had been with HENRIOD in Paris. He immediately designed a small high performance car, three of which were nominated for the Dieppe GP des Voiturettes of 1908. The tiny 8hp 4-cylinder engine of 62 × 90mm and 1086cc was one of the first to have a shaft-driven ohc and the slanted valves allowed for a nearly hemisperical chamber. In fact its design was quite similar to the famous voiturettes of Bugatti and Isotta Fraschini. Lubrication was by pump under pressure and the crankshaft had ball bearings. Ignition was by high tension magneto and the carburettor was fitted directly to the engine. Pump cooling was supported by the flywheel which formed a fan. Power was transmitted through a multi-plate clutch, a 3-speed gearbox, and the driving shaft to the differential of the rear axle. Although Beck finished only in 12th position in Dieppe, the team was more successful in

1897 Martini 2-cylinder 4-seater.
ERNEST SCHMID

1903 Martini 2-seater.
ERNEST SCHMID

the Coupe des Voiturettes race of Compiègne, winning the Delage team cup. The production version of 10hp had a slightly increased capacity of 1194cc, later 1269cc, and sold for SFr6850.

In 1910 Martini had an output of 260 chassis but nevertheless the year ended with a substantial loss and when the house bank went bankrupt, serious financial problems loomed. One action to cut further losses was to drop the advanced, but expensive to make, voiturette from the programme. Towards the end of 1911, financial arrangements were finalised and BAYARD-CLEMENT became one of the main shareholders and took over the technical management. Staff totalled about 250 workers. Adolf von Martini moved to Italy and was connected with the new short-lived venture of the ADEM car, which he intended to market in Great Britain. His brother Max apparently also left the company as his name no longer figured in the starting lists of regional and national sporting events. The chief designer, Charles Baehni, also left St Blaise to set up his own operation in Geneva to produce the YAXA.

In 1912 Martini, under the new management, offered for sale three models – 12/16hp, 16/24hp and 25/35hp with 2412cc, 3561cc and 5319cc respectively. A large order, for 53 motorcars, was received from the United States. The annual result was positive, allowing for a 5 per cent dividend to be paid to the shareholders. In 1913 the programme was changed again and five models were on the market. Most surprising, a 15hp Sport with a new high-performance 4-cylinder ohc-

1904 Martini 16hp tourer.
NATIONAL MOTOR MUSEUM

1932 Martini Model NF6 saloon.
ERNEST SCHMID

engine and four valves, set at an angle said to deliver 50bhp, was produced. Experiments with Knight engines had been conducted in 1911 and now the 25hp, with a fashionable 4-cylinder sleeve-valve engine of 4396cc producing slightly more than 35bhp, was launched. With 539 cars registered on Swiss roads, Martini was by far the most popular make. At the Swiss National Exhibition of 1914 in Berne, Martini displayed various cars with coach-built bodies by Geissberger, of Zürich, Gygax, of Biel and Gangloff, of Geneva. Several more were shown on the stands of the coachbuilders. The new small Martini 8/22hp with a monobloc 4-cylinder engine of 1356cc was, however, not yet ready. Obviously Martini was not very happy with the sleeve-valve engine and the 25hp was silently dropped from the programme.

The 1914 range comprised two conventional 4-cylinder models of 10/28hp 2612cc and 18/24hp 3561cc and the slightly de-tuned 15hp Sport as the 11/35hp with 2995cc. With the outbreak of World War I, Martini, like other Swiss manufacturers, exported cars and commercial vehicles to one or the other of the belligerent nations. By 1915 the private bank O. Guhl of Zürich had secured a majority shareholding and the factory of Frauenfeld was renamed Motorenwerke Frauenfeld AG in which BERNA and Martini each had a 50 per cent interest. Production in 1916 totalled 276 chassis and was increased to 345 in 1917, the highest ever output of the company. Substantial orders for lorries were filled for the Dutch Army. The end of the war brought a sharp decline of production. In 1919 Martini adopted a one model policy with their 'TF' which was an improved 18/24hp now with 3815cc capacity and an output of 45bhp. There was an increasing flow of US and European cars imported into Switzerland, but because many countries had introduced high or prohibitive import duties and there were now more advanced designs from the big foreign companies, exportation was made more difficult. Martini had a bad year with a considerable loss. Rootes Brothers took over the Martini branch in London but the interest they had shown for the St Blaise factory ended when they became

aware of the company's difficult situation. Despite the second highest production on record, 1920 did not bring any improvement, and high costs and low market prices led to another loss. The company could no longer cope with its obligations and although additional capital had been raised; the board had no choice but to declare its position and to request a moratorium from its creditors early in 1921. The company was in very low water and neither a change in management nor a planned increase in capital did any good. There was no money to develop the desperately-needed new models and despite severe cost-cutting, 1921 ended with a loss of nearly SFr1 million.

In an advertisement offering the TF with various body styles the text ended with the desperate slogan 'Support Swiss industry'. No doubt the TF was a good car built to high standards but at SFr17,000 for the chassis, it was too expensive. The Studebaker Big Six with its touring body, and offering 65bhp at a top speed of 65mph (105km/h) could be bought for SFr13,000. A small order by the Swiss Army for ten of the small 'Martineli' 10/12hp of 1356cc was filled but hopes for more substantial contracts came to naught. On the private market, this model did not stand any chance against the mass-produced Citroën, Renault and others. Martini struggled on but did not come up with any new ideas during 1921–24. Of the 20,028 passenger cars registered in Switzerland, Martini contributed 755 but had definitely lost its leading position to Fiat, Citroën and Peugeot. Cost saving and restructuring production and welcome export orders to England, Spain and Argentina kept the company barely afloat.

In 1924 the two Swiss brothers Walter and Robert STEIGER, who had produced machinery and cars in southern Germany, acquired the majority of the share capital and secured seats on the board of directors. Walter Steiger charged himself with the technical management of Martini and heavily invested into the modernisation of the tool machinery and equipment of the factory. It was not until 1926 that the brand new Martini Six Typ FU was exhibited at the Geneva Show. Walter Steiger was responsible for the design. The 6-cylinder L-head side-valve monobloc was a conventional engine with 74 × 120mm, 3096cc and a respectable 70bhp. The crankshaft had four white bearings, piston rods were made of light alloy and pistons by Nelson-Bohnalite were used. The 3-speed gearbox with direct top was flanged to the engine. Top speed was about 60mph (97km/h). The chassis was conventional with semi-ellipitic springs and 4-wheel servo brakes. Most cars had Rudge wire wheels and bodies made by Martini. Its strong points were reliability, durability and high quality and it was specially adapted for the mountainous roads of Switzerland. Until early 1927 the old TF remained available; obviously the company had not sold all stocks prior to launching the new 'U'. The old Martini badge showing the logo and a rifle was replaced by a new design with a climbing chamois on a multicoloured shield. Later a proud ibex would embellish the Martini radiators. With the new model, sporting success returned and various Swiss competitions, including the famous Klausen hill climb were won in the touring class by works cars. Top speed was measured at 79mph (127km/h). Early in 1928 the model 'FUG' with the engine enlarged to 4397cc and offering 90bhp became available. Both models could also be ordered with coach-built tourer, limousine or coupé bodies by Gangloff, Gygax, Hess of Solothurn, and others. In the newly furbished St Blaise factory, the production capacity amounted to 300 to 400 chassis per year.

The financial situation of the company was not very strong despite no losses being declared during 1924–27. The cost of tooling up for the new models, the limited sales on a small home market flooded with less expensive imported cars and the failure to export in substantial numbers led to another painful loss in 1928. Martini was not only one of the best cars available but also one of the most beautiful. Late in 1929 both models were improved in details and received Perrot brakes with Westinghouse vacuum servo assistance. Business was dragging along. The labour force was reduced considerably, working hours were reduced, capital once again lowered in a dramatic fashion and the management resigned, but at the end of the year losses had accumulated to nearly half a million francs.

In this perilous situation, Martini decided early in 1930 to take out a licence for the WANDERER 10/50hp model W11 which was launched as the model 'KM'. The 6-cylinder ohv-engine had 2523cc and top speed of the car was about 60mph (97km/h). The price of SFr15,000 was quite reasonable but it had a rather difficult start, was never considered a true Martini, and was nicknamed 'German Helvetia'. The programme was supplemented by the type 'OK' which had a new 4-speed gearbox with two silent ratios. The annual result of 1930

1931 Martini Model NF6 all-weather tourer by Wenger.
NATIONAL MOTOR MUSEUM

showing a critical loss of nearly one million francs made it very difficult to continue and the board of directors decided in May 1931 to cease car production. As the manufacturing of the improved big Martinis had just begun and as there were considerable stocks of raw material and parts, the final decision was delayed. Production was to continue on a very limited scale and only according to orders received.

For 1931 the books were closed with another loss of half a million francs. Instead of assembling the parts of the KM, the Wanderer cars, albeit with the Martini badge on the radiator were now imported in a finished state. In 1932, after a total of 440 cars had been sold, the KM model was dropped. The Depression had by now reached disastrous dimensions and Martini was hit particularly hard. Its sales in Switzerland had dwindled from 87 in 1930 to a mere 27 in 1932. The end was near. In 1933 only the NF with the 4379cc engine remained available. The staff was cut once more to a ridiculous 30 workers, some of the few remaining assets were sold, repair work was sought, co-operation with other manufacturers planned – all to no avail. In June 1934 the shareholders' general meeting approved the liquidation of the Martini company, the oldest, most important and proudest of all Swiss motorcar manufacturers. The very last of the Martini NF Six chassis were taken over by Swiss coachbuilders and some of the most handsome luxury cars of purely Swiss manufacture resulted from this transaction. BERNA, Olten took over the factory and made certain that all repairs and overhauls of Martini cars could still be performed at least for the next five years. Fortunately a handful of Martini cars of various models were saved by museums and by private collectors.

FH

Further Reading
Friedrich von Martini (1833–1897), Christopf Bischof,
Verein für wirtschaftshistorische Studien, Meilen, 1992.
Automobiles Martini, Saint-Blaise (Suisse), R.G. Friedli, St Blaise, 1993.
Martini – Geschichte eines Unternehmens, H.-J. Seifert,
PR Martini, Frauenfeld, c.1970.
Die Entwicklung der schweizerischen Automobilindustrie, Walter Schürmann,
Dissertation, University Berne, 1952.
'Martini', J.-P. Thévoz, *Fanatique de l'Automobile*, Oct.-Nov., 1974.
Lost Causes of Motoring, Europe, Lord Montagu of Beaulieu, Vol. 1,
Cassell, London, 1969.

MARTINIQUE *see* CUMBERFORD

MARTINOT ET GALLAND (D) 1898–1899
Ateliers de Construction de Bitschweiler, Thonn, Alsace.
This Alsatian make, the first in the province, built a light car with 5hp horizontal single-cylinder engine, wire wheels and solid tyres. Various designs of 2- or 4-seater bodywork were offered. It was followed by more famous marques such as Mathis and Bugatti which became French after 1918.
HON

MARTINS (DK) 1944
This was a plan to create a Danish equivalent of the Volkswagen. The prototype had streamlined bodywork, a rear-mounted engine with between 28bhp and 35bhp and independent suspension using rubber springing. The 700kg car was 165in (4200mm) long.
CR

MARTIN & WALKER *see* TECHNIC

MARTLET (GB) 1980s
A classic car restoration company offered a basic sports car throughout the 1980s.
CR

MARUTI (IND) 1973–1974; 1982 to date
1973–1974 Maruti Ltd, Gurgaon, Harayana.
1982 to date Maruti Udyog Ltd, New Delhi.
Named after an Indian sacred monkey, the original Maruti was an attempt to build an Indian people's car. It was a 2-door saloon powered by a rear-mounted 676cc 2-cylinder air-cooled engine with a 4-speed gearbox and spur gear final drive. The 4-seater body was of monocoque construction. The prototype was built in 1973, and there were ambitious plans for mass production, 10,000 cars in 1974/5 and 60,000 per annum from 1977 onwards. However, very few were made. The project was backed by Sanjay Gandhi, son of Mrs Indira Gandhi, who was killed in a plane crash in 1980.

The name was revived in 1982 when the new factory of Maruti Udyog (now a 50/50 joint venture between Suzuki and the Indian Government, originally

1973 Maruti 676cc saloon.
MARUTI

1999 Maruti Zen hatchback.
MARUTI

74 per cent Government-owned) began to make the SUZUKI Fronte under licence, selling it under the name Maruti 800. In 1989 exports to France began, this being the first Indian-built passenger car (as opposed to Jeeps) sold in Western Europe. Favourable Government treatment enabled the Maruti to be sold at a very reasonable price (the equivalent of £3428 in 1998) and to gain 80 per cent of the domestic market. 1999 models included the 796cc 3-cylinder 800, based on a discontinued Suzuki Alto, the 993cc 4-cylinder Zen, based on the current Suzuki Alto, and the 1299cc Esteem based on the Suzuki Swift.

NG

MARVEL (i) (F) 1905–1908
Automobiles Marvel, Paris.
This was a conventional car powered by 4-cylinder engines of 15, 20/24, 25/30 and 30/40hp. The latter was chain-driven, but all the smaller models used shaft drive.

NG

MARVEL (ii) (US) 1907
Marvel Motor Car Co., Detroit, Michigan.
This was a light runabout powered by a 14hp 2-cylinder engine with shaft drive. The only model was a 2-seater selling for $800, but very few were made, It was built in the same factory as the PARAGON (i) although there was no link between the two companies. In late 1907 there were plans to revive the Marvel as the CRESCENT (i).

NG

MARVIA (RI) 1990s
P.T. Marvia Graha Motor, Jakarta Pusat.
This company bravely produced fibreglass replicas based on the Suzuki SJ410 chassis. These included a Mercedes SSK replica and an A.C. Cobra replica (which could also be based on the Suzuki Carry van).

CR

MARYLAND (i) (US) 1900–1901
Maryland Automobile Co., Luke, Maryland.
This company made tubular shell boilers as well as a wide range of steam cars, from a runabout at $900 to an omnibus at $2500. All had vertical 2-cylinder engines and chain drive. The company was in receivership in May 1901, and in 1902 the factory was taken over by a beverage bottling company.

NG

MARYLAND (ii) (US) 1907–1910
Sinclair-Scott Co., Baltimore, Maryland.
The Sinclair-Scott company had been makers of food-canning machinery for about 70 years when they turned to producing car parts for other firms soon after the turn of the century. One of the companies they supplied was ARIEL (i), and when they failed to pay for their components Sinclair-Scott took over the design and, with rebadging and only minor changes, put it into production as the Maryland. The engines was the same single-ohc four made by the Trebert Auto & Marine Co. of Rochester, New York. Tourer, roadster and limousine models were made, the latter an expensive car at $3450. During their four years' production 871 Marylands were sold, but apparently Sinclair-Scott lost money on every one of them, so at the end of 1910 they decided to concentrate on food-processing machinery.

NG

MAS (US) c.1982
MAS Racing Products, Minneapolis, Minnesota.
The MAS Super-T kit car used Ford Pinto running gear to build a Ford Model T hot rod.

HP

MASANO (US) c.1953
Tom Masano, Reading, Pennsylvania.
Tom Masano was a Kaiser dealer who built a fibreglass body for the Henry J chassis. It had central tail fin and high mudguards with a low, wide grill. The prototype was fitted to a new Henry J with a 6-cylinder engine. Trim and seats were standard Henry J. Masano planned to put it into production in 1953.

HP

MASCOT (S) 1920
Raverken, Hälsingborg.
The Mascot provided an ingenious way of converting a motorcycle to a car. The frame was supplied complete with body and two wheels, to which the motorcycle could be fitted, its rear wheel acting as the offside rear wheel of the car. The passengers sat in tandem and it had wheel steering. Thus a customer already in possession of a fairly powerful motorcycle could, at a cost of 1700 Skr, obtain a car.

NG

MASCOTTE (GB) 1919–1921
Mascotte Engineering Co. Ltd, London.
The Mascotte was one of many attempts to cater for the burgeoning light car market, which was eventually dominated by William Morris and, to a lesser extent, Clyno. When it appeared at the 1919 Olympia Show it was described as 'the only entirely new light car to be seen at the Show', but it was a pretty conventional machine, powered by a 1496cc Dorman 4MV 4-cylinder engine, with 3-speed gearbox and worm drive. The 2/3-seater body was made by Mascotte themselves in their small factory in Kensal Road, but it was not a handsome car, with large radiator of Rolls-Royce shape mounted rather far forward, and disc wheels. Only 11 Dorman engines were bought by Mascotte, then they turned to the Belgian-built Peters engine in two sizes, 1645 and 1820cc. Probably not many of these were bought either, and Mascotte was out of business before the end of 1921. Dorman records show that one further engine was delivered in 1924, probably a replacement unit rather than for an attempted revival.

NG

M.A.S.E. (F) 1921–1925
Manufacture d'Autos, Outillage et Cycles, St Étienne, Loire.

1947 Maserati A6-1500 coupé by Pinin Farina.
NICK BALDWIN

This was a quality small car powered by a 904 or 1108cc ohv engine of the company's own manufacture and designed by Nemorin Causan. The man behind the company was René Le Grain-Eiffel, grandson of Gustave Eiffel who built the Eiffel Tower. He and Causan had worked on the AJAM cyclecar which never went into production, and which, like the M.A.S.E, had ifs by transverse semi-elliptic springs which took the place of a front axle. Attractive bodies, either coupés or pointed-tail sports coachwork, were made by Desfilhes of Montbrison. In 1924 the Causan engine gave way to a 1098cc ohv C.I.M.E. power unit, and a more reliable and easy to operate gearbox was provided. However this did not help sales, and at the end of 1924 the St Étienne company sold the rights to M. Degoutte who made a few more up to the end of 1925.

NG

Further Reading
'La MASE 1100', Jacques Rousseau, *l'Album du Fanatique*.

MASERATI (I) 1926 to date

1926–1938 Officine Alfieri Maserati SpA, Bologna.
1938 to date Officinc Alfieri Maserati SpA, Modena.

There were six Maserati brothers: Carlo, Bindo, Alfieri, Ettore, Mario and Ernesto. With the exception of Mario, who became an artist, all were to devote their lives to cars and motor racing.

In the mid–1920s, Diatto was in financial difficulties and withdrew from racing whereupon Alfieri took over the GP project. He converted the supercharged 2-litre straight-8 engine to 1500cc, to comply with new regulations and, in 1926, formed Officine Alfieri Maserati SpA Bologna. The former Diatto was renamed the Maserati 26 and, with Alfieri at the wheel, it won its class on its debut, in the Targa Florio.

Maserati cars were not an instant success but they began to make a mark from about 1929. Both Alfieri and Ernesto drove works cars in the early days, but from 1931 on, they were content to leave the driving to others. Then, in 1932, tragedy struck the young company when Alfieri had an operation from which he did not recover.

In Ernesto, however, there was a successor as chief designer and Maserati thrived. Its Grand Prix efforts were restricted by financial constraints, although Maserati replaced Bugatti as the first choice of the privateer and, from 1936, Maserati was often outstanding in voiturette racing.

1964 Maserati Quattroporte saloon, with Omer Orsi.
NICK BALDWIN

Maserati also made a few sports cars which enjoyed some success in the 1100cc class, mainly in Italy, but they were not for everyday use.

In 1938, the brothers were persuaded by Commendatore Adolfo Orsi to sell the company. Orsi was particularly interested in buying the successful spark plug business, but also felt that the competition arm could be a prestigious flagship to his industrial combine. The brothers were retained on a ten-year service contract, although the company was run by Orsi's son, Omer, with Alberto Massimino as head of the racing division. Maserati moved from Bologna to Modena.

War soon intervened but, afterwards, Ernesto created his first road-going sports car, the Tipo A6. Its straight-six single-ohc 1488cc engine was similar to the prewar Tipo 6CM voiturette unit. With a single twin-choke Weber carburettor, it gave 65bhp (and rising) and was fitted in a ladder frame with two large diameter side members. Front suspension was by coil springs and unequal wishbones, and the live rear axle was suspended on coil springs.

It appeared at the 1947 Geneva Show with a simple, clean, coupé body by Pinin Farina. Although intended as a road car, it formed the basis for some competition versions.

1966 Maserati Ghibli coupé.
NICK BALDWIN

1970 Maserati Mexico coupé.
NICK GEORGANO

At the end of 1947, the Maserati brothers, having honoured their ten-year contract, returned to Bologna to found OSCA. Their decision was partly prompted by the fact that Omer Orsi wished to concentrate on road cars while the brothers were interested only in racing. Road vs racing cars would become a theme in the Maserati story for the next 12 years, but Maserati could never get the balance right in the way that, say, Ferrari and Porsche did. Ironically, the GP car the brothers left behind, the 4CLT/48, briefly put Maserati at the very pinnacle of motor racing, but there was no follow-through.

Meanwhile, Maserati made further developments of the A6 series, including a 2-litre version but, by 1957, after 12 years in production, only 138 had been made. Cars were a mere fraction of Maserati's portfolio: spark plugs, batteries and car horns were bigger money spinners, as was the manufacture of machine tools.

In 1952, Maserati entered the World Championship, but its campaign was hampered by the late arrival of the car and by an accident to Juan-Manuel Fangio, its lead driver. Between September 1953 and September 1957, however, Maserati won seven World Championship races to the five of Lancia (run by Scuderia Ferrari) and the three of Ferrari.

A Maserati 250F won the first race of the 2½-litre World Championship, in 1954, and one ran in the last race of the formula in 1960. Without Maserati, the privateer's friend, Formula One might not have flourished in the late 1950s.

From 1955, Maserati sports racing cars were outstanding, class by class, and were often superior to Ferraris of similar capacity.

Maserati's competition history reached its peak in 1957 when Fangio won the World Driver's Championship in a works Maserati 250F, and Maserati also came within a whisker of winning the World Sports Car Championship. Then it abruptly withdrew from competition.

Orsi had invested heavily in Argentina and, after the overthrow of President Juan Péron in 1955, it was financially embarrassed. In a bid to generate cash, the outstanding engineer, Giulio Alfieri, set to work on a GT car. The engine of the 3500GT was a 3486cc double-ohc straight-six unit derived from the sports racing 350S (which was related to the 250F engine) and it drove through a 4-speed ZF gearbox (5-speed optional from 1960, standard from 1961). The chassis was recognisably the descendent of the A6/1500, but the live rear axle was suspended on semi-elliptics.

Standard bodies were a 2+2 hard-top by Touring and a slightly shorter Vignale convertible, but there were some bespoke confections. Front disc brakes were

NATIONAL MOTOR MUSEUM

MASERATI, ALFIERI (1887–1932)

Alfieri Maserati was the third son of a railway-engine driver, Rodolfo Maserati and his wife Carolina, née Losi. Rodolfo was one of the few Italians who could truly master the crude Krupp steam locomotives of that age.

When Alfieri was 16, his older brother Carlo arranged for him to begin work in the Isotta Fraschini factory in Milano, where their brother Bindo was also working. In 1910 he was sent to Argentina, with his younger brother Ettore, as a service representative, but he spent most of his time rebuilding cars for racing. They returned to Italy in 1912. In 1914 Alfieri and Ettore formed the Officine Alfieri Maserati and in 1916 began making spark plugs in Milano, moving to Bolgona in 1919.

In 1920 he race-tuned a Nesselsdorfer (NW), and then a SCAT. In 1921 he built his own racing car, with an Isotta Fraschini chassis, Hispano-Suiza V8 engine, SCAT gearbox, and Itala rear axle.

After that, Alfieri was approached by Isotta Fraschini with an offer to join their racing team. He turned this to his advantage by agreeing to drive, but talked Isotta Fraschini into giving him a contract also for the construction of a new racing car. To build it, he found new and larger premises at Ponte Vecchio on the outskirts of Bologna. The car had a 4500cc 4-cylinder engine and met with considerable success.

In 1923 Alfieri signed a contract with Diatto to modify their cars to make them more suitable for racing. In the following years he raced Diatto cars extensively, and won the Susa-Moncenisio hill climb in 1923.

As the GP formula in force during 1922–25 called for a maximum weight of 1430lb (650kg), Diatto assigned Maserati to design and develop a Grand Prix racing car. It became a very fast but unreliable supercharged straight-8. The first one was ready just in time for the 1925 Italian GP, where it broke down with blower trouble. Diatto decided they had been in racing long enough.

Alfieri Maserati decided he had learned a lot from his time with Diatto and started to make an improved machine in his Ponte Vecchio workshop. The 1926 formula called for a 1500cc engine and a minimum weight of 1100lb (500kg), two seats and a minimum body width of 31.5in (800mm).

For this formula Alfieri created a beautiful but simple straight-8 1491cc (60 x 66mm) supercharged engine with gear-driven twin-ohcs. Its peak output was 125bhp at 5300rpm. It was named Tipo 26 for the year 1926 and was the first car to carry the Maserati trident (borrowed from the Neptune statue in the city centre square at Bologna). The design was by one of Alfieri's brothers, the artist Murio (1890 – 1981).

In 1927 he had a racing accident which left him with some injuries that later demanded minor surgery. He died from side effects of the surgery on 3 March 1932.

JPN

NATIONAL MOTOR MUSEUM

NATIONAL MOTOR MUSEUM

MASERATI, CARLO (1881–1910)

Carlo was the oldest of the six Maserati brothers and instilled in all of them (except Mario, who was an aspiring artist) a passion for machinery.

He was still a schoolboy when he built his own steam engine. His career started in a bicycle factory, and he raced the 2-wheelers to such good effect that he attracted the attention of Marquis Carcano di Anzani del Parco, who volunteered to finance Carlo's experimentation with internal combustion engines. Carlo designed the 4-stroke single-cylinder engine that powered the first Carcano motorcycle, and for two years he was a regular competitor in road races, riding Carcano machines.

When he was 20, he was hired by Fiat as No.1 test driver, but left soon afterwards to join Bianchi in a similar capacity. He raced Bianchi cars in the 1907 Coppa Florio and the Kaiserpreisrennen, but had already gone to work for Isotta Fraschini as a test engineer. In 1907 he signed up with Junior in Milano, and was named managing director of the small firm when he was only 26. He was just beginning to design a family of aircraft engines when he died in 1910.

JPN

NATIONAL MOTOR MUSEUM

MASERATI, BINDO (1883–1980)

Bindo served an apprenticeship in a local machine shop and was a highly regarded technician when he went to work for Isotta Fraschini in Milano. He stayed there until 1932, when his brothers asked him to join them in Bologna after Alfieri's death. He became a partner in the Officine Alfieri Maserati and served as sales manager, not just for cars but mainly for the Maserati range of high-precision machine tools, which gave them the cash-flow they needed to maintain a racing team.

In 1947 he joined Ettore and Ernesto in starting OSCA, where he played an active part on the commercial side until the factory was sold. He died on September 1980.

JPN

MASERATI, ETTORE (1894–1990)

Ettore's first job was with Junior in 1908-10, and next he accompanied Alfieri Maserati to Argentina in 1910-12, and worked for Isotta Fraschini after their return to Italy, before being assigned in 1914 to the Franco Tosi works, which assembled the 12-cylinder Isotta Fraschini engines for Captroni airplanes.

He became the business administrator and money-manager for the family, running the affairs of Officine Alfieri Maserati from 1930 to 1947, and those of OSCA from 1947 to 1963, when the company was sold to MV Agusta.

He died on 4 August 1990.

JPN

NATIONAL MOTOR MUSEUM

MASERATI, ERNESTO (1898–1975)

Ernesto Maserati was the secret weapon, first of the Officine Alfieri Maserati, and later of OSCA. He had a more innovative, more intellectual, more scientific approach to car engineering than his brothers. Born on 4 April 1898, he was the youngest of them all. In 1914 he was the manager of a garage in Bologna, and began his racing career as a riding mechanic for Alfieri.

He joined Officine Alfieri Maserati in 1926 and was named supervisor of engine design in 1932. He created engines with 4, 6, 8 and 16 cylinders prior to 1936, and designed the OSCA V12 in 1949. He pioneered two-stage supercharging, and in 1940 he was experimenting with a supercharged 1500cc 4-cylinder engine having a built-up crankshaft and one-piece con-rods, which ran very well at 7000rpm. He invented the MAER rotary-valve engine in 1965, unique in being applicable to both 2-stroke and 4-stroke engines.

He died on 1 December 1975.

JPN

1973 Maserati Bora coupé.
NICK BALDWIN

1993 Maserati Biturbo saloon.
NICK BALDWIN

1993 Maserati Shamal coupé.
NICK BALDWIN

optional in 1959, standard in 1960 and, while most had disc wheels, Borrani wire were a 1959 option. In 1961, three twin-choke Webers gave way to Lucas fuel injection, power increased by 15bhp and the 3500 GT became the 3500 GTI.

Alfieri was more open than most Italians to developments such as disc brakes and fuel injection. He was also responsible for the outstanding Tipo 60/61 'birdcage' sports racers of 1958 to 1960, which Maserati sold to privateers.

Between 1957 and 1964, 2223 examples of the 3500 GT were made and, often, Maserati outsold Ferrari mainly because they made the more practical road car.

In 1957, Maserati nearly won the WSCC with its 450S sports racer which used a 4.5-litre 'quad cam' V8 which had originally been commissioned by an American enthusiast for an Indianapolis car. The commissioner, who was rumoured to be associated with organised crime, vanished overnight. Maserati did not return to Indianapolis, but it was left with a superb engine. A 330bhp

5-litre version was fitted to a 3500 GT chassis to become the 5000 GT and 34 owners enjoyed a 2+2 coupé which would touch 168mph (270km/h), and sprint, 0–62mph (0–100km/h) in 6.5 seconds

The Sebring, of 1962, was a short wheelbase 3500 GTI, with a body by Michelotti. As the name implies, America was the target market and options included air conditioning and automatic transmission – Ferrari did not offer such luxury. Three engine options were available and, from 1962 to 1966, the Sebring sold 444 examples.

Another 3500 GT derivative was the Mistral, made from 1963 to 1970, which had a shorter, stiffer, and lighter, Sebring chassis. Frua styled the body, which had a lifting tailgate, and 948 were made, mostly in the first five years of production.

Another arrival in 1963 was the first Quattroporte (4-door), a 5-seat saloon built on a tubular frame, boxed for stiffness. A De Dion rear axle suspended on coil springs was fitted until 1966, when it was replaced with a live axle and semi-elliptics. At first, the Quattroporte was fitted with a 4136cc version of the V8 engine and it fed its 260bhp through either a ZF 5-speed gearbox, or a Borg-Warner automatic. It would propel the car to 130mph (209km/h). In 1967 came a 290bhp 4.7-litre engine.

Not until 1965 did a sports car, the Mexico, use the V8 engine. The Mexico was a close-coupled 4-seater which used the Quattroporte chassis with a live rear axle. It was not, however, significantly shorter, or lighter, but with the 4.2-litre engine, it was good for 149mph (240km/h) and a 4.7-litre version was an option from 1969.

It sold slower than the saloon (about 250 made) largely because America thought its styling, by Frua, was bland. The exercise more or less marked Frua's exit from the stage.

The 2-seat Ghibli of 1966 to 1973, succeeded where the Mexico had failed, on style, and it was the work of Giugiaro, who was then at Ghia. The Ghibli had a shortened Mexico chassis and most of the 1274 built were fastback coupés – there were 125 open cars.

A 330bhp 4.7-litre engine was fitted to the Ghibli until 1970 when it was replaced by a 4.9-litre unit which produced only five extra horses but delivered 354lb/ft torque at 4000rpm.

Another significant newcomer in 1966 was the Indy – Maserati won the Indianapolis 500 in 1939 and 1940, so the name had been earned. In fact, on more than one occasion, Ferrari mounted an abortive campaign on the Indianapolis 500 simply because Maserati had won the race. The Indy was a 2+2 coupé on a Quattroporte chassis, slightly shortened, with a slightly wider track. The Indy completed Maserati's range for the late 1960s, and it replaced the Sebring, thus phasing out the 6-cylinder cars which were the last vestiges of the influence of the Maserati brothers.

The Indy's steel body, styled by Vignale, was welded, not bolted, to the frame. Initially, it had the 4.1-litre V8, but the 4.7-litre came in 1970 (155mph (249km/h), 0–62mph (0–100km/h) in 7.5 seconds), and 1973 saw a 4.9-litre version. There were some years when the Indy outsold the Ghibli, and 1136 had been made by the time production ended in 1974.

During the 1960s, Maserati's success as a maker of road cars contrasted with low-key involvement in competition. After the Tipo 60/61 'birdcage' sports racers, and its unsuccessful mid-engined derivatives, Maserati's main competition involvement was the supply of V12 Formula One engines to Cooper – an engine which had first run in 1957.

In January 1968, Maserati began a co-operation with Citroën, which was interested in exploiting Maserati's engine expertise and, by March 1968, Citroën had taken a majority shareholding. The most public expression of the partnership was the Citroën SM which combined a Citroën chassis – with hydro-pneumatic suspension and power-assisted everything, with a 3-litre V6 Maserati engine. It has since appeared in both 'Best Car' and 'Worst Car' polls in motor magazines.

It was possibly the influence of Citroën which led Maserati to go against its fundamental design philosophy and, in 1970, it introduced two mid-engined cars, the Bora and Merak. The case for mid-engined GT cars was not strong in 1970 – the Lotus Europa was considered inferior to the Elan and Maserati and Ferrari front-engined cars comfortably out-sold the Lamborghini Miura, the only mid-engined car in their class.

Giugiaro's new Ital Design studio both styled the Bora and designed the steel unitary construction. Alfieri Giulio was responsible for the layout and the all-round independent suspension by coil springs and double wishbones. The

1999 Maserati 3200GT coupé.

MASERATI

Bora began with the 4.7-litre engine (4.9-litre from 1975) and, since Maserati was married to Citroën, it had the French maker's 'no travel' braking system and hydraulic pedal adjustment. Top speed was 158mph (254km/h), with 0–62mph (0–100km/h) in 6.5 seconds.

On sale between 1971 and 1980, 571 Boras were made. The most popular new model, however, was the 3-litre Merak (1832 made, 1972 to 1983) which, as was becoming usual, was a parts bin cocktail. The ex-Citroën SM engine was fitted to a Bora chassis, so 190bhp had to propel an apparently small car which was actually only 150lb lighter than the Bora.

A 220bhp SS version came in 1974. Until 1979, a 170bhp 2-litre 'tax bracket' Merak was made for the Italian market. Also in 1974, a new front-engined 2+2 coupé, the Khamsin, replaced the Ghibli and Indy. Styling was by Marcello Gandini at Bertone, and Bertone also designed, and made, the steel floorpan. Suspension was similar to the Bora/Merak: independent all-round by coil springs and double wishbones, but rack and pinion steering was a new departure, and the Khamsin used Citroën hydraulic steering and brakes. A 320bhp 4.9-litre engine was used and 149mph (240km/h) was possible.

By Maserati standards, the Khamsin was disappointing with only 431 made, 1974 to 1982, but there was a mitigating circumstance, the OPEC oil crisis. Even so, the Khamsin was a hot property compared to the Quattroporte II which found only five buyers. The Quattroporte II used the 3-litre V6 allied to Citroën transmission, front-wheel drive, power steering and hydro-pneumatic suspension. The Bertone body was anonymous and its 190bhp was inadequate.

In 1974, Peugeot bought 38.2 per cent of Citroën, as a first step to a take-over. In the wake of the OPEC oil crisis, Maserati's trading losses were more than the company was worth so it was effectively bankrupt. Under Peugeot's influence, Citroën came close to closing Maserati, but it was saved by the Argentine former racing driver, Alejandro de Tomaso. De Tomaso owned his eponymous company, plus Innocenti and other Italian automotive firms and he bought Maserati with the aid of a government grant.

When de Tomaso bought Maserati, he eliminated Citroën's influence and introduced badge-engineering until he could phase out the old range. So, the 1977 Kyalami 4-seater sports saloon was a de Tomaso Longchamps with styling changes and a 255bhp 4.1-litre Maserati V8 instead of a Ford V8. In 1978, a 280bhp 4.9-litre engine was an option but, though the car was quick (146mph (235km/h), 0–62mph (0–100km/h) in 7.6 seconds), it had few buyers.

The last of the traditional Maseratis was the Quattroporte III which had a stretched Kyalami floorpan with styling by Ital Design and either a 4.1 or a 4.9-litre V8. From 1976 the trim was upgraded and it was re-named the Royale. It was made in small numbers until the early 1990s.

In 1981, Maserati introduced the Biturbo which was a sporting saloon with steel unitary construction and, as the name implies, twin turbo-chargers. It had MacPherson strut front suspension, independent rear by trailing arms and coil springs, and 4-wheel disc brakes. It was also a car whose style was anonymous – it could have been made by almost anyone and what followed was a nightmare of identification. The Biturbo, with V6 and V8 engines (in 3- and 4-valve per cylinder versions) was made in 2.0, 2.5, 2.8 and 3.2-litre editions and there were 2- and 4-door models. Thus, a Maserati 420 was a 4-door car with a 2-litre engine while a 228 was a 2-door with a 2.8-litre unit. Some of the 4-valve models were identified along the lines: 2.24v or 4.24v.

Other versions were given names such as Racing, Karif, Shamal and Ghibli. There were saloons, coupés and body kits – and there were also many quality control problems because Maserati was not geared for mass production. Production peaked in 1984 at 6365 cars when Chrysler bought five per cent of Maserati in return for a design contract. There did not, however, appear to be much original thought coming from the company and, in 1993, de Tomaso sold Maserati to Fiat Auto – sales had dipped to under 1000 units a year. By then the Maserati brothers were dead, Ettore out-lived his brothers to die in 1990, aged 96.

After the take-over, Fiat decided that it had to carry through most of the models in the pipeline. So, in 1994, came the fourth model to be called Quattroporte, and it did have four doors, but it had no relationship at all with previous cars of the same name, and neither did a model which revived the name, Ghibli. They were variants of the Biturbo and some mainstream manufacturers could offer equal performance with better, much better, quality and reliability plus a pan European network of dealers and support.

Under the new regime, the 330bhp 2-litre Barchetta Cup of 1994, a 2-seater sports car, was built for a one-make racing series, centred on Italy. A detuned version, Barchetta Stradale, was sold as a road car in some countries.

By the end of 1996, Fiat Auto had invested nearly $170 million in Maserati and, in January, 1997, the factory was closed for several months to be refurbished. Fiat said that it expected Maserati would reach a ceiling of about 3500 units a

1906 Mass 18hp tourer.
NICK BALDWIN

year and would be 'Italy's Jaguar', making 4-seat high performance saloons with sporting cars in a subsidiary position.

By mid–1997, Ferrari SpA had bought 50 per cent of Maserati, with the rest owned by Fiat Auto (Ferrari is not owned by Fiat Auto, but by a Fiat holding company). Thus, the two companies which had been fierce rivals on the race track in the 1950s, and in the market place in the 1960s, were joined.

The Maserati factory was refitted and, in 1998, a new 2+2 front-engined coupé, with a 370bhp 3.2-litre twin-turbo V8, was announced. It had a new, independently-sprung, platform and a body by Giugiaro, and it could deliver 168mph (270km/h) with 0–62mph (0–100km/h) under 5 seconds. It also had some of the advanced electronic systems denied to Maserati during its de Tomaso days, but off-the-shelf at Fiat. It was placed in the market against cars like the Aston Martin DB7, and a cabriolet was planned for the new century.

MJL

Further Reading
Maserati, a History, Anthony Pritchard, David & Charles, 1976.
Maserati Road Cars, Richard Crump and Rob de la Rive Box, Osprey, 1979.
Maserati Heritage, David Sparrow and Ian Ayre, Osprey, 1995.
Maserati Bora and Merak, Jan P. Norbye, Osprey, 1982.
Illustrated Maserati Buyer's Guide, Richard Crump and Rob de la Rive Box, Motorbooks International, 1984.

MASON (US) 1906–1914
1906–1908 Mason Motor Car Co., Des Moines, Iowa.
1908–1909 Mason Automobile Co., Des Moines, Iowa.
1909–1910 Maytag-Mason Motor Co., Waterloo, Iowa.
1912–1914 Mason Motor Co., Waterloo, Iowa.

The Mason was made as a tourer or runabout powered by a 24hp flat-twin engine with epicyclic transmission. It was designed for Edward R. Mason by Fred S. Duesenberg. In 1909 the company was bought by washing machine maker F.L. Maytag and production moved to Waterloo, where the 2-cylinder cars were continued as Masons, and a four was marketed as a MAYTAG. For 1911 both cars were named Maytag, but the following year the Maytag family pulled out, and 2- and 4-cylinder cars were made under the Mason name up to the end of 1914. The Duesenberg brothers, Fred and August, left in 1913 to make racing cars in St Paul, Minnesota, and were later famous for their luxury cars built in Indianapolis.

NG

MASS (F) 1903–1923; PIERRON (F) 1912–1923
Automobiles Mass (L. Pierron), Courbevoie, Seine.
Like the Marlborough, the Mass was built in France but sold largely on the British market, and indeed its name came from the British importer Mr Masser-Horniman. The first cars were assembled voiturettes typical of their period, with 4½hp Aster or 6hp De Dion-Bouton engines and tubular frames, many components coming from Lacoste et Battmann. A 10hp 2-cylinder De Dion with

twin carburettors was offered in 1904. Though a single-cylinder 8hp 2-seater was still offered in 1906, larger cars were made from 1905, including a T-headed twin with auxiliary transverse rear suspension, and a 3.8-litre 18/24hp with chain drive and Mercedes-like radiator. Engine sizes grew still further, to 5.6 litres in 1906 and 8 litres on the 1907 40/50hp. These were all 4-cylinder units by Gnome or Ballot, and there were also cars with smaller Ballot engines, the 2.4-litre 15 and 3.4-litre Special 15 with pump cooling. The 2-litre 10/12 of 1910 represented a step forward in design, with monobloc engine, unit construction of engine and gearbox, and pressure lubrication. For some reason it reverted to a separate gearbox for 1913.

Ownership of the company is somewhat uncertain; Masser-Horniman was described as the proprietor in 1904, with premises in Ladbroke Road, north London, and the 'principal' in France was Léon Pierron. From 1912 his name was used for the cars sold on the French market. The manager of the Courbevoie factory in 1907 was Englishman J.R. Richardson, whose Lincolnshire-based company also sold Masses and made RICHARDSON (i) cars. It is possible that the Richardson was, in fact, a Mass; certainly the smallest Richardson of 1905 had a 6½hp single-cylinder, as did the smallest Mass.

In 1911 the biggest Mass had a 4.9-litre 4-cylinder engine, and for 1913 came the first six, with very long stroke (80 × 180mm) and capacity of 5426cc. By then it was becoming difficult to sell the cars in England, and Mass Cars Ltd took on agencies for American R.C.H. and Paige cars, selling the latter under the name of Mass-Paige.

Pierrons sold in France had slightly different engine sizes from those exported to England; for example the smallest Mass for 1913 had dimensions of 75 × 100mm = 1766cc, while Pierron's bore and stroke were 68 × 130mm = 1887cc. All 1914 Masses had 4-cylinder Ballot engines, from the 1766cc 10hp to the 5338cc 20/30hp. Only one model was revived after the war, the 2812cc 15.9hp, which was offered up to 1923, though how many were sold is not known.

NG

MASSILLON (US) 1909
W.S. Reed Co., Massillon, Ohio.
W.S. Reed was nothing if not ambitious, making for his first car a large 60hp 6-cylinder engine of 7.8-litres capacity, with twin sparking plugs for each cylinder. It was offered in two wheelbases, 118in (2995mm) for the 2-seater roadster and 124in (3147mm) for the 5-seater tourer. They were priced at $1750 and $2000 respectively, and Reed said he would make 35 cars in his first year. However, he was in financial trouble before many cars were made, and sold out to C.P. Munch who built the car as the KEYSTONE from 1909 to 1910.

NG

MASTER (US) 1917–1918
Master Motor Car Co., Cleveland, Ohio.
This company was formed to make a 6-cylinder 100bhp car in limousine, runabout and tourer models, to sell for the high price of $5000. Few, if any, cars were built for sale.

NG

MASTERBILT SIX (US) 1926
Govro-Nelson Engineering Co., Detroit, Michigan.
The Masterbilt Six was a 6-cylinder air-cooled car which never made it to the marketplace. Designed by Victor Govreau, who had previously served as chief engineer of the ill-fated PAN car of St Cloud, Minnesota, the prototype(s) consisted of a modified Franklin 6-cylinder engine and a Marmon chassis and closed coachwork, identified by a wide belt moulding but otherwise similar to other cars of its period. The Masterbilt Six could be readily distinguished by its false front which was mounted ahead of the front axle. 'Production', such as it was, included one 4-door sedan and possibly one or two other similar prototypes.

KM

MASTERCO (GB) 1991–c.1993
Masterco, Bolton, Lancashire.
This was essentially a revival of the PANACHE LP400. Body/chassis kits retailed for only £2550 and the company claimed that complete cars could be on the road for a mere £8000.

CR

MATADOR *see* AMERICAN MOTORS

MATAS (E) 1919–1921
Fábrica de Automóviles Matas & Cía, Barcelona.
Joaquín Matas prepared small cars using MAG, Dorman and Continental engines. These cars had a special front suspension with large travel, due to the front leaf spring being fixed in a central pivot just in front of the radiator.
VCM

MATCHLESS (GB) 1913–1924
H. Collier & Sons Ltd, Plumstead, London.
Matchless was one of the best-known names among British motorcycles. They had only two short-lived involvements with cars, the first in 1912 when they produced a 3-wheeled cyclecar powered by a 8/10hp V-twin engine, with 3-speed gearbox and, very unusually for a 3-wheeler, shaft drive to the single rear wheel. It was not revived after the war, but in 1923 they announced a 4-wheeler with some advanced features. These included ifs by double transverse springs, unitary construction steel body and front-wheel brakes. The latter were beginning to catch on, but not usually on such a small car as the Matchless. The engine was a 1250cc air-cooled flat-twin, and final drive was by shaft to a worm rear axle. Unfortunately the Matchless 10 was expensive at £225, and even a reduction to £185 for 1924 did not help the company to sell more than about 50 cars.
NG

MATCO (US) c.1974–1986
Matco, Inc., Ventura, California.
The Matco Diamante was a neoclassic luxury car similar to the EXCALIBUR and CLENET. It could be built on a 1977 or later Cadillac chassis or a custom chassis was available that used Chevrolet, Cadillac or Buick engines. When first introduced, it was only sold in assembled form for over $100,000, but a kit version was added later. It had long running boards and a 'rumble seat' for extra passengers. They were available in roadster or longer phaeton form. Matco also made the California High Boy, a replica of a 1932 Ford hot rod that used a custom frame and Ford or Chevrolet V6 or V8 engines.
HP

MATFORD *see* FORD (iv)

MATHESON (US) 1903–1912
1903 Matheson Motor Car Co., Grand Rapids, Michigan.
1904–1905 Matheson Motor Car Co., Holyoke, Massachusetts.
1906–1910 Matheson Motor Car Co., Wilkes-Barre, Pennsylvania.
1910–1912 Matheson Automobile Co., Wilkes-Barre, Pennsylvania.
The Matheson was a high-grade and well-built car made in comparatively small numbers. The company was founded by two brothers, Charles Walter (1871–1940) and Frank F. Matheson (1876–1967) who bought up the HOLYOKE Motor Works and the services of Holyoke's chief engineer Charles R. Greuter. The first few cars were assembled in Grand Rapids, but the engines and gearboxes came from Holyoke, and early in 1904 they moved the whole operation to Holyoke. The first car had a 24hp 4-cylinder engine with ohvs which were Greuter's speciality, chain drive and a 7-seater tourer body. It sold for $5000, putting it among the most expensive American-built cars, up with the Locomobile and Pierce Great Arrow. Nevertheless 60 cars were sold in their first fiscal year, and for 1905 a 40hp limousine at $6000 joined the 24hp tourer. The company moved to a new, purpose-built factory at Wilkes-Barre in March 1906, and production rose encouragingly to about 300 cars in 1907. They were financed partly by New York financiers Henry U. Palmer and Charles A. Singer, who agreed to buy all their output. In 1907 they set up the Palmer & Singer Manufacturing Co. of Long Island offering cars under their own names which were in fact built by Matheson. In 1906 the most expensive Matheson was a 60/65hp 4-cylinder tourer at $7500.

Charles Greuter left in 1908 to design a car of his own which never went into production, though he would be famous in the 1920s for the Stutz Vertical Eight. He was replaced by French-born L.C. Kenan who designed Matheson's first six. This appeared for 1909, and also marked a change from chain to shaft drive, though a few chain-driven fours were made up to 1910. Kenan was replaced

1924 Matchless 10hp tourer.

1911 Matheson Silent Six tourer.

1902 Mathieu 9hp tonneau.

by A.M.Dean who designed the 1911 Silent Six, a 50hp car made with touring and limousine bodies on 125 or 135in (3172 or 3426mm) wheelbases. However Matheson was in receivership in July 1910, and although it was reorganised as the Matheson Automobile Co., it survived for little more than two years before a second receivership in December 1912 ended production. About 100 sixes and 800 fours had been made altogether. The factory was later used for production of the OWEN MAGNETIC, and after the failure of that company Frank Matheson bought it back to use as a distributorship for Oakland, Dodge and GMC trucks. Charles was also involved with Dodge, becoming a vice-president of sales, and later in the same capacity at Oakland when they were launching the Pontiac. He was general sales manager for Graham when he died in a car crash in 1940. Frank lived on until 1967.
NG

MATHIEU (B) 1902–1906
1902–1903 Éts de Construction d'Automoteurs Eugène Mathieu, Louvain.
1903–1906 Usines de Saventhem, Brevets E. Mathieu, Saventhem.
At the beginning of 1902 French-born Eugène Mathieu bought up the works where the DELIN car had been made, and began production of motorcycles

1913 Mathis tourer.
NATIONAL MOTOR MUSEUM

1923 Mathis 8/15CV coupé.
NICK GEORGANO

1929 Mathis 14CV saloon.
NICK BALDWIN

and cars with single-cylinder 6 and 8CV engines. In January 1903 he brought out a more powerful single of 9CV, then in 1904 launched two 4-cylinder models, the 8/12 and 15/30, the latter with a system of changing engine speed by altering the movement of the camshaft. At the end of 1903 they moved to a factory at Saventhem where the EXCELSIOR would be made a few years later. There he made three 4-cylinder models, 14/16, 24/30 and 35/45CV, and also made marine engines and electric generating units. Eugène Mathieu patented the torque tube in 1903, and these were used in the Saventhem-built cars which were sometimes known as U.S. Brevets Mathieu.

NG

MATHIS (D) 1910–1914; (F) 1919–1935; 1945–1950
1910–1914 E.E.C. Mathis, Strasbourg.
1919–1950 SA Mathis, Strasbourg.

Émile Mathis (1880–1956) was born in Alsace of French stock but with German nationality as a result of the German possession of Alsace and Lorraine between 1871 and 1918. His father Charles was a hotelier who owned the hotel Ville de Paris in Strasbourg, and Émile trained in this business before travelling to England for technical and business training. It has been said that he built an experimental car in 1898 and he himself used an illustration of a '1900 Mathis' in 1920s advertising, but it seems that the earliest cars that he was associated with were De Dietrichs. He was a friend of the De Dietrich family from about 1897, and was also friendly with Ettore Bugatti who was responsible for De Dietrich design from 1902 to 1904. He went into partnership with Bugatti on April 1st 1904 to build a large car of Bugatti's design, which was marketed as the HERMÉS (i). He also sold several makes including Panhard, De Dietrich, Rochet-Schneider, Minerva and Fiat, all quality makes which enhanced Mathis' reputation. He managed to sell two Fiats to the Kaiser, these being the only non-German cars in the Imperial garage. By 1905 his Auto-Mathis-Palace in Strasbourg was the largest sales organisation in Germany and the third largest in the world.

In 1910 Mathis launched the first car for sale bearing his name. This was the 2025cc 8/20PS, a straightforward design with monobloc side-valve 4-cylinder engine, 4-speed separate gearbox and shaft drive. To supplement this car he bought the 2544cc Typ PK4 from STOEWER, which he sold in Germany as a Stoewer-Mathis and in France simply as a Mathis. He was good at forgetting the origin of the cars he was connected with; by the mid–1920s he was describing the Type 13 Bugatti, made several years after he had severed his links with Ettore, as a Mathis, while his personal Fiat racing car, which he sold to Sir Frederick Richmond, he described as a 100-120hp Mathis!

Mathis production was limited to start with, amounting to only 75 cars in 1911. The following year he brought out a smaller car, the 1132cc Babylette with vertical gate change, which was made mostly in 2-seater form, and there were several larger 4-cylinder models, up to the 3435cc 14/35PS, as well as a 4396cc Knight-engined model which was probably a Minerva with a Mathis radiator, or possibly a Fiat with Minerva engine and Mathis radiator. Apart from the Babylette it is difficult to sort out exactly what was a genuine Mathis-built car at this time. Production was increased for 1912, with 200 cars promised for the UK market alone, and 600 in 1913. Mathis cannot have pleased the British agent, Gordon Marshall, when he concluded a deal with Harrods whereby the London store would take 175 cars direct from Strasbourg, bypassing Marshall altogether.

By 1914 Mathis was deputy chairman of the DAHV, the German motor trade association, similar to Britain's Society of Motor Manufacturers & Traders, and an important figure in the industry, though only 34 years old. During the war he was sent to Switzerland to try to purchase tyres that Germany desperately needed for the war effort. On one of these journeys he slipped into France, and never returned to Germany. In 1918 Alsace became French once more, and Mathis was able to return to his factories. These were completely rebuilt in the early 1920s, and Mathis soon became one of the leading manufacturers of popular cars. Production rose from under 2000 in 1920 to more than 20,000 in 1927, putting the Alsatian make in fourth place among French car makers, beaten only by Citroën, Renault and Peugeot.

The Babylette was revived in 1919, now called the 8/15hp, and was joined for 1921 by a 6/8hp with a tiny 4-cylinder engine of only 760cc. This was in the cyclecar class, but was greatly superior in having four cylinders, with aluminium pistons, a 4-speed gearbox, an electric starter and shaft drive. The oil was circulated by the flywheel, as on the Model T Ford. Also in 1921 there was an anglicised version of the 8/15 called the B.A.C., though few were sold, and later B.A.C.s were not Mathis-based. Up to the mid-20s Mathis made nothing over 1½ litres, and his small fours were characterised by differential-less rear axles, splash lubrication and although they had 4-speed gearboxes, top gear was very low to cope with the limited power output. In 1923 they brought out two small sixes, the 1140cc Type PS and the 1187cc Type L. The latter had a detachable head and single-ohc, with some sporting pretensions, but the PS was a strictly touring model with fixed head side-valve engine and neither front-wheel brakes nor differential. Like the fours, both sixes had 4-speed gearboxes and could be quickly distinguished by their vee-radiators.

QUELQUES MODÈLES 1933
MATHIS

4 CYLINDRES

Coupé 2/3 pl. TY - 5 CV ou PY - 6 CV
ou PY Sport 8 CV « ROUE LIBRE »

Cond. Int. 4 portes TY - 5 CV et PY - 6 CV

EMYQUATRE

Cond. Int. 4/5 places 8 CV 4 Cyl.

Cond. Int. «Dynamic» 4/5 pl. 8 CV - 4 Cyl.

EMYSIX

Cond. Int. 4/5 pl. 11 et 14 CV - 6 Cyl.

Cond. int. 6/7 pl. 14 CV - 6 Cyl.

EMYHUIT

Faux-Cabriolet «Deauville» 4 pl. FOH - 3 litres - 8 Cyl.

Cond. Int. 4/5 pl. FOH - 3 litres - 8 Cyl

VEHICULES INDUSTRIELS

Fourgon PUF
Charge totale 1200 kgs

Camionnette bâchée QGUN
Charge totale 1600 kgs

Autocar U 2 - 17 places
Charge totale 3000 kgs

Camion Brasseur U 6 F
Charge totale 4750 kgs

17247. 100.000) 28 9 32. L R

R. C. Strasbourg B 68

1931 Mathis Type MY coupé.
NICK BALDWIN

1932 Mathis Emyhuit Deauville coupé.
NICK BALDWIN

1946 Mathis VL 333 coupé.
NATIONAL MOTOR MUSEUM

For 1926 Mathis brought out a larger family car, the 1616cc Type GM with pressure lubrication, front-wheel brakes and a differential. This was clearly aimed at the Citroën C4 market, just as the 1829cc EMY6 was a competitor for the Citroën C6. This had coil ignition and hypoid rear axle, and was made from 1928 to 1932, though enlarged to 2179cc in 1929 (Type SGM and SMY) and to 2443cc in 1930 (Type SG and SGF). Another new model for 1927, when Mathis was making 75 cars a day, was the 1168cc Type MY which was good value at 15,950 francs, when the comparable Renault NN cost 17,450 francs. Fabric saloons were among the most popular body styles and justified Mathis' slogan 'Le Poids-Voilà l'Ennemi' (Weight is the Enemy).

Mathis moved up market in the early 1930s with a series of straight-8s, the 3050cc FOH, which used an enlarged version of the six, and the 5298cc KFON for which Mathis bought in Continental engines. Only six KFONs were made, one of which became the personal car of Mathis' wife.

Mathis was a great admirer of American mass-production methods, and in 1930 he planned a deal with William C. Durant whereby a slightly enlarged version of the 1062cc Type PY would be made in Durant's factory at Lansing, Michigan. Prototypes were shown at the 1931 New York and Chicago Shows,

and there was talk of 100,000 cars a year being made to sell at $455 each. In fact the project never got off the ground, but it would probably have met with no more success than the American Austin, as Americans were just not interested in small cars at that time.

Mathis' sales began to drop in the early 1930s, despite such advances as hydraulic brakes in 1931, synchromesh in 1932 (a year before Citroën or Renault), and transverse ifs on the 1933 1445cc EMY4. This and the companion 2288cc EMY6 made up the range until 1935 when Fords began to appear on the Strasbourg production lines (see FORD (iv)). Apart from a hybrid called the Quadriflex which combined a Ford V8 engine with the all-independent suspension Mathis chassis, of which very few were made, the Mathis factories made only Ford-based products, cars and commercial vehicles, which sold under the Matford name.

Unhappy at playing second fiddle to Ford, Mathis sold his shares in Matford in 1938 and moved to the United States, where he made marine engines during the war under the name Matam. He returned to Strasbourg in 1946 and planned a completely new car. Designed by Jean Andreau, it was a highly aerodynamic 3-wheeler powered by a 700cc flat-twin engine driving the front wheels. It was called the VL333 (voiture légère, 3 litres to 100km fuel consumption, 3 wheels, 3 seats). The egg-shaped coupé body was an electrically-welded unitary structure. Though it appeared at several shows Mathis could not obtain government permission to put it into production. In 1947 he tried again, with the 666 (6 seats, 6 cylinders, 6 speeds), a 2.2-litre horizontally-opposed 6-cylinder saloon with curious angular styling, panoramic windscreen and all-round independent suspension. Capacity was raised to 2840cc in 1948, and the 666 was still around in 1950, but nobody bought one.

Mathis kept his factory going by making light aero engines and components for Renault. The last vehicle to bear his name was a Jeep-type powered by the 666's 2840cc engine, of which just three were made in 1951. In 1954 Mathis sold the Strasbourg factory to Citroën. He died two years later after a fall from a hotel window.
NG

Further Reading
Émile Mathis, Constructeur Automobile Alsacien, J.F. Blattner,
Édifrée, Paris, 1990.
Lost Causes of Motoring: Europe, Volume 2, Lord Montagu of Beaulieu,
Cassell, 1971.

MATHOMOBILE (B) 1980–c.1994
Mathomobile Replicars, Brussels.
Created by an engineer called Claude Mathot, this was a Bugatti Type 35 replica based on a shortened VW Beetle platform. Air cooled engines from Volkswagen or Porsche could be installed, or alternatively a Kaylor 22kW electric motor which could achieve a range of 100 miles at speeds up to 77mph (124km/h). Most production was exported to the USA.
CR

MATRA (F) 1965–1984
1965–1967 Matra Sports, Champigny-sur-Seine.
1967–1969 Matra-Sports sarl, Romorantin, Loir-et-Cher.
1969–1979 Matra-Simca Division Automobile, Velizy-Villacoublay,
Seine et Oise.
1979–1984 Automobiles Talbot, Velizy-Villacoublay, Seine-et-Oise.
Engins Matra (Mécanique Aviation Traction) were a large aerospace and armaments concern who took over the assets of the small sports car company run by René Bonnet, who was a friend of Matra's founder Marcel Chassagny. They continued with the René Bonnet theme of a Gordini-tuned 1108cc Renault engine in 70 or 94bhp forms, with disc brakes all round and fibreglass coupé bodywork. Called the Matra Djet, the car was made by a separate division called Matra Sports. The first cars were made at Bonnet's factory at Champigny-sur-Seine, but in 1967 Matra transferred production to their premises at Romorantin and introduced a new model, the M530 coupé powered by a mid-mounted 1.7-litre German Ford V4 engine. Though a twin-carburettor version arrived in 1969 and improved performance, the M530 never became a best-seller, perhaps because of its odd styling, and also a poor dealer network. It was listed up to 1973 (9690 built), but in 1969 Matra-Sports was taken over by SIMCA which became fully Chrysler-owned in 1970. This led to the Bagheera (named after

the panther in Kipling's *Jungle Book*) introduced in 1973. It had an 84bhp 1294cc Simca engine inclined and mounted transversely at the rear, with power-assisted disc brakes all round, and all-independent suspension. The fibreglass coupé body set on a steel spaceframe was unusual in seating three in line, though not, as in the McLaren F1, with the driver in the middle. It gained a 90bhp 1442cc engine in 1977, and was made up to 1980, becoming a Talbot-Matra in 1979 as a result of Peugeot-Talbot's takeover of Chrysler. By the time it was withdrawn, Bagheera sales had reached 47,802, a high figure for a specialised car. It was replaced by the Murena, another coupé but with a steel body and 2-seater layout. The basic engine was a 1.6-litre Simca, but there was the option of a 118bhp 2156cc Chrysler unit which gave it a top speed of 121mph (194 km/h). Like the Bagheera it was badged as a Talbot-Matra, and 10,613 were made before Matra was bought by Renault in 1983, which led to the marque being discontinued. The factory was then used for manufacture of the Renault Espace. A non-sporting Matra made from 1977 to 1984 was the Rancho, an estate which looked like a cut-price Range Rover, but had only front-wheel drive and was powered by a detuned version of the Bagheera's 1442cc engine.

Apart from their road cars Matra had a very successful career in racing, starting with Formula 3 in 1965 and winning the Formula 1 Constructors' Championship in 1969 with a Ford-Cosworth engined car driven by Jackie Stewart. They also won at Le Mans in 1972, 1973 and 1974 with V12-powered sports/racing cars.

NG

Further Reading
Matra, Toute l'Histoire, Gérard Crombac, E.P.A., 1982.
'Matra: The most improbable Champion', Karl Ludvigsen,
Automobile Quarterly, Vol. 12, No. 1.

MATTHEWS *see* SOVEREIGN

MATTHEY ET MARTIN (F) 1924–1925
Matthey et Martin, Paris.
This was a shaft-driven light car powered by an 894cc side-valve S.C.A.P. engine.
NG

MATULA *see* SPORTSCAR

MAUDSLAY (GB) 1902–1923
Maudslay Motor Co. Ltd, Parkside, Coventry.
This company was descended from one of Britain's most distinguished engineering businesses, which had been founded in London by Henry Maudslay (1771–1831). He worked with Joseph Bramah where he perfected the Bramah patent lock, developed a hydraulic seal that made Bramah's press successful and invented the micrometer, slide rest and screw-cutting lathe. The steam engine works that he set up in Lambeth, South London, Maudslay Son and Field, made many marine engines, and built a steam carriage in 1835. Shortly before they discontinued steam engine manufacture in 1900, Walter H. Maudslay set up a new company in Coventry to make internal combustion marine engines, but did not find many customers at first. He was joined by his sons Cyril and Reginald, though the latter soon left to start the STANDARD Motor Co. They engaged Alexander Craig to design a 20hp 3-cylinder car engine which was fitted in a chain-drive chassis and marketed during 1903 after the prototype had put up a good performance at the 1902 Welbeck Speed Trials. Craig's engine was remarkable for having a single ohc and pressure lubrication. It also had large inspection covers in the crankcase to allow the withdrawal of pistons and con rods. In December 1903 Maudslay launched a 40hp 6-cylinder car which was almost certainly the world's first ohc six. Also in the 1904 range were 3-cylinder models of 18 and 25hp, and a 9.6-litre 60hp six. This cost £1260 or £1470 with racing bodywork, and was among the most expensive cars on the British market. Very few were made. These early Maudslays had various types of radiator, some a tubular type, slung beneath the De Dion-type bonnet, some with a higher tubular type and from 1906, a conventional honeycomb in a Delaunay-Belleville-like circular shell. A number carried bodies with sideways facing passenger seats which were convertible from an open brake for summer use to a station omnibus.

In 1905 some 2-cylinder engines with pushrod ohv were made, but these mainly powered commercial vehicles. The staples of the Maudslay range were a 25/30hp four and the two sixes, the last of the latter being made in 1909. By

c.1969 Matra M530 LX coupé.
GILES CHAPMAN

1976 Matra Bagheera S coupé.
GILES CHAPMAN

1981 Matra Murena coupé.
GILES CHAPMAN

then annual production was about 100 cars, double what it had been in 1905. In 1910 came the best known Maudslay passenger car, the 3308cc 17hp four, still with single-ohc, known as the Sweet Seventeen. Bodies included 2- and 5-seater tourers, a limousine and a landaulet. Late in 1910 a petrol-electric version was tried but not proceeded with, but a constant-mesh silent chain gearbox was available for 1912. A Colonial version with higher ground clearance was available; this had bevel drive in place of the underslung worm of the home market car. For that year a 27hp six joined the Sweet Seventeen, but was made in smaller numbers. Electric lighting and starting were offered on 1914 models.

A 3-ton truck of standardised design was made in large numbers during the war, and solely commercial vehicles were made after the war. The only exception was an advanced sports car chassis which appeared at the 1923 Olympia Show.

1903 Maudslay 20hp tonneau.
NICK BALDWIN

1904 Maudslay 40hp tourer.
NICK BALDWIN

1910 Maudslay 17hp limousine.
NICK BALDWIN

Known as the 15/80, it had a 1991cc twin-ohc 6-cylinder engine with inclined valves in hemispherical combustion chambers, a 7-bearing crankshaft and 4-wheel brakes. Only two chassis were made, the second being destroyed by fire at the coachbuilders. It is thought that the show chassis never received a body. Fletcher's *Motor Car Index* listed it for 1924 and 1925, but under 1926 they recorded 'Manufacturers state that they are not marketing the 6-cylinder car at present, but are concentrating on Safety Passenger Coaches'. These and other commercial vehicles kept the Maudslay name going up to 1957, latterly part of the A.C.V. (Associated Commercial Vehicles) Group which also included A.E.C. and Crossley.

NG

Further Reading
'Maudslay Memories', Nick Baldwin, *The Automobile*, June 1993.
'The Maudslay Motor Co. Ltd', Nick Baldwin, *Old Motor*, Vol. 9, No. 6.

MAUMEE *see* CRAIG-TOLEDO

MAURER (D) 1908–1909; 1923–1924
1908–1909 Johanna Maurer, Nuremberg.
1923–1924 Automobilfabrik Ludwig Maurer, Nuremberg.
The friction drive pioneer Ludwig Maurer left MAURER UNION in 1908, and wanting to make cars on his own he registered a new company in his wife's name as he was forbidden to use his own. Small 2-cylinder cars with friction drive were made for a few months only. He then concentrated on making engines, and in 1923 launched a 199cc motorcycle and a cyclecar powered by a 2/6PS flat-twin 2-stroke engine, with chain drive. Neither lasted more than a year.

HON

MAURER UNION (D) 1900–1910
1900–1908 Nürnberger Motorfahrzeuge-Fabrik 'Union', Nuremberg.
1908–1910 Automobilwerk Union AG, Nuremberg.
The characteristic of all cars made under this name was the friction drive invented by Ludwig Maurer. The first cars had 1140cc 6hp single-cylinder engines and proved quite popular, although they suffered from the usual problems associated with friction drive, slipping when the discs were wet. Final drive was by chain or shaft. A 1526cc V-twin joined the single in 1904, and a few 4-cylinder cars were made from 1906. Some cars and commercial vehicles of Maurer design were made in England by Dougill of Leeds.

HON

MAUSER (D) 1923–1929
Mauser-Werke AG, Oberndorf.

The famous armaments factory of Mauser turned to new products after World War I, and started with an unusual car called the Einspur-Auto. This had two wheels, with small retractable wheels at the side for starting and stopping. A single-cylinder engine of 498 or 510cc was used, with 3-speed gearbox and chain drive to the rear wheel. The body was a quite roomy 3-seater, with two passengers sitting behind the driver. The steering wheel was of exceptionally large diameter. The prototype appeared at the 1921 Berlin Show, but production did not start until two years later. It lasted until 1925, and a few examples by another firm in Oberndorf were made up to 1929, while it was made under licence in France as the MONOTRACE. In 1923 Mauser brought out a conventional 4-wheeled car with 1568cc 6/24PS ohv 4-cylinder engine and 4-wheel brakes. It was used as a taxi as well as a private car. Total production of the Einspur-Auto and the 6/24PS was about 1000 cars.

HON

MAUVE (F) 1922–1924
Cyclecars Mauve, Levallois-Perret, Seine.

Eugène Mauve built and raced the unconventional ELFE cyclecar from 1919 to 1921, and the following year turned to a more conventional car powered by a 1086cc single-ohc 4-cylinder Anzani engine. He raced the first under the name Anzani or Mauve-Anzani, which has led to Anzani being listed as a make of car. Production cars, however, were always called Mauve, and were typical small 2-seater sports cars. Even the tuned models, which gave 31bhp, had rear-wheel brakes only.

NG

M.A.V.A. (GR) 1980–c.1987
M.A.V.A. SA, Athens.

The Greek Renault importer, M.A.V.A., offered its own unique model called the Farma from 1980. Designed by Georgios Mihail, it was a Renault 4-based leisure car with a 2-seater plastic body not dissimilar to the Renault Rodeo. The production rate was as high as four units per day.

CR

MÁVAG (H) 1938–1942
Magyar Királyi Állami Vas-, Acél- és Gépgyárak, Budapest.

The Machine Factory of the Hungarian Railways built many trucks and buses from the 1920s on. In 1938 the son of the governor, István Horthy was elected as managing director. He decided to buy the licence for the German FORD Eifel and V8 types. The Eifel even had a local version, with lengthened wheelbase for use as a taxi. It was not too popular as the structure was not rigid enough and the car collapsed. The V8 was equipped with hydraulic brakes, unlike their German counterparts. Car production soon ended, but truck and bus production continued after World War II. MÁVAG continued in various forms until the 1990s.

PN

MAVERICK (US) c.1952
Maverick Motors, Mountain View, California.

The Maverick was an early fibreglass-bodied kit car that fitted full-size American sedan chassis. Designed by company president Sterling Gladwin and fabricated by James Nolan and Jim Rae, the Maverick was a clean and smoothly rounded 2-seat roadster. Factory assembled cars were built on 1953 Cadillac chassis and cost $3800. The $950 bodies could be fitted on 1936 to 1953 Cadillac, Hudson, Packard, Buick or Chrysler frames. Standard Maverick bodies had no doors, boot or bonnet, although doors were supposedly optional. Factory literature showed the one-piece body as being quickly removable for easy maintenance, but they had two small access panels on the bonnet. A modified LaSalle grill and bumpers were used up front. Less than 10 complete cars are believed to have been built.

HP

MAX (i) (F) 1927–c.1929
Mourlot et Cie, Billancourt, Seine.

Not to be confused with the later LÉON MAX, this was a small cyclecar powered by 2-stroke engines of 350cc (single-cylinder) and 514 or 617cc (2-cylinder). The

c.1901 Maurer Union 6hp 2-seater.
NICK GEORGANO/NATIONAL MOTOR MUSEUM

c.1925 Mauser Einspur-Auto 2-wheeler.
NATIONAL MOTOR MUSEUM

1938 Mávag-Ford V8 saloon.
NICK GEORGANO

smaller car had friction transmission, the larger models a conventional 3-speed gearbox. Though of diminutive size, the Max had a long bonnet which gave it a sporty appearance.

NG

1904 Maxim 16hp landaulette.
NICK GEORGANO

1927 Maximag 7CV sports car.
ERNEST SCHMID

MAX (ii) (NL) 1988–1990

Max Motors BV, Helmond.

With smart, compact, upright styling, the Max Roadster was a promising steel-bodied 2-seater cabriolet with speedster-style rear head fairings and mechanicals derived from the Peugeot 205. With an 83bhp 1360cc engine fitted, a top speed of 118mph (190km/h) and 0–62mph (0–100km/h) in 9.0 seconds was claimed. Planned production did not apparently begin.

CR

MAXIM (GB) 1902–1905

London General Automobile Co. Ltd, London.

This car was designed by Hiram Stevens Maxim, inventor of the Maxim gun, and father of Hiram Percy Maxim who was chief engineer for COLUMBIA (i). It was a medium-sized car powered by a 16hp 2-cylinder T-head Fafnir engine, with 3-speed gearbox and double-chain drive. The first model had an armoured wood chassis and gilled-tube radiator, but later cars had steel frames and honeycomb radiators. The Maxim was on the market up to 1905, but by this time their main activity was the supply of lighting equipment for cars.

NG

MAXIMAG (CH) 1922–1928

SA Motosacoche, Carouge, Geneva.

Motosacoche was the leading motorcycle manufacturer of Switzerland, with an annual production (1914–22) of up to 5000 vehicles and 4000 engines for other companies. In 1914 a high-performance 4-cylinder in-line engine with a shaft-driven ohc,1093cc and producing a very creditable 33bhp, was completed. It was offered to various foreign companies for their racing voiturettes and most satisfactory tests were conducted but the outbreak of the World War I intervened.

At the Paris Automobile Show of 1922, the 5hp Maximag super cyclecar was shown for the first time. It had a conventional side-valve 4-cylinder engine of 1093cc with a combined pressure/splash lubrication and thermo-syphon cooling. Power was transmitted via multiple-plate disc, a 3-speed gearbox and shaft to the rear wheels.

On the early models brakes were on the rear wheels only but soon 4-wheel brakes were fitted. The early tourers were supplemented with various 2- and 4-seater body styles and Brichet of Geneva coach-built a very neat Grand Sport version. Apparently the branch factory at Lyon, France also built some of the Maximag cyclecars. The market was not as interesting as expected and in 1928 production of cars, which had totalled about 200 vehicles, came to a close – but Motosacoche remained and was active in the motorcycle field.

FH

MAXIM-GOODRIDGE (US) 1908

Maxim & Goodridge, Hartford, Connecticut.

This was an attractive-looking electric car of which only a prototype was built. It was the work of Hiram Percy Maxim, who had been chief engineer for COLUMBIA (i), and T. W. Goodridge, former general manager of STUDEBAKER. It was a tiller-steered 2-seater victoria phaeton, with worm drive and a top speed of 18mph (29 km/h). A price of $1800 was fixed, but before it went on the market the name was changed to Lenox, and soon after that Maxim lost interest, preferring to follow in his father's footsteps and make guns. Goodridge sold the patented worm drive to WAVERLEY of Indianapolis, who also made electrics, and joined the sales office of MATHESON.

NG

MAXIM TRI-CAR (US) 1911–1914

1911–1912 G.H. Bushnell Press Co., Thompsonville, Connecticut.
1912–1914 Maxim Tri-Car Manufacturing Co., Port Jefferson, New York.

This was a fairly close copy of the PHÄNOMOBIL 3-wheeler with engine above the front wheel which it drove by chain, and steering by a long tiller. The prototype had a single-cylinder engine, but production Maxims used an 8hp 2-cylinder unit. They were intended for carriage of passengers or goods, and more of the latter were made. In 1912 they moved into the Port Jefferson factory formerly occupied by the makers of the ONLY car. There was no link with any other car called Maxim, the name coming from one of the co-designers, French-born Maxim Karminski.

NG

MAXTON (US) 1991 to date

Maxton Concessionaires Ltd, Englewood, Colorado.

With an unlikely name like the Maxton Rollerskate, this kit car had to be good. Initially designed by Chris Lawrence, it was intended to be a sophisticated small sports car with a Datsun 6-cylinder engine and De Dion rear suspension. By the time it got into production, it had been redesigned by Ben Vanderlinder and was a Lotus 7-type sports car with Mazda RX-7 engine, transmission and rear axle. It was first sold in turn-key form, but low demand prompted a kit version that could be purchased in stages. It had a narrow wedge-shaped body with wide wheel flares. Total weight was 1680lbs. A longer version was offered for taller drivers. Plans for a more sophisticated version and an aluminium-bodied coupé were not realised.

HP

MAXWELL (US) 1904–1925

1904–1912 Maxwell-Briscoe Motor Co., Tarrytown, New York.
1913–1920 Maxwell Motor Co., Detroit, Michigan.
1920–1925 Maxwell Motor Corp., Detroit, Michigan.
1925 Chrysler Corp., Detroit, Michigan.

Thanks to radio comedian Jack Benny, the Maxwell is among the best known of automotive lost causes. Benny's cantankerous, fictitious Maxwell continued to entertain listeners (and television viewers) into the 1970s. The car was named for Jonathan Maxwell (1864–1928), an Indiana machinist who had worked on the car developed by Elwood HAYNES and the APPERSON brothers. Later, at Olds Motor Works, he had a part in creation of the curved-dash OLDSMOBILE and the silent NORTHERN.

Jonathan Maxwell met Benjamin and Frank Briscoe while working at Olds. He came to their shop looking for help in building a radiator for the Oldsmobile, which he got, and was sufficiently impressed with the product that the Briscoe firm became a major supplier of sheet metal parts to Olds. Benjamin Briscoe then decided to enter the automobile business himself, and, after an aborted venture with David BUICK, approached Maxwell, luring him away from

Northern in 1903 with the promise that the car he designed would bear his name. Maxwell had the car ready by the following Christmas. A three-way partnership, among Maxwell, Briscoe and a C.W. Althouse, had been formed in July, but Althouse left at year's end, at which time Maxwell-Briscoe Motor Co. was formed. With money raised on Wall Street, Maxwell-Briscoe leased a factory at Tarrytown, New York, formerly home to the MOBILE steamer.

Production of the Maxwell started in June 1904, but only ten cars were built that year. The first Maxwell was a jaunty little tourabout built on a 72in (1827mm) wheelbase. Power came from a twin-cylinder side-valve engine located up front, under a bonnet, mechanically-operated inlet valves, thermosyphon cooling and a 2-speed planetary gearbox. The 2-passenger tourabout sold for $750; a larger 5-passenger model was listed for $1400. A further 823 cars followed in 1905, and a 4-cylinder model appeared the next year. Thereafter fours and twins were sold side by side, and production was meteoric, some 9460 cars being built in 1909.

As the firm grew, it branched out, establishing works at Newcastle, Indiana, and Pawtucket, Rhode Island. Its popularity was enhanced by the efforts of sales manager C.W. Kelsey, later to build his own KELSEY automobile. Kelsey promoted the Maxwell with publicity stunts such as teeterboard contests, driving up the steps of public buildings, and participation in the Glidden Tours. At Kelsey's instigation, Alice Huyler Ramsey became the first woman to drive across the American continent in 1909, accompanied by three female friends in a Maxwell. In 1910, over 20,000 were sold.

Benjamin Briscoe, however, lusted after a larger automobile company, and felt that a combine of existing manufacturers was the best route. Talks with FORD, Olds, and William Durant came to naught, as Ford and Olds bowed out. A merger of Buick with Maxwell-Briscoe, as United Motors Co., almost came about, then died, after which Durant struck out on his own to form General Motors. Briscoe's United States Motor Co. finally came into being in January 1910, consisting of Maxwell-Briscoe, Columbia, truck builder Alden-Sampson, and, later, Stoddard-Dayton and Brush. Maxwell was now the third-best-selling American car, behind Ford and Buick, but this did not sufficiently gild the fortunes of U.S. Motor Co. By September 1912 the firm was insolvent, due to a complicated series of transactions and misadventures. The only make to survive the U.S. Motor collapse was Maxwell. The company was reorganised and renamed Maxwell Motor Co. in January 1913, under the management of Walter Flanders, late of Ford and the Everett-Metzger-Flanders (E-M-F)/STUDEBAKER group. The geographically distributed plants were sold, and Jonathan Maxwell, along with the Maxwell car, relocated to Detroit.

The twin-cylinder cars were dropped after 1912, and a 6180cc six, basically former Flanders Six, was added the following year, cars now selling for $785 to $2200. The six was short-lived, and the staple model was the 3045cc 4-cylinder Model 25, on a 103in (2614mm) wheelbase. This continued for several years, 100,000 Maxwells (75,000 cars and 25,000 trucks) being sold in 1917. In 1917, Maxwell allied itself with CHALMERS, as Walter Flanders took the helm of both companies. This gained Maxwell needed production space, as the Chalmers plants were underutilised. Banking that the end of World War I would improve the fortunes of the auto industry, Maxwell poised to increase production yet again, but was caught off guard. Only slightly over 34,000 cars were sold in 1920, and debts were mounting, partly due to an even more precarious situation at Chalmers. Maxwell quality, at least its reputation for same, had suffered, too, making the cars difficult to sell. The fact that no significant design changes had been made for three years did not help, either.

The bankers brought in a new manager, Walter P. Chrysler, who had excelled at Buick, General Motors, and Willys-Overland. Initially Chrysler was reluctant, feeling, as he would remember in his autobiography, 'I would not touch it with a ten foot pole'. Chrysler put Maxwell into a 'friendly receivership', and purchased the assets of the two firms, which he renamed Maxwell Motor Corp. He investigated the reliability problems with the cars, discovering that most were traceable to weak rear axles, for which a fix was engineered. Chrysler cut the price of the 1921 model, now called, to distinguish it from the troublesome car, the Good Maxwell. A redesigned car for 1922 was dubbed the New Series Maxwell, and quality and reputation had improved such that 67,000 were sold. Walter Chrysler's own 6-cylinder CHRYSLER, however, substantially outsold Maxwell for 1924, much to Chrysler's delight. Moreover, the Chrysler sold for about twice the price of the Maxwell. Taking a cue from this success, he reorganised the company yet again in 1925, renaming it Chrysler Corp. The

1908 Maxwell-Briscoe 14hp 2-seater.
NICK BALDWIN

1915 Maxwell Model 25 town car.
NICK BALDWIN

1924 Maxwell showroom display.
NATIONAL MOTOR MUSEUM

Maxwell survived that year only, and in 1926 became the 4-cylinder Chrysler 58, using the same engine as its predecessor. By 1928, the 4-cylinder Chrysler, née Maxwell, had become the PLYMOUTH. In retrospect, Walter Chrysler recalled that the Maxwell turned out to be 'the greatest opportunity in my whole life'.

KF

Further Reading
'U.S. Motor – Ben Briscoe's Shattered Dream', Anthony J. Yanik,
Automobile Quarterly, Vol. 36, No. 2.
Life of an American Workman, Walter P. Chrysler,
Curtis Publishing Co., 1937; Dodd, Mead & Co., 1950.

1925 Maybach W.5 limousine.
NATIONAL MOTOR MUSEUM

MAXWERKE (D) 1899–1903

Elektrizitäts- und Automobil-Gesellschaft Harff & Schwartz AG, Cologne.
This company made electric vehicles which were more often seen as delivery vans and trucks, though some passenger models were made. They also experimented with petrol and petrol-electric drive.

HON

MAYA *see* CAMBER

MAYBACH (D) 1921–1941

Maybach Motoren-Werke GmbH, Friedrichshafen.
Wilhelm Maybach (1846–1929) had been Gottlieb Daimler's partner in all his experimental and early production cars, and was responsible for many of the important developments in early Daimler cars. He left the company in 1907 to make engines for Count Zeppelin's airships, which were built at Friedrichshafen on Lake Constance (Bodensee). In 1912 he moved his factory to be closer to the Zeppelin works, and during the war made large numbers of engines for Zeppelins and Gotha bombers. He retired in 1914, handing over to his son Karl (1879–1960) who turned to making engines for cars and commercial vehicles after the war, as under the Treaty of Versailles German companies were not allowed to make aero engines.

About 150 examples of the W.2 5.7-litre 6-cylinder engine were sold to SPYKER between 1920 and 1925, and other customers included truck makers Faun of Nuremberg, and the Berlin bus company ABOAG. However these contracts did not provide enough work to keep the factory busy, so in 1921 Karl launched the Maybach car. This used an improved version of the W.2 engine, a 6-cylinder side-valve unit with light alloy pistons and dual ignition. The 5740cc engine gave 72bhp, and unless saddled with too heavy a body, the W.3 could reach nearly 80mph (130km/h). The chassis had 4-wheel brakes, the first use of these on a German car, and transmission, most unusually for such a large car, was a 2-speed epicyclic one. In fact, the higher speed was suitable for all normal work once the car had moved off from rest. The lower gear was for starting and steep gradients only, and was actuated by its own pedal, known as the hill pedal. A separate pedal actuated reverse gear.

Launched at the 1921 Berlin Show, the W.3 was one of the most expensive cars on the German market, costing more than the Mercedes 28/95PS. Coachwork was supplied by several well-known German firms such as Auer, Erdmann & Rossi, Kellner, Neuss and Papler, though Spohn soon became the favoured coachbuilder, providing most Maybach bodies from the late 1920s onwards.

Given Germany's harsh economic climate in the early 1920s, culminating in the runaway inflation of 1922/23, it is surprising that many W.3s were sold. Western Europe took hardly any, due to anti-German feeling, though a few were sold to the USA, and in 1929 the Emperor Haile Selassie of Ethiopia bought a W.5 landaulet. About 700 W.3s were sold between 1922 and 1928. They were joined in 1926 by the W.5 which had a larger engine due to its exceptionally long stroke (dimensions were 94 × 168mm) Capacity was 6995cc which gave 120bhp. The cylinder heads were now detachable The chassis was generally similar to that of the W.3, though the running boards and wheel arches were integral with the frame, a feature shared with the 30hp Armstrong-Siddeley. The gearchange pedal was power assisted.

In 1928 came the first sign of Maybach's obsession with the multi-speed gearbox. A separate overdrive (Schnellgang or fast speed) unit was mounted behind the main gearbox, giving four forward speeds. It was selected by a separate right-hand lever on the floor, and engaged by depressing the accelerator, so the clutch was not used. It was an optional extra on the W.5, which was called the W.5SG when so equipped, and was also sold to a number of other German car makers including Hansa, Hansa-Lloyd, Mannesmann, Opel and Wanderer.

1929 was a year of triumph and sadness for the Maybach Motorenwerke; in August the Graf Zeppelin airship powered by five 570bhp 12-cylinder Maybach engines flew round the world (Maybach V12 engines were also used in the US Navy's airships 'Akron' and 'Macon'), and in November appeared the company's first 12-cylinder car, but at the end of December Wilhelm Maybach died at the age of 84. He had been retired for many years, but took a keen interest in the activities of the company, and must have been especially pleased with the Graf Zeppelin's achievement and the new luxury car. Known as the DS, this had a 6962cc 150bhp V12 engine with ohvs operated by pushrods and rockers from a centrally-mounted camshaft. The gearbox was now a straightforward 3-speed

NICK BALDWIN

MAYBACH, KARL WILHELM (1879–1960)

Creator of the Maybach automobile, Karl Wilhelm Maybach's claims to fame also included the 410hp V12 diesel of 1933, which gave the Fliegende Hamburger train a top speed in excess of 112mph (180km/h), and the 750hp spark-ignition V12 for the Königstiger 68-ton military tank of 1944, among other engineering accomplishments.

He was born in Cologne on 6 July 1879, the elder son of Wilhelm Maybach and his wife Bertha née Habermass. In elementary school, he was characterised as 'difficult and headstrong' by the teachers, who gave him only average grades. His grades did not improve when he attended the Realschule in Cannstatt, leaving at the age of 17. He reported for military service, but was declared unfit due to a heart flutter. He did not like the idea of studying at the Stuttgart Polytechnic Institute, as suggested by his father, and instead got his permission to work for the Daimler Motoren Gesellschaft as a trainee; he soon revealed himself to be a superb draftsman.

In 1897 his father arranged an educational programme for him at Maschinenfabrik Esslingen, an engineering company with 2500 workers, going through the shops and getting hands-on experience of patterns and templates, jigs and fixtures, blacksmithing and boiler-making, operating and setting drills and lathes, toolmaking and fitting. He stayed there for 3½ years, the final year in the electro-technical department.

sliding pinion one with central change, but behind it was the Schnellgang, now operated by a selector lever on the steering column, with kickdown actuation. The DS was a very large car, with a wheelbase of 144in (3655mm) and weight of about 2¾tons. Bodies, mostly by Spohn, were usually traditional limousines or 4-door cabriolets, though a few 2-door roadsters were made by Erdmann & Rossi.

In 1930 the DS was renamed the DS7 (Double Six, 7 litres), and for the first time the name Zeppelin was applied to the cars. The ultimate development of the series was the DS8 with 7978cc 200bhp engine and a gearbox giving eight forward speeds. Known as the Doppelschnellgang, it featured two low speeds, 1a and 1, followed by three higher speeds, each of which had two ratios, thanks to the overdrive which was now incorporated in the gearbox. A large floor-mounted lever gave the choice of reverse 1a or main drive (1-4), while altering the position of two small levers on the steering wheel gave the choice of four speeds in either 1a or 1. After selecting the required speed the driver lifted his foot from the accelerator and the change was made automatically, the clutch being vacuum-controlled. This made for very smooth driving, though one wonders if all the complexity was worth while, given the great flexibility of the 200bhp

1932 Maybach Zeppelin D58 cabriolet.
NICK GEORGANO

In 1901 he presented himself for examination at the Königliche Baugewerkschule (Royal Construction Trades School) in Stuttgart, and obtained a diploma as a mechanical technician. To broaden his experience, he went to Berlin and worked in the drawing office of Ludwig Löwe & Co., an arms and munitions contractor with a 4000-strong workforce. Here, he also gained an understanding of mass production and industrial finance. After six months with the Löwe enterprise, his father's friend (and fellow-board member of Daimler Motoren Gesellschaft) Max Wilhelm von Duttenhofer, hired him as a test engineer for a techno-scientific research institute in Neubabelsberg, which Duttenhofer had founded.

However, his experience so far was confined to Germany, and he wanted to work in the French auto industry. During the Universal Exposition in Paris in 1889, where Daimler and Maybach (Sr) had shown the wire-wheeled car, the latter had formed a personal friendship with Count Henri de Lavalette, whose machine works were to evolve into a major supplier to the industry. For two years, 1906-08, Karl Maybach was a member of a research group given the task of designing an advanced high-performance car in the shops of the Société des Ateliers de Construction de Lavalette at St Ouen, a suburb on the northern doorstep of Paris. This project he discussed at length in correspondence with his father, and it formed the core of their plan to sell a ready-made car design to Opel.

In 1908, after his return to Stuttgart, the Opel project was his main occupation. Then his father became involved with Count Zeppelin, and founded Luftahrzeug-Motorenbau GmbH at Bissingen on the river Enz, with Zeppelin's financial backing. Karl Maybach became its chief engineer in 1909, and designed the 6-cylinder L-head AZ engine for airships.

The engine company moved into more spacious premises in Friedrichshafen in May 1912, and its title was shortened to Motorenbau GmbH, as its product range widened to include airplane and marine engines.

After Count Zeppelin's death in 1917, Karl and Wilhelm Maybach bought the engine company, which became Maybach Motorenbau GmbH in March 1918. By the end of the year, however, the German market for aircraft engines no longer existed. Karl Maybach spent 18 months designing and testing an automotive engine, which went into production in 1920 as the W.2, an in-line six of 5740cc, producing 70hp at 2200rpm. It found a steady clientele with truck makers Magirus, Faun, Krauss-Maffei, NAG, and Vomag.

Towards the end of 1918, Karl Maybach became interested in the high-speed diesel engine, and built his first diesel test engine. But it was to take five years of development work before a production engine was ready.

During the years 1919–23 the company was not making a profit. The factory was overmanned, there was no proper cost-accounting, and new-product lead-times were too long. In 1923, Maybach Motorenbau GmbH came under the control of the Zeppelin company, which was back in the business of building airships.

Maybach built the 420hp V12engines for the ZR III airship, constructed in 1923 and sent to the US as part of Germany's war reparations. Diesel engine production began in 1924 with a 150hp unit, first demonstrated in a railway locomotive built by Waggonfabrik Wismar. Financially, however, the company was heading for disaster. An annual loss of Rm1.3m was reported for 1929, and the company went into liquidation. It was still a subsidiary of Luftschiffbau Zeppelin GmbH, whose management wanted to maintain the skilled workforce and protect the industrial investment and the goodwill of the Maybach name.

In March 1930 Zeppelin authorised the production of 100 bus engines (type OS-5), 70 cars, and 30 airship engines. The income stemmed the tide, and the market for railway locomotive power units revived.

Germany began re-arming in 1933, but it was 1935 before Maybach received its first military order (500 engines for half-tracks). From then on, military orders dominated, but in 1942-43 Karl Maybach occupied himself mainly with the design of new engines for postwar railway locomotives. Aerial bombardment destroyed 70 per cent of the factory in 1944, and Karl Maybach moved with his family to a small farming village in Allgäu.

In May 1946, he offered his services to the French occupation authorities, and before the end of the year he moved, with a staff of 60 volunteers from the engine company, to an engineering office at Vernon on the river Seine, leaving his family in Wohmbrechts (Allgäu). He shuttled back and forth until mid-year 1951, when he left Vernon for good, and retired to Garmisch in 1952.

Maybach Motorenbau GmbH later came under the control of Friedrich Flick who also became the biggest shareholder in Daimler-Benz AG and linked the two companies, organisationally, industrially, and commercially.

Karl Maybach died suddenly in Friedrichshaften during the night before Sunday 6 February 1960.

He married Käthe Lewerenz in Hamburg-Altona on 2 August 1915. Her father, Alfred Lewerenz, was an export trader and partner in the firm of Deurer & Kaufmann, which had a business connection with the engine company. Karl and Käthe had five children: Liselotte born in 1916, Walter born in 1920, Marianne born in 1922, Irmgard born in 1923, and Günter born in 1927.

Liselotte married a lawyer, Dr Ludwig Hengstl in 1941. Walter was a lieutenant in the Afrika-Korps under General von Arnim when killed in action on 14 February 1943. Marianne married Heinz Gessler, head of the Robert Gessler publishing company in 1951. Irmgard cut short her schooling to work as her father's secretary until 1957.

Günter studied engineering at the Stuttgart Technical University and graduated in 1952 with a thesis on turbocharging, then attended Penn State University. He held a seat on the Maybach board from 1962 but became seriously ill and died on 18 June 1963.

JPN

c.1937 Maybach SW38 cabriolet.
NICK GEORGANO/NATIONAL MOTOR MUSEUM

engine. The Doppelschnellgang was offered to other manufacturers, but the only one to take it up was Lagonda who offered it on their 3-litre Selector Special in 1932 and 1933.

The Maybach Zeppelin appealed to the wealthy conservative buyer who thought a Mercedes-Benz or Horch too flashy, and whose patriotism prevented him from buying a Rolls-Royce or Hispano-Suiza. They were not much favoured by the Nazi hierarchy, who preferred Mercedes-Benz, although the Reichsminister of Transport, Dr Dorpmüller, had an Erdmann & Rossi-bodied cabriolet, and the German ambassadors in London and The Hague both used Maybachs. At a chassis price of RM29,500 (RM36,500 to 38,500 for a complete car), the DS8 was second only to the Grosser Mercedes 770K in price. About 25 per year were made up to 1937, but thereafter only about another 25 more were made up to the end of production in 1940.

An improved W.5 called the W.6 or W.6DSG when fitted with the Doppelschnellgang, was made up to 1935, selling for appreciably less than the Zeppelin, RM15,000 to 23,000. They used the same wheelbase as the 12-cylinder cars, as did a smaller six, the 5184cc DSH, of which about 50 were made between 1934 and 1937. Both these models looked very similar to the Zeppelin until one opened the bonnet. In order to widen their market, Maybach brought out a brand new, considerably smaller car for 1935. The SW35 (Schwingachse 3.5 litres) had a 3435cc single-ohc 6-cylinder engine with square dimensions (90 × 90mm), giving 140bhp. Transmission was by Doppelschnellgang, but the chassis was thoroughly up-to-date, electrically welded and cruciform-braced, with coil-and-wishbone ifs and swing axles at the rear. The original SW35, of which about 50 were made, had flat, leaf-type valve springs, but these were replaced by conventional coil springs on the later SW38 (1936–39) and SW42 (1939–41). These had larger engines of 3817 and 4197cc respectively. About 615 of all SW models were made.

Maybach were kept very busy during the war, when they turned out some 140,000 engines for half-track vehicles and tanks. After the war they were successful making big diesel engines for use in railcars and boats. In 1960 Maybach merged with Daimler-Benz, making the Stuttgart firm's larger diesel engines. The name was revived in 1998 for a projected super-luxury saloon with V12 engine, to be introduced as a model of Mercedes-Benz in 2001.

No exact figures are available for Maybach production, but estimates for the total are around 2100 to 2300, of which 135 are thought to survive.

NG

Further Reading
Geschichte der Maybach Automobile, Michael Graf Wolf-Metternich, Automuseum, Nettelstett, c.1968.
Lost Causes of Motoring: Europe, Volume 1, Lord Montagu of Beaulieu, Cassell, 1970.
'Modest by Comparison: Maybach SW Series', Karla A. Rosenbusch, *Automobile Quarterly*, Vol. 33, No. 3.
'Zeppelin, the Landship from Friedrichshafen', Stan Grayson, *Automobile Quarterly*, Vol. 12, No. 2.

MAY CORP (GB) 1991

May Corp, Totnes, Devon.
Chris Field, an ex-Vauxhall stylist and creator of the MIRACH, designed a new sports car called the ECU. Looking somewhat like the 1990 Lotus Elan, it was however mid-engined with rear-wheel drive. Its clever open roof arrangement consisted of a retractable rear screen and targa top. It was engineered to accept virtually any front-wheel drive 1.6–2-litre engine, for May Corp hoped to find a major manufacturer to take up the design, which debuted at the 1991 Frankfurt motor show. Despite intentions of currying Ford and GM interest, neither a sponsor nor an outside manufacturer could be found.

CR

MAYER (D) 1899–1900

Hugo Mayer, Berlin.
Mayer made a single-wheeled *avant train* with the Belvalette engine mounted above the wheel. It was available as a separate attachment or as a complete 3-wheeler with 2-seater or delivery van body.

HON

MAYFAIR (i) (GB) 1900–1907

1900–1901 Sports Motor Car Co., Ltd, Kilburn, London; Kensington, London.
1906–1907 G.L.M. Dorwald & Co., Putney, London.
The first Mayfair was an imported car, and very probably so was the second. The Sports Motor Co. advertised various models which they sold under the names Mayfair or Sports. The Mayfair was a 2-seater voiturette with single- or 2-cylinder engine, and was imported from Belgium where it was made by LINON. The 1906/07 Mayfair was sold by the makers of the CRAIG-DORWALD, and was

available in four models, the smallest with a 6hp De Dion- Bouton engine, the others being a 10hp twin and two fours, of 15 and 28hp. Their origins are unknown, though the 6hp may well have been another of LACOSTE ET BATTMANN's efforts.

NG

MAYFAIR (ii) (US) 1925

Mayfair Manufacturing Co., Jamaica Plain, Massachusetts.

This was a Model T Ford, rebuilt with disc clutch and conventional gearbox. The radiator was restyled and the only body was a 3-door sedan at $485. This was $100 cheaper than a new Ford sedan, because Mayfairs were made from second-hand Fords. However, its appeal was limited, and not more than 10 were made.

NG

MAYO (S) 1996

Autobil Mayo AB, Boras.

The Mayo P1 was a mid–engined sports car styled in the familiar mid–1990s junior supercar mould. Intended for series production, but never developed beyond a single running prototype, the 2-seater P1 used a mixture of Saab 900 and 9000 componentry, with a transverse mid-mounted Saab 2.0-litre turbocharged engine, claimed to develop 250 bhp with a maximum speed of 174mph (280km/h).

CR

MAYRETTE (D) 1921–1924

Karl Mayer Kraftfahrzeugbau, Munich.

This was a small car made in single- or 2-seater form and powered by a 500cc flat-twin BMW engine. A second version was a 3-wheeler and used a 200cc J.A.P. engine driving the single rear wheel. A few dozens of each version were built, all by hand.

HON

MAYTAG (US) 1910–1911

Maytag-Mason Motor Co., Waterloo, Iowa.

In June 1909 Senator Fred Maytag and his son Harold purchased the MASON Automobile Co. of Des Moines, Iowa, removed the plant to Waterloo and reorganised as the Maytag-Mason Motor Co. The 2-cylinder Mason cars were unchanged, but the Maytags added a 32/35hp 4-cylinder tourer. For 1911 this was made in five body styles, two roadsters, a tourer, toy tonneau and torpedo. In January 1912 the Maytags left, and Edward R. Mason regained control. The cars were named Mason again, though the factory remained in Waterloo. Total production under the Maytag name was 765 cars. The Maytags continued in their business of agricultural equipment and washing machines, the latter still made under the Maytag name today.

NG

MAZDA (J) 1960 to date

1960–1984 Toyo Kogyo Co. Ltd, Hiroshima.
1984 to date Mazda Motor Corp., Hiroshima.

In terms of passenger car manufacture, Mazda is younger than the two giants of the Japanese motor industry, Nissan and Toyota, but it has grown rapidly to become, in the late 1980s, the fourth largest Japanese car producer, and the tenth largest in the world. In addition, Mazda has made more Wankel rotary engines than any other company.

Mazda's history dates back to 1920 when Toyo Cork Kogyo (Eastern Cork Industries) Ltd was formed in Hiroshima to make gaskets and cork insulated wooden panels. In 1921 Jujiro Matsuda became president, and it was from his name that the company's products were named. The Japanese pronunciation is 'Mahtsuda', and as the Zoroastrian Lord of Light was Mazda it seemed an appropriate name for his products. The company name became Toyo Kogyo Ltd in 1928, and it was not until 1984 that it was renamed Mazda Motor Corp. Three-wheeled delivery trucks were added to the company's products in 1931, followed by 4-wheelers in 1958. A prototype passenger car was built in 1940 – it was a small 2-door saloon not unlike a Datsun in appearance, but it did not go into production because of the outbreak of war with the United States in December 1941.

It was another 19 years before a Mazda car appeared. This was the R-360, a small 2+2-seater coupé powered by a rear-mounted 356cc air-cooled V-twin

1968 Mazda 1200 saloon.
NICK GEORGANO

1973 Mazda RX4 2.6 saloon.
NICK BALDWIN

1976 Mazda 1300 hatchback.
NICK BALDWIN

1980 Mazda 323 1500GT hatchback.
NICK BALDWIN

1987 Mazda Luce V6 sedan.
MAZDA

1990 Mazda 121 hatchback.
MAZDA

1990 Mazda 626 GT coupé.
MAZDA

1990 Mazda RX-7 Turbo cabriolet.
MAZDA

engine. This gave 16bhp and a top speed of 60mph (96km/h). An unusual feature for such a small car was an optional automatic transmission. Mazda sold 23,417 R-360s in their first year of production, and was encouraged to follow with larger cars. These were the Carol 360 and 600, made in 4-door saloon and estate car models. The Carol's engine was an air-cooled flat-4 transversely mounted behind the passenger compartment, at first of 358cc, later of 596cc. The latter was capable of 65mph (104km/h) from an engine that revved up to 9000rpm. By 1962 the 600 was being built at the rate of 1000 per month.

At the Tokyo Show in November 1962 Mazda exhibited their first front-engined car, the 1000. This was a 4-door saloon with more modern lines than the rather dumpy 600. It did not go into production immediately, but appeared in 1963 as the Familia 800, made as a 2-door saloon, coupé or estate car, with styling by Bertone. The engine was a 782cc water-cooled four, and Mazda now had a car suitable for attacking the European and North American markets. The one millionth Mazda was delivered in March 1963, but most of these were commercial vehicles. However the second million came during 1966, and a much higher proportion of these were passenger cars. The Familia 800 grew up into the 1169cc 1200 in 1968, made as a 4-door saloon or estate car, while in 1966 came a larger 4-door saloon, the Luce 1500 powered by a 1496cc single-ohc 4-cylinder engine. In 1968 these were joined by the 1796cc 1800 with front disc brakes as standard. The Bertone styling gave these Mazdas a slight resemblance to contemporary BMWs.

The Wankel Era
In October 1960 Mazda's president Tsunedji Matsuda, son of the founder Jujiro, visited the NSU factory at Neckarsulm, Germany. He had already studied the rotary engine which Dr Felix Wankel was developing with NSU, and was anxious to see it in action, although NSU would not launch the Wankel-engined car on the market for another three years. In November 1961 Mazda signed an agreement for the licence production of Wankel engines, and a prototype Mazda-built rotary was tested in a car in 1963. This was a twin-rotor unit, as Mazda engineers found that the single-rotor engines as used by NSU caused too much vibration.

In 1966 they were ready to test the market for rotary-engined cars, and launched the Cosmo 110S. This was an attractively-styled 2-seater coupé powered by a twin-rotor engine which developed 110bhp. Top speed was 98mph (157km/h), which was not really adequate for a sports car, but the 110S was not initially planned as a sports car, though it looked like one, but rather as a test bed for the radical new engine. Indeed the 1966 models, of which 80 were made, were not for sale. They were loaned to selected customers for long-term evaluation, in the same way that Chrysler's gas turbine cars were in the United States. The difference was that the 110S *did* go on general sale the following year. By then it had a more powerful engine which gave a top speed of 112mph (179km/h). The specification included a De Dion rear axle, 5-speed gearbox and, from 1969, front disc brakes. Production was never large, only 1176 being sold between 1967 and 1972, but the 110S earned Mazda much prestige for its engineering, and it also provided the company with its entry into sport, when one finished fourth overall in the 1968 Marathon de la Route at the Nürburgring.

Once the rotary engine had been proved in the 110S, Mazda tried it in a mass-produced car. In 1968 they put an improved version of the 0813 engine that powered the 110S into the 1200 bodyshell to make the R100 saloon/coupé/estate car. This had an exceptional performance for a car of its size, with a top speed of 105mph (168 km/h). It was made up to 1973, production totalling 95,706, and it was joined in 1970 by the larger RX-2.

Mazda hedged their bets in the 1970s by offering a line of conventionally powered cars in the same bodyshells as the rotary ones. Thus the Capella or 616 was a saloon or coupé driven by single-ohc 4-cylinder engines of 1490, 1586 or 1769cc. With the twin-rotor engine the car was called the RX-2. This had a higher performance than the Capella, and was more expensive, but sales were not far behind those of the conventional car, at 225,004 between 1970 and 1978, compared with 254,919 of the Capella over the same period. The next Mazda was the 818, a smaller saloon/coupé/estate with 1272, 1490 or 1586cc engines, offered in rotary form as the RX-3. The third, and largest, generation of 1970s Mazdas was the 929, a 4-door saloon/2-door coupé/estate car of the same size as the Ford Cortina or Opel Rekord. It had a 1769cc 4-cylinder engine and, with rotaries of nominal 2292 or 2616cc, was known as the RX-4. The conventionally powered cars outsold the rotaries, but the latter were by no means negligible, totalling more than 750,000 during the 1970s.

1994 Mazda Xedos V6 saloon.
NICK BALDWIN

The small 1200/1300 was made in very large numbers between 1968 and 1977, being joined by the 985cc 1000. Also made in coupé or estate car forms, this series of utterly conventional family cars sold 980,968 units. Historian Graham Robson summed it up well: 'No frills, nor meant to be, but it earned Mazda's bread and butter for years'. In 1977 it gave way to the 323 which used the same 985 or 1272cc engines in a restyled bodyshell made in 3- or 5-door hatchback versions. An entrant in the highly competitive market of the Toyota Starlet/Ford Fiesta/Opel Kadett, the 323 sold very well; in four years nearly as many were made (904,573) as the earlier cars had achieved in 11 years. For 1981 a completely new car bore the 323 designation, a 4-door saloon/5-door hatchback with transverse engine driving the front-wheels. Three engines were offered, 1071, 1296 and 1490cc, while manual or automatic transmissions were available. The 323 estate was continued with rear drive into 1983.

1997 Mazda 323 5-door hatchback.
MAZDA

The RX-7

In the spring of 1978 Mazda brought out their first sports car since the 110S. This had a twin-rotor Wankel engine of the same size as the larger one used in the RX-2 and RX-3. It developed 105bhp, later increased to 115bhp. A 5-speed gearbox was standard, but automatic could be had on cars sold on the US market. The body was an attractively-styled 2+2 coupé, and the RX-7 quickly established itself as an alternative to the Datsun Z cars or Porsche 924. Top speed was 118mph (190km/h) and 0–60 took (0–96km/h) 10 seconds. The maximum safe engine speed was 7000rpm, so to avoid expensive damage there was a buzzer which warned the driver when the revs had reached 6800rpm. Various turbocharged models were made, raising power to up to 200bhp. Among the most popular was the Elford Engineering version offered by former British racing driver Vic Elford, whose Garrett-turbocharged engine gave 160bhp and a speed of 145mph (232km/h). Nearly 500,000 RX7s were made up to theend of 1985, when a new version came out. This had a restyled body which gave the car some resemblance to a Porsche 944, all-independent suspension and a more powerful engine developing 150bhp. It was made throughout the 90s, though withdrawn from European markets in 1995 as slow sales made it impossible to justify the expense of overcoming emission problems. Only 192 were sold in Britain between 1992 and 1995. A new RX-7 with 280bhp twin-turbo engine with catalytic pre-heater in a completely restyled body with four doors was launched at the Tokyo Show in October 1999.

New Models and International Links

In line with other manufacturers worldwide, Mazda turned to front-wheel drive in the 1980s. After the 323 came the 626 which had been a medium-sized rear-driven saloon since 1978. From 1983 the 626 used transverse single-ohc engines of 1587 or 1998cc driving the front wheels. Body styles were a 4-door saloon, 5-door hatchback or 2-door coupé. These were made with little change

1999 Mazda MX-5 hard-top.
MAZDA

until a new series appeared in the summer of 1987. The same body styles were offered, updated in appearance, and there were now five engines, from a 1597cc single-ohc with two valves per cylinder, through a 1789cc single-ohc with three valves per cylinder to a 1998cc twin-ohc with four valves per cylinder, as well as a single-ohc 1998cc diesel. The new 626 also had 4-wheel steering on the 5-door hatchback. This used mechanical, electronic and hydraulic components to vary the relationship of the steering between front and rear wheels according to the

1999 Mazda Premacy MPV.
MAZDA

2000 Mazda Tribute 4 × 4 estate car.
MAZDA

speed of the car. The hatchback was also offered with the option of full-time 4-wheel drive.

The 323 was redesigned in 1985 with new bodies giving better accommodation, though the same engine options and body styles were offered. In 1986 came an important new 323, the 4×4 Turbo which had a 1597cc twin-ohc 16-valve engine developing 140bhp. This significant contender in the hot hatchback market had a top speed of 127mph (203km/h), with 0-60mph (96km/h) in just under 8 seconds. It gave Mazda a suitable car to go rallying with. In 1987 Timo Salonen won the Swedish Rally to give Japan their first major rally victory in Europe for 11 years. The 323 was still made in 1999, with 1324, 1498 and 1840cc 16-valve engines as well as two diesels.

The largest car in the range was the 929 which had been made in various forms since 1966, though it was seldom seen in Europe. It was a conventional rear-drive saloon which used a 2-litre 4-cylinder engine for years, but in 1986 Mazda brought out their first 6-cylinder engine for the 929. This was a 1997cc V6 with or without turbocharger, and an alternative was the in-line four or a twin-rotor engine as used in the RX-7. In 1991 a 2954cc V6 became the only engine available in the 929, which was still made in 1999. Originally known in Japan as the Luce, it has more recently borne the name Sentia.

Mazda had links with Ford for many years (in 1999 they were one-third Ford owned), and this led to international connections in a number of countries. The 323 and 326 were made by Ford of Australia, where they were sold under the names Laser and Telstar. Mazda played an important part in setting up Ford's Mexican factory where the Mercury Tracer, based on the Mazda 323, was made. Mazda also had an interest in the Korean manufacturer Kia which they set up jointly with Ford in 1985. Kia made the Festiva, sold on the US market as the Ford Festiva. A similar model was made by Mazda and sold on Japanese and European markets as the Mazda 121. In 1985 work started on a large factory at Flat Rock, Michigan, which came on stream in 1987. It made the Mazda-based Ford Probe coupé, and more recently has built the 626 for the North American market. The American Escort made from 1990 onwards was a rebodied Mazda 323. From March 1996 121s for the European market were made at Ford's British plant at Dagenham.

In 1989 Mazda took a significant step into the popular sports car market, filling the gap vacated by the MG Midget nine years earlier. The MX-5,

known as the Miyata on the US market, and the Eunos in Japan, was a simple front-engine/rear-wheel drive 2-seater powered by a 115bhp 1598cc twin-ohc engine, with 5-speed gearbox and disc brakes all round. For those who felt that the chassis could handle more power a 150bhp turbocharged version was offered in Britain, which raised to speed from 114 to 130mph (182 to 208km/h). In the summer of 1993 Mazda offered an 1840cc engine giving 140bhp. This and the smaller unit were available on the 1999 MX-5. The second generation MX-5 came in 1998, when the retractable headlights of the original were dropped. By February 1999 500,000 MX-5s had been made, making it the most popular 2-seater sports car in the world. The 10th Anniversary Edition had a 6-speed gearbox. There were plans to extend this gearbox, which is also used in the Lexus IS200, to regular MX-5s. Mazda also made another sports car in the 1990s, the MX-3 coupé, based on the 323 but with a 1598cc 4-cylinder or 1840cc V6 engine. Introduced in 1991 it was discontinued in January 1999.

The 1991 Tokyo Show saw a new upmarket saloon, the 1598cc Xedos 6 (Eunos 500 in Japan), which was based on the 626 but had fresh styling which set it apart – and it was considerably more expensive. In 1993 it was joined by the Xedos 9 (Eunos 800) with the same bodyshell but powered by a 2497cc V6. Both models of Xedos had 5-speed manual or 4-speed automatic transmissions. They were continued into 1999, and a successor was planned to share technology with the forthcoming small Jaguar, code-named X400, and a new Ford Mondeo.

Mazda entered the MPV market in September 1988 with a car simply called the MPV, powered by a 2954cc V6, originally driving the rear wheels but with 4-wheel drive from spring 1989. It was also available with a 2500cc 4-cylinder diesel engine, and was still made in 1999, together with a new, smaller MPV, the Premacy with 1840cc twin-ohc 16-valve petrol, or 1998cc single-ohc diesel engine. A smaller car on the same lines was the Demio, with 1298 or 1498cc engines. An entry in the 4 × 4 market was the Tribute, a 5-door estate with 2-litre 4-cylinder or 3-litre V6 engines. It made its European market debut at the 2000 Geneva Show.

In addition to the Mazdas sold internationally, there were several home market-only models. These included the Carol, a 657cc 3-cylinder town car catering to Japan's K Class and using Suzuki Alto running gear, the similarly-powered AZ Wagon which was almost identical to the Suzuki Wagon R, the Sentia and RX-7, and the Marvie, a large 4 × 4 estate based on the Ford Explorer. In addition, two off-road Suzukis, the Jimny and the Vitara, were sold as the Mazda AZ-Offroad and Levante respectively.

NG

MAZZIERI (I) 1993–1994
Officine Mazzieri Pacifico, Cingoli.

The Mazzieri Micron PMCEP was an electric passenger vehicle. In form it was a monobox 3-door 4-seater hatchback with a fibreglass body. It used a steel ladder chassis with MacPherson strut front and interconnected rear suspension, plus all-round disc brakes. The front-mounted 8kW (11bhp) electric motor was powered by twelve 6-volt batteries and drove the front wheels. A top speed of 43mph (69km/h) was claimed, with a range of 50 miles.

CR

M.B. (i) (US) 1909–1911
Motor Buggy Mfg Co., Minneapolis, Minnesota.

Originally known as the Acme (ii), this 22hp 2-cylinder motor buggy was renamed M.B. in 1909. A larger 4-seater touring body was offered, and when this did not improve sales, the company turned to a 45hp 4-cylinder tourer which they named the Renville. This did not survive beyond 1911.

NG

M.B. (ii) (GB) 1919–1921
Merrall-Brown Motors Ltd, Bolton, Lancashire.

Designed by Louis Merrall Brown, this light car had the appearance of a 3-wheeler as the rear wheels were set very close together, so that the effect was that of a twin-tyred single wheel. It was powered by an 8hp V-twin J.A.P. engine driving through a 2-speed gearbox with chain final drive. Within a few months of its announcement in May 1919 the air-cooled J.A.P. had given way to a water-cooled 10hp Precision V-twin, and in November 1919 a 4-cylinder 10/12hp Coventry-Simplex engine was available in addition to the twin. Customers were hard to find, though, and not more than 25 cars had been sold by the end of the year. Towards the end of 1920 a more conventional 4-wheeler was announced, still with the Coventry-Simplex engine but with a normal rear axle, though without differential. The company was out of business by May 1921 and later the premises were acquired by Hardman's Funeral Services who were still there in 1997.

NG

Further Reading
'Four into Three', M. Worthington-Williams, *The Automobile*, October 1997.

M.B. (iii) (I) 1924
Motta & Baudo, Turin.
This was a light car powered by a 4-cylinder Chapuis-Dornier engine, with independent suspension front and rear, and a chassis sharply upswept at both ends. It did not go into production.

NG

M.B. (iv) (GB) 1984–1986
Ribble Publishers, Preston, Lancashire.
The M.B. 750 was marketed as a plans set for home builders to create a plywood body on an Austin 7 chassis. A Reliant 700/750/850 engine was used in conjunction with modified Austin 7 brakes, suspension and steering. Alternatively a Vauxhall Viva could donate its mechanicals.

CR

MBC see EMBEESEA

M.B.M. see MONTEVERDI

M.C. (GB) 1984–c.1994
1984–1989 M.C. Cars, Sheffield, Yorkshire.
1989–c.1994 Carlton Automotive, Barnsley, West Yorkshire.
c.1994 Ian Birks, Sheffield, Yorkshire.
The first of several British 1960s nostalgia kit revivals, the M.C. Acer was a Turner re-engineered by Mark Clarkson to use modern mechanicals. It was designed for either Vauxhall Viva or Ford Escort parts, although many other donors were quoted, including Hillman Avenger, Datsun 120Y, Morris Marina and Triumph Spitfire/Dolomite. The tubular steel chassis formed the basis for the fibreglass bodywork, which had two or 2+2 seating. Only eight cars were ever supplied.

CR

M.C.A. (i) (D) 1962–1964
M.C.A. Automobile Ulrich Otten, Bremen.
This company made sports cars with Volkswagen engines and fibreglass bodies. Models included the 1198cc Jetstar roadster and the 1493cc Jetkomet coupé. The engines were tuned to give 45 and 65bhp, respectively.

HON

M.C.A. (ii) (GB) 1983–1995
1983–1990 M.C.A., Bognor Regis, West Sussex.
1990 Minari Engineering, Ranton, Staffordshire.
1990–1994 Dash Sportscars, Eardisley, Hereford.
1994–1995 I.P.S. Developments, Hadleigh, Suffolk.
Ex-patriot Italian ex-racing driver Aurelio Bezzi's M.C.A. was a simple but charming rear-engined sports coupé. It used a steel tube chassis, angular fibreglass body panels and all Fiat 126 parts including its 594cc twin-cylinder engine. After Bezzi emigrated, Dash Sportscars offered the M.C.A. as a Cabriolet version too. See also MONTE CARLO.

CR

McBURNIE COACHCRAFT (US) c.1982–1989
McBurnie Coachcraft, Santee, California.
Tom McBurnie built one of the first quality Ferrari Daytona replicas, and based it on the Chevrolet Corvette. It was quite convincing, and one was featured in the popular series *Miami Vice*. McBurnie added two other Ferrari replicas that were based on the Datsun 240Z chassis. One replicated the 250GTO, while the

other was a convertible version of the same car. The company shut down after being sued by Ferrari for having copied their designs. McBurnie later started THUNDER RANCH.

HP

M.C.C. see KRIT and VAPOMOBILE

MCC see SMART

McCLUSKEY (US) c.1995 to date
McCluskey Ltd, Torrance, California.
Mike McCluskey had been restoring original Cobras for years when he started making exact reproductions of the Cobra Daytona Coupé. As of 1999 they had built nine examples at $220,000 each.

HP

McCORD (US) 1913
McCord Automobile Co., Chicago, Illinois.
This obscure car was made by a group of businessmen who hoped to profit by an implied association with the well-known radiator makers, the McCord Manufacturing Co. The radiator firm denied any such association and very few McCord cars were built, though one found its way to a British Army depot during World War I. They were conventional tourers with 4-cylinder Rutenber engines.

NG

McCORMACK (US) 1956–1960
Henry McCormack, Orange, California; Track Kraft, Los Angeles, California.
The McCormack Coupé started life as a custom car shown at the Los Angeles car show. It received favourable attention and the body was offered in kit form. The prototype had a Corvette V8, electric doors, roll up windows and a 4-speed transmission. It was a striking convertible with a removable hard-top. The headlights were set in vertical housings and a low, wide grill was used. Built on a 106in (2690mm) wheelbase, it could be fitted to sedan chassis or a custom frame was available. It was sold in kit form only at $695. By 1960 it was being sold by Track Kraft and had been renamed the Comet.

HP

McCOY (GB) 1984 to date
1984–c.1988 Birchall Automotive, Barnham Broom, Norfolk.
c.1988–1990 N.G. Wynes Fibreglass (McCoy Cars),
North Tuddenham, Norfolk.
1990 to date Neville Wynes Fibreglass Products (McCoy Cars),
Fakenham, Norfolk.
If the McCoy looked rather like a Clan Crusader on stilts, that should come as no surprise, since the same person was responsible for both (ex-Lotus man John Frayling). Unlike the rear-engined Clan, the McCoy used a front-mounted Mini in a fibreglass monocoque body. There was even an estate version with a full four seats, bizarrely called the McIVoy. An alternative power source was the Metro. From 1992 McCoy also offered an abortive Triumph TR2/3 replica which had a box section steel chassis, Ford Cortina front uprights, Sierra rear hubs and double wishbone suspension all round. McCoy offered three body styles: TR2, TR3 and TR3A.

CR

McCUE (US) 1909–1911
The McCue Co., Hartford, Connecticut.
Made by a former manufacturer of carriage fittings and motor accessories, the McCue was a medium-sized car in the medium price range, from $2000 to $2450. It had a 30hp 4-cylinder engine, 3-speed gearbox and shaft drive, and was offered with the usual range of open body styles, runabout, tourer and 'gentleman's roadster'. In the summer of 1911 Charles T. McCue ended production of complete cars and turned to the manufacture of axles.

NG

1912 McFarlan Model 40/45 roadster.
NICK BALDWIN

1924 McFarlan SV Six sedan.
NICK BALDWIN

McCULLOUGH (US) 1899–1900

Back Bay Cycle & Motor Co., Boston, Massachusetts.
W. T. McCullough built an unusual car powered by two 2-cylinder engines, each driving a rear wheel by chain. He probably made only one of these, and was soon offering another design with one engine, a 4½hp twin. He also advertised that he rented cars 'with competent instructors', and presumably dealt in bicycles as well, so car manufacture must have been very limited.

NG

McCURD (GB) 1923–1927

McCurd Lorry Manufacturing Co. Ltd, Hayes, Middlesex.
Scots-born Wallace Atherton McCurd was a pioneer used car dealer, setting up in this business in London in 1898, when there cannot have been many used cars around to sell. He continued in this line up to, and possibly beyond 1912, when he started to make a 3½ ton truck. The works at Dollis Hill, London, were occupied with munitions manufacture during the war, and afterwards McCurd found it hard to re-establish truck production as there were so many ex-War Department vehicles on the market. He began testing a car of his own manufacture in 1921, and it was launched at the White City Show in November 1922 from a new factory at Hayes, a few miles south west of Dollis Hill. Unlike many light cars of the period, it did not use proprietary components, but had a 1645cc 4-cylinder monobloc engine of McCurd's own design and manufacture. The specification also included a modern-type single-plate clutch and electric starter. An unusual feature was a watch in the centre of the steering wheel, which acted as a horn. Although a quality product, the McCurd was expensive at £485 for a 2- or 4-seater, and probably not many were sold, though no production figures survive. Commercial vehicle production was suspended while the cars were being made, but was resumed in 1925 and mostly coaches were made for a further few years.

NG

Further Reading
'The Story of the McCurd', M. Worthington-Williams,
The Automobile, February 1997.

McCURDY (US) 1922

The Hercules Corp., Evansville, Indiana.
Named after the president of the Hercules Corp., builder of petrol engines and bodies for cars and trucks, the McCurdy was a stillborn attempt by the company to widen its sphere by automobile manufacture. The several prototypes completed were all touring cars with a wheelbase of 127in (3223mm) and wire wheels as standard equipment. The engine was a Continental 6-cylinder L-head. Listed price for this car which failed to make it to the marketplace was $2095 for the touring version. Whether plans had been made for other body options during its first year in business is unknown.

KM

McCUTCHEN (US) c.1984

McCutchen Manufacturing, Inc., Englewood, Colorado.
Just when all Cobra replicas were being built alike, the McCutchen came a long with something different. Although any engine could be installed, the McCutchen was specifically designed to accept the 426 Chrysler Hemi. Rear suspension could be a simple live axle or a Corvette irs system. The doors, bodywork, bonnet and boot were composite sandwiches of fibreglass and balsa wood for more strength.

HP

McFARLAN (US) 1910–1928

1910–1913 McFarlan Carriage Co., Connersville, Indiana.
1913–1928 McFarlan Motor Car Co., Connersville, Indiana.
The McFarlan automobile was introduced in 1910, work on the initial car having been underway since the late summer of 1909. It was the result of the plan by Harry McFarlan to augment the existing line of horse-drawn vehicles made by the McFarlan Carriage Co. which had been founded in 1856 by his grandfather, English-born John McFarlan. To prove their worth, two McFarlans were entered in a two-day racing event at the Indianapolis Motor Speedway on 3–4 September 1910. The cars performed well and resulting publicity helped promote the make and the re-organisation of the company as the McFarlan Motor Car Co. in 1913, the carriage building activities being terminated shortly thereafter. The first five years of production were successful in a small way, McFarlan cars being equipped with a variety of 6-cylinder engines by Brownell, Buda, Continental, Wisconsin and possibly others.

In 1916, the company switched to the larger 6-cylinder engine of Teetor-Hartley and with it the McFarlan became a larger, heavier and, year after year, more expensive automobile. A line of commercial vehicles, considered during this period, failed to materialise except for three pieces of fire apparatus made on special order for the local fire department. And like its East Coast stablemate, the Cunningham, almost all McFarlan coachwork would be of in-house construction. A few McFarlan funeral cars would be built in the mid–1920s.

The zenith of McFarlan production began with the huge Model TV (for Twin-Valve) series which was introduced for 1922. Powered by an improved Teetor-Hartley engine developing 120bhp at 2400rpm, the cars featured a 140in (3553mm) wheelbase and a line of open and closed coachwork priced from $6300 to $9000 weighing 5000lbs (2½ tons) for the 7-seater touring car and considerably more for the closed offerings. These cars would be the hallmark of McFarlan – the cars for which the company would be generally known. Among its galaxy of owners were Governors Trinkle and Trumbull of Virginia and Connecticut respectively; heavyweight boxing champion Jack Dempsey, silent film actor Wally Reid and band leader Paul Whiteman. The McFarlan was highly publicised at the New York City Automobile Show of 1922 featuring a custom-built cabriolet with coachwork by Brooks-Ostruk, its engine with its triple-ignition and 18 sparking plugs emphasised in the display. The car's largest production of 235 units completed and sold occurred in 1922.

In 1924, the company introduced a lower-priced six with an engine by Wisconsin, a 127in wheelbase and prices from $2600 to £4600. The smaller car proved unsuccessful and was phased out of production during 1926, replaced by the new Line-8 with an 8-cylinder engine by Lycoming, developing 79bhp at 3000rpm, and featuring a wheelbase of 131ins (3325mm) and prices from $2650 to $4000. The new eight attracted a successful clientele of its own and, with the TV, would be continued until McFarlan closed its doors in 1928.

During its last years, the McFarlan Motor Car Co. also built bodies for several other cars and upon its demise, the assets of McFarlan were acquired by E.L. Cord.

1923 McFarlan TV Six roadster with boxer Jack Dempsey.
NATIONAL MOTOR MUSEUM

Approximately 3600 automobiles were built during the company's 19 years of production. More than 20 have survived.

KM

Further Reading
What was the McFarlan?, Keith Marvin, Alvin J. Arnheim and Keith Blommel, published privately by Alvin J. Arnheim, 1967.
'Monster from the Mid-West', Arch Brown,
Special-Interest Autos, February 1990.

McGILL (US) 1921–1922
McGill Motor Car Co., Fort Worth, Texas.
George McGill had been interested in 4-wheel drive for several years before he formed his company, and had built a prototype in 1917. Only two cars were built after he formed the company; one was a 1920 Elcar Six converted to 4-wheel drive and fitted with a McGill radiator badge and hubcaps, while the other may have been a Lexington which had received similar treatment.

NG

McINTYRE (US) 1909–1915
W.H.McIntyre Co., Auburn, Indiana.
This was a continuation of the KIBLINGER, the new company being formed by Kiblinger's factory manager, W.H. McIntyre. At first the same range of high-wheelers was made, but in 1911 McIntyre added a line of conventional 4-cylinder cars previously made as the AMERICA by the Motor Car Co. of New York City. A 6-cylinder tourer was added for 1913, and the company also made the IMP cyclecar in 1913 and 1914. Some models of the high-wheeler were made under licence in Canada by TUDHOPE.

NG

McKAY (i) (US) 1899–1902
Stanley Manufacturing Co., Lawrence, Massachusetts.
The McKay steamer was built by Frank F. Stanley who was no relation to the well-known Stanley brothers, who were also making light steam cars in New England at the same time. With a vertical engine and chain drive, it was built under licence from George Whitney, and in 1899 was known as the Stanley-Whitney. Frank Stanley chose the name McKay 'in honour of the well-known inventor', omitting to mention that the invention was in the field of sewing machines rather than cars. At least 25 cars were built in 1900, but figures for the next two years are not known.

NG

1921 McGill Model 5-6 tourer.
KEITH MARVIN

1910 McIntyre M-40 30hp tourer.
NICK BALDWIN

McKAY (ii) (CDN) 1910–1914
1910–1912 Nova Scotia Carriage Co., Kentville, Nova Scotia.
1913–1914 Nova Scotia Carriage & Motor Car Co., Amherst, Nova Scotia.
The Nova Scotia Carriage Co. was founded in 1868, and when demand for horse-drawn vehicles began to slow down they turned to cars. The first was based on the American PENN, and was a conventional machine powered by a 30hp

1922 McKenzie 10.8hp 2-seater.
DR K MCKENZIE

1995 McLaren F1 coupé.
NATIONAL MOTOR MUSEUM

4-cylinder Buda engine. About 25 were made at Kentville, after which the McKay brothers moved to Amherst which was said to be the industrial centre of Nova Scotia. They hoped to make 1000 cars a year, as well as commercial vehicles, but the collapse of the Penn company in 1912 was a severe blow, and the McKay did not survive 1914. As well as the 30, a larger 40hp car was made; total production in Amherst was about 200 cars.

NG

McKEE (US) 1967–1981
McKee Engineering Corp., Palatine, Illinois.
Robert McKee had been fabricating successful racing cars for some time when he began building prototype electric cars and sports cars for specialist companies. Among his best known racing cars were the McKee Can-Am and F5000 cars and the Howmet Turbine endurance racing cars. One of the first street cars was the MACH 1, a mid-engined sports car. McKee built a series of experimental electric cars for GLOBE-UNION and USB.

HP

McKENZIE (GB) 1913–1926
1913–1920 Thomas McKenzie, Birmingham.
1920–1926 McKenzie Motors Ltd, Birmingham.
Thomas McKenzie began making light cars in a small works in a side street half a mile from the centre of Birmingham. He had moved into these premises in about 1904, to make sidecars and car bodies. The first complete car, which appeared at the 1913 Olympia Show, had a 1098cc 4-cylinder side-valve engine, but by early 1914 the stroke had been lengthened, increasing capacity to 1162cc. The cylinder block was stamped 'Thos McKenzie, Birmingham' and it may well have been made by, or specially for, him. A 3-speed gearbox was used, and final drive was by worm gear. 2- and 4-seater cars were made up to the end of 1915, and the 1916 model was listed as having a 4-speed gearbox, though it is not certain that any were made because of the war.

Re-launched in 1919, and made in a larger factory, the McKenzie now had a proprietary engine, a 1330cc Alpha. A limited company was formed in 1920, and for 1921 the Alpha engine gave way to a 1498cc Coventry Simplex. A smaller engine of 1074cc, also by Coventry Simplex, was added to the range in 1924

and this was used in a 4-seater which had only one door on the nearside. The McKenzie was a quality small car, described as 'being eminently suitable for doctors, government and municipal officials and business men, and with easy gear changing is equally suitable for the lady motorist'. They had a number of successes in trials and hill climbs, and at least one sports model was made. Production figures are not known, but pre-World War I output could not have been more than one car per week.

NG

Further Reading
'The History of McKenzie Cars', T.I. McKenzie and Kenneth McKenzie, *The Automobile*, July and August 1989.

McLACHLAN (GB) 1899–1900
1899 E.A. McLachlan, Stoke Newington, London.
1900 McLachlan Engine Co., Hackney. London.
Mclachlan was a builder of engines running on heavy oil, and fitted a few of his engines to light cars. In 1899 he built a 3-wheeler with a rear-mounted horizontal single-cylinder engine, which cost only £75. In 1900 he made a 4-wheeler with 3½hp single-cylinder engine.

NG

McLAREN (GB) 1969–1970; 1993–1998
1969–1970 Trojan Ltd, Croydon, Surrey.
1993–1998 McLaren Cars Ltd, Woking, Surrey.
Although catapulted to fame by the 1993 F1 road car project, McLaren had a historical precursor for this most complete of supercars. Trojan Ltd built the M6 GT racer for McLaren, but homologation obstacles prevented its racing prospects. So Trojan made a roadgoing version for Bill Bradley, followed by another for Bruce McLaren. These were virtual racing cars, with Bartz-tuned Chevrolet 5.0-litre V8 engines, unequal-length wishbone suspension and lightweight 41in (1041mm) high glassfibre bodywork. A top speed of 180mph (290km/h) was estimated for these road racers, but any production future the M6 might have had was scotched by Bruce McLaren's death.

Two decades later came the McLaren F1. Formerly chief designer at Brabham, Gordon Murray was the driving force behind the F1, a car that qualifies as the fastest, most involving, most expensive road car ever made. Murray was in charge of design and development, while Lotus stylist Peter Stevens created the car's shape. Lightness was a crucial goal and the F1 would tip the scales at not far above 1000kg, due largely to the all-carbon fibre bodywork. Part of the unique package was the 3-seater cabin with the driver sitting in the middle ahead of the two passengers. Entry was via dihedral hinging doors.

BMW's Motorsport division agreed to design an all-new V12 engine from scratch. With no less than 627bhp on tap from the 6064cc engine, performance was truly explosive. Ex-Formula One driver Jonathan Palmer achieved an incredible 231mph (371km/h) at the Nardo test track in Italy in August 1993. Tests uncovered more amazing figures: 0–60mph (0–96km/h) in 3.2 seconds, 0–100mph (0–160km/h) in 6.3 seconds and 30–70mph (48–112km/h) in just over 2 seconds. The F1 was also a successful racer-an F1 GTR came first in virtually every GT Endurance race it entered, and the F1 was triumphant at Le Mans in 1995.

The transmission was a compact 6-speed rear-mounted gearbox that also acted as a mounting point for the rear suspension. Highly sophisticated double wishbone suspension employed a subframe for each suspension unit, a 'Ground Plane Shear Centre' system, and a rear 'Inclined Axis Shear Mounting' system.

At £635,000 tax-paid in the UK, the F1's cost reflected its cost-no-object development budget (the engine bay was lined with gold for its heat insulation properties), ultra-high technology, and the fact that each one took 6000 man-hours to build. As part of an unrivalled back-up, if you had a problem with your car, McLaren would jet out a mechanic on the next available flight. The first customer car was finished on Christmas Eve 1993, and over the next four years and a couple of evolutions (including the F1 LM and the long-tail F1 GTR), a total of 100 cars were made, well short of the initial target of 300. In 1999 the company was reportedly working on a much cheaper roadgoing sports car project.

CR

Further Reading
Driving Ambition: The Official Inside Story of the McLaren F1,
Doug Nye and Gordon Murray. Virgin Publishing, 1999.

McLAUGHLIN; McLAUGHLIN-BUICK (CDN) 1908–1922; 1923–1942
1908–1918 McLaughlin Motor Car Co. Ltd, Oshawa, Ontario.
1918–1942 General Motors of Canada Ltd, Oshawa, Ontario.
The McLaughlin Carriage Co. was founded in 1867, the same year as the Canadian nation. Formerly it had consisted of British Upper Canada and French Lower Canada. McLaughlin's first products were sleighs, but they soon added carriages, and by 1907 they had made more than 25,000 horse-drawn vehicles. In that year R. Samuel McLaughlin (1871–1972) decided to enter the motor business. After examining and testing some American cars, he decided he could do better himself, and built a 2-cylinder tourer with a round radiator. However, his chief engineer became seriously ill, and McLaughlin turned to Billy Durant for a supply of Buick engines and other components. They signed a 15-year contract, which was to outlast Durant's presidency of General Motors.

The first McLaughlin went into production in December 1907 as a 1908 model. Called the Model F, it had a 22hp 2-cylinder engine and was made as a 5-seater tourer selling for $1400. Mechanically it was almost identical to the Model F Buick, but it had a McLaughlin-built body, and this pattern was followed over the next few years. The cars were generally called McLaughlin, though they were also advertised as McLaughlin-Buick; some cars carried the McLaughlin name on the radiator and McLaughlin-Buick on the hub caps. Model names followed Buick practice, with the Model S being a 4-cylinder roadster and Model 5 a 4-cylinder tourer. The Model 7 of 1909/11 was the largest 4-cylinder McLaughlin, with a 6432cc T-head engine designed originally for the WELCH. It may have been built in larger numbers than the equivalent Buick, which did not last beyond the 1910 season, and of which only 85 were made. McLaughlin's first six was the B-55 for the 1914 season. As before it had a Buick chassis but McLaughlin body of higher quality. The story goes that A.P. Sloan, then president of General Motors, saw a McLaughlin outside the New York City Buick showroom and flew into a rage, fearing lest Buick owners should see it and demand similar quality.

Buick dropped their 4-cylinder cars in 1916, and McLaughlin were not happy with losing a cheaper line of car. They imported the OAKLAND Light Six, which they sold as the McLaughlin Light Six at a lower price ($1085) than the previous 4-cylinder car. To obtain an even cheaper line, they made CHEVROLETS under licence, but these did not carry the McLaughlin name. In 1916 the factory produced 7796 Chevrolets and 2859 McLaughlins. Another import, though short-lived, was the RAUCH & LANG electric, which they fitted with their own bodies.

In 1918 the McLaughlin business was sold to General Motors and became General Motors of Canada. Five years later the agreement that Sam McLaughlin had made with Billy Durant ran out, and all cars were called McLaughlin-Buicks from then onwards. Differences between the Canadian and American cars became minimal, though Mclaughlin built some 'specials' from time to time. Two special tourers with canework at the tops of the doors and lizard-skin upholstery were built for the visit of the Prince of Wales in 1927, and two convertible limousines on the 1939 Series 90 chassis lengthened by 18in (457mm) for the visit of King George V1 and Queen Elizabeth. They were still called McLaughlin-Buicks up to 1942, but when production resumed after the war the McLaughlin name was dropped. The Oshawa plant continued to make Buicks in large numbers, and from 1962 to 1971 made the ACADIAN. Sam McLaughlin remained on the board of GM Canada until the age of 97.
NG

McLEAN see NIMBUS

M.C.M. (AUS) 1945
J. McMahon, Sydney, New South Wales.
Jim McMahon, assisted by another speedway driver, Ray Revell, took the cue from the then wide interest in Australian car production, to begin work on a sports car. It was intended to have a 2-litre air-cooled V8 engine, with the initial example using a Ford V8-60 crankshaft and Triumph Speed Twin cylinders. The tubular chassis, with a wheelbase of 88.5in (2250mm) used some Morris 8/40 components. Its body was a sports tourer with flush headlamps and cutaway doors, which was ready before its engine, and so test runs were made with other power. The death of its instigator, however, brought about the end of the project.
MG

c.1909 McLaughlin Model G roadster.
NATIONAL MOTOR MUSEUM

1915 McLaughlin Model B-55 tourer.
CARS OF CANADA

McRAE (NZ) 1990 to date
McRae Cars, Auckland, North Island.
Racing driver Graham McRae made his first competition car in 1961 and the McRae GM series of Formula 5000 cars was constructed in England in the 1970s. Production of fibreglass-bodied replicas of Porsche 356 Speedster and 550 Spyder models began in 1990, with Volkswagen, Porsche and Subaru power packs. Exports were made to Australia, Japan and the United States.
MG

MCV (CDN) 1999 to date
Motion Concept Vehicles, Toronto, Ontario.
Canada's first mid-engined supercar, the MCV, had a carbonfibre monocoque frame with carbon-Kevlar body panels. The prototype used a turbocharged General Motors 4.6-litre V8 giving 500bhp, but production models were planned to have a 400bhp normally-aspirated Ford V8. These engines were to run on natural gas, a first for a supercar with a top speed in the region of 200mph (322km/h) and 0–60mph (0–96km/h) in under 5 seconds. The anticipated price was £125,000.
NG

MD (F) 1953–1954
Marcel Dubois.
There is one survivor from the production run of seven of these attractive 2-seater sports cars. The tubular chassis frame was clothed with bodywork styled by Frua and much of the running gear, including a supercharged version of the 203 engine, was supplied by Peugeot.
DF

1928 M.E.B. 3-wheeler.
MICHAEL WORTHINGTON-WILLIAMS

1913 Médinger cyclecar.
NATIONAL MOTOR MUSEUM

MEAD (US) c.1994

Mead Automotive, Houghton Lake, Michigan.
The 1957 Thunderbird was replicated by this kit car company. It used Ford V8 running gear and a ladder frame with Ford suspension.

HP

MEADE see THOMASSIMA

MEADOWS see FRISKY

MÉAN (B) 1964–1974

1964–1971 Méan Motor Engineering SA, Liège-Guillemins.
1971–1974 Liberta Engineering SA, Liège.
Founded by an ex-Ford France engineer called Jacques d'Heur, Méan's first car was the Sonora. This was a kit-form open sports car with a removable top and bodywork in fibreglass. Into a complex tubular steel chassis were installed Volkswagen running gear, Renault disc brakes on some models and various engines, including Renault, Ford Anglia, Cortina GT, Ford V4 and V6, NSU and Peugeot 404. The Aquila, presented in 1966, was a variation on the same theme with a rear-mounted Ford engine. Racing versions were marketed under the name Barquette. A new Liberta racer was shown at the 1970 Brussels motor show, and the company was renamed Liberta in 1971. The new Liberta Funcar was a roadgoing model using a strong box-section chassis with an integral roll-over bar that looped around a 'breadvan' style rear end with a central T-bar over the open roof. It could be powered by Renault 8/10/12 or Simca 1000 engines and could be bought fully-built or in kit form. Almost 120 cars were made in 1972 alone.

CR

M.E.B. (GB) 1928–c.1934

Bromilow & Edwards Ltd, Bolton, Lancashire.
The M.E.B. was a redesigned version of the Royal Ruby 3-wheeler which never went into production. It was powered by a 980cc air-cooled V-twin JAP engine driving through a conventional 3-speed gearbox with chain final drive to the single rear wheel. The first body was a 2-seater, but it seems that a family model was offered later and for 1931 there was a fixed head coupé. A 1932 model was sold as a B/E in 1936 for the modest price of £15.

In 1929 three of the Edwards brothers broke away from the parent firm to form Edbro Ltd which has made tipping gear for trucks up to the present day.

NG

MEBEA (GR) 1970s–1980s

Mebea S.A., Athens.
Greece was one of the largest markets for 3-wheeled Reliants outside Great Britain, so much so that licensed production was undertaken by Mebea in Athens. It also made a version of the Reliant-conceived TW9 3-wheeled truck, and produced the Reliant Fox utility car.

CR

MÉCANIQUE ET MOTEURS (B) 1903–1906

Sté Mécanique et Moteurs, Liège.
Founded by M. Martiny, this company made not only cars but also motorcycles, engines and components for other car builders. Their 1903 car had a 16hp 4-cylinder engine with ohvs, unusual for that date, Although advanced it was either not very satisfactory or too expensive to make, for the 1904 16hp had side-valves. The frame was of armoured wood. For 1905 they offered a wider range, from a 10hp 3-cylinder to several fours of up to 35hp. These had steel frames. In 1906 they built a 12/14hp, later 16/18hp, to be sold by HERMÈS (ii).

NG

MECCA (US) 1915–1916

Mecca Motor Car Co., Teaneck, New Jersey.
The Mecca was made to the order of the Times Square Motor Co. of New York City, first by a company in Teaneck, New Jersey, and secondly by the PRINCESS Motor Car Co. of Detroit. The Teaneck product was a 4-cylinder cyclecar to sell for $450, while Princess made a full-size car with 23hp engine, though called the Mecca Thirty, selling for $695 in tourer, runabout or roadster forms. This was in fact the Princess Thirty with Mecca nameplate.

NG

MECCANICA MANIERO (I) 1967

Michelotti designed the bodywork for the high-performance MM 4700 coupé. Using Ford Mustang components, including its 4.7-litre V8 engine, it had a square-tube steel chassis with all-independent suspension. Apparently it remained a prototype.

CR

MECHALEY (US) 1903

Mechaley Brothers, Stamford, Connecticut.
Mechaley Brothers were agents for Rambler cars and Brennan engines. In 1903 they built a 4-seater tonneau powered by a 15hp 2-cylinder Brennan engine. It was on the market for less than a year, and few, if any, were sold, though the $1500 price included delivery to anywhere in the United States.

NG

MECHANIX ILLUSTRATED SPORTSTER see WHITEHEAD (ii)

MED-BOW, MEDCRAFT see SPRINGFIELD (ii)

MEDIA (i) (US) 1899–1900

Media Carriage Works, Media, Pennsylvania.
Founded in 1895, this carriage builder made an electric car for a New Jersey doctor in 1899, and encouraged by its success, started a small line of similar cars in 1900. The high-built 2-seater sold for $1100, had a range of 35 miles (56km) per charge and a top speed of 12mph (19km/h). Production, such as it was, was

1994 Mega Track 4 × 4 coupé.

limited to 1900, though as Media continued in the carriage business they may have made one or two cars later than that.

NG

MEDIA (ii) (GB) 1912–1916
Mead & Deakin, Tyseley, Birmingham.

F.W. Mead and Harry Deakin started building a car in 1904, but it was not completed until 1907. It had a 6hp single-cylinder Fafnir engine and was sold to a local doctor in 1909. With the arrival of the cyclecar craze in 1912 they tried again, and listed cars powered by a 750cc Salmon or 1244cc Chapuis-Dorner 4-cylinder engine. They probably made only one of each, or perhaps two of one model, as *Fletcher's Motor Car Index* in the 1920s carried this pathetic reference under Medea (an alternative spelling): 'The makers inform us that only two of these cars were ever made, and as they are both now derelict there is no object in giving their specification'. By then Mead and Deakin had more important matters on their hands, for in 1921 they started to make the RHODE car.

NG

MEDICI *see* LEONARD

MÉDINGER (GB) 1913
Médinger Car & Engine Co., Southall, Middlesex.

This car's name came from Émile Médinger, the French-born Sunbeam team driver, who designed it. The prototype had a 1005cc 2-cylinder 2-stroke engine and chain drive, and was said to run quite satisfactorily on paraffin, once it had been primed with a little petrol. It was built at Wolverhampton, possibly in the Sunbeam works, but production was to take place in the Phonophore Works at Southall, also the home of the L.E.C. cyclecar. These Médingers were to have shaft drive, but few, if any, were made.

NG

MEGA (F) 1992 to date
Aixam-Mega, Aix-les-Bains.

Few people could have expected the leading maker of the smallest vehicles in France, AIXAM, to diversify to such an extreme extent as it did when, in 1992, it launched a new marque under the name Mega. The group became France's third-largest car producer after Renault and PSA. Its first commercial product was the Club. This was a rugged looking and practical car range, using Peugeot

1994 Mega Club 4-seater.

engines (1.1, 1.4 or diesel 1.5). There were 2-wheel drive or 4-wheel drive models (the 4 × 4 system coming from the Citroën AX 4 × 4), and the rear of the plastic bodywork could be changed from a convertible to a hard-top to a pick-up. Quite at the opposite of the Aixam microcar range was Mega's next model, the stupendous Track, also launched in 1992. Described by the manufacturer as 'a high technology Behemoth on wheels', this was one of the largest cars in the world, measuring 200in (5080mm) long and 87.4in (2220mm) wide and weighing 2.28 tonnes – yet it was a sports coupé. It used a mid-mounted 395bhp Mercedes-Benz 6-litre V12 engine coupled with a 4-speed automatic transmission and permanent 4-wheel drive. The suspension height was hydraulically controlled to make it suitable for rough terrain work. The 4-seater cabin was luxuriously trimmed in leather and the problem of rear vision was solved by installing a rear-view video camera. The Track was finally productionised in 1995 with a very high price tag. The same year Mega took on the MONTE CARLO and made numerous alterations prior to an intended production run, though by the end of 1998 it had still not succeeded. At the 1998 Paris Mondial, a new 'Concept' range replacing the Club was launched. As before, three versions were offered: pick-up, cabriolet and hard-top estate – all interchangeable – but on a longer wheelbase and with power steering, central locking and larger wheels and tyres. An LPG option was also offered alongside the standard Peugeot 1.4-litre model.

CR

1969 Meister G5N microcar.
HANS MEISTER

MÉGY (F) 1901–1903
L. Mégy, Paris.
The Mégy was a remarkably simple car to drive, for it had an automatic transmission in which the 'gear ratio changed according to the conditions of the road surface', according to press reports. The clutch was operated by moving the steering wheel down, while an upward movement worked the brake. Mégy showed three cars at the 1903 Paris Salon, a tonneau, a limousine and a racing car. The latter does not seem to have competed in any major events.
NG

MEILUO (CHI) 1987 to date
State Operated Jiangbei Machinery Works, Jilin City, Jilin Province.
The SHENJIAN JJ 7060 was also sold as Meiluo JJ 7060. In the mid–1990s a Chinese CKD-assembled 4-door Opel Corsa appeared under the name Meiluo JJ 7090.
EVIS

MEISENHELDER (US) 1919–1924
Roy M. Meisenhelder, York, Pennsylvania.
The Meisenhelder was not a brand of automobile itself but was, rather, a standard make with an abundance of extra gadgets. These included stylised lanterns, metal bars to keep luggage apart from the finish, elaborate running boards, conical wheels and other fanciful additions completely obscuring the identity of the make. The first of the Meisenhelder creations shrouded a 1919 Paige, giving it its own individuality in a curious manner. Subsequent customised cars followed, until 1924. The last Meisenhelder survives in a private collection. Every Meisenhelder carried its own serial number plate.
KM

MEISTER (A) 1969–c.1971
Hans Meister, Graz.
The Meister G5N Mopedkabine was a tandem 2-seater 3-wheeler with the most basic plastic bodywork over a tubular frame. Steering was by handlebars and the engine (a 49cc Puch 3.5bhp moped unit), was sufficient for a top speed of merely 25mph (40km/h). It drove only one rear wheel and the driver had to kick start it into life.
CR

MEIWA (J) 1952–c.1956
Meiwa Automobile Manufacturing Co.
A range of 3-wheeled body styles was offered by the Meiwa Automobile Manufacturing Co., including a 7-seater people carrier. It followed standard Japanese trike practice in having the driver seated alone up front, but the bodywork was all-enclosed and the rear passengers had doors for access. The front-mounted engine was a 744cc, 16bhp single-cylinder 4-stroke unit.
CR

MELDI (I) 1927–1933
Giuseppe Meldi, Turin.
Meldi had worked for the Moto Borgo motorcycle company from 1923 to 1926, and also made sidecars. When Moto Borgo went out of business in 1926 he started to make cars on his own. They were cyclecars, rather late for such a type to appear, powered by a 1-litre Della Ferrera air-cooled V-twin, or 4-cylinder units by Chapuis-Dornier (750cc) or Citroën (855cc). They had independent suspension all round, by Lancia-type sliding pillars at the front and swing axles at the rear. The Meldi was made in 2- or 4-seater forms, but only 12 cars were completed in a six year period.
NG

MELEN (GB) 1913–1914
F. & H. Melen Ltd, Birmingham.
This was a light car powered by a 1103cc 2-cylinder Alpha engine, with shaft drive. Though experimental models were air-cooled, the Alpha unit used in production cars was water-cooled.
NG

MELKUS (DDR) 1969–c.1980
Heinz Melkus KG, Dresden.
The Melkus was the only sports car made in the German Democratic Republic. It was based on the WARTBURG, using the 992cc 3-cylinder 2-stroke engine with three carburettors. The engine was placed ahead of the rear axle, with the 5-speed all-synchromesh gearbox behind. The body was a fibreglass coupé. A larger engine of 1119cc giving 70bhp was adopted from 1972, and by 1978 the Melkus had disc brakes all round. Annual production was seldom more than 20 cars.
HON

MEMORY MOTORS (US) c.1994
Memory Motors, Inc., Conroe, Texas.
The M-53 was a fibreglass replica of the 1953 Corvette, which was the first year the Corvette was built. The kit car used Chevrolet running gear and V8 engine.
HP

MENARA (MA) 1993 to date
Canam SA (Automobiles Menara), Casablanca.
King Hassan II himself supported the Menara, named after a historic site in Marrakesh. Morocco's only current sports car was a neo-classic built entirely by hand. It used Ford 2-litre 4-cylinder or 3-litre V6 engines with a 4-speed automatic or manual transmission and front suspension from the Ford Granada. As well as a 2-seater, a 2+2 was under development for launch in 1999.
CR

MENARD (CDN) 1908–1910
1908–1909 Windsor Carriage & Delivery Wagon Works, Windsor, Ontario.
1909–1910 Menard Auto Buggy Co., Windsor, Ontario.
The Menard was the first high-wheeler to be made in Canada. It was built by wagon maker Moise Menard and designed by M.B. Covert, who had previously been responsible for the Detroit-built COVERT car. It had a 16hp air-cooled flat-twin engine under the seat, with friction transmission and chain drive. A water-cooled engine was adopted in 1910. Business was good for a while and Menards were sold as far east as Quebec and as far west as the Prairies, but with the waning popularity of the high-wheeler Menard decided to concentrate on trucks and fire engines which were made until 1919.
NG

MENDELSSOHN see PASSY-THELLIER

MENDIP (GB) 1913–1922
1913–1919 Mendip Engineering Co., Chewton Mendip, Somerset.
1919–1921 Mendip Motor and Engineering Co. Ltd, Southmead, Bristol.
1922 New Mendip Engineering Co. Ltd, Atworth, Melksham, Wiltshire.
In 1908 Charles Wesley Harris started to produce steam wagons from the small but fully-equipped Cutlers Green Ironworks, and petrol-engined commercials were also available from 1911 onwards. Announced in 1913, the first light car

had a T-head engine of 1094cc imported from Belgium, overhead worm rear drive, and a conventional mechanical specification, noteworthy mainly for the number of components made on the premises. This was to become a Mendip hallmark. The engine size was increased slightly to 1311cc for production models and only 2-seater bodywork was ever available. World War I prevented development and the works was devoted to fine machine work, such as carburettors and other parts for aircraft engines. This presented problems, not least in completing and getting paid for Government orders after the Armistice, and it was at this time that the Thatcher family (father and two sons) became involved, as office administrator, general manager, and designer, respectively. Alterations were made to the transmission to improve reliability and after the stock of Belgian engines was finished, alternatives were offered from Chapuis-Dornier, Dorman, and (mostly) the 67 × 95mm (1340cc) Alpha. In March 1919 the price was £255 without lights – lighting sets were in short supply – rising to £360 (with Tredelect lighting) in November 1920, which was hardly competitive with MORRIS. A controlling interest was purchased in 1914 by H. Bateman Hope, a local barrister and later M.P., and he instigated the move to Bristol after World War I to enable larger scale production. Harris re-located at Weston-super-Mare, and built a few vehicles there under his own name. It had proved necessary to farm out some work, such as some bodywork to Fullers of Bath, and this had led to problems. Unfortunately, Hope died in 1921, at a time of difficulty in the trade with strikes and recession, and this combination of misfortunes led to the firm's demise. The works were auctioned, spares and service being taken on by Baines Manufacturing Co. Ltd of Westbury-on-Trym. George Thatcher took some of the machinery and parts and assembled a few more cars near Melksham, whilst his brother Arthur moved to LAGONDA. Total production was less than 400, of which only one survivor is known.

DF

MENGES (US) 1907

Menges Motor Co., Grand Rapids, Michigan.

Albert C. Menges had designed the HARRISON car which featured a clutch-operated electric starting motor, and used the same device on the car he tried to make under his own name. It was a large car, with 4-cylinder engine said to develop 100bhp, on a 122in wheelbase and with an 8-seater tourer body. The price was $5000, but only prototypes were made. One further prototype was made by the Sterling-Hudson Whip Co. of Elkhart, Indiana.

NG

MENLEY (GB) 1920

Menley Motor Co., Stoke-on-Trent, Staffordshire.

This was a simple cyclecar powered by a 999cc air-cooled 2-cylinder Blackburne engine, with 3-speed Juckes gearbox and chain drive to a countershaft, with final drive by belts. It had an ash frame and electric lighting was extra. It was a rare example of a car from the potteries town of Stoke-on-Trent, but only 16 Menleys were made.

NG

MENOMINEE (US) 1915

Menominee Electric Co., Menominee, Michigan.

The main business of Menominee was the manufacture of electric motors and telephones, but they had a few ventures into car making. The first, in 1902, was the building of one car to test their battery, and in 1912 they experimented with a children's electric car. They controlled the company making the DUDLY BUG cyclecar, and this car experience led them to put an electric car on the market in 1915. This was a 2-seater cabriolet on a 108in (2741mm) wheelbase, with a range of 50–60 miles (80–96 km) and a top speed of 20mph (32km/h). The price of $1250 included a recharging outfit. A run of 150 cars was planned, but actual output was fewer, and the make did not survive the year 1915. There was no connection with the Menominee truck, which was made in Clintonville, Wisconsin.

NG

MENON (I) 1897–1902

Carlo Menon, Roncade di Treviso.

Menon made light voiturettes powered by single-cylinder engines using air-cooling for the block and water-cooling for the head, although the first models

1914 Mendip 11hp 2-seater, second prototype.
MICHAEL WORTHINGTON-WILLIAMS

c.1898 Menon 3¹/₂hp *vis-à-vis*.
NATIONAL MOTOR MUSEUM

were entirely air-cooled. The chassis was unsprung as the *vis-à-vis* 4-seater body was suspended on the chassis by four full-elliptic springs. Menon made about 20 of these cars, before giving up in the face of competition from De Dion-Bouton. There was a Menon motorcycle made from 1925 to 1928, but it is not certain if these were made by the same man.

NG

MENTASCHI (I) 1924

Ditta Mentaschi & Cia, Milan-Lambrate.

A light electric car with tandem seating was exhibited at the 1924 Milan Show, but did not go into production.

NG

M.E.P. (F) 1952–1959

Maurice Émile Pezous, Albi.

The brainchild of an aeronautics engineer, the M.E.P. D7 coupé used a Citroën Traction Avant power train, its engine modified to produce 78bhp and mounted in a steel tube chassis. Suspension was independent by torsion bars at either end, with adjustable damping. The transmission was a 4-speed Cotal electromagentic or conventional type, and the brakes were large hydraulic drums all round (revolutionary ventilated discs were also developed). The 2-door coupé bodywork was in steel and could seat four passengers. In 1954 a more streamlined 170SL coupé was launched, again based on Citroën parts, but in all only seven cars were made up until 1959, including one cabriolet. From 1965 to 1971, M.E.P. then made a string of single-seater racing cars.

CR

1929 Meray 3-wheeler.
PAL NEGYESI

1903 Mercedes 18/22PS tonneau, with J. J. Astor.
NATIONAL MOTOR MUSEUM

1903 Mercedes 18/22PS limousine by Rothschild.
NICK GEORGANO

MERA (US) 1987–1988

Corporate Concepts, Capac, Minnesota.

The Mera was the first Ferrari 308 replica built on a Pontiac Fiero chassis, and there were a number of things that set it apart from the army of imitators that sprang up later. Meras were only sold through Pontiac dealers, and they were all built on new Fiero V6 chassis. They retailed for $26,000 to $28,000, which was only a little less than a Corvette. The quality of the fibreglass body was very good, and they came with a standard Pontiac warranty. The 1987 models had Pontiac wheels, while the 1988 models had cast alloy wheels by Cromodora in Italy. There were 247 built before production was halted due to legal action from Ferrari, and Pontiac's decision to discontinue the Fiero. The moulds were sold to AMERICAN FIBERGLASS. Corporate Concepts showed a prototype of

a rebodied Ford Probe in 1991, but the outlandish rear wings and vents apparently doomed the effort.

HP

MÉRAY (H) 1923–1934

Méray Motorkerékpárgyár Rt, Budapest.

The Méray-Horváth brothers Lóránd and Endre established the first Hungarian motorcycle company in 1923. It was a small workshop but after 1925 when MAGYAR ACÉLÁRUGYÁR obtained it, production continued on a grander scale. In addition to motorbikes a 3-wheeler van was constructed, using motorcycle accessories and the well-proven 500cc and 600cc JAP engines. After their parent company failed to achieve any success with passenger car development they designed their own small car based on the van, in 1929. The mechanics were the same, but the car had an enclosed body. Despite big plans the economic crisis hit them hard and few people chose the freedom which their slogan promised: 'Who possesses a Méray small car, owns total freedom as well'. Around 1934 another attempt was made with a 3-cylinder engine arranged in a star shape, probably of aircraft origin. Out of the ten chassis made, only one received a passenger car body (the others carried lorry coachwork), as family cars such as the FIAT Balilla flooded the market. The Méray company became the ADLER distributor in 1936 and that spelled the end of other activities. The company was nationalised in 1948 and the buildings were used as a party garage.

PN

MERCEDES (D) 1901–1926

1901–1903 Daimler Motoren-Gesellschaft, Bad Cannstatt.
1903–1926 Stuttgart-Untertürkheim.

One of the most famous names in automobile history, the Mercedes was designed and built in Germany, but owed its existence and name to an Austrian businessman resident in Nice. Emil Jellinek bought his first Daimler car in 1896, and over the next four years sold quite a number to wealthy motoring enthusiasts living on the French Riviera. He was frequently in contact with the Daimler Motoren-Gesellschaft, regularly requesting cars with greater power and more up-to-date design. In March 1900 one of the 24hp Daimler racing cars crashed in the La Turbie hill climb, killing its driver Wilhelm Bauer. Jellinek blamed Daimler for making a high and unstable car, Daimler blamed Jellinek for demanding too much power. Out of the acrimony came a request from Jellinek for an all-new car, longer and with a lower centre of gravity. If Daimler would build a car along these lines, Jellinek promised to take 36, but he expected delivery of the first car by October 1900, six months after he placed the order. He also insisted that he have the sole agency for France, Belgium, Austria-Hungary and the United States. Cars sold by him would have a new name, for which he chose that of his 11-year old daughter, Mercédès. Those not sold by him would continue to be called Daimlers, though in fact the Mercedes name was soon adopted everywhere; however, the company remained Daimler Motoren-Gesellschaft, becoming Daimler-Benz AG in 1926.

During the summer of 1900 rumours began to emerge from Cannstatt of a remarkable new car which would instantly make all its rivals seem old-fashioned. In July, Paul Meyan, editor of *La France Automobile*, wrote 'French factories would do well to get busy extremely quickly in order that Daimler should not set the fashion in France'. The first Mercedes was not completed until November, and Jellinek did not take delivery until 22 December. It did not perform well initially, and had to be withdrawn from its first competition, the Grand Prix de Pau in February 1901, but it was clear to all that a remarkable new car had been born. Wilhelm Maybach, aided by Gottlieb Daimler's son Paul, had transformed the old Phoenix-Daimler out of all recognition.

The 5913cc 4-cylinder engine had mechanically-operated inlet valves. A gate-type gearchange enabled the driver to engage any speed at will. A longer and lower frame gave the Mercedes a completely fresh appearance, aided by the honeycomb radiator which was fully framed by the bonnet instead of being slung between the dumb irons at the front of the frame. The chain drive of the earlier cars was retained. The engine developed 35bhp, 11 more than the Phoenix racing car. After the unfortunate incident at Pau, the Mercedes redeemed itself during the Nice Speed Week in March. Wilhelm Werner beat all the petrol-engined cars, being defeated only by the Serpollet steamer. He was also fastest in the La Turbie hill climb and won the Nice-Salon-Nice race held in the same week. Although the new car made its name in competition, as any self-respecting make had to do

c.1910 Mercedes 45hp sporting tourer by Gordon Watney.
NATIONAL MOTOR MUSEUM

at that time, Mercedes were also sold as touring cars. Indeed the only difference between a tourer and a racer was the presence of lights, wings and a 4-seater tonneau body.

The 5.9-litre 35PS was made in 1901 only, and was followed by the 40PS whose stroke was lengthened from 140 to 145mm, to give 6129cc. There was quite a complex range of Mercedes in the years 1901 to 1903, from the 1760cc 8PS to the 9235cc 60PS. All had basically similar characteristics, although the 60 had overhead inlet valves in place of the side-valves in a T-head of the other cars. The best known were the 40 and the 60, which set the standard for the highest class of car for the next few years. Many foreign companies modelled their cars more or less on the Mercedes; among these were Berliet and Rochet-Schneider in France, Fiat and Itala in Italy, Ariel and Star in England, and Locomobile in the USA. Like the original 35PS, the 60 was equally at home on the boulevard or the race track. When the team of three 90PS racing cars built for the 1903 Gordon Bennett Race were destroyed in a factory fire, the Paris agent secured three 60 tourers, stripped them of their coachwork, and entered them in the race. Camille Jenatzy finished first, and Baron de Caters fifth.

The 60 was made up to 1905, followed by a redesigned model with the same cylinder dimensions but the valves in a T-head; this was sold as the 36/65PS. It was backed up by a complex range of smaller cars starting with the 2610cc 15/20PS (1905–1909) which was the first Mercedes to have shaft drive. This feature gradually spread up the range, so that after 1909 the only chain-drive Mercedes were the large 28/60, 38/70 and 37/90PS. In 1903 a new factory was opened at Untertürkheim, near Stuttgart, and production reached 853 vehicles, including commercials, in 1905. This was followed by a slump, so that 1909 saw only 109 cars and 122 commercials built. This was brought about by a worldwide overproduction of cars, and led to many manufacturers bringing out smaller and more up-to-date designs over the next few years. Daimler already had such a car in the 15/20PS, which was re-issued as the 10/20PS from 1909 to 1912, and as the 10/25PS from 1912 to 1915. From 1910 to 1913 there was also a smaller 1846cc 8/18PS.

1907 Mercedes Electrique brougham.
NICK BALDWIN

1910 Mercedes-Knight 16/40PS tourer.
NICK BALDWIN

c.1914 Mercedes 90hp sporting tourer.
NATIONAL MOTOR MUSEUM

1914 Mercedes 22/50PS limousine.
NICK BALDWIN

By 1908 Mercedes was well-established as the leading make of European car. Royal owners included Kaiser Wilhelm II of Germany, King Leopold of Belgium and England's King Edward VII who, although he used British-built Daimlers for official engagements in his own country, was said to prefer his Mercedes, which he always travelled in during his many visits to the Continent. In the United States the Mercedes was favoured by many celebrated millionaires, including members of the Astor and Vanderbilt families (William K. Vanderbilt was a keen racing driver and took several records at Daytona in his 90hp Mercedes), Henry Clay Frick and Isaac Guggenheim who gave their names to famous art galleries, and racing drivers Foxhall Keene and Clarence Gray Dinsmore. America was the best export market for Mercedes cars, and 25 per cent of the 1904 production crossed the Atlantic. In that year manufacture of the 45PS began in a factory at Long Island City owned by a subsidiary of the Steinway piano company. The car was called the American Mercedes, though a high proportion of the chassis components were imported; indeed advertising stressed that 'most of its vital parts are formed in our parent company's own dies'. It was only made up to 1907 when the factory was destroyed in a fire. In 1909 Daimer applied for registration of the now famous 3-pointed star as a trade mark. It was registered and used from 1911 onwards.

The Paul Daimler Era

After the departure of Wilhelm Maybach in 1907, design was in the hands of Paul Daimler who was chief engineer up to 1922. He was responsible for the development of the new, smaller cars and also for the introduction of a range using the Knight sleeve-valve engine. These were made from 1910 to 1915 in three sizes, the 2610cc 10/30PS, 4080cc 16/40PS and 6330ccc 25/65PS. The 16/40 was revived after the war, and with slightly more power, as the 16/45 and 16/50PS, was made up to 1924.

Also designed under Paul's direction were the large chain-driven sporting models, the 9530cc 37/90PS and the 9850cc 38/100PS. Unlike the touring cars which had side-valves in a T-head or L-head, the 37/90 had ohvs, one inlet and two exhaust per cylinder. These gave a sufficient opening area, but kept the size of each valve small enough not to cause a build up of heat on the surface. Unlike earlier Mercedes, the 37/90 carried its gearbox halfway down the frame, in unit with the differential from which drive was taken by countershaft and chains to the rear wheels. The 37/90 was made from 1910 to 1914, and a few of the 38/100s with larger engines were made in 1915. Also between 1913 and 1918 seven very large cars were made, with airship engines of 12,100cc (4-cylinders), 20,500cc (6-cylinders) and 24,030cc (8 cylinders). Rivals to the 200PS Benz, they were not regular catalogued models, though three of the 20.5-litre 79/200PS were sold to Italy. These were the last chain-driven Mercedes cars.

Most 37/90s had open sporting bodywork, 2- or 4-seaters, but there were a few limousines as well. The sharply pointed radiator which characterised Mercedes and the larger Mercedes-Benz up to the early 1930s, was first seen on the 1912 37/90, and soon extended to most of the larger models, including the Mercedes-Knights. In 1914 the 37/90 was replaced by a more modern car, the 28/95. This had a 6-cylinder single-ohc engine of 7280cc and shaft drive. Output was 90bhp, the same as the 37/90 though the capacity was smaller by more than 2 litres. The ohvs were inclined in the cylinder head, a practice derived from the engine of the 1913 Grand Prix Mercedes. The aluminium water jacket which surrounded the cylinders was derived from aero engine practice. The 28/95 was the first of a long line of sporting 6-cylinder cars which culminated in the Mercedes-Benz SSKL of 1929–1932. Not more than 25 were made before the war, but the 28/95 was reintroduced in 1920, and a further 565 were made up to 1924.

Mercedes contested several major races in the years up to 1914, and had some spectacular successes. As in more recent times they tended to hold back until they were sure of their cars. Thus they ignored the first two Grands Prix of 1906 and 1907, but entered the 1908 event with three 12.8-litre cars, victory going to Christian Lautenschlager. The 1912 Grand Prix they kept away from, and they finished no better than third, fourth and sixth in 1913, but for the 1914 Grand Prix they entered five of the new 4½-litre 4-cylinder single-ohc cars. They went in for more meticulous practice than any other team, as well as taking replacement axles and other components, and were rewarded with the first three places, by Lautenschlager, Wagner and Salzer. One of the Grand Prix cars was taken to America and was raced by Ralph de Palma, winning the 1914 Chicago Cup and Elgin Trophy, and the 1915 Indianapolis 500.

From the Armistice to the Merger

The first two years after the war were very grim times in Germany, with acute shortages of coal, petrol and rubber. Some cars were sold without tyres, which the buyer was expected to find as best he could. Only 621 cars were made at Untertürkheim in 1919, all of them 16/45PS Mercedes-Knights. A merger with Benz was first considered that year, but it was to be another seven years before this came about. In 1920 production was 1616 cars, again mostly Mercedes-Knights, though the 28/95 was reintroduced that year. For 1921 came a new range of poppet-valve cars with single-ohc 4-cylinder engines of 1568 and 2614cc. They were known as the 6/25 and 10/40PS, and from the spring of 1923, when superchargers became available, as the 6/25/40 and 10/40/65PS. The first figure represented the taxable horsepower, the second and third the brake horsepower without supercharger and with it. They were the first cars in the world to be catalogued with superchargers, which differed from most other systems in that the blower forced air into the carburettor, instead of being placed between the carburettor and inlet manifold. It was not permanently engaged, but could be activated by additional pressure on the accelerator. Relatively few of the 6/25 and 10/40 models were equipped with superchargers, and it was not widely

NICK BALDWIN

NICK BALDWIN

JELLINEK, EMILE (1853–1918)

One of the most influential figures in the early history of motoring in Europe, Emile Jellinek will be better remembered for the name of his daughter than for anything else. He was born in Leipzig, the son of a Bohemian rabbi (some sources say he was a professor of Oriental studies), and on leaving school was sent to the Austro-Hungarian embassy in Tetuan, the capital of Spanish Morocco. He married into a prominent business family, later moving to Oran where he prospered in the tobacco trade, then to Algiers where he worked for a large French banking house, and then back to Austria. In Vienna he became a successful entrepreneur, and in the early 1890s was sent to be his country's consul in Nice. This was very pleasing to him as he hated cold weather and loved high society. He soon took up motoring, first with a De Dion-Bouton tricycle, and then with Benz and Daimler cars. He found the Daimler well-built but too slow for his taste, and asked the Cannstatt company to make a faster car with a front-mounted 4-cylinder engine of sufficient power to propel the car at 30mph (48km/h). Because he ordered four cars at a time, they were willing to meet his requests.

In 1899 they built a massive and high 24/28hp car with which Jellinek won the touring class at the La Turbie hill climb. This spurred the wealthy amateur driver Baron Arthur de Rothschild to forsake his Panhard and order a similar Daimler. This started Jellinek on his career of selling Daimler cars on the Riviera, although he must have had this in mind when he ordered four. Within twelve months he had sold about 34 cars from Cannstatt, but this success was clouded by the death of Wilhelm Bauer at the 1900 La Turbie hill climb. Jellinek blamed the Daimler company for sending him such a top-heavy car. 'One of our best men was the victim of your ill-designed monster', he said, and Wilhelm Maybach countered by saying that it was Jellinek's insistence on power that produced the monster. The result was a new design, to Jellinek's general specifications and worked out in detail by Maybach and Paul Daimler. "Build me a car exactly after my specifications, and I will take a whole series', said Jellinek. True to his word, he ordered 36 of the new cars, with a value of 550,000 marks, almost certainly the largest single order in the motor trade at that time.

MERCEDES JELLINEK

The new car was called Mercedes after Jellinek's 11-year old elder daughter, although from about 1898 he had used the pseudonym 'M. Mercedes' when he raced. A lover of all things Spanish (his first wife Rachel was Spanish), he called his house at Nice the Villa Mercedes, and in 1903 officially changed his surname to Jellinek-Mercedes. He remained the company's representative up to 1907, but relations with the Daimler Motoren Gesellschaft became increasingly strained, as Jellinek wanted to receive credit for everything that the cars did, and claimed that any faults were because the company did not listen to him. The departure from Daimler of his friend Wilhem Maybach was the last straw. However, he had plenty of other irons in the fire. From 1904 he became involved in property development, building the Hotels Astoria and Mercedes in Paris, and the Scribe in Nice. In 1907 he became honorary vice-consul in Monaco, a more important post than that in Nice, as Monaco was a sovereign state. He was entitled to wear an ostrich-plumed hat and to carry a sword, which must have delighted him. Also in 1907 a car was named after another of his daughters, Maja, and built by the Austrian Daimler company, but it lasted only two seasons. He continued to live in state in Monaco until the outbreak of war when, as a prominent citizen of an enemy country, he was no longer *persona grata*. Suggestions that he was involved in spying are unfounded. He moved to Switzerland, and died in Geneva in March 1918.

And Mercedes? An artistic child, fond of acting and parties, she had no interest in motor cars. In 1909, when she was 20, she married Baron Charles Schlosser, but the marriage was not happy. She married another Austrian baron in the 1920s, and died in Vienna in 1929, aged 40.

Emile Jellinek had at least five children, Mercedes, Maja, Guy, Didier and Andrée.

NG

Further Reading
My father, Mr Mercedes, Guy Jellinek-Mercedes, G.T. Foulis, 1961.

1924 Mercedes 24/100/140PS tourer.
NICK BALDWIN

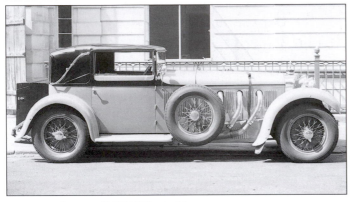

1928 Mercedes-Benz (i) SS 38/250 coupé.
NICK BALDWIN

1929 Mercedes-Benz (i) Mannheim 15/75PS limousine.
NICK BALDWIN

1932 Mercedes-Benz (i) Typ 170 saloon.
NATIONAL MOTOR MUSEUM

adopted until the arrival of the big 6-cylinder cars in 1924. Total production of the 6/25 was about 360 cars, and of the 10/40, about 200.

The 28/95 was made up to 1924, gaining front-wheel brakes in 1923, though these had been fitted to some cars earlier, including the one with which Max Seiler won the 1921 Coppa Florio and came second in the Targa Florio. This was a remarkable feat, for it had been made in 1914, and Sailer drove it all the way from Untertürkheim to Sicily, competed in the races and then drove home again, single-handed and on one set of tyres because a second set could not be spared. Mercedes won the Targa in 1922, with a 1914 Grand Prix car driven by Count Masetti.

In 1923 Ferdinand Porsche came to Untertürkheim from Vienna where had worked for Austro-Daimler. Paul Daimler moved on to Horch for whom he designed a series of straight-8s. Porsche's first designs for Mercedes were the 3920cc 15/70/100PS and 6240cc 24/100/140PS. They featured light metal cylinder blocks, engines and gearboxes in unit, dual ignition and 4-wheel brakes. Cantilever springs were retained for the rear suspension, but later both models were fitted with semi-elliptics all round. Porsche's engines had single-ohcs, but with vertical valves rather than the inclined valves favoured by Paul Daimler. The supercharger was standard, although the cars were not initially particularly sporting. Most carried fairly heavy touring or limousine coachwork, and it was not until the arrival of the shorter chassis Modell K that sports cars were made. This was after the merger with Benz. Plans for this were revived in 1923, and the following year the two companies signed an agreement of mutual interest The full merger was masterminded by Wilhelm Kissel, financial director for Benz, in conjunction with the Deutsche Bank who held the majority of Benz shares and a large number of Daimler shares. On 1 July 1926 a new company, Daimler-Benz AG, with a capital of RM36.36 million, was formed with Kissel as general manager, a post he held until his death in 1942.

NG

Further Reading
see Mercedes-Benz.

MERCEDES-BENZ (i) **(D)** 1926 to date

Daimler-Benz AG, Stuttgart-Untertüurkheim; Mannheim; Bremen.

The new company of Daimler-Benz was well provided with designers and models of car. Three brilliant engineers joined the board, Hans Nibel (1880–1934) and Friedrich Nallinger (1883–1937) from Benz, and Ferdinand Porsche (1875–1951) from Daimler. Two Benz designs were continued with Mercedes-Benz badges, the 2610cc 10/35PS and 4160cc 16/50PS, but they were discontinued in 1927. From Daimler came the big Porsche-designed 6-cylinder cars, the 3920cc 15/70/100PS which was renamed the Mercedes-Benz Typ 400, and the 6240cc 24/100/140PS which became the M-Benz Typ 630. A short-wheelbase sports chassis, the Modell K, was added in 1926, and less than a month after the merger the new company had its first team success. Three Modell Ks finished 1-2-3 in the Grand Prix de l'Europe at San Sebastian, Spain. The Modell K was not an ideal competition car, having a high centre of gravity and inadequate brakes. To improve on this, Porsche designed a new car for 1927, known as the Typ S. This had a lower chassis than the K, although the wheelbase was unchanged at 134in (3410mm), Bosch-Dewandre servo-assisted brakes (also available on the K from 1928) and an engine enlarged to 6800cc. This gave 120bhp, or 180bhp when the supercharger was in use. The S was the first of the classic Mercedes-Benz sports car which have come to epitomise the German sports car in the same way that Bentley does the British or Alfa Romeo the Italian. Its top speed approached 90mph (144km/h), and among its many successes were the first three places in the 1927 German Grand Prix. The standard body was an open 4-seater made by Daimler-Benz' own coachworks at Sindelfingen, but custom bodies were also made by other firms including Erdmann & Rossi, who made a 4-door tourer, and Freestone & Webb who made a 4-door saloon.

The Typ S was listed from late 1926 to 1930, and during these years it was joined by more powerful models. In 1928 came the SS, with a slightly larger engine of 7065cc, which developed 200 or 225bhp. The bonnet was a little higher, giving the SS a more aggressive appearance than the S. The wheelbase was unchanged, and the factory-bodied 4-seater tourer was very similar to that of the S. A greater variety of coachbuilders worked on the SS chassis, including Erdmann & Rossi, Glaser, Neuss, Papler and Reutter in Germany, Armbruster in Austria, Saoutchik in France, Freestone & Webb in England, Castagna in

1934 Mercedes-Benz (i) Typ 150 sports car.
NICK BALDWIN

Italy and Murphy in the USA. Most of these bodies were open tourers, cabriolets or coupés. The SS had a fine performance, with a top speed of 115mph (184km/h) with the highest axle ratio. But for the more ambitious sportsman there was the SSK with a wheelbase reduced to 116in and engines in three degrees of tune, giving 200, 225 or 250bhp. Three sizes of supercharger were used on these big Mercedes-Benz, with a compression of 0.6kg/sq.cm which was available on all SS and SSK models, the larger (0.7kg/sq.cm) optional on SS and SSK, and the competition version, nicknamed the 'elephant blower' (0.85kg/sq.cm). This was only available on works-sponsored cars driven by selected men. Private owners, even one as well-known as Malcolm Campbell, were not granted an elephant blower. The elephant blower was used mainly on the formidable SSKL (Super-Sport-Kurz-Leicht), a works competition car whose frame was drilled in side and cross members in order to get the weight down to a minimum. However, the elephant blower occasionally found its way onto other models, notably the SS which Caracciola took to the 1930 Tourist Trophy and was not allowed to start on the grounds of having a non-standard supercharger. Similarly equipped SSs ran at Le Mans in 1930, without much success.

Le Mans apart, the big Mercedes-Benz had many successes, of which the most celebrated was Caracciola and Werner's win in the 1928 German GP (SS), Caracciola's wins in the 1929 TT (SS), 1930 Irish GP (SSK), 1931 German GP (SSK) and 1931 Mille Miglia (SSKL). The big blown cars also had many successes in hill climbs, the leading driver being Hans Stück. He was a wealthy amateur who purchased his SSKL from the company and paid for the factory assistance that he received.

The fame of the S series cars was quite out of proportion to the numbers made. Of more than 49,000 Mercedes-Benz cars built between 1927 and 1933, only 297 were of the S series. These were made up as follows:

S	1926–1928	146	*(although catalogued up to 1930,*
			apparently none was delivered after 1928)
SS	1928–1933	111	
SSK	1928–1932	33	
SSKL	1929–1932	7	

They were essentially publicity gatherers, 'the best megaphones that Kissel could produce to shout the Mercedes name around the world' (Beverly Rae Kimes), and as such they succeeded admirably.

Touring Cars 1926–1940

While the big sports cars were gaining publicity for Mercedes-Benz, a wide range of lesser machinery was earning the company's profits. Soon after the merger two 6-cylinder touring models were introduced, the 1988cc 8/38PS and the 2968cc 12/55PS. Designed by Hans Nibel, they had side-valve engines, flat radiators and artillery wheels, and were made with a wide variety of open and closed bodies including taxicabs, delivery vans and hotel buses. Made up to the mid–1930s, their engines were gradually enlarged over the years, and from 1929 they were given names from the towns where they were made, the smaller being the Stuttgart and the larger the Mannheim. From 1930 to 1933 the latter was made as an attractive-looking sports roadster with twin carburettors, shorter wheelbase and wire wheels. With 3969cc engine, it was known as the 370S. 193 of these were made, out of a total Mannheim production of 1623. At the top of the touring car range were the straight-8 Nürburg, made in 4622 and 4918cc models, and the enormous Typ 770 Grosser Mercedes. The Nürburg was re-named the Typ 500 in 1931, and made up to 1939. Wood spoked wheels were available to the end, making the 500 probably the last car in the world to be catalogued with wooden wheels.

The Grosser Mercedes had a 7655cc straight-8 engine which developed 150bhp, and could propel the 3½-ton car at up to 100mph (161km/h). It was seen by Daimler-Benz management as a competitor for the Maybach Zeppelin, and indeed could be had with Maybach's Schnellgang supplementary gearbox giving six forward speeds as an alternative to the Mercedes-Benz gearbox. Prices ran from RM41,000 for a pullman-limousine to RM47,000 for a 6-seater cabriolet, making the 770 Germany's most expensive car. Only 113 were made between 1930 and 1938. Owners included the former Kaiser Wilhelm II who took delivery of his in Holland where he was living in exile, Kings Farouk of Egypt and Faisal of Iraq, and Emperor Hirohito of Japan who had seven of them, some of which were still in use in the 1960s.

In 1938 came a new 770, which used the same engine in a new chassis, a lengthened version of the 540K with all-independent suspension. Mostly made as 7-seater limousines or cabriolets, the second series Typ 770s were 245in (6218mm) long, and weighed up to 4.75 tons in armoured form. While the earlier 770s were bought by private individuals, nearly all the later models went to Nazi leaders, or to a few foreign rulers of whom Hitler approved. These included Stalin (after the 1939 Nazi-Soviet pact), Finland's Field Marshal von Mannerheim, Spain's General Franco and Portugal's Antonio Salazar. A total of 88 were made, the last being completed in 1943.

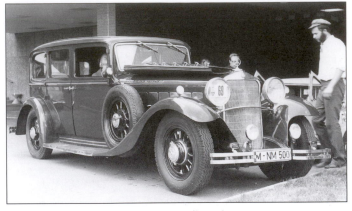

1933 Mercedes-Benz (i) Nürburg Typ 500N limousine.
NICK BALDWIN

1935 Mercedes-Benz (i) Typ 500K roadster.
NICK BALDWIN

At the other end of the scale, Mercedes-Benz' bread-and-butter was earned by the 170. The first car to bear this name was a small six with 1692cc side-valve engine developing 32bhp, hydraulic brakes and independent suspension all round, by twin transverse springs at the front and twin coil springs and swing axles at the rear. It was another design from the versatile Hans Nibel, an underrated engineer whose cars ranged from the 1908 Grand Prix Benz through the rear-engined Benz Tropfenwagen, the Mercedes-Benz SSKL to the first of the famous Grand Prix cars of 1934. Despite an unexciting performance with a top speed of only 55mph (88km/h), the 170 sold well, a total of 13,775 finding buyers between 1931 and 1936. It was followed by a series of larger 6-cylinder cars, the 1961cc 200, 2229cc 230 and 3208cc 320. All had all-round independent suspension and conventional box frames, though the last of the short-chassis 230s had tubular frames, as did the 4-cylinder 170V. This was the most successful prewar Mercedes-Benz, with sales of 71,973 cars and 19,075 military *Kübelwagen* between 1936 and 1942. It was revived after the war, and a further 49,367 were made up to 1953.

Two unusual avenues explored by Daimler-Benz in the 1930s were those of rear-engined and diesel cars. At the end of 1933 they launched the 130H, a 2-door saloon and cabriolet with a 1308cc 4-cylinder engine mounted behind the rear axle, driving forward by an underslung worm gear. The frame was a forked backbone design, and the usual Mercedes swing axle suspension was used. With only 26bhp the 130H was seriously underpowered, taking more than 37 seconds to reach its maximum speed of 56mph (90km/h). This was perhaps no bad thing as the concentration of weight on the rear axle made handling somewhat alarming. A 2-seater roadster with 55bhp 1498cc engine ahead of the rear axle was a more desirable proposition, but only five of these 150Hs were made. There were also six coupé versions of the 150H which took part in the 1934 ADAC 2000km Trials. A total of 4298 130Hs were made between 1933 and 1935, followed by 1507 of the 170H, which used the 38bhp 1697cc engine of the 170V. The letters indicate front (*Vorn*) or rear (*Heck*) engine location.

In 1936 Daimler-Benz introduced the 260D, the world's first diesel-engined passenger car. They already had a lot of experience with diesel-powered trucks, and their car used a 4-cylinder 2545cc ohv engine in a 230 chassis. Body styles were also from the 230, though there was not such a wide range, the choice being limited to tourer, saloon or landaulet. As with all diesels, specific output was on the low side, the engine developing 45bhp as against 55bhp from the smaller 230 petrol engine. However, the combination of cheap fuel and an economical engine were attractive to many customers including taxi drivers. Between 1936 and 1940 Daimler-Benz sold 1967 260Ds. By the time of the company's 100th anniversary in 1986, more than three million diesel cars would be built. Demand exceeded supply; in 1939 the waiting list for a 260D was 15–18 months, more than for any other model. For a 170V the time was 12–15 months, while a 540K could be delivered in four months.

The Big Straight-8s

In 1933 Daimler-Benz announced the first of a new line of fast cars which was to take over the mantle of the S series, yet to be a very different type of machine. The big Mercedes-Benz of the 1930s were to their predecessors as the Derby Bentleys were to the Cricklewood models, quieter and more comfortable though with less drama about their performance. Hans Nibel's intention was to combine high performance with the handling of his recently-introduced all-independent Typ 170, so he used all-independent suspension again on his new model, which bore the type number 380. The engine was a 3823cc ohv straight-8 which developed 90bhp unblown and 140bhp with the supercharger. The 380 was a good-looking car, especially in cabriolet form, which accounted for most of the 150 cars made. Other body styles were an open tourer (11 made), 2-seater roadster (7) and 4-door saloon (6), while 19 chassis were supplied to outside coachbuilders. Unfortunately the power was insufficient for the 2-ton weight, and top speed was an uninspiring 84mph (134km/h).

To improve matters Nibel enlarged the engine to 5018cc, giving 100bhp unblown and 160bhp with supercharger. Introduced in 1934 the new model was called the 500K, the K standing for *Kompressor*. Although the 380 was also supercharged, it was never called the 380K. The wheelbase of the 500K was slightly longer at 130in (3299mm), but the 500K's appearance was similar to the smaller car, and the same range of cabriolets, roadsters and saloons was offered, although the saloons had two doors rather than four. A special model, not seen on the 380 chassis, was the Autobahn-Kurier, an aerodynamic coupé designed for high-speed cruising on Germany's new motorways. Perhaps it was too advanced for public taste, for only four were made, out of a total 342 500Ks.

In 1936 the engine was enlarged to 5401cc, and power was now 115bhp unblown and 180bhp blown. The new model was called the 540K, and came in the same wheelbase lengths as the 500K. There was also a longer chassis (149.6in/ 3797mm) which carried large 7-passenger bodies and looked not unlike a Grosser Mercedes. Otherwise the same body styles were available as on the 500K, and the two models were almost indistinguishable. Bodies peculiar to the 540K were the Aktion P 2-door armoured saloons made in 1942/43. Twenty of these were made, 18 on confiscated chassis whose bodies were removed and scrapped, and two on new chassis. Total production of the 540K was 419.

The 500K and 540K were very popular with the Nazi hierarchy, owners including Hermann Goering, Josef Goebbels, Robert Ley and Adolf Hühnlein, the NSKK Korpsführer who organised motor sport in Germany. Hitler was more often seen in a Grosser Mercedes cabriolet, and it is likely that, despite all the claims for surviving examples to be 'Hitler's car', he did not actually own any, but used cars from a pool which was always available.

In 1939 an enlarged engine of 5800cc was tested in a 540K chassis. It has been said that 12 were built, under the name 580K, and that one was supplied to Hühnlein, but company records do not bear this out, and possibly only one was made. More substantial were the 6020cc V12 Typ 600V and 600K. These were made with cabriolet, limousine and tourer bodies in 1940/41, and might well have replaced both the 540K and 770 had the war not intervened. Exact numbers are not known, but there were not more than 10 of the 600V and seven of the 600K, which was supercharged and developed 240bhp.

Though not the province of this book, it must be mentioned that Daimler-Benz had a very successful career in Grand Prix racing between 1934 and 1939, with straight-8 and V12 cars which dominated the sport. They scored 33 wins in major races, together with one (the 1939 Tripoli GP) with the 1½-litre V8 voiturettes.

The Three-Pointed Star Rises from the Ashes

The Daimler-Benz factories suffered very seriously during the war; the Untertürkheim plant was 70 per cent destroyed and the Sindelfingen body plant 85 per cent. When workers were allowed back to Untertürkheim in May 1945 their first task was to clear away the rubble. Fortunately the production line for the 170V, which had lain idle since 1942, was relatively undamaged. The first engine was built in February 1946, and complete vehicles began to emerge from the factory in June. Commercial vehicles were more essential to economic recovery than cars, so all the 214 170Vs built in 1946 were bodied as delivery vans, pick-up trucks or ambulances. The first passenger car was delivered in May 1947, and production that year was 1045, of which 381 were cars.

Up to 1949 the only model made was the utilitarian 170V, but in that year it was joined by a diesel version with the same bodywork, the 170D, and a more luxurious saloon, the 170S. This had a body similar to that of the prewar 230. Among its features not found on the 170V (until 1950) was external access to the luggage boot. Also available in 2-door cabriolet and roadster forms, the 170S was made up to 1955. It was joined in 1951 by the 220 which had a new oversquare (80 × 72.8mm) 2195cc 6-cylinder engine with single-ohc. The saloon and cabriolet bodies were similar to those of the 170S, but the 220 had a more modern front end with headlamps faired into the wings. With 80bhp it could easily reach 90mph (144 km/h). A total of 18,514 220s were made from 1951 to 1954, when they were rebodied.

The recovery of Mercedes-Benz was very dramatic. From the paltry 214 utility vehicles made in 1946, production rose to 5116 in 1948, 17,417 in 1949 and 33,906 in 1950. This easily beat the best prewar figure of 28,039 in 1937, and from then on there were substantial increases almost every year, with six figures being reached in 1959, when 108,440 cars were delivered, as well as 23,945 trucks, 3364 buses and 6766 Unimog 4 × 4 tractors.

A return to the luxury market came with the launch of the 300 at the Frankfurt Show in April 1951. This had a new 2996cc single-ohc 6-cylinder engine developing 115bhp mounted in a 120in wheelbase and available as a 6-light saloon or 4-light cabriolet. At DM19,900 and 23,700 respectively they were the most expensive German-built cars at the time of their introduction, though soon surpassed by the 300S which made its debut at the Paris Show in October 1951. This was a short wheelbase coupé or cabriolet at DM34,500. It used a twin-carburettor version of the 300 engine which gave the handsome 2-seaters a top speed of 110mph (176km/h). The 300 was made up to 1962, improvements including servo-assisted brakes in 1955 (300B), and optional automatic transmission in 1956 (300C). Although the size of the engine was unchanged the 300C had more power thanks to twin carburettors, and the final 300D (1957–62) had fuel injection and gave 160bhp. In 1960 a very small number of pullman-landaulets were made on an extended wheelbase, which anticipated those on the 600 chassis a few years later. A special 300 pullman-landaulet throne car was supplied to Pope John XIII.

The 300S had a shorter life because its place was taken by the 300SL in the mid–1950s, but it remained in production until 1958. The only major change was the adoption of fuel injection in 1955, which increased power to 175bhp. A total of 760 300S cars were built, while the 300 in its various forms accounted for 11,430.

Return to Sport

In January 1947 racing chief Alfred Neubauer wrote to the Caracciolas: 'We think very little about racing around here'. Understandable in the austere atmosphere of the time, yet little more than five years later the three-pointed star was again seen winning on the race tracks. The resurrected Grand Prix cars had not been very successful, and to develop a brand new Formula One machine would be too expensive and time-consuming, though they did it in the end. First, though, a sports car would be developed around the existing 300 engine. By using three carburettors, an improved camshaft and better inlet and exhaust manifolds, DB engineers managed to raise power to 175bhp. This engine was mounted at an angle of 45 degrees so that it would fit under the very low bonnet. The transmission and axles came from the production 300, but the coupé body was all new, and of very advanced design. Largely the work of Rudi Uhlenhaut, it consisted of a multitube space frame clad in light aluminium panels. Because of the prevalence of tubes in construction, the body could not have doors extending down to the sills, so a compromise was made in which the sills were about half way up the body side, and above them were doors which opened vertically, being hinged in the centre of the roof. When viewed from the front,

1935 Mercedes-Benz (i) Typ 500K cabriolet A.
NICK GEORGANO

1953 Mercedes-Benz (i) Typ 220 cabriolet A.
NICK BALDWIN

1960 Mercedes-Benz (i) 220SE saloon.
NICK BALDWIN

1960 Mercedes-Benz (i) 190SL roadster.
NICK GEORGANO

1957 Mercedes-Benz (i) 300SL 'Gullwing' coupé.
NICK BALDWIN

the open doors bore some resemblance to a seagull in flight, which led to the car being described as the 'gullwing coupé', though this term was not applied to the original competition coupés.

Known as the 300SL (Sport-Leicht), the new cars made their competition debut in the 1952 Mille Miglia, where they finished second and fourth (Kling and Caracciola). In the Berne Grand Prix they finished 1-2-3 (Kling, Lang and Riess) and six weeks later they went to Le Mans where, against the best opposition that Jaguar, Ferrari and Talbot could provide, they finished first and second (Lang/Riess and Helfrich/Niedermayer). Another 1-2-3-4 victory at the Nürburgring – with open roadsters – was followed by what was probably the most significant success of the season, first and second for Kling and Lang in the Carrera Panamericana in Mexico. This brought the Mercedes name to Americans who, at that time, paid little heed to what went on at European venues like Le Mans and the Mille Miglia.

The 300 SL had served its maker's purpose in showing the world that they were back in business, and they were prepared to drop it in order to concentrate on the Grand Prix car. However, the New York distributor, Austrian-born Max Hoffmann, thought he could sell the car in America, and offered to take 1000 of them. The production 300SL, which made its debut at New York's International Motor Sports Show in January 1954, differed considerably from the competition cars of 1952. The body was chunkier in appearance, and considerably strengthened. This added nearly 400kgs to the weight, but there was more power (215bhp) too, thanks to the fuel injection system that replaced the three carburettors. This gave the 300SL a top speed of 145 to 160mph (232 to 256km/h), according to the rear axle ratio. The tilting of the engine made maintenance awkward and ruled out right-hand drive, but this did not deter a number of customers in left-driving countries such as Great Britain and Sweden. In all, 1,400 gullwing coupés were sold between 1954 and 1957, and the 300SL was continued in roadster form until 1962, 1858 of these being sold. They were easier to get into, thanks to deeper doors, and the last models (1961 onwards) had all-disc brakes. However, they lacked the charisma of the gullwing coupé, and fetch about 20 per cent less on the collector's market today.

A year after the appearance of the production 300SL came a smaller version, the 190SL, which used the 1897cc 4-cylinder engine from the 190 saloon, in a 2-seater sports body which bore some resemblance to the 300SL, though there was never a coupé version. The 190SL has suffered in comparison with its more powerful sister, but it was popular when new, and sold 25,881 units between 1955 and 1963. The price was little more than half that of a 300SL, DM16,500

compared with DM29,000 for the gullwing and DM32,500 for the roadster.

The launch of the 300SL was delayed by the necessity to prepare a team of Grand Prix cars for the 1954 season. Known as the W196, they had 2496cc twin-ohc straight-8 engines with fuel injection, desmodromic valve gear, 5-speed gearbox, space frame construction and inboard brakes. Two body styles were made, a conventional open wheeler for twisty courses, and an enclosed streamliner for high speed circuits. The streamlined cars finished first and second (Fangio and Kling) on their first outing in the French GP, and went on to win three more Grands Prix before the end of the season.

In 1955 with Stirling Moss in the team they had a marvellous season, with five GP victories, four by Fangio and one by Moss. The Argentine won the World Drivers' Championship, and MB the Constructors' Championship. They also won the Sports Car Constructors' Championship with the 300SLR, a streamlined roadster powered by a 2979cc version of the W196 engine. With this Moss won the Mille Miglia, with Fangio second place, and stock 300SLs in fifth, seventh and tenth places. Other victories included the TT, Targa Florio and Swedish Sports Car GP, but the year was overshadowed by the appalling accident at Le Mans involving Levegh's car, in which the French driver and 82 spectators died. DB withdrew the other cars at once, giving victory to the D-type Jaguar of Hawthorn and Bueb. The 300SLR's season was remarkable – it had won five of the six races it had entered, and was leading when withdrawn from the sixth (Le Mans). None had retired through component failure during the 1955 season. Yet after the Targa Florio victory in September, Daimler-Benz announced that they were pulling out of racing altogether.

Unitary-Construction Touring Cars

In 1953 came a new saloon body which was not only slab sided in the modern manner, but was of unitary construction. Two models were made at first, the 180 which was powered by the familiar 1767cc engine of the 170V and S, and (from 1954), the 220 which used the 2195cc six of the earlier 220. The 180 was made in diesel form, and for the first time in Mercedes history, sales of diesels exceeded those of the petrol-engined version, by 152,000 to 118,000. Many of these were for taxi use, and the 180D began Mercedes' domination of the cab ranks which has continued up to the present day, not only in Germany but all over the world. From 1956 an additional model was the 190, powered by a 1897cc petrol or diesel engine. This had an all-synchromesh gearbox with column change. While the 180 was only made as a 4-door saloon, the 220 could be had as a 2-door cabriolet or coupé. With twin carburettors it became the 220S, and with fuel injection the

1969 Mercedes-Benz (i) 600 Pullman limousine.
NATIONAL MOTOR MUSEUM

220SE. These were attractive and fast cars, with a top speed of 100mph (161km/h). Servo-assisted brakes were standard on the S and SE, while a Hydrak automatic clutch was available from late 1957. From 1956 to 1959 there was a cheaper variant, the 219, which used the single-carburettor 220 engine in the 180 bodyshell. This was similar in size and shape, but less luxuriously trimmed.

In 1959 the first generation unitary bodies gave way to a re-styled version with more regular styling at the rear, incorporating small fins, though they were very restrained compared with the contemporary transatlantic excesses. The track was wider and the bodies roomier. The first cars to receive this new body were the 220S and SE, followed in 1961 by the 190 and 190D, and the 300. This used the 2996cc fuel-injected engine and self-levelling air suspension, and most 300s were sold with automatic transmissions. Both 220 and 300 were made in coupé and cabriolet forms when they bore the suffix SEC. From 1963 there was a longer wheelbase 300 called the 300SEL. In 1965 the 190 received a 1988cc engine, becoming the 200 or 200D – again the latter sold better, nearly 162,000 in four seasons compared with 70,207. Dual-circuit servo disc brakes were standard on the 200s, having been introduced on the 220SEC in 1961 and on the saloons in 1962. In 1967 a number of 200Ds were made with 7-passenger limousine bodies and extended wheelbases, mainly for taxi work. This style was continued on the smaller Mercedes (200D, 240D) through the 1970s and 1980s.

Although they were out of racing, MB had an active rallying history up to 1965. The 300SL won the European Rally Championship in 1956, and from 1961 to 1964 there was a works-sponsored team whose successes included 1-2-3 in the 1960 Monte Carlo, and wins in the 1960 and 1961 East African Safari and 1962 and 1963 Liège-Sofia-Liège. Cars entered included the 219 and 220 saloons and the 230SL sports car (see below). After 1964 rallies were left to private entrants and no notable successes were achieved.

From the mid–1960s the MB range expanded by the familiar process of mixing engines and bodyshells. The 230 and 230S (1965–68) saloons used a 2281cc engine in the 220 bodyshell, while two new engines, the 2496cc 240 and 2778cc 280, were used in a new, larger and lower body to make the 250S/250SE/250SEC and similar models in the 280 range. All of these were available in 4-door saloons and 2-door coupés and cabriolets. The same bodies were used with the old 2996cc engine to make the 300SE saloon, though the long wheelbased 300SEC used the smaller 280 engine. At the top of the range was the 300SEC 6.3, a very rapid luxury saloon powered by the 6330cc V8 designed for the 600 limousine. Only 6526 of these 134mph (214km/h) saloons were made, though the theme of large engines in medium-sized bodyshells was continued in the 450SEL 6.9 of the 1970s.

1971 Mercedes-Benz (i) 350SL coupé.
NICK BALDWIN

The Mighty 600

In 1956 the go-ahead was given for a new Grosser Mercedes, a prestige car to rival the best that Rolls-Royce or Cadillac could make. Friedrich van Winsen, later chief of body development at Daimler-Benz, was entrusted with the project, watched over by Fritz Nallinger, son of Friedrich Nallinger who had come to the company at the time of the merger in 1926. Several engine configurations were considered, V12, V16 and even 24 cylinders, but they finally settled for a 6330cc V8 with one camshaft per bank of cylinders, developing 250bhp. Transmission was by a 4-speed automatic box, and the specifications included disc brakes all round and air suspension. Two models were announced in August 1963, the saloon on a 126in (3198mm) wheelbase, and the pullman limousine on a 153.5in (3896mm) wheelbase. Overall lengths were 218 and 245.6in (5533 and6233mm). In 1965 they were joined by an even more exclusive landaulet on the long wheelbase. The saloon cost DM56,500, and the limousine DM 65,500 (a 300SE saloon cost DM53,350). By 1978 inflation had raised these prices to DM144,100 and 165,500. Although the 600 was made up to 1981, no prices were quoted after 1978. Production peaked in 1965, when 408 were made, and dwindled to less than 100 per year after the fuel crisis of 1973/4. Sales were

1977 Mercedes-Benz (i) 230T estate car.
NICK BALDWIN

1981 Mercedes-Benz (i) S Class saloon.
NICK BALDWIN

undoubtedly hit by the 300SEL 6.3 which used the same engine, had more performance because of a lighter body and was considerably cheaper. Total production of the 600 was 2677, of which 2190 were 'short' saloons, 428 pullman limousines and 59 landaulets. The latter were supplied almost exclusively to Heads of State – among owners of the long-wheelbase 600 were Pope Paul VI, Mao Tse-Tung who had eleven, and Uganda's Idi Amin. There were a few 'specials' on the short chassis 600 – two 2-door saloons on a wheelbase shortened to 117.3in (2977mm), and one hearse which was still used in Hanover in the early 1980s, while one of the last to be delivered was bodied by B & B in 1930s style with separate wings and headlamps, reputedly for King Khaled of Saudi Arabia.

Sports Cars and Coupés: the New Generation

The 190SL was phased out in February 1963, and the following month's Geneva Show saw its replacement, the 230SL. This had a new wider and more spacious body, though still only a 2-seater, and was powered by a 2281cc 6-cylinder engine that later went into the 230 saloon. This 150bhp fuel injection unit gave the 230SL a top speed of 124mph (198km/h), or 121mph (195km/h) with the optional automatic gearbox. Soon after the car was launched Eugène Bohringer won the Spa-Sofia-Liège Rally in one, which gave the 230SL some sporting credibility, though many people felt that it was not powerful enough.

To remedy this, Daimler-Benz installed a 2496cc engine in 1966 (250SL), followed by the 2778cc 280SL which was made from 1967 to 1971. This developed 180bhp, and gave the car a top speed of 121mph (195km/h). 4- or 5-speed gearboxes were available as well as a 4-speed automatic. The 5-speed box was also available on the 230SL and 250SL, though not very often bought. Coupé or roadster bodies could be had, the latter with a detachable hard-top. Production figures for this series of sports cars were 19,831 230SLs (1965–67), 5196 250SLs (1966–68) and 23,885 280SLs (1967–71), making it by far the most popular Mercedes Benz sports car.

The replacement for the 280SL was a larger car, heavier by 364lbs and less sporting in appearance, more of a high performance motorway express. This was the 350SL powered by a 3499cc V8 engine, and its companion the 4520cc 450SL. The V8 engines and the suspension were those of the S Class saloons. Most were supplied with automatic transmission, four speeds up to July 1972, thereafter three speeds. They were made up to 1980, the majority with the 4½-litre engine (66,298 compared with 15,304). In 1972 the 2-seater SLs were joined by the SLC 4-seater coupés, also available with 3½ or 4½-litre V8 engines. They had longer wheelbases and were intended as replacements for the 220/250/280SEC coupés of the 1960s. Top speed was 130mph (208km/h) with the smaller engine, 134mph (214km/h) with the larger (about 3mph (5km/h) less with automatic transmission). From 1974–82 there was a 280SLC with twin-ohc 6-cylinder engine, and from 1977-81 a 5-litre model known first as the 450SEC 5.0, and then more simply as the 500SEC. These were not supplied with manual gearboxes, and had a top speed of 140mph (224km/h). Only 2769 were made, with two sizes of engine, 4990 and 4973cc.

The SL roadsters were continued into the 1980s with different engines, but little changed in appearance. In 1988 models were 2962cc 6-cylinder 300SL, 4196cc V8 420SL and 4973cc 500SL. They were not sports cars, but as British journalist John Simister summed them up: 'Cars to appeal to lovers of beautifully made artefacts who want to enjoy some wind in their hair'.

The 4-seater coupés were extensively restyled in 1980, with body lines derived from the W126 saloons, yet with a horizontal grill to proclaim them as part of the sporting range. They were only available with V8 engines, the 3839cc 380SEC, and 4973cc 500SEC. In 1999 the latter still was being made, but the smaller engine had grown to 4196cc (420SEC) and for the highest performance the range included the 5547cc 560 SEC. This developed 300bhp and gave the 4-seater coupé a top speed of 148 mph (238km/h).

Saloon Development 1968 Onwards

The story of Mercedes-Benz saloons over the past thirty years is one of continuous improvement rather than any dramatic changes. 1968 saw new, more aerodynamic bodies distinguished by vertical headlamp units. They were known as the W114/115 bodies, and came with a wide variety of engines, 200, 200D, 220, 220D, 230, 240D, 250, 280. As well as the saloons, there were 2-door coupés with the 250 and 280 engines, and two limousines with 220D or 230 engines. The larger saloons of 1968–72 had similar bodies (code number W108), and the 6-cylinder 280 engine or the 3499cc V8 350 engine. Some had longer wheelbases (300SEL), and the top of the range was the 300SEL 6.3.

The W114/115 bodies were replaced in 1975 by the W123, restyled with horizontal headlamp clusters, and available with five different engine sizes (200, 230, 250, 280, 300) in carburettor and fuel-injected versions, and four diesels, 200D, 220D, 240D, and 300D. The 300D was the largest diesel passenger car made by Daimler-Benz, and had a unique 5-cylinder engine, effectively the 240D plus one extra cylinder. As before, coupés and limousines were available in the W123 range and, from 1978, estate cars. The W123 bodies were made until 1984, when they were replaced by the more aerodynamic W124s powered by 200, 230, 260 and 320 petrol engines, and 200D (4-cylinder), 250D (5-cylinder) and 300D (6-cylinder) diesels. From 1985 the 300D was turbocharged, a feature also found on the earlier 5-cylinder 300D for the American market.

The larger Mercedes saloons received a new W116 body in 1972, engine options being the 6-cylinder 280 and V8 350 or 450. The SEL models had an extra 4in (102mm) of wheelbase, and while the 280 offered a choice of manual or automatic transmission, the larger models were available only with automatics. They were superb cars, enabling Mercedes-Benz to make a very real challenge to Rolls-Royce for the title 'The Best Car in the World'. For those who wanted the ultimate in performance there was the 450SEL 6.9 which used the 450 engine enlarged to 6834cc in the 450SEL bodyshell. Unlike the 'ordinary' 450 it had the hydro-pneumatic suspension of the 600. Top speed was 143mph (229km/h), quite remarkable for a 5-seater saloon, but one paid for the experience – 1977 prices were DM45,800 for a 450SEL, and DM73,100 for the 6.9. A total of 7380 were made between 1975 and 1980, compared with 44,274 of the SEL. James Hunt, former British Formula One champion, owned two 6.9s.

The 1979 Frankfurt Show saw a further development for the large Mercedes saloons in the shape of the W126 body. This was lower and more aerodynamic, with a 14 per cent better drag co-efficient than the W116. It was made in seven models and two wheelbases, from the 6-cylinder 280 to the V8 500. In 1980 the range was augmented by the coupés, 380SEC and 500SEC, and in 1985 more V8 engines were available, the 4196cc 420 and 5547cc 560. The latter was available only in the 560 SEC coupé and 560SEL long wheelbase saloon.

In December 1982 Daimler-Benz brought out a new car, smaller than their existing models, to give them an entry into a market dominated by BMW. The 190 was powered by a 1997cc 4-cylinder single-ohc engine developing 90bhp. The 4-door saloon body (W201) was a smaller version of the W126, and there was a choice of manual (4 or 5 speeds) or automatic (4 speed) gearboxes. It had irs, the first non-swing axle from Mercedes-Benz. The first 100,000 190s were built in twelve months, and production was increased further when a new factory was opened at Bremen in 1984. The 190 range was soon extended by a number of different engines. A 1997cc 4-cylinder diesel was available from the start, followed by a 2497cc 5-cylinder diesel in 1984, while the high-performance model was the 190E 2.3-16, with a Cosworth-developed 16-valve 2299cc engine developing 186bhp. Capacity went up to 2498cc (195bhp) in 1988, and 1990 saw a limited edition Evolution 11 version with 235bhp and a large rear wing.

The mid-range W124 saloons (200–300 and 300E) received new bodies and irs in 1985 and 1988, and were available in estate car form and with 4-wheel drive. There were also coupés on a shortened W124 floorpan, while the big SL roadsters were continued to 1989 when they were replaced by new SLs with 2960cc V6 or 4973cc V8 engines. In 1992 the SL was available with the 5987cc V12 engine also used in the top-of-the-range S-Class saloons, and in 1998 new V6 (2799 and 3199cc) and 4966cc V8 engines were adopted. These and the V12 made up the SL's engine range for 1999.

The big S Series saloons were continued through the 1980s, with new V8 engines of 4196 and 5547cc from 1985. The 48-valve 5987cc V12 with 408bhp was added to the engine options in 1992. During the decade the S Series came to seem overlarge and out of step with current green thinking. The new S, introduced in October 1998, was considerably lightened and slimmed down, being shorter and narrower and weighing 660lb less than its predecessor. The V12 engine was no longer an option on the S, though a new V12 with three valves per cylinder was promised for early 2000. The V6 and V8 engines had the 3-valve layout from October 1998. In 1993 the 190 was renamed the C Class, and the 200/400 Series (W124) the E Class. Both were available with a wide range of petrol and diesel engines, the E Class having seven petrol and four diesels, from a 1996cc four to a 4973cc V8 in petrol units, and 1997 to 2996cc diesels. An estate car joined the C range in June 1997, and a 2398cc V6 engine in the autumn. In the spring of 2000 a new C-class range appeared, with lower, restyled bodies. Power options included four petrol engines, two fours and two V6s, and three common-rail diesels.

An entry in the smaller sports car class came in 1996 with the SLK roadster. This came with 1998 or 2295cc 4-cylinder engines. The smaller unit gave 136bhp, or 192bhp with Roots-type supercharger and for 2000 a 218bhp 3199cc V6 was available. At the other end of the scale was the CLK GTR coupé. A road-going version of Mercedes' 1998 GT Championship winning cars, it had a mid-mounted 6998cc V12 giving 612bhp and a top speed of 200mph (320km/h); 0–60mph (0-96km/h) took 3.9 seconds and 0–125mph (0-200km/h) 9.9 seconds. A very limited production run of 25 cars was planned, selling for around £1.1 million each. It was assembled by AMG who also prepared tuned versions of lesser Mercedes, and hand-built a very small number of SL Gullwings and 600 Pullmans with modern engines. Other AMG-prepared models included a 4×4 E Class saloon with 354bhp 5.4-litre V8 engine, the same engine in the CLK55 coupé, and an S Class limousine with wheelbase stretched to 161in (4085mm) and overall elngth of 242.4in (6158mm).

In 1997 Mercedes-Benz entered completely fresh territory for them with the A Class, a 4-door 'one box' saloon only 140in (3553mm) long, with engine and gearbox housed under the floor and driving the front wheels. There were three 4-cylinder engine options, 1397 and 1598cc petrol and 1689cc diesel, and a choice of 5-speed manual or 4-speed automatic gearboxes. The rear suspension was redesigned after a media-hyped incident in which an A Class overturned during a high-speed reversing test. Though expensive for its size, the A Class has proved very popular, and more than 400,000 had been sold by March 2000. A twin-engined A Class, with one 1.9-litre 16-valve engine at the front and another at the rear, was shown at the 1999 Geneva Show, with the possibility of a limited production run of 300 cars.

The 1999 Mercedes-Benz line-up was a large one, with A, C, E and S saloons, estates in the C and E ranges, the CLK cabriolet and coupé, CL coupé based on S Class, SLK and SL roadster, and CLK GTR. There were also separate off-roaders described below. Future plans included coupé and hatchback in the

1982 Mercedes-Benz (i) 500SEL coupé.
NICK GEORGANO

1990 Mercedes-Benz (i) 300/500SL sports car.
DAIMLER-BENZ

1992 Mercedes-Benz (i) 190D saloon.
NICK BALDWIN

re-styled C Class, the 557bhp 5496cc V8-engined SLR coupé developed in conjunction with McLaren, and the range-topping Maybach luxury saloon, to be powered by a V12 engine.

The Off-road Cars

In 1979 Daimler-Benz entered the growing market for 4×4 passenger vehicles. The G-Wagen, or Geländewagen to give it its full name, originated as a military vehicle, but when it was rejected by the German Army in favour of the VW Iltis, the makers offered it to civilian buyers. Made in two wheelbases, 94.5 (2398mm) and 112in (2843mm), and with a variety of engines from the 230 to the 300, in petrol and diesel form, the G-Wagen could be had with estate car bodywork, as an open pick-up or panel van. The engines and transmissions were made in Germany, and the chassis and bodies by Steyr-Daimler-Puch in Austria, where final assembly took place. They were marketed by Mercedes-Benz dealers, except in Austria, Switzerland, Yugoslavia and East European countries, where they were sold by Steyr dealers, and badged as a Puch. It was also made under licence by Peugeot for the French Army. Design changed little over the years, though a 2996cc 300D turbo diesel was available from 1996, and a 4966cc petrol V8 from 1998.

1998 Mercedes-Benz (i) A160 hatchback.
DAIMLER-BENZ

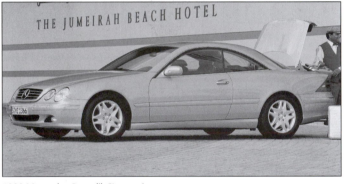

1999 Mercedes-Benz (i) CL coupé.
DAIMLERCHRYSLER

1999 Mercedes-Benz (i) SLK roadster.
DAIMLERCHRYSLER

If the G Class was Mercedes' Land Rover Defender, the M Class introduced in 1997 was their Range Rover, and a rival to BMW's X5. It had a 5-door body and offered a choice of three engines, 2295cc four, 3199cc V6 and 4266cc V8. A 5.5-litre AMG-prepared V8 was planned for a late 1999 introduction.

In May 1998 Daimler-Benz merged with Chrysler, having the larger share (57 per cent) in the £24 billion group
NG

Further Reading
Mercedes-Benz Personenwagen 1886–1986, Werner Oswald, Motorbuch Verlag, 1986.
The Star and the Laurel, Beverly Rae Kimes, Mercedes-Benz of North America, 1986.
Mercedes-Benz, the Supercharged 8-cylinder cars of the 1930s, Jan Melin, Johnson & Co., Gothenburg, 1990.
Mercedes-Benz Production Models, 1946–1983, W. Robert Nitzke, Motorbooks International, 1983.
Mercedes-Benz Since 1945, a Collector's Guide (3 volumes), James Taylor, Motor Racing Publications, 1985, 1986.
Mercedes-Benz Roadsters, L.J.K. Setright, Osprey, 1979.
Mercedes-Benz Saloons, F. Wilson McComb, Osprey, 1981.
Mercedes-Benz Diesel Automobiles, W. Robert Nitzke, Motorbooks International, 1981.

MERCEDES-BENZ (ii) **(BR)** 1999 to date
Mercedes-Benz, Juiz de Fora, Minas Gerais.
Mercedes-Benz were the first commercial vehicle manufacturers who started production in Brazil, under the auspices of the government, in 1956. They built a new industrial plant in Juiz de Fora, near São Paulo, in the Minas Gerais State. This plant cost $820 million and they planned to make 40,000 of the small Class A 4-door saloons in 1999, reaching a yearly production of 70,000 in 2000. They aimed to sell these vehicles in Argentina, Brazil, Uruguay, Paraguay, Chile, Venezuela, Colombia, and Mexico.
ACT

MERCER (US) 1910–1925; 1930
1910 Mercer Autocar Co., Trenton, New Jersey.
1910–1919 Mercer Automobile Co., Trenton, New Jersey.
1919–1925 Mercer Motors Co., Trenton, New Jersey.
1929–1930 Elcar Motor Car Co., Elkhart, Indiana.
Named after Mercer County in New Jersey, where the car was made, the Mercer was one of the two most celebrated American sporting cars, the other being the Stutz Bearcat. In fact, the Type 35 Raceabout which earned the make's fame only made up a small proportion of the total output of Mercers.

The Mercer company grew out of the short-lived ROEBLING-PLANCHE company which had made cars in Trenton in 1909, backed by the wealthy Roebling family (who amongst other engineering work had built the Brooklyn Bridge), and designed by Étienne Planche (who later helped Louis Chevrolet with his first car). They used the factory occupied by the makers of the WALTER car, for which Planche worked, but in 1909 William Walter moved back to New York, and the Roeblings decided to make a new car which they called the Mercer. Unlike the Roebling-Planche it had shaft drive, used a proprietary engine by Beaver, and was made as a tourer, toy tonneau and speedster. Planche may have had a hand in its design, but he soon left Mercer and was replaced by Finlay Robertson Porter (1872–1964). It was Porter who set the new company on its path to fame by designing a 4916 cc 4-cylinder T-head engine which went into a toy tonneau and raceabout for 1911. The latter had a robust but light frame and sketchy body consisting of two seats ahead of a bolster fuel tank, behind which was a small toolbox and two spare tyres. There was no windscreen, although some cars were fitted with a monocle screen for the driver, but this cannot have afforded much protection, and a pair of goggles was much more effective. The Raceabout was capable of about 75mph (120km/h) and was widely used for racing, often being driven to the venue with its wings and lights in position. These would be removed for the race, then re-installed for the return home. The Raceabout was known by different suffixes during the years that it was made, 35R for 1911, 35C for 1912, and 35J for 1913 and 1914. At the same time there were other Type 35s, a Runabout which was a much staider vehicle with windscreen, doors and a hood, a tourer and a limousine which was used as a taxicab as well as for private service.

The driving force behind the Raceabout's development was Washington A. Roebling, and his death on the Titanic in April 1912 marked the end of the best days of Mercer. Other members of the family felt that the 35 needed replacing with a more up-to-date design, but could not convince Porter of the necessity of this. He left in early 1914 and moved to Long Island where he built the F.R.P. His replacement at Mercer was Erik H. Delling, who had built a successful racing car called the Deltal. The car he designed for Mercer was based on this, a 4-cylinder L-head engine with a very long stroke (95 × 171mm) and a capacity of 4846cc. Though about the same size as Porter's T-head engine, it gave 72bhp against 60bhp from the older design. Like the Type 35, the new 22/70 came with a variety of bodies, from Raceabout to limousine, though the latter did not reach the catalogue until 1916. Delling's Raceabout was less stark than Porter's, with sides to the body (though no doors yet), wire wheels and electric starting. A windscreen was standardised from 1919. It was faster than its predecessor, but was raced less, largely because the era of the privately-entered car which could be driven home after the event was practically over by 1915.

By 1918 all three founding members of the Roebling family had died, and the heirs put Mercer up for sale the following year. It was bought by a Wall Street investment group headed by Emlen S. Hare who dreamed of an empire of upmarket cars, and also bought LOCOMOBILE and CRANE-SIMPLEX. He planned to increase Mercer production to 50,000 cars per year, which was an idea doomed from the start given the car's price and the fact that they made no more than 857 cars in 1919. Hare sold Mercer back to the Kuser family, who had been original investors with the Roeblings, and production of the Delling design continued, now called the Series 5. However the cars grew less interesting. Up to 1922 the Raceabout had staggered seating, to give the driver ample elbow room for fast manoeuvring, but this was replaced by an ordinary bench seat. For 1923 the 4-cylinder engine gave way to a proprietary unit, a 5429cc 6-cylinder ohv Rochester giving 84bhp. The only 4-cylinder cars made after 1922 were completed from left-over components. The so-called Raceabout was now a sedate-looking 2-seater with dickey seat, no more sporting in appearance than the old Runabout. A new 6-cylinder line with front-wheel brakes was introduced in September 1924, and they managed to make 287 cars in 1925. That was the end, though, and in 1926 the Trenton factory was sold to the Roller Bearing Co. of America. The name was acquired by former Chevrolet manager Harry M. Wahl, who hoped to have a new Mercer built at the Elkhart, Indiana factory of ELCAR. In 1929 Mercer's chief designer Mike Graffis came up with a new car to be powered by a 140bhp straight-8 Continental engine, with bodies by Merrimac. A change of plan led Wahl to consider manufacture in part of the Standard Steel Car Co.'s factory at Butler, Pennsylvania, where the AMERICAN AUSTIN was being made, but this never came to fruition, and the two cars that were built came from Elcar. A chassis and a convertible were shown in New York in January 1930, but Wahl had spent all his available money on them, and with a deepening depression he could obtain no more.

NG

1999 Mercedes-Benz (i) S500L saloon.
DAIMLERCHRYSLER

1915 Mercer 22-70 sedan.
NICK BALDWIN

1921 Mercer Series 5 tourer.
JOHN A. CONDE

Further Reading
'The remarkable Roeblings and their Raceabouts', Tony Muldoon, *Automobile Quarterly*, Vol. 34, No. 3.
The One and Only 1931 Mercer, Ken Gross, SIA, December 1982.

MERCILESS (US) 1906–1907

Huntington Automobile Co., Huntington, New York.
The curious and unsympathetic name of this car (would even Mr Toad have called his car a Merciless?) was apparently chosen because it resembled Mercedes, and the car was also Mercedes-like, with a 70hp 6-cylinder engine. It was designed by John F. McMulkin, a former engineer with American Mercedes, which had recently ceased production due to a factory fire. At least four cars were made before bankruptcy ensued in December 1907.

NG

MERCUR *see* EGO

1918 Mercury (iv) chassis.
NICK BALDWIN

1941 Mercury (vi) coupé.
NATIONAL MOTOR MUSEUM

1953 Mercury (vi) Monterey convertible.
NATIONAL MOTOR MUSEUM

MERCURY (i) (US) 1903–1904
Mercury Machine Co., Philadelphia, Pennsylvania.
The first of many makes to bear the name Mercury was a light 2-seater powered by a 7hp single-cylinder engine, with 3-speed gearbox and shaft drive. It had an angle-iron frame and semi-elliptic springs all round. The price was $925.
NG

MERCURY (ii) (GB) 1905
Ivanhoe Motor Co., Cricklewood, London.
This company made a small number of 24hp 4-cylinder cars which also went under the name Ivanhoe. In 1906 they became agents for WEIGEL and planned to show these cars on their stand at Olympia, though they had applied to show Ivanhoes. For this they were refused permission to exhibit the Weigels, and only second-hand cars were seen on their stand.
NG

MERCURY (iii) (US) 1913–1914
Mercury Cyclecar Co., Detroit, Michigan.

This cyclecar was quite typical in its engine and transmission, a 9.8hp V-twin De Luxe with drive via friction transmission and belt final drive. Less usual was its body which was of unitary construction suspended by a transverse semi-elliptic spring at the front and two quarter-elliptics below the axle at the rear. It was made in three styles, a tandem 2-seater, a single-seater with space at the rear for traveller's samples, and a single-seater delivery van. The company gained a boost when their cyclecar was chosen by the Michigan State Automobile School for driving instruction, but still went under in August 1914. The factory was later owned by the makers of the STORMS electric cyclecar which had an even shorter life.
NG

MERCURY (iv) (GB) 1914–1923
1914–1919 Medina Engineering Co. Ltd, Twickenham, Middlesex.
1919–1923 Mercury Cars Ltd, Twickenham, Middlesex.
This Mercury was a good example of the 'large car in miniature' theme exemplified by better-known makes such as Calcott and Singer. It was powered by a 1298cc 4-cylinder engine said to be of Medina-Hastings manufacture, i.e. in their own works. A new company was formed after the war, operating from a different address but still in Twickenham. A 2-seater with the same engine was shown at Olympia in 1919, and another Mercury appeared on the stand of coachbuilders W.H. Arnold with 2-door all-weather saloon body. Apart from this, most coachwork on Mercury chassis was made by Mercury themselves. By April 1920 they claimed that 200 cars were on the road. A new model with larger engine of 1794cc joined the smaller cars at the 1920 White City Show, but seems only to have been listed for the 1921 season. It was Mercury's last Show appearance, and the cars were not made after 1923. Like many others, the company was a victim of competition from mass-production cars like Morris.
NG
Further Reading
'Distant Memory', M. Worthington-Williams, *The Automobile*, June 1997.

MERCURY (v) (US) 1918–1920
Mercury Cars, Inc, Hollis, New York.
The Mercury was a low-production car featuring a Weidely 4-cylinder engine, a 114in (2893mm) wheelbase and a complete line of open and closed bodies. The Mercury was a light car and promoted as economical in operation and maintenance which was probably true, the 4-seater touring model weighing only 2800lbs. Among its features was a door mounted on the floor for ready access to the brake mechanism. The Mercury was priced from $2750 to $3900 and production was small. The Mercury should not be confused with either the Mercury of Cleveland, Ohio, announced in 1920 or the Mercury of Belfast, New York, rumoured to feature a 4-cylinder Rochester-Duesenberg engine. In all probability, neither of these Mercurys went beyond the planning stage.
KM

MERCURY (vi) (US) 1938 to date
Ford Motor Co., Dearborn, Michigan.
It is one of the ironies of history that Edsel Ford should have his name linked with the disastrous Edsel car, made fourteen years after his death, when the car he was really responsible for was the Mercury, a success from the start. At the end of the 1930s everyone at Ford was aware that there was a big gap between the low-priced Ford V8 and the upper-medium-priced Lincoln Zephyr V12. This meant that Ford owners who wanted to trade up but could not afford a Lincoln inevitably went to a rival make, probably a Dodge or Pontiac. Edsel was determined to plug this gap, and gathered a team of engineers and stylists led by E.T. (Bob) Gregorie. The car had to have its own name, and of the 103 suggestions, Edsel himself selected Mercury.
Launched in November 1938 as a 1939 model, the Mercury bore a strong family resemblance to the 1939 Ford, with a touch of Lincoln Zephyr about it as well. However, there were no body panels common to Ford and Mercury, and the latter had an extra 4in (101mm) in the wheelbase. Importantly the extra inches were not in the bonnet or engine compartment but in the passenger area. The Mercury's engine was a larger and more powerful V8 which had already been supplied in Fords used by police forces, and in some trucks. It had an extra 3.175mm bore, giving a capacity of 3917cc and 95bhp, compared with the Ford's 3622cc and 85bhp. The 4-door sedan at $917 cost $167 more than a De Luxe

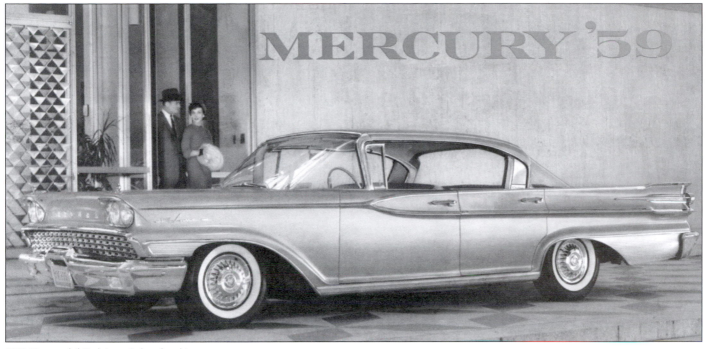

1959 Mercury (vi) Park Lane 4-door hard-top.
NICK BALDWIN

Ford, but was $40 less than Buick's cheapest 4-door sedan. The Mercury shared the hydraulic brakes introduced on the 1939 Fords. Four body styles were offered in the 1939 line-up, 2- and 4-door sedans, coupé and convertible.

Production during the first season was an encouraging 70,835. This figure included US and Canadian output, and manufacture in a surprising number of Ford's overseas plants, including Mexico, Brazil, France, Holland, Denmark, Belgium and Rumania. The Mercury was little changed for 1940, though there was a new body style in the shape of a 4-door convertible sedan. This was the most expensive of the line, at $1212. Few American firms were offering this style by 1940 (Ford had just dropped it at the end of the 1939 season), and Mercury listed it only for one season. Only 1083 were made, and Ford did not offer a 4-door convertible again until the 1961 Lincoln Continental. A longer wheelbase and boxier styling following that of Ford identified the 1941 models, while the 1942s were slightly restyled, had 100bhp engines and the option of Liquimatic drive, an automatic transmission also offered on Lincolns. It was not very satisfactory, and Mercury did not offer an automatic again until 1951.

There were few changes in the 1946–48 Mercurys, apart from a restyled grill and one new body style, the Sportsman convertible. This had mahogany panelling with maple or yellow birch framing, and cost $200 more than the companion Sportsman made by Ford. Only offered for the 1946 season, just 205 were sold, making it one of the rarest Mercury styles. Overall sales for the 1946 season were 86,597, and for 1947, 85,378. The all-new 1949 models were launched, very early, on 29 April 1948. For the first time their styling was more reminiscent of Lincoln than of Ford, a reflection of the fact that a separate Lincoln-Mercury Division had been set up in 1947. Indeed the Mercury shared body panels with the smaller Lincolns. Although the wheelbase was unchanged at 118in (2995mm), the new Mercurys looked longer than their predecessors, and were among the sleekest of the 1949 US cars. Engine capacity was increased to 4185cc and power to 110bhp. Other features included ifs and hypoid rear axles. Production rose sharply to 301,307, though this covered a longer model run than usual, from April 1948 to August 1949. There were few styling changes for 1950 or 1951, and the main technical development was the adoption for 1951 of Merc-O-Matic automatic transmission, a 2-speed system developed in co-operation with Borg-Warner. New styling shared with Lincoln appeared on the 1952 Mercurys; they had flatter topped bonnets giving a wider look, and wrap-around rear windows on the coupés. New Lincoln-Mercury assembly plants opened at St Louis, Los Angeles and Metuchen, New Jersey. The first two were dedicated to Mercury production, but at Metuchen this was shared with the smaller Lincolns.

1967 Mercury (vi) Cougar coupé.
LINCOLN-MERCURY

Two series of Mercury were offered for 1953, the Custom sedans and hard-top, and the Monterey convertible, hard-top, station wagon and sedan. Although using the same bodies and engines, the Montereys were better equipped and came in dual colour schemes. In 1954 the Sun Valley transparent-topped coupé was offered in the Monterey line. This was similar to Ford's Sunliner, having a plastic roof tinted at the front. Customers complained that it heated up like an oven, and it was dropped at the end of the 1955 season after 11,528 had been made. A more important development for 1954 was the adoption of an ohv V8 engine in Mercurys and Fords. Only slightly larger than the side-valve unit (4195 against 4185cc), it had oversquare dimensions and more power, 160bhp. No soon than it was introduced than the new engine was enlarged, 1955 units having 4785cc and 188 or 198bhp. A new top-of-the-line model appeared called the Montclair, which used the more powerful engine and was available only with automatic transmission.

In line with other American makes Mercurys grew ever larger in the 1950s, with a new 122in (3096mm) wheelbase for 1957, and two engines, a 5113cc for 1956 joined by a 6030cc for 1957. Mercury's largest engine ran to 7046cc and 360bhp, and was made from 1958 to 1960 only. The most dramatic-looking model of the period was the Turnpike Cruiser, a convertible or hard-top with retractable reverse-slant rear window, air ducts mounted on top of the windscreen, push-button control for the Merc-O-Matic transmission, and Seat-O-Matic power-operated seats with 49 pre-set positions held in a memory bank. It was the kind of car which symbolises the gadget-laden 1950s to today's collectors, but did not sell well. Prices ran from $3758 to $4103, several hundred dollars

1969 Mercury (vi) Colony Park station wagon.
NICK BALDWIN

1978 Mercury (vi) Monarch Ghia sedan.
NICK BALDWIN

1987 Mercury (vi) Sable sedan.
LINCOLN-MERCURY

1989 Mercury (vi) Cougar coupé.
LINCOLN-MERCURY

above other Mercurys. Production boomed in the mid–1950s, peaking at 328,778 in the 1955 model year. However, they dropped dramatically to 133,271 in 1958. The middle of the market, which Mercury occupied, was shrinking, and a new line was urgently needed.

Ford introduced their Falcon compact at the end of 1959, and Mercury followed with their version in March 1960. The Comet was a dressed up Falcon, sharing the same 2365cc 6-cylinder engine, though styling was on the lines of the larger Mercurys, and the wheelbase was 5in (127mm) longer. Three body styles were offered, 2- and 4-door sedans and a station wagon. Prices ran from $1998 to $2365. The Comet sold well, first year figures being 116,331. Added to 155,010 larger Mercurys, this made for a much more encouraging picture. A more sporty Comet sedan with bucket seats was introduced for 1961 under the name S-22, when all Comets were available with a 2785cc engine. Hard-top and convertible versions of the S-22 were available in 1963, and for 1964 it was renamed the Caliente. More powerful V8 engines became available in all Comets. These were the famous 260 and 289 units used in Mustangs and the early Cobras, so they gave the Comet plenty of performance. By 1966 it was no longer a compact, but became an intermediate, sharing the Ford Fairlane's bodyshell.

A 3654cc 6-cylinder engine was also used in the full-size Mercury Meteor and Commuter for 1961, when the largest standard engine was a 4785cc V8. Optional engines went up to 6390cc. The Monterey and Montclair were continued through the 1960s, part of an increasingly complex range of full-size cars. More expensive than either of these, though on the same wheelbase and offered with the same engine options, were the Park Lane sedan, hard-top and convertible, and the Marquis made only as a hard-top until 1969, when it was offered with a variety of bodies, replacing the Park Lane.

For 1967 Mercury introduced their version of the highly successful Ford Mustang. Named the Cougar, it was a 4-seater coupé on a shorter wheelbase than any other Mercury, although 3in (76mm) longer than a Mustang, with a choice of engines, the 4736cc 289 as standard, with the 6390cc unit as an option. From 1968 there were higher performance Cougars, the GT and GTE which used the 6997cc 427 engine giving up to 390bhp. A variety of options to improve handling and performance was available on Cougars of this period. The XR-7 was the luxury version, with leather interior and simulated walnut dashboard. 1969 saw the Cougar Eliminator, a high-performance model offered with a choice of high-revving Boss 302 engine from the Boss Mustang or the 351 or 428 (5752 or 7014cc) engines, with or without Ram Air induction. Disc brakes on front wheels and a choice of wide or close ratio 4-speed manual gearboxes were features of the Eliminators, which gave 400bhp in their most powerful form. This made them, like the contemporary Mustangs, muscle cars rather than the pony cars from which they were developed.

The first Cougars sold the best, with 123,672 standard models and 27,221 XR-7s finding customers in the 1967 model year. The next season saw 81,014 regular Cougars and 32,712 XR-7s sold, while in 1969, when a convertible was offered for the first time, the figures were 72,127 Cougars and 27,942 XR-7s. Total Cougar production was only 72,363 for 1970, of which 20,542 were XR-7s, and 2200 Eliminators. Emission regulations caused the Eliminator to be dropped after 1970, and subsequent Cougars were less powerful. The last convertible was made in 1973, and for 1974 the Cougar became a sporty coupé version of the Montego 4-door sedan. Three years later the Montego name was dropped, and the entire range of intermediate Mercurys acquired the Cougar name.

In the 1970s the Mercury range became wider and more complex than ever. The German-built Ford Capri was sold by Lincoln-Mercury dealers from the summer of 1970, while another import handled by them was the De Tomaso Pantera mid-engined coupé, of which about 4000 were sold between 1970 and 1974. Of the domestically-built cars, the Comet name was revived in 1971 for Mercury's version of the Ford Maverick 2-door sedan. The standard engine was a 2785cc six, but 3277 and 4096cc sixes or the 4949cc 302 V8 were options. Later Comets had 4- as well as 2-door sedan bodies, and were made up to 1977. The next size up was the Montego (1968–77), an intermediate car made in sedan, coupé and station wagon forms from the 4096cc six to the 7014cc V8. The more expensive Montego sedans were called Broughams and the station wagons Villagers, though not for every year that they were made.

For 1975 Mercury brought out a 'precision-size luxury car' named the Monarch. About the same overall size as the Comet, the Monarch was better trimmed,

2000 Mercury (vi) Cougar coupé.
FORD MOTOR CO.

particularly in its Ghia versions, had completely different styling closer to that of the full-size Mercurys, and was quite a bit more expensive. Ford's version was the Granada.

The big Mercurys of the early 1970s were quite similar to Lincolns in appearance, with concealed headlamps. They were large cars, with 124in (3147mm) wheelbases and overall lengths of 225in (5710mm), made in two series, the Monterey and the more expensive Marquis. Automatic transmission was standard and engines were V8s up to 7538cc. Because of emission controls even this largest engine gave only 275bhp in 1974 and 216bhp in 1975. The Marquis became the Grand Marquis in 1978, but despite the name it was a smaller car with 114in (2893mm) wheelbase, 214in (5431mm) overall length and the largest engine was a 5751cc V8.

In the 1950s and 1960s the Mercury was definitely a 'junior Lincoln' rather than a 'senior Ford', but from the mid–1970s onwards the Mercury range came closer to Ford's. The Bobcat, introduced in 1976, and the Zephyr of 1978 were more luxurious versions of Ford's Pinto and Fairmont. The latter replaced the Comet, and was listed with the Bobcat's 2294cc 4-cylinder engine, 3277cc six or 4949cc V8 options. The 1981 Mercury Lynx was the Division's version of the international front-drive Ford Escort. From 1982 to 1984 Mercury offered the LN7, Ford's Escort-based sporty coupé under another name.

The later 1980s Mercury range was Ford-based throughout: the Lynx in 3- or 5-door hatchback versions, the Topaz 2- or 4-door sedan (Ford Tempo), the Sable, a very aerodynamic 4-door sedan or station wagon (Ford Taurus), the Cougar sports coupé (Ford Thunderbird) and the Grand Marquis sedan or station wagon (Ford LTD Crown Victoria). The Cougar and Grand Marquis drove on the rear wheels, all the others were front-driven. Mercury also sold the Tracer hatchback which was a Mazda 323 assembled in Mexico, and the German-built Merkur XR4Ti and Scorpio. In 1990 they began to sell the Capri coupé, also Mazda-derived but built in Australia. These models were continued through 1994, when the Capri was dropped, joined in 1993 by the Villager MPV (also sold under the name Nissan Quest) which was Ford-built even though it carried the Nissan name. In 1998 the Topaz gave way to the Mystique (Ford Contour, which was the American version of the European Mondeo). The first Mercury-badged 4×4 appeared in 1996 under the name Mountaineer, being a slightly restyled Ford Explorer. Otherwise the Tracer, Mystique, Sable, Grand Marquis

2000 Mercury (vi) Grand Marquis LS sedan.
FORD MOTOR CO.

and Villager were still offered in 1999. The rear-drive Cougar disappeared at the same time as the Ford Thunderbird, but the Cougar name went onto a front-drive Mondeo-based coupé. The Contour/Mystique was dropped during 2000, as Ford no longer saw the Mondeo as a world car.

NG

Further Reading
The cars of Lincoln and Mercury, George Dammann and James K. Wagner, Crestline Publishing, 1987.
'Genesis of Mercury', James K. Wagner, *Automobile Quarterly*, Vol. 35, No. 1.

MERCURY (vii) **(GB)** 1991 to date
1991–1993 KaRa Sports Cars, Southend, Essex.
1993–1998 Mercury Motorsport, Shoeburyness, Essex.
1998 to date R.S. Ltd, Shoeburyness, Essex.
This kit car started life in 1991 as the KaRa 430, but from 1993 became the Mercury Motorsport EVO 200. It was plainly inspired by the Group B Ford RS200

1921 Merit Model B tourer.
KEITH MARVIN

1982 Merlin (iii) sports car.
NICK GEORGANO

racer, even though every panel of its fibreglass body was in fact different. The space frame chassis had a 6-point roll-over cage and side impact bars built in, and was designed for Ford Sierra-based suspension, steering and brakes. Engine choices spanned Ford 4 cylinder or V6 engines (up to Cosworth), Renault V6, and even V8s, with optional Sierra 4×4 transmission.

CR

MERIT (US) 1921–1922

Merit Motor Car Co., Cleveland, Ohio.

The short-lived Merit was a victim of the 1920–21 postwar recession and only produced 150 cars before its failure. The Merit had 129in (3274mm) and 119in (3020mm) wheelbases and was powered, first, by a Walker 6-cylinder engine through 1921 and, subsequently, by a Continental 7R, also a six. The earlier cars which were longer, were priced at $2245 for the coupé and touring car, the only body styles offered during the first year. With the shorter wheelbase in 1922, the price was $1985 for the same models plus a roadster. The last cars were sold in early 1923 and as 1923 models.

KM

MERKEL (US) 1905–1907; 1914

1905–1907 Merkel Motor Co., Milwaukee, Wisconsin.

1914 Joseph F. Merkel, Middletown, Ohio.

Joseph Merkel was a well-known maker of bicycles and motorcycles, in business from 1901 to 1917, who had two ventures into car production. The first was a shaft-driven runabout or tourer offered with three different sizes of 4-cylinder engine, 14/16, 20/24 and 35/40hp. He offered air- or water-cooling. In 1911 he moved to Middletown and three years later joined the cyclecar craze with a tandem 2-seater with 12hp 4-cylinder engine, 3-speed gearbox and shaft drive. This was unsuccessful even by the standards of cyclecar manufacture, and only two were made. After that Merkel abandoned 4-wheelers for good.

NG

MERLIN (i) (GB) 1913–1914

New Merlin Cycle Co., Birmingham.

This company specialised in supplying components 'for the construction of perfect Miniature or Light Cars', the catalogue claimed. Every component could be provided, including chassis for belt or shaft drive, and two sizes of engine, a 1099cc vertical twin or a 1098cc four, although they admitted that they did not make the engines, nor springs, tanks, radiators or mudguards. They also supplied a complete car under their name, which used a 9hp 2-cylinder Blumfield engine, so it is very likely that the engines which Merlin supplied separately were also Blumfields. They were priced at £33 or £48, and touring, sporting, coupé or cabriolet bodies with a framework of best selected ash cost from £10.

NG

MERLIN (ii) (AUS) 1955

Merlin Fibreglass Co., South Melbourne, Victoria.

The M.-M. Special of Massola and Molina was an early example of successful Holden-based competition cars and Silvio Massola saw it as the basis for a fibreglass-bodied sports car. He teamed up with Tom Hollinrake of Aviation Electroplating to get his design into production. On a chassis of 3in (76mm) tube with a 92in (2337mm) wheelbase and normal Holden track, all mechanicals were Holden, although the engine was modified and fitted with two carburettors. Weight was 1684lbs (764kg), but, for a sports car, it was wide and the 3-speed gearbox, with column shift, unusual. Six complete cars were sold and a further six shells sold for buyer fitting. Merlin concentrated on boats during the 1960s, since when, as Merlin Trans-electrics, it has produced industrial vehicles.

MG

MERLIN (iii) (GB) 1980 to date

1980–1985 Thoroughbred Cars, Shoeburyness, Essex.

1985–1992 Paris Cars, Southend, Essex.

1992 to date Merlin Sports Cars, Southend, Essex.

The rakish 1930s-style Merlin roadster originated in the USA under the name Witton Tiger and suffered with a VW Beetle engine stuck in the tail. Although briefly offered here in that guise, the definitive UK version was more suited to the domestic market. It had its own separate chassis and Ford Cortina MkIII/IV/V parts (with special trailing arm and Panhard rod rear suspension). A 2+2 version called the Monro in 1983 was soon renamed the +2, and a Ford Sierra-based chassis option arrived in 1992. Lotus had some input on chassis design after early criticisms.

CR

MERRALL-BROWN *see* M.B. (ii)

MERRY '01 (US) 1958–1962

American Air Products Corp., Fort Lauderdale, Florida.

Also known as the Merry Olds, this was a replica of the Curved Dash Oldsmobile. It used a 4hp single-cylinder air-cooled Clinton engine.

NG

MERZ (US) 1914

Merz Cyclecar Co., Indianapolis, Indiana.

Charles Merz was a former racing driver who joined the ranks of the cyclecar makers in 1914. Like so many of their kind, his car had a 9hp V-twin De Luxe engine, with transmission by friction discs and final drive by belt. The body seated two in tandem, and its most unusual feature was a single cyclops headlamp incorporated in the head of the dummy radiator.

NG

MESERVE (US) 1901–1904

W.F. Meserve, Canobie Lake, New Hampshire.

William Forest Meserve built a few cars of different designs to sell to friends, and although he said that he would build additional cars 'after designs suited to the individual taste of purchasers', he certainly never set up regular manufacture. His first, made in 1901, had a single-cylinder 2-stroke engine, and was followed by a steam truck which was in use locally for 20 years. He formed a company for truck manufacture, the Meserve Auto Truck Co., but built no further examples. His most ambitious car was a large tourer powered by a 32hp 4-cylinder 2-stroke

1960 Messerschmitt Tiger Tg500.
NATIONAL MOTOR MUSEUM

engine of his own design and manufacture. Completed in 1904, it seems to have been his last vehicle. He later ran a business assembling jail cells.

NG

MESSERSCHMITT (D) 1953–1964

1953–1956 Regensburger Stahl- und Metallblau GmbH, Regensburg.
1956–1964 Fahrzeug- und Machinenbau GmbH, Regensburg.

The Messerschmitt Kabinenroller (cabin scooter) was one of the first and among the most successful of the many minicars which enlivened the motoring scene in the 1950s. Although it bore the name of the famous aircraft builder, Willy Messerschmitt, he had little to do with the car's design. This was the work of the aeronautical engineer Fritz Fend who entered the road vehicle business in 1946 when he began the manufacture of a hand-propelled invalid car in a small works at Rosenheim in Upper Bavaria (see FEND).

By the end of 1951 Fend wanted to make an enclosed tandem 2-seater. Lacking the facilities in his small factory, he approached the Messerschmitt company, with which he had connections as an aeronautical engineer, and which was anxious to find work as aircraft manufacture was still forbidden to them. During 1952 Fend worked with Messerschmitt on his design. This was launched on the market in the Spring of 1953 under the name Messerschmitt KR175 (Kabinenroller 175cc). The 2-stroke Fichtel & Sachs engine actually had a capacity of 173cc, and developed 9bhp at 5250rpm. It drove through a 4-speed unsynchronised gearbox and chain to the rear wheel. The tubular steel chassis was combined with a monocoque tub which formed the lower part of the body. The upper part was a sheet metal pressing topped by a plexiglass canopy hinged at the side which opened to allow driver and passenger to get in. Steering was by handlebars and was very high geared, ¾ of a turn from lock to lock. At the 1954 Milan Fair the KR175 was offered for the Italian market under the name Mivalino, to be made by Metalmeccanica Italiana Valtrompia (MI-VAL), but few were built.

The KR175 sold well, appealing to motorcyclists who wanted more weatherproof transport, and to many customers who could afford its DM2470 price tag, but could not raise the DM4150 needed for the cheapest Volkswagen. Among the

1954 Messerschmitt KR175 3-wheeler.
NATIONAL MOTOR MUSEUM

many extras offered on the KR175 were a spare wheel, a jack, a luggage rack and a heater. From 1954 an electric starter was standard equipment, but no reverse gear was provided until the advent of the KR200 in 1955. This was not, in fact, a gear but a lever which reversed the running of the engine, only possible in a 2-stroke. The engine had to be switched off, then restarted after the lever had been actuated, when, theoretically, all four gears were available, with top being even faster than when the car was travelling forwards, thanks to better aerodynamics! It is not known if anyone was brave or foolish enough to put this into practice.

1925 Messier 1.6-litre tourer.
NICK BALDWIN

1909 Métallurgique 12/14hp coupé.
NICK BALDWIN

1914 Métallurgique limousine by Miesse.
NICK BALDWIN

Other improvements on the KR200 were a slightly larger engine of 191cc (10.2bhp), a foot throttle in place of the handlebar twist grip of the KR175, improved rear suspension and hydraulic shock absorbers on all three wheels. In 1957 a soft-top convertible version appeared, followed by a starker model without sidescreens, the only weather protection coming from a windscreen, folding top and side curtains. This was called the KR201 roadster. Later versions of this dispensed with the hinged top, entry being effected by climbing over the sides.

In 1956 the ban on German aircraft production was lifted, and Messerschmitt quickly became involved in important aviation work. Sales of the 3-wheeler were declining, due to competition from the BMW Isetta and Heinkel which offered more sociable side by side seating. The Messerschmitt directors were happy to sell the car project to Fritz Fend. He was allowed to keep the name and emblem, but he formed a new company, Fahrzeug- und Maschinenbau GmbH, Regensburg. Officially, the cars were now called FMR, though the public still thought of them as Messerschmitts.

The 3-wheelers were continued, but in 1958 Fend introduced the formidable Tg500, generally known as the Tiger, though he was not able to copyright this name. Externally it looked like a 4-wheeled KR200, and indeed the nose, front suspension and monocoque tub were taken from the 3-wheeler. The engine, however, was a 493cc vertical twin designed by Fichtel & Sachs but built by FMR, which developed 19.5bhp and gave the Tiger a top speed of 78mph (125km/h). The gearbox was still an unsynchronised 4-speeder, now with two overdrive speeds, but there was a conventional reverse gear. Available with cabin top or as an open roadster, the Tiger had considerable appeal to the sportsman, and its reputation in Britain was sharply boosted when one won the 1958 London Motor Club's Cats' Eyes Rally. However, its market was limited, and sales were only about 400, compared with about 8000 KR175s and 25,000 KR200s. The Tiger was dropped after 1961, but the KR200 continued to be made, in declining numbers, up to June 1964. In 1962 Fend built a prototype 4-wheeler.

NG

Further Reading
'Ist Das Nicht ein Kabinenroller?', Carl Wagner,
Automobile Quarterly, Vol. 11, No. 2.

MESSIER (F) 1924–1931

Georges Messier, Montrouge, Seine.
Georges Messier invented a compressed air suspension system in which the air was compressed by a small engine-driven pump and stored in a central reservoir before being distributed to columns on each of the four wheels. He fitted it first to a S.L.I.M.-Pilain chassis before starting small-scale manufacture under his own name. He used 4-cylinder C.I.M.E. engines to start with, the 1494cc ohc unit for competition cars and the 1598cc pushrod ohv unit for tourers and saloons. Later, he used American engines of 2770 and 3310c (6-cylinders), and 3692 and 4850cc (8-cylinders). The big straight-8 was a Lycoming, and the smaller engines probably were as well. The Lycoming 8 was used in the Type H chassis which came in two wheelbases, 134in (3401mm) and 142in (3604mm). Of the 50 Type H chassis made, more were bodied as ambulances than as private cars, as their suspension made them ideal for ambulance work. Georges Messier died in a riding accident in 1933, but his company later became an important manufacturer of hydraulic aircraft landing gear, while his air suspension provided the basis for the hydro-pneumatic system used in the Citroën DS from 1955 onwards.

NG

METALINE (GB) 1983 to date

Metaline Ltd, Wisbech, Cambridgeshire.
Metaline was one of the earliest British AC Cobra replicators and it had the unique feature of an all-aluminium body. However most production cars had a semi-space frame powder-coated chassis fitted with a semi-monocoque one-piece body in fibreglass with carbonfibre strengthening. Jaguar running gear was used, with optional anti-roll bars, and there were custom-made steering rack and pedals. Any small or big-block V8 engine was suitable, including very high output units. The company also operated under the name Brooker Automotive Developments.

CR

MÉTALLURGIQUE (B) 1901–1927

1901–1907 SA La Métallurgique, Marchienne-au-Pont.
1907–1927 SA L'Auto Métallurgique, Marchienne-au-Pont.
The parent company was founded in 1860 and became a prominent manufacturer of railway locomotives and rolling stock. By the 1890s they had three factories, but when they decided to venture into car manufacture none was suitable, as they were geared to heavy engineering. A new factory was built at Marchienne-au-Pont, and they showed their first cars at the 1901 Paris Salon. These were voiturettes, one with a 4½hp vertical twin engine under the seat, with a *vis-à-vis* body, and the other a similar engine but front mounted under a bonnet, and

with a 2-seater body. A larger car with vertical-twin engine appeared in 1902, but only about 25 cars were made that year. It was the arrival from Germany of Ernst Lehmann in 1903 which put Métallurgique on the map. A former Mercedes engineer, Lehmann designed for Métallurgique a range of engines, two twins and two fours, from 7 to 20CV, with mechanically operated inlet valves, high-tension magneto, steel frames and shaft drive. The twins were dropped at the end of the 1905 season, though two models were revived briefly in 1907/08. Métallurgique were mainly known for well-built 4-cylinder cars in the medium to large class. There were seven models in the 1907 range, from a 2798cc 16/20hp to a 9890cc 60/80hp. Their first monobloc four came in 1908, and their engines were unconventional in having *désaxé* crankshafts, that is, mounted slightly offset to the pistons, which was claimed to reduce friction and give a better balanced engine. Métallurgique never made a six, though they considered a V8 in 1914.

Foreign Connections

Although plans to build Métallurgiques in England came to nothing, they were made in France by GILLET-FOREST who wanted a more modern design to replace their horizontal-engined cars. From 1905 to 1907 they made several models of Métallurgique type, from an 8CV twin to a 40CV four. More important were Métallurgique's links with the German BERGMANN company. They had strong connections with Germany, thanks to Ernst Lehmann and Hans Aschoff who was their German agent. Bergmann were looking for a quality car to make under licence and built various sizes of Métallurgique from 1909 to 1914. They ranged from the 1696cc sold in Germany as the 6/18PS, to the 7.3-litre 38/90CV, which was a 29/70PS by German rating. Both German- and Belgian-built cars were sold in England, the chassis prefixes being BM and MM.

Métallurgique were one of the first companies to adopt the vee-radiator, which came on their 1908/09 models. They retained these up to the end of car production. By 1913 they all had monobloc engines, and electric lighting was optional for the first time that year. Most of the cars sold in England had Vanden Plas bodies. They were the third most important Belgian car maker, after F.N. and Minerva, though production never exceeded 1000 per year.

Postwar

Despite losing all their machinery to the German army, Métallurgique were among the first Belgian makes to get into production again, and in November 1919 the first postwar car was reported to be on its way to England. The 1919 models were 14 and 18hp cars assembled from prewar stock, and were joined by a 26hp which had 4-wheel brakes and a more pointed radiator. A new model for 1921 was a 3-litre sports model with the same dimensions as the 3-litre Bentley and, like the Bentley, a single-ohc. Only three of these were made. For the 1923 season all these designs gave way to a single model which was to last Métallurgique for the rest of its life. Designed by Paul Bastien, it had a 1969cc single-ohc engine, 4-speed gearbox with central lever and Adex-type 4-wheel brakes, as made by Excelsior. It was a quality fast tourer in the same class as the Ballot 2LTS or Delage DIS, but did not find many buyers. Exact figures are not known, but probably they did not exceed 150, of which 100 were made in the first season, 1923. Faced with declining sales, Métallurgique closed their car factory at the end of 1927, and sold it to IMPÉRIA.

NG

Further Reading
'Métallurgique – a quality car from Belgium', Nick Georgano, *The Automobile*, February 1993.

METEOR (i) (US) 1900–1901

Springfield Cornice Works, Springfield, Massachusetts.

The first of ten makes to carry the Meteor name, this was a spindly-looking runabout powered by a single-cylinder De Dion-Bouton or Aster engine, with drive by a long chain to the rear axle. Prices were $800–850 according to the engine. At the end of 1901 the name of car and company was changed to AUTOMOTOR.

NG

METEOR (ii) (US) 1902–1903

Meteor Engineering Co., Reading, Pennsylvania.

This company took over the assets of the Steam Vehicle Co. of America, which had made the READING (i) steamer. They continued the Reading design and also made a larger car with 4-cylinder horizontal engine under a bonnet, which resembled a petrol car and sold for $2000. They planned to make a petrol car

1926 Métallurgique 2-litre saloon.
NICK BALDWIN

powered by a De Dion-Bouton engine, but the contract from their selling agent was cancelled, and only one petrol-engined car was ever made.

NG

METEOR (iii) (GB) 1903–1905

Pritchett & Gold Ltd, Feltham, Middlesex.

This company made two models of Meteor, with 12hp Blake engine or 24hp Mutel. Both were 4-cylinder units, and both cars had shaft drive. Pritchett & Gold also made electric cars, but these more commonly went under the name PRITCHETT & GOLD or P & G.

NG

MÉTÉOR (iv) (B) 1903–1906

Felix Hecq, Brussels.

A few cars were made under this name, beginning with a voiturette powered by a 9hp De Dion-Bouton engine, which was joined in 1905 by a 16/20hp four with armoured wood frame. This survived into 1906, after which the make disappeared.

NG

METEOR (v) (US) 1904–1905

Federal Manufacturing Co., Cleveland, Ohio.

When C.C. Woerhington bought up the BERG Automobile Co. of Cleveland, he continued that car, and also introduced a new one to which he gave the name Meteor. It had an 18hp 4-cylinder engine, 3-speed gearbox and shaft drive. The only body style was a 4-seater tonneau, but it was offered in either wood or aluminium, the latter being $200 more expensive. For 1905 only the wooden version was made, and later that year that cars were re-named CLEVELAND (iii).

NG

METEOR (vi) (US) 1907–1910

Meteor Motor Car Co., Bettendorf, Iowa.

Made by Bodo Liebert and Arno Petersen, whose family money came from the largest department store in Davenport, Iowa, this Meteor was a large car powered by a 50hp T-head 4-cylinder engine offered as a runabout, tourer or limousine at between $3000 and $4000. 25 cars were completed in 1908, and a run of 50 was planned for 1909. Probably they were not all made, as a fire destroyed the factory in the summer of 1909. There were plans to re-start production in Davenport, but these came to nothing.

NG

METEOR (vii) (US) 1914–1933

Meteor Motor Car Co., Shelbyville, Indiana and Piqua, Ohio.

The Meteor was the continuation of the CLARK (iv) that had been built since 1912. Maurice A. Wolfe, who headed Meteor, moved the operations to Piqua, Ohio shortly after his acquisition of the Clark interests and it may be presumed that the few Meteor cars dating to Shelbyville were, in effect, rebadged Clarks. Once established in Piqua, production was limited to roadsters and touring cars equipped with 6-cylinder Continental or Model engines culminating with an ambitious, if short-lived, V12 powered by a Weidely engine in 1916. At this point, Wolfe decided to concentrate his efforts in the ambulance and funeral car field with passenger cars available on special order, including sedans and limousines, ostensibly for professional car use. Meteor ambulances, hearses and

1920 Meteor (vii) 7-seater sedan.
KEITH MARVIN

1926 Meteor (vii) 7-seater sedan.
NICK GEORGANO/NATIONAL MOTOR MUSEUM

the occasional pleasure cars were well regarded by a satisfied clientele and during the decade of the 1920s the Meteor factory operated at full strength. One reason for its success was the experimentation by Wolfe of a cooling system which could operate equally well at high speed or at prolonged low speed without overheating, an important consideration in the cases where a vehicle was used for both rescue and funeral purposes. Continental engines were used exclusively by Meteor including the 9N, 8R and 6J. Wheelbase was 127in (3223mm). The Meteor Co. was accommodating to the less affluent funeral director by augmenting the Meteor line with a smaller, less expensive line of vehicles badged 'MORT' – ironic in that *mort* is the French word for dead or death – and including both funeral cars and closed sedans and limousines for pallbearers' use. After about 1930, Meteor, like other professional car manufacturers, began to rely increasingly on standard chassis for their coachbuilding with Buick as its major chassis and, although by accepted practice the chassis was slightly changed to accommodate the coachbuilders' individuality and carry its nomenclature, the last Meteor-badged chassis were marketed in 1932 or early 1933. As an added point of interest, Maurice Wolfe also spread his manufacturing expertise into motor boats, phonographs, records and radios, all of them bearing the same trademark as that used on all of the Meteor motor vehicles. The insignia gained particular prominence during the Democratic Presidential Nomination at San Francisco, California in 1920. For this occasion, Maurice Wolfe, a Democratic Party member, sent the brass band of the Meteor Motor Car Co. which performed musical selections during the convention, the Meteor-in-Flight insignia prominently displayed on the bass drum! Meteor eventually ecame the Miller-Meteor Division of the Divco-Wayne Corp. which failed in 1979.

KM

METEOR (viii) (US) 1919–1922
Meteor Motors Inc., Philadelphia, Pennsylvania.
The Meteor was a powerful, expensive motor car of top quality which was built for affluent sporting car fanciers who wanted a handsome automobile with high-performance regardless of cost. Powered by a 4-cylinder Rochester Duesenburg engine, it featured a 4-speed transmission with its own design of direct drive in third gear and with a vee-radiator similar to Austro-Daimler. The Meteor featured custom coachwork by Fleetwood and a 129in (3274mm) chassis, and wire wheels, including two side-mounted spares ahead of the cowl. The majority of its parts were of the highest quality available by specialists in their respective fields, and the Meteor, in effect an 'assembled car' was seldom if ever regarded as such.

Introduced during the summer of 1919, the intial Meteor was introduced as a 4-passenger sports touring model, the rear seat disappearing into the rear deck when not in use. This was priced at $4850. The price was increased to $5000 for 1920, and the line was augmented by a 2-passenger roadster at $5500. For 1921–22, the line was further extended with a town car priced at $6500, plus the availabilty of a bare chassis at $4000. At least one collapsible town car, designed by coachbuilder Karl H. Martin, manufacturer of the WASP automobile, was also built on special order in 1921.

Meteor, unable to survive the 1920s Depression, ceased manufacturing in early 1922. Production is estimated at 75 to 125 completed cars.

KM

METEOR (ix) *see* FORD (ii)

METEOR (x) (US) 1952–1962
Meteor Sports Cars, El Segundo, California and Lakewood, Colorado.
Dick Jones formed a partnership with Jim BYERS in the early 1950s. They built an attractive fibreglass kit car body inspired by Vignale-bodied Ferraris of that time. The first car was built on a cut-down 1939 Ford chassis with a Ford Flathead, although subsequent cars had Chevrolet V8 engines. The new body was shown at the 1953 Los Angeles Motorama. In 1955 Jones bought out Byers and moved the Meteor operation to Colorado. The Meteor bodies were well built and Jones included specially fabricated door hardware, glass and detailed instructions. About 25 cars were built.

HP

METEORITE (GB) 1912–1924
1912–1921 Meteor Motors Ltd, London.
1921–1924 Meteorite Cars Ltd, London.
The first Meteorite was a light car powered by a 8hp air-cooled V-twin J.A.P. engine, with 3-speed gearbox and shaft drive. It sported a Rolls Royce-type radiator which characterised the make for the rest of its life. A 10hp 4-cylinder model joined the twin for 1915, with a 1328cc engine said to be of the maker's own manufacture, and there was also a larger car with 2914cc 20/28hp 6-cylinder Aster engine. This was called a Meteor rather than a Meteorite, and did not reappear after the Armistice. The J.A.P.-engined car was listed in 1919, but was quickly replaced by a new model using a 1498cc 10.8hp Coventry-Simplex engine. They had now moved to Uxbridge Road, Shepherd's Bush, where they were neighbours of the coachbuilders Strachan and Brown who provided their bodies. These were a 2-seater, 4-seater tourer and coupé, priced from £450 to £575. Like the other London makes beginning with 'M', Mascotte and Mercury, the Meteorite had little to offer the public which they could not obtain elsewhere at a lower price. At the 1923 Show they exhibited two models with coachbuilt bodies by the Albany Carriage Co., a coupé and a saloon. There was also a new chassis powered by a 1696cc 6-cylinder engine, but this may never have reached the market at all. 1924 was the last year for the Meteorite. For 1925 they said 'manufacture of the Meteorite is postponed until times become normal'. Alas, they never did. The stock of spare parts and drawings was bought by C. H. Humphreys of Bedford, who are sometimes erroneously listed as makers of the car. In 1930 they sold what was left on to Elephant Motors of London, who actually listed the 14hp six.

NG

1919 Meteor (viii) sports tourer.
KEITH MARVIN

METHVEN (NZ) 1903

G. Methven, Dunedin, South Island.

One of the early locally-made motor vehicles, Methven's effort was a high-wheeled wagonette with fully elliptic springs. It had a 4hp petrol engine, tiller steering and was said to have been able to achieve a speed of 24mph (39km/h). He used it until 1906, when he purchased a Locomobile.

MG

METISSE see RICKMAN

METROPOL (US) 1913–1914

Metropol Motors Corp., Port Jefferson, New York.

If the size of the company did not live up to its grand title, the car it produced was quite spectacular, with a 4-cylinder engine of 7325cc, and a very long stroke (dimensions were 108 × 200mm). The engine was a T-head design, rather old-fashioned for 1913. It was designed by François Richard, and was made in the factory previously occupied by the ONLY Motor Car Co. who had made a single-cylinder car with an even longer stroke. With a claimed top speed of 75mph (120km/h), the Metropol was good value at $1475 for a 2-seater speedster. For 1914 they offered three styles, speedster, racer and 5-seater tourer. The make did not survive into 1915, and Richard moved to Cleveland where he made the RICHARD.

NG

MÉTROPOLITAINE (F) 1911–c.1913

Jossu, Jannel et Cie, Paris.

When they announced their car in 1911 this company said that their name was not unknown, as they had made bicycles for a long time. The car was a light 2-seater of Renault-like appearance, with a dashboard radiator and coal-scuttle bonnet. It was powered by an 850cc single-cylinder engine, had a 3-speed gearbox with direct drive in top gear, and shaft drive.

NG

1922 Meteorite 10.8hp tourer.
NICK BALDWIN

METROPOLITAN (i) (GB) 1901

Metropolitan Motor Manufacturing Co., Fulham, London.

The Metropolitan had an unusual engine with two vertical cylinders spaced apart so that they looked almost like two separate motors, with the flywheel between them. It was quoted as a 7/8hp and lived in front of the frame under a short bonnet. Transmission was by belts from the transverse crankshaft to a countershaft on which a complicated system of two rocking pulleys provided two forward speeds. Final drive was by chain from the countershaft to the rear axle. The car had cycle-type wheels and solid tyres. The makers exhibited two cars at London's Agricultural Hall Motor Show in May 1901, a 2-seater and a 4-seater tonneau. G.R. Doyle, in the first edition of *The World's Automobiles*, noted of this make, 'Made only two cars, neither of which would work'. These were presumably the two show cars. Perhaps their problems lay in the transmission.

NG

1958 Metropolitan (iii) convertible.
NATIONAL MOTOR MUSEUM

1922 Metro-Tyler 5/6hp cyclecar.
NATIONAL MOTOR MUSEUM

METROPOLITAN (ii) (US) 1922–1923

Metropolitan Motor, Inc, Kansas City, Missouri.

The Metropolitan was the successor to the SEVERIN (1920–1921) under new management. The first Metropolitans were little more than the Severins, as the majority of components of the Severin were used in the new Metropolitan M-61 which was offered as a touring car and a sedan at $1500 and $2000 respectively. For 1923, the company introduced a 4-cylinder car – the M-41 – with an in-house ohv engine, and a 2⅝ × 4in bore and stroke. A light car weighing 1600lbs, the M-41 had a 100in (2538mm) wheelbase with open body styles priced at $600 and closed ones at $100 more.

KM

METROPOLITAN (iii) (US/GB) 1954–1961

American Motors Corp., Kenosha, Wisconsin.

Developed from a 1950 prototype called the NX-1, the Metropolitan was a sub-compact car rivalling European imports such as the VW Beetle. It was built

by Austin at Longbridge, Birmingham, and used the 1200cc 4-cylinder ohv engine that powered the Austin A40 Somerset, with a unitary construction convertible or coupé body by Fisher & Ludlow styled to look like a baby Nash. They were sold in America with both Nash and Hudson badges. Capacity went up to 1489cc in 1956. Advertised as 'milady's perfect companion for shopping trips', the Metropolitan sold well, 97,000 of them up to 1961. Most went to America, though they were on the UK market from 1957.

NG

METRO-TYLER (GB) 1922–1923

Metro-Tyler Ltd, London.

This company was formed from the merger of the Birmingham-based Metro Manufacturing & Engineering Co. and the Tyler Apparatus Co. of London, both of which had made motorcycles before the war. Tyler was also the sole concessionaire for the DEWCAR cyclecar. They merged in 1919 and continued to make motorcycles, adding a cyclecar in 1922. This was a very light machine powered by a 550cc 5/6hp 2-cylinder engine which was basically two of their motorcycle engines on a common crankcase. They had 3-speed gearboxes and belt drive, with the option of chain for 1923. The chassis price was a low £125; with a 2-seater body it was £149. With the 758cc Blackburne engine available in 1923, the price was £155.

NG

METZ (i) (US) 1909–1921

1909 Waltham Mfg Co., Waltham, Massachusetts.
1909–1921 The Metz Co., Waltham, Massachusetts.

This was the third make of car built by Charles Herman Metz (1863–1937), his previous efforts being the Orient Buckboard and Waltham Orient, both described under WALTHAM (ii). In 1909 he started to make a car under his own name which was marketed in an unusual way. It was sold in kit form, and in stages, so that the buyer completed Parts Group One before taking delivery of Parts Group Two. The packages came in 14 parts and sold for $25 each, so the cost of purchase was spread over several months. The scheme had the advantage for Metz of disposing of a large quantity of parts left over from the old Waltham Manufacturing Co. without the capital outlay of paying a workforce to assemble

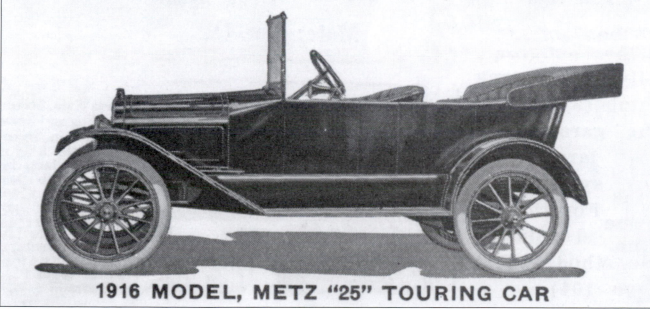

The Quality Car

1916 MODEL
METZ "25" ROADSTER

METZ

1916 models. Price, $600 each, completely equipped. Both Roadster and Touring Car built on same chassis, 108-inch wheel base, and carry identical equipment, including electric starter and electric lights, 25 h.p. water-cooled motor, large wheels and tires, rain vision wind shield, instant one-man top, speedometer, built-in gasoline gauge, signal horn, etc. Write for DEALER particulars and new illustrated catalog "P."

METZ COMPANY, WALTHAM, MASS.

1916 MODEL, METZ "25" TOURING CAR

1924 MG (i) 14/28hp sports tourer.
NICK BALDWIN

them. Once he had obtained a reasonable sum for the sale of parts he began to offer the cars fully made up as well.

The car had a 12hp 2-cylinder engine, with friction transmission and chain drive, and was offered only as a 2-seater. Metz promoted the friction transmission, which was of course used by many other car manufacturers, as 'a speed for every need'. The only body style was a 2-seater roadster until 1915, when a tourer was added. By then the original 2-cylinder engine had been replaced by a 22 or 25hp four. The last year for the kit scheme, or Metz Plan, was 1912, when a 4-cylinder Plan Roadster cost $495 and an Assembled Roadster $600. Sales reached their peak in the mid-teens, 7163 in 1915 and 6130 in 1916. Metz enjoyed a flourishing export market, selling to Europe, Australia and Thailand.

In 1919 a completely different Metz appeared. The Master Six was a conventional tourer powered by a 45bhp Lycoming or Rutenber engine, with 3-speed gearbox and shaft drive. Sedan, tourer and roadster bodies were added to the range for 1920, but only 851 cars were sold, including 100 coupés and just one sedan. The Metz had little to offer the public in a market where many makes were struggling for position, and the lead was passing to large producers like Buick. For 1922 the name was changed to Waltham Six, but only six cars were sold under that name.

NG

Further Reading
'One Piece at a Time – The Cars of C.H. Metz', Thomas S. Lamarre, *Automobile Quarterly*, Vol. 32, No. 3.

METZ (ii) (NL) 1909

Built in Amsterdam, the Metz 3-wheeler resembled the German Phänomobil, with a 3½hp 2-cylinder Minerva engine mounted over the front wheel. The body was a 2-seater, but an additional seat was available.

NG

MEYER (i) (CH) 1884–1889

1884–1889 Gottfried and Heinrich Meyer, Horgen.
The two brothers Meyer built their first steam tricycle in 1884 for their personal use. It was 2-seater, had a rear-mounted boiler and chain drive to the large rear wheels. Steering was by lever on the smaller front wheel. Four more steam vehicles of heavier construction were completed, seating up to five persons.

FH

MEYER (ii) (US) c.1919

J. Meyer Corp., Chicago, Illinois.
The Meyer may have existed as a lone prototype, a large disc-wheeled touring car which was featured in the March 1919 issue of *Motor Age Magazine*. If the marketing plan for the Meyer was curious, it certainly did not lack in ambition. Plans included a 'tailored to order' car which could be specified by the owner to have two to 12 cylinders and virtually any type of open or closed coachwork.

If this was not enough of a novelty, the wheel, welded to the hub with a protective leather shield between and a tyre with two separate hollow sections completed the 'advantages'. Whether 'production' followed the pilot model is doubtful. The Meyer, so went the advertisement, would cost as high as $7000 depending on the desires of the purchasers.

KM

MEYERS (US) 1963–1971

B. F. Meyers Co., Fountain Valley, California.
Bruce Meyers made the first successful fibreglass-bodied dune buggy and launched a craze that dominated the American kit car market for a decade. The first Meyers Manx was a distinctive roadster design that used a fibreglass monocoque with integral steel frame to which the builder attached Volkswagen suspension and running gear. This design proved difficult to manufacture and assemble, and only 12 were built. Meyers eliminated the monocoque and fitted the body to a shortened VW floorpan. At $298, they sold thousands of kits. However, they were also easy to replicate and competitors turned out copies that were cheaper, if flimsy. There were several versions of the Manx, including a utility version for lifeguards and Forest Service Rangers to use on beaches and unimproved roads. Meyers added a 4-seat dune buggy that looked like a longer Manx called the Turista or Resorter. It was primarily designed for hotel chains to carry tourists, and the sides were low enough to step over. The Meyers Tow'd was a buggy designed for off-road use. It had a steel frame and rudimentary body, and was intended to be flat towed (Tow'd) to off-road events. About 850 were sold. The last Meyers product was the Manx SR, or street roadster. It was a sports car based on the same shortened VW floorpan as used by the Manx buggy, but it had an attractive body with a 'Targa' style top and basic street equipment. Between 400 and 600 of these were built. By 1971 Meyers had lost a critical patent infringement case against a rival dune buggy builder, and financial problems forced them out of business. The Manx SR project was picked up by KARMA Coachworks. In 1991 Meyers announced he would resume production of a new Manx, which was to be wider than the originals but with a strong family resemblance. However, production had not begun as of 1999. In all, Meyers produced around 7000 cars.

HP

MEYRA (D) 1948–1956

Meyra-Werke, Vlotho.
Founded by Wilhelm Meyer, this company was a well-known maker of invalid cars, making the first examples in Germany after World War II. The 3-wheeler of 1948 had a 197cc Ilo single-cylinder engine and single front wheel. It was a 2-seater, but sales were initially restricted to those who had been injured in the war. In 1953 came the 200, an Isetta-like car with single rear wheel and entrance at the front. Unlike the Isetta, though, only half of the front opened, which must have restricted the car to relatively slim owners. The 200 was powered by a 197cc Ilo engine, and the fully enclosed body had a steel framework covered by fabric, later by steel panels. Shortly before production ended in the middle of 1956, a few examples were made of a more powerful version with 350cc Ilo engine. Total output of the Meyra 200 was about 530 cars.

HON

MEYRIGNAC (F) 1977–c.1982

Denis Meyrignac, Paris.
Launched at the 1977 Geneva Motor Show, the Meyrignac was a striking 2-seater coupé based on an Alpine-Renault backbone chassis. The rear-mounted engine could be either a 1.6-litre 95bhp 4-cylinder or a 2.7-litre 150bhp V6, mated to a 5-speed manual gearbox. The entire upper centre body section, including the windscreen, lifted for access to the interior.

CR

M.F.E. (GB) 1984–1996

1984–1988 Metro Fibre Engineering (Motorspeed), Tangmere, West Sussex.
1988–1992 Scorhill Motors, Godalming, Surrey.
1992–1993 Scorhill Motors, Walton-on-Thames, Surrey.
1993–1996 Scorhill Motor Co., Chertsey, Surrey.
Designed by MG specialists Motorspeed, the M.F.E. Magic was a kit-form sports car that blurred the distinction between 1930s styling and fun cars. In its original

form it accepted MGB components but in 1985 a chassis was offered for Ford Cortina MkIII suspension and power train. The open fibreglass bodywork featured a forward-hinging bonnet and a gelcoat finish.

CR

MG (i) (GB) 1923 to date

1923–1928 Morris Garages Ltd, Oxford.
1929–1970 MG Car Co. Ltd., Abingdon, Berkshire.
1970–1975 Austin-Morris Division, British Leyland Motor Corp., Abingdon, Berkshire.
1975–1978 Leyland Cars, British Leyland UK Ltd, Abingdon, Oxfordshire.
1978–1980 Jaguar Rover Triumph Ltd, Abingdon, Oxfordshire.
1982 to date Austin Rover Group Ltd/Rover Group Ltd, Birmingham.

Arguably the world's most famous sports car, the MG has shadowy beginnings, and historians have difficulty in establishing which car was in fact the first MG. One certainty is that without the imagination and drive of Cecil Kimber the MG would never have come into being. Kimber joined Morris Garages, the group of retail outlets owned by William Morris, as sales manager in 1921, becoming general manager a year later.

He quickly began to design special bodywork for the Morris Cowley. This was the Chummy, a 2-seater with space in the back for two additional passengers, with a hood covering all four seats, unlike the usual dickey seat arrangement where the rear passengers sat unprotected. The rear of the car was lowered by the simple expedient of mounting the auxiliary quarter-elliptic spring above the frame instead of below it. Kimber ordered the bodies from Carbodies of Coventry, where they were mounted on Cowley chassis, and finished off in one of the Morris Garages, in Longwall Street, Oxford. They were sold under the name Morris Garages Chummy, and cost about the same as a standard Cowley 4-seater tourer.

In February 1923 assembly was moved to a tiny workshop measuring 19 × 100ft (6 × 30m) in Alfred Lane, Oxford. With only three men working for him, Kimber managed to produce as many as 20 Chummys per week. With a mildly tuned model, he won a Gold Medal in the 1923 Land's End Trial, and this must have encouraged him to build a more sporting version of the Cowley. This had a 2-seater body by Raworth of Oxford, with a raked windscreen. Six bodies were ordered, and the first car delivered in August 1923. At £350 it was very expensive compared with £198 for the Morris 2-seater Cowley, and it was a year before the six cars were sold.

Kimber's next car was a Chummy body on the Morris Oxford chassis, followed by a saloon on the 14/28 Oxford chassis. This was advertised in the first issue of *The Morris Owner* magazine (March 1924) as 'the MG vee-front saloon'. This was the first use of the MG name, and two months later, the Raworth-bodied Cowley was advertised as the 'MG Super Sports Morris'.

During 1924 Kimber built at least two special cars to individual order. One had a polished aluminium 4-seater body by Carbodies, with discs covering the ugly artillery wheels. Built for trials driver Billy Cooper on the 14/28 Oxford chassis, it attracted a lot of attention at Brooklands and elsewhere, leading to requests for replicas. At least 13 had been made by October 1924, when a longer wheelbase Oxford enabled better-looking cars to be made. Kimber's advertising referred to them as MGs though the press tended to call them special bodied Morrisses, a practice that continued for some time.

The 14/28 tourer can be regarded as the first production MG. In 1925 Kimber issued his first catalogue, in which the car was called the MG Super Sports, with no more mention of Morris. Modifications to the chassis (which had been introduced in 1924) included a steeply raked steering column, flattened springs, more direct steering, handbrake moved from centre to right, and a higher final drive ratio. Clearly, the MG was no longer a special bodied Morris, though its ancestry was still proclaimed by the bullnose radiator. This did not yet carry the MG Octagon badge, though octagons were used on the doorplates mounted on the running boards. Three body styles were offered, the 4-seater at £375, a 2-seater at £350, and the Salonette, a 2-door saloon with a 2+2 seating and a little duck's tail for luggage at £475.

In the twelve months following the announcement of the new cars, 135 were built, 93 4-seaters, 36 2-seaters, and six salonettes. The little workshop in Alfred Lane also built 25 closed bodies on unmodified Morris chassis. It is worth mentioning that the stark 2-seater, registered FC 7900, which still exists and has featured so often in advertising as the first MG, or 'Old Number One', was

1927 MG (i) 14/40 2-door salonette.
NICK BALDWIN

1929 MG (i) 18/80 Mk I tourer.
NATIONAL MOTOR MUSEUM

1932 MG (i) C-type Midget sports car.
NICK GEORGANO

by no means the first, and it was not a standard model. It was not even built at Alfred Lane, being assembled at Longwall Street and powered by an ohv Hotchkiss engine. Kimber took a Gold Medal with it in the 1925 Land's End Trial, and sold it shortly afterwards.

Conditions at Alfred Lane were very cramped, and in September 1925 Kimber persuaded William Morris to let him have part of the Morris Motors radiator factory. Staff now numbered about 50, and a further move towards individuality was that Morris engines were now dismantled and carefully checked before being reassembled and installed in the chassis. In September 1926 Morris replaced the bullnose radiator with a flat one, at the same time making the chassis wider and shorter. MG followed suit, the new car being available with the same bodies as the bullnose, although there were two models of Salonette, the 2+2 with duck's tail luggage compartment, and a 4-seater with conventional D-back saloon body. From late 1927 they were called 14/40, and carried an enamelled MG radiator badge. The stock of 14/28s carried over into the 1928 season and, sold as 14/40s, were rebadged with octagons. Production was 235 cars in the 1927 season, and 399 in the 1928 season.

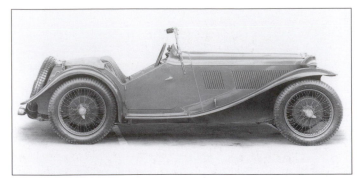

1933 MG (i) L2 Magna sports car.
NICK BALDWIN

1933 MG (i) J1 Midget 4-seater sports car.
NICK GEORGANO/NATIONAL MOTOR MUSEUM

1939 MG (i) VA drop-head coupé.
NATIONAL MOTOR MUSEUM

In July 1927 Morris Garages was registered as a limited company, and two months later they moved into their first purpose-built factory, at Edmund Road, Cowley. Chassis now carried an MG car number, as well as a Morris chassis number. Another landmark of 1927 was the first of MG's countless racing successes, when Alberto Sanchez Cires drove a 14/40 to victory in a touring car race outside Buenos Aires.

In October 1928 MG had their first stand at London's Olympia Motor Show. Three models were exhibited, the familiar 14/40 and two completely new cars which marked a further step towards individuality. The little M-type Midget became the more popular, but it was less innovative than the 6-cylinder 18/80, for most of its components came from William Morris' new Minor. This was unusual for a mass-produced small car in having an ohc engine, a Wolseley design available to Morris as he had purchased the Wolseley company in 1927. Kimber used this 847cc unit in the Minor's chassis with a few modifications such as a lowered suspension, increased steering column rake and altered

gearchange and pedal layout. It was very much the same treatment as he had given to the Morris Cowley four years earlier. The body was a light 2-seater with pointed tail, consisting of an ash frame panelled in fabric-covered plywood. Built by Carbodies, these bodies cost £6.50 each, and the Midget was put on the market at £175. With a top speed of nearly 60mph (97km/h) it was not a sparkling performer, but it provided sporting motoring at a low price, and in this lay its significance. *The Autocar* said 'The MG Midget will make sports car history', while with hindsight the great MG enthusiast Rivers Fletcher described it as a car whose importance is almost impossible to over-estimate. Many motorists who felt that a sports car was beyond their means or their driving ability became eager customers for the M-type, and then for its successors, the J-types, P-types and T-types.

The M-type brought about a dramatic increase in sales, which rose to about 900 cars in 1929. Of these, the Midget accounted for about 58 per cent, the 18/80 for 30 per cent and the 14/40, in its last year, no more than 12 per cent. The success of the Midget meant that the two-year old factory in Edmund Road was no longer big enough, and at the end of 1929 MG moved for the fourth time, to the surplus part of a leather factory in Abingdon, seven miles from Oxford.

The other new model at the 1928 Motor Show was the 18/80 which used a modified form of the 2468cc single-ohc 6-cylinder engine from the Morris Light Six. Kimber was not at all impressed with the Morris chassis, so he designed a completely new frame with a new front axle and rebuilt rear axle. Modified Marles steering was used, the wheels were the handsome Rudge Whitworth centre-lock type, and in place of the Morris radiator there was the definitive MG design with vertical centre rib which characterised the make up to the 1950s. The engine had twin carburettors, and a new block and head – it developed 50bhp and gave the car a top speed of 78mph (125km/h). Four body styles were originally offered, open 2 or 4-seaters, a 2-door Salonette and a 4-door saloon.

Total production of the 18/80 was 741 cars, of which 500 were the Mk I (1928–31), 236 the Mk II (1929–33) and 5 the Mk III or Tigress. The Mk II was not a very different car apart from a 4-speed gearbox, bigger brakes and a track wider by 4in (101mm). Some new body styles were offered, including a drophead Coupé De Luxe, and a Speed Model tourer with cutaway doors and Dewandre servo brakes. The Mk III was a competition car with a tuned engine incorporating a new camshaft, crankshaft and pistons, cross-flow head, dual ignition and dry sump. Output was 90bhp and top speed nearly 110mph (177km/h). It was built with the 1930 Double Twelve Hour Race at Brooklands in mind, but the only one entered retired, and it was clear that a lot more work would need to be done to make the car competitive. Kimber decided, probably wisely, that the money would be better spent on the racing Midget, and the Tigress was never raced again. 25 were laid down but only five completed, the remaining bodies which had been ordered from Carbodies being mounted on Mk I chassis. Most 18/80s were bodied by Carbodies, the bare chassis being driven from Abingdon to Coventry.

A racing engine formed the basis of the C-type or Montlhéry Midget, a limited production sports car with cowled radiator, fold-flat windscreen, twin scuttle cowls and undershield. Its price was £295 unsupercharged, and £345 with a Powerplus blower. However, within six months the prices had risen to £490 and £575, which perhaps explains why only 44 C-types were sold.

The M-type Midget remained in production until 1932, gaining a coupé version in 1930, and a metal-panelled body for the open car, which sold alongside the fabric bodied car for £20 more. In 1931 came the D-type which had a close-coupled 4-seater body, open or closed, on a lengthened chassis having the C-type's underslung frame, though not its engine. This was only made from late 1931 to mid 1932, production being 250 cars. By contrast, the M-type accounted for 3235 cars. Both were replaced by the J-types, the 4-seater J1 and the 2-seater J2. They used the 847cc engine with the C-type's cross-flow head, with new bodies having cutaway doors and spare wheel mounted in the tail in the manner of all the smaller MGs up to the 1950s. Cycle-type wings were featured at first, replaced by full length ones. There was a new 4-speed gearbox with central remote control.

The competition models of the J series were the J3 and J4. These used supercharged 746cc engines in a J2 chassis with C-type gearbox. The J4 was the fastest as it used a larger Powerplus blower with up to 1.2kg/cm2 boost. Obviously, the market for the J3 and J4 was limited, only 22 J3s and 9 J4s being sold, compared with 380 J1s and 2083 J2s. Even more specialised were the Q and R

1948 MG (i) TC Midget sports car.

CHARLES, H.N. (1893–1982)

An automotive engineer of unusually broad experience, Charles was equally at home with suspension design as with engine projects. Born at Barnet in Hertfordshire on 22 November 1893, he was educated at Highgate School and University College, London, graduating with a BSc in engineering.

In 1914 he was a part of a racing team preparing a Triumph motorcycle with a fuel-injection engine for a Brooklands speed-record attempt, and then served in the Royal Naval Service as a mechanic in 1914-15. Transferred to the Royal Flying Corps, he worked on the development of fighter-plane engines until the end of World War I and was discharged with the rank of captain.

In 1919 he joined Zenith carburettors as a sales engineer, and in 1921 signed up with Automotive Products for a position in the sales department's technical branch.

In 1925 he went to work for Morris Motors as a technical assistant in the production department, where he met Cecil Kimber who talked him into devoting most of his spare time to design work for MG. At Kimber's request, he was attached to the Abingdon factory in 1930, where he developed the ohc MG family and broke new ground in chassis design with the all-independent torsion-bar suspension and fork-shaped frame of the R-Type, appearing in 1935.

Its racing career was cut short when Lord Nuffield sold the MG Car Co. to Morris Motors Ltd and the racing department at Abingdon was closed. Given the title of chief engineer for MG, Charles then returned to Cowley to develop a new family of pushrod-operated ohv engines for MG, one of which was used in the TA. He left the Nuffield organisation in 1938 and became chief engineer of Rotol airscrews, where he developed a reversing gear and a blade-feathering device.

During 1943 he joined Austin as a development engineer at Longbridge Works, and designed the independent coil-spring front suspension for the postwar models, beginning with the A40. He invented a two-part valve guide which Austin patented, and was co-inventor, with C.F. Nossiter, of a dish-and-dowel mounting for rocker arms (eliminating the rocker-shaft), patented in 1946.

He was a member of the British Intelligence Sub-Committee investigating the German motor industry in 1945.

He served as chief engineer for the Sheerline and Princess until he left Austin in 1946, becoming a consultant to Cam Gears Ltd, where one of his assignments was to help Joe Craig develop an exhaust-pressure-controlled carburettor for Norton motorcycles. He retired to Teddington, Middlesex, in about 1961, and died in an Oxford hospital on 18 January 1982.

JPN

1949 (i) MG YA saloon.
NICK BALDWIN

types. The former used a heavily modified 746cc engine with Zoller blower having a 1.8kg/cm2 boost giving up to 113bhp, in a K3 chassis. Top speed was nearly 120mph (193km/h), and the Q sold for £650, excluding wings and lights. In its final 'sprint' form of 1936 the Q engine gave 146.2bhp, or almost 200bhp per litre. This was a higher specific output than any other engine in the world, and is all the more remarkable as its engine was developed from the M-type whose 20bhp from 847cc represented only 23.6bhp per litre.

The R-type used the Q's engine in a completely new chassis with backbone frame and all-round independent suspension by wishbones and torsion bars. It was available only with single-seater racing body at £750. Ten were made, in 1935.

The last of the ohc Midgets was the P-Series, made from 1934 to 1936. The PA (1934–5) had the same size engine as the J2, but with three main bearings in place of two, giving greater smoothness and tuning potential. The wheelbase was lengthened by just over an inch, and there were improvements in steering, clutch and brakes. The PA had the flowing wings of the later J types (although cars used for trials had cycle wings, as did the trials TAs), and could be had with open 2 or 4-seater bodies, or a neat 2-seater Airline coupé. These were made for MG by Allingham in London. Most other MG coachwork now came from Morris Motor Bodies branch, as Kimber had ended his connection with Carbodies in 1933. The PB (1935–6) was essentially the same car, but with a larger engine of 939cc, a vertically-slatted radiator as opposed to the previous honeycomb type, and higher first and second gears. The same bodies were available, at prices from £222 to £290. 2000 PAs were built, of which 27 were converted to PB specification, and 526 PBs including the converted cars.

Kimber was not immune to the fashion for the small 6-cylinder engine, and in 1931 he brought out the F-type Magna. This had the 1271cc single-ohc six from the Wolseley Hornet, fitted with twin carbs which still gave it only 37.2bhp. A longish wheelbase enabled 4-seater bodywork to be fitted, an open sports tourer, and a Salonette. In 1932 the F Magna was also available with the 2-seater sports body of the J2 Midget. This was known as the F2, the 4-seater cars becoming the F3. After 1250 F Magnas had been made they were replaced by the L Magna which had a smaller engine (1087cc) but a crossflow head, giving slightly more power at 38.8bhp. The L1 was a 4-seater, the L2 a 2-seater, while there were two closed bodies, the Salonette and a curiously styled Continental coupé.

At the same time as the Magnas, MG was building the Magnettes, which initially used the 1087cc engine, although later they were available with the 1271cc as well. Known as the K Series, the Magnette range was very complex, with three chassis (K1, K2, K3), four engines (KA, KB, KD and K3), three gearboxes and at least five different bodies. The K1 was an open 4-seater or saloon, K2 a 2-seater, K3 the competition 2-seater, while the KA engine was the triple carburettor 1087cc, the KB, the same engine with twin carburettors, the KD the 1271cc, and the K3 a highly tuned version of the KD.

The K3 was one of the most remarkable cars of the 1930s. The engine had a machine-balanced crankshaft, straight-cut bevel gear drive for the camshaft

and a Number 9 Powerplus blower. Output was 120bhp. Among countless racing successes was Nuvolari's win in the 1933 Tourist Trophy, in which he set a lap record not broken until Stirling Moss' victory in 1951, and this was with a C-type Jaguar of nearly three times the K3's capacity.

The last Magnettes were the KN and N series. The KN was only made as a saloon, using the K1 body, now with a sunshine roof, and a 1271cc N engine, essentially a KD uprated to 56bhp. Only 201 were made, from mid–1934 to late 1935. The N used the same engine in a shorter chassis, and came in a choice of four bodies, open 2, 2/4 and 4-seaters, and Airline coupé. Production was 738 cars, plus five NE competition 2-seaters.

A New Era

On 1 July 1935 Lord Nuffield, as William Morris had become the previous year, sold the MG Car Co. to Morris Motors, so that it was now a wholly-owned subsidiary of the larger concern. He appointed Leonard Lord as Managing Director, and Kimber was retained in the subordinate post of Director and General Manager. Nuffield had little love of racing, and Lord none at all. The competition department was abruptly shut down.

It was not only the racing department that was swept away by the new regime. Within a year all the ohc Midgets and Magnettes had been replaced by new cars which used pushrod ohv engines from other models in the Nuffield range. First to appear was the SA, a long-bonnetted 4-door saloon powered by the 2062cc Wolseley Super Six engine. Although it disappointed the diehard MG enthusiast, the SA was a very handsome car, and a direct competitor for the new SS Jaguar which had been announced only ten days earlier. Before it went into production, the engine was enlarged to 2288cc, bringing it closer to the 2664cc Jaguar. Another change between the car as announced and the production model was the replacement of the crash gearbox with one boasting synchromesh on top and third. As well as the factory-built 4-door saloon, there was a drophead coupé by Tickford and an open tourer by Charlesworth.

Two more touring MGs followed the SA, with a strong family resemblance in their styling, the VA with 1548cc 4-cylinder Wolseley Twelve engine, and the WA with SA engine enlarged to 2561cc. This was the most luxurious MG made, yet not overpriced at £442 for a saloon, £450 for a Charlesworth tourer (only five made) and £468 for a Tickford drophead coupé. All these touring MGs had Lockheed hydraulic brakes, a design distrusted by Kimber. The SA was made in the largest numbers, 2738, followed by the VA (2407) and the WA (369).

The PB Midget was continued to the spring of 1936, then replaced by the first of the T series. This was a larger car than the PB, closer to the Magnette in size, powered by a 1292 pushrod ohv engine closely related to that of the Wolseley Ten. Like the SA, it had synchromesh on the two upper ratios, and hydraulic brakes. MG purists bewailed the disappearance of the ohc engine, but really the TA was a great step forward, roomier and faster, with a smoother and more flexible engine. Most of the 3003 made between 1936 and 1939 were open 2-seaters, but a very small number of Airline coupés were made in 1936, and a few Tickford dropheads were made throughout the model's life. This style was continued on the TB, of which 379 were made during 1939. It was similar to the TA in appearance, but had a new 1250cc XPAG engine as used in the Morris Ten. With a shorter stroke it proved more suitable for tuning than the TA engine, a fact that was to be of immense value after the war.

As soon as war broke out in September 1939, Kimber stopped car production in anticipation of important contracts for war work. These took some time to arrive, and the most important one, the assembly of the front section of the Albemarle bomber, led to Kimber's dismissal by Miles Thomas.

Sports Cars for the World

MG was back in production quicker than most British firms, but like their fellows, with a prewar design. The TC Midget was very similar to the TB, but had a cockpit 4in (101mm) wider, while the sliding trunnion suspension was replaced by conventional shackled springs. The price had jumped from £225 to £480, and was to rise again to £528 in 1946, but that was in line with the rest of the industry. The first TCs came off the line in October 1945, 81 being completed by the end of the year. 1946 saw more than 1500 built, over a third going for export. By the time production ended in late 1949, exactly 10,000 had been made, more than any previous model of MG. Of these, 3408 were sold in Britain, 6592 went to export markets, including 2001 to the USA.

There it became the archetypal fun car. Its top speed of 78mph (125km/h) was slower than a Buick or Oldsmobile sedan but owners found sheer joy in driving the little cars, flinging them through corners as fast as they would go. For this joy

SAFETY FAST!

The M.G. Magnette K3 Racing Model. Unsupercharged £595. Supercharged £695
With Pre-selector Gearbox.

THE 1933 M.G. MAGNETTE 'K' SERIES

1952 MG (i) TD Midget sports car.
NATIONAL MOTOR MUSEUM

1954 MG (i) TF Midget sports car.
NATIONAL MOTOR MUSEUM

1957 MG (i) ZB Magnette saloon.
NICK BALDWIN

they were prepared to forgive the harsh springing, lack of a heater or the fact that it could not be had with lhd. Keen drivers such as Briggs Cunningham, Phil Hill and John Fitch bought TCs, and out of the Boston branch of the MG Owners' Club grew the Sports Car Club of America, which was later to organise such important events as the Trans Am and Can-Am races. As the SCCA was formed in 1944 the TC itself had no part in its formation, but postwar MG enthusiasm undoubtedly swelled the club's ranks.

TCs were raced widely not only in the USA and Britain but all over Western Europe, Africa and Australia. In response to requests for more power the factory supplied a manual of tuning instructions in 1949, which listed various stages of tuning to raise output from 54 up to 97bhp, the latter with a supercharger.

In December 1949 the TC gave way to the TD, which had the same engine but was updated with coil and wishbone ifs, rack and pinion steering, and a hypoid axle. Its appearance was considerably changed by the presence of bumpers, and the replacement of the traditional wire wheels with discs. Enthusiasts

complained as loudly as they had done when the PB was replaced by the TA, and they were to complain even more when the TF arrived. However, the TD sold very well, 29,664 being made up to late 1953. Of these 23,500 were sold in the USA, more than ten times the number of TCs, so many more Americans owed their introduction to sports cars to the TD. Unlike its predecessor it was supplied with lhd, which doubtless increased its popularity. New York dealer Jack Inskip lengthened the chassis of about a dozen TDs, and added a rear seat. This did not please Abingdon, and when they had been sold no more were made. In 1952 42 TDs were sold abroad for every one purchased in Britain. That year the power of the standard engine went up to 57bhp, while factory-backed tuning could give up to 90bhp.

In 1951 a TD with aerodynamic body ran at Le Mans, and although engine trouble forced George Phillips to retire, the car recorded a speed of 118mph (190km/h), a gain of 50 per cent over the regular TD. This was largely thanks to the body, for the engine received little attention. Another car with similar body on a lower frame was built in 1952, and MG hoped to put this into production as the TD's replacement. However, their masters, the newly-formed British Motor Corp., preferred the Austin Healey 100 which Leonard Lord had just sanctioned, and all MG could do was to make a facelifted TD. This appeared in October 1953 as the TF. It had a sloping radiator grill and fuel tank, headlamps partially faired into the wings and bucket seats in place of the TD's one-piece squab. Wire wheels were back as an option. It was so obviously a stop-gap car that there was much criticism, especially from foreign journalists. Even the provision of a 1466cc engine in 1954 (TF 1500) failed to satisfy them very much. Yet today the TF is the most sought after of the postwar Midgets. Its appearance is just as acceptable to the classic car collector as the TC or TD, and in 1500 form it is that much faster. When Alistair Naylor decided to build an MG replica in 1980, it was the TF shape that he chose, while the RMB Gentry kit car and the Brazilian Avallone were also TF-based.

Touring MGs
Before looking at the next generation of sports cars, we need to back-track to 1947 when the first postwar MG saloon appeared. This was the Y-type, which would have been launched in 1941 had it not been for the war. Smaller than the SA or WA saloons, the Y had a single carburettor version of the TC engine in a box section frame with ifs by coil springs and wishbones. The body was a six-light saloon of distinctly prewar lines, but well finished. Top speed was 70mph (113km/h), but the tuning available to TC owners could also be applied to the Y, and tuned cars were entered in events such as the Monte Carlo Rally and Production Touring Car Race at Silverstone. A total of 7459 YA and YB saloons were made, the YB having improved brakes and a hypoid rear axle. There were also 877 YT 2-door tourers which used the TD's twin carburettor engine. The TD owed a great deal to the Y, including its suspension and chassis which was of similar design, though five inches shorter.

For 1954 the YB was replaced by the ZA Magnette. This shared a 4-door saloon bodyshell with the Wolseley 4/44 introduced the previous year, and was the first car to use the 1489cc BMC 'B' engine which later powered the Farina-bodied Austin Cambridge/Morris Oxford, etc saloons and the early MGA sports cars. It was replaced by the ZB in 1956, basically the same car but with a more powerful engine (69bhp), higher rear axle ratio, dual tone colour schemes and a wider rear window. A few ZBs were made with Manumatic automatic transmission. Production of these Magnettes was 18,076 ZAs and 18,534 ZBs.

Though the Z series was criticised for its Wolseley bodyshell and BMC engine, it had more individuality than its successor, the Magnette III. This was simply the B series body also made as an Austin Cambridge, Morris Oxford, Riley 4/68 and Wolseley 15/60, fitted with an MG radiator grill and, as Michael Sedgwick inimitably observed, 'the odd octagon or two dotted around the scenery'. The B series engine had an extra carburettor, as did the Riley version. The Magnette III was not even made at Abingdon, but at Cowley where it shared an assembly line with the Morris, Riley and Wolseley versions. It was sold until 1961 when it was succeeded by the Magnette IV, the same car with a 1622cc engine. This lasted until 1968, total production being 16,676 Mk IIIs, and 14,320 Mk IVs.

The last MG saloons, before the 1980s range of Austin-based cars, were another example of badge engineering. They were MG versions of the BMC 1100/1300 range, distinguished by twin carburettor engines, plusher interiors with wooded fascia boards and, usually, dual colour schemes. The 1100 was made from 1962 to 1968 and the 1300 from 1967 to 1971. Early 1300s had the

KIMBER, CECIL (1888–1945)

Renowned throughout the world as the father of the MG marque, Cecil Kimber was born in London on 12 April 1888, the son of a printing engineer, Henry Francis Kimber, and his wife, the former Fanny Matthewman. He was educated at Stockport Grammar School, afterwards joining his father in the printing ink business. While still in his teens he became a keen motorcyclist, but a serious accident while riding a friend's machine left him with a damaged leg for the rest of his life, and turned him to four wheels, in the shape of a 10hp Singer. In 1914 he left his father's firm, and soon afterwards joined Sheffield-Simplex as a personal assistant to the chief engineer.

During World War I he moved to AC Cars at Thames Ditton, then to components makers, E.G. Wrigley of Birmingham. He invested most of his savings in this company, and lost them through Wrigley's involvement with the Angus-Sanderson car, whose radiator was styled by Kimber. Although it was a financial disaster, his connection with Wrigley led to his life's work; Wrigley had been among the original component suppliers to William Morris, and were bought by him in 1923. This was the connection which led Kimber to take the position of sales manager of Morris Garages in Longwall Street, Oxford, in 1921, and it was here that he built his first special, a close-coupled 4-seater by Carbodies of Coventry mounted on a stock Morris Cowley chassis. These were assembled in a tiny works at Alfred Lane, and sold under the name Morris Cowley Chummy. More specialised models followed.

There has been much debate about the origin of the octagon badge. Some say that it was not Kimber's idea but came from Ted Lee, an accountant with Morris Garages. Another source claims that it came from an octagonal dining table at Kimber's home, which had been made by Kimber's father. The earliest known use of the badge dates from 2 March 1923, although it was not formally claimed as a trade mark until 1 May 1924.

In September 1925 Kimber moved production of MGs from Alfred Lane to a bay in the Morris Motors radiator factory in Bainton Road. He clearly had the support of William Morris in this, although both men must have been aware of the conflicting claims on Kimber's time between managing Morris Garages and making MG cars. He continued with both for several years; the MG Car Co. came into being in January 1928 and in September 1929 they left Oxford for new premises at Abingdon-on-Thames. At this point Kimber resigned from Morris Garages, becoming managing director of the MG Car Co. Ltd in July 1930. The governing director was Sir William Morris without whose encouragement and financial support Kimber could clearly never have set up as a car manufacturer. An indication of Morris' financial significance is that in the distribution of £1 shares, Kimber and three others received one each, and W.R. Morris/Morris Industries, 18,996.

With the introduction of the £175 M-type Midget in the autumn of 1928 Kimber moved into a popular market, and his cars could no longer be thought of simply as improved Morrises. Indeed he began to buy components from other sources, including axles from Wolseley. MGs had been raced almost from the first examples, and from 1930 to 1935 Kimber supported an active racing programme. This brought great publicity and established the MG name as a leader among British sports cars, but it did not help the balance sheet. The practical Morris was not impressed with the racing programme, although not actively opposed to it, but the crunch came in July 1935 when he sold MG to Morris Motors. He brought in as Managing Director the hard-headed Leonard Lord, later to head Morris' arch-rival, Austin. Lord was hostile to anything which sapped profits, and when he visited Abingdon he is said to have looked at the racing shop and remarked 'Well, that bloody lot can go, for a start'.

This was the beginning of Kimber's disillusion with his position at MG. He no longer had absolute control over the design and components that went into new MGs. Increasingly, they were designed at Cowley, and individual aspects such as the ohc engines gave way to pushrod units shared with Morris and Wolseley cars. He was approached by a group of London financiers to form a new company, the G.K. Car Co, in which he would have full control of design and marketing, but he declined the offer.

When World War II broke out production of MGs naturally came to an end, and the factory had little to do. They were reduced to making fish-frying pans for a local army depot. Kimber managed to secure a contract to make frontal sections for the Albemarle bomber, but he did this without consulting his masters at Morris. Miles Thomas, Managing Director of Morris, asked him to resign in the autumn of 1941. It was a terrible blow and friends suggested that he sue Lord Nuffield, as William Morris had become, for wrongful dismissal. Kimber, characteristically loyal, said "I don't think I could do that to him, not to Morris, not after all this time. He gave me a chance to be someone in the motor trade, none of us would have been up to much without him'.

Kimber soon found other work, first with coachbuilders Charlesworth, for whom he organised aircraft production, and then with Specialloid Pistons. He was approached by John Black, who had recently bought up Triumph, but was not happy with Black's plans. These were not unlike those of Morris in 1935; to use components from a mass-production saloon (Standard) in a sports car. He was considering retirement after the war, but never lived to enjoy it. He died in a freak railway accident at King's Cross station in February 1945, one of only two people killed when a train ran backwards and overturned.

Opinions differ on Kimber's skill as an engineer; he was President of the Institute of Mechanical Engineers, Automobile Division, a position not earned easily, yet he undoubtedly relied a great deal on his colleagues, in particular his chief engineer H.N. Charles, and long-term colleagues such as Cecil Cousins, Syd Enever, and Reg Jackson. His gifts lay more, perhaps, in his artistic eye and flair for colour and line which made many of his 1930s cars among the best-looking on the market. His contribution to the world of motoring can be summed up in a letter he wrote to a friend after his enforced resignation in 1941, 'I have the satisfaction of having created a car that has given lots of fun and pleasure to thousands'.

Cecil Kimber was married twice: first to Irene Hunt, who died in 1938, and second to Muriel Dewar. By his first marriage he had two daughters, Lisa who married Dean Delamont of the RAC, and Jean, who married first Eric McGavin, and secondly Dennis Cook, and who is a tireless ambassador for the MG marque around the world.

NG

Further Reading
The Cecil Kimber Centenary Book, ed. Richard Knudson, The New England MG T Register Ltd, 1988.
Oxford to Abingdon, Robin Barraclough and Phil Jennings, Myrtle Publishing, 1998.

1958 MG (i) A twin-cam sports car.
NICK BALDWIN

1964 MG (i) Magnette IV saloon.
NICK BALDWIN

[image of cars including MGB and Midget]

1976 MG (i) B (foreground) and Midget sports cars.
NICK BALDWIN

single carburettor engine, and AP automatic transmission was available on the 1300 from 1968 to 1969 only. Production figures were 124,860 of the 1100 and 32,549 of the 1300.

The MGA

The streamlined body first seen at Le Mans in 1951 finally went into production in 1955, powered by the 1489cc 'B' engine in 72bhp twin carburettor form, and known as the MGA. For the first time since 1928 there was no Midget in the range, though the name would be revived later. The MGA was an instant success, being up to date in appearance and with excellent performance and handling. Top speed was 96mph (155km/h) and, as MG expert F. Wilson McComb observed 'to lose an MGA on a corner called for the most outrageous lack of discretion'. More than 13,000 MGAs were sold in the first year of production,

and total sales of the A between mid–1955 and mid–1962 were 101,081. This figure included 2111 of the Twin Cam 1600, and 40,220 of the pushrod 1600 which was made from 1959 to 1962. An attractive closed coupé was offered from 1956 onwards, slightly faster than the open cars because of better aerodynamics.

The Twin Cam MGA had a 1588cc engine which developed 108bhp compared with the 72bhp of the 1500, giving a top speed of 113mph (182km/h). Disc brakes were provided on all four wheels, and an identifying feature was the use of centre-lock disc wheels. If the engine had been reliable the Twin Cam would have been a worthy rival to the Porsche 356 or Alfa Romeo Giulietta. In skilled hands and with the right octane of petrol it was all right, and there were a number of race successes to prove it, but less experienced drivers frequently over-revved it, burning out pistons in the process, and the necessary 100 octane fuel was not always available. Problems with the cars in America were said to be earning MG a bad reputation as a whole, so in April 1960 the Twin Cam was dropped. Several hundred chassis were left over, and these were fitted with 1588cc or 1622cc pushrod engines, and sold as 1600 De luxe (82 made) or Mk II De Luxe (313 made) respectively. They were very desirable cars, combining the pushrod engine's reliability with the disc brakes of the Twin Cam.

Return of the Midget

The Austin Healey Sprite had been styled by Healey, but was developed and built at Abingdon. When the time came for the 'Frogeye' to be updated, the front end was restyled by Healey in a more conventional manner, with wing-mounted headlamps, while the tail design was the work of MG stylists. The Sprite II was announced in May 1961, and in the following month came its MG version for which the name Midget was revived. Apart from the MG radiator grill, chrome strips along the sides, different instrument faces and seats with contrasting piping, the Midget was the same car as the Sprite, but cost £38.50 more. Both cars were made side by side in the MG factory, but Sprite sales outstripped those of the Midget (31,665 Sprite IIs, 25,681 Midget Is). Both cars received a 1098cc engine and front disc brakes in 1962, and were revised in 1964 as the Sprite III and Midget II, with semi-elliptic rear suspension in place of quarter elliptics and radius arms, and wind-up windows. The Midget III (1966–69) had a detuned Mini Cooper S engine of 1275cc and 65bhp, while the Mk IV (1969–74) had a new grill shared with the Sprite, Rostyle spoked wheels (although wire wheels could be had as an option) and black sills and windscreen surrounds. British Leyland lost the right to the Healey name in December 1970, and after a few Austin Sprites had been made in 1971 the name was dropped, and all the same small sports cars were badged as MG Midgets. Nomenclature is confusing, for some sources refer to the 1969–74 cars as Mark IVs, others as Mk IIIs with the works number GAN5. The last Midgets, 1974–79, were either Midget 1500s or Mk IIIs (GAN6). They had the Triumph Spitfire's 1493cc engine, increased ride height and large black plastic bumpers front and rear, to meet US safety regulations. On the credit side, top speed was over 100mph (160km/h), but the Midget was by now woefully old-fashioned, and because the corporate policy of BL favoured the Triumph sports cars no funds were made available for updating the Midget or its larger companion, the MGB. The last Midget came off the line in late 1979, about twelve months before the last MGB.

The MGB and its Variants

The MGA was a hard act to follow, but the company came up with an even more successful car in the MGB. Introduced in September 1962, the B used a modified and enlarged (1798cc) A engine, transmission and front suspension in an all-new chassis. This was a steel monocoque lower than the A by 1in (25mm), and wider by 2in (50mm). The B was 5in (127mm) shorter in overall length. Visibility was much improved, and although initially the B was not much faster than its predecessor, 104mph (168km/h), it was more comfortable and capable of higher cornering speeds. It reached a wider market and in its first full year of production, 1963, it helped towards a 75 per cent increase in MG output, to around 30,000 cars. 1964 was even better, with sales approaching 38,000 of which more than 30,000 were exported. It is worth noting that actual car production at Abingdon was considerably higher than this, because Austin Healey Sprites were also built there as well as Morris Minor Travellers and vans from 1960 to 1964. In 1965 an attractive coupé, the MGB GT, joined the open model, and was available in all subsequent variants of the B. After 115,898 roadsters and 21,835 coupés had been made, the original B was replaced by the Mk II in 1967. This had an all-synchromesh gearbox with the option of automatic from 1967 to 1973. A new grill and Rostyle wheels did not improve its appearance, though wire wheels could be had as an option.

1980 MG (i) B GT coupé .
NICK GEORGANO

A new model in 1967 was the MGC, which was seen as a replacement for the ageing Austin Healey 3000, using that car's 6-cylinder 2912cc engine in the MGB hull. The larger engine gave a top speed of 118mph (190km/h), but its penalty was a heavier front end which necessitated a redesigned front suspension, in which torsion bars replaced the B's coils. Handling was not as good as on the B, and there was a notable lack of torque at low speeds. The MGC was not well received by the press who felt that it lacked the sporting character of the B. Few customers were prepared to pay £154 more than for a B, and the C was quietly dropped towards the end of 1969, after 8999 had been made. The MGB, on the other hand, enjoyed evergreen popularity, and was made up to 23 October 1980, when the Abingdon production line closed down for ever. It was not greatly changed in the 1970s, as MG was starved of development funds. Its appearance was altered, and not for the better, in 1974 when, to meet US safety regulations, large black bumpers replaced the slim chromed ones, and the ride height was raised, the same modifications that the Midget suffered. Engine output declined as well, because of emission controls. Total production of all MGB Mk IIs was 375,147.

A short-lived but exciting MGB was the V8, which was powered by the 3528cc Rover V8 engine, itself developed from a Buick design. Apart from the V8 badge on the radiator grill and new wheels similar to those of the Reliant Scimitar GTE, there was no external difference between the V8 and the 4-cylinder MGB. This was perhaps unfortunate, for owners wanted to advertise the fact that they had paid £529 more for a car capable of more than 125mp (200km/h). The main reason for limited production was that MG could not get enough of the V8 engines, particularly after the introduction of Rover's SD1 saloon in June 1976. Only 2591 MGBs were made with the V8 engine, all of them GT coupés, although a few have been privately converted to roadsters.

Rebirth in the 1980s
When British Leyland announced the closure of the MG factory, a consortium led by Alan Curtis of Aston Martin showed interest in buying MG to continue production at Abingdon. However, they were not allowed to use the name, which BL wanted to keep for future models, and the deal never went through. Their retention of the name became clear in May 1982 when they announced a high-performance version of the Metro which carried the MG name and famous octagon badge. Special wheels, a rear spoiler and a new interior also

1993 MG (i) RV8 sports car.
NICK BALDWIN

distinguished the car which had a tuned version of the 1275cc engine, giving 72bhp and a top speed of 100mph (160km/h). October 1982 saw the arrival of the Metro Turbo, whose Garrett turbocharger boosted power to 93bhp, with a top speed of 112mph (180km/h). When the MG Metro was launched it was estimated that it would account for around 8 per cent of all Metros, but the reality was 15 per cent or more. These two models remained in production until 1991, along with the MG-badged versions of the Maestro and Montego. The latter had a fuel-injected 2-litre O series engine, giving a top speed of 115mph (185km/h). A highly specialised Metro Turbo was the 6R4 (6-cylinders, Rally car, 4-wheel drive) built for Group B rallying in 1984. This bore little resemblance to any Metro you could buy, apart from the general shape of the body, being powered by a mid-mounted 2½-litre V6 engine developing 240bhp, and driving all four wheels via a 5-speed gearbox.

The MG badge returned to sports cars in 1992 on the RV8. This was a stop-gap model, using an MGB body shell and power from a 3.9-litre Rover V8 engine. Top speed was 135mph (217km/h) and it had a certain nostalgic charm, but it was hopelessly outdated for the 1990s. No more than 2000 were sold before a

1998 MG (i) F Abingdon Limited Edition sports car.
ROVER GROUP

more original car appeared under the MG name. This was the MGF, which used a mid-mounted 1.8-litre twin-cam Rover K series engine available in two versions, standard and VVC, the latter with variable valve control. Outputs were 120 and 145bhp respectively. With the more powerful model anti-lock braking was available. For 2000 a supercharged version was offered as well, with power as high as 230bhp, and semi-automatic transmission was available.

In May 2000 BMW sold the Rover Group to the Phoenix consortium, who continued the MG name on high-performance versions of Rover models, and planned a 160mph (257km/h) coupé based on the QVALE Mangusta platform.

NG

Further Reading
MG by McComb, F. Wilson McComb, Osprey, 1984.
Oxford to Abingdon, Robin Barraclough and Phil Jennings, Myrtle Publishing, 1998.
The MGA, MGB and MGC, Graham Robson, MRP, 1980.
MGB, the Complete Story, Brian Laban, Crowood, 1990.
Sprites and Midgets, the Complete Story, Anders Ditlev Clausager, Crowood, 1991.
MG Saloon Cars, Andrew Ditlev Clausager, Bay View Books, 1998.
The MGA, First of a Line, John Price Williams, Veloce, 1999.
Early MG, Phil Jennings, Published by the author, 1989.

MG (ii) (RA) 1966–1967
Compania Industrial de Automotores SA, Monte Chingolo, Buenos Aires.
Derived from the Di Tella 1500, the MG was produced at the Monte Chingolo plant which Compania Industrial de Automotores SA took over after SIAM Di Tella ceased production there. The MG, with its larger engine capacity developed 75bhp instead of the Di Tella's 55bhp. Only 235 cars with the MG badge were made before production ceased in April, 1967.

ACT

M.G.P. (F) 1912
Automobiles Jean Margaria, St Cyr, Seine.
One model of the M.G.P. was listed, with 12hp monobloc 4-cylinder engine of 2.3-litres capacity.

NG

MIAMI UNICORN (US) c.1990
Miami Unicorn, Miami, Florida.
The Pegasus Countach and Testarossa were kit cars built by this Florida company.

HP

MIARI E GIUSTI (I) 1896–1899
Miari, Giusti et Cia, Padua.
Professor Enrico Bernardi was a pioneer Italian car maker, building a tiny car for his 4-year old son as early as 1884. In 1892 he built a full-size 3-wheeler for two adults, and two years later this was put into production by Miari e Giusti. It had a 624cc horizontal single-cylinder engine with detachable head, and hot tube ignition. Final drive to the single rear wheel was by chain.

NG

MICHEL (F) 1926–1927
Aviation Michel, Strasbourg.
After World War I Auguste Michel set up a business reconditioning aero engines, including such famous models as Mercedes, Gnome-Rhône, Fiat, Hispano-Suiza Liberty, Renault and Maybach. From this he proceeded to making aero engines destined for light aircraft designed by Vaslin, then to a proprietary car engine of 1017cc and then to a complete car, the 6CV which was powered by the same engine. It had coil ignition, a 4-speed gearbox and front-wheel brakes, and the small disc-wheeled tourer looked not unlike a Mathis. Few were made, and Michel returned to general engineering, although his light aero engines were still offered in 1933.

NG

MICHEL IRAT (F) 1929–1930
Automobiles Michel Irat SA, Paris.
Michel Irat was the son of the better-known car maker, Georges Irat. In 1929 the latter acquired the Chaigneau-Braiser company (see BRASIER) and reorganised it under his son's name. The Type CB2 Michel Irat was very similar to the small Chaigneau-Brasier, with a 1086cc side-valve engine. After Georges Irat decided there was no point in running two separate companies, and absorbed Michel Irat into his own. He did not continue the design.

NG

MICHEL UN (F) 1926
Automobiles Michel Un, Neuilly-sur-Seine.
The Michel Un used the engine and chassis of the 2120cc 11CV DONNET-ZÉDEL, but the conventional gearbox was replaced by a ZF-Soden 4-speed preselector, with push-button control. Forward and reverse were selected by a lever on the steering wheel. They advertised that 'changing speeds is no longer a chore, but child's play'. Tourer and saloon models were offered, but they were considerably more expensive than a standard Donnet-Zédel, the saloon costing 10,000 francs more at 48,000 francs, which probably explains why the Michel Un did not survive more than a year.

NG

MICHIGAN (i) (US) 1901
Michigan Automobile Co., Grand Rapids, Michigan.
This was an attractive-looking little tiller-steered steam car. Alternatively called the Carter Steam Stanhope, it was the first automotive effort of Byron J. Carter, who later made the JAXON steamer, JACKSON petrol car, and best known of the four, the friction-drive CARTERCAR.

NG

MICHIGAN (ii) (US) 1903–1907
Michigan Automobile Co., Kalamazoo, Michigan.
Made by the Blood brothers, Maurice and Charles, the first of this series of Michigans was a light car powered by a 3$\frac{1}{2}$hp single-cylinder engine with tiller steering, on a wheelbase of only 48in (1218mm) on the prototype and 54in (1370mm) on production cars. About 100 of these had been made by the end of 1904, together with about 30 of a larger car with 12hp 2-cylinder engine and rear-entrance tonneau body. The Blood brothers then left Michigan and formed the Blood Automobile & Machinery Co. to make a car under their own name. What were essentially the same designs were made by Michigan up to 1907, being 16hp twins with side-entrance tonneau bodies.

NG

MICHIGAN (iii) (US) 1904–1913
Michigan Buggy Co., Kalamazoo, Michigan.
This company entered the motor trade with a motorised version of their horse-drawn buggy, using a 3$\frac{1}{2}$hp single-cylinder engine and a transmission which gave two forward speeds but offered no reverse. They were made in very small numbers, and car production proper did not start until 1911 when they brought out a conventional car with 40hp 4-cylinder Buda engine and roadster or tourer bodies. This was joined by a 33hp for 1912, and they were made up to 1913, when financial mismanagement brought the company to a close.

NG

MICHIGAN (iv) (US) 1910

Michigan Motor & Manufacturing Co., Detroit, Michigan.
This company exhibited a roadster with 33hp 6-cylinder engine at the Detroit
Show in January 1910, and promised production of 500 cars from a large factory
at Rochester. This turned out to be a small shed, and the grandly-named company
to be a stock promoting scheme. The show car was probably the only Michigan
Six ever made.

NG

MICHIGAN (v) (US) 1916

Michigan Hearse & Motor Co., Grand Rapids, Michigan.
This company specialised in hearses, but made a few 6-cylinder limousines which
could be used by undertakers as mourners' cars in funeral processions.

NG

MICRO see CITY MOBILE

MICROBOND (NZ) 1957

Weltex Plastics Ltd, Christchurch, South Island.
The Mistral, built under licence from Micron Plastics in England, was New
Zealand's first successful fibreglass car project. Bob Blackburn headed the
enterprise and the fibreglass work was directed by Bill Ashton, formerly the
body designer of the English company. Although the body was sold for fitting
to such chassis as the Austin A40, Ford Prefect and Singer 9, a complete car was
also offered, which had a tubular chassis, swing-axle ifs and a hotted Ford Ten
engine coupled to a close-ratio gearbox. A Mistral body was also fitted to a
prominent competition car, the 'Cropduster', a name which derived from its
Gipsy Major aero engine.

MG

MICROCAR (i) (F) 1957

An expansive Plexiglass 'bubble' top distinguished the curious Microcar 3-wheeler.
It had a tubular steel chassis and plastic lower bodywork, with two hoops
supporting the dome top, behind which were sited the headlamps. A 125cc
single-cylinder or 250cc engine powered the single front wheel.

CR

MICROCAR (ii) (F) 1980 to date

1980–1988 Constructions Nautiques Janneau, Les Herbiers, Vendée.
1988–1997 Microcar sarl, Les Herbiers, Vendée.
1997 to date Janneau New Co., Les Herbiers, Vendée.
The Janneau boatbuilding firm took over the rights to the MINI-CAT, gave
it four wheels and repositioned the 49cc Peugeot engine to the front. It was
renamed the Microcar RJ49 and adopted a position at the absolute cheapest
end of the market. It was joined by the DX49 coupé in 1981 and a convertible
RJ in 1983. For 1984 the new Microcar 50 range was launched, engines ranging
from 50cc to 600cc, and the marque became France's best-selling microcar
brand, with 20,000 cumulative sales by 1987 thanks to a huge distribution
network. A new model in 1988 was the Spid, with 273cc Yanmar or 654cc
Ruggerini diesel engines. The new Lyra of 1990 slotted in below it in price and
was also sold, from 1992, with electric power. The 1994 Newstreet was a stylish
open fun car aimed at the 14–18 year-old age group, and was powered by a rear-
mounted 50cc Yamaha moped engine. In 1998 the range comprised the Lyra
and Newstreet.

CR

MICRODOT (GB) 1976–1981

Mallalieu Engineering Ltd, Abingdon, Oxfordshire.
Aston Martin designer William Towns first expressed his passion for city cars
in the Mini-based Minissima (initially called the Townscar) of 1973, which was
even given to British Leyland for evaluation. Three years later came the even
smaller Microdot, which he described as 'a bubble car for the 1980s'. It was
a tiny car with a large glass area (incorporating glass gullwing doors) and seating
for three abreast. Towns found a backer for the project in the Bentley Mk VI
sports car makers Mallalieu in 1980, who were to build a batch of cars with
a petrol engine (Mini, Reliant and marine 2-strokes were suggested). To be offered
in two versions, an economy and a luxury, at prices from £4000 to £7000, the

1913 Michigan (iii) Forty tourer.
NICK GEORGANO

c.1994 Microcar (ii) Spid 30SR.
NICK GEORGANO

Microdot would surely have been too expensive. As it was, Mallalieu's bankruptcy
in 1981 put paid to the plan. The Microdot was eventually acquired by Daihatsu
GB, which installed a 547cc Domino (Mira) engine in place of the original electric
powerplant.

CR

MICRON (F) 1925–1930

Automobiles Micron, Castanet-Tolosane, Toulouse.
This was one of the smallest of 1920s French cyclecars, powered by single-
cylinder engines of 350 or 500cc. Designed and manufactured by Henri Jany, it
was made mostly as a single-seater, and was unusual in having front-wheel drive.

NG

MID-AMERICA (US) c.1994

Mid-America Industries, Milan, Illinois.
Mid-America built a Corvette Grand Sport replica that was sold in kit form.
They were available in coupé or roadster form to replicate the lightweight
Corvette racing cars built in 1963. Built on a 1963–67 Corvette tub, they had
either a Corvette chassis or a special Mid-America tube frame with Corvette
suspension.

HP

1982 Midas Gold coupé.
NICK BALDWIN

1990 Midas Gold convertible.
PASTICHE CARS

1912 Midland 25/30hp tourer.
BRYAN K. GOODMAN

MIDAS (GB) 1978 to date

1978–1982 D&H Fibreglass Techniques, Greenfield, Oldham, Greater Manchester.
1982–1989 Midas Cars, Corby, Northamptonshire.
1989–1990 Pastiche Cars Ltd, Rotherham, South Yorkshire.
1991 to date G.T.M. Cars, Loughborough, Leicestershire.
Harold Dermott took over production of the Mini-Marcos in 1975 but his intention was always to move up-market. So he asked Richard Oakes to design a new Mini-based coupé called the Midas. This was an unusually competent kit car with a chassis-less monocoque body made entirely of fibreglass. It housed a complete Mini front subframe, a steel rear beam, and B.M.C. A-series engine. Kits were mostly very up-market compared to the standards of the day. Later cars – by now dubbed Midas Bronze – had revised bumpers incorporating foglamps. The concept was developed further with the 1985 Midas Gold, which was based on Austin/MG Metro parts. Richard Oakes restyled it with blistered

wings, a new frogeye front end and larger side windows, while McLaren F1 designer Gordon Murray contributed to under-car aerodynamics. A convertible Gold was launched in 1989. Midas suffered a factory fire in 1989 and was forced to liquidate. All Midas products were briefly revived by Pastiche Cars, but in 1991 GTM bought the Gold Convertible project, going on to add many changes, like Hydragas suspension and an optional hard-top. Meanwhile the Midas Bronze was produced by MIDTEC from 1992 up until 1997. Proving that the concept was still fresh, a new model in 1995 was the Midas 2+2. Once again Richard Oakes was responsible for the styling, which was longer and wider and boasted a cleaner front end and a bustle back. Under the skin it used post–1990 Rover Metro or 100 mechanicals.
CR

MIDDLEBRIDGE (GB) 1987–1990

Middlebridge Scimitar Ltd, Beeston, Nottinghamshire.
Middlebridge took on the defunct RELIANT Scimitar GTE and modified it in over 450 different ways to become the Middlebridge Scimitar. Notable among the changes were a rear anti-roll bar and modified springing and damping. The Ford V6 power route was kept, using the 2.9-litre Scorpio unit. As with the Reliant, its most famous customer was H.R.H. Princess Anne, but the company was liquidated before it had a chance to relaunch the GTC convertible as well as the sports estate. About 80 were made.
CR

MIDDLEBY (US) 1909–1913

Middleby Automobile Co., Reading, Pennsylvania.
Charles Middleby made his cars in the factory recently vacated by the Duryea Power Co., and used much of the same machinery. Unlike the Duryea, the Middleby was a conventional car, unusual only in its use of air-cooling. The engine was a 25hp four, and it was offered in various open body styles, tourer, runabout and surrey. The cars were distinguished by their peaked bonnets. For 1911 Middleby brought out a larger car, with 40hp water-cooled engine and wheelbase lengthened from 108 (2741mm) to 122in (3096mm). This was less successful than the air-cooled models.
NG

MIDDLETOWN (US) 1909–1911

Middletown Buggy Co., Middletown, Ohio.
Founded in 1901 as the New Decatur Buggy Co., this was one of the largest horse-drawn vehicle manufacturers, with an output of more than 20,000 per year. Falling sales of horse buggies led them into the motor field and, reorganised as the Middletown Buggy Co., they launched a car in 1909. Its Rutenber engine had four cylinders, which was unusual for a motor buggy, but it did not sell at all well, and by 1911 the new company was bankrupt. Owner Harry Elwood leased part of the buggy factory to make a forward-control truck called the Crescent, but this venture lasted only two years.
NG

MIDLAND (US) 1908–1913

Midland Motor Co., Moline, Illinois.
This company succeeded DEERE-CLARK, though the 1908 Midland was not related in design to the 1907 Deere, apart from the fact they both had medium-sized 4-cylinder engines. The Midland was made initially with a 30/35hp engine and 118in (2995mm) wheelbase, joined in 1909 by a 25/30hp on a 112in (2843mm) wheelbase. By 1911 the largest had a 50hp engine, still with 118in (2995mm) wheelbase, and five styles of open body were offered. All the 4-cylinder engines were made by Milwaukee, and possibly the 50hp six introduced for 1912 was as well. The company's slogan was 'Unusual Cars at Common Prices', and if their design was nothing out of the ordinary, they were apparently well made and well liked. About 600 were made each year in 1911–12–13, but mismanagement led to a massive bankruptcy in 1914, and the end of the Midland car.
NG

MIDSTATES (US) 1982 to date

MidStates Classic Cars and Parts Inc, Hooper, Nebraska.
The Cobra replica made by MidStates was available with a variety of frame and suspension options. A simple ladder frame could be adapted to Ford or Chevrolet

running gear, and Ford, Corvette or Jaguar suspension could be ordered. Also, special suspension from VSE could be specified. They were sold in kit and turnkey form.

HP

MIDTEC (GB) 1992–1997
Midtec Sports Cars, Leicester.
This project originated as the NOBLE Midtec Spyder and was an attempt to offer a lightweight mid-engined sports car in kit form. A huge variety of powerplants could be fitted, from Renault to Ford Pinto to Fiat twin-cam, in all cases mounted longitudinally behind the driver. Adjustable double wishbone suspension was used all round. Midtec assumed the MIDAS Bronze in 1992 and a small Ford-engined open 2-seater sports prototype called the Calico was displayed in 1994 but did not proceed further.

CR

MIELE (D) 1911–1913
Miele & Cie Maschinenfabrik, Gütersloh.
Renowned today for high-quality washing machines and dishwashers, Miele had a short-lived venture into car production. There were two 4-cylinder models, the 1568cc 6/17PS and the 2292cc 9/22PS, both designed by Professor Klemm who was later well-known for his light aircraft. They had monobloc engines, 4-speed gearboxes and shaft drive.

HON

MIER (US) 1908–1909
Mier Carriage & Buggy Co., Ligonia, Indiana.
Mier was an established buggy manufacturer when they decided to make a motorised version in 1908. It had the usual 2-cylinder engine under the seat, with friction transmission and double-chain drive, but a frontal bonnet gave it a different appearance from the average high-wheel buggy. About 100 were sold in the first season, and a longer wheelbase and slightly more powerful engine were offered in 1909, but it was a very crowded market, and Mier could not compete. At the end of 1909 they abandoned motor vehicles for horse-drawn buggies, which they continued to make up to the 1920s.

NG

MIESSE (B) 1896–1926
Jules Miesse et Cie, Brussels.
In 1894 Jules Miesse left his job as foreman in a steel stamping works to start his own engineering business in the Brussels suburb of Anderlecht. Two years later he built a steam car with 3-cylinder horizontal engine fired by paraffin in an armoured wood frame. After two further years of trials he put it on the market. By 1902 he was making cars with two sizes of engine, 6 and 10CV, increased to 10 and 15CV, when he went over to all-steel chassis. Their flash boilers were housed under a bonnet and final drive was by chains.

In the spring of 1902 the Miesse Steam Motor Syndicate Ltd was formed to exploit the patents in England, and later in the year a manufacturing licence was sold to the TURNER Motor Manufacturing Co. of Wolverhampton. For two years the cars were sold as Miesse, then as Turner-Miesse. They also built steam trucks, and continued production of Miesse-type steamers until 1913, seven years after the Belgian parent company had given them up. The cars sold in England had a variety of bodies, 'all by English carriage-builders of the highest repute', 4- and 6-seater tonneau, 5-seater stanhope (with dickey seat for footman behind), and closed coupé. It is interesting that the 1902 catalogue criticised the petrol engine, saying that its action resembled the blow of a hammer, and praised steam to the skies, yet Jules Miesse started experimenting with internal combustion in 1900, and put a light car on the market in Belgium in 1902. A taxicab chassis was made in 1904, and this became an important part of the business. Miesse showed a large petrol car with Goldschmidt-Direct gearless transmission at the 1904 Brussels Salon, but it seems that, apart from the taxis, very few petrol cars were made until 1906. In that year steamers were given up, and two petrol models with T-head engines, a 24hp four and a 35hp six, were made. In 1907 the largest engine was a 60hp six with monobloc construction, unusual for a six at that date. The works were more than doubled in area in 1906, enabling production to exceed 200 per year.

By 1909 all models had monobloc engines, and in 1912 there was a 20hp

1912 Miele 9/22PS tourer.
GILES CHAPMAN

1902 Miesse 10hp Class E steam coupé.
NICK BALDWIN

1909 Miesse 24/30hp landaulet.
NICK BALDWIN

so-called 'valveless' engine which used a combination of piston and slide valves. The 1914 range had 4-cylinder L-head engines of 2813 and 4396cc, dry-sump lubrication, 4-speed gearboxes, electric lighting and vee-radiators which characterised Miesse cars up to 1924. In the middle of the 1914 season they brought out an advanced four with single-ohc, but World War I prevented development.

Two new models with single-ohc derived from the 1914 design were introduced after the war, a four and a straight-8. They had the same cylinder dimensions, 69 × 130m, giving 1943 and 3886cc. The same dimensions were used for a 2915cc six in 1923, and there was also a smaller six of 1356cc. A flat radiator replaced the vee in 1924, and front-wheel brakes were offered as standard in

1035

1917 Milburn light electric brougham.
NATIONAL MOTOR MUSEUM

1925, when the larger straight-8 went up to 4.6 litres. A large factory extension in 1919 was given over to commercial vehicles, and these gradually took over in importance By the mid 1920s no more than 100 cars were being made per year, and in 1926 they were dropped. There had been plans in 1923 for the DUNAMIS straight-8, sponsored by tobacco maker Theo Verellen, to be made in the Miesse factory, but nothing came of these. Truck and bus production flourished though, and in 1926 Miesse made what was probably the first straight-8 engine to be used in a commercial vehicle, They adopted Gardner diesel engines in 1932, and continued to make commercials up to 1972. From 1946 to the mid-50s they assembled NASH cars for the Belgian market, and also made a few MAICO-CHAMPIONs under licence.

NG

MIEUSSET (F) 1903–1914

Ateliers de Construction Mécanique et d'Automobiles Mieusset, Lyons.
This company was founded in 1867 to make fire-extinguishing equipment, and continued in this business long after car manufacture ended. They began with an ambitious range of five cars, a 6hp single-cylinder with the option of chain or shaft drive, an 8/12hp twin and three 4-cylinder models, of 12/16, 16/20 and 20/25hp, all with double-chain drive. Larger fours of 40 and 60hp joined the range in 1906, and were made without great change until 1914. From 1906 to 1908 Mieusset made a concerted drive to sell cars in the United States, being imported by J.P. Bruyère, but this business did not last long.

The 1914 range consisted of eight models, all with 4-cylinder engines, from a 12/16 to a 60/80hp. Car production was never more than a sideline for Mieusset. It was not revived World War I, though trucks were made until 1925.

NG

MIG see MONTE CARLO

MIGNON (F) 1908

C.E. Chepke, Paris.
The few cars made under the Mignon name were 8hp 2-cylinder voiturettes or 12/14hp 4-cylinder tourers.

NG

MIGNONETTE (F) 1900

Wehrle et Godard-Desmaret, Neuilly, Seine.
The Mignonette was a light voiturette powered by a rear-mounted engine geared to the rear axle. 3hp De Dion-Bouton or Aster engines could be had, and the car had a 2-seater body and wheel steering.

NG

MIGNONETTE-LUAP (F) 1899–1900

Jiel-Laval et Cie, Bordeaux.
This car had no known connection with the Mignonette from Neuilly, though it was also a light voiturette powered by a rear-mounted De Dion-Bouton engine, in this case, of 2¼hp. In the event of engine failure, the car was provided with pedals, and it was said to be sufficiently light to be pedalled to the nearest garage. It had tiller steering.

NG

MIJMAR (NL) 1972–1973

Mijmar, Aalsmeer.
This company was a maker of hard-tops (for example, for the Fiat 850 Spider) before launching into production with the Mijmar Martare GT. This was a very low-slung sports coupé with fibreglass bodywork that vaguely resembled a Ford GT40. The entire front half of the car hinged forward for passenger entry. Two versions were offered: one with a VW Beetle chassis and engine and one with its own chassis and a Fiat 125 engine. In both cases the engine was rear-mounted.

CR

MIKASA (J) 1957–1961

Okamura Manufacturing Co. Ltd, Yokosuka.
Having made a torque converter and aeroplanes, Okamura turned to the manufacture of the Mikasa light car in 1957. There were two models: the Mk I (a 2-door estate car) and the Touring (an open sports car). The former was powered by an 18-21bhp air-cooled 2-cylinder 4-stroke 585cc boxer engine driving the front wheels, although that in the Touring developed slightly more at between 21 and 23bhp. The transmission was a 2-speed fluid torque converter and drive went to the front wheels. The box-section chassis had ifs by quarter-elliptic leaf springs, while the rear axle was suspended on semi-elliptic springs.

CR

MIKROMOBIL (D) 1922–1924

1922–1924 Automobile-Gesellschaft Thomsen KG, Hamburg-Wandsbek.
1924 Mikromobil AG, Hamburg-Wandsbek.
Despite its name this was not the smallest of cars, having a 6/18PS 4-cylinder 2-stroke engine and a 4-seater body.

HON

MIKRUS (PL) 1958–1960

Wytwornia Sprzetu Komunikacyjnego, Mielec.
This was a 2-door saloon with a rear-mounted 2-cylinder air-cooled engine developing 14bhp at 5000rpm.

NG

MILANO (i) (I) 1906–1907

Stà Milanese d'Industria Meccanica, Milan.
The Milano was typical of many Italian makes which tried to establish themselves on an overcrowded market. It had a 22/28hp 4-cylinder engine and shaft drive. Its only unusual features were water-cooled brakes and a turbine fan mounted on the periphery of the flywheel. It had a Hotchkiss-like circular radiator.

NG

MILANO (ii) see J.W.F.

MILANO (iii) see S&J

MILBURN (US) 1914–1923

Milburn Wagon Co., Toledo, Ohio.
This wagon maker was founded in 1848, and in 1909, while they were still in the horse-drawn business, they leased part of their plant to the Ohio Electric Car Co. who made the OHIO Electric there until they moved into their own factory in 1911. This presumably turned the thoughts of Milburn's directors towards the electric vehicle, and in September 1914 they began production of their own version. It was lighter-looking than many contemporaries, with wire wheels and an attractive curved front. In addition to the usual coupé they made a roadster and a delivery van. The Model 36L limousine of 1919 had a bonnet which made it look just like a petrol-engined car, but this attempt at disguise was not popular, also perhaps because it cost $900 more than the traditional coupé. Milburns were used by President Wilson's secret service staff.

A disastrous fire in December 1919 seriously damaged the company's finances, but the electric car was on the way out anyway. Milburn were re-capitalised in 1921, but by then three-quarters of their workforce was building bodies for Oldsmobile. This GM link was strengthened when the Corporation bought the factory in February 1923. A few last electrics were assembled for a month or two, then the factory was used for the assembly of Buicks.

NG

MILDÉ; MILDÉ-GAILLARDET (F) 1898–1909; 1907–c.1912

Mildé et Cie, Levallois-Perret, Seine.

Charles Mildé was one of the leading makers of electric vehicles in France. His first effort, in 1898, was a 3hp power pack and drive system which could be bolted onto any horse-drawn vehicle. In November 1898 he advertised a light postal delivery van, and made a number of commercial vehicles from then onwards. At the 1900 Paris Salon he displayed five vehicles including a cab, an omnibus, a fore-carriage or *avant-train* for motorising horse-drawn vehicles, and a 3-wheeled car. The latter was called the Mildé et Mondos and used two motors on the rear axle.

In 1901, in partnership with Michel Ephrussi who was related to the Rothschild family, Mildé took over the ailing Société l'Électromotion which imported COLUMBIA electrics, their support enabling Électromotion to continue in business until 1907. By 1903 Mildé design had settled down to a conventional range of electric cars and vans, with single, compound-wound motors on the rear axle, seven to nine forward speeds, the highest giving 22mph (35km/h), and two or three speeds in reverse. Like his rival Charles Kriéger, Mildé became interested in petrol-electric drive but had no experience of the internal combustion engine. He asked Frédéric Gaillardet, who had been chief engineer for DOCTORESSE and La Française (DIAMANT), to look after the petrol-electric cars. The first of these, made in 1904, used a 6hp De Dion-Bouton engine, but larger 4-cylinder engines were used later. From about 1907 they were called Mildé-Gaillardets and had Renault-type bonnets, engines up to 30/35hp and shaft drive. The pure electrics were dropped in 1909, but Mildé-Gaillardet carried on, two new models being announced at the 1911 Paris Salon, with 6-cylinder engines of 18/20 and 35/40hp. Mildé's name was not seen again until World War II when it was combined with Kriéger in the Mildé-Krieger electric conversions of La Licorne cars and Chenard-Walcker vans.

NG

MILES; MILO (GB) 1910–1912

Joubert Miles, Sharpness, Gloucestershire.

Miles set himself up in business as a cycle manufacturer at the age of 12 in the 1880s and later contracted to manufacture frames for other firms, such as Pedersens in nearby Dursley. His first involvement with the motor trade came with a batch of frames built for Fée (later Fairy and Douglas) motorcycles in Kingswood, Bristol, before they developed their own facilities. When he saw the increasing popularity of light cars, he went into limited production with a tricar of his own design, predictably with tubular frame and chain drive. He always used JAP engines for these, air- or water-cooled, which he deemed to be the most reliable available. 4-wheeled versions were available later, and one or two conventional full-sized cars were also built. With the advent of mass-produced cars he ceased development and concentrated again on cycles. He was still producing specialist machines such as circus unicycles up to his retirement in the 1960s at the age of 92.

DF

MILLARD-LE GUI see LE GUI

MILLER (i) (US) 1911–1914

Miller Car Co., Detroit, Michigan.

This company made a very conventional car with 4-cylinder engines of 30 or 40hp, shaft drive and tourer or roadster bodies. The company also made the Kosmath delivery van, and when this design was bought up by Elmore Gregg of Pittsburgh, a number of Miller employees moved there. In 1916 Gregg launched the PENNSY car, which incorporated much of the Miller's design.

NG

MILLER (ii) (US) 1928–1932

Harry Miller, Los Angeles, California.

Harry Armenius Miller (1875–1943) was the most famous builder of racing cars in America between the wars, his cars dominating racing at Indianapolis and on the board tracks in the 1920s, while every Indy winner from 1930 to 1938 was powered by a Miller engine. His road cars were few and far between; he built one for family use in 1905, but apparently it did not work very well. In 1922 he announced plans to build a $2000 4-cylinder car and a $10,000 car to be powered by his 2-litre straight-8 racing engine, but he was too busy even to build

1919 Milburn Model 36B electric sedan.
NICK BALDWIN

1900 Mildé et Mondos electric 3-wheeler.
NATIONAL MOTOR MUSEUM

prototypes. However, in 1928 he built a made-to-order roadster powered by a 5080cc V8 engine specially built for this car, with 4-wheel drive. It was delivered to wealthy California sportsman Philip Chancellor. Four years later Miller received another commission, this time from a New York diplomat, William A. Burden. Also a roadster and also featuring 4-wheel drive, it had a supercharged V16 engine of 4965cc, and cost $35,000 (about $950,000 in today's money). That was the last of Harry Miller's road cars.

NG

MILLER-QUINCY (US) 1922–1924

The Miller Quincy Co., Quincy, Illinois.

Miller-Quincy was a specialist in the manufacture of funeral cars which, between 1922 and 1924, built a few large sedans and limousines, ostensibly for funeral use, on its own chassis. Like other specialists in this field, the cars were built on special order and there was no 'production' as such. The cars were powered by a Continental 6-cylinder 8R engine, were equipped with disc wheels, rode on a 130in (3299mm) wheelbase and were priced at $2780.

KM

MILLOT (i) (F) 1901–1902

Millot Frères, Gray, Haute-Saône.

This company was founded in 1805 to manufacture agricultural equipment, and turned to stationary engines in 1892. These were soon made in a great variety. By 1900 Millot were making engines in 22 models, running on petrol, paraffin or heavy oil, and used as marine engines, for generating electricity, for powering lighthouses as well as portable agricultural engines. In about 1900 they began making a self-propelled mobile saw bench, with 9hp single-cylinder engine under the seat, and followed this with a car having a 6 or 8hp 2-cylinder engine under the bonnet, with chain drive to the gearbox and chain final drive. A 12hp 4-cylinder tonneau was also made and, in 1902, an 8hp 4-cylinder car. Millot's cars formed a small part of their activities, and were quickly given up. At least three of the saw benches survive, having been fitted with *vis-à-vis* passenger bodies in the intervening years.

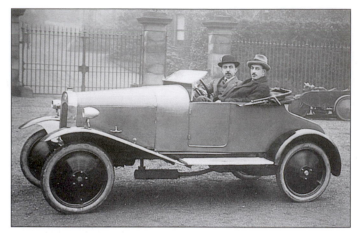

1920 Milton (i) 2-seater.
MICHAEL WORTHINGTON-WILLIAMS

1900 Milwaukee steam stanhope.
NICK BALDWIN

Engine production continued at Gray, and in 1925 an estimated 25,000 Millot engines were in service all over the world. Business declined after World War II, and the works were bought by the truck and tractor makers, Labourier. Millot retained a small part of the premises for maintenance and repair work. In 1987 the company, which had employed 1000 men at the turn of the century, had a staff of ten.

NG

MILLOT (ii) (CH) 1906–1907
1906–1907 Automobile Millot AG, Zürich.
Eugen KAUFMANN made passenger cars and some buses under his own name in Tägerwilen and founded this new company to produce powerful and expensive luxury cars in Zürich. The programme centred on two 4-cylinder models of 25/30hp and 40/50hp and two 6-cylinder models of 35/50 and 70/80hp. Prices ranged from SFr15,000 to 30,000. The T-head engines had separately cast cylinders and the crankshaft turned on ballbearings. Double ignition with magneto and coil, multiple-plate clutch and 4-speed gearbox were standard. The two smaller models were shaft-driven, whereas the larger models had chain drive. At an extra cost of SFr1000, an automatic starter was available and transmission brakes were water-cooled. A beautiful 70/80hp double phaeton coach-built by Geissberger, Zürich was exhibited at the Paris Show. Apart from the Dufaux cars from Geneva, this must have been the most powerful and costly Swiss passenger car of the period. After a very limited production the marque ceased to exist.

FH

MILNES (GB) 1901–1902
G.F. Milnes & Co. Ltd, Wellington, Shropshire.
Although sold under the name Milnes, these cars were made in Germany by the Berlin branch of the DAIMLER (i) company, and were sold in Germany under the name M.M.B. The chassis available had engines of 12, 16 and 24hp, to which Milnes-built bodies were fitted. They had four separately-cast cylinders with shaft drive on the 12 and 16hp, and chain drive on the 24hp. In 1902 M.M.B. stopped making passenger cars, which naturally brought the Milnes car to an end, but commercial vehicles were continued under the name Milnes-Daimler up to 1914. They supplied large numbers of buses to various London operators. G.F. Milnes were also well-known makers of tramcars.

NG

MILO (GB) c.1904–1907
Lambert Bros, Snodland, Kent.
Six cars were built by the Lambert brothers, including a rear-entrance tonneau powered by a 4-cylinder engine designed by Arthur Lambert. Castings for this were made by the Tilling-Stevens works at Maidstone. The name Milo was also used for the tricars made by Joubert MILES at Sharpness, Gloucestershire.

NG

MILTON (i) (GB) 1920–1922
Belford Motor Co., Edinburgh.
Named after Argentine-born Hangel Jacque Milton, who sponsored the make, the Milton was a light car powered by a 1088cc 4-cylinder Alpha engine, with friction transmission and final drive by single chain. The body was hinged at the rear, and could be lifted up for maintenance, a practice more familiar on American cars such as the Gale. In November 1921 Milton showed four cars at Olympia, 2- and 4-seater tourers, a coupé and a Special Sports. The engine was now a 1592cc Decolange. The company was liquidated early in 1922, and chassis numbering would indicate that no more than 12 Miltons were made. However, it is possible that a few more were assembled by the liquidator, one with a Dorman engine.

NG

MILTON (ii) (E) 1967–1968
Carrocerias Milton, Villafranca de Panadés.
This was a special convertible on a Seat 600D base using a tuned engine of 42hp and a strengthened chassis. The good-looking body was of fibreglass. A total of 36 cars were made for a price close to that of the 850 coupé.

VCM

MILWAUKEE (US) 1900–1902
Milwaukee Automobile Co., Milwaukee, Wisconsin.
When the Milwaukee company launched its steam cars it made no great claims for originality. 'It is not a radical departure from all other types, and will not revolutionise the whole automobile industry', they said. It was indeed like many others of its kind, with a 5hp vertical 2-cylinder engine, single-chain drive and tiller steering. Three body styles were listed, a 2-seater stanhope, 4-seater surrey which could be steered from the rear seat, and a delivery van. The same models were listed in 1901, at slightly higher prices, but for 1902 there was a more substantial-looking 4-seater rear-entrance tonneau with wheel steering and a small frontal bonnet. Milwaukee was bankrupt by June 1902.

NG

MILWAUKEE STAR (US) 1903
Milwaukee Auto Engines & Supply Co., Milwaukee, Wisconsin.
Ass their name implies, this company was mainly engaged in engine manufacture, but in 1903 they made five cars under the name Milwaukee Star. They had 13hp engines under the seat and rear-entrance tonneau bodies.

NG

MINARI (GB) 1990 to date
1990–1993 Minari Engineering, Ranton, Staffordshire.
1994 to date Minari Engineering, Seighford, Staffordshire.
Designed by ex-Rover and Panther engineers, the Minari sports car was a smart-looking convertible kit designed for Alfa Romeo parts. The mechanical basis was

1910 Minerva 26hp tourer.
NICK BALDWIN

Alfasud or Alfa 33, from which was taken the engine, 5-speed gearbox, steering, brakes, suspension, wiring, instruments and so on. The fibreglass body was a monocoque, and the styling was revised in 1992 when the model was renamed Road Sport: the changes included deeper doors and winding windows. A lightweight racing RSR version arrived in late 1994. Licensed production also took place in Belgium.

CR

MINELLI (CH) 1998 to date
1998 to date Minelli AG, Pfäffikon, Zürich.
This company, founded in 1961 by Italo Minelli, originally was a cylinder grinding works, expanding its activities to repairing and tuning of engines, importing of industrial products and Perkins diesel engines. When his son Reto Minelli (born 1958) took over, he had a solid professional education and a great love for traditional British sports cars. In 1995 the idea was born to produce a truly worthy replica of the famous MG TF. The chief designer, Hans Peter Sutter, had been working in the development department of Daimler-Benz. The two prototypes of the Minelli TF 1800 Mk I were shown for the first time at the Geneva Show of 1998 and were well received. The car, which was mostly hand-built and assembled, was powered by a Ford Zetec 4-cylinder double-ohc engine of 1796cc yielding 115bhp. The body was made of reinforced fibreglass, the steel-spoke wheels and the seats were imported from England, and finest walnut was used for the dashboard. The first small production run of 10 cars is planned to be increased to 30 vehicles per year. The price was SFr62,500.

FH

MINERVA (B) 1899–1939
1899–1902 S. de Jong et Cie, Antwerp.
1903–1934 Minerva Motors SA, Antwerp.
1934–1935 Société Nouvelle Minerva, Antwerp.
1935–1939 SA des Automobiles Impéria-Excelsior, Antwerp; Nessonvaux.
The Minerva was probably the finest car to come out of Belgium; certainly the company made high-quality cars for longer than any other firm. It was founded by a Dutchman, Sylvain de Jong (1868–1928), who started work as a journalist, then set up a cycle-making business in Antwerp in 1897. The cycles were sold under the names Minerva and Romania, but only the first was ever used for cars. Motor

1904 Minerva 10hp tonneau.
NICK BALDWIN

1914 Minerva 26hp landaulet.
NICK BALDWIN

1921 Minerva 30hp landaulet.
NICK BALDWIN

1930 Minerva AKL 32/34hp saloon by Victor Broome.
NICK GEORGANO

tricycles followed in 1899, and at that year's Antwerp Cycle Show de Jong showed a prototype voiturette and light van. However, he was too busy with bicycles and engines to bother with cars for several years. His engines were used by 75 motorcycle makers, including such well-known names as Humber, Royal Enfield and Triumph in England, Cottereau in France, and Adler and Opel in Germany. From 1901 to 1910 complete Minerva motorcycles were made.

A few heavy-looking Panhard-type cars with 2-, 3- and 4-cylinder engines were made between 1902 and 1904, but the first important product was the Minervette introduced in 1904. This had a 636cc single-cylinder engine mounted transversely at the front, with a 2-speed constant-mesh gearbox and final drive by single chain to the offside rear wheel. It was sold on the British market by a different firm from the larger Minervas, which were handled by C.S. Rolls & Co. De Jong formed a new company with greater capital in 1903, and proceeded to make larger cars with 3.6-litre 4-cylinder or 6250cc 6-cylinder engines. These were introduced in 1906 and 1907 respectively, when Minerva had 1200 employees turning out 600 cars and 1500 motorcycles per year. In 1909 they adopted the Knight sleeve-valve engine, being only the second European company (after Daimler) to do so. Both sleeve-valve and poppet-valve engines were made in 1909, but thereafter Minerva remained loyal to the Knight to the end of its life.

In 1910 King Albert of the Belgians bought a Minerva and drove it himself on a tour of the Tyrol, while by 1914 other royal owners included the Kings of Norway and Sweden. The latter had a striking limousine with non-standard vee-radiator and a wrap-around windscreen. Another famous Minerva owner was Henry Ford. 1913 was the last full year of prewar production, when Minerva built 3000 cars, more than any other Belgian manufacturer. Four models were listed, of 14, 18, 26 and 38hp. Electric lighting was available in 1912, and for 1914 electric starting was an option and wire wheels were standardised. The company also started to make heavy commercial vehicles, which would become of growing importance between the wars. The factory kept going for as long as possible after the outbreak of war in August 1914, building armoured cars on the 38hp chassis until Antwerp was invaded in October by the German army, which used the factory for repair work.

In 1919 De Jong visited America to study the latest production methods and to buy the latest machine tools. By the end of the year he was making a 3560cc 20CV monobloc four in respectable numbers, followed in 1920 by a 30CV six with the same cylinder dimensions, giving 5341cc. Smaller models followed, a 1978cc four which was made up to 1927, and a 2967cc six, again with the same dimensions. This had 4-wheel brakes as standard, and in 1926 all Minervas had these, with Dewandre servo assistance on the larger models. A new body department was opened at Mortsel, an Antwerp suburb, so Minerva could make all their own coachwork, as well as most of the rest of the car, apart from chassis frames, magnetos, carburettors and tyres. Previously most of their bodies had been bought from coachbuilders, and this practice continued on a number of the luxury chassis.

The 1920s were successful years for Minerva, with 2500 cars made in 1925 and nearly 3000 in 1926. They also supplied engines to other firms, notably MORS in France and CROWN MAGNETIC in England. Minerva had a financial interest in Mors, and in 1923 there were plans to assemble Minervas in the Mors factory, though nothing seems to have come of this. To gain additional factory space they bought up two rival car makers, S.A.V.A. in 1923 and PIPE in 1924. For 1927 the 30CV was replaced by the 5934cc AK with alloy pistons, light steel sleeves and a wheelbase of 149.5in. This was followed in 1929 by the even more magnificent 6616cc straight-8 AL, whose engine was designed by Alexis Vivinus who had made cars of his own before World War I. This was one of Europe's finest cars, as well as having one of the largest sleeve-valve engines of the period, but it appeared at the wrong time and not more than 50 were made. The last ones were laid down in 1933, but they were not all sold until 1936. There was also a smaller straight-8, the 3958cc AP, of which several hundred were made from 1931 to 1937, and the 2000cc 6-cylinder AB to provide the firm's bread and butter, but Minerva was failing in the early 1930s. De Jong's death in January 1928 had deprived the firm of strong leadership, and, like other Belgian marques, Minerva could not compete with imports, especially from the United States. They tried to reach a more popular market with the 2000cc 4-cylinder M4 of 1934-36, but although this was the first Minerva to have synchromesh, it was sluggish in performance, while its looks were no more distinguished than a contemporary Citroën or Renault. Nevertheless about 250 were sold, all with 6-light saloon bodies.

Minerva was reorganised in 1934, but the following year the new company became part of Mathieu van Roggen's Imperia-Excelsior group. A handful of APs continued to be made at Antwerp, as were commercial vehicles, but the rest of the prewar Minerva-Impérias were no more than front-wheel drive Impéria TA9s. They were sold as Minervas on the French and British markets, to cash in on the prestige of the name.

In 1937 Van Roggen had one last fling with an advanced car having unitary construction, all-independent suspension by torsion bars, and automatic transmission by torque converter. Just about the only conventional part of this Minerva TAM–18 was its Ford V8 engine, and even this was mounted transversely and driving the front wheels. It was displayed at the 1937 Brussels Salon, but only three prototypes were made.

Ettore Bugatti considered transferring his production from Molsheim, where he was plagued by strikes, to one of the Minerva factories, but news of the death of his son Jean in August 1939 recalled him to Molsheim, and less than a month later war broke out. Minerva continued to make commercial vehicles up to 1948, and from 1950 to 1953 made Land Rovers under licence. There were two more attempts at car production, in 1952 with the Italian Cemsa-Caproni design which eventually became the Lancia Flavia, and in 1953 with a luxury car using Armstrong Siddeley Sapphire components. Nothing came of either scheme, though Minerva did assemble 49 6-light Sapphires in 1953. The last vehicles made by Minerva were a few jeep-type vehicles powered by 4-cylinder Continental engines, made from 1953 to 1956. The Mortsel factory was sold off in small lots during 1957, although the street that runs alongside it is still called Minervastraat.

NG

Further Reading
'Minerva – the Life and Death of a Goddess', Michael Sedgwick,
Automobile Quarterly, Vol. 22, No. 1.
Minerva Vandaag (Minerva Today), Philippe Boval and Albert Valcke,
Groeninghe Drukkerij N.V., 1998.

1976 Mini 850 saloon.
NICK BALDWIN

MINEUR (B) 1924–1925
Automobiles Mineur, Marchienne-au-Pont.
The Mineur was one of several transformations of the Model T Ford that were fashionable in Belgium for a short time. It had a handsome vee-radiator.
NG

MINI (GB) 1970 to date
1970–1975 Austin-Morris Division, British Leyland Motor Corp. Ltd, Birmingham.
1975–1980 Leyland Cars, British Leyland UK Ltd, Birmingham.
1980–1988 Light Medium Cars Division, BL Cars Ltd, Birmingham.
1988 to date Austin-Rover Group Ltd (1988–1990); Rover Group Ltd, Birmingham.
In 1970 the former Austin and Morris Mini models were given a marque status of their own, although Austin badges were seen on some export Minis until at least 1986. The 1275cc Cooper S variant was discontinued after 1971, but the other models, 848, 998 and 1275cc were continued. The 4 millionth Mini was delivered in November 1976, a record for a single model of British origin, and the 5 millionth in 1986. By the summer of 1999 sales had exceeded 5.3 million. Heated rear windows came in 1975, and 12in wheels were optional from mid–1974 and standard from mid–1977, but otherwise there were no major changes in the 1970s. The advent of the Austin Metro (for a short time called Mini-Metro) led to changes in the Mini line, with the 1275cc engine being dropped, leaving all models, the City saloon, de luxe HL and the HL Estate, with the 998cc engine. Front disc brakes and 12in wheels were standard on all models from 1984, and various special edition models were made from time to time. 1989 saw a return of the Mini Cooper name on a 1275cc 63bhp model with John Cooper's signature on white bonnet stripes, and an even more powerful model was the E.R.A. which had a 93bhp MG Metro Turbo engine. A Mini cabriolet developed by Karmann in Germany went on sale in 1993, at £12,000, but only 414 were made.

1999 Mini 1275 saloon.
ROVER GROUP

From 1992 the only engine available in the Mini was the 1275cc unit, fitted with catalytic converter. A new Cooper version, the Mini Cooper S Works with 90bhp engine, was launched in March 1999. It had a driver's airbag and optional 5-speed gearbox. By the late 1990s the Mini had become a niche product rather than the mass-produced car it had been originally. Fewer than 400,000 had been made since 1986, though demand in Japan grew over the period, so that they took around 8000 in 1998. The Mini continued in production until September 2000, when it gave way to the all-new MINI powered by a 4-cylinder 16-valve engine developed by a joint BMW/Chrysler team and made in Brazil. Planned engine options were 1.4-litre, 1.6-litre and supercharged 1.6-litre, the latter giving 155bhp, and featuring Steptronic 6-speed transmission.

2000 Mini 1.3i saloon.
ROVER GROUP

2001 MINI Cooper saloon.
ROVER GROUP

c.1968 Minijem MkII coupé.
NICK GEORGANO

As a result of BMW's decision to sell the Rover Group in Spring 2000, production of the new MINI was transferred to Cowley from Longbridge, delaying the start of deliveries for six months. It went on sale in July 2001.

NG

Further Reading
The Complete Mini, Chris Rees, Motor Racing Publications, 1991.
Mini, James Ruppert, Crowood AutoClassics, 1997.
Mini Cooper and S, Jeremy Walton, Osprey, 1989.
The Sporting Minis, a Collector's Guide, John Brigden,
Motor Racing Publications, 1989.

MINICAR (US) 1969
3-E Vehicles, San Diego, California.
The Minicar was a curious doorless 3-wheeler produced in kit form. Of rigidly

square appearance, it lacked any roof, had a single headlamp and a Perspex windscreen. The company later produced an aerodynamic electric 3-wheeler design called the XEP-100 but this did not enter production.

CR

MINICARS (US) c.1969–1980
Minicars, Inc., Goleta, California.
Prototype safety cars were the products of this company. They built a number of them in the 1970s which were purchased by the US government to tout automobile safety. The same company also operated as PACIFIC COACHWORKS, builder of the DiNapoli neoclassic car. The designer for both this car and the safety cars was Nick DiNapoli.

HP

MINI-CAT (F) 1978–1980
1978–1980 Mini-Cat, Valence, Drôme.
1980 Mini-Cat, Tain l'Hermitage.
The Mini-Cat microcar was designed by Serge Aziosmanoff, who created the G.R.A.C. racing cars. It had a single front wheel and a rear-mounted 49cc Peugeot GL10 engine mated to a continuously variable automatic transmission. All three wheels were braked, the steering was by handlebar and the rear suspension was by swinging arms. A smart-looking 4-wheeled model called the AZ49 was presented in 1979, again with all-wheel disc braking and independent suspension. In 1981 the rights were taken up by the boatbuilder Janneau, which produced a revised version under the name MICROCAR.

CR

MINI-COMTESSE *see* ACOMA

MINIJEM (GB) 1966–1975
1966–1968 Jem Developments Ltd, London.
1968–1971 Fellpoint ltd, Penn, Buckinghamshire.
1971–1972 High Performance Mouldings, Cricklade, Wiltshire.
1973 High Performance Mouldings, Wombwell, Barnsley, Yorkshire.
1974–1975 Malcolm Fell, Barrow-in-Furness, Lancashire.
This firm produced a 2+2 fibreglass body/chassis unit to take B.M.C. Mini mechanical parts. A MkII version was introduced in 1968, and by mid-1970 total production exceeded 350. Final versions of the Minijem were monocoques, the tubular back-bone chassis having been dispensed with.

NG

MINILUX (F) 1981–1982
Éts Difauto, Châtellerault.
The Minilux was a typical *sans permis* 2-seater microcar powered by a 49cc Motobécane engine. It had four wheels and very compact enclosed bodywork.

CR

MINIMA *see* BOUFFORT

MINIMA (i) (F) 1911
Éts Leroy, Levallois-Perret, Seine.
A voiturette powered by a 6/8hp single-cylinder Zedel engine was briefly offered under the Minima name.

NG

MINIMA (ii) (I) 1935
Antonio Passarin, Milan.
Passarin was a boat-builder who made a single-seater coupé powered by a 120cc 2-stroke motorcycle engine driving the single rear wheel by chain. He also made a tandem 2-seater with 250cc engine. Neither went into series production.

NG

MINIMOBIL (D) 1984–1987
M.W. Kleinwagen GmbH, Wielenbach.
One of the few German microcars, the Minimobil was powered by a 50cc Sachs 2-stroke engine, and was made in two forms, the Cityboy coupé and Sunnyboy cabriolet. About 600 were made.

HON

MINIMOBIL SIGMA (H) c.1986

Túrkevei Autójavító Vállalat, Túrkeve.

While Hódgép readied his PULI city car, two friends, József Csathó and Attila Baráth who worked at a small repair shop thought about redesigning the Polski-Fiat 126p. Their dream was a practical city car which was easy to park, but also very agile. Their Sigma used a converted 126p floorpan, with a tiny BMW engine and a one-off frame and body construction. It was 98in (2500mm) long. The steering wheel was located in the centre and there was the capability to fit invalid chairs, so even a disabled person was able to drive the car. There were two seats in the second row, a similar arrangement to the McLaren F1. The finished prototype was exhibited at the Budapest International Fair, but it became obvious that no-one could buy it at the price they proposed, so the project was abandoned.

PN

MINI MOTORS see STIMSON

MINIMUS (D) 1921–1924

Minimus Fahrzeug GmbH, Pasing.

The Minimus cyclecar had an air-cooled V-twin engine of 4PS and seated two passengers in tandem. A 4-cylinder version was offered later in the make's short life.

NG

MINION (GB) 1983–1987/1995 to date

1983–1985 Minion Cars Ltd, Bexhill-on-Sea, East Sussex.
1985–1987 Imperial Specialist Vehicles, Eastbourne, East Sussex.
1995 to date Jackal Cars, Pevensey, East Sussex.

The brainchild of school teacher Peter Fairhurst, the Minion Jackal was a 1930s style kit car that was unusual in that it was a 4-seater fixed hard-top coupé, although that hard-top could be ordered as a removable item. Another unusual point was the mechanical basis: Vauxhall Viva (or, later, Ford Cortina). It was renamed Imperial in 1985, and then, after a long absence from production (Eagle Cars retained the jigs and moulds), it returned to production in 1995 as the Jackal Sports and Imperial Saloon and was offered with Ford Sierra mechanicals.

CR

MINI SCAMP see SCAMP

MINK (BERMUDA) 1968

A more saucer-like microcar than the Mink has never been built. The prototype was built by an engineering company in the Midlands of Great Britain for an intended production run in Bermuda. Using a 198cc Lambretta scooter engine sited in the rear, the Mink was capable of 55mph (88km/h) and 70mpg. Weighing only 530lbs, it was built on a backbone chassis, and the tiny fibreglass body featured a precipitous front overhang in the effort to retain a saucer-like shape.

CR

MINO (US) 1914

Mino Cyclecar Co., New Orleans, Louisiana.

When this car was in the planning stages its name was to be the New Orleans Cyclecar, but it bore the shorter and catchier name Mino when it appeared on the market, which was not for long. It was a single-seater, powered by an air-cooled V-twin engine, with epicyclic transmission and vee-belt drive.

NG

MINOTAUR (GB) 1998 to date

Minotaur Cars, Sheerness, Kent.

Although it first appeared in prototype form at a kit car show as early as 1993, the definitive Minotaur was presented in 1998. This was a heavily sculpted high performance coupé with racing inspiration behind its styling and engineering. It used a multi-tubular space frame chassis with independent suspension and a mid-mounted Rover V8 engine. It was offered in kit form.

CR

1990 Mirach V8 sports car.
LORENZ & RANKL

MINUS (GB) 1982 to date

1982–1984 Status Motor Co. (Design & Moulding), Wymondham, Norfolk.
1984–c.1987 Minus Cars, Wymondham, Norfolk.
c.1987 to date Minus Cars, New Buckenham, Norfolk.

This kit car was originally launched as the STATUS Mini Minus but was productionised under the Minus Cars banner. It was a fibreglass reinterpretation of the lowered Minisprint of the 1960s. It naturally used Mini mechanicals as well as its interior trim, glass, lights and opening panels, including shortened doors. As the Minus was to the Mini, so the next model – the Minus MkIII or Maxi – was to the Mini Clubman estate. It looked like a miniature Matra Rancho and benefited from a lift-up tailgate. The Maxi was then made by P.S.R. Fabrications but production had ceased by 1992. The third Minus model was the 4R2, launched in 1992 and based on Mini Minus but boasting a mid-mounted engine and body styling that aimed to do to the Mini what Rover had done with the Metro 6R4 – in other words, a rear aerofoil, fat wheel arches and air dams behind the doors.

CR

MINUTOLI-MILLO (I) 1902–1903

Stà Minutoli Millo & Cia, Lucca.

Vittorio Millo's first car was a 3-wheeler made in 1896, and in 1902 he formed a company to make a 4-seater tonneau powered by a 2.4-litre 4-cylinder engine with automatic inlet valves, with shaft drive. Millo died before any serious number of cars could be made. The prototype survives in the Museo dell' Automobile in Turin.

NG

MIOLANS (F) 1910

Valade et Guillemand, Neuilly, Seine.

The Miolans made an appearance at the 1910 Paris Salon, but little was heard of it subsequently. It was a light car with gearbox mounted on the rear axle.

NG

MIRA (F) 1906

Made at Neuilly the Mira was offered in two models, a single- and a 4-cylinder, both using De Dion-Bouton power units.

NG

MIRABILIS (I) 1906–1907

Giuseppe de Maria, Turin.

De Maria built a light voiturette powered by a $3\frac{1}{2}$hp single-cylinder engine designed and built by himself. The motor industry crisis of 1907 killed it before many could be made.

NG

MIRACH (GB) 1988–1997

1988–1994 Leopard Cars Ltd, Totnes, Devon.
1996–1997 Clive Robinson Cars, Totnes, Devon.

Ex-Vauxhall stylist Chris Field created the Mirach as a larger, more modern version of the Lotus 7. Its minimal doorless bodywork was realised in fibreglass

1909 Mitchell Model K 30hp tourer.
NICK GEORGANO

1913 Mitchell Forty roadster.
NICK BALDWIN

1922 Mitchell Model F-50 tourer.
JOHN A. CONDE

and carbon fibre over a tubular space frame chassis, and featured advanced aerodynamics. It was powered by a bored-out 4-litre Rover V8 engine. After only ten cars had been built, production was suspended. A later plan to market the car in kit form using Ford Sierra running gear and a variety of engine choices (including Rover V8, Ford Cosworth, Ford V6 and Vauxhall Astra) never came to fruition.

CR

MIRAGE (i) (GB) 1988 to date
Mirage Replicas, Wellingborough, Northamptonshire.
One of the leaders in the Lamborghini Countach kit replica market, the Mirage was a fairly conventional blend of a space frame chassis, fibreglass body, Ford Granada/Scorpio running gear, Renault V6, Rover V8 or small block V8 power and a Renault 30 transaxle. A Jaguar V12 powered version was also offered.

CR

MIRAGE (ii) (US) c.1993
Mirage, Montour Falls, New York.
In addition to a line of Ferrari replicas, Mirage offered armour plating services. The Spirite was a Ferrari 308 replica, the Ninja duplicated the F-40 and the Ghost did likewise with the 512BBi. All appear to have been Fiero-based.

HP

MIRELI (P) 1987–c.1994
Fibromireli, Coimbra.
In the breach created by the demise of the Citroën Méhari and Renault Rodéo, the Mireli was a fibreglass open jeep-style car with soft side screens, based on Renault 4 or 6 mechanicals.

CR

MIRROR IMAGE (US) c.1994 to date
Mirror Image Motor Works, Burleson, Texas and Round Rock, Texas.
This company made very high quality reproductions of the Lamborghini Countach, the 25th Anniversary Countach and the Koenig-modified version. All Mirror Image cars were based on a sophisticated space frame with fabricated suspension and Corvette brakes. Turn-key cars were equipped with new Chevrolet Corvette LT-1 5700cc V8 engines and modified Porsche 911 transaxles. They were also sold in kit form.

HP

MISTRAL (B) 1932
M. Houdret, Brussels.
Houdret built an advanced car which he exhibited at the 1932 Brussels Salon. It was a long, low 4-seater sports car powered by a 3050cc straight-8 Ballot engine which developed 95bhp. A supercharged version giving 200bhp and a top speed of 120mph (193km/h)was announced, but probably never built. In fact, the show car was almost certainly the only Mistral ever made. It took part in the 1932 Liège-Madrid-Liège rally.

NG

MITCHELL (US) 1903–1923
1903–1904 Wisconsin Wheel Works, Racine, Wisconsin.
1904–1910 Mitchell Motor Car Co., Racine, Wisconsin.
1910–1916 Mitchell-Lewis Motor Co., Racine, Wisconsin.
1916–1923 Mitchell Motors Co., Racine, Wisconsin.
The ancestry of this company dates back to the foundation of the Mitchell Wagon Co. at Fort Dearborn, which later became Chicago, in 1837. The company moved to Kenosha in 1845 and to Racine in 1857. It became the Mitchell & Lewis Co. in 1884 after William T. Lewis had married Henry Mitchell's daughter, and a subsidiary called the Wisconsin Wheel Works began bicycle manufacture in the 1890s. They made an unsuccessful motorcycle in 1900, and built their first car in 1903. It was a light 2-seater powered by a 4hp single-cylinder engine, with epicyclic transmission and single-chain drive. There was also a 7hp, and for 1904 this and a 16hp four with 5-seater tourer body made up the Mitchell range. The Mitchell Motor Car Co. was formed that year, when 82 cars were made. Conventional 3-speed gearboxes were used, and in 1905 customers could have a choice of air- or water-cooling. By 1907 all engines were water-cooled fours and shaft drive was standard. There were three models, 20, 24/30 and 35hp, all tourers or runabouts, and sales reached four figures for the first time, with 1377 Mitchells finding buyers. At about this time Mitchell's New York branch set up a hire department, whereby a car and driver could be hired for $5.00 an hour, or $500 a month.

Mitchell's first six was announced for the 1910 season. It had a 50hp engine and used the same cylinder dimensions as the 30hp four, capacities being 4651 and 6977cc. In 1912 Mitchell made over 6000 cars, and were the leading car makers in Wisconsin. A new range of T-head engines, two fours and a six, was introduced for 1913, designed by French-born René Pétard. They were called 'The American-built French car' and had high-cowled torpedo-style bodies and electric starters. Sales dipped to 3913, and worse was to follow when only 2253 Mitchells were sold in 1914. William Mitchell Lewis (son of William T.) and René Pétard left to make a new car, also in Racine, called the LEWIS. Mitchell was reorganised as Mitchell Motors Co., and sales began to pick up again, reaching a record 10,938 in 1917. The four was not made after 1915, and a 29hp V8

1044

lasted only one season (1916). Thereafter Mitchells were conventional 6-cylinder cars offered with a wide range of bodies. The larger of the 1918 sixes, the 29.4hp Model C-7-42, came in 12 styles from a speedster to a 7-seater town car. The only distinction of the later Mitchells was an unfortunate one. In an attempt to modernise what was a very upright style, they sloped the radiator backwards on the 1920 models; unfortunately the rest of the car remained resolutely vertical so the radiator looked quite out of place, and gave rise to the epithet, 'the drunken Mitchell'. The matter was put right on the 1921 models, but sales were declining anyway. Like so many other well-made but relatively small production cars, Mitchell could not compete with the big manufacturers. Their place as Wisconsin's leading car makers had been taken over by NASH, who bought the Mitchell plant as well in 1924 as a location for their new AJAX car. Mitchell production ended in mid–1923, only 713 cars being made that year.

NG

Further Reading
'Mitchell: The car you ought to have', Bob Hall,
Automobile Quarterly, Vol. 32, No. 1.

MITCOM (US) c.1982

Mitcom Inc., Hollywood, California.
The Chalon was a popular conversion for the Porsche 914. It was an attractive fibreglass body kit with a longer and more graceful nose, wide wheel flares for fitting wider tyres and an air dam.

HP

MITSUBISHI (i) (J) 1917–1921; 1959 to date

1917–1921 Mitsubishi Kobe Dockyard Works, Kobe.
1959–1970 Mitsubishi Heavy Industries (Reorganised) Ltd, Tokyo.
1970 to date Mitsubishi Motors Corp., Tokyo.
The history of the Mitsubishi company dates back to 1870 and the foundation of the Tsukomo-Shokai shipping company, renamed Mitsubishi-Shokai in 1873. Mitsubishi is the Japanese word for 'three diamonds', the symbol used on today's cars. In 1917 a branch of what was by then a large conglomerate, Mitsubishi Shipbuilding Co. of Kobe, built a 4-cylinder car based on the Fiat Tipo 3, though all the components were Japanese made. About 20 of these cars, known as the Mitsubishi A, were built up to 1921, but competition from cheaper cars imported from America made the project uneconomic. Truck production began in 1930, and after World War II the enormous Mitsubishi group was split into three parts. The trucks and buses, named Fuso, were made by Mitsubishi Nippon Heavy Industries, and Mitsubishi Heavy Industries (Reorganised) made Kaiser Henry J cars under licence from 1950 to 1953, followed by Jeeps. It was this company that built the first mass-produced cars, starting in 1959.

The first was a small 2-door 4-seater saloon powered by a rear-mounted 493cc 2-cylinder engine developing 20bhp. Known as the 500, its engine was enlarged to 594cc and 25bhp in 1961. The following year it was renamed the Minica, and was joined by the first front-engined Mitsubishi, and the first to bear the name Colt, which was widely used in later years. By 1966 there were three Colts, the 800 with 3-cylinder 2-stroke engine of DKW type, and the 1000 and 1500 with 4-cylinder oversquare pushrod ohv engines. The 800 had fastback styling, but the larger Colts were conventional notchbacks; all had four doors. At the bottom of the range was the Minica, and above the Colts was the Debonair, a 6-cylinder saloon on American lines.

In 1965 the three separate companies were amalgamated once more, making a vast conglomerate, one of the biggest companies in the world, with interests in aircraft, locomotives, earth-moving machinery, nuclear fuels and beer. In 1970 Mitsubishi Motors Corp. was formed as a wholly-owned subsidiary of Mitsubishi Heavy Industries, and in the same year the Chrysler Corp. took a 15 per cent holding in the company, increased to 35 per cent in 1971. A new range of medium-sized cars called Galant appeared in 1970 – these had 4-cylinder single-ohc engines of 1.4- and 1.6-litres, and were made as 4-door saloons or 2-door coupés. The pushrod-engined Colts were continued in 1.1- and 1.2-litre forms, as were the Minica and Debonair. From 1970 Colts were sold on the US market as Dodge Colts, and later Galants were imported as well. They were sold as Dodge Colt Galants; as Mitsubishi's exports expanded the name Colt was increasingly used, so that it became almost a marque name rather than a model.

Exports to Britain, the Netherlands, Belgium and Luxembourg began in 1974, followed by Finland and Norway in 1976, Denmark, West Germany, Switzerland and Austria in 1977, and France in 1979.

1917 Mitsubishi (i) Model A limousine.
NICK BALDWIN

1960 Mitsubishi (i) 500 saloon.
NICK BALDWIN

1966 Mitsubishi (i) Minica saloon.
NICK BALDWIN

Car production rose by 270 per cent in the 1970s, from 457,160 in 1970 to 1,158,600 in 1981, when Mitsubishi was the fourth largest Japanese manufacturer.

The Minica and Debonair remained in the range, both gaining ohc engines. Capacity and power of the Minica was steadily increased, so that by 1981 it was giving 32bhp from 546cc. It was little sold outside Japan, and neither was the large Debonair. The models which provided the base of Mitsubishi's successful export drive were the Lancer, Galant and Sigma saloons, and the Celeste and

1974 Mitsubishi (i) Colt 1600 saloon, badged as a Dodge.
NICK BALDWIN

1979 Mitsubishi (i) Sigma 2000 saloon.
NICK BALDWIN

1983 Mitsubishi (i) Starion 2+2 coupé.
NATIONAL MOTOR MUSEUM

1989 Mitsubishi (i) Galant saloon.
MITSUBISHI

Sapporo coupés. The saloons were conventional rear-drive cars with a permutation of four engines, 1238, 1439, 1597 and 1995cc, of which the Lancer used the first three and the Galant and Sigma the two larger units. The Celeste was a 2-door hatchback coupé with Lancer floorpan and running gear, though the 2-litre engine was an option. With twin carburettors and a 5-speed gearbox, the top of the range Celeste could exceed 100mph (161km/h). It was not widely sold in Europe, but was marketed in America as the Plymouth Arrow. The Sapporo, named after the city where the 1972 Winter Olympics were held, was also marketed as a Plymouth, but they retained the Japanese name. It was a more stylish coupé than the Celeste, using the floorpan, suspension, transmission and 2-litre engine of the Galant. This was replaced by a new short-stroke engine of almost the same capacity (1995cc) in 1980, and a turbocharged version was introduced in 1982.

Turbocharging

Turbocharging became something of a Mitsubishi speciality in the 1980s, encouraged by their development chief Shinji Seki. The first to achieve popularity in Europe was the Lancer Turbo, a 5-seater saloon whose 2-litre engine gave 145bhp and a top speed of 112mph (180km/h). By 1982 practically all models in the Mitsubishi range could be had with turbochargers, except for the Minica and Debonair. An important new model in 1982 was the Starion, a powerful coupé to compete with the Datsun Z series or Mazda RX-7. It was powered by a 168bhp turbocharged version of the 1997cc engine, driving the rear wheels by a 5-speed gearbox. Top speed was 133mph (214km/h), and in 1985 the addition of an intercooler increased this to 137mph (220km/h).

In 1978 Mitsubishi announced their first front-wheel drive car, variously known as the Mirage (in Japan) 1400 or Colt 1400. This was made in 3- or 5-door hatchback versions, powered by 1244 or 1410cc 4-cylinder engines mounted transversely. The transmission was unusual in having two ratios, economy and performance, with a total of eight forward speeds, and an automatic option became available later. A 1597cc engine was added to the range in 1981, supplemented by a 105bhp turbo version of the 1400 during 1982. A booted version of the Mirage was known as the Fiore. For the domestic market, a number of Mirages were sold with Modular Displacement engines in which two cylinders (numbers 1 and 4) could be de-activated automatically when the car was travelling slowly, and when the accelerator was pressed hard for overtaking or hill climbing, they were brought back into use. Because of the expense of developing them thoroughly, the MD engines have not been widely used by Mitsubishi.

In 1982 the front-drive, transverse engine theme was extended to two larger cars, the Tredia saloon and Cordia coupé. The Tredia was offered with 1400, 1600 or 1800 engines, with a turbocharged 1600 being the most powerful, while the Cordia had the two larger engines, also with the turbo 1600. In 1983 the Galant also went front-drive, with 1800 or 2000 engines, both available in turbo versions. A 2-litre V6 engine was available in the Galant from autumn 1986.

The two domestic market Mitsubishis, Minica and Debonair, also adopted front-wheel drive, the Minica in 1984 and the Debonair a year later. The Minica was a tiny 4-door saloon, still powered by an engine of only 546cc, while the Debonair now had V6 engines of 1998 or 2972cc. Most Debonairs were saloons, but a long-wheelbase 8-seater limousine was also made in small numbers.

People carriers and cross-country

In February 1983 Mitsubishi entered the market for high-roofed estate cars, sometimes called 'people carriers' or MPVs (Multi Purpose Vehicles), competing against the Nissan Prairie and Toyota Space Cruiser. Mitsubishi's contribution was called the Chariot in Japan, the Colt Vista in America and the Space Wagon in Europe. It was powered by 1600, 1800 or 2000 engines driving the front wheels through a 5-speed gearbox, and had seating accomodation for six to seven passengers. An 1800 turbo diesel engine was added to the range in 1984, and a 4-wheel drive version was also announced the same year.

Mitsubishi have been making 4 × 4 cross-country vehicles ever since they acquired a licence for Jeep production in 1953. These are still made today, looking much more like the original World War II Jeep than the current American-built models. In addition Mitsubishi launched in 1981 a range of larger and more luxurious 4 × 4 machines named the Pajero (Shogun in the UK). They were made in short and long-wheelbase versions, the latter being in the same class as the Range Rover. Engine options were 1997cc, with or without turbocharger, 2555cc and 2477cc turbo-diesel.

1989 Mitsubishi (i) Colt 1.3 hatchback.
MITSUBISHI

International links

Like most other Japanese firms, Mitsubishi has established a number of manufacturing links with companies in different countries. The Chrysler connection became less important during the late 1970s, for once Chrysler began to make their own small cars such as the Horizon they were less anxious to push Mitsubishi products. In 1982 Mitsubishi set up their own dealer network in North America, though some badge-engineered models were also sold by Chrysler, such as the Colt 1400 which carried the name Plymouth Champ. In 1988 Chrysler and Mitsubishi set up the Diamond Star factory at Normal, Illinois, to build the Eclipse which was sold under the names Mitsubishi Eclipse and Plymouth Laser. The 2+2 coupé was offered with a 1.8-litre single-ohc or 2-litre twin-ohc 4-cylinder engine. The chief difference between the Mitsubishi and Plymouth versions was that the former had front and rear spoilers, giving a better Cd figure of 0.29, compared with the Plymouth's 0.33. 4-wheel drive versions appeared in 1989, called the Eagle Talon GSi (see EAGLE (x)) or Mitsubishi Eclipse GSX.

A new Eclipse styled in Mitsubishi's Californian studio, with corrugated door mouldings, was announced at the New York Show in April 1999. Longer, wider and taller than the previous Eclipse, it was offered with a choice of 155bhp 2.4-litre 4-cylinder, or 205bhp 3-litre V6 engines. The 4 × 4 option was dropped.

1993 Mitsubishi (i) 3000 GT coupé.
NICK BALDWIN

In 1980 Mitsubishi bought Chrysler's Australian factory and began to build Sigmas and Galants there (see MITSUBISHI (ii)). A more recent international link has been with Volvo in production of the Carisma (see below). Mitsubishi has also been active in helping developing countries to set up motor industries. In 1973 they began to supply engines, transmissions and suspension units to the Korean company, HYUNDAI, for their Pony cars, and they also have a 30 per cent interest in the PROTON company of Malaysia.

The Minica was given turbo power in 1989 in the Dangan ZZ, the world's smallest turbocharged engine at 547cc. With twin ohc and 5-valves per cylinder, output was 64bhp, the highest permitted in a Japanese K Class minicar. A 1990 derivative was the Toppo with 660cc and a very high roofline. This and the Minica were continued through the 1999 season. The Mirage was replaced in 1984 by restyled and longer cars with conventional 5-speed gearboxes under the Colt name. They were made in 3-door hatchback form initially, later in saloon and 5-door hatchback layouts, with a 160bhp twin-cam 16-valve engine in the hottest model, the GTi-16V. The mid-sized Galant received a transverse engine

1999 Mitsubishi (i) Shogun 3-door 4x4.
MITSUBISHI

1999 Mitsubishi (i) Evo VI saloon.
MITSUBISHI

and front-drive for 1984, and in 1989 the top model was offered with 4-wheel drive and steering, powered by a 145bhp twin-cam 2-litre engine. At the top of the saloon range were the 3-litre V6 Diamante with 4-wheel drive, and the Debonair V, a continuation of the traditional large car theme with front-drive since 1986 and a choice of 2- or 3-litre V6 engines. These were still offered, mainly on the home market, in 1999.

The sporting side was represented by the 2-litre turbocharged Starion coupé introduced in 1982 and replaced in 1990 by the 3000GT with 300bhp twin-turbocharged 3-litre V6 engine, and 4-wheel drive and steering. It was sold in the USA as the Dodge Stealth; both models were still made in 1999. A high-performance saloon was the Lancer Evo VI GSR with 276bhp turbocharged 2-litre engine. The hottest model, called the Extreme and launched in October 1999, gave 340bhp, and a 0-60mph (97km/h) time of 4 seconds.

The MPV line was expanded in 1991 with the addition of the Space Runner, a small version (8in/200mm shorter) of the Space Wagon, but with the same choice of engines, 1.8-litre petrol and 2-litre turbo diesel. Both were still offered in 1999, the Space Runner with 250bhp and 4-wheel drive (the Sportsgear) at the top of the range. The 4 × 4 Shogun was still made in short and long-wheelbase forms, with two turbo diesel fours, of 2.5- and 2.8-litres and a 3.5-litre petrol V6. For 2000, monocoque construction was adopted for a new Shogun with all round independent suspension. In 1994 Mitsubishi extended the 4 × 4 range further, with the Space Gear, a monobox design similar to the Renault Espace and also made as the Hyundai H-i. In 1996 came the Challenger (Montero in the US), a luxury 4-door 7-seater with the same engine options as the Shogun but with lower, more car-like, lines. Several variations on the Shogun/Pajero theme were offered in 1999, from the 659cc Pajero Mini and 1095cc Junior (Japanese market only) to the Pinin, a short-wheelbase 3-door with 118bhp 1.8-litre engine aimed at the Toyota RAV4 and Honda HR-V market, and assembled by Pininfarina in Italy.

A new international project was launched in 1996 with the Mitsubishi Carisma saloon and Volvo S40 saloon and V40 estate being built on the same production lines at Volvo's Dutch plant at Born. The Carisma was offered with 1.6- and 1.8-litre engines, the latter a turbodiesel made by Renault, and a new engine for 1998 was the GDI (Gasoline Direct Injection), a 1.8-litre unit giving diesel-like economy at part throttle, and good acceleration at full throttle. The joint project, called NedCar, gave Mitsubishi a valuable entry into the European manufacturing scene.

In Japan Mitsubishi has five factories for car production, and three for trucks. The Okazaki plant is particularly advanced; four completely different models can be produced on the same production line, with anything up to 2500 different specifications. The use of robots enables completely different bodies to be welded up on the same line, a batch of 3000GT coupés followed by a batch of Colt saloons.

In March 2000 DaimlerChrysler took a controlling stake in Mitsubishi worth £1.3 billion.

NG

MITSUBISHI (ii) (AUS) 1980 to date
Mitsubishi Motors Aust. Ltd, Clovelly Park, South Australia.

The sharp rise in fuel prices, in the wake of the mid–1970s energy crisis, badly affected CHRYSLER Australia, which had concentrated on full-sized cars but could not then gain support from the US parent due to its own problems. Mitsubishi models which were produced by Chrysler Australia, however, thrived and the Sigma, with its smooth balance-shaft engine, became the prime choice of big car owners moving down to a four. In 1980 Mitsubishi purchased Chrysler's holding and the Chrysler Sigma was immediately badged Mitsubishi. The introduction of the Colt with front-wheel drive, catered for the small car market while the Magna of 1985 was a uniquely Australian model. Although based on a Japanese type, it was 2.5in (65mm) wider, 1.5in (40mm) longer and the 2555cc Astron engine was reworked for mating with the front drive. It met with strong demand, and the resulting full utilisation of production capacity delayed a station wagon until 1987.

With the 1991 release of a new body, the 4-cylinder Magna was joined by an upmarket Verada with a 3-litre V6 engine and the first standard fitting in Australia of an anti-lock braking system. The Australian production of the station wagon was the sole source for export markets. The new body shell of 1996 had a very close affinity with the Japanese Diamante model, with Australia supplying the export markets. The long-running 2.6-litre engine was phased out of production in favour of the V6, an imported 2.4-litre becoming the base engine. The V6 was made in 2972cc and 3497cc sizes, the larger for the Verada and export Diamante.

MG

MITSUI see HUMBEE SURREY

MITSUOKA (J) 1981 to date
Mitsuoka Motor Co. Ltd, Toyama City.

Obtaining an official licence to produce cars in Japan is a very difficult task, but Mitsuoka – a large automotive company founded in 1968 – succeeded in becoming Japan's 10th car constructor in 1993. It had started out in 1981 producing a miniature enclosed 50cc trike called the Bubu Shuttle (later referred to as the 501 Cabin Scooter). As many as 300 units per year were made but a change in the law regarding driving licences for 50cc vehicles forced the company to branch out, choosing to enter neo-classic territory. First came a VW Beetle based Mercedes SSK replica in 1987. Then came the Bubu 356 Speedster, a Porsche replica; the Le Seyde, another 'replicar' based on Nissan Silvia mechanicals; and the Dore, a large American neo-classic design using a Ford Mustang engine. Seemingly frivolous was the Viewt, an absurd attempt to rebody a Nissan March/Micra to look like a parody of the Jaguar Mk2, but it sold an incredible 80 units per month. This success inspired further pastiches, including the Galue (a Bentley lookalike based on the Nissan Crew taxicab), the Ray (a retro styling exercise on a Mazda Carol) and the Ryoga (another Jaguar Mk2 lookalike, this time on the Nissan Primera).

The 1994 Zero 1 was its most serious product, a Caterham 7 inspired sports car based on Mazda MX-5 mechanicals, including its 120bhp 1.6-litre engine. All-independent suspension fitted into a tubular chassis clothed in aluminium panels, much like the Caterham. This successful model was followed up in 1996 by the Classic Type F, an updated version of the Zero 1 with an Alfa Tipo-style front end. The 740kg heavy car was fitted with a 130bhp Mazda 1.8-litre engine.

In a historic move, Mitsuoka became Japan's first ever kit car maker with two new designs launched in 1998. These were the K-2 (a miniature roadster with styling inspired by the Messerschmitt KR201) and the K-1 (a single-seater microcar with open sides and a clutchless transmission). The K-1 was also sold fully-built as the MC-1. In all cases, a 49cc air-cooled single-cylinder twin-stroke 6.1bhp engine of Mitsuoka's own design was used.

CR

MIURA (BR) 1977–c.1987
Aldo Auto-Capas, Porto, Alegre.

Aldo Auto-Capas were an accessory manufacturer who decided to go into car building, producing a rear-engined sports coupé with Brazillian Volkswagen engines and running gear. A roadster was also available. The car featured retractable headlamps and an electrically-adjustable steering column. The Miura met with some success, and in 1980 production was running at 45 units per month. It survived until around 1987.

NG

MIVAL *see* MESSERSCHMITT

M.J. (F) 1920
This obscure company made a few cars with 1¹/₂-litre 4-cylinder engines.
NG

M&L (US) c.1985
M&L Automotive Specialties, Manitowoc, Wisconsin.
This company built the first aluminium-bodied Cobra replica in the United States. The chassis and suspension were also identical to the original except for thicker tubing. It was sold in kit or turn-key form, with kits starting at about $70,000 in 1985.
HP

M.L.B. (F) 1894–1902
Compagnie des Moteurs et Autos M.L.B., Hondouville, Eure; Passy, Seine.
The partners in this company were Messrs J. Landry and G. Beyroux, and the cars were sometimes known by their names. Their first products had a 4hp vertical single-cylinder engine mounted at the rear, with 3-speed gearbox and double-chain drive. Various bodies were fitted, including a 4-seater *vis-à-vis* and an enclosed cab. In 1901 a lighter car with wire wheels was built.
NG

M.L.T. (F) 1900
Molas, Lamielle et Tessier, Paris.
Named after its makers, the M.L.T. was a heavy-looking 6-seater brake with double-chain drive. It had a 20hp 4-cylinder single-acting engine of steam type but actuated by compressed air which was stored in reservoirs at a pressure of 200 atmospheres. The air was heated by gas burners, then admitted to the cylinders at varying pressures to give power ranging from 1 to 35hp. A 12-seater wagonette was also made, and possibly some trucks, but the system was probably not efficient enough to be a serious form of transport.
NG

M&M (US) c.1996
M&M Auto, Fort Lauderdale, Florida.
The M&M Vetper was a Dodge Viper replica built on a Chevrolet Corvette chassis. It was sold in kit and fully assembled form.
HP

M.M.B. (D) 1899–1902
Motorfahrzeug- und Motorenfabrik Berlin AG, Berlin-Marienfelde.
This company was set up by former directors of DAIMLER (i) to make cars of Daimler design but to avoid paying royalties to Gottlieb Daimler. They were not equal to the Cannstatt-built Daimlers in quality or finish, and after Gottlieb's death in 1900 there was no need for this independent company, so it was merged with the main Daimler company. The factory was retained for manufacture of commercial vehicles which were sold in England as the Milnes-Daimler. M.M.B. also made electric cars under licence from Columbia in America, and petrol-electrics of Austro-Daimler design.
HON

M.M.C. (GB) 1897–1908
1897–1898 The Great Horseless Carriage Co. Ltd, Coventry.
1898–1907 The Motor Manufacturing Co. Ltd, Coventry.
1907–1908 The Motor Manufacturing Co. (1907) Ltd, Clapham, London.
This marque had its origins in the Great Horseless Carriage Co. Ltd, one of the creations of the celebrated company promoter Harry J. Lawson who had floated the English Daimler company in 1896. In the summer of that year he floated the Great Horseless Carriage Co. with grandiose plans to make cars and commercial vehicles in large numbers. His premises were part of the Motor Mills at Coventry, which also housed Daimler as well as seeing manufacture of tricars under licence from LÉON BOLLÉE and some of Edward PENNINGTON's odd creations. Neither Daimlers or M.M.C.s were made until the summer of 1897, when, according to A.C. Brown who joined the company as an apprentice fitter, four or five chassis were under construction. They were similar to the Daimlers being made next door, with 4hp vertical-twin engines, tube ignition and tiller steering. The

1899 M.L.B. 4-seater *vis-à-vis*.
NATIONAL MOTOR MUSEUM

1900 M.M.C. 6hp Daimler-type 2-seater.
NICK BALDWIN

1902 M.M.C. tonneau
NATIONAL MOTOR MUSEUM

1900 Mobile (i) steam runabout.
NICK BALDWIN

engines and gearboxes were made by Daimler, with the bodies and wheels by the Great Horseless Carriage Co.

In 1898 the firm was reorganised as The Motor Manufacturing Co., and new designs were produced the following year. These were the work of George Iden, who came from the London, Brighton & South Coast Railway. They broke away completely from the Daimler layout, having rear-mounted horizontal-twin engines. Several types were made, such as the Princess 4½hp 2-seater, Sandringham 6hp phaeton and Balmoral 11hp charabanc. They were apparently not very successful. A.C. Brown said 'I worked on most of George Iden's "Flight of Fancy" designs. Some did not go at all, some went a bit, and most of them were flops'. While waiting for these to be ready, some of the crypto-Daimlers were made, and also some motorcycles, tricycles and quadricycles with M.M.C.-built De Dion-Bouton engines. In 1898 75 cars and 31 engines were made, the figures for the first ten months of 1899 being 163 cars and 92 engines. By then all engines were made by M.M.C., whether of Daimler, De Dion-Bouton or Iden design. Alfred Burgess, who had joined the company as a clerk in 1896, became company secretary in 1901 –he was later to run one of the re-formed M.M.C. companies.

The first reorganisation took place in 1902, when the complex range was reduced to three models, with front-mounted vertical engines of 1-, 2-, or 4-cylinders. The single was a light car with 5hp M.M.C.-De Dion-Bouton engine, the others were on Panhard lines. They looked rather ungainly, with large gilled-tube radiators. They must have sold reasonably well, for M.M.C paid a dividend for the first time in 1903. That year's cars had lower bonnets, some with honeycomb radiators, and used the Iden constant-mesh gearbox. The largest chassis was a 25hp four, on which a very luxurious touring saloon was shown at the Paris Salon.

Despite some success in the period 1903–05, M.M.C. cars did not have a very good reputation, particularly with regard to spare parts. One owner said that he could never get parts that would fit. 'No two cars were exactly alike. Things were done in a haphazard fashion by individually good workmen.' George Iden resigned in December 1903, later making a few cars under his own name at Parkside, Coventry. The M.M.C. range continued through 1904 with little

change, though on the 8hp single-cylinder model the buyer could have mechanical or automatic inlet valves. The company was in receivership at the end of 1904, and their part of the Motor Mills was taken over by Daimler. Several times since 1900 M.M.C. had approached Daimler about some form of reunion, but they had always been rebuffed. They moved to new premises in Parkside and announced an ambitious range of six models, from a 9hp single to a 35hp four, but few were made.

Two years later the company was reorganised again, and moved to London under the management of Alfred Burgess. *The Automobile Owner* was enthusiastic about the new company's prospects: 'I have spoken of the revival of M.M.C., but it has more than revived, for under keen business management and the guidance of councillors whose names have become synonymous with success in the industry … the M.M.C. firm is not merely reviving but has already passed the stage of probation and has achieved position'. Burgess announced that he would make 104 cars in 1907, large machines with 35/45hp 6-cylinder engines of 8550cc on a 126in (3198mm) wheelbase, and with a Delaunay-Belleville-type radiator. Sadly, the works at Clapham were never completed and only one 35/45hp was made. According to a company report it was not a success, although an employee, writing many years later, said that it was a very satisfactory job. By December 1908 M.M.C. was in liquidation again, and the machinery at Clapham was sold the following year.

In 1910 Burgess joined Frank Wellington in the Wellington Motor & Aerial Navigation Co. Ltd, described as 'a car manufacturing concern with aerial aspirations as an extra object'. This was still located at the Clapham works, but not a single car, let alone an aeroplane, was made there. Two years later Burgess surfaced again, once more using the name Motor Manufacturing Co., but his Finchley premises only provided spare parts for M.M.C. cars and sold, so it was claimed, 'all makes of new and second-hand cars'.

NG

M.M.F. (F) 1912

Muller, Mignot et Cie, Levallois, Seine.

This company made several cars with 2120cc 4-cylinder engines.

NG

M.M.W. (D) 1901–1903

1901 Magdeburger Motor & Motorfahrzeugfabrik GmbH, Magdeburg.
1901–1903 Magdeburger Motor-Werke Max Stang & Co., Magdeburg.

This company built one basic chassis to which either passenger or goods vehicle bodies could be added. The whole body could be lifted for easy access to the works. Mechanical details are not known.

HON

MOBBEL *see* PICCOLO

MOBILE (i) (US) 1900–1903

Mobile Co. of America, Tarrytown, New York.

This company was founded by John Brisben Walker, editor and publisher of *Cosmopolitan* magazine, and asphalt tycoon Amzi Lorenzo Barber, who put up most of the $250,000 which the partners offered to the STANLEY twins for their patents. In June 1899 they set up the Automobile Co. of America, only to find that another firm had already claimed that name, so they changed it to Locomobile Co. of America. Their partnership did not last long, and when they broke up Barber kept the factory which had made Stanleys and would henceforth make Locomobiles, which seems only fair since he had put up the money. However he allowed Walker to make cars of the same design, which he did, under the name Mobile, at a new factory at Tarrytown on the banks of the Hudson river. The first Mobile did not leave the factory until March 1900, which gave Barber a good start. The models in common between the two makes were much the same in price, but Walker offered many more models, 28 in all between 1900 and 1903, including heavy commercial vehicles which Barber did not make. Walker's prices ran from $550 for a 'special runabout' to $3000 for a 'Model 50 9-passenger coupé'.

Walker gave up his steamers at the end of 1903, but Locomobiles were made for a further season, during which they were joined by petrol cars which lasted until 1929. Walker sold his factory to MAXWELL-BRISCOE.

NG

MOBILE (ii) **(GB)** 1903–1907

Mobile Motor & Engineering Co. Ltd, Birmingham.

Mobile's first venture was the sale of the De Dion-Bouton or Aster-powered WADDINGTON light car, and the first Mobiles were similar. They used the 6hp single-cylinder De Dion-Bouton or Aster engine in a 2-seater, the 8hp De Dion single also in a 2-seater, and the 9hp Aster twin in a 4-seater tonneau. All the Mobiles had shaft drive. In 1907 their assets were acquired by CALTHORPE, Mobile's manager Louis Antweiler becoming a director of Calthorpe, which he remained until that company's closure in 1926. Mobile owners were assured by Calthorpe of a supply of spare parts, but the cars were not continued.

NG

MOBILEK **(GB)** 1979

Doreen Kennedy-Way, Dudley, West Midlands.

The Mobilek was the brainchild of a female inventor who hoped to launch her electric trike in 1979, intending it for shopping trips and commuting by businessmen. It was to cost £1000, but there were problems with the Ministry of Transport's type classification for the car and it never went into production.

CR

MOCHET **(F)** 1924–1958

Charles Mochet, Puteaux, Seine.

Charles Mochet was France's best known maker of pedal cars as a practical means of transport for adults. He made these from 1927 until well into World War II, but he also had two periods of powered vehicle manufacture. From 1924 to 1930 he made a cyclecar under his initials, C.M. This had a rear-mounted 350cc single-cylinder 2-stroke engine, with 3-speed gearbox and chain drive. It had a kick-starter and a boat-shaped plywood body which was similar to that fitted to the pedal-operated Vélocars. In 1929 he offered a cyclecar with 142cc engine, but after 1930 he seems to have concentrated on the Vélocar which was made in four models, a standard 2-seater called the Série, a similar car with small box behind the seats, called the Camionette, a streamlined 2-seater called the Confort, and the Confort Familial with accommodation for two adults and two children. The specification included ifs, four speeds by *dérailleur* gear and electric lighting. The empty weight of a Vélocar was about 110lb. They came into their own during World War II, when they were much in demand, being used by doctors, priests and commercial travellers for their regular work.

In 1945 Mochet returned to the powered vehicle with the Vélocar Type H, a simple 2-seater powered by a 100cc single-cylinder Zürcher engine, with auxiliary pedals for the driver. (On the unpowered Vélocars, both driver and passenger had pedals). It rode on bicycle wheels, and only the rear ones had brakes. It evolved into the Type K (1947–49) which did away with pedals, and this gave way to the slightly more civilised CM Luxe with 125cc engine, also by Zürcher, which raised maximum speed from 25 to 30mph (40 to 48km/h). It received full-width bodywork on the CM Grand Luxe, and a coupé body arrived with the CM 125Y of 1953, which used an Ydral engine. This was continued until the end of car production in 1957 or 1958, being slightly re-styled in 1955 and again in 1956. With 125cc engine no driving licence was needed, but there was also a 175cc model for those with licences. These later Mochets had roll-top coupé bodies and full electrics including windscreen wiper and trafficators. With 175cc engine, top speed was 37mph (59km/h). At his peak in the early 1950s, Mochet was making 40 cars a month. In addition to these derivations of the Vélocar, Mochet made a small sports car with 750cc CEME motorcycle engine and Antem body, which appeared at the 1953 Paris Salon. Only two were made.

After ending car production, Mochet made bicycles with reclining seats for many years.

NG

MOCK **(D)** 1924

Gebr. Mock, Tübingen.

This small car made by the Mock brothers had a 1330cc 5/20PS 4-cylinder engine. It was made in only limited numbers, but some competed in local race meetings.

HON

1904 Mobile (ii) 12hp tourer.
NICK BALDWIN

1932 Mochet Vélocar Modéle Confort Familiale.
NICK GEORGANO

MODEL **(US)** 1903–1907

1903–1904 Model Gas Engine Co., Auburn, Indiana.
1904–1906 Model Gas Engine Works, Auburn, Indiana.
1906–1907 Model Automobile Co., Peru, Indiana.

This company was run by E.A. Myers, who began making engines and complete cars in 1903. The cars had 12hp flat-twin engines and 2-seater runabout or 4-seater detachable tonneau bodies. They had three forward speeds and two reverse, final drive being by single-chain. They were joined by a 16hp in 1904, and the flat-twin engines grew in size to reach a peak of 24hp in 1906, though a smaller 6/18hp was still made. In 1906, when he had made more than 300 cars, Myers separated the Automobile Co. from the Gas Engine Works, which supplied engines to a number of other manufacturers, and in 1908 he renamed the cars STAR (iv). The last Model was made in 1907 and had a 45hp 4-cylinder engine.

NG

MODENA **(US)** c.1985

Magnum Design and Development, El Cajon, California.

The Modena 250 Spyder California was a replica of the 1960–61 long wheelbase Ferrari 250GT Spyder California. The Modena kit car was based on a backbone-style tube frame with Ford V8 running gear. The fibreglass body had plexiglass-covered headlights and a Fiat 124 windscreen. They were sold in kit and completely assembled form. This project was later sold to PRECISION DESIGN.

HP

MODERN *see* PAYNE-MODERN

MODERN CLASSICS **(US)** c.1994

Modern Classics, Inc, Atlanta, Georgia.

The LeMans 427 was a Cobra replica with a ladder frame and Ford suspension. It was designed to take Ford or Chevrolet V8 engines and had a longer 94in (2386mm) wheelbase for extra cockpit room.

HP

1968 Mohs Ostentatienne Opera sedan.
NICK GEORGANO

MODOC (US) 1912–1914

Modoc Motor Co., Chicago Heights, Illinois.

Named after an Indian tribe, the Modoc was built by the mail order company Montgomery Ward, who ran their own factory. It was an assembled car, with 30/40hp 4-cylinder Continental engine, Brown-Lipe clutch and gearbox, Gemmer steering gear, Rayfield carburettor and A.O. Smith frame. A 5-seater tourer was the only body style. It failed to find many buyers because of the complete lack of repair and service facilities for a mail order car.

NG

MODULO (I) 1988 to date

Italian Car, Ronco Briantino (MI).

The Modulo 3-wheeler was first seen as early as 1988, although it took some time for production to begin. Designed by ex-Alfa Romeo engineer Carlo Lammattina as a high performance fun machine, its exposure was helped by appearances at the 1994 and 1995 Geneva Motor Shows and the fact that F1 and Indy champion Nigel Mansell bought one. BMW K-75, K-1100 or other motorbike engines such as Moto Guzzi could be fitted centrally (unusually, BMW's 12 month drive train warranty still applied if fitted). The steel tube space frame chassis was clothed with aluminium side panels and a carbon-fibre and Kevlar reinforced fibreglass tandem 2-seater open bodywork. Rack-and-pinion steering, independent suspension and hydraulic disc brakes all round completed the mechanical picture. The distinctive styling featured pop-up headlamps, a low-level windscreen, hinging front and rear upper bodywork and steel roll-over bars.

CR

MOHAWK (i) (US) 1903–1905

Mohawk Auto & Cycle Co., Indianapolis, Indiana.

This company grew out of the Mohawk Cycle Co. which made bicycles under the name Rumsey. Their first cars came in two versions, a tiller-steered 7hp single-cylinder runabout and an 18hp 2-cylinder tonneau with wheel steering. They also built two large racing cars with 70hp 4-cylinder engines for cycle racing champions Carl Fisher and Earl Kiser. Both men would later help to set up the Indianapolis Motor Speedway. Production of the smaller cars lasted into 1905.

NG

MOHAWK (ii) (US) 1914–1915

Mohawk Motor Co., Boston, Massachusetts.

This was a light car powered by a 4-cylinder ohv Farmer engine, with shaft drive to a semi-floating rear axle. The only body style was a 2-seater.

NG

MOHAWK-MANON *see* MANON

MOHLER *see* ROCKAWAY

MOHS (US) 1967–1978

Mohs Seaplane Corp., Madison, Wisconsin.

It was a good thing that Mohs did not have to make a living on sales of their cars. Their seaplane and motor scooter business carried their unlikely car line-up.

They were among the most ungainly, and expensive, cars on the market. The Mohs Ostentatienne opera sedan was built on an International Harvester chassis with a truck engine. A large, chrome grill was tacked to a long, low and graceless body. Steel safety beams running down the sides excluded normal doors, so entry was by a large door at the rear that hinged upward to the roof. There was a long list of options that included a refrigerator, and the 20in tyres were filled with nitrogen. Velvet upholstery was standard as was gold trim in the interior. At a price of $25,000, only one is believed to have been built. The next Mohs vehicle was the Safarikar, a boxy convertible with padded naugahyde bodywork. This model had doors, but they slid in and out on linear bushings. It also had a bed in the back. A handful of Safarikars were sold.

HP

MOKE (P/I) 1983–1993

1983–1990 Austin-Rover Ltda, Vendas Novas.
1990–1993 Moke Automobili SpA, Varese.

Having ceased production at Longbridge in 1968 and in Australia in 1981, Austin-Rover produced the Mini Moke utility/leisure vehicle at its Portuguese plant from 1983 to 1989, but falling sales forced it to close. In 1990 the whole project, including the factory and Moke name, was sold to the Italian motorbike manufacturer Cagiva and initially production continued at the Vendas Novas plant in Portugal. There were some detail changes in 1991 but in 1993 the production tooling was removed from Portugal to Italy, though apparently production never recommenced. The parent company, Piaggio, also made Daihatsu vans and in 1990 presented a prototype called the Scooter, a very small car that trod the line between motor-scooter and car.

CR

MOKO (GB) 1984–1985

Moko Component Cars, Camborne, Cornwall.

This BMC 1100 based kit inspired by the Mini Moke was unusual in that it had aluminium bodywork. The steel chassis was pre-drilled to accept BMC 1100 or Austin Allegro subframes and incorporated a roll cage, while the floor was of marine ply wood. A 5-door hard-top was optional.

CR

MOLINE; MOLINE-KNIGHT (US) 1904–1919

Moline Automobile Co., East Moline, Illinois.

This company grew out of the Root & Vandervoort Engineering Co. which had made stationary and portable engines since 1899. The men behind it were Orlando J. Root and W.H. Vandervoort whose names would appear in the R. & V. KNIGHT which succeeded the Moline-Knight in 1920. The first Moline car had a 12hp 2-cylinder engine, epicyclic transmission, chain drive and 4-seater tonneau body. It was joined by the 18/20hp 4-cylinder Model B for 1905, and the cars gradually grew in size, reaching a 40hp four by 1909. The last year for the twins was 1907. Because of their performance in reliability trials, the 1912–13 models, tourers and a roadster, were known as Dreadnoughts

For 1914 Moline adopted the Knight sleeve-valve engine, and the cars were henceforth known as Moline-Knights, though a poppet-valve Moline was made alongside the new model in 1914 only. The Knight engine was a 50hp monobloc 4-cylinder unit, used in conjunction with a 4-speed gearbox. At the time the Moline's Knight was the only American sleeve-valve engine to be cast en bloc. For the first time, Moline offered closed bodywork on this model, a sedan and a limousine. The Moline-Knights were made with little change to 1919, in two sizes of engine, 3.6 and 5 litres. For 1920 the design was continued as the R. & V. Knight.

NG

MÖLKAMP (D) 1923–1926

Möllenkampwerke AG für Fahrzeugbau, Düsseldorf; Cologne.

When PRIAMUS ended car production their factory was taken over by Möllenkamp who started manufacture of a 2590cc 10/50PS 6-cylinder car. They followed this with a 4-cylinder 6/30PS of 1460cc, which was, in fact, a CEIRANO S.150 built under licence. Neither of these cars was made in large numbers, and all production ended in 1926.

HON

MOLL (D) 1922–1925

Moll-Werke AG, Chemnitz.

The Moll was a light car powered by a 1595cc 6/30PS 4-cylinder Siemens & Halske engine, with 4-speed gearbox and shaft drive to a bevel rear axle. It was sold in England by L.G. Hornsted under the names Hornsted or Summers. It was followed by the Mollmobil cyclecar, designed by Fritz Görke. This was a tandem 2-seater powered by a DKW engine of 164cc, later replaced by a slightly larger one of 198cc.

HON

MOLLA (F) 1922

Molla et Cie, Paris.

The Molla cyclecar was powered by a 2-cylinder engine and had belt final drive.

NG

MOLLE (F) 1907–1910

Émile Molle, Riom, Puy de Dôme.

Molle made a very small number of cars all using 2-stroke engines of his own construction. His total output was nine cars, of which seven had 1525cc 2-cylinder engines, and two had single-cylinder engines of 1330cc.

NG

MOLLER (US) 1920–1922

Moller Motor Car Co., Lewistown, Pennsylvania.

The Moller was a small rhd specifically targeted to the export market, differing from its peers in that field by offering custom bodies by prominent coachbuilders as an option. Marketed without fanfare in 1920, the Moller was introduced to the motoring public at the New York Auto Show in January 1921, at which a chassis, priced at $1500 plus a phaeton and a sedan with Healey bodies, were shown. The Moller was powered by a 4-cylinder engine and rode on a chassis with a 100in (2538mm) wheelbase. All Mollers were not surprisingly built with right-hand steering. Production was terminated in 1922 although some of the unsold cars were marketed in 1923 as that year's models. A specially-equipped Moller was badged as the Falcon in October 1921 and this name was continued until production ceased – but not without confusion. In 1922, the Halladay – then in its death throes – introduced a small car which it also named the Falcon, probably unbeknownst of what was transpiring in Lewistown, which has been the bane of automotive historians in latter years. The confusion was augmented by the introduction of the Möller taxi by the H.P. Möller of Hagerstown. The Mollers of both Lewistown and Hagerstown were both natives of Denmark. An interesting point – the Mollers can be differentiated by the Hagerstown family's use of the umlaut in the 'o' of Möller. The Lewistown Mollers did not use it.

KM

MOLSHEIM II (US) c.1976

Molsheim, Pasadena, California.

Unlike the vast numbers of Volkswagen-based, fibreglass-bodied Bugatti replicas built by American kit car companies, the Molsheim II was a well-built and designed replicar. Built by Tim Barton and Paul Barkman, it used quality aluminium body panels that could be used for restoring original cars. The radiator shell and wheels were also identical to original, as were many of the brackets and trim parts. The engine was a turbocharged 2000cc Ford Pinto. Suspension was live axle at both ends and the automatic transmission was converted to clutchless manual operation. The price in 1976 was $19,500.

HP

MOM (F) 1906–1907

Ateliers de Construction Mécanique 'Mom', Paris.

Like many small French manufacturers of the period, Mom listed two small cars as production models, a 6hp single-cylinder voiturette and a 10/12hp 4-cylinder, but added that they would make cars of any size from 20 to 120hp. They were also marine engine manufacturers, so presumably they had a supply of these larger engines which could have been used in a car, if any customers ordered one.

NG

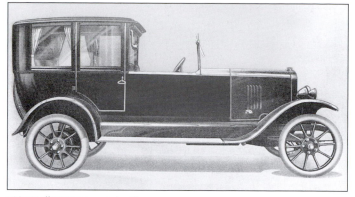

1921 Moll 6/30PS coupé de ville.
HANS-OTTO NEUBAUER

c.1924 Mollmobil 200cc cyclecar.
NATIONAL MOTOR MUSEUM

1971 Momo Mirage sports sedan.
NATIONAL MOTOR MUSEUM

MOMO (US) 1971

The Momo Corp., Forest Hills, New York.

The Momo Mirage was a stylish sports sedan with impeccable parentage. The handsome, angular body was designed by Gene Garfinkle and Peter Kalikow, and was refined and built by Pietro Frua. The tubular chassis with all-independent suspension was built by former Formula Junior constructor Stanguellini, and Alfred Momo oversaw the project from his base in New York. Momo had worked with Briggs Cunningham on racing Jaguars. All workmanship and materials were of highest quality, and a Chevrolet 5700cc V8 was used with 5-speed Z-F manual or automatic transmissions. Brakes were Girling discs and much of the suspension was fabricated.

HP

Further Reading
'Momo Mirage', Winston Goodfellow, *Automobile Quarterly*, Vol. 39. No. 2.

c.1926 Monet Cyclecarette 3-wheeler.
NATIONAL MOTOR MUSEUM

MONARCH (i) (US) 1903–1904
Milwaukee Motor Manufacturing Co., Milwaukee, Wisconsin.
The company specialised in engine manufacture, but made some cars as well. They were 2-seater runabouts with single-cylinder engines, epicyclic transmission and single-chain drive. A total of 48 were made in 1903 and 12 in 1904, when they went under the name New Monarch.

NG

MONARCH (ii) (US) 1905–1908
Monarch Automobile Co., Aurora, Illinois.
This was a light 2-seater runabout powered by a 7hp air-cooled single-cylinder engine. It was advertised by P.J. Dasey of Chicago as early as 1903, but apparently he could not get any to sell, and it was only when the makers moved from Chicago to the suburb of Aurora that production began. The first Monarchs had wire wheels and tiller steering, but by 1907 they had wood-spoked wheels and wheel steering, although the engine and wheelbase remained unchanged.

NG

MONARCH (iii) (US) 1906
Joseph S. Heller, New York City, New York.
Broker's secretary Joseph Heller made a small runabout with 7hp air-cooled single-cylinder engine, with 3-speed epicyclic transmission at his home on West 75th Street. He advertised replicas at $500 each, but it is not known if he received any orders.

NG

MONARCH (iv) (US) 1906
Monarch Motor Car Co., Cleveland, Ohio.
This Monarch was a 2-seater roadster described as a 90hp, built by W.D. Drown who crashed the prototype in a hill climb, but interested a group of businessmen who formed a company to make other roadsters with 120hp engines, as well as more modest tourers of 40/45hp. Their plans called for 50 tourers and 10 'racers' as they called them, although they carried road equipment, in 1907. Space was hired in the factory of the Broc Carriage Co., but it seems that no cars were made there. Probably Drown's crashed prototype was the only Monarch made.

NG

MONARCH (v) (US) 1907–1909
1907 Monarch Motor Car Co., Franklin Park, Illinois.
1908–1909 Chicago Heights, Illinois.
This company started out with a 2-seater runabout and 4-seater surrey powered by a 12/14hp 2-cylinder engine, with epicyclic transmission and shaft drive. They were priced at $600–900. They showed four at the Chicago Automobile Show in January 1907 and were in production by the spring. The factory burnt down in May, destroying, as well as machinery, 176 runabouts awaiting delivery. This put paid to the 1907 season, and when they found new premises at Chicago Heights they decided on a more ambitious car. This had a 40hp 4-cylinder engine and was made as a tourer or gentleman's roadster selling for $2500. Probably no more than 25 were made, and the company was bankrupt by the summer of 1909.

NG

MONARCH (vi) (US) 1908
Monarch Machine Co., Des Moines, Iowa.
This was another engine manufacturer who motorised a few buggies with their 20hp 2-cylinder engines. Transmission was by epicyclic gears and final drive by chain. They called the result the Road King, and sold it for $750.

NG

MONARCH (vii) (GB) 1912–1914
R. Walker & Sons, Tyseley, Birmingham.
The Birmingham Monarch was a cyclecar powered by an 8hp V-twin Precision engine with 2-speed epicyclic transmission and shaft drive. The frame was of pressed steel and suspension by four quarter-elliptic springs. It was priced at 110 guineas (£115.50) with air-cooled engine, and 120 guineas (£126) with water-cooled engine.

NG

MONARCH (viii) (US) 1913–1916
Monarch Motor Car Co., Detroit, Michigan.
Designed by Robert C. Hupp, who achieved much greater fame with his HUPMOBILE, the Monarch was a 16hp 4-cylinder car with Renault-type bonnet and 2- or 4-seater bodies, both selling for $1050. About 150 had been made by May 1914, when a cheaper car with the same engine but shorter wheelbase was added at $675. Both were made into 1915, when Hupp became more ambitious and launched a car with a 29hp V8 engine. This was only made for a short time as the Monarch company went bankrupt in early 1916. Rights to the V8 and a new 12hp four were bought by the Carter brothers of Hyattsville, Maryland. They were marketed in 1917 under the name C.B.

NG

MONARCH (ix) (GB) 1925–1928
Monarch Motor Car Co., Castle Bromwich, Birmingham.
The mid–1920s was an unusual time to be launching a medium-sized family car, but the makers of the Monarch hoped to penetrate a market dominated by such well-known cars as the Austin Twelve, Humber 14/40, Standard 14hp and Vauxhall 14/40. The prototype Monarch had a 13.9hp ohv Meadows engine, although the makers said that production cars would have their own 2121cc engine. The specification included a 4-speed gearbox in unit with the engine and a Salisbury spiral bevel rear axle. The only body style offered was a Mulliner saloon priced at £525. Though the Monarch was carried by some lists up to 1928, it received very little publicity. Possibly the 1925 prototype was the only one made.

NG

MONARCH (x) see MERCURY (vi)

MONCRIEF see PAWTUCKET

MONDEX MAGIC (US) 1914
The Aristos Co., New York City, New York.
This short-lived car used a slide-valve engine invented by the Swiss, Martin Fischer, who also made FISCHER cars in his native land. The engines were of 40 and 60hp, the cars selling for the high prices of $4500 and $6500. They were made for the Aristos company by Palmer & Singer of Long Island City. Mondex was a trade name for various products made by Aristos, such as the Mondex Helix Mixture, to improve carburation, and Mondex body polish.

NG

MONET (F) 1920–1939
Éts Monet et Goyon, Mâcon, Saône-et-Loire.
Monet et Goyon were well-known makers of motorcycles from 1917 to the mid–1960s who built some unusual cyclecars for a few years. These were generally known as Monets, the name Monet-Goyon being reserved for the motorcycles. Joseph Monet's first vehicle was a tricycle with hand propulsion intended for war wounded. Called the Vélocimane, it was motorised in 1920, with a 117cc single-cylinder engine with no clutch or gearbox. The engine was started by pedalling. Called the Auto Mouche, it was made in this form until 1923, when it was enlarged, with a 147cc Villiers engine, Albion 2-speed gearbox and kick-

1972 Monica 590 sedan.
NICK BALDWIN

starter. A seat for a second passenger was available. The design was lowered in 1928, and in 1930 the 147cc engine was replaced by a 250cc unit, also by Villiers. The second seat could be facing forwards, or in *dos-à-dos* form, like the contemporary POIRIER. This improved Auto Mouche was made with little change up to 1939.

Alongside the Auto Mouche, Monet made several types of cyclecar, both 3- and 4-wheeled. The V2 of 1920 to 1923 had a 500cc Anzani single-cylinder engine mounted over, and driving the single front wheel by chain. It was made in passenger- and goods-carrying forms and latterly had a 750cc V-twin MAG engine. Steering was by a long tiller which, when raised, lowered the engine and acted as a clutch by loosening the chain, and thereby, as the catalogue said 'liberating it from all work'. Another 3-wheeler was the Cyclecarette, derived from the 2-wheeled Vélauto scooter and powered by a 270cc Villiers engine mounted under the seat. The passenger sat ahead, in a cane seat between the front wheels, in a configuration similar to the LÉON BOLLÉE voiturette made 30 years earlier. In this form it was known as the VT3 Paris-Nice, while the single-seater and goods versions were the VT1 and VT2 respectively. The lights were mounted on the wheel hubs, and turned with the steering. A later and more sophisticated version of the VT3 had side by side seating, a hood and a boat-like pointed front. In 1929 there appeared yet another 3-wheeler, called originally the Tricar, and later the Tri-Monet. This was motorcycle-based, using the seat, tank, engine and drive of the firm's 500cc MAG-powered machine, but in place of the front forks was an axle with two wheels, Between them was mounted a streamlined sidecar for a single passenger. Made from 1929 to 1931, the Tri-Monet could also be had with a 350cc Villiers 2-stroke engine.

The 4-wheeled Monet was derived from the Cyclecarette 3-wheeler, and used the 270cc Villiers engine, rear-mounted and driving through a 2-speed gearbox and chain drive to the centre of the rear axle. The wheels were very close together so a differential was not necessary. There was also a front-engined version with lower lines. These 4-wheelers were made up to 1928, and there was a final attempt at a car in 1935. This had a streamlined body with a 350cc Villiers engine mounted just ahead of the driver and passenger. Only one prototype was made.

NG

Further Reading
'Monet & Goyon et le cyclecar', J. Godard,
l'Album du Fanatique, November 1970 and May 1973.

MONICA (F) 1971–1975
Compagnie Française de Produits Métallurgiques, Balbigny, Loire.
The Monica GT was the idea of Jean Tastevin who made a fortune from leasing railway rolling stock. France had no luxury car maker and Tastevin saw a gap in the market. The name came from his second wife, Monique. Chris Lawrence designed both the 4-door 4-seat body and the chassis. The latter was part space frame, part sheet steel floorpan and had a De Dion rear axle. Originally, a Triumph 2.5-litre engine was intended, but prototypes were made with 3.4-litre V8 engines, designed by Ted Martin, which drove through a 5-speed ZF gearbox. It was decided not to proceed with the Martin unit because of the danger of warranty claims, and cars were offered with either a 5.6 or 5.9-litre Chrysler engine with automatic transmission as an option.

Production began in 1973 and the first eight cars had been completed when work was halted because of the OPEC Oil Crisis. The parent company's leasing business took a sudden dive as most of its oil tanker wagons were idle and with fuel prices spiralling, it was a bad time to launch a thirsty car.

There were 30 cars on the production line, ranging from 99 per cent complete to a bare chassis. They were acquired by Guy Ligier, but few were completed. A proposal for the project to be taken over by Panther came to nothing.
MJL

MONITOR (i) (US) 1909–1911
1909–1910 Monitor Automobile Works, Chicago, Illinois.
1910–1911 Janesville, Wisconsin.
The Monitor was a solid-tyred high-wheeler which was more car-like than many of its kind, with a bonnet in front, though the 18/20hp flat-twin engine was mounted under the seat. After the move to Janesville they brought out a 4-seater surrey with the same engine and wheelbase. This could be converted to a truck by removing the rear seats, and was called the Milk Wagon/Pleasure Car. After 1911 they decided that wagons were more profitable than pleasure cars. Monitor trucks were made up to 1916.
NG

c.1926 Monotrace 2-wheeler.
GILES CHAPMAN

1914 Monroe 14hp roadster.
NICK GEORGANO

MONITOR (ii) (US) 1915–1922

1915–1916 Cummins-Monitor Co., Columbus, Ohio.
1916–1922 Monitor Motor Car Co., Columbus, Ohio.

Monitor started its manufacturing with a typical 4-cylinder car, advancing quickly into offering both a six and a V8, although the latter may never have actually surfaced. Both fours and sixes were produced during 1917 and, starting in 1918, the company phased out the four and produced 6-cylinder cars exclusively throughout the remainder of its life. Power plants varied with Continental, G. B. & S., and Herschell-Spillman engines in various models. Monitor's production was largely targeted to roadsters and touring cars with a sedan, introduced in 1917, as its only closed body types. The G. B. & S. and Continental 7R engines would remain in use until the end of production, although the company had planned to re-introduce a Herschell Spillman type for 1922. Unfortunately, the company failed before the contract could be filled and before the ending of 1922, the Monitor had become history. More than 5000 Monitors had been sold during the company's eight years of activity.

KM

MONITOR (iii) (F) 1920–1922

Charles Rouquet et Cie, Suresnes, Seine.

The Monitor cyclecar was made originally with a rear-mounted 747cc V-twin Train engine with chain drive running in an oil-bath case. For 1922 the engine was at the front, and two models were offered, a 2-seater with staggered seating, and a single-seater for commercial travellers, in which the area for goods and samples replaced the second seat and extended to the rear of the car. The frame was of armoured ash.

NG

MONK & LONSDALE see LONSDALE

MONNIER (F) 1908

Monnier et Cie, Juvisy-sur-Orge.

Two models were listed by this regional car maker, a 6/7hp single-cylinder and a 10/12hp 4-cylinder. Though they claimed that the carburettor on the larger car was their own, the engines were probably of proprietary make such as Aster or De Dion-Bouton.

NG

MONO (D) 1909–1912

Mono-Werke Roger & Niebuhr, Automobil- und Maschinenfabrik, Hamburg.

This company made a single model with 6/16PS 4-cylinder engine, but its sales did not extend beyond the local area.

HON

MONOCAB (F) 1952–1954

Éts. Fouga SA, Paris.

This was an ultra-light car made under patents of Armand Citroën, who was a cousin of the much better known André. A 3-wheeler with single rear wheel, it was powered by a 50cc single-cylinder 2-stroke VAP engine mounted alongside the wheel which it drove via a cone clutch and single chain, with only one speed. The engine was started by a pedal which was also used to help it on steep hills, or when driving into a strong head wind!. Under favourable conditions, a top speed of 25mph (40km/h) was claimed. The tiny headlamps were placed on the cycle-type mudguards, which turned with the steering. A slightly more refined car, also called Monocab, was offered by another Citroën, Joseph, in 1954. This had a 70cc Lavalette engine and Weymann-type body, and a top speed of 31mph (50km/h).

NG

MONOCOQUE ENGINEERING (US) c.1978–1979

Monocoque Engineering, Costa Mesa, California.

The Monocoque Box was an unusual minivan-type vehicle that looked like a shoebox with four cycle-type mudguards attached to the outside. The body was reinforced plastic and it used a perimeter steel frame with a Honda 1600cc engine. Price in 1979 was an expensive $18,000. Options included amphibious drive gear and aluminium wheels.

HP

MONOS (D) 1928–1930

Monos Fahrzeug-Gesellschaft mbH, Berlin-Lichtenberg.

Like earlier designs by Fritz Görke (GÖRKE, MOLLMOBIL), the Monos 3-wheeler had a side-mounted engine with chain drive to one of the rear wheels. The body was a tandem 2-seater.

HON

MONOTRACE (F) 1924–1930

Ateliers du Rond Point, St Étienne, Loire.

The Monotrace was a 2-wheeled car based on the MAUSER Einspur-Auto, but production lasted longer than its German prototype. It had a 510cc single-cylinder engine, with 3-speed motorcycle gearbox and chain drive. Two auxiliary wheels supported the car when it was at rest The wide body seated two people behind the driver.

NG

MONROE (US) 1914–1924

1914–1916 Monroe Motor Co., Flint, Michigan.
1916–1918 Monroe Motor Co., Pontiac, Michigan.
1918–1922 William Small Co., Flint, Michigan.
1923–1924 Premier Motor Corp., Indianapolis, Indiana.

The Monroe was a well-regarded, low-priced car which, despite its well-built construction and reliability, remained a low-production automobile with an average of about 1500 units annually. The Monroe used 4-cylinder engines throughout its eleven years of activity – a Mason or a Sterling for its first four years and an in-house motor thereafter. Offering open cars exclusively during its first five years of production, a sedan was added in late 1918.

It was rumoured that the company would be taken over by PREMIER (i) in 1923 but instead Strattan Motors obtained the Monroe and continued production briefly. Shortly after, Premier obtained control of both Monroe and Strattan and marketed the Monroe briefly in a redesigned model which featured a flat, squared radiator in place of its earlier rounded type. Production was brief and small, the final cars rebadged and sold as the Model B Premier.

KM

MONSTER MOTORSPORTS (US) 1992 to date
Monster Motorsports, Escondido, California.

For those to whom too much horsepower is still not nearly enough, Monster Motorsports installed Ford 5000cc V8 engines and transmissions into new Mazda Miatas (MX-5). The suspension was reworked with larger brakes and a Ford differential. The Monster Miata had a 225hp engine, while the Mega Monster Miata had a supercharged 400hp version of the same engine. Both used 5-speed Ford transmissions. The Mega Monster Miata had a top speed of 174mph (280km/h) and was faster than a Dodge Viper or Chevrolet Corvette. The price in 1999 was $50,000 for the Mega, which included a new Miata and custom bodywork including mudguard flares and spoilers. The standard Monster Miata kit did not include body modifications and could be fitted to a customer's car. A third model was the F/XR Monster Miata, which had a 178hp turbocharged Miata engine and upgraded suspension, bodywork and brakes. Before getting into the Miata modification business, Monster Motorsports had built Cobra replicas, including an aluminium-bodied version. In 1999 they were working on a conversion to install Ford 4600cc 4-cam V8s into the BMW Z3.

HP

MONTE CARLO (MC/GEORGIA) 1990 to date
1990–1993 Monte Carlo Automobile, Monaco.
1993 Tako Industries, Georgia.
1996 to date Aixam-Mega, Aix-les-Bains.

Monaco has rich motoring connections but is such a small nation that manufacturing is rarely a possibility. The M.C.A. Centenaire (so called because 100 cars were planned to be built) was a notable and extraordinary exception. A mid-engined supercar designed to compete with Ferrari, it used F1 technology. In particular it featured a carbon fibre central monocoque with aluminium and tubular front and rear subframes, plus carbon fibre/Kevlar body panels. The suspension was fully adjustable all round. Prototypes used Lamborghini V12 engines with 455bhp and a top speed of over 190mph (306km/h) was quoted, though a Carlo Chiti-developed 4-litre V12 with twin turbochargers and 720bhp was introduced on the production version, called the GTB, at the 1992 Detroit Show. The original car had been launched to a private gathering on the eve of the 1990 Monaco Grand Prix and two years later at the same event, a less expensive open-topped model called the Beau Rivage was launched with a non-turbocharged 3.5-litre 450bhp V12 engine. The rights were sold in 1993 to a Georgian company that also owned Russian aircraft maker MiG. It planned to offer three versions under the MiG name: the M100 2-seater, M200 2+2 and M300 4-door, all based on the Monte Carlo. One example appeared at the 1993 Le Mans 24 Hours test day, but things went quiet thereafter and in 1996 the Monte Carlo was acquired by MEGA. It was considerably re-engineered and restyled, gaining a 395bhp Mercedes V12 engine and optional carbon brakes. However, it had still not entered production by the end of 1998.

CR

MONTE CARLO see DARRIAN

MONTEROSA (I) 1959–1961
Carrozzeria Monterosa, Moncalieri, Turin.

Giorgio Sargiotti's coachbuilding concern was founded in 1946 but it took until around 1959 for his first true cars to arrive. These were based on either the Fiat 500 or 600 and were available in three forms: a 2+2 sports coupé, a saloon and a luxury saloon. The engines were available tuned by Abarth or Stanguellini. Very few cars were built.

CR

MONTEVERDI (CH) 1956–1992
Automobile Monteverdi AG, Binningen.

Peter Monteverdi (1934–1998) was trained as an automobile mechanic at the famous Saurer works in Arbon. He wanted to become a racing driver. In 1951,

1962 M.B.M. (Monteverdi) Osca engined sports car.
ERNEST SCHMID

1962 M.B.M. (Monteverdi) Ford 105E coupé.
NATIONAL MOTOR MUSEUM

1971 Monteverdi 375L coupé.
NICK BALDWIN

even before he obtained his driver's licence, he had built his first small racer based on the Fiat Balilla, and which he called Monteverdi Special. It had a space frame, axles, aluminium 2-seater body and many other parts designed and made by himself.

In 1956 his father died and he took over his automobile repairshop in Binningen. He was successfully racing Fiat, Porsche and Ferrari sports cars and converted his Ferrari Monza 750 into a gull-winged road car for his own use. He then built his first single-seater, a formula Junior racer with a tuned DKW 3-cylinder 2-stroke engine placed midships in the space frame. The next model, which he named MBM (Monteverdi-Basle-Motors) still had the DKW engine,

1972 Monteverdi 375/4 saloon.
NICK BALDWIN

which delivered 85bhp. It cost SFr17,000 and at least one was delivered to the USA. The bodies, originally made of aluminium, were now of fibreglass. In 1960 he shared the exhibition stand of Italsuisse at the Geneva Autoshow and displayed one of the MBM racing cars next to a go-kart which he had meanwhile added to the manufacturing programme. In 1961 an open 2-seater version, MBM Sport with a 4-cylinder Osca engine of 1100cc and 100bhp was completed. It was a very handsome sports-racing car, a sort of miniaturised Testarossa. Peter Monteverdi had chosen a very unorthodox set-up for the rear axle. The driver, apart from making use of the original Osca 4-speed gearbox, could select from his seat no less than five different final-drive ratios. A Lotus 5-speed gearbox was connected to the differential. In 1962 a neat little sports coupé with a Ford Anglia engine was presented but no production resulted. The racing cars now also obtained tuned Anglia engines.

Monteverdi's ambition for some time had been to build a Formula 1 racing car. In 1961 this dream was realised. It was a scaled-up model D Junior racer with space frame and a Porsche flat-four engine of 145bhp, normally built into the RSK. Results were quite promising but in October, Peter Monteverdi suffered a serious accident driving this car on Hockenheim-Ring, and this brought about the end of his career as a racing driver.

Business, however, continued to be very good and Monteverdi was agent for top marques such as Lancia, Ferrari, Jensen and BMW. By now he had realised that making Junior racing cars was not really earning him a great deal of money and he turned his attention to luxurious and fast touring cars. He was convinced that among his well-to-do customers some would prefer more personalised and individual cars. In 1967 the first model of the new generation, the Monteverdi High Speed 375S, was launched. It was a beautiful 2-seater GT coupé designed and also produced by Pietro Frua and reminiscent of the Maserati Ghibli, which is considered by many as one of the truly outstanding designs of the 1960s. It was presented to the Swiss press and at the International Automobile Exhibition at Frankfurt in September, and was well received. The space frame made of square tubes, the De Dion rear axle, disc brakes and a lockable differential gave proof of an advanced technical concept. Interior and finish were of the top standard. Making use of the Chrysler V8 engine of 7206cc, there was plenty of power available – 380 SAE bhp to be exact. Customers looking for the ultimate power parcel could order the 400SS version with 406 SAE bhp.

In spring 1969 an additional model, the Monteverdi 375L with the wheelbase increased by 15cm was shown at the Geneva Show. Its 2+2 body was again designed by Frua, which hence turned to Fissore but this did not please Frua, which demanded a licence for every car built. Peter Monteverdi therefore decided to design himself a new range of models which were in fact bearing out even better the individual lines. There were again the 375S 2-seater coupé and the 375L 2+2 which was selling well, accounting for 50 per cent of the total Monteverdi production over the years. In 1970 there was an attempt to produce a smaller coupé, the Monteverdi 2000 GTI, which was based on the BMW 2000ti, but this did not materialise. In the following years new exciting versions of the 375 theme followed – the High Speed 375C was a convertible, the High Speed 375/4, a beautiful 4-door saloon which could even be had with a glass partition and the 375 Berlinetta, a 2-seater coupé to replace the 375S. The most breathtaking Monteverdi was undoubtedly the Hai 450SS presented at the Geneva Show of 1970 (Hai means Shark). The ultra-low 2-seater mid-engined coupé was designed by Peter Monteverdi and produced by Fissore. The Chrysler Hemi V8 engine of 6974cc offered 450bhp and top speed was an indicated 175mph (282km/h). The price of about SFr90,000 was considerably higher than for the Ferrari 365GTB/4 or the Lamborghini Miura, both with V12 engines. This mirrors the luxurious interior and finish but also accounts for the fact that only two Monteverdi Hai 450 were ever built. The second, made in 1973, was designed Hai 450GTS and with this model, apart from small modifications on the body, the engine was tuned and developed 450 DIN bhp, increasing top-speed to 183mph (295km/h). In 1975 the Monteverdi 375 Palm Beach, a handsome 2-seater convertible was presented. Then Peter Monteverdi turned his attention to 4×4 vehicles for which there was a new and potential market not only in the Arabian countries.

The Monteverdi Safari was launched in 1976. It made use of the International Scout chassis fitted with Chrysler V8 engines and a Monteverdi designed body and interior. It cost SFr40,000, which was more expensive than the prices of the competitors. Nevertheless, Monteverdi sold by far more cars then ever before and in 1978 added the slightly less expensive Sahara, which sold equally well. It was available with American 4-cylinder or V8 engines or by request with the Nissan 6-cylinder diesel. By this time the manufacturing programme (production was near Turin), had changed considerably with off-road vehicles.

The only passenger cars were the 4-door saloon and convertible of the new Sierra range, which was launched in 1978. For the saloon, Monteverdi made use of the Dodge Aspen body shell which was highly modified. Chrysler V8 engines of 5210cc or 5898cc and 168 or 180bhp respectively, were mounted. Plans and prototypes of a modified Opel Diplomat, of the Turbo coupé based on a Ford chassis, and of various military vehicles did not result in production. This held true also for the Monteverdi Tiara, a modified Mercedes S-class (380SEL/500SEL) with V8 engines, which was shown in 1982. This was the end of the production of Monteverdi cars–at least for some time.

In 1985 Peter Monteverdi opened his automobile museum, which contained the largest Monteverdi collection in the world including even the Hai 450GTS. Ten years later, he astonished the motoring world once more by presenting at the 1992 Geneva Show, a fabulous 2-seater racing coupé, which could not be driven on public roads. In memory of his earlier supercars he named it Monteverdi Hai 650 F1. Its technical concept is indeed pure Formula 1 with carbon, kevlar and epoxi used for the monocoque chassis and body. The Ford Cosworth Formula 1 engine is a V8 of 3491cc offering not quite the 650bhp the name would make believe, but still 578bhp at 11000rpm, and would propel the rocket in 8 seconds from standstill to 125mph (201km/h) and give a top speed of 210mph (338km/h). A small series of 12 of these supercars was envisaged at the price of SFr850,000 but no sales are recorded and consequently there was no production. Peter Monteverdi, who had been one of the outstanding designers of Switzerland and bravely produced extraordinary vehicles when most others had given up, died in July 1998.

FH

Further Reading
'Monteverdi Hai: Peter Monteverdi's done it again', Michael Lorrimer, *Automobile Quarterly*, Vol. 9, No. 2.
'What a car! Monteverdi high-speed', Michael Lorrimer, *Automobile Quarterly*, Vol. 8, No. 1.

MONTIER ET GILLET; MONTIER (i) (F) 1895–1898

1895 Voiturette à Vapeur Système Montier et Gillet, Richelieu, Indre-et-Loire.
1897–1900 Charles Montier, Paris.
The first vehicle built by this family was the work of the father, Élie Montier, with a partner, Gillet, and aided by Montier's 16-year old son Charles. It was a steam car with 4-seater *vis-à-vis* body and an elaborate detachable canopy top. Although a company was formed for its production, only one was made. Soon afterwards Charles Montier went to Paris and made one petrol-engined car in the works of the Établissements Pinède. Exhibited at the 1897 Paris Salon, it was also a *vis-à-vis* and bore some resemblance to his father's steamer, though of much lighter appearance with wire wheels, and shorter in the wheelbase. The same vertical tiller steering was used. He was unable to put it into production as the Pinède works closed down, but he found a very small workshop where, aided by his father, he made a number of light 2-seaters powered by front-mounted flat-twin engines. A vertical single-cylinder was also seen on a few cars. He did not have the resources to continue for long, and later worked for Darracq before making Ford-based Montier (ii) cars in the 1920s.

NG

MONTIER (ii) (F) 1920–1934

Charles Montier et Cie, Courbevoie; Levallois; Asnières, Seine.
Charles Montier (1879–1952) began selling Model T Fords shortly before World War I. He quickly became an enthusiast for the car, and in 1916 designed a conversion set for making an agricultural tractor out of the T. The war over, he set up a factory to make conversions of the T, including saloons and town cars on the standard chassis, and lowered the frame for sports and racing cars. These also received ohv engines, conventional 3- or 4-speed gearboxes and front-wheel brakes. By 1926, all Montier-Fords had front-wheel brakes. Other ways in which Montier improved the appearance of the humble Model T included replacing artillery wheels with wire, raising the radiator and using more attractive bodies including some saloons by Weymann. He made most bodies in his factory, using the best local artisans. Because of demand he moved twice to larger premises, first to Levallois and then to Asnières.

When the Model A arrived in 1928, Montier turned his attention to that car, again lowering the chassis and fitting some attractive *faux-cabriolet* bodies as well as standard American bodies on the lowered frames. He had an active

1931 Montier Model A-based faux cabriolet.
NATIONAL MOTOR MUSEUM

1909 Moon Model D landaulet.
NICK BALDWIN

sporting career with racing cars based on the Model A, including a two-car entry in the 1929 French Grand Prix, in the 1930 GP de l'Europe at Spa and 1930 Circuit des Routes Pavées in which he finished second. In 1932 he prepared a special car with two Model A engines in line using the chassis of a 1927 single-seater. The 'straight-8' had a top speed of 112mph (179km/h), but it was not easy to maintain equal running of both engines. Montier's son Guy drove this car in the Circuits of Dieppe and La Baule in 1933, though without great success. The arrival of the Ford V8 in 1932 presented Montier with problems as he knew that there would be annual changes which he would have difficulty keeping up with. Nevertheless, he designed a twin-barrel carburettor for the 1932 V8-18, and built at least one Montier Special on the 1934 V8-40. This was a roadster with cycle-type wings and headlamps mounted behind the grill in the manner of the Peugeot 402.

NG

Further Reading
'L'Épopée Ford/Montier', Georges Montier, *l'Album du Fanatique*, Feb-May 1976.

MONZA *see* FIEROSSA

MOON (US) 1905–1929

1905–1907 Joseph W. Moon Buggy Co., St Louis, Missouri.
1907–1929 Moon Motor Car Co., St Louis, Missouri.
Joseph Moon (1850–1919) was a carriage builder. After selling his half interest in the Moon Brothers Carriage Co. to his brother in 1893, Moon set up the Joseph W. Moon Buggy Co. It was under this name that he built his first automobile in 1905. Shown at the New York Automobile Show in January 1906, the car, called Moon Model A, was a 5-passenger touring car with a front-mounted 30hp Rutenber 4-cylinder engine driving through a leather-faced, multiple-disk clutch and a sliding gear transmission. By this time Moon was using the name

1923 Moon Model 6-40 tourer.
NICK BALDWIN

1927 Moon Model 6-60 Royal roadster.
NICK BALDWIN

1928 Moon Model 6-72 sedan.
JOHN A. CONDE

Moon Motor Car Co., although the firm was not incorporated until 1907. That year, the Model C was offered in limousine, runabout, and 7-passenger touring forms, as well as the 5-passenger touring. In 1906, Moon had hired Louis P. Mooers, formerly with PEERLESS. Mooers designed an ohc 4-cylinder engine, which used a unique single rocker arm per cylinder. Cars also featured aluminium bodies and 4-speed transmissions. A 7-passenger Model D was added in 1908, at which time Moon cars sold in the eastern United States were badged HOL-TAN, from the name of the New York dealer. That arrangement was dissolved in 1909.

Mooers left Moon after two years, and as new features were warranted they were drawn in from outside sources. Thus, Moons gradually became assembled

cars. Mooers' engine was dropped in 1912 in favour of a T-head valve-in-block design, and some proprietary power units were bought in from Continental. The Models C and D were supplanted by the 30 and 45 in 1910, and a 40 was added in 1912. A 6-cylinder 65 came in 1913, as did a Wagner electric starter. The lesser series were now called 39 and 48. Closed coupé bodies had been offered since 1911. 'The Moon policy invariably delivers more than the buyer expects or pays for', read the company's advertising. The Joseph W. Moon Buggy Co. continued to manufacture horse-drawn conveyances until 1916, and many of its officers also held stock in Moon Motor Car Co.

From 1916, 6-cylinder engines were offered exclusively, and bodies featured concealed door hinges and locks. A handsome Delaunay-Belleville-type dual-cowled touring body was introduced. In 1919 came what would be Moon's hallmark, a Parthenon-roofed, sharp-edged radiator shell that unashamedly aped that of ROLLS-ROYCE. Joseph Moon died that same year, and was succeeded by vice-president Stewart McDonald, who also happened to be his son-in-law. The 1920s would be Moon's bread-and-butter years, its cars selling in the $1500 to $2500 range, competitive with BUICK and OLDSMOBILE, and the firm turned a tidy profit for the first half of the decade. Peak production, slightly more than 10,000 cars, occurred in 1925. The cars were stylish, the Rolls-like radiator co-ordinating nicely with handsome bodies produced by Pullman, Rubay, and Murray. Colours were touted by the company as 'brave', and included such imaginative hues as 'Mist-o-Marne', 'Versailles blue', 'milori green', and 'lake maroon'. The modern 'Duco' finishes were adopted, but were further embellished with a finish coat of varnish. Interior fabrics included broadcloth, mohair, and 'high grade corduroy'.

For 1924, low-pressure balloon tyres were offered, and Lockheed hydraulic brakes, an external-contracting design, were optional. Later they would become standard fare. 'The old mechanical brakes have to go', said a Moon advertisement 'They are not safe enough for modern traffic strains'. The 1925 promotional patter advised that 'you can hold your speedometer at 50 to 60 (80 to 97km/h) – or better if you dare – without vibration', the benefit of the car's four main bearings and pressure-fed lubrication.

Moon cars sold best in the midwestern United States, and in 1923 the company claimed to be outselling most other makes in Chicago. This was no doubt owing to the efforts of super salesman Erret Lobban Cord, later famous for the front-wheel drive CORD car, who worked there for distributor Quinlan Motor Co. Exports begun in 1908 had burgeoned by the 1920s, by which time 47 countries were importing quantities of the marque. Cars were shipped in crates until 1928, when open shipments commenced, the first leg of their journey being on barges floated down the Mississippi River to New Orleans. Other cars were shipped by rail to New York, whence they were loaded aboard ships.

A significant departure from Moon's previously successful formula came in July 1925, with the introduction of the DIANA, a low-priced 8-cylinder car intended to be a stylish market leader. A subsidiary firm, Diana Motors Co., was set up to build the new car, although its kinship was obvious from the fact that the parent and offspring companies shared the same officers. Reliability problems with the Diana, combined with payment of a claim to the US government dating from World War I, caused Moon Motor Car Co. to post a near-million dollar deficit in 1926. In the last quarter of that year, Moon missed a dividend to its shareholders. Another trouble for the company was that its scheme to take 'in-house' the big city distribution network was running in the red. In fact, the Moon Motor Car Co. would never see another profit.

The failed Diana experiment, though, did not dissuade Moon from further ventures. President McDonald engaged designer Howard 'Dutch' Darrin, then practising in Paris, to conjure up a Diana replacement. The Moon Aerotype of 1928 was the result. This was a hastily-produced design rushed to completion because Moon could not afford Darrin's $1000 per day fee for very long. Although 'filled in' by in-house staff, the Aerotype was attractive, in part because it 'borrowed' from another timeless icon, the HISPANO-SUIZA. The Aerotype appeared first in 8-cylinder form, the 8-80, and later as a 6-72.

Another ill-fated venture was Moon's attempt to spin off another 'paper' subsidiary, the Windsor Corp., in 1929. Trying to capitalise on the image of the Prince of Wales, the company introduced the WINDSOR White Prince automobile, which caused immediate problems with export and relations with the United Kingdom. These Windsors were sold, not surprisingly, as Moons in British territory. However, in the United States the Moon badge was laid to rest, with the 'old' Moon model 6-72 being redesignated a Windsor 6-72.

The New Six-68 Sedan

MOON
MODERN MOTOR CARS

Character is built up in the Moon from the very foundation. A perfect balance and lasting freedom from rumbles and squeaks are conceived in the design of the extra heavy frame —the backbone of a motor car, where faults soon show up in a warped and rattling body.

The new Moon Six-68 Sedan is a big brother of the Moon Six-48. A Sedan of amplified roominess and motor power, it retains the typical lightness and compactness that give the Moon mastery of all sorts of highways. Elegance is summed up in coach work and interior finish that are a heritage from the days of fine Moon carriages.

Selling at a price that appeals to your reason, the Six-68 Sedan is a soft answer to yearnings for extraordinary motor car luxury.

MOON MOTOR CAR COMPANY, ST. LOUIS, U. S. A.

1919 Moore (iii) Model 30 tourer.
NICK BALDWIN

1910 Mora Light Four tourer.
NICK BALDWIN

The final fling of Moon Motor Car Co. ended up being the firm's most bizarre period. In search of new work, it had built some cotton-picking machinery in 1929, and was pursuing ventures with taxicabs and aviation. Neither bore fruit. Then along came Archie Andrews, president of New Era Motors, searching for facilities in which to build the RUXTON automobile. A series of intricate negotiations resulted in the acquisition by New Era of 150,000 shares of Moon stock in exchange for Ruxton 'rights . . . plant equipment, engineering data, and finished and unfinished cars'. Moon president Carl Burst, who had risen to the helm in 1928 when McDonald rose to chairman of the board, was ousted, along with other old-guard officers. The Ruxton venture was doomed, however, and the 1930 bankruptcy of New Era Motors spelled the end also for Moon. The final distribution of assets of Moon Motor Car Co., however, did not occur until 1966.

KF

Further Reading
Great Cars of the Great Plains, Curt McConnell,
University of Nebraska Press, 1995.
'The Moon in all its Phases', C. Burst III and A.D. Young,
Automobile Quarterly, Vol. 25, No. 4.
Recollections of a Moon Man, Ralph Atkinson, SIA, April 1999.

MOORE (i) (US) 1906

Moore Automobile Co., Walla Walla, Washington.
This car was unusual in that the sole purpose of setting up a company and making the car was to protest against the big manufacturers' failure to make cars of 60in (1523mm) track. This was standard in Washington State, though 56in (1421mm) was the norm in the rest of the country. Only the frame was built by the Moore company, the other components, including a 4-cylinder engine, were bought from outside sources. It was made for one season only, and when Franklin started the ball rolling by making cars with a 60in (1523mm) track, the Moore Automobile Co. was dissolved.

NG

MOORE (ii) (US) 1906–1907

Moore Automobile Co., Bridgeport, Connecticut.
The designer of this car made lavish use of ball bearings, so that it was called 'The Ball Bearing Car'. Only one chassis was offered, a 40hp 4-cylinder available with three styles of body, tourer, runabout and limousine. They were very expensive at $6500 for the runabout to $8000 for the limousine, putting them up against top price cars like the Locomobile. It is hardly surprising that the company lasted less than two years.

NG

MOORE (iii) (US) 1916–1920

Moore Motor Vehicle Co., Minneapolis, Minnesota (1916–1918);
Danville, Illinois (1919–1920).
This was one of several attempts to rival the Model T Ford, though unlike the Ford it was an assembled car, using a 30hp 4-cylinder G.B. & S. engine, Pontiac Chassis Co. frame and Wayne body. Made only as a tourer up to 1919, when a 5-seater 'Sport Model' was offered as well, it changed mainly in price. This rose from $550 in 1916 to $1095 in 1920. A total of 1186 Moores were made.

NG

MOORE (iv) (US) 1917

Moore Car Corp. of America, Indianapolis, Indiana.
This was a hybrid car/motorcycle, with two large wheels and two tiny stabilisers close to the rear wheel which could be raised or lowered 'at the touch of a button'. It was powered by a 22hp 2-cylinder Sinclair engine and had a 3-speed gearbox and shaft drive. Speeds of 3 to 90mph (5 to 144km/h) were quoted, the latter seeming most improbable. The Moore-Car as it was sometimes called, was advertised as 'the car for every man, and every woman too, who does not like a motorcycle and cannot afford an automobile'. However, it failed to last out the year of its introduction, and production was probably minimal.

NG

MOOSE JAW STANDARD (CDN) 1916–1917

This car is sometimes thought of as a successor to the CANADIAN STANDARD, but this is only geographical in that both makes came from the Saskatchewan town of Moose Jaw. A few years after the closure of the Canadian Standard Auto & Tractor Co. in 1913, a group of citizens hired an engineer, acquired a factory and bought enough components from American suppliers, including 6-cylinder Continental engines, to make 25 luxury cars. Only five were completed, one going to each of the backers. The remaining parts were sold, the engineer paid off and the project was wound up. It is thought that no company was ever formed. One of the five cars survives today in Saskatchewan.

NG

MOPS (D) 1923

Schmidt & Bensdorf GmbH, Mannheim.
This was a 3-wheeled cyclecar with tandem seating and a 350cc engine driving the single rear wheel.

HON

MORA (US) 1906–1911

Mora Motor Car Co., Newark, New York.
The Mora was introduced as a 24hp 4-cylinder car on two wheelbases, 98 (2487mm) and 103in (2614mm), as a 5-seater tourer, 4-seater surrey and 2-seater 'racy type roadster'. The latter was also made on the 42/50hp 6-cylinder chassis offered from 1908 to 1909, and on the 60hp Large Four of 1909. The company said that they would not make more than 100 racy type roadsters per year. They were bankrupt by November 1911, when the company inventory included 50 unsold cars. The assets were acquired by the Frank Toomey Co. of Philadelphia, who sold off the cars, but they probably did not make any more. Mora also built the BROWNIEKAR under the name of a subsidiary company, the Omar Motor Co.

NG

MORAIN SYLVESTRE *see* M.S.

MORALY (F) 1956

The most unusual thing about the Moraly microcar was its seating layout: the four passengers sat in diamond formation, with the driver alone up front and rearmost passenger behind the middle pair. It was powered by a rear-mounted 250cc single-cylinder 18bhp 2-stroke engine and its bodywork was made of fibreglass over a tubular chassis.

CR

MORAVAN *see* AVIA (ii)

MORETTI (I) 1945–1984

1945–1961 Fabbrica Automobili Moretti SpA, Turin.
1962–1984 Moretti Fabbrica Automobili e Stablimenti Carrozzeria SAS, Turin.
Giovanni Moretti was eight years old when, in 1912, his father died and he had to go to work. He was just 21 when he set up his company and, from 1925 to 1945, Moretti specialised in racing motorcycle engines and 3-wheeled commercial vehicles. In 1945, Moretti began to build small-engined cars at a rate of about one a week – Moretti's 4-cylinder single-ohc engines should not be confused with the many Fiat-based units which were made in Italy.

Moretti's first model was the 'La Cita' minicar which had a front-mounted 14bhp vertical-twin engine, first of 250cc, then of 340cc. It had a tubular chassis with hydraulic brakes and independent suspension by transverse leaf springs and lower wishbones and was available as a saloon, an estate, and a coupé.

By 1950, the single-ohc 4-cylinder engine was ready and, in 600cc and 750cc versions, was fitted to a new backbone chassis, with, on the sporting models, independent suspension all round. It was available with a variety of body styles, including a coupé. 1954 saw a wide range of Morettis which had power outputs between 27bhp (single-ohc two-bearing 750cc engine) and 51bhp (double-ohc three-bearing 750cc engine) plus a special 52bhp double-ohc 1.2-litre engine. The latter was fitted in a coupé, with styling by Michelotti, which sold mainly in America.

In 1957 Moretti made a special coupé body on a Fiat Nuova 500 but continued to offer a wide range of engines: there were 27bhp and 43bhp versions of the single-ohc 750cc engine; a 55bhp double-ohc 750cc unit; an 820cc single-ohc engine; and a one-litre single-ohc version. By then suspension was by coil springs and double wishbones and disc brakes were fitted to the front wheels of the most powerful model.

Despite the wide range of engines, and models, production was tiny; only 118 cars in 1958, for example, and hardly any two were alike. From 1960 Moretti turned its attention to Fiats and dropped its original designs.

Most Morettis thereafter were new bodies on standard chassis, in fact, after 1970, the company officially listed itself as a coachbuilder. Most notable of the sports Morettis was the 2.5-litre Spyder which was made between 1960 and 1963; it was based on the running gear of the Fiat 2300, but the engine was enlarged and tuned to give 163bhp. Most models, however, were based on the smaller Fiats.

In 1961 Fiat contracted Moretti to build special examples of its range and the subsequent vehicles were sold through Fiat agencies. The company ceased making cars in 1984, when it made convertible versions of such Fiats as the Uno and Regata. It continued to make light commercial vehicles for some years afterwards but now specialises in the manufacture of industrial plant.

MJL

MORFORD (GB) 1993 to date

Morford Motor Co., Whaddon, Cambridgeshire.
Created by two Morgan enthusiasts, the Morford was an aluminium-bodied trike which looked like it had been made by folding cardboard. It was much larger than most contemporary trikes, with a long wheelbase which helped stability. All mechanical items were taken from the Renault 5, although the rear suspension was supported on a Jaguar spring and shock absorber. On the same steel tube chassis, the designers came up with an all-new more curvaceous Mk2 body in 1995.

CR

MORGAN (i) (GB) 1905–1906

Morgan & Co. Ltd, Leighton Buzzard, Bedfordshire.

1953 Moretti 750cc coupé.
NATIONAL MOTOR MUSEUM

1963 Moretti 2500SS sports car.
NATIONAL MOTOR MUSEUM

Morgan & Co. were much better known for their coachwork than for their cars, starting in London in 1795 and moving to Leighton Buzzard in 1886. In 1905 they built a car powered by a 5.8-litre 4-cylinder T-head Mutel engine, with Sparkes-Boothby hydraulic clutch. This was evidently not very satisfactory as the following four cars had conventional leather cone clutches. Morgan later became agents for ADLER cars; those fitted with Morgan coachwork were sometimes sold as Morgan-Adlers.

NG

MORGAN (ii) (GB) 1910 to date

Morgan Motor Co. Ltd, Malvern Link, Worcestershire.
The Morgan is unique among the world's cars on several accounts. Apart from the power unit the design has changed little in over sixty years, and by today's standards it is frankly hard riding and uncomfortable, yet it has a longer waiting list than any other car. The company is run by the son of the man who founded it ninety years ago.

Henry Frederick Stanley Morgan (1881–1959), was the son of the vicar of Stoke Lacey, Herefordshire, who, unlike his father and grandfather, decided not to go into the Church, but became an engineering apprentice with the Great Western Railway. (Other car makers who were ex-railway apprentices included W.O. Bentley and Henry Royce.) After this he opened a garage in Malvern Link, and in 1908–9 he began to build, in the engineering workshop of Malvern College and helped by engineering teacher Mr Stephenson-Peach, a single-seater 3-wheeler. It was powered by a V-twin Peugeot engine, transmission being by dog clutches and two chain drives of different ratios. Its most remarkable feature was the ifs by coil springs and sliding pillars, the basic principle of which is still used in Morgan cars today.

In 1910 Morgan formed the Morgan Motor Co. Ltd, and with the aid of £3000 from his father he built a small factory in Malvern Link. In November of that year he exhibited two single-seaters at the Motor Cycle Show, powered by 961cc JAP V-twin engines. Their lack of an extra seat limited their appeal, and in 1911 he began to make 2-seaters. Orders for these came in very satisfactorily, and the make's first sporting success was achieved with a Gold Medal in the Land's End Trial. In 1912 a Morgan covered 58.96 miles (94.95km) in an hour at Brooklands, setting a new cyclecar record. The first major success came in 1913

1911 Morgan (ii) Runabout.
NICK BALDWIN

1912 Morgan (ii) prototype 4-seater.
NICK BALDWIN

c.1920 Morgan (ii) Grand Prix 3-wheeler.
NICK BALDWIN

when W.G. McMinnies won the Cyclecar GP at Amiens, though he was subsequently disqualified as the 3-wheeled Morgan was held to be a sidecar. This led to the marketing of three sporting models, the Grand Prix No.1 with side-valve engine and narrow body, the Grand Prix No.2 with the same engine and wider body, and the Grand Prix No.3 with an ohv engine which was almost identical to the car which won at Amiens. Touring 2-seaters were also made, and an experimental 4-seater was running in 1915. At the outbreak of World War I annual production was nearly 1000 cars.

Manufacture was soon resumed after the war, additional assembly space being acquired in 1919 in Pickersleigh Road, Malvern Link. Four years later all production was transferred there, and it is still the home of Morgan today. As early as March 1919 Morgan were turning out 20 cars per week. The touring model, confusingly called the Sports, had a Swiss-built MAG V-twin air-cooled engine, while the sporting Grand Prix was powered by a water-cooled JAP engine, and was joined by the faster Blackburne-engined Aero for 1921. This long-tailed model was re-named Super Sports Aero in 1929, while the Sports was logically re-named the Standard in 1922. In 1921 came the Family Model, the first production 4-seater, which was also available as a 2-seater. The Family Models, which were made until 1936, could be distinguished by the dummy radiators in front of their air-cooled V-twin engines. Sporting Morgans, on the other hand, displayed their engines proudly ahead of the short bonnet, which made for excellent cooling, though they were vulnerable to flying stones. By 1925 water-cooled JAP engines were available on the Family models, at a higher price. Refinements such as front-wheel brakes and electric starting arrived in the later 1920s, and in 1931 a 3-speed gearbox was an optional alternative to the 2-speeder, being standardised after 1932. The sporting Aero models were offered with a choice of 980cc side-valve JAP, 1078cc ohv Anzani or 1096cc ohv JAP engines, the latter capable of 71mph (115km/h). The Super Sports Aero of 1929-32 with the larger JAP engine and a lower chassis, had a top speed of 80mph (130km/h).

In 1933 Matchless engines became available in the Family and Sports models, the latter being the Aero's replacement. Capacity was 990cc, a side-valve unit for the Family and (from 1934) an ohv for the Sports. These were available in addition to the larger JAP units, but the latter were gradually phased out after 1935. A new model was the 4-seater Sports Family, which was available with any of the four engines, sv or ohv, JAP or Matchless. The Super Sports, with barrel-backed body and spare wheel recessed in the tail, was made in dwindling numbers up to 1939. It offered speed at a remarkably low price (over 80mph (130km/h) for £135 in 1934), but was too spartan for most people's tastes.

To reach a wider market for their 3-wheelers, Morgan introduced in 1934 the F series, powered by 4-cylinder Ford engines of 933 or 1172cc. These had channel section steel frames in place of the tubular frames of previous Morgans, and conventional accelerator pedals, whereas earlier models had throttle controls on the steering wheel. The first was the F4 4-seater, joined in 1936 by the F2 2-seater and in 1937 by the F Super which had the barrel-backed body of the Super Sports, though the exhaust pipe ran beneath the car rather than along the side. At 75mph (120km/h), it was a slower car than the Super Sports, and not highly regarded by Morgan aficionados. The F4 and F Super were revived after the war, and made with little change until 1952. Total postwar 3-wheeler production was 265.

Four Wheels, Four Cylinders

By the mid–1930s it was becoming clear that the 3-wheelers could no longer keep the company going, so a prototype of a small 4-wheeled sports car in the MG Midget class was tested during 1935. It was powered by the Ford Ten engine used in the F 3-wheeler, but when the car was launched in December 1935 a 1122cc Coventry-Climax inlet-over-exhaust-valve engine was used. Front suspension was by sliding pillars as on the 3-wheelers, and rear suspension was by semi-elliptics. 2- and 4-seater bodies were offered, with a 2-seater drophead coupé joining the range for 1939. In that year the Climax engine was replaced by a 1267cc ohv built by Standard to Morgan's specification. The 4/4 did not catch on straight away, as traditional Morgan enthusiasts thought it too soft, while for the other customers the MG was well established in that particular market. However, the fact that the 4/4 was actively campaigned in rallies and trials by H.F.S. Morgan and his son Peter helped its popularity, and the respectable number of 812 were sold up to the outbreak of war. In 1938 and 1939 a 4/4 ran at Le Mans; this had a 1098cc Climax engine and cycle-type wings. A very small number of Le Mans replicas were sold to the public.

"MOTORING *for the* MILLION"

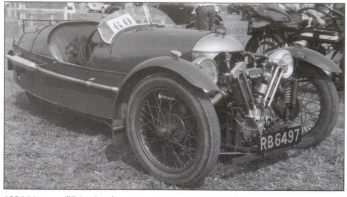

1931 Morgan (ii) 3-wheeler.
NICK BALDWIN

1948 Morgan (ii) 4/4 4-seater.
NICK BALDWIN

1960 Morgan (ii) Plus 4 2-seater.
NICK BALDWIN

1964 Morgan (ii) Plus 4 Plus coupé.
NICK BALDWIN

A few cars were assembled from prewar components in 1945, and production got under way in 1946. The postwar 4/4 was virtually unchanged from the 1939 version, and the same body styles were offered. Only the prices were very different, up from £199–236 to £499–557. Most of the 4/4s made up to 1950 went for export, as did their successor, the Plus Four. This had a generally similar appearance, but the wheelbase was 4in (101mm) longer, and the engine was a 2088cc Standard Vanguard unit. New features on Morgans were hydraulic brakes and a hypoid rear axle. In 1954 the 1991cc engine used in the Triumph TR2 supplemented the Vanguard unit, and replaced it after 1958; this not only gave more power, but put the Plus Four inside the 2-litre class for competitions. The chief external sign of the new engine was a radiator grill rounded at the top, which is still used on Morgans today.

In 1956 the 4/4 name was revived for a 2-seater of Plus Four appearance powered by the 1172cc side-valve Ford Ten engine. This was replaced four years later by the 997cc oversquare ohv engine of the Ford Anglia. Only 59 of these were made. Since then the 4/4 has been progressively updated with newer Ford engines, the 1340cc unit from the Classic 315 saloon (1961-63), the 1498cc Cortina GT (1963–68), the 1599cc Kent (1969–82), the 1598cc CVH (1982–93) and the 1796cc Zetec from 1994 to date. 93 4/4s were fitted with twin-cam 1600 Fiat engines from 1985 to 1987. Total production of the different models up to 1968 was 1298, with about 3000 being made in the 1970s. Changes were few, apart from front disc brakes in 1961 and an all-synchromesh gearbox in 1963.

The Plus Four remained in production until 1969, with few changes apart from a 105bhp 2138cc engine from 1962, and the option of disc brakes in 1959, standardised two years later. 143 competition models with more power was obtained by fitting the 4-branch force-flow exhaust system used on the Super Sports. These engines gave 120bhp and 118mph (190km/h), and were made between 1961 and 1969. The Plus Four Super Sports used the same engine which was Lawrence-tuned. 104 Super Sports were made between 1961 and 1969, plus 11 others not classed by the works as Super Sports. There was also a curious coupé called the Plus Four Plus, of which 26 were made between 1964 and 1967. Under its all-enveloping body it was a standard Plus Four, and it was not well received. Of the regular Plus Fours, 783 were made with the Vanguard engine, and 3850 with the Triumph. The Plus Four name was revived in 1988 in what was a 4/4 with twin-ohc 16-valve 2-litre Rover engine. This was still made in 1999, in 2 and 4-seater models.

The Plus 8

When Triumph dropped their 4-cylinder sports car engine in 1968, Morgan had to shop elsewhere for their power unit. They chose the 3528cc V8 which Rover were using in their 3500 saloons, and which was itself based on the Buick Special engine of 1961. The Morgan Plus Four became the Plus Eight, with little external change, though to cope with the greater power (160bhp) the track was increased, and fatter tyres with wider wheel rims were introduced. The traditional wooden plank floor was replaced by steel, but the ash-framed body was continued, with steel or aluminium panels. Top speed was 125mph (200km/h), and when the 190bhp Rover Vitesse engine was available in 1984, the maximum went up to 130mph (210km/h). A Rover 4-speed gearbox replaced the Moss unit in 1973, and was in turn replaced by a 5-speeder in 1975. Apart from the introduction of rack-and-pinion steering in 1983, the Plus Eight has been made with very little change up to the present day. Capacity of the V8 engine went up to 3948cc and there was a 4552cc (220bhp) option from 1997. Because Land Rover are unable to supply the 4.6-litre engine with a manual gearbox, Morgan's V8 is assembled for them by PTP of Coventry. Twin air bags are an option on the latest Plus 8.

In 1999 production was running at about ten cars per week (all models) and demand greatly outstripped supply. At one time the waiting list for a Plus Eight was six years, but Peter Morgan was not happy with this. The ideal would be about eighteen months, and he would begin to worry if it went below six months. Some 45 per cent of Morgan production was exported, with Germany being the biggest customer. A completely new Morgan was launched at the 2000 Geneva Show. Called the Aero 8, it was powered by a 286bhp 4398cc BMW V8 engine, giving a top speed of 160mph (257kn/h). It had a light weight aluminium chassis based on that of the works GT2 racing car. The aluminium body was more streamlined than that of its predcessors, yet was still instantly recognisable as a Morgan.

NG

1997 Morgan (ii) 4/4 2-seater.
MORGAN

Further Reading
Morgan to 1997, a Collector's Guide, Roger Bell,
Motor Racing Publications, 1997.
Completely Morgan, the 4-wheelers 1936–1968, Ken Hill, Veloce, 1994.
Morgan, First and Last of the Real Sports Car, Gregory Houston Bowden,
Haynes, 1986.

MORGAN (iii) (D) 1924–1925

Morgan Auto-AG, Berlin.
The German Morgan was an unusual cyclecar in which the four wheels were
arranged in diamond pattern, as in the earlier SUNBEAM-MABLEY. The rear
wheel was driven by shaft and bevel gear from a 500cc 2/12PS 2-cylinder engine.
HON

MORGAN-MONOTRACE *see* MONOTRACE

MORIN (F) 1948; 1957

Sté de Production A. Morin, Paris.
Morin's first design was the Aérocar of 1948, a very small 3-wheeled microcar whose
open 2-seater Duralinox bodywork was perversely inspired by the contemporary
Buick. It had a rear-mounted 125cc engine and 4-speed gearbox, and was intended
for home construction using Morin plans and key components. Nine years later
Morin presented another microcar prototype, this time a 4-wheeler with very narrow-
set rear wheels. A twin-cylinder 400cc engine was mounted in the tail, between
sizeable tailfins. The enclosed 2-seater coachwork featured a forward control driving
position.
CR

MORISSE (F) 1899–1914

P. Morisse et Cie, Étampes, Seine-et-Oise.
The first Morisse was a voiturette typical of its time, with a 3hp single-cylinder
engine under the seat. Where it differed from most was that the belt drive was to
the front wheels. The engine could be started from the driver's seat. Morisse did
not stick to front drive for long, and his 1901 models had 5½hp vertical or
horizontal engines driving the rear wheels. By 1904 he was using vertical engines
exclusively, 6 and 9hp De Dion-Bouton singles, 10hp twins by De Dion or Tony
Huber, and 24hp fours by Tony Huber or Fossier. The fours had double-chain
drive but the smaller cars were shaft-driven.

2000 Morgan (ii) Aero 8 sports car.
MORGAN

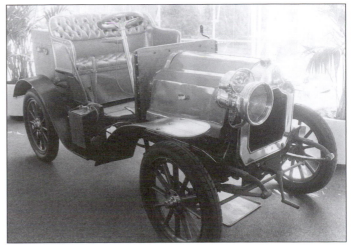

1904 Morisse 2-seater.
JAN P. NORBYE

1914 Morris (i) Oxford 9hp De Luxe 2-seater.
NICK BALDWIN

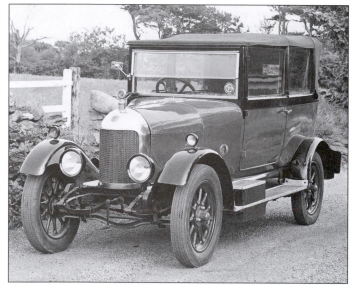

1924 Morris (i) Oxford 14/28hp cabriolet.
NATIONAL MOTOR MUSEUM

1930 Morris (i) Minor 2-seater.
NATIONAL MOTOR MUSEUM

The 1912 range consisted of monobloc fours of 9/11, 10/12, 14/16 and 16/20hp, all with shaft drive. These later cars were often called S.E.M., though still made by Morisse.
NG

MORLOCK (US) 1903

Morlock Automobile Co., Buffalo, New York.
When J.F. Morlock bought the SPAULDING (i) Automobile & Motor Co. he sold off the few remaining Spaulding cars and then produced a basically similar design under his own name. It was a tiller-steered 2-seater runabout or 4-seater *dos-à-dos* powered by a 6hp single-cylinder engine mounted under the seat and driving the rear wheels by single chain.
NG

MORRIS (i) (GB) 1913–1983

1913–1919 W.R.M. Motors Ltd, Cowley, Oxford.
1919–1970 Morris Motors Ltd, Cowley, Oxford.
1970–1975 Austin-Morris Division, British Leyland Motor Corp. Ltd, Cowley, Oxford.
1975–1978 Leyland Cars, British Leyland UK Ltd, Cowley, Oxford.
1978–1980 Austin Morris BL Cars Ltd, Cowley, Oxford.
1980–1983 Light Medium Cars Division, BL Cars Ltd, Cowley, Oxford.
The Morris was one of the most popular British cars for all of its 70-year history, yet it never made a great impact on export markets. When its maker, Lord Nuffield, was introduced in the 1930s to a foreign audience as the builder of Morris cars, he was greeted blankly. Then someone mentioned that he also owned MG, and broad smiles broke out; who had not heard of the little English sports car, MG?

In 1910 William Morris (later Lord Nuffield), began to plan a light car which would sell at a low price because of large scale production. As he had very small premises he would have to buy practically all of the components from outside sources. The prototype Morris Oxford was assembled at the Morris Garages in Longwall Street, Oxford, but for production Morris acquired a former military college at Cowley. The 1018cc 4-cylinder T-head engine was made by White & Poppe of Coventry to Morris' specifications, while the gearbox also came from W & P. Steering and axles came from E.G. Wrigley of Birmingham, and the bodies from Raworth of Oxford, who later made some of the earliest MG bodies. Docherty of Coventry made the rounded radiator, originally nicknamed the 'bullet nose' because of its resemblance to a 0.303 bullet, and later changed to 'bullnose', possibly because the radiator badge featured a cow, symbol of the city of Oxford. The prototype was exhibited (with a wooden engine!) at the Manchester Show in February 1913, and production began at Cowley in March. At £175 it was good value, being a substantial 2-seater far removed from the cyclecars which were attempting to dominate the cheaper end of the market. By the end of the year 393 had been sold, followed by 909 in 1914 when drophead coupé, sports and delivery van bodies were also offered. The Oxford chassis was too short to carry 4-seater bodies, and Morris knew that he could never achieve the volume of sales he dreamed of unless he had a 4-seater to offer. The prices quoted by his suppliers for enlarged engine and chassis were too high, so Morris went shopping across the Atlantic, and soon found what he wanted.

The Continental Manufacturing Co. of Detroit offered him a 1496cc engine for the equivalent of £18 (White & Poppe charged £50 for their 1018cc unit), while he was able to buy gearboxes, steering and axles from other American firms at equally good prices. World War I broke out while negotiations were going on, but Morris did not cancel his orders, and the first of the new cars was completed in April 1915. Known as the Cowley, it was originally priced at £169 for a 2-seater and £194 for a 4-seater, but import duties quickly raised these to £199 and £222, which prices applied during the 1916 season. Half of the 3000 engines Morris ordered from Continental were lost at sea, and demands for military production reduced car output, so that only 1344 Cowleys were made between 1915 and 1918. Oxford production during the same period was 173.

New Engines and Mass Production

Morris had to look for a new engine supplier after the war, as Continental had no other customers for their small unit, and it was not economical to make it only for Morris. The Coventry branch of Hotchkiss, the French car and armaments company, were looking for work, and agreed to make a copy of the Continental engine. The first postwar cars used left-over Continental engines, but by September 1919 the Hotchkiss unit was in production. Two models of Morris were offered, the basic Cowley and the better-equipped Oxford, which cost about £50 more. Sales were slow to start with, because of rapidly escalating prices; a Cowley 2-seater cost £295 in 1919 and £465 in October 1920. Morris then took the bold step which was to make him a millionaire within a few years. He cut his prices dramatically, even though the cars sold at a loss for a while.

NICK BALDWIN

MORRIS, WILLIAM (1877–1963)

He has been described as 'the man who put Oxford on wheels' but it would be fairer to say that he put Britain on wheels, for he made more cars than any native producer for many years. William Richard Morris was born in Worcester on 10 October 1877, the eldest of seven children of farm bailiff Frederick Morris and the former Emily Pether. The family moved back to Oxford, where both sides had farmed for generations, and settled on Emily's father's farm at Headington, just outside Oxford.

William (he was generally known as Will) left the Church School at Cowley at the age of 14, and was apprenticed to a bicycle repairer. He soon realised that he could make more money by working for himself, so, with a capital of £4 he set up business at his parents' home – the showroom and shop were in a front room and the workshop was a shed at the back. Repairing bicycles soon led to building them and his first customer was the rector of St Clements who ordered a special 27in frame. This was in 1892, and nine years later Morris had substantial premises at 48 High Street, Oxford. He assembled his first motorcycle in 1901 and planned to go into partnership with a cycling friend, Joseph Cooper, to manufacture them, but Cooper became nervous about the expenditure of capital on the newfangled device, when bicycles were selling so well. The partnership was dissolved and Morris had to return Cooper's share of the capital, although the men remained friends. More than 10 years later Cooper returned to help Morris with his first car, and subsequently was in charge of the Axle Department of the Nuffield Organisation.

The Morris motorcycle lasted only three years, from 1902 to 1905, but Will expanded his business into Longwall Street where car repairs were carried out. He obtained financial support from a wealthy undergraduate Launcelot Creyke, and he soon took the agencies for a variety of cars and motorcycles. Gradually sales and repairs took over from cycle manufacture, and in 1910 he registered the name, The Morris Garage, which became The Morris Garages three years later. In 1913 he introduced motor buses into Oxford, against the will of the council, which favoured horse-drawn trams. He brought six Daimler double-deckers from London overnight, and began to operate them by selling tickets from shops along the route, as collecting fares on the buses would have been illegal. Eventually the council admitted that motor buses were best, and bought their own fleet, although people preferred Morris' buses. Finally he sold his fleet to the council.

In 1912 he turned motor manufacturer when he announced the Morris Oxford 2-seater at the Motor Show. He had no car to exhibit, only blueprints, but London dealer Gordon Stewart was sufficiently impressed with the design (and a subsequent road test) to promise to take 400 cars as soon as they could be made. The deposit he paid helped Morris to obtain a factory at Cowley. This was located in the former Hurst's Grammar School, where his father had been educated, and which had been enlarged to become a military training college. The buildings had been empty for 21 years, which enabled Morris to buy them at a very reasonable price. The training college buildings became the factory, the school was the office. A complete car was ready in

time for the North of England Motor Show at Manchester in February 1913, although like the 1919 Bentley and other show cars it was not truly complete as it lacked an engine. However, production was soon underway, and 393 cars were sold in 1913. By the end of the year Morris had 99 agents, and by the end of 1914, 909, including outlets in Holland, Belgium, Denmark, Italy, Scandinavia, and Uganda.

The Oxford was an assembled car, but one using British-made components, apart from the German Bosch magneto. For his next model, the Cowley, which was to be made in much larger numbers, Morris went shopping in Detroit, buying engines from Continental, gearboxes from the Detroit Gear Machine Co, and axles and steering gear from other sources. Cowley production was interrupted by the war, but the Morris factory was kept very busy making trench howitzers, mine sinkers and other equipment. The factory expanded and at the end of the war Morris received the first of his honours, with an O.B.E. He had also become seriously rich, which enabled him to expand production and in the 1920s to buy up many of his suppliers such as Osberton Radiators, body builders Hollick & Pratt, and the Hotchkiss engine works. All three of these firms were bought by Morris personally, and sold a few years later to Morris Motors. In 1923 he bought axle makers E.G. Wrigley, and in February 1924 used their factory for the newly formed company, Morris Commercial Cars Ltd. This remained his personal property until 1936, the year after he sold MG to Morris Motors. In 1927 he bought Wolseley Motors, which brought him particular satisfaction as Wolseley had turned him down as an agent 20 years before. He described the Wolseley purchase as 'the most thrilling day of my life'.

Unlike Herbert Austin who was a Member of Parliament, Morris showed little interest in politics. In 1923 he was asked to stand as the Conservative candidate for Oxford, but declined. He did, however, act at the candidate's chief spokesman. They were defeated by the Liberals, who made contemptuous remarks about Morris' abandonment of the free trade principle which he had embraced so enthusiastically when he bought American components for the Cowley. From the 1920s onwards Morris was a great patriot, adopting the slogan 'Buy British and be Proud of it'. He had some grandiose ideas, such as his claim that he could have stopped Hitler if only he [Hitler] had spoken English.

In 1926 Morris made two donations of £10,000 each, one to a scheme to enable parents to visit their children in borstal institutions, and the other to Oxford University to found the King Alfonso Chair of Spanish Studies, appropriate in view of the King's enthusiasm for motoring. These were the first of many benefactions, which made him one of the greatest philanthropists of the inter-war years. In particular he gave large sums to hospitals in Oxford, making the University prominent in the medical field, which it had never been before. He also supported Guy's Hospital in London to the tune of nearly £168,000, and contributed to hospitals in Banbury, Exeter, and Worcester, as well as founding Nuffield College, Oxford, and the Nuffield Nursing Homes. It is estimated that he gave away £30 million in his lifetime. He became Sir William Morris in 1929, Baron Nuffield in 1934, and Viscount Nuffield in 1938.

He remained Chairman of the Nuffield Organisation, which controlled all the vehicle companies, Morris, Morris Commercial, MG, Wolseley, and Riley, as well as making tanks, aero-engines, and complete Spitfires, up to the merger in 1952 with Austin to form the British Motor Corp. Six months after the merger he retired, handing over to his erstwhile employee, Leonard Lord. He lived simply in retirement, preferring to drive his 1939 Wolseley Eight to any grander cars, and playing golf as long as his health permitted. He died on 22 August 1963.

William Morris married Elizabeth Anstey, daughter of an Oxford furrier, in 1904. They had no children.

NG

Further Reading
The Life of Lord Nuffield, P.W.S. Andrews and Elizabeth Brunner, Basil Blackwell, 1955.
The Nuffield Story, Robert Jackson, Frederick Muller Ltd, 1964.
William Morris, Viscount Nuffield, J. Overy, Europa, 1976.
Lord Nuffield, Peter Hull, Shire Publications, 2nd edition, 1993.

1931 Morris (i) Cowley saloon.
NATIONAL MOTOR MUSEUM

1931 Morris (i) Isis saloon.
NICK BALDWIN

By the Motor Show in October 1921 Cowley prices were 35 per cent lower than they had been in February, a greater cut than any other manufacturer had made. Up to 1925 Morris continued to slash his prices and to increase production. Sales jumped from 6937 in 1922 to 20,024 in 1923, 32,939 in 1924, and 54,151 in 1925, giving Morris 41 per cent of all British car registrations, and putting them in first place among British manufacturers.

During 1923 the Oxford ceased to be merely a more luxurious version of the Cowley, being given a larger engine of 1802cc, and, in 1924 a longer wheelbase for the 4-seaters. The smaller engine (1548cc) was still available. Although several coachbuilders had made closed bodies on the Oxford chassis, the first factory saloon did not appear until the 1924 season. This had two doors, but a 4-door

saloon, together with a landaulet, arrived for 1925. In 1922 there appeared a 6-cylinder car known as the Oxford Silent Six, with 2355cc Hotchkiss engine, but it was not a success, quickly gaining a reputation for broken crankshafts. Not more than 50 were made, up to the middle of 1924. Front-wheel brakes were introduced on the Oxford for 1925, and for the Cowley a year later. Like the Oxford, the Cowley gained saloon bodies, though only with two doors, the 1925 models being conventionally located, and the 1926 on the nearside of the body only.

In September 1926 the familiar 'bullnose' radiator was replaced by a flat design, cheaper to make but with less character. William Morris is said to have disliked it, comparing it to a tombstone, so the original design was replaced by one 2.2in wider. At the same time the chassis was considerably redesigned, being wider and upswept at the rear, with long semi-elliptic springs in place of the ¾-elliptics of the earlier models. The Cowley and Oxford were continued, and there was also a new model in the shape of the Empire Oxford. This had a larger engine of 2513cc designed for Morris Commercial light trucks, four forward speeds in place of three, and a worm-drive rear axle. As its name implied it was intended for the British colonies, but was not sufficiently robust to stand up to overseas conditions. The vast majority of those exported to Australia had to be returned to Cowley. Only 1742 were made in three seasons; some were used by the Royal Air Force and some supplied to the Anglo-Persian Oil Co.

A more significant new model, launched for the 1928 season, was the Light Six. This had a completely new 2468cc single-ohc engine designed by Frank Woollard and Arthur Pendrell at Morris Engines Branch in Coventry. (William Morris had bought up Hotchkiss as he did most of his component suppliers.) The body was completely new too, being an all-steel design made by the newly built Pressed Steel Co.'s factory set up next to the Morris factory at Cowley. For a while, this was the largest body plant in Europe. The original Light Six used an elongated Oxford chassis, but after only 11 had been made, a new longer and wider chassis was provided. Saloon, tourer and coupé models of the Light Six were made, 3650 being built up to the summer of 1929 when it was replaced by the Isis. This used the same engine, but had a new Pressed Steel body also employed on

NICK BALDWIN

1938 Morris (i) Eight saloon.
NATIONAL MOTOR MUSEUM

1938 Morris (i) Twenty-five Series III 3½ -litre saloon.
NATIONAL MOTOR MUSEUM

THOMAS, MILES WEBSTER (1898–1980)

From 1940 to 1947 Miles Thomas was the man who held the reins of the Nuffield group, co-ordinated its war-production programme and masterminded its return to the automobile market after World War II. His career began as a journalist with Temple Press in London, the publishing house which owned *The Motor*, *The Light Car* and *The Commercial Motor*. During his four years with Temple Press he developed numerous contacts in the motor industry and among its suppliers, and in 1925 he became managing director of Morris Press Ltd, with responsibility for all the group's publications.

After four years in that capacity, he was promoted to sales manager and director of Morris Motors Ltd, and shepherded the sales organisation through the lean years of the economic depression. When the truck and bus branch got too deeply into trouble, he was given the task of nursing it back to health, as director and general manager of Morris Commercial Cars Ltd in 1934.

A year later it was Wolseley's turn, and Thomas took over as director of Morris Motors Ltd. He was responsible for the sacking of Cecil Kimber from MG in 1941.

Miles Thomas became chairman of the Cruiser Tank Production Group in 1941 and a member of the British Government's advisory panel on tank production. Beginning in 1943, he developed a master plan for bringing order to the car-manufacturing activities of the Nuffield Group, which gave more importance to Wolseley at the commercial level while diluting its technical independence by increasing the component-sharing with Morris-badged cars.

He put all his energy behind the project which led to the modern Morris Minor in 1948, but left the Nuffield Group before it went into production. After more than 20 years of exercising tact and diplomacy in his relationship with Lord Nuffield, he got into a bitter quarrel with the chairman in 1947 and walked out.

He was appointed deputy chairman of British Overseas Airways Corp. in 1948, and chairman on 1 July 1949. Ennobled in 1943 as Lord Thomas of Remenham, he led BOAC's modernisation with considerable flair and success. In 1955, however, he left to become chairman of Monsanto Chemicals. He retired in 1971 and died in 1980.

JPN

the Wolseley 21/60; Morris had bought up the Wolseley company in 1927. The body pressings were identical to those used by Dodge on their Victory Six as Pressed Steel used dies from their parent company, Budd of Philadelphia. The Isis also had a new chassis, with Bishop cam steering and hydraulic brakes, the first use of these on a Morris. This Isis was continued to 1935, but from 1932 had traditional ash frame construction instead of pressed steel, and a 4-speed gearbox. Total production of the Isis was 7406, much less than the cheaper side-valve Oxford Six which sold 32,282 units between 1930 and 1933, and a further 6308 under the names Sixteen and Twenty in 1934 and 1935. In addition to these there was a complex range of other Morrises in the early 1930s, including the old 1548cc Cowley (up to 1934), the 1938cc 6-cylinder Major, renamed Cowley Six in 1934 and Fifteen Six in 1935, the 1292cc Ten-Four (1933–35) and 1378cc Ten-Six (1934–35) which shared the same bodies, and the large 3485cc Twenty Five (1933–35). Apart from the Isis, all these cars had side-valve engines.

The smallest Morris was the Minor which was launched as a direct competitor for the Austin Seven in 1928. It had an 847cc single-ohc engine developed by Wolseley, and a 6-cylinder version was used in the Wolseley Hornet. The Minor was made as a 4-seater tourer at £125, or a fabric saloon at £135. In 1930 a coachbuilt saloon at £140 was added, and there were also 2-seater and commercial versions. In 1932 came the 4-door Family Eight saloon on a longer wheelbase, and a companion Sports Coupé; though using the same ohc engine as the Minor, they were officially not called Minors but Eights. A simplified Minor with side-valve engine was launched in February 1931 at the magic figure of £100. It did not sell very well as equipment was very basic, with no bumpers, and head and sidelights combined in one shell. Most customers preferred to spend another £25 for better equipment. The side-valve engine was also used in saloons and tourers; these Minors were made up to 1934, the last ones having synchromesh, four speeds and hydraulic brakes. The Minor was Morris' best-selling model in the early 1930s: 39,087 ohc cars (and commercials), 47,231 side-valve versions. They helped to pull the company out of a bad patch, brought about by the Depression and the unnecessarily complex range.

1939 Morris (i) Eight Series E tourer.
NATIONAL MOTOR MUSEUM

1939 Morris (i) Series M Ten saloon.
NICK BALDWIN

The 1934 London Motor Show saw a replacement for the Minor in the shape of the Eight, a freshly styled car with 918cc side-valve engine boasting a three-bearing crankshaft. Four body styles were offered, 2- and 4-door saloons, and 2 and 4-seater tourers. Of about 218,000 Morris Eights made up to autumn 1938, around 15 per cent were open models. In June 1935 the title Series was used, to fit in with the larger Series II Morrises which were part of Leonard Lord's standardisation plan. Eights built before this date were retrospectively called the pre-series, though they were almost identical in design.

Leonard Percy Lord was appointed Managing Director of Morris Motors in 1933, as Sir William Morris was spending an increasing amount of time abroad. Lord was determined to streamline production, and to this end he installed a moving assembly line at Cowley, and commissioned a new range of cars to be built on it. The Series II Morrises all had similar bodies, 6-light saloons with sloping backs, 2-light coupés on the smaller models, and 4-light coupés on the larger. No open models were offered in the Series II. There were three sizes of body and no fewer than seven engines, from the 1292cc 4-cylinder Ten to the 3485cc Twenty Five, 59,364 of the 4-cylinder cars were made and 18,391 of the sixes. October 1937 saw the introduction of the Series II Eights and the Series III of the larger models. These had generally similar lines to the previous Series, but could be distinguished by their Easyclean pressed steel wheels and painted radiator shells. Under the bonnet there were now ohvs, and the number of engines was reduced to four, two fours and two sixes. The Series II Eights still had side-valve engines but shared the larger cars' wheels and other styling changes.

Two new models were announced for 1939, the year in which the millionth Morris car was delivered (May 22). The Series E Eight received a completely new body, with waterfall grill, recessed headlamps and no running boards. The same styles were offered as before, 2 and 4-door saloons, and two tourers. The 918cc engine was unchanged, but there was now a 4-speed gearbox. The Series M Ten looked less modern, with separate headlamps, but it had a new 1140cc ohv engine shared with the Wolseley Ten, and integral construction. Only one body style was available, a 6-light saloon. After the war the same models were re-introduced, though there were no more Series E Tourers.

The Ten received a new radiator grill in September 1946, which had been first seen on the Indian-assembled Hindustan Ten. By the time the Eight and Ten were discontinued in the autumn of 1948 production had reached more than 114,000 Series E Eights and 80,596 Series M Tens.

The Issigonis Era

Alec Issigonis joined Morris in 1936 as a development engineer, and during the war designed the independent suspension for the Mk I Morris light reconnaissance car. In 1943 he began work on a postwar replacement for the Series E which was provisionally named Mosquito. This had a streamlined body with wings faired into the doors, and torsion bar ifs. Various engines were tried, including an unconventional 3-cylinder double-piston two-stroke, and a horizontally-opposed flat four. In the end it was decided to use the familiar 918cc side-valve unit which dated back to 1934. The new car, now called the Minor, was launched at London's first postwar Motor Show in October 1948, together with a new Oxford 4-door saloon powered by a 1476cc sv engine, and the Six, which used the Oxford bodyshell and a longer bonnet to house the 2215cc single-ohc 6-cylinder engine which it shared with the Wolseley Six-Eighty.

The first Minors were 2-door saloons or tourers, but in October 1950 a 4-door saloon was added to the range, and three years later came an estate car called the Traveller. In February 1952 the Nuffield Organisation (which now included Morris, MG, Riley and Wolseley) merged with Austin to form the British Motor Corp. This resulted in much rationalisation between the various makers, not all of it happy, but a good result was the replacement of the old side-valve Morris engine by Austin's smaller but more powerful 803cc ohv A Series engine from the A30. In 1956, when Austin brought out the 37bhp 948cc engine this went into the Minor to make the Minor 1000. In 1962 capacity went up to 1098cc and power to 48bhp, giving the little car a top speed of nearly 81mph (130km/h). Few changes were made thereafter, and the Minor carried on until April 1971, by which time 1,583,622 had been made. No tourers were made after June 1969. One final Traveller was assembled from spares at a customer's request, and delivered in October 1974. The Minor had become one of Britain's best-loved small cars, and in its early years enjoyed much success in export markets. Today it is more eagerly collected than any of its contemporaries, and several firms specialise in restoring Minors to as-new condition, even adding improvements such as 5-speed gearboxes.

The Six was dropped in 1953 after 12,400 had been made, but the Oxford survived in name until 1971. It gained a new and more bulbous body in 1954, together with the 1489cc ohv B Series engine, and in 1959 became part of the Farina-styled range which included the Austin Cambridge, MG Magnette, Riley 4/68 and Wolseley 15/60. In its various forms the Oxford accounted for 601,673 cars. It was a reliable workhorse but had none of the appeal of the Minor,

and there is no interest among collectors today. The Isis name was revived for the Six's replacement, made from 1955 to 1958. Like its predecessor it had an Oxford bodyshell with a longer bonnet which housed a 2639cc BMC C Series 6-cylinder engine. It was made in saloon and estate versions, production totalling 12,155.

In 1959 the Issigonis-designed Morris Mini Minor appeared, with its almost identical twin the Austin Se7en. These and subsequent Mini variations are described under the Austin entry. The Morris version of the 1100, essentially an enlarged Mini with Hydrolastic suspension, came in 1962, a year before the Austin, while another model shared with Austin was the 1800, made from 1966 to 1975. A small number of the wedge-shaped 18/22s also carried the Morris badge, before being renamed Princess in 1976.

NICK BALDWIN

LORD, LEONARD (1896–1967)

A brilliant production engineer and the architect of the merger which formed the British Motor Corp. Leonard Percy Lord was born in Coventry and educated at the Bablake School in the city. His first job was as a draughtsman at Courtaulds, where one of the directors asked him what he was going to do when he grew up: 'Sit in your chair', he replied. He soon moved on to Vickers and then, during World War I, to the Coventry Ordnance Factory where he worked under Carl Engelbach, later to be one of Herbert Austin's right-hand men. He worked briefly for Daimler and then in 1920, moved to the Coventry factory of Hotchkiss which was making engines for William Morris. He made a very useful contribution there when he suggested producing metric thread bolts with Whitworth heads, to fit British spanners. This enabled the French-designed machinery to be adapted quickly to British engineering requirements. In 1923 Morris bought up Hotchkiss and invited Lord to Cowley as manager, at the age of 27. He attracted the attention of Frank Woollard, who Morris had 'acquired' when he purchased E.G. Wrigley & Co, and who was to be one of the guiding spirits in the adoption of mass production. This was also Lord's forte, and he was soon transferred to Wolseley to modernise their factory. In 1932 he was brought back to Cowley as Managing Director of Morris Motors.

His forceful manner ('If the door isn't open, then you kick it open' was one of his favourite sayings) made more enemies than friends; among senior Morris personnel who clashed with him were Oliver Boden and Miles Thomas. The latter said that everyone admired Lord's methods if not his manners. 'He frightened the living daylights out of them. If he wanted a thing done there were no quibbles, that was done. Lord said and Lord had it done'.

From 1932 to 1936 Lord reorganised Cowley from end to end, introducing flow-line production and overseeing the very successful Morris Eight which, like the larger cars, was made in a Series rather than a model year. This was to avoid sales tailing off dramatically before the Motor Show, as purchasers awaited the announcement of new models. This was another of Lord's ideas, and one that undoubtedly appealed to Morris, although he never got on with his Managing Director. The break came in 1936 when Lord argued that he should have a percentage of the profits he had generated, instead of a straight salary. Morris violently disagreed, and Lord left Cowley in August 1936. However, Morris' admiration led him to offer Lord a post as administrator of his Special Areas Trust, a charity for what today would be called Regional Development. Lord had no love for Morris by this time, and threatened to 'take that business at Cowley apart brick by brick', but he accepted the job to tide him over until he found other work in the motor industry. Apart from anything else, it was very well paid; £10,000 a year was more than he received as Managing Director of Morris Motors.

In February 1938 Lord became Works Director at Austin, replacing his former boss Carl Engelbach, and on Lord Austin's death three years later he became Joint Managing Director (with Ernest Payton). In 1945 he became Managing Director. He was responsible for the re-styled Austin Eight and Ten of 1939, for shadow factory aircraft production during the war, and for such important postwar models as the Austin-Healey 100 and Sprite, Farina-styled A40, and, most important of all, for inviting Alec Issigonis back to design the Mini.

When Lord told Morris that he was joining Austin, the older man said 'Go ahead, I don't see why we shouldn't have a lot of fun cutting each others' throats'. Lord certainly priced Austin models very keenly against their rivals from Cowley, but by 1950 co-operation seemed more attractive than throat-cutting. Lord phoned Morris suggesting a merger, but the idea was turned down by the Morris board, although the two men did meet eventually. The actual merger between the Austin Motor Co. and the Nuffield Organisation took place over the winter of 1951-52, and was finalised in February 1952. Lord became Chairman on the retirement of Lord Nuffield six months later. He retired as managing director himself in 1956 at the age of 60, handing over to George Harriman, but remained as Chairman until his 65th birthday in1961. He received a knighthood in 1954, and was created Lord Lambury ('Lord Lord would sound bloody stupid', he said) in January 1962. When he died five years later, George Harriman paid tribute to him: 'He was always a man of decision – indeed a top line man if ever there was one. Because he was so often forthright and outspoken the world may have regarded him as tough, but with his abundant qualities went a heart of gold which conditioned all his plans and decisions, however, swift and penetrating they might be'.

Lord was married, with two daughters.

NG

Further Reading
' The Classic Tycoons – Leonard Lord,
Thoroughbred & Classic Car, January 1980.

NICK BALDWIN

ISSIGONIS, ALEC (1906–1988)

One of the most inspired designers of small cars, Alexander Arnold Constantine Issigonis was born in Smyrna, (now Izmir), Turkey, the only child of a Greek-born British subject, Constantine Issigonis, and the daughter of a German brewery owner, Hulda Prokopp. By a strange coincidence her cousin was Bernd Pischetsrieder, who was head of BMW at the time that they acquired Rover, maker of Issigonis' Mini.

Young Alec was educated privately in Smyrna, and lived an idyllic life until the outbreak of World War I. His father ran an engineering works, and he spent hours there, being particularly fascinated by a large steam engine. Although Turkey was an ally of Germany, the war did not impinge on their lives too much at first, but later the German army occupied Smyrna, interned the Issigonis family, and confiscated their property. At the end of the war the area was given to the Greeks, but in 1922 the Turks reclaimed the territory and the family was driven out. His father stayed in Malta, where he died later that year, and Alex and his mother arrived in England virtually penniless. He spent three years at Battersea Polytechnic, just scraping through his exams in mechanical engineering. After completing a European tour in a Singer Ten with his mother, who had by then managed to obtain some compensation for their confiscated property, Alec took a job with a London consultancy which was working on a semi-automatic transmission. The work took him to the Midlands frequently, and this resulted in a post in the drawing office at Humber, where he worked in the suspension department under William Heynes, later to become engineering chief at Jaguar. Alec worked on an ifs system for the Hillman Minx; it was not adopted, although some of his ideas went into the ifs used on the Hillman Hawk and Humber Snipe.

In 1936 he moved to the Morris factory at Cowley, his mother taking a house at Abingdon. He worked on an ifs system for the M-Series Morris Ten, buy the war prevented it from going into production, although the same design was used on the postwar MG Y-type saloon. While working on the Morris, he learnt the importance of adequate weight on an independently sprung front axle. 'I found that cars ran much straighter and were more directionally stable if I put a couple of sandbags on the front bumper', he said. He decided that if he ever designed a complete car it must be nose heavy, even at the expense of traction on the rear wheels. During his time at Morris he built the very advanced Lightweight Special, a single-seater racing car with monocoque stressed-skin construction of plywood faced on both sides with aluminium sheets, and powered by an Austin Seven Ulster engine. In 1939 it beat a works Austin with the same engine at Prescott Hill Climb.

During World War II Issigonis worked on a number of strange projects for Morris, including a motorised wheelbarrow that could be dropped in a cylinder by parachute, and assembled on the ground; also an amphibious version with four wheels and oars for propulsion on water. None of them came to production, but their creator found the challenges interesting. Before the end of the war he began work on the new small car, code-named Mosquito, which was to become the Morris Minor. He felt very strongly that a car had to be designed as an integrated whole, and managed to get together a team of colleagues including draughtsman Jack Daniels who had worked with him on the M-Series Morris before the war. He was responsible for the body design, being influenced by American ideas such as the flaring of wings into doors, and a generally bulbous look. When Lord Nuffield saw the prototype he was furious; 'We can't make that, it looks like a poached egg!' He had little time for its designer, whom he referred to as 'Issy wassy' and in fact it is believed that the two met only twice, first on the occasion of the showing of the prototype, and again in 1960, when Nuffield finally acknowledged that the Minor was a good design, and thanked Issigonis for his contribution to the company's success. Issigonis wanted the Minor to incorporate a flat-4 engine and front-wheel drive, but because of cost, the production car had the old side-valve engine from the Series E Morris, and rear drive.

The merger that formed the British Motor Corp. made Issigonis unhappy, for he distrusted a mixture of engineering and politics. In 1952 he moved to Alvis, for whom he designed an advanced, lightweight luxury saloon powered by an all-aluminium $3\frac{1}{2}$-litre V8 engine with an ohc for each bank of cylinders. A prototype was built and extensively tested, reaching 110mph (177km/h), but the cost of tooling for the body was beyond Alvis' resources, and the project was dropped.

Unlike Nuffield, Leonard Lord had a high regard for Issigonis, and in 1956 he invited him back to Longbridge. The respect was mutual; Issigonis said 'I was glad to be back with Lord – a tough, wonderful man with a fantastic personality, a born businessman and a great production engineer'. The two men saw eye to eye on the need for a small car, Lord because he anticipated drastic fuel shortages due to the Suez crisis, Issigonis because he was a keen apostle of the 'small is beautiful' philosophy. He said that a small car presented a tremendous design challenge non-existent with a large one: 'Mr Royce had nothing to do'.

In 1950 he had built an experimental Morris Minor with transverse engine and front-wheel drive, but had left for Alvis before it could be thoroughly tested, The idea was revived when he began to design Project ADO15, which became the Mini. Lord gave the go-ahead to the project in March 1957, and by October two prototypes were on the road. The car was not consciously styled; one of Issigonis' many aphorisms was 'Styling is designing for obsolescence'. Rather it was designed logically as clothing for the mechanical elements, with no overhand at front or rear, the simplest and smallest shell to house four people and an engine.

Alex Issigonis was awarded a CBE in 1964 and a knighthood in 1969, and was particularly gratified by being elected a Fellow of the Royal Society and being awarded its Leverhulme medal for 'Services to Science and its Application'. He retired in 1971, but continued to be active in scientific work, which included hot-air balloons, up to his death at the age of 82. He never married.

NG

Further reading

'Alec Issigonis', Jonathan Wood, *Automobile Quarterly*, Vol. 40, No.1.

1948 Morris (i) Minor saloon.
NICK BALDWIN

British Leyland policy in the 1970s dictated that the innovative front-drive cars should carry Austin badges, while Morris would cater for the traditional market so successfully held by the Ford Cortina and Vauxhall Victor. Announced in April 1971, the Morris Marina was offered with two sizes of engine, the 1275cc A Series and 1798cc B Series. Body styles were a 4-door saloon and a 2-door coupé, with an estate being added at the end of 1972. There was a high-performance model in the shape of the 1.8TC which used the B Series engine in MGB tune, and was capable of 100mph (161km/h), but handling was never up to performance, and the car did not appeal to sporting motorists. The Marina was well summed up in a report by the Automobile Association: 'One of the most blatant current examples of the family car as a domestic utensil. It is devoid of any real flair or enthusiastic appeal but eminently practical, safely and effectively designed for its job, and offered at a keen price'. 953,576 were made between 1971 and 1980, including 3870 diesel versions which all went for export.

When the Marina was restyled by Ital Design, it was given the name Ital, though the conception was the same, and similar bodies were offered. Engine options were the 1275cc A Series, and the 1695cc single-ohc O Series which had been adopted on the Marina since 1978. In October 1980 the Ital range was extended by the 2.0HLS which used the O Series engine enlarged to 1993cc. Automatic transmission was standard on this model. Itals were made in the Austin factory at Longbridge up to December 1983 when the model was discontinued, and the Morris name was no more. The following year the Ital dies were sold to Pakistan.

NG

Further Reading
Morris Minor, a Collector's Guide, Guy Saddlestone, Motor Racing Publications, 1997.
The Morris Motor Car, 1913–1983, Harry Edwards, Moreland Publishing, 1983.

1949 Morris (i) MS Six saloon.
NICK BALDWIN

The Bullnose and Flatnose Morris, Lytton Jarman and Robin Barraclough, David & Charles, 1976.
Morris Minor, the World's Supreme Small Car, Paul Skilleter, Osprey, 1981.

MORRIS (ii) (AUS) 1958–1973

British Motor Corp. Australia, Zetland, New South Wales.
Leyland Motor Corp. Australia, Zetland, New South Wales.
When manufacturing began in the new plant built on the Victoria Park racecourse site purchased by Lord Nuffield, it was run by B.M.C. and a badge-engineered unified range was the programme. The Marshal was a cosmetic twin of the AUSTIN A95 Westminster, while the Major was a WOLSELEY 1500 with a horizontal grill. An Australianised Major, with tail fins, appeared in 1959, while the Farina-line Oxford used a 1622cc engine to improve its competitive position

1962 Morris (i) Oxford VI saloon.
NICK BALDWIN

1971 Morris (i) Marina 1300 saloon.
NICK BALDWIN

against the similarly priced Holden. The 1961 Mini-Minor was the only Morris in Australia and was designated 850, because the Mini name was thought to be derogatory. The 1962 Major Elite, with 1622cc, became the sole model in its series and the Oxford was discontinued with the end of badge engineering. The Major Elite had a good warranty claim record but was superseded by the front-driven 1100, sold only as a Morris. Complete manufacture of the front-drive cars was underway, the A-series engine for the Mini and 1100 having provision for a mechanical fuel pump. Extensive outback endurance testing ensured that the 1100 was right from the beginning and it was accorded a great reception, being the best-selling 4-cylinder model for several years but, apart from a two-carburettor option, it remained unaltered and sales sagged.

Australian body shells for the Mini differed in several ways from the imported version and the 1965 Mini De-Luxe had a 998cc engine, 'wet' suspension and wind-up windows. Cooper models were also offered and the Mini retained its market position. Production of the 1275cc engine saw it in the 1967 1100S and the Mini-matic automatic became available. The Mini-Moke was introduced but was reworked for local manufacture as the Moke in 1968 with 13in wheels, and Australia became the sole production centre. In 1969 the Mini K (kangaroo) and Moke had an 1100cc engine and an all-synchromesh gearbox. The 1100 body was finally restyled, fitted with a 1485cc ohc E-series motor and was joined by a station wagon, named Nomad, with automatics retaining the 1275cc engine. An upmarket 1500 OD5, with 5-speed gearbox, followed in 1970. The long-nosed Mini Clubman was on sale in 1971 in forms up to the 1275 GT, a Cooper replacement. The conventional Marina, fitted with 1485 and 1750cc E-series engines replaced the 1500 in 1972. This was initially a Morris wearing the Leyland badge. That name applied to the whole range from 1973.

The Australian-made Austin Freeway with Farina-styled body and 2449cc 6-cylinder Blue Streak engine, was sold in New Zealand, badged as a Morris, from 1962 to 1965.

MG

MORRIS (iii) (RA) 1966–1967

Compania Industrial de Automotores SA, Monte Chingolo, Buenos Aires.
Morris saloons and Morris Travellers were produced by Compania Industrial de Automotores SA after they took over the SIAM Di Tella operation in Monte Chingolo. These cars were derived from the Di Tella 1500, but had a larger engine. Thus they were known as Morris 1650 and Morris Traveller 1650, with their engines developing 75bhp. Production started in 1966 and ceased in April, 1967. 3027 saloons and 847 Traveller station wagons were made.

ACT

MORRIS & SALOM (US) 1894–1897

1894–1895 Morris & Salom, Philadelphia, Pennsylvania.
1895–1897 Electric Carriage & Wagon Co., Philadelphia, Pennsylvania.
Henry G. Morris and Pedro G. Salom built their first electric car in 1894. Called the Electrobat, it had two 1½hp Lundell electric motors, each geared directly to one front wheel. These were considerably larger than the rear wheels, by which the car was steered. They applied for a patent on this design in January 1894, but may not have had a car running before 1895. They entered three cars in the Chicago *Times-Herald* Race that November, but only one was ready for the start, and could not do so as the horse-drawn wagon bringing the batteries could not navigate the snowy streets. It was, however, awarded a prize on account of its design. Several other cars were built during 1895, each with its own name in the manner of railway locomotives or ships. The Skeleton Bat was a light bodyless 2-seater with drive to the front wheels, though these were nearly equal in size to the rear wheels. The Fish Wagon also had front-wheel drive and a closed rear portion for four passengers, while the Crawford Wagon was an open 2-seater with the motors driving the rear wheels. The names probably refer to the purchaser as each car was made to order. In 1896 Morris and Salom began series production of a hansom cab with the driver perched high behind his passengers, still with front-wheel drive and rear-wheel steering. A fleet of these took to the streets of Philadelphia in 1896, and were adopted in New York in 1897. They performed so well that Isaac L. Rice, president of the Electric Storage Battery Co., bought up the Electric Carriage & Wagon Co. It became the cornerstone of his Electric Vehicle Co., whose production was taken over by Colonel Pope's COLUMBIA Automobile Co.

NG

MORRIS-COMMERCIAL (GB) 1930–1931

Morris-Commercial Cars Ltd, Birmingham.
This company was formed in 1924 to make a 1-ton van with which William Morris could compete with American imports. Larger commercial vehicles soon joined the range, and the first 6-wheeler came in 1927. A saloon version of this was launched in 1930, powered not by the truck's 2513cc 4-cylinder engine, but by a 4256cc six which gave the heavy car a top speed of over 70mph (112km/h). Known as the 6D, the design featured wire wheels and hydraulic brakes. It was expensive at £866 for a chassis, and fewer than 20 were made.

NG

Further Reading
'Six of the Best', Norman Painting, *The Automobile*, December 1999.

MORRISON (i) (US) c.1888–1895

William Morrison, Des Moines, Iowa.
There is no doubt that William Morrison built the first successful electric car in America. What is less certain is exactly when he did it. 1888 and 1890 have both been claimed as the date when his heavy wagon first rolled onto the streets of Des Moines. It was a 6-seater with a 4hp motor and 24 battery cells under the seat. The motor was geared to the rear axle. Steering was by a handlebar connected to a pivot on each front wheel. The wheels were linked by a yoke bar. The car attracted the attention of Harold Sturges of the American Battery Co. who bought it from Morrison and entered it in modified form in the 1895 Chicago *Times-Herald* Race. Sturges was a more active promoter than Morrison, and the car was sometimes known as a Sturges. Morrison built a few more electric cars, but he was really more interested in battery design than in complete cars.

NG

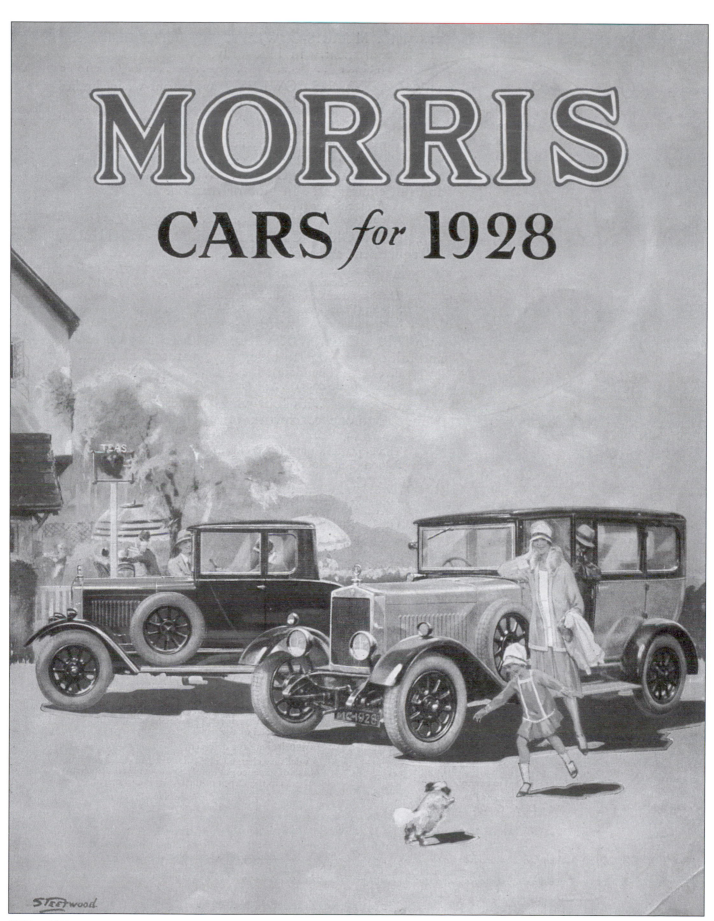

1965 Morris (i) 1100 saloon.
NICK BALDWIN

1922 Morriss-London 17.9hp all-weather tourer.
NICK BALDWIN

MORRISON (ii) (GB) 1904–c.1905
Krupkar Ltd, London.
This was a 2-seater 3-wheeler powered by a 6hp 2-cylinder engine driving the front wheels. Its origin is uncertain as it was exhibited at the 1904 Crystal Palace Show by Krupkar who imported various German makes including Cudell, Horch and Opel. None of these made anything like the Morrison at that time. The name Krupkar came from the use of metal from Krupp of Essen.

NG

MORRISS (GB) 1908–c.1910
H.E. & F.E. Morriss, London.
Frank Morriss had a long involvement with the motor industry, having sold Benz and Daimler cars at King's Lynn (see SANDRINGHAM) at the turn of the century, and after World War I being involved with the MORRISS-LONDON. In 1908

he and his brother brought out a steam car with 2-cylinder slide-valve engine mounted under the floorboards, with single-chain drive to the rear axle. The pilot light burnt petrol, but the fuel in the main burner was paraffin. The boiler was located under the bonnet. A 4-seater tourer was ready for demonstration at the time of the 1908 Olympia Show. The Morriss brothers said that the only reason it was not at Olympia was that they feared it would not be completely ready. In 1909 they announced a 2-seater on similar lines, and said that several of the 4-seater cars had given much satisfaction to their owners. One source said that only four Morriss steamers were made; the figure was probably a little higher, but serious production never took place.

NG

MORRISS-LONDON (US/GB) 1919–1923
Century Motors Co. (Crow-Elkhart Motor Car Co.), Elkhart, Indiana.
The Morriss-London was the final automotive venture of Frank Morriss, who imported chassis made by CROW-ELKHART with the intention of equipping them with English bodies. A few cars may have been imported complete to start with, but Morriss' bankruptcy in 1920 meant that a consignment of 69 chassis was left unclaimed at the docks. Saunders Motors of Golders Green, North London bought the chassis for what seemed the bargain price of £75 each, but they were in poor condition, having crossed the Atlantic as deck cargo and then remained untouched for more than 12 months. However Saunders refurbished them, fitted them with tourer or landaulet bodies and sold them as the 17.9hp Saunders, at £285 for the tourer and £375 for the landaulet. The announcement in *The Motor* in September 1923 said 'the chassis is the same as at one time utilised for the Morriss-London car'. It is most unlikely that any fresh chassis were imported from America, especially as Crow-Elkhart went out of business in 1923. Century Motors was the subsidiary under which the Morriss-London was built. The 69 chassis, less a few which were dismantled for parts, represented the total of Saunders cars sold.

NG

Further Reading
'Fragments on Forgotten Makes', W. Boddy, *Motor Sport*, July 1969.

1901 Mors 60hp Paris - Berlin racing car, with C.S.Rolls at the wheel.
NICK BALDWIN

MORS (F) 1895–1925; 1941–1943

1895–1907 Sté d'Électricité et d'Automobiles Mors, Paris.
1908–1943 Sté Nouvelle d'Automobiles Mors, Paris.

The Mors was one of France's better-known cars in the pre–1914 era, and for a while had a distinguished sporting record. The origins of the company dated back to 1851 when a M. Mirand set up a company to make artificial flowers, with paper-wrapped wire stems. It was the use of the wire-wrapping machinery which led Mirand into electrical work, including telegraph and railway signalling equipment. His firm was taken over by the Mors family in 1874, and later branched out into steam-powered launches and, in the 1890s, petrol-engined railway inspection cars. One of their employees was Henri Brasier, later to become a well-known car manufacturer. In 1895 Émile Mors built a Brasier-designed car using his low-tension coil-and-dynamo ignition. Two years later he put into production a series of cars using V4 engines with water-cooled heads and air-cooled barrels. The engines were rear-mounted, and drove through a Benz-like belt-and-pulley system.

Mors' business grew rapidly, and in 1898 they turned out about 200 cars. The rear-engined V4 was joined by a Petit Duc with front-mounted 850cc flat-twin engine and final drive by side chains. Steering was by handlebar on the first models, but before Petit Duc production ended in 1901 wheel steering had been introduced. Like the V4, the Petit Duc's flat-twin engine had partial water-cooling, but full water-cooling was adopted in 1902. Vertical engines appeared in 1899, and from 1903 were standard. Low-tension magneto ignition was adopted from 1900, and the 1901 cars had what amounted to one carburettor per cylinder, with a large central float chamber. 1903 models had 4-cylinder T-head engines, Mercedes-like honeycomb radiators, chain drive and pressed steel frames. They lost Henri Brasier to Georges Richard in 1901, and in 1904 another leading designer, Charles Schmidt, crossed the Atlantic to join Packard. Also in 1904 Mors adopted the shouldered radiator which, in various forms, characterised the make for the rest of its life. 1904 models consisted of five 4-cylinder cars,

1897 Mors 6hp *dos-à-dos*.
NATIONAL MOTOR MUSEUM

from a 2.3-litre 12hp to an 8.1-litre 40/52hp, the latter with an auxiliary transverse spring at the rear. From 1906 to 1909 three models of Mors were made in St Louis, Missouri by the St Louis Car Co., and sold under the name American Mors.

1904 was the last year in which Mors achieved anything in sport, and even this was only seventh place in the Gordon Bennett Race. However they had had many successes earlier, with wins in the Paris-St Malo and Bordeaux-Biarritz races of 1899, Paris-Bordeaux and Paris-Berlin in 1901 and Paris-Madrid in 1903, though the latter was stopped at Bordeaux. They entered a team of three cars in the 1908 French Grand Prix, but achieved nothing.

1904 Mors touring limousine.
NATIONAL MOTOR MUSEUM

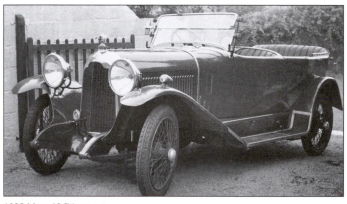

1923 Mors 12CV tourer.
NICK GEORGANO/NATIONAL MOTOR MUSEUM

From 1904 to 1908 Mors was in frequent financial difficulty due to lax management, an unfortunate venture into taxicabs and falling sales. In 1907 chairman Léopold Bellan sold the electricity part of the business to Émile Mors' brother Louis, then sold the land on which the factory was built and leased it back. When even this failed to help the cashflow he proposed to liquidate the company, but a prominent stockholder opposed this step and brought in his son-in-law's brother André Citroën into the business. Under his management sales doubled from 1909 to 1910 to 647, helped by new models such as the shaft-drive 10 and 15hp with L-head monobloc engines, which had appeared in 1907. As with many car makers, these smaller, more up-to-date designs gradually took over from the chain-driven dinosaurs, though there was still a 9182cc 50/60hp six with chain drive in the 1912 catalogue.

Sleeve-valve engines were offered as well as poppet-valves from 1913. They were bought from Minerva and came in four models from a 2120cc 14/16hp to a 7360cc 35/40hp, all 4-cylinder units. After the war all Mors used Minerva sleeve-valve engines. The Belgian firm had a financial interest in Mors, and in 1923 there was talk of assembling Minervas in the Mors factory, though this did not come about. It would have been a helpful way of utilising factory space, for Mors' own cars sold in declining numbers in the 1920s. There were two models, a 3306cc (3560cc from 1922) 14/20, joined for 1923 by a 1978cc 12/16hp. Panhard called their sleeve-valve cars SS (sans soupapes), so Mors went one better with SSS (sans soupapes silencieuse). They were sold in England by Malcolm Campbell who raced one at Brooklands, but despite front-wheel brakes from 1921, a handsome vee-radiator and wire wheels, they did not find many buyers in either England or France. Imports ended in 1924 and all production in 1925. Citroën, who was now mass-producing cars of his own, took over the factory.

A subsidiary of Émile Mors' electrical business built a few small electric cars during World War II. From 1952 to 1956 they made the Speed motor scooter.
NG

MORSE (i) (US) 1905–1906
Morse Motor Vehicle Co., Springfield, Massachusetts.
Designed by Sewell Morse, this was a steam car with 20hp horizontal 3-cylinder single-acting engine with flash boiler, and direct drive to the rear axle. The only body style offered was a 5-seater tourer.
NG

MORSE (ii) (US) 1910–1916
Easton Machine Co., South Easton, Massachusetts.
Alfred G. Morse started experimenting with cars in 1904, but was not ready to put one on the market until 1910. The 24hp 4-cylinder Model D was expensive at $3900-4000. 1911 models were larger at 34hp and even more expensive, from $4000 for a tourer or roadster to $5200 for a limousine. The Morse was practically out of production by the end of 1913, though a few more cars were delivered up to 1916.
NG

MORSE (iii) (US) 1914–1916
Morse Cyclecar Co., East Pittsburgh, Pennsylvania.
This was a typical cyclecar with tandem seating, a V-twin Spacke engine, 2-speed epicyclic transmission and chain drive. The only unusual feature was that the chains drove the front wheels. The tandem roadster and a light delivery van were both priced at $350.
NG

MORSE-READIO (US) 1909–1910
Morse-Readio Auto Co., Springfield, Massachusetts.
Built by Glenn E. Morse and George N. Readio, this car had a 36hp 4-cylinder engine, and was made in one body style only, a 4-seater roadster without doors. It was priced at $2500. A number were sold in the Springfield area, and they had a good reputation, but the partners lacked the financial backing to start large-scale production.
NG

MORT (US) 1923–1926
Mort Motor Co., Piqua, Ohio.
The Mort Motor Co. was a sub-division of Meteor Motors of Piqua, Ohio, a leading manufacturer of ambulances and funeral cars. The Mort was introduced as a less expensive line to the Meteor, available at approximately $750 to $1000 less than the senior car and received singular attention because of its name, *mort* being the French word for 'dead', a curious name for a funeral car specialist. Like Meteor, Mort made some 7-seater limousines and large sedans, primarily intended as mourners' cars. The Mort sedan was priced at $1850 to $2000. Power was by a 6-cylinder Continental engine.
KM

MORTON (US) c.1984
Morton Car Co. Inc., San Leandro, California.
The Morton 3 was a 3-wheeler kit car with a distinctive fibreglass coupé body sporting a Kamm-tail. The single front wheel was covered by a long, pointed nose and the gullwing doors were removable for open-air motoring. It had a steel tube frame with independent suspension and VW or Porsche running gear. Other engines could be fitted on special order.
HP

MORVI (IND) 1911–1912
Morvi Motor Works, Morvi State.
Designed by Ralph Ricardo who had previously been responsible for the DOLPHIN (i), the Morvi was a light car with a single-cylinder T-head engine and shaft drive. It was built in the workshops of the Morvi State Railway, Ricardo's employers, but he left before production could begin, and possibly only one Morvi was made.
NG

MOSELLE (US) c.1980

Moselle Motor Coach, Tarzana, California.

Moselle made a neoclassic car that was sold in assembled form. There were three versions of the Mercedes SSK-inspired design, including roadster, 4-seater and limousine bodywork. There were four engine choices, starting with a Ford 4-cylinder and progressing to a V8. They carried a five-year warranty.

HP

MOSER (CH) 1914–1924

1914–1920 Moteurs Moser, St Aubin, Neuchâtel.

1920–1924 Fritz Moser, Fabrique d'Automobiles et Motocyclettes, St Aubin.

At the turn of the century, Fritz Moser, a trained mechanic, worked for the Zürcher-Lüthi (ZEDEL) company in St Aubin, which produced proprietary engines. Soon he started his own workshop building motorcycles, in which he was most successful. He built a new factory, employing about 100 workers and by 1914 he began manufacturing in small batches cyclecars with water-cooled V2 engines and chain drive. At the same time he started co-operation with Rudolf EGG, who had prepared prototypes of light touring cars with 4-cylinder Zürcher engines of about 1000cc. Moser built a small number of these cars, with 2- and 4-seater open bodies. World War I interrupted production but in 1919, Moser launched a new 3-wheeler with an air-cooled V2 engine of which a handful was made. One year later Moser opened a branch factory in Pontarlier, France, supplying engines to various French motorcycle manufacturers. The production of cyclecars and voiturettes was again commenced. The former obtained an air-cooled V2 engine of 8–10hp and the latter a 4-cylinder engine, probably again from Zürcher. By 1923 the cyclecar was discontinued and the light tourer obtained a L-head 4-cylinder engine of Moser design of 1327cc and 12–15hp.

Strong competition by the big companies which offered up-to-date models at lower prices brought about the end of small volume production. From 1924 Moser concentrated on producing motorcycles. By 1930 Ernst Moser had retired and five years later the factory closed.

FH

Further Reading

'Schweizer Autopionier Rudolf Egg', Ferdinand Hediger, *Automobil Revue*, February 1965.

MOSKVITCH *see* MZMA

MOSLER *see* CONSULIER

MOSQUITO (i) **(GB)** 1976–1977

Mosquito, Hereford, Herefordshire.

Only six examples of the Mosquito Mini-engined trike were made but the model achieved much greater success when it was revived in 1992 as the TRIAD.

CR

MOSQUITO (ii) **/ MOUNTAINEER (GB)** 1989–c.1993

C.L. Hollier Services, South Ruislip, Middlesex.

This was an ugly dual-purpose sand-rail style car with a rear-mounted Mini engine. The Mountaineer was a 1992 evolution, powered by an Austin Maxi engine.

CR

MOSS (GB) 1981 to date

1981–1985 Moss Motor Co., Sheffield, Yorkshire.

1985 Moss Sportscars Ltd, Handsworth, Sheffield, Yorkshire.

1985–1987 J.C. Autopatterns Ltd, Sheffield, Yorkshire.

1987 C.S.A. Character Cars, Radstock, Bath, Avon.

1987 Hampshire Classics, Basingstoke, Hampshire.

1987 to date Moss Cars (Bath) Ltd, Radstock, Bath, Avon.

An accomplished specials builder, John Cowperthwaite scored great success with his Moss range of kit cars. He was the first person to satisfy a latent demand for cheap kit-form Morgan-style cars. Based on a lightly modified Herald/ Vitesse chassis, the Moss Roadster was good value, pretty and easy to build. A 2+2 Malvern version arrived in 1983 and the same year there was a Moss Triumph replacement chassis or an all-new chassis for Ford engines. The second Moss model was the Mamba, a recreation of the 1960s specials-era A.K.S. Continental.

1918 Moser 2-seater, badged as an Egg, but made in the Moser factory.
NICK GEORGANO/NATIONAL MOTOR MUSEUM

c.1983 Moss Malvern sports car.
CHRIS REES

1984 Moss Mamba sports car.
NICK BALDWIN

1984 Moss Monaco sports car.
CHRIS REES

1902 Motobloc 10hp tonneau.
NATIONAL MOTOR MUSEUM

1905 Motobloc tourer in Coupe des Pyrénées.
NATIONAL MOTOR MUSEUM

It too used a Triumph Herald or Vitesse chassis or could be fitted on Moss' own Ford-based chassis. It was unpopular, and was only briefly revived by C.S.A. in 1987. The 1984 Monaco was a great fun car that was extremely cheap. Its fibreglass barrel body mounted on a Herald/Vitesse floorpan (a Ford-based box section chassis was also available and other engines were possible – up to a Rover V8). Moss production faltered around a factory fire in 1985 and eventually the project settled with three Moss club members in Bath. A brand new chassis arrived in 1992, also able to take Rover V8 engines and Ford Sierra parts.

CR

MOTA (US) c.1953
Banning Electric Products Corp., New York, New York.
This small fibreglass-bodied roadster used an early version of hybrid electric power. A small petrol engine drove an alternator, which in turn provided power to an electric motor that propelled the car.

HP

MOT ET SARALEGUI (F) 1902
This was a very light 2-seater with seats in tandem and the driver in front.

NG

MOTOBÉCANE (F) 1958
Motobécane SA, Pantin, Paris.
The well-known motorcycle manufacturer Motobécane, a prodigious supplier of engines to the microcar industry, itself produced some prototypes of a 4-wheeled microcar. The 125cc air-cooled 9bhp single-cylinder engine was placed in the rear, driving the rear wheels via an infinitely variable transmission. The 2-seater bodywork was open and featured removable soft doors and a fold-flat windscreen. The chassis was a simple tubular affair. A later enclosed prototype gained a 4-cylinder 300cc engine with an extremely short block, plus sliding doors. The prototypes were still testing in the mid–1960s but the success of the Mobylette motorcycle and the general decline of the microcar sealed their fate. Motobécane was taken over by Moto Guzzi in 1974.

CR

MOTOBLOC (F) 1901–1930
1901–1902 Automobiles Schaudel, Bordeaux.
1902–1930 Automobiles Motobloc, Bordeaux.
Charles Schaudel was a Bordeaux gunsmith who made bicycles from the mid–1890s, and in 1900 built a car which he exhibited at the Paris Salon. It was unusual in several ways, having two vertical cylinders mounted transversely in the frame, with the gearbox in the sump. This was the same layout that Sir Alec Issigonis used in the Mini nearly 60 years later. The engine was integral with the gearbox, which led to the name motobloc; this was originally a description of the design, and only became the name of the make when Schaudel was bought out by his brother-in-law Émile Dombret. The rest of the car was conventional enough, with tubular frame, single-chain final drive and a rear-entrance tonneau body. It was made until 1904, when completely new cars designed by Dombret appeared. These had 2- or 4-cylinder engines, with inlet-over-exhaust valves and pressed steel frames. Their most distinctive feature, introduced in 1906, was the placement of the flywheel between the cylinders rather than at the end of the crankshaft. In 1907, when shaft drive began to replace chains, there were five 4-cylinder models, from a 2798cc 18/22hp to a massive 11,655cc 60 with oversquare cylinder dimensions of 160 × 145mm. This was offered for only one season (1907–08). A light car with 9hp 942cc single-cylinder engine was offered in 1909, but thereafter Motoblocs were fours, joined in 1911 by their first six, the 3316cc Type AN. Two larger sixes followed, of 3617 and 4460cc, There were also fours of 1592, 2412, 3306 and 4070cc. They were well made and very conventional-looking, and could easily be mistaken for a small Lancia or Mercedes. More distinctive was the 20hp six which had a vee-radiator and electric lighting. Motobloc also made trucks and engines for motor boats. During the war they made shells and Salmson aero engines.

Times became more difficult after the war, as they had factory capacity to make 1500 cars a year, yet struggled to sell 300. Two models were offered initially, a 2412cc 12CV and a 2974cc 15CV, with pushrod ohvs and, from 1922, front-wheel brakes. They had vee-radiators and most came with disc wheels, but were not sufficiently distinctive to compete with many other makes offering similar cars. By 1924 there was a smaller car of 1323cc with single-ohc engine, which was enlarged to 1450cc in 1927. Following a reorganisation of the firm, a new all-independently sprung chassis was announced for 1930. Three 6-cylinder engines were planned for it, of 1.7-, 2-, and 2.3-litres, but it is not certain that all were made. A saloon and a cabriolet were shown at the 1930 Bordeaux Fair, alongside a light truck, a tractor and a motor boat, but that was the last gasp of Motobloc. There was a Motobloc motorcycle made at Vichy after World War II, but it is not thought to be connected with the Bordeaux car.

NG

MOTOCAR (F) c.1898

Voitures Automobiles Motocar, Courbevoie, Seine.

This was an unconventional steam car powered by a 3-cylinder radial engine under the seat, with the boiler at the rear. The only evidence for its existence is a catalogue, which made no mention of the final drive or any other mechanical details. It did, however, list the partners in the company, who were a pretty aristocratic group, the Comte L. Dalla Décimas, the Baron de la Grange, O'tard A. Chagneaud, R. Dupuy d'Augéac and A. Kécheur. The latter was described as the designer, the car being built according to the 'système A. Kécheur'. It was displayed at a Paris Salon, but as the catalogue is undated, it is not certain when.

KB

MOTOCOR (I) 1921–1930

Motovetturetta Carrozata Originale Resistentissima, Turin.

This was a 3-wheeler with single front wheel which could be powered by a variety of motor-cycle engines, according to the customer's choice. The driver sat alone in front, with two passengers behind him. A delivery version and motorcycles were also made.

NG

MOTOFLITZ (D) 1949

Made at Kleve, this was a minicar powered by a 500 or 600cc single-cylinder air-cooled Columbus engine. Rear-mounted, it was unusual for so small a car in driving through an automatic transmission. The Motoflitz had an American-style grill and vee-windscreen.

NG

MOTOR CLASSICS (US) c.1982

Motor Classics Ltd, Pomona, California.

This kit car company built a very accurate replica of the 1937 Cord 812. It was built on a stretch 1980 Pontiac chassis with a V8 engine. The interior was upholstered to match the original, and an engine-turned dashboard included modern instruments, a stereo system and air conditioning. Motor Classics also built a replica of the 1936 Auburn Speedster with a Ford LTD chassis and Chevrolet V8 power.

HP

MOTORCAR CLASSICS (US) c.1979–1985

Motorcar Classics, North Hollywood, California and San Rafael, California.

The Piper Lance was a kit car copied from the CMC Gazelle. It was a neoclassic design that fitted a VW floorpan or a special frame with Ford Pinto or Mustang mechanicals. The Seneca was a replica of the MG-TD based on Ford Pinto or Mustang running gear, including an optional V8 engine. It was slightly larger than an original MG, providing more interior room. They also sold a Bugatti replica. Company owners Tom and William Piper were grandsons of the founder of the Piper aircraft business.

HP

MOTOR CRIOLLO see HISPANO-ARGENTINA

MOTORETTE (i) (US) 1910–1914

C.W. Kelsey Manufacturing Co., Hartford, Connecticut.

Kelsey had built a 3-wheeled car called the Auto-Tri in 1898, and possibly for this reason he chose the same layout for the Motorette. Built in a section of the Cheney Silk Mill in Hartford, it had a 7hp air-cooled 2-cylinder 2-stroke engine made by a local firm, and final drive was by chain to the single rear wheel. Kelsey built up a good export market, with Motorettes being sold as far afield as Denmark and Japan, as well as in Canada. The Japanese model was made as a rickshaw.

In 1911 a number of faulty engines were delivered, and Kelsey changed his supplier and went for a 4-stroke design, but the damage to the Motorette's reputation had been done. It was only partly redeemed by a coast-to-coast run. About 210 Motorettes were made. There were plans to make an electric version co-designed by Kelsey and his friend Thomas A. Edison, but this model was never built.

NG

1912 Motobloc 12/16hp 2-seater.
NATIONAL MOTOR MUSEUM

1921 Motobloc 15hp coupé de ville.
NICK BALDWIN

MOTORETTE (ii) (US) 1946–1948

Motorette Co., Buffalo, New York.

This was a light (420 lbs) 3-wheeler with single front wheel and chain drive to the left rear wheel, powered by a single-cylinder Wisconsin engine giving 4hp.

NG

MOTORMOBILE see VILAIN

MOTORVILLE (GB) 1987–c.1994

1987–1989 Motorville, Denham, Buckinghamshire.
1989–c.1994 Motorville (Watford) Ltd, Watford, Hertfordshire.

The famous FAIRTHORPE marque stopped making cars in 1976, but the Denham factory was kept going to support existing cars. In the hands of Motorville, the time was judged right to launch an updated version of the classic Faithorpe EM. It had a semi-space frame chassis with a longer wheelbase than original, a fibreglass body with flared arches and numerous detail changes to the design. The donor car was a Cortina Mk III/IV. The 2+2 version could be had with a Rover V8 engine and gearbox, while a 2-seater 'S' model was also made for Ford Escort running gear.

CR

MOUETTE (F) 1923–1925

Automobiles Mouette, Paris.

L. van der Eyken, who made the FOX (i), was also the manufacturer of the Mouette, a conventional small car with a resemblance to the Citroën. Various proprietary

c.1923 Mourre 1-litre 2-seater.
NATIONAL MOTOR MUSEUM

1912 Moyer 30hp roadster.
NATIONAL MOTOR MUSEUM

engines were used, including Ruby and S.C.A.P. in 1100 and 1500cc forms, and the specification included a multi-plate clutch and 4-speed gearbox. Most Mouettes were touring cars, but there was a *Grand Sport* as well.

NG

MOURRE (F) 1920–1923

Antoine Mourre, Paris.

This car is sometimes described as one of Marcel Violet's efforts, but it was not made by him. Antoine Mourre bought the rights to Violet's 1058cc 2-cylinder 2-stroke engine, which was made for Violet by SICAM, and installed it in his 2-seater cyclecar. This had an aluminium bonnet, with the rest of the body made of mahogany and the wings of steel. Violet drove one of these cars into second place in the 1921 Cyclecar Grand Prix. Despite the good performance of the Violet engine, (even the road cars were capable of 70mph or 112km/h), Mourre turned to a 950cc 4-cylinder Fivet engine for his final cars, made in 1923.

NG

MOUSTIQUE (B) 1925–1927

Autos Moustique, Brussels-Etterbeek.

The Moustique (mosquito) was a light car powered by a 2.75CV flat-twin engine which gave it a top speed of 47mph (75km/h). Final drive was by chains,

and the chassis had cantilever springs all round. For 1927 the twin was joined by a 6CV 4-cylinder model available with open or closed bodies. It cost more than double the price of the flat-twin, and by the end of the year all Moustique production had come to an end.

NG

MOVEO (GB) 1931–1932

Moveo Car & Engineering Co., Preston, Lancashire.

The Moveo was the work of motorcycle racer and manufacturer Bert Houlding (1882–1955), who had used the name on a motorcycle in 1910, and made Matador motorcycles in Preston from prewar days up to 1925. Work on the Moveo car began in 1929, and it was two years before it was announced, in August 1931. It took another six months for it to be ready for the road. Houlding's recipe was a powerful proprietary engine, a 2973cc 6-cylinder ohv Meadows giving 74bhp, a 4-speed Moss gearbox and a deep channel-section frame swept down behind the engine and up over the rear axle. This gave very low lines which were complimented by an attractive 2-door coupé body by Jensen.

The Moveo was priced at £785, and more powerful engines, also by Meadows, of 3280 and 4430cc were promised, the smaller with optional supercharger. However only the one coupé and another chassis were ever made, as Houlding lacked financial backing, and when his tiny staff asked for a pay rise, they were made redundant.

NG

Further Reading
'Moveo Premier – the Preston Grand Tourer', Martyn Flower,
The Automobile, October 1989.

MOVILUTIL (E) 1957

Movilutil, Barcelona.

This was an attractive 4-seater using a 2-cylinder 350cc engine of 15bhp. It also had a 4-speed gearbox and hydraulic brakes on all four wheels.

VCM

MOYEA (US) 1903–1904

1903–1904 Moyea Automobile Co., New York, New York.
1904 Consolidated Motor Co., New York, New York.

This car, whose name was an Indian word for 'swift running', was a licence-built ROCHET-SCHNEIDER 12/16hp 4-cylinder chain-drive chassis with 5-seater tonneau body. Moyea planned a factory at Rye, New York, but while this was being built, they had their cars made, first in Middletown, Ohio, and then by Alden Sampson in Pittsfield, Massachusetts, with bodies coming from the Springfield Metal & Body Co. The 1904 Moyea had a larger engine of 25hp and a three inches longer wheelbase, but at $4000 it cost $1000 less than the 1903 car, which was probably overpriced. They changed their name to Consolidated in January 1904, and before the year was out Alden Sampson had bought up Consolidated and marketed the car as an ALDEN SAMPSON.

NG

MOYER (US) 1911–1915

H.A. Moyer, Syracuse, New York.

Harvey Allen Moyer was a wagon builder, originally in Cicero, New York, and from 1875 in Syracuse. In 1909 he announced that he would make 200 cars that year, but it seems that no Moyer cars were made until 1911. His first were runabouts and tourers with 29.4hp 4-cylinder engines, and in 1912 these were joined by a 38.4hp six made only as a tourer. These cars featured full-pressure lubrication. Moyer seems never to have formed a company, yet he built about 400 cars before lack of capital forced him out of business. His slogan was 'All Roads Are Level to a Moyer'.

NG

MOZOTA (F) 1906

B. de Mozota, Paris.

This obscure manufacturer listed three models for one season only, a 10/12, 24/30 and 40/60hp, all with 4-cylinder engines.

NG

MP (U) 1962–1964
Mutio, Passadore & Co., Montevideo.
The MP was a rather boxy 2-door saloon powered by French Panhard mechanical components. Production was handled between messrs Mutio and Passadore and a company called Carmeta. Mutio and Passadore had raced Panhards extensively and with some success in Uruguay, particularly in the El Pinar Autodrome, before embarking in the MP venture, which lasted until 1964, when production stopped. 100 MPs were made, and the manufacturers lost money in each car they produced.
ACT

M.P. (GB) c.1909
These initials were used for two distinct cars, one a French-built product with Barriquand et Marre engine to be sold in England by J.E.H. Moneypenny of Hanover Square, London. The other was built by Feest & Sons of Goswell Road, London, for sale by the Harrington Garage of South Kensington. An M.P. is reported to have run at Brooklands in 1908.
NG

M.P.M. (US) 1915
Mount Pleasant Motor Co., Mount Pleasant, Michigan.
The M.P.M. was built in two models, a 4-cylinder roadster and a V8 tourer, priced at $1085 and $1095. Ten were made before the man behind the car, Louis J. Lampke, ran out of money and asked for $10,000 more from the citizens of Mount Pleasant. They did not have enough confidence in the project to agree, so he tried again in Saginaw, but with no more success. However, he stayed in Saginaw, and in 1916 he started a company to build another V8, the YALE (ii).
NG

MR see PULSAR

MROZ (US) c.1986
Mroz Coachbuilders, Fullerton, California.
The Glockler-bodied Porsches of the early 1950s were beautiful racing cars, and Mark Mroz decided to base his kit car on these examples. He restyled the body to fit the standard length VW chassis. The one-piece body had no doors and the kit was inexpensive and easy to assemble.
HP

M.R.R. (I) 1904–1907
Count Michelino Rodocanacchi Ralli, Livorno.
This was a 4-seater rear-entrance tonneau of Mercedes appearance, with 4-cylinder engine and double-chain drive.
NG

M.S. (F) 1919–1928
Automobiles M.S., Sèvres, Seine-et-Oise (1919–1924);
Suresnes, Seine (1924–1928).
Morain Sylvestre built a cyclecar which was on the market by the end of 1919. It had a 998cc vertical-twin Train engine with aluminium pistons developing 20bhp, a differential-less rear axle and a 2-seater body with radiator in the style of a Rolls-Royce or Sizaire. He made this car, sometimes known by his full name rather than his initials, until 1921, and in 1922 sold about 25 chassis to DELFOSSE who fitted their own bodies.
In 1924 Sylvestre brought out a new M.S. which was in fact made by MARGUERITE. He bought 50 or 60 of their Model BO with 961cc Chapuis-Dornier engine, and mounted his own bodies which included open sports and a 2-seater cabriolet with canework body.
NG

M.S.L. (GB) 1911–1912
Motor Showrooms Ltd, London.
The M.S.L. was assembled from French components at premises off Long Acre, near London's theatreland. Two models were made, a 10/14 and a 12/16hp, both with 4-cylinder monobloc engines. 2- and 4-seater tourer bodies were offered. In September 1911 plans were announced for the whole car to be manufactured in England, but nothing came of these. M.S.L. advertising ended during 1912.
NG

1955 MT 125cc 3-wheeler.
NICK GEORGANO

MT (E) 1957
Maquinarias y Transportes SA, Barcelona.
This company specialised in light vans with motorcycle engines and offered, under the name Maquitrans, an open 3-wheel minicar with single wheel at the rear. It used a single-cylinder 175cc 6.9hp engine and hydraulic brakes on the front wheels. An electric starter and a folding roof were also available.
VCM

M.T.C. (NL) 1993–c.1994
Maharishi Technology Corp. NV, Amsterdam.
The M.T.C. Pushpak Electric was a multi-purpose jeep-type vehicle with electric propulsion. It had a steel chassis and bolt-on fibreglass bodywork that could be adapted between numerous styles. A special tray with all the batteries on board was located between the axles, enabling battery transfer rather than recharge. A top speed of 55mph (89km/h) and a range of 75 miles was claimed.
CR

MUELLER (US) 1896–1899
Mueller Manufacturing Co., Decatur, Illinois.
This company dated back to 1861 and was run by Hieronymus A. Mueller and his six sons. They made water and gas meters, valves and other plumbing items. In 1895 Mueller imported a single-cylinder Benz which he modified, boring out the cylinder from 130 to 140mm, giving it three forward speeds instead of two, and adding a reverse, as well as improving the cooling system and using his own sparking plug and carburettor. He entered this car, under the name Mueller-Benz, in the 1895 Chicago *Times Herald* Race. The Muellers subsequently made three or four more cars, all on Benz lines. A reporter said in 1896 that they had just made a 'strictly American motor carriage, with four seats facing forwards and a double-cylinder motor'. Benz did not make a 2-cylinder engine until 1897, but perhaps Mueller was just anticipating Karl Benz' next move. Hieronymus was killed in a workshop explosion in 1900, and his sons made no more cars. They concentrated on brass forgings and automobile products, and were still in business in 1952.
NG

MUELLER-NEIDHART (S) 1952
This was a 2-seater light car with tubular backbone frame and triple headlamps. It had Swiss-designed Neidhart suspension of compressed rubber in vertical tubes. No details of the engine were given. It was to have been made in Sweden and Holland, but never left the prototype stage.
NG

MULFORD (US) 1915; 1922
1915 Ralph K. Mulford Co., Brooklyn, New York.
1922 Mulford Motors Co., Brooklyn, New York.
Designed and built by the famous racing driver, Ralph Mulford, these were advanced sporting cars powered by 16-valve 4-cylinder engines. Mulford had

1912 Multiplex (i) 50hp tourer.
NATIONAL MOTOR MUSEUM

helped to build a number of racing cars, including one which was raced under the name Mulford Special. This was later converted to a road car, and may have been one of the 1915 Mulfords. Their engines were patterned on the Duesenberg 'walking beam' unit. Mulford built only seven cars in all, two in 1915 and five more in 1922. The two 1915 cars were taken by the bankers who had backed him, and he made no profit at all; it seems that he fared no better with the second batch. He was a much better driver than a businessman.

NG

MULLNER (A) 1913–1914

In contrast to France, Britain and the United States, and later Germany, cyclecars were rare in Austria. The Mullner was one of them, though, with a 6/7hp 2-cylinder Zedel engine and single-chain drive to one rear wheel.

NG

MULTIPLEX (i) (US) 1912–1913

Multiplex Manufacturing Co., Berwick, Pennsylvania.
The Multiplex was a large high-quality car powered by a 50hp 4-cylinder Waukesha engine, and offered in three body styles on a 134in (3401mm) wheelbase, tourer, roadster and raceabout. Prices were $3125 to $3600. A lighter and more sporting car on an 85in (2157mm) wheelbase was planned, but the company failed before it could be made. Only 14 Multiplexes were made.

NG

MULTIPLEX (ii) (US) 1953–1954

Multiplex Manufacturing Co., Berwick, Pennsylvania.
The Multiplex was an early American experiment in small-displacement sportscars. The prototype was designed and built by Fritz Bingaman, and had a tubular chassis with double a-arm front suspension. It was fitted with a homely aluminium body and a Singer 1500cc engine. After developing it at race tracks, production models of the Multiplex 186 were sold. They had Willys 4- or 6-cylinder engines with more attractive fibreglass coupé or roadster bodies styled after the Italian Cisitalia sportscars. Price in 1954 was in the $4000 range. Multiplex would also sell bare chassis without engines.

HP

MUMFORD (GB) 1973–1978/1983 to date

Mumford Engineering, Nailsworth, Gloucestershire.
Brian Mumford's unique trike was based on Vauxhall Viva parts and attracted some attention from the Luton manufacturer. In design it had aircraft-inspired

ideals, including a riveted aluminium monocoque chassis, specially-designed suspension and an aerofoil-type aerodynamic shape with a flat undertray and concealed headlamps. There was diff-less shaft drive to the single rear wheel. After a faltering 1973 launch, the Mumford was revived in 1983 in Series 2 form with a few improvements. Only around ten cars had been built by 1998. Mumford also manufactured the LOMAX between 1984 and 1986.

CR

MUMFORD-SYME (AUS) 1905

Mumford-Syme Motor Pty Ltd, Fitzroy, Victoria.
This firm followed F.G. Mumford, who had made motor-cycles, and it offered automobile engines, gears, axles and castings. Late in 1905 it revealed its own car, a 2-seater with a 6hp single-cylinder water-cooled engine and a 3-speed sliding gear transmission, which was wholly Australian made. By the following year, Mumford was missing when Syme Engineering & Motor Co. showed a car with the same mechanicals in an ash frame with final drive by chain to a live rear axle.

MG

MUNICH (US) c.1982

Munich Motor Works, Cupertino, California.
Ford Mustangs from the 1979–81 era were transformed into Mercedes 450SL replicas with kits from this company. They also converted mini-pick-up trucks into convertibles.

HP

MUNSON (US) 1896–1900

Munson Electric Motor Co., La Porte, Indiana.
The Munson was a petrol-electric car, probably the first in America. The prototype was made in Chicago, but all production, such as it was, took place in La Porte. Although John W. Munson gave his name to the car, the engineering was by P.M. Heldt. The vehicle was powered by a horizontal 2- or 4-cylinder engine which drove a generator providing power to an electric motor which drove the rear wheels. The makers claimed that as the petrol engine turned at a constant speed, unpleasant exhaust gases were eliminated. At least four vehicles were made in La Porte, a 2-seater buggy, a 4-seater surrey, an 11-seater omnibus and a 3000lb delivery wagon. Production of all four types was promised, but there is little evidence that many were made. Heldt later became a well-known technical journalist.

NG

MUNTZ (US) 1950–1954

Muntz Car Co., Glendale, California and Evanston, Illinois.
In 1949 Earl 'Madman' Muntz bought a custom-bodied Buick from Frank KURTIS. When he arrived he saw the Kurtis sports car that Kurtis had been building in small numbers with Ford V8 power. Muntz, who had made a fortune in new and used cars and television sets, liked it so much he bought the Kurtis factory and started building a redesigned version he called the Muntz Jet. Muntz changed the car into a 4-seater with first Cadillac, then Lincoln V8 engines and quickly moved the factory to Illinois. In 1951 Muntz switched from aluminium to steel for the body panels. The weight increased substantially from the Kurtis design, however, the Jet was still pretty quick by Detroit standards. The metal top was removable, but no soft-top was offered. At $5500 it was too expensive, and yet Muntz lost money on each one. Less than 400 were sold before production stopped in 1954.

HP

Further Reading
'Muntz Jet', Michael Lamm and Paul Sable,
Automobile Quarterly, Vol. 39, No. 3.

MURAD (GB) 1948–1949

1948–1949 Murad Machine Tool Co. Ltd, Aylesbury, Buckinghamshire.
1949 Murad Developments Ltd, Aylesbury, Buckinghamshire.
Wadia Hanni Murad, born in Jamaica of Lebanese descent, was an accomplished engineer whose company flourished during World War II producing precision lathes for armaments manufacture and other purposes. Thereafter he suffered the machinations of bureaucracy and was impeded from developing his proposed car-producing factory for two critical years and the first prototype was not completed until 1948. This featured a carefully balanced 1.5-litre inclined-ohv

1952 Muntz Road Jet convertible.
NATIONAL MOTOR MUSEUM

engine with hydraulic tappets, set in an underslung frame with coil ifs, and the individualistic body styling attracted much interest. A 2-litre option was to have been available. An order for 50 was received from Scandinavia, where it is believed a prototype was sent, and an initial batch of 100 cars was put in hand. A letter of October 1949 asserts that the car was then 'in production'. However, continual government-induced delays caused cashflow problems and escalating costs, which led to receivership, and to Murad at last succumbing to pressure to move to a 'development area' – in this case, the Isle of Sheppey. Then the government pulled the plug on aid promised for that area, and most of the parts stayed there until the 1980s. It is uncertain whether any other cars were completed, but Murad's own car, which is alleged to have exceeded 400,000 miles in his hands, survives him and is in safe custody.

DF

Further Reading
'The Bourne Jinx', M. Worthington-Williams,
Classic and Sports Car, July and November 1983.
'Muradacity', M. Worthington-Williams,
Classic and Sports Car, November 1983.

MURDAUGH (US) 1901

Burton Murdaugh, Oxford, Pennsylvania.
Murdaugh built three light cars powered by 3½hp single-cylinder engines, with shaft drive to a rear axle without differential. Steering was by tiller. Each was a slight improvement on the previous one, and after the third had been made Murdaugh indicated that he would make more, to sell at $600 each. He described himself as 'The Murdaugh Automobile Co.', but there is no evidence that he formed a company or sold any cars.

NG

MURENA (US) 1969–1970

Murena Motors Ltd, New York, New York.
The Murena 429GT was a sports station wagon with a 7033cc Ford V8 engine and a 3-speed automatic transmission. Conceived by Murena president Joseph Vos, Charles Schwendler and Jeremy Fell, the prototype was built in Italy by Intermeccanica, who had also built the ITALIA, OMEGA and APOLLO sports

1948 Murad 1½-litre saloon.
BRYAN K. GOODMAN

cars. It was a large car with a 118in (2995mm) wheelbase and an overall length of 205in (5203mm). It had a live axle at the rear with 4-wheel Girling disc brakes. The styling was clean and sleek, with two doors and plenty of interior room. With a price tag of $14,950 in 1970, sales were slow–estimates vary from 11 to 40 cars.

HP

MURRAY (i) (US) 1902–1903

Church Manufacturing Co., Adrian, Michigan.
Willis Grant Murray had been manager of the car department at the Olds Motor Works, and the car that he designed for the Church Manufacturing Co. was not unlike a Curved Dash Oldsmobile without the curved dash. The single-cylinder horizontal engine, epicyclic transmission and suspension by springs extending from front to rear axle were similar to the Oldsmobile though Murray claimed more power. The Church company hoped for mass production, but could not raise enough capital. Murray left, and the cars were renamed CHURCH for 1903. In 1904 a larger car called the LENAWEE was made by the same company.

NG

1926 Murray (iii) Six sedan.
KEITH MARVIN

1917 Murray (ii) Eight roadster.
KEITH MARVIN

MURRAY (ii) (US) 1916–1920

Murray Motor Car Co., Pittsburgh, Pennsylvania.

The Murray – or Murray Eight – made its debut at the New York Show in December 1916 in touring car form, featuring a Herschell-Spillman V8 engine and a Rolls-Royce-type radiator. During 1917, a series of additional body types were added including a roadster, coupé, sedan and town car at prices ranging from $2500 and up. The Murray Eight was considered a prestigious automobile and its clientele included members of many leading Pittsburgh families. One of the more prominently noted Murray cars was a phaeton designed along ultra-modern art deco lines with sharply-angled fenders, built for W.C. Carnegie of Pittsburgh. It enjoyed wide display in contemporary automotive journals. Despite its appeal and reasonable price scale, the Murray did not receive the enthusiasm and purchasers which had been predicted for it and, following an abortive move to Newark, New Jersey, it changed hands – (see MURRAY (iii)) with less than 200 cars completed.

KM

MURRAY (iii) (US) 1920–1931

1920–1921 Murray Motor Car Co., Newark, New Jersey.
1921–1931 Murray Motor Car Co., Boston and Atlantic, Massachusetts.

The Murray (iii) was the continuation of the earlier Murray (ii) or Murray Eight which had been built in Pittsburgh, Pennsylvania since 1916, William N. Murray having announced that he was moving his operations to Newark, New Jersey. The Murray company was forced into receivership before any production could be attempted and the Murray assets and machinery were taken over by John J. McCarthy who moved the operations to Boston, Massachusetts. Facts surrounding the cars which subsequently appeared under the Murray badge are nebulous. The Boston-based car was occasionally listed on rosters as the 'Murray Six'. This was a misnomer as McCarthy was apparently using any engines he could lay his hands on in a strictly hand-to-mouth business. A handsome, if archaic, sedan was reported and illustrated in 1926 by the local press but, from its appearance, it was probably a rebadged chassis dating back to the Murray Eight days which ended in 1920. Murray cars are known to have been completed and sold during the 1920s but such information known indicates that there were no two cars alike. Murray did built one handsome roadster which he used as his personal car and for promotion. The cars were built as late as 1928 and possibly 1931. In 1929, Murray announced plans for a new Murray to be priced at $6500 and up and, in an attempt to attract financial support, issued a prospectus listing some of the outstanding names comprising Murray clientele. Among those listed were W.C. Carnegie, M. Gugenheimer and Mrs William Thaw of Pittsburgh; Mrs A.J. Vanderbilt, Allison V. Armour, Pliny Fisk and Julius Fleischman, all of New York City; silent screen star Mae Murray of Hollywood, California; author Mary Roberts Rinehart of Sewickley, Pennsylvania, and Mrs L.E. Harriman and Mrs L. Harriman, both of Brockton, Massachusetts. There were others comprising top positions in their respective fields or in Social Register listings. The listing, taken from one of Murray Eight owners of a decade earlier, fooled few. Murray continued to promote the car as late as 1931.

KM

MUSCHANG (B) 1965–1969

Muschang, Arlon.

Citroën pioneered the idea of a twin-engined 4-wheel drive car with its 2CV Sahara in the 1950s, and the Belgian Renault concessionaire, Muschang, repeated the exercise with the Renault 4. From 1967, it offered its own open doorless bodywork with very narrow-set headlamps mounted on a separate pod. Versions were also offered with only one engine and 4×4 or 4×2 transmission. Léopold Muschang sold his designs to APAL in 1969.

CR

MUSTANG (US) 1948
Mustang Engineering Corp., Renton, Washington.
This rear-engined sedan seated six and had a bus-like aluminium body. It had centre side doors like a van. The engine was a 596bhp 4-cylinder Hercules, and the car was designed by a former Lincoln service manager, Roy C. McCarty.

HP

MUSURUS (F) c.1921–1922
Janvier, Sabin et Cie, Chatillon-sur-Bagneux, Seine.
Janvier were mainly engine manufacturers who made a few complete cars. Some were listed under their own name (see JANVIER (i)) but the Musurus was named after Musurus Bey, a wealthy Turkish enthusiast who commissioned the cars. They were powered by 4-cylinder T-head Picker-Janvier engines, and had rounded vee-radiators similar to the contemporary Delaunay-Belleville or NAG.

NG

MUTEL (F) c.1902–c.1906
Mutel et Cie, Paris.
This company was a well-known maker of proprietary engines which were used in a large number of French makes as well as some in England. Among firms using Mutel engines, usually for their larger models, were Century (i), La Licorne, Dorey, Elswick, Lacoste et Battmann, Meteor (iii), Morgan (i), Prunel, Regal (i), Sage and Wasp (i). They also sold a few cars under their own name, using their engines in chassis by M.A.B. These seem to have been special orders rather than production cars. An example was a large, chain-driven touring limousine of 1903, with electric interior lighting and movable tables, powered by a 30hp 4-cylinder engine. They were listed in L'Annuaire Général de l'Automobile for 1902 as makers of 2-, 3-, and 4-seater cars, running on petrol or alcohol fuel.

NG

M.V. see VAGHI

M.V. AUGUSTA (I) 1965–1966
Meccanica Verghera, Gallarate.
This well-known motorcycle manufacturer produced its first prototype car, which failed to reach production, in the early 1950s, a curious-looking aircraft-influenced 4-wheeler with a 350cc boxer engine and a Perspex dome roof. Then at the 1965 Geneva Salon, it presented a 4 × 4 all-terrain utility car with all-flat panels, six seats (plus a single central driver's seat) and Lypsoid balloon tyres. Called the Diana, it was licensed version of the German KRAKA. This was abandoned in 1966 in favour of a utility car using a Ford 1.7-litre engine.

CR

M.V.M. (GBG) 1956
Manor View Motors, Catel, Guernsey, C.I.
The M.V.M. was the only car to have been built for sale in the Channel Islands (though there was a Guernsey-built motorcycle, the Pacer, in 1914). It was a light 2-seater sports car with ladder-type tubular frame, independent suspension all round and a fibreglass body. Only three cars were made, two with 325cc 2-cylinder 2-stroke Anzani engines and one with a 1100cc 4-cylinder Coventry-Climax, which gave a top speed of 100mph (161km/h). A credit squeeze by the bank prevented builder Leslie Le Tissier from making any more.

NG

M.V.S. see VENTURI

MW (i) see WEGMANN

MW (ii) (D) 1985–1988
MW Kleinwagen GmbH, Wielenbach.
This microcar appeared in two versions. The CityBoy was fitted with a rear-mounted 50cc 2-stroke Sachs engine. Three models were available, restricted to speeds of 6, 15 or 28mph (10, 25 or 45km/h), according to the type of licence held by the driver. There was also an electric version, the SonnyBoy, with a range of 40–80 miles. The cars were intended for use by handicapped people or those who only held a moped licence. More than 1000 were made.

HON

MWD (D) 1911–1912
Motoren-Werke mbH, Dessau.
This firm made two models of touring car which sold mainly to a local market. The 8/22PS was taken over by Anhaltische Automobile- und Motorenfabrik AG and sold under the name DER DESSAUER.

HON

MWF (A) 1905–1907
Maschinen- und Waggonbaufabrik AG, Simmering.
Specialists in railway carriages and wagons, MWF took over production of the WYNER which they built in their own works. Like Wyner they used mainly 8/10hp single-cylinder De Dion-Bouton engines.

HON

MYERS (US) 1911
Consolidated Motor Car Co., Atlanta, Georgia.
The short-lived Myers was an assembled car which featured a 4-cylinder engine and three body types – roadster, touring car and a light delivery commercial vehicle, also available as a chassis. Despite the novelty of interchangeable bodies, few were completed and the company was out of business in a few months.

KM

MYMSA (E) 1957
Motores y Motos SA, Barcelona.
Mymsa was a small 4-seat 3-wheeler with folding roof, four doors and a single wheel at the front. It used a single-cylinder 175cc 8.8bhp engine.

VCM

MYSTIQUE (GB) 1985
This was a BMW M1 replica with mid-mounted Rover V8 power, but it was never officially launched.

CR

MYTHOLM (GB) 1899–1901
Yorkshire Motor Car Manufacturing Co. Ltd, Hipperholme, Yorkshire.
This company took over the works of Brown & Buckton who had made an experimental car in 1896. They made a new 4hp 2-cylinder water-cooled engine which they called the Mytholm, this being the name of their workshops and an area near Bradford. They fitted this engine to the JACKSON (i) Doctor's Car and changed the name of the car to Mytholm. Production was very slow, each car taking three to four weeks to complete, as the 'works' consisted of just one small room in the Mytholm Mills. With orders for 22 cars in 1900, the directors hoped to buy the rest of the Mills, but the shareholders would not agree. Reynold Jackson left for London in July, and the final Mytholm car was made in May 1901.

NG

MZMA (SU) 1947 to date
1947–1968 Moskovskji Zavod Malolitrashnykh Avtomobiley, Moscow.
1968 to date Avtomobilnji Zavod imjeni Leninskogo Komsomola.
At the end of World War II, the victorious Russians dismantled the Opel production lines and transferred them to Moscow, the prewar 4-door Kadett becoming the basis for the first successful Soviet 'people's car'. The machinery was installed at the premises of the former KIM factory and the Kadett, re-badged, wearing a red star on top of the grill, was called a Moskvitch (a Muscovite, inhabitant of Moscow). The initial model Moskvitch-400 had an even smaller engine and

1950 Moskvitch (MZMA) 400 saloon.
MARGUS H. KUUSE

1959 Moskvitch (MZMA) 407 saloon.
NICK BALDWIN

1980 Moskvitch (MZMA) 2141SL saloon.
MARGUS H. KUUSE

1988 Moskvitch (MZMA) 2141 hatchback.
MARGUS H. KUUSE

3bhp less than KIM-10, but the modified model 401 of 1954 had the same 26bhp and the second to third gear was synchronised, along with a column change.

In April 1956 the first original Moskvitch replaced the outdated model – after about a quarter of a million had been manufactured. The Moskvich-402 was a rather modern looking small family saloon even by contemporary Western European standards, furnished with a 1220cc, 35bhp engine and capable of 65mph (105km/h). Derivatives included the first ever Russian estate car, the Moskvich-423 and an early 4 × 4 SUV, numbered as the Moskvitch-410. A model with a new ohv engine of 1358cc and 45bhp, doing 71.4mph (114.8km/h), was called Moskvitch-407. Novelties included a 4-speed gearbox and hypoid final drive, not to mention a 2-tone bodywork. The model 403 of 1962–1965 followed with its reinforced front suspension, new steering, hydraulically actuated clutch and pendant pedals. Such attributes were also used on the next model, Moskvitch-408, which acquired boxcar styling, with rear end paying tribute to the BMW 700. This new body style was introduced in May 1964. The Moskvitch and Ish cars for the following three decades were based on this particular body. On 18 May 1967 the one millionth Moskvitch was completed and a few months later there came a brand new ohc engine of 1478cc and 75bhp. This rather advanced aluminium unit was built at Ufa Motor Works (UMZ) and the Moskvitch-412 was capable of reaching 87mph (140km/h). The speedy model was rather successfully used in the following year's London–Sydney Rally and two years later in the London–Mexico Rally.

In a country where political overtones were attached to almost everything it was not surprising that the MZMA was re-named AZLK–Avtomobilnji Zavod Leninskogo Komsomola (Auto Works named after Lenin's Communist Youth). Further sporting laurels were achieved in the 1974 Tour d'Europe and in the 1973 East African Safari. By now the Moskvitch make was known in some 70 countries of the world. The production number surpassed the magic 100,000 in 1969. From 1976 the model acquired the number 2140 which was also produced with a low compression (7.2:1) 68bhp engine for rural usage where 76 octane petrol still dominated. With export in mind a deluxe model Moskvitch-2140-117 appeared.

The first front-wheel drive model was larger, 171in (4350mm) long and weighing 1070kg, the Moskvich-2141 of 1986. The 6-light, 5-door hatchback bodywork was copied from that of the SIMCA 1307/1308. The 1.6-litre engine came from a VAZ-2106, by just 1.4bhp more powerful than the evergreen Ufa unit. A 5-speed gearbox, rack and pinion steering and strut-type front suspension were technically the most important novelties. The car had a top speed of 96.25mph (154.86km/h). In 1988 the model 2140 was dropped altogether. In the early 1990s Ishmash built about 134,000–168,000 cars of Moskvitch origin and AZLK was capable of only 105,000–106,000, mainly due to complications with the model 2141. By the second half of the 1990s production figures collapsed to the unheard level of 2929 in 1996, but increased to 20,000 plus in 1997, and to twice that figure in 1998.

The technical advances were mostly in installing a new Ufa (UZAM) engine of 1702cc and 85bhp in the Moskvitches since 1994, the quantity of VAZ engines used coming down to 4096 that year. Ford diesel engines were also tried in a few hundred Moskvitches. There is a 2-litre UZAM-3320 engine of 100bhp in the pipeline

The *dernier cri* is a model called Svjatogor, boasting a 1998cc Renault powerplant of 112bhp. The Moskvitch Works now belong now to the city of Moscow and there are plans for further co-operation with Renault. After going full circle, the works may end in the position in which KIM started decades ago – assembling foreign components.

MHK

NACIONAL (MEX) 1949–1952
Fabrique DM-Nacional, Mexico City.

Mexico has become an important location for manufacture of foreign designs, in particular the VW Beetle, Ford Escort/Mercury Tracer, Plymouth Neon and Nissan Sentra, but the Nacional was a rare example of a home-grown design, though using an American engine. It was built in part of the factory of Distribuidora Mexicana, a big furniture making company, and designed by Antonio Ruiz Galindo, son of the owner of DM. Convertible bodies to customers' designs were built on American chassis, mainly Mercury. After about 15 had been made, Galindo turned to selling imported Fiats.

NG

NACIONAL CUSTALS (E) 1919
Joaquín Custals, Barcelona.

Custals left T.H. and formed his own company, building a cyclecar. Very little is known about this car, which had no success.

VCM

NACIONAL G (E) 1939–1940
Natalio Horcajo, Zaragoza.

This was a serious project to build the first mass-produced people's car in Spain after the Civil War. The engineers Martin Gomez and Natalio Horcajo prepared, with the help of important members of the armed forces, several prototypes of a 2-doors sedan and a good-looking 2-seater spider, which used a 2-cylinder 2-stroke 700cc engine, a 3-speed gearbox, tubular backbone frame, and independent suspension. One prototype was air-cooled, the other water-cooled. Both technicians also patented a rotary motion engine (Wankel) with ellipsoidal rotor. In spite of military acceptance, the plans were stopped without explanation and all the prototypes destroyed.

VCM

NACIONAL PESCARA (E) 1929–1932
Fábrica Nacional de Automóviles SA, Barcelona.

This is the story of a very rich man, the Marquis de Pescara, who wanted to build one of the most singular luxury cars in his country. Raul and his brother Enrique Pateras Pescara first prepared a helicopter which had numerous vanes, a very strange design, shown at Paris and perfected at Barcelona. At the end of the 1920s, Pescara decided to build his own car near Barcelona. He looked for the best engineers in the country, paying three times more than any other company, and in 1930 introduced a very advanced car powered by a 2960cc straight-8 engine with one ohc and 80bhp at 3600rpm, using a lot of aluminium and Electron alloy in engine and chassis components. The strangest item was a 2-speed gearbox with the direct gear up to 40mph (65km/h) and the second starting from 2.4mph (4km/h) up to 75mph (121km/h), nearly an automatic drive system. It also had four hydraulic lifting jacks, only four points of lubrication, a very low chassis and hydraulic brakes.

The Pescara brothers bought the Terramar race track near Sitges, where they tested the car. In July 1930 the Nacional Pescara was entered in the Peña Rhin hill climb with a simple, stripped down body, winning in its category with Enrique Pescara the driver. The next evolution of the car had two ohcs with 125bhp at 4800rpm, equipped with a shorter platform with a racing-body and a 3-speed gearbox. In 1931 this car participated at the German Kesselberg hill-climbs, beating famous cars and drivers, and was proclaimed European Mountain Champion at the end of that year. The car participated in other championships until 1936.

In 1932/33 the same 8-cylinder engine used a supercharger that raised power to 180bhp at 5500rpm. The company also worked on a unique 4100cc 10-cylinder in-line engine, expecting 100bhp, also equipped with a supercharger in a racing version, but never finished it due to political problems in Spain. Pescara continually requested the help of the Spanish Government to develop an important car industry, but never received either assistance or money. Pescara entered discussions with Voisin to develop a 16-cylinder 4-litre engine, but this car was finally built in Switzerland with the 150bhp engine made by SLM. This car with a convertible body, was used by Pescara himself, who already lived in Switzerland. It seems that about five Nacional Pescara were built, and two survive. The Marquis of Pescara died in Paris in 1966.

VCM

1931 Nacional Pescara at Zbraslav Jiloviste hill climb.
NATIONAL MOTOR MUSEUM

1948 Nacional R.G. saloon.
NICK BALDWIN

NACIONAL R. G. (E) 1948–1949
Fábrica Nacional de Automóviles, Aviones y Motores de Aviación, Barcelona.

Ramón Girona Guillaume, born in Cuba, decided to start as an aircraft and car manufacturer in Barcelona. In 1948 he presented two small aeroplanes using its own engines and a 2-door 4-seater good-looking car with his own 2-cylinder 692cc 6hp engine. This was capable of 50mph (80km/h). One of these cars survives at the Salvador Claret Motor Museum in Sils (Gerona).

VCM

NACIONAL SITGES (E) 1935–1937
Fábrica de Automóviles Nacional-Sitges, Sitges.

Little is known about this company situated at the famous summer resort near Barcelona. It seems that only one type of car was finally built, using different bodies and a 4-cylinder 1235cc engine of 36bhp. During the Spanish civil war the company prepared armoured bodies for cars and trucks.

VCM

NACKE (D) 1901–1913
Automobilfabrik E. Nacke, Coswig.

Emil Hermann Nacke was already a manufacturer of machine tools when he started car making. Early models were called Coswiga after their home town. By 1906 Nacke was making two large 4-cylinder cars of 5192cc (20/45PS) and 6782cc 26/55PS, with chain drive. He was a personal friend of August Horch, and there was some technical collaboration between the two companies. By 1910 Nacke was making smaller cars with pair-cast cylinders and overhead inlet valves such as the 2612cc 10/25PS (1910–1913) and 2071cc 8/22PS (1912–1913). The last passenger car was the 3564cc 14/35PS, made from 1912 to 1913. Production of commercial vehicles became increasingly important, and led to the abandonment of passenger cars. Truck chassis were made up to 1931.

HON

1902 NAG-Klingenberg tonneau.
HANS-OTTO NEUBAUER

1911 NAG electric coupé.
HANS-OTTO NEUBAUER

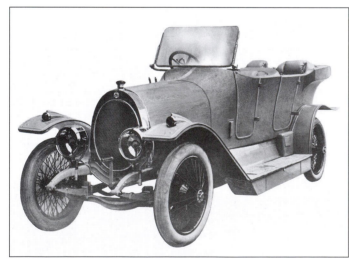

1913 NAG K5 25hp tulip sports tourer by Kellner.
NATIONAL MOTOR MUSEUM

NAF (US) c.1979–1993
North American Fiberglass, Tempe, Arizona.
In addition to their successful line of 289 and 427 Cobra replicas, NAF built other kit cars of interest. The Dolphin looked like a Lotus 7 Series IV, but the resemblance ended at the bodywork. The tubular frame mounted a Datsun 210 engine and transmission with Datsun 510 irs and Opel 1900 front suspension. It was sold in kit or assembled form. The Shrike GT was an attractive mid-engined sports car that accepted transverse GM 4- and 6-cylinder engines as well as V8s on Oldsmobile Toronado transaxles. Front suspension could be Opel, Ford Mustang or custom fabricated units. Brakes were 4-wheel discs. The low and racy coupé body was an original design. The NAF Cobra replicas used MGB front suspension combined with a Jaguar irs unit. In 1984 they added a Cobra Daytona Coupé replica that fitted the same chassis. This was an unusual 'replica', in that they started with an unused extra body from the Willment Cobra coupé built in England, and changed the nose to match the Pete Brock Daytona coupé design. Supposedly, only three bodies were made. This same body was later resurrected by Johnex in Canada. In 1992 NAF introduced a racing version of their 427 Cobra replica with huge wheel flares to cover larger tyres, and a Fiero-based Ford GT-40 replica.
HP

NAG (D) 1901–1934
1901–1908 Allgemeine Elektrizitäts-Gesellschaft, Berlin.
1908–1915 Neue Automobil-Gesellschaft, Berlin.
1915–1934 Nationale Automobil-Gesellschaft, Berlin.
The Neue Automobil Gesellschaft was a division of the famous electrical firm AEG (Allgemeine Elektrizitäts-Gesellschaft). In 1900 Emil Rathenau, a director of AEG, acquired the rights to manufacture a small car which had been designed by Professor Georg Klingenberg of Berlin-Charlottenburg's Technical High School. A few of these had already been made and sold under the names AAG or Klingenberg. It was a light car for two or four passengers powered by a 5hp single-cylinder engine. An unusual feature was that the engine, gearbox and differential were mounted in a single unit on the rear axle. By December 1901 cars of this type were being marketed under the name NAG-Klingenberg, and front-engined developments followed. In 1902 there were 10PS 2-cylinder and 20PS 4-cylinder cars with rear-entrance tonneau bodies and double-chain drive. Designed by Joseph Vollmer, formerly chief engineer of the Kühlstein; in Wagenbau, these were simply called NAGs.

Helped by successful commercial vehicle sales, NAG prospered over the next few years, making ever larger cars up to the 33/75PS 8½-litre K8 which was made from 1905 to 1914. The valves were in a T-head up to 1912, thereafter L-head. An unusual feature of the 1904 20/24PS Typ B was the use of ¾-elliptic front suspension and semi-elliptics at the rear. This does not seem to have been used on later NAG models. Among distinguished owners of NAG cars were the Kaiser, who ordered one for himself in 1905 and another for his wife two years later, and the King of Rumania who bought 17 NAGs between 1905 and 1914. In 1908 NAG adopted a graceful oval radiator that characterised their cars up to 1914, and also introduced an important new model, the 1570cc 4-cylinder Puck. This was an up to date design with a monobloc L-head engine, detachable artillery wheels and shaft drive. It sold in larger numbers than the bigger NAGs, so well in fact that NAG ordered a batch of G4 chassis from Stoewer. These were very similar to the Puck, having the same cylinder dimensions. They were bodied by the NAG at their Berlin factory, and sold under the name NAG Puck. In 1911 the Puck was replaced by the Darling; this had the same size engine but a 3-bearing crankshaft and an output of 18bhp, 6bhp more than the Puck had offered. One of these cars, driven by Karlsson, dominated the light car class of the Swedish Winter Trials for three years in succession. The last of the T-head cars was made in 1912, and thereafter all NAGs held 4-cylinder L-head engines. In 1914 there were five models, from the 6/18PS Darling to the 33/75PS K8. They also made a small number of light electric cars with Renault-style bonnets, and electric taxicabs. NAG was now one of the largest vehicle manufacturers in Germany with annual production of over 2000. A considerable number of these were trucks and buses. In 1907 NAG became a wholly-owned subsidiary of AEG, and the company name was changed to Nationale Automobil Gesellschaft in 1915. They prospered during the war making trucks and 200hp Benz aero-engines, and in 1919 combined with Brennabor and Hansa to form the GDA (Gemeinschaft Deutscher Automobilfabriken); this was a sales organisation, and there was no interchange of design between the three makes. In 1914 NAG acquired the services of Christian Riecken who had worked as a designer for Métallurgique and Minerva. It was he who produced their single postwar model, the 2553cc C4 4-cylinder car. It had an attractive rounded vee-radiator not unlike that of the contemporary Delaunay-Belleville, but was a conservative design with fixed cylinder head and separate four-speed gearbox. It was followed in 1923 by the D4 which boasted an ohv engine of 2598cc, and a detachable head. It also had Perrot 4-wheel brakes as standard, being the first medium-priced German car to be so equipped. The C4 and D4 had a very staid appearance, with their artillery wheels and upright lines, but they sold well, finding about 5000 customers between 1920 and 1927.

From the C4 was derived an attractive and successful sports car, the C4b. The tourer's 30bhp at 1700 rpm was raised to 45bhp at 2700rpm, and the axle ratio was also raised. This gave a top speed of around 75mph (120km/h), a good 25mph (40km/h) more than the C4. These cars had wire wheels in place of the artilleries of the tourers. Riecken was not only a designer but a very able driver, and had many successes with sports and racing versions of the C4b. A 24-hour record at Monza, earned the name Monza for subsequent examples of the C4b. Four cars were entered in the 1926 German GP, and Riecken finished 2nd at 83.95mph (135.1km/h), being defeated only by Caracciola on a 2-litre straight-8 Mercedes which gave 160bhp against the nominal 45bhp of Riecken's car.

The GDA was disbanded in 1926, the year in which NAG bought the Protos company from another electrical firm, Siemens-Schuckert. In 1927 they bought up the Presto company of Chemnitz which also owned the moribund Dux Automobilwerke of Leipzig. These acquisitions resulted in a new range of cars to replace the D4, and not before time. The new models were known as NAG-Protos, and had pushrod ohv 6-cylinder engines in 3075cc (Typ D6) and 3594cc (D7) sizes. In 1928 these were renamed the Typs 201 and 204, and were joined two years later by the 3963cc Typs 207 and 208. These larger models had hydraulic brakes and centralised chassis lubrication. The 208 was a sports cabriolet and was slightly lower and lighter than the 207s, although overall dimensions were the same. There were also two models of NAG-Presto in 2613 and 3119cc sizes with 6-cylinder side-valve engines. These were inherited from the Presto range, and were made with the NAG name in 1928 only. They had flat radiators, and looked not unlike the Fiat 525. About 1000 Presto and NAG-Presto cars were made, compared with 2000 NAG-Protos, which ran from 1926 to 1934.

In 1929 NAG gained a new designer in Paul Henze who had previously worked for Imperia, Steiger, Simson and Selve. He designed for NAG a 4508cc 100bhp V8 engine which was installed in the Typ 207/208 chassis, the new model being called the Typ 218/219. With bodies by Drauz they were handsome machines, competing with the Mercedes-Benz Mannheim, but cost RM3000–4000 more. Prices were sharply reduced in 1934, but by that time NAG was practically out of business. Not more than 50 V8s were sold. In 1930 the front-wheel drive expert Richard Bussien joined NAG and used Henze's V8 engine turned round and installed in a backbone frame chassis with all-round independent suspension. This Typ 212 was too advanced to sell in the Depression years, and only the one prototype was made. NAG then changed tack altogether and produced the NAG-Voran 220, a small front-drive car with a flat four air-cooled engine of 1484cc developing 30bhp. It had a DKW-like chassisless construction with wooden body panelled in steel and covered in fabric. Front suspension was of the Lancia-type coil and sliding pillar, and the brakes were hydraulic. It was an advanced little car, and in the hands of another firm might have done well, but NAG's finances were shaky and their works old-fashioned and ill-equipped. Only 383 NAG-Vorans were made in 1933 and 1934. Most had 2-door cabrio-limousine bodies, but there were some 4-door taxicabs on a longer wheelbase. In August 1934 NAG withdrew from car manufacture, although the name survived for a further 15 years on Büssing-NAG trucks and buses, as they had merged with the heavy vehicle firm in 1931. NAG's Berlin factory was used by the parent company, AEG, for electrical work up to 1945 when it was nationalised by the East German government.

NG

Further Reading
Autos aus Berlin, Protos und NAG, Hans-Otto Neubauer, Kohlhammer, 1983.

NAGANT (B) 1899–1929

1899–1928 Fabrique d'Armes et d'Automobiles Nagant Frères, Liège.
1928–1929 SA des Automobiles Imperia-Excelsior, Liège.
Established by the brothers Léon and Maurice Nagant, this company made armaments, electrical equipment and machine tools, turning to cars in 1899 when they began to make the French GOBRON-BRILLIÉ opposed-piston engine under licence. This licence was in fact handled by Albert Roland who operated an agency from the same address as Nagant Frères. They made 2- and 4-cylinder versions of this, in passenger and goods-carrying forms, up to 1904, selling them under the name Gobron-Nagant. About 150 per year were made up to

1925 NAG D4 10/45PS coupé de ville by Kühlstein.
HALWART SCHRADER

1928 NAG-Presto Typ F 10/50PS tourer.
NICK GEORGANO

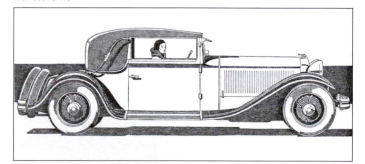

1930 NAG Typ 208 sport-cabriolet.
HANS-OTTO NEUBAUER

1932 NAG Typ 212 V8 front-wheel drive saloon.
NATIONAL MOTOR MUSEUM

1907 Nagant-Hobson 35/40hp tourer.
NICK BALDWIN

1927 Nami-1 tourer.
MARGUS H. KUUSE

the end of 1904, when Roland took out another licence, to make ROCHET-SCHNEIDER cars. These were built to be sold under the Nagant name and also as LOCOMOTRICE.

The first Nagant cars proper were designed by the German engineer Ernst Valentin, and marketed from 1907. These had 4-cylinder L-head engines and chain drive, being made in 24 and 40hp models. These cars were sold in France under the name Busson-Dedyn and in England as Nagant-Hobson, while the German company, Achenbach of Hamburg, made them under licence as the HEXE. Valentin left in 1909 to join PROTOS, and was replaced by Dufresne. He was responsible for the range made up to the outbreak of war. In 1913 there were six models, from a 1855cc 10/12CV to a 5292cc 30/40CV, all with 4-cylinder engines and shaft drive. The last prewar design was the 4534cc 20/25CV, with monobloc 4-cylinder engine. This was the basis of the engine used in Nagant's two cars entered in the 1914 Grand Prix, though these had inclined ohvs operated by ohcs. Considering the relatively small size of Nagant, Esser did well to finish sixth, behind three Mercedes, a Peugeot and a Sunbeam.

The Nagant story in the 1920s was similar to most Belgian makes; despite well-made cars there was a gradual decline in sales due to foreign competition and the inability to make economies which were available to the mass producers. At the 1919 Paris Salon they showed a 3014cc car derived from prewar designs, at first with a side-valve engine, but with ohvs and a detachable head from 1921. It was replaced by smaller models, the 1953cc 10CV and 2120cc 15CV. From 1923 the 15CV became the sole model. It was quite a modern design, with hemispherical combustion chambers, 4-speed gearbox and 4-wheel brakes on the Adex system made by Excelsior.

At the 1925 Brussels Salon Nagant announced a 2930cc 6-cylinder model, and in 1926 a small six of 1982cc, but few were made as Nagant production was winding down. At the 1927 Paris Salon Nagant showed a 1¹/₂-litre straight-8 2-stroke engine but it was never put into a car. In 1928 they were bought up by

the Imperia group and production ended. A few cars were still being sold off in 1929.
NG

NAGIL (F) 1980–1983
Nagil S.A., Sete.
Gilbert Nadal built a Citroën Méhari-inspired open-top 4-seater based on the chassis and running gear of the Renault 4. The Nagil (an abbreviation of Na(dal) Gil(bert)) had a fibreglass body and a full-length detachable roof. Nadal built around 80 Nagils, a handful of which were fitted with Renault 5 Alpine 1.3-litre engines.
CR

NAIG (D) 1909–1911
Neue Automobil-Industrie GmbH, Berlin-Charlottenberg.
This company made a small number of voiturettes, whose technical details are not known.
HON

NALLE MOTORS (US) c.1988
Nalle Motors, Richmond, Virginia.
Tom Nalle noted the similar shapes of the Datsun 240Z and the Cobra Daytona Coupé and did something about it. Nalle sold a simple conversion kit with fibreglass panels to convert the inexpensive Datsun to Cobra looks. Original Datsun engines could be used, or Nalle offered an engine swap kit to install a Ford 5000cc V8. The lines were not too convincing.
HP

NAMCO (GR) 1976–1985
Namco SA, Thessaloniki.
The Pony was a rustic leisure/work vehicle with open steel bodywork. It used the Citroën 2CV floorpan unchanged and was offered in 2- and 5-seater forms, as well as commercial variants. A fibreglass hard-top was offered as an option. As many as 4000 units were produced annually, leading to a grand total of around 17,000 2CV-based cars built in all. The company later collaborated with the German-sponsored INTHELCO operation to produce a Ford Fiesta-based model.
CR

NAMELESS (GB) 1908–1909
Nameless Motor Car Co., Hendon, London.
The founders of this company either lacked the imagination to think up a name for their car, or perhaps believed that Nameless would attract more attention. It was a conventional machine powered by a 15.9hp 4-cylinder White & Poppe engine. The chassis price was £290.
NG

NAMI-1 (SU) 1927–1931
Spartak Works, Moscow.
Designed at the scientific Auto-Motor Institute (the NAMI) under Konstantin Sharapov, this model was a Russian equivalent to Hans Ledwinka's TATRA Type 11/12. The NAMI-1, a light 4-seater with a touring bodywork, had a backbone chassis and a 2-cylinder, 1.16-litre air-cooled engine, developing 20bhp. For better traction there was no differential in the transmission, but even at the moderate speeds this model was capable of (43.5mph (70km/h) maximum) its handling was hampered due to this simplification. There were other problems, like high fuel consumption and breakdowns were common. In 1927 just three cars were completed, but over the three following years something production-like was organised at the former P. Iljin works of Moscow, re-named Spartak by the Communists. The auto industry bosses at Avtotrest decided to close the production down for 1931 and Spartak was given a task to supply various parts, including radiators, for use at the KIM and another assembly works where Ford cars and trucks were made. By most optimistic estimates about 360 to 400 NAMI-1 were assembled. Sharapov and his team worked at the following model NATI-2, this time with a 4 cylinder, 1.2-litre engine. A few prototypes were completed, including a 2-seater and a pickup, but the project was quietly closed down.
MHK

NANCE *see* TOURAINE

NANCÉIENNE (F) 1900–1903

Sté Nancéienne d'Automobiles, Nancy.

This company built cars and commercial vehicles powered by the opposed-piston engine made under licence from GOBRON-BRILLIÉ. Most were commercials but some cars were made with engines designed to run on alcohol fuel. A Nancéienne won the 1901 Paris-Roubaix Race for alcohol-fuelled cars, and a 10hp 4-seater averaged 27mph (43km/h) in the Paris–Berlin race, also in 1901.

NG

NAPIER (GB) 1900–1924

1900–1903 D. Napier & Son Ltd, Lambeth, London;
1903–1924 Acton, London.

The engineering firm of D. Napier & Son had a distinguished history dating back to 1808, when Scots-born David Napier set up his business in London's Soho, moving to Lambeth in 1830. Among their products were gun-finishing and bullet-making machinery, and machines for printing stamps and banknotes and for minting coins. However the company was in decline by the 1890s, and when James Murdoch Napier, son of the founder, died in 1895, there were only seven employees at Lambeth. James' son Montague was a keen cyclist, and his hobby brought him in contact with Selwyn Francis Edge, also a racing cyclist and a budding motorist. He asked Napier to make improvements to his 1896 Panhard, which included replacing the tiller with a steering wheel, adding a radiator and replacing the hot-tube ignition by battery and coil. Edge was sufficiently impressed to promise Napier that he would buy his complete output of cars, should he go into production, and so long as he had exclusive rights. It was the same arrangement as that reached by Rolls and Royce a few years later.

The first Napier car was made in 1900, using a similar engine to Edge's 'improved Panhard'; with it Edge won a Bronze Medal in the Thousand Miles Trial, and it was followed the same year by a larger car with 4.9-litre 4-cylinder engine which developed 24hp, though Napier only called it a 16hp. This and the 8hp twin were made into 1901, when there was also a monstrous car with 16,304cc 4-cylinder engine (165.1 × 190.5mm), which developed 103bhp, though Napier designated it a 50hp. It took part in the Paris-Bordeaux and Paris-Berlin Races of 1901, although without success, and was actually catalogued at £1500, but only two were built. Napier and Edge redeemed themselves in 1902 when Edge won the Gordon Bennett Race in a 30hp 4-cylinder car, the first win for a British car in a major international event. Sales of the 16hp began in 1900, and hire purchase was available from November 1901. Early customers included Prime Minister Arthur Balfour and Mrs Edward Kennard, wife of the owner of the Thousand Miles Trial car. She was enthusiastic about her 1902 Napier: 'she answers to the change speed lever as does a high-mettled hunter to the touch of a spur'.

Napier built 250 cars in 1903, but this strained the premises at Lambeth to the seams, and in the summer of that year they moved to a new factory built on a 4-acre site at Acton in West London. In October they announced an 18/30hp 6-cylinder car, which Edge proclaimed as the first of its kind in the world. Counter claims have been made, particularly for the Spyker racing car (which also had 4-wheel drive), but this was a one-off competition car, whereas the Napier went into production and led to an all 6-cylinder range within a few years. The Napier's image was so linked to the 6-cylinder theme that when they built three 4-cylinder cars for the 1908 Tourist Trophy Race, they were entered under the name Hutton.

The 18/30hp six joined chain-driven fours of 15 and 24hp, and a shaft-driven 30hp four, but by 1906 they were making only two chassis, the 4998cc Forty and 7750cc Sixty, both with 6-cylinder engines and shaft drive. In 1907 a workforce of 1200 men turned out only two cars per week. This labour-intensive work inevitably made the cars very expensive. A 60hp chassis cost £1200, making it the most costly British car. The years 1906 to 1911 saw Napier's reputation at its peak; the 1910 catalogue listed more than 160 members of the aristocracy, army and church among Napier customers, and the make was particularly popular with Indian rulers. The largest chassis was the 14,184cc, called an 80hp in 1907/08 and a 90hp from 1909 to 1912. It was built largely for India, some were 240in (6091mm) long and had three or even four rows of seats. Some were also made for competition, including the two survivors.

In July 1907 Edge re-organised his company as S.F. Edge (1907) Ltd, promising

1902 Nancéienne tonneau.
NATIONAL MOTOR MUSEUM

c.1901 Napier 16hp 2-seater. Charles Jarrott at the wheel.
NICK BALDWIN

c.1907 Napier 60hp tourer.
NICK BALDWIN

not to handle any other make of car (he had been selling Gladiators up to then), so long as Napier provided him with at least £160,000 worth of cars per year. This worked for a while, but in 1911 Edge complained that the cars were old-fashioned and of poorer quality than before. Napier retorted that Edge was not taking up the agreed minimum. In 1912 Edge issued a writ accusing Napier of supplying unsatisfactory cars. A series of actions followed which culminated in Napier buying up Edge's company for £152,000. Edge agreed not to engage in the motor trade for seven years; he kept to this and in 1919 became involved with AC.

Despite Edge's misgivings, Napier production was at its peak in the years 1909–1913. About 600–750 cars were made annually, compared with only 100 in 1907. The all-6-cylinder policy had been well and truly abandoned, with

1913 Napier 15hp Colonial tourer.
NICK BALDWIN

small 2- and 4-cylinder chassis being offered, although the former were mostly bodied as taxicabs. London had more than 600 Napier cabs in 1912, and cab production exceeded that of cars in 1910, being 556 compared with 356. In 1912 the figures were reversed, deliveries being 574 passenger cars, 122 cabs and 95 commercial vehicles. One of the best prewar Napiers was the 4738cc 30/35hp six which was made from 1909 to 1915. There was also a 2680cc 4-cylinder 15hp which was made in Colonial forms with higher ground clearance, as the

'Colonial' or 'Extra-Strong Colonial' models. Car production dropped to 300 in 1914, while demand from the cab trade almost completely dried up.

Napier had two foreign operations during the Edwardian period. From 1904 to 1912 the Napier Motor Car Co. of America built about 100 4- and 6-cylinder cars, at first in Boston and from mid–1905 at Jamaica Plain, Massachusetts. They had either locally-built bodies or, at a higher price, bodies imported from Britain. One model, the 18hp 4-cylinder Nike roadster, had no British equivalent. From 1906 to 1909 Napiers were also made in Italy under the name SAN GIORGIO.

During the war Napier made about 2000 trucks for the War Department, but more important in the long term was their introduction to aero-engines. They made the Sunbeam Arab V8 and RAF 3a V12 under licence, and in 1916 developed their own Napier Lion, a 500bhp broad-arrow 12 which not only poweredmany aeroplanes but also 1920s Land Speed Record cars such as Campbell's Bluebirds and the 1931 Golden Arrow driven by Sir Henry Segrave.

In 1919 Montague Napier returned to car production with a 6175cc single-ohc six designed by A.J. Rowledge. It had monobloc casting with aluminium cylinders and steel lining, and dual ignition. Chassis features included a 4-speed separate gearbox with central change, cantilever suspension and a foot transmission brake. Known as the T75, it was more advanced than any prewar Napier and beautifully built, but at £2100 for a chassis, it cost the same as a Silver Ghost but somehow lacked the cachet of the car from Derby. Bodies were mostly by Cunard which was a subsidiary of Napier. Planned production was 500 chassis, but only 187 were made, production ending in November 1924. Of the total of 187, 120 were the T75, 17 the T77 which was a Colonial model with different

NICK BALDWIN

EDGE, SELWYN FRANCIS (1868–1940)

Selwyn Francis Edge was always ambitious. An astute businessman, he was also a dauntless racing driver of enormous mental and physical strength, and his will-power dominated every aspect of his activity. Such a man made many enemies and few friends.

Born in Sydney, New South Wales, Australia, he cut short his formal schooling, went to England as a youth, and staked his future on an ability to propel any kind of bicycle faster than anyone else. An affinity for motor cars came to life in 1895 when Fernand Charron took him for a ride in a Panhard-Levassor.

He had a comfortable income as manager of Dunlop's London Branch at 14 Regent Street in 1896, when he bought a De Dion-Bouton tricycle and began entering it in races.

In 1899 he formed a partnership with Charles Jarrott and Herbert Osbaldestan Duncan in founding the De Dion-Bouton British & Colonial Syndicate, with a capital of £10,000. Along with other importers of motor vehicles, this company had to pay royalties to H.J. Lawsons' British Motor Syndicate. That ended in Edge's favour when Lawson's syndicate went into liquidation and its assets were taken over by a new company, British Motor Traction Co. Ltd. To retain their stake, the shareholders in Lawson's syndicate had to make fresh cash payments, which deterred many of them. S.F. Edge stepped in to snatch up all the options for a relatively minor outlay and took control of the British Motor Traction Co.

Edge had made a friend of Montague Stanley Napier when both were members of the Bath Road Club as amateur cyclists, and in 1898 Edge asked Napier to make some modifications to his Panhard-Levassor in the Napier works at Lambeth, London. The job was so well done that Edge went to inspect the Napier works and decided that the factory had all that was needed to make complete motor cars.

In October 1899 Edge and Harvey du Cros Sr announced that they had founded The Motor Vehicle Co. to distribute a car, designed to resemble the successful Panhard, manufactured by D. Napier & Son, with bodies built by Mulliner's of Northampton. Edge drove Napier cars in races, and even won the Gordon Bennett cup in 1902. He also set a world's record for a one-man 24-hour run at Brooklands in 1907 which stood for 17 years. He entertained a busy correspondence with the press and all rivals, in business and in the sport, defending his interests in fearless and forthright terms.

In 1913 he was elected President of the Society of Motor Manufacturers and Traders.

In 1912 he sold his holdings in S.F. Edge Ltd to D.Napier & Son Ltd and resigned from his position as its chief executive officer.

During World War I he served in the Ministry of Munitions, where he first came in contact with Autocarriers Ltd.

His contract with Napier, however, precluded him from any work for a motor vehicle manufacturer for seven years. It eventually ran out in October 1919, and Edge began buying shares in A.C., initially at a modest level, but by 1921 he held so big a stake that he was invited to join the A.C. board of directors. A year later, he took complete control of A.C. and served as its chief executive until 1929.

He sold his interest in A.C. and played no further part in the motor industry. He died in February 1940.

JPN

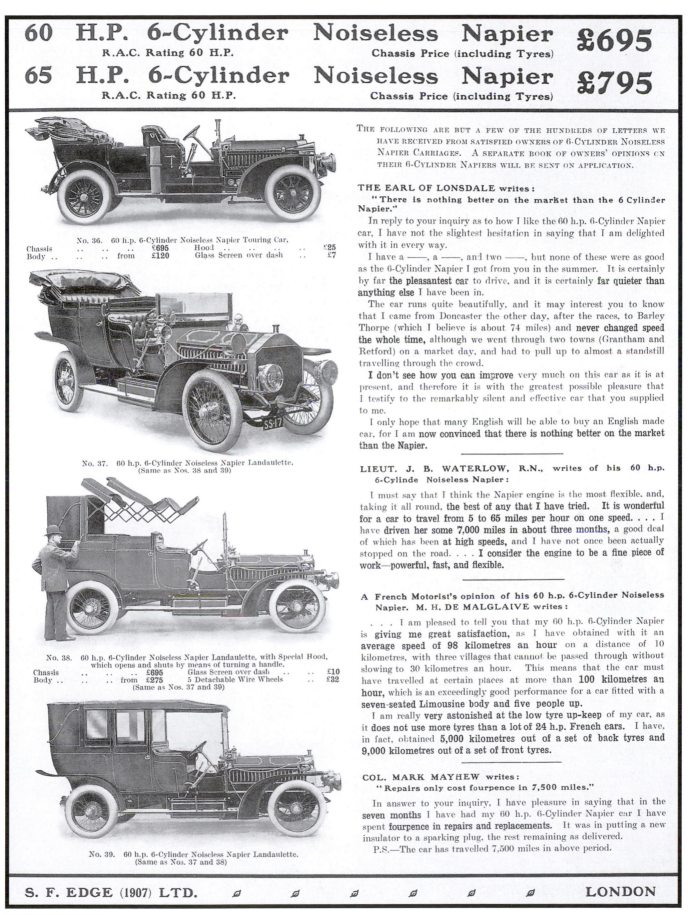

60 H.P. 6-Cylinder Noiseless Napier £695
R.A.C. Rating 60 H.P.   Chassis Price (including Tyres)

65 H.P. 6-Cylinder Noiseless Napier £795
R.A.C. Rating 60 H.P.   Chassis Price (including Tyres)

No. 36. 60 h.p. 6-Cylinder Noiseless Napier Touring Car.

| Chassis | .. | .. | £695 | Hood .. | .. | .. | £25 |
| Body .. | .. | from | £120 | Glass Screen over dash | .. | £7 |

No. 37. 60 h.p. 6-Cylinder Noiseless Napier Landaulette.
(Same as Nos. 38 and 39.)

No. 38. 60 h.p. 6-Cylinder Noiseless Napier Landaulette, with Special Hood,
which opens and shuts by means of turning a handle.

| Chassis | .. | .. | £695 | Glass Screen over dash | .. | £10 |
| Body .. | .. | from | £275 | 5 Detachable Wire Wheels | .. | £32 |

(Same as Nos. 37 and 39.)

No. 39. 60 h.p. 6-Cylinder Noiseless Napier Landaulette.
(Same as Nos. 37 and 38.)

THE FOLLOWING ARE BUT A FEW OF THE HUNDREDS OF LETTERS WE HAVE RECEIVED FROM SATISFIED OWNERS OF 6-CYLINDER NOISELESS NAPIER CARRIAGES. A SEPARATE BOOK OF OWNERS' OPINIONS ON THEIR 6-CYLINDER NAPIERS WILL BE SENT ON APPLICATION.

THE EARL OF LONSDALE writes :

" There is nothing better on the market than the 6 Cylinder Napier."

In reply to your inquiry as to how I like the 60 h.p. 6-Cylinder Napier car, I have not the slightest hesitation in saying that I am delighted with it in every way.

I have a ——, a ——, and two ——, but none of these were as good as the 6-Cylinder Napier I got from you in the summer. It is certainly by far the pleasantest car to drive, and it is certainly far quieter than anything else I have been in.

The car runs quite beautifully, and it may interest you to know that I came from Doncaster the other day, after the races, to Barley Thorpe (which I believe is about 74 miles) and never changed speed the whole time, although we went through two towns (Grantham and Retford) on a market day, and had to pull up to almost a standstill travelling through the crowd.

I don't see how you can improve very much on this car as it is at present, and therefore it is with the greatest possible pleasure that I testify to the remarkably silent and effective car that you supplied to me.

I only hope that many English will be able to buy an English made car, for I am now convinced that there is nothing better on the market than the Napier.

LIEUT. J. B. WATERLOW, R.N., writes of his 60 h.p. 6-Cylinde Noiseless Napier :

I must say that I think the Napier engine is the most flexible, and, taking it all round, the best of any that I have tried. It is wonderful for a car to travel from 5 to 65 miles per hour on one speed. . . . I have driven her some 7,000 miles in about three months, a good deal of which has been at high speeds, and I have not once been actually stopped on the road. . . . I consider the engine to be a fine piece of work—powerful, fast, and flexible.

A French Motorist's opinion of his 60 h.p. 6-Cylinder Noiseless Napier. M. H. DE MALGLAIVE writes :

. . . I am pleased to tell you that my 60 h.p. 6-Cylinder Napier is giving me great satisfaction, as I have obtained with it an average speed of 98 kilometres an hour on a distance of 10 kilometres, with three villages that cannot be passed through without slowing to 30 kilometres an hour. This means that the car must have travelled at certain places at more than 100 kilometres an hour, which is an exceedingly good performance for a car fitted with a seven-seated Limousine body and five people up.

I am really very astonished at the low tyre up-keep of my car, as it does not use more tyres than a lot of 24 h.p. French cars. I have, in fact, obtained 5,000 kilometres out of a set of back tyres and 9,000 kilometres out of a set of front tyres.

COL. MARK MAYHEW writes :

" Repairs only cost fourpence in 7,500 miles."

In answer to your inquiry, I have pleasure in saying that in the seven months I have had my 60 h.p. 6-Cylinder Napier car I have spent fourpence in repairs and replacements. It was in putting a new insulator to a sparking plug, the rest remaining as delivered.

P.S.—The car has travelled 7,500 miles in above period.

S. F. EDGE (1907) LTD.   **LONDON**

1910 Napier 40hp Purdah Wagon for the Nizam of Hyderabad.
NICK BALDWIN

1919 Napier T75 40/50hp tourer.
NICK BALDWIN

frame, 45 the T79 with a 144in (3655mm) wheelbase and five the T80 with a 137in (3477mm) wheelbase. The T81 and 82 were to have been 4-wheel braked versions of the T79 and 80, but they were never built.

There were rumours of a Napier-Bentley in 1931, when Napier showed an interest in buying Bentley, but they were outbid by Rolls-Royce. At the same time they developed a 3-wheeled mechanical horse, but their heart was not in such mundane work, and they sold the project to Scammell who produced it successfully for many years.

Napier continued to be very successful in the aero-engine field, notably with the H-formation engines of 16- and 24-cylinders designed by Major Frank Halford who had raced a 1 1/2-litre Grand Prix car of his own design at Brooklands. In 1945 Napier was taken over by English Electric.

NG

Further Reading
Lost Causes of Motoring, Lord Montagu of Beaulieu, Cassell, 1960.
The 40/50 Napier, Ronald Barker, Profile Publications, 1966.
The First to Wear the Green, David Venables, Haynes, 1998.
'Edwardian Giant: The Napier Story', Ronald Barker,
Automobile Quarterly, Vol. 17, No. 3.

NAPOLEON (US) 1916–1919
1916–1917 Napoleon Motor Car Co., Napoleon, Ohio.
1917–1919 Traverse City Motor Car Co., Traverse City, Michigan.
This was a conventional light car powered initially by a 17hp 4-cylinder engine, although it was also quoted as a 30hp, and the rating was increased to 37hp in 1918 after the move to Traverse City. Although launched in Napoleon, most of the cars were made in Traverse City. Also in 1918 a 45hp 6-cylinder car was added to the range. Bodies were tourers and roadsters, with a 6-seater tourer only on the 45hp chassis. About 300 Napoleons were made up to 1919 when they began making trucks, which lasted until 1923.

NG

NARDI (i) (I) 1947–1964
1947–1950 Nardi-Danese, Turin.
1951–1964 Officine Enrico Nardi, Turin.
Enrico Nardi began his career as an engine tuner and special builder in the 1930s and, helped create the Auto Avia 815, Enzo Ferrari's first car. From 1947, Nardi made tuning equipment, accessories and, occasionally, cars. Until 1950, Nardi was in partnership with Renato Danese and the cars were called Nardi-Danese.

An attempt to break into the 500cc Formula 3 market in 1951 was a failure, but Nardi had better luck with dual-purpose specials, each with a multi-tubular frame and Fiat suspension. Engines included Panhard, BMW, Universal, Alfa Romeo, Lancia, Crosley, Giannini, and Fiat. An eccentric twin-boom Nardi ran at Le Mans in 1955, entirely without distinction.

Nardi largely gave up on cars after 1957 although, in 1959, he attempted to market a Fiat 600 with a Vignale body and, in 1964, built a coupé for Chrysler with a Michelotti body and a 350bhp Plymouth V8 engine.

Nardi's reputation, however, rests on his hand-crafted steering wheels and works-approved equipment such as the floor-change conversion for the Lancia Aurelia D20.

MJL

NARDI (ii) (E) 1959–1966
Nardi Española SA, Zaragoza.
The Italian Enrico Nardi was one of the four partners of Nardi Española, preparing modified Seat 600s with excellent sporting bodies, designed by Michelotti. The

engine of the 600 was enlarged to 750cc, 850cc and 952cc, and the compression raised from 7.5:1 to 9.5:1, and the cars used a 2-barrel Weber carburettor. The Spanish Nardi also formed an official competition team and entered the Nardi 1000 in several races, with great success.

VCM

NARDINI (F) 1914

This was a light car built in France to the order of a Monsieur Nardini who sold it in England from premises in London's Shaftesbury Avenue. The engines were 4-cylinder Altos units of 1094 and 1778cc, and it has been suggested that the chassis were also made by Altos, but there is no proof of this. However, an alternative London address was Altos Ltd, Vauxhall Bridge Road, which was perhaps the depot, while Shaftesbury Avenue was the showroom. The bodies were conventional 2- and 4-seaters.

NG

NASH (US) 1917–1957

1917–1954 Nash Motor Co., Kenosha, Wisconsin.
1954–1957 American Motors Corp., Kenosha, Wisconsin.
The Nash Motor Co. was incorporated in July 1916 as a result of the take-over of the Jeffrey Motor Co. by Charles W. Nash. Nash had been President of General Motors for four years, but resigned after disagreements with Billy Durant. For more than a year he continued production of the Jeffrey, a conventional 6-cylinder car, although by the summer of 1917 they were carrying Nash nameplates. The first Nash car proper arrived in the autumn of 1917 as a 1918 model. It had a 6-cylinder ohv engine designed by Finnish-born Nils Erik Wahlberg. The 4080cc engine developed 67bhp and the rest of the design was conventional enough. Five body styles were offered during the first year at prices from $1295 for a 4-door tourer to $2085 for a 2-door 4-seater coupé. Despite his factory's preoccupation with making 4-wheel drive trucks for the US Army, Nash delivered 10,283 cars during the first year. This figure rose to 27,081 in 1919, and 35,084 in 1920. To ensure an adequate supply of bodies Nash bought a 50 per cent interest in the Seaman Body Corp. of Milwaukee, and in 1936 this became 100 per cent Nash-owned.

Nash quickly began to expand his range, bringing out in 1921 a 4-cylinder car powered by a 2718cc engine which was essentially his six with two fewer cylinders. For 1923 Nash had three models, from the 4-cylinder Model 41 starting at $1395 up to the LAFAYETTE priced at between $5025 and $7500. This luxury car did not last beyond 1924, though 1859 were built. Both this and the Nash Four were made in Milwaukee; the machinery from the original Lafayette plant at Mars Hill, Indiana, was shipped to the old Mitchell factory in Racine, Wisconsin where Charlie Nash was to begin building the AJAX (vi) car in 1925.

After a dip in production to 20,850 in 1920, due to a nationwide recession, profits picked up, and by 1925 Nash was making 85,428 cars, 50 per cent up on the 1924 figure. There was little change in design during these years, although a taller radiator and drum headlamps identified the 1922 cars and nickel radiator shells were featured. In May 1925 the Ajax was announced as an independent marque made in a separate factory at Racine. It had a 2786cc side-valve 6-cylinder engine, and was available in two body styles only, a five-passenger tourer at $865 and a sedan at $995. First year sales were quite encouraging at 22,122, but Charlie Nash hoped for more and felt that perhaps the Ajax lacked appeal because it did not have a Nash nameplate. Consequently, a year after its introduction, the Ajax was re-named Nash Light Six. New nameplates and hub caps were made available to Nash dealers so that they might update any Ajaxes they might have on hand. As the Light Six, it was continued to 1927, when a slightly larger Standard Six replaced it. There were also the larger 3400cc Special Six and 4652cc Advanced Six. Front-wheel brakes were introduced on all Nashes in 1925. Sales reached six figures (122,606) in 1927, rising to 138,137 the following year.

The Nash was now a well-respected car in many parts of the world (exports accounted for 10.8 per cent of production in 1927). Several foreign monarchs were Nash customers, including King Carol of Rumania, Queen Alexandrine of Denmark, Prince Wilhelm of Sweden and King Ghazi I of Iraq. In America, such distinguished families as the Rockefellers and the Vanderbilts owned Nashes.

Twin ignition was introduced on the 1928 models; this was not the dual ignition involving magneto and coil that some expensive European cars featured, but simply the employment of two sparking plugs per cylinder. It also featured

1927 Nash Advanced Six sedan.
NATIONAL MOTOR MUSEUM

1934 Nash Lafayette Six brougham.
NICK GEORGANO/NATIONAL MOTOR MUSEUM

on Nash's first straight-8 which was introduced for the 1930 season. This had a 4893cc engine developing 100bhp, and was offered on two wheelbases, 124 and 133in (3147 and 3375mm). There were seven body styles. Prices were fairly reasonable, $1625 to $2260. Nash sales were inevitably hit by the Depression, but thanks to Charlie Nash's careful management, not so seriously as some other firms. In 1932 Nash was the only American car maker apart from General Motors to register a profit, despite poor sales of only 20,233 cars.

Smaller straight-8s were introduced for 1931, a 3922cc ohv and a 3719cc side-valve. This gave Nash three eights and only one six in their range. For 1932 capacities of the big eights went up to 4260 and 5276cc, with power outputs of 100 and 125bhp. 1932 also saw considerable restyling with handsome vee-radiators.

Nashes were restyled again for 1934 when the Russian-born Count Alexis de Sakhnoffsky helped in the design of the new Speedstream models. These had sloping vee-radiators, large built-in luggage boots and rear wheel spats on the more expensive models. The 1934 range included a new lower-priced car for which Nash revived the Lafayette name. Priced at $595–695, the Lafayette had a 75bhp 3569cc 6-cylinder side-valve engine, and a wheelbase of 113in (2868mm). Eight body styles were offered, from a two-passenger coupé at $585 to a five-passenger town sedan brougham at $715. Although sometimes listed as a separate marque, the Lafayette was marketed only through Nash dealers.

The 1935 and 1936 Nashes had curious styling, with sharply sloping grills and fastback sedan bodies. The 5276cc straight-8 engine was dropped after 1935, and the largest Nash was then the 4260cc Ambassador Eight, which was made up to 1942. There was also the 3848cc Ambassador Six and a new model, the 400, which used the same engine as the Ambassador Six but a shorter wheelbase and different styling.

George Mason Takes Over

In 1936 Charlie Nash was 72 years old and looking for someone to take over the helm of his company. The man he wanted was George Mason (1891–1954) who had worked wonders with the Kelvinator refrigerator company. In order to get Mason Nash had to buy up the Kelvinator Corp., which he did in April 1937. People made jokes about the unlikely alliance between refrigerator and car manufacturers, prophesying that the 1937 Nashes would come equipped with ice cube trays, and that the Kelvinators would have 4-wheel brakes, but in fact the merger was very good for both companies. The 1937 Nashes were more conventionally styled than their predecessors, and production was up from 53,038 to 85,949 as the industry climbed out of the Depression. 1938 models offered the 'Weather Eye' heating/air conditioning system by which the interior climate could be controlled by a radio-like dial, while since 1936 Nash had made a reclining front seat which could join up with the rear seat to make a comfortable double bed. The Lafayette lost what individuality it had in 1937, becoming the Nash Lafayette 400. 1939 Nashes had fresh styling, with faired-in headlamps and three-piece grills, while for the British market the Ambassador Six could be had with a 4730cc Perkins diesel engine.

NICK BALDWIN

NASH, CHARLES (1864–1948)

Many successful businessmen like to represent their lives as a rags to riches story, but the rags are sometimes more fiction than fact. This was not so with Charles Warren Nash, who was born on 28 January 1864 in DeKalb County, Illinois. His parents separated when he was six; neither, it seems, wanted to look after him, and his grandparents were unable to, so he was 'bound out' to a Michigan farmer to work for him until he was 21, with no more than three months schooling a year, and home and clothing provided. At the end of the time he was to receive three suits and $100. In fact the schooling turned out to be less than the promised three months, and the little boy sometimes worked 20 hours a day. At the age of 12 he left the farm, and after working on another, and then for a carpenter he managed to amass enough money to buy ten sheep. It is not known what happened to them, but, knowing Nash's later career, he probably made a profit out of them. By the age of 18 he owned a hay baling machine which he hired out to farmers, followed by a threshing machine. His next job was a clerk in a hardware store in Flint, Michigan, where his life was changed for ever when he met William Crapo Durant. At that time Durant was running the Flint Road Cart Co., later to become the Durant Dort Carriage Co., and he hired Nash to work, first of all in the blacksmith's shop, and then stuffing upholstery. He stuffed to such good effect that he soon became a department superintendent, and then vice-president and general superintendent of the newly formed Durant Dort Co.

When he first saw one, Nash was unimpressed with the motor car, as were Durant and his partner Joshua Dallas Dort. However, by 1904 Durant was involved with David Buick, and in 1908 he formed General Motors. Two years later he was ousted by the controlling banks. The general manager of Buick, William Little, left with him and his place was taken, on the banks' recommendation, by Charles Nash. He was a good businessman but admitted that he was not yet an automobile man, so he hired Walter Chrysler as works manager. Chrysler said of him later 'Nash may have known little about automobiles when he began in 1910, but he did know how to handle men, he knew how to run a factory. He was never the sort of fellow to become reckless with someone's money'. In December 1912 Nash became president of General Motors. Nash liked Durant personally; after all he owed his start in business to him, but he felt that they could not work together. As Beverly Rae Kimes put it, Nash's guiding maxim was a dollar saved is worth two earned, while Durant preferred earning two and spending three. Nash's maxim was the wiser, for he left $20 million while Durant died in poverty.

When he saw that Durant was going to regain control Nash resigned, on 1 June 1916, together with James Storrow, the banker was also on the GM board. Together they planned to buy Packard in partnership with Walter Chrysler, but he elected to stay on with Durant. This plan was very short-lived, but in August 1916 Nash and Storrow, aided by the Boston bankers, Lee, Higginson & Co., bought the Thomas B. Jeffery Co. o f Kenosha, Wisconsin, for a reputed $10 million. The company was immediately renamed the Nash Motors Co., but cars of Jeffery design with Nash nameplates were made until the autumn of 1917, when the Nash Model 681 was introduced as a 1918 model. In July 1918 Nash was chosen to serve as assistant director of aircraft engineering and production, which post he held until the end of the war four months later. His company also made large number of 4x4 trucks, originally a Jeffery design, for the US Army.

Nash made a number of purchases in the postwar period, to expand production of the Nash car and to widen its range. In 1919 he obtained a valuable body supplier when he bought into the Seaman Body Corporation, and when he decided to move into the luxury market he considered buying Pierce-Arrow. When this failed to materialise he turned to a smaller maker of expensive cars, Lafayette, although he did not continue this line for more than one season. In 1925 he launched the lower-priced Ajax, but after one season it was absorbed into the regular Nash line. He retained a hands-on approach to the business right up to his retirement in 1932, and devoted a lot of his time to visiting Nash dealers right across the United States. When he was as the factory he always ate his lunch with the workers in their cafeteria. He and his wife were generous in their donations to charity. In particular they founded the Kenosha Youth Foundation and eventually gave half a million dollars to it. They also supported Boy Scout camps, Nash being a keen outdoorsman himself. He was particularly fond of fishing, and in 1922 he landed the largest halibut ever caught in the state of Maine.

In January 1932 he resigned as president of Nash Motors, taking on the less arduous post of chairman of the board. Former vice-president Earl H. McCarthy took Nash's place, but four years later he resigned, and Nash brought in George Mason from the Kelvinator Corporation. This involved a merger with Kelvinator, and Nash remained as chairman of the board of the new company, with Mason as the active president. Nash died on 6 June 1948, at the age of 84.

Charles Nash married farmer's daughter Jessie Hallock in 1884. They had three daughters, of whom two married Nash Motors executives.

NG

Further Reading
'Climbing his own Ladder, the Elevation of Charles Nash', Karla A. Rosenbusch, *Automobile Quarterly*, Vol. 35, No. 3.

Hier is nu een ideale wagen voor U, de nieuwe

Victoria-Cabriolet

de meest geschikte wagen voor ons land.....!

Gesloten zijnde is de Victoria-Cabriolet absoluut rammel- en tochtvrij en niet van een normaal gesloten model te onderscheiden. Het is de meest ideale en bovendien volmaakte carrosserie die men zich kan voorstellen.

In enkele seconden, met een paar eenvoudige handgrepen is de Victoria-Cabriolet van een open in een gesloten wagen en van een gesloten in een open wagen te veranderen. Door het vaste verband, waarin de ramen gevat zijn, bestaat het eenvoudig niet, dat de carrosserie zal gaan rammelen. Alle ramen zijn neerlaatbaar.

LAAT U DEZE PRACHTIGE KAPCONSTRUCTIE EENS DEMONSTREEREN.
CABRIOLET-SEDANS KUNNEN WIJ U DIRECT UIT VOORRAAD LEVEREN!

NASH

IMPORTEUR VOOR GEHEEL NEDERLAND
N.V. H. ENGLEBERT'S AUTOMOBIELHANDEL - THERESIASTRAAT 145 - TEL. 772085 - DEN HAAG

AGENTEN IN ALLE GROOTE PLAATSEN VAN NEDERLAND

Coil and wishbone ifs arrived on the 1940 models, and for 1941 there was a new model with integral construction. Made in eight closed body styles, the new car was called the 600 for its fuel consumption of 600 miles (965km) on a 20 gallon (75-litre) tankful. During the 1930s Nash usually held 12th or 13th place in the American production league, but they were 11th in 1941, with 80,428 cars delivered. Apart from styling changes the 1942 models were similar to the 41s, but war halted production on 1 February after 5428 had been made that year.

Nash were quickly off the mark with their postwar cars, and actually came 3rd in the production league after Ford and Chevrolet in 1945. Once the big firms got going Nash fell back, but they were still 8th in 1946 and 11th in 1947, when output was well above prewar levels, at 113,315 cars. In appearance the early postwar Nashes were warmed-over 1942 designs, and the Ambassador Eight was not revived. 1949, however, saw completely new styling with the controversial Airflyte design, nicknamed the 'bathtub'. This was an all-enveloping sedan body with fastback rear end and partially-enclosed front as well as rear wheels. The body was largely the work of Nils Wahlberg, who had designed the first Nash engine in 1918, and who shared with George Mason a fascination with aerodynamics. Its drag coefficient of 0.43 was better than any other contemporary American car. Underneath its advanced body, which brought integral construction to the

HENRY FORD MOTOR MUSEUM AND GREENFIELD VILLAGE

de SAKHNOFFSKY, ALEXIS (1901–64)

Count Alexis de Sakhnoffsky was genuine Russian nobility, born in Kiev on 12 November 1901. His father was an advisor to Czar Nicholas II. Growing up in a household of German nannies, French tutors and a British nurse, young Alex became proficient in four languages.

When Alex was 12, an uncle gave him a ride in a French Serpollet steamcar, one of the faster vehicles of that day. His cousin owned Mercedes, Austro-Daimlers and Opels, and his father bought a new Mercedes touring car in 1913 with a muffler cutout. Sakhnoffsky later wrote, '...when this monster moved along at 65 mph, flames shooting out of the cutout, it was a sight to behold. I knew then and there that...my future would be closely connected with big, fast, beautiful cars.'

In 1917, the Bolsheviks seized the Sakhnoffskys' property, whereupon Alex's father committed suicide. Sakhnoffsky joined the White Russian army in 1919 but immediately recognized that the plight was hopeless. He fled first to Paris and then to Brussels, where he enrolled in the School of Arts and Crafts. He also took an $18-a-month job as an apprentice draftsman and test driver for the Brussels coachbuilder Van den Plas.

As the company's test driver, Alex could try out freshly coachbuilt cars on weekends. Aristocratic, good-looking and always fashionably dressed, he and his latest girlfriend would drive to the poshest hotels in Belgium and France, where people might talk and wonder about the dashing young couple in their stylish motorcars, but no one questioned Sakhnoffsky's status as a nobleman.

Meanwhile, he so impressed Van den Plas management, first by translating for foreign clients and then by doing quick design sketches as customers explained their personal wants and needs, that in late 1924, the 23-year-old count became the company's official 'art director'. This put him in contact with European royalty and the sorts of people with whom he felt comfortable.

Sakhnoffsky/Van den Plas designs won the prestigious Monte Carlo Grand Prix for four years running: 1926 through 1929. In 1928, at the Earls Court salon in London, Sakhnoffsky met a representative of the Hayes Body Company in Grand Rapids, Michigan, who offered him a two-year contract at roughly double his Van den Plas salary.

Hayes was America's fourth largest maker of automobile bodies and supplied Chrysler, Willys, Reo, Marmon and others. Hayes needed an 'art director' in answer to the styling departments recently set up by rival bodymakers Fisher, Briggs and Murray. Sakhnoffsky arrived in November 1928.

Sakhnoffsky's first task at Hayes was to style a new Marmon Model 78 for 1930. Marmon used this body until the company went out of business, whereupon the dies were sold to Peerless, then DeVaux and finally Continental Motors. Meanwhile Sakhnoffsky also styled the baby 1930 American Austin.

But his crowning design for Hayes was the famous Cord L-29 coupe that won the Grand Prix at Monte Carlo in 1930 (Sakhnoffsky's fifth win in a row) and first prize in the Bournemouth Elegance Contest as well as that season's Le Tourquet Rallye. The L-29 was something of a concept car for Hayes and, incidentally, was eventually purchased by Brooks Stevens.

Hayes' fortunes sank in the early Depression and, by 1931, Sakhnoffsky was virtually penniless and threatened with deportation. He went to Canada and petitioned the U.S. immigration service to let him return to the States as a resident alien. Permission arrived when Sakhnoffsky took a job with Auburn in July 1931.

Auburn, though, soon let him go, whereupon Sakhnoffsky opened a private industrial design office in 1932–33. He promptly became a design consultant to–among others–Packard, Nash, Studebaker, Continental Motors and the White Motor Company. He styled the flamboyant 1934 Nash and contributed significantly to White's 1936 trucks. White continued to use Sakhnoffsky designs until 1960.

The count, meanwhile, had a roller-coaster career. His clientele grew through the 1930s and ranged from auto- and truckmakers to manufacturers of home appliances, furniture, bedding, clothes and packaging. He enhanced his reputation on the pages of Esquire magazine with illustrations that had the instantly recognizable 'Sakhnoffsky sweep', a technique that had spiral-nebula swirls coming off a car or truck. These swirls became his hallmark. He also used this technique to create several classics of advertising art, including ads for the 1935 Auburn and 1939–1940 American Bantam.'

Sakhnoffsky became an American citizen in 1939. His career oscillated between feast and famine, he married twice, moved from Michigan to New York, Los Angeles, Chicago, back to Michigan and finally to Georgia. He contributed to Esquire for 20 years; designed, built and sold 10 or 11 copies of a 1940 Nash convertible that resembled the Packard Darrin; served on Averill Harriman's staff as an Air Force lieutenant colonel and Russian translator in World War II; worked with Brooks Stevens briefly during 1948-50; and continued to consult for White and Mack trucks until arthritis got the better of him in 1960. He passed away in 1964.

ML

1949 Nash 600 sedan.
NATIONAL MOTOR MUSEUM

whole Nash range, the 'bathtub' was conventional, with a choice of 6-cylinder engines, 2828 or 3848cc. Known as the 600 and the Ambassador, these Nashes were made with little change, apart from updated styling, until 1952, when completely redesigned bodies appeared, partly the work of Pinin Farina. These still had the partially-enclosed front wheels, a pet idea of George Mason's, but the fastback was replaced by a sizeable projecting boot, and there was much more glass area, with a wrap-around window.

Compacts and Sub-compacts

Although postwar sales continued to be very good, with a record 142,592 cars delivered in 1949, Mason felt that an independent car maker should have something different to offer compared with the Big Three. His answer appeared in 1950 in the shape of the Rambler. This was what would later be called a compact car, with a 100in (2538mm) wheelbase and the 2.8-litre 6-cylinder engine of the 600. Launched in March 1950 as a 2-door convertible, the Rambler line gained a station wagon in June, and a 2-door hard-top coupé called the Country Club for 1951. At $1808 the Rambler was a little more expensive than the cheapest 600, but its compact size earned it considerable popularity. More than 20,000 were sold in 1950, out of a record overall production of 189,534 cars. When the larger Nashes received Pinin Farina styling for 1952, the Ramblers followed for 1953.

Following his philosophy of the 'different car', Mason explored the sub-compact field as well. In the winter of 1950 he exhibited at New York's Waldorf Astoria Hotel a small 2-seater of typical Nash lines but only 145in (3680mm) long. The prototype was powered by a Fiat 500 engine, but when it went into production in 1954 it was Austin-powered (see METROPOLITAN (iii)).

American Motors Corporation

Although the independent manufacturers had flourished in the car-hungry postwar years, their share of the market dropped from 18.6 per cent in 1946 to less than 5 per cent six years later. George Mason realised that a company with annual sales of less than 200,000 could never compete in research and development, nor in price, with the giants who were making over a million. He therefore decided

1956 Nash Ambassador Custom sedan.
NATIONAL MOTOR MUSEUM

on a merger with Hudson, which came into effect on 1 May 1954, the new company being called American Motors Corp. Mason became president, but died suddenly less than six months later, so his place was taken by his deputy George Romney.

Production of Hudsons was moved from Detroit to Nash's Kenosha plant, and for the next three years Hudsons were merely badge-engineered Nashes. For 1955 Nash added a V8 to their Ambassador range, the 5244cc engine being made by Packard. The automatic transmission also came from Packard. In mid–1956 AMC brought out their own 4.1-litre V8, although the larger Packard unit, now 5768cc, was also listed up to the end of the season. There was also a new Rambler for 1956, with a longer wheelbase, 4-door sedan and station wagon bodies (four doors had first been offered in the Rambler range in 1954) and a 3205cc 6-cylinder engine, now with ohvs. 1957 was the last year for the

1952 Nash-Healey coupé by Pinin Farina.
NATIONAL MOTOR MUSEUM

1913 National (i) Series V semi-racing roadster.
NICK BALDWIN

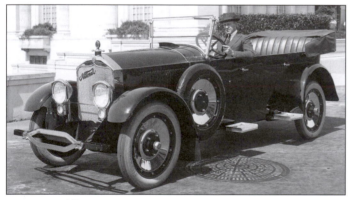

1922 National (i) Sextet Newport tourer.
JOHN A. CONDE

Nash name; the Ambassador had an AMC-built 5358cc V8, while Ramblers had their own styling and a choice of three engines, the 3205cc six and two V8s, of 4097 and 5358cc. From 1958 to 1968 all American Motors cars were marketed under the RAMBLER name and then as AMERICAN MOTORS.

NG

Further Reading
'Blueprints and Balance Sheets, the Cars that Charlie Built', Beverly Rae Kimes, *Automobile Quarterly*, Vol. 15 No.2.
'Refrigerators and Two Georges', Sam Medway, *Automobile Quarterly*, Vol. 15, No. 2.

NASH-HEALEY (US/GB) 1951–1954
Nash Motors Co., Kenosha, Wisconsin.
The Nash-Healey was the result of a chance meeting between Nash president George Mason and British sports car builder Donald Healey in 1949 when they were passengers aboard the *Queen Elizabeth*. By the time they docked in the US, a deal had been hatched to build Healey sportscars, with Nash 6-cylinder engines, to be sold through the Nash dealer network. The first ones were built in

1951, and had modified 3848cc engines with 125hp in simple ladder frames. The Nash six had been treated to twin SU carburettors, a hotter cam and an aluminium cylinder head. The first bodies were built by Panelcraft in England, and were a bit plain and slabsided. They received good reviews, and in 1952 the Nash-Healey received a makeover in the form of a new Pinin Farina body with handsome, rounded contours and headlights inset into the grill. Coupé and roadster versions were available. Power rose to 135hp with the introduction of a larger engine with Carter carburettors. There were several successful Nash-Healey racing cars, but they were based on Healey Silverstone chassis, not the production version. However, by 1954 Nash was failing and production was halted after 506 cars had been built.

HP

NATAL JEEPS (ZA) 1990s
Natal Jeeps, Durban.
This company offered fibreglass replicas of the Jeep CJ6 and CJ7 Wrangler based either on a custom chassis designed for Ford Cortina parts or a proprietary one-ton 4 × 2 or 4 × 4 chassis.

CR

NATIONAL (i) (US) 1900–1924
1900–1902 National Automobile & Electric Vehicle Co., Indianapolis, Indiana.
1902–1904 National Vehicle Co., Indianapolis, Indiana.
1904–1916 National Motor Vehicle Co., Indianapolis, Indiana.
1916–1924 National Motor Car & Vehicle Corp., Indianapolis, Indiana.
The first National was a light, tiller-steered electric runabout, also sometimes called the Electrobile. The Style A runabout cost $900, but there were more expensive electric vehicles including a Style E New York Trap at $1650 and a Style F Stanhope at $1750. National also made horse-drawn carriages, but sold this business to the Gates-Osborne Carriage Co. in 1902. A variety of electric vehicles was made up to 1906, joined in 1903 by two petrol-engined cars, an 8hp 2-cylinder and a 16hp 4-cylinder. They had Rutenber engines and shaft drive. The engines apart, practically the whole car was made in National's factory. The guiding spirit behind the move to petrol engines was Arthur C. Newby, who was one of the men who backed the Indianapolis Motor Speedway which opened in 1909. The 2-cylinder car lasted only one year, and by 1905 Nationals were larger cars with a 4-cylinder engine of 35/40 and a six of 50/60hp, characterised by round radiators which were entirely swept by the large fan. The six was one of the first to be made in America. National acquired its own engine plant in 1907, leasing premises from the Indiana Chain Co. It would be ten years before National turned again to a proprietary engine maker. Cylinders were cast separately until 1908, when pair-casting was adopted and there were four models, fours of 40 and 50hp and sixes of 50 and 75hp, the latter on a 127in (3223mm) wheelbase and costing $5000–6500. Production had risen from 150 cars in 1901 to 1313 in 1908, and was to rise to 1816 in 1915, before dropping because of the war and, later on, the challenge of the mass-produced cars.

National had many sporting successes, particularly in the years 1909 to 1912; winning the Elgin and Illinois Trophies in 1911 and the Indianapolis 500 in 1912. This was particularly appropriate as Arthur Newby was a director of the Speedway. However, they withdrew from works-sponsored racing after 1912. There were important developments for the 1916 season; at the lower-end of the scale there was a new six with 29hp monobloc Continental Red Seal engine, selling in the $1690 to $2900 range, and at the opposite end was a V12 of National's own design and manufacture. This went into a 128in (3249mm) chassis, the same as the Continental-engined models, and was priced modestly at $1990 for a tourer, rising to $3200 for a 5-seater sedan. The Highway Twelve was cheaper than the old six, which was called the Newport Six, and sold for $2560 to $3400.

In 1916 National was bought by a New York concern and the name changed to National Motor & Vehicle Co. They never made other vehicles of their own design, although they did build a number of Jeffery Quad 4x4 trucks for the US Army in 1917/18. The Highway Twelve was dropped at the end of 1919, and the only model from 1920 to 1922 was a six powered by National's own 4.9-litre engine, called the National Sextet. It was made in five or six body styles, the 1921 sedan being priced as high as $4950. In 1922 National became part of Associated Motor Industries, a combine headed by Clarence Earl who had recently resigned from EARL Motors. The other makes in the group were DIXIE FLYER and JACKSON (ii). For 1923 the 4-cylinder Dixie Flyer was badged as the National 4-H, while the National 6-51 was the former Jackson Six. The National Sextet was continued as the 6-71. Although they now covered a wider segment of the market than ever before, from $975 to $3285, sales did not benefit, dropping from 615 in 1921 to 215 in 1923 and only 183 in 1924, the last year for the once mighty National.

NG

NATIONAL (ii) **(GB)** 1902–1906
Rose Bros, Gainsborough, Lincolnshire.
Rose Brothers was founded in 1895 to make machinery for packaging cigarettes, butterscotch and chocolate. They turned to cars in about 1902, with a 10/12hp 2-cylinder and 18/22hp 3-cylinder chassis, both with shaft drive. They were designed by the Baines brothers, Edward and Frank. In 1905 they were joined by a 20/24hp 4-cylinder model, but a projected six announced in 1906 was never marketed and may not even have been made as a prototype. Rose Brothers made the whole of the chassis and engine, but bodies came from outside suppliers, notably Hamshaw of Leicester.

There is a suspicious lack of press material after 1906, though Paul Hasluck's book, *The Automobile*, listed the 18/22hp 3-cylinder and fours of 24 and 40hp 'on Mercedes lines' as current in 1909, and company publicity claimed that cars were made until 1912. A realistic estimate of production is 50 cars, of which most were the 3-cylinder model. They were sometimes referred to as Rose National. Rose Brothers later became part of Rose Forgrove Ltd which was taken over by Baker-Perkins. Curiously they had absorbed another packaging machinery company which had formerly made cars, DAY LEEDS.

NG

NATIONAL (iii) **(GB)** 1904–c.1905
National Motor Co., Manchester.
Designed by two members of the Manchester Motor Club, this was a wheel-steered tricar powered by a 4hp water-cooled M.M.C. single cylinder engine with 2-speed transmission and direct drive on top gear. The driver sat in a bucket seat, with a wicker seat ahead of him for his passenger. This could be replaced by a tradesmans's van body, or removed if the machine was to be used as a single-seater.

NG

NATIONAL MOTORCAR **(US)** c.1990
National Motorcar Corp., Davie, Florida.
The NMC Phantom Classic Coupé was a neoclassic kit car based on a Chevrolet Camaro or Pontiac Firebird body and running gear. A long bonnet and flowing fibreglass running boards gave it a 1930s classic look. It was designed by Norman and Bruce Johnson.

HP

NATIONAL SHOWCARS **(US)** c.1994
National Showcars, Montville, New Jersey.
The Morocco II was a styling and performance kit for the 1980s Chevrolet Corvette. It included an extended nose with exposed headlights and a bonnet scoop like a 1965 396 Corvette. Engine options included a supercharger and other performance modifications.

HP

NATIVE AMERICAN CRAFTSMAN **(US)** 1996–1997
Native American Craftsman Co., North Highland, California.
The NAC Tomahawk was a Cobra replica kit that was grafted onto a cut-down Datsun 240/260/280Z. It was developed from a STALLION body shell by former Kellison employee Rory Bateman.

HP

NAVAJO (i) **(US)** c.1954
Navajo Motor Car Co., New York, New York.
This fibrelass-bodied sports car was visually similar to the Jaguar XK-120. The early models had Ford V8 engines, but Studebaker engines were also considered. The Navajo was sold in 2-seat and 5-seat versions. Total weight was said to be 2300lb (1045 kg) and a removable fibreglass hard-top was standard equipment.

c.1906 National (ii) 20/24hp tourer.
NATIONAL MOTOR MUSEUM

1984 Naylor TF 1700 sports car.
NAYLOR CARS

The bodies were made by Jim Craig in New Jersey. Price for the 2-seater was $2700, with the 5-seater priced below $3200.

HP

NAVAJO (ii) **(GB)** 1984–1986
Alan Langridge Engineering, Chichester, Sussex.
Goodwood-based ex-racing car constructor Alan Langridge created a sort of modern Mini Moke with the Navajo. He designed and built a monocoque in zinc-plated Zintec; the only fibreglass part being the forward-hinging bonnet. Any BMC 1100/1300 could donate its components for the kit, the Hydrolastic suspension being replaced by coil spring/dampers. It was a slow seller and Langridge soon emigrated to South Africa.

CR

NAVARRE **(US)** 1921
A.C. Schulz, Springfield, Massachusetts.
The Navarre, the prototype a large sedan, was launched at Hotel Astor in New York City during the New York Automobile Show week in January 1921. This was a handsome car to sell in the $6000 to $6500 price range, having been designed by A.C. Schulz, formerly associated with Locomobile and Mercer. It was powered by a 6-cylinder ohv engine, designed by Schulz and featured a wheelbase of 131in (3325mm). The car was widely acclaimed at the time of its introduction as the shape of things to come by Navarre. Unfortunately, due to insufficient financing, the Navarre went no further.

KM

NAYLOR **(GB)** 1984–1986
Naylor Brothers, Bradford, Yorkshire.
Established MG restorers the Naylor Brothers created the Naylor TF as an accurate MG TF replica which stayed true to MG practice of using Morris mechanicals (in the form of Morris Ital front suspension, rear axle, engine and gearbox). Its

1913 Nazzaro Tipo 2 roadster.
NICK BALDWIN

1913 N.B. 12hp tourer.
NATIONAL MOTOR MUSEUM

form of construction was authentic, too – steel panels over an ash frame, with beaten steel wings. Some modernities were fitted, though: rocker switches and recessed door handles, for instance. When Naylor hit financial trouble in 1986, Maurice HUTSON revived the model.

CR

NAZZARO (I) 1912–1923
1912–1916 Fabbrica Automobili Nazzaro, Turin.
1919–1923 Automobili Nazzaro, Florence.
Felice Nazzaro (1880–1940) was a rival to Vincenzo Lancia in Fiat's racing team between 1900 and 1908. More successful than Lancia on the racetracks, his cars were far fewer in number and made relatively little impact on the market. He set up Nazzaro & Cia, Fabbrica di Automobili early in 1911, but no cars were made until he moved to larger premises the following year. His first car had a 4398cc monobloc 4-cylinder engine and a 4-speed gearbox. Considering its builder's racing background the Nazzaro carried surprisingly unsporting bodywork, mostly solid-looking tourers and closed cars. Radiators were not unlike the touring Fiats or Lancias, though the Tipo 2 roadster had a pear-shaped radiator like the more sporting Fiats, and a stark 2-seater body. Nazzaro built a special 4½-litre 16-valve single-ohc engine for his 1914 French Grand Prix cars, but they achieved nothing, and cost the company a lot of money. About 230 cars and 50 commercial vehicles had been made by 1916 when the firm was liquidated and Nazzaro returned to Fiat. There he had one more major victory, in the 1922 French Grand Prix, and then managed the competition department up to his death in 1940.

The factory was bought by Tosi of Legnano and used for aero-engine manufacture during the war. In 1919 a new company based at Florence revived the Nazzaro car. The Tipo 5 had a 3½-litre single-ohc 4-cylinder engine and a more sporty appearance than the prewar models, with a sharp vee-radiator. From 1922 they had two exhaust valves per cylinder. About 210 had been made when production ended in 1923.

NG

N.B. (I/GB) 1913–1915
John Newton Fabbrica Automobili, Turin.
Though made in Italy, the N.B. was designed by Englishmen, John Newton and R.O. Harper, and sold mainly in Great Britain by Newton & Bennett of Manchester. Newton was the sole owner of the Turin factory, which had previously housed the makers of the VALT car. The first N.B.s were essentially Valts with N.B. badges on their flat, Fiat-like radiators but production N.B.s had a 2155cc 12hp long-stroke four (dimensions were 70 × 140mm). They were bodied in England, mainly as tourers although there were also 2-seaters and fully-enclosed saloons. Unlike the Valt-derived cars, the N.B. had a vee-radiator reminiscent of the Prince Henry Vauxhall. Estimates of production vary between 500 and 1000 cars. In November 1914 the name was changed to Newton but very few were made because of difficulties in obtaining components, particularly Bosch magnetos and also because the British government imposed a 33 per cent tax on imported cars. In 1915 the factory was bought by DIATTO.

After the war Newton & Bennett sold the CEIRANO under the name Newton-Ceirano, while Harper designed the HARPER Runabout.

NG

Further Reading
'The story of Newton-Bennett', Dennis Harrison,
The Automobile, December 1991.

N.C.F. (GB) 1985 to date
1985–1990 N.C.F. Motors Ltd, Newcastle-on-Tyne, Tyne & Wear.
1990–1997 N.C.F. Motors Ltd, Bishop Auckland, Co. Durham.
1997 to date N.C.F. Motors Ltd, Great Whittington, Newcastle, Tyne & Wear.
Metal-bodied kit cars are rare and that was a major strength of Nick Findeison's rugged Diamond estate, which had aluminium panels over a tubular steel chassis and frame. Ford Cortina mechanicals were used but later developments allowed Toyota Hi Lux or Sierra 4 × 4 drive trains. After 300 had been built, a MkII model was launched in 1990, based on the Granada Mk2. A MkIII version arrived in 1993, more smoothly styled and with a shorter tail. The idea of a Fiat Panda-based utility kit first appeared in 1992 as the Road Rat, but it took two years for the more sophisticated Torino to reach production. Virtually everything came from the donor Fiat Panda and either front-wheel drive or 4 × 4 versions could be built. The bodywork was welded galvanised steel mounted on a tough steel frame chassis. Kits could be bought in pick-up or estate styles, the latter with a side-hinged tailgate. The Blitz of 1996 was so successful that it displaced the company's other models. It was an ultra-simple, very cheap single-seater buggy designed for off-road and on-road use. Initially it used a rear-mounted Fiat 126 engine but it soon switched to Mini power.

CR

NEALE (GB) 1897
Douglas Neale, Edinburgh.
The Neale was a very high dogcart with *dos-à-dos* seating for four passengers, powered by an electric motor driving by chain to one rear wheel. The body and wheels were made by Drew, also of Edinburgh. Only four were sold, at £150 each.

NG

NEANDER (D) 1934–1939
Neander Motorfahrzeug GmbH, Düren-Rolsdorf.
Ernst Neumann-Neander was an artist who took an interest in car styling before World War I. He designed some striking bodies for Austro-Daimler and Benz, while in the 1920s his work was seen mainly on SZAWE cars. From 1923 to 1931 he made a number of unorthodox motorcycles with Duralumin frames, and in 1928 built a few prototypes of a single-seater cyclecar with 350cc engine mounted at the side. In 1934 he began to make the Pionier, a tandem 2-seater with aluminium body powered by a front-mounted 1000cc J.A.P. 2-cylinder

engine driving the front wheels without the need for a differential. It had independent suspension all round, and was followed by the 'Kurvenleger' in which the wheels alone tilted while cornering, the body remaining stable. In 1937 Neander built a monoposto racing car. This was a one-off but a small series of Pioniers was made and took part in competitions.

HON

N.E.C. (GB) 1905–1920

New Engine Co. Ltd, Acton, London.

This company was founded in 1903, to make 2-stroke aero-engines, designed by G.F. Mort. The first premises were a tiny workshop in Reading, with staff of four, including G.F. Mort and his brother J. Charles Mort. In 1904 they moved to larger premises at Acton. Aero-engines were made at least until 1913, and were supplied to a number of aircraft manufacturers including A.V. Roe and Shorts, who built a Wright biplane with 50hp V4 N.E.C. engine in 1910.

The first N.E.C. car was marketed in 1905; like all its successors, it had a horizontal engine under the floor and a flat front with no bonnet. It had a 2-speed gearbox, but from 1906 onwards, three speeds were provided. The engine was a 24hp 4-cylinder, but 15 and 20hp twins were made between 1906 and 1911, and 30 and 40hp fours from 1907 to 1914. Only two sizes of cylinder were used for all N.E.C.s, 114 × 114mm and 127 × 114mm. These gave capacities of 2326 and 2886cc for the twins, and 4652 and 5773cc for the 4-cylinder engines. The longest wheelbase was 138in (3503mm), and as all seating was within the wheelbase, the car gave a very comfortable ride. In 1906 *Country Life* described its as '... possibly the most comfortable motor carriage on the market'. They had worm-drive rear axles. Most N.E.C.s were tourers or town cars with limousine or landaulette bodies, but a few 2-seaters were made on the smaller chassis. All coachwork was made at the Acton works. A 30hp tourer competed in the 1907 Scottish Reliability Trial.

N.E.C. production was quite limited, probably not above 100 cars per year, although they exhibited regularly at Olympia. G.F. Mort died in 1911 and the business was carried on by his brother. The 30 and 40hp models were carried on some lists up to 1922, but any postwar N.E.C.s were probably assembled from prewar stock. They did not exhibit at any postwar motor show. By 1921 the company was involved in making drilling machine tables, general engineering and component manufacture. In 1938 the works were occupied by Norton & Gregory Ltd, makers of mathematical instruments.

NG

NECKAR (D) 1959–1967

Neckar Automobilwerke AG, Heilbronn.

When NSU resumed car production the NSU-FIAT marque had to find a new brand name. They chose the name of the Neckar river near their works at Heilbronn. It was used for assembled Fiat cars up to 1967, when it was dropped in favour of Fiat for the cars assembled at Heilbronn.

HON

NEGRE (F) 1897

H. Negre, Amiens, Somme.

This was a steam car with Serpollet-type boiler, horizontally-opposed 4-cylinder engine and chain drive. It had a 2-seater body with an extra forward facing seat at the front, ahead of the engine and boiler. Only one or two prototypes were made.

NG

NEIMANN (D) 1931

Made by Abram Neimann, this was a 3-wheeler powered by a rear-mounted 600cc Triumph engine which drove the single rear wheel. Serious production never started.

HON

NELSON (i) (US) 1917–1921

1917–1920 E.A. Nelson Motor Car Co., Detroit, Michigan.
1920–1921 E.A. Nelson Automobile Co., Detroit, Michigan.

Emil A. Nelson had worked in a number of automobile companies when, in 1916, he decided to form his own company to build a light car of his own design. The E.A. Nelson Motor Car Co. was organised in 1917, the Nelson being fitted

1939 Neander Pionier tandem 2-seater.
NATIONAL MOTOR MUSEUM

1911 N.E.C. 30hp torpedo tourer.
NICK BALDWIN

1921 Nelson (i) Model E tourer.
JOHN A. CONDE

with an in-house ohc 4-cylinder engine developing 29bhp at 2200rpm and a 114in (2893mm) wheelbase. The car was available in three body styles – a roadster at $1200; a touring car at $1500 and a sedan at $2200 and was distinguished by its clean-cut body design including a prominent coachbuilders' curve. The company, although a relatively small operation, was able to market all cars it produced and, following bankruptcy in 1920, was re-organised with production continuing into 1921. The Nelson failed to ride out the economic setback caused by the 1921 depression and went out of business, having produced about 1000 cars in its five years of existence.

KM

NELSON (ii) (GB) 1989–1994

Nelson Motors, Shepperton, Middlesex.

The Nelson S350 was a rather attractive classic cigar-shaped sports kit in the Ronart mould. It had a steel backbone chassis, fibreglass bodywork, Jaguar suspension and a Rover 3.5-litre V8 engine. Some 14 examples were built in all.

CR

NEMALETTE (D) 1923–1925
Netzschkauer Maschinenfabrik Franz Starke & Söhne, Netzschkau.
This was a 2-seater 3-wheeler with single front wheel and transmission to the rear wheels.

HON

NEMBO (I) 1970
This was a sharply-styled coupé based on the VW Beetle floorpan, featuring quad headlamps and a panoramic rear screen.

CR

NEMESIS see RV

NEREIA (US) c.1994 to date
Nereia Cars, Wilmington, North Carolina.
This company built a continuation of the AMORE CIMBRIA kit sports car. It had gullwing doors and hinged side windows for ventilation. Nereia based their kit on Volkswagen floorpans or a custom tube frame that mounted either V6 or V8 engines. They were sold in kit or completely assembled form.

HP

NESSELSDORF see NW

NESTOR see PIRAT

NETHKIN (US) c.1988–1995
Nethkin Associates, Fishersville, Virginia.
In the 1980s this kit car company made a line of neoclassic kits that resembled dehydrated Duesenbergs. They used a box frame that could mount a Volkswagen engine at the rear or a 4, 6 or V8 engine up front. They made convertibles, sedan deliveries, dual cowl phaetons and sedanca de ville body styles. By 1993 they had added the Palermo Coupé and Spyder, which were Ferrari Testarossa replicas based on Pontiac Fiero chassis. All Nethkin cars could be purchased in kit or ready-to-drive condition.

HP

NEUSTADT-PERRY; NEUSTADT (US) 1901–1908; 1915
1901–1904 Neustadt-Perry Co., St Louis, Missouri.
1904–1908 Neustadt Automobile & Supply Co., St Louis, Missouri.
J.H. Neustadt was a supplier of components to those who wished to assemble their own cars, providing a series of kits for different sizes and styles of car. He advertised them as 'The Machine You Can Put Together Yourself', although it appears that he did supply some complete cars as well. One style was a 4-seater with folding front seat and tiller steering, another, called the J.H.N., was more up-to-date, with an inclined steering column and small frontal bonnet. Kits were available for steam cars up to 1903 and petrol models were made with 1, 2 or 4 cylinders, air- or water-cooling, epicyclic or friction transmissions and single- or double-chain drive. In 1904 he bought out his partner Perry and from then on used his own name solely. Kits were offered at least as late as 1908, and from 1911 to 1914 he made a truck in complete form. Neustadt's last creations were three 4-wheel drive cars which he built for a single customer in 1915.

NG

NEVCO see GIZMO

NEW-AXA (F) c.1902–1904
Louis Herlicq, Paris.
This was a light 2-seater voiturette powered by a 4¹/₂hp De Dion-Bouton engine under a bonnet. A honeycomb radiator gave it quite a modern appearance. Apparently only 13 were made, but one survived in daily use until 1923.

NG

NEW BRITISH (GB) 1921–1923
Charles Willets Jnr Ltd, Cradley Heath, Staffordshire.
This company's main business was the manufacture of heavy lifting tackle (Cradley Heath was a leading centre of chain making), and made a few cars when other work was slack. The New British light car used 998cc V-twin Blackburne engines in air- or water-cooled form, with friction transmission and chain final drive to a differential-less rear axle. The only body style was a 2-seater, which cost £195 in air-cooled form, or £215 with water-cooling. Probably fewer than 100 were made.

NG

NEW CARDEN see CARDEN

NEW CENTURY (i) (GB) 1902–1903
Suffield & Brown, Willesden, London; Poplar, London.
This company showed two cars at the Agricultural Hall Motor Show in 1903. One was a steam car called the Hythe with tubular boiler under the bonnet, 3-cylinder compound engine and chain drive. The other was the New Century petrol car with a very large 2-cylinder horizontal engine. They also advertised electric cars with Joel motors.

NG

NEW CENTURY (ii) (GB) 1902–1904
Hoyle Bros & Co. Ltd, Brighouse, Yorkshire.
Announced in the same year as the London-built New Century, the Yorkshire variety was a light 2-seater with a single-cylinder engine mounted at the front of the frame, at 25 degrees from the horizontal and inclined towards the front of the car. The gearbox gave speeds of 8mph (12km/h) and 18mph (29km/h), and final drive was by chain. The bicycle-type wheels could be shod with solid or pneumatic tyres.

NG

NEW ENGLAND (i) (US) 1898–1899
New England Motor Carriage Co., Boston; Waltham, Massachusetts.
This company announced that they would make steam and electric cars, but it seems that only the steamer was built. The prototype was completed in Boston, but production, such as it was, took place in Waltham where two other makes of generally similar light steam carriage, the WALTHAM and AMERICAN WALTHAM were being made at about the same time. The New England had a vertical 2-cylinder engine, chain drive and tiller steering. In September 1899 the makers started to make the Comet bicycle, and cars were given up soon afterwards. This was the reverse of the traditional practice, in which bicycle making preceded that of cars.

NG

NEW ENGLAND (ii) (US) 1899–1901
New England Electric Vehicle Co., Boston, Massachusetts.
New England Electric Vehicle Transportation Co., Camden, New Jersey.
These companies were both subsidiaries of the better-known Electric Vehicle Co. of Hartford, Connecticut, makers of the COLUMBIA (i) electric cars and trucks. They made various designs of passenger electrics, including the 3-wheeler designed by Charles BARROWS of Willimantic, Connecticut. In 1901 both companies started to dispose of their stock, and the following year they were closed down by the parent company.

NG

NEW ENGLAND EXOTIC REBODIES (US) c.1996 to date
New England Exotic Rebodies, Haverhill, Maine.
The 308 GTSi was a kit car replica of that Ferrari model, designed to fit on a Chevrolet Camaro or Pontiac Firebird chassis. They also sold the Exotic SL, which was a Mercedes 500SL replica scaled to fit a Chrysler LeBaron convertible chassis.

HP

NEW ERA (i) (US) 1901–1902
Automobile & Marine Power Co., Camden, New Jersey.
This was a 2-seater runabout of rather ungainly appearance, due to its high build and short wheelbase. It was powered by a 7hp single-cylinder engine under the seat, with double-chain drive and tiller steering. Its initial price of $700 was soon raised to $850.

NG

NEW ERA (ii) (US) 1916

New Era Engineering Co., Joliet, Illinois.

This New Era was a conventional light car powered by a 16hp 4-cylinder engine, and made as a 2-seater roadster or 5-seater tourer. It lasted a very short time, and company president Forrest J. Alvin moved to Harvey, Illinois where he made the GENEVA (ii) car.

NG

NEW ERA (iii) (US) 1933–1934

New Era Motors Corp., New York, New York.

This was a Ford V8 with LeBaron body, made as a taxicab, 7-seater sedan and 7-seater limousine. Most were sold to the taxi trade, but among buyers of the sedan was Mrs Eddie Cantor, wife of the well-known comedian. She paid $975 for her New Era, getting on for double the price of a regular Ford Fordor sedan.

NG

NEWEY (GB) 1913–1921

Gordon Newey Ltd, Birmingham.

This company sold an assembled car under the name Newey-Aster in 1907, but seems to have been dealers rather than manufacturers until 1913 when they launched a light car with 10hp 4-cylinder Aster engine. This was revived briefly after the war, joined by a 12/15 with 1750cc Chapuis-Dornier engine. When French engines were unobtainable during the war, Newey imported a 2.4-litre American unit, possibly a Continental, which he put in a car he called the G.N.L., with British-built 2- and 4-seater bodies. Newey's ill health brought car making to an end in 1921.

NG

NEW HUDSON (GB) 1912–1924

New Hudson Cycle Co. Ltd, Birmingham.

New Hudson was a well-respected name in the motorcycle world for many years. In business from 1909 to 1957, they had two brief periods of car manufacture. The first was in 1912, at the beginning of the cyclecar boom, when they launched a very small 2-seater powered by a 737cc 4½hp single-cylinder engine, with epicyclic transmission and shaft drive. It was listed up to 1915.

A new car carried the New Hudson name after the war, this time a 3-wheeler powered by a 1250cc V-twin engine with 3-speed gearbox and chain drive to the single rear wheel. In 1922 the engine was replaced by a slightly smaller V-twin, this time made by M.A.G. and with inlet-over-exhaust valves. This was made up to 1924. Motorcycles were made up to 1933 after which there was a gap until the name was revived by B.S.A. who continued the marque to 1957.

NG

NEW IMPERIAL (GB) 1914

New Imperial Cycles Ltd, Birmingham.

New Imperial was another well-known motorcycle maker who had a brief involvement with cars. Like the New Hudson, theirs was also a cyclecar, but with a small 4-cylinder engine, 3-speed gearbox and shaft drive. It was listed only in 1914.

NG

NEW MAP see ROLUX

NEWMOBILE (GB) 1906–1907

Newmobile Ltd, Acton, London.

This company listed a 24hp 6-cylinder car of unknown origin. It is possible that it was their own product, but this is not likely. Newmobile Ltd was founded in March 1906 'to take over the business of motorcar manufacturer and dealer P.G. Tachi', but he has not been recorded as a car maker in any published lists. They also advertised small commercial vehicles.

NG

NEW MONARCH see MONARCH (i)

1919 Newey 10hp 2-seater.
NICK BALDWIN

1900 New Orleans voiturette.
NATIONAL MOTOR MUSEUM

NEW ORLEANS (GB) 1900–1910

1900–1901 Burford, Van Toll & Co., Twickenham, Middlesex.
1901–1905 New Orleans Motor Co. Ltd, Twickenham, Middlesex.
1905–1910 Orleans Motor Co. Ltd, Twickenham, Middlesex.

The first, and most popular, New Orleans was a Belgian VIVINUS voiturette made under licence in England. It was made by H.G. Burford who was to have a long career in the motor industry, with Milnes-Daimler and later making commercial vehicles under his own name, and Dutch-born Johannes Van Toll who sold Daimler engines in Holland, and drove a German-built Daimler in the 1896 Emancipation Run. They chose the name New Orleans after Orleans Road in Twickenham, site of their factory, which was itself named after Orleans House, so called because a former owner had been the exiled Duc d'Orléans. The car had a front-mounted 3½hp single-cylinder engine with transmission by belt to fast and loose pulleys on a countershaft, and thence by spur gears to the rear axle. Two forward speeds were provided.

It is likely that the first few New Orleans, launched in February 1900, were imported Vivinus. Indeed New Orleans' design over the next few years followed that of the Belgian cars very closely and it may be that there was more importation, or assembly of imported components, than actual manufacture at Twickenham. A 6hp 2-cylinder car was available from October 1900, and the following spring

1908 Orleans 40hp limousine.
NATIONAL MOTOR MUSEUM

came a 7hp version with water-cooling and, for the first time, three forward speeds. A 9hp twin and 14hp four came in 1903, the former with a tubular frame, the latter with a flitch-plate chassis.

Although the 3hp single-cylinder voiturette was still available in 1905, the company's attention was turned to much larger cars with 4-cylinder T-head engines of 22 and 25hp (3498 and 4560cc), and a 30/35hp six of 6840cc. In 1907 the 25hp was replaced by a 40hp with 8712cc 4-cylinder L-head engine. These larger cars were called Orleans rather than New Orleans, it is said in order to dispel any suggestion of American origin. They were described in 1906 as being the first Orleans cars of all-British construction, and certainly their specifications do not tie up with Vivinus models of the period. The 1910 30/35hp six had pair-cast cylinders. 1910 was the last year in which the big Orleans were listed, and they did not appear at any shows that year. Although large and imposing cars, they were not well-known on the British market, and were probably made in very small numbers. One loyal owner was Earl Cairns whose 35hp six of 1908 was his third example of the make.

NG

Further Reading
'The New Orleans – Fact or Fiction?' David Hales,
The Automobile, May 1995.

NEW PICK *see* PICK

NEWPORT (US) c.1994
Newport Car Conversions, Norwalk, California.
The Ponari was a Pontiac Fiero-based kit car that looked like a Ferrari 308. It had been built by ZMC. Three body variations were sold, a coupé, Targa and convertible. They were sold in kit and turn-key form.

HP

NEW WAVE AUTO (US) c.1994
New Wave Auto, Altamonte Springs, Florida.
The New Wave Ziero was a conversion kit for the Pontiac Fiero. It added a Corvette-style nose and tail along with side scoops and ground effects panels to the standard Fiero chassis. A tail spoiler and revised dashboard were included in this low-cost kit.

HP

NEW YORK SIX (US) 1927–1929
New York Motors Corp., Baltimore, Maryland.
The New York Six is a curio in US automotive history as it may not have built at all – even in prototype form. As there is room for doubt, it is included here. The New York Six was unique in one respect – as a car which was equipped with the Parkmobile, a device which, by the use of hydraulic sets of small wheels, expedited parking into small spaces. The Parkmobile had been invented and patented by Villor P. Williams of Baltimore, Maryland, and first appeared before the public through illustrated news items in the automotive press. These gave an erroneous impression of what the Parkmobile was all about as it depicted the front of a car on the Parkmobile captioned as 'The Parkmobile', the implication being that the car and the device itself comprised a single unit. The photo undoubtedly was the personal car of Mr Williams as it showed a 1925 Velie with a Maryland licence plate. This was soon dispelled by the release of folders printed to promote the Parkmobile and which included a sketch of a car purported to be the New York Six, astride the Parkmobile and instructions on how the device was operated. The folders also included the design of the car's radiator badge, at once elaborate and attractive. The car itself featured a radiator and bonnet similar to the Reo Wolverine car. Wheels were wood, with disc wheels optional and wire wheels at slight extra cost. The Parkmobile was also reportedly to be included on all Davis Eight cars which were to be introduced in 1928 as 1929 models. The Davis Eight failed to get into regular production and whether the pilot models carried the Parkmobile attachment is unknown. Williams followed an irregular course during the promotional days centring his operations in various parts of Illinois, Indiana and New York, as well as the listed headquarters in Baltimore.

KM

NFS INDUSTRIES (US) c.1986
NFS Industries, Lake Orion, Minnesota.

The General Jr was a kit that converted a 1978 to 1986 GMC pick-up truck into a scaled-down semi-tractor truck cab. It had a tall, vertical cab with a squared-off bonnet similar to a full-size GMC semi. The kit included a fibreglass nose, bonnet, doors and rear deck.

HP

N.G. (GB) 1979 to date

1979–1989 N.G. Cars Ltd, New Milton, Hampshire.
1987–1989 T.A. Motor Car Co., Rotherham, South Yorkshire.
1989–1990 Pastiche Cars Ltd, Rotherham, South Yorkshire.
1991–1993 G.T.M. Cars, Loughborough, Leicestershire.
1993 to date N.G. Cars Ltd, Epsom, Surrey.

Nick Green's first project was the Tycoon sports coupé but this did not enter production. Instead Green turned the clock back and produced a kit car called the N.G. TA, which turned out to be very popular. Vaguely influenced by the prewar Aston Martin International, it was initially offered for MGB mechanicals, which fitted in a steel cruciform chassis, to which a one-piece fibreglass body and aluminium bonnet were fitted. The inspiration for the 1982 TC came from Aston's prewar Ulster, and the basis remained MGB with optional Rover straight-6 or V8 power. From 1985 there was a lightweight TCR version intended for racing. The 1983 TD was a 2+2 version which did away with the TC's boat-tail rear, while the TF was a TD with flowing wings. The TA departed in 1987 to the T.A. Motor Car Co. (TAMCC) who developed a Marina-based chassis. This company changed its name to Pastiche in 1989 and took on the entire NG range. The models were renamed: the TA became the International, the TC and TD were dropped and the TF became the Ascot, while a new Marina-based version was also available. With optional Rover V8 power it became the Gladiator, while NG's new Cortina/Sierra chassis model was dubbed the Henley. GTM bought the lot but sold the Henley to CHALLENGER in 1992. Another abortive NG was the 1988 Sedan, a Rover V8 powered luxury 4-seater sports saloon with flowing wings and a fixed roof.

CR

NIAGARA (i) (US) 1900–1902

Niagara Automobile Co., Niagara Falls, New York.

The prototype of this car was completed in 1900, but the company was not formed until March 1901. The car had a 4hp engine and seated four passengers, which sounds quite a load for so small an engine. Few were made, and the company was out of business by the autumn of 1902.

NG

NIAGARA (ii) (US) 1903–1905

Wilson Automobile Co., Wilson, New York.

The Niagara was powered by a 5hp single-cylinder engine mounted under the seat, from which it could be started by a lever. It was a 2-seater with folding front seat to accommodate two more passengers. For 1905 engine power was raised from 5 to 8hp and the price went up by $50 to $900. In the spring of that year the company's assets and equipment were acquired by the La Salle-Niagara Automobile Co. who made a car under their own name from 1905 to 1906.

NG

NIAGARA (iii) (US) 1915–1916

Mutual Motor Car Co., Buffalo, New York.

The Niagara Four was, on the surface, a car of mixed parentage, sponsored by the Mutual Motor Car Co. of Buffalo and the Poppenberg Motor Co., a Buffalo dealership managing its sales and service. The car actually was a rebadged CROW, the product of the Crow company of Elkhart, Indiana. The car's specifications comprised standard components throughout and was otherwise devoid of any originality. Perhaps it was best known as an object of humour at the time for, although the car used a Lycoming engine, the remark of the day was that if it had used a Falls motor instead it might have been called the Niagara Falls, evoking visions of countless honeymooners, tourists and tight-rope walkers, all of whom seemed to gravitate to Niagara Falls, a dual community in both New York State and Ontario, Canada. The 500 or so Niagara Four cars were all 5-seater touring cars without change in the two years of the car's existence. Price was $740.

KM

1980 N.G. TA MkII tourer.
NATIONAL MOTOR MUSEUM

1983 N.G. TF sports car.
NICK BALDWIN

1990 N.G. Pastiche Henley roadster.
PASTICHE CARS

NICE CAR COMPANY (US) c.1990–1997

Nice Car Co., Glyndon, Minnesota.

The Reflection Series I was a replica of the 1967 Corvette Sting Ray that fitted on a mid-sized General Motors sedan chassis. Any Chevrolet engine could be used and it was a relatively simple kit to build. In 1997 the Nice Car Co. was bought by CK3 Design Corp. in Las Vegas, Nevada.

HP

NICLAUSSE (F) 1906–1914

J. et A. Niclausse, Paris.

Like Delaunay-Belleville, Niclausse, founded by Jules and Albert Niclausse in 1890, were well-known boiler makers for whom cars were a sideline, and like the firm from St Denis, they chose a round shape for their radiator and bonnet. Cars were made in a factory separate from the main boiler works. Their first car

1917 Nike 12/15hp sports car, designer Antonia Riera Cordoba at the wheel.
NATIONAL MOTOR MUSEUM

1913 Niclausse 35CV limousine.
NICK BALDWIN

had a 6330cc 30/40hp 4-cylinder T-head engine with separately-cast cylinders and shaft drive. This model was continued throughout the make's lifetime, though the designation changed to 35/50hp in 1908. The following year two smaller models of 12/16 (2437cc) and 20/30hp (4082cc) were introduced. The 12/16 had monobloc cylinders, while the cylinders of the 20/30 were pair-cast. The 1909 models had universal joints between the differential and the wheel hubs. The three models, 12/16, 20/30 and 35/50, were continued without great change up to 1914, but Niclausse did not return to car manufacture after the war. Their boiler work continued; in 1924 their works occupied 30 acres, three times its area in 1914.

NG

NIELSEN (DK) 1957

Jens Nielsen intended to produce a series of his miniature roadsters but ultimately only one was ever made. It was an ultra-compact open-topped car weighing only 100kg (220lbs) and powered by a front-mounted engine driving the front wheels.

CR

NIELSON (US) 1906–1907

Neilson Motor Car Co., Detroit, Michigan.

This was a light runabout powered by a 12hp air-cooled single-cylinder engine, with friction transmission and double-chain drive. Although the car had a short bonnet, the engine was located under the seat. E.A. Nielson built a prototype truck in 1906, and it is possible that only a single example of his car was made as well.

NG

NIGERS (US) 1911

Consolidated Motor Car Co., Atlanta, Georgia.

In June 1911 *The Sportsman and Motorist* announced a new car from this company. No technical details were given, but the photo showed a 2-seater roadster with, presumably, a 4-cylinder engine, not unlike a Hupmobile Model 20 in appearance.

NG

NIKE (E) 1917–1919
Automóviles Nike, J. Alejandro Riera SC, Barcelona.
This was a short-lived car prepared by an industrial components specialist. The Nike was shown at Barcelona Motor Fair in 1919, using an own 4-cylinder engine with 12/15hp and aluminium pistons. There exist photos of a prototype that used a curious panoramic windscreen not seen on the cars shown.

VCM

NIKKEI-TARO *see* N.J.

NILE BRUNEL *see* BELGA

NIMBUS (GB) 1984–1987
1984–1986 Nimbus Projects, Whitchurch, Hampshire.
1986–1987 Nimbus Cars (Custom Moulds), Andover, Hampshire.
The Nimbus was a 2-seater kit-form coupé whose most notable feature was fibreglass monocoque bodywork that featured an early use of Kevlar reinforcement. Balsa sandwich bulkheads, sills and pillars were also employed. The front suspension and brakes were modified Vauxhall Viva items, while a complete Mini front subframe was installed at the rear to create a mid-engined package. A convertible body was also offered. When Nimbus failed, the sub-contracted body moulders Custom Moulds of Andover took it on.

CR

NIMROD (GB) 1973/1979/1981–1986
1973 Nimrod Engineering, Hunston, Chichester, Sussex.
1979 Nova Cars Ltd, Bradford, Yorkshire.
1981–1986 Talbott Alternative Car Co., Wincanton, Somerset.
1986 Fibreglass Applications, Westbury, Wiltshire.
The Nimrod was an original-looking buggy-type machine with a targa roof, and used a Mini front subframe and rear trailing arms in a space frame chassis. Only five kits were sold before the project folded. It was twice revived, latterly with an optional transparent soft-top but by then was very outdated in style. About 20 cars were built in all.

CR

NINON (F) c.1930
G. Vincent, Nantes.
Better known for their motorcycles, this firm briefly marketed a light 3-wheeler, using mostly cycle parts, which they called the Mototri.

DF

NISSAN (i) **(J)** 1937–1942; 1960–1966; 1984 to date
Nissan Motor Co. Ltd, Yokohama.
The Nissan Motor Co. was founded in December 1933, when the name was changed from the former Jidosha Seizo Co. Ltd. This company's products were already being sold under the name DATSUN which was carried by the majority of cars made by Nissan up to the end of 1983. During this period a few cars were badged as Nissan, notably the 6-cylinder saloon based on the GRAHAM, made from 1937 to 1940, and the smaller Opel-like 4-cylinder saloon made from 1940 to 1942. In the 1960s some Datsun-built models were called Nissans, notably the 1488 and 1883cc Cedric saloons, 1595cc Silvia sports coupé, and President saloon and limousine with 3988cc V8 engines. An extended wheelbase version of the latter, called the Prince Royal, was made for the Japanese Emperor in 1966. These Nissans were integrated into the Datsun range in 1967, and the name was not seen again on cars until 1 January 1984 when, as part of a worldwide corporate image change, all Datsuns were re-named Nissan. The range at that time consisted of the 988cc Micra, 1171cc Cherry, 1270 or 1488cc Sunny, 1590 or 1890cc Stanza, 1809 or 1973cc Bluebird and 1488cc Prairie MPV, all with front-wheel drive, and the rear-drive 280ZX sports car and President V8 saloons. The 280ZX was rapidly replaced by the 2960cc V6-engined 300ZX, available with or without supercharger; this in turn gave way in 1989 to a new 300ZX with up to 300bhp in twin-turbocharged form, 4-wheel steering and active suspension. There was also a smaller and less sophisticated 4-cylinder 200SX coupé. This was still available in 1999. The Micra's range was widened to a 1235cc engine and 5- as well as 3-door models, with a 930cc turbocharged version for the home market in 1985. A greatly improved Micra appeared in

1981 Nimrod roadster.
NICK GEORGANO

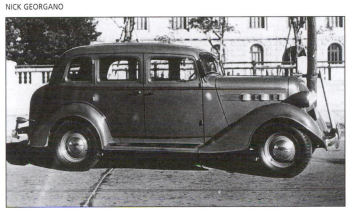
1937 Nissan (i) Model 70 sedan.
NATIONAL MOTOR MUSEUM

1963 Nissan (i) Cedric 1900 sedan.
NICK BALDWIN

1992, with 998 or 1275cc petrol engines with 16-valves and twin-ohc, or a 1597cc 8-valve single-ohc diesel engine. These were still made, in 3- or 5-door versions, in 1999. For the home market there was also the Micra-based Cube, a high-roof 5-door monospace in the Daihatsu Move class, with 1275cc engine.

The Japanese market received a new Bluebird in 1987 with turbo and 4 × 4 versions, while the older export Bluebird was replaced in 1990 by the Primera saloon with 1883cc 16-valve engine. This was still made in 1999, with 1597 or 1998cc twin-ohc 16-valve engines or a 1974cc 8-valve turbo diesel. An estate car joined the Primera range in 1997. One size below the Primera was the Almera, launched in 1995, and with 1392 or 1998cc petrol or 1974cc turbo diesel engines. These followed the pattern of other Nissans, with 16-valve twin-ohc in the petrol engines and 8-valve single-ohc in the diesel.

Among the larger Nissan saloons were the rear-drive Laurel with 1998 or 2499cc V6 engines plus a 2826cc diesel, the front-drive Maxima with 1995 or

1986 Nissan (i) Prairie MPV.
NISSAN

1992 Nissan (i) 3000ZX coupé.
NISSAN

1995 Nissan (i) Micra Wave hatchback.
NISSAN

1998 Nissan (i) Primera estate.
NISSAN

2496cc V6s, with different dimensions even though the engines were so close in size, the rear-drive Cedric and Gloria, whose name dated back to the 1960s and which evolved only gradually over the years, and the 4494cc V8 President, again an elderly design which continued to satisfy a demand on the home market. There were also the INFINITI models which were marketed under their own name.

The Prairie was updated in 1995 and again in 1998, with a 1998cc 4-cylinder engine and permanent 4-wheel drive. It was joined in 1998 by a smaller MPV using Almera running gear, the Tino, while a more upright and van-like MPV was the 1597cc Serena, the European market models of which were built in Spain. This and the Detroit-built Quest, also badged as the Mercury Villager, were rear-driven, while the Prairie and Tino had transverse engines and front-wheel drive. Nissan has a long history of 4×4 off-road vehicles, dating back to the Patrol which first appeared in 1951 as a quasi-Jeep, evolved into a Range Rover rival in the 1970s, and was still made in 1999, in 3- and 5-door versions, with 2826 or 4169cc 6-cylinder turbo diesels or a 4479cc petrol engine. A smaller 4 × 4, developed in conjunction with Ford and made in Spain, was the Terrano. Launched in 1986, this was made in 3- and 5-door models, like the Patrol, but had 4-cylinder engines in the Terrano II, made from 1992. These were a 12-valve 2389cc petrol and 8-valve 2664cc turbo diesel. The larger Terrano, sold in America as the Pathfinder, had a 3275cc V6 engine as well as the Terrano II's 4-cylinder diesel. A different type of 4 × 4 was the Rasheen, a 5-door developed from a concept car, powered by 1498, 1839 or 1998cc 4-cylinder engines. Introduced in 1995, it was a less practical machine than the Terrano and was available only on the Japanese market.

On the sporting side there was the Skyline coupé, derived from a saloon which dated back to 1957. The saloon and standard coupé had 1998 or 2499cc 24-valve 6-cylinder engines, but there was also a series of higher-performance Skyline GT-R coupés. This appeared in 1989 as the R32 with 2569cc twin-turbo engine giving 277bhp, with 4-wheel drive and hydraulically-operated 4-wheel steering, and evolved into the R33 (1995–98) with revised engine and electronically-controlled 4-wheel steering. The latest version, the R34 introduced in 1999, was smaller and lighter by 132lb (60kg), and the engine still gave 277bhp, though with only a single turbocharger. It now had a 6-speed gearbox. A totally different sports Nissan was the R390, a road-going version of the sports/racing coupé which ran at Le Mans in 1997. It had a mid-mounted 3.5-litre twin-turbo V8 developing more than 600bhp, with a carbon/Kevlar body. Its price was approximately $840,000.

A field which Nissan pioneered and largely made its own was the retro-styled small car. This started with the BE-1 which appeared as a concept car at the 1985 Tokyo Show, but soon went into production. It was based on the Micra, but had styling somewhat recalling that of the Mini, which had cult status in Japan. The BE-1 cost nearly twice as much as the Micra on which it was based, but sold very well, though production was limited to 10,000 units. It was replaced in 1989 by the Pao which took the concept a stage further back, resembling one of the first Japanese small cars of the 1950s, and by the S-Cargo, a curious little van with exaggeratedly rounded lines. Pao production was also limited to 10,000 examples. The fourth design to emerge from the Pike Factory, as the department for these retro cars was called, was the Figaro, a Micra-powered 2-seater sports car with 1960s styling.

A new project in 1998 was the Altra, a station wagon powered by lithium-ion batteries which gave a range of 120 miles per charge. In 1998 30 were supplied to California fleet users, with a further 90 in 1999, and general sales starting in 2000. Though aimed at California, these were made in Japan.

International Links

Nissan has more international manufacturing sites than any other Japanese company, and several of these make their own models. The first to be opened was in Mexico in 1961, followed by Australia in 1976, where they took over the former Volkswagen plant at Dandenong, Victoria. In January 1980 they began to buy into the Spanish Motor Iberica SA, and started production of the Patrol in the Barcelona factory in 1983. This continued in 1999, together with the Serena MPV and Terrano 4 × 4. The second European factory was in Italy, where a joint company was set up with Alfa Romeo to make a hybrid car called the Arna, using Alfasud engines and transmissions in a Nissan Cherry body shell. It did not sell particularly well, and was made only from 1984 to 1986. The third European involvement was in England, where in 1986 a factory was set up in Washington, Tyne & Wear, to assemble the Bluebird. This led to full-scale

1997 Nissan (i) Primera 2.0 Sri hatchback.
NISSAN

manufacture two years later, followed in 1990 by the Primera and in 1992 by the Micra. In 1998 the Washington plant turned out 288,838 cars, making it the largest car maker in Britain.

Another important international connection is in the USA where in 1983 Nissan Motor Manufacturing Corp. USA set up a plant at Smyrna, Tennessee. Initially this made pick-up trucks, but has since produced a variety of passenger cars including the Altima, a medium-sized sedan for the US market only, derived from the Primera but with a larger engine of 2389cc. Also made at Smyrna in 1999 were the 200SX coupé and Frontier pick-up. An international link in reverse came in 1984 when Nissan began building the Volkswagen Santana in their factory at Zama, Japan.

Further international co-operation will result from the acquisition by Renault of a 36.8 per cent stake in Nissan, announced in March 1999. This £3.3 billion investment was likely to put the new group in fourth place in world wide output, after General Motors, Ford and Toyota/Daihatsu, with annual sales of around four million vehicles.

NG

NISSAN (ii) (AUS) 1977–1992
Nissan Motor Co. (Australia) Pty Ltd, Clayton, Victoria.
Nissan established a presence in Australia in 1966 after the Hartnett Holdings representation was terminated following government rejection of its plan to produce a 6-cylinder model in Australia. Arrangements were made for the 4-cylinder models to be assembled by the Pressed Metal Corp. at Enfield, New South Wales. Full local manufacture followed the purchase of the former VOLKSWAGEN plant by Nissan Motor Manufacturing. The export of castings, to gain export credits against imported components, was underway by 1978 and bodies were being welded by robots. The Bluebird, introduced in 1981, was the 1983 4-cylinder sales leader and the Pulsar was a joint operation with the HOLDEN Astra in 1984.

1999 Nissan (i) Almera Tino MPV.
NISSAN

2000 Nissan (i) Almera hatchback.
NISSAN

1962 Nobel 200 3-wheeler.
NICK GEORGANO

1913 Noel cyclecar.
BRYAN K. GOODMAN

The Nissan design used Holden pressed body panels and fitted Holden's Family 2 power pack, and further co-operation followed when the HOLDEN Commodore was fitted with the 3-litre Skyline engine. In 1986 the 2-litre class was catered for by the Pintara, an Australian model with the 4-cylinder twin-spark engine installed in the Skyline body shell. By 1989, however, model sharing was being carried on with FORD (vi), and the front-drive 2389cc Pintara also wore a Ford Corsair label, while Falcon commercials were also sold with the Nissan nameplate. The Pintara was available in TRX performance form and as a 'super-hatch' station wagon. Despite heavy capital outlay, this Australian operation was not profitable and was closed in 1992.

MG

N.J. (J) 1952–1956

Nippon Keijidosha Co., Kawaguchi, Saitama.

This was a very small 2-seater open car resembling a Crosley, with its full share of American-style chromework. Originally called Nikkei-Taro, it was designed around new Japanese small car tax laws. Its 12bhp 4-stroke 2-cylinder 360cc engine sat in the tail, driving through a 3-speed unsynchronised gearbox. Commercial vehicles were also constructed.

CR

N.M.C. (AUS) 1915

Norton Manufacturing Co. Ltd, Darlinghurst, New South Wales.

A cyclecar with a 9hp water-cooled 2-cylinder engine coupled to a 2-speed gearbox and belt drive, the NMC was accompanied by a 4-cylinder 9.5hp 3-speed, shaft drive De Luxe model.

MG

NOBEL (GB) 1959–1962

York Noble Industries Ltd, London.

The German FULDAMOBIL S-7 came to Britain thanks to Cyril Lord's York-Noble Industries. The Nobel 200 was produced under licence in factories in Bristol and Newtownards, Northern Ireland, in most respects identical to the Fuldamobil, although it was also available with three wheels as well as a close-set 4-wheeler. The box-section steel chassis was fitted with fibreglass-and-plywood bodywork, a 191cc Fichtel & Sachs single-cylinder engine and a 4-speed gearbox (integral with the engine and incorporating an electric reverse). Cars could be bought either fully-built or in kit form. Ambitious plans anticipated weekly production of no less than 400 cars but it quickly became obvious that the demand for the Nobel was nowhere near that sort of figure. Moves to merge York-Noble with Lea-Francis, itself in the process of winding up, sealed the Nobel's fate. In all, about 1000 Nobels were made, including an alternative utility version called the Nobletta, also made with a sun canopy for hot countries. The Nobel was also manufactured abroad in several countries (in Belgium by Belgian Automobile Industries of Olsene, in Chile by Autos Nobel Sudamericana of Santiago and in India by a subsidiary of Bombay businessman Murari Vaidya). Later a licence was also sold to an Austrian firm.

CR

NOBLE (i) (US) 1902

Noble Automobile Manufacturing Co., Cleveland, Ohio.

This company was formed to make a 2-seater runabout with chain drive, powered by a 6½hp single-cylinder engine to sell for $800. A few were made, including one for a scissors grinder in Washington. D.C. in which belts from the engine shaft drove his tools and grindstones. The company planned to make larger cars, and may have turned out one or two with 10hp 2-cylinder engines, but they were out of business within a year.

NG

NOBLE (ii) (GB) 1985–1992/1998 to date

1985–1988 Kitdeal Ltd (Noble Motorsport), Narborough, Leicestershire.
1988–1992 Noble Motorsport, Narborough, Leicestershire.
1998 to date Noble Moy Automotive, Cosby, Leicestershire.

Lee Noble has become one of the most respected names in the specialist car industry; his career began here. Working under the name Kitdeal before becoming Noble, he introduced an amazing Group C-inspired coupé in 1985. The main attraction was a fabulous space frame chassis, with double wishbone front suspension, Cortina Mk III steering, front uprights, hubs and discs, Renault 20/30 driveshafts and gear lever and complete drive train also from the big Renault. It won the kit car race series twice. Only one Ultima Mk2 was ever made. A more curvaceous Mk3 model in 1987 gained a revised chassis and extra engine options, encompassing Rover and small block V8s. More interested in other projects, Lee Noble took it out of production in 1990, but it craved resurrection and it was revived by ULTIMA Sports in 1992. Another model was an exacting replica of the Ferrari P4 racer, recreated in every detail in fibreglass and Kevlar. The space frame chassis, developed from the Ultima, could accept Renault V6 or Rover/Chevrolet V8 power. There was race-derived purpose-built suspension and a choice of open or enclosed roofs. In 1992 the P4 passed on to J.H. Classics to become the DEON MkIV, but that was quickly acquired by Neil Foreman, whose company (N.F. Auto Development of Staplehurst, Kent) returned the model to production as the Foreman P4 in 1995, adding a Can-Am roofless version in 1997. Noble also developed the MIDTEC Spyder and produced a Lotus 23 replica that was quickly taken over by AURIGA, and it also imported the BECK 550 Porsche Spyder replica. Lee Noble was also behind the ASCARI. A new product for 1998 was the Noble M10, a convertible 2-seater sports car with double wishbone suspension and vented disc brakes all round, and a mid-mounted Ford 2.5-litre V6 engine. It won great praise in the press – one magazine even pronounced it as superior to the Lotus Elise.

CR

NOBLE (iii) (US) c.1992–1994

Noble Motor Cars Corp., Penn Yan, New York.

Noble bought the TF-1800 and TF-V8 MG TF replica kits from GREAT LAKES. These were very accurate replicas with MGB or Chevrolet engines and suspension was MGB-derived.

HP

NOEL (F) 1913–c.1921

Lucien Noel, Courbevoie, Seine.

The first of Lucien Noel's cyclecars was powered by an 8.9hp 2-cylinder engine. with an underslung frame and tandem seating in which the driver sat at the rear, as in the contemporary Bédélia. Noel drove one in the 1913 Cyclecar GP, in which he finished eighth. The postwar Noel had side by side seating and a 904cc 4-cylinder Ruby engine. Lucien and his brother entered two cars, one air-cooled and the other water-cooled, in the 1920 Coupe des Voiturettes. The water-cooled car was probably Ruby-engined, the air-cooled possibly a prewar model.

NG

NOEL BENET (F) 1900

Noel Benet, Offranville, Seine-Maritime.

This was a typical voiturette powered by a single-cylinder De Dion-Bouton engine, unusual only in that drive was to the front wheels. This was one of the first complete front-drive cars, as opposed to *avant-train* attachments for horse-drawn vehicles. Few Noel Benets were made, but one survives.

NG

NOGUEIRA (P) 1989

Hermengildo Nogueira developed a Mercedes SSK replica with its own chassis and a VW-Porsche engine but it is believed no production run was secured.

CR

NOMA (US) 1919–1923

Noma Motors Corp., New York, New York.

The Noma was a typical assembled car tailored with an ovoid radiator, low slung coachwork and wire wheels, giving it a sporting appearance. It made its debut at the New York Auto Show in January 1919, and received favourable attention from the public and reasonable copy by writers for the automotive press. The 1920 Noma was available only as a 2-seater speedster at $2900 and a 4-seater close-coupled phaeton for $300 less. It was fitted with a Continental 7R 6-cylinder L-head engine as standard equipment, or optionally, at the same prices, a 6-cylinder Beaver engine. The sporty Noma with its aluminium step plates was continued in 1921 with prices increased to $3000 and $3200 respectively for the speedster and the phaeton, these dropping to $2000 and $2100 in 1922 augmented by a 6-seater touring car at $2200 and a sedan for $3200. The last Nomas were built in 1923 with a further change in prices – the speedster and 4-seater both at $2500, the 6-seater touring car at $2600, and the sedan at $3500. The Noma wheelbase measured 125in (3173mm). During 1922, the Noma was available with a choice of engines – both Continental L-head sixes – the 3670cc 7R which had been used in 1919, 1920, and 1921 and the 4965cc 9N. Apart from a variety of engines, the only other changes in Noma production appears to have been in an ever-changing price list for its models. An estimated 625 Nomas were completed in the car's five year existence.

KM

NOMAD (i) *see* GNOME (ii)

NOMAD (ii) *see* FOERS

NO NAME *see* HORLEY

NORCROSS *see* NOR-X

NORDEC (GB) 1949

North Downs Engineering Co., Whytleafe, Surrey.

Nordec manufactured the Ballamy (L.M.B.) split-axle ifs and Marshall-Nordec (Rootes-type) superchargers. In 1949 Nordec attempted to market a sports car which used a supercharged Ford 10 engine in a modified Ford 8 chassis with L.M.B. ifs. The body looked like a scaled-down Allard, but the prototype was dumpy and unprepossessing. A sleeker production model was promised, but the damage was done. The arrival of Dellow, offering superior cars for the same small market niche, killed any prospects that Nordec may have had.

ML

1900 Noel Benet voiturette.
NATIONAL MOTOR MUSEUM

1920 Noma Model 1 speedster.
NATIONAL MOTOR MUSEUM

1904 Norden 6½hp runabout.
NATIONAL MOTOR MUSEUM

NORDEN (S) 1902–1905

AB Södertälge Verkstäder, Södertälge.

In 1901 this company signed an agreement with the German firms, NAG and PROTOS, to make some of their designs in Sweden under the name HELIOS.

1904 Norfolk 10hp double phaeton.
NATIONAL MOTOR MUSEUM

In 1902 they made a similar arrangement with NORTHERN of Detroit, Assembled from American-made components, the Norden had a 5hp single-cylinder engine, tiller steering and a 4-seater *dos-à-dos* body. For 1904 engine power went up to 6½hp, in line with the American car, but in 1905 the directors of AB Södertälge Verkstäder decided that railway products were more profitable than cars, and the Norden was discontinued. The stock of completed cars was sold off in 1906. Production figures are not known, but only three Nordens were registered in Stockholm in 1905. As this was Sweden's principal city, the numbers in the rest of the country are not likely to have been many more. Total output may not have exceeded ten cars.

NG

NORDENFELT (B) 1906–1909

This is something of a mystery make as it was said in the British press that it used many components by the steel firm John Cockerill of Liège, yet that company denied any involvement with this or any other make of car. The chassis was apparently by Barriquand et Marre, a well-known supplier of steel frames, and the cars shown at Olympia had English-built bodies by Hewers or Withers. The 1906 show car had a 24/30hp 4-cylinder engine, and later cars had 16, 30/35 and 40/45hp engines. The Nordenfeldt had a round bonnet and radiator in the style of the Delaunay-Belleville. It is not mentioned in the comprehensive *Histoire de l'Automobile Belge*.

NG

NORFOLK (GB) 1904–1905

A. Blackburn & Co., Cleckheaton, Yorkshire.
This company made light cars with two sizes of 2-cylinder engine, 10 and 12hp. They differed only in the cylinder bore, 88mm in the 10hp and 95mm in the 12hp. Capacities were 1460 and 1700cc respectively. The rest of the specification included 3-speed gearboxes and chain drive, with 2- or 4-seater bodies. Only 12 Norfolks were made, of which one survives today, but the company made one further car which they called the Northern.

NG

NORIS (D) 1902–1904

Süddeutsche Motorwagen Industrie Noris Gebr. Bauer, Nüremburg.
Noris cars used French-built proprietary engines in their three models, single-cylinder 6PS, 2-cylinder 12PS and 4-cylinder 24PS. Although apparently of good quality, the Noris cars could not compete against many other makes, and production lasted little more than a year.

HON

NORMA (GB) 1912–1914

Norma Motor & Engineering Co. Ltd, Hammersmith, London.
The first product of this company was an unusual cyclecar called the Pinnace, which had a streamlined boat-shaped body and was powered by a rear-mounted J.A.P. V-twin engine. Drive was taken forward by chain to a 3-speed gearbox in the centre of the armoured ash frame, and thence by another chain to the rear axle. It was designed by A. Percy Hann who drove one in the 1912 London-Exeter Trial, and was priced at £130, but few were sold. The company's next products were conventional light cars with 10.4 or 11.8hp 4-cylinder engines of 1460 and 1740cc, which they sold under the name Norma.

NG

NORRIS (GB) 1914

Stockport Garage Co., Stockport, Cheshire.
This was a light car powered by a 966cc 4-cylinder engine, with 3-speed gearbox and shaft drive. The price of 165 guineas (£173.25) included genuine leather upholstery. It was introduced in June 1914, so had only a short life before the outbreak of World War I in August.

NG

NORSJO *see* SHOPPER

NORSK (N) 1908

Norsk Automobil & Vognfabrik, Christiania.
This company was financed by a bicycle dealer, C.E. Sontum, who planned to produce cars designed by a German engineer, Carl Hantsch. The first appeared in the Spring of 1908, and had an 8hp single-cylinder engine and friction transmission. Only three more were made before the company folded, the last having a 4-cylinder engine.

NG

NORSK GEIJER (N) 1923–1930

C. Geijer & Co. Bilfabrik, Oslo.
This company took over Den Norsk Jernsenfabrik (Norwegian Iron Bed Works) in 1923, and built five cars with 4-cylinder Lycoming engines, which were used as taxicabs. Production seems to have been sporadic, but in the late 1920s they made a larger car powered by a 65bhp straight-8 Lycoming engine, with hydraulic brakes on a 127in (3223mm) wheelbase. The total output was not more than 30 cars.

NG

NORTH AMERICAN ARKLEY (US) c.1995 to date

North American Arkley, Asheville, North Carolina.
The English Arkley kit was built under licence by this company. This was a kit body for the MG Midget/Austin Healey Sprite chassis. North American Arkley also engineered engine conversions for Datsun 4-cylinder and Mazda rotary engines. They were sold in kit and turn-key form.

HP

NORTH BRITISH *see* DRUMMOND (i)

NORTHEAST EXOTIC CARS (US) c.1988

Northeast Exotic Cars, Mayfield, Pennsylvania.
The Scorpion was a Lamborghini Countach replica based on a Pontiac Fiero or a custom tube frame. Coupé and convertible versions were available on either chassis. The tube chassis version used Corvette running gear and Chevrolet engines with GM, Porsche or Z-F transaxles.

HP

NORTHERN (US) 1902–1908

1902–1906 Northern Manufacturing Co., Detroit, Michigan.
1906–1908 Northern Motor Car Co., Detroit, Michigan.
This company was founded in the summer of 1902 by two ex-Olds men who were to become famous as separate car makers later on. They were Charles Brady King (1868–1957) and Jonathan Dixon Maxwell (1864–1928). The first Northern was a single-cylinder runabout designed by Maxwell, and with a strong resemblance to the Curved Dash Olds, though without the characteristic curved dash. Early

1922 North-Lucas saloon.
MICHAEL WORTHINGTON-WILLIAMS

versions were called the Silent Northern, and about 300 were sold in 1903. Maxwell left that year to join Benjamin Briscoe in making the MAXWELL-BRISCOE, but King stayed with Northern until the end of car production.

A 15hp 2-cylinder tourer on an 88in wheelbase joined the runabout for 1904, and by 1906 the 20hp 2-cylinder Type C could be had with limousine body, as well as a tourer on a 106in (2690mm) wheelbase. There was also a 30hp 4-cylinder tourer with air-operated brakes and clutch on a 112in (2843mm) wheelbase. An even larger four was made in 1907, the Type L with 50hp engine on a 119in (3020mm) wheelbase, with a 6-seater limousine body costing $4500. The little single-cylinder runabout was still made, selling for $650, and this and a 24hp 2-cylinder Model C and 40hp 4-cylinder Model L made up the Northern range for 1908, which was the make's last year. In June they merged with the WAYNE Automobile Co., and soon afterwards both Northern and Wayne factories were taken over by E.M.F. Charles King left at the end of the year, and set up his own car manufacturing company in 1911.

NG

NORTH LUCAS (GB) 1923

Robin Hood Engineering Works, Putney, London.
This was a highly unusual car made by Ralph Lucas who had built the LUCAS Valveless earlier in the century, and Oliver D. North who was Chief Engineer at Scammell Lorries from 1920 to 1948. It seems that the design of the car was largely his, with Lucas providing the finance. The Robin Hood works, where it was made, was the home of KLG sparking plugs. The car was inspired by the streamlined designs of Edmund Rumpler, and had a unit-construction body clad in a streamlined saloon envelope of aluminium (body) and fabric (roof). It

was built by the Chelsea Motor Building Co. Although nominally a 4-seater, the rear seat was hardly wide enough to seat one person, due to the narrowing of the body in the interests of streamlining. The rear-mounted engine was a 1460cc 5-cylinder radial with vertical crankshaft, the cylinders being J.A.P. motorcycle units. Power was taken by a 3-speed gearbox to a worm final drive. Front suspension was independent by coil springs and dashpot pistons operating in aluminium cylinders.

North and Lucas had no production facilities for their car, and no replicas were made. In 1928 North took it to the Scammell works where it was eventually broken up.

NG

Further Reading
'Unorthodox Evolution', M. Worthington-Williams,
The Automobile, March 1997.

NORTH STAR (GB) 1920–1921

Shand Motor & Engineering Co. Ltd, North Star Works, Lee Green, London.
This very simple cyclecar shared an address with the EDMOND, which was slightly larger, having a 2-cylinder 688cc Coventry-Victor, whereas the North Star made do with one cylinder, a 4hp Blackburne unit (or optional Precision 2-stroke) with Gradua variable belt gear and single belt drive. It was advertised as 'the finest and cheapest town runabout and holiday tourer in existence for the small family', saying that a child could be carried in the passenger's lap. How happy the 4hp Blackburne would have been with such a load was not explained, although purchasers were warned 'not to overload the car to the extreme'. Not many North Stars were made, although some took part in light car trials.

1911 Norwalk 35 torpedo tourer.
NICK BALDWIN

Both makes, as well as the larger CARROW and SWALLOW (i) were part of the automotive empire of coal mine owner Sir John Payne-Gallwey.

NG

Further Reading
'Mining Motors', M. Worthington Williams, *The Automobile*, April 1997.

NORTHWAY (US) 1921–1922

Northway Motor Sales Co., Natick, Massachusetts.
Ralph E. Northway had been an engine manufacturer in Detroit, Michigan who sold his company – subsequently to supply engines for Oldsmobile – to General Motors in 1912 and, for two years headed the Crescent Motor Co. plant in Carthage, Ohio. He formed the Northway company in 1918 for the manufacture of a line of trucks named after himself. In 1921, Northway decided to augment his truck production with a quality passenger car. The car was launched at Hotel Astor in New York City during Auto Show week in January 1921. The car, designed by A.J. Romer, featured a wheelbase of 128in (3249mm), a 6-cylinder ohv engine of its own design, and a complete line of open and closed bodies, aimed at the upper-class market price range of $2800 to $4950. Plagued by financial difficulties, the Northway failed to achieve more than token production. For 1922, the engine was replaced with a less powerful Herschell-Spillman L-head six, but operations of Northway passenger cars were discontinued on 30 April. Shortly thereafter, Ralph Northway left the company for the Maxim Motor Co. of Middleboro, Massachusetts, builders of fire apparatus, and Romer left to set up a company in nearby Danvers, Massachusetts to built a car under his own name. The Northway truck operations failed in 1926. Despite its attractive lines, enhanced by a Rolls-Royce-shaped radiator, overall production of the Northway car was minimal.

KM

NORTHWESTERN *see* HAASE

NORTON (GB) 1913

Tom Norton Ltd, Llandrindod Wells, Radnorshire.
This was an unconventional cyclecar which had two separate sidecar bodies. It was powered by a front-mounted air-cooled V-twin engine, with epicyclic transmission and shaft drive to the rear axle. Very few were made. Tom Norton was a well-known motor dealer, and had no connection with Norton motorcycles.

NG

NORWALK (US) 1910–1922

1910–1911 Norwalk Motor Car Co., Norwalk, Ohio.
1911–1922 Norwalk Motor Car Co., Miamiaburg, West Virginia.
The Norwalk Motor Car Co. grew out of the AUTO BUG company, and was formed when Auto Bug's owner, Arthur E. Skadden, realised that the day of the high-wheeler had come to an end. The Norwalk was a conventional car with 35hp 4-cylinder Model engine, made initially as a 2-seater roadster or 5-seater tourer. 137 were made in 1910, but Skadden soon got into difficulties and moved to West Virginia where a new group of backers helped him get into production again. The 1912 Norwalks had underslung frames and included a 38hp six as well as a 45hp four. For 1913 still larger cars were made, all sixes, of 40/60hp on 127 (3223mm) and 136in (3452mm) wheelbases and 50/70hp on a 144in (3655mm) wheelbase. The latter had one of the largest engines of its day, with a capacity of 8603cc, yet it was not excessively expensive at $3750 for a 6-seater tourer. Probably the cars were underpriced, for though 1913 was Norwalk's best year, with 412 cars made, they were soon in difficulties again, with receivership in 1914 and the factory closed in February 1915.

Norwalk production was not resumed until 1918 when a completely different car carried the name. This was a modest tourer, with 3153cc 4-cylinder Lycoming engine. They were sold not only as Norwalks, but also with BUSH, MARSHALL and STORK-KAR badges. Of the 103 cars which left the factory in 1918, only 50 were Norwalks. From 1920 to 1922 the Norwalk was built by PIEDMONT. In 1922 they made 127 cars, of which 25 were badged as Norwalks.

NG

NORWOOD (US) c.1979 to date

Bob Norwood Autocraft Inc., Dallas, Texas.
Norwood Autocraft was a tuning shop catering to modified Ferraris, Porsches and similar exotics. Bob Norwood has been involved in numerous racing projects, and his turbocharged street cars were well known. In addition to twin-turbocharged Ferrari 308, Testarossa and F-50 conversions, Norwood also made several series of complete cars. He started with a short run of Ferrari TR59 replicas. These were aluminium-bodied copies of the Ferrari Testarossa racing cars using Ferrari 250 GTE or 330 GT 2+2 running gear. The engines were brought up to TR specifications with 6 carburettors. They also sold a number of 330 P4 Ferrari replicas. The first one was based on 365 Boxer running gear, but subsequent models had proper V12 engines by Ferrari or custom engine builder Batten. They had aluminium bodies on a tubular steel chassis with fabricated suspension and Porsche G50 transaxles. These P4 replicas were priced at $350,000 in 1993. Norwood also built a prototype of a supercar called the Norwood A-12. It had a futuristic body with a 12,742cc Batten V12 engine with 3 plugs per cylinder producing 1240hp. Priced at $450,000 in 1993, it did not make it into production.

HP

NOR-X (US) 1907

United Electrical Manufacturing Co., Norcross, Georgia.
Sometimes called the Norcross, this car is believed to have been a KNOX renamed for sale to a local market. It had a 4-cylinder engine and models offered were 4- and 5-seater tourers and a 2-seater roadster. Prices were $800–850.

NG

NOSTALGIA MOTORCARS (US) 1991 to date

Nostalgia Motorcars Ltd, Rock Hill, South Carolina.
Jim Harrell, owner of Nostalgia Motorcars, designed the Aquila to resemble a 1950s sports-racing car without being a copy of any particular car. It was a beautiful roadster with an aluminium body and tube frame with a late-model Chevrolet V8 engine. Suspension was fabricated and a 5-speed transmission was used. The Aquila was well balanced and usable with its stock running gear. It was only sold in turn-key form for $68,867. Harrel later assembled SHELBY 4000-series Cobras.

HP

NOTA (AUS) 1957 to date

Nota Engineering Co., Parramatta, New South Wales.
Guy Buckingham made specials in England and continued in Australia, with the assistance of two countrymen, Michael Martin, a chassis and suspension man, and Jack Whiffen, a coachbuilder, to turn out one-off competition cars.

The Nota name arose when Buckingham's son, Chris, could say notacar but not motorcar. The 1957 Streamliner sports/racing car was almost a production item with 11 made. It was also known as the Nota-Mazengarb because of the ohv conversion head for the Morris 8/40 engine. In 1960 a clubman was introduced, with a 90in (2286mm) wheelbase, to accept BMC A-series and Ford 105E 4-cylinder engines. In later years a 92in (2337mm) wheelbase version

1980 Nova (iii) coupé.
NATIONAL MOTOR MUSEUM

was made to accept 6-cylinder Holden or Triumph engines. A competition type, the Sportsman was developed which took its drivers to five championships. 64 clubmen were made by 1972. Chassis frames were supplied to fibreglass body producers K.M. and J.W.F., while a variety of competition cars, including Formula Junior and Formula Vee, were constructed. With a total of 250 built, it was the next most prolific Australian racing car builder after ELFIN.

The first road car was a curvaceous 1959 VW-based roadster, which remained a sole example. The Sapphire of 1964 was the first model to which schoolboy Chris had an input with regard to its body styling and six were made. In the early 1970s Guy returned to England and Chris carried on, introducing the 1971 Type 4 Fang with mid-engined Mini power and a Hillman Imp front end. 62 were made by 1978. The introduction of a successor, the Marauder, was foiled by problems with component supply. The 1996 F1, a high-tech design weighing only 1115lbs (560kg), used Toyota V6 power.

MG

NOVA (i) (B) 1914
Florimond Lenaerts, Tirlemont.
This was an assembled car made in the garage owned by Florimond Lenaerts, with financial backing from industrialist Gustave Van Wilderode. Very few were made because of the outbreak of World War I.

NG

NOVA (ii) (NZ) 1968–1970
Anziel Group Ltd, Auckland, North Island.
The Nova project had its origins in 1963 when Ian Gibb visited the RELIANT works in England and there learned of its technical support for car-making projects in Israel and Turkey. He then formed the opinion that, by adopting a similar approach, New Zealand could produce a national car. In 1967 a prototype 2-door saloon, similar to the Turkish ANADOL, arrived and negotiations commenced to obtain licences to import sufficient components to allow an economic annual production rate of 3000 units.

In 1968 a 1500cc Ford Cortina powered model, with disc front brakes, appeared to be on track as 1969 information suggested that a 4-door car was expected to be on sale within a year. The Government, however, not wishing to appear as favouring one particular firm, would only approve import licences for one third of the volume of components required for a viable operation.

MG

NOVA (iii) (GB) 1971 to date
1971–1973 Automotive Design & Development Ltd, Woolston, Southhampton, Hampshire.
1974–1975 Automotive Design & Development Ltd, Accrington, Lancashire.
1978–1979 The Nova Shop, Cricklade, Wiltshire.
1978–1980 Nova Cars Ltd, Bradford, Yorkshire.
1980–1982 Nova Cars Ltd, Ravensthorpe, Dewsbury, Yorkshire.
1982–1990 Nova Sports Cars Ltd, Mirfield, West Yorkshire.
1990–1993 Nova Kit Cars Ltd, Southend, Essex.
1993–1997 Nova Developments (Cobley Engineering), Newquay, Cornwall.
1997 to date Aerotech Ltd, London.
Designer Richard Oakes' second project (after the Tramp beach buggy) was the amazing Nova, which was conceived by Phil Sayers. Dramatic styling incorporated a clamshell canopy for entry and was so good-looking that buyers forgot the humble Volkswagen Beetle floorpan sitting underneath it. Kits were dear at £750 but quality was high. The poor economy saw Nova go to the wall, but a number of firms resurrected it in the late 1970s. Vic Elam emerged as the main maker through the 1980s, and he added body modifications in 1981 and a Bermuda targa-topped version in 1984. The Nova became one of the most prolifically licence-produced cars of all time, with production taking place in the USA (Sterling and Sovran), France (Défi), Italy (Totem and Puma), South Africa (Eagle), Zimbabwe (Tarantula), Australia and New Zealand (Purvis Eureka), Austria (Ledl) and Switzerland (Gryff). The Canadian prototype firm Concordia also built a car based on the Nova.

CR

NOVAL (F) 1982–1984
Noval, Reuilly.
One of the better-looking French microcars, the Noval was fairly conventional. It had a steel tube chassis, polyester bodywork, all-independent suspension, hydraulic brakes and automatic transmission. Numerous power options were listed, including 50cc and 125cc petrol units, a 231cc diesel and 2.4kW electric versions.

CR

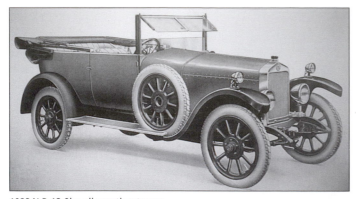

1923 N.P. 13.9hp all-weather tourer.
NICK BALDWIN

1908 NSU (i) 20PS tourer.
NICK BALDWIN

1912 NSU (i) 8/24PS tourer.
NICK BALDWIN

NOVARA (US) 1916–1917

Herreshoff Manufacturing Co., Bristol, Rhode Island.
The Herreshoff company were well-known yacht builders responsible for several America's Cup contenders, who were in business from 1863 to 1946. The Novara car was the idea of Sidney DeWolf Herreshoff (1886–1977), and was a roadster powered by a 1969cc ohv 4-cylinder engine by Sterling (some sources say Scripps-Booth). It was very sporty in appearance, with a curved, Fiat-like radiator, cycle-type wings and a 2-seater body planked with cedar on the inside and mahogany on the outside, with an oak frame. The body side sills were bolted to a nickel steel frame which was curved to correspond to the lower curve of the body. This and the nickel frame were made in Herreshoff's boatworks. The Novara was priced at $2750, and might well have found eager

buyers among wealthy young socialites but they were going off to war by the time it came onto the market. Matters were not helped by the death in a car accident of the New York distributor Gorham N. Thurber. Estimates of Novara production range from one to three cars.

NG

NOWA (D) 1924–1926

Nowa-Werke, Nowawes, Potsdam.
Two models of light car were made by this small firm, a 1.3-litre 5/18PS and a 1.6-litre 6/28PS, but production was very limited.

HON

N.P. (GB) 1922–1925

S.L.C. Co. Ltd, Newport Pagnell, Buckinghamshire.
The N.P. light car took its name from its place of manufacture, and the initials of the makers stood for Salmons Light Car. It was built by the well-known coachbuilders, Salmons & Sons, who had been in business at Newport Pagnell since 1820 (see Salmons in coachbuilding section). Two sizes of Meadows 4-cylinder engines were used, a 1795cc 11.9hp and a 2120cc 13.9hp, together with a 4-speed Meadows gearbox, and Timken rear axle. The bodies were made by Salmons of course, mostly open 2-seaters, tourers and coupés, although a few saloons were made as well. Prices were high, at £520 for a tourer and £650 for a coupé, both with the smaller engine. It is claimed that 395 cars were made, but this seems on the high side, given that there was no production line, and that N.P. manufacture was slotted in between coachbuilding on other chassis. They were withdrawn at the end of 1925, just at the time when Salmons had brought out their Tickford all-weather saloon which was to keep them fully occupied for many years.

NG

NSU (i) (D) 1905–1977

1905–1913 Neckarsulmer Fahrradwerke AG, Neckarsulm.
1913–1926 Neckarsulmer Fahrzeugwerke AG, Neckarsulm.
1926–1929 NSU Vereinigte Fahrzeugwerke AG, Neckarsulm.
1958–1969 NSU Motorenwerke AG, Neckarsulm.
1969–1977 Audi NSU Auto Union AG, Neckarsulm.
The roots of NSU reach back to 1873 when Christian Schmidt and his partner, Heinrich Stoll, set up an engineering shop at Riedlingen on the upper Danube. Their first product was a knitting machine. The partnership broke up in 1880 when Schmidt found a more suitable location for the plant, with room to expand, in the town of Neckarsulm. He named his enterprise Neckarsulmer Strickmaschinen Union, but did not at that time use the initials as a trade mark.

The first penny-farthing bicycle, appearing in 1886, was named Germania. Schmidt adopted the safety bicycle in 1888, and the NSU trade mark was first used in 1892, when the company was re-organised as Neckarsulmer Fahrradwerke AG.

Motorcycle production began in 1901, with Zedel air-cooled 1-cylinder engines, but they were advertised as Neckarsulmer Motorrad, not NSU. Two years later, the company began producing its own engines, designed by Karl Schmidt (1875–1954), son of Christian, who had served his apprenticeship with Gottlieb Daimler.

He was *de facto* chief engineer, and wanted to build cars, but preferred to begin with a ready-made design. He chose the Pipe, paid for the manufacturing rights, and began making the 28/32PS and the 50PS models in 1905. They were too expensive to sell locally, and only a few were produced.

Karl Schmidt then designed a small, low-priced car, the 6/10 which went into production in 1906. The 4-cylinder 1420cc T-head engine put out 10 to 12bhp at 1650rpm, driving the rear axle via a 3-speed gearbox and propeller shaft.

The companion-model 15/24 had a 4-cylinder 4-litre engine and 6-seater touring car body. But they were not yet badged as NSU. They were marketed as the Original Neckarsulmer Motorwagen. The first NSU-badged cars appeared at the Berlin motor show in December 1907, where NSU introduced the 5/12 with an 1132cc 4-cylinder T-head engine (cast in pairs) and a 10/20 car with a 2608cc engine for which the makers claimed 20hp at 1400rpm.

NSU entered a team of three 10/20hp cars in the Prince Henry Trials in 1909, and all three completed the 1140-mile tour without penalty points. The team was awarded a silver medal.

1965 NSU (i) Prinz 4 saloon.
NICK BALDWIN

The first popular NSU was the 5/12 of 1909, which was in such demand that factory expansion was started. The car was upgraded to 5/15 in 1914, with pressure lubrication and automatic spark advance. In 1919 the engine was redesigned with a one-piece cylinder block, becoming the 5/20, which was kept in production until 1926.

Christian Schmidt had died in 1908, and his son left the company in 1909 to set up an aluminium foundry in Heilbronn and began producing pistons and other parts for the motor industry.

It was Arthur Hardt, serving as technical director from 1909 to 1912, who designed the 3.3-litre 13/35, built from 1911 to 1914, and the remarkable 8/24, a highly durable rugged 2.2-litre. An 8/24 took part in the Moscow-Berlin-Paris road rally in 1913. It was the lowest-powered car entered, but it finished without trouble and won three awards for its performance.

Georg Schwarz replaced Hardt on 1 October 1912. Schwarz hailed from Bolheim, where he was born on 20 December 1862, and had designed the Wartburg and Dixi cars. His first designs for NSU were a single-cylinder motorcycle and a 2½-ton truck. In 1914 NSU produced 900 cars, 3600 motorcycles, and 27,000 bicycles. Truck production began in 1914 as military orders flowed in, but NSU also built cars and motorcycles throughout World War I.

The 8/24 was kept in production, alongside the 5/20, until 1925. A heavy touring car with 4-wheel brakes, the 14/40 had a slow-running (2000rpm max) 3.6-litre 4-cylinder engine rated at 54hp, was launched in 1921 and also discontinued in 1925. Built on a 126in (3198mm) wheelbase, it weighed 3792lbs (1720kg) and had a top speed of 62mph (100km/h).

The new model range was composed of the 5/25 with its 5/30 Sports derivative, and the 8/40, both having 4-cylinder L-head engines of 1.3 and 2.1 litres, respectively.

In 1925 Schwarz designed a racing car with a 6-cylinder 1500cc supercharged engine rated at 60hp at 3000rpm. The car weighed only 1822lbs (828kg) and

1958 NSU (i) Prinz 1 saloon.
NATIONAL MOTOR MUSEUM

had a top speed of 109mph (175km/h). He must have been as surprised by its success as the Bugatti and Mercedes drivers in the 1925 German Grand Prix when he saw August Momberger streak home to win, with the brand-new and untested NSU. It was no fluke. Four of these cars were built and entered in the first international German Grand Prix at Avus in 1926. Result: first, second, third, and fourth, in front of 19 other competitors.

These successes came too late to boost NSU's car sales. The year 1925 was a disaster, while the demand for bicycles soared, and motorcycle sales had a small

1965 NSU (i) Wankel spyder.
NATIONAL MOTOR MUSEUM

upturn. One of the big shareholders in NSU was Jacob Schapiro, managing director of Karosseriewerk Schebera in Berlin-Tempelhof, which produced most of the bodies for NSU cars.

Schebera was also the main body supplier to Benz, and set up a branch factory at Heilbronn for deliveries to Mannheim. The Benz contract was cancelled in the merger with Daimler, which led Schapiro to suggest a merger of Schebera and NSU. It came about in 1926, with the establishment of NSU Vereinigte Fahrzeugwerke AG.

NSU had bought a tract of land at Heilbronn in 1924 and set up a factory where its car production was transferred in 1927, as the full capacity of the local Schebera plant became available. Schapiro also ran driving schools, a taxicab fleet and auto retail agencies. Distribution and sales of NSU products now became his responsibility.

For the first time, NSU was in the market with a 6-cylinder model. The 6/30, introduced in 1928, had an L-head engine with 1567cc displacement (later raised to 1781cc). It put out 30hp at 3000rpm (34hp in the bigger version). Georg Schwarz retired in 1927, due to ill health and died in 1929.

As for the alliance with Schapiro, it proved to bring NSU's downfall. As losses mounted in several of Schapiro's businesses, two banks forced him to repossess over RM 20 million in property that nobody wanted. To make matters worse in Heilbronn, Schapiro forced NSU to raise its dividends to shareholders. To keep NSU from going under, the management decided to stop car production and raise cash by selling the Heilbronn plants.

Fiat not only purchased the plants for RM 1 million, but also RM 5 million in NSU shares, with the understanding that Fiat would complete all NSU cars in process of assembly before starting to build its own models in Heilbronn. NSU-Fiat Automobil-AG was established on 1 January 1929, while the NSU company was re-organised as NSU Motorenwerke AG, concentrating on motorcycle production. The body factory at Tempelhof was closed.

NSU had no further involvement with cars, except for accepting a Porsche contract in 1932 to build three test cars belonging to the People's Car Project. The company prospered with its motorcycles, and in World War II, with the Kettenrad, half crawler tractor, half motorcycle-sidecar. The factories were destroyed by repeated air raids in 1944–45. Yet by the mid–1950s, NSU was the world's biggest motorcycle maker. At the same time, the president of NSU, Gerd Stieler von Heydekampf, foresaw the end of the motorcycle boom in Europe. His solution: build cars.

In 1955 the NSU engineering department was instructed to develop a small 4-seater car, with a dry weight of approximately 1100lbs (500kg) and a top speed of at least 62mph (100km/h). NSU had to dig deep in its financial reserves and borrowed $7.5 million to set up a new plant for the car.

The concept came from Ewald Praxl who had joined NSU in 1939 and worked on tactical vehicles during the war. Born in Postelberg, Bohemia, on 5 July 1911, he held an engineering diploma from the Prague Technical Institute, graduating in 1937. He became chief draughtsman, then deputy chief engineer, for NSU motorcycles, and directed the NSU racing team in its most successful years.

The transversely mounted, air-cooled 2-cylinder engine was designed by Albert Roder, an engine expert who had come to NSU from Zündapp in 1935. Overall responsibility fell to Viktor Frankenberger, technical director of NSU since 1951,

NICK BALDWIN

WANKEL, FELIX (1902–1988)

Renowned as the father of the rotary piston engine, to which he gave his name, Felix Wankel was born at Lahr in the Black Forest where his father was a ranger. He never attended university, but showed an early interest in mathematics and engineering, particularly in the field of the motor car, although it is believed that he never drove one. He conceived the idea of the rotary piston engine which could be used for both car and aircraft propulsion in 1929, although it was to be many years before the idea saw practical application. This was because he could not find funding from any major organisation. However, in 1936, as the Luftwaffe expanded rapidly, he was invited by Hermann Goering's Air Ministry to set up the Wankel Test Institute. This worked on a number of aircraft projects which were said to have contributed to the Luftwaffe's superiority in the early years of World War II.

In 1945 he was captured by the French and imprisoned for a while, and his Institute was dismantled. In 1951 he was contacted by the NSU company in connection with a problem with the rotary valves on its racing motorcycles. He developed very efficient superchargers for use in record-breaking NSU motorcycles, and in 1957 the first rotary engine ran at the NSU factory. The company's rights to the engine led to some speculation in their shares, and they sold a manufacturing right to Mazda who nearly beat them into production with a rotary-powered car. However, NSU launched theirs in the Sport Spider in 1963, putting it on sale in 1964. Mazda who, like NSU had experienced many problems in refining the engine for production, launched their twin-rotor 110S coupé in May 1967. NSU made 2375 Wankel Spiders and 33,910 of the Ro80 twin-rotor saloon, and Mazda has made more than one million rotary engined cars, the design still being continued in the revived RX-7.

Felix Wankel died in October 1988.

NG

1969 NSU (i) Ro80 saloon.
NICK BALDWIN

whose background was production engineering. He was born on 19 August 1910, attended schools in Ulm and Munich, worked as a trainee for two years prior to being enrolled at the Munich Technical University, from which he graduated in 1937 with a degree in mechanical engineering. His first job was as tool designer with NSU, where he was to spend his entire career.

The first NSU Prinz cars rolled off the line in 1957, but motorcycle sales were still going so well that in 1958, the 13,017 cars produced accounted for only 27 per cent of the income.

In 1957 NSU approached Bertone with a design contract for a sports coupé on the Prinz platform, and the Sport-Prinz went into production at Neckarsulm in 1959. It was discontinued in 1967 after a production run of 20,831 cars.

In 1959 and 1960, NSU car production topped 30,000 units. Motorcycle production was halted in the autumn of 1963, and the tooling, drawings, and parts on hand were sold to Tito's government in Yugoslavia who wished to start making motorcycles in Sarajevo.

A completely new model, the Prinz 4, with 4-cylinder transverse rear engine, went into production in June 1961, with styling inspired by the Chevrolet Corvair. NSU car production soared to 87,257 units in 1964 and 91,973 in 1965. In order to gain self-sufficiency, NSU bought the stamping plant and body shop from Karosseriewerk Drauz of Heilbronn on 1 July 1965.

NSU had been experimenting with Wankel-patent rotary engines for over a decade when the Wankel-spider was announced in 1964 (a single-rotor engine in a roadster version of the Sport-Prinz). NSU sold 2181 of them in a 3-year period. The Prinz 4 led to a number of high-performance derivatives, first the Prinz 1000, then the TT and the TTS with 78 and 83bhp respectively.

NSU produced 625,171 basic Prinz 4 from 1961 to 1973 plus 207,428 1000 C and 2402 TTS4s. The 1200 TT was made from 1967 to 1972, with a total of 52,082 units, and the 1200 reached 267,660 units in six years of production, 1967–73.

The Prinz 4 evolved into a refined compact family car, Type 110 (later renamed NSU 1200) in 1966. Ewald Praxl had been working for years on a truly advanced front-wheel drive saloon, which went into production as the Ro-80 in 1967. It combined a twin-rotor Wankel engine with front-wheel drive and semi-automatic transmission (3-speed gearbox and hydraulic torque converter), a spacious interior and a low-drag body shape. The architecture was Praxl's to the smallest detail, although the final styling touches came from Klaus Luthe.

The chassis engineers were Herbert Brockhaus and Rudolf M. Strobel, while the engine was developed by Walter Forede and Georg Jungbluth. Over its 10-year production life, NSU made 37,395 Ro-80s.

The last NSU car was the K-70, designed by Hans Georg Wenderoth, who left a good job with Deutsche Shell in Hamburg to complete his studies at the Berlin Technical University, before joining NSU as director of testing in July 1961. The K-70 was a modern front-wheel drive family saloon with a 4-cylinder 1500cc engine, first shown at the Geneva Show in March 1969. But all plans for its production were shelved when Volkswagenwerk's offer to take over NSU was accepted on 26 April 1969. The Wolfsburg giant merged NSU with its Auto Union GmbH subsidiary to form Audi NSU Auto Union AG. Since the end of NSU Ro-80 production, the Neckarsulm plant has been building certain Audi and Porsche models.

JPN

Further Reading
NSU 1873–1984 (in German), Peter Schneider,
Motorbuch Verlag, Stuttgart, 1985.

NSU (ii) (U) 1967–1970
NSU, Montevideo.
The boxy NSU P6 was designed and built in Uruguay, using German mechanical components. The 4-seat, 2-door sedan had been approved by the Technical Institute at Lindau, Germany. A larger model, called the P10 was also made. The 1969 merger of NSU of Germany with Audi, which brought the former under VW control, led to the demise of the Uruguayan P6 and P10 models.
ACT

NSU-FIAT (D) 1929–1967
1929–1959 NSU-Fiat Automobil AG, Heilbronn.
1959–1967 Neckar Automobilwerk AG, Heilbronn.
In 1929 NSU made an agreement with FIAT whereby it would cease to make cars of its own design, and would use its new Heilbronn factory for licence manufacture of various Fiat models. In fact NSU had no financial stake in the new business, of which 50 per cent was held by Fiat and 50 per cent by the Dresdner Bank. The first Heilbronn-built cars were called NSU-Fiat Standards, and used the 2516cc Fiat 521 engine in the shorter wheelbase 522 chassis, with

1930 NSU-Fiat Type 514 cabriolet.
NATIONAL MOTOR MUSEUM

1959 NSU-Fiat 500 Weinsberg coupé.
NICK GEORGANO/NATIONAL MOTOR MUSEUM

1961 NSU-Fiat 770 Jagst coupé.
NATIONAL MOTOR MUSEUM

local bodywork. Only 548 were made in 1932, being outnumbered by the 990 Fiats imported complete from Italy. In 1934 the Balilla went into production at Heilbronn, with bodies by two local firms, Drauz and Weinsberg, 1704 were made that year, and more than 3000 in 1935. From 1936 to 1941 several other Fiat models were made, including the 500, of which about 7000 were made, 1100 (about 5000) and 1500 (about 4000). Again, bodies were by Drauz and Weinsberg, and followed Fiat styling very closely, apart from a small run of 2-seater sports bodies on the 500, which were quite unlike anything from Turin.

Production did not get underway after the war until 1950, when the 500C coupé and estate car were made. Like their Italian equivalents, they had ohv engines. By the time they were replaced by the 600 in 1955, 11,974 had been made. Other Fiat models made at Heilbronn included the 1100 in various forms from 1953 to 1968, and the 1400/1900 series.

In 1958, NSU of Neckarsulm, who had made motorcycles in the intervening years, returned to car manufacture, and to avoid confusion between the two products, NSU-Fiat changed its name to Neckar Automobilwerk AG, although the cars often carried the NSU-Fiat name as well as the new one. They made the 600 saloon in large numbers, the peak year being 1962 when 50,297 were delivered. These included some examples of a design peculiar to Neckar, the Weinsberg coupé using Fiat 500 mechanical units. 6190 of these were made between 1959 and 1963. After 1967 the Neckar name was dropped, and cars were sold as Fiats up to 1973 when the factory was closed. It was cheaper to import cars complete from Turin. The name was changed to Deutsche Fiat AG, and the Heilbronn factory was used for repair work.

NG

NUG (D) 1921–1925

Nug Kraftfahrzeugwerke Niebaum, van Horn & Co., Herford.
Unlike so many small German makes of the 1920s, the Nug made its mark in sporting events, including the first Avus race in 1921. It had a 960cc 4-cylinder engine with inlet-over-exhaust valves, which developed 18bhp. Saloon as well as open sports models were made, and the cars were distinguished by a sharply-pointed vee-radiator and wire wheels.

HON

NU-KLEA (US) 1959–1960

Nu-Klea Automobiles Corp., Lansing, Michigan.
The tiny Nu-Klea electric car was available in convertible or hard-top form. A fibreglass body was fitted to a steel chassis that they planned to change to aluminium later in the production run. A 2-position switch, marked forward and reverse, took the place of a transmission. It had conventional hydraulic brakes and two electric motors, one at each rear wheel. It could be recharged from household current.

HP

NW (A/CS) 1897–1918

Nesselsdorfer Wagenbau-Fabriksgesellschaft, Nesselsdorf (now Koprivnice).
The company now known as Tatra became an automobile maker in 1897, but its history stretches to 1850 when Ignaz Schustala (1822–1891) set up a wagon shop in the small Moravian town of Nesselsdorf. After 1881 with a request for railway cars, Schustala decided to convert his facilities to railway equipment production. He then, in 1890, brought on an engineer Hugo Fischer von Roslerstamm (1856–1917) to serve as technical director. The next year, Schustala died and the company was managed by von Roslerstamm.

In 1897, Nesselsdorfer obtained a Benz automobile and 2-cylinder engine for investigation by its engineers. The interest in possible automobile production seemed to have been sparked by the exploits of Baron Theodor von Liebieg (1872–1939), a textile magnate from Reichenberg (now Liberec). Engineers Edmund Rumpler and Karl Sage, works manager Leopold Svitak, and von Roslerstamm conducted a detailed analysis of the Benz; as a very young student Hans Ledwinka (19 at the time) looked on from a distance. It was decided to construct a car, to be called Präsident, based on the design of the Benz. The 6bhp at 600rpm 2714cc water-cooled 2-cylinder Benz engine was mounted in the rear of the chassis, power being transmitted by two belts to a differential-gear-equipped countershaft, which drove rear wheels by chains. The Präsident with a top speed of 22mph (35km/h), was shown in 1897 at an exhibition in Vienna, and a decision was made to build ten more cars with some modifications. With Rumpler and Sage having left NW, Ledwinka got the job of re-designing the transmission. In 1899, cars called Meteor, Nesselsdorf, Wien, Bergsteiger, Versucher, Auhof and Spitzbub with the same Benz engines were built.

The 1900 Type A, of which 22 were made, was the first true Nesselsdorfer production car. Designed by Ledwinka, its rear-mounted 2714cc engine produced 9bhp at 1400rpm, top speed 25mph (40km/h). After this Ledwinka designed the B which was capable of 28mph (45km/h) from a centrally mounted 12bhp 3190cc engine. It went into production in 1902 just as Ledwinka left the company to work with steam. Until 1904 38 Type B units were made. Two examples of the C Type with 5881cc 24hp flat-4 engines were built in 1902. The D of 1904 was equipped with a similar engine, 12 were produced. Then came 8 examples of the E with a 18bhp 3775cc 2-cylinder engine, followed in 1906 by 3 examples of the F with a 35bhp 7550cc flat-4 engine.

1897 NW Präsident 4-seater.
NICK BALDWIN

During those years there was more and more criticism of the Nesselsdorfer vehicles, largely due to the unreliable central placement of the engine which was practically inaccessible without taking the car to pieces. To solve this problem, two engineers were hired with the task of designing a better NW. Kronfeld designed the J (with front-mounted 35bhp 5881cc engine – 11 were made between 1906 and 1908), and Lang designed the L (with front-mounted 29bhp 4503cc SV four). Both the J and L were very heavy and therefore underpowered.

Upon his return to NW in late 1905, Ledwinka, as the director of the car division, decided to design a completely new car, the Type S. This one was powered by an advanced 3308cc ohc 4-cylinder engine with 30bhp output and a top speed of 56mph (90km/h) (37 examples were made until 1909). A more powerful version of the S with 4962cc 50bhp 6-cylinder engine, 68mph (109km/h), was produced from 1911 in a quantity of 10.

1912 was a dark year for NW, due to a 23-week labour strike from May to October. L. Svitak left NW in November 1912, and Hugo Fischer von Roslerstamm in April 1913.

The Type S was replaced by the T in 1914 (44bhp 3562cc monobloc four), later renamed T 21 and produced until 1922. In 1915 came the Type U propelled to 75mph (121km/h) by a 5343cc 55bhp 6-cylinder engine. This remained in production until 1925 as type T 10.

When Erhard Kobel, the new chief since 1916, built a railroad car factory instead, Ledwinka once again left NW, this time for the Steyr.

After World War I, in 1918–19, the NW marque was replaced by the Tatra.
MSH

NYBERG (US) 1903–1904; 1911–1913

1903–1904 Nyberg-Waller Automobile Co., Chicago, Illinois.
1911–1913 Nyberg Automobile Works, Anderson, Indiana.
Swedish-born Henry Nyberg built a 2-cylinder runabout soon after arriving in Chicago, and followed this with a single-cylinder model, unlike nearly all other car makers who progressed from singles to twins. He went into partnership with a Mr Waller to make his runabout, but it seems that most of their business was in repair work. No more cars were made in Chicago, though Nyberg remained there until 1911 when he moved to Indiana. There he moved into the former RIDER-LEWIS factory and began manufacture of a 35/40hp 4-cylinder car selling for $1250. A 60hp six was added for 1912, and two sizes of six for 1913, a 45 and a 60hp. These were more ambitious cars, selling for up to $3250 for a 7-seater limousine on a 138in (3503mm) wheelbase. However, the company was seriously under-capitalised, and closed in November 1913. The factory re-opened in March 1915 to make the MADISON, with Henry Nyberg as the manager. This venture lasted until 1919.
NG

1905 NW Typ B 8hp break.
NICK BALDWIN

1911 NW 40hp limousine.
NICK BALDWIN

1914 NW Typ S tourer.
NATIONAL MOTOR MUSEUM

NYMPH (GB) 1975–1977

Bohanna Stables, Cadmore End, High Wycombe, Buckinghamshire.

Peter Bohanna and Robin Stables were behind the 1972 Diablo prototype, which eventually became the A.C. ME3000. Their later Nymph was a very different project: an economical open fun car. The bodywork was a fibreglass monocoque based on a moulding taken from a Hillman Imp floorpan, and the mechanicals were all Imp. There was some interest from Chrysler UK to produce the car but the demise of the Imp in 1976 scotched any such plans and 34 Nymphs were eventually produced independently as kits.

CR

NYVREM (GB) 1986

Nyvrem Cars, Weston-super-Mare, Avon.

Designed by a man called Mervyn (hence 'Nyvrem' in reverse), the Nirvana was an execrable Ford Cortina-based 2-seat coupé. A space frame chassis housed any of a variety of engines mounted in a centre-transverse position, with provision for Ford V6 engines mounted longitudinally. Because of half-baked styling, the car was withdrawn for redevelopment but nothing more was ever heard.

CR

OAKLAND (US) 1907–1931

Oakland Motor Co., Pontiac, Michigan.

The Oakland Motor Car Co. had its origins in the Pontiac Buggy Co. established in 1893 in the city after which it was named. Because there was already an existing PONTIAC (i), a new name had to be found when Edward G. Murphy of the buggy company decided to go into the automobile business. The name chosen was Oakland, which had also been borne by the buggies, after Oakland County in which the city of Pontiac was located. The first Oakland car was designed by Alanson P. Brush (1878–1952) who had already helped the Lelands with the early Cadillacs, and was later to design the Brush Runabout. The Oakland was a relatively small car with a 20hp vertical-twin engine which rotated counter-clockwise, planetary transmission and shaft drive. The prototype appeared in late 1907 and during 1908 four body styles were offered, including a 2-seater with dickey, a 5-seater touring car, a landaulet and a taxicab. About 200 of the 2-cylinder Oaklands were made in 1908, and the model was continued into 1909. The last 2-cylinder models had a different design of engine, and were built by a company within the General Motors group, probably the Seager Engine Co. of Lansing, Michigan. 1909 saw the adoption of a conventional 5213cc 40hp 4-cylinder engine. About 700 of these were made during 1909 out of a total of 1035 Oaklands that year. The 2-cylinder car was dropped at the end of the season after about 750 had been made in all.

Towards the end of 1908 Oakland had attracted the attention of William C. Durant, and in April 1909 it was absorbed into Durant's General Motors Corp. The 40 was continued for 1910, and was joined by a 3295cc 30hp. These were produced in much larger numbers, 1910 figures being 4049 cars, 1911, 3386 and 1912, 5838. Oakland, whose slogan was 'The Car With a Conscience', earned themselves a good reputation in motor sport, particularly reliability runs and hill climbs. In 1912 Oakland were in 8th place among American car producers. The largest model was now the 5473cc 45, and there was also a 4160cc 40, in addition to the 3295cc 25.

Oakland introduced their first 6-cylinder car for 1913. This had a 6246cc engine and a 130in (3299mm) wheelbase. It was known as the Greyhound 6-60 line, and was offered with a choice of Delco electric lighting and ignition combined with a compressed air starter or the full Delco electric lighting, ignition and starter. 1913 Oaklands were distinguished by handsome vee-shaped German silver radiators. Engines, now and for many years to come, were made by Northway, while bodies came from Budd. The 6-cylinder engine was enlarged to 7233cc for 1914, this being the largest engine ever installed in an Oakland. About 100 of these were built, selling for $2450 for each of the four body styles. There was also a new 4727cc 6-48 Light Six. The 6-60 was dropped for 1915 when two models were offered, the 3154cc Light Four and the 4727cc Light Six. A new chief engineer joined Oakland that year, Finnish-born Nils Eric Wahlberg who later worked for Nash from 1918 to the early 1950s. Charles W. Nash was general manager of Oakland as well as president of General Motors until he resigned both jobs in the Spring of 1916. A new model for 1916 was the Model 50 V8 powered by a 5675cc engine also used by Oldsmobile and Scripps-Booth. This developed 71bhp and helped Oakland to a record production of 25,675 in the calendar year 1916. The following year was even better with 33,171 cars made, giving Oakland 8th place in the US industry. Another new model for 1916 was the Model 32; this had a small 2900cc 6-cylinder engine and a flat radiator. For 1917 it gained ohvs and an increase in power from 35 to 41bhp. It was known as 'The Sensible Six' and was made until 1924. The flat radiator was standardised on the 1918 Oakland range which no longer included a V8. Sales that year were 27,757 because of war contracts, but in 1919 they jumped to 52,124, a figure not beaten until the arrival of the Pontiac seven years later. 1916 was the last year for the 4-cylinder Oaklands, and the ohv six was the only model up to the end of the 1923 season. A copper-cooled 6-cylinder engine, on the same lines as Chevrolet's copper-cooled four was planned for the 1922 season, but after disappointing tests it was dropped. The 1922–23 sixes were called the 6-44 and the 1924 models were designated 6-54.

The Oakland 6-54A marked a number of changes from the previous models; although the engine was the same size it now had side-valves as these made the engines cheaper to produce. An improvement was the use of 4-wheel brakes, but Oakland's most important step forward for 1924, and one which earned it a place in history, was their use of the Duco nitro-cellulose lacquer paint which was developed for General Motors by the DuPont laboratories. The use of this air-dried material cut the time required to paint an Oakland body from 36 to

1911 Oakland 15hp coupé.
NICK BALDWIN

1915 Oakland 25hp tourer.
NICK BALDWIN

1921 Oakland Model 34-C tourer.
NICK BALDWIN

13½ hours, with a great reduction in labour costs. The Duco finish eventually became available in almost any colour, thereby greatly expanding the public's choice of car colours, but the 1924 Oaklands were finished in a single shade of blue, the cars being advertised as the True Blue Oakland Six. Five body styles were available, from $995 to $1445. 37,080 cars were produced in the 1924 model year, but GM's president Albert P. Sloan was not happy with Oakland's position in the line-up. He dismissed general manager George W. Hannum, replacing him with Alfred R. Glancy, who was given the task of supervising the introduction of a new line of cars to be called Pontiac. This went into production in 1926, and is described in its own entry.

The 6-cylinder Oakland was called the 6-54B for 1925, and 6-54C for 1926 while in 1927 it became the Greater Oakland Six, and for 1928 the All-American Six. Engine capacity was slightly increased to 3032cc from 1925, while a new 3474cc engine powered the All-American Six. The increase in size was necessary in order to mark out the Oakland line from the smaller and cheaper Pontiacs.

1929 Oakland All-American sports phaeton.
NATIONAL MOTOR MUSEUM

Oakland prices ran from $1045 to $1265, compared with $745 to $925 for the Pontiacs. The All-American Six had the same cylinder bore as the Pontiac, and identical pistons. More than 60,000 All-American Sixes were made between June 1927 and June 1928, compared with just over 130,000 Pontiacs. New styling, including a horseshoe-shaped radiator grill with dividing line down the centre, appeared on the 1929 Oaklands and Pontiacs.

For 1930 Oakland introduced a 4113cc 85bhp V8 engine. This was installed in the All-American Six chassis with similar body styles, although the new engine reduced overall weight of the cars by about 1500lbs (682kg). Top speed of the Oakland V8, which replaced the All-American Six for 1930, was around 72mph (115km/h). Only 24,443 V8s were made in the calendar year 1930, as against more than 188,000 Pontiacs. The V8 Oakland was continued into 1931, but the public saw it merely as a big Pontiac, which indeed it was. Appearance was very similar, and the same body styles, all made by Fisher, were offered. One of the main differences was that the 1931 Oakland had a synchromesh gearbox and also 5in (127mm) longer wheelbase. However, these were not enough to sell the car, only 12,985 Oaklands finding buyers during the 12 months January to December 1931. For the New York Show in January 1932 the Oakland V8 was rebadged as a Pontiac, and six months later the name Oakland Motor Car Co. was changed to Pontiac Motor Co. The Oakland's fate was unique in that, whereas other GM divisions had spawned new sub-makes such as Buick's Marquette, Cadillac's La Salle and Oldsmobile's Viking, the sub-makes eventually dying, in Oakland's case the parent firm was killed off, and Pontiac survives successfully up to the present day.

NG

Further Reading
Seventy Five Years of Oakland – Pontiac, John Gunnell, Crestline, 1981.

OASIS *see* SCORHILL

O&C (GB) 1984–1988
O&C Products (W.V. Engineering), Peterborough, Cambridgeshire.
One of the early Lotus 7 inspired replicas which proliferated in the 1980s was the O&C Sport, which was a dual purpose road/race car. The basis was one of three: Morris Marina, Ford Escort or Toyota Celica/Carina. It had a removable windscreen for competition work. The Super Sport was similar to the Sport, except for its massive front wings/spoiler and the option of a Rover V8 engine. A more practical road car proposition was the Sprint, with its 1930s style flowing front and rear wings, small doors and full windscreen. A further model, the Sonnet was similar in conception to the Sport, sharing the pressed steel body/chassis construction and roll-over frame, but it had more stylised front and rear body sections, and could be either Marina or Minor based. Oldham & Crowther's Thruxton was more of a racer, using a pressed steel main body/chassis unit as per normal O&C practice, but designed to accept a variety of coil/spring and wishbone suspensions systems, with a live rear axle or optional irs. A further Toyota Celica-based coupé model, the Serac SS, was presented but probably did not enter production.

CR

O'CONNOR (US) 1916
O'Connor Corp., Chicago, Illinois.
The O'Connor was announced in six different models, the largest having a 25hp 6-cylinder engine. It is likely that only one prototype was built, or possibly no cars at all, the photograph being a retouched version of another car, as with the OWEN (i). The promoters, neither of whom bore the name O'Connor, also floated the O'Connor Aeroplane Co. and the O'Connor Hydroplane Co.
NG

OCTO (F) 1921–1928
L. Vienne, Courbevoie, Seine.
The Octo was a light car of no great originality which managed to survive for eight years in a highly competitive market. The first model used a 1590cc side-valve 4-cylinder Ballot engine and friction transmission, and this was followed in 1922 by a 972cc Ruby engine, also with side-valves, but with a conventional 3-speed gearbox. Most were sold with 2-seater bodies, but there was also a delivery van and a Grand Sport model which had an ohv Ruby engine, flared wings and, from 1926, front-wheel brakes. From 1927 a larger Ruby engine of 1097cc was adopted, but the Octo was practically at the end of its life by then.
NG

OD (D) 1933
OD-Werke, Dresden.
The OD was largely seen as a 3-wheeled delivery van or truck, in which the single front wheel was driven by a 200cc DKW engine. However a few were made with 2-seater passenger bodies, or as Kombinationswagen, an early form of estate car. The manufacturer, Willy Ostner, later made 4-wheeled vans under his own name which were built up to 1957.
HON

ODELOT (US) 1915
Lawrence Stamping Co., Toledo, Ohio.
The Odelot was made in only one style, a 2-seater doorless raceabout powered by a 20hp 4-cylinder engine priced at a modest $450. A tourer was promised, but the company did not remain in business for long enough for it to appear. The name was the reverse of the city where the car was made.
NG

ODETTI (I) 1922–1923
SA Automobili Odetti, Genoa.
This company made a light car powered by a 8.9hp vertical-twin 2-stroke engine, with 3-speed gearbox and shaft drive. Chassis and body were of integral construction. Probably only a few prototypes were made.
NG

ODIN (US) c.1982
Odin, Cambridge, Indiana.
The Odin Cyclecar was a 3-wheeled sports car with a motocycle running gear. A steel tube frame used two wheels in front. The fibreglass body had a 1920s look with small windscreen, exposed engine and a short, stubby tail. They were sold in kit and assembled form.
HP

OFELDT (US) 1899–1902
1899–1900 F.W. Ofeldt & Sons, Brooklyn, New York;
1901–1902 Newark, New Jersey.
Ofeldt & Sons were well-known makers of steam launches who put one of their V-twin marine engines in a car in 1899. 'It is not a thing of beauty' observed *Horseless Age*, but the second car was perhaps better looking; anyway it incorporated a surrey fringe 'to look as much like a horse-drawn vehicle so that it wouldn't scare horses'. Only two cars were built at Brooklyn, and at least one more and a large delivery wagon with a 4-cylinder engine at Ofeldt's other factory at Newark.
NG

OFFORD (GB) c.1903

Offord & Sons, South Kensington, London.

Like THRUPP & MABERLY, Offord was a well-known coachbuilder who made a small number of electric carriages based on their horse-drawn vehicles.

NG

OGLE (GB) 1960–1972

David Ogle Ltd, Letchworth, Hertfordshire.

David Ogle set up a design company in 1954, undertaking industrial design work such as television and radios. He hoped to rival the Italian carrozzeria and offered his first car for sale in 1960. This was a rounded 4-seater fibreglass-bodied coupé with tailfins. Its basis was the Riley 1.5, from which the platform was taken and then reinforced by a tubular structure by Tojeiro. The suspension and 68bhp 1.5-litre engine were taken directly from the Riley. Only eight were made up until 1962, when a new Ogle appeared, the SX1000. This was one of the first attempts at rebodying the Mini, in this case with a dumpy fibreglass coupé shell seating 2 to 4 passengers in a luxurious interior. The high cost of manufacture, coupled with David Ogle's death at the wheel of an SX1000, brought production to a halt. However, the design was later revived as the FLETCHER GT. Two examples of the Daimler V8-powered SX250 were also built, the design later forming the basis of the Reliant Scimitar. Ogle also offered an estate version of the Scimitar with glass rear bodywork. The last commercially-available Ogle model was the Aston Martin 'Sotheby Special' of 1972, of which two examples were built. Ogle continued as a design company, with strong automotive links: it designed the Reliant Scimitar GTE, Bond Bug and Reliant Robin, and continues to exist today.

CR

OGREN (US) 1915–1923

1915 Ogren Motor Car Co., Chicago, Illinois.
1916–1917 Ogren Motor Car Works, Waukegan, Illinois.
1920–1923 Ogren Motor Car Co., Milwaukee, Wisconsin.

Designed by Hugo W. Ogren, who had been responsible for the COLBY, the first Ogren was a 34hp 6-cylinder tourer. For 1917 the range was expanded to include five body styles, at prices from $2500 to $3750. No cars were made between 1917 and 1920, when Ogren reorganised with a new factory in Milwaukee, adapted from an ice skating rink. The new Ogren used a 4965cc 65bhp Beaver 6-cylinder engine, replaced for 1922 by a 5327cc 70bhp Continental. Prices were now considerably higher, running from $4250 to $5500. Although it was a handsome car, with round-topped radiator, disc wheels and step plates, it was overpriced, and only 26 were sold in 1922 and five left-overs in 1923. Meanwhile Hugo Ogren had left to make the COMMANDER. Total Ogren production was 306 cars.

NG

OGSTON see DEEMSTER

O.H.B. see CRESTMOBILE

OHIO (i) (US) 1909–1912

1909–1912 Jewell Carriage Co., Carthage, Ohio.
1912 Ohio Motor Co., Carthage, Ohio.

Often rendered OhiO, this was a conventional car with 4-cylinder engines quoted variously as 35/40hp (1910) and 40hp (1911–1912), although they were probably the same units. There was also a smaller 28hp roadster listed for 1911 only. Seven body styles were listed in 1912, some having distinctive names, such as the Euclid torpedo and Grand Prix Bullet roadster. The vice-president of the company was Ralph E. Northway who was better-known for his engine company, which he sold to General Motors in 1912. This gave him enough money to buy out the Ohio Motor Co. and rename it the Crescent Motor Co. The OhiO designs were continued under the name CRESCENT (iv) but only up to 1914.

NG

OHIO (ii) (US) 1910–1918

Ohio Electric Car Co., Toledo, Ohio.

Advertised as 'The only car for the woman of refinement today', the Ohio was

1903 Offord electric victoria.
NICK BALDWIN

1962 Ogle SX-1000 coupé.
NATIONAL MOTOR MUSEUM

1910 Ohio (i) Forty-A tourer.
NICK BALDWIN

1938 Ohta Model OD saloon.
NATIONAL MOTOR MUSEUM

1914 Old Mill 10hp coupé.
NICK BALDWIN

a fairly typical electric car made mostly in coupé form, with steering from the front or rear seats, though an open victoria or a roadster were listed up to 1916. Crocker-Wheeler motors were used, with 4-speed controllers. In its first year the company shared a factory with the makers of the MILBURN electric and built only 12 cars, but once they were in their own premises, production rose to 300 in 1915 and 650 in 1916. The decline in popularity of the electric car brought about the end of the company, though they tried to diversify by making bodies for other car makers.

NG

OHLSEN (NZ) 1990–1998
John Ohlsen Developments Ltd, Auckland, North Island.
A former Shelby racing team mechanic, who had a special affinity with the 1964 FIA 289 Cobra, Ohlsen resolved to build a replica of that particular version. The completed Shelby FIA 289 Cobra was a Shelby-authorised and authentic replica with transverse front suspension, hand-beaten aluminium-alloy body and Halibrand-pattern wheels. In 1995 a Shelby Daytona coupé replica was also offered.

MG

OHMIC (J) 1950s
The Ohmic was an extremely compact open 4-wheeled microcar with a sporting touch. It sat on tiny 8in wheels and was powered by a 356cc 2-cylinder engine developing 11.5bhp. It is unknown if a production run was undertaken.

CR

OHTA (J) 1922; 1934–1957
1922; 1934–1935 Ohta Jidosho Seizosho Co. Ltd, Tokyo.
1936–1945 Kosoku Kikan Kogyo Co. Ltd, Tokyo.
1947–1957 Ohta Jodosha Kogyo Co. Ltd, Tokyo.
Founded in 1912, the Ohta Jidosho Seizosho Co. built a prototype 4-seater car in 1922, but did not go into production until 12 years later. The 1934 Ohta was powered by a 736cc 4-cylinder side-valve engine, and was very much the same type of car as the DATSUN. Open tourers, saloons and roadsters were made, as well as light trucks. After the war production was restarted with the Model PA. This used the same engine enlarged to 903cc but with independent suspension and updated bodies. Some of the saloons were used as taxis and there was also a Model OE with prewar styling, a 2-door roadster with cut-away doors. Again, this was similar to a contemporary Datsun model.

In the 1950s Ohta made the VK-2 with a 5-seater closed body behind which was a pick-up, what would in later years be called a crew-cab pick-up. Their final model was the PK-1, a 4-door saloon with 25bhp engine. In 1957 Ohta was absorbed by KUROGANE who had made cars but by then were making only 3-wheeled trucks.

NG

OKEY (US) 1896–1908
1896–1906 Perry Okey, Columbus, Ohio.
1907 Okey Motor Car Co., Columbus, Ohio.
Perry Okey built his first car in 1896 when he was only 16, and over the next ten years he made at least nine cars, gradually improving the design and selling them when they were completed. In 1905 he made four of the same kind, with 2-cylinder 2-stroke engines, epicyclic transmission and shaft drive. He was encouraged by the journalist Hugh Dolnar to form a company to make these in larger numbers, and in January 1907 the Okey Motor Car Co. was formed. However, financing was insufficient, and by November the company was in receivership. The receiver was allowed to borrow $2000 to enable orders on hand to be completed, so it is possible that an Okey or two was sold into 1908.

NG

OLDFIELD (US) 1924
Oldfield Motors Corp., Los Angeles, California.
Racing driver Barney Oldfield had divested his holdings in the Oldfield tyre, a division of Firestone, in 1924 and this was the ideal opportunity for a group who saw a success in marketing the Oldfield name for a new make of automobile, theorising that the Oldfield magic would be an instant winner in the marketplace with Barney Oldfield himself heading the new concern. The idea seemed sound enough, with Barney's career on the track seemingly sufficient to automatically give the car a sort of built-in promotion. The corporation was duly organised and a prototype convertible coupé built in the Los Angeles factory of the Kimball truck company. This pilot model was ahead of its time in design featuring 4-wheel hydraulic brakes and integrally-built bumpers. Balloon tyres were fitted to the Oldfield's wire wheels and power was from a Wisconsin 6-cylinder engine developing 75bhp at 2500rpm. Listed price of the model was $3550 and Oldfield himself was assigned to drive the car to Indianapolis for the 1924 Indianapolis 500. While the car was being exhibited in and around the Indianapolis area, a showroom was set up in Los Angeles. Upon his return from Indiana, an 8-cylinder engine was substituted for the six and the car then placed on display in the showroom where it attracted considerable attention. But Oldfield had fallen in love and he and his bride chose the time to go an extended honeymoon in Europe. In Oldfield's absence, interest in the new car flagged and upon his return it was decided to abandon the project entirely. Thus the handsome car with its high fluted radiator turned out to comprise the complete output of the Oldfield automobile.

KM

OLD MILL (GB) 1914
Albert Lambourne Ltd, Brighton, Sussex.
Albert Lambourne built an experimental car or two at the beginning of the century, and in 1914 made a light cars for sale under the name Old Mill. It was a well-made machine, with 1093cc 10.2hp Dorman engine, shaft drive and a mechanical starter operated from the dashboard. An open 2-seater and coupé were made, but they were expensive at £220–£242, and only 13 were sold. They

were made at the Old Mill Works, on the site of Black Mill which had been demolished in 1906.

NG

Further Reading
'The Cars of Albert Lambourne', *Old Motor*, January 1964.

OLDSMOBILE (US) 1896–2001

1897–1899 Olds Motor Vehicle Co., Lansing, Michigan.
1896–1943 Olds Motor Works, Lansing;
Michigan (Detroit, Michigan 1899–1907).
1943–2001 Oldsmobile Division of General Motors Corp.,
Lansing, Michigan.

Ransom Eli Olds (1864–1950) was unusual in having two well-known makes of car named after him, the Oldsmobile and later, the Reo. He built a 3-wheeled steamer in 1887, followed by a 4 wheeler in 1893. These were purely experimental, although it is reported that he sold one of the steamers to India. In 1895 and 1896 he obtained patents for internal combustion engines, and not wishing to risk the success of his father's company, Pliny F. Olds & Son, he sought financial backing to start a new company for the manufacture of petrol-engined cars. The Olds Motor Vehicle Co. was formed in August 1897, although at least one car had been completed before the end of 1896, and four more were completed in 1897. They were 4-seaters powered by 5hp single-cylinder engines, with a top speed of 18mph (30km/h). Olds also built at least two electric cars at about this time, although little is known about them. Olds appears to have built no cars in 1898, the year in which one of his backers persuaded him to move to Detroit, where there was a much greater supply of labour, as well as buyers, than in the small town of Lansing.

A new company, the Olds Motor Works, was incorporated in May 1899, and Olds began work on a new car which appeared in 1901 as the Oldsmobile Runabout (earlier cars were simply called Olds). It had a horizontal single-cylinder engine of 1565cc, two-speed planetary transmission and single-chain final drive. The engine turned at no more than 500rpm ('one chug per telegraph pole'). The front of the body curved up to form the dash, hence the name Curved Dash which was adopted in later years. Suspension was by two long springs which ran from the front to the back of the frame, reinforcing the wooden side members. The Olds factory in Detroit was almost destroyed by fire in the spring of 1901, and only one car, a prototype Curved Dash, was rescued. It has been claimed that because this was the only one of several different designs to survive, Olds was forced to base his future production on this car, but it seems that he and his management had already decided that the Runabout was the model they would put into production. By the end of 1901 they were being sold to the public for $650, which price did not include mudguards of any kind – these were $10 extra. Other extras included a rear-facing seat for two more passengers ($25), a hood and additional lighting.

425 cars were made in 1901, production rising to 2100 in 1902, 4000 in 1903, 5500 in 1904 and 6500 in 1905. These figures made Oldsmobile the largest car maker in the world in the years 1903 to 1905. From 1904 other models as well as the Curved Dash contributed to the total, though the little Runabout was the best seller; it has been credited with being the first mass-produced car, although there was no moving assembly line as at Ford's Highland Park factory ten years later. However, the cars were pushed along on their wheels so that successive groups of workmen could add components. Olds was more of an assembler than a manufacturer, for several major mechanical components were bought in, engines from Leland & Faulconer, transmissions from the Dodge brothers and radiators from the Briscoe brothers. Although its light construction might have made the Curved Dash seem more of a town car, examples made a number of long distance runs. The first to arrive in New York was driven there by Roy Chapin for exhibition at the city's second annual show in Madison Square Gardens in October 1901. The 632-mile (1017km) journey took seven days. In 1903 L.L. Whitman and Eugene Hammond drove a Curved Dash from San Francisco to New York, calling at Olds' Lansing factory on the way. This journey took 73 days.

Few changes were made during the Curved Dash's six-year production run, and the basic price of $650 was maintained throughout. From 1903 wood-spoked wheels became more common than wire, though the latter were still available. The wheelbase was extended from 60 to 66in (1524 to 1676mm) in 1904. An alternative runabout with straight dash was offered in 1906–07, still at

1902 Oldsmobile curved-dash runabout.
NATIONAL MOTOR MUSEUM

1910 Oldsmobile Limited 60hp tourer.
NICK BALDWIN

1920 Oldsmobile Model 37-A tourer.
NICK BALDWIN

the $650 price set in 1901. The Curved Dash sold well abroad, and was one of the first American cars to become popular in Europe. Many were sold in Britain, Germany and Scandinavia, while of the 150 new car registrations in Moscow in 1905, 80 were Oldsmobiles. The design was made under licence in Germany as the Polymobil and Ultramobil. The former had a extra seat in place of the curved dash.

Ransom Olds Departs
Like many makers of a successful design, Henry Ford and William Morris included, Ransom Olds was reluctant to change his car, and particularly to

1923 Oldsmobile Model 30-A sedan.
JOHN A. CONDE

1931 Oldsmobile F-31 Six sedan.
NICK BALDWIN

1938 Oldsmobile L-38 Eight sedan.
NICK GEORGANO

there were many other cars in this price range, and Oldsmobile production fell to 1600 cars in 1906 and 1200 in 1907. Up to that year Oldsmobile had maintained factories in both Detroit and Lansing, but they consolidated production in the latter town, which was expanding rapidly. In 1908, undeterred by the poor sales of the larger cars, Oldsmobile brought out their first six, the Model Z with 7836cc engine and a price tag of $4500. There was only one body style, a 7-seater touring car, and sales were just 55 in 1908, out of 1055 for all Oldsmobiles.

In November 1908 the company was bought by William C. Durant for $3 million, his first step towards founding his General Motors empire. For the following season he brought out a new Oldsmobile, the Model 20 with 22hp 2713cc 4-cylinder engine. This was no more than a lengthened version of the small Buick, but it gave Durant a cheaper Oldsmobile, selling for $1250. About 500 were sold in 1909, together with 150 Model Zs and 1100 of the other models. A small number of closed cars, coupés and limousines were built in 1908 and 1909.

One of the most impressive Oldsmobiles ever, and certainly the largest, was a new model for 1910. The Limited had a 8272cc 6-cylinder engine derived from that of the Model Z, and the same wheelbase of 130in (3302mm). The wheels, however, were larger at 42in (1067mm), giving the car a distinctive appearance, high and yet with an apparently low bonnet level because of the enormous wheels. Priced at $4600 to $5800 in 1910, the Limited's prices rose to between $5000 and $7000 the next year, when engine capacity went up to an enormous 11,570cc. Total production of the Limited over three seasons was 825 cars. The other Oldsmobiles at this time were all 4-cylinder cars, the 4375cc Defender, 5506cc Special and 7718cc Autocrat.

Charles W. Nash, president of General Motors, was named general manager of Oldsmobile in 1913, and started a policy of smaller cars, just as William Durant had done. The 1914 range included the Model 42, or Baby Olds, powered by a 3146cc 4-cylinder engine, selling for $1450. Top of the range was the 7319cc 6-cylinder Model 54, which had Delco electric lighting, starting and ignition. This had been first used by Oldsmobile on their 1913 Model 53. Thanks to the Model 42, sales picked up well in 1915, to 7696 from 1400, and in 1916 were even better, at 10,142. The company gained a new chief engineer in 1914, Italian-born Fabio Segardi who had worked for Darracq and Fiat. He was responsible for Oldsmobile's first V8 engine, a 40bhp 4031cc L-head unit. This was actually manufactured by Northway, a Detroit company owned by General Motors, who also supplied engines to Oakland and Scripps-Booth. It is possible that Northway built most Oldsmobile engines at this time. Segardi's influence was also seen in the Fiat-like pear-shaped radiator adopted by Oldsmobile on some 1916 and all 1917 models. The Model 44 V8 was renamed Model 45 for 1917 becoming the most popular model, with 13,440 out of a total of 22,613 cars made that year. Sales were down a little in 1918, to 19,169, but this was inevitable as the factory was busy making kitchen trailers and Liberty aero-engines. However, the 1919 figure was the best yet, with 39,042 cars selling to a car-hungry public.

A new general manager, A.B.C. Hardy, took over in 1921, when two new models appeared, the 3670cc 4-cylinder Model 43 and the 3834cc V8 Model 47. The slightly larger Model 46 V8 was continued to the end of the 1922 season when only the four and the V8 were made. Then in mid–1923 came a new six, the 2785cc Model 30 which was made up to 1927, and which replaced both the 4- and 8-cylinder cars. It was priced initially from $750 to $1095, and for the first time Olds used bodies by Fisher, a GM-owned company. Part of Fisher's manufacturing plant was in Oldsmobile's Lansing premises, but in 1929 Fisher moved to the former Durant factory in Detroit.

Among the more important improvements during the Model 30's lifetime were Duco paint and chrome or nickel plated radiators for 1925, mechanical pump feed and 4-wheel brakes for 1927. Disc or artillery wheels were used, with a very small number of customers going for wire wheels. Engine capacity went up to 3031cc for 1927, and to 3228cc on the new 1928 F-28 engine which was to power Oldsmobiles well into the 1930s, with only minor changes. Sales boomed during the 6-cylinder car's lifetime, from 44,854 in 1924 to 86,593 in 1928 and 101,579 in 1929. These put Oldsmobile around 12th place in the production league most years, rising to 9th in 1929. They were 4th among GM products, behind Chevrolet, Pontiac-Oakland and Buick.

The F-28s were completely restyled, with longer bonnets and lower bodies, and were available with disc, artillery or wire wheels. Five body styles were

move into a different market. However, he was only a very minor stockholder in the company, and when the Smith family, who owned the majority of the shares, insisted on making larger and more expensive cars, Olds left. This was in January 1904 and before the end of the year he had set up another company, also in Lansing, to make a car bearing his initials, the Reo. From 1906 to 1917 Reo outsold Oldsmobile every year, so perhaps the Smiths were sorry they allowed Olds to go.

The Curved Dash was joined by a Touring Runabout in 1904. Selling for $750 this looked very different, having a frontal radiator and bonnet, but the engine was still a single cylinder unit under the seat, and the same suspension system was used, on a longer wheelbase. There was also a 10hp model with detachable rear-entrance tonneau body, selling for $950.

A 20hp 2-cylinder car with side-entrance tonneau selling at $1400 appeared in 1906, and the following year, which was the last for the Curved Dash Runabout, saw a considerably larger car, with front-mounted 28hp 4-cylinder engine and 106in (2692mm) wheelbase, selling for $2250. This was the Model S, made as a 5-seater Palace Touring or a two-seater roadster. It did not sell well, as

1950 Oldsmobile 98 sedan.
NATIONAL MOTOR MUSEUM

1966 Oldsmobile Toronado coupé.
NATIONAL MOTOR MUSEUM

1980 Oldsmobile Delta 88 sedan.
NICK BALDWIN

offered, but there were many sub-varieties, standard and special models, so that the total number of models offered was 18. Closed bodies predominated, although there were also roadsters, and a 5-seater tourer was offered up to the end of the 1930 season. There were no major changes on the 1929 F-29s (models were named after their year of production up to 1938), nor in the appearance of the 1930s, but these offered synchromesh on the two upper ratios.

Oldsmobile had made a return to 8-cylinders with the V8 VIKING marketed as a separate make in 1929–30, but for 1932 they launched a brand new 3933cc straight-8 which developed 87bhp. Known as the L-32 it was installed in the same chassis as the 6-cylinder F-32, and there was little to distinguish the two cars externally. One noticeable feature was that the L Series had twin windscreen wipers, while the F Series had only one. The same body styles were offered, prices for the eight being around $50 higher, not very much considering the extra performance offered. Nevertheless fewer eights were sold, 5329 against 13,797 sixes. A free wheeling unit was fitted to all 1932 Oldsmobiles, but only for one season.

The 1933 Oldsmobiles were restyled, with sloping vee-grills and more rounded body lines. Different grill designs distinguished the two series. Capacity of the six was increased to 3621cc (80bhp) while the eight remained the same at 3933cc, though quoted power was up to 90bhp. As America climbed out of the Depression, car sales improved dramatically. In the 1933 model year Oldsmobile sold 36,648 cars, nearly double the 1932 figure, but this was easily beaten by 1934's figure of 79,814, while the 1935 season saw 126,768 cars delivered. For several years in the mid–1930s Oldsmobile held 5th place among American car makers.

1934 Oldsmobiles received hydraulic brakes and 'knee-action' coil-and-wishbone ifs, while the 1935 models had freshly styled bodies which Fisher called 'turret tops'. These had a one-piece steel roof over a composite frame, becoming all steel in 1937. This year also saw larger engines, the F Series now being 3769cc and 95bhp, while the L Series ran to 4211cc and 110bhp. In the middle of the 1937 season the Safety Automatic Transmission was offered as an option on the L Series. Made by Buick though not offered on their cars until the 1938 season, this was not an automatic in the modern sense, but a steering column gearchange which allowed the driver to keep both hands on the wheel while changing gear, hence

NICK BALDWIN

OLDS, RANSOM ELI (1864–1950)

Son of Pliny F. Olds, a machine-repairshop owner in Geneva, Ohio, Ransom Eli Olds was born on 3 June 1864. The family moved to Cleveland, Ohio, in 1870, and in 1873 settled on a farm 10 miles south of Cleveland. After graduating from high school, he took a book-keeping course at Bartlett's Business College. Pliny Olds gave up farming and returned to Cleveland in 1878, having found a job as a pattern-maker. The family moved again in 1880, when Pliny Olds set up his own mechanical workshop in Lansing, Michigan. Ransom's older brother, Wallace, went into partnership with their father, and by 1984 P.F. Olds & son were dealing in steam engines as well as undertaking a variety of foundry and machine work. Ransom went to work in the family shop in 1883 as one of seven full-time employees, and two years later bought Wallace's stake in the business.

In 1886-87 he built a 3-wheeled steam car (with a single tiller-steered front wheel) but no production ensued. At the same time, P.F. Olds & Son was advertising 'gasoline' engines of their own make. They were in fact steam engines, using boilers heated by gasoline-fueled burners. In 1890 the company was incorporated as the Olds Gasoline Engine Works, Pliny and Ransom holding 1450 shares each, and Wallace a token 100 shares.

In 1892 Ransom completed a new steam carriage, with the engine and boiler standing on a low platform behind the seats, driving the small-diameter wide-tracked rear wheels. The front wheels were much bigger, and were mounted close together under the seat. It was sold and shipped to Bombay, marking the start of an export trade in Automobiles from America.

He was co-inventor, with Madison F. Bates, of an internal combustion engine for which they applied for a patent in August 1895. In the summer of 1896 one such engine was mounted in a 4-wheeled carriage, and a demonstration run was made in Lansing on 11 August 1896.

Engine production began in March 1897,after Ransom had taken majority control of the firm, with 2600 (out of 3000) shares.

Several motor carriages were built that year, and on 9 September 1897, the Olds Motor Vehicle Co. was incorporated by R.E. Olds, Edward L. Sparrow, Samuel L. Smith, and others. In 1898 the Olds Gasoline Engine Works purchased the Anderson Road Cart Co. in Lansing, planning to use its plant for car production.

On 8 May 1899, the Olds Gasoline Engine Works and the Olds Motor Vehicle Company were merged to form the Olds Motor Works with Samuel L. Smith as president and majority shareholder. He had made a fortune in copper-mining and lived in Detroit. He bought a tract of land on Jefferson Avenue in Detroit and erected a factory for making cars, adopting the name Oldsmobile in December 1900. Ransom E. Olds held the title of Vice President and General Manager.

The Detroit factory proved too small, and when it burned down, R.E. Olds made a deal with the Lansing Businessmen's Association to get a parcel of land, ten times bigger than the Detroit site, for a token $4750, on condition of moving all Olds operations to Lansing. Construction began in 1901 and the first cars were shipped on 22 February 1902.

Frederic L. Smith (son of Samuel) was secretary of the Olds Motor Works and had frequent quarrels with R.E. Olds. Smith saw the need to modernise the 'curved dash' model earlier than Olds, and also urged Olds to develop a new, smaller engine for a lower-priced companion model. R.E. Olds left the company on 4 January 1904, and later sold his shares in the Olds Motor Works.

A group of 11 businessmen in Lansing petitioned him to go back to making cars, promising strong financial backing. That led to the founding of the Reo Motor Car Co. in August 1904. Olds wired Horace T. Thomas, who had worked closely with him at the Olds Motor Works from 1900 to late in 1903 (when he joined Columbia in Hartford, Connecticut) to come to Lansing as chief engineer of Reo. He leased factory space in a food-processing plant and rolled out the first Reo car on 1 January 1905.

A new factory, purpose-built for car assembly, was erected, and Olds quickly founded several other companies to supply Reo with parts, such as the Atlas Drop Forge Co. and the Michigan Screw Co., each one becoming a profit centre.

R.E. Olds made an extensive tour of Europe in 1907, to research the market potential for Reo cars as well as to look at the trends in automotive engineering. In1908 he refused a $4 million offer from the Morgan investment bankers for the Reo Motor Car Co. (an offer made on behalf of Benjamin Briscoe and W.C. Durant).

He became president of the Capital National Bank in Lansing and chairman of the board of the Peoples State Savings Bank.

He served as president of the Reo Motor Car Co. until 1923, while Horace Thomas directed the product engineering and Richard H. Scott ran the production side. Olds had lured Scott away from the Toledo Machine & Tool Co. to run the plant of the Olds Gasoline Engine Works in 1898. He transferred him to the Olds Motor Works in 1900 and made him factory superintendent of Reo in 1904. Scott was named vice president and general manager of Reo in 1914 and succeeded Olds as president in 1923.

In 1912 R.E. Olds combined all his investments into one holding, the R.E. Olds Co., with a full-time attorney, secretary, and treasurer. He financed the building of Hotel Olds, opposite the state capitol in Lansing and sailed around the world with his wife in 1927.In 1928-29 he financed construction of the Olds Tower Building, a 26-storey office building, and in 1930 decided to withdraw from the chair of the Reo board. But the depression forced him back into harness in 1934, when he steered Reo out of the passenger-car industry and expanded its truck-building activity. Horace Thomas left for health reasons in 1935 and retired to Florida, and Richard Scott retired in 1934, handing over the Reo presidency to D.E. Bates. R.E. Olds finally went into retirement in 1937, keeping busy with investments, charities, and donations to education institutions. He spent his winters n Daytona Beach, Florida, and most of his summers at Charlevoix, Michigan.

He died on 26 August 1950.

He was married in 1889, and had two daughters.

JPN

1980 Oldsmobile Omega sedan.
NICK BALDWIN

1989 Oldsmobile Cutlass Supreme International coupé.
OLDSMOBILE

the 'Safety' part of the name. It was semi-automatic in that some changes could be made without using the clutch. In 1938 this transmission was an option on all Oldsmobiles. This was the last year for the designations F and L series; although the 6- and 8-cylinder engines were continued they were called the 70 and 80 for 1939. There was also a 60 with the 6-cylinder engine on a shorter wheelbase, and there were no longer styling distinctions between the sixes and eights.

Automatic Transmission and the Return of the V8
General Motors engineers had been working on automatic transmissions for several years, and as Oldsmobile had offered their semi-automatic in 1937, it was only appropriate that when a fully-automatic 2-pedal system had been perfected, it was Oldsmobile that should get it first. Christened Hydramatic transmission, it offered four forward speeds with a steering column shift for neutral and reverse. Available on all 1940 Oldsmobiles, Hydramatic cost only $57, less than the Safety Automatic Transmission of 1937. Not many 1940 models had Hydramatic because production was slow to start, but nearly 50 per cent of the 1941 models were automatic. This was a record year for Oldsmobile,

with 270,040 sold for the model year, and calendar year production of 230,703. The range was more complex than before, with four series, 60, 70, 80 and 90, and two engines, a 3900cc six and a 4211cc eight. Body styles included fastback coupés and sedans as well as the older-style notchbacks, a 4-door convertible phaeton of which only 119 were made, and a station wagon. The 1942 range was simpler, with 60, 70 and 90 models. The 4-door convertible phaeton was no longer made, and even 2-door convertibles were rare, as were station wagons. The war halted all production on 5 February 1942, after 67,999 of the 1942 models had been made, only 12,230 actually in the year 1942.

Oldsmobile were quickly back in production after the war, with new cars in the showrooms as early as July 1945. Like nearly all American cars they were similar to the 1942s, with updated grills. The same models were made for 1947, and for the first part of the 1948 season, but in February of that year Oldsmobile brought out the restyled 98 series. The bodies were throughly up-to-date, with a straight line from wings through to the rear; they were lower and looked longer, though the wheelbase was actually 3in (76mm) shorter. Three body styles were available in the 98 series, 4-door sedan, 2-door club sedan which looked like a fastback coupé, and convertible. The only engine available in the 98 was the straight-8. The 60 and 70 series were still made with the old styling, but for 1949 all Oldsmobiles followed the lines of the 98. Hydramatic transmission was standard on the 98, and by 1949 90 per cent of all Oldsmobiles sold were automatics.

The main news for 1949 was a return to the V8 engine, in the shape of the Futuramic Rocket which replaced the old straight-8. The Rocket was one of the new generation of high compression ohv engines from GM, with a cr of 7.25:1, and gave 135bhp from its 4965cc. It powered the 98 and also a new model called the 88, which was essentially the shorter and lighter 76 with the V8 engine. Made in sedan and convertible models, the 88 was the highest performance Oldsmobile, with a top speed well over 100mph (160km/h). It soon became popular on the stock car racing circuits, winning six of the nine NASCAR championship events in 1949. They dominated the 1951 season, winning twice as many points as their nearest rival, Plymouth. An 88 convertible was chosen as the Pace Car for the 1949 Indianapolis 500, and in 1950 the first Carrera Panamericana was won by an Oldsmobile.

1950 was the last year for the 6-cylinder engine, and for 1951 the Rocket V8 was made in two versions, 135bhp for the 88, and 160bhp for the Super 88 and 98. Outputs went up to 150 and 165bhp respectively for 1953, while other improvements included power-assisted steering for 1952 and 12-volt electrics for 1953. Oldsmobile stood higher in the sales league than they had ever done before the war, 7th from 1951 to 1953, 4th in 1954 and 5th from 1955 to 1957. The 1954 models had wrap-around windscreens and engines enlarged to 5309cc, with outputs of 170 and 185bhp. For the rest of the 1950s Oldsmobile followed the development of other GM cars, with ever larger and more powerful engines, 6079cc and 277bhp in 1957, while in 1959 two sizes were available, 6079cc in the Dynamic 88 and 6456cc in the Super 88 and 98. 1958 saw GM's X-frame standardised, and also the option of air suspension. This was no more successful than it had been on other GM cars, for the compressors were liable to fail, when, in the words of Oldsmobile historian Dennis Casteele, 'the car assumed the posture of a lowered hot rod'. In 1959 Olds dealers were quietly offered a kit to remove the New-Matic suspension.

The Compact F-85 and Performance 4-4-2

During the 1960s the big Oldsmobiles began increasingly to share body panels with other GM makes, beginning with Buick. This was the start of the process which, in the 1990s, has resulted in a series of different sized and styled bodies being used by four, and sometimes five makes. However, in the l960s Oldsmobile also made some individual cars. 1961 saw their offering in the compact market, the unitary construction F85 with aluminium block 3523cc V8 engine and coil suspension all round. Made as a 4-door sedan and station wagon, or 2-door coupé, the F85 sold for $2384–$3091, about $600 less than the comparable full-size cars. Oldsmobile sold 76,394 F85s in the 1961 model year, out of total sales of 318,550. A convertible was added to the F85 range for 1962, and from 1964 Buick's 3684cc V6 engine was used in the economy model, with a 5408cc V8 in 230 or 290bhp versions as well. In mid-season the F85 was offered with the 4-4-2 (4-barrel carburation, 4-speeds and 2-exhaust pipes) high-performance pack which raised power to 310bhp. The F85 was not just one model but a whole series, and accounted for about one third of all the 546,112 Oldsmobiles sold in 1964. For 1966 there were four sub-groups in the F85 series, Standard, De Luxe, Cutlass and 4-4-2, the smallest being a new 4097cc in-line six made by Chevrolet.

Oldsmobile Adopts Front-drive

A completely new model for 1966 was the Toronado, America's first front-drive car since the Cords of the 1930s. Engineered by John Beltz and styled by David North, the Toronado was a 5-seater coupé powered by a 6960cc V8 engine developing 385bhp. The engine was mounted slightly to the right of centre so that the Turbo Hydramatic transmission could be mounted alongside it, facing forward. The torque converter was behind the engine, and drive from it to the transmission was by chain. The Toronado was not cheap, costing $4585 in standard form and $4779 in de luxe form (the most expensive 98 cost $4413), but more than 40,000 were sold in the first year, 34,630 being de luxe models. They certainly performed, with a top speed around 130mph (210km/h) and handled well, despite an unladen weight of nearly 4410lbs (2000kgs). Capacity went up to 7546cc for 1968, although power was down to 375bhp. 143,134 first series Toronados were made which were replaced for 1971 by a restyled model with longer wheelbase and squarer lines at the front. This continued up to 1978, with minor styling changes, and progressive downsizing of engines to 6604cc and 200bhp. Up to that time all Toronados were built at Olds' main plant at Lansing, but the new, smaller Toronados from 1979 onwards were built by a GM Assembly Division at Linden, New Jersey.

Meanwhile the F85 range was separated into the base F85 with 6-cylinder engine, and the more powerful Cutlass, which in 1967 was available in five models from the 150bhp six to a 320bhp V8. A full range of body styles was available in the Cutlass series, 2- and 4-door sedans, coupés, convertibles and station wagons. In 1968 the 4-4-2 became a true muscle car, with 360bhp 6551cc V8 engine (7456cc and 370bhp in 1970). Although it could be had with automatic transmission, the 4-4-2 was aimed at the enthusiast, and the standard transmission was a Hurst 3-speed floor change. Other features included disc brakes at the front, anti-spin differential and rally stripes. The most powerful of all was the Hurst Olds, which was designed by Jack Watson of Hurst Motors and put together by industrialist John Demmer who had been a supplier of components to Oldsmobile for a long time. He set up a limited production area in his Lansing factory, where the basic cars off the assembly line were given

2000 Oldsmobile Bravada 4x4 station wagon.
OLDSMOBILE

many finishing touches, including tuning the engine to give 390bhp with a forced air induction system, heavy duty transmission and larger tyres. Only 515 Hurst Olds were made in 1968, and 906 in 1969. The 4-4-2 was dropped after 1971 as the muscle car market was hit by a move towards unleaded fuel, although the Hurst Olds was revived in 1972, based on the Cutlass Supreme hard-top and convertible. 600 were made that year, one of which was chosen as the Pace Car for the Indianapolis 500. The 4-4-2 continued in name, but only as an option on the Cutlass and Cutlass Supreme.

Badge Engineering Takes Over

The 1970s saw greater rationalisation within the General Motors companies, so that by the end of the decade individuality was largely a thing of the past. In 1973 the F85 was replaced by the Omega, a compact which was a thinly disguised Chevrolet Nova. Two engines were offered, Chevrolet's 4097cc six and a 5735cc Oldsmobile Rocket V8. Three bodies were available on the Omega, 4-door sedan, 2-door coupé and 3-door hatchback coupé, the first of this style to be offered by Oldsmobile. The next small car was the Starfire introduced in 1975; made only as a 4-seater 2-door coupé, its body was shared with the Buick Skyhawk and Chevrolet Monza, and the engine was a 3785cc V6. In 1977 the standard engine in the Starfire became a Pontiac-built 2294cc 4-cylinder, with the V6 as an option. The Starfire was phased out during the 1980 season.

The larger Oldsmobiles continued in production through the 1970s, with gradual reduction in power output due to emission controls. The last convertible for several years, a Delta 88 Royale, came off the line in July 1975, and the full-size 98, which had been made in various forms since 1941, was discontinued in 1976. The name was continued on a shorter car. The Cutlass was nearly as large as the 98 by the mid–1970s, but came with a much wider choice of engines, a 3791cc six and five V8s from 4093 to 7456cc, whereas the 98 was powered only by the largest of the V8s. The Cutlass, too, was down-sized after 1977, being 660lbs (300kg) lighter than before, with the largest engine a 4998cc V8. Body shells were shared with Buick's Century Limited.

An important development in 1978 was the introduction of GM's first diesel engine, a 5731cc V8 with similar dimensions to the petrol unit; both were installed in the 88/98 series, and a year later diesels were available in the Cutlass (4257cc) and in a smaller and lighter Toronado. Oldsmobile became the maker of diesel engines for the whole GM Corporation; in 1980 they made 126,853 for their own cars, and 152,000 for other GM divisions. Oldsmobile sales had risen dramatically from the mid–1970s, exceeding the million mark for the first time in 1977, when 1,135,909 cars were sold. From around 6th place they moved up to 3rd in 1972, behind mass-producers Chevrolet and Ford. In the 1980s Oldsmobile production was spread over a number of factories. The 88/98 models were made at the old Lansing plant, while the Cutlass came from a newer Lansing plant, and the Toronado from Linden, New Jersey. The models shared with other GM divisions, such as the Omega and Starfire, were made at a number of different locations, coming down the same production line as equivalent Buicks, Chevrolets and Pontiacs. This rationalisation became more noticeable as the decade continued; in 1980 the Omega became part of the front-drive compact X-car range, similar to the the Buick Skylark, Chevrolet Citation and Pontiac Phoenix, while 1981–2 saw the sub-compact J-cars, of which Oldsmobile's Firenza version was launched in May 1982. All Oldsmobiles

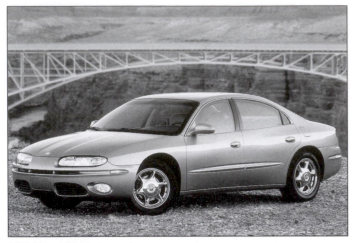

2001 Oldsmobile Aurora sedan.
OLDSMOBILE

c.1990 Oltcit hatchback.
CHRIS BACKLUND

from then onwards had their equivalents in other GM ranges. The X-car was the Omega and the A-car the Cutlass Ciera, while the big rear-drive sedans were the 88/98 series with V8 engines up to 5-litres (petrol) or 5.7-litres (diesel). Unlike Chevrolet and Cadillac, Olds dropped their classic rear-drive sedans after 1985, when the 88 Royale and 98 Regency became front-drive cars, part of the C-range. Only the Custom Cruiser station wagon was still rear-driven, and this was dropped after 1992.

The Toronado name was continued on a luxury coupé which shared body and running gear with Buick's Riviera and Cadillac's Eldorado. The Firenza was dropped at the end of the 1988 season, leaving the Cutlass Calais as the smallest Oldsmobile, with a 2474cc four, 2966cc V6 or a high-performance twin cam 16-valve 2261ccc four which gave 180bhp. A new model for 1990 was the Silhouette, a front-drive MPV with 3130cc transverse V6 engine, also made as the Chevrolet Lumina and Pontiac Trans Sport. Also new for 1990 was the Bravada, Olds' version of the Chevrolet Blazer 4 × 4 station wagon.

In 1991 Oldsmobile followed Buick's Roadmaster and Chevrolet's Caprice in returning to the large rear-drive theme; although Olds did not make a sedan, only the Cruiser station wagon with a 4998cc V8 engine and an overall length of 218in (5530mm). This was continued until 1994, although the Buick and Chevrolet models lasted until 1996 when GM abandoned the large rear-drive theme, probably for good.

For 1992 the Cutlass Calais was replaced by the Achieva as Olds' smallest car. Like its predecessor it was a front-drive sedan or coupé with four engine options, three versions of the 2261cc four and a 3343cc V6. Cousin to the Buick Skylark and Pontiac Grand Am, it was made up to January 1998, when it was replaced by the Alero. This had the same V6 and a slightly larger four of 2392cc, and was made as a 4-door sedan and 2-door coupé. This was made into 1999, along with the 3135cc V6 Cutlass sedan, 3791cc Intrigue and 3791cc 88 and Regency, the latter being the 98 renamed. At the top of the range, although it did not carry Oldsmobile badging, was the Aurora, an aerodynamic sedan powered by a 253bhp

3995cc 32-valve V8 similar to the Northstar used by Cadillac. A restyled Silhouette and the 4 × 4 Bravada were still in the Oldsmobile range. General Motors discontinued the Oldsmobile name at the end of 2001.
NG

Further Reading
The Cars of Oldsmobile, Dennis Casteele, Crestline, 1981.
Oldsmobile, the First 75 Years, Beverly Rae Kimes and Richard M. Langworth, Automobile Quarterly Publications, 1972.
Illustrated Oldsmobile Buyer's Guide, Richard H. Langworth, Motorbooks International, 1987.

OLGA (F) c.1900
L. Lemaire, Puteaux, Seine.
This was a voiturette offered with a 1¾hp single-cylinder De Dion-Bouton engine, though other engines were said to be available. A 'progressive transmission' without belts or chains gave two forward speeds, of 5 and 20mph (8 and 32km/h). The 2-seater body was suspended on the chassis frame by large C-springs.
KB

OLIVER (US) 1905
Oliver Trackless Car Co., South Bend, Indiana.
Frederick William Oliver started with a conventional car powered by a 12hp 2-cylinder horizontal engine with double-chain drive and a 5-seater tonneau body. He showed it at the Chicago Automobile Show in 1905, but perhaps finding insufficient interest in what was a very ordinary car, he came up with an idea completely out of the ordinary. Instead of driving through any of the wheels, the Oliver Trackless Car transmitted power to the road through a large drum centrally mounted under the chassis, which could be raised or lowered to give the action of a clutch. The other wheels were wider than normal, being more like rollers. In fact, Oliver said that his car would act as a roller, improving the road surface wherever it went. Needless to say, he found no buyers, and though he planned commercial and agricultural vehicles, his company was soon out of business.
NG

OLLEARO (I) 1934
Fabbrica Motoleggere Ollearo, Turin.
This company built motorcycles from 1925 to 1952, and briefly offered a 3-wheeler in which the front portion was a motorcycle with driver seated on a saddle, and the rear was a cabriolet body for two passengers. Like the motorcycles, the Ollearo car had shaft drive.
NG

OLTCIT (RO) 1981–1994
1981–1989 Oltcit SA, Craiova.
1989–1991 Oltena, Craiova.
1991–1994 Automobile Craiova SA, Craiova.
Rumanian Government officials realised after the introduction of the DACIA 1300 the need for a smaller model. In 1977 an agreement with the French CITROËN was reached. The new company was named Oltcit, after the name of the county where the plant was located, and Citroën. The plant, which was ready in 1981, was the equal of Western European factories, but the quality of work ranked far behind. The Citroën Visa was made in three versions: Club, Special and Axel 12 TRS (the latter for export). The Club with 1.1-litre, 57bhp engine was the best known. Only one body style, a 3-door hatchback, existed.

After the Rumanian revolution the car and the company were renamed Oltena, and in 1991 became Automobile Craiova. In 1994 an agreement with Daewoo spelled the end of Oltcit and the beginning of Rodae.
PN

OLYMPIAN (US) 1917–1920
Olympian Motors Co., Pontiac, Michigan.
The Olympian was built in the plant of the former CARTERCAR Co. Its builder R.A. Palmer had been general manager of Cartercar, and when General Motors, who had used it for two years for OAKLAND manufacture, put it up for sale, Palmer bought it for manufacture of his own car. This was a conventional low-priced vehicle with a 23hp 4-cylinder engine and tourer or roadster bodies in the

c.1923 O.M. Tipo S305 torpedo cabriolet.
NICK BALDWIN

$795 to $850 range. Unlike Ford, Palmer offered his cars in a variety of bright colours. A sedan at a considerably higher price of $1565 was listed in 1918 and 1919, and the factory was turning out 15 cars a day in early 1919. However production ended in 1920, and the factory was taken over by Otis C. FRIEND who made a car under his own name for a year. Total production of the Olympian was 2070 cars.

NG

O.M. (I) 1918–1934
1918–1928 SA Officine Meccaniche, Brescia.
1928–1934 OM Fabbrica Bresciana di Automobili, Brescia.
The Officine Meccaniche was a locomotive-building firm dating back to 1899, although its antecedents had made carriages from 1849. In 1917 they took over the Fabbrica Automobili ZÜST, and the first cars made under the O.M. name were similar to the 25/35hp Züst. These were made up to 1923, but a completely new design appeared in 1921. The work of the Austrian-born engineer Barratouche, it had a 1327cc side-valve 4-cylinder engine with monobloc casting and detachable head. It developed only 18bhp, but was gradually developed during the 1920s, and although O.M. always stuck to side-valves on their standard models, output was as high as 80bhp (with supercharger) by 1930. The original model was called the 465 (4-cylinder, 65mm bore) and was followed by the 467 and 469 models, with capacities of 1410 and 1496cc respectively. Introduced in 1924, the 469 had 4-wheel brakes and was very successful in competitions. Their achievements included first three places in the 1927 Mille Miglia and team prize in the 1928 Coppa delle Alpi. With 119 first, second and third places in the 124 races O.M. entered between 1921 and 1931, many people wondered why other makers such as Alfa Romeo went in for the

1927 O.M. Tipo 469S tourer.
NICK BALDWIN

complexities of overhead valves and camshafts. In his *Lost Causes of Motoring* Lord Montagu titled his chapter on the O.M. 'Why Put the Camshaft Upstairs?'

In 1923 O.M. introduced their first six, the 1990cc Tipo 665, which became more popular in England than the fours. It was handled by L.C. Rawlence whose chief engineer R.F. Oats tuned the competition cars and fitted some of them with Ricardo ohv heads, as well as rebuilt gearboxes and stronger crown wheels and pinions. The ohv conversion was catalogued in England, although never in Italy. In 1930 capacity went up to 2220cc on the Tipo 667; the sports models had sloping radiators and underslung frames and looked very like the contemporary Alfa Romeo 6C, although touring 667s retained the vertical radiator. The 665 as well as the 4-cylinder 469 was listed to 1934, but commercial

1928 O.M. Tipo 665 tourer.
NATIONAL MOTOR MUSEUM

1929 O.M. Tipo 665 coupé.
NATIONAL MOTOR MUSEUM

1933 O.M. Tipo 665 Superba cabriolet.
NICK BALDWIN

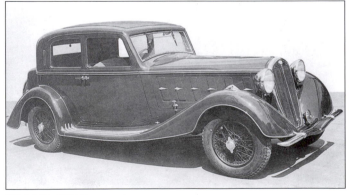

1934 O.M. OMV Alcyone saloon.
NICK BALDWIN

vehicles assumed more importance at Brescia, particularly after they took out a licence from Saurer to build diesel-engined trucks and buses. The stock of O.M. cars and parts was bought by the Esperia company in 1930, run by two former O.M. executives, Coletta and Mangano.

O.M. was bought by Fiat in 1933, a further nail in the coffin of the cars though, surprisingly, a new model appeared in 1934, built by Esperia. This was the Tipo OMV or Alcyone, with 2.3-litre 6-cylinder engine with overhead exhaust valves, synchromesh gearbox and hydraulic brakes. It had something of the appearance of a Fiat Ardita. Although it appeared at a number of shows it never went into production.

O.M. made a wide variety of commercial vehicles, though from the late 1960s they became increasingly badged-engineered Fiats. The name no longer appears on any vehicles.

NG

Further Reading
'*Lost Causes of Motoring Europe, Volume 1*', Lord Montagu of Beaulieu, Cassell, 1970.

OMAHA (US) 1912–1913
Omaha Motor Car Co., Omaha, Nebraska.
This car was designed by David W. Henry, former chief engineer of the COLBY Car Co. It was a conventional tourer with 3818cc 4-cylinder engine, unusual only in having an underslung frame, and even that was not unique, being featured by the better-known AMERICAN UNDERSLUNG and NORWALK cars. The proposed price was $1250, but very few Omahas were made.
NG

OMAI (I) 1988–c.1991
OMAI sas, Ortona.
The OMAI Sheverò was a 4 × 4 vehicle in the same vein as the Fiat Campagnola. It was powered by a 2445cc, 72bhp SOFIM diesel 4-cylinder engine and was available in two body styles, both in steel: an open-top model and fixed-roof estate.
CR

OMÉGA (i) (F) 1900
Kreuzberger Frères, Paris.
The Oméga voiturette featured horizontal single-cylinder engines with opposed pistons in the Gobron-Brillié style. The two crankshafts were geared to a common shaft, from which final drive was by chain to the rear wheels. Two sizes of engine were offered, 3½ or 5hp.
NG

OMEGA (ii) (D) 1921–1922
Omega Kleinautobau GmbH, Berlin-Charlottenburg.
This was one of many German small cars of the period, powered by a 3/10PS 4-cylinder engine. In 1922 the name was changed to OMIKRON.
NG

OMÉGA (iii) (F) 1922–1930
1922–1925 Automobiles Oméga-Six, Pantin, Seine.
1925–1930 Automobiles Oméga-Six, Boulogne-sur-Seine.
The Oméga-Six was a high-quality sports car built without regard to commercial profit as its founder, Jules Daubeck supported the company with a fortune made from the manufacture of railway sleepers. He engaged the engineer Gadoux to design the car, which had a 2-litre 6-cylinder single-ohc engine not unlike a smaller Hispano-Suiza H6. This was not surprising as Gadoux had worked for Hispano. The engine developed 50bhp and gave the car a top speed of 75mph (121km/h) with an open body. Two wheelbases were offered, 120 and 130in (3046 and 3299mm), and bodywork included an open tourer, a saloon and a coupé de ville. For 1924 twin Solex carburettors were adopted, boosting power to 55bhp, and a 4-speed gearbox replaced the original 3-speed unit.

The original premises were very small, limiting output to 50 cars a year at best. In 1925 Daubeck moved to the rue de Silly in Boulogne, the same street where the FARMAN was made. Oméga-Six cars competed at Le Mans in 1924 and 1925, and in the Circuit des Routes Pavées from 1925 to 1928, but without great success in either. Their best places were Boyriven's fourth overall in the 1925 and 1926 Circuits, though Bonne won the 3-litre class in the 1928 Circuit.

2·200 LITRE SIX O.M. SUPERCHARGED CHASSIS

ENGINE 6-cylinders in line, vertical, 67 m/m bore by 105 m/m stroke, R.A.C. rating 16.7 h.p. cast en bloc, detachable head, inlet and exhaust valves in line and interchangeable. Engine specially constructed and fitted with vibration damper and Roots's type blower.

PISTONS Special aluminium alloy, low co-efficient of expansion, ensuring silent working.

CRANKSHAFT Machined throughout and balanced, ground journals and crank pins.

CRANKCASE Aluminium, and so constructed as to provide water cooling to centre bearings, three point suspension, bearings carried in the top half. Filter entire area of sump. Oil reading level fitted.

LUBRICATION SYSTEM By submerged rotary pump delivering oil at pressure to main bearings, crankshaft drilled to supply connecting rod bearings, bye pass to timing gears. Adjustable pressure valve is provided.

COOLING SYSTEM Thermo syphon, large capacity, honeycomb radiator.

CARBURETTOR Memini or R.A.G.

PETROL SUPPLY 16-gallon tank carried at rear of chassis frame, petrol drawn to Autovac or Autopulse apparatus attached to dashboard under bonnet and thence delivered to engine. Nivex level gauge fitted on instrument board.

STEERING GEAR Worm and wheel. Universal ball joints to all steering connections.

REAR AXLE. Semi-floating type, spiral bevel final drive, differential of the bevel type.

BRAKES Front and rear wheel brakes. All brakes fully compensated

GEAR BOX & CLUTCH Gear box cast in one piece, with clutch and flywheel casing, and bolted to the engine to form one complete unit. Four speeds and reverse are provided, with either central or right hand change. A gear drive is provided to couple up to the flexible shaft of the speedometer. Clutch of dry single plate type fitted to flywheel.

SPRINGS Semi-elliptic, front and rear of ample dimensions. Underslung.

SHOCK ABSORBERS Hartford or Houdaille.

CHASSIS LUBRICATION Enot's gun.

ROAD WHEELS Rudge-Whitworth's detachable wire well-base for straight-sided tyres.

TYRES Dunlop 28 × 5.25 straight-sided, well-base rims.

ELECTRICAL INSTALLATION Bosch. *Dynamo* Fitted on off-side of engine, gear driven from timing wheels.
Starter Motor Fitted on near-side of motor to top half of crank chamber, easily removable and adjustable.
Ignition Bosch coil.
Accumulators 12 volt large capacity, enclosed in box hung in chassis frame.

EQUIPMENT Dynamo, battery, electric horn, full kit of tools, lifting jack, tyre pump, spare wheel and tyre, full set of lamps, speedometer, petrol gauge and revolution counter.

GENERAL

Capacity, c.c.	-	-	-	-	2200
Treasury rating	-	-	-	-	16.7
Tax	-	-	-	-	£17
Overall length	-	-	-	-	12' 10"
Overall width	-	-	-	-	5' 7"
Wheelbase	-	-	-	-	9' 2"
Track	-	-	-	-	4' 6"
Axle clearance	-	-	-	-	8½"
Chassis weight	-	-	-	-	16½ cwts

c.1925 Oméga (iii) Six torpedo by Gaston Grummer.
NICK BALDWIN

1924 Omikron 4/12PS coupé.
HANS-OTTO NEUBAUER

A larger engine of 2660cc was used from 1926, and in 1927 a 4280cc straight-8 was announced. Very few were made, although one was driven by Roost in the Circuit. The six was made in normal and low-chassis models, and a variety of striking bodies were fitted, including a pointed-tail 6-light saloon by Holvoet, and coupés by Gaston Grummer and Maurice Proux. In 1929 there appeared a twin-ohc 3-litre engine with a superb and expensive 8-bearing crankshaft which gave 150bhp with twin Cozette carburettors and considerably more in supercharged form. An extra injection of finance from Boyriven, who was a rich manufacturer of accessories as well as a racing driver, helped with the launch of these cars, but very few were sold. Most went to Daubeck's friends or business associates, sometimes in exchange for materials. A disagreement between Daubeck and Boyriven did not help matters, and the financial crisis of 1929 was the last straw. Daubeck lost all his money in the crash and committed suicide in 1932. His strongbox, reputed to represent his last assets, was found to contain some bread and a Camembert cheese.

NG

Further Reading
'Oméga Six', Serge Pozzoli,
l'Album du Fanatique, December 1974–February 1975.

OMEGA (iv) *see* PREMIER (iv)

OMEGA (v) **(GB)** 1925–1927
W.J. Green Ltd, Coventry.
The Omega motorcycle was made from 1909 to 1927, originally in Wolverhampton, but a few cars were made in the last years of the company's life. They were 3-wheelers powered by a 980cc V-twin JAP engine, driving the single rear wheel by chain. The price was only £90.

NG

OMEGA (vi) **(US)** 1967–1969
1966–1967 Suspensions International Corp., Charlotte, North Carolina.
1967–1969 Genser-Foreman, New York, New York.

When the GRIFFITH sports car project ran out of money, it was taken over by former magazine editor Steve Wilder. He switched from the bulky Chrysler V8 to a lighter Ford engine, and had AUTOMOBILI INTERMECCANICA in Italy continue with body and chassis production. Initially they were shipped to race car builders Holman & Moody in North Carolina for assembly, although Wilder later set up his own assembly line. About 36 cars were constructed before Wilder halted production and sold the Omega name for Oldsmobile. Production resumed with backing from Genser-Foreman, the New York Triumph distributors. Production was moved entirely to Italy, where Intermeccanica completed each car before shipping. These cars were identical to the Omega but were called GFX, for Genser-Foreman Experimental. They were soon renamed Torino, although Ford objected since they were making a sedan by that name. This necessitated yet another renaming to Italia. About 125 cars were built from 1966 to 1969. During this time engine size grew from 4700cc to 5000cc and finally 5700cc. Reisner replaced the Italia in 1969 with the INDRA.

HP

OMIKRON **(D)** 1922–1925
1922–1924 Omikron Kleinautobau GmbH, Berlin-Charlottenburg.
1924–1925 Berlin-Forster Automobilfabrik GmbH, Berlin-Charlottenburg.
This was the OMEGA (ii) renamed, but slightly larger engines were used, of 4/16 and 5/20PS, made by Steudel.

HON

OMNA-AUTO **(US)** c.1980–1985
Omna-Auto Inc, Seattle, Washington.
Industrial designer Alan Gerard started this company with his sons to build inexpensive Volkswagen-based kit cars. Their most distinctive model was the Rumbleseat Roadster, a rebody kit that made a VW resemble a 1910-era Renault. It included brass-finished trim, a windshield, fibreglass body and upholstery. Completed bodies, as well as kits, were available. The Oldbug was a nostalgic kit resembling a 1900-era truck that fitted on a VW chassis. It was an open-sided design with large brass headlights and tall, skinny tyres. A more modern kit was the Bugbox, which added a delivery-truck rear end to a VW Beetle. The body was cut away behind the doors and a fibreglass box tail added. The Flatbed was another Beetle conversion, but this one attached a flat truck bed to the back of a truncated Beetle body. Omna-Auto was replaced by GERARD COACH in 1985.

HP

OMNIA **(NL)** 1907–1911
1907–1908 Houwing & Co., Stompwijk.
1908–1911 NV Omnia Motoren, Voorburg.
Before entering the car business the firm of Houwing & Co. manufactured boats and marine-engines at the Omnia Engineering Works in Rotterdam. Around 1906 they planned to build cars under licence from an unknown Belgian car factory, and displayed a number of chassis at the R.I.A. show, of which one had a 2-seater body of their own make. The smallest one had a 10/12hp 2-cylinder engine and a 3-speed gearbox. A 12/15hp 3-cylinder engine was available; an exception in those days. Today called square-engines, these had a bore and stroke of 110 &mult 110mm. A third model was a 4-cylinder 16/20hp, with thermosyphon cooling. The heaviest chassis had a 45/55hp 4-cylinder engine with a displacement of 8012cc. Most of the cars were ordered by the H.A.T.O. taxicab organisation at The Hague, who preferred the Landaulet body style.

In 1909 the Omnia management took the decision to standardise the production on one type of chassis, using the 15/20hp 4-cylinder monobloc with a bore and stroke of 85 × 110mm and Bosch magneto ignition. It seemed that this chassis was a licence-built SPYKER, and it has been claimed that Omnia was finally only an assembly plant, with frames delivered by the French firm Dyle et Bacalan. After building about 100 cars, Omnia closed its doors in 1911.

FBV

OMNIMOBIL **(D)** 1904–1910
Aachener Stahlwarenfabrik AG, Aachen.
This company supplied sets of components to would-be car makers, particularly those who were bicycle manufacturers and had the basic factory equipment. The kits included engine with gearbox, chain or shaft transmission, axles, steering

gear etc. At first a 6PS 2-cylinder engine was supplied, later a 16PS 4-cylinder. Among their customers was CITO. In 1908 the company started to make complete cars under the name FAFNIR, and production of the Omnimobil sets ceased two years later.

HON

OMNIUM (GB) 1913–1914
Omnium Motor Co. Ltd, London.
The first Omnium cyclecars were almost identical to the EAGLE (vi) made in Shepherds Bush, with water-cooled 2-cylinder engines, 3-speed gearboxes and shaft drive to a worm rear axle. They probably were Eagles, as the Omnium address in Great Portland Street was clearly an office and showroom and not a factory. A later Omnium had a 4-cylinder engine which was also offered by Eagle. At least six were registered in Australia in 1914.

NG

OMNOBIL (D) 1922
Deutsche Elektromobil- und Motorenwerke AG, Wasseralfingen.
This short-lived firm offered electric cars in single or tandem 2-seater forms.

HON

ONE OF THE BEST see ADAMS (i)

ONFRAY (F) 1899–c.1905
Compagnie Française de Cycles et Automobiles, Paris.
This company were first and foremost cycle makers. Their 1899 catalogue featured six models of bicycle, a motor tricycle called the Gaulois and a 3-wheeled car with a horizontal single-cylinder engine, chain drive to the single rear wheel and bodies for two, three or four passengers. Later cars sold by this firm were vertical-engined 4-wheelers mostly with shaft drive. The 6 and 8hp models had radiators mounted at the side of the bonnet, Renault style, while the 9 and 10hp cars had frontal radiators. The 10hp was chain driven.

NG

ONLY (US) 1909–1913
Only Motor Car Co., Port Jefferson, New York.
This make owed its name to the fact that the car had only one cylinder, and it was an enormous one, with bore of 127mm and stroke of 254mm, giving a capacity of 3294cc. The crankshaft had a flywheel at each end. Designed by François Richard, it was offered in 2-seater roadster form only, at a price of $700, although at least one 4-seater car was built. Few of the single-cylinder models were made. In 1912 Richard produced a new design, with four cylinders in another long stroke layout, 114.3 × 200mm, and a capacity of 8204cc. With a raceabout at $1000 and a tourer at $1250 it was not expensive for such a large car, but few customers came knocking at the door, and the directors decided to rename the car the METROPOL and offer it in raceabout form only. This venture lasted only into 1914. Meanwhile Richard moved on to Cleveland, where he made the RICHARD car.

NG

ONNASCH (D) 1924
Traugott Onnasch, Oslin.
The Onnasch 3-wheeler was named the 'Taschen-Auto' (Pocket Car) as it could be easily dismantled for storage or transport in a bag. 2½hp single-cylinder or 8hp 2-cylinder engines by Bekamo were available. Onnasch also announced a 4-cylinder car but it did not go into production.

HON

ONYX (GB) 1993 to date
1993–1995 Onyx Automotive, Mildenhall, Suffolk.
1995–1998 Onyx Automotive, Grimsby, Lincolnshire.
1998 to date Onyx Sports Cars, Grimsby, Lincolnshire.
1998 to date Formby Kit Cars, Formby, Merseyside.
Basing a kit-form sports car on Fiat Panda parts sounded unpromising, but the recipe of compact dimensions, simple lines, steel tube chassis and agile handling made the Fire-fly a hit. Later versions could have the Fiat 127, Lancia Y10/Y10 Turbo or Fiat Uno power, all in a semi-monocoque chassis. There was also a

1914 Omnium 10hp 2-seater.
MICHAEL WORTHINGTON-WILLIAMS

1924 Onnasch 8hp tourer.
HANS-OTTO NEUBAUER

stripped-out ER model with a cut-down windscreen. A slightly larger model, the Firecat, arrived in 1994, using Fiat Uno or twin cam power. A new model in 1998 was the Tomcat, a Mini- or Metro-based fun car designed for road use and grasstrack racing; sharing some of the same ancestry was another new car, a 3-wheeler called the Bobcat. At the same time the Fire-fly was pensioned off to Formby Kit Cars.

CR

O.P. (F) 1921–1924
Automobiles O.P., Levallois-Perret, Seine.
This was a light car powered by side-valve Chapuis-Dornier engines of 898 or 1095cc, or a long-stroke 1093cc ohv unit of unknown provenance, possibly made by O.P. themselves. The smaller car had a conventional 3-speed gearbox, the larger used friction transmission, which was a reversal of the usual practice of using friction discs with relatively low power. The O.P. still used acetylene lighting in 1922, possibly later.

NG

OPEL (D) 1898 to date
1898–1928 Adam Opel, Rüsselsheim.
1928 to date Adam Opel AG, Rüsselsheim.
Adam Opel (1837–1895) was Germany's leading maker of sewing machines from the 1870s and began bicycle manufacture with his five sons in 1886. After his death in 1895, and with the cycle market shrinking, his widow and sons looked for fresh fields. In 1897 they bought the rights to the LUTZMANN, and the following year they put the Benz-like design into production as the Opel-Lutzmann. Friedrich Lutzmann had moved from Dessau to Rüsselsheim with his machinery and workforce. The first model had a 1545cc 3½hp single-cylinder, engine, and was made in 2- or 4-seater versions, followed by 5 and 8hp cars. They did not sell well, only 11 in 1899 and 24 in 1900. The Opels ended their agreement with Lutzmann during 1900, and that might have been the end of the Opel car. However, they took on the concession for selling DARRACQ cars in Germany, and soon began to fit German bodies to the French chassis,

1899 Opel System Lutzmann 4PS *vis-à-vis*.
OPEL

1904 Opel System Darracq 10/12PS tonneau.
OPEL

1909 Opel 4/8PS 'Doktorwagen' 2-seater.
OPEL

selling them as Opel-Darracqs. This continued until 1906, after they began to make their own cars, which first appeared at the Hamburg Show in 1902. They had 2-cylinder engines of 1884cc and shaft drive. The first 4-cylinder Opel, the 4715cc 20/24PS, appeared in 1903. Two years later it had been joined by the 6880cc 35/40PS, although the largest car in the range was a Darracq design, the 8012cc 45/50PS.

From 1907 Opel made their own designs exclusively; the most popular, and largest-selling prewar Opel, was the 1029cc 4/8PS 4-cylinder light car, known as the *Doktorwagen* because of its suitability for medical men. Introduced in 1909, its capacity went up to 1128cc in 1910 and several thousand were made up to 1914, including its successor, the 1320cc 5/12PS *Puppchen* (doll). It was part of a wide range which included two other small cars with monobloc engines, the 1592cc 6/12PS and 1848cc 8/16PS, as well as several bigger cars with pair-cast cylinders, of which the largest was the 10,200cc 40/100PS which had one overhead inlet and two side-exhaust valves. It had a top speed of 78mph (125km/h) even with a 5-seater tourer body.

The Opel factory was almost destroyed by fire in 1911, but they turned this to advantage by re-building with the latest machinery. Sewing machines were dropped, with exactly one million having been made, but bicycles were continued, as well as motorcycles which were made from 1901 to 1925. Shortly after car production resumed, early in 1912, the 10,000th Opel was made. During 1913 they made 3200 cars, the largest output in Germany and the sixth in Europe, and also started production of heavy trucks. These were made during the war for the Army, and also BMW aero-engines were made at Rüsselsheim.

The factory was occupied by French forces at the end of the war, and with raw material in very short supply, it was some time before production restarted, although new cars were listed from May 1919. They were of prewar design in six sizes, from the 1570cc 4-cylinder 6/16PS to the 7790cc 6-cylinder 30/75PS. The early 1920s, especially the period September 1922 to June 1923, saw drastic inflation in Germany, so that an 8/25PS Opel, which cost RM 115,000 in January 1921 was priced at RM 156 million in June 1923. In modern terms this would be equivalent to the price of a Mini at £9325 rising to £12,644,700! When prices settled down with the introduction of the more realistic gold mark, the 8/25PS cost RM 10,500, though tyres were extra. These early 1920s Opels were rather cumbersome-looking cars, with typical German vee-radiators and artillery wheels, although a sports model was offered with disc wheels.

In 1924 the factory was re-equipped with moving assembly lines and a new range of smaller cars was introduced. The first was the 951cc 4/12PS which was based on the CITROËN 5CV and was made in bright green finish, from which came its nickname *Laubfrosch* (tree frog). Unlike the Citroën, it was developed into a number of slightly larger cars, the 1018cc 4/14 and 4/20PS, of which there were several different body styles, chummy 4-seater, 2-seater cabriolet with dickey seat, and 2-door saloon. This 4PS series was made in larger numbers than any previous Opel, 119,484 between 1924 and 1931. There were several larger models made over the same period, including the 1916cc 8/40PS and 2620cc 4-cylinder 10/40PS and several sixes from the 3160cc 12/50PS to the 4170cc 16/60PS. A short-lived venture into the luxury market was the 24/110PS Regent, with 5970cc straight-8 engine. Several body styles were offered, including a pullman-limousine, tourer, roadster and coupé, but only 25 were made, from April to October 1929. By 1928 Opel's 8000 employees were making 250 cars a day, of which about half were 4/12s, for a 37.2 per cent share of the German market. They were the leading German make and also the world's largest producers of bicycles.

In January 1929 the Opel family interests were reorganised into a joint-stock company, Adam Opel AG, and in March General Motors purchased 80 per cent of the stock, increasing their holding to 100 per cent by October 1931. The total cost of $66.7 million made the Opels one of the richest families in Europe. The first GM-inspired Opel was the 1790cc 1.8-litre six, made from 1931 to 1933. It was sold in France under the name GM 108; apart from the replacement of the Opel badge by one reading General Motors 108, there was no change. Presumably this was to counter any lingering anti-German feelings in France, for it was billed as combining American performance with European economy. It was joined by the 1193cc 1.2-litre, these two models being the starting point for the range over the next few years, with gradual increases in engine capacity. In 1935 came the 1279cc Olympia, named for the 1936 Olympic Games held in Berlin. It was the first Opel to have integral construction and was made as a 2-door saloon and cabrio-limousine with roof that folded right back to make an open 4-seater. In 1938, with a larger engine of 1488cc, a 4-door saloon was made as well. A junior version of the Olympia was the Kadett, made from 1937 to 1940. This had generally similar styling, also in 2-door saloon and cabriolet-limousine styles, with a 4-door from 1938. A total of 107,608 Kadetts were made, and nearly 120,000 Olympias.

There were also two 6-cylinder Opels of the later 1930s, the 2473cc Super Six and the 3626cc Admiral. The latter shared an engine with the Blitz 3-ton truck, and was made as a 4-door saloon and tourer with factory bodywork, and also a pullman-limousine and 2-door cabriolet by Hebmüller. A total of 6404 Admirals were made, including 590 chassis supplied to outside coachbuilders. The Super Six, originally called the 2 litre, came in a variety of 2- and 4-door coachwork, open and closed, and was made from 1934 to 1938, when it gave way to the Kapitän. This had the most advanced bodywork of any prewar Opel, and featured the extension of the wings into the front doors that was seen on some American GM cars just before World War II. Opel had them first, as a smaller production run allowed stylist Frank Hershey more flexibility than he had at Detroit. Another advanced feature of the Kapitän was fully-faired rectangular headlamps. Combined production of the 2 liter and Super Six was 96,453, and of the Kapitan, 25,374 up to October 1940, though it was revived after the war. Dubonnet-type ifs was introduced on the 2 litre in 1934, and was standard on all models by 1939. Kapitäns and Olympias from 1938 to 1940 had ohv engines.

c.1912 Opel 40/100PS tourer owned by Prince Michael of Russia.
NATIONAL MOTOR MUSEUM

MICHAEL LAMM

CHERRY, WAYNE (born 1937)

Wayne K. Cherry was born in Indianapolis on 3 September 1937. As a youngster, he developed an interest in auto racing and concurrently began to draw cars and trucks. During his teen years, he drag-raced a 1955 Chevrolet and became an excellent motor mechanic.

After he graduated from high school, he put together a portfolio, which he sent to just one school: Art Center College of Design in Los Angeles. Art Center accepted him in 1959, and he immediately drove his Chevrolet out to California looking, according to a classmate, 'Just like Harrison Ford in American Graffiti'. Wayne finished Art Center in 1962 and was immediately hired by General Motors Design Staff.

In 1965, at the age of 27, he was sent to Vauxhall, GM's British subsidiary, an assignment he says he enjoyed immensely, partly because it allowed him to see European motor racing first-hand. Cherry expected the assignment to last just a short time, but as the months turned into years, he found himself more and more at home in England. And Vauxhall gave him a chance to take on ever-increasing design responsibilities.

Meanwhile, his passion for motor racing grew stronger. He followed Formula One with avid interest, attended Jim Russell's Formula Ford driving

school at Snetterton, and took competition lessons from Motor Racing Stables at Silverstone and Brands Hatch, 'mostly', he said, 'to get a chance to drive on those famous race tracks'.

In 1970 he was named Vauxhall/Bedford's assistant design director, a position he continued to hold under Ed Taylor. When Taylor returned to the U.S. in 1975, Cherry became Vauxhall/Bedford's director of design.

In 1983, after GM combined Vauxhall and Opel styling activities, Cherry moved to Opel in Germany to oversee all European GM car and truck design. As Cherry's first designs came to market, Opel began to blossom and soon ranked as Europe's top-selling marque. By 1987, Opel had become a major GM profit centre, attributable in some measure to Cherry's work - a notion not lost on Opel management, which at the time included Jack Smith and Bob Eaton. Smith ended up as GM chairman and Eaton went on to become chairman of Chrysler Corp.

In 1991, Chuck Jordan asked Cherry to return to the States to become executive designer for Chevrolet/Geo and GM Canada. He had spent 26 years in Europe and enjoyed a terrific record there. He wasn't anxious to leave, but understanding that after Jordan's retirement he might be considered for the GM Design Staff vice presidency, he moved back to the U.S.

Jordan had favoured Cherry's candidacy initially when he brought him over, but then suddenly changed his mind and endorsed his second-in-command, Jerry P. Palmer. But because Jordan had a volatile temper, and because he tended to be autocratic in the manner of Earl and Mitchell, and perhaps especially because Palmer was now viewed as 'Jordan's man', Cherry got the vice presidency. Then, too, there was his previous connection with GM chairman Jack Smith. Smith and the GM board apparently wanted someone more predictable than Jordan and felt that Cherry, with his proven international track record, could help steer the company in new directions.

Cherry made monumental changes within what came to be called the General Motors North American Operations Design Center. The former system of 27 separate studios, including one or more for each GM car division, plus advanced, plus interiors, gave way to eight Brand Character Centers. Inside these, themes and identities were created and then transferred, along with some of the people who produced them, into one of four mega-studios. These large studios saw GM cars and trucks into production. Designs done under Cherry and Palmer, his second-in-command, tended toward the conservative side. In 2000 Cherry was leaving day-to-day design responsibilities to Palmer and devoting himself mostly to brand-character issues and corporate portfolio development.

Cherry married Rowena Dobson in 1984. They have a daughter.
ML

1931 Opel 1.8-litre saloon.
NATIONAL MOTOR MUSEUM

1937 Opel Super Six cabriolet.
NATIONAL MOTOR MUSEUM

1938 Opel Admiral saloon.
NICK BALDWIN

By the late 1930s Nazi control of the motor industry was making GM's position very difficult, and in October 1940 they relinquished control to the government. The factory was heavily bombed during the war, and was taken over by the American military administration in May 1945, initially making spare parts. Complete vehicles began to leave the factory in July 1946, at first trucks, and from December 1947 the Olympia, followed a few months later by the Kapitän. The dies for the Kadett had been taken by the Russians, and it

appeared later as the MZMA/MOSKVITCH 400. General Motors formally resumed control in November 1948. The first postwar Olympia and Kapitän had prewar styling, though the latter lost its rectangular headlamps, but they were restyled in 1950 and 1951 respectively, and in 1953 and 1954 they gained completely new slab-sided styling. The 1953 Olympia was called the Olympia Rekord, the latter a name which stayed in the catalogue for many years, long after the Olympia had disappeared. Capacity went up to 1680cc in 1959 and 1897cc in 1965, when it gained a single-ohc engine. The Kapitän also grew in body size and engine capacity, reaching 2605cc in 1959 and 2784cc in 1965. The same engine was used in the revived Admiral from 1965 to 1968. Both Rekord and Admiral shared a 4-door saloon body with Chevrolet-like styling. The same bodies were used for the Diplomats which had Chevrolet V8 engines of 4636 or 5354cc. A 2-door coupé was a style unique to the Diplomat whose mechanical elements also provided the basis for the BITTER CD coupé.

In 1962 Opel brought out a new small car for which they revived the name Kadett. Made in a new factory at Bochum, it had a 993cc oversquare ohv engine, and was made originally as a 2-door saloon only, joined in 1963 by a coupé and an estate car called, like the larger Opel estates, the Caravan. A 4-door saloon arrived in 1965, when capacity went up to 1078cc. Production was going from strength to strength, 649,542 of the first series Kadett were made, and by October 1966 Bochum had produced its millionth car. Overall Opel production reached five million during 1965. A sports coupé called the GT was made from 1968 to 1973 using either the 1078cc Kadett or 1897cc Rekord engine. It had front disc brakes and fresh styling with retractable headlamps, and with the larger engine could do 115mph (185km/h). Understandably, this was a more popular option and of nearly 104,000 GTs sold, only 3573 had the Kadett engine. The majority of GTs, about 80,000, were sold in the United States.

Another move into sporting territory came with the Manta coupé which was Opel's answer to the Ford Capri. Introduced in 1970 with a choice of three single-ohc engines from 1584 cc and 60bhp to 1897cc and 90bhp, though later models had engines both less and more powerful, 60bhp (1196cc) and 105bhp (1897cc). It shared the floorpan, suspension and running gear of the Ascona saloon which was introduced a few weeks later. By the time Manta production ended in 1975, 498,533 had been made. The Ascona was introduced to bridge the gap between the Kadett and the Rekord, and was made in 2- and 4-door saloon models and the Caravan estate car. It was a great success, selling 641,438 units before it was replaced by a new longer and wider Ascona of which 1,512,971 were made up to 1981. There was also a second generation Manta, again derived from the Ascona, and with the same engines. These included special rally versions, with 2410cc Cosworth-developed twin-ohc 16-valve engines and 5-speed gearboxes. Only 448 Asconas and 256 Mantas were made in this form. Walter Röhrl won the 1982 Drivers' and Manufacturers' Rally Championships in a Manta 400.

From the 1970s the Opel range was increasingly similar to that of GM's British company, VAUXHALL, though it took 20 years for the models to be totally integrated. Even in the 1960s the Kadett was the German equivalent of the Vauxhall Viva, though they shared no mechanical parts, and styling was only superficially similar. The 1972–77 Rekord 11 shared floorpan and suspension with the Vauxhall Victor FE, though the Opel offered a wider range of engines, including a 2068cc diesel. The next Rekord had completely new styling and a wider range of engines; it was made in England as the Vauxhall Carlton. The 1973 Kadett L included a hatchback in the range (from 1975) and came with five engine options, two with pushrod ohv and three with single-ohc units, though the latter was available only in the Rallye coupés. It was one of the international T-car range, and was the basis of the 1975–1984 Vauxhall Chevette. In 1979, after 1,701,075 had been made, it gave way to a new Kadett which used some of the engines from the previous models but mounted transversely and driving the front wheels. 4-speed gearboxes were used at first, later mostly 5-speeds, and it was even more successful than its predecessor, with 2,092,140 made before it was replaced by a third generation Kadett in 1984. The Kadett was replaced in 1991 by the Astra, a name which had been used by Vauxhall for their version of the Kadett since 1980. It was made in 3- and 5-door hatchback and estate forms, with engines from 1398 to 1998cc, the latter a 16-valve unit giving 150bhp. It was completely restyled and given new engines in 1998, though of roughly the same sizes as before. For 2000 there was a coupé and a high-performance 3-door hatchback called the GSi, with more than 160bhp from its 1998cc 16-valve engine, and a 6-speed gearbox.

1937 Opel Olympia saloon.
OPEL

1953 Opel Olympia Rekord saloon.
OPEL

1962 Opel Kadett A saloon.
OPEL

Among the larger Opels, the 1967-72 Commodore had the same basic body shells, styling and suspensions as the 1966–72 Rekords, but used 6-cylinder ohc engines of 2490 or 2784cc, and many were sold with automatic transmission. It was replaced by the second generation Commodore with new styling but the same engines (1972–1977), which in turn gave way to the Senator for 1978. This was an impressive large 4-door saloon or 2-door coupé with a 2197cc 4-cylinder petrol or 2260cc diesel engine, or sixes of 2490, 2784 and 2969cc. The coupé was called the Monza and was good for 133mph (214km/h). A 5-speed gearbox was optional from 1979, though most were sold with automatics. The UK-market equivalents were called Vauxhall Royales or Senators, but all were made in Germany.

In 1982 Opel brought out a new car below the Kadett in size, called the Corsa, (Vauxhall Nova) with 993, 1196 or 1297cc 4-cylinder transverse engines, the two larger with single ohc and electronic ignition. Later a diesel and high-performance GSi models were offered. Made in GM's Spanish factory at Zaragoza, the Corsa came in 3- and 5-door versions, and was still the base model of the Opel range in 1999. It was completely restyled in 1993, and in 1999 engine options ran from a 973cc 3-cylinder through three sizes of 16-valve 4-cylinder, 1199, 1398 and 1598cc and two diesels.

In 1988 the Ascona was replaced by the Vectra, a similar-sized car with a family resemblance to the larger Omega. Made in saloon and hatchback versions, the Vectra came with seven engine options, from 1.4 to 2-litres, the latter available in twin-ohc 16-valve form. There was also a 4 × 4 version. It was restyled in August 1996 and February 1999, when it was made with 4-cylinder engines of 1598 and 1998cc, and a 2498cc 24-valve V6, as well as a 1995cc turbo-diesel. The Omega was the top of the Opel range, introduced in 1986 with 1796 and 1998cc fours and a 2594cc six, joined in 1989 by the Lotus Omega with 3617cc engine tuned by Lotus to give 360bhp and a top speed of 170mph (274km/h). Its spiritual successor, announced in 1999, used a 339bhp 5665cc V8 from the Corvette. Like its predecessor it had a 6-speed manual gearbox, though a 4-speed automatic was an alternative, and Lotus was heavily involved in the suspension, steering and brakes. As with less powerful Omegas, it was sold in the US as the CADILLAC Catera. Other engines available in the 1999 Omegas included 1998 and 2198cc fours, 2498 and 2962cc V6s, 1995cc four and 2496cc in-line six turbo-diesels. Unlike other Opels, the Omegas had rear-wheel drive.

Opel made several sporting models in the 1990s. First was the Calibra, launched in 1989, a 2-door 4-seater coupé based on a Vectra floorpan with 1998cc engine in 8- or 16-valve forms, and the next was the Tigra launched in 1993. This was a Corsa-based 2+2-seater coupé, a rival for Ford's Puma, and powered by a 1389cc 16-valve engine in 90 or 100bhp forms. More than 100,000 were sold in the first 18 months, and it was still in the range in 1999. The Calibra was made until 1997, with the addition of a 2498cc V6 engine and a 4×4 model, and was due to be replaced by a new Astra-based coupé in 1999. The latest sporting Opel is the Speedster, a mid-engined 2-seater in the Lotus Elise mould, with lightweight fibreglass panels and a transversely-mounted 2198cc 16-valve engine, a version of which is already used by SATURN in America. Production was due to start in July 2000 at Lotus' Norfolk factory.

Opel also offered the Isuzu-derived Frontera 4×4 estate car, and two MPVs, the Sintra with 2198cc 4-cylinder and 2962cc V6 petrol or 2172cc diesel engines, introduced in 1996, and the slightly smaller Astra-derived Zafira introduced in 1999. This had a unique flexible seating system, in which each of the two third row seats disappeared into the floor at the touch of a button.

Another new model was the Agila, a 5-door high-roof city car to be built at a new plant at Gliwice, Poland, offered with a choice of 1- or 1.2-litre engines. It was due to go on sale in the summer of 2000.

NG

Further Reading
'*Alle Opel Automobile*', W. Schmarbeck and B. Fischer,
Motorbuch Verlag, 1992.

OPES (I) 1946–1949
Officine Precisione e Stampaggio, Turin.
The Opes Ninfea was quite a grown-up project, a Ford-inspired 2-door saloon car with a light alloy underbody joined in unit with the main body. The front suspension was independent by lower wishbones and upper transverse arms, with swing rear axles. A 3-cylinder air-cooled alloy-head radial engine, initially of 702cc but later 784cc, drove the front wheels.

CR

OPESSI (I) 1935–1936
This was a prototype 3-wheeler powered by a Lynx motorcycle engine, Piero Opessi being the Milan agent for Lynx. It was exhibited at the 1936 Milan Motorcycle Show, and both side-valve and ohv versions were planned.

NG

OPHIR see CENTURY (i)

OPPERMAN (GB) 1956–1959
S.E. Opperman Ltd, Elstree, Hertfordshire.
This tractor manufacturer commissioned Lawrie Bond (of BOND Minicar fame) to design a new microcar. Bond duly created the Unicar in 1956, a car which was to combine 'big car comfort with small car economy'. This was a conventional looking machine with a steel-reinforced fibreglass body seating 2+2. Its 328cc Excelsior engine was placed in between the two rear seats, just in front of the rear axle. Its 18bhp could take the car to 60mph (97km/h). The two rear wheels were placed close together, avoiding the need for a differential. To buy new, it cost £399 10s or, from 1958, you could build one from a kit and some 200 Unicars were sold. Opperman's new model for 1958 was the Stirling 2+2 coupé, with smart fibreglass bodywork. It shared the same mechanical layout as the Unicar but had a wider rear track and a differential. Its engine was the 424cc Excelsior Talisman 25bhp twin, but a second (and final) prototype was built in conjunction with Steyr-Puch of Austria with a 493cc flat-twin engine from the Austrian version of the Fiat 500.

CR

OPPERMANN (GB) 1898–1907
1898–1902 Carl Oppermann, Clerkenwell, London.
1902–1907 Carl Oppermann Electric Carriage Co. Ltd, Clerkenwell, London.
Carl Oppermann began his motor vehicle career by fitting an electric motor to a horse-drawn victoria made by Arthur Mulliner. It had centre-pivot steering, with batteries and motor hidden under the body. Top speed was only 8mph

1995 Opel Tigra coupé.
OPEL

1999 Opel Astra Silver Edition hatchback.
OPEL

1958 Opperman Stirling coupé.
NATIONAL MOTOR MUSEUM

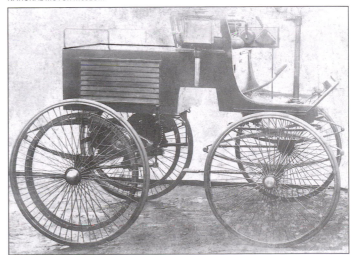
1900 Oppermann electric dog-cart.
NATIONAL MOTOR MUSEUM

1908 Orel 12hp tourer.
NATIONAL MOTOR MUSEUM

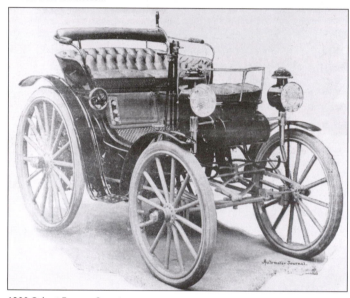

1900 Orient Express 2-seater.
NATIONAL MOTOR MUSEUM

(13km/h). By 1900 he was making complete cars, with tubular frames and worm drive, and by 1901 he was sufficiently well-known for *The Motor-Car Journal* to remark in their report on the Agricultural Hall Show 'We generally expect to find something interesting at the exhibit of Mr Carl Oppermann…' What they found was a victoriette with 2-seater body, 3hp motor and full elliptic springs mounted on a flexible subframe with universal joints '…to allow the wheels to suit themselves to any inequalities of the road surface'. It had a 2-seater body, but a third seat for an attendant could be fitted without difficulty. The second Oppermann exhibit was a 3-seater dog-cart called the Lucania, with similar frame and a 3hp motor which could be arranged to drive either the front or rear wheels, while a third was a simple 2-seater runabout priced at the modest sum of £160. It had a 1hp motor driving the rear wheels directly by worm gear.

In 1905 Oppermanns were available with bonnets under which the motors were mounted, with four forward speeds and shaft drive to a worm rear axle. A 4-seater tonneau of this pattern was sold to the King of Siam. For 1906 single chain drive was an alternative to the worm rear axle. Oppermann ended car manufacture in 1907; five years later he was reported to be running a garage in Kensington.

NG

OPUS (i) (GB) 1966–1972

1966–1970 Rob Walker Corsley Garage Ltd, Warminster, Wiltshire.
1970–1972 H.S.P. Motor Co., Bristol.
The Opus H.R.F. (Hot Rod Ford) was a strange aberration produced by racing team owner Rob Walker. Neville Trickett designed it according to the American Model T dragster idiom. It was marketed for just £99 for the body/chassis kit, and earned a reputation for precarious road manners; it was tiny, weighing just 8cwt (400kg). The suspension was a mixture of Ford Popular and Anglia, the front wheels were Mini and the recommended engine was a Ford Cortina (1300 or 1600). Over 200 examples were made in total. A company called Lambert Services, who made the chassis for later cars, also built an all-metal Mini Moke replica kit for a Minivan floorpan from 1970 to 1972.

CR

OPUS (ii) (GB) 1998 to date

Opus Cars, Ringwood, Hampshire.
Lotus Seven lookalikes were commonplace in the 1990s and the Opus Sprint was one of the more obscure ones. It used a space frame chassis, metal main body panels and fibreglass or carbonfibre cycle wings and nose cone. The usual engine fitment was Ford crossflow.

CR

OREL (F) 1905–1914

Automobiles Orel, Argenteuil, Seine-et-Oise.
The first Orel was a light car powered by an 8hp V-twin engine, and in 1907 the makers added a 7hp single and a 12hp four. Two of the singles ran in that year's Coupe des Voiturettes, but without success. Orels grew larger over the next few years, and by 1912 the range consisted of 8/10hp 2-cylinder and 14 and 18hp fours, all made by Buchet. For 1913 Orel joined the ranks of the sleeve-valve brigade, using a 2½-litre 20/24hp Knight 4-cylinder engine.

NG

ORIA see LENTZ

ORIAL (F) 1923–1924

The Orial was a light car made at Lyons under licence from SÉNÉCHAL, who presumably preferred to sell the licence rather than to transport the cars from their factory at Courbevoie. A 904cc Ruby engine was used.

NG

ORIENT see WALTHAM (i)

ORIENT EXPRESS (D) 1895–1903

Bergmann's Industriewerke, Gaggenau.
This car was the first automobile product of Bergmann's Industriewerke who later made cars under the names BERGMANN and GAGGENAU. Theodor Bergmann made vending machines and entered car manufacture with a design by Josef Vollmer. It was on Benz lines, with a single horizontal-cylinder engine of 1924cc developing 4bhp, and final drive by belts. A 4-seater *vis-à-vis* body was the most popular, though 2-seaters were made as well. Later, 2-cylinder engines were used, and a 4-cylinder model appeared in 1903. This was more often marketed under the Bergmann name.

HON

ORION (i) (CH) 1900

1900 Zürcher & Huber, Automobilfabrik Orion, Zürich.
Alfred Zürcher had been with the MARTINI company of Frauenfeld before he founded in 1898 the company in Zürich together with his friend Huber, who financed the venture. In 1900 they launched their first model, a *vis-à-vis* with a front-mounted, water-cooled single-cylinder engine. Before many of these had been completed, Orion started the production of commercial vehicles which they continued successfully until 1910. From 1903 to 1905 Orion was representing OLDSMOBILE in Switzerland and sold about 50 curved-dash models. Fom 1910 onward, Orion concentrated on repairing commercial vehicles and manufacturing radiators.

FH

ORION (ii) (A/CS) 1906, 1930
Vilem Michl, motocykly 'Orion', Slany.

Vilem Michl, founder of the first Czech cycle firm in 1894, built the 'Orion' motorcycles from 1902, and from 1906, some tens of voiturettes with engines placed under the floor were sold. His son Vilem Michl Jr constructed a 3-wheeler in 1930 powered by a 500cc SV engine at rear. The other features were two wheels with independent suspension in front, 3-speed gearbox, battery ignition and a body styled to customer's demands. Only a few were sold, but his 2- and 4-stroke motorcycles were more popular being exported to Germany, Russia, Italy, Hungary and even South Africa.

MSH

ORION (iii) (GB) 1914
This was a light car powered by an 8.9hp 4-cylinder engine with final drive by belts. It was sold from an address in Gloucester Road, South Kensington, but the maker is uncertain.

NG

ORIX (E) 1952–1954
Juan Ramírez, Barcelona.

Juan Ramírez was a well-known tuning specialist for racing cars. In 1952 he built his first car, the Orix, a small convertible with a 2-cylinder, 610cc boxer engine of 27bhp, mounted at the rear. This car won at the Rabassada circuit in 1953. The car looked so good that twelve friends ordered a closed version. This second car was as good as the first creation, but Ramírez had no space in his small workshop to start serious production. In 1954 he introduced an ugly copy of the VW Beetle, but thereafter he dedicated himself exclusively to tuning.

VCM

ORLEANS see NEW ORLEANS and OWEN (i)

ORLO (US) 1904
Jackson Automobile Co., Jackson, Michigan.

The Orlo was a product of the same company that made the better-known JACKSON (ii). It had a 16hp flat-twin engine mounted under the front seat and driving through a single chain. Advertising made much of the side-entrance tonneau body, at a time when many, though not all, 4-seater cars had rear-entrance tonneaus. A single-cylinder runabout and delivery van were announced at the same time, but may not have been built. The Orlo lasted only one year, and thereafter the Jackson Automobile Co. made only Jacksons.

NG

ORMOND (US) 1904–1905
United Motor & Vehicle Co., Boston, Massachusetts.

This was a short-lived and expensive steam car powered by a 25hp 4-cylinder single-acting engine with flash boiler. The 5-seater tourer had a canopy top, and the steering column could be swung to ease the seating of portly drivers. Its price of $3000 was way above that of popular steamers such as the Locomobile, and anyway 1904 was late to be launching a steamer, when the type was going out of fashion.

NG

ORPINGTON (GB) 1920–1924
Smith & Milroy Ltd, Orpington, Kent.

Smith & Milroy were motor engineers who announced a light car in August 1920. It was powered by a 1505cc 4-cylinder Coventry Simplex engine, driving through a Moss 3-speed gearbox and shaft to a bevel rear axle. This was conventional enough, but the axle, brakes and steering gear were said to be interchangeable with those of the Ford Model T, and the chassis was designed to take a Ford radiator if the Orpington one was damaged in an accident. The headlamps were mounted on top of the wings, and the only body was a 2-seater, advertised as 'The Business Man's Light Car' or 'A Business Man's Car'. A new model appeared in 1922, little changed except for a slightly smaller engine of 1368cc and more conventional position of the headlamps. A sports model was added in 1922 and a 4-seater tourer in 1923, by which time capacity had reverted to 1505cc. Estimates of production, taken from chassis numbers, run from 200 to 300, but a former employee said that no more than 11 or 12

1900 Orion (i) 3-seater *vis-à-vis*.
NATIONAL MOTOR MUSEUM

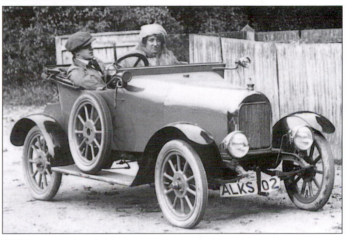

1920 Orpington 2-seater.
NICK BALDWIN

Orpingtons were made. The company later held a BRITISH SALMSON agency, and as engineers and car repairers survived into the 1950s.

NG

Further Reading
'High Street Trader', M. Worthington-Williams,
The Automobile, March and December 1998.

O.R.S.A. (I) 1973–1975
O.R.S.A. SpA, Turin.

This was a revival of the SIATA Spring, the least deserving of all Siata's models for such treatment. It retained its specification almost entirely, including the MG TD pastiche styling, but swapped the now defunct Fiat 850 for Spanish-built SEAT 850/133 mechanicals.

CR

ORSON (US) 1910–1911
Brightwood Manufacturing Co., Springfield, Massachusetts.

The Orson was a conventional enough car, with a 40hp 4-cylinder engine on a 130in wheelbase, but its method of financing was unusual. It was built by a co-operative of 100 of Wall Street's most prominent bankers, who would share the costs and receive a car each, at the cost price of $4000, no profit being made. The organiser was Horace M. Kilborn, president of the National City Bank of New York, and whose son Orson gave the car its name. The subscribers were said to have a combined wealth of $250 million, The car was built in Springfield, the chassis by the Brightwood Manufacturing Co., the body by the Springfield Metal Body Co.

In the event only 80 cars were made, at an average cost of $7000, and not all the wealthy owners were pleased. Daniel M. ('Brass Dan') Brady, brother of the

1954 Osca1100 sports car.
NATIONAL MOTOR MUSEUM

1965 Osca 1600 coupé by Fissore.
NICK GEORGANO/NATIONAL MOTOR MUSEUM

more famous 'Diamond Jim', claimed that he had to spend $1000 on repairs to his Orson. Plans to build the cars for general sale fell through, and the Orson Automobile Co., which was set up in 1912, never made a car.

NG

ORYX (D) 1907–1922

1907–1909 Berliner Motorwagen-Fabrik GmbH, Berlin-Reinickendorf.
1909–1922 Oryx Motorenwerk, Zweigniederlassung der Dürkoppwerke AG, Berlin Reinickendorf.
The Berliner Motorwagen-Fabrik (BMF) was a well-known maker of commercial vehicles from 1900, who made the friction-drive ERDMANN or FEG cars, and launched cars under the name Oryx, while from 1907 the commercials were called Eryx. The first Oryx car had a 1555cc 6/10PS 4-cylinder engine. In 1909 the factory was taken over by DÜRKOPP, but Oryxes continued to be made

under their own name. They were relatively small fours with monobloc engines; the 6/10PS was continued to 1918, joined by the 1830cc 7/21 PS (1913–1914) and 2610cc 10/30PS (also 1913–1914). After the war the works were fully integrated into Dürkopp's activities, and used for the manufacture of components, although some Oryx cars may have been made up to 1922.

HON

O.S. (US) 1914–1915

The Owen-Schoeneck Co., Chicago, Illinois.
John L. Owen and George Schoeneck organised this company to make a car designed by Schoeneck. It was a conventional machine, with 4-cylinder Herschell-Spillman engine, and was listed at $2350. Very few were sold under this name, however, as the partners separated. Schoeneck later designed a 6-cylinder car which was marketed as the GENEVA (ii).

NG

OSCA (I) 1947–1967; 1998 to date

1947–1967 Officina Specializzata Costruzione Automobili, Bologna.
1998 to date G.M.P. Automobili.
This company was founded by the three surviving Maserati brothers, Ernesto, Ettore and Bindo, in December 1947. They had sold their own business to the Orsi family in 1938, but remained with the firm until 1947. They left because Omer Orsi was pressing them to make road cars which he saw as more profitable than competition cars. Although they had different talents, Ernesto being the designer, Bindo the businessman and Ettore the workshop supervisor, they were united by their love of racing. Their first product was a sports car with 1100cc single-ohc 4-cylinder engine, tubular frame and coil-and-wishbone ifs. The engine gave 71bhp, and with a weight of only 895lbs performance was excellent. Twin-ohcs were used from 1950 onwards, and this engine was made in a number of different sizes. They included fours of 749 and 1453cc, and a 2-litre six. Road-going models, with open and closed bodywork, were catalogued, but most Oscas were intended for competitions. Successes were scored mainly in Italian events, though international fame came when Stirling Moss and Bill Lloyd won the 1954 Sebring 12 Hour race.

Sports cars were made in small numbers through the 1950s and 1960s, not more than 20 or 30 cars per year from a workforce of about 40. Bodies came mostly from Fissore, Vignale and Zagato. The best-known Osca was the 1600 which used a 1.6-litre twin-ohc 4-cylinder engine developing 140bhp, and had the unusual feature for its time of a 6-speed gearbox. The brothers had developed this engine for Fiat who used it in their 1500S sports car, though its power was held back to 80bhp.

In 1963 the brothers sold their company to Count Domenico Agusta's MV-Agusta motorcycle company. The twin-ohc fours were continued for three years, then replaced by a German Ford V4 engine which went into the PR2 coupé. Few of these were made, and Osca production was discontinued in 1967.

In 1998 the name was revived for a limited-production sports coupé powered by a mid-mounted 2457cc 16-valve flat-4 SUBARU engine, with 5-speed gearbox. The body was styled by Ercole Spada and carried the emblem of Carrozzeria Touring, although it was built by Nino and Mario Marazzi. The chassis and suspension were designed by Mario Colucci of ABARTH fame.

NG

O.S.I. (I) 1963–1968
Officine Stampaggi Industriali, Turin.
Founded in 1960, O.S.I. was affiliated to Ghia, being used as its pressings and production wing, making the bodies for cars such as the Innocenti S and Fiat 2300 coupé. Gradually it asserted its independence and from 1963 it made a Spider and Coupé based on the Fiat 1200, which was subsequently marketed by Neckar. It also displayed a coupé on the Fiat 850 under its own name and produced a 4-door version of the Alfa Romeo 2600. Perhaps its most famous work was the Ford O.S.I. 20M coupé produced by O.S.I. and sold through Ford of Germany dealerships. Launched in 1966 on O.S.I.'s Geneva show stand, it used a standard Ford Taunus platform and engine and a 4-seater coupé body. Around 3500 of these cars were made. O.S.I. also displayed the Cross Country in 1966, a jeep-style open 4-seater using Fiat 124 parts. In 1967 a similar style vehicle called the Week-End based on Fiat 850 parts was announced, but this never advanced beyond the prototype stage and O.S.I. was wound up in 1968.

CR

OSTERFIELD (GB) 1907–1909
Douglas S. Cox, West Norwood, London.
Douglas Cox was a well-known car dealer who listed two models under his own name, a 19.6hp four and a 40hp eight. He also made, or sold, the EMERALD light car, and bought John Weller's premises, where the WELLER car had been made.

NG

OTAS (I) 1969–1971
Otas Costruzioni Automobilistiche, Turin.
Otas offered two Fiat-based sports cars. First was a variation of the Lombardi Grand Prix fitted with a linered-down Giannini engine. Then came an Aldo Sessano-designed 2-seater coupé based on the front-wheel drive Autobianchi A112, whose 903cc engine was uprated from 44 to 59bhp so that a top speed of 100mph (161km/h) could be achieved. At 1,400,000 lire, it was more costly than Fiat's 850 Coupé, but far more exclusive.

CR

O.T.A.V. (I) 1905–1908
Officine Turckheimer Automobili e Velocipede, Milan.
This company was founded by German-born Max Turckheimer who set up a business in Italy dealing in, and later manufacturing, bicycles. In 1902 he began to make motorcycles, and three years later launched a light car. It was powered by a 4hp air-cooled single-cylinder engine with two fans, one in the normal position ahead of the engine and the other in a housing in the crankcase and driven by the crankshaft. It had a 2-speed epicyclic transmission and final drive by belts. Weighing only 440lbs, it had a top speed of 22mph (35km/h), and was said to climb any hill. It was made up to 1908, when power was quoted as 5½hp, and was joined by a 10hp twin with three speeds and a 2.8-litre 4-cylinder car. The latter may have been made in the JUNIOR factory in Turin, for Frederico Momo had substantial share holdings in both companies. The O.T.A.V. was discontinued at the end of 1908, and the Junior closed down two years later. However, Turckheimer regained control of the Milan factory where he made industrial engines and components for motorcycles. His son and nephew were Italian concessionaires for British Ariel motorcycles up to the 1950s.

NG

1966 O.S.I.-Ford 20M/TS coupé.
NICK GEORGANO

1907 Osterfield 18hp tourer.
MICHAEL WORTHINGTON-WILLIAMS

1908 O.T.A.V. 5½hp 2-seater.
NATIONAL MOTOR MUSEUM

O.T.I. (F) 1956–1959
1956 Office Technique International, Paris.
1959 Éts Bugatti, Molsheim.
This obscure 3-wheeler, of which very few were made, nevertheless involved three famous names. It was designed by Lucien Rolland, one of the partners in ROLLAND-PILAIN, and after his death in 1957, the rights passed to the DECAUVILLE company. They, in turn, sold them to BUGATTI who planned to make the car with body by Gangloff. Originally known as the Microcar, the O.T.I. was a very light open 2-seater powered by a 125cc single-cylinder SNECMA engine driving the single front wheel. The 1956 prototype had a doorless body, but the 1959 Bugatti/Gangloff model had doors and more adequate weather protection.

NG

1910 Otto (ii) 30/33hp demi-tonneau.
NICK BALDWIN

OTOKART (F) 1966
Otokart, Bezons.
In some ways, the Otokart models produced by Jean-Pierre Ponthieu can be treated as precursors to the great French microcar boom. Powered by 50cc Sachs engines, they did not require a driving licence to run. There were two models: the Valérie, a very plain, doorless utility machine; and the Eugénie, an extraordinary doorless cabriolet designed to evoke the style of veteran Renaults.
CR

OTO MELARA (I) 1984–c.1991
Oto Melara SpA, La Spezia.
An engineer called A. Costa was behind the Oto Melara Gorgona, a robust-looking saloon car designed for the armoured vehicle market. In profile the aluminium 4-door bodywork recalled the Lamborghini LM002 and it too had 4-wheel drive, but was powered by a 100bhp 2.4-litre VM turbodiesel engine mounted in the rear. The chassis was a mix of steel and aluminium and featured MacPherson strut suspension front and rear.
CR

OTOMO (J) 1924–1927
Hakuyosha Ironworks, Tokyo.
The engineer Junya Toyokawa, who had invented a gyro-compass for boats and aircraft, built several prototypes of the ALES light car at the Hakuyosha Ironworks, and put into production an improved version called the Otomo. It had a 944cc air-cooled 4-cylinder engine and 3-speed gearbox. All components, including the bodies, were made in the factory; body styles included open 2- and 4-seaters, saloons and delivery vans.

Tokoyama estimated that production would need to exceed 1000 cars per year to undercut imported products, but only 270 Otomos were made altogether. A water-cooled ohv engine was introduced in 1926. Although it was not a success, the Otomo has the distinction of being the first of the millions of Japanese cars to be exported, when one was sold to Shanghai, China.
NG

OTOSAN see ANADOL

OTOSANTARU (J) 1947–1954
Japan Auto Sandal Motors, Tokyo.
The Otosantaru Auto-Sandal was a very small and basic microcar reminiscent of the 1920s Hanomag. The 2-seater boasted a single headlamp and sat on motorcycle wheels. A 5bhp single-cylinder 350cc engine was rear-mounted and suspension was by leaf springs all round.
CR

OTTERCRAFT see STEADMAN

OTTO (i) (F) 1900–1914
Sté Générale des Voitures Automobiles Otto, Paris.
This company gained its name from the German-designed Otto stationary engine which they imported and then made under licence from the late 1870s. Another German connection was with the Diesel engine, for which Otto held the rights and which they announced that they would put into a car, in about 1900. Nothing came of this, understandably, as even trucks were not to use diesel engines for another 20 years or more. There seems to be some confusion about

the first Otto cars which were shown in Paris in August 1900. One report gives them as having front-mounted 7 and 12hp vertical-twin engines, though another says the engines were a horizontal 6hp and a vertical 10hp. In February 1901 they moved to a new address and showed four cars. These had 10hp horizontal 2-cylinder engines and 20hp vertical fours, both with armoured wood frames. For 1903 they offered a 10hp single-cylinder car with regulation of engine speed by variable lift exhaust valve. It had a rear-entrance tonneau body and a De Dion-Bouton-type bonnet.

There seems to be little trace of Otto cars until 1909 when they announced the F.L. These cars, made under licence from Serex, made up the bulk of production up to 1914, although there is a surviving car, dated 1909 bearing the name O.T.T.O. on its radiator. This is curious, as there is no suggestion that initials were ever used at the time when the cars were new. Another make built, or sold by Otto was the CULMEN.
NG

OTTO (ii); OTTOMOBILE (US) 1910–1912
1910–1911 Otto Gas Engine Works, Philadelphia, Pennsylvania.
1912 Ottomobile Co., Mount Holly, New Jersey; Philadelphia, Pennsylvania.
Like the French Otto, this company owed its name to the original Otto gas engines patented by Nicolaus August Otto in 1867. The Otto car was a conventional one, with 3950cc 30/35hp 4-cylinder engine, though it was lower and longer-looking than many contemporaries, as they had a long wheelbase with no overhang at front or rear. Three body styles were offered in the 1910 season, eight in 1911 and ten in 1912, by which time the name of company and car had been changed to Ottomobile. The cars continued to be made in Philadelphia, as the Ottomobile Co. of Mount Holly was a sales organisation. Larger engines of 4686 and 5211cc were used on the 1912 Ottomobiles, but sales were few, and the make did not survive into the 1913 season.
NG

OTTO (iii) (D) 1923–1924
Otto-Werke GmbH, Munich.
This make was also linked with the famous Otto Gas Engine company in that the car's designer Gustav Otto was the son of Nicolaus August. His company built a light motorcycle called the Flottweg from 1919 to the early 1930s, and in 1923 launched a large car powered by a 27/85PS 4-cylinder engine. It took part in competitions, often with Gustav or his wife Ada at the wheel.
HON

OTTOKAR (US) 1902–1904
Otto Königslow Machine Co., Cleveland, Ohio.
Usually rendered OttoKar, this was a light 2-seater powered by a 6hp single- or 14hp 2-cylinder engine, with epicyclic transmission and single-chain final drive. The 1902/03 model had tiller steering and a Renault-type bonnet, while for 1904 there was wheel steering and a squarer bonnet with Vauxhall-like flutes at each side. Königslow made about 75 cars, most of them in 1903. After making ten in 1904 he sold his business to the Globe Machine & Stamping Co. in June.
NG

OTTOLINI (I) 1900–1901
Fabbrica Automobili Ottolini, Milan.
This was a short-lived company which made a few light cars with 5hp single-cylinder engines, four forward speeds and belt drive.
NG

OTTOMOBILE see OTTO (ii)

OURS (F) 1906–1909
SA des Automobiles Ours, Paris.
The main product of the Société Ours was taxicabs, of which 150 were running in Paris in 1908, but they also made some cars with 10/12hp 3-cylinder or 14/16hp 4-cylinder engines. They had round radiators in the style of Delaunay-Belleville, and some carried a bear on the badge, 'ours' being French for bear.
NG

OUZOU (F) 1900–1901

Émile Ouzou et Cie, Levallois-Perret and Poissy, Seine.

It is not certain if Émile Ouzou was a person or not, as the company behind this car was called Émel Cuzon et Cie, and it may be that Émile Ouzou was simply thought to be a more attractive name. The cars used single-cylinder Soncin engines made by Émel Cuzon, which, in 1901 became Sonçin, Grégoire et Cie, and later made the GRÉGOIRE (i) car. The Ouzou voiturette was made in two models, with 4 and 6hp single-cylinder engines, 2-speed epicyclic transmission and single-chain drive. The smaller had two seats, while a third passenger could be accommodated in the 6hp. Production was sporadic, and did not last beyond the end of 1901. GrÉgoire left in 1903 and the company was renamed Bellamy-Sonçin. M. Bellamy became famous for the enormous racing car he built in 1904, a straight-8 with separately-cast cylinders whose dimensions were 183 × 183mm, giving a capacity of 38 litres, and an output of 200bhp.

NG

OVERHOLT see ILLINOIS (ii)

OVERLAND (US) 1903–1926

1903–1905 Standard Wheel Co., Terre Haute, Indiana.
1905–1909 Overland Auto Co., Indianapolis, Indiana.
1909–1926 Willys-Overland Co., Toledo, Ohio.

The first Overland was built by the Standard Wheel Co. who were major suppliers of wheels to the carriage and wagon industry. When they decided to enter the motor field they sent their young engineer Claude E. Cox around several other companies to learn about the latest ideas. When he returned he designed a 2-seater runabout which was unusual in having its 5hp vertical single-cylinder engine in front under a bonnet, rather than under the seat as in the OLDSMOBILE and most contemporary American light cars. The drive was taken by a 2-speed epicyclic transmission and single chain to the rear axle. The prototype ran in February 1903, and about 12 more were built that year, selling for $595. In 1904 output doubled to 25, and a 2-cylinder model joined the single. They were both tiller-steered 2-seaters, but for 1905 Cox came up with wheel steering and added a shaft-driven 4-seater with 16hp 4-cylinder engine, selling for $1500. The twins were continued in two sizes, 7 and 9hp, but the single was dropped.

As space in the Terre Haute factory was cramped, Cox moved production to Indianapolis, where the Standard Wheel Co. had another factory. One of their customers, buggy builder David M. Parry, financed the launch of the Overland Auto Co. Standard Wheel then withdrew, and the Overland was made in an extension of Perry's buggy factory. Two models were made for 1906, a 9hp twin and a 16hp four. Output was only 47 cars, and all were bought by a dealer from Elmira, New York, named John North Willys. He was sufficiently pleased with them to place an order for 500 1907 models, securing his order with a $10,000 deposit. By November he had still received no cars, so he travelled to Indianapolis to find Parry bankrupt, having lost not only his factory but also his home. There were no complete cars, and only parts for assembling two or three. However, Willys still believed in the Overland, and lacking a factory he started production in a circus tent, where 465 cars were made in 1908. They were 20/24hp 4-cylinder cars of conventional design, with Ford-like epicyclic transmission, selling for $1250. By 1909 Willys had a proper factory, and turned out 4907 cars. There were now four models, on two wheelbases, with 30hp 4-cylinder and 45hp 6-cylinder engines and conventional 3-speed gearboxes. The six lasted only one year, and Willys did not make another six until 1915. Instead, he concentrated on reasonably priced fours, from a 20hp starting at $775 to a 40hp from $1350 to $2750.

In April 1909 Willys purchased a large factory at Toledo, Ohio, which had formerly been used for making the POPE-TOLEDO. His company was to remain in Toledo for the rest of its existence. Willys had considered buying the MARION Motor Co., of Marion, Ohio, but instead he acquired the majority of Marion shares, and sold Marions until 1912. In October 1909 he formed the Willys-Overland Co., and the following year he made 15,598 cars with a workforce of 5000 men. When he took over in Indianapolis there were only 15 men on the payroll. By now he had lost Claude Cox, who was not happy with Willys' brash, risk-taking methods. Cox went on to a successful career in the motor industry, but never spoke to Willys again.

1908 Ours 14/16hp limousine.
NICK BALDWIN

1914 Overland Model 79 tourer.
NATIONAL MOTOR MUSEUM

1918 Overland Big Four 35hp tourer.
NICK BALDWIN

Despite Cox's disapproval, Willys clearly had the formula for success, and Overland sales boomed over the next ten years. They were already third in the industry in 1910, behind Ford and Buick, and in 1912 they moved up into second place. They held this until 1919, when they were edged down to fifth, behind Ford, Chevrolet, Buick and Dodge. The peak year was 1916, when 142,779 cars were delivered, although this figure included a number of WILLYS-KNIGHTS. There were 13 models on four wheelbases in 1911, but gradually the range was streamlined, and in 1914 there was only one Overland model, the 3983cc Model 79 made as a roadster, tourer or coupé. The range expanded again in 1915, with two sizes of four, 30 and 35hp, and a new 45/50hp six sold only in tourer form for $1475. The 1915 models were the first to have lhd.

1920 Overland Four sedan.
NATIONAL MOTOR MUSEUM

In 1919 Willys announced a new, low-price Overland Four. The plan was to sell it for $500, challenging the Model T Ford ($525) and Chevrolet 490 ($735). However, a disastrous strike closed the factory from Spring 1919 until just before Christmas, which delayed the introduction of the Four and pushed its prices up to $945-1575, at which it was no competitor at all for Ford. Willys lost control of his company between the end of 1919 and the end of 1921 (see WILLYS), but on his return he deliberately moved the Overland up-market, realising that he could never compete with Ford. For 1923 two wheelbases were offered, the 100in (2538mm) Model 91 and the 106in (2690mm) Model 92. The latter range included better-equipped models such as the Redbird, Blackbird and Bluebird. Sales rose from 50,000 in 1921 to 150,000 in 1925. That year an Overland Six appeared, with 2780cc engine and on a 113in (2868mm) wheelbase, but 1926 was the last year for the Overland. For 1927 it gave way to a new smaller and more up-to-date car called the Whippet. The Overland name was revived for the single year 1939, but as a model name, not a make.

NG

Further Reading
'John North Willys, his Magnetism, his Millions, his Motorcars',
Beverly Rae Kimes, *Automobile Quarterly*, Vol. 17, No. 3.

OVERMAN (US) 1895–1898

Overman Wheel Co., Chicopee Falls, Massachusetts.
The Overman Wheel Co. was a manufacturer of bicycles sold under the name Victor. To get into the car business A.H. Overman hired Harry A. Knox who produced several designs for him, including one in 1895 which had three small 2hp air-cooled engines. Others followed at the rate of about one per year, but in 1898 Overman decided to make a steam car. This did not suit Knox, who left to make petrol cars of his own at Springfield, Massachusetts. In 1899 Overman launched his steamer under the name VICTOR (i).

NG

OWATONNA (US) 1903

Virtue & Pound Manufacturing Co., Owatonna, Minnesota.
This company seems to have been mainly a maker of engines for workshop and farm use. They built at least three cars, principally to demonstrate the efficiency of their 10hp engine, though a price of $1250 was quoted. It is not certain how many more were made, if any, but Virtue and Pound continued in business as stationary engine makers up to about 1917.

NG

O-WE-GO (US) 1914

O-We-Go Car Co., Owego, New York.
This cutely-named cyclecar was similar to many, with tandem seating for two, friction transmission and belt drive. The makers planned to build their own engines, but thought better of this ambition, and bought a 10/12hp 2-cylinder motorcycle unit from Ives. A prototype reached 58mph (93km/h) on test, and production began in April 1914. It lasted until the end of the year, when bankruptcy put an end to the O-We-Go.

NG

OWEN (i) (GB) 1899–1935

Automobile Transport Co., London.
Twentieth Century Travel Co., London.
Orleans Car Co., London.
Shadowy makes of which there is little hard evidence of manufacture are not unknown in the car world, particularly when they were linked with stock market promotions. The Owen was something else, a 'make' with at least six alternative names, listed on and off for 36 years, yet with no press descriptions (after 1902), road tests, advertising or even photographs on which a serious historian can rely. Two addresses crop up again and again in references to the cars, Nos. 6 and 72 Comeragh Road, West Kensington. At one time it was suggested that these were the same, due to re-numbering of the road after World War I, but

a study of street directories shows the intersecting roads appearing at the same numbers in 1905 as in 1920.

The first contemporary press reference is found in *The Motor Car Journal* for 30 March 1901, when The Automobile Transport Co. of Comeragh Road were said to be making a 3½hp voiturette called the Twentieth Century. A drawing accompanied the article, but was too vague to give a clear idea of how the car worked, showing no gears, pedals or handbrake. The 3½hp engine was standard, but '...the company are building cars with 5 and 7hp engines' said the *Journal*. The drawing showed a 2-seater, but the article concluded by saying 'The main underframes are designed so that almost any description of body can be built on them'. This vagueness was typical of the early announcements of the cars. By December 1901 Mr E.H. Owen told the *Journal* that he was prepared to take orders for Twentieth Century cars of 9, 12, 16 or 24hp 'for delivery in the New Year'.

Only a month later the company name had changed to the Twentieth Century Travel Co., and the cars were called Lococars. Only one model was now described, with 24hp 4-cylinder engine, four or more forward and reverse speeds, and a 'transmission which obviates the use of chains which, however, can be fitted if desired'. The body was said to be far removed from the ordinary type in that it resembled the cab of a locomotive with a saloon attached. Alas, there was no illustration of this intriguing vehicle.

No more was mentioned of the Twentieth Century Travel Co. or Lococars, but in the 1905 *Autocar Buyers Guide* the Automobile Transport Co. listed cars under four different names, the 10hp Parisia, the 20hp Londonia, the 30hp Twentieth Century and the 40hp Owen's Gearless. Some of them occur again over the next three years in *The Autocar* lists, along with the Atalanta and the Owen Petelectra with petrol-electric drive. The same illustrations, side and front views, are used to illustrate the 10hp 2-cylinder and 35hp 4-cylinder Londonia. They show a very conventional 5-seater tourer and could easily be from a 'borrowed' printing block. Models of up to 60hp are listed up to 1913, and a few Models A, B and C were said to have been made between 1914 and 1917. Owen provided detailed lists of chassis numbers, but this in itself is no evidence of manufacture.

An intriguing reference appears in *The Car to Buy* published in 1908. This illustrates a limousine of indeterminate make, and lists four models from a 20hp four to a 60hp six. Among distinctive features are mentioned 'Owen's improved hook-jointed live axle', special 'Cab' screen, and 'special dashboard honeycomb cooler', which would indicate a Renault-type radiator, yet the photo shows a conventional radiator at the front of the bonnet! The address is given as The Owen Motor Co., 1 Long Acre, London, almost the only variation from Comeragh Road. Under 'Records', we are informed that Owen was the maker of the first English motor-driven vehicle in 1887! This contrasts with the claim made to the editors of *Automobiles of the World*, published in 1921, that the first Owen car was made in 1895. Another section in *The Car to Buy* gives space for 'A Few Users'. Most makers list their quota of aristocrats, generals and the like, but Owen conveniently says 'On Application'.

The picture is no less complex after World War I, with the appearance of the Orleans, a smaller companion make listed in 10, 15 and 20hp models, the latter with a long-stroke engine of 76 × 165mm, giving a capacity of 2994cc. This is given in *The Autocar Buyers' Guide* as the 20hp Orleans, yet the same dimensions are listed in *Fletcher's Motor Car Index* for the 20hp Owen Dynamic whose chassis price is £300 higher. In 1921 Owen listed the first of his 8-cylinder cars, the Model OE with 5302cc V8 engine, 2-speed gearbox and Owen's own starter and carburettor. A chassis price of £2250 was quoted, more expensive than a Rolls-Royce Silver Ghost at £2100. The car was actually illustrated in the 1921 *Buyers' Guide*, but the side view is suspiciously like the KENWORTHY, with slight retouching. The Kenworthy was never on the British market and was sufficiently obscure to be unknown to most British readers. Another example of Mr. Owen's cunning.

In 1925 the V8 gave way to a 7634cc straight-8 on a 150in (3807mm) wheelbase, with a chassis price of £1850, reduced to £1750 for 1927 and 1928, then raised to £1775 in 1929, which price was maintained up to 1935, when the Owen 'MM' disappeared from all lists. *The Autocar* had already dropped it after 1928.

Turning from what is clearly fantasy, what facts are there about this shadowy empire? Three Owens were associated with Comeragh Road: John Pugh Owen, BA, who was in the Post Office Directory at No. 72 from 1899 to at least 1905, E.H. (Edward Hugh) Owen, the most persistent name to appear, and the one

1920 Owen (i) Eight tourer, the only known photograph of an Owen.
NICK BALDWIN

linked with the cars, and Edward David Griffith Owen who was on the voter's list at No. 6 until 1934. A Hugh Owen was the first starter at Brooklands, having formerly been a starter for the Jockey Club. He lasted only one season, possibly because of his attachment to horse racing tradition, which was rapidly being abandoned at Brooklands. Could he be the same as 'E.H.'?

Of the buildings, No. 72, which appears in all the pre–1914 listings, is part of a terrace of late Victorian houses with no commercial premises whatsoever. No. 6 consists of a small shop with two flats (or a maisonette) above. In 1905 it was occupied by Charles Lock, upholsterer, and in the early 1920s it was registered to Robert Saunders, furniture dealers, who also had No. 8. In 1929 Saunders had No. 8, and No. 6 is not mentioned at all. In 1930 Nos. 4A and 6 were occupied by the South Western Sanitary Laundry Ltd, with Robert Saunders still at No. 8. There is no mention of the Owens at all, yet they gave No. 6 (sometimes grandly called Carrick House) as their address throughout the 1920s. If they rented the upstairs premises, they would not have appeared in the Street Directory. It is interesting that they never took paid advertising in any known magazine. All the lists are in buyers' guides and insurance manuals, which would have been free insertions.

Attempts to link the cars with other makes do not really stand up. The NEW ORLEANS from Twickenham was called Orleans in its later days, but was Belgian in origin. Admittedly, a Twickenham garage run by the Jenner family who were involved with the New Orleans, was listed in 1939 as holding Owen and Orleans spares, but this may have been slipped in by a clerk on the Stone & Cox insurance manual. Certainly when the author visited Jenner's garage in 1958, the widow of E.H. Jenner, who had driven a New Orleans in the 1905 T.T., knew absolutely nothing about the Owen. There have also been suggestions of a link with the OWEN MAGNETIC, on the strength of one of E.H. Owens' cars, the 1920 Owen Dynamic, having a magnetic clutch which sounds similar to the Entz transmission used by the American car. But the Owens of the latter were Raymond M. and Ralph R., both Americans born and bred, and it is not a particularly unusual name.

The most plausible explanation is that E.H. Owen was a fantasist in the Walter Mitty mould, and judging by all the contradictions in his history and specifications, not a particularly good one.

NG

Further Reading
'Comeragh Road Mystery', M. Worthington-Williams, *The Automobile*, October 1989.

OWEN (ii) (US) 1910–1911

Owen Motor Car Co., Detroit, Michigan.

This was a large car powered by a 6965cc 4-cylinder engine, with an early example of a central gearchange. It had a 120in (3046mm) wheelbase and rode on 42in (1066mm) wheels, which gave it something of the appearance of the Oldsmobile Limited. Four body styles were listed, tourer, close-coupled tourer, runabout and berline limousine. In October 1910 the partners sold the business to REO in exchange for Reo stock. Reo completed the 35 cars for which parts were on hand, but did not make any more Owens. Ralph Owen marketed some of the last cars as the R.O. He and his brother Raymond later made the OWEN MAGNETIC.

NG

1911 Owen (ii) 50 tourer.
NICK BALDWIN

OWEN (iii) (GB) 1973–1983

H.R. Owen, London.

Chris Humberstone designed the Sedanca for the luxury car dealer H.R. Owen as a sports coupé with generous space for four passengers. The elegant bodywork was realised in aluminium over a Jaguar XJ6 floorpan and featured pop-up headlamps, rubber bumpers and a hatchback. A luxurious interior boasted Dralon and suede upholstery, and a silver notepad and hairbrushes! Owen planned to make 100 cars per year but Jaguar's refusal to supply mechanicals effectively scuppered the project. However, two further cars were built for an Arabian customer in 1978 and 1983 by Robert Jankel of PANTHER.

CR

OWEN MAGNETIC (US) 1915–1922

1915–1916 R.M. Owen & Co., New York.
1916–1919 Baker R. & L., Inc, Cleveland, Ohio.
1919–1921 Owen Magnetic Automobile Co., Wilkes-Barre, Pennsylvania.
1921–1922 Owen Magnetic Motor Car Corp., Wilkes-Barre, Pennsylvania.

Raymond M. Owen (1873–1943) built his first horseless carriage, with the help of his brother Ralph, in 1899. Thereafter the brothers manufactured delivery trucks in Cleveland, Ohio, under the name Phoenix Motor Vehicle Co. for a few years, before selling the company and taking on an OLDSMOBILE sales franchise. R.M. Owen & Co. was organised in New York City in 1906, to serve as Olds distributors and dealers, later taking on FRANKLIN, PREMIER, MITCHELL, RAUCH & LANG and DORRIS as well. The firm also served as exclusive national distributor for Ransom Olds's new REO car for the make's first ten years. Raymond Owen also collaborated with his brother in the Owen Automobile Co., builder of the OWEN (ii) automobile.

Roy Rainey was responsible for getting Raymond Owen interested in the Entz electro-magnetic transmission, the centrepiece of what would become the Owen Magnetic. Justus Bulkley Entz had invented the device, the first patent for which dated from 1898. In place of gears, the transmission utilised electrical field windings in place of the engine flywheel. These windings created electrical force, which acted upon armature windings attached to the driveshaft. The force generated was varied by an electrical controller which provide a theoretically infinite number of speed ratios and also furnished electric braking on deceleration. Reversing was accomplished by a small mechanical gearset. The electrical transmission components also served to start the engine, power the car's electrical accessories and recharge its storage battery.

Owen founded the Entz Motor Car Corp. in New York City, an adjunct to R.M. Owen & Co., to put such a car into production. The Owen Magnetic debuted at the 1915 New York Auto Show. Offered either as a 7-passenger tourer or cloverleaf roadster (both cars priced at $3750), the Model O-36 used a 5973cc Buda side-valve 6-cylinder engine of 48bhp. Built on a 136in (3452mm) wheelbase, the 'Car of a Thousand Speeds' made a big hit with press and public. Bodies were by the Rauch & Lang Carriage Co. of Cleveland.

The Entz Motor Car Corp. was disbanded, and manufacture was entrusted to R.M. Owen & Co., which expected to build 250 cars a year. Owen's New York facilities, however, were inadequate, so an alliance was contemplated with the Cleveland-based BAKER Electric Vehicle Co., then in the process of merging with former rival Rauch & Lang to form the Baker R. & L. Co. The Baker division would manufacture the cars, whose bodies would continue to come from the R. & L. coachbuilding division. R.M. Owen & Co. would sell them. Further potential assistance in production was to come from the General Electric Co. (not connected to the British firm of the same name), which acquired a major interest in the Entz patents and would manufacture the transmissions at Fort Wayne, Indiana. Owen desired a larger engine, and had helped his friend George Weidely set up the Weidely Motor Co. in Indianapolis, Indiana, to design and build such a power unit.

Additions to the Owen Magnetic line for 1916 included a landaulet body in the O-36 series, priced at $5000, and a slightly smaller M-25 series, which used a 4969cc Continental 6N 6-cylinder engine of 45bhp. The M-25 sold for $3150 to $4400. Production of both models, however, suffered repeated delays; fewer than 800 cars were built in 1916.

Owen Magnetics for 1917 were unchanged, except for price increases of $150 to $200. Despite the initial optimism, production fell, to under 500 cars. A new, larger model, the W-42 was readied for 1918, using the long-awaited Weidely engine. An ohv 6-cylinder unit, it displaced 6798cc and much aluminium was used in its construction. The M-25 was discontinued and production of the O-36 interrupted, ostensibly to concentrate on the W-42. Production, however, fell even further, to barely 200 cars.

1917 Owen Magnetic Model 0-365 cloverleaf roadster.
JOHN A. CONDE

For 1919 the O-36 was revived and the W-42 continued. In mid-year, Raymond Owen severed his ties with Baker R. & L., moving production of the Owen Magnetic to Pennsylvania, where it would be carried out in the Wilkes-Barre plant of the International Fabricating Co., with final assembly at a factory in Forty Fort, formerly home to the MATHESON automobile. Bodies were now by the Ohio Body & Blower Co. of Cleveland and bore the firm's Lind badge. But production did not start in Pennsylvania until March 1920, and consisted of the W-42 only. The company had become Owen Magnetic Automobile Co., and was reincorporated in June as the Owen Magnetic Motor Car Corp. Cash flow continued to be a problem, seemingly solved by an order from exporter J.L. Crown for 500 chassis to be sold overseas as CROWN-MAGNETICs. However, the production problems continued, and Owen was unable to fulfill the Crown order. A voluntary receivership was granted in August 1920, and, under supervision of the receivers, assembly resumed at a limited pace. Model for 1921 were unchanged except for model designation, which was now simply 60. A November auction of the company's assets was briefly stayed, and then in March 1922 it was all over.

Raymond Owen had kept his other business interests separate from Owen Magnetic, so was largely unaffected by the firm's collapse. R.M. Owen & Co. became the New York distributor for HUDSON, and Owen himself bought into STEVENS-DURYEA Inc. of Chicopee Falls, Massachusetts. He accumulated great wealth after his Owen-Dyneto Electric Corp. of Syracuse, New York, became the sole supplier of electrical components to PACKARD.

KF

Further Reading
'Owen & Entz: An Electrifying Combination', Karl S. Zahm,
The Bulb Horn, Vol. 52, Nos 1, 2, 3.
'The Entz System and Owen Magnetic', Stuart W. Wells,
Automobile Quarterly, Vol. 36, No. 3.

OWEN-SCHOENECK *see* O.S.

OWEN-THOMAS (US) 1908–1910
Owen-Thomas Motor Car Co., Janesville, Wisconsin.

1920 Owen Magnetic Model Six tourer.
NATIONAL MOTOR MUSEUM

W. Owen Thomas designed a most unusual 6-cylinder engine which was billed as having 'no starting handle, no water jackets, no carburettor and no electrical distributor'. What it did have was direct-injection based on aviation practice, rotary valves in the cylinder head, air-cooling and continuously-operating sparking plugs. The 60hp 6-cylinder engine was built in-unit with the gearbox and final drive was by shaft. Thomas planned to build the car in a disused shed belonging to the Chicago & North Western Railroad, and made at least three before the money ran out. The Wisconsin Engine Co. bought the rights and planned to make the car at Corliss, Wisconsin, but dropped the idea before a single car was made.

NG

OWOSSO (US) c.1982–1987
Owosso Motor Car Co., Owosso, Michigan.
The Owosso Pulse was a tandem 2-seater that looked like a renegade jet fighter cockpit missing its tail. It had four wheels arranged diamond-pattern with one in front, one in back and two outboard at the ends of vestigial winglets. Headlights

were enclosed under glass and power came from a Yamaha motorcycle engine. The cockpit bubble canopy slid back fighter-plane style. They were sold in kit or assembled form, and an estimated 250 were made. The Pulse was later returned to production by WARP FIVE as the Starship.

HP

OXFORD (i) (US) 1900
Oxford Automobile Co., Everett, Massachusetts.
This was a typical light steam car whose makers boasted that 'the steam is so condensed within the vehicle that none is visible without'. It was made as a 2-seater runabout, 4-seater family carriage and victoria stanhope at prices from $850 to $1200.

NG

OXFORD (ii) (US) 1905
Detroit-Oxford Manufacturing Co., Oxford, Michigan.
Sometimes referred to as the Detroit-Oxford, this car had a 16hp 2-cylinder engine, friction transmission and shaft drive. Only one prototype was built, with a doorless 4-seater tourer body. In January 1906 its builder William Radford moved to Fostoria, Ohio, and made the car for a year as the FOSTORIA.

NG

OXFORD (iii) (CDN) 1913–1915
Oxford Motor Cars & Foundries Ltd, Montreal, Québec.
This English-sounding car was made by a French-Canadian family called Pontbriand who set up a machine shop in Sorel, Québec, in 1882. When they decided to enter the car business they hired an American, H.M. Potter as designer. They planned to make the D-Four and the C-Six, but only the latter was built, and then only in four examples, two tourers, a roadster and a chassis on which the buyer built a truck body. Almost all the components were imported from America, and when the war made these hard to obtain, the Pontbriands left the car business.

NG

Glossary

A guide to some of the more frequently used technical and general terms which may not be familiar to the reader.

ALAM formula rating. *See* horsepower.

All-weather. In the immediate post-World War 1 period this name was applied to cars which could be opened to the elements, but which had comprehensive arrangements against wind and rain when they were closed. This would normally have included glass windows in metal frames, which either folded down into the doors or were stowed away in a special compartment. This was in contrast to a tourer, which had only a rudimentary hood and, possibly, canvas side-curtains which rolled down. The complexity and expense of these systems meant that all-weather bodies were confined to expensive chassis. In America such a design was known as a Springfield Top.

Automatic inlet valves (aiv). Inlet valves opened atmospherically, without any mechanical control. A primitive system, soon replaced by mechanical actuation (*see also* moiv).

Avant-train. A 2-wheeled power unit consisting of engine, gearbox, final drive, steering wheel, and other controls, which could be attached to a horse-drawn vehicle, or to enable various bodies to be used with the same engine. *Avant-train* units were the earliest examples of front-wheel drive, but were outmoded soon after 1900. Electric as well as petrol engines were used.

Belt drive. A system whereby the final drive is a conveyed from countershaft to rear axle by leather belts.

bhp. *See* horsepower.

Blower. *See* supercharger

Brake. *See* shooting brake.

Brougham. Based on its horse-drawn forerunner, the brougham was a highly formal design, distinguished by the separate nature of the passenger compartment, which often retained its own carriage lamps. Even when the chauffeur's area became enclosed the passenger saloon was made wider, usually by use of a 'D-front' - so called because of its shape as seen from above. Another distinguishing feature was the brougham's sharp-edged appearance in profile; this applied both to the roof-line and to the shape of the door, and the 'brougham door' - curved forward at the toe - continued to appear as a feature of otherwise conventional designs well into the thirties.

Cabriolet de Ville. This version of the cabriolet implies merely that the front portion of the folding head can be opened separately into the de ville position, usually by being rolled up; the later term for a similar, although less formal, design was a three-position drophead coupé. *See also* Salamanca.

Cabriolet. Of all coachbuilding terms, this is the one whose meaning has evolved the most over the years. Originally a cabriolet was a four-door, four- or six-light drophead body with a division, and without even having enclosed drive. Soon, however, the requirement for the division was dropped, and it came to mean the same as an all-weather; it began to replace that name during the mid-twenties. (A variation, the coupé cabriolet, had only two doors.) The increasing popularity of the style in the thirties, and some borrowing of features from Germany where it was even more popular, led to a further widening of its definition; it could now, for example, describe a body (sometimes known as a saloon cabriolet) where only the fabric roof itself opened, leaving windows and frames standing, and indeed some commentators tried to restrict its use to such bodies (leaving drophead coupé for the alternative type). Later, the requirement for four doors evaporated, and a cabriolet came to be synonymous with a drophead coupé.

Cardan (shaft). The driving shaft which conveys power from gearbox to rear axle. More usually known as the propeller shaft, the word was widely used in France (transmission à cardan) in the early days to distinguish shaft drive from chain drive. The principle is said to have been invented by the Italian philosopher Girolamo Cardano (1501 – 1576).

Catalytic Converter or **Catalyst.** A device in which a chemical reaction is induced in order to change the chemical composition of the gases flowing through it. The automotive catalyst consists of a 'washcoat' usually containing platinum and rhodium, on a ceramic or metallic core, fitted into the exhaust system in order to clean up exhaust gases after they leave the engine. Two types are commonly used. The two-way catalyst removes half to two-thirds of CO and HC and can be retrofitted relatively easily. It is commonly used on diesel engines. The three-way catalyst in addition removes NOx, but this requires it to be 'regulated' and integrated with the engine management system as this can only be achieved when the engine is run at a relatively rich stoichiometric mixture. It can then remove up to 95% of toxic emissions under ideal conditions. Both types are damaged by lead and require the use of unleaded fuel.

Chain drive. A system whereby the final drive is conveyed from countershaft to wheels by chains. Double-chain drive was widely used on powerful cars until about 1908, but could still be found on some old-fashioned machines as late as 1914. Indeed, Frazer-Nash used three chains, one for each forward speed, as late as 1939. A number of light cars used a centrally-mounted single-chain drive to a live axle.

Close-coupled. Originally, implied that all seats were within the wheelbase (often to make more luggage space), and that rear seating room was therefore limited. Later, when engines had been moved forward and seating within the wheelbase had become the norm, the term came to mean merely that the body was shorter than normal.

Clover-Leaf. An arrangement of three seats, usually in an open car or coupé, where the third seat is placed behind and between the two front ones so that its occupant's legs are between the front seats. In vogue during the twenties.

Common rail. A type of direct injection diesel engine developed by Fiat and Bosch in the 1990s. It achieves the very high injection pressures needed in two stages. The first stage pressurises a tube-like chamber – the common rail – from which the injectors build up the remainder of the required pressure before injection into individual cylinders. It is technically less demanding than the alternative unit injector approach whereby very high technology injection pumps - the unit injectors - build up the required pressure for each cylinder individually.

Continental Coupé. A popular style in the late-1920s and early 1930s. The intended image was of a fast, close-coupled car which would be ideal for Continental touring; it was reinforced by making the luggage container in the form of a separate trunk rather than an integral part of the body, since this was perceived to be a French style of the time.

Convertible. An all-embracing term which has come to mean any car with a folding head. *See also* all-weather.

Coupé de Ville. Similar to a cabriolet de ville, but the rear part of the head is fixed instead of folding. Where it was intended to make clear that the design had only two doors and no division, it was sometimes called a sedanca coupé.

Coupé. The French word coupé means 'cut'. As applied to coachbuilding, it originally referred to the centre part of a horse-drawn carriage, between the 'box' in front and the 'boot' at the rear. Thus for a car it also means foreshortened - ie close-coupled - but it is applied specifically to a 2-door, 2- or 4-light, close-coupled body with either a fixed or an opening head; in the latter case it must have normal glass windows - fixed, lifting or sliding - otherwise it becomes a sports body. A coupé can have two or four seats enclosed under the head.

Cowl. A scuttle, 'cowl' being the preferred term in America. A dual-cowl design (usually a phaeton) had a second cowl in front of the second row of seats.

CV. *See* horsepower.

Cycle Wing. A wing on the front wheel which closely follows the wheel's curvature, like the mudguard on a bicycle. Sometimes actually turned with the wheel. *See also* helmet wing.

Cyclecar. A simple light car whose design owed much to motorcycle practice, of which a large variety were made from 1912 until about 1922. The typical cyclecar had an engine of fewer than four cylinders, was often air-cooled, and final drive was by belts or chains. Cyclecars flourished in England, France, and the US, but disappeared with the coming of mass-produced 'genuine light cars', such as the Austin Seven and Citroën 5CV.

De Dion axle. A system of final drive in which the rear axle is 'dead', or separate from the driving shafts. The drive is transmitted by independent, universally-jointed half-shafts. The system was first used on the De Dion-Bouton steamers of the 1890s, but was abandoned by the firm after 1914. It is, however, used on a number of modern sports cars.

De Ville. Implies a body style where the front (ie driver's) compartment is either open to the skies or can be made to be. Originally all 'de ville' designs had four doors.

Dickey-Seat. Usually found on two-seater coupés of the twenties; a lid behind the hood lifted up to form an additional seat.

Dos-à-dos. A 4-seater car in which the passengers sat back to back. Seldom seen after about 1900, this lay-out was revived briefly in the Zundapp Janus of 1956.

Drophead Coupé. A coupé with an opening head.

Drophead. A design where the head can be folded flat to make the car open.

Epicyclic gearbox. A form of gear in wehich small pinions (planetary pinions) revolve around a central or sun gear, and mesh with an outer ring gear or annulus. Bset known for their use on the Ford Model T, epicyclic gearboxes were found in a wide variety of early US cars. In the US they are known as planetary transmissions.

Estate car. *See* shooting brake.

Fast and loose pulleys. A system of transmission in which the countershaft carried a loose pulley for neutral, and two fixed pulleys meshing with spur gears of different ratios on the axle. Moving a belt from loose to fixed pulley provided a clutch action. The system was used on early Benz, New Orleans, and other cars.

Faux-Cabriolet. The French word 'faux' means false; these bodies looked like dropheads because they had fabric-covered roofs, and often dummy hood-irons, but in fact their roofs were fixed.

F-head. Cylinder head design incorporating overhead inlet and side exhaust valves. Also known as inlet-over-exhaust (ioe). *See also* L-head; T-head.

Fixed-head Coupé. A coupé with a solid, immovable head (although it might possibly be fitted with a sunshine roof).

Flexible Fuel Characteristics. Ability of an engine type to run on more than one type of fuel. External combustion engines often have this advantage; it means an engine is less dependent on a possibly finite fuel source.

Friction transmission. A system of transmission using two disks in contact at right angles. Variation in gear ratio was obtained by sliding the edge of one disk across the face of the other. This theoretically provided an infinitely variable ratio, although in some systems there were a limited number of positions for the sliding disk.

GDI. Gasoline direct injection, the term used by Mitsubishi for its direct injection petrol engine, the first of a new generation of such engines, which promise greater fuel efficiency and lower emissions.

Helmet Wing. Similar to a cycle wing, but the bottom kicks backwards away from the wheel rather in the manner of a Roman helmet.

HEV or **Hybrid-electric Vehicle**. A vehicle which has a dual powertrain one of which is electric. In practice most examples have a heat engine – usually internal combustion – generating electricity, which is then used to power electric motors which drive the wheels. Two types exist, parallel hybrid in which either the heat engine or full electric drive from batteries can be used allowing the vehicle to operate in zero emissions mode in urban areas and as a normal internal combustion car elsewhere. More elegant is the series hybrid, which uses the advantages of internal combustion and electric vehicle in order to create a more efficient powertrain than in a conventional car.

High-wheeler. A simple car with the appearance of a motorised buggy, which enjoyed a brief period of popularity in the US and Canada between 1907 and 1912. Over 70 firms built high-wheelers, the best known being Holsman, International, and Sears.

Horsepower. (hp, bhp, CV, PS) The unit used for measuring the power output of the engine, defined mechanically as 33,000 foot-pounds per minute. Up to about 1910 the horsepower quoted by makers was meant to correspond to the actual output, although it was often used with more optimism than accuracy. Sometimes a double figure would be quoted, such as 10/12 or24/30; here the first figure represented the power developed at 1000rpm, while the second was the power developed at the engine's maximum speed. In 1904 the Automobile Club of Great Britain & Ireland's rating of horsepower (the RAC rating from 1907 onwards) was introduced, calculated on the bore of the engine only, and as engine efficiency improved the discrepancy between rated and actual horsepower grew. Thus, by the mid-1920s a car might be described as a 12/50 or a 14/40, where the first figure was the rated hp, and the second the actual hp developed at maximum revs. RAC ratings were widely used until after World War II, but when taxation by horsepower was abandoned in January 1948, manufacturers soon stopped describing their cars as Eights or Tens.

The American ALAM (later NACC) horsepower rating followed the British system of calculation on the cylinder bore alone, but French (CV) and German (PS) ratings were based on different formulae, with the result that a 15hp British car might be called an 11CV in France or a 9PS in Germany. The French rating was introduced in 1912 and the German at about the same time. Prior to this the terms CV and PS were used to denote actual brake horsepower. Today horsepower rating has largely been abandoned; engine capacity is indicated in litres, and power in developed or brake horsepower.

Hot-tube ignition. An early system in which the mixture was ignited by a small platinum tube, open at its inner end, which was screwed into the cylinder head. The outer, closed end was heated to red heat by a small petrol-fed burner, and when the mixture passed into the tube, it ignited. The system was outdated by 1900, although some firms continued to fit tubes as an auxiliary to electric ignition.

Indirect Injection Diesel. This is the traditional diesel engine, where the actual combustion process is started in a pre-chamber connected to the combustion chamber itself. Combustion then spreads to the combustion chamber itself in a controlled manner. It offers reduced engine noise at the expense of higher fuel consumption, compared to the alternative direct injection diesel engine, where the combustion process is started in the conventional manner within the actual combustion chamber.

Inlet-over-exhaust valves (ioe). *See* F-head.

Landaulet. (*Also spelt* landaulette.) A very popular style amongst the moneyed classes before and after World War I. Based on a well-known style of horse-drawn carriage, its distinguishing feature was that only the rear portion of the roof opened - ie that part covering the back-seat passengers. Originally it was assumed not to have an enclosed driving compartment, so in later years the term enclosed landaulet (or sometimes limousine landaulet) made the distinction. It was further assumed to have a division; when this was omitted, it became a saloon landaulet. Finally, it might be a three-quarter, single or coupé landaulet (this last sometimes shortened to coupélette), according to whether it had six, four or two lights.

Lean-burn. A process whereby the amount of fuel burnt in the engine is minimized in favour of air, leading to hotter and more efficient combustion with a useful reduction in emissions of CO and HC, although NOx emissions increase, as the air is heated to higher temperatures. Diesel engines are naturally lean-burn.

L-head. Cylinder head design in which inlet and exhaust valves are mounted on one side of the engine. It was the most commonly-used design for all but high-performance engines from about 1910 until after World War II. Also known as side valves (sv), *See also* T-head.

Light. A light in coachbuilding terms is a side-window; hence it is convenient to classify a saloon, for example, as 4-light or 6-light.

Limousine de Ville. A limousine with a folding roof extension above the driver's seat.

Limousine. The essential qualities of a limousine are that it should be roomy (usually through having a long wheelbase), its roof should be fixed, and it should have a division. The driver's compartment may not have been enclosed in the early days, but the passenger compartment always was. The massive leg room in the rear usually permitted the addition of two further 'occasional', i.e., folding, seats. What was not normal was a luggage compartment, since a limousine was used for town work rather than touring; there was often, however, a folding luggage grid. Later, a demand grew for a dual-use body which could combine both formal and touring requirements, which became known as a sports limousine or later touring limousine; this retained the division, but sacrificed some rear leg-room, and usually the occasional seats, to permit the addition of a luggage-boot. The sports limousine often dispensed with a quarter-light.

Live axle. An axle which transmits power, as opposed to a dead axle, where the power is either carried by separate half-shafts (*see* De Dion axle) or by side chains.

Mechanically operated inlet valves (moiv). *See* automatic inlet valves.

Monocar. Single-seater car. The expression is never used for racing cars, most of which have been single-seaters since the late 1920s (these are sometimes known as *monopostos*), but for ultra-light single-seater cyclecars of the 1912 to 1915 period.

Motor buggy. *See* high-wheeler.

Overhead valve. Cylinder head design in which the valves are mounted above the combustion chamber, either horizontally or inclined at an angle. Generally abbreviated to ohv.

Over-square. An engine in which the cylinder bore is greater than the stroke (e.g., 110mm × 100mm). A 'square' engine is one in which the bore and the stroke are identical (100mm × 100mm).

Phaeton. An alternative term for a tourer. This was the preferred description in America, where the dual-cowl phaeton was particularly popular.

Pillarless. A fixed-head body where there is no obstruction above the waist-line between the windscreen pillar and the rear quarter. Can apply to both two- and four-door designs.

Planetary transmission. *See* epicyclic gearbox.

Power-train. Term commonly used for the subassemblies of the car that make it move; i.e. engine, clutch, gearbox and final drive.

PS. *See* horsepower.

Quarter-light. Originally a light, or window, alongside the rear seat which was fixed in the rear quarter of the car rather than being part of a door. Later, when it became common to arrange swivelling ventilation windows in the front section of front doors, these also became known as quarter-lights, and it became necessary to distinguish between front and rear ones.

RAC rating. *See* horsepower.

Roadster. The term originated in America, and meant an open body with one wide seat capable of taking two or three abreast, possibly also having a dickey-seat. It was the American equivalent of the British 2-seater. In recent years it has come to mean the same as a two-seater sports car.

Roi des Belges. A luxurious type of open touring car, named after King Leopold II of Belgium. The style is said to have been suggested to the King by his mistress, Cléo de Mérode. The style was sometimes also known as the Tulip Phaeton.

Rotary valves. Valves contained in the cylinder head whose rotary morion allows the passage of mixture and exhaust gases at the appropriate times.

Runabout. A genereal term for a light 2-seater car of the early 1900s, especially those made in the US.

Salamanca. Sometimes called a salamanca cabriolet, this design was conceived by Count de Salamanca who was the Rolls-Royce agent in Madrid. It was no more than a formal, four-light cabriolet de ville, but luxurious in execution; the term was used exclusively in connection with Rolls-Royce chassis.

Saloon Limousine. Similar to a Sports Limousine, in that it had a division but being built on a shorter chassis than a normal limousine had to sacrifice some rear leg-room. Unlike a sports limousine, however, it normally had a quarter-light - ie it was a six-light design - and would not have had a luggage-boot.

Saloon. Probably the term which has least changed in meaning over the years. It has always meant a vehicle which has a fixed roof (although possibly with a sunshine roof fitted), which is completely enclosed, and which does not have a division. It can have four lights or six, and either four doors or two, although during the thirties the last type became increasingly difficult to distinguish from a fixed-head coupé, and indeed was sometimes named saloon-coupé.

Scuttle. That part of the bodywork between the engine compartment and the windscreen, forming an apron over the legs of the front passengers.

Sedanca de Ville. The word sedanca is in theory synonymous with de ville, so to describe a body as a sedanca de ville is illogical in the extreme. In practice it implied a de ville design with a large, saloon-like rear compartment often having four side-windows.

Selective transmission. The conventional transmission in which any gear mey be selected at will, as distinct from the earlier progressive transmissions, where the gears had to be selected in sequence.

Shooting brake; brake; estate car; station bus; station wagon. The original brake or shooting brake was similar to the wagonette (*qv*), and was used on large estates to carry members of shooting parties. The station bus was used for conveying guests and servants, and was usually a closed vehicle, whereas early brakes were open. After World War I both types declined in use, but the names were reincarnated in the wood-panelled station wagon which US manufacturers

began to offer as part of their ranges in the 1930s. By 1941 all the popular makers were listing station wagons, and the fashion spread to Europe, where the name estate car was more often used, after World War II.

Side valves. Cylinder head design in which the valves are mounted at the side of the combustion chamber. They may be side-by-side (L-head), or on opposite sides of the engine (T-head). The usual abbreviation, sv, applies to the L-head design; the rarer T-head design being specifically mentioned.

Sleeve valves. Metal sleeves placed between the piston and the cylinder wall. When moved up and down, holes in them coincide to provide passage for gases at the correct times.

Speedster. An American term for a sporting open car with sketchy bodywork, usually no doors, a raked steering column and bolster fuel tank behind the seats.

Spider. A French term for a very light sporting voiturette, often with a sketchy dickey seat, around the turn of the century. It was revived by Alfa Romeo for their sports cars in the 1950s, and by Porsche as the Spyder.

Sportsman's Coupé. A 2-door, 4-light fixed-head coupé with built-in luggage-locker. The provision of covered luggage accommodation was quite an innovation in Europe in 1927, when the intense but short-lived fad for this type of design started. It was achieved by 'close-coupling', ie moving the rear seats forward so that the rear passengers' feet were in floor wells under the front seats.

Sportsman's Saloon. This was a 4-door, 4-light close-coupled saloon; the craze for this type of body took over, around 1929-30, from that for the sportsman's coupé. The name was later shortened to sports saloon.

'Square' engine. *See* over-square.

Station bus; station wagon. *See* shooting brake.

Sunshine Saloon. During the latter half of the twenties, particularly in the UK, numerous styles were named 'sunshine saloons' by their builders. They ranged from saloons with what we would now call a sliding or sunshine roof, to semi-cabriolet designs where the whole roof folded back.

Supercharger. A compressor (colloquially a 'blower') fitted to an engine to force the mixture into the cylinders at a pressure greater than that of the atmosphere. First seen on the 1908 Chadwick, the supercharger was widely used on sports and racing cars in the 1920s and 1930s, and on Formula 1 racing cars until 1954. Differs from a turbocharger (*qv*) in that it runs at a constant speed.

Surrey. An open 4-seater car, often with a fringed top.

T-head. Cylinder head design in which inlet and exhaust valves were mounted on opposite side of the engine. Two camshafts were needed, and in order to make do with only one, the L-head (qv) design was developed. The T-head was outmoded after about 1910.

Three-quarter. An older coachbuilding term, little used after the twenties. A three-quarter body had a quarter-light; its opposite, a single body, did not; thus a 4-door, 6-light landaulet would be referred to as a 'three-quarter landaulet', whereas a 4-door, 4-light version would be a 'single landaulet'.

Tonneau Cover. A covering for an open tourer or sports car for use when no sidescreens have been erected. It comes from a very early motoring term describing the passenger-carrying part of a body (from the French word for a barrel).Because they were built on a short chassis, early tonneaus had a door at the back, between the two seats, these being known as rear-entrance tonneaus. These gave way to the side-entrance tonneau, which was in fact, synonymous with the tourer, though early examples would have had doors for the rear seats, but not for those at the front.

Torpedo. An early term for what was in effect a large 4- or 5-seat tourer. Although bearing little resemblance to a torpedo, its name came from its smooth contours, free from intricate mouldings, and from the continous horizontal line formed by the bonnet and waist-line, often accentuated by a secondary scuttle or cowl between the two rows of seats.

Tourer. Always an open body with a collapsible hood, and usually having four or five seats. The feature which distinguishes it from a cabriolet or drophead coupé is that its side windows - if it has any at all - are in the form of lightweight detachable side-screens which can be removed and stowed in a locker.

Trembler coil ignition. Ignition by induction coil and electromagnetic vibrator, which broke the primary circuit and induced the high-tension current in the secondary windings. Used by Benz and many other pioneers, but superseded by the De Dion-Bouton patent contact breaker, invented by Georges Bouton in 1895.

Turbocharger. A compressor fitted to an engine to force mixture into the cylinders at a pressure greater than that of the atmosphere. Unlike a supercharger, a turbocharger is usually driven by exhaust gases from the engine, so that the faster the engine is running, the greater the boost provided by the turbocharger, and vice versa. First seen on a production car in the Chevrolet Corsair Monza Spyder in 1962, the system became well-known in the BMW 2002 Turbo (1973), and Porsche 911 Turbo (1975). It was introduced to ordinary production saloons by Saab on their 99 of 1977.

Vee-radiator. A honeycomb radiator coming to a more or less sharp point. The first production car to use the design was probably the Métallurgique in 1907, and by 1914 a large number of makes had vee-radiators. They were especially popular in Germany, and from 1919 to 1923 there was hardly a single German or Austrian car without a vee-radiator. They should not be confused with the vee-shaped grill found on many cars of the later 1930s, whose flamboyant design concealed an ordinary, flat radiator.

Victoria Hood. A type of hood which is cantilevered out from its point of attachment to the front of the seat it is intended to cover, with no support from the windscreen. Only feasible for 2-seaters (although at least one 4-seater design had two such hoods, one for each row of seats).

Vis-à-vis. A 4-seater car in which two passengers sat facing the driver.

Voiturette. A French term for a light car, initially used by Léon Bollée for his 3-wheeler of 1895, but soon applied by manufacturers and journalists to any small car.

Waggonette. A large car, usually for six or more passengers, in which the rear seats faced each other. Entrance was at the rear, and the vehicles were usually open. See also shooting brake.

Further reading.
The Complete Book of Automobile Body Design, Ian Beattie, Haynes Publishing. 1977.

Contributors

NICK GEORGANO

Editor in Chief

Nick Georgano was born in London in February 1932. He began his career as a motoring writer at the age of 7 when he prepared a truck catalogue which was typed out by his long-suffering mother. He was 16 when he first attempted to write an 'encyclopedia'.

On coming down from Oxford in 1956 he became a preparatory schoolmaster during which time he helped his friend Ralph Doyle to revise his *The World's Automobiles* – Nick completed this after Ralph's death in 1961, an invaluable apprenticeship for editing the *Complete Encyclopedia of Motorcars*, first published in 1968. On the strength of this he abandoned the schoolroom for the typewriter and has since edited or written 31 titles including *The Complete Encyclopedia of Commercial Vehicles* (editor), *The Encyclopedia of Motor Sport* (editor), *A History of Transport* (editor), *History of Sports Cars, History of the London Taxicab, Early Days on the Road* (with Lord Montagu of Beaulieu), *The American Automobile – a Centenary, The Art of the American Automobile, Britain's Motor Industry – The First 100 Years* (editor). For the latter and for *The Complete Encyclopedia of Motorcars* he was awarded the Montagu Trophy of the Guild of Motoring Writers. He was Head Librarian at the National Motor Museum from 1976 to 1981. He is a member of the National Motor Museum Advisory Council and Trustee of the Michael Sedgwick Memorial Trust and the Horseless Carriage Foundation, California.

KENNETH BALL

Born in August 1929, Kenneth Ball attended Accrington Grammar School and studied engineering at Blackburn Technical College. He has an HNC in Mechanical Engineering and in Automobile Engineering, and is a graduate of the Institute of Mechanical Engineers.

Since his youth, Kenneth Ball has collected and dealt in rare motoring publications. He also founded Autobook Publishers Ltd, which, during the 1960s and early 1970s, was the world's largest publisher of motor car workshop manuals. He sold his publishing interests in 1972 to concentrate on collecting and dealing in rare motoring publications.

DAVID FILSELL

Born in March 1934, David started collecting material for a motor encyclopaedia soon after. When he went to Bryanston he was delighted to find a like-minded pupil in Nick Georgano. David chose a career in hospital administration, but his pervasive interest in all things motoring manifested itself in a variety of ways – rallying, marshalling, cigarette cards, model collecting and so on, as well as motoring history. He was a major contributor to *The Complete Encyclopedia of Motorcars* and *The Encyclopedia of Motor Sport*. He has been an active Vintage Sports Car Club (V.S.C.C.) member since 1954. Having recently retired, he intends to spend more time with his Barrington motors, his collection of Clynos and on original research.

CHRISTOPHER
'KIT' FOSTER

Holding BSc and MSc degrees in Electrical Engineering, 'Kit' Foster served as engineer and project manager for the US Department of Defense for over 25 years. He is currently a freelance motoring journalist and contributing editor to *Special Interest Autos*. He has contributed regularly to *Automobile Quarterly*, *Collectible Automobile*, and *Classic Car Mart*. Previous credits also include *Classic and Sportscar*, *The Automobile*, *Old Cars Weekly* and *Car Collector*. From 1989 to 1995 he was editor of the *Society of Automotive Historians' Journal* and *Automotive History Review*.

AUSTIN MAXWELL
'MAX' GREGORY

Max Gregory was born in March 1935. After a long career as a dairy farmer in Australia, he was forced to retire in 1995 following a motor accident. Since then, he has concentrated on his hobby as a motoring writer and historian. He has been a contributor to *Restored Cars* magazine since 1974, and has also had articles published in New Zealand and the US.

PAUL FERDINAND
HEDIGER

Born in February 1934 in Switzerland, Ferdinand Hediger's interest in engines and motor vehicles started in his childhood. He became sales manager, and later general manager, of a target arms factory exporting pistols worldwide, from which he retired in 1995.

From 1965 his freelance articles, mainly on motoring history, were published by the Swiss weekly *Automobil Revue*, as well as various German, Austrian, British, US, and Spanish magazines. His first book *Klassische Wagen Vol. II* was published in 1972, followed by *Oldtimer* in 1978, and *Klassische Wagen 1919-1939* in 1988, for which he obtained the Award of Distinction by the SAH.

ERIK H. F. van INGEN
SCHENAU

Erik van Ingen Schenau was born in April 1947. Following an early career in social work, he has worked in the tourist industry since 1982 and is currently director of a travel agency in The Netherlands. In 1966 he began researching automotive developments in the People's Republic of China, travelling extensively in China and developing his specialism in Chinese automobiles. He founded the China Motor Vehicle Documentation Centre, a large library of Chinese automobile reference material, based in The Netherlands. His freelance writing has been published across the European motor press and he is a correspondent for the German *Auto Katalog*.

MARGUS HANS
KUUSE

Margus Hans Kuuse was born in December 1943 in Tartu, Estonia, and trained as an engineer at Tallinn Technical University. Since 1971 he has held the position of editor for numerous motoring magazines, including *Tehnika Ja Tootmine*, *Autorev__*, *Autoposter*, and *Autopluss*. He is currently news/contributing editor for *Eesti Ekspress*, *Autoleht*, and *Motor News* in Russia, Ukraine and Belorussia.

As a freelance writer, his work has appeared in leading motor magazines and newspapers internationally, including a period in the 1970s and 1980s as Soviet correspondent to the British *Autocar* magazine. Book credits include Estonia's main auto history book *Sada Autot*. He has also worked as a consultant for Estonian television.

MICHAEL LAMM

Born in February 1936, Michael Lamm has followed a career as a publisher, writer and editor in the US. From 1959, his early work as an editor included the *Foreign Car Guide*, *Motor Life*, and *Motor Trend*. He turned to freelance work in 1965, in 1970 became founder and editor of *Special-Interest Autos*, and since 1971 has been a contributing editor to *Popular Mechanics*. Michael is owner of the Lamm-Morada Publishing Co. Inc. which he founded in 1978. He has authored and published many articles and books, including *A Century of Automotive Style*.

MIKE LAWRENCE

Mike Lawrence was a teacher until 1982, when, at the age of 40, he became a motoring journalist. He has been editor of *Motor Sport*, motoring editor of the *Portsmouth News*, and has contributed to many journals internationally. He was the historical consultant to BBC2's history of motor racing, *The Power And The Glory*, and consultant to the Goodwood *Festival of Speed* videos. Mike has written, or co-written, more than 25 books, and is a consultant to Brooks the Auctioneers. Living near Goodwood, he masterminded the campaign to support the return of racing to the circuit.

Mike's poetry and plays have won awards and, in 1996, he gained a PhD for his research into Shakespeare's dramatic techniques. As Dr Lawrence, he teaches courses on Shakespeare for the Universities of Sussex and Gothenburg.

VOLKER CHRISTIAN
MANZ

Born in January 1956 in Hamburg, Germany, Christian has lived in Spain for the last twenty years. He published his first story at the age of 13, but entered professional journalism in 1982, after a career in hotel management. He is a correspondent for *Automobil-Revue* and other German language magazines, and contributes to several Spanish car magazines. His articles have been translated into 16 languages and published in 22 countries. Christian is co-editor of *Hispano-Suiza/Pegaso, A Century of Trucks and Buses*, and editor of electric car bulletins.

KEITH MARVIN

Keith was born in July 1924, and followed a career in the newspaper industry in the US between 1948 and 1974. He then turned to freelance writing and editing, his publications including several books on automotive history, with indepth studies of Dagmar, Wasp, and McFarlan cars, and two books on number plate history. His articles and book reviews have been published widely in the US, Canada, and the UK. He has also had several books of verse published.

Keith was a founding member of the Society of Automotive Historians, and has worked as a designer of number plates for various governments.

PÁL NÉGYESI

Pál was born in Hungary in November 1973, and is a graduate in librarian and communication studies. He has contributed to various Hungarian car magazines, including *Autô-Motor*, *Sport Auto*, and *4 × 4 Magazin*. He wrote for the short-lived *British Alternative Car World*, and several articles for *Classic Car Mart*. In 1997 he became editor of *AutoClassic*, Hungary's premier classic car magazine. His first book, which covers the history of the first Hungarian motorcycle factory, Méray, was published in 1998.

HANS-OTTO NEUBAUER

Hans-Otto was born in July 1929 in Altona, Germany. After working with BP in Germany, he became a freelance writer and editor, specialising in all German makes and aspects of the automobile in social history. He contributed to the first edition of the *Encyclopedia of Motorcars*, and was editor of *Die Chronik des Automobils* and *Die Geschichte des Automobils*. His articles have been published in numerous magazines and the press. Hans-Otto is a founder member of the Automobilhistoriche Gesellschaft, and is editor of the *Automobilhistorische Nachrichten*.

PAUL NIEUWENHUIS

Born in May 1954 in The Netherlands, Paul was educated in Australia, Belgium, Spain, and the UK. He graduated from the University of Edinburgh with an MA and PhD in General Linguistics. Paul joined the Motor Industry Research Unit in Norwich in 1986, followed by the Centre for Automotive Industry Research at Cardiff Business School in 1990. His publications include *Japanese Commercial Vehicles*, as well as co-authoring *The Green Car Guide* and *The Death of Motoring?*, and co-editing *Motor Vehicles in the Environment*. He has contributed to a number of magazines and journals, particularly on environmental and strategic issues affecting the motor industry.

JAN P. NORBYE

Jan Norbye was born in August 1931 in Oslo, Norway. He graduated from Oslo Commercial College in 1951, and held positions with Esso and Volvo up to 1961. He became technical editor of *Car and Driver* in 1961 until 1964, followed by automotive editor of *Popular Science* until 1974, and international editor of *Automotive News* until 1980. Jan then turned to freelance writing and has authored many books including *Autos Made in Japan*, *The Complete History of the German Car*, *The Wankel Engine*, *The Gas Turbine Engine*, *Modern Diesel Cars*, and *The 100 Greatest American Cars*.

HAROLD W. PACE

Harold Pace was born in July 1952 in the US. He has been a freelance commercial photographer in the advertising industry since 1980. He began writing for automotive publications in 1993, and has been a contributor to many motor magazines including *Automobile Quarterly*, *Excellence*, *Forza*, *Vintage Motorsports*, and *Sports Cars International*. His specialist interest is in limited-production kit, sports and racing cars. In 2000 he published a comprehensive survey of these machines, *The Big Guide to Kit and Specialty Cars*. Harold has also competed in drag, slalom, SCCA and historic racing.

ROBERT PRZYBYLSKI

Robert was born in August 1962 in Poland. In 1991 he became a freelance writer, working for car-enthusiast magazines. He moved to Motomagazyn in 1993 as a staff writer, and is currently editor-in-chief. He has also been a contributor to newspapers and yearbooks. Other publications include *A Big Three – A 100 Years of the American Automobile*.

CHRIS REES

Born in October 1963, Chris Rees is a full-time motoring journalist and author with a passion for specialist cars. He has been editor of *Alternative Cars* magazine, and has worked on the staff of numerous specialist, mainstream, internet and classic car titles. Books to his credit include *British Specialist Cars, Three-Wheelers, Microcar Mania, Classic Kit Cars, Caterham Sevens, Original Alfa Romeo Spider*, and the annual *Classic Car Buyers Guide*.

HALWART SCHRADER

Halwart Schrader was born in February 1935 in Germany, and is a graduate of Art History and Commercial Graphics. He started work in the advertising department of *Der Spiegel*, then moved to the editorial staff of Auto Union customers' magazine *Copilot*. He launched the *BMW Journal* in 1962, staying three years. In 1973 he started his own publishing business, becoming editor/publisher of Germany's first classic car magazine *Automobil Chronik*. He has written more than 50 books on motoring history and related subjects.

MARIAN
ŠUMAN-HREBLAY

Born in March 1950, Marian graduated from Charles University in Prague with an MA in Librarianship. He worked as a librarian before moving into motor bookselling in 1990, and is now owner of the Autoantikvariat bookselling and consulting firm. He has been a member of the Society of Automotive Historians since 1985.

ALVARO CASAL
TATLOCK

Born in January 1940, Alvaro has been a journalist in Uruguay since 1962. From 1971 he spent four years as the South American correspondent of the *Veteran and Vintage Magazine*. He has had numerous books published since 1982, on motoring and other subjects. His latest book, *The Automobile in South America*, was published in 1996. With support from the Uruguayan Automobile Club, he founded Uruguay's first motor museum in 1983.

FRANS B. VRIJALDENHOVEN

Born in October 1928, Frans received technical training at Saurer, Jaguar Cars, and Daimler-Benz. In 1951 he became service manager for Holland for Mercedes-Benz cars and trucks. This was followed by similar positions with Skoda, IFA, Steyr, OM and Büssing trucks, and Adler motorcycles. In 1955 he became vice-managing director of a General Motors dealership in The Hague. Prior to retirement, he held the position of adviser at the National Association for the Dutch car trade.

Frans is currently an automotive historian and freelance publisher. His published work includes books on the cars of Prins Bernhard of The Netherlands, and Dutch royal motoring in general since 1904. He has written other specialist publications on Dutch coachbuilders, assembly plants in Holland, and the cars of the German Kaiser Wilhelm II.

NICK WALKER

Nick Walker was born in August 1936. Although trained as an engineer, he spent most of his career in marketing and general management. After retiring early, he took up writing on motoring matters, concentrating on coachbuilding and coachbuilders. He has written regularly for *Classic Car Mart* and also for *The Automobile*. Other published work includes the *A-Z of British Coachbuilders*. Nick is honorary librarian for the Vintage Sports Car Club (V.S.C.C.), and honorary archivist of IBCAM. An Alvis owner for many years, he is Midlands Chairman of the Alvis Owners Club.

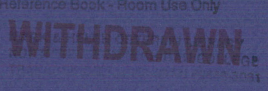